HARROD'S LIBRARIANS' GLOSSARY

of terms used in librarianship, documentation and the book crafts

AND REFERENCE BOOK

HARROD'S LIBRARIANS' GLOSSARY

of terms used in librarianship, documentation
and the book crafts

AND REFERENCE BOOK

Seventh Edition

Compiled
by
RAY PRYTHERCH

Gower

Published by
Gower Publishing Company Limited
Gower House
Croft Road
Aldershot
Hants GU11 3HR
England

Gower Publishing Company
Old Post Road
Brookfield
Vermont 05036
USA

British Library Cataloguing in Publication Data
Harrod, Leonard Montague
Harrod's librarians' glossary of terms used in librarianship, documen-
    tation and the book crafts and reference book. – 7th ed.
1. Library Science – Dictionaries
I. Title   II. Prytherch, R.J.
020′.3′21   Z1006

ISBN 0 566 03620 7

Printed and bound in Great Britain by
Billing and Sons Limited, Worcester.

Contents

Preface to the seventh edition

It is over fifty years since the first Edition of *Harrod's Glossary* was published; in those years the structure and attributes of librarianship, archive work, publishing, and the book trade have changed superficially to an extent that makes them almost unrecognizable. However, the basic principles of the professions – assembling and organizing information to meet the needs and demands of users for whatever purpose – have not changed, and this fundamental continuity has made it possible to undertake regular revisions of the *Glossary*, preserving the professional ethos and the foundation skills whilst constantly updating and revising the means through which these skills operate and the styles in which the end-product is delivered.

The purpose of the *Glossary* is to explain and define terms and concepts, identify techniques and organizations, provide up-to-date summaries of the activities of associations, major libraries, Government and international bodies; the boundaries of the subject area have expanded so widely in recent years that decisions on what to include and what to exclude are increasingly difficult to make. Within the traditional fields of information work, librarianship, authorship, publishing, archive work, printing, binding, conservation and the book trade, developments in each field and in their inter-relationships have been profound, and new technologies have transformed methods of work. The simplest guide to whether a term or organization should be included has remained the likelihood or otherwise that anyone reading the literature of these fields will find the term or body regularly mentioned. It is clearly impossible to trace everything, and comments from reviewers and readers are a valuable source of new leads for future editions.

The international nature of the *Glossary* has been retained, although there is a British emphasis; it remains true that no other similar work is currently available in any country, and thus the wide scope, currency, compact format and depth of coverage remain unique. For this edition, over 700 organizations were contacted for up-to-date information; over 2,000 entries in the previous edition have been updated or revised to some extent, and there are over 800 completely new entries and references totalling over 30,000 words of text. That the *Glossary* is of similar size to its predecessors is explained by the quantity of older material that has been removed; older technology terms cannot be discarded wholesale as much is still in use somewhere in the world; historical developments in organizations and professional associations helps our understanding of the present situation; the means by which books were printed and bound over hundreds of years remains fascinating and important. Thus it is necessary always to strike a balance between discarding superseded terms and retaining those of continuing value. New entries, particularly for databases, networks, and computer terminology, have to be introduced with an eye on their probable long-term importance; inclusion of new material merely because it is new is not a safe criterion. Increasingly, brief entries in the *Glossary* will need to be seen as a starting point; once the context is clear, further information can be sought from more detailed, specialist sources. This is especially the case where new technology is concerned: computer jargon and the myriad of new networks and databases cannot be effectively traced through a volume published every four or five years. Only major items and established terms can be included, and the rapid rate of change renders currency difficult.

The relevance and usefulness of the *Glossary* should nonetheless remain of high value to all involved in the information handling industries, the book trade, bibliographers, and those who use their services.

Ray Prytherch
May 1990

Historical Note

In the mid-1930s the Library Association (which was then the only British examining body in librarianship apart from the Library School at London's University College) proposed that an examination paper in library terminology should be set. As there was no publication which was suitable for students studying for this paper, L. M. Harrod immediately set about compiling *The Librarians' Glossary* which when published in 1938 by Grafton was a rather small book of 176 pages. A decision on the setting of such a paper by the Library Association was deferred for two years and then the proposal was not accepted, but in the meantime the *Glossary* apparently filled a need, for it sold steadily and in August 1954 the copy for a revised edition (which was about twice the size of the first edition) was sent to the publisher. This edition however was not published until 1959 owing to the death of Miss Frank Hamel who was the owner of Grafton. Very soon afterwards André Deutsch took over the Grafton publications and new updated editions were called for, prepared and published in 1971 and 1977.

Ever since the end of the Second World War there had been considerable developments in library services, practices and techniques, not only in public services but also in commercial, industrial and university library provision. Not only were librarians expected to know about the various aspects of book production and library services, but also about library co-operation both national and international, all of which were developing rapidly. New technical inventions and developments in non-library fields were influencing the mechanics of library practice, and certain branches of library work were becoming more highly specialised. The *Glossary* endeavoured to cover these in each of the succeeding and greatly enlarged editions of 1971 and 1977, each of which became out of print in a shorter time than had the earlier editions. The basic content of the 4th edition was still the glossary proper, and a rough count indicated that 310 terms had been expanded and 690 terms were defined; of other types of terms, there had been 130 amendments and 400 additions. In order to keep that edition a reasonable size physically, the Latin names of towns used on the title pages of books, the classified list of terms and the précis of the Public Library and Museums Act of 1964 were omitted. Even so, the text occupied 903 pages compared with 694 in the third edition.

The Gower Publishing Company acquired the Grafton Series in 1981, and wished to see a fifth edition published with a minimum of delay. Ray Prytherch, at that time Senior Lecturer at Leeds Polytechnic, was asked to prepare this, and L. M. Harrod acted as Advisory Editor. The fifth edition was published in 1984, which was also the year in which L. M. Harrod died; the foundations which he laid in the *Glossary* have been of enormous value to the profession, and his influence still underlies editions published since his death.

Advice on using the *Glossary*

The word-by-word method of filing is used; acronyms and abbreviations, whether pronounceable or not, are treated as words and filed in the alphabetical sequence in their appropriate place.

Where there is a choice between a full term and an acronym, the entry appears under whichever is likely to be more commonly sought, with a reference from the alternative expression.

Glossary

36-Line Bible. Printed in Latin anonymously at Bamberg *c.* 1460, probably by Heinrich Keffer. It has 882 printed leaves, two columns to a page, 36 lines in each column.

42-Line Bible. *See Mazarin Bible.*

48-Line Bible. The Bible printed by Johann Fust and Peter Schöffer at Mainz on 14 August 1462. The type, a medium gothic of humanistic design, was probably cut specially for this work in which it first appears. Many copies were printed on vellum.

3M/JMRT Grant. A grant system to encourage participation by new librarians in ALA and JUNIOR MEMBERS ROUND TABLE (*q.v.*) activities.

3M/Library Association Library Research Bursary. An annual award given to develop the best research outline submitted on a given theme. The award is intended to fund a six-month programme, with a personal prize also for the winner.

A4 Size. A European standard size of paper, 210 × 297 mm (8.27 × 11.69 inches). *See also DIN, Paper Sizes* for a complete table of sizes.

A5 Size. A European standard size of paper, 148 × 210 mm (5.83 × 8.27 inches). *See also DIN, Paper Sizes* for a complete table of sizes.

A7 Library Card. Standard size card of 74 × 105 mm (2.91 × 4.13 inches), eight of which can be cut from a DIN A4 sheet of 210 × 297 mm (8.27 × 11.69 inches). Also called 'A7 size card'. *See also Card, DIN, Paper Sizes* for a complete table of sizes, *Standard Size Card.*

AACR. Acronym for Anglo-American Cataloguing Rules; the first edition appeared in 1966 (North America) and 1967 (UK). A second edition (AACR 2) published in 1978, is the product of a Revision Committee including representatives from the British Library, the Library of Congress, the British and American Library Associations and the Canadian Committee on Cataloguing. AACR 2 is jointly published by the ALA, LA and Canadian LA. Documents used as a foundation include ISBD(M), ISBD(G) and the PARIS PRINCIPLES (*qq.v.*). The 1988 revision contains an extensive re-drafting of the chapter on computer files.

AAL. Association of Assistant Librarians (*q.v.*).

AALL. American Association of Law Libraries (*q.v.*).

AAP. Association of American Publishers, Inc. (*q.v.*).

AASL. American Association of School Librarians (*q.v.*).

AASL Distinguished Service Award. An annual award to recognize an outstanding contribution to national or international school librarianship or school library development; administered by the AMERICAN ASSOCIATION OF SCHOOL LIBRARIANS (*q.v.*).

ABACUS. Acronym for Association of Bibliographic Agencies of Britain, Australia, Canada and the United States. Holds annual meetings to exchange information and discuss topics of mutual concern.

Abbreviated Catalogue Entry. A catalogue entry (title, subject, translator, etc.) which does not give as much information as the main entry card. *See also Added Entry.*

ABC. Abridged building classification for architects, builders and civil engineers. *See International Council for Building Research, Studies and Documentation.*

Aberrant Copy. One in which binding or machining errors, and not merely defects, occur, and the correct state of which can be recognized.

ABHB. Acronym for *Annual Bibliography of the History of the Printed Book and Libraries*; a series of annual volumes covering output from 1970, issued under the auspices of the IFLA Committee on Rare and Precious Books and Documents. Volume 17A is a cumulated subject index covering 1970–1986.

ABLISS. Association of British Library and Information Studies Schools (*q.v.*).

ABN. Acronym for Australian Bibliographic Network; set up in 1981 this is the major automated cataloguing, search and location system in Australia, and is based on the National Library. Online access is offered by 24 major state and university libraries and 120 smaller libraries, and altogether 230 institutions contribute data; there are 600 registered users, and the network carries some 5 million bibliographic records.

Abridged Decimal Classification. An abridgement of Dewey's *Decimal Classification* intended for use in small libraries.

Abridged Edition. An edition in which the author's text is reduced in length, or which summarizes the original text of a work. *See also Expurgated Edition.*

Abridgement. *Synonymous with* Epitome (*q.v.*).

Absolute Location. *See Fixed Location.*

Absolute Size. *See Exact Size.*

Absorbency. The ability of paper to absorb printing ink. This quality varies widely between different papers.

Absorbent Paper. Paper having the quality of absorbing and retaining ink or other liquid.

ABSTI. (Canadian) Advisory Board on Scientific and Technological Information. Set up in 1969 by the National Research Council to create an information system for engineering and the natural sciences.

Abstract. 1. A form of current bibliography in which sometimes books, but mainly contributions to periodicals, are summarized: they are accompanied by adequate bibliographical descriptions to enable the publications or articles to be traced, and are frequently arranged in classified order. They may be in the language of the original or be translated. Periodicals which contain only abstracts are known as journals of abstracts or abstract journals. Abstracts may be *indicative*, mainly directing to the original; *informative*, giving much information about the original, summarizing the principal arguments and giving the principal data; or *evaluative*, when they comment on the worth of the original. A *general* abstract is one which covers all essential points in an article, and is provided where the interests of readers are varied and known to the abstractor only in general terms. A *selective* abstract contains a condensation of such parts of an article known to be pertinent to the needs of the clientele and is prepared by a librarian (i) for the executives, research workers and specialists within the organization or those normally making use of library services, (ii) in response to a request for a literature search, or (iii) to keep the staff of the organization or users of the services informed of developments in their field as revealed in the daily or periodical press, documents or reports. An *author* abstract is one written by the author of the original article. A *comprehensive abstracting service* endeavours to abstract every publication and article appearing in its subject field, whereas a *selective abstracting service* selects for abstracting only those publications and articles which it considers are likely to be of use to a specific class of reader.   2. The individual entry in an abstract journal. 3. In law libraries two further types of abstract are found: a *locative* abstract, which specifies where the original document can be traced, and an *illative* abstract which specifies the general nature of the material in the document. 4. Printers' type, the design of the face of which is based on mechanical drawing, with more or less straight edges and lines of uniform thickness, having no serifs (sans-serif) or square serifs of the same weight as the letter (block-serif). Futura, Lydian and Optima are examples of sans-serif, and Beton, Cairo, Karnak and Memphis of block-serif. *See also Pseudo Abstract, Synopsis, Type Face.*

Abstract Bulletin.   A publication, produced by any duplication, printing, or other means, which consists of abstracts. Also called 'Abstract journal'.

Abstract Card.   A card, on which is entered an abstract of a document or of an article in a periodical.

Abstract Journal.   *See Abstract.*

Abstracting Service.   The preparation of abstracts, usually in a limited field, by an individual, an industrial organization for restricted use, or a commercial organization; the abstracts being published and supplied regularly to subscribers. Also the organization producing the abstracts. Such services may be either comprehensive or selective. Also called 'Secondary service'.

Abstraction.   The mental process of dividing and grouping which is involved in classifying.

ABTAPL.   Abbreviation for Association of British Theological and Philosophical Libraries. Founded in October 1956 on the recommendation of the International Association of Theological Libraries to promote the interests of libraries, scholars and librarians in these fields and to foster co-operation between them. One of its main objects is to make the bibliographical resources of constituent members as widely known as possible. Publishes *Bulletin* (q.). *See also SCOTAPLL.*

ACA.   Association of Canadian Archivists (*q.v.*).

Academic Libraries.   Those of universities, polytechnics, colleges, schools, and all other institutions forming part of, or associated with, educational institutions.

Acanthus.   An ornament, representing two acanthus leaves pointing different ways, used in tooling book-bindings.

Accent.   A mark used in typesetting to indicate a stress or pitch in spoken language.

Access.   1. (*Information Retrieval*) (i) a device or method whereby a document may be found; (ii) permission and opportunity to use a document; (iii) the approach to any means of storing information, e.g. index, bibliography, catalogue, computer terminal.   2. (*Archives*) Availability of government archives to the general public; such documents are subject to restrictions of confidentiality for a specified number of years. Similar restrictions are also sometimes applied to donations or bequests of other kinds of documents to archive depositories or libraries. Such documents are said to be 'closed' until their access date is reached and 'open' when the period of restriction has expired.

Access Point.   (*Indexing*) Any unique heading, or heading with its QUALIFIER (*q.v.*) in an index. An element used as a means of entry to a file.

Accession.   1. To enter in an ACCESSIONS REGISTER (*q.v.*) particulars of each book in the order of its acquisition.   2. (*Archives*) The act of taking documents into physical custody in an archival agency, records centre, or manuscript repository, and recording same. In some cases transfer of legal title may also be involved.

Accession Book.   *See Accessions Register.*

Accession Card.   *See Accessions Register.*

Accession Date.   The date on which a publication is entered in the ACCESSIONS REGISTER (*q.v.*).

Accession Department.   *See Accessions Section.*

Accession Number.   The number given a book from the ACCESSIONS REGISTER (*q.v.*).

Accession Order.   The arrangement of books on the shelves according to the order of their addition to a class; a numerical and chronological, as distinguished from a classified, arrangement.

Accession part of the Criticism Number.   *See Associated Book.*

Accession Record.   *See Accessions Register.*

Accession Slip.   *See Process Slip.*

Accession Stamp.   A rubber stamp which is impressed on the back of a title page; when the information is written in the appropriate panels of which the stamp is comprised, it gives much information concerning the records, and processing, of the individual book.

Accessions.   A group term indicating additions to the stock of a library.

Accessions Catalogue.   *Synonymous with* ACCESSIONS REGISTER (*q.v.*).

Accessions List.   *See Accessions Register.*

Accessions Register.   The chief record of the stock added to a library. Books are numbered progressively as they are added to stock and entered in the register. It may be in book form, on cards, or on a computer database, and may give a condensed description of the acquisition and history of each book from its reception to its withdrawal.

Accessions Section. A section of a cataloguing or processing department which is concerned with accessioning library materials.

Accident. *See Predicables, Five.*

Accompanying Material. (*Cataloguing*) Material such as an atlas, portfolio of plates, videotape, software, etc., which is intended to be kept in physical conjunction with a publication, and to be used with it.

Accordion Fold. Paper used on line printers or teletypewriters is stored in page lengths that are folded so that each fold is in the opposite direction to the previous fold, in the manner of the bellows of an accordion. Also termed 'Zigzag fold', 'Concertina fold'.

Accreditation (USA). The procedure operated by the American Library Association for approval of schools running courses in library science.

ACHLIS. *See Australian Clearinghouse for Library and Information Science.*

Acid Blast. The spraying of half-tone and zinc plates with acid as part of the etching process. This results in a sharper image.

Acid-Free Paper. In principle, paper which contains no free acid or having a pH value (when determined by the standard method) of 7 or more. Commercial practice permits a limited amount of acid under this designation. *See also pH Value.*

Acid Resist. An acid-proof protective coating which is applied to metal plates before etching.

Ackerley (Joe) Prize. An annual prize awarded by the English Centre of PEN INTERNATIONAL (*q.v.*) for a literary autobiography written in English.

Acknowledgement. Characters sent between receivers and senders of data to indicate readiness to proceed.

ACLIS. Acronym for the Australian Council of Library and Information Services: formed 1988 to 'offer advice to governments and other authorities responsible for libraries, facilitate co-operation and co-ordination of library services in the national interest, and speak for libraries on matters of common concern'. ACLIS will have a State and Territory Infrastructure and is initially supported by the National Library. The successor body to the Australian Advisory Council on Bibliographic Services (AACOBS) and the Australian Library and Information Council (ALIC).

ACORDD. Acronym for the Advisory Committee for the Research and Development Department (of the British Library).

Acoustic Coupler. A computer and a remote terminal connected by a telephone line require an acoustic coupler to receive and transmit sound tones.

Acquisition. The processes of obtaining books and other documents for a library, documentation centre or archive.

Acquisition Department. The department of a library concerned with the ordering of books and possibly their cataloguing and processing also. Often other functions such as obtaining books by exchange or gift, administration of serials and binding are undertaken. *See also Cataloguing Department, Order Department, Technical Services Department.*

Acquisition Record. A record of all books and other material added or in process of being added; it is usually kept in alphabetical order. It may be (1) in two parts consisting of (i) a file of orders completed and of orders outstanding, and (ii) a register of periodicals – including government publications – received, or (2) separate files for each of these records. If a DEAD FILE (*q.v.*) is kept this would also be considered a part of the acquisition record.

Acquisitions Officer. An assistant who undertakes the duties necessary for acquiring new books for a library.

ACRILIS. Acronym of the Australian Centre for Research in Library and Information Science which has been established to pool the resources of documents, reports, theses, expertise and international contacts available at the Information Resources Centre and the Department of Library and Information Science at the Riverina College of Advanced Education at Wagga Wagga, and to collect research reports world-wide with the objects of making them available throughout Australia, promoting research, maintaining indexes to research methodology and abstracts, etc.

ACRL. Association of College and Research Libraries (*q.v.*).

ACRL Academic or Research Librarian of the Year Award. An annual award for outstanding contribution to academic or research librarianship administered by the ASSOCIATION OF COLLEGE AND RESEARCH LIBRARIES (*q.v.*).

Acrography. A method of producing relief surfaces on metal or stone by means of tracing with chalk, for making electrotype or stereotype plates.

Acronym. A word formed from the initial letter or letters of each of the successive parts of the name of an organization, group or term, e.g. IMCE (International Meeting of Cataloguing Experts), Unesco (United Nations Educational Scientific and Cultural Organization), FLIP (Film Library Instantaneous Presentation), WISI (World Information System on Informatics).

Acrophony. In pictographic writing, the principle that the value of each consonant is the value of the first letter of its name, as the *b* of *beth*, the *g* of *gimel*, and the *d* of *daleth*.

ACSI. Association Canadienne des Sciences de l'Information. *See Canadian Association for Information Science.*

Acting Edition. An edition of a play which gives directions concerning exits, entrances, properties, etc. It is intended for actors and is often published in a limp cover, usually of paper.

Action Plan. *See Plan of Action* (EC).

Active Records. *See Current Records.*

Activity. (*Information Retrieval*) A term which indicates that a record in a MASTER FILE (*q.v.*) is used, referred to or altered.

Activity Ratio. (*Information Retrieval*) The ratio of the number of records in a file which have ACTIVITY (*q.v.*) to the total number of records in that file.

Actual Arrangement. *See Ideal Arrangement.*

ACURIL. Acronym for THE ASSOCIATION OF CARIBBEAN UNIVERSITY, RESEARCH AND IINSTITUTE LIBRARIES (*q.v.*).

Ad loc. Abbreviation for *ad locum* (*Lat.* 'At the place cited').

Adams Report. The 'Report on library provision and policy' by Professor W. G. S. Adams to the Carnegie United Kingdom Trustees (CUKT, 1915). The Report, which contained much statistical information, related especially to grants made by Andrew Carnegie to develop public libraries, and presented a view of future policy.

ADAPSO. Association of Data Processing Service Organizations (US), represents some 750 corporate members who provide various computer services – software products, software services, processing services, integrated systems, training, and consultancy.

Adaptation. 1. A book that has been re-written or edited, wholly or in part, for a particular purpose such as for reading by children when the original was intended for adults, or a novel adapted for dramatic presentation. Not to be confused with an abridgement or EPITOME (*q.v.*). 2. A work re-written or presented in another intellectual form to serve a different purpose from the original version, or converted into a different literary form.

Adapter. One who adapts a literary work by simplifying the text, omitting passages, or changing its form, e.g. novel into play.

ADBPA. Association pour le Développement des Bibliothèques Publiques en Afrique. *See Association for the Development of Public Libraries in Africa.*

ADC. Association of District Councils (*q.v.*).

Add Instructions. In the 18th, 19th and 20th edns of Dewey's Decimal Classification, 'add instructions' which specify exactly what digits should be added to a base number, replaced the 'divide-like' notes. *See also Divide Like the Classification.*

Addams Award, Jane. Awarded annually by the Jane Addams Peace Association and the Women's International League for Peace and Freedom to the children's book of the year best combining literary merit, themes of brotherhood, and creative solutions to problems.

Added Copies. Duplicate copies of titles already in stock. Not to be confused with ADDED EDITION (*q.v.*).

Added Edition. A different edition from the one already in the library.

Added Entry. 1. A secondary catalogue entry, i.e. any other than the MAIN ENTRY (*q.v.*). Where printed cards are used, it is a duplicate of the main entry, with the addition of a heading for subject, title, editor, series, or translator. When printed cards are not used, the added entry is formed from the main entry by the omission of all or part of the imprint and collation, and sometimes of sub-titles, and the addition of an appropriate heading. It must not be confused with a CROSS REFERENCE (*q.v.*). Added entries may be made for editor, title, subjects, series, illustrator, translator, etc., and in the case of music, for arranger, librettist, title, medium, form, etc. additionally. *See also General Secondary.* 2. The heading chosen for an added entry.

Added Title Entry. An entry, not being a main entry, made under the title for books with distinctive titles or in cases where title entries would be an advantage, such as anonymous works.

Added Title-page. A title-page additional to the one from which a main entry for a catalogue entry is made. It may precede or follow the one chosen and may be more general, such as a series title-page, or may be equally general, as a title-page in another language, and placed either at the beginning or end of a book. *See also Parallel Title.*

Addendum (*Pl.* Addenda). 1. Matter included in a book after the text has been set. It is printed separately and is inserted at the beginning or end of the text; it is less extensive than a SUPPLEMENT (*q.v.*). 2. A slip added to a printed book. *See also Corrigenda.*

Addition. 1. (*Classification*) The simple extension of an existing Array (*q.v.*), either by interpolation or extrapolation. 2. (*Noun*) A book or other item that has been obtained for addition to the stock of the library. This term is sometimes used to refer to such items before they have been accessioned.

Additional Designation. (*Cataloguing*) Explanatory information, e.g. dates, place of birth or residence or a HONORIFIC TITLE (*q.v.*) added to a name for purposes of distinguishing it from other identical names. *See also Descriptor.*

Address. 1. A label, name or number which designates a register, a location, or a device in a computer where information is stored. 2. That part of an instruction in a computer program which specifies the register, location or device upon which the operation is to be performed.

Address Table. (*Information Retrieval*) A list that links the leading term of each entry to the location, or address, of an entry made in connection with RANDOM ACCESS STORAGE (*q.v.*) in which a fixed location is assigned to each entry.

Adequate Description, principle of. The provision of enough information in a catalogue entry to enable a reader to make a right choice of books. *See also Cataloguing, Principles of.*

ADI. American Documentation Institute (*q.v.*).

Adjacency. The proximity of two or more words specified as a requirement in an online search statement; thus a phrase can be sought, where individual words by themselves would be irrelevant.

Adjustable Classification. A scheme of classification designed by James Duff Brown in 1897. It was superseded by his SUBJECT CLASSIFICATION (*q.v.*).

Adjustable Shelving. Shelves which may be raised or lowered at will. *See also Bracket Shelving, Cantilever Shelving, Slotted Shelving.*

ADLIB. Acronym for Adaptive Library Management System, developed by LMR Information Systems, Maidenhead, UK. A software package for storage and manipulation of bibliographic data, with modules for the various functions – cataloguing, circulation, acquisition, etc. The package is used by several UK public, academic and special libraries; with the SB Telepen system and a Prime minicomputer a total system can be assembled. There is also an ADLIB User Group.

Adolescent Library. *See Teenage Libraries.*

ADONIS. Acronym for Article Delivery Over Network Information Systems; launched in 1981 following a two-year study by Elsevier Science Publishers into the problem of photocopying as it affects commercial publishers, based on a survey of photocopy requests to the British Library Lending Division. It was anticipated that electronic document delivery by the publisher would be cheaper than the present system via libraries, and allow the publishers to receive a royalty. In 1986 it was agreed to run a two-year trial of storing and supplying 219 high-use biomedical journals on CD-ROM. During 1987 and 1988 the contents of the journals were indexed each week (bibliographic details, not subject indexing) at Excerpta Medica in Amsterdam, and each item indexed (articles, letters, abstracts and other material of lasting editorial interest, but not announcements, contents pages or advertisements) was identified by a unique ADONIS article number. The index information was sent in machine-readable form (ASCII) to the Scanmedia Ltd bureau in the UK where the content of the articles was scanned. The scanned contents, together with the ASCII index information were then preformatted and a weekly master disc was produced by Philips and DuPont Optical Company (PDO) in Hanover, from which copies were prepared and dispatched to the participating document supply centres. The main objective of the project was to learn about the impact of such a service on the document fulfilment centres and their customers. Major cost savings were identified, and a commercial service is planned to begin in January 1991.

Adopt a Book Appeal.   Launched 1987 by the National Preservation Office of the BRITISH LIBRARY (*q.v.*) to raise funds for conservation treatment of stock. Major sponsors receive an illuminated scroll, and the conserved item carries a bookplate with the sponsor's name.

Adoption of the Public Libraries Acts.   The decision of the local authority to take the necessary administrative and legal steps to provide library facilities as permitted by law.

ADP.   1. Abbreviation for automated (or automatic) data processing.   2. *See Association of Database Producers.*

ADRIS.   Acronym of Association for the Development of Religious Information Services which was founded to promote co-ordination and co-operation among existing and new information services pertinent to religion by sharing relevant information, identifying needs, considering proposed projects, and developing co-operative ventures. Functions from Fordham University, Bronx, NY. Publishes *ADRIS Newsletter.*

ADRS.   *See Automatic Document Request Service.*

Adult Department.   The department of a library which provides books for the use of adults.

Adult Independent Learners.   *See Adult Learners.*

Adult Learners.   People who are following organized or independent courses of study, but who are not enrolled in an educational establishment. Usually, but not always, people who are older than the conventional 'student' age group. The term Adult Independent Learner (AIL) is also used.

Adult Literacy Project (UK).   A BBC project, begun in 1975, aimed at reducing adult illiteracy in the United Kingdom. A national campaign to reduce the difficulties of an estimated two million adults with serious difficulties in reading, writing and spelling. It was a direct response to the main recommendation of the Russell and Alexander Committees on Adult and Community Education.

Advance Copy (Sheet).   A copy of a book, usually bound, but sometimes in sheets, to serve as a proof of the binder's work, for review, notice, advertising or other purposes.

Advancement of Librarianship in the third World (ALP).   An IFLA core programme established in 1984 to plan a cohesive strategy to create the best possible conditions for self-development of library services. In the programme the following tasks are emphasized: enlargement or participation of the Third World countries in IFLA's work; support and advice to librarians, library schools, and library associations in those areas; the strengthening of regional co-operation by establishing regional standing committees and information centres; the furthering of professional education and training by special seminars and through exchange of librarians within Third World countries. The ALP programme is located within IFLA headquarters in The Hague. An explanatory paper *IFLA and the Third World* was published by IFLA in 1987. Abbreviated ALP.

Advancement of Literacy Award.   An annual award of the PUBLIC LIBRARY ASSOCIATION (*q.v.*) of the ALA to an American publisher or bookseller who has made a significant contribution to literacy advancement.

Advertisement File.   A file of advertisements, usually arranged by the name of firm or of product. Such files are most often maintained in a firm's library or advertising agency.

Advice Centre.   An area in a central, branch or mobile library, or in non-library premises, devoted to the provision of advice, usually on social issues.

Adviser, Readers'.   *See Readers' Adviser.*

Advisory Group for Aerospace Research and Development.   *See AGARD.*

Advisory Group on National Bibliographic Control.   Established in the USA through the joint effort of the National Science Foundation, the National Commission on Libraries and Information Science (NCLIS) and the Council on Library Resources (CLR), with the responsibility of advising the sponsoring agencies on how best to co-ordinate their programmes and recommending priorities for action.

Advocates' Library, Edinburgh.   *See National Library of Scotland.*

Aerial Map.   A map made from one or more photographs taken from above the surface of the earth.

Aerograph.   An instrument, which by means of compressed air, blows a fine spray of liquid colour onto a lithograph stone or drawing, or when re-touching photographs.

Aerospace/Defence Librarians Sub-Group.   Formed 1988/89 as a part of the Library Association Industrial Group.

AETLTA (U.K.).   Acronym for the Association for the Education and Training of Library Technicians and Assistants. Formed in 1981 from the Library Assistants' Certificate Tutors' Group. Unites those actively concerned with the development of sub-professional qualifications.

Affective Relation.   One of the ten analytical relations used in the SEMANTIC CODE (*q.v.*) in which one concept is influenced or determined by another.

Affiliated Library. One which is part of a library system, but has its own board of management and is not administered as part of the system.

AFIPS. American Federation of Information Processing Societies (*q.v.*).

AFNOR. Acronym for Association Français de Normalisation, the French equivalent of the BRITISH STANDARDS INSTITUTION (*q.v.*).

Afro-Caribbean Library Association. *See National Afro-Caribbean Library Association.*

Against the Grain. Said of paper which has been folded at right angles to the direction in which the fibres tend to lie. In a well-printed book the back fold of the paper is never 'against the grain'; the grain direction should run from head to tail in the finished book in order that the pages will lie flat when the book is opened. *See also Cross Direction, Grain Direction, With The Grain.*

AGARD. Acronym of the Advisory Group for Aerospace Research and Development, an organization within the North Atlantic Treaty Organization (NATO), which exists to bring together the leading personalities of the NATO nations in the fields of science and technology relating to aerospace for the following purposes, amongst others: (a) to exchange scientific and technical information; (b) to continuously stimulate advances in the aerospace sciences relevant to strengthening the common defence posture; (c) to provide assistance to member nations for the purpose of increasing their scientific and technical potential; (d) to recommend effective ways for member nations to use their research and development capabilities for the common benefit of the NATO community. A number of AGARD publications are useful in the field of general documentation and librarianship.

Agate. 1. (*Binding*) A bloodstone or agate used in hand binding to burnish gold or coloured edges. 2. (*Printing*) Used to denote 5½ point type.

Agate Line. An American standard of measurements for the depth of columns of advertising space in a newspaper. Fourteen agate lines make one column inch.

Agent. An individual or firm acting as a middleman between librarian and publisher in the acquisition of material. An agent is commonly used in connection with periodical subscriptions, back numbers of periodicals, and foreign publications. *See also Literary Agent.*

Agglutinative Symbol. A symbol, in a system of NOTATION (*q.v.*) in a classification scheme, two or more parts of which have a constant and inflexible symbol.

AGLINET. Abbreviation for Agricultural Libraries Information Network which was established within the framework of the International Association of Agricultural Librarians and Documentalists (IAALD), for the purpose of organizing co-operation among agricultural libraries at regional and international levels.

AGRA. Association of Genealogists and Record Agents (*q.v.*).

AGRALIN. National Agricultural Bibliographic Network for the Netherlands; established 1980 at Wageningen. Fifty members at present.

AGREP. Permanent Inventory of Agricultural Research Projects; an EC databank of on-going research relevant to agriculture in its widest sense.

AGRICOLA. *See National Agricultural Library.*

Agricultural Librarians in Colleges and Universities. A subject interest group (UK) associated with Aslib's Biological and Agricultural Sciences Group. Abbreviated ALCU.

Agricultural Libraries Information Network. *See AGLINET.*

AGRIS. Abbreviation for International Information System for the Agricultural Sciences and Technology, which was adopted in November 1971 at the 16th Conference of the Food and Agricultural Organization (FAO) of the United Nations. Collects information on the agricultural literature of the world through 120 national, regional and international centres co-ordinated by the AGRIS Centre at FAO Headquarters, Rome. The data is processed at the AGRIS Processing Unit in Vienna and made available monthly in two formats – the printed AGRINDEX, and the on-line AGRIS database.

AID. Association Internationale des Documentalists et Techniciens de l'Information. *See International Association of Documentalists and Information Officers.*

AIDBA. Association Internationale pour le Développement de la Documentation des Bibliothèques et des Archives en Afrique. *See International Association for the Development of Documentation, Libraries and Archives in Africa.*

AIESI. *See Association Internationale des Écoles des Sciences de l'Information.*

AIIM. *See Association for Information and Image Management.*

AIInfSc. Associate of the INSTITUTE OF INFORMATION SCIENTISTS (*q.v.*).

AIL. Adult independent learners. *See Adult Learners.*

AIL. Association of International Libraries (*q.v.*).

AIM. Advanced Information in Medicine; a European Community programme developing a framework for medical informatics. Initial phase 1988-90.

Air Brush. *Synonymous with Aerograph* (*q.v.*).

Air-dried. Hand-made, or good machine-made paper or brown paper which is hung over lines and dried slowly in air at a uniform temperature, as distinct from paper which is machine-dried in heat.

Aisle. The passageway between two parallel bookcases.

AITRC. *See Applied Information Technologies Research Center.*

AJL. Association of Jewish Libraries (*q.v.*).

Ajouré Binding. A style of binding practised in the last third of the fifteenth century in Venice. It was in the traditional Eastern manner with arabesques, gilding, and cut-out leather, over a coloured background.

A.L. *See A.L.S.*

ALA. *See American Library Association* or *Associateship.*

ALA Trustee Citations. Two annual awards to recognize efforts of library board members; administered by the AMERICAN LIBRARY TRUSTEE ASSOCIATION (*q.v.*).

ALAG. *See Asian Librarians and Arts Officers Group.*

ALANET. Electronic mail and information service of the American Library Association. Features XMAIL ('Cross Mail') to provide a direct connection between the electronic service and telex networks. *See also LA-NET, LIBNET.*

Alaska Seal. Sheepskin or cowhide made to imitate sealskin.

ALBA/DASP/SAMKAT. Danish research library bibliographic network, administered at the National Library, Copenhagen. Established 1978; 30 full members, but 200 other libraries use the network for searching.

Albertype. A process of making pictures with a gelatine-covered plate, the printing being a variety of photogravure.

Albion Press. Invented in 1823 by R. W. Cope of London; it was an improvement on the STANHOPE PRESS (*q.v.*) and enabled sufficient pressure for printing to be achieved with a single pull on the spindle bar. It was simple in construction, durable, cheap, and easy to work. Its American counterpart was the Washington Press, and its German one, the Hagar Press. The Albion and COLUMBIAN (*q.v.*) presses were used commercially well into the twentieth century; several British private presses used the Albion.

Album. 1. A book of envelopes or jackets for holding gramophone records, usually with a decorative cover and sometimes with descriptive notes. 2. A book of blank leaves in which literary extracts, quotations, poems, drawings, photographs, autographs, newspaper cuttings, stamps, etc. are written, inserted or fixed.

Albumen Process. The most commonly used sensitizer for coating photo offset plates.

ALCL. Association of London Chief Librarians (*q.v.*).

Alcophoto. A photo-mechanical process for making zinc, aluminium or other litho plates.

Alcove. A recess formed by placing two presses at right angles to a wall, and touching it at one end. Also called a CELL (*q.v.*).

Alcove Mark. In an old library, the mark used to indicate in which alcove any particular book may be found. Books in such libraries are arranged according to location and not classification. *See also Fixed Location.*

ALCU. *See Agricultural Librarians in Colleges and Universities.*

ALCTS. *See Association for Library Collections and Technical Services.*

Aldine (Italian) Style. 1. (*Printing*) Ornaments of solid face without any shading whatever, used by Aldus and other early Italian printers. The ornaments are Arabic in character, and are suitable for early printed books. 2. (*Binding*) Late fifteenth and early sixteenth century Venetian bindings in brown or red morocco which were carried out for Aldus Manutius. They had the title, or the author's name in a simple panel in the middle of the front cover of a book so that it could be seen when the book lay on a shelf or table. Early examples were decorated in blind with an outer frame and a central device. It is assumed that as Aldus was the leading printer in Venice he would supervise the binding of his books which was done by the Greek binders he employed.

Aldine Leaves. Small binders' stamps bearing a leaf and stem design; used on books bound for ALDUS (*q.v.*) *c.* 1510.

Aldine Press. The Italian press which achieved fame for introducing italic type in 1501. The Press was founded by Aldus Pius Manutius. *See also Aldus, Italic.*

Aldus. An Italian publishing firm founded at Venice in 1495 by Teobaldo Manucci (Aldus Pius Manutius; Aldo Manuzio) 1450–1515. Aldus specialized in small-size editions of Greek and Latin classics which were published between 1494 and 1515, and the first Italic (*q.v.*) type, which was cut for Aldus by Griffi, was first used for a small format edition of the classics. Aldus's printer's device of anchor and dolphin has frequently been used by other printers, e.g. William Pickering for the Chiswick Press in the late nineteenth century. Between 1515 and 1533 the press was managed by his brothers-in-law, the Asolani, during which time the work of the press deteriorated. In 1533 his youngest son Paulius Manutius (1512–74) took over the press and concentrated on Latin classics.

ALEBCI. Acronym of Asociación Latinamericana de Escuelas de Bibliotecologia y Ciencias de la Información. Established in 1970 at Buenos Aires to further library education in Latin America.

Alexander Prize. An annual award for a historical essay; administered by the Royal Historical Society.

Alexandrian Library. The greatest library of the ancient classical world; founded in the fourth century BC at Alexandria which was then a pre-eminent international meeting point for trade and culture. By the first century BC the library held over 500,000 manuscripts, catalogued in the 'Pinakes' of Callimachus – a form of bibliography giving names of author and a summary of the text. The materials were lost and the library destroyed during the civil wars of the third and fourth century AD. In 1987 Unesco launched an appeal to re-establish a library at Alexandria, to be operated by the government of Egypt as part of an Arab and Middle Eastern research centre.

Alfa. An alternative name for esparto grass. *See Esparto.*

Algol. Acronym for Algorithmic Language, an international algebraic, procedure-oriented language which is similar in concept and content to Fortran.

Algorithm. (*Indexing*) Instructions for carrying out a series of logical procedural steps in a specified order.

Algorithmic Code. One that has rules for converting source (i.e. common language) words into code equivalents.

Algraphy. The process of printing from aluminium plates by lithographic and offset printing. Also called 'Aluminography'.

ALIA. *See Australian Library and Information Association.*

ALIC. *See Australian Library and Information Council.*

Alienation. (*Archives*) The act of transferring, or losing, custody or ownership of documents to an agency or person not officially connected with the organization whose documents are involved.

Alignment. 1. The exact correspondence in a straight line of the top and bottom of the letters and characters in a fount. 2. The arrangement of type in straight lines. 3. The setting of lines of type so that ends appear even at the margins.

ALIS. Automated library information system; a bibliographic network providing a union catalogue for the Scandinavian technological university libraries, and based at the Danish National Library of Technology. Established 1970; 18 members.

ALISA. Australian Library and Information Science Abstracts, an annual subject index to Australian literature in the fields of LIS, published by the AUSTRALIAN CLEARINGHOUSE FOR LIBRARY AND INFORMATION SCIENCE (*q.v.*) from 1982. Covers monographs, research reports, conference papers, periodical articles and unpublished material from Australian sources; articles and reports by Australian authors from other sources are also included. Online access is available.

ALISE. *See Association for Library and Information Science Education.*

ALJH. Association of Libraries of Judaica and Hebraica in Europe (*q.v.*).

All Along. The method of sewing by hand the sections (usually on cords or tapes) of a book, when the thread goes 'all along', or from KETTLE STITCH (*q.v.*) to kettle stitch in each section. Also used to describe machine book-sewing when each section is sewn with the full number of stitches. *See also Two Sheets On.*

All-over Style. The style of book decoration which covers the whole of the side of a binding, as distinct from a corner, centre or border design, whether made up of a single motif, different motifs, or a repeated motif.

All Published. Used in a catalogue entry and in other connotations, concerning a work, the publication of which has been started but is not completed. Also relates to all the issues of a periodical, publication of which has ceased. *See also Ceased Publication.*

All-purpose Linotype. A machine similar to the LUDLOW (*q.v.*).

All Rights Reserved. A phrase placed in a book usually on the back of the title-page, signifying that the copyright is reserved, and that proceedings may be taken against any person infringing that copyright.

All Through. *Synonymous with* Letter by Letter alphabetization. *See Alphabetization.*

All-Union Institute of Scientific and Technical Information. *See Viniti.*

Allocate, to. The process of deciding into which department or library of a library system books and other material shall be allocated.

Allocation. The act of allocating books. *See also Allocate, to.*

Allonym. A false name, especially the name of some person assumed by an author to conceal identity or gain credit; an alias; a pseudonym.

Allusion Book. A collection of contemporary allusions to a famous writer.

Almanac(k). A publication, usually an annual, containing a variety of useful facts of a miscellaneous nature, and statistical information. It was originally a projection of the coming year by days, months, holidays, etc.

ALP. Advancement of Librarianship in the Third World (*q.v.*).

Alphabet Length. (*Printing*) The length, usually stated in points, of the twenty-six letters of the alphabet. The relative compactness of a type face is determined by the comparison of alphabet lengths. The alphabet length in points, divided into 341, gives the number of 'characters per pica'. *See also Type Face.*

Alphabet Mark.   A mark, such as the CUTTER AUTHOR MARK (*q.v.*), which is incorporated in the call number of a book to enable alphabetic order to be maintained on the shelves without the use of abnormally long symbols.

Alphabet of Symbols.   A set of distinct recognizable and repeatable characters or symbols which are used for identifying documents, as the notation used in a scheme of classification, e.g. the figures, capital letters and lower case letters used in Bliss's Bibliographic Classification, or the 10 numerals, 26 capital letters, 26 lower case letters, 8 Greek letters and 9 punctuation marks used in the Colon Classification. Also called 'Base of Symbolism'.

Alphabetic Subject Catalogue.   One arranged alphabetically by subjects, usually without subdivisions.

Alphabetic Writing.   The third, and final, stage in the development of writing, in which a single symbol was used to represent a single distinctive sound feature in the spoken language, rather than ideas or syllables. *See also Phonetic Writing, Pictography.*

Alphabetical Arrangement.   The systematic arrangement of entries in a catalogue, index, bibliography or other list of items, or of books on the shelves of a library in alphabetical order of authors, subjects, titles or other distinguishing characteristics. *See also Alphabetization.*

Alphabetical Catalogue.   One in which the author, title, and/or subject entries are arranged alphabetically.

Alphabetical Collateral Search.   An examination of entries under headings alphabetically adjacent to, or near to, the headings covered in a HIERARCHICAL SEARCH. (*q.v.*). *See also Substitution Generic, Systematic Collateral Search.*

Alphabetical Device.   One of the principles used in the Colon Classification for determining the sequence of subjects. It is used only when no better systematic order is apparent, e.g. proper names, trade names, etc.

Alphabetical Subject Index.   An alphabetical list of all subjects named, or dealt with, in a book classification scheme, or classified catalogue, together with reference to the place(s) where each subject occurs.

Alphabetico-classed Catalogue.   An alphabetical subject catalogue, in which entries are not made under specific subjects, as in the dictionary form, but under broad subjects arranged alphabetically, and each sub-divided alphabetically by subject to cite more specific sub-divisions. Author and title entries may be included in the same alphabet under the appropriate subject headings.

Alphabetico-direct Catalogue.   One in which 'direct' headings, i.e. consisting of natural language and the natural form of phrases, as 'stamp collecting', 'subject cataloguing', are used, the headings being arranged in alphabetical order. *Synonymous with* ALPHABETICO-SPECIFIC CATALOGUE.

Alphabetico-specific Catalogue.   *Synonymous with* ALPHABETICO-DIRECT CATALOGUE (*q.v.*).

Alphabetico-specific Subject Catalogue.   One in which alphabetically arranged headings state precisely the subject of the literary unit indexed, whether it is a whole document or only a portion such as a chapter, section or paragraph of it. Also called 'Dictionary index'. *See also Basic Analysis, Collateral Reference, Downward Reference, Qualified List, Upward Reference.*

Alphabetization.   Arranging a list of words, names, or phrases according to the letters of the alphabet. In the main there are two methods in use: 1, 'word by word', or 'nothing before something';   2, 'letter by letter' strictly according to the letters irrespective of their division into words, or of punctuation. In 1969 the British Standards Institution issued a Standard (no. 1749) on *Alphabetical arrangement* in which it recommends the 'word by word' or 'nothing-before-something' method whereby items which have the same first or second words are arranged in the alphabetical order of the subsequent word, e.g.

Black Acts	Blackberry
Black Book	Blackburn
Black Earth	
NSW	Newcastle (NSW, Australia)
New Castle (Pa., U.S.A.)	Newels
New Haven (Conn., U.S.A.)	Newhaven (England)
New Testament	News-room
New York	Newton
Newark	

If the 'letter-by-letter' or 'follow-through' method were used these words would be arranged

Black Acts	Blackburn
Blackberry	Black Earth
Black Book	
Newark	News-room
(Newcastle (NSW, Australia)	New Testament
New Castle (Pa., U.S.A.)	Newton
Newels	New York
New Haven (Conn., U.S.A.)	NSW
Newhaven (England)	

Alpha-Numerical Indexing.   An indexing scheme which uses a combination of the alphabet and numbers, broad subjects being listed in alphabetical order and the subdivisions under them being given numbers. No attention need be paid to the first letter of the first word, and there may or may not be a hierarchical significance. The documents are identified with the number and filed according to it.

ALS.   Automated Library System Ltd. Company producing automated library circulation control systems. Various packages are available.

A.L.S.   (Autograph letter signed). A letter entirely in the handwriting of the signer. If unsigned it is referred to by the letters 'A.L.'; if written by someone else but signed, by 'L.S.'; if typed and signed by hand, by 'T.L.S.'.

ALSC. *See Association for Library Service to Children.*

ALTA. American Library Trustee Association (*q.v.*).

ALTA Literacy Award. An annual award made in recognition of a significant contribution to the literacy problem in the US, administered by the AMERICAN LIBRARY TRUSTEE ASSOCIATION (*q.v.*).

ALTA Major Benefactors Honor Award. An annual award of recognize outstanding gifts, administered by the AMERICAN LIBRARY TRUSTEE ASSOCIATION (*q.v.*).

Alterations. (*Printing*) Changes made in a PROOF. (*q.v.*).

Alternative Locations. Bliss considers that one of the principles of classification is to provide alternative locations for certain studies or sciences regarded from different points of view or preferred in other allocations.

Alternative Title. 1. A secondary title following the words 'or', 'a', or 'an'. More commonly known as the SUBTITLE (*q.v.*). 2. One of several titles, which in particular circumstances (e.g. in multi-language publications with titles in the languages of the text) could be used as the MAIN TITLE (*q.v.*).

Aluminium Plates. Extremely flexible plates used in OFFSET PRINTING (*q.v.*).

Aluminography. *Synonymous with* ALGRAPHY (*q.v.*).

Alvey Programme. The Alvey Committee (chairman John Alvey, of British Telecom) was established in 1982 by Kenneth Baker, the then Minister for Information Technology. Its report – *Programme for Advanced Information Technology* (HMSO 1982) – the 'Alvey Report', proposed a programme of collaborative research in four main areas: software engineering; man-machine interfaces; intelligent knowledge-based systems; very large-scale integration. The British Government devoted some £350 million to the programme over a five year period.

AMA. Acronym of the (British) Association of Metropolitan Authorities which was formed on 31 July 1973 to watch over, protect and promote the interests, rights, powers and duties of its member authorities; also to provide a forum for the discussion of common concern, and to provide such central services for its member authorities as it may consider appropriate. Members were the Greater London Council, the Inner London Education Authority, the City of London Corporation, the 32 London Borough Councils, the 6 Metropolitan County Councils and the 36 Metropolitan District Councils. The Association was financed by subscriptions of the member Authorities. Published *Municipal Review* (m.). *See also Association of District Councils.* The Authorities were disbanded in March 1986.

Ambiguous Title. One which is so vague that it may be misunderstood. In a catalogue, amplification may be made in brackets immediately following the title, or in a note.

Ambrogal Printing. An offset printing process invented by Ambrosius Galetzka; it is reminiscent of American aquatone printing. Sheets of celluloid are prepared for lithographic printing. *See also Aquatone.*

AMCL. Association of Metropolitan Chief Librarians (*q.v.*).

American Association of Law Libraries. Established 1906. Aims 'to promote librarianship, to develop and increase the usefulness of law libraries, to cultivate the science of law librarianship and to foster a spirit of co-operation among members of the profession'. Publishes *Law Library Journal* (q.). Abbreviated AALL.

American Association of School Librarians.   A Division of the American Library Association since 1 January 1951; became an associated organization of the National Education Association in 1969. It is concerned with the improvement and extension of library services in elementary and secondary schools. Abbreviated AASL. Publishes *School Media Quarterly* (q.)– formerly *School Libraries* until Fall 1971.

American Book Award.   This award made by the Association of American Book Publishers is for a book written, translated or designed by an American Citizen during the preceding year.

American Booksellers Association.   A trade association with an overall membership of some 6000 firms. Actively seeks membership of librarians and links with the profession.

American Braille.   An obsolete variation of BRAILLE (*q.v.*).

American Documentation Institute.   *See American Society for Information Science.*

American Federation of Information Processing Societies.   Founded in the USA in 1961 to serve as a national voice for the computing field; to advance knowledge of the information processing sciences. Abbreviated AFIPS.

American Finish.   *See Paper Finishes.*

American Library Association (ALA).   The American Library Association, founded in 1876, is the oldest and largest national library association in the world. Its concern spans all types of libraries: state, public, school and academic libraries; special libraries serving persons in government, commerce and industry, the arts, the armed services, hospitals, prisons, and other institutions. With a membership of libraries, librarians, library trustees, and other interested persons from every state and many countries of the world, the Association is the chief advocate for the people of the United States in their search for the highest quality of library and information services. The Association maintains a close working relationship with more than 70 other library associations in the United States, Canada, and other countries, and it works closely with many other organizations concerned with education, research, cultural development, recreation, and public service. On 31 August 1987, the Association had 2772 organization members and 42,373 personal members – a total of 45,145. The Headquarters are in Chicago. The mission of the American Library Association is to provide leadership for the development, promotion, and improvement of library and information services and the profession of librarianship in order to enhance learning and ensure access to information for all. There are 15 Round Tables. Specialized offices within the ALA are: Office for Intellectual Freedom; Office for Library Outreach Services; Office for Library Personnel Resources; Office for Public Information; Office for Research; and the Washington Office. There are eleven divisions: American Association of School Librarians, American Library Trustee Association, Association for Library Collections and Technical Services, Association for Library Services to Children, Association of College and Research Libraries, Association of Specialized and Co-operative Library Agencies, Library Administration and Management Association, Library and Information Technology Association, Public Library Association, Reference and Adult Services Division, Young Adult Services Division (*qq.v*). Extensive programmes of monograph and serial publications, including *American Libraries* (11 p.a.).

American Library Trustee Association. A Division of the American Library Association since 1 September 1961; founded in 1890 to study and encourage the development of libraries in all types of community and all types of library services in the USA and Canada; to study the library programmes of the several states and of Canada, and to disseminate the information gained from such study; to strengthen state trustee organizations. Abbreviated ALTA. Publishes *The Public Library Trustee* (4 p.a.).

American Merchant Marine Library Association. Founded in 1921 to maintain a library for the free use of the officers and crews of American ocean-going vessels of passenger, freight, tramp and tanker fleets, Great Lakes fleets, Coast Guard personnel and other members of the armed forces, lighthouses, lightships, etc. More than a million volumes are in circulation in American ships; six shore libraries are maintained. Abbreviated AMMLA.

American National Standards Institution, Inc. The USA organization for issuing recommendations as to the production, distribution and consumption of goods and services; it is the American equivalent to the BRITISH STANDARDS INSTITUTION (*q.v.*) and is the United States member of the INTERNATIONAL ORGANIZATION FOR STANDARDIZATION (*q.v.*). Standards issued by the Institute are known as American National Standards. From 1918, when it was founded, until 1966 it was known as the American Standards Association (ASA) and from then until October 1969 as the United States of America Standards Institute (USASI) its Standards being known as USA Standards. Abbreviated ANSI. *See also International Standards, National Information Standards Organization, National Institute of Standards and Technology, Z39.*

American Russia. Cowhide used for bookbinding.

American Society for Information Science. Founded in 1937 as the American Documentation Institute; expanded in 1952 to permit personal membership, and changed to its current name from 1968. It aims to improve the provision of knowledge, leadership and development opportunities for information professionals and organizations, to enhance and advance the state of the art of information science and its applications; stimulates discussion, professional development, research, and policy formulation. There are 21 special interest groups: Arts and humanities; Automated language processing; Behavioural and social science; Biological and chemical information systems; Classification research; Computerized retrieval services; Education for information science; Foundations of information science; Information analysis and evaluation; Information generation and publishing; International information issues; Law and information technology; Library automation and networks; Management; Medical information systems; Numeric data bases; Office information systems; Personal computers; Storage and retrieval technology; Technology, information and society; User online interaction. Publishes *Journal of the American Society for Information Science* (6 p.a.), *Bulletin of ASIS* (6 p.a.), *Annual Review of Information Science and Technology* (ARIST), conference proceedings, handbook, and monographs. Co-sponsor of INFORMATION SCIENCE ABSTRACTS (*q.v.*). Abbreviated: ASIS.

American Society of Indexers. Founded 1968 with the following objectives: to (a) improve the quality of indexing and to secure useful standards for the field; (b) act as an advisory body on the qualification and remuneration of indexers to which authors, editors, publishers and others may apply for guidance; (c) issue from time to time books, articles and other material on the subject of indexing and to co-operate with other societies and organizations in such publication; (d) defend and safeguard the professional interests of indexers; (e) co-operate with other societies and organizations in the field of indexing and information science and especially with The Society of Indexers (Great Britain). It is affiliated to the Society of Indexers, whose journal, *the Indexer* (2 p.a.), serves as the journal of both societies. Publishes *Newsletter* (irreg. membs.). Abbreviated ASL.

American Standard Code for Information Interchange. *See ASCII.*

American Theological Library Association. Founded 1947 to bring its members into closer working relations with each other and with the American Association of Theological Schools; to study the distinctive problems of theological seminary libraries; to increase the professional competence of the membership; and to improve the library service to theological education. Publishes *Proceedings* (a.), *Newsletter* (q. to membs.), *Index to Religious Periodicals Literature*, 1949 to date. Abbreviated ATLA.

American Trust for the British Library. Formed 1979 primarily to fill the gaps in the British Library's collections of American materials during the period 1880–1950 when funds were small. Encourages private donations and sales, and liaises with American booksellers.

Americana. Material relating to the Americas,,whether printed about or in, the Americas, or written by Americans or not.

Amigos. A southwestern US consortium with extensions into Mexico; mainly academic library members. Based in Dallas, Texas.

AMMLA. American Merchant Marine Library Association (*q.v.*).

Ampersand. The abbreviation, sign or character for the word 'and', thus: &. Also called 'Short and'.

A.Ms.S. (*Pl.* A.Mss.S.) (autograph manuscript signed). A manuscript wholly in the handwriting of the signer.

-Ana (often with the euphonic *i* added: IANA). A suffix to names of persons or places, denoting a collection of books, anecdotes, literary gossip, or other facts or pieces of information, e.g. Americana, Johnsoniana, Lincolniana.

Analects.   A collection of literary fragments, gleanings or other miscellaneous written passages.

Analet.   A 'small analysis' or statement of the (*classification*) steps taken to analyse a complex subject.

Analphabet.   A person who did not have the opportunity to learn to read (for whatever reason) but would be able to learn to read if the opportunity were given. One who is totally illiterate.

Analogue Computer.   A computer which operates by directly representing changes in one phenomenon by changes in another. *See also Digital Computer.*

Analysis.   1. (*Cataloguing*) A book is said to be 'analysed' when any part of it is recorded separately in a catalogue by means of an ANALYTICAL ENTRY (*q.v.*).   2. (*Classification*) Breaking down a subject into its facets. *See Facet.*   3. (*Information retrieval*) (i) The perusal of source materials and the selection of analytics (e.g. index entries, subject headings, keywords and descriptors) that are considered to be of sufficient probable importance to justify the effort of rendering them searchable in an information-retrieval system. (ii) A detailed examination of a document to determine and state its characteristics, including abstracting, classifying and indexing.

Analytic.   *See Analytical Entry.*

Analytical Bibliography.   The kind of bibliography which determines facts and data concerning a publication by examining the signatures, catchwords, cancels and watermarks, and making a record in an approved form of the results. Also called 'critical' or 'historical bibliography'. *See also Bibliography, Descriptive Bibliography.*

Analytical Cataloguing.   The branch of cataloguing which is concerned with making analytical entries. *See Analytical Entry.*

Analytical Entry.   An entry in a catalogue for part of a book, periodical or other publication, article or contribution of separate authorship in a collection (volume of essays, festschrift, serial, volume of musical compositions, etc.). The entry includes a reference to the work containing it. The entry is supplementary to the comprehensive, or MAIN ENTRY (*q.v.*), for the whole work. Such entries, called 'Analytics', may be made under authors, subjects or titles. In special libraries they are often made for significant paragraphs, sections, tables, etc., and occasionally for particular facts or figures, in addition to parts or chapters of books, units of a series and of a collection.

Analytical Index.   1. An index in which the entries are not arranged in one straightforward alphabetical sequence, but the subject of the work is divided into a number of main headings and these in turn are subdivided as necessary, each sequence of entries being arranged alphabetically. The abstracts (or papers) included in the volume to be indexed are then classified according to these main headings and so placed in their appropriate places in the analytical index.   2. An alphabetical subject index to information in articles of broader connotation than the subject index headings, as in an encyclopaedia.   3. A classified index to material under specific subjects, as in a reference book.

Analytical Method.   In classification, the breaking down of a specific subject into constituent elements according to a given formula, these elements then being reassembled in a predetermined order designed to give the most useful arrangement.

Analytical Note.   1. That part of an analytical entry containing the reference to the document for which the entry has been made.   2. A note following a MAIN ENTRY (*q.v.*) detailing the separate items which comprise the whole document.

Analytical Relations.   The ten relations used in the SEMANTIC CODE (*q.v.*) developed by the Center for Documentation and Communication at Western Reserve University, to link words to descriptors (here called semantic factors), to control the descriptor language. They are: categorical, intrinsic, inclusive, comprehensive, productive, affective, instrumental, negative, attributive, and simulative relation. *See also Semantic Factor.*

Analytico-synthetic Classification.   A scheme which gives the classifier the maximum autonomy in constructing numbers for new specific subjects not enumerated in the schedules. Ranganathan's *Colon Classification* was the first scheme of this kind. A FACETED CLASSIFICATION (*q.v.*).

Anastatic Printing.   A process or method of obtaining facsimile impressions of any printed design or engraving by transferring it to a plate of zinc, which, on being subjected to the action of an acid, is etched or eaten away, with the exception of the parts covered with ink. These parts are left in relief and can be printed from readily.

Anastatic Reprint.   An unaltered reprint made in the mid nineteenth century, especially in France, by making an inked offset of the type of metal plates which were etched in relief.

And others.   When there are more than three joint authors, collaborators, etc., a catalogue entry may be made only under the first to be mentioned followed by *and others*, or by *et al.* (*q.v.*).

ANDBP.   Acronym of the Association Nationale pour le Développement des Bibliothèques Publiques, which was formed in July 1971 to give all French people easier access to information, culture and life-long education by promoting the development of networks of modern public libraries.

Andersen (Hans Christian) Medals.   In full, the International Hans Christian Andersen Youth Book Awards. First awarded in 1956 (to Eleanor Farjeon for *The Little Book Room*), now awarded to a living author, and to an illustrator as well, whose complete work has made 'a lasting contribution to literature for children and young people'. the Awards take the form of medals and are made every two years by the INTERNATIONAL BOARD ON BOOKS FOR YOUNG PEOPLE. *See IBBY.*

Anepigraphon.   A publication whose title-page is missing.

Angel Literary Prize.   An annual award offered for a book written by authors living and working in East Anglia, UK.

Angle Brackets.   *See Brackets.*

Anglo-American Cataloguing Rules. *See AACR.*

Angular Marks. *See Brackets.*

Anhydrous. Water-free. Normally used with reference to chemical salts and solvents.

Animal Tub-sized. *See Tub-sizing.*

Animals in Foliage Panel. A panel in a book-binding decoration which is divided vertically into two, each half containing curving foliage with an animal within each curve. It is the characteristic Netherlands design.

Annal. An entry in a record of events in their chronological order year by year.

Annalistic Arrangement. A bibliography of an author's writings arranged in order of publication.

Annals. A record of events arranged in chronological order.

Annexe. 1. Supporting contributions to a main report, thesis, or other work. 2. A document usually attached to, but not physically a part of, that to which it is attached.

Annotate. To make an annotation.

Annotated. Said of a catalogue or bibliography entry which has been provided with an ANNOTATION (*q.v.*).

Annotating. The act of preparing an ANNOTATION (*q.v.*).

Annotation. A note added to an entry in a catalogue, reading list or bibliography, to elucidate, evaluate or describe the subject and contents of a book; it sometimes gives particulars of the author.

Annual. A serial publication, e.g. a report, year book or directory issued once a year. *See also Bi-Annual, Year Book.*

Annual Bibliography of the History of the Printed Book and Libraries. *See ABHB.*

Anonym. 1. An anonymous publication. 2. An anonymous person or writer. 3. A pseudonym.

Anonymous. A publication is said to be anonymous when the author's name does not appear anywhere in it, either on the title-page or cover, or in the preface, introduction or foreword. According to some authorities, if the authorship can be traced in catalogues or bibliographies it may be considered not to be anonymous. The opposite of onymous.

Anonymous Classic. A work of unknown or doubtful authorship, commonly designated by title, which may have appeared in the course of time in many editions, versions, and/or translations.

Anonymous Entry. An entry in a catalogue for a book the author of which is not mentioned on the title-page.

Anopisthographic Block Book. One that is printed on only one side of the paper.

Anopisthographic Printing. The manner of printing early block books, using writing ink and printing on only one side of the leaf. *See also Block Books, Opisthographic.*

ANRT. Acronym for Association Nationale de la Recherche Technique. A French association which is particularly concerned with problems of technical information.

ANSI. American National Standards Institute (*q.v.*).

Ante-dated. A book which bears a date of publication which is earlier than the actual date. The opposite of 'Post-dated'.

Anterior Numeral Classes. The first group of the main classes of Bliss's *Bibliographic Classification*. They are bibliothetic in character and conform to the generalia classes of other schemes. Three of the nine divisions accommodate general works (2 bibliography, 6 periodicals, 7 miscellanea); the remainder provide for special collections of books which for some reason it is preferred to shelve apart from the main collection. *See also Systematic Auxiliary Schedules*.

Anteriorizing Digit. (*Classification*) The digit which, when added to a class number, causes the resulting class number to have precedence over the number to which it was added. For example the *a* in the class number X*a* is the anteriorizing digit. Also called 'Anteriorizing common isolates'.

Anteriorizing Value. (*Classification*) Said to be possessed by a digit which, when added to a class number (and which is then said to be the 'host class number'), causes the resulting class number to have precedence over the host number. For example, in the Colon classification, class numbers containing lower case roman letters, or arrows, have precedence over class numbers without them, as: X*a*, precedes X, B63*a* precedes B63, L23: 45*a* precedes L23: 45, N← M precedes N.

Anthology. A collection of choice extracts, usually of poetry, or on one subject, from the writings of one author, or various authors, and having a common characteristic such as subject matter or literary form.

Antiope. A French videotex system: l'Acquisition Numerique et Televisualisation d'Images Organisées en Pages d'Ecriture. The trade name Teletel is more common.

Antiphonary. A liturgical book intended for use in a choir. Generically it includes antiphons and antiphonal chants sung at Mass and at the canonical Hours, but now refers only to the sung portions of the BREVIARY (*q.v.*).

Antiqua. A German name for Roman types. A small book hand based on the Caroline minuscule, called *lettera rotonda* or *lettre ronde* (round letter) in Italy and France. Type based on this writing is now known as Roman, and is the usual kind of type (as distinct from *italic*) used for book work.

Antiquarian Bookseller. One who deals in old books, which are rare enough to command higher prices than ordinary second-hand books.

Antique. 1. (*Paper*) The name given to printing papers made from esparto grass. They usually have a rough surface, and the poorer qualities are called *featherweight*, so loosely woven that 75 per cent of the bulk is air space. The term originally referred to machine-made paper made in imitation of hand-made paper. Antique papers have a matt or dull finish and are neither calendered nor coated. They are suitable for printing type and line engravings, but not for half-tones, and are used for most books without blocks. 2. (*Binding*) Designates blind tooling. *See Tooling*.

Antique Finish. (*Paper*) A rough surface, suggestive of old hand-made printing paper. Generally used to indicate an 'unfinished' paper, i.e. one not calendered, and usually of the FEATHERWEIGHT PAPER (*q.v.*) class.

Antique Gold Edges. *See Gilt Edges.*

Antique Laid.   Originally, paper made on moulds of which the chain wires were laced or sewn direct to the wooden ribs or supports of the mould, thus causing the pulp to lie thicker along each side of every chain line in the sheet of paper. Now, any rough-surfaced laid paper. *See also Mould.*

Antique Tooling.   A form of blind tooling.

Antonym.   A word having the opposite meaning of another. The opposite of synonym.

Antonymous Catchwords.   Headings used in an index, which are exactly opposite in meaning.

AP.   Abbreviation for AUTHOR'S PROOF (*q.v.*).

Aperture Card.   A card with one or more openings (the number depending on the amount of space required for identifying stored document images) into each of which is mounted a 'frame' cut from a strip of microfilm. The identification on the card can consist of written information, punched holes, or characters on film. Also called PEEPHOLE CARD (*q.v.*).

Apocalypse of St. John.   *See Block Books.*

Apoconym.   A name changed by the cutting off or elision of letters or syllables.

Apocryphal.   Of unknown authorship or doubtful authenticity.

Apograph.   A copy of an original manuscript.

APOLLO.   Article Procurement with On-Line Local Ordering; a project of the Commission of the European Community, offering a highspeed data transmission system by which documents are requested and retrieved electronically, but with the actual document delivery achieved by conventional means. Lack of funding makes the future uncertain, and technological advances may overtake APOLLO. *See ADONIS and ISDN.*

Apostil (Apostille).   An annotation, or marginal note (archaic).

app.   Abbreviation for APPENDIX (*q.v.*).

Apparatus Criticus.   The sources of information and the existence of manuscripts, letters and other material used by an author, and enumerated by him in footnotes, marginalia and commentary in support of his text, and thus associated with the preparation of the definitive edition of a work. Includes particularly, information concerning variant readings, doubtful texts and obscurities.

Appendix.   Matter which comes at the end of the text of a book and contains notes which are too long for footnotes, tables of statistics, or other items for which there is no room in the body of the book, which, from the nature of the information, is more suitably placed at the end of the text.

Applied Bibliography.   *Synonymous with* HISTORICAL BIBLIOGRAPHY (*q.v.*).

Applied Information Technologies Research Center.   AITRC is a consortium, including OCLC and Chemical Abstracts, formed to develop knowledge delivery systems for the 1990s. The Center is located at Ohio State University.

Appraisal.   1. An estimate of the value of a book as a contribution to a subject.

2. (*Archives*)   (i) The process of determining the value, and so the disposition, of documents, based upon: (a) their current legal fiscal or administrative use; (b) their research or information use; (c) their arrangement; or (d) their relationship to other records. Also called 'Selective retention'. (ii) The monetary value of gifts of manuscripts. *See also Intrinsic Value.*

Approach Term.   The word which a catalogue-user seeks in a catalogue, in anticipation that it will lead him to a statement in SUBJECT HEADING LANGUAGE (*q.v.*) of a required compound subject.

Aquatint.   1. A process of etching on copper or steel plates by means of nitric acid, producing an effect resembling a fine drawing in water colours, sepia or India ink. It is used to render tonal effects rather than lines. Now supplanted commercially by lithography.   2. A print made by this method.

Aquatone.   A photographic printing process which is similar to collotype, but is used with offset presses.

Arabesque.   A species of decoration consisting of interlaced lines and convoluted curves arranged in more or less geometrical patterns; so-called because it was brought to its highest perfection by Arabian or kindred artists. Also applied to a fanciful mixture of animals, birds, and insects, and of plants, fruit and foliage, involved and twisted; but pure arabesque has in it no representation of living forms, as this is forbidden by the Koran.

Arabic Figures.   The numerical characters 1, 2, 3, etc., as distinct from roman numerals I, II, III, etc., so called from having been introduced into European from Arab use: they have been used for foliation since the last quarter of the fifteenth century. Arabic numerals first appeared in European MSS in the twelfth century, although the Arabs probably brought them from India in the eighth century. Arabic is used for numbering the text pages of books. 'Old Style' numerals are as follows 1, 2, 3, 4, 5, 6, 7, 8, 9, 0 and have ascenders and descenders, although tabular work makes it desirable to have 'lining figures' (1, 2, 3, 4, 5, 6, 7, 8, 9, 0) as an alternative. These are also known as 'Modern'. It is the presence or absence of ascenders and descenders which indicates whether the figures are 'Old Style' or 'Modern'. This distinction applies to italic as well as to roman: Old Style – *1, 2, 3, 4, 5, 6, 7, 8, 9, 0.* Modern – *1, 2, 3, 4, 5, 6, 7, 8, 9, 0. See also Foliation, Hanging Figures, Lining Figures, Pagination, Roman Numerals.*

ARBICA.   Acronym of the Arab Regional Branch of the International Council on Archives. *See International Council on Archives.*

Arbitrary Code.   *Synonymous with* TABULATED CODE (*q.v.*).

Arbitrary Symbol.   (*Classification*) A symbol, e.g. a punctuation mark, used in a NOTATION as a FACET INDICATOR (*qq.v.*).

Arbuthnot Honor Lecture, May Hill.   An endowed annual lecture, established by Scott, Foresman and Company in tribute to May Hill Arbuthnot, one of the foremost authorities on literature for children. The Association for Library Service to Children of the ALA administers the selection of the lecture series.

Archbishop Parker's Bible.   *See Bishops' Bible.*

Archetypal Novel. Commonly used to describe the earliest romances, tales and works of fiction; the fore-runner of the modern novel.

Architectural Binding. A sixteenth-century style of book cover decoration which consisted of columns supporting an arch under which was a panel to contain the title. The contents of the books so decorated seldom related to architecture.

Archival Description Project. *See Manual of Archival Description.*

Archival Document. A document which it is expected will be kept permanently, as near as possible in its original form, for the evidence which it might afford both in itself and within its context.

Archival Integrity. The standard of administration and preservation that requires that archive holdings are identified and arranged as originally compiled, assembled and administered, kept in their original filing sequence, and preserved in their entirety without mutilation, alteration or destruction of any portion of them.

Archival Quality. (*Reprography*) The degree to which a processed film or print will retain its characteristics without loss of quality over an indefinite period of storage under controlled conditions.

Archival Value. The decision, after appraisal, that documents are worthy of indefinite or permanent depository.

Archive Administration. The collection and conservation of ARCHIVES (*q.v.*), their organization for use, and the theoretical and practical studies of such procedures.

Archives. 1. Public records or historical documents kept in a recognized repository. 2. Documents which formed part of an official transaction and were preserved for official reference; these include documents specially made for, and those included in, an official transaction. 3. The repository itself. 4. Colloquially a collection of old books or documents. 5. Written documents, or annexures to them, compiled for the purposes of, or used during, a public or private business transaction of which they themselves form a part; and which are preserved by the persons concerned with the transaction, or their successors, in their own custody for their own use. Similarly, any records of the activities of societies or groups. 6. A collection of original records assembled in the course of the normal activities of a person or persons, or of a public or private organization; or such records from a number of different sources, and kept together to ensure their preservation. *See also International Council on Archives, Records, Modern Public Records.*

Archives of Electronic Publications. *See Knowledge Warehouse.*

Archivist. A person who has the care of archives, and also makes them available under proper safeguards to historians and researchers.

Area. 1. (*Public Libraries*) A geographical part of the Library system, not as extensive as a region, served by a number of branches and/or centres, and forming a library unit for administrative purposes. 2. (*Cataloguing*) A major section of a bibliographic description (forming a part of a catalogue entry) which comprises data of a particular category or set of categories.

Area Headquarters. (*Public Libraries*) The premises from which the Libraries in an Area are administered, which may or may not be a library to which the public has access.

Area Librarian. One who is in charge of a library area, and responsible for a small number of branches and other service points in that area.

Area Search. Examination of a large group of documents to segregate those documents pertaining to a general class, category or topic. Screening.

Area Table. A common geographical facet based on the geographical numbers used in the Dewey Classification in order to provide geographical arrangement of material classified primarily by subject.

Aristo Paper. A photographic copying paper, the colloid being gelatine.

Aristonym. A title of nobility converted into, or used as, a surname.

Arithmetical Notation. *Synonymous with* INTEGRAL NOTATION (*q.v.*).

ARL. Association of Research Libraries (*q.v.*).

ARLIS. Abbreviation for The Art Libraries Society founded in 1969; this Society exists to promote art librarianship, particularly by acting as a forum for the interchange of information and materials. ARLIS is affiliated to its American counterpart ARLIS/NA. It regularly organizes social functions and professional visits for its members. It publishes *Art Libraries Journal* and *Newsheet* (6 p.a.).

ARLIS/NA. The Art Libraries Society of North America; founded 1972 and now having 1250 members worldwide, comprising individuals, institutions, and business affiliates. ARLIS/NA has similar objectives to ARLIS (*q.v.*), and functions via regional chapters, special interest groups, and type of library groups. Publishes *Art documentation* (q.) *ARLIS/NA Newsletter* (q.), handbook, occasional papers, etc. Sponsors two annual awards: George Wittenberg Award (for an outstanding art publication) and the Gerd Muehsam Award (for an exceptional student paper in the field).

Arm. The projecting, or unclosed, horizontal or upward-sloping stroke of a type of letter.

Armaria. *See Armarium.*

Armarian. A worker in a monastic library whose duty it was to prevent the books under his charge from being injured by insects, to look after bindings, and keep a correct catalogue. He presided over a SCRIPTORIUM (*q.v.*) and supplied the scribes with parchment, pens, ink, knives, awls and rulers. Also called an 'Armarius'.

Armarium. A wardrobe, or cupboard, possibly a separate piece of furniture in which scrolls, or subsequently books, were kept. Closed armaria apparently developed in Imperial times and survived in monastic libraries until the Renaissance or later.

Armarius. *See Armarian.*

Armenian Bole. A bright-red clay which is used as a colouring material and also to dust on to the edges of books before gilding to act as a base for the gold, to which it gives a greater depth and lustre. It is obtained mainly from Bohemia, Italy and Silesia.

Arming Press.   A hand blocking press used now only for short runs but originally for impressing armorial bearings.

Armorial Binding.   One decorated with the arms or other device of royalty or nobility. Generally applied to bindings earlier than the mid nineteenth century.

Arms Block.   An engraved brass block or binder's ZINCO 2 (*q.v.*) made by a line-block maker and used in an arming or blocking press to impress a coat of arms on leather bindings.

ARPANET.   *See INTERNET.*

Arrangement.   The adaptation of a whole musical work, or an integral part of a musical work, to a medium of performance other than that for which it was originally written, e.g. the casting of a song as a piano piece, or of an orchestral overture as an organ piece. Sometimes also, a simplification or amplification, when the musical structure and the medium of performance remain the same.

Arranger.   One who transcribes a whole musical work, or a part of a work, for a medium of performance other than that intended by the composer. The arrangement may be a simplification or amplification, the medium of performance and the musical structure remaining the same.

Array.   1. In classification, the series of co-ordinate subdivisions which are obtained by dividing a class or a division according to a single characteristic: e.g. Literature divided according to characteristic *Form* gives the array Poetry, Drama, Novel, Essay. Each co-ordinate division in an array should exclude all of the others, and the whole array should be exhaustive of the contents of the class. The order of the divisions in an array should be that deemed most helpful to users.   2. A set of co-ordinate terms (i.e. terms subordinate to the same genus). Also used in information retrieval for a sequence of headings in a file and as a set of search terms. An ordinal arrangement of informational materials.   3. A set of mutually exclusive co-ordinate subclasses totally exhaustive of a class, derived by its division according to some one characteristic.

Arrester.   (*Classification*) The second curve; used in the Colon Classification to enclose the Subject Device Number. The first, or opening, curve is called the 'Starter'. *See also Brackets, Circular Brackets, Curves.*

Ars Memorandi.   *See Block Books.*

Ars Moriendi.   A mediaeval block book setting forth by means of pictures and text the art of dying becomingly.

Art.   The name given to papers coated on one or both sides after the paper is made by brushing on China clay, sulphate or barium, or sulphate of lime and alumina (the last for the 'satin-white' finish) and afterwards polished. In *imitation art* the paper is 'loaded' (i.e. the China clay is mixed in with the fibre) not 'coated'. *Matt art* is unglazed coated paper with a smooth, soft, egg-shell finish.

Art Canvas.   A cloth for bookbinding, also known as light-weight buckram.

Art Libraries Society.   *See ARLIS.*

Art Paper.   *See Art.*

Art Parchment. *See Vellum Parchment.*

Art Vellum. 1. A brand name for a lightweight book cloth. 2. A fabric used for classes of works which do not require a very strong cloth.

Art Work. A term covering all forms of illustrative matter (line drawings, photographs, paintings, diagrams, hand lettering, etc.) used in a printed publication to distinguish it from type-set matter. In America the term is used to distinguish any material prepared by hand as camera copy.

Artefacts. (*Classification*) A group of 'artificial' entities, i.e. those which do not occur naturally, and which are 'concrete', e.g. chairs, automobiles. The other group is known as MENTEFACTS (*q.v.*).

ARTEMIS. Automatic Retrieval of Text through European Multipurpose Information Services. A report published by the European Community in 1981 which examined the concept of a document delivery system. *See also DOCDEL.*

Article. A contribution written by one or more persons for publication in a PERIODICAL (*q.v.*); such a contribution when so published. *See also Work.*

Articulated Indexing. A method of producing computer generated subject indexes from a sentence-like title statement without complex subject analysis.

Artificial Characteristic. *See Characteristic of a Classification.*

Artificial Classification. One in which some accidental thing is adopted as the 'difference'. *See Predicables, Five.* Classification by analogy, i.e. by external or accidental likeness, unlikeness, or apparent purpose. *See Characteristic of a Classification.*

Artificial Indexing Language. (*Information Retrieval, Indexing*) A group of signs, symbols or digits (or of phrases, or words arranged in an inverted order according to rules and so becoming 'controlled' language) to represent facts and ideas. An index language. The opposite of NATURAL LANGUAGE (*q.v.*). *See also Indexing Language.*

Artificial Intelligence. The branch of computer science that is attempting to replicate some aspects of human intelligence, for example solving problems, and drawing conclusions and voice recognition. *See also Expert Systems.*

Artistic Manuscript. A record or document produced by hand, and decorated or illustrated in such a way as to achieve distinction as a work of artistic merit. Illuminated manuscripts are the most important examples. *See also Literary Manuscript.*

Artistic Map. One made by an artist rather than by a cartographer; such maps consequently appeal to the eye and are often not correct cartographically. They are used as illustrations, endpapers, and for advertisement.

Artist's Proof. A proof of an engraving or etching, usually with the signature of the artist in pencil, and sometimes with a small sketch, known as a remarque, in the margin. Used as a model or sample. Also called 'Remarque Proof'.

Artotek. A picture and art library.

Artotype. A photo-engraved picture made by one of the gelatine processes.

Arts Council of Great Britain Writers' Awards.   Three awards available annually to UK resident authors of known literary achievement needing financial support for research or writing of their next book.

ARTTel.   Automated request transmission by telephone. Name adopted in 1982 for former Telephone Access Service at the British Library Document Supply Centre. Extensively used by customers preparing requests on microcomputers or intelligent terminals, which are transferred to a microcomputer at the Centre.

Artype.   Type letters which are printed on acetate sheets gummed on the back. Those required are cut out of the sheet and pressed in the required position to form 'copy' which is photographed for printing by the offset process.

Arundel Psalter.   Two Psalters bound together, and each illuminated in a distinct style. The first, containing many miniature-filled initials was probably by an early fourteenth-century court artist. The second is typical of the East Anglian School and is probably earlier. It has full-page scenes from the Passion and a large number of allegorical scenes. It is held in the British Library.

Arvon Foundation Observer International Poetry Competition.   A UK biennial award for poetry in English not previously published or broadcast.

'As If' Filing.   The filing alphabetically of abbreviations as if they were spelled out, e.g. St. as Saint, Mr. as Mister, 1001 as One thousand and one.

As Issued.   Indicates that a book offered for sale secondhand is in its original format.

As New.   Used in secondhand booksellers' catalogues to indicate that the physical condition of a book offered for sale is 'almost indistinguishable from the condition of newness'.

ASA.   American Standards Association. *See American National Standards Institute, Inc.*

Ascender.   The vertical ascending stem of lower-case letters such as b, d, k, etc.; that part which extends above the x-HEIGHT (*q.v.*). *See also Descender.*

Ascender Line.   (*Printing*) The imaginary line which runs along the top of ascenders. This will be above the CAP LINE (*q.v.*) in the case of types the capitals of which are lower than the ascenders. *See also Ascender, Base Line, Cap Line, Mean Line.*

Ascetonym.   The name of a saint used as a proper name.

ASCII.   American standard code for information exchange; a character coding system widely used as an agreed framework for computer communication.

ASCLA.   *See Association of Specialized and Co-operative Library Agencies.*

ASD.   1. Acronym for Association Suisse de Documentation. The Swiss Association for Documentation; it was formed in 1939 after having been in existence as a study group since 1930. Publishes *Kleine Mitteilungen/Petites Communications* (irr.).   2. Acronym for the Automated Services Department (of the British Library).

Ashendene Press.   One of the most distinguished British private presses. It was founded in 1895 by C. H. St. John Hornby, a partner in the firm of W. H. Smith & Son, and undertook fine printing at the instance of Sydney Cockerell in 1900.

Ashley Library (UK). Started in the late 1920s by W. E. Ashley Brown, a former deputy editor of the *Sunday Express*, the library comprises more than a million newspaper cuttings concerned exclusively with strange and peculiar facts. The library was sold in 1983 to G. Nown of Southport, who intends to maintain and revive it.

ASHSL. *See Association of Scottish Health Sciences Librarians.*

ASI. American Society of Indexers (*q.v.*).

Asian Librarians and Arts Officer Group. An informal UK group established in 1988 with participants from all types of people active in cultural affairs in the UK Asian community.

ASIDIC. Abbreviation for the (American) Association of Information and Dissemination Centers, the purposes of which are to recommend greater efforts at standardization, and promote more efficient use of data resources. It is composed of organizations which offer two or more current awareness and/or retrospective search services processed by computer, for data bases from a variety of sources. It was established in 1969; publishes *ASIDIC Newsletter* (q.).

ASIS. American Society for Information Science (*q.v.*).

Aslib. Aslib, an independent, autonomous organization, assists companies and other bodies, in many different ways, to manage their information. It provides a unique focal point for all concerned with the management of information. Its 2000 member organizations include industrial and commercial companies, academic and research institutions, central and local government and international bodies in more than 70 countries. Aslib is also a strong voice in representing the views of its members at regional, national and international level. An extensive training programme is operated, and an Information Resource Centre offers fast advice on areas such as online methods, LANS, software, etc. Special interest groups are as follows: Audio-visual; biosciences; chemical; computer; economic and business information; electronics; engineering; informatics-advanced information systems; one-man-bands; planning and environment, transport information; social sciences information; technical translation. There are numerous publications, including *Aslib Information* (m) *Aslib Proceedings* (m) and *Journal of Documentation* (q). The subtitle *Association for Information Management* was added in 1983.

Aslib Cranfield Research Project. An investigation into the comparative efficiency of four indexing systems; it consisted of the preparation – and subsequent testing – of four separate indexes for which 18,000 documents were indexed by the Universal Decimal Classificaiton (using conventional card catalogues), an alphabetical subject index, a special facet classification, and the Uniterm system of co-ordinate indexing (for which alphabetical and facet aspect cards posted with document numbers were used). The project was undertaken by means of a National Science Foundation grant which was offered to Aslib in July 1957; it was undertaken at the College of Aeronautics, Cranfield, under the direction of the Librarian, Cyril Cleverdon.

Aslib/ISI Award for Innovation in Information Management. An annual award for the most outstanding contribution to the development of information management by an individual, or named members of a team, based in the UK. First awarded in 1984.

Asociación Latinamericana de Escuelas de Bibliotecologia y Ciencias de la Informacion. *See ALEBCI.*

Aspect Card. A record used in an ASPECT SYSTEM (*q.v.*) of recording information for retrieval. A separate card is used for one subject or point of view and entered on it are the numbers or other identification symbols of each document which has this quality. The number is entered on as many cards as are necessary to record every aspect of the document.

Aspect System. A method of indexing which assumes that a Discrete Record represents a single subject (or aspect) and contains, in searchable form, information as to which documents in a file have this subject in common. Also called 'Inverted' or 'Term entry' system. *See also Document System, Term Entry.*

ASSASSIN. Agricultural System for the Storage and Subsequent Selection of Information. A software package developed by the Agricultural Division of ICI. Includes modules for index production, thesaurus control, and SDI. A microcomputer counterpart is known as HOMER (*q.v.*).

Assembler. (*Information retrieval*) The program which converts the symbolic language program, written by the programmer, to a machine-language program.

ASSIA. *Applied Social Sciences Index and Abstracts;* a bi-monthly indexing and abstracting service covering a wide range of journals in the broad field of the social sciences. Produced by Library Association Publishing Ltd., and launched in 1987; transported to Bowker-Saur Ltd. in 1990.

Associate Librarian. American term for a deputy librarian.

Associated Book. As used in connection with the Colon Classification, a book which is written about another book, as e.g. a criticism of, or reply to, it. The book which is the subject of the criticism or reply is called a 'Host book'. The BOOK NUMBER (*q.v.*) of an Associated Book should consist of that of the Host Book followed by ':g'. The number so added is called the 'Criticism number'. Where there is more than one Associated Book of the same Host Book, a digit, 1,2, etc., representing each additional Associated Book, may be added to the Book Number and so becomes part of it. The number added in this way may be called the 'Accession part of the Criticism number'.

Associateship (UK). The basic stage in professional qualification. Associates are admitted to the Register of Chartered Librarians maintained by the Library Association, and may use the post nominal letters ALA.

Association. *See Links.*

Association Book. One having an autograph inscription or notes by the author, or which was in any way intimately connected with a prominent person who may have owned or presented it, or which had belonged to someone connected with its contents. Evidence in or on the book of the association is essential. If there is no signature or presentation inscription there should be a bookplate, or binding stamp, or marginal or other notes to indicate the association.

Association Canadienne des Sciences de l'Information. *See Canadian Association for Information Science.*

Association Copy. *Synonymous with Association Book.*

Association des Bibliothécaires Français. *See Association of French Librarians.*

Association for Information and Image Management. A UK trade association principally concerned with micrographics, but intending to market its relevance to the whole of the information industry. Abbreviated: AIIM.

Association for Information Management. *See ASLIB.*

Association for Library and Information Science Education. Formed in 1981 as a development of the Association of American Library Schools; seeks to promote excellence in professional education, provide a forum for the interchange of ideas, promote research and formulate policy. Publishes *Journal of Education for Library and Information Science* (q.). Abbreviated ALISE.

Association for Library Automation Research Communications. *See LARC Association.*

Association for Library Collections and Technical Services. The new name, adopted 1989, for the Resources and Technical Services Division (RTSD) of the American Library Association. Major concerns include collection development, acquisition, cataloguing, automation, preservation, etc. Abbreviated ALCTS.

Association for Library Service to Children (ALSC). Division of the American Library Association. Founded 1957, present title 1977. Aims to improve and extend library services to children in all types of libraries. Publishes *Journal of Youth Services in Libraries* (q.) jointly with the Young Adult Services Division. Operates several award systems: Newbery-Caldecott, M. L. Batchelder, Laura Ingalls Wilder. (*qq.v.*).

Association for the Development of Public Libraries in Africa. Founded in Dakar, 13 September 1957 and renamed the INTERNATIONAL ASSOCIATION for the DEVELOPMENT of LIBRARIES in AFRICA (AIDBA) in 1960 and the INTERNATIONAL ASSOCIATION FOR THE DEVELOPMENT OF DOCUMENTATION, LIBRARIES AND ARCHIVES IN AFRICA (*q.v.*) in 1967. Abbreviated ADBPA.

Association for the Development of Religious Information Services. *See ADRIS.*

Association for the Education and Training of Library Technicians and Assistants. *See AETLTA.*

Association Française des Documentalist etc. Bibliothécaires Spécialisés. A major French professional association, based in Paris, and organizing major conferences every 2 years (Bordeaux, 1991). Membership organized in regional groups and subject divisions. Several publications including *ADBS Informations* (m).

Association Internationale des Documentalistes et Techniciens de l'Information. *See International Association of Documentalists and Information Officers.*

Association Internationale des Écoles des Sciences de l'Information. Formed in 1977 in Geneva, aims to bring together French-speaking information professionals, to encourage professional development, and stimulate research in professional matters. A major conference is held every two years. Secretariat in Montreal.

Association Nationale de la Recherche Technique. *See ANRT.*

Association Nationale pour la Développement des Bibliothèques Publiques. *See ANDBP.*

Association of American Publishers, Inc. Formed in May 1970 by a merger of the American Book Publishers Council and the American Educational Publishers Institute. The Association aims to promote and expand the market for American books, journals, software, databases, audio-visual materials etc., and has a membership of some 250 firms. Divisions include general publishing, higher education, international activity, paperback publishing, professional and scholarly publishing, and school publishing. Current programmes include copyright, book distribution, freedom to read, and new technologies. Abbreviated: AAP.

Association of Assistant Librarians. A group of the (British) Library Association; it caters for members of a particular status rather than, as in the case of other groups, for those engaged in a particular branch of librarianship. It is organized in Divisions which operate at local level. Originally known as the Library Assistants Association, it was formed on 3 July 1895 at a meeting convened by Mr. W. W. Fortune; the name was changed to the Association of Assistant Librarians in June 1922. It was an independent association until 1 January 1930 when it became a Section of the Library Association. Publishes *Assistant Librarian* (11 p.a.). Abbreviated AAL.

Association of British Library and Information Studies Schools. Founded 1962 as the Association of British Library Schools to further the work of the full-time schools of librarianship by affording heads of such schools, and some representatives of the library and professional organizations opportunities of meeting to discuss education in librarianship. Abbreviated ABLISS.

Association of British Theological and Philosophical Libraries. *See ABTAPL.*

Association of Canadian Archivists. The Association was founded in 1975 and exists to provide an effective agency of communication and professional leadership among all persons who are engaged in the discipline and practice of archival science. It also encourages co-operation of archivists with all those concerned with the preservation and use of the records of human experience through: a regular, informative and scholarly programme of publication; prescription of the highest standards in the conduct of archives administration and development of a code of professional responsibility; representation of the needs of the archival profession before governments and other regulatory authorities; co-operation, exchange and contact with regional, national and international organizations and related professional disciplines; promotion of public knowledge and appreciation of archives and the function of archival institutions in preserving cultural heritage and identity; investigation, promotion and approval of academic programmes leading to professional qualification in archival science and to advancement of general education in the preservation and use of documentary materials. Currently there are 600 members; publishes *Archivaria* (2 p.a.) and *Bulletin*. Abbreviated ACA.

Association of Caribbean University Research and Institute Libraries. Formed in 1968 to foster and improve contact and collaboration between members; holds conferences and seminars, encouurages co-operative initiatives, and exchanges of staff. There are currently 50 members. Publishes *Caribbean Education Bulletin* (q.). Abbreviated ACURIL.

Association of College and Research Libraries. A Division of the American Library Association since 1938; founded in 1889 to represent and promote 'libraries of higher education (institutions supporting forml education above the secondary school level), independent research libraries, and specialized libraries'. Has 13 sections. Publishes *College and Research Libraries* (17 issues p.a., 11 being *C&RL News*). Abbreviated ACRL.

Association of Database Producers. A UK trade organization aiming to represent the interests of commercial and non-commercial organizations developing and selling databases.

Association of Data Processing Service Organizations. *See ADAPSO.*

Association of District Councils. Formed on 30 November 1973, this Association became operative on 1 April 1974 to: '(a) protect and further the interests of the district councils as they may be affected by legislation or proposed legislation or otherwise and to promote a high standard of administration of the public services in the district; (b) join, where appropriate, with other local authority Associations; (i) promote the interests of local government in general and (ii) provide such central services for the district councils as may be considered to be appropriate.' The Association consists of the non-metropolitan district councils in England and the district councils in Wales; these range in size and character from authorities which are substantially rural to large cities and towns. Members of the Council of the Association are elected from the districts and from the counties by formulae based on population. Financed by members' subscriptions. The Association superseded the Rural District Councils Association and also the Urban District Councils Association when these ceased to exist on 1 April 1974 due to the alteration of local authority boundaries and the reorganization of local government in England and Wales. Publishes *The District Councils Review* (m.). Abbreviated ADC. *See also AMA.*

Association of EDC Librarians. Formed 1981 by UK librarians responsible for EUROPEAN DOCUMENTATION CENTRES (*q.v.*). Meetings, conferences, and visits are organized, and the Association issues a quarterly *EDC Newsletter*.

Association of French Librarians (Association des Bibliothecaires Français). Founded 1906. Based in Paris. Aims to unite librarians, promote library services and represent France in international gatherings. Publishes

Bulletin d'Information de l'A.B.F., (q.) monographs, handbook and reports.

Association of Genealogists and Record Agents. Founded in 1968 to promote and maintain high standards of professional conduct and expertise within the spheres of genealogy, heraldry and record searching and to safeguard the interests of members and clients. Members are subject to a Code of Practice with which they agree to comply when accepting membership. This is open to well-qualified professional researchers who have been engaged as genealogists or record agents for a number of years. The Association does not undertake research but publishes an informative booklet listing members with details of their special interests and the areas where they work. Publishes *Newsletter* (3 p.a.). Abbreviated AGRA.

Association of Information and Dissemination Centers. *See ASIDIC.*

Association of International Libraries. Founded in September 1963 at the Sofia meeting of the International Federation of Library Associations, of which it is a Section. Aims: to facilitate co-operation between international libraries. Membership is open to (a) individuals capable of promoting co-operation between international libraries, (b) libraries of international organizations, in particular the libraries of inter-governmental organizations, (c) all other libraries whose international character is recognized by the Executive Committee. It is financed by members' dues. Abbreviated AIL.

Association of Jewish Libraries. Formed in June 1966 by the amalgamation of the Jewish Librarians Association and the Jewish Library Association 'to promote and improve library services and professional standards in all Jewish libraries; to serve as a centre of dissemination of Jewish library information and guidance; to encourage the establishment of Jewish libraries; to promote publication of literature which will be of assistance to Jewish librarianship; to encourage people to enter the field of librarianship'. An American association. Publishes *Bulletin* (2 p.a.). Abbreviated AJL.

Association of Librarians in Schools. An informal association of school librarians in Nottinghamshire (UK). Abbreviated ALIS.

Association of Libraries of Judaica and Hebraica in Europe. Founded in Paris, 28 April 1955, to facilitate the use of literature on Judaica and Hebraica in European libraries; to create a catalogue of such literature in Europe; to give bibliographical and other help to affiliated libraries and others. Has an information bureau and arranges training courses in Jewish librarianship. Abbreviated ALJH.

Association of London Chief Librarians. The organization which was formed in succession to the ASSOCIATION OF METROPOLITAN CHIEF LIBRARIANS (*q.v.*) when the boroughs of greater London were reconstituted as from 1 April 1965. The objectives of the Association are to promote discussion and exchange of views, better management, co-operation, joint action etc. Abbreviated ALCL. *See also FOLACL.*

Association of Metropolitan Authorities. *See AMA.*

Association of Metropolitan Chief Librarians. An advisory body to the Metropolitan Boroughs Standing Joint Committee (MBSJC) which was composed of representatives of the Metropolitan Borough Councils and the Corporation of the City of London until 31 March 1965. It consisted of the respective chief librarians who met regularly to consider mutual library problems, advised on library developments in the area and managed the LONDON UNION CATALOGUE (*q.v.*). *See also Association of London Chief Librarians.*

Association of Metropolitan District Chief Librarians. The organization representing the librarians of the (UK) Metropolitan districts, formed after local government reorganization in 1974. *See also FOLACL.*

Association of Northern Ireland Education and Library Boards. Formed on 24 October 1973 to: (a) seek to achieve the highest standards in education and library services for all the people of Northern Ireland, and to co-ordinate the efforts of the Education and Library Boards to that end; (b) promote and encourage the interchange of ideas on questions relating to the education and library services and to provide a forum for debate on such matters; (c) supply information and advice to member Boards on education and library matters; (d) exercise vigilance in relation to all proposed legislation, regulations and administrative arrangements affecting education and library services and to take action, where deemed necessary, for the safeguarding or improvement of standards in the services affected; (e) provide a collective voice for the education and library services in relations with the government and the community. Financed by the Department of Education (NI) and controlled by the five Area Boards in membership.

Association of Research Libraries. Founded in 1931 to develop and increase by co-operative effort, 'the resources and usefulness of the research collections in American libraries'. Membership is institutional, by invitation only, and currently stands at 118 United States and Canadian libraries. The Association represents research libraries in the professional and scholarly communities, in the government and private sectors. It is a forum for discussion, and a centre for studies, planning, and collective action. A five-year plan 1983–1988 laid emphasis on scholarly communication, access to research materials, preservation, information policy, staffing needs, and management. The Association's Office of Management Studies (*q.v.*) operates the North American Collections Inventory (NCIP) – an online project based on work started by RLG in 1979. The Association is also closely involved in development of CONSPECTUS (*q.v.*), the National Register of Microform Masters (NRMM) and retrospective conversion programmes, stemming from the RECON Project 1985–87. Publishes *ARL Newsletter* (5 p.a.).

Association of Scottish Health Sciences Librarians. The principal Scottish organization of library and information workers in health care disciplines. It acts as a single, authoritative and independent voice for the views of this group of health care staff; offers opportunities for conference and discussion; and provides services which promote the efficient flow of information in the health sciences. ASHSL started informally in 1970 and became a formally constituted body in 1974. In December 1988, membership stood at 100. This figure includes members working in Colleges of Nursing and Midwifery, Postgraduate Medical Centres, University Medical Schools, the Royal Colleges, the National Library of Scotland, the Scottish Office, the Health Boards and the Common Services Agency. ASHSL is independent of other profesional associations, but it maintains links with the Library Association and its Medical Health and Welfare Libraries Group, with the Scottish Library Association, the NHS Regional Librarians' Group and the University Medical School Librarians' Group. Publishes *Interim* (2 p.a.), *Union List of Periodicals*, and *Directory*.

Association of Specialized and Co-operative Library Agencies.   Division of the American Library Association. Founded in 1977 by the merger of the Association of State Library Agencies and the Health and Rehabilitative Library Services Division. The Association represents the interests of state library agencies, specialized library agencies, and multi-type library co-operatives. Publishes *Interface* (q). Abbreviated ASCLA.

Association of Swiss Librarians.   (Association des bibliothécaires suisses/ Vereinigung schweizerischer Bibliothekare/Association dei Bibliotecare Svizzeri). Founded 1897, based in Berne, the Association has 1400 individual and 300 institutional members. Publishes *ARBIDO-Bulletin*, *ARBIDO-Revue,* and various professional documents.

Association of UK Media Librarians.   Formed in 1986, the AUKML expanded in 1988 by merging with the National Association of News Librarians. Aims to create links between people working in media libraries (newspapers, broadcasting, etc.) and develop international comparisons. Publishes *Deadline* (q.).

Association of Visual Science Librarians.   An international organization, composed of professional librarians, or persons acting in that capacity, whose collections or services include the literature of vision. Among current members are individuals who work within libraries that serve educational institutions, eye clinics and hospitals, and private companies with an interest in eye or vision-related products and services. The Association encourages co-operation, fights for improved access, develops services, and promotes standards. Publishes *Union List of Vision-related Serials* and *PhD Theses in Physiological Optics* (a).

Association pour l'Advancement des Sciences et des Techniques de la Documentation.   *See ASTED.*

Association Suisse de Documentation.   *See ASD.*

Associative Indexing.   Automatic (i.e. computer) indexing, which records association between terms, or words in a text, without there necessarily being a specified functional relationship between them.

Associazione Italiana Biblioteche.   *See Italian Libraries Association.*

ASTED.   Abbreviation for Association Pour l'Advancement des Sciences et des Techniques de la Documentation, a Montreal organization which in 1974 replaced l'Association Canadienne des Bibliothécaires de Langue

Francaise (ALBLF). Publishes *Documentation et Bibliothèques* (4 p.a.); *Nouvelles* (10 p.a.).

Asterisk (*). The first and frequently most used reference mark for footnotes, technically known as a 'Star'. *See also Reference Marks.*

Asterism. 1. A group of asterisks, as in a triangle, $\ast\ast\ast$ or $\ast\ast\ast$ drawing attention to a following remark, passage or paragraph. 2. The use of a number of asterisks instead of a proper name, as Mr. T******; a form of pseudonym.

ASTIA. Armed Services Technical Information Agency; now the DEFENSE TECHNICAL INFORMATION CENTER (*q.v.*).

Astra Prize for Medical Writing. An annual award for a medical textbook published in the UK, administered by the MEDICAL WRITERS GROUP OF THE SOCIETY OF AUTHORS (*q.v.*).

Astronomical Map. One showing the stars. Also called a 'star map'.

Asyndetic. Without cross-references. The reverse of SYNDETIC (*q.v.*). *See also Syndetic Catalogue.*

Atkinson (Hugh C.) Memorial Award. An award to recognize outstanding accomplishments by academic libraries that have advanced library automation, management, or research. Administered by ACRL, LITA, LAMA and ALCTS divisions of ALA.

Atkinson Report (UK). The report *Capital Provision for University Libraries*, prepared by a working party of the University Grants Committee (HMSO 1976) Chairman: Prof. R. Atkinson. *See also Self-Renewing Library.*

ATLA. American Theological Library Association (*q.v.*).

Atlas. A volume of maps, with or without descriptive letterpress. It may be issued to supplement or accompany a text, or be published independently. Also, a volume of plates, engravings, etc., illustrating any subject; a large size of drawing paper measuring 26½ × 34 inches; a large folio volume, resembling a volume of maps, sometimes called 'Atlas folio'. The word 'atlas' was first used in the title of the first collection of maps – Gerardus Mercator's *Atlas sive cosmographicae meditationes de fabrica mundi*, Düsseldorf, [1585]–1595, which was composed in three parts in 1585, 1590 and 1594, and issued after his death by his son Rumold Mercator in 1595.

Atlas Folio. The largest size folio. About 25 inches by 16 inches. *See also* ELEPHANT FOLIO.

Atlas Size. A large square folio book, size about 25 × 16 inches.

ATS. Abbreviation for Animal Tub-sized. *See Tub-Sizing.*

Attaching. (*Binding*) The process of attaching the boards to the sewn sections after rounding and backing. The attaching joint is a strip of tough paper pasted on to the outside of the end leaf to serve as a connecting link with the boards. Not to be confused with CASING (*q.v.*).

Attention Note. A note, sometimes combined with a ROUTEING SLIP (*q.v.*), attached to a periodical in order to draw the attention of users to specific articles or items of information in which they may be interested. It is individual with respect of items to which attention is drawn and the individual addressed.

Attribute. In co-ordinate indexing, a characteristic mentioned as subject-matter. *See also Characteristics of a Classification.*

Attributed Author. The person to whom a book is attributed, because of doubt as to the authorship. *See also Supposed Author.*

Audio Charging. A form of Transaction Charging in which the loan serial number, and the essential details of the book and of the reader are spoken into a microphone and recorded on a tape. When all the Transaction Cards representing returned books have been sorted into serial number order, any missing ones represent overdue books. *See also Charging Methods, Transaction Card Charging.*

Audio Library. A collection of sound recordings, including compact discs, tapes and records.

Audiotape. A generic term designating a sound recording on magnetic tape. Also called 'Phonotape'.

Audio-Visual Aids. Material such as records, tape recordings and various VISUAL AIDS (*q.v.*) used as an adjunct to teaching. *See also Media.*

Audio-Visual Area. An area within a library building, or serving as an adjunct to a library, which is equipped with apparatus for screening or listening, and for storing materials used in connection with the apparatus.

Audio-Visual Group. A Group of the (British) Library Association, formerly known as the SOUND RECORDINGS GROUP (*q.v.*). Publishes *Audiovisual Librarian* (q.).

Audio-Visual Materials. Non-book materials such as records, tapes, slides, filmstrips and video-tapes. *See also Non-Book Materials.*

Audit. Checking accounts for accuracy and to see that expenditure is authorized by the appropriate authority.

AUKML. *See Association of UK Media Librarians.*

Aurianne Award. Established in 1956 by the Executive Board of the American Library Association, and made under the will of Miss Augustine Aurianne. Awarded annually 'to the author for a book published in the preceding year but one, which is considered the best book of the year on animal life which helps to develop a humane attitude in the young'. It is administered by the Association for Library Service to Children, and the selection of the book to receive the award is made by the Aurianne Award Committee.

Australian Bibliographic Network. *See ABN.*

Australian Bibliographical Centre. The Centre, which was established in 1956, was administratively part of the National Library of Australia; all its functions have been taken over by the National Library and it has ceased to be administered as a separate unit.

Australian Centre for Research in Library and Information Science. *See ACRILIS.*

Australian Clearinghouse for Library and Information Science. ACHLIS was established in 1982 as a non-profit service to the library profession to collect systematically and record all Australian documentation in library and information science. Publishes *ALISA*. (*q.v.*). Currently based at South Australia College of Advanced Education.

Australian Library and Information Association. Known until 1988 as the *Library Association of Australia*, ALIA is an Australia-wide organization first incorporated by Royal Charter in 1964 and supplemented in 1988. It has c.7500 members, of whom c.5500 are professional members. Institutions may also become members of the Association. The objects of the Association are to promote and improve the services of libraries and other information agencies; to improve the standard of library and information personnel and foster their professional interests; to represent the interests of members to governments, other organizations and the community and to encourage people to contribute to the improvement of library and information services by supporting the Association. There are branches in each state and over twenty-five divisions comprising members interested in various aspects of library and information work from cataloguing and special libraries to rural and isolated libraries and conservation. The Association provides services to members on industrial matters and organizes workshops, conferences and seminars on new developments within the industry. The governing body of the Association is the General Council. It publishes the *Australian Library Journal*, the newsletter *InCite*, as well as a range of specialist publications to cater for the interests of members.

Australian Library and Information Council. Set up in 1981 to advise the government at all levels on library and information matters. Reported to the Cultural Ministers Council, and included representatives of State and Territory Librarians, Directors of the Australian Archives and National Library, and of the education and science communities. Abbreviated ALIC. *Now see ACLIS.*

Australian Library and Information Science Abstracts. *See ALISA.*

Australian School Library Association. Established 1969. Based at Goulburn, NSW. Aims to promote development and improvement of school libraries and librarianship. Publishes *School Libraries in Australia* (q.).

Authentication. 1. (*Archives*) The act of determining that a document, or a reproduction of a document, is what it purports to be. *See also Certification.* 2. Confirmation that a record entered on a database is of the approved standard.

Author. The person, persons or corporate body, responsible for the writing or compilation of a book or other publication not a periodical. Usually to be distinguished from an editor, translator, compiler, etc., although, failing any alternative, these may be regarded as authors for purposes of cataloguing. In a wider sense, an artist, a composer of a musical work, and a photographer are authors to whom would be attributed work which they had created.

Author Abstract. *See Abstract.*

Author Affiliation. The organizations with which an author is affiliated, as indicated on the title-page, or in a periodical article or proceedings, and appearing after the author's name in a library catalogue.

Author Analytic. *See Analytical Entry.*

Author Authority List. *See Name Authority File.*

Author Bibliography.   One listing books, articles, or other contributions to knowledge made by, or by and about, a particular author. It may include biographies and criticisms of his work as well as works by him.

Author Card.   A catalogue card bearing an author entry; usually the main entry card. *See also Main Entry.*

Author Catalogue.   A catalogue of author entries arranged alphabetically under authors' names; it usually includes entries under editors, translators, composite authors, corporate bodies, first words of titles, or any other words or names used as headings for the main entries.

Author Entry.   A catalogue entry under the name of the person or body responsible for the writing, or compilation, of a published work. Failing one or more real names, the author entry may have to be made under a pseudonym, initials, or some other heading. For music, it is generally an added entry under the name of the author of the text accompanying a musical work, e.g. librettist, or author whose work served as the basis or inspiration for a musical work, the main entry being made under the composer's name.

Author Heading.   The heading under which an author entry is made.

Author Indention.   *Synonymous with* FIRST INDENTION (*q.v.*).

Author Mark.   Symbols (letters, figures, or other signs) used to represent authors and so individualize books having the same class, subject, or shelf number, in order to simplify the arrangement of books and catalogue entries. *See also Book Number, Cutter Author Marks, Merrill Alphabeting Numbers, Three Number Author Table.*

Author Number.   *Synonymous with* AUTHOR MARK (*q.v.*).

Author Order.   Said of books, or of entries relating to books, which are arranged in alphabetical order of authors' names.

Author–Publisher.   The writer of a work who is his own publisher.

Author Statement.   That part of a catalogue entry which mentions the author when transcribing the title. It is usually omitted unless it contributes data which is essential in some way to the entry, e.g. it would be given for joint authors.

Author Style.   The usual combination of block capitals and lower-case letters which is used for author headings in a catalogue. *See also Subject Style.*

Author Table.   A printed list used in assigning author numbers, e.g. the CUTTER AUTHOR MARKS (*q.v.*), or the CUTTER–SANBORN THREE-FIGURE TABLE (*q.v.*).

Author–Title Added Entry.   An added entry which involves two elements, placed in a TRACING (*q.v.*) and also at the top of a secondary entry. It would be given for the author's name followed by the title of a book when an adaptation, supplement, etc., is involved, or in a subject heading for a commentary on an individual work.

Author–Title Index.   One which has entries under authors' names and under titles, either in one or in two alphabetical sequences.

Authoritative Edition.   *See Definitive Edition.*

Authorities.   *See Primary Sources, Secondary Sources.*

Authority Card. 1. A card which gives the form selected for a heading in a catalogue. If a personal name is used as a heading, references to sources and records of variant forms are given; if a corporate name, sources, brief history and any changes of name are given. 2. A card which bears the classification number given by the classifiers to a subject, and also the subject index headings for entries made out for it. Where chain indexing is undertaken, a separate entry would be made for each step taken in determining the number. *See also Authority List, Chain Indexing, Name Authority File, Subject Authority File.* 3. In acquisition work, a term sometimes used to denote a request, requisition or recommendation card, so named because it bears the signature or authority for an acquisition transaction.

Authority Entry. An entry for a society or institution, giving such particulars as the date of founding, date of incorporation, changes of name, and affiliation or union with other societies.

Authority File. *Synonymous with* AUTHORITY LIST (*q.v.*).

Authority List. 1. A list of all personal and corporate names, names of anonymous classics and sacred books, the titles of anonymous books and the headings for series cards, which are used as headings in the catalogue; sometimes references are given to books in which each name and its variants were found, and in the case of corporate entries, sources, a brief history and particulars as to changes of name. The entries are made when a heading is first decided upon. It gives the cataloguer a record in the forms used in the public catalogues. If the list is kept on cards, one entry to a card, each card is known as an 'authority card'. 2. A list in classified order of classification symbols or numbers which have been allocated to books, with their corresponding index entries. Also called 'Authority file'. *See also Authority Card, Chain Indexing, Name Authority File, Subject Authority File.* 3. Also called, in the context of indexing documents, CLOSED INDEXING SYSTEM; CONTROLLED TERM LIST (*q.v.*). *See also Open-Ended Term List, Term, Thesaurus.*

Authorized Edition. An edition issued with the consent of the author, or of his representative to whom he may have delegated his rights and privileges.

Author's Agent. *See Literary Agent.*

Author's Alterations. *Synonymous with* AUTHOR'S CORRECTIONS (*q.v.*).

Author's Binding. A superior binding used on a few copies of a book as presentation copies from the author.

Author's Club First Novel Award. An annual award for the most promising first novel published in the UK.

Author's Copies. The complimentary copies of a book, usually six in number, presented on publication to its author by the publisher.

Author's Corrections. Deviations from the original copy, as distinct from corrections by the author of printer's errors marked on a printer's proof. *See also Author's Revise.*

Author's Edition. 1. The collected or complete edition of an author's works, uniformly bound, and indicating on the title-page that it is the complete works of the author. 2. An edition the publication of which has been authorized by the author. *See also Definitive Edition.*

Authors' Foundation. A UK grant-making fund administered by the Society of Authors (*q.v.*).

Author's Proof. The clean proof sent to an author after the compositor's errors have been corrected. Abbreviated AP.

Author's Revise. A proof bearing the author's or editor's corrections as distinct from one corrected by the printer.

Author's Rights. Those secured to an author under a copyright act.

Author's Signature. A quantity of 40,000 ems of type (about sixteen printed pages) used as a basis for calculating author's royalites in the Soviet Union. The number or roubles paid per 'author's signature' varies with the quality or importance of the work.

Auto-Abstract. 1. (*Noun*) The resulting product of a machine preparing an extract consisting of complete sentences from a document which is so abstracted. *See also Abstract.* 2. (*Verb*) To select an assemblage of keywords from a document, commonly by an automatic or machine method, in order to form an abstract of the document.

Auto-Bias Device. The linking, when determining notation in the Colon Classification, of two foci within the same facet by the use of a hyphen. *See also Facet, Focus.*

Autobiography. The life of a person written by himself/herself.

Auto-Encode. To select keywords from a document, by a machine method, in order to develop search patterns for information retrieval.

Auto-Encoding. The process of producing either auto-abstracts or automatically generated index entries on the basis of word frequency.

Autograph. A person's signature. In the book trade, a description of cards, documents, letters, manuscripts, etc., written or signed with the writer's own hand.

Autographed Edition. An edition of a work, copies of which are signed by the author. *See also Limited Edition.*

Autography. 1. The author's own handwriting. 2. Reproductions of the form or outline of anything by an impression from the thing itself. 3. A lithographic process of reproducing writing, drawing, etc., in facsimile. 4. That branch of diplomatics which is concerned with autographs.

Auto-Index. To prepare an index by a mechanical method.

Autokerning. In computer typesetting, the automatic reformatting of text to remove unsightly white spaces between characters or words. *See also Kern.*

Auto-Lithography. A lithographic method in which the artist draws in reverse directly on to the stone or medium.

Automated Library Systems Ltd. *See ALS.*

Automatic Abstracting. The selection by machine of words and phrases from a document for quotation in order to describe its content. *See also Automatic Indexing.*

Automatic Assignment Indexing. The process of using machines to assign index entries in respect of the text of a document, such entries being obtained from a standardized list such as a subject heading list, a thesaurus, or a dictionary which exists independently of the text of the document being indexed.

Automatic Derivative Indexing. The process of using machines to extract, or derive, index entries from the text of a document without human intervention once procedural rules or programs have been formulated.

Automatic Dictionary. The component of a language translating machine which provides a word for word substitution from one language to another. In automatic searching systems, the automatic dictionary is the component which substitutes codes for words or phrases during the encoding operation.

Automatic Document Request Service. A service operated by the British Library Document Supply Centre via the BLAISE network which enables libraries to identify a document and submit an interloan request in one single operation. Abbreviated ADRS.

Automatic Format Recognition. (*Information retrieval*) The automatic recognition by a computer of the structure of a record in terms of fields, element, etc., without the need for tagging (*See Tagged (Tagging) 2*).

Automatic Indexing. 1. The selection of keywords from a document by a machine method in order to develop index entries. 2. The use of machines to extract and assign index terms without human intervention once programmes or procedural rules have been established. *See also Automatic Abstracting, Mechanized Indexing.*

Automatic Routeing. *See Routeing.*

Automation. The organization of machine handling of routines or operations, requiring minimal human intervention.

Autonym. The real name of an author.

Autotype. To make a copy by a carbon process.

Autotype Reproduction. One reproduced by the autotype process, which is a variety of the collotype process, in which the plate is coated with a light-sensitive resin instead of a gelatine.

Autotypy. The process of making copies by the carbon process.

Auxiliaries. *See Universal Decimal Classification.*

Auxiliary Number. One placed after the class number in order to group the books by some method, such as alphabetically or chronologically. The OLIN BOOK NUMBER (*q.v.*) and CUTTER AUTHOR MARKS (*q.v.*) are auxiliary numbers.

Auxiliary Publication. The process of making data available by means of specially ordered microfilm or photocopies. Auxiliary publication usually presupposes that the materials have not been published before, although it is sometimes applied to publication of microcard copies of out-of-print books.

Auxiliary Schedules and Tables. Tables of subdivisions which are appended to schedules of all schemes of classification. They consist of items of relationship, time, locality, etc. and the symbols of the different items can be added to book classification numbers. Broadly, they fall into three groups: those which (a) are common and can be used with the same meaning throughout the classification, e.g., the common subdivisions of Dewey's

Decimal Classification; (b) are common to, and may only be applied to, certain subjects, e.g. the Systematic and Auxiliary Schedules of Bliss's Bibliographic Classification; (c) can be applied in only one place as in most of the Library of Congress Classification Schedules. *See also Systematic Auxiliary Schedules.*

Auxiliary Syndesis.   The accessory apparatus, e.g. cross reference, which is used to supplement indexing sequence so as to reveal other relations.

Auxiliary Tables.   In the Universal Decimal Classification tables of secondary aspects of subjects which may be applied to primary aspects to qualify them, and are distinguished by a special symbol, or 'facet indicator'. For a synopsis of auxiliaaries, *see Universal Decimal Classificaion.*

Average Slope Map.   One which indicates the average steepness of land slopes.

AVMARC.   The AVMARC file is part of the British Library Automated Information Service (BLAISE) and consists of bibliographic records for audiovisual materials. It became part of BLAISE in late 1979 and at that time contained just over five thousand records. The original input to AVMARC, which excluded music recordings and 16mm films, came from the Learning Materials Recording study which was sponsored by the Inner London Education Authority (ILEA) and the British Library Research and Development Department (BLRDD). The setting up of the file involved the conversion to machine-readable form of part of the catalogue of the ILEA Central Library Resources Service Reference Library. Further records for the file were created from information supplied by the British Universities Films Council (BUFC) and publishers of audio-visual materials. Records for all this material were published in 1979 as the *British Catalogue of Audiovisual Materials 1st Experimental Edition.* The AVMARC file was updated in April 1981 bringing the total number of records to nearly eight thousand. These new records were published as the *British Catalogue of Audiovisual Materials Supplement 1981.* Records are now continually added to the file, but no printed version is produced, and access is via BLAISE-LINE (*q.v.*) only.

Azerty.   The standard typewriter keyboard arrangement used in continental Europe, placing the letters a.z.e.r.t.y. from the left on the top row. *See also Qwerty.*

Azure Tooling.   (*Bookbinding*) Tooling in which horizontal lines are shown close together.

Azured Tool.   A bookbinder's tool with close parallel lines running diagonally across its surface. Derived from the use of thin horizontal lines used in heraldry to indicate blue.

Babel.   Conferences organized by BEDIS (*q.v.*) in 1986 and 1989 have sought to avoid an 'electronic Babel' and have become known as Babel 1 and Babel 2.

Baber Award, Carroll Preston.   An annual cash award presented for the encouragement of research in library science, improvement in services to specific user groups, and new uses for technology. Administered by the American Library Association Awards Committee. First awarded in 1986.

Back. 1. The 'back' or inside margins of pages. 2. *Synonymous with* SPINE (*q.v.*). 3. The surface of a piece of movable type parallel to the BELLY (*q.v.*).

Back Board. The piece of millboard or strawboard which is used for the back cover of a book.

Back Cornering. (*Binding*) The cutting off of a small portion of the inner corners of the boards near the headcaps in order to improve their setting.

Back Cover. *Synonymous with* REVERSE COVER (*q.v.*).

Back File. The file or 'back numbers' (i.e. those preceding the current issue) of a periodical.

Back Fold. *See Bolt.*

Back Issue. *Synonymous with* BACK NUMBER (*q.v.*).

Back Lining. A piece of material (paper, cloth, calf skin) glued to the back sections of a book after sewing, before securing the cover.

Back List. The titles which a publisher keeps in print.

Back Margin. The margin of a printed page which is nearest the fold of the section. Also called: 'Gutter', 'Gutter margin', 'Inner margin', 'Inside margin'.

Back Mark. A small oblong block or number printed in such a position on the sheet that when the sheets of a book are folded and placed together for casing, the oblongs or numbers will follow each other in a slanting and/or numerical sequence down the spine and thus show if any section has been duplicated, misplaced or omitted. Also called 'Collating mark', 'Quad mark'. *See also Black Step.*

Back Matter. Matter which is published at the end of the text, e.g. addenda, appendix, author's notes, bibliography, glossary, index, reference matter. Also called 'End-matter', 'Subsidiaries'. *See also Preliminaries.*

Back Number. An issue of a periodical which precedes the current number.

Back Order. An uncompleted order which is held back for future delivery.

Back Page. The verso, even-numbered, side of a leaf of a book or sheet of printed paper or manuscript. The back of a page.

Back-Projection Reader. A reader in which an enlargement of a microform image is projected on to the back of a translucent screen for reading from the front by transmitted light.

Back Title. The title which is placed on the spine, or back, of a book. *See also Binder's Title, Cover Title.*

Back-Up. To print the second side of a sheet after the first has been printed.

Back-Up Services. 1. The services provided by libraries in support of a central loan collection. 2. Those providing documents, or substitutes for documents, in support of a literature survey, reading list or some similar information service.

Backbone. *Synonymous with* SPINE (*q.v.*).

Backed. 1. A damaged leaf of a book, whether text or plate, which has been 'laid down' on, or pasted on, to paper, gauze or linen. 2. The spine of a book which is covered with a different material to the sides, as 'marbled boards backed with leather'. 3. The spine of a book which has been re-covered with a different material to the original, a 're-backed' one having been re-covered with similar material to the original.

Backing. The bookbinding operation whereby the sewn sections of a book, after glueing, are placed securely between backing boards after ROUNDING (*q.v.*), and hammered to splay them outwards from the centre of the book. It adds permanence to the rounding, and forms an abutment, or ridge, into which to fit the boards: the ridge so formed is called a 'joint'. This operation is carried out in Britain and America after ROUNDING (*q.v.*): in most Western European countries rounding only is done. *See also Flat Back, Round Back.*

Backing Boards. (*Binding*) Boards used when backing and forming the groove or joint. They are made of very hard wood and sometimes faced with iron. The edge intended to form the groove is thicker than that which goes towards the fore-edge, so that when placed on either side of the book in the lying press the power of the press is directed towards the back.

Backing Machine. A machine for backing books, generally used for publishers' binding and cheap work.

Backing Store. *See Memory.*

Backing Up. *See Perfecting.*

Backless Binding. A volume which is bound in such a way that the spine is flat or concave, covered with paper and gilt, and probably tooled, so as to look like the fore-edge which is itself finished in a similar manner.

Backlining. The material, usually paper, pasted on the inside of the SPINE (*q.v.*) of a book.

Backs. The back margins of pages, i.e. those nearest the fold of the section. *See also Back.*

Backslide. The block which is placed behind the cards in a catalogue drawer, and is moved backwards and forwards according to the quantity of cards in the drawer to prevent them from falling out of an upright position. It is usually made with its front sloping back at the top to permit of easy consultation.

Backstrip. *Synonymous with* SPINE (*q.v.*).

Baconian Classification. The scheme propounded by Francis Bacon in his *Advancement of Learning* (1605), which more than any other philosophical scheme of thought, or classification of knowledge, has had the greatest influence on library classification. It was based on the three faculties, Memory, Imagination, and Reason, and these produced the three main headings, History, Poetry and Philosophy. The scheme was used for the arrangement of books, and its inversion is the basis of Dewey's *Decimal Classification.*

Bad Break. Incorrect line end hyphenation, or the start of a page of text with a WIDOW (*q.v.*) or the end of a hyphenated word.

Bad Copy. 'Copy' which is difficult to read. This reduces the speed, and increases the cost, of typesetting. *See also Copy 1.*

Bad Letter. *Synonymous with* DAMAGED LETTER (*q.v.*).

Bains Report. *The New Local Authorities: Management and Structure.* The report of a study group appointed jointly by the Secretary of State for the Environment and local authority associations to examine principles and structures in local government at both elected member and officer levels. The Group was set up in May 1971, chaired by M. A. Bains, Clerk of the Kent County Council, and its Report was published in 1972.

Baker Report. The Report of the Working Party appointed by the Minister of Education in March 1961, *Inter-Library Co-operation in England and Wales,* 1962. E. B. H. Baker was Chairman of the Working Party. *See also Bourdillon Report.*

Ball. 1. *See Ink Ball.* 2. In typography, the finishing element at the top of the strokes of the type letter *a* and *c.*

Ball Local History Awards. The Alan Ball Local History Awards, of which two are made each calendar year (an author award, and a book production award) were instituted in 1985 by the Library Services Trust (of the London and Home Counties Branch of the Library Association). Alan Ball, Chief Librarian of the London Borough of Harrow, had been active in the Branch for over 20 years. The Awards are to encourage UK library activity in the area of local history.

BALLOTS. Acronym of Bibliographic Automation of Large Library Operations using a Time-sharing System, the on-line interactive library automation system that supported the acquisition and cataloguing functions of the Stanford University libraries' technical processing operations. A grant from the Council on Library Resources, Inc. in 1975, enabled new development tasks toward a California automation network to be undertaken. This project eventually formed the basis for RLIN (*q.v.*).

BAND. Acronym for Book Action for Nuclear Disarmament, a London-based group of independent writers, booksellers, publishers, librarians and literary agents. Responsible for the organization of the National Peace Book Week.

BANDS. The cords or strings whereon the sheets of a book are sewed. With FLEXIBLE SEWING (*q.v.*), the bands appear upon the back. When books are sewn so as to embed the cord in the back, or in modern books sewn on tapes, the appearance of raised bands is sometimes produced by narrow strips of leather or cardboard glued across the back before the volume is covered. The space between the bands is called 'between bands'.

Bangladesh National Scientific and Technical Documentation Centre. *See BANSDOC.*

Bank Letter. A bulletin or other periodical publication issued by a bank primarily to give information on current industrial, business and financial conditions in general.

Banned. Prohibited from sale by ecclesiastical or secular authority.

BANSDOC. Abbreviation for the Bangladesh National Scientific and Technical Documentation Centre which developed in Dacca from the East Pakistan branch office of PANSDOC and is now a part of the Bangladesh Council of Scientific and Industrial Research (BCSIR). BANSDOC operates from the premises of the Bangladesh Council of Scientific and Industrial Research, based in Dacca, and functions 'to serve as an infrastructure for an effective research and development programme as a part of the overall development of the country'.

BAPLA. The British Association of Picture Libraries and Agencies is the only trade association in Britain that represents UK picture libraries and agencies holding stock photographs. Each one of the 200 full members is a commercial library or agency and together they handle more than 100 million images. The membership embraces almost all the major commercial libraries and agencies and many of the smaller, specialist ones. There is a separate category for national and regional museums. Members are asked to adhere to a Code of Conduct which ensures that the membership acts in an ethical manner. Applicants for membership are asked to supply referees. Election is by the Executive Committee on payment of the entry fee and subscription. BAPLA maintains close contact with other trade associations with similar aims, such as the Association of Photographers (AFAEP), British Institute of Professional Photographers (BIPP), Society for Picture Researchers and Editors (SPREd), Professional Sports Photographers Association (PSPA), American Society of Magazine Photographers (ASMP), Picture Council Agency of America (PACA), German BVPA and Italian GADEF. BAPLA has also been an active member of the Committee on Photographic Copyright. Publishes *BAPLA Journal* (q.) and a *Directory* (a.).

Bar. The horizontal stroke of letters; e.g. A, H and e.

Bar-Code. A code arranged in a series of parallel lines or bars, representing data that is transferred by a *bar-code scanner* into digital signals for a computer store.

Bargate (Verity) Award. An annual UK award for a new and unperformed play.

Barnard Memorial Prize, (Cyril). This Prize was established by the Medical Section of the Library Association in 1960 to commemorate one of the founders of the Section.

Barnes Report (UK). The Report of the Commission on the Supply of and Demand for Qualified Librarians. The Chairman was M. P. K. Barnes, and the Report was published by the Library Association in 1977.

Barrow Process. (*Archives*) A process of document repair and restoration which involves de-acidification, the use of tissue to strengthen the original, and thermoplastic lamination. It is named after William J. Barrow (1904–67).

Bartlett (Alice Hunt) Award. An annual UK award made by the Poetry Society to a living poet whose work the Society wishes to honour and encourage.

Baryta Paper. A form of metallic paper, consisting of a suitable body paper coated with barium sulphate; marks can be made on this with a metal point or stylus. It is used in some types of automatic recording apparatus and also for text impressions on photocomposing machines.

BAS. *See Bowker Acquisition System.*

Basan Skin. Sheepskin tanned with the bark of oak or larch.

Base. The range of characters of a NOTATION 1, (*q.v.*). The total number of such characters is known as the base length.

Base Line. (*Printing*) The lowest limit of the body of a piece of type; the imaginary line on which the bases of capitals rest. *See also Cap Line, Mean Line.*

Base Map. One on which additional information may be plotted for a particular purpose.

Base of a Notation. (*Classification*) The series of symbols used. Their number is the length of base, or its first dimension. In the Dewey *Decimal Classification* it is ten – the ten arabic numerals, in Bliss's *Bibliographic Classification* it is thirty-five – the twenty-six letters of the English alphabet combined with the nine arabic numerals.

Base of Symbolism. *See Alphabet of Symbols.*

Base of Type. The feet, or lowest part, on which the base of a capital letter rests.

Base Paper. *Synonymous with* BODY PAPER (*q.v.*).

Base Stock. The material, such as plastic, paper or cloth, used as carrier for a photosensitive emulsion.

Basic Analysis. The citation in upward hierarchical order of the constituent elements of a composite subject. It is the first stage in converting a classification symbol into a verbal subject heading for an alphabetico-specific subject catalogue. The second stage is producing the Qualified List (*q.v.*).

Basic Class. (*Classification*) *Synonymous with* MAIN CLASS (*q.v.*).

Basic List. (*Information retrieval*) An alphabetical or classified list of terms from which a thesaurus may be construed.

Basic Stock. Standard books which it may be considered should form the basis of a well-balanced and authoritative book stock.

Basic Weight. (*Paper*) The substance of paper is expressed as the weight of a given superficial area, the units most commonly used being either pounds per ream or grammes per square metre. For example '20 × 30 inches 36 lb 480s' means that if the paper were cut into sheets measuring 20 × 30 inches, then 480 sheets would weigh 36 lb.

Basil. A thin sheepskin not suitable for library bookbinding. It is mostly used for binding account books.

Basis. Danish library bibliographic network for public and school collections. Based at the Central Library, Ballerup; established 1974, with 90 members at present.

Baskerville. A typeface named after John Baskerville (1706–75) of Birmingham, famous printer and type-founder who was printer of Bibles and prayer books to the University of Cambridge 1758–68. His folio Bible of 1763 was his masterpiece. The type is a modification of Caslon. For a specimen alphabet, *see Transitional, Type Face.*

Bas-Relief Printing. *Synonymous with* EMBOSSING (*q.v.*).

Basso Continuo. Italian for continued bass, or FIGURED BASS (*q.v.*).

Bastard Title. *Synonymous with* HALF-TITLE (*q.v.*).

Bastard Type. Type having the face larger or smaller than the size proper to the body, as a nonpareil face on a brevier body, or 10 point face on 12 point body, used to give the appearance of being leaded. *See also* Gothic Type.

Bastarda. *See* Gothic Type.

Batch Processing. A technique by which items to be processed in a data processing machine must be collected into groups prior to their processing; contrasted to on-line processing.

Batchelder Award, Mildred L. Awarded, for the first time in 1968, to an American publisher for the most outstanding of those books originally published in a foreign language in a foreign country, and subsequently published in English in the United States during the calendar year preceding the appointment of the Mildred L. Batchelder Award Committee which is appointed annually. This Committee nominates from three to five books, the final choice is made by the membership of the Association for Library Services to Children.

Bath University Comparative Catalogue Study. *See BUCCS.*

Batten Cards. Cards used in the Batten retrieval system, which represent the presence or absence of each document by a hole or no-hole in a specific position. *See also Peek-a-Boo.*

Batten System. A method of indexing, invented by W. E. Batten, utilizing the co-ordination of single attributes to identify specific documents. Sometimes called the 'peek-a-boo' system because of its method of comparing holes in cards by superimposing cards and checking the coincidence of holes.

Battered. Type matter or electros when accidentally injured, or so worn that they give defective impressions, are said to be battered.

Battered Letter. *Synonymous with* DAMAGED LETTER (*q.v.*).

Battledore. *See Horn Book.*

Baud. Measurement, in bits per second, of the speed at which data can be transmitted by a terminal. Slow terminals operate at speeds up to 300 baud. Telephone lines will accept speeds of up to 5000 baud maximum with a usual maximum of 2400 baud.

Bay. A U-shaped arrangement of shelving. *See also Press, Stack, Tier.*

Bay Guide. A guide to the subjects of the books shelved in a BAY (*q.v.*).

Bay Psalm Book. *The whole Book of Psalmes faithfully translated into English metre*; the first book printed in Cambridge, Mass., in what is now the USA, in 1640 by Stephen Day, on the first press introduced into English-speaking America in 1638.

BB&O. Berkshire, Buckinghamshire & Oxfordshire Branch (*q.v.*) (of the Library Association).

B.Bibl. Bachelier en Bibliothéconomie et en Bibliographie. A degree of librarianship awarded in Canada.

BBK. Bibliotechno-bibliograficheskaya Klassifikatsiya; the principal classification scheme used by libraries in the USSR.

BBS. *See Bulletin Board Systems.*

BCM. *British Catalogue of Music (q.v.).*

BCOP. Birmingham Co-operative Project; established 1977 by the major libraries in the Birmingham (UK) area to investigate economies through resource sharing.

BCR. *See Bibliographic Center for Research.*

Beard. That part of the shoulder of a piece of movable type that slopes down from the 'face', or bottom of the printing surface of the letter to the front of the 'body', but more particularly that portion sloping from the bottom serifs of the face to the 'belly'. It consists of the BEVEL *(q.v.)* and the SHOULDER *(q.v.).*

Bearers. *(Printing)* Type-high strips of metal placed around pages of type when locked in formes from which electrotype plates are to be made. They appear as black borders on proofs. *See also Forme.*

Beater. *Synonymous with BREAKER (q.v.).*

BEC. *See Business Education Council.*

Beckett (Samuel) Award. Two UK annual awards for a first play for the stage and for television, professionally performed in the current year. Jointly sponsored by Channel 4, the Royal Court Theatre, and Faber and Faber.

Bed. The flat steel table of a printing machine or press on which the *forme* of type is placed for printing. When the forme has been secured, it is described as having been 'put to bed'. *See also Chase.*

Bedford Bindings. Bindings by Francis Bedford (1799–1883) an Englishman who succeeded to the business of Charles Lewis. He was the greatest English binder of his time, but his work has little artistic merit and little originality. He attained good results by imitating early Venetian work, with twisted or Saracenic ornament, as well as the later Veneto-Lyonese style, practised in England in Queen Elizabeth's time.

BEDIS. Booktrade Electronic Data Interchange Standards; a working party set up in 1987 by the UK MARC Users Group to investigate the current state of standards used for the electronic transmission of bibliographic data. A preliminary discussion paper was issued in April 1988, and overviews all kinds of data transferred between publishers, booksellers and librarians. *See also BTECC Babel.*

Beirut Agreement. The 'Agreement for facilitating the international circulation of visual and auditory materials of an educational, scientific and cultural character' was intended essentially to promote social and cultural progress in all countries. The purpose of the Agreement is to facilitate the despatch from country to country of (i) films, filmstrips and microfilms; (ii) sound recordings; (iii) glass slides, models, wall charts, maps and posters. At a meeting of international experts held at Geneva in 1967 (the Agreement had been adopted at the Third Session of Unesco held at Beirut in 1948 and came into force on 12 August 1954) it was agreed that the term 'audio-visual' should be liberally interpreted to include the various types of such equipment which had been introduced in the intervening years.

Belles Lettres. Polite literature, or works of literary art showing grace and imagination, as poetry, drama, criticism, fiction and essays. From the French; literally 'beautiful letters'.

Bellows Press. A small flat-bed platen press used for jobbing work, e.g. envelopes, broadsides, cards, hand bills, etc. The presses manufactured by the Adana Company are of this kind.

Belly. The front of the part of a piece of movable type called the body.

Beltel. The South African videotex service.

Bembo. A Roman type face cut originally by Francesco Griffi for Aldus and first used by him in Cardinal Pietro Bembo's *Aetna*, 1495–6. It was the model followed by GARAMOND (*q.v.*) and was re-cut by the Monotype Corporation in 1929. It is regarded by many as the most beautiful of the old-face designs; the modern 'Monotype' Bembo is one of the best book types available. It is relatively condensed, a good space saver, and having long ascenders, is legible and pleasant even when set solid. For a specimen, *see Type Face.*

Ben Day Process. A process invented by Ben Day to produce shaded tints or mottled effects by transferring various inked designs in relief on a gelatine film to the metal plate which is later etched.

Bench Press. A small press, resting on a work bench and used by bookbinders to press cased books. *See also Standing Press.*

Beneventan Handwriting. A beautiful minuscule handwriting used in Southern Italy and Dalmatia which survived a number of national varieties developed from the Italian semi-cursive minuscule, itself a descendant of the Roman cursive. *See also Cursive, Handwriting.*

Benson Medal. An occasional award made by the Royal Society of Literature for an exceptional literary work.

Berghoeffer System. A filing system first used by Prof. Dr. Christian W. Berghoeffer who compiled the Frankfurter Sammelkatalog in 1891. *See also Finding List Catalogue.*

Berkshire, Buckinghamshire and Oxfordshire Branch. A branch of the (British) Library Association; formed on 1 January 1963, having been from 1956 a Sub-branch of the London and Home Counties Branch. Abbreviated BB & O.

Berne Convention. In full, Berne Convention for the Protection of Literary and Artistic Works. *See Berne Copyright Union.*

Berne Copyright Union. The International Convention for the Protection of Literary and Artistic Works, known as the 'Berne Convention', was adopted by an international conference held at Berne in 1886. Designed to protect effectively, and in as uniform a manner as possible, the rights of authors in their literary and artistic works, the Berne Convention was originally signed on 9 September 1886, and completed in Paris on 4 May 1896; it was revised in Berlin on 13 November 1908, completed at Berne on 20 March 1914, revised at Rome on 2 June 1928, at Brussels on 26 June 1948, at Stockholm on 13 July 1967, and at Paris on 24 July 1971. The United Kingdom has been a party to the Convention from 5 December 1887, but the USA, although bound by the Universal Copyright Convention since 16 September 1955, joined only in 1988. The protection of the Berne Convention applies to authors who are nationals of one of the countries of the Union established by that Convention, for their works whether published or not, and to authors who are nationals of non-Union countries, for their works first published in one of those countries, or simultaneously in a country outside the Union and in a country of the Union. The duration of the protection provided by the 'Paris Act' of the Berne Convention is for the author's life and fifty years after his death. *See also Copyright, International; IGC, WIPO.*

BEST. British Expertise in Science and Technology; a database intended to promote collaboration between academic institutions and industry. Set up in 1985 at St. Andrews University.

Best Seller. A book which is so popular that unusually large numbers are sold.

Besterman Medal. Awarded annually by the Library Association for an outstanding bibliography or guide to the literature first published in the United Kingdom during the preceding year.

Beta Phi Mu Award. A cash award presented to a library school faculty member, or anyone making an important contribution to education for librarianship. Administered by the American Library Association Awards Committee.

Betamax. Half inch video-cassette format manufactured by Sony and aimed mainly at the domestic market.

BETI. *British Education Thesis Index. See British Education Index.*

Between Bands. *See Bands.*

Bevel. The part of the shoulder of a piece of movable type immediately sloping down from the 'face'. The distance from the face to the bottom of the bevel is known as the 'depth of strike'. Also called 'Neck'.

Bevelled Boards. Heavy boards with bevelled edges principally used for large books in imitation of antique work.

b.f. Abbreviation for BOLD FACE type.

BHI. *British Humanities Index (q.v.).*

BIALL. *See British and Irish Association of Law Librarians.*

Biannual. A publication which is issued twice a year. This word is sometimes used synonymously with *Biennial* which strictly means 'published every two years'. To avoid misunderstanding, the terms 'Half-yearly' or 'Twice a year' are tending to be used instead of Biannual. *See also Bi-monthly.*

Bias Phase. 1. In classification, where one topic is described (usually in a relatively elementary manner) for the benefit of those working in, or concerned with, another field, a document is classified under the topic introduced, not under the persons for whom it is written, e.g. anatomy for speech therapists would go under anatomy, not speech therapists. 2. The treatment of a subject generally and fairly completely, if concisely, from the point of view of a class of users whose primary interest is in another subject. It is one of Ranganathan's three chief 'phase relations', the other two being INFLUENCE PHASE and TOOL PHASE (*qq.v.*).

BIB. Biennale of Illustrations Bratislava (*q.v.*).

BIBDES. Bibliographic Data Entry System: a Software package used by the British Library to organize input to the BLAISE systems.

Bibelot. An unusually small book, valuable as a curiosity because of its format or rarity. Also called 'Dwarf book', 'Thumb book'.

Bible. *See Bishops' Bible, Complutensian Polyglot, 40-Line Bible, Geneva Bible, Mazarin Bible, Polyglot, 36-Line Bible, Vinegar Bible, Vulgate.*

Bible Paper. A very thin tough opaque paper used for Bibles or other lengthy books which are required to have little bulk. It is made from new cotton or linen rags. Often erroneously referred to as INDIA PAPER (*q.v.*). Also called 'Bible printing'. *See also Cambridge India Paper, Oxford India Paper.*

Bible Printing. *See Bible Paper.*

Biblia Pauperum. A type of mediaeval picture book of scriptural subjects, with descriptive vernacular text. Very popular among clergy and laity in continental countries before the Reformation. Many manuscript copies are preserved in different languages. It was one of the first books printed in the Netherlands and Germany, originally from blocks and then from type. It was reprinted several times in later years, most recently in 1884, with a preface by Dean Stanley.

BIBLID. Bibliographic identification; the International Standards Organization has agreed on a unique identification code for contributors to serials and monographs with several authors. This is similar to the US equivalent and it is intended to produce a common international draft scheme. The ISO version was used experimentally during 1986.

Biblio. The bibliographical note and/or imprint which is placed on the back of the title-page. *See also Preliminaries.*

Biblioclasm. The destruction of books, or of the Bible.

Biblioclast. A destroyer of books.

Bibliofile. The entire Library of Congress MARC database stored on three compact laser discs, with a monthly update that comprises a cumulative replacement disc. Retrieval is possible by author, title, ISBN, etc. and can be limited by various features. The system, which will also print cards and labels, is marketed by Library Corporation of Washington DC.

Bibliogenesis. The production of books.

Bibliognost. One versed in knowledge about books and in bibliography.

Bibliogony. The production of books.

Bibliograph. A bibliographer.

Bibliographee. A person concerning whom a bibliography has been made.

Bibliographer. 1. A person who is able to describe the physical characteristics of books by recognized methods. 2. One able to prepare bibliographies by recognized principles.

Bibliographic. *Synonymous with* BIBLIOGRAPHICAL (*q.v.*).

Bibliographic and Information Technology and Standards Committee. *See BITS.*

Bibliographic Automation of Large Library Operations using a Time-sharing System. *See BALLOTS.*

Bibliographic Centre. An organization, often a department of a library, which maintains a collection of Reference books from which it is possible to give information concerning the availability of books. In the USA, some of these centres are providing general reference information services. Also, a centre which acts as a depository for books and an agency for organizing book exchanges. *See also Bibliographical Centre.*

Bibliographic Center for Research. A Rocky Mountain/Midwest US co-ordinator of automated library services. Based in Denver, Colorado. Abbreviated BCR.

Bibliographic Classification. A scholarly and detailed scheme devised by H. E. Bliss and first applied in the College of the City of New York where the author was librarian in 1902. In addition to normal sub-division there are Systematic Auxiliary Schedules which are used on similar lines to Dewey's common sub-divisions: these provide for sub-division by form, geography, language, historical period, and of the philology of any language, of an author's works, etc. Apart from these schedules and the Anterior Numerical Classes, the notation is alphabetical, and although not extending beyond four letters, tends to be complete. The publication of a totally radical revision and expansion of the scheme was commenced in the summer of 1976. Every class has been gutted and reconstructed but the basic structure remains intact. This new edition has been prepared by Jack Mills and published by Butterworth. *See also Bliss Classification Association.* It is usually referred to as the Bliss Classification. The Bliss Classification Working Party operates in England and has prepared *The Abridged Bliss Classification; the Bibliographic Classification of Henry Evelyn Bliss revised for school libraries* which was published by the School Library Association in 1967 (reprinted with minor corrections, 1970).

Bibliographic Control. The creation, development, organization, management and exploitation of records prepared firstly to describe items held in libraries or on databases, and secondly to facilitate user access to such items.

Bibliographic Coupling. Comparison of articles and books cited in references and bibliographies appended to documents, as an indication of likely overlap or identity of subject coverage in the documents.

Bibliographic Database. A database containing records made up of BIBLIO-GRAPHIC INFORMATION (*q.v.*) and designed to identify and locate relevant items.

Bibliographic Index. A subject index to current bibliographies, whether published separately as books, or pamphlets, or bibliographies appearing in books and pamphlets, or as periodical articles. Published thrice annually, with annual cumulations, by the H. W. Wilson Company. Available on-line via WILSONLINE, and on CD-ROM.

Bibliographic Index. 1. A systematic list of writings or publications (e.g. of books or periodical articles) with or without annotations. 2. An index of publications or articles which contains no material descriptive of their contents other than bibliographical references. Also called 'Bibliographical index'.

Bibliographic Information. Details concerning a publication which are sufficient to identify it for the purpose of ordering. They may include the following: author, title, publisher, place of publication, edition, series note, number of volumes, parts and/or supplements, and price; editor, translator or illustrator may also be necessary in the case of certain books. Sometimes called 'trade information'.

Bibliographic Item. An article in a periodical, a technical report, a patent, a monograph, or a chapter in a symposium, which is capable of being given a separate bibliographic entry in a catalogue or bibliography. Also called 'Bibliographical item'.

Bibliographic Processing. *See Processing.*

Bibliographic Unit. 1. Any document, part of a document, or several documents, forming a bibliographic whole which is treated as a single entity in a system of bibliographical description. A BIBLIOGRAPHIC ITEM (*q.v.*). 2. More commonly, a group of people working together as a team in some bibliographic work.

Bibliographic Volume. A unit of publication distinguishable from other units by having its own title-page, half title, cover title, or portfolio title. If a periodical, all the parts which comprise the publisher's volume. Also called 'Bibliographical volume'.

Bibliographical. Of, or relating to, or dealing with, bibliography.

Bibliographical Centre. A place where bibliographies and catalogues of libraries, and those issued by publishers, are assembled, and information on books is given. They are usually associated with book-lending agencies, co-operative book stores, or national libraries, and may or may not be intimately connected with the lending of books. In the USA they also serve as bureaux organizing the inter-lending of books between libraries. *See also Bibliographic Centre.*

Bibliographical Classification. One designed for the classification of books and other literary material, and for the entries in bibliographies and catalogues. *See also Knowledge Classification.*

Bibliographical Description. The description of a published work of literary or musical composition, giving particulars of authorship, of others who have contributed to the presentation of the text (editor, translator, illustrator, arranger, etc.), title, edition, date, particulars of publication (place and name of publisher and possibly of printer), format, etc. In the case of music it may relate to a single recording or to an album of the same, as well as to printed music, and is concerned only with the publication *per se*, not its musical content. Not to be confused with MUSICAL DESCRIPTION (*q.v.*).

Bibliographical Index. *Synonymous with* BIBLIOGRAPHIC INDEX (*q.v.*).

Bibliographical Information in Printed Music. The presentation of bibliographical and related information in printed music, for the guidance of editors and publishers of music, is specified in BS 4754: 1971.

Bibliographical Item. *Synonymous with* BIBLIOGRAPHIC ITEM (*q.v.*).

Bibliographical Note. 1. A note, often a footnote, containing a reference to one or more books or periodical articles, etc., as sources for the work. 2. A note in a catalogue or in a bibliography relating to the bibliographical history of, or describing, a book. 3. A note, often a footnote or annotation, in a catalogue, mentioning a bibliography contained in a book.

Bibliographical References. References to books and parts of books (including articles in books), to periodicals and other serials, and to articles in periodicals. BS 1629: 1976 *Bibliographical references* gives rules and examples for entries in bibliographical lists and for identifying works or parts of works, quoted or referred to, in reviews, abstracts, etc.

Bibliographical Scatter. The appearance of an article on one subject in a periodical devoted to a totally different subject. Their oversight can be avoided by providing entries in KWIC (*q.v.*) and similar indexes, current awareness lists, subject indexes to periodical articles, etc., and by analytical subject entries in library catalogues.

Bibliographical Service. The facilities, procedures and devices which are employed to produce a bibliography consisting of a continuing series of publications, or bibliographical information as requested.

Bibliographical Society. The leading bibliographic society in the United Kingdom. It was founded in 1892. Publishes *The Library* (q.). The aims of the Society are, first, to promote and encourage study and research in the fields of historical, analytical, descriptive and textual bibliography, and the history of printing, publishing, bookselling, bookbinding and collecting; second, to hold meetings at which papers are read and discussed; third, to print and publish works concerned with bibliography; and fourth, to form a bibliographical library. The Society awards, from time to time, a gold medal for services to bibliography.

Bibliographical Society of America. The leading bibliographical society in America. It was founded in 1904 to promote bibliographical research and to issue bibliographical publications. Publishes *Papers* (q. to memb.). Abbreviated BSA.

Bibliographical Society of Canada. Founded in May 1946 to promote bibliographical publication, encourage the preservation of printed works and manuscripts, and extend knowledge of them, particularly those relating to Canada, and facilitate the exchange of bibliographical information. Membership is open to individuals and to institutions. Publishes *Papers* (a.), and a six-monthly *Bulletin*.

Bibliographical Society of the University of Virginia. Founded in 1950, this Society represents an advanced school of thought in modern bibliography.

Bibliographical Tool. A publication, such as a list of books, which is used by a bibliographer in the course of his work.

Bibliographical Unit. A document (*Fr.* ouvrage) which is an independent unit and described in a separate main entry in a catalogue.

Bibliographical Volume. *Synonymous with* BIBLIOGRAPHIC VOLUME (*q.v.*).

Bibliographing. The action of consulting bibliographies.

Bibliographize. To make a bibliography concerning some person and/or his writings, or of some subject.

Bibliography. 1. The compilation of *systematic* or *enumerative* bibliographies – books, MSS, audio-visual formats and other publications arranged in a logical order giving author, title, date and place of publication, publisher, details of edition, pagination, series and literary/information contents. Such a bibliography might be of works by one author, or on one subject, or printed by one printer, or in one place, or during one period. The term is also applied to the whole of the literature on a subject. A bibliography may be complete/general/universal (i.e. including all formats, periods, subjects, etc.) or national (material emanating from one country), or select (rated by quality or relevance to a purpose) or special (limited to one aspect) or trade (compiled for commerical purposes in the booktrade). 2. The art or science of describing books, especially their physical make-up or literary contents; consideration of books as physical objects, and the history of book production. Often in this sense the terms *critical, analytical, historical,* or *physical* bibliography are used. *See also Bio-bibliography, Cartobibliography, Textual Bibliography.*

Bibliography Note. *Synonymous with* BIBLIOGRAPHICAL NOTE (*q.v.*).

Bibliography or Bibliographies. An extensive list of bibliographies.

Bibliokleptomaniac. A book-thief who is regarded as insane.

Bibliolater. One who exercises BIBLIOLATRY (*q.v.*); one who has excessive admiration or reverence for books. Also called a 'Bibliolatrist'.

Bibliolatrous. Given to, or characterized by, BIBLIOLATRY (*q.v.*).

Bibliolatry. Book-worship.

Bibliological. Pertaining to bibliology.

Bibliologist. One versed in bibliology.

Bibliology. The scientific description of books, dealing with their construction from the beginnings to the present day, including paper and other materials, typography, illustration and binding. Also called 'Analytical, 'Critical', 'Descriptive' or 'Historical' bibliography. *See also Bibliography.*

Bibliomancy. Divination by books, generally by verses of the Bible.

Bibliomane. An indiscriminate collector of books.

Bibliomania. A mania for collecting and possessing books. Also called 'Bibliomanianism', 'Bibliomanism'.

Bibliomaniac. One affected with a mania for collecting books, particularly old or rare editions. Also called 'Bibliomanist'.

Bibliomanist. A BIBLIOMANIAC (*q.v.*).

Bibliometrics. The application of mathematical and statistical methods to the study of the use made of books and other media within and between library systems.

Bibliopegic. Relating to the binding of books.

Bibliopegist. A bookbinder.

Bibliopegistic. Of, relating to, or befitting, a bookbinder. Also called 'Bibliopegistical'.

Bibliopegy. The art of bookbinding.

Bibliophagic. Of, or pertaining to, a BIBLIOPHAGIST (*q.v.*).

Bibliophagist. One who 'devours' books.

Bibliophegus. The name used in early Christian times for a bookbinder.

Bibliophile. A lover of books who knows how to discriminate between good and bad editions. Also called 'Bibliophilist'.

Bibliophile Binding. A special binding such as might be used by a bibliophile.

Bibliophile Edition. A specially printed and bound edition of a book which is published for sale to bibliophiles. *See also Fine Paper Copy.*

Bibliophilic. Of, or pertaining to, a BIBLIOPHILE (*q.v.*).

Bibliophilism. The love of books.

Bibliophilist. *Synonymous with* BIBLIOPHILE (*q.v.*).

Bibliophilous. Addicted to BIBLIOPHILY (*q.v.*).

Bibliophily. A love of books; a taste for books.

Bibliophobia. A dislike, or dread, or books; an aversion to books.

Bibliopoesy. The making of books.

Bibliopolar. Of, or belonging to, booksellers. Also called 'Bibliopolic', 'Bibliopolical'.

Bibliopole. One who deals in books, especially rare or curious ones.

Bibliopolism. The principles, or trade, of bookselling.

Bibliopolist. A bookseller.

Bibliopolistic. Of, pertaining to, or befitting, a bookseller.

Bibliopoly. The selling of books. Also called 'Bibliopolery'.

Bibliopsychology. The study of books, readers and authors and their mutual relationships. It was formulated by Nicholas Rubakin in his Institute of Bibliopsychology in Switzerland, 1916–46.

Bibliosoph. One who knows, or knows about, books.

Bibliosophist. A BIBLIOPHILE (*q.v.*).

Bibliotaph. One who keeps his books under lock and key. Also called 'Bibliotaphist'.

Bibliotaphic. Of, or belonging to, a bibliotaph.

Bibliotekstjänst. The Swedish library supply agency (a company since 1960) which developed from a central selling agency founded in 1936 by the Swedish Library Association (Sveriges Allmanna Biblioteksforening). It publishes lists of recommended new publications and binds them when ordered by public and school libraries, supplying them through local booksellers. It also publishes indexes of newspapers and periodicals, publications including book lists and library guides on behalf of the Swedish Library Association, schedules of the Swedish Classification scheme, and printed catalogue cards. Other activities are designing and manufacturing furniture and giving advice on library planning.

Bibliothec. Belonging to a library or librarian. A librarian.

Bibliotheca. 1. A library. 2. A bibliographer's catalogue.

Bibliothecal. Belonging to a library.

Bibliothecal Classification. A classification scheme for the arrangement of books on the shelves of a library.

Bibliothecal Schemes. *See Bibliographical Classification.*

Bibliothecar. A librarian. *See also Bibliothecarian.*

Bibliothecarian. 1. A librarian. 2. Of, or belonging to, a library, or a librarian.

Bibliothecary. 1. A librarian. 2. A library. 3. Of, or belonging to, a library.

Bibliothèque de France. The new French national library under construction at Tolbiac in Eastern Paris; scheduled to open in 1995 and to take over to a large extent the functions of the Bibliothèque Nationale.

Bibliothèque Nationale.　The oldest of the European national libraries; it has existed in Paris since the fourteenth century, although in its early days as the personal library of the sovereigns. It posseses over 7,000,000 volumes of printed books, 5,000,000 prints and 175,000 mss. It is the French legal deposit library. Abbreviated BN. *See also Bibliothèque de France.*

Bibliotherapist.　A person skilled in BIBLIOTHERAPY (*q.v.*).

Bibliotherapy.　The use of selected reading and related materials for therapeutic purposes in physical medicine and in mental health. As an aspect of hospital and institution librarianship it requires an acquaintance with a wide range of literature and a knowledge of the techniques of group leadership and individual guidance.

Bibliothetic.　Pertaining to, or based on, the placing or arrangement of books.

Biblio-train.　A railway coach fitted up as a mobile library.

BIBOS.　Bibliotheksverbund; a library bibliographic network, based in Vienna. Began in 1981; currently 22 members.

Bibsys.　Bibliographic network for Norwegian university libraries. Established 1976 and based at Trondheim; 5 members.

Biennial.　A publication issued every two years; but *see also Biannual.*

Biennale of Illustrations Bratislava.　An international exposition of children's book illustrations which, with the co-operation of the Unesco national commissions, seeks to develop this art-form by creating a suitable environment for their evaluation. The Grand Prix BIB and many other prizes are awarded on the recommendation of an international jury, which judges the illustrations alone without the text. The exposition is organized by the Slovak National Gallery and the Czechoslovak Committee for Co-operation with Unesco. The first BIB was held in Bratislava, Czechoslovakia, in September 1967, and the first recipient of the Grand Prix BIB was Yasuo Segawa of Japan for his illustrations for *Taro and the bamboo shoot* by Masako Matsuno. Abbreviated BIB.

Bifurcate Classification.　1. A classification branching in pairs, positive and negative, such as the Tree of Porphyry. Also called classification by dichotomy.　2. The bifurcate division of a genus by a single significant difference into a species and a residuum, which may or may not be disregarded in further division.

Bifurcation.　A method of subdivision in classification whereby every class is divided into two only, a positive and a negative group. Also called 'Dichotomy'.

Bigram.　Any group of two successive letters.

BII–CIC.　Abbreviation for Bureau Intergovernmental pour l'Informatique – Centre International de Calcul. *See* IBI–ICC.

Bildschirmtext.　Austrian and West German videotex system. Abbreviated BTX.

Bill.　1. A written complaint at law.　2. A draft of a proposed law introduced in a legislative body.

Bill Book.　A book in which invoices or bills (accounts) are entered as received. The entries are usually arranged alphabetically under the suppliers' names (American).

Bill of Middlesex.   A precept having the same force as a writ, but with the formal opening omitted.

Bill of Type.   1. A complete assortment of any fount of type.   2. The plan or ratio by which founts of type are made up by type founders in order to provide the correct proportion of each letter or character, as ascertained by experience as to probably requirements. Also called 'Fount Scheme', 'Scheme'.

Bi-monthly.   A serial publication issued in alternate months.

Binary.   (*Information retrieval*) 1. A number system using only two symbols, the digits one and zero.   2. A number system where quantities are represented in base 2 rather than base 10.

Binary Code.   (*Information retrieval*) A code that makes use of only two characters, usually 0 and 1.

Binary Number System.   A system, used in many electronic computers and in information theory, which has only one digit, 1, and a zero. Thus the first ten whole numbers of this system, together with their decimal equivalents, which consist of nine digits and a zero, in parentheses, are: 0(0), 1(1), 10(2), 11(3), 100(4), 101(5), 110(6), 111(7), 1000(8) 1001(9), 1010(10).

Binary Search.   (*Information retrieval*) A search in which a set of items is divided into two parts, where one part being rejected, the process is repeated on the accepted part until the item having the required property is found. *See also Fractional Scanning.*

Bind, to.   To assemble and fasten securely printed or manuscript SHEETS (*q.v.*) within a cover which may be made of wood or board covered with leather or cloth, plastic, stiff card (board) or paper. *See also Boards 1, Sheets.*

Bind In.   To fasten supplementary material securely into a bound book.

Binder.   1. A person who binds books.   2. A case, or detachable cover, for filing magazines, pamphlets, etc., usually on wires or cords, one for each publication.

Binder's Block.   *See Binder's Brass.*

Binder's Board.   *See Millboard, Strawboard.*

Binder's Brass.   A design, or letters of the alphabet, cut in brass and used by a bookbinder's finisher in lettering book covers. When a BLOCK (*q.v.*- 2) is used it is called a 'Binder's block'. *See also Arms Block, Zinco.*

Binder's Dies.   (*Binding*) Lettering or designs cut in brass and used for decorating book covers by stamping or embossing them. Also called 'Panel stamps'.

Binder's Ticket.   A small engraved or printed label, usually fixed to the top outside corner of one of the front end papers between about 1750 and 1825, and giving the name of the binder. These tickets were superseded by the binder's name stamped in gilt, ink, or blind, on one of the inside boards, usually on the extreme lower edge: this is called a 'name pallet'.

Binder's Title.   The title lettered on the back of a book when re-bound, to distinguish it from the publisher's title on the cover or title-page. *See also Back Title, Cover Title.*

Binder's Waste.   Printed sheets which are surplus to a bookbinder's needs and which are sometimes used in bookbinding for lining purposes.

Bindery. A place in which books are bound or re-bound.

Binding. 1. The cover of a volume. 2. The finished work resulting from the processes involved in binding a book. 3. Colloqually, a number of books in a library which are waiting to be re-bound, or those which bave been re-bound. *See also Bookbinding.*

Binding Book. A book in which are entered particulars of books sent to a binder for re-binding. It may vary in information given, from a title list to full binding instructions.

Binding Cloth. *See Book Cloth.*

Binding Copy. A book which is so worn as to need rebinding.

Binding Department. The department of a library or printing establishment in which books are bound or re-bound.

Binding Edge. A back edge of a volume, or the folded edge of a section; the edge opposite the FORE-EDGE (*q.v.*). *See also Ridge.*

Binding from Sheets. Purchasing books in unfolded sheets and having them bound by the library binder.

Binding Record. A record of books sent to the binder. This may consist of the book-cards, a duplicate of the binding slips, or a special record kept on a card or in a BINDING BOOK (*q.v.*).

Binding Rub. *See Rub.*

Binding Slip (Sheet). The form on which instructions for binding are written for the binders' guidance. A slip relates to one book only and is usually inserted in a book before it leaves the library and remains in it throughout all the binding processes.

Binding Variations. The bindings of books, which, although published in the same edition, vary in colour or type of book cloth, tooling, etc. This may arise through a number of manufacturing causes, especially if the whole of an edition is not bound at the same time, or through storage under unsatisfactory conditions, e.g. dampness.

Binomial. (*Classification*) A name which consists of two, and occasionally three, terms.

Bio-bibliography. A bibliography which contains brief biographical details about the authors.

Biographee. A person who is the subject of biography.

Biographee Entry. The entry in a catalogue (dictionary, name, or subject) under the name of the BIOGRAPHEE (*q.v.*); the subject entry for a biography.

Biographer. A person who writes a biography of another.

Biographical Dictionary. A collection of lives of people arranged in alphabetical order.

Biography. 1. A written account of a person's life. 2. The branch of literature concerned with the lives of people.

Biography File. A file of records on cards, or of cuttings, giving information about individuals. Also called a 'Who's who' file.

Birmingham and District Library Association. An autonomous Association founded in 1895, which became the Birmingham and District Branch of the (British) Library Association on 1 April 1929. *See West Midlands*

Branch to which the Birmingham and District Branch of the Library Association changed its name in 1964.

Birmingham Libraries Co-operative Mechanization Project. *See BLCMP.*

Birmingham Notation. *See GKD Notation.*

BIRS. British Institute of Recorded Sound Ltd (*q.v.*). *See British Library.*

Birth and Death Dates. The years of birth, and possibly of death, given in personal name entries in catalogues.

Biscoe Time Numbers (Biscoe Date Table). A table (designed by W. S. Biscoe) which allocates letters to year periods in order to arrange books in chronological, rather than alphabetical, order both on the shelves and in the catalogue. The full table is as follows:

A	B.C.	J	1830–1839	S	1920–1929
B	0–999	K	1840–1849	T	1930–1939
C	1000–1499	L	1850–1859	U	1940–1949
D	1500–1599	M	1860–1869	V	1950–1959
E	1600–1699	N	1870–1879	W	1960–1969
F	1700–1799	O	1880–1889	X	1970–1979
G	1800–1809	P	1890–1899	Y	1980–1989
H	1810–1819	Q	1900–1909	Z	1990–1999
I	1820–1829	R	1910–1919		

Examples of use: a book published in 1676 would be lettered E76, a book published in 1916 would be lettered R6.

BISG. *See Book Industry Study Group, Inc.*

Bishops' Bible. A Bible printed [1568] in London by Richard Jugge, senior Queen's Printer to Elizabeth I. Sometimes called 'Archbishop Parker's Bible'.

Bishop's Rules. A set of rules for abbreviating periodical titles: (1) if the journal title consists of a single word, the first four letters are taken; (2) if of two words, the first two letters of each word; (3) if of three words, the first letter of each of the first two words and the first two letters of the last word; (4) if of more than four words, usually the first letter of each of the first four words. *See also Coden.*

Bit. A contraction of 'binary digit'. The smallest unit of information; a zero or a one; a 'yes' or 'no'.

Bite. The term given to the action of acid eating into metal in the process of block making or plate engraving.

BITS. Bibliographic and Information Technology and Standards Committee; a standing committee of the (British) Library Association, which notes and comments on current work, and legislative issues, and prepares policy statements on such topics as videotex, downloading, cable services, electronic publishing, etc.

BIVA. *See British Interactive Video Association.*

Bi-Weekly. *Synonymous with* FORTNIGHTLY (*q.v.*) and 'Semi-monthly'.

BL. *See British Library.*

Black.   A mark made unintentionally on a sheet of paper by a lead, space or piece of furniture which has risen. Also called 'Work up'.

Black Face.   *Synonymous with* BOLD FACE (*q.v.*).

'Black' Headings.   Headings, other than subject headings, in a dictionary catalogue. The term has its origin in the fact that it was the practice in many libraries to use red for the subject headings and black for all the others.

Black (James Tait) Memorial Prizes.   Annual UK awards for fiction, and for biography; administered by the University of Edinburgh and supplemented by the Scottish Arts Council.

Black Letter.   A term used to indicate old English, text, or church type, which was based on the writing in mediaeval manuscripts.*Synonymous with* GOTHIC TYPE (*q.v.*).

Black Step.   A rule about 6 points thick and up to 24 points long printed between the first and last pages of a section so as to show on the spine of the section when folded. In the first forme it is positioned opposite the top line of text, and about 24 points lower in each successive forme, so that when all the sections of a book have been gathered and placed together a diagonal line is seen across the spine. Any error in gathering is immediately apparent. Also called 'Back mark', 'Collating mark' (*qq.v.*), 'Quad mark'.

Blackwell/North America Scholarship Award.   An annual award administered by the RESOURCES AND TECHNICAL SERVICES DIVISION (*q.v.*) of the ALA for an outstanding book or paper on acquisition or collection development.

Blad.   A mock-up of a book used for advertising purposes, including covers, wrappers and maybe preliminaries to give an idea of the finished appearance.

BLAISE.   Acronym for British Library Automated Information Service; marketed by the Bibliographic Services Division of the British Library. A computerized online interactive information system and a central cataloguing service, which in 1982 split into BLAISE-LINE and BLAISE-LINK (*qq.v.*). *See also BLAISE/LOCAS.*

BLAISE-EDITOR.   A suite of computer programs enabling BLAISE subscribers to copy records from central databases and transfer them to a subfile. Now titled BLAISE-RECORDS (*q.v.*).

BLAISE-LINE.   From July 1982 the BLAISE online service was split into two services; BLAISE-LINE and BLAISE-LINK (*q.v.*). BLAISE-LINE offers the standard bibliographic database, including BNBMARC, Whitaker, BLISS (*q.v.*), British Library Catalogue Preview, Document Supply Centre (monograph) catalogue, Humanities and Social Science catalogue. SRIS (*q.v.*) catalogue. LCMARC, University of London catalogue; also includes AVMARC (*q.v.*), Cartographic materials, HELPIS (*q.v.*), Music Library catalogue, Conference Proceedings Index, SIGLE (*q.v.*), Eighteenth Century Short Title Catalogue, Incunable Short Title Catalogue, HMSO Publications Catalogue.

BLAISE-LINK.   From July 1982 the BLAISE online service was split into two services: BLAISE-LINK and BLAISE-LINE (*q.v.*). BLAISE-LINK operates in collaboration with the National Library of Medicine (US), and includes access to the databases MEDLINE, TOXLINE and many others in the life sciences field. Subscribers to BLAISE-LINK have direct access to the NLM computer at economic cost, and can access other networks through it.

BLAISE/LOCAS. An automated external cataloguing service which is administratively part of the British Library. BLAISE/LOCAS evolved from the Library Software Package (LSP) developed by the British National Bibliography (BNB) and continued by the Bibliographical Service Division of the British Library on its establishment in 1974.

The package consisted of computer programs which facilitated the maintenance of a local MARC file, the retrieval of records from that file, the creation of new MARC records and the production of a local catalogue, LSP was offered for sale to libraries, many of which lacked the computer resources to make use of it. As a result, BNB itself decided to use the package to produce local catalogues via a computer bureau. The system then became known as LOCAS (Local Cataloguing Services).

In 1977 LOCAS became part of BLAISE (*q.v.*) and was run on the same computer. Although the programs were still based on the original LSP, they had been enhanced and now differed greatly from the package first offered for sale to libraries. In February 1979, BLAISE decided to withdraw LSP from sale. In April 1979, BLAISE/LOCAS progressed from being a batch system and became an on-line service. Libraries of any size and type may join BLAISE/LOCAS and the membership is representative of a wide range of organizations.

BLAISE-Records. British Library on-line service offering authoritative machine-readable records from the MARC database for use on automated cataloguing, acquisitions, circulation and other stock-control systems. Covers books, serials, maps, music, grey literature and audio-visual materials. Operated in conjunction with OCLC (*q.v.*). The software access package is known as BLAISE-Recorder.

Blank. An unprinted page which is part of a Signature (*q.v.*) and is consequently recorded when making a bibliographical description of a book in the form 'bl.' following the unprinted signature or page number in [].

Blank Book. A bound book consisting of blank leaves only; used for notes, records, accounts, etc.

Blank cover. The cover of a bound book which is devoid of lettering or ornamentation.

Blank Leaves. The unprinted leaves to be found at each end of a book. If these are conjugate with printed leaves they should be included in a bibliographical description of the book, but if only binder's fly-leaves, ignored.

Blank Page. A page of a book on which nothing has been printed.

Blanket. 1. The packing used on the impression cylinder of a printing machine; it may consist of cloth, rubber or paper. 2. The resilient rubber sheet attached to a cylinder on to which the image to be printed is transferred, or offset, from the inked lithographic plate, and then offset on to the paper.

Blanket Cylinder. *See Offset Printing.*

Blanking. (*Binding*) An impression made on the cloth cover of a book with a heated brass stamp as a base for lettering or decorative stamping.

BLBS(D). *See British Library Bibliographic Services (Division).*

BLCMP. BLCMP (Library Services) Ltd, originally the Birmingham Libraries Co-operative Mechanization Project, was formed in 1969 by the Universities of Aston and Birmingham and Birmingham Public Libraries. Financial support was provided by OSTI. Accommodated in turn by Aston University, and then the University of Birmingham, BLCMP became a completely independent company in 1977. Registered under the Industrial and Provident Societies Act, BLCMP is controlled by directors elected from a Council of Members and aims to make minimal profits. Active user groups meet in many areas. A full range of services is offered – cataloguing, OPAC's, serials control, acquisitions, circulation control, and management information.

BLDMARC Record. A bibliographic record in UKMARC format produced by or for a department of the British Library primarily for use in the catalogues of the British Library's own collections (BLD being an abbreviation for British Library Departmental). *See MARC.*

Bleach. The process of whitening pulp or cellulose, usually with a solution of chlorine.

Bleached Kraft. A white paper made from bleached sulphate wood pulp and used for a variety of purposes when strength is required, e.g. as a body paper for coating. *See also Kraft Paper.*

Bled. A book the letterpress or plates of which have been cut into by the binder is said to have been 'bled'. *See also Cropped.*

Bled Off. Said of a book when the illustrations have been intentionally printed across the normal margins so that the final trim has brought some of the illustrations to the outside edges of the page.

Bleed. 1. To trim printed matter so close that the text or plates are cut into. *See also Cropped, Cut, Trimmed, Uncut.* 2. In the diazotype process of reproduction, the dye image which has run or spread.

Bleeding. The diffusion of printing inks or colours into surrounding areas.

BLEND. Acronym for Birmingham and Loughborough Electronic Network Development. In 1980 the British Library made grants to both Birmingham and Loughborough Universities to facilitate a programme of research into communication through electronic networks. Loughborough began by investigating the feasibility of setting up an electronic Journal. The first community to use the systems were researchers interested in the field of computer/human factors. Several BLEND reports were issued by BLRDD during the funding period (1980–1984). *See Project Quartet.*

BLICAD. British Library Interim Committee on Art Documentation – an advisory group set up in 1984 to review the national provision for art information and documentation.

Blind. Lettering on a book or other article without using gold leaf or colour.

Blind-blocked. Lettering on book covers not inked or gilt, only embossed or impressed.

Blind Embossing. Raising paper in a pattern, or in the shape of letters, by means of dies but not using ink on the raised (i.e. embossed) parts. *See also Embossing.*

Blind Index. A form of indexing equipment in which the headings on cards or slips cannot be seen until those immediately in front are turned over. The opposite of VISIBLE INDEX. (*q.v.*).

Blind P. The paragraph mark ¶. *See also Paragraph Mark, Reference Marks.*

Blind Page. An unnumbered, and usually blank, page which is included in the overall pagination. These usually occur in the PRELIMINARIES (*q.v.*).

Blind Reference. A reference in an index to a catchword which does not occur in the index, or a reference in a catalogue or bibliography to a heading under which no entry will be found.

Blind Stamping. Embossing lettering or a design on to book covers, whether by hand or in a press, without using gold leaf or colour. Also called 'Antique', 'Blind blocking' and 'Blind tooling'.

Blind Tooling. *See Tooling.*

Blinded-in. A design which is impressed on a book cover with heated tools but not coloured or gilt.

BLISS. The British Library Information Sciences Services; a new title adopted 1988 for the library formerly known as the Library Association Library. The library was started in 1933, and financial responsibility passed to the BL in 1974. At present still housed at LAHQ but expected to move to the new BL building in the early 1990s. Stock comprises 85,000 books and pamphlets, 1250 current journals; thesis collection. BLISS database from 1976 is available on BLAISE-LINE (*q.v.*). Current awareness offered by the monthly newsletter *CABLIS* (*q.v.*).

BLISS Bibliographic Classification. *See Bibliographic Classification.*

BLISS Classification Association. Formed in May 1967 to replace the former British Committee for the Bliss Classification consequent upon the receipt of the copyright of the BC from the H. W. Wilson Company. Publishes *BC Bulletin* (a.). In 1987 it became an organization in liaison with the (British) Library Association.

BLMARC Record. A bibliographic record in the UKMARC format produced within the British Library, being either a BNBMARC or a BLDMARC record. *See MARC.*

Block. 1. To print with a solid shading at the bottom or sides, as a second impression in a different colour and in a projecting position. 2. In bookbinding, to emboss or letter book covers with a block or frame containing the entire device, and at one operation, as distinguished from die stamping. 3. A large stamp without a handle used in a blocking press by bookbinders for impressing a design on a book cover. 4. A type-high piece of wood, plastic or metal, bearing a design from which an impression can be made. A general term which includes line-blocks, half-tones, electros, etc. 5. To secure a plate to its proper position for printing. 6. A piece of wood or metal on which a stereotype, electrotype or other plate is mounted to make it type high. 7. A piece of hard wood used by engravers. 8. The core of a roller on a lithographing press.   9. In photography, to paint over a part of a negative to prevent or modify its printing.   10. A stop in a catalogue drawer. *See also Backslide.*

Block Books.   Those printed from engraved blocks of wood. Block books originated in the Netherlands and in Germany after about 1410; most are dateable from 1460 to 1480. They were printed on one side of the leaf in a thin brownish ink. Generally they may be divided into three groups: 1. those which have pictures and words descriptive of the pictures engraved at the foot of the picture or in cartouches proceeding from the mouths of the principal figures;   2. those which have pictures on one page and a full page of explanatory text opposite, or form distinct and separate units on the same page;   3. those with xylographic text only. The *Biblia pauperum* and *Apocalypse of St. John* are well-known examples of Group 1; *Ars memorandi, Ars moriendi* and *Speculum humanae salvationis* of Group 2; and the *Donatus de Octo Partibus Orationis* of Group 3. Block books continued to be printed well into the sixteenth century and several of the later ones were printed on a press with printer's ink, in such instances often on both sides of the paper. Those printed on one side only of the paper are called 'anopisthographic'. Books printed from engraved wood blocks, are called 'xylographic' books. *See also Opisthographic, Wood Block, Woodcut, Xylography.*

Block Indexing.   1. A system of indexing wherein 'blocks' of materials are collected, each block being small enough to permit easy manual search of the group contained therein.   2. A system for separation of information on microfilm into groups or 'blocks' identified by readily distinguishable numbers to facilitate reference.

Block Printing.   Making an illustration, or printing a design on paper or material, from wood or metal blocks with the design in relief.

Block-pull.   A proof of an illustration or text engraved on a block as distinct from type.

Blocking.   The impressing of a gold leaf, metal foil, or other graphic medium into a book-cover by means of a stamp, 'brass' or BLOCK 3 (*q.v.*) having a raised surface. The term is also applied to the impressing of type, blocks, etc., without any intervening media, this operation being known as 'blind-stamping'. Called 'Stamping' in the USA.

Blocking Foil.   A paper foil coated with gold, white metal or coloured pigment which is transferred to the leather or cloth cover of a book by means of a heated die used in a blocking press. The process using these materials is known as 'foil blocking'.

Blocking Press.   A press using heated blocks to impress, or stamp, lettering, designs, etc., on the book covers and cases. In machine bookbinding, ribbons of blocking foil of varying widths are used; these contain their own glair or adhesive. The press is also used for blind or ink blocking, no heat being necessary for the latter process.

Blotting Paper.   Absorbent paper made from specially prepared rags, and unsized.

Blow Up. 1. A photograph, jacket, book review, specimen page of a book, etc., greatly enlarged for exhibition or advertising purposes. *See also Giant Book.* 2. In documentary reproduction a copy having a larger scale than the original; an enlargement or PROJECTION PRINT (*q.v.*).

BLRD. *See British Library* (Reference Division).

BLRDD. *See British Library* (Research and Development Department).

Blue Book. A more lengthy British Government official publication of similar character to a WHITE PAPER (*q.v.*), printed with a blue paper cover. (The traditional blue cover is now used principally for Select Committee Reports and for certain Accounts and Papers presented to Parliament under statute). The French colour is yellow; German, white; Italian, green. *See also Green Paper, Parliamentary Publications, White Paper.*

Blue-line Print. 1. A positive print made by the DIAZOTYPE PROCESS (*q.v.*). 2. A blue-print with blue lines on a white field, made by printing from a negative master.

Blueprint. A blue on white, or white on blue, print submitted by a blockmaker as a rough proof before blocks are supplied. Also, a print produced by the BLUEPRINT PROCESS (*q.v.*).

Blueprint Process. A method of reproducing documents whereby a sheet of paper, which has been treated with a preparation mainly consisting of ferro prussiate, together with the document, are exposed to powerful arc lamps. The paper is then developed by placing it in running water. A blue and white negative results and this can be used to produce a blue and white positive. Only single-sided documents which are perfect (having no creases or alterations) are suitable for reproduction by this process.

Blundell (K) Trust. A system of annual grants made by the SOCIETY OF AUTHORS (*q.v.*) to young writers needing funds for research.

Blurb. The publisher's description and recommendation of a book, usually found on the front flap of a book jacket. *See also Puff.*

Blyton Handi-read Centre. *See National Library and Information Centre on Books, Reading and the Handicapped Child.*

BN. Bibliothèque Nationale (*q.v.*).

BNB. *British National Bibliography* (*q.v.*).

BNBC. British National Book Centre (*q.v.*).

BNBMARC Record. A bibliographic record in UKMARC format produced by British Library Bibliographic Services for the British National Bibliography (BNB) and associated databases and services. *See MARC.*

Board Label. The label pasted on the inside of the front board of a library book to show ownership, and usually bearing a few of the more important rules. Also called a 'Book plate' or 'Book label'.

Board of Directors. *Synonymous with* BOARD OF LIBRARY TRUSTEES (*q.v.*).

Board of Library Trustees. The committee responsible for the control of an American library system. Also known as 'Library Board', 'Board of Directors', 'Library Trustees' and occasionally, 'Library Commission'.

Board Paper. *Synonymous with* PASTE DOWN (*q.v.*).

Boards. 1. The sheets of millboard, pasteboard or strawboard used for bookcovers. When covered with paper, a book so bound is said to be bound in 'paper boards', when covered with cloth, in 'cloth boards'. 2. So named because wood was used originally. 3. A general term which includes pulp, index, paste, ivory and other forms of card used for printing. *See also Bristol Board, Ivory Board.* 4. The pieces of wooden board used by a binder to grip a book when pressing, cutting, backing, burnishing, etc.

Boar's Head Press. A private printing press founded in 1931 by Christopher Sandford who afterwards acquired the GOLDEN COCKEREL PRESS (*q.v.*).

Bodoni. An early Modern Face (*q.v.*) roman type designed in 1790 by Giambattista Bodoni (1740–1813) of Parma, the most celebrated printer of his day. It was re-cut for contemporary printing in 1921. Characteristics are vertical stress, long ascenders and descenders, fine straight-line serifs, and thin hair lines. For a specimen alphabet, *see Type Face.*

Body. 1. (*Printing*) (i) The measurement (or thickness) from back to front of a type letter, slug, rule, lead etc. (ii) The part of a piece of movable type from the foot to the flat surface at the upper end, above which is the 'SHOULDER' (*q.v.*) and from which the moulded letter rises. It comprises the 'BELLY', 'BACK', 'FEET', 'SIDES', 'PIN MARK', 'NICK' and 'GROOVES' (*qq.v.*). Also called the 'Shank' or 'Stem'. 2. (*Paper*) The apparent weight of a sheet of paper.

Body Matter. (*Printing*) The text, as distinct from display matter, or illustrations.

Body of the Book (Work). The main part of the book, commencing at the first page of the text and including any illustrations or foot-notes which may accompany it, and excluding any preliminary or appended matter.

Body of the Entry. The part of a catalogue entry which describes a publication. It usually follows a heading (thus beginning with the title) and ends with the imprint. *See Imprint 1.*

Body Paper, or Board. The foundation for art, chromo, coated, blueprint, gummed, photographic and other papers which are made by coating or treating with a composition of any kind. Also called 'base' or 'raw' paper.

Body Size. *See Type Size.*

Body Type. Type, of 14 point or less, used for the main body of a composition, as distinguished from the display type used in headings, etc. It also includes sizes of type up to 24 point which may be used in book work. Display type may begin at 18 point.

Bogle International Library Travel Fund Award. An award made by the International Relations Committee of the ALA to enable an ALA member to attend an international conference for the first time.

Boiler. The part of paper-making machinery in which the raw material is boiled in water before it goes into the BREAKER (*q.v.*). Also called 'Kier'. *See also Digester.*

Bold Face. Heavy-faced type, also called 'Full face' and 'Black face'. **This is bold face**, and is indicated in a MS. by wavy underlining〰〰. Bold face is usually used to give emphasis to certain words, and for headings. In machine setting, bold characters can normally be set or tapped in the same line as the roman and italic. Most FOUNTS (*q.v.*) have a bold face based on the same design as the medium weight as well as the roman and italic. Bold face developed from the CLARENDON (*q.v.*) face which has only slight contrast in the up and down strokes and was used, with other type faces, for emphasis. Clarendon grew out of the Antique face, cut by Vincent Figgins prior to 1815, believed to be the earliest of the designs now generally known as Egyptian. It is peculiar in giving equal emphasis to the up and down strokes and serifs. *See also Egyptian, Type Face.*

Bole. (*Printing*) To reduce the height of type by shaving the feet. *See also Armenian Bole.*

Bolognese Letters. Manuscript lettering which originated at the legal school of the University of Bologna and was used as the basis for the Gothic types known as 'Rotunda'. It was introduced into Germany from Venice and was consequently often called 'Litterae Venetae' by the early German printers.

Bolt. The folded or doubled edge of paper at the head, tail or fore-edge of a sheet in an uncut or unopened book. These are known as head bolts, tail bolts or fore-edge bolts. The folded edge at the back of a sheet is referred to, not as a 'bolt', but as the 'last fold' or 'back fold'. *See also Fold to Paper, Fold to Print, Open Edge.*

Bom Proof. A proof which is specially printed and bound for submission to a book club.

Bone Folder. A flat piece of bone 6 to 9 inches long, about 1 inch wide and ⅛ inch thick with rounded corners and edges which is used for rubbing along the fold of a sheet of paper to bend the fibres of the paper firmly into position, and in book repairing. *See also Folding Stick.*

Bonnange Card Catalogue Tray. An obsolete form of tray invented by M. F. Bonnange. The cards are hinged near the bottom, the lower piece (which is thicker than the upper) having shoulders which fit into grooves in the sides of the tray.

Book. 1. A set of blank sheets of paper bound along one edge and enclosed within protective covers to form a volume, especially a written or printed literary composition presented in this way. 2. A division of a literary work, which is separately published and has an independent physical existence, although its pagination may be continuous with other volumes. 3. At a Unesco conference in 1964 a book was defined as 'a non-periodical printed publication of at least forty-nine pages, exclusive of cover pages'. *See also Pamphlet.* 4. A collection (*Fr.* assemblage) of manuscript or printed leaves fastened together to form a volume or volumes, forming a BIBLIOGRAPHICAL UNIT (*q.v.*). (It is distinct from periodicals, and from other forms of material, such as films, prints, maps, etc.). *See also Adaptation, Document, Fascicle, Part, Printed Book, Publication, Version, Volume, Work.*

Book Action for Nuclear Disarmament. *See Band.*

Book Auction Sale. A method of selling second-hand books; it dates from the early seventeenth century, and is the usual method of selling large libraries or individual copies of rare or valuable books. The prices realized are recorded in *Book auction records* or the American *Book prices current.*

Book Band. A narrow strip, or band, of printed paper placed round a jacketed book to advertise it by drawing attention to it, e.g. its cheap price, an award which had been made in respect of it, the 'book of the film', etc.

Book Boat. A common means of providing a library service to residents on islands and land masses accessible only by boat, for example in Norway, Sweden and Denmark.

Book Boxes. Boxes in which books are transported.

Book Capacity. *Synonymous with* SHELF CAPACITY (*q.v.*).

Book Card. A piece of card or plastic material on which are written the means of identifying a particular book (usually some or all of the following: charging symbol, accession number, class number, author, title) and which is used in charging (i.e. recording) the loan of the book. Book cards are usually made of manilla, of different colours for different departments or classes of books, but plastic is often used because of its better handling properties and greater durability. Also called 'Charging card', and in America 'Book slip', 'Charge slip' and 'Charging slip'.

Book Carrier. *See Book Conveyor.*

Book Catalogue. A catalogue produced in book form. Also used as a synonym for PRINTED CATALOGUE (*q.v.*). Sometimes used synonymously for PAGE CATALOGUE (*q.v.*) and 'Book form catalogue'.

Book Classification. A general term covering bibliographical and bibliothecal classifications.

Book Cloth. Cotton or linen cloth (usually coloured) used for book covers.

Book Club. A publishing activity issuing to subscribing members, specially, and cheaply, printed books of merit. The subjects of the books published may be restricted to one subject; the books have usually been published before, although in some cases very recently, and are limited in number in any one year.

Book Club Edition. A book sold by a Book Club to its members. Such books may not be the same edition, reprint, issue or impression as are normally available through trade channels to the public; they are usually specially printed and bound, and except in the cases of clubs or societies whose purpose is to supply books of exceptional quality, may be of inferior materials.

Book Collecting. The assembling of books which because of their bibliographic interest, their contents (historic or factual), the history of the individual copies, or their rarity, have some permanent interest to the collector.

Book Collection. *Synonymous with* BOOK STOCK (*q.v.*).

Book Collector. One who purchases books systematically often in a given field of knowledge or within the limits of some branch of historical bibliography.

Book Conveyor. A system of metal or other containers joined to an endless chain, or other device, which is capable of conveying books, correspondence, papers, etc., either horizontally or perpendicularly between the various parts of a large library on different flloors. They are usually electrically operated, and push button control ensures the automatic discharge of the containers' contents at specified service points. Also called 'Book carrier', 'Book distributor'.

Book Coupon. *See Unesco Coupons.*

Book Cover. *See Cover.*

Book Crafts. The operations which are carried out in producing books and which require varying degrees of skill in their performance; these include paper-making, printing, design of books, design and production of illustrations, and binding.

Book Decoration. The impressing of a design on the cover of a book, often by gold (but sometimes blind) tooling. The design so impressed.

Book Development Council. The export division of the Publishers Association which provides a comprehensive information service to publishers on conditions in overseas markets. It also answers queries about British publishing from potential customers abroad.

Book Display. A small exhibition of books usually on one or several related subjects, in (and sometimes outside) a library.

Book Distributor. *See Book Conveyor.*

Book Drop. A box or chute provided so that readers can return books when a library is closed or where drive-in facilities are available.

Book End. *See Book Support.*

Book Fair. 1. An exhibition of books and of book-making, sometimes including talks by authors, illustrators, booksellers and publishers. 2. Trade exhibitions of books with the object of selling and exchanging books. Some, particularly those held at Frankfurt and Leipzig before the Second World War, became world famous. The Frankfurt Book Fair has in recent years developed into an important international means of selling books and encouraging translation of books into other languages.

Book Form. Said of a work published as a book but which has been issued previously in serial form, usually in a periodical.

Book Fund. The fund, or amount of money, which is available for the purchase of books, and possibly of non-book materials.

Book Hand. A style of artificial, calligraphic handwriting used for books (as distinct from the cursive styles used by individuals for records, memoranda, correspondence, etc.), before the introduction of printing. Uncial, Caroline minuscule, Gothic, and Humanistic are book hands. Bastard, and Chancery are not.

Book Hoist. *See Book Lift.*

Book Holder. (*Reprography*) A device for holding open a bound volume in a level or near-level plane so that all parts of the image are in focus during reproduction.

Book Hunter. One whose occupation is the tracing of specific titles in the second-hand market, sometimes at the request of a would-be purchaser.

Book Illustration. The making of drawings or paintings to illustrate the text of a book. The resulting illustration.

Book Industry Study Group, Inc. A voluntary research organization with some 250 members from all sectors of the US book trade. Aims to increase readership, improve distribution of books, and examine the market. Promotes and supports research into reading and the book and publishing industries. Major trade and professional organizations are members. Abbreviated BISG.

Book Jacket.   The paper wrapping covering a book as issued by the publisher. It serves the purposes of protecting the book, and if illustrated (as it usually is), of attracting attention. It bears the name of the author, the title, and usually has a BLURB (*q.v.*) on the first flap, and elsewhere, particulars of other books by the same author or issued by the same publisher. Also called 'Dust cover', 'Dust jacket', 'Dust wrapper', 'Jacket', 'Wrapper'.

Book Label.   *See Board Label, Book Plate.*

Book Lift.   A small device for carrying books perpendicularly from one floor to another. Usually electrically operated. A hand-operated lift is sometimes called a book hoist.

Book List.   A list of books, usually on some specific subject and arranged in classified or author order.

Book Number.   1. The number, letter, or other symbol or combination of symbols used to distinguish an individual book from every other book in the same class, and at the same time to arrange books hearing the same class number in the desired order on the shelves, by author, title, edition, date of publication, etc. It usually consists of the (a) Author Mark, (b) Work Mark, (c) Volume Number. Also called 'Book mark'. *See also Call Number.*   2. In the Colon Classification it follows the class number and precedes the COLLECTION NUMBER (*q.v.*) to form the CALL NUMBER (*q.v.*); it is the symbol used to fix the position of a book in relation to other books having the same ULTIMATE CLASS (*q.v.*). The Book Number individualizes the document among the documents having the same class number, and is used to mechanize the position of a document among those having the same ultimate class. *See also Associated Book.*

Book of Armagh.   Written by Ferdomnach, a scribe, who died in 844, this MS contains portions of the New Testament. It is the first example of the Irish pointed hand to which a definite date can be given, and resembles the English pointed hand of the period.

Book of Hours.   The name given to books of private devotions designed for the laity; they were very popular and in general use throughout the Catholic Church from the fourteenth to the sixteenth centuries. Both before and after the discovery of printing they were often beautifully illuminated, and fine examples of them are today much coveted by collectors. Great personages were fond of having these books made specially for themselves, with decorations and illustrations of an individual appeal.

Book of Kells.   *See Kells, Book of.*

'Book of the Year for Children' Medal.   A bronze medal awarded by the CANADIAN ASSOCIATION OF CHILDREN'S LIBRARIANS (*q.v.*) for outstanding children's books, one in English and one in French, published in Canada during a calendar year and written by a Canadian or resident of Canada.

Book Paper. A name given to paper manufactured for books to distinguish it from newsprint, cover paper and writing paper.

Book Plate. A label pasted in a book to mark its ownership and sometimes to indicate its location in a library. Private book plates are often ornate or artistic: simpler and smaller ones bearing merely the owner's name are called 'book labels'.

Book Pocket. The strong paper receptacle like the corner of an envelope pasted on the inside of the board of a book to take the book card. The BOARD LABEL (*q.v.*) frequently serves this purpose.

Book Post. A postal rate applying to the carrying of books: it is usually cheaper than the ordinary parcel rate providing the packages are made up in such a way that the postal authorities may examine then at will without breaking any seals and without inconvenience.

Book Preparation. *See Processing.*

Book Press. A press, usually of wood or steel, into which books are placed during binding or repairing processes. *See also Book Stack, Bookcase, Press, Tier.*

Book Processing. *See Processing.*

Book Processing Center. A co-operative organization operated for a group of libraries where the ordering and processing of books (cataloguing, preparation) is undertaken for all the participants, whether as a separate service or as one of other services. (American.)

Book Production. The art and craft of making books including designing, choice and use of materials, illustration, printing and binding.

Book Rack. A shelf or small group of shelves used for displaying books.

Book Railbus. A means of taking books to isolated residents in northern Sweden. The railbus stops at every house alongside the railway.

Book Rarities. Books of which few copies are known to exist; scarce books.

Book Rest. A portable fitting similar to the music rest of a piano which is placed at a convenient angle for reading on a table or desk to hold a book when notes are being made from it.

Book Review. An evaluation of a book published in a periodical or newspaper.

Book Sale. A sale organized by a library to dispose of surplus and out-of-date stock. Prices at such a sale are generally very low.

Book Satchel. A bag used in mediaeval times for carrying books. It frequently hung from a cleric's habit cord or on a warrior's belt.

Book Selection. The process of choosing books for inclusion in a library with a view to providing a balanced increase to the stock.

Book Shrine. A box or chest, usually ornamented, in which valuable books were placed in mediaeval times. *See also Cumdach.*

Book Sizes. Traditional British sizes, in inches, are as follows:

Pott	$6\frac{1}{4} \times 4$	8	$\times 6\frac{1}{4}$
Foolscap	$6\frac{3}{4} \times 4\frac{1}{4}$	$8\frac{1}{2}$	$\times 6\frac{3}{4}$
Crown	$7\frac{1}{2} \times 5$	10	$\times 7\frac{1}{2}$
Large Crown	$8 \times 5\frac{1}{4}$	$10\frac{1}{2}$	$\times 8$
Large Post	$8\frac{1}{4} \times 5\frac{1}{4}$	$10\frac{1}{2}$	$\times 8\frac{1}{4}$

	Octavos	Quartos
Demy	$8\frac{3}{4} \times 5\frac{5}{8}$	$11\frac{1}{4} \times 8\frac{3}{4}$
Post	8×5	10×8
Small Demy	$8\frac{1}{2} \times 5\frac{5}{8}$	$11\frac{1}{4} \times 8\frac{1}{2}$
Medium	$9 \times 5\frac{3}{4}$	$11\frac{1}{2} \times 9$
Small Royal	$9\frac{1}{4} \times 6\frac{1}{8}$	$12\frac{1}{2} \times 10$
Royal	$10 \times 6\frac{1}{4}$	$12\frac{1}{2} \times 10$
Super Royal	$10\frac{1}{4} \times 6\frac{3}{4}$	$13\frac{1}{2} \times 10\frac{1}{4}$
Imperial	$11 \times 7\frac{1}{2}$	15×11

See also Octavo, Paper Sizes, Size. American book sizes are given below: in several instances there are minor differences between these and the British sizes with a common name. The sizes are not absolute.

Name	*inches*
Thirty-sixmo	$4 \times 3\frac{1}{3}$
Medium Thirty-twomo	$4\frac{3}{4} \times 3$
Medium Twenty-fourmo	$5\frac{1}{2} \times 3\frac{5}{8}$
Medium Eighteenmo	$6\frac{2}{3} \times 4$
Medium Sixteenmo	$6\frac{3}{4} \times 4\frac{1}{2}$
Cap Octavo	$7 \times 7\frac{1}{4}$
Duodecimo	$7\frac{1}{2} \times 4\frac{1}{2}$
Crown Octavo	$7\frac{1}{6} \times 5$
Post Octavo	$7\frac{1}{2} \times 5\frac{1}{2}$
Medium Duodecimo	$7\frac{2}{3} \times 5\frac{1}{8}$
Demy Octavo	$8 \times 5\frac{1}{2}$
Small Quarto (usually less)	$8\frac{1}{2} \times 7$
Broad Quarto (varies up to 13×10)	$8\frac{1}{2} \times 7$
Medium Octavo	$9\frac{1}{2} \times 6$
Royal Octavo	$10 \times 6\frac{1}{2}$
Super Royal Octavo	$10\frac{1}{2} \times 7$
Imperial Quarto	11×15
Imperial Octavo	$11\frac{1}{2} \times 8\frac{1}{4}$

(*The first column gives the vertical height.*)

For metric book sizes, *See Metric Book Sizes.*

Book Slip. *See Book Card.*

Book Slip. *See Book Card.*

Book Stack. A room closed to the public, which is equipped to shelve large numbers of little-used books in as small a space as possible. *See also Book Press, Bookcase, Press, Tier.*

Book Stamp. An ownership mark made by means of an ink impression from a metal or rubber stamp, embossed, on the title-page, cover or end-paper of a book.

Book Stand. A small portable stand for displaying books.

Book Stock. The whole of the books comprising a library.

Book Store. 1. A room or stack in which books are kept.   2. A book shop.

Book Support. An 'L' or 'T' shaped piece of steel or wood placed at the end of a row of books to keep them upright. Also called 'Book end'.

Book Token. A greetings card to which stamps of various values can be attached; the stamps are purchased from, and exchanged at, bookshops for books of the appropriate value.

Book Trade. The organized business of selling books. The term usually relates to the whole national organization involving booksellers and their organizations together with the publishers and their organizations.

Book Tray. A tray for carrying books. It has three sides no more than about 4 inches high provided with slots or handles to facilitate carrying.

Book Trolley. *Synonymous with* BOOK TRUCK (*q.v.*).

Book Trough. A short V-shaped shelf for displaying books on a counter or desk.

Book Truck. A wheeled trolley about 3 feet long, with two or three shelves accessible from each side which is used for conveying books to different parts of a building. Special adaptations are made for taking books to patients in hospital wards.

Book Trust. The National Book League, founded as the National Book Council in 1924, was reconstituted as Book Trust in 1986. It is an independent body that promotes books and reading, supported by the book trade, the Arts Council and subscription income. Operates an information service, library, reference collection of recent children's books; organizes exhibitions, issues booklists and guides, and administers several literary prizes. The CHILDREN'S BOOK FOUNDATION (*q.v.*) is a new development.

Book Week. A local or national event in which librarians, often with the co-operation of booksellers and publishers, arrange book displays and lectures, with the object of stimulating interest in books, particularly amongst children. These are arranged on a national scale less often in England than in America, where in addition to the general book week, others dealing with a particular type of book are arranged, as Religious Book Week, Catholic Book Week.

Bookamatic. The trade name for a method of TRANSACTION CARD CHARGING (*q.v.*). Embossed plastic book cards and readers' cards are used to print the name and address of the reader and the author and title of the book on a transaction card which is kept in the library. A transaction card bearing the same number and date due for return is placed in the book. The book-card is kept always in the book and is only taken out to place it in the recorder so as to print the details of loan on the transaction card. *See also Charging Methods.*

Bookbank. A CD-ROM service of J. Whitaker & Sons Ltd; developed over a 3-year period 1984–1987, with the full service being marketed from 1988. Disks are replaced monthly and contain the bibliographic data previously recorded in the printed and microfiche versions of *British Books in Print.*

Bookbinder. A person whose occupation is the binding of books.

Bookbinding. 1. The act or process of binding a book, whereby the sheets are sewn or otherwise fastened into a permanent cover of book-binder's board, the sides and back of which are covered with leather or cloth, or other suitable material. 2. The strong covering of the book.

Bookbinding Board. A 'board' used as a component in making covers of hardback books.

Bookbinding Stamp. A tool with an embossed design which is used to impress a design on the cover of a book.

Bookbus. A bus converted into a mobile library service vehicle. Considered to be more eye-catching, attractive and appropriate for some types of provision than a specially built mobile library, and much cheaper as a second-hand vehicle is usually converted.

Bookcase. A case with shelves for books; it may or may not have doors. *See also Book Press, Book Stack, Press, Tier.*

Booker Prize for Fiction. An annual prize for a novel written in English by a citizen of Great Britain, Eire, Pakistan or South Africa. Administered by the Book Trust, and sponsored by Booker McConnell plc.

Booketeria. A self-service library, mainly of novels, placed in a modern store in parts of American towns which are not served by branch libraries. Borrowers issue books to themselves, place returned books in special parts of book shelves for assistants who attend each morning to discharge them, and leave any fines due.

Bookform Index. An index having the physical form of a book, the terms, or headings, followed by their appropriate references, being printed and bound up in the form of a book.

Booklet. A small book in a paper cover or in very light binding.

Bookmark. A piece of paper or other material placed between the leaves of a book to mark a place. Bookmarks are frequently used as a means of advertising. It may take the form of a piece of ribbon fastened in the 'hollow' back of a book, i.e. between the back folds of the sections and the spine. Also called 'Book marker'.

Bookmark List. A list of books printed in the form of a bookmark.

Bookmobile. A large van, equipped with shelves and a book-issuing desk, which the public may enter to select books for home reading. Also called a MOBILE LIBRARY or TRAVELLING LIBRARY (*qq.v.*).

Booknet. A service of the British Library Document Supply Centre, introduced late 1988, to co-ordinate disposal of surplus items of library stock. Items are sent to BLDSC by participating libraries, and lists of material are circulated twice a month. Replaces the earlier Gift and Exchange service.

Bookseller. A retail dealer having a varied selection of books covering a wide range of subjects. Sometimes second-hand or antiquarian books may be stocked.

Booksellers Association of Great Britain and Ireland. Founded in 1895, the Association exists to promote and protect the interests of 3400 bookselling businesses of all sizes, including independent, chain and multiple bookshops. The Association aims to help booksellers become more profitable and efficient by assisting them to increase sales and develop the market; by helping them to reduce costs, by fighting for better distribution in the trade; b giving advice on all aspects of bookselling, including training, trade practice, marketing and starting a bookselling business. It provides a forum for booksellers and represents their interests on a national and international level. The Book Token and Booksellers Clearing House schemes are administered by their subsidiary companies.

Bookshelf. A micro-computer based library automation package, providing circulation, cataloguing, periodicals, ordering and membership-file functions. Popular with small independent libraries.

Bookshop. A retail outlet specializing in books.

Bookstall. A 'stand', of temporary or permanent design, at which books are sold, the vendor usually being on the inside and the purchaser on the outside of the stand.

Booktrade Electronic Communications Committee. *See BTECC.*

Booktrade Electronic Data Interchange Standards. *See BEDIS.*

Bookwork. The branch of the printing industry, particularly typesetting, which is concerned with book production.

Bookworm. 1. The larva of a moth or beetle which burrows into the covers and pages of books. 2. A person who reads voraciously.

Boolean Logic. A technique of using the most basic conceivable forms of expression to represent any logical possibility, i.e. a thing either exists or does not exist, is either present or not present, operative or not operative, etc. It was first developed and codified by the English mathematician George Frederick Boole (1815–1864). The use of the terms 'and', 'or', 'not' in formulating online search commands is based on Boolean logic.

Border. 1. (*Bibliography*) An ornamental enclosure of a title-page or a substantial part of it, or of a page of type, illuminated manuscript or body of printed matter; or merely an ornamental design placed on one or more sides of the above. *See also Block 4, Compartment, Frame, Rule Border.* 2. (*Binding*) Ornamentation placed close to the edges of the sides of a book-cover or the spine of a volume. To be distinguished from FRAME (*q.v.*). 3. (*Printing*) A continuous decorative design arranged around matter. It can consist of continuous cast strips of plain or patterned rule, or be made up of repeated units of FLOWERS (*q.v.*).

Borrower. *See Reader.*

Borrowers' Index. *See Borrowers' Register.*

Borrower's Number. The registration number assigned to a member of a library.

Borrowers' Register. A list of members of a library.

Borrowers's Ticket (card). The membership card entitling the holder to borrow books from a library.

Boss. A metal knob, often ornamented, fixed upon the covers of books, usually at the corners and centre, for protection and embellishment.

Bottom Edge. The Tail (*q.v.*) of a book. Also called 'Lower edge', 'Tail edge'.

Bottom Margin. *Synonymous with* TAIL MARGIN (*q.v.*).

Bottom Note. *Synonymous with* FOOTNOTE (*q.v.*).

Bound. 1. A book which is sewn or otherwise fastened into stiff boards. 2. (*Adj.*) In Co-ordinate Indexing (*q.v.*) joined in modification of the meaning of a commonly used term; e.g. 'Free Energy' is a *bound* term (unit concept) while 'Free' and 'Energy' may be *free* terms in the same co-ordinate indexing system.

Bound Term. (*Indexing*) A heading, or term, consisting of more than one word. *See also Collateral Term, Generic Term.*

Bound-to-Stay-Bound Scholarships. Two annual awards to support students of library work with children; administered by the Association for Library Service to Children (*q.v.*).

Bound Volume. Any book that is bound; usually a number of issues of a periodical comprising a volume and bound.

Bound With. A term used by cataloguers when referring to books published separately but subsequently bound together. When such a volume has been supplied with a collective title-page the main catalogue entry may be made from this, the individual publications being entered in a contents note and given analytical entries. Otherwise each item would be given its own entry 'Bound with . . . ' and the first item in the collection quoted. In each case there would be only one Call Number (*q.v.*).

Boundary Straps. *Synonymous with* Deckle Straps (*q.v.*).

Bourdillon Report. The Report of the Working Party appointed by the Minister of Education in March 1961, *Standards of Public Library Service in England and Wales*, 1962. H. T. Bourdillon was Chairman of the Working Party. This, together with the Baker Report (*q.v.*), formed the basis of parliamentary discussions and the framing of the Public Libraries and Museums Act of 1964.

Bourgeois. An obsolete name for a size of type equal to 9 pt.

Boustrophedon Writing. Derived from *boustrophedon*, Greek for 'as the ox ploughs'; refers to primitive writing in which alternate lines run from left to right and then from right to left–the pattern that would be made by an ox ploughing a field. The letters in the lines commencing at the right are reversed as if mirrored.

Bow Bracket. *Synonymous with* Brace (*q.v.*).

Bowdlerized. A text which is altered by changing or omitting words or passages considered offensive or indelicate: after Thomas Bowdler who in 1818 published an expurgated edition of Shakespeare.

Bowker Acquisition System. An online system operated by the US Bowker company, designed to simplify the ordering of books and other materials in libraries and bookshops. It is based on the Bowker compilations *Books in Print*, etc. Abbreviated BAS.

Bowker Bibliography Prize. Offered annually by the Bowker Publishing Company Ltd., beginning in 1975, to a student or a group of students, at the College of Librarianship Wales for an original work of scholarly bibliography. The Prize takes the form of a bursary and travel to complete the work, which is later published by Bowker jointly with the College.

Bowker/Ulrich Serials Librarianship Award. An annual award instituted 1985 by the R. R. Bowker Company and presented under the auspices of the American Library Association. Rewards outstanding service in the field of serials librarianship.

Bowl. The full rounded and entirely enclosed portion of a type letter as in O, B, D, b, a; the part enclosing a closed COUNTER (*q.v.*).

Box. (*Printing*) 1. An area within a larger type area, or within or between type columns, formed by rules or white spaces with the object of emphasizing what is printed within. 2. A rectangular or square border of one or more lines placed around type matter, and made up of rules which may be mitred or butted.

Box File. A container made to stand on a shelf, and intended primarily to contain flimsy material such as correspondence or newspaper cuttings. The most durable kinds are those with wooden sides, board base and hinged lid, the whole being covered with cloth and/or paper and lined with paper. A spring clip is usually provided to keep the contents in position. *See also Pamphlet Box.*

Box-in. To place rules around type matter so that the characters when printed appear in a frame or box.

Box Library. Boxes containing standard sets of books catering for different tastes and supplied in developing countries by community development organizations to community centres in rural areas for circulation from village to village.

Boxed. A work in two or three volumes inserted into a container to display them, keep them together, or protect them.

Boxhead. 1. A series of printed or ruled lines for headings in a ruled table. 2. A cut-in head with a frame around it. Also called 'Box heading'.

Boxhead Ruling. The space at the top of a ruled column for the insertion of hand-written headings for each column.

Boyet Style. A style of book decoration practised by Luc Antoine Boyet, who worked in France in the eighteenth century for Count Hoym. It is characterized by a plain border, ornamental corners and edges, and a central monogram or device. Boyet is sometimes credited with introducing DOUBLURES (*q.v.*).

Boys and Girls House, Toronto. Established in 1922 by the Toronto Public Library as a library for children, it is now an international centre for those concerned with library work for children. It includes the Osborne and Lillian H. Smith Collections.

BRA. British Records Association (*q.v.*).

Brace. (*Printing*) A bracket } cast on its own body, usually to a definite number of ems. Formerly called 'Vinculum'. A *sectional brace* is made of several parts which can be assembled to the length required; the middle position is called a COCK (*q.v.*).

Bracket Shelf. A shelf secured temporarily or permanently for display purposes at the end of a bookcase.

Bracket Shelving.   Adjustable shelving where the shelves rest, or are fixed, on brackets, which are secured to the rear upright stanchions of steel shelving fixtures, and which also serve as book supports. Also called 'Suspension shelving'. Sometimes the brackets simply support the shelves from underneath; this type is also called 'Cantilever shelving'.

Brackets.   Rectangular enclosing marks [ ]. Used in cataloguing to indicate something which does not appear in the original but is added by the cataloguer. To be distinguished from CURVES ( ), (*q.v.*). Angle brackets < > are used to enclose matter which itself appears in [ ] on the title-page. Also called 'Angular marks', 'Square brackets'. *See also Circular Brackets, Curves.*

Bradel Binding.   A type of temporary binding said to have originated in Germany, and first adopted in France by a binder named Bradel.

Bradford's Law of Scattering.   *See Law of Scattering.*

Braille.   A system of reading and writing for the blind in which the letters are formed by raised dots embossed into the paper in groups of six, three high and two wide. Named after the inventor Louis Braille (1809–52), a blind Frenchman.

Braille Book Bank.   *See NBA.*

Branch.   1. A section of the (British) Library Association's membership, admission to which is dependent on the place in which a librarian is resident or works. Membership of only one branch is permitted. Aslib also has geographical branches. *See also Division, Group, Library Association, Section.* 2. In a college or university, a collection of books and other materials on one subject, housed in a separate area and serviced by its own staff. It is centrally administered and is usually on the same campus as the main library.

Branch and Mobile Libraries Group.   A Group of the (British) Library Association; it was formed in January 1966 and is concerned with the particular outlook and needs of such kinds of service point. Publishes *Service Point* (3 p.a.); *Occasional Paper Series* (irreg.); *Fiction Guides Series* (irreg.).

Branch Librarian.   The librarian in charge of a branch library. *See also Departmental Library.* The librarian in charge of a branch library not covered by the definitions of AREA LIBRARIAN, DISTRICT LIBRARIAN, REGIONAL LIBRARIAN, REGIONAL OFFICER (*qq.v.*).

Branch Library.   A library other than the main one (called the 'Central') in a syst. It usually comprises adult lending and children's departments, a quick-referenceecollection and possibly a news-room, and is intended to meet the library needs of the surrounding population, particularly in the matter of books for home-reading. It is housed in premises set aside for the purpose, is specially equipped and furnished, and staffed by trained assistants. The book stock is a permanent one. Sometimes called a 'District Library'.

Branching Classification.   A classification with two or more sub-classes, or main branches, each subdivided again, and perhaps again and again. It may be converted into a TABULAR CLASSIFICATION (*q.v.*). Also called a 'Ramifying classification'.

Brass Rule. *See Rule.*

Brayer. Formerly a wooden pestle, round in shape and flat at one end with a handle on the other, used to spread ink on the block to an even depth and consistency before being taken up by the ink balls. Later, a hand-roller for distributing the ink before it is taken up by forme rollers. Also used when making a galley proof.

Brazilian Institute of Bibliography and Documentation. *See IBBD.*

Break (Break up). (*Printing*) To dispose of a forme of printing matter by separating material to be re-melted from furniture, blocks, rules, foundry type, etc. *See also Distributing.*

Break-line. The last line of a paragraph where quads are needed to fill out the last space. In good typesetting it does not begin a new page. *See also End a Break, End Even, Run On.*

Breaker. A part of the machinery used to make paper; it is a tub-like vessel into which the raw material is placed after boiling in the 'boiler' or 'kier' in order that it may be washed and further broken to reduce and separate the fibres. Also called 'Beater' or 'Hollander'.

Breeches Bible. *See Geneva Bible.*

Breviary. The book of daily Divine Office used in the Roman Catholic Church. It contains: 1. Calendar; 2. Psalter; 3. Proprium de Tempore (collects and lessons); 4. Proprium Sanctorum (collects, etc., for Saints' Days); 5. Commune Sanctorum (collects, etc., for Saints without special services); 6. Hours of the Virgin, burial services, etc., i.e. Small Offices. It contains neither the Communion Service nor the Mass.

Brevier. An obsolete name for a size of type equal to about 8 pt.

Bridge. A connection between two or more LOCAL AREA NETWORKS (*q.v.*). *See also Gateway.*

Brief. 1. A letter of authority. 2. A letter of the pope to a religious community, or an individual upon matters of discipline, and differing from a BULL (*q.v.*) by being less solemn and ample, and in the form in which it is written. 3. A letter patent which used to be issued by the sovereign as head of the church, licensing a collection to be made in churches for a specified object or charity. 4. A written description of the requirements for a building to be designed, and supplied to an architect so that he may prepare plans. It sets out the purpose of the building and its various rooms or departments, indicating their size, shape and juxtaposition, and any special features to be provided.

Brief Cataloguing. Simplified cataloguing, especially in respect of details after the imprint and including the tracing, for books that are likely to go into a storage centre, for pamphlets, and for other special categories. *See also Limited Cataloguing, Simplified Cataloguing.*

Brieflisting. (*Cataloguing*) A method of briefly cataloguing books which pose problems for the cataloguer, as a means of temporarily reducing a backlog of cataloguing arrears. The books are numbered and arranged numerically on the shelves of the cataloguing department, and an author entry is prepared for the catalogue. Once a brieflisted book is asked for it is catalogued fully; in the meantime, the service to readers is inadequate due to the absence of subject and added author and other entries.

Brighton/MARC.   *See BRIMARC.*

Brilliant.   An obsolete name for a size of type about 4 pt.

BRIMARC (UK).   An experiment to test the feasibility of a full catalogue service using MARC tapes was carried out with Brighton Public Libraries. Proved to be cost-effective; BLAISE/LOCAS (*q.v.*) evolved from BRIMARC.

Bring-up.   To bring a block up to the correct printing height by using underlay or interlay.

Briquet.   A conventional representation on a bookbinding of a steel used with tinder for striking a light.

Brisch-Vistem System.   A system of recording information on punched cards (called 'characteristics cards'), each of which has a thousand numbered squares and is reserved for a particular subject in accordance with a coded scheme of classification appropriate to the general subject area. Holes are punched to record information, each numbered square being allocated to a particular document or item of information; these are indexed alphabetically. Information is obtained by superimposing cards allocated to the appropriate subjects, the coincident holes indicating the items possessing the characteristics required. This system is sold under the trade name VISIscan. *See also Peek-a-Boo.*

Bristol Board.   A fine quality board made from rags and used for drawings or paintings. It is made by pasting two or more sheets of paper together, the substance being determined by the number of sheets.

British and Irish Association of Law Librarians.   Founded 1969; the principal aim of the Association is to promote the better administration and exploitation of law libraries and legal information units, by further education and training, through the organization of meetings and conferences, the publication of useful information, the encouragement of bibliographical study and research in law and librarianship, and co-operation with other organizations and societies. The Association is self supporting and draws its income chiefly from subscriptions. There is no affiliation to any other professional association, or legal body, and control is in the hands of the membership. The affairs of the Association are managed by its Council, which consists of four annually elected officers, assisted by an elected committee of five members, with the power to co-opt experienced non-elected members. Publishes *Law Librarian* (3 p.a.), *Manual of Law Librarianship* (1987), *Directory of Law Libraries* (1988), etc. Abbreviated BIALL.

British Architectural Library.   A national collection maintained by the Royal Institute of British Architects (RIBA).

British Association of Picture Libraries and Agencies.   *See BAPLA.*

British Book Design and Production Awards.   Various annual prizes awarded by the British Printing Industries Federation.

British Catalogue of Music. A catalogue of music and books about music published in Great Britain and consisting of entries made from material deposited under the Copyright Acts at the Copyright Receipt Office at the British Library. Publication began in 1957 under the auspices of the Council of the British National Bibliography. A faceted scheme of classification, drawn up by E. J. Coates, former Editor of the *Catalogue*, was used for arranging entries until 1981. From 1982 arranged by the Dewey Decimal Classification *Revision of 780 Music* (Forest Press, 1980). Originally published quarterly, now three times p.a. Abbreviated BCM.

British Catalogue of Music Classification. The scheme, drawn up by E. J. Coates, which was used to classify the entries in the BRITISH CATALOGUE OF MUSIC (*q.v.*).

British Copyright Council. Founded in 1954 as the British Joint Copyright Council. The name was altered and the scope and membership greatly increased in 1965. The aims of the Council are briefly (a) to defend and foster the true principles of copyright; (b) to cherish as an ultimate aim the acceptance of those principles throughout the world; (c) to bring together the bodies who speak for authors, artists, composers, actors, musicians and all others who are partners in or justly interested in the protection of copyright; (d) to keep a vigilant watch on any changes in law, administration, social practice, or mechanical contrivance which may require an amendment to the law; (e) to give attention to any matter relating to copyright brought to notice by a member; (f) to increase public knowledge of the principles, problems and importance of copyright law and practice. The membership of the Council is composed of British societies of authors, artists, actors, musicians and others who are concerned with creative activity. The Council has strongly promoted the COPYRIGHT LICENSING AGENCY (*q.v.*).

British Council. Established in 1934, and incorporated by Royal Charter in 1940, the Council promotes a wider knowledge of Britain abroad, develops cultural relations with other countrires, and administers educational aid programmes. It maintains 116 libraries overseas and is the agent for the low-priced books scheme (enabling students overseas to buy British textbooks on special terms), the books presentation programme (gifts of books to institutions in developing countries) and the library development scheme (advice on the establishment and improvement of libraries). A review of its libraries overseas was published in 1977 (*The Library and Information Services of the British Council*, British Council, 1977).

British Education Index. An index to articles in the field of education taken from over 250 periodicals. Founded in 1972 and operated in the British Library until 1985. The University of Leeds (UK) took over compilation from 1986. The British Education Thesaurus which is used in BEI is also published. *British Education Thesis Index* (BETI) is also now available from the same source. Online access is available via DIALOG.

British Film Institute (UK). The British Film Institute is a grant-aided cultural and educational organization which is responsible to the Department of Education and Science. The BFI was founded in 1933 and its aims

include the stimulation of appreciation and study of the cinema and television as art, and entertainment, and as a record of contemporary society. A
further aim is to maintain and preserve a national repository of films of
permanent value and this has now been extended to include television. This
custodial function is carried out by the National Film Archive which is a
major department of the British Film Institute. The BFI offers many
services to its members and to the general public. These include an advisory
service, an extensive and well-developed library service and lectures and
courses on film and television. Among its notable publications are the
British National Film Catalogue, Sight and Sound, and *BFI News* (members
only).

British Humanities Index.   A quarterly index, with annual cumulations, of
articles appearing in nearly 450 British, and a few Commonwealth periodicals; it is published by the Library Association. Prior to January 1962 it was
known as the *Subject Index to Periodicals*, and first appeared in 1915; no
volumes were issued in the years 1923 to 1925 inclusive. Abbreviated BHI.

British Institute of Recorded Sound Ltd.   *See National Sound Archive.*

British Interactive Video Association.   A grouping of some 30 companies
active in the commercial IV market. Established 1985, aims to develop
public awareness and co-ordinate technological advances. Abbreviated
BIVA.

British Jig-saw Puzzle Library.   Founded in 1933 the library has a stock of
4000 puzzles, all wooden and hand cut. Based at Leamington Spa, UK.

British Library.   The National Library of the UK; the Dainton Report (*q.v.*) of
1969 suggested the creation of a national library by the amalgamation of the
British Museum Library (including the National Reference Library of
Science and Invention), the National Central Library, the National Lending
Library for Science and Technology, and the British National Bibliography.
This suggestion was confirmed in the White Paper *The British Library*
(Cmnd. 4572) presented to Parliament in January 1971, and the *British
Library Act* (1972 Chapter 54) received Royal Assent on 27 July 1972.
The Act establishes the British Library, establishes the British Library
Board as the controlling authority, and sets out the broad aims of the
service; it also transfers the British Museum Library to the new body, and
with it the right to copyright deposit. The Act took effect in July 1973. The
British Library comprises:

1. The Board and Corporate Services (including the Chief Executive's
    office, finance, marketing, press and public relations, and central
    administration.)
2. Humanities and Social Sciences, which is responsible for Collection
    Development (the former Department of Printed Books, India Office
    Library and Records, Oriental Manuscripts, and Printed Books),
    Special Collections (Maps, Western Manuscripts, Music, Philatelic),
    the National Sound Archive, Public Services (General reading rooms,
    North library, Official Publications and Social Sciences Service, BLISS
    (*q.v.*), Newspaper Library, Exhibitions and Education), Planning and

Administration, and the Preservation Service (including the NATIONAL PRESERVATION OFFICE (*q.v.*).

3. Science Technology and Industry (including the Science Reference and Information Service, Business Information Service, Online Search Service, Japanese Information Service, and the Document Supply Centre).

4. Research and Development Department; (a document outlining priorities for research 1989-1994 emphasizes the importance of electronic publishing; industrial, commercial and business information research; information policy research; information handling and the new technologies; educational research and research into professional teaching; research into the needs of users.)

5. Bibliographic Services (including the Automated Services Department, Record Creation Unit with the Copyright Receipt Office and the CIP Programme, and the Editorial Control Group, including the UK National Serials Data Centre). BLAISE (*q.v.*) is the responsibility of this Service. The Marketing Office handles licensing schemes for the use of records in automated formats by other libraries and networks. The Library issued a paper *Currency with Coverage, the Future Development of the British National Bibliographic Service* in 1987; this explains how Bibliographic Services will meet the targets set in the strategic plan.

6. Publications Sales Unit.

Most of these components are based at central London addresses, but the Document Supply Centre, Bibliographic Services, Research and Development Department, and Publications Sales Unit are located at Boston Spa, West Yorkshire. A new building is under construction in central London; work began in 1981 and the first stage will open in 1991. The project should be complete in 1996.

As well as BLAISE services, an enormous quantity of serial and monograph publishing is undertaken by the Library, and numerous reports appear from Research and Development. Major publications include *British National Bibliography, Serials in the British Library, British Catalogue of Music, Current Research in Britain, General Catalogue of Printed Books* (and supplements), which is now also available on CD-ROM.

In 1985 the Library issued *Advancing with Knowledge* – a strategic plan for 1985-90. In 1989 a further plan was published to cover 1989–94: *Gateway to Knowledge* outlines the Library's strategy during the period of removal to the new Central London building, and states that the primary purpose is to advance knowledge by giving ready access to collections and databases, and by pursuing and promoting research about the collection, preservation, communication and exploitation of knowledge. User needs, efficient cataloguing, co-operation and use of new technologies are cited as key areas.

British Library Interim Committee on Art Documentation.   *See BLICAD.*

British Museum Library.   This Library ceased to exist as a part of the British Museum on its incorporation as a major part of the BRITISH LIBRARY (*q.v.*).

The British Museum (Natural History) Library was not so transferred. Abbreviated BML.

British National Bibliographic Service. The title given to the range of bibliographic publications and aids produced by the Bibliographic Services of the BRITISH LIBRARY (*q.v.*).

British National Bibliography. An organization which has issued since 4 January 1950 a weekly printed list of books published in Great Britain. Full catalogue entries are made from books received at the Copyright Office of the British Library, classified by Dewey's *Decimal Classification* and published each week in classified order, but with appropriate subject headings. The last issue each month contains a monthly index. Annual cumulations are made. The publications are known as '*BNB*' or *British National Bibliography*. This organization was incorporated in the activities of the BRITISH LIBRARY (*q.v.*) in 1974, becoming a major part of the Bibliographic Services Division. From early in 1977, *BNB* entries include records of items catalogued in advance of publication (CIP). From 1988 a CD-ROM version has been available. In 1989 other copyright libraries began to contribute cataloguing data in machine-readable format.

British National Bibliography Research Fund. The fund exists to support research into the book trade and related library activities in the UK. Administered by the British Library Research and Development Department, through a Committee which includes representation from ASLIB, the Booksellers Association, British Council, Library Association, Book Trust, Publishers Association and the Royal Society.

British National Book Centre. This Centre and the National Central Library became a part of the BRITISH LIBRARY (*q.v.*) when this was formed in 1974; the centre continued to function, but as the 'Gift and Exchange Section', housed with the Document Supply Centre. In 1988 it was re-launched as BOOKNET (*q.v.*).

British National Committee on Palaeography. A sub-committee on manuscripts of the Standing Conference of National and University Libraries (SCONUL). *See also Sconul.*

British Paper and Board Industry Research Association. This Association was concerned with research on pulping, and paper-making processes, the assessment of raw materials, performance of paper-making machinery, performance testing of paper and effluent treatment. It was grant-aided through the Ministry of Technology. Abbreviated BPBIRA. But since the Ministry of Technology was dissolved and its research responsibilities distributed, research in the field of printing, paper and board is being undertaken by PIRA. *See entry under Printing and Allied Trades Research.*

British Record Society. Formed in 1889 with the object of preserving records and making them accessible to scholars by the publication of indexes in a series known as the *Index Library*. Over 80 volumes have been published relating to various categories of record, and in the last few decades they have been concerned almost exclusively with indexing testamentary records.

British Records Association.   Inaugurated November 1932 to co-ordinate the work of the many individuals, authorities, institutions and societies interested in the conservation and use of archives in the United Kingdom. It aims to co-ordinate and encourage the preservation and exploitation of all records of the past; to act as a forum for users, custodians, and owners of records; and to campaign on archival issues.

The Records Preservation Section is largely funded by a range of grants and donations, including a grant-in-aid from HM Treasury (administered through the Historical Manuscripts Commission).

The Association has 1000 members, and organizes an Annual conference, and regional meetings. Publishes *Archives* (two p.a.). Abbreviated BRA.

British Society for International Bibliography.   Founded in 1927 as the British section of the Institut de Bibliographie, known as BSIB, and amalgamated in 1948 with Aslib.

British Standards Institution.   The approved British body for the preparation and promulgation of national standards covering, inter alia, methods of test; terms, definitions and symbols; standards of quality of performance or of dimensions; preferred ranges; codes of practice. A selection of Standards of interest to librarians, information officers and documentalists include the following:

BS1000 :	*Universal decimal classification (q.v.).*
1629 : 1989	*Recommendations for references to published materials.*
1749 : 1985	*Alphabetical arrangement.*
2509 : 1970	*(1983) Presentation of serial publications, including periodicals.*
3700 : 1988	*Preparing indexes to books, periodicals and other documents.*
4187 :	*Specification for microfiche* Part 1: 1981; Part 3: 1978 (1985).
4191 : 1976	*(1985) Microform readers.*
4748 : 1982	*Format for bibliographic information exchange on magnetic tape.*
4754 : 1982	*Presentation of printed music and scores.*
4971 :	*Repair and allied processes for the conservation of documents* Part 1: 1973 (1988); Part 2: 1980.
5261 :	*Copy preparation and proof correction* Part 1: 1975 (1983); Part 2: 1976.
5513 : 1977	*(1983) 35 mm microcopying of newspaper cuttings.*
5525 : 1977	*(1983) 35 mm microcopying of maps and plans.*
5644 : 1978	*(1985) Computer output microfiche.*
5723 : 1979	*(1984) Guidelines for the establishment and development of monolingual thesauri.*

5847 : 1980	*35 mm microcopying of newspapers.*
5999 : 1983	*Serials holdings statements for libraries.*
6054 :	*Glossary of terms for micrographics.*
	Part 1: 1981; Part 2: 1983; Part 3: 1984.
6313 : 1982	*35 mm microcopying of serials.*
6371 : 1983	*Citation of unpublished documents.*
6474 :	*Coded character sets for bibliographic*
	information exchange. Part 1: 1984;
	Part 2: 1985; Part 3: 1984.
6478 : 1984	*Filing bibliographic information in libraries.*
6529 : 1984	*Selecting indexing terms.*
6568 : 1984	*Basic reference model for OSI.*
6723 : 1985	*Guide to the establishment and development of*
	multi-lingual thesauri.
6868 : 1987	*Standard Generalised Markup Language.*
6879 : 1988	*Codes for the representation of names of*
	countries and similar areas.
8205 : 1985	*Design of learning spaces with a/v equipment.*

Standards information can be accessed online via Pergamon-Infoline. Abbreviated BSI. *See also Standards, Z39.*

British Talking Book Service for the Blind. *See NTBL.*

British Technology Index.   A current subject guide to the major articles published in 400 British technical journals; published monthly since January 1962, each twelfth issue being an annual cumulation. Published by the Library Association. Abbreviated *BTI.* From 1982 retitled Current Tech-nology Index (*q.v.*).

British Theatre Association Library.   A London-based, international centre for theatre research; founded in 1919 as the British Drama League, and containing the largest collection of play texts in Europe. The libraries of many theatrical families are represented in its holdings. In 1989 its future became uncertain after various small grants were discontinued, but the Robert Holmes à Court Foundation agreed to underpin its finances, and a move to new premises is anticipated in 1991. Abbreviated BTA.

British Union Catalogue of Periodicals.   A list of over 140,000 titles of periodicals of the world, from the seventeenth century to the present day, together with particulars of the holdings of over 440 British libraries. Compiled with funds made available by the Rockefeller Foundation, it was published in four volumes between 1955 and 1958. It was kept up-to-date by the Bibliographical Services Division of the British Library (*q.v.*), additions and amendments being recorded in the quarterly *BUCOP: new periodical titles* and annual cumulations. Familiarly called *BUCOP.* Replaced in 1982 by *Serials in the British Library.*

British Universities Film and Video Council.   Exists to encourage the use, production and study of audio-visual media, materials and techniques for teaching and research in higher education. It provides a forum for the exchange of information and experience in this field. Founded 1948 (as the British Universities Film Council) and based in London. Operates a reference library, and an audio-visual reference centre; publishes an annual *Catalogue* on microfiche, and various reports and newsletters. Abbreviated BUFVC.

BRITS Index. British Theses Service – a 3-volume index to the British Theses Collection at BLDSC and the University of London, covering the years 1971–1987. Annual supplements are to be issued. Published by IPI Ltd. in association with the British Library.

Broad. Applies to a sheet of paper which is divided by halving the long side (i.e. across the narrow way). This is the regular or common way of dividing a sheet. Hence a *broad folio*, quarto, or octavo. The opposite of OBLONG (*q.v.*). A *broad fold* is a sheet folded so that the longest dimension is horizontal; the grain then runs with the shorter dimension of the paper.

Broad Classification. 1. Use of only the more inclusive classes of a classification scheme, omitting detailed subdivision. Also called 'Reduction of numbers'. 2. A classification scheme which does not provide for minute subdivision of topics. 3. An arrangement of books in main classes with little or no sub-division. *See also Close Classification.*

Broad Folio. *See Folio.*

Broad System of Ordering. *See BSO.*

Broader Term. (*Information retrieval*) A term which denotes a concept which is broader than one with a more specific meaning, e.g. Science is broader than Anthropology. *See also Narrower Term, Related Term.*

Broadsheet. A long, narrow advertising leaflet; usually the long quarto of the sheet of paper from which it is cut. It may be printed on both sides. Sometimes used synonymously with BROADSIDE (*q.v.*).

Broadside. A large sheet of paper printed on one side right across the sheet, for sheet distribution, and usually intended to be posted up, e.g. proclamations, ballad sheets, news-sheets, sheet calendars, etc. *See also Broadsheet.* Also used of a poster of which the width is greater than the depth.

Broadside Page. *Synonymous with* LANDSCAPE PAGE (*q.v.*).

Brochure. Literally 'a stitched work' (from the French 'brocher', to stitch). A short printed work of a few leaves, merely stitched together, and not otherwise bound, a pamphlet.

Broken Back. A book whose back has broken open from head to tail. Also called 'Broken binding'.

Broken Letter. One, the face of which is damaged and cannot give a complete impression. Indicated in a proof by placing a small × in the margin. Also called 'Bad letter', 'Battered letter', 'Damaged letter', 'Spoiled letter'.

Broken Order. The removal of a section, or sections, of the book stock from its proper sequence in the classification in order to facilitate use.

Broken-over. A PLATE (*q.v.*) or other separate sheet which is to be inserted in a book, and is given a narrow fold near the back, or binding, edge before sewing, etc., to ensure that it will lie flat and turn easily when the book is bound.

Bronzing. Dusting with a fine metallic powder over a sheet freshly printed with ink, varnish or size to give a brilliant, lustrous effect.

Bronzing Size. A printing ink made specially for bronzing. The term is sometimes used for printing ink for subsequent printing with metallic ink.

Brothers of the Common Life. Monks who maintained monasteries in various parts of Germany and the Low Countries in the last quarter of the fifteenth century and set up printing presses in about sixty of them between 1475 and 1490. Their first dated book was issued in 1476 from the 'Nazareth' Monastery at Brussels.

Brown Classification. The familiar name for James Duff Brown's SUBJECT CLASSIFICATION (*q.v.*). *See also Adjustable Classification.*

Brown Library, John Carter. A collection of 30,000 books dealing with the discovery and settlement of America to 1800; assembled by John Carter Brown (1797-1874) who was one of America's best-known book collectors. The library was passed on to Brown University, Providence, Rhode Island, USA, in 1900, since when it has grown considerably and is one of the finest collections of Americana in existence.

Brown Mechanical Woodpulp. A woodpulp for papermaking obtained by grinding steamed or boiled logs.

Browne Book Charging System. A system of book charging which is attributed to Nina E. Browne, an American librarian, who described it in 1895. It is, however, very little different from the method adopted about 1873 by L. G. Virgo, Librarian of Bradford Public Library. The reader has a limited number of tickets, each of which is available for one book only at a time, and which are given up when books are borrowed and handed back when the books are returned. This simple, reliable and speedy method was replaced in America by the Newark and Detroit methods and others based on them, but, until photo-charging and computerized methods were introduced, was the most universally used method in Great Britain. 'Reverse Browne' uses a pocket book-card and a card ticket: this was described by Jacob Schwartz in 1897 and had been in use for a number of years. *See also Charging Methods, Token Charging.*

Browsability. The ability of an indexing system to lend itself to unsystematic or random searches. This ability is of interest or use to the searcher even though it may not produce a logical answer to the search question.

Browse. To investigate, without design, the contents of a collection of books or documents.

Browsing Room. A room provided in an American college, university, or public library which contains novels and non-fiction books on all subjects, but no text books. It is intended for recreational reading and not for study, in order to help achieve which, furnishings are bright and informal. Books may or may not be borrowed for home reading. A development of the POPULAR LIBRARY (*q.v.*).

BRS Europe. A commercial provider of information retrieval software, training support, and CD-ROM products. Publishes *BRS Europe Update* (q.) and runs a BRS European User Group. An off-shoot of Bibliographic Retrieval Services, USA.

Brush Coated. (*Paper*) Paper given a smooth printing surface by applying the clay, or other, coating substance as a separate and later operation to the actual paper making, in order to make it perfectly smooth so as to take a high degree of finish. *See also Art, Coated Paper, Machine Coated.*

Brush-Pen. A pen, with a fibrous point, made of reed, used for writing on papyrus.

Brussels Convention. Popular name for the revision (signed on 26 June 1948) of the BERNE COPYRIGHT UNION (*q.v.*). *See also Copyright, International.*

Brussels Expansion. A familiar name for the UNIVERSAL DECIMAL CLASSIFICATION (*q.v.*).

Bryant Memorandum. The *Memorandum on the present program of the Library of Congress and related agencies.* It comments on the Federal and research library situation and the role of the Library of Congress. It was written in 1962, by Douglas Bryant, Associate Director of the Harvard Library, at the request of Senator Claiborne Pell of Rhode Island who introduced it into the *Congressional Record* for 24 May 1962. The reply by the Librarian of Congress, L. Quincy Mumford, appeared in the *Congressional Record* for 2 October 1962.

BS. British Standard. *See entry under British Standards Institution.*

BSA. Bibliographical Society of America (*q.v.*).

BSD. *See British Library (Bibliographic Services Division).*

BSI. British Standards Institution (*q.v.*).

BSIB. *See British Society for International Bibliography.*

BSO. Acronym for Board System of Ordering, a system (within the UNISIST (*q.v.*) programme) being developed to serve as a switching mechanism, between individual classifications and thesauri in the process of information transfer, rather than as a new classification system. It will be an essential tool for systems interconnection and will play an essential part in ISDS (*q.v.*), the referral network, and the operation of information systems. *See also SRC.*

BTA. *See British Theatre Association Library.*

BTEC. *See Business and Technical Education Council.*

BTECC. Booktrade Electronic Communications Committee; set up in 1988 with representation from the Publishers Association, the Booksellers Association, and the Library Association. Funding is provided by the BNB Research Fund, and co-ordination provided by the British Library Research and Development Department. The Scot Report from the Booksellers Association, and the Cullen Report from the Publishers Association (both described in *The Bookseller*, April 3, 1987, pp. 1285–6, 1308–15) recommended such a body, and its initial concerns are to examine the common concerns of various sectors of the book world, to encourage standardization, and to develop electronic exchange of data. BTECC focuses on the role and needs of participants; BEDIS (*q.v.*) is concerned more with the technical requirements.

BTI. *British Technology Index* (*q.v.*).

BTX. *See Bildschirmtext.*

BUCCS. Acronym of the Bath University Comparative Catalogue Study which was carried out with a grant from OSTI in 1972 to determine which form (card, printout, COM., rollfilm, or fiche), and which order (name, title, classified, or KWOC) (a) best meets demands on the catalogue; (b) is easiest to use; (c) is most cost-effective. *See also Centre for Bibliographic Management.*

Buckle-Folder. A machine which folds printed sheets by passing them between two continuously revolving rollers placed one above the other until the leading edge touches a stop bar. The rollers continue to impel the rear half of the sheet until it is folded and so carried down between the lower revolving roller and a third one which is parallel to it. *See also Knife-Folder.*

Buckles. (*Binding*) Severe wrinkles near the head and back of the folded sections. *See also Section.*

Buckram. A strong textile, either of linen or cotton, used for covering books. *See also Art Canvas.*

BUCOP. Abbreviation for BRITISH UNION CATALOGUE OF PERIODICALS (*q.v.*).

Budget. The total amount of money which is available for library purposes after the estimate of anticipated needs has been approved by the appropriate authority.

Buds. In bookbinding, an ornament filling a small panel on some rolls: it is a conventionalized form of a spray bearing buds.

Buffer. 1. A substance, or mixture of substances, which in document preservation is used to control the acidity or alkalinity of a solution or paper at a pre-determined level, e.g. the use of chalk in the manufacture of paper. 2. A temporary memory data store, typically between two devices when input and output speeds differ.

BUFVC. *See British Universities Film and Video Council.*

Building-in Machine. A machine which, in book production, dries cased books in a matter of seconds by means of several applications of heat and pressure. This is an alternative to the slower method of the STANDING PRESS (*q.v.*).

Bulk. 1. The thickness of a book exclusive of its covers; this will be less after, than before, binding. Book papers are measured by the thickness of a number of pages. The extremes between which papers of the same weight, but of a different class, vary in bulk may be seen from the following figures, based on 320 pp. of quad crown 100 lb.

Featherweight	53/32 in.	Pure Super – calendered	22/32 in.
Esparto M.F.	29/32 in.	Coated Art	21/32 in.
Pure M.F.	24/32 in.	Imitation Art	20/32 in.

2. The thickness of a sheet of paper related to its weight and measured in thousandths of an inch. 3. To 'bulk' a book is to make it appear bigger than it need be by using a thick but lightweight paper.

Bull. A formal papal letter under the leaden seal (Bulla).

Bulletin. 1. A publication, generally a pamphlet, issued by a government, society or other organization at regular intervals and in serial form. 2. A periodical or occasional publication containing lists of books added to a library, and other library information.

Bulletin Board. A notice board in a library on which are exhibited lists of books, announcements of forthcoming events, jackets of new books added to the library, and miscellaneous library information.

Bulletin Board Systems. An online message system which can 'post' notices and general information onto the terminals of users of a network.

Bullock Report. *A language for life, report of the Committee of Inquiry appointed by the Secretary of State for Education and Science under the Chairmanship of Sir Alan Bullock* published in 1975. The Committee was set up by Mrs Thatcher in 1972 when Secretary of State for Education and Science, to inquire into the teaching of reading and the other uses of English in British Schools.

Bumped Out. (*Printing*) 1. Matter which is widely leaded. 2. A line of characters in which extra spacing has been inserted to square it up with the measure of a longer line.

Bumper. A machine used to compact the sections of a book after they have been sewn together. Also called a 'Nipper' or 'Smasher'.

BUMS. Bibliographic network providing a computerized cataloguing and circulation control system for Swedish public libraries. Based at Biblioteks-jänst, Lund; founded 1974, and currently having 88 members.

Burin. An engineer's tool.

Burnished Edges. Coloured or gilt edges which have been made smooth and bright by a polishing tool.

Bursting Strain. The measurement, expressed in pounds per square inch, of pressure required to rupture paper when being tested on a Mullen or Ashcroft machine.

Business and Technical Education Council. Established 1983 from the merger of the Business Education Council (BEC) and the Technician Education Council (TEC). A UK validating body for a range of career-related courses, offered in a variety of study modes. Scotland is covered by SCOTVEC. Abbreviated BTEC.

Business Archives Council. A non-profit-making body supported by voluntary contributions from business firms, universities libraries and record offices, and managed by a committee representing all of these interests. Its objects are to preserve business records and encourage interest in business history. Publishes *Business Archives* (2 a year).

Business Education Council (UK). *See Business and Technical Education Council.*

Business Information Service. Set up to promote awareness of the British Library's holdings on business information, to act on a national focus, and to liaise with librarians; based at the Science Reference and Information Service (SRIS).

Butt Splice. *See Splice.*

Butted. (*Printing*) Lines of type, or rules, placed end to end to make larger lines. Also called 'Butted slugs'.

Butted Slugs. *See Butted.*

Butterfly Plan. An arrangement of bookstacks in a butterfly or fan shape. *See also Radiating Stacks.*

Butting. 1. To produce a line of type in the form of a slug (using a Linotype, or similar machine), which is longer than the machine normally makes (30 picas); the line is set on two slugs which are butted together – placed end to end. 2. To place two pieces of paper, cloth or leather with edges touching.

Bye-laws. Bye-laws may be made under the provisions of the (British) Public Libraries and Museums Act 1964, s. 19, regulating the use of facilities provided by the authority under this Act and the conduct of persons in premises where those facilities are provided. Bye-laws may include provisions enabling officers of a local authority to exclude or remove from premises maintained by the authority any person who contravenes the bye-laws. A set of model bye-laws has been prepared at the Department of Education and Science. Before bye-laws can be effective they must be submitted by local authorities in England and Wales to the Secretary of State for confirmation. Bye-laws must be displayed in any premises maintained under the Act to which the public ha access. The provisions in Northern Ireland and in Scotland are slightly different.

Byline. The line of type at the head of a newspaper or magazine article indicating its authorship. *See also Masthead.*

Byname. *See Nickname.*

Byte. The space occupied in a computer memory by one character or by one space; consists of eight binary digits. A kilobyte is 1000 bytes, and a megabyte is 1,000,000 bytes.

Byzantine Bindings. Book covers, rather than true bindings, finely wrought in gold and silver, and often inlaid with precious stones. They date from the foundation of Byzantium by Constantine the Great in the fourth century.

c. Abbreviation for CHAPTER (*q.v.*), caput or *circa* (*q.v.*). Also for the word 'copyright' when used in descriptive notes, though not legally valid in a copyright notice when © should be used.

©. The symbol claiming copyright under Article III (1) of the Universal Copyright Convention (*see Copyright, International*); it is required by law to be placed before the name of the copyright proprietor and the year of first publication. The Intergovernmental Copyright Committee, meeting in Washington in October 1957, recommended positions in various kinds of publication where the symbol might be placed: amongst these was the title-page or the page immediately following, or at the end of a book or pamphlet; under the main title or the MASTHEAD (*q.v.*) of a newspaper, magazine or other periodical; on the face side of a map, print or photograph, either on the actual map or picture (but near the title or the margin) or on the margin.

ca. Abbreviation for *circa* (*q.v.*).

CAB. *See Citizens Advice Bureau.*

CAB. Commonwealth Agricultural Bureaux (*q.v.*).

Cabinet. 1. An enclosed rack or frame for holding type cases, galleys, etc.; made formerly of wood but now also of pressed sheet steel. 2. A standard size of card, 4¼ × 6½ inches.

Cabinet Edition. *See Library Edition.*

Cabinet Size. *See Oblong.*

Cable Systems. Cable television was originally developed to provide good quality reception to homes which could not be served adequately by domestic antennae. The UK market stagnated as the UHF transmitter network improved reception via antennae, and Government regulations prevented the introduction of new channels. In 1980 a small number of pilot services were licensed, and the ITAP Report on Wideband Cable Systems (1981) suggested that IT based services could be financed by the private sector. This led to the setting up of the Hunt Committee and the HUNT REPORT (*q.v.*) which proposed a liberal framework of regulations to encourage private investment. The Cable and Broadcasting Act was passed by Parliament in 1984.

Cable Television. *See Cable Systems.*

CABLIS. A monthly Current Awareness Bulletin for Librarians and Information Staff, compiled by the British Library Research and Development Department, and based on the resources of BLISS (*q.v.*). Redesigned and re-launched in 1989.

CACL. Canadian Association of Children's Librarians (*q.v.*) (a Section of the Canadian Association of Public Libraries).

CACUL. Canadian Association of College and University Libraries (*q.v.*) (a Division of the Canadian Library Association).

Cadastral Map. One drawn on a large scale to show ownership, extent and value of land for purposes of taxation.

CAIRS. Computer-Assisted Information Retrieval System; a software package for text information management, storage and retrieval, suitable for a wide variety of computers of all sizes. Developed by the Food Research Association, Leatherhead, UK.

CAIRS LMS. A fully integrated library management system, covering all aspects of library housekeeping, developed from the above.

CAIS. Canadian Association for Information Science (*q.v.*).

CAITS. An online information retrieval service for trade unions, community groups and local authorities. The service is operated by the Centre for Alternative Industrial and Technological Systems, at the Polytechnic of North London, UK and covers social policy, social services, public expenditure, commercial and economic issues, and technological references.

Calcography. *See Chalk Drawing.*

Caldecott (Randolph) Medal. This medal is awarded annually under the auspices of the Association for Library Services to Children of the American Library Association. The award is made each January to the illustrator of the most distinguished picture book for children published in the United

States during the previous year. Donated by the Frederic G. Melcher family, the medal has been awarded since 1938 and recipients must be citizens of or resident in the United States. *See also Newbery Medal.*

CALDIS.   Calderdale Information Service for Business and Industry; a service to local firms offered by Calderdale Business Information Centre Ltd., based on Calderdale College Library, Halifax, UK, and featuring access to books, journals, standards, and online searching facilities. Issues *CALDIS News* (q.).

Calendar.   1. A chronological list of documents in a given collection, e.g. charters, state papers, rolls, etc., giving the date, and with annotations indicating or summarizing the contents of each.   2. An almanack giving lists of days, months, saints' days, etc., for a given year, or a special list of important days for certain purposes throughout the year, e.g. a university or gardening calendar.

Calender.   A machine consisting mainly of metal rollers between which paper is passed to give it a smooth surface. The degree of smoothness depends on the pressure of the rollers and the extent to which they close the pores.

Calendered Paper.   Paper that is given a smooth surface by rolling, when newly-made, between smooth cylinders under pressure. Paper which receives a minimum of calendering emerges as an antique. With more calendering it acquires a machine finish, then an English finish, and it finally becomes a super-calendered, glossy sheet. *See also Super-Calendered Paper.*

Calf.   A bookbinding leather made from calfskin and so used since at least 1450. It may have a rough or a smooth (the more usual) finish. Books which are full-bound can be further described as being diced, grained, marbled, mottled, scored, sprinkled, stained, or tree, according to the form of decoration used. Special styles are known as antique, divinity, law, reversed or roughened.

CALL.   Canadian Association of Law Libraries (*q.v.*).

CALL.   *Current Awareness Library Literature* (irreg.) presents the tables of contents of over 300 issues of more than 200 library and library-related periodicals. Compiled by Goldstein Associates.

Call Card.   *Synonymous with* CALL SLIP (*q.v.*).

Call Number.   As the term implies, the number by which a reader requisitions a book. Usually the classification number (or in fixed location, shelf number) followed by the BOOK NUMBER (*q.v.*) or simply the AUTHOR MARK (*q.v.*). It is used to identify a particular book, and to indicate both its position on the shelves and its position relative to other books; it is marked on the spine of a book as well as on catalogue cards and other records. In the Colon Classification, the call number consists of the class number, book number and COLLECTION NUMBER (*q.v.*). The class number fixes the position of a book's specific subject relative to other subjects.

Call Slip.   A printed blank on which are entered the author, title and call number for books required in a reference or university library. Also called 'Call card', 'Readers' slip'; 'Requisition form'.

Calligraphic Initial. An initial in a mediaeval illuminated manuscript made by a scribe rather than an artist. Such initials are in ink, and rarely brushed with colour or touched with gold.

Calligraphy. The art of fine handwriting: penmanship. A calligrapher is a trained penman. Calligraphic types are those designed in close sympathy with the spirit of good handwriting.

Calotype. An early photographic process invented (c. 1839) by W. H. F. Talbot. Paper sensitized with silver iodide was brushed over with a solution of silver nitrate, acetic acid or gallic acid and exposed while wet. Translucent paper permitted a positive to be printed and led to the use of the glass plate. Also called 'Talbotype'.

Cambridge India Paper. Trade name for a grade of paper used for Bibles; made by James R. Compton & Bros. Ltd., Bury, Lancashire. So named to distinguish it from OXFORD INDIA PAPER (*q.v.*). *See also India Paper.*

Cambridge Style. The English style of book decoration characterized by double panels with a flower tool at each of the outer four corners.

Cameo. A die-stamping process which results in the design being in plain relief on a coloured background.

Cameo Binding. A binding having the centre of the boards stamped in relief, in imitation of antique gems or medals. Also called 'Plaquette binding'.

Cameo-coated Paper. An American dull-finished coated paper suitable for printing half-tones with a non-lustrous surface: it is particularly suitable for artistic engravings. The English equivalent is matt-finished art paper. *See also Art.*

Cameo Stamp. The earliest form of tool for blind tooling used between the eleventh and early sixteenth centuries. It was oval in shape and engraved with a pictorial design; when impressed on the side of a book it resembled a cameo.

Camera Copy. Material (e.g. table, diagram, photograph, etc.) which is ready for photographing for reproduction, usually by lithography, in a publication.

Camera Microfilm. The developed microfilm used in a camera to photograph a document; so used to distinguish the film from a microfilm copy made therefrom. Also called 'First generation microfilm'. *See also First Reproduction Microfilm.*

Camera Ready. Typescript which is ready to be photographed as part of a book production process.

Campbell Citation, Francis Joseph. A citation and medal awarded by the ALA for outstanding contributions to library services for the blind.

CAN/SDI. Abbreviation for Canadian Selective Dissemination of Information; a network for which the National Library of Canada operates an automated retrieval system that regularly scans thousands of publications, searching for titles in the fields of the social and behavioural sciences and the humanities of interest to the system's subscribers. CISTI (*q.v.*) is concerned with the scientific fields.

Canada Institute for Scientific and Technical Information. *See CISTI.*

Canadian Association for Information Science.   Association Canadienne des Sciences de l'Information. Formed in 1970 to promote the development of information science in Canada by bringing together persons in the many disciplines engaged in the production, storage, retrieval, and transmission of scientific and other information. Financed by membership dues, annual conferences of the Association, and publications. Publishes *Newsletter* (q.), *Canadian Journal of Information Science* (a.). Abbreviated CAIS/ACSI.

Canadian Association of Children's Librarians.   Formed 1939. Agreed, consequent upon the restructuring of the Canadian Library Association, to become a Section of the CANADIAN ASSOCIATION OF PUBLIC LIBRARIES (*q.v.*). Publishes *CACL Bulletin*. Abbreviated CACL.

Canadian Association of College and University Libraries.   A Division of the CANADIAN LIBRARY ASSOCIATION (*q.v.*). Exists to further the interests of librarians and libraries in institutions which offer formal education above the secondary level, and to support the highest aims of education and librarianship. There are three sections: Small Universities Libraries, Community and Technical Colleges, and Canadian Academic Research Libraries (CARL). Publishes *CACUL Newsletter* (6 p.a.) and reports. Abbreviated CACUL.

Canadian Association of Law Libraries.   Founded in July 1962 as a Chapter of the American Association of Law Libraries with the objects of fostering a spirit of co-operation among Canadian law libraries and increasing their usefulness and efficiency. Publishes *CALL newsletter, Index to Canadian legal periodical literature*. Abbreviated CALL.

Canadian Association of Library Schools.   Established in 1966 at the Canadian Library Association Conference, after informal meetings the previous year. Aims to promote the development of library education in Canada. Based at the University of Western Ontario. Publishes *Newsletter* (q.).

Canadian Association of Public Libraries.   A Division of the CANADIAN LIBRARY ASSOCIATION (*q.v.*). Founded in June 1972 at the Canadian Library Association's annual conference; it incorporates three former sections of the Canadian Library Association – Adult Services, Canadian Association of Children's Librarians, and Young People's, and aims to further public library service to all Canadians. Provides sections and committees to encourage interchange among public librarians who serve various groups. Publishes a newsletter. Abbreviated CAPL.

Canadian Association of Research Libraries.   *See CARL.*

Canadian Association of Special Libraries and Information Services.   A Division of the CANADIAN LIBRARY ASSOCIATION (*q.v.*). Membership is open to special librarians, librarians from subject divisions of academic and public libraries, and specialists in information science. Publishes a newsletter *Agora* (q.) and directories, etc. Abbreviated CASLIS.

Canadian Book Exchange Centre.   The Centre is a clearing-house service provided by the National Library of Canada, for the distribution and exchange of publications which are deemed surplus by some institutions but would be of use to others. The Centre was established to provide an efficient and practical method of handling surplus publications in Canada. Not only does it ensure that the nation's collective surplus holdings of Canadian and foreign publications are accessible to all, it also helps ease space and staffing problems of institutions since surplus materials are put back into circulation instead of being kept in storage. Since its inception in 1974, the Centre has received about 21 million publications and distributed about 6.5 million.

Canadian Library Association (CLA).   Formed in 1946, and incorporated in 1947; headquarters in Ottawa. Bilingual title dropped in 1968, but bilingual programmes continue. In 1975 a new constitution was adopted. CLA works to improve the quality of Canadian library and information services, encourage professional conduct, and promote public support for libraries. There are five divisions: Canadian Association of College and University Libraries (CACUL); Canadian Association of Public Libraries (CAPL); Canadian Association of Special Libraries and Information Services (CASLIS); Canadian Library Trustees Association (CLTA); Canadian School Library Association (CSLA). Publishes *Canadian Library Journal* (6 p.a.), *Feliciter* (12 p.a.), *Canadian Periodical Index* (12 p.a.).

Canadian Library Trustees' Association.   A Division of the CANADIAN LIBRARY ASSOCIATION (*q.v.*). Its main objective is to educate members in the principles of trusteeship; membership is open to all library trustees interested in promoting better public library services. Publishes a *Newsletter* (4 p.a.). Abbreviated CLTA.

Canadian National Science Library.   *See National Science Library* (of Canada).

Canadian School Library Association.   Founded in 1961; became a Division of the Canadian Library Association in 1973. Aims: to improve the quality of school library service by stimulating interest at all levels of the education system. Publishes a newsletter – *Moccasin Telegraph* (3 p.a.). Abbreviated CSLA.

Cancel.   This term is loosely given to a part of a book (leaf, part of a leaf or leaves) on which there is a major error which cannot be allowed to remain, and to the leaf which is printed to take the place of the original. The original leaf, which would be more accurately described as the 'Cancelled leaf' (Cancellandum), is cut out by the binder and the corrected one (cancel, cancelling leaf, cancellans) pasted to its stub. Occasionally both leaves are found in a book, the binder having omitted to remove the cancelled leaf.

Cancel a Loan.   To record the return of a borrowed book; to cancel the record of its loan.

Cancel Title.   A reprinted title-page to replace one cut out.

Cancelland.   *Synonymous with* CANCELLANDUM (*q.v.*).

Cancellandum.   *See Cancel.*

Cancellans.   *See Cancel.*

Cancellation.   The removal of a leaf of a section of a book because of textual error, or for some other reason, leaving a portion of the leaf in the form of a stub. The portion left is known as a disjunct leaf. The portion of the leaf removed is known as the cancellandum and a leaf inserted to take its place is known as the cancellans. *See also Cancel.*

Cancellation Mark. *Synonymous with* DELETION MARK (*q.v.*).

Cancelled Leaf. *See Cancel.*

Cancelling Leaf. *See Cancel.*

Canevari Binding. A style of binding named after Demetrio Canevari (1539–1625), physician to Pope Urban VII, and usually consisting of a blind-tooled centre panel enclosing a sunken portion bearing a large cameo either glued to the leatheer or impressed on it.

Canon. An obsolete name for a size of type equal to about 48 pt. The name is probably derived from the use by early printers of this size of type for printing the Canon of the Mass.

Canonical Class. (*Classification*) Traditional sub-class of a main class, enumerated as such in a scheme of classification, and not derived on the basis of definite characteristics.

Canonical Order. 1. (*Cataloguing*) An order fo arranging a group of entries, other than by alphabetical sequence, which derives from a convention associated with the material to which the entries refer, as for example, the order of the books of the Bible. 2. (*Classification*) A possible order for terms in an array forming a series of co-ordinate classes. Order by means of a notation. *Synonymous with* MATHEMATICAL ORDER (*q.v.*).

Cantilever Shelving. Shelving in which the shelves rest on cantilever brackets having lugs at the back which engage in slots in the upright. No uprights support the shelves at the front, all the weight being carried on the brackets. This provides a long line of shelving without the obstructions caused by the supporting brackets of the bracket type shelving. *See also Bracket Shelving, Shelving.*

Caoutchouc Binding. A method of binding which was introduced in about 1840 whereby the spine folds of a book were cut off and the resulting separate leaves attached to each other and to a backing strip by a coating of flexible rubber solution and cased in the ordinary way. The rubber solution eventually perished and the leaves fell out. The process was abandoned about 1870, the method being revived in the late 1940s when the so-called PERFECT (*q.v.*) method was used.

Cap. 1. Abbreviation for capital. 2. (*Binding*). Protection given to the leaves of a book while being tooled by hand, by wrapping and pasting brown paper around all the book except the boards. When so protected, the book is said to be capped.

Cap Line. (*Printing*) 1. A line of type which is set in capital letters. 2. An imaginary line which runs along the top of capital letters. *See also Ascender Line, Base Line, Mean Line.*

Capacitance Disk. In optical disk technology, a system of signals encoded in the disk to guide the stylus, which touches the surface. An alternative system is VHD (*q.v.*).

Capitales Quadrata. *Synonymous with* SQUARE CAPITALS (*q.v.*).

Capitalization. The use of capital letters.

Capitals. The largest letters of any size of type: those kept in the upper of the two cases of printer's type. Sometimes call 'full capitals' to distinguish them from SMALL CAPITALS (*q.v.*). THIS IS AN EXAMPLE. The use of capitals is indicated in a MS. or proof by a treble underlining. Abbreviated caps, *See also Lower Case Letters, Small Capitals, Upper Case Letters.*

CAPL. Canadian Association of Public Libraries (*q.v.*) (a Division of the Canadian Library Association).

Capped. *See Cap.*

Capsa. A cylindrical box used in Roman libraries to hold one or more rolls standing upright.

Capstan. (*Binding*) An ornament, roughly resembling a capstan, which was common on English and French heads-in-medallions rolls.

Caption. 1. The heading at the beginning of the text or of a chapter, section, etc. 2. The wording which appears immediately underneath, or adjacent and relating to, an illustration. This is sometimes called 'Cut line', 'Legend', or 'Underline'.

Caption Title. The title printed at the beginning of a chapter or section, or at the top of a page. Where the title-page of a book is missing, this may be used to provide a title for the entry in a catalogue or bibliography; in such case a note 'caption title' is normally used. Also called 'Head title', 'Drop-down title', 'Text title'.

Caravan Libraries. Mobile libraries drawn by tractor units or other vehicles which may perform other duties after taking the library to its site. They may be caravans or other trailers adapted for use as mobile libraries. Sometimes these libraries provide static library services in urban areas in emergency or until a permanent branch can be opened or erected. *See also Mobile Library.*

Carbonized Forms. Paper so coated with a pressure-transferable pigmented layer so that copies of all or part of original typescript or manuscript can be obtained without inserting separate sheets of carbon paper, and made up into unit books or used in sets or continuous forms.

Card. A rectangular piece of card (*see Boards 3*) of international standard size, usually 5 × 3 inches, 12.5 cm × 7.5 cm (7.5 cm × 12.5 cm in continental countries), having a surface suitable for writing or typing on, and used for entries in catalogues and similar records. *See also A7 Library Card.*

Card Cabinet. The case of drawers for accommodating a Card Catalogue (*q.v.*). Also called a 'Card Catalogue Cabinet'.

Card Catalogue. A catalogue, the entries of which are made on cards of uniform size and quality, and stored in any desired order on their edges in drawers or other form of container, each card being restricted to a single entry and with details of class number or call number to enable the item to be found. *See also A7 Library Card, Main Entry, Standard Size Card.*

Card Charging. The recording of issues of books by means of book-cards associated with readers' tickets or identification cards.

Card Drawer. A drawer for holding cards in a CARD CABINET (*q.v.*). Also called 'Card tray'.

Card Fount. The smallest complete fount of type stocked and sold by a typefounder.

Card Index. An index made on cards usually of standard size (5 × 3 inches) and kept on their edges in a drawer. *See also Card, Standard Size Card.*

Card Number. A symbol consisting of numbers, or a combination of letters and numbers, and possibly the date, used to identify particular entries on centrally produced printed catalogue cards such as those of the British National Bibliography or the Library of Congress.

Card Stock. A 'board', or heavy weight paper, usually over .006 inch in thickness made to withstand heavy wear in tabulating or punched card machines, or catalogues.

Caret. (*Lat.*: 'it needs'). The mark ($\wedge$) used in a MS. or proof to signify that something is omitted and indicate where an addition or insertion is to be made. Also called 'Insertion mark'.

Carey Award. An occasional award made by the Society of Indexers for outstanding services to indexing, and named in honour of Gordon V. Carey, the Society's first president. Awarded to G. Norman Knight (1977), L. M. Harrod (1982), Margaret Anderson (1983).

CARL. Canadian Association of Research Libraries. An association of 30 academic research libraries having responsibility for post-graduate studies and research programmes. Formed in 1976.

Carnegie Library. A library built with the financial assistance of funds given by Andrew Carnegie.

Carnegie Medal. An award made by the (British) Library Association to the writer of an outstanding book for children. The book must be written in English and have been published in the United Kingdom during the year preceding the presentation of the award. Named after Andrew Carnegie (1835-1918) the ironmaster and philanthropist, it was first awarded in 1936 to Arthur Ransome for *Pigeon Post.*

Carnegie Reading List Awards. An award made to ALA constituent units to encourage the preparation of information and dissemination literature.

Carnegie United Kingdom Trust. The Carnegie United Kingdom Trust was inaugurated under the auspices of Andrew Carnegie in 1913 and incorporated by Royal Charter in 1917. Its aim is the improvement of the well-being of the masses of the people of Great Britain and Ireland by such means as are embraced within the meaning of the word 'charitable' according to Scottish or English law. The work of the Trust operates on a five-yearly cycle and is particularly concerned with innovatory schemes in community service, amateur participation in the arts and nature conservation. Grants are not normally made to individuals.

The Trust initially continued Carnegie's own policy of giving library buildings to local communities; these were once-and-for-all gifts, requiring the community to stock the building with books and pay for the maintenance. Although several hundred such buildings are still to be found in use in the United Kingdom, the Trust's work has now largely moved into other community projects for which there is no clear statutory provision.

Carolingian. A minuscule book hand developed in France in the eighth century from the Roman cursive, much influenced by the English half uncial. The Carolingian minuscule is the prototype of the modern styles of penmanship, and of lower case roman type. It belongs to the second dynasty of French Kings founded by Charlemagne and much of its success was due to Alcuin of York, a distinguished English scholar, churchman and poet, who took charge of the Abbey of St. Martin at Tours at his invitation. It was the dominant book hand for nearly three centuries.

Carrel. A small room connected with a reference library, which is set aside for continuous research work by one reader and in which books, note-books, etc., may be securely locked during the temporary absence of the reader. This word is now used to indicate any table or other space reserved for one reader which provides by means of front and side screening a more or less secluded study and writing area, whether or not facilities are provided for locking up books. *Closed carrels* are cubicles which give complete seclusion. *Open carrels* give partial seclusion. *Suspended carrels* are those which are provided by fitting (suspending) writing areas similar to table tops into the uprights of steel shelving to give writing space in stack rooms. *Wet carrels* are those equipped with an electricity supply for using audio-visual equipment; *dry carrels* are without such facilities. *See also Oasis.*

Carriage. A flat frame bearing the guide rails on which the plank (supporting the stone on which rests the forme) of a hand printing machine moves to its printing position.

Cart. A small book box, not on wheels, but divided into sections to display children's books face up (American). Called in Europe a KINDERBOX (*q.v.*).

Carter G. Woodson Book Award. *See Woodson Book Award, Carter G.*

Cartier Diamond Dagger Award. *See Crime Writers' Association.*

Cartobibliography. A bibliography of maps.

Cartogram. A highly abstracted, simplified map the purpose of which is to demonstrate a single idea in a diagrammatic way. In order to do this outlines of land or the exact locations of other features are often altered.

Cartographer. A maker of maps.

Cartographer Entry. An entry under a cartographer's name.

Cartography. The science and art of making maps.

Carto-net. A software system developed for the use of graphics to retrieve maps from automated catalogues. Supported by the British Library Research and Development Department.

Cartouche. 1. A frame, either simple or decorative, or a scroll, in which the title, name of the cartographer, and other particulars relating to a map are placed. The cartouche usually appears in a corner of the map, and in old maps was frequently adorned with country scenes, animals, human figures, armorial or architectural designs, etc. 2. A drawn framing of an engraving, etc. 3. (*Binding*) A small rectangular ornament formed on blind rolls by one or more lines, generally with a plain centre.

Cartouche Title. The title which appears within the cartouche or scroll-like design on a map or engraving.

Cartridge.   1. A single-core container enclosing processed microforms, for insertion into readers, reader-printers and retrieval devices, the film requiring no threading or rewinding.   2. A plastic box containing a continuous loop of sound tape for insertion into a sound reproducing machine, thus providing continuous playback without rewinding.

Cartridge Paper.   A hard, tough paper made with a rough surface and in a number of grades; used for drawing upon. Also a grade of paper used as an ENDPAPER (*q.v.*).

Cartulary.   *Synonymous with* CHARTULARY (*q.v.*).

Case.   1. (*Binding*) The cover for a book which is made completely before being attached to a book by means of the endpapers and sometimes tapes in addition.   2. (*Printing*) In hand composition, a tray divided by 'bars' into compartments in which printer's individual letters, numerals and spaces are kept and which is placed on the FRAME (*q.v.*) when in use, and in a cabinet when idle. The arrangement of the compartments is the same for all types and sizes. Cases may be in pairs, an upper and a lower containing respectively the capitals and small letters (hence *upper* case (u.c.) and *lower* case (l.c.)) or the whole fount may be in a double unit. *See also Casing.*

Case Binding.   *See Case.*

Case Book.   A book bearing a cloth cover, as originally issued by the publisher. Thus 'cased'.

Cased.   *See Case Book.*

Casing.   The operation of inserting a sewn book into its case, or cover, which is made separately from the book, and pasted to the book by means of endpapers.

CASLIS.   Canadian Association of Special Libraries and Information Services (*q.v.*) (a Division of the Canadian Library Association).

Caslon.   A type face designed and cut in 1722 by William Caslon (1692–1766). It is an OLD FACE (*q.v.*) type and is one of the most widely used of all type faces in American and British printing. For a specimen alphabet, *see Type Face.*

Cassette.   1. A double-core container enclosing processed roll microfilm for insertion into readers, micro-printers and retrieval devices.   2. A container for videotape or audiotape for insertion into a camera, projector, reader, recorder or play-back unit.

Cassie.   An old term, derived from the Fr. *cassé* (broken), for the outside and frequently damaged sheets of a ream of good paper. 'Cassie quires' are the two outside quires of a ream, also called 'Coding quires'.

Cast Coated Paper.   A very expensive American art paper with an exceptionally soft, absorbent and uniformly flat surface.

Cast-up.   To calculate the cost of composing type.

Casting Box.   (*Printing*) A machine, or device, for casting stereos.

Casting Off.   The process of estimating the amount of space COPY (*q.v.*) will occupy when set up in a given size of type.

Casual Mnemonics.   Characters used mnemonically in a scheme of classification where letters in the notation are used to indicate subjects, the notation letter being the same as the first letter of the name of the subject.

They are used in particular circumstances and not as part of the normal method of notation. *See also Mnemonics.*

CAT. Computer-aided translation, or computer-assisted translation. *See Machine Translation.*

Catalogue. 1. (*Noun*) A list of books, maps, or other items, arranged in some definite order. It records, describes and indexes (usually completely) the resources of a collection, a library or a group of libraries. To be distinguished from (i) a list, which may or may not be in any particular order and may be incomplete, and (ii) a bibliography, which may not be confined to any one collection of books or to a particular group of libraries. Each entry bears details of class number or call number to enable the item to be found, as well as sufficient details (such as author, title, date of publication, editorship, illustrations, pagination and edition) to identify and describe the book. 2. (*Verb*) To compile a list of documents according to a set or rules so as to enable the consulter to know what items are available, and from the class number, call number or other means of identification, where they may be found. In a special library, in addition to entries under authors, subjects, and possibly titles, it may include (a) analytical entries; (b) abstracts – especially in scientific and technical libraries; (c) annotations indicating the treatment or coverage of the subject; (d) entries under subjects for work in progress and for individuals who are authoritative sources of information on specific subjects; (e) entries for pertinent information material in other parts of the organization or in other libraries.

Catalogue Card. 1. A plain or ruled card on which catalogue entries may be made. 2. A card containing such an entry. *See also Standard Size Card.*

Catalogue Code. A set of rules for guidance of cataloguers in preparing entries for catalogues so as to ensure uniformity in treatment. Such codes may include rules for subject cataloguing, and for filing and arranging entries.

Catalogue Drawer, Catalogue Tray. One of the drawers of a card catalogue, in which catalogue cards are kept.

Catalogue Raisonné. A catalogue of an author's work, especially of an artist's pictures, engravings, etc., usually arranged by subjects, with comments, elucidations, appraisals, and bibliographical details. Also called CLASSED CATALOGUE and CLASSIFIED CATALOGUE (*q.v.*).

Cataloguer. A librarian who prepares an entry for a catalogue.

Cataloguing. Strictly, the process of making entries for a catalogue; it may also cover all the processes involved in preparing books for the shelves, or simply the preparation of entries for the catalogue.

Cataloguing, Principles of. There may be said to be seven basic principles of cataloguing, five (multiple approach, unique entry, inevitable association, probable association, specific entry) common to all types of entry, and two (adequate description, concise description) relating to book description. See under the names of the various principles.

Cataloguing and Indexing Group. A Group of the (British) Library Association. It was formed in 1964 and came into official existence on 1 January 1965. Aims: to unite members of the LA engaged in, or interested in, the planning, production or maintenance of library catalogues, and of bibliographies and indexes, and to promote the study and discussion of questions relating to those activities. Publishes *Catalogue and Index* (q.) Abbreviated CIG.

Cataloguing Department.   The department of a library which deals with the ordering, cataloguing and classification of books, together with their processing, i.e. preparation for issue to the library users. Where there is no ORDER DEPARTMENT (*q.v.*), the work of ordering and processing books is also done here. In some American libraries, the work of preparing the books for the shelves, other than cataloguing and classification, is carried out in a separate department.

Cataloguing-in-Publication. (CIP)   CIP was pioneered in the Library of Congress in 1971, and the British programme which closely resembles the US system became fully operational in 1977. The aim of the programme is to provide bibliographic data for new books in advance of publication, and it depends heavily on the voluntary co-operation of publishers. Records are compiled from information supplied by publishers on a standard data sheet submitted to the Library of Congress or the British Library Bibliographic Services. In the UK a UK MARC CIP entry appears in the printed BNB and on BLAISE-LINE, and after receipt of the published book in the Copyright Receipt Office an amended entry may appear. The record also appears in the book itself, usually on the verso of the title-page.

Cataloguing in Source.   Cataloguing books before they are published, the entries being compiled from proof copies made available by the publishers, and the work being carried out by a centralized agency so that full cataloguing information is printed in the books concerned. *See also Cataloguing-in-Publication.*

Cataloguing Rules.   *See Catalogue Code.*

Catch.   A metal plate secured to a book cover and having a bar, over which the clasp fits. Sometimes a pin is used instead of there being a bar.

Catch Letters.   Groups of letters (usually three in a group) appearing in dictionaries, gazetteers, etc., at the tops of pages to indicate the first or last words of a page or column. Those on *verso* pages represent the first three letters of the first word on that page, those on the *recto* represent the first three of the last word on that page. Sometimes two groups of letters joined by a hyphen indicate the first and last words on a page.

Catch Stitch.   *Synonymous with* KETTLE STITCH (*q.v.*). Also a stitch made when sewing on tapes by passing the needle (after it comes out of the right side of the tape and before it goes across the tape) eye-end down under three or four threads below it and then into the loop so formed. The thread is then pulled up tight to form a knot in the centre of the tape before being drawn back into the middle of the section. This is done to avoid too great looseness.

Catch Title.   *Synonymous with* CATCHWORD TITLE (*q.v.*).

Catchline.   A line of type inserted temporarily at the top of matter by the compositor in order to identify it, and so printed on proofs. Also the name given to a short line of type in between two large displayed lines.

Catchment Area. In library planning, denotes the area from which readers may be expected to be drawn to a given library service point.

Catchword. 1. The word occurring at the bottom of a page after the last line, such word being the first on the following page. Catchwords originally appeared at the last page of a quire of a MS. and served as a guide to the binder. Later, they appeared at the foot of every verso, sometimes every page, but in conjunction with the signature served no useful purpose and were discontinued in the nineteenth century. Also called 'Direction word'. 2. A word at the top of a page or column in encyclopaedias and works of a similar nature, denoting the first or last heading dealt with on the page. 3. In indexing, the word or words which govern the position of an entry in the index.

Catchword and Trade Name Index. *See Current Technology Index.*

Catchword Entry. An entry in a catalogue, bibliography or index under some striking word in a book's title, other than the first, which is likely to be remembered, and so selected as entry word.

Catchword Index. One which uses a significant word from a title or text to index an item.

Catchword Title. A PARTIAL TITLE (*q.v.*) consisting of some striking or easily remembered word or phrase. It may be the same as a sub-title or the ALTERNATIVE TITLE (*q.v.*). Also called 'Catch title'.

Categorical Tables. In J. D. Brown's *Subject classification*, tables representing forms, standpoints, qualifications and other modes of dividing subjects. Each term in the tables is given a number (0 to 975). These are added (after a point which is used as a separating device) to subject numbers in any part of the classification:

> e.g. .1 Bibliography.
> .2 Dictionaries.
> .10 History.
> .33 Travel.
> .57 Museums.

Category. (*Classification*) 1. A 'point of view' according to which a subject can be divided. Considered by some to be synonymous with FACET (*q.v.*). 2. A concept of high generality and wide application which can be used to group other concepts. 3. A comprehensive class or description of things. 4. A logical grouping of associated documents. 5. A class or division formed for purposes of a given classification. In faceted classification, special distinctions are made between categories, classes, facets and phases. *See also Fundamental Categories.*

Catena. A series of extracts from the writings of the fathers, arranged with independent additions to elucidate scripture and provide a commentary thereon.

Catenati. Chained books.

Cater-Cornered. Paper which is cut diagonally, not square.

Cathedral Binding. One decorated with Gothic architectural motifs, often including a rose window, done between 1815 and 1840 in England and

France. In England the decoration was sometimes built up of large single tools; in France it was normally stamped on the covers. This was a revival by the nineteenth century binder Thouvenin of the ARCHITECTURAL BINDING (*q.v.*) style.

Catholic Library Association.   Founded 1921 in the USA to initiate, foster, and encourage any movement toward the development of Catholic literature and Catholic library work. Publishes *Catholic Library world* (10 p.a.); *Catholic periodical and literature index*(6 p.a.); *Handbook and membership directory* (a.). Abbreviated CLA.

CATLINE.   Catalog-on-line; the database representing the general book and journal catalogue of the National Library of Medicine (US).

CATNI.   *See Current Technology Index.*

Cat's Paw Calf.   (*Binding*) An acid strain pattern on a calf binding which resembles the paw marks of a cat.

CATV.   *See Community Antenna Television.*

Caucus.   A short-term interest group set up within an organization to respond to pressing needs without establishing a permanent group or committee.

CAV.   Constant Angular Velocity; a mode of operation of optical disk equipment in which one frame is recorded on each circular track, and each frame can be separately accessed. *See also CLV.*

Cawthorne Prize.   An award instituted in memory of the late Albert Cawthorne, formerly Chief Librarian of Stepney, London. UK. Awarded to the candidate obtaining the highest marks in Part I of the Library Association's professional examinations, and now discontinued.

CBC.   Children's Book Council (*q.v.*).

CBI.   *See Cumulative Book Index.*

CCC.   Acronym for the Central Classification Committee of FID; it is responsible for the UNIVERSAL DECIMAL CLASSIFICATION (*q.v.*).

CCC.   *See Copyright Clearance Center.*

CCITT.   Comité Consultatif International Télégraphique et Téléphonique (International Consultative Committee for Telephones and Telegraph) was formed in 1956, and is one of the members of the International Telecommunications Union. CCITT's members are the telecommunication authorities in the various nations; its recommendations are issued in four-yearly periods (the *Red Book* 1984, the *Blue Book* 1988) and are most commonly seen in the digital communcation 'x' series (eg. x.400 on message handling) and its OSI work (*see Open Systems Interconnection*).

CD.   Compact disk (*q.v.*). *See also CD–ROM.*

CDAC.   *See Computer Database Advice Centre.*

CD–I.   Compact Disc Interactive; the use of a compact disc in an INTERACTIVE VIDEO (*q.v.*) context. Commercial CD–I machines became available late 1988.

CDNL.   *See Conference of Directors of National Libraries.*

CD–ROM.   Plastic disks with a reflective metal coating which are read by a small laster beam. CD–ROM compact disks have the same dimensions (12 cm diameter) as audio compact disks and their contents are read in the same way; the differences lie in the way that the signals are processed after being read. The capacity of a single disk can be 650 megabytes, equivalent to 1500 floppy disks, or 250,000 sheets of A4 paper. Linked to personal computers CD–ROM have rapidly become a major publishing medium for distributing databases, directories, and catalogues. Many CD–ROM databases were originally available on-line. Users of the CD–ROM versions often find significant economic benefits over on-line access: a fixed, one-time payment gives unlimited use of data held on a CD–ROM, aiding accurate budgeting and extending the service to a wider range of users. In comparison, every call to a remote, on-line database involves multiple variable costs that need to be balanced against continued use of the data. Since a common technical standard is in use, there are no problems with differing national telecommunication systems, and data can be retrieved in the native language of the user. *See also WORM.* Erasable, re-usable disks may become available soon, but their potential for library use seems limited.

CD–ROM Standards and Practices Group. Formed in the UK in 1990 by ten CD–ROM application developers to devise and promote international standards for CD–ROM-based systems of information handling, for the benefit of the user community.

Ceased Publication. A work in several volumes, the publication of which was not completed, or a periodical, the publication of which has been discontinued.

CEC. Commission of the European Community; *see European Community.*

CEDAR. Computer Enhanced Digital Audio Restoration; a low-cost digital signal processing software package which allows old audio recordings to be re-mastered without extraneous noises, scratches and crackling. Developed for the NATIONAL SOUND ARCHIVE (*q.v.*).

Cedilla. The mark under the letter ç to indicate that it has a sound other than that of k; in French it has the sound of *s* and in Spanish of *th*.

CEEFAX. The TELETEXT (*q.v.*) service provided by the British Broadcasting Corporation.

Cel. Generally a sheet of transparent acetate on which letters, characters or objects are printed or painted. They are used as overlays on top of an opaque background, and can be exchanged for other cels over the same background.

CELIM. Continuing Education for Library and Information Management – a research programme studying the relationship between the need for continuing education and the impact and effectiveness of courses and provision. The programme is based at Ealing College of Higher Education (UK).

Cell. An area in a library formed by placing two free-standing bookcases against wall shelving. This arrangement was used by Sir Christopher Wren at Trinity College, Cambridge, in 1676. Usually called 'Alcove'.

Cellulose. The common term for chemical wood pulp, the basic substance of paper manufacture. It is the predominating constituent of plant tissues from which it must be separated before it can be used.

Cellulose Acetate. *See Film Base.*

Cellulose Triacetate. *See Film Base.*

CEN.   *See European Committee for Co-ordination of Standards.*

CENELEC.   *See European Committee for Co-ordination of Standards.*

Censorship.   Prohibition of the production, distribution, circulation or sale of material considered to be objectionable for reasons of politics, religion, obscenity or blasphemy. This action is usually taken by persons empowered to act by federal, national, state or local laws, and takes the forms of preventing publications passing through the Customs of through the post, or of action in a law court to prevent their sale. *See also Index Librorum Prohibitorum.*

Center for Paper Permanency.   Formed 1988 at the New York Public Library as a clearing house for information about the efforts of various bodies and agencies advocating the use of permanent/durable, alkaline paper.

Center for Research Libraries.   An American co-operative scheme to house little-used materials integrated into a collection in which duplicates are eliminated in order to sponsor broader co-operation, including co-operative acquisition. It started in 1949, and now has 138 members. It is situated in Chicago, and was known as the Midwest Inter-Library Center, abbreviated MILC until the Spring of 1965 when, because it served institutions in eleven States and the University of Toronto in Canada, it was decided to change its name. Its scope now extends to all research libraries in the USA and Canada, and potentially, Mexico. The Center's official mission states that it is a not-for-profit corporation established and operated by scholarly and research institutions to strengthen the library and information resources for research and to enhance the accessibility of those resources. It functions as a co-operative, membership-based research library that acquires, stores, preserves, provides bibliographic access to and lends/delivers from its collections of 3.6 million volumes and 1.1 million microforms. Collections include foreign newspapers, foreign dissertations and state documents. Publishes various catalogues, and contributes to the OCLC database. Abbreviated CRL.

Center for the Book.   Established 1977 in the Library of Congress to organize, focus, and dramatize the US's interest in books, reading and the printed word. The Center involves authors, publishers, booksellers, librarians, scholars, readers and educators in improving the quality of book production, encouraging the international flow of printed material, encouraging the study of books, promoting books and reading, and generally raising 'book awareness'. *See also Centre for the Book.*

Centesimal Device.   A method used in the Universal Decimal Classification to lengthen arrays where nine divisions are inadequate; the digits 11–99 are used to represent co-ordinate subjects instead of 1–9.

Central Catalogue.   1. A catalogue placed in the central library of a library system but containing entries for books in all the libraries.   2. A catalogue of the central library of a library system.

Central Library.   The chief library in a system, maybe containing the office of the chief librarian, the administrative department, and the largest collections of books. Sometimes called the 'Main Library'; if a public library it is usually situated in the centre or busiest part of a town, if a non-public library it would be at the most important or effective place in the organization, possibly at the headquarters.

Central Music Library. A limited company which is housed at the Buckingham Palace Road Branch of the Westminster City Public Libraries and administered by the Westminster City Council, UK. Founded on 21 October 1948 by an original donation of £10,000 from Winifred Christie Moor, it includes the former collections of Gerald Cooper, Edwin Evans and his father, Charles Woodhouse and Eric Blom. The large collection of sheet and bound music, as well as the books, are available for loan through public libraries. From 1 January 1974 this Library became a back-up library of the British Library Document Supply Centre. Abbreviated CML.

Central Processing Unit. The centre of any digital computer system; it co-ordinates and controls the activities of all the other units and performs all the logical and arithmetic processes to be applied to data. Abbreviated CPU.

Central Shelf List. 1. A shelf list recording all the books in the central library of a system of libraries. 2. A combined shelf list, housed in the central library, but recording all books in all the libraries of a library system.

Centralized Cataloguing. 1. The cataloguing of books by some central bureau, and the distribution therefrom, of printed entries on catalogue cards, or in machine readable form. 2. The cataloguing at one library of all the books of a library system comprising more than one library, thus achieving uniformity throughout the system.

Centralized Processing. In the USA, the Library Services Act has stimulated the setting up of processing centres for the purchase, cataloguing, classifying and processing of books, audio-visual and other material for a number of libraries.

Centralized Registration. The registering of readers at one library in a system, comprising several libraries, rather than at those at which the application forms are handed in.

Centre. 1. In an English county library, a small static library service point, provided in premises which may at times be used for other purposes, open less than ten hours a week, having a stock which is changed from time to time, and staffed by voluntary or paid librarians. 2. An organization, with or without a building for its exclusive use, which makes available at one central point a pool of specialized personnel and information, or services for the benefit of other organizations or individuals. *See also Advice Centre, Referral Centre, Research Library.*

Centre for Bibliographic Management. Name adopted 1987 by the Centre for Catalogue Research; funded by British Library grants from 1977, with the present grant valid until 1991. It is the focal point in the United Kingdom for research, information and instruction in the field of bibliographic record research and development. It is not only concerned with the use of bibliographic records for cataloguing, acquisitions, issue systems and resource sharing schemes, but also with subject access provision. It monitors the performance of both the UK MARC record service and the Whitaker database and links are maintained with the publishers, booksellers, library suppliers, and library systems' suppliers. Issues a *Newsletter* (2 p.a.). From 1990 the Centre also houses the OFFICE FOR LIBRARY NETWORKING (*q.v.*).

Centre for Catalogue Research. *See* the above entry.

Centre for Episcopal Acta. Established at the Borthwick Institute of the University of York, UK; the Centre has taken over a central index of English episcopal *acta* relating to the twelfth and thirteenth centuries which had been established at the Institute, and with the assistance of The British Academy is publishing volumes of bishops' *acta*.

Centre for Information Science. A department of the City University, London.

Centre for Library and Information Management. *See Claim.*

Centre for Research in User Studies (UK). The Centre came into operation in 1976; it was set up to re-examine the fields of user studies, evaluate the methods used in surveys, indicate gaps in knowledge and act as a clearing-house for information. The Centre is based at the University of Sheffield, and was funded by the British Library Research and Development Department. Publishes *CRUS NEWS* (3 p.a.). Abbreviated CRUS. In 1985 the role of the Centre broadened beyond user studies, and whilst the acronym remains, the British Library funding has ceased, and the Department of Information Studies is responsible for it as the 'Consultancy and Research Unit'.

Centre for the Book. 'To promote the significance of the book in all its forms, as a vital part of the cultural, commercial and scientific life of the country' the British Library opened a Centre in autumn 1990. The Deutsche Bibliothek has a similar scheme. *See also Center for the Book.*

Centre National de la Recherche Scientifique et Technique. *See CNRS.*

Centre Note. (*Printing*) A note, or reference, placed between columns of text as in a Bible. *See also Incut Note.*

Centred Dot. (*Printing*) A period placed higher than the base line of a piece of type, as, c·e·n·t·r·e·d, to show multiplication (1·2 = 2), or to separate roman capitals in the classic form of inscriptions (M·A·R·C·V·S). Also called 'Space dot'.

Centred Heading. (*Classification*) A typographical device used in the Dewey Decimal classification. It consists of a range of notation numbers and a heading, which are centred on the page instead of the numbers being in the usual column, and represents a concept for which there is no specific number in the hierarchy of notation, and which therefore covers a span of numbers.

Centrepiece. (*Binding*) An ornament, usually ARABESQUE (*q.v.*), placed in the centre of the cover of a bound book and often used with cornerpieces, or cornerstamps. It was a favourite style of binding in the late sixteenth and early seventeenth centuries. Also used of a piece of metal usually embossed and engraved, and fastened on to the cover. Also called 'Centrestamp'.

Centrestamp. *Synonymous with* CENTREPIECE (*q.v.*).

Centro de Documentaçao Cientifica.   The Portuguese Scientific Documentation Centre, formed to survey the country's library resources and to
rationalize holdings.

Centro de Documentación Cientifica y Técnica.   The Mexican Centre of
Scientific and Technical Documentation.

CERN.   European Organization for Nuclear Research (*q.v.*).

Cerne, Book of.   An illuminated MS. of the Passion and Resurrection portions
of the Gospels, written at Lichfield in the early ninth century, so named as it
was formerly kept at Cerne Abbey, Dorset; it is now in the Library of
Cambridge University. The style of decoration is severely calligraphic and
the colours used are light shades with only occasional gold; some pages are
enlivened with beasts.

Cerograph.   A wax engraving process usually used for making maps. A
drawing is made direct on wax spread over a copper plate which is then used
as a mould from which an electrotype is made. Also called 'Cerotype'.

Cerography.   The process used for making cerographic priints. *See also
Cerograph.*

Cerotype.   **A print made by the cerographic process.** *See also Cerograph.*

Certificate of Issue.   The statement, printed in a LIMITED EDITION (*q.v.*),
certifying the number of copies printed and sometimes bearing the
autograph of the author and/or illustrator.

Certification.   (*Archives*) 1. The act of attesting that a document, or a reproduction of a document, is what it purports to be.   2. The document
containing such an attestation. *See also Authentication.*

cf.   Abbreviation for *confer* (*q.v.*) (*Lat.*, meaning 'compare').

CFSTI.   Abbreviation for Clearinghouse for Federal Scientific and Technical
Information. A section of the US Department of Commerce; its function is
to make available particulars of unclassified (i.e. non-secret) reports in the
USA, which it does by publishing a list *United States Government research
and development reports* (USGRDR). This clearinghouse was transferred to
the National Technical Information Service (*See NTIS*) when this was
formed in 1970, and its functions merged with the broader mission of NTIS.

ch.   Abbreviation for CHAPTER (*q.v.*).

Chain.   (*Classification*) The succession of divisions subordinate one to another
expressing the relation 'A includes B, which in turn includes C' (or,
conversely, 'C is part of B, which is part of A'), e.g. Literature, English
Literature, English Poetry, Shakespeare's Poetry, *Adonis*, constitute a
chain of divisions in the class Literature. A hierarchy of terms, each
containing or including all which follow it in the same series: a hierarchy of
sub-classes of decreasing extension and increasing intension, devised by
successive division. The chain of progression in a scheme of classification
from general to specific may be:

    780 Music
      782 Dramatic music
        782.1 Opera
          782.154 Wagner *Die Meistersinger*

The indexer, using the principle of chain indexing, works his way back from the most specific step to more general terms, and in this case would provide these entries:

Operas by individual composers	782.154
Opera	782.1
Music: Dramatic	782
Music	780

Chain Indexing. An alphabetical subject indexing system, originally devised by S. R. Ranganathan, wherein a heading is provided for each term, or link for all the terms, used in a subject heading or classification. Each term represented by a given part of the classification symbol, followed by the term for each other part, appears as a heading in the reverse order of the symbol, so that the last term in the symbol becomes the first. If the symbol is comprised of four parts, there will be four entries: the first consisting of four terms; the second, of three after the first term of the previous entry has been omitted; the third, of two, and so on. The final one is the heading for the symbol with the widest connotation, and the most extension, relating to the subject in question. *See also Correlative Index, Relative Index.*

Chain Line. *See Laid Paper.*

Chain Mark. *See Laid Paper.*

Chain Procedure. 1. (*Cataloguing*) A method of constructing subject index entries, without permutation of components, by citing terms contained in particular chains. *See also Chain.* 2. (*Classification*) The procedure for determining the class index entries, the specific subject entries, the *See also* subject entries for a document from its class number and the class numbers of the cross-reference entries provided for it. *See also Chain Indexing.*

Chain Stitch. *See Kettle Stitch.*

Chained Books. Books chained to shelves or reading desks in libraries of the fifteenth to early eighteenth centuries to prevent theft. The practice began to die out by the middle of the seventeenth century when it became customary to shelve books upright.

Chained Library. One in which the books were chained to shelves or reading desks.

Chalcography. Engraving on copper or basss.

Chalk Drawing. One executed in crayon or pastel. The art of drawing with chalks or pastels is called calcography.

Chalk Engraving. *Synonymous with* CRAYON ENGRAVING (*q.v.*).

Chalk Overlay. A method of overlaying whereby an impression is taken on paper having a thin coating of chalk. This coating is then washed off the non-inked parts with diluted acid, thus leaving the inked design in relief. The resulting outline is then fitted as an overlay to the cylinder or platen so as to decrease or increase pressure. Also called 'Mechanical overlay'.

Champlevé. Enamelled bindings made by craftsmen between the eleventh and thirteenth centuries. Designs were cut into a thin sheet of gold or copper which formed the cover, the cavities being filled with enamel. On other bindings the enamel was limited to the decoration of borders and corners. This kind of binding was mainly carried out at Limoges. *See also Cloisonné.*

Chancery. The department of the Lord Chancellor, from which issue documents under the Great Seal, such as Charters, Letters Patent, writs and the like, also the place where Charters, Letters Patent and documents of a like nature are enrolled.

Chancery Liberate. *See Liberate Roll.*

Chap. Abbreviation for CHAPTER (*q.v.*).

Chap-Book. A small, cheap book, in a paper binding, and of a popular, sensational, juvenile, moral or educational character. These were popular in the seventeenth and eighteenth centuries, and contained tales, ballads, historical incidents, biographies, tracts, interpretations of dreams, palmistry, astrology, etc. They were sold by chapmen, i.e., pedlars, hawkers. The word comes from the Anglo-Saxon root *ceap* (trade).

Chapel. An association of journeymen in the printing and binding trades. Chapels usually exist in printing works of medium and larger size. The secretary, or leader, called the Father of the Chapel, is appointed by the members and one of his duties is to collect and forward trade union dues. To 'call a chapel' is to hold a chapel meeting of the journeymen.

Chapman Codes. Two- or three- letter code abbreviations for British county and regional names. Generally in agreement with BS 6879; issued by the Federation of Family History Societies, 1980.

Chapter. A division of a book, usually being complete in itself in subject matter but related to the preceding and following ones.

Chapter Heading (Head, Headline). The heading placed at the text beginning a chapter. It is usually set below the normal top of the type area of the other pages; the type used is normally larger than that used for running titles, and is of a uniform size and position for each chapter.

Character. 1. A letter of the alphabet, numeral, punctuation mark, or any other symbol cast as a type. Also called 'Sort'. 2. A personage, real or fictitious, figuring in an opera or work of imaginative literature, especially a novel or play. 3. A style of handwriting. 4. (*Information retrieval*) A symbol which is used in a data processing system; it may be a numeral, a letter of the alphabet, punctuation mark or space.

Character Count. A count of every letter, number, punctuation mark, word or sentence space, etc., in a piece of prose copy.

Character Reader. (*Information retrieval*) A specialized device which can convert data represented in a type fount or script directly into machine language. Such a reader may operate optically or, if the characters are printed in magnetic ink, the device may operate either magnetically or optically.

Character Recognition. (*Information retrieval*) The use of a machine to sense and encode into a machine language characters which are written or printed to be read by human beings.

Character Significance Sequence. An order applied to symbols forming headings which are used as filing media and indicating the precedence each normally arranged in their conventional order in the character significance sequence, but numerals and other non-alphabetic symbols may be arranged in their own conventional order (or if contractions or abbreviations, to be filed as if in full) or be arranged to precede or follow the alphabetic sequence.

Characteristic of a Classification. A distinctive property, element, or feature, inherent in a character by which a class is defined. A *typical characteristic* is one by which an individual of a class is representative of that class. A *type* is a typical individual, one that has most distinctly the typical characteristic, or characteristics, distinctive of the class. A class may be a type, or *typical class*, if it is representative of a *class of classes* (*Bliss*). The attribute which forms the basis of division. Language, form, and historical period are common characteristics in the classification of literature. A term used to express the principles by which a group is divided (as, genus into species), e.g. the characteristic that divides the animal kingdom into two parts is the absence or presence of a backbone. The characteristic is said to be 'natural' when it exhibits the inherent properties of the things classified. When it does not affect the structure, purpose, or intrinsic character of the things to be divided, but separates according to an accidental quality it is said to be 'artificial'. Thus, in zoology, the presence of a backbone is a natural characteristic, while the habitat (land, sea, or air) is an artificial characteristic. The characteristics chosen as the basis of arrangement must be essential (i.e., the most useful) for the purpose of the classification. They must be used consistently, i.e. it is impossible to classify a subject by two characteristics at once. *See Cross Classification.* Ranganathan's characteristics are: differentiation, concomitance, relevance, ascertainability, permanence, relevant sequence, consistency. Also called a 'Principle of division'.

Characters in Pica. *See Alphabet Length.*

Charcoal Drawing. One made with a charcoal crayon on paper with a rough surface. Such drawings are easily smudged, and to prevent this they are sprayed with a fixative.

Charcoal Paper. A soft, rough-surfaced paper used for making charcoal drawings.

Charge. 1. A payment made to a library or information service for the use of its stock or facilities; charges are particularly levied for the use of non-traditional services, for example the searching of on-line databases. Public libraries in the UK may only make a charge for services under Section 8 of the Public Libraries and Museums Act 1964. 2. The record of a loan, giving particulars of the item lent and the borrower's details. 3. The process of issuing an item for loan is also termed 'charging'; it is to this activity that the following eight entries relate.

Charge a Book. The action of recording the loan of a book, or making a 'charge'.

Charge Slip. *See Book Card.*

Charging Card. *See Book Card.*

Charging Desk. *Synonymous with* CIRCULATION DESK (*q.v.*).

Charging Machine. A machine used for recording the loan of books to readers.

Charging Methods. The methods by which loans of books are recorded. *See also ALS, BLCMP, Bookamatic, Browne Book Charging System, Cheque Book Charging Method, Detroit Self-Charging System, Dickman Charging System, Newark Charging System, Photocharging, Plessey, Punched Card Charging, Telepen, Token Charging, Transaction Card Charging.*

Charging Slip. *See Book Card.*

Charging System. The method used in keeping records of the loan of books. *See Charging Methods.*

Chart. 1. A map for the use of marine navigators showing the coastline, the position of rocks, sandbanks, channels, anchorages, and the depths of water in different parts of the sea expressed in feet or fathoms. 2. A graphical representation by means of curves, or the like, of the fluctuation of statistical records of such items as population, prices, production, barometric presure, temperature, etc. 3. Information of any kind arranged in tabular form, or graphically by means of curves. 4. A map designed for aeronautical navigation.

Chart Paper. A hard, tub-sized paper which must be strong, tough, pliable and subject to folding without cracking. It should be liable to stretch as little as possible during printing, smooth without gloss, suitable for pen and ink charting and therefore able to withstand erasure. *See also Plan Paper.*

Charter. An instrument whereby a sovereign or legislature grants rights to a person or corporation.

Charter Bookseller. A retail bookseller who satisfies certain conditions laid down by the (British) Booksellers Association with regard to service to the public.

Charter of the Book. A declaration of the principles which should guide the treatment of books both nationally and internationally, was approved in 1971 by the international professional organizations of authors, publishers, librarians, booksellers and documentalists, in association with Unesco and in connection with International Book Year, 1972. The theme of each of the articles was: (1) everyone has the right to read; (2) books are essential to education; (3) society has a special obligation to establish the conditions in which authors can exercise their creative role; (4) a sound publishing industry is essential to national development; (5) book manufacturing facilities are necessary to the development of publishing; (6) booksellers provide a fundamental service as a link between publishers and the reading public; (7) libraries are national resources for the transfer of information and knowledge, and for the enjoyment of wisdom and beauty; (8) documentation serves books by preserving and making available essential background material; (9) the free flow of books between countries is an essential supplement to national supplies and promotes international understanding;

(10) books serve international understanding and peaceful co-operation. The full text of each article is given in *Unesco Bulletin for Libraries*, **26** (5) Sept.–Oct. 1972 pp. 238-40. *See also London Declaration.*

Charter Roll. A parchment roll upon which charters were enrolled at the Chancery.

Chartered Librarian (UK). One who has become fully qualified professionally, and been admitted to the Register of Chartered Librarians maintained by the Library Association.

Chartulary. 1. A keeper of archives. 2. A place in which records or charters relating to a religious, civil or private state are kept. 3. The book in which they are listed or copied. Also called 'Cartulary'.

Chase. (*Printing*) A rectangular iron frame in which, by means of wedges, composed matter is secured and rendered portable. The wedges are called side- and foot-sticks and quoins. When they are adjusted, between the type matter and the chase, the whole becomes a forme, and is said to be 'locked up'. In SHEET WORK (*q.v.*) the forme which contains the text which will be on the inside pages of a printed sheet when folded, is called the 'inner forme' and that which contains those on the outside, the 'outer forme'.

Chased Edges. *Synonymous with* GAUFFERED EDGES (*q.v.*).

Chaucer Type. A re-cutting, in 12-point, of the TROY TYPE (*q.v.*) designed by William Morris. It was first used in 1892. *See also Golden Type.*

Cheap Edition. An edition of a book issued at a cheaper price. Usually it is a reprint of an earlier edition, printed on poorer paper and bound in a cheaper cover.

Check Digit. A digit added to a sequence of digits intended for computer input purely to check the accuracy of the main sequence; it is related arithmetically to the sequence and thus an error is automatically noticed. The final single digit of an ISBN is a check digit.

Check-list. 1. A record on which is noted each number, or part, of a work 'in progress' as it is received. 2. A list of items giving brief information sufficient only for identification. 3. An enumeration of documentary holdings with a minimum of organization and bibliographic information.

Check Marks. Indications made by cataloguers on title-pages of books, as a guide to assistant cataloguers or typists, of items to be omitted in the entries, e.g. ( ) may mean, 'omit from all cards', [ ] may mean 'omit from title card but include on subject cards'. They are pencilled on by the cataloguer as a guide to assistants.

Checkout Routine. 1. A procedure used in machine documentation systems to determine the correctness of answers, involving the use of sample inquiries, the aanswers to which are known. 2. The necessay procedures demanded before removing a document from a collection.

Checkpoint. A library security system manufactured by Plessey. A non-magnetic method of reliably detecting library materials which have been pre-conditioned with pressure-sensitive detection labels: a thin paper-like label concealed in book, periodical or audio-visual items disturbs a low energy field between two sensing screens and activates an alarm signal and locks a gate or turnstile.

Cheltenham. A type face designed by Bertram G. Goodhue (1869–1924) in 1896 and widely used by jobbing printers as it is a FOUNDERS' TYPE (*q.v.*).

Cheltenham Classification. A system devised for the library of the Ladies' College, Cheltenham, and used in a number of schools. The tables were published under the editorship of Miss E. S. Fegan and Miss M. Cant who were successive librarians of the College. Being aligned closely with the school curriculum, the contents of the main classes correspond with the traditional coverage of subjects as taught.

Chemac. A kind of copper line block used for blocking. *See also Block 2.*

Chemical Wood. Wood reduced to pulp by a chemical process, cooking in acid (sulphite process), or an alkaline liquor (soda process), for use in the manufacture of paper. This produces a purer pulp than that obtained by the MECHANICAL WOOD (*q.v.*) process. A combined chemical and mechanical wood process results in a paper which is intermediate in quality between the two.

Chemise. A loose cover for a book with pockets for boards. These were sometimes used in the Middle Ages instead of binding.

Cheque Book Charging Method. An adaptation of the BROWNE BOOK CHARGING SYSTEM (*q.v.*) to enable it to deal more rapidly with great pressure at the entrance side of the circulation desk. With this system a reader is issued with a small book of perforated slips of paper, similar to a small cheque book, and each bearing the same number. When a book is borrowed, a slip torn from the cheque book by an assistant is placed with the book card to form a CHARGE (*q.v.*). On discharging a book, the numbered cheque book slip is destroyed. When writing overdue notices, the name and address of the borrower is obtained by referring to the list of cheque book numbers against which names and addresses have been entered. Delayed discharging (i.e. cancelling the loan record at a less busy time) is possible with this method. *See also Charging Methods.*

Chequering. (*Binding*) To divide a surface into squares of alternately different ornament or colours, by equidistant vertical and horizontal lines like a chess-board.

chi. (*Bibliography*) The Greek letter χ used to denote an unsigned gathering or leaf in respect of which no signature can be inferred and which is not the first gathering. *See also pi.*

Chiaroscuro. 1. A black and white sketch. 2. A method of printing engravings, usually wood-engravings, from blocks representing lighter and darker shades, used especially in the fifteenth and sixteenth centuries. 3. A print produced by this means. 4. The earliest form of colour printing. It was a woodcut method, the colours being successively printed in register from separate blocks after an impression from the master block had been made.

Chiffon Silk. A thin, strong and durable silk material which can be used for mending and strengthening paper, especially of valuable books.

Children's Book Award. An award founded in 1980 and given to authors of fiction for children under the age of 14 by the Federation of Children's Book Groups.

Children's Book Circle. An informal group of children's book editors and those who work in publishers' children's book departments. It was started in 1962 to provide an opportunity for such persons to exchange ideas on the publication of, and publicity for, children's books. The Eleanor Farjeon Award 'for distinguished services to children's books in the past year' was first made in 1966 (to Mrs. Margery Fisher for her reviews of children's books in *Growing Point*) in memory of Eleanor Farjeon, one of the greatest children's writers, who died in 1965. Anyone doing outstanding work for children's books, whether librarian, teacher, author, artist, publisher, reviewer, television producer is eligible for the award.

Children's Book Council. A non-profit making organization, encouraging the reading and enjoyment of children's books. The Council consists of American publishers of trade books for children. It organized the first National Children's Book Week in 1945 and has continued to do so each year since; it is also concerned with projects involving the annual Children's Book Showcase. The Council acts as the US section of the International Board on Books for Young People (IBBY) (*q.v.*) and participates in this connection by making an annual donation of a selection of children's books to twelve repositories throughout the world. Abbreviated CBC. *See also Book Week, Trade Book.*

Children's Book Foundation. Inaugurated 1986, this major part of the BOOK TRUST (*q.v.*), promotes broad-based educational activities. Operates the Children's Book Library, liaises with schools and libraries, and runs courses and workshops.

Children's Book Group. A specialist publishers' group of the PUBLISHERS ASSOCIATION (*q.v.*); regular meetings of members are held for the common interest of the kind of publishing with which they are concerned. A fairly regular and close contact is maintained with the Youth Libraries Group of the (British) Library Association.

Children's Book Groups. Unofficial groups of persons concerned with furthering the use of books for children by means of story telling, children's activities, talks, book exhibitions and book sales, co-operation with public libraries and with schools and booksellers. The usefulness of the groups was recognized in the BULLOCK REPORT (*q.v.*). *See also Federation of Children's Book Groups.*

Children's Book of the Year Award. An annual award made by Lancashire County Library, UK, for the best work of fiction for 11–14 year-old readers.

Children's Book Trust. A non-profit-making Indian publishing venture inspired by Shankar Pillai, the Indian cartoonist. Situated in Delhi, it publishes books in English and Hindi which are sold at subsidized prices.

Children's Book Week. *See Book Week.*

Children's Library. The department reserved for the exclusive use of children. It usually contains lending and reference sections and periodicals.

Children's Literature Association. Essentially a university-oriented organization, formed in the USA to advance the scholarly and critical teaching of children's literature, especially at college level. Works in conjunction with other organizations, with publishers and with the public to disseminate information about children's literature. Membership is open to anyone interested in children's books. Publishes a quarterly newsletter (members only) and an annual journal *Children's Literature: The Great Excluded*. Abbreviated ChLA.

China Clay. A substance (SiO_2) found in large quantities in Cornwall and used in paper making to obtain finish, consistency and opacity, it is also used for coating papers.

China Paper. Very thin, silky and costly, waterleaf paper used for proofs for woodcuts and for woodcuts to be mounted on stronger paper. Also called 'Chinese paper' and 'Indian proof paper'.

China Society of Library Science. Founded 1979, based in Beijing; a new constitution was adopted in 1987. Aims to promote library science, and unite professional librarians through conferences and symposia. There are 7000 members in 28 geographical units; publishes *Bulletin of Library Service* (q.).

Chinese Science and Technology Information Association. Founded 1978 in Beijing. Aims to sponsor exchanges of information at national and international level. Publishes *Library and Information Service* (6 p.a.) with English contents page.

Chinese Style. A book printed on double leaves, i.e. with unopened folds at the fore-edges and the interior pages blank. 'Japanese style' refers to a Japanese book printed in the same manner.

Chip. A term denoting a single integrated electronic circuit, also called a 'microchip', or 'silicon chip'. Provides the calculating functions of a computer.

Chip Board. (*Binding*) A less expensive material than MILLBOARD or STRAW-BOARD (*qq.v.*) used for covering books.

Chi-Rho. Sacred monogram formed by the first two letters of the Greek word for Christ ☧

Chirograph. A formal handwritten document.

Chiroxylographic. A mediaeval block book in which the illustrations are printed from blocks and the text added by hand.

Chiswick Press. The printing press founded by Charles Whittingham the Elder (1767–1840) in 1811, and continued even more successfully by his nephew of the same name (1795–1876) who controlled the Press from 1840. The elder Whittingham was famous for his attractive, popularly priced classics and for his handling of woodcuts; the nephew was well known for his association with the publisher William Pickering, whose printing he did after 1830. The name of the Press was first used in an imprint in 1811 and persisted for 150 years.

ChLA. *See Children's Literature Association.*

Chloride Paper. Sensitized photographic paper with an emulsion of gelatin-silver chloride of medium sensitivity. Mainly used for contact printing.

Cholmondeley Awards. Annual awards made by the SOCIETY OF AUTHORS (*q.v.*) for the encouragement of poets.

Chorochromatic Map. One in which areal distribution is shown by distinctive colours or tints. This method is used for most geological, soil or political maps.

Chorographic Map. One representing a large region, country, or continent, on a small scale.

Choropleth Map. One showing 'quantity in area' calculated on a basis of average numbers per unit of area, such as population in a country, by tinting civil divisions by graduated lines or colours, the degree of darkness of which is proportionate to the value represented.

Choroschematic Map. One in which small semi-pictorial symbols such as dots or lines of various shapes, sizes and density are used over the area of the map to represent distribution without indication of quantity, of land utilization or vegetation.

Chorus Score. *See Score.*

Chrestomathy. A collection of excerpts and choice selections, especially from a foreign language, with notes of explanation and instruction.

Chromium-Faced Plates. Printing plates upon which chromium has been deposited electrolytically.

Chromo. Pertaining to colours. 1. In colour printing there are many terms prefixed by this word, the combining word often giving the particular definition, such as chromo-collotype, chromo-lithography, chromo-xylography. 2. (*Paper*) A heavily coated paper used for chromo-lithography; it is more heavily coated than art paper.

Chromography. A reproduction of a coloured illustration by lithography, or one of the many photo-mechanical processes.

Chromo-lithography. *See Colour Lithography.*

Chromo-xylography. Coloured woodcuts. *See also Chiaroscuro.*

Chronfile. (*Archives*) *See Reading File.*

Chronicles. These differ from annals in being more connected and full, though like annals, the events are treated in the order of time.

Chronogram. A phrase, sentence or inscription, in which certain letters (usually distinguished by size or otherwise from the rest) express by their numerical values a date or epoch, e.g. stVLtVM est DIffICILes habere nVgas, which is:

V L V M   D I I C   I L V
5 50 5 1000 500 1 1 100 1 50 5 = 1718.

See also Roman Numerals.

Chronological Device. One of the distinctive principles for determining the sequence of subjects in the Colon Classification. It is a notational device which ensures chronological order by using a symbol to represent a date or origin.

Chronological File. (*Archives*) *See Reading File.*

Chronological Order. Arrangement in order of date. Applies to order of entries in a catalogue (date of publication – imprint or copyright) or of the material itself (books, pamphlets or cuttings).

Chrysography. The art of writing in gold letters, as practised by mediaeval writers of manuscripts.

Church and Synagogue Library Association. Formed 1967 in Philadelphia for librarians of all church and synagogue libraries. Membership is open to voluntary and professional librarians, to library committee members, ministers, priests, rabbis, directors of Christian education, principals of synagogue schools, Sunday school superintendents, churches, publishers, booksellers and others interested in church and synagogue libraries. It is an ecumenical association, having Chapters based on geographic areas. Publishes *Church and Synagogue Libraries* (6 p.a.), and guides to practice. Abbreviated CSLA. Currently located in Portland, Oregon, and having over 800 members.

CIA. Conseil International des Archivés. *See entry under International Council on Archives.*

CIB. Conseil Internationale du Bâtiment pour la Recherche, l'Étude et la Documentation. International Council for Building Research, Studies and Documentation (*q.v.*).

Cicero. A continental unit for measuring the width of a line of type. One Cicero equals 4.511 mm, or 12 Didot points. The name is said to be derived from the size of type used in Schoeffer's edition of Cicero's *De Oratore* in the late fifteenth century. *See also Didot System, Measure, Point.*

CICI. Confederation of Information Communication Industries; formed 1984 by trade associations and professional bodies in the information industry – UK organizations are well represented (LA, IIS, Aslib, BL) together with publishing associations, broadcasters, music and recording industries, computer services, software publishers. Major industrial companies provide financial support; CICI offers a forum for discussion of common concerns, and represents the industry's view to Government.

CICIREPATO. Committee for International Co-operation in Information Retrieval among Examining Patent Offices; a committee of ICIREPAT (*q.v.*).

CICRIS. The Commercial and Industrial Co-operative Reference and Information Service; aims to share information on mutually beneficial topics, run training courses, arrange visits, and advise on the setting-up of library and information services. Taken over by the Hammersmith and Fulham Council Library Service in 1988 with its HQ at Hammersmith Central Library. The creation of the single European market in 1992 is a particular focus of present activity. Over 70 industrial and library members.

CIDB. International Council for Building Documentation. *See entry under International Council for Building Research, Studies and Documentation.*

CIDESA. The International Centre for African Social and Economic Documentation (Le Centre International de Documentation Économique et Sociale Africaine). Set up in January 1961. Aims to collect and co-ordinate documentation on economic and social subjects concerning Africa with a view to furthering the progress of the continent in these fields. Membership is open to scientific and philanthropic institutions. Financed by members' dues. Publishes an annual bibliographic index; a bulletin of information on studies and theses in course of publication, or planned.

CIDST. *See Committee for Information and Documentation on Science and Technology.*

CIG. Catalogue and Indexing Group (of the Library Association). Co-ordinate Indexing Group (of Aslib) (*qq.v.*).

CILLA. Acronym for Co-operative of Indic Language LASER libraries. A co-operative group set up by five LASER (*q.v.*) members – Brent, Camden, Ealing, Hackney and Wandsworth – to acquire, process and interlend materials in the five Indic languages.

CIM. Abbreviation for computer input microfilm; the use of microformat for the very high speed entry of information into a computer. *See also COM.*

CIM SIG. Acronym of the Computerized Information Management Special Information Group, a sub-group of the Institute of Information Scientists.

CINDEX. Camden Community Information Index and Exchange; a 6000 entry community information directory available in all libraries in the London Borough of Camden.

CIMTECH. *See National Centre for Information Media and Technology.*

CIP. 1. Cataloguing-in-publication (*q.v.*). 2. Community Information Project (*q.v.*).

Cipher. 1. The initials of a name, or the arrangement of its letters in an ornamental manner, but disposed in such a way that it becomes a kind of private mark. 2. In machine searching as part of information retrieval, the codes whose notations, whether alphabetic or other symbols, are intentionally scrambled so as to keep the system of rules, and thus the common or source language, a secret.

circa. (*Lat.* 'about') Used to indicate uncertainty in a date, as *c.* 1934, about 1934. Usually abbreviated to *c.* or *ca.*

Circle of Officers of National and Regional Library Systems. *See CONARLS.*

Circle of State Librarians. The organization to which those employed in British government libraries and information bureaux may belong. It had its beginnings in 1914 when the PANIZZI CLUB (*q.v.*), named after Sir Anthony (Antonio) Panizzi who was Director of the British Museum, was formed. In those early days government librarians were only a minority of the membership of the Club, the objects of which were 'to provide opportunities for social intercourse between the Senior Officers of Reference and Research Libraries and to promote all measures tending to their higher efficiency'. After the First World War, the then Treasurer of the Panizzi Club, A. E. Twentyman, Librarian of the Board of Education, took the initiative of reviving the Club and associating State Librarians as such with it. The name 'Circle of State Librarians' was used; it was an informal organization limited to officers-in-charge of Government libraries. The circle was revived in 1946 and membership was widened to admit 'those employed in a State Library or Information Service, who possess such professional qualifications or experience as will satisfy the Committee', and who were engaged in the storing and dissemination of knowledge, such as archivists, intelligence officers of research departments and others whose interests and problems were similar to those of librarians. In 1953 the function of the Circle was again widened 'to cultivate a common interest in bibliographical problems arising in Government service' and the membership opened 'to all members of the Government service who are interested in the activities of the Circle'. Publishes *State Librarian* (3 p.a.). Abbreviated CSL.

Circuit Edges. The edges of a book-cover which overlap the edges of the book. Used mostly for Bibles. Also called 'Divinity circuit', 'Divinity edges', 'Yapp edges'.

Circular Brackets. CURVES (*q.v.*), or Round Brackets, used in the Colon Classification to enclose the SUBJECT DEVICE NUMBER (*q.v.*) which forms part of the CLASS NUMBER (*q.v.*). The first '(' is called 'Starter' and the second ')' 'Arrester'. *See also Brackets.*

Circulating Library. A library which lends books for use outside the building. In England, the term usually indicates a commercial library where payment has to be made for the use of the books. *See also Subscription Library.*

Circulation. The total number of books issued from a library in a given period.

Circulation Control System. An automated package available to libraries for the routines of the circulation system. Software will record loans using a stock database and a user database, generate overdues warnings, trap reserved items, etc.

Circulation Department. The American term for the department of a public library which lends books for home-reading. Called a 'Lending department' in England.

Circulation Desk. The area of a library in which the staff handle the loans procedure. Also called 'Charging desk', 'Counter', 'Delivery desk', 'Discharging desk', 'Issue desk', 'Lending desk', 'Loan desk', 'Receiving desk', 'Return desk', 'Slipping desk', 'Staff enclosure'.

Circulation Record. A record of the books issued for home-reading.

Circulation Statistics. A record of the number of books circulated (issued) for home-reading.

Circulation Work. The American term indicating the work of a department issuing books for home-reading.

Circumflex. A typesetter's accent, shaped like an inverted 'v' or 'u' and placed above the appropriate letter.

CIS. Cataloguing in Source (*q.v.*).

CISE. Colleges, Institutes and Schools of Education (*q.v.*) (a Group of the Library Association).

CISTI. Acronym of Canada Institute for Scientific and Technical Information which was formed in Ottawa in 1974 by combining the National Science Library (NSL) and the Technical Information Service (TIS). Funded by the

Canadian government through the National Research Council, CISTI promotes the use of scientific and technical information by the people and government of Canada to meet economic, regional and social development. Functions through branches, and a series of sections including Document Delivery; Reference and Referral; CAN/OLE CAN/SDI (Online Enquiry Service); Health Sciences Resource Centre; Acquisitions; Cataloguing; Scientific Numeric Database Service; Policy, Planning and Systems; Publicity and Communications; Administration. An extensive publishing programme operates.

CISTIP. Acronym of the Committee on International Scientific and Technical Information Programs, which was established within the Commission on International Relations of the National Academy of Sciences – National Research Council. Its function is to provide continuing reviews, analyses and information to the Academy, the National Science Foundation and other bodies on issues and activities relating to US participation in the planning, development, co-ordination, operation and financing of international scientific and technical information programmes.

Citation. A reference to a text or part of a text identifying the document in which it may be found. *See also References.*

Citation Index. A list of articles that, subsequent to the appearance of the original article, refer to, or cite, that article. This method is particularly applicable to scientific literature. *See also Science Citation Index, Social Science Citation Index.*

Citation Order. The order of application of principles of division in determining an appropriate class number for a document. Also called 'Facet formula'.

Citizens' Advice Bureau (UK). Over nine hundred Citizens' Advice Bureaux give explanations and advice to people who are in doubt about their rights or who do not know about the state or voluntary services available. The service is free as each bureau receives a grant from the local authority in whose area it operates and most of the staff are volunteers. Service founded 1939; each bureau is expected to attain a certain level of work and of staff training in order to become a member of the National Association of Citizens' Advice Bureaux, which co-ordinates the organization's work, provides a central consulting service, and disseminates via its monthly information service new information on legal affairs, social security, housing, consumer complaints, etc. Abbreviated CAB(x).

City and Guilds of London Institute. *See Library and Information Assistant's Certificate.*

Civilité. A group of gothic cursive printing type faces, the earliest and best of which was cut by Robert Granjon in the mid sixteenth century. They were based on a relatively informal hand, closely related to the English 'secretary'.

CJK. Chinese, Japanese, Korean; Abbreviation registered by RLG (*q.v.*) to indicate East Asian language materials in the RLIN DATABASE (*q.v.*).

CLA. 1. Canadian Library Association (*q.v.*). 2. Catholic Library Association (*q.v.*). 3. *See Copyright Licensing Agency.*

Claim.   Any communication sent to a bookseller or other supplier to hasten the delivery of overdue material.

CLAIM   (UK). Acronym for the Centre for Library and Information Management, based at Loughborough University of Technology. A research organization that specializes in the field of library management. Carried out several projects for the British Library Research and Development Department. Published reports, directories, surveys, etc. *Now see Library and Information Statistics Unit.*

Clandestine Literature.   Publications which are printed, published, and circulated secretly. They are usually of a political nature and seek to overthrow the government, or in time of war, act against the power in authority. Also called 'Secret literature', 'Underground literature'.

Clandestine Press.   A printing press which operates secretly.

Clapp–Jordan Formulae.   Formulae devised by Verner Clapp and Robert T. Jordan, and stated in 'Quantitative criteria for adequacy of academic library collections' (*College and Research Libraries* **26** (5) September 1965). They attempt to identify the principal factors affecting the academic needs for books and to ascribe suitable weights to each.

Clarendon.   The name of a particular type face, and also of a group of faces characterized by little difference between thick and thin strokes, narrowness, and angular semi-Egyptian serifs. 'Consort' and 'Fortune' are of this kind. They were originally designed to give bold emphasis, particularly for dictionaries so that the word defined stood out clearly, and although still used for this purpose are now being used in their own right. For a specimen alphabet, *see Type Face.*

Clarendon Press.   Edward Hyde, first Earl of Clarendon (1609–74), gave the profits of the copyright of his *History of the Rebellion* to the University of Oxford to erect the first building in which the University's business of printing was wholly carried on – hence the name Clarendon Press. The business was transferred from the Sheldonian Theatre to this new building in 1713.

Clark Award, Daphne.   Daphne Clark was a founder member of the Library and Information Research Group, and was its Chairman at the time of her death, in September 1983. LIRG agreed to make an annual award in her memory towards the research expenses of an approved project, the first award being made in 1985.

Clarke (Arthur C) Award.   An annual UK award for the best science fiction novel published in the UK.

Clasp.   A metal fastening hinged to one booard and made to clip or lock into a loop or bar on the other board of a bound book or album. *See also Catch.*

Class.   (*Classification*) (*Noun*) 1. A group of concept, or of things, assembled by some likeness which unifies them. This likeness is called the 'characteristic of a classification'. A class consists of all the things that are alike in essentials, characters, properties and relations, by which it is defined.   2. A group having the same or similar characteristics.   3. A major division of a CATEGORY(*q.v.*). *See also Form Classes, Main Class, Summum Genus.*   4.

(*Verb*) To classify books according to a scheme of classification.   5. (*Archives*) A self-contained unit within an archive group.

CLASS.   *See Co-operative Library Agency for Systems and Services.*

Class Catalogue.   *Synonymous with* CLASSIFIED CATALOGUE (*q.v.*).

Class Entry.   An entry in a catalogue under the name of a class, as distinct from one under a specific subject.

Class Guide.   A guide to the shelves which gives the main class symbol and subject, and perhaps the same information for the main divisions of the class.

Class Letter.   The first letter of a main class or division of a classification scheme the notation of which begins with a letter of the alphabet; it is used to designate a particular main class of the classification.

Class Library.   The class room library in a primary school, so called to distinguish it from the 'general' or 'central' library provided in the same school for all to use.

Class List.   A list of the books in a particular class, usually arranged in classified order. In archive administration, a list of the documents in a CLASS (*q.v.*), the entries being arranged in numerical order with enough detail to distinguish one document from another.

Class Mark.   The classification symbol placed on the spine of the book, on the title-page and added to a catalogue entry to indicate the book's place in the classification and on the shelves.

Class Notation.   *Synonymous with* CLASS MARK (*q.v.*).

Class Number.   One or more characters showing the class to which a book belongs in the scheme of classification in use. In a RELATIVE LOCATION (*q.v.*), this number also shows the place of the book on the shelves and in relation to other subjects. It translates the name of its specific subject into the artificial language of the notation of the scheme of classification. The class number may be compounded of a variety of symbols used in a specific sequence, and followed by certain signs or symbols the purpose of which is to separate the constituent parts of the Class Number and/or to indicate the characteristic of the following symbol.

Class Symbol.   *Synonymous with* CLASS MARK (*q.v.*).

Classed Catalogue.   *Synonymous with* CLASSIFIED CATALOGUE (*q.v.*). Also called 'Class catalogue'.

Classed Library.   *Synonymous with* CLASSIFIED LIBRARY (*q.v.*).

Classer.   As used by Bliss and Savage, one who allocates class numbers to books according to an existing scheme of classification. *See also Classing, Classifier.*

Classic.   An outstanding work, usually appearing in several versions and in translation, and sometimes adapted, being the subject of commentaries and other writings, and continuing in print even long after first publication.

Classic Device.   (*Classification*) In the Colon Classification, the digit *x* which is put after the class number to which a CLASSIC (*q.v.*) should be assigned and which precedes a Work Facet or Author Facet. This is done to bring together the different editions of a classic in a class, also the different editions of each of its commentaries, and to keep a classic and the commentaries thereon in juxtaposition. Also to keep each classic and its associated commentaries in juxtaposition to other classics in the same class.

Classical Author. For the purposes of the Colon Classification, an author, one at least of whose works is a classic. The Classic Device, consisting of the digit *x* placed after the number representing the ultimate class to which the classic should be otherwise assigned and adding asfter it an Author Facet, is employed to bring together the different editions of a classic in a class and also the different editions of commentaries on the classic.

Classification. 1. The arrangement of things in logical order according to their degrees of likeness, especially the assignment of books to their proper places in a scheme of book classification. 2. A scheme for the arrangement of books and other material in a logical sequence according to subject or form. 3. A 'coding' system within which the series of symbols indicating a concept, or semantemes, are subject to certain order relationships. *See also Broad Classification, Close Classification, Enumerative Classification, Hierarchical Classification, Summum Genus.* 4. 'Any method of recognizing relations, generic or other, between items of information, regardless of the degree of hierarchy used and of whether those methods are applied in connection with traditional or computerized information systems' – the definition adopted in the terms of reference of the FID Committee on Classification Research (FID/CR) in 1973.

Classification Code. A scheme of classification.

Classification Decimale Universelle. *See Universal Decimal Classification.*

Classification for Social Sciences. Compiled by Barbara Kyle for the Unesco Social Science bibliographies at the request of the INTERNATIONAL COMMITTEE FOR SOCIAL SCIENCES DOCUMENTATION (*q.v.*). Referred to as the KC (Kyle Classification).

Classification Mark. *See Class Mark.*

Classification of Library Science. A faceted scheme which was prepared by the CLASSIFICATION RESEARCH GROUP (*q.v.*) and published in 1965. The Scheme is in two sections; the first (sections A/Z) contains the 'core' subjects of library science, while the second (classes 1/8) contains 'fringe' subjects which are disciplines in their own right but are of concern to librarians and information scientists. A revised version of this scheme is used in *Library and Information Science Abstracts.* A second edition appeared in 1975.

Classification Research. A Committee on Classification Research (FID/CR), based on the Documentation Research and Training Centre, Indian Statistical Institute, Bangalore, India, has classification matters constantly under review. Publishes *FID/CR Newsletter* (q.).

Classification Research Group. An unofficial group of British librarians who have been meeting since February 1952 to discuss the theory and practice of classification. Abbreviated CRG. *See also Classification of Library Science.*

Classification Schedule. The printed scheme of a system of classification.

Classification Scheme. A scheme by which books are classified or arranged in systematic order. The following are some of the better known schemes, the authors' names being given in brackets: Bibliographic Classification (Bliss); Colon Classification (Ranganathan); Decimal Classification (Dewey); Expansive Classification (Cutter); Library of Congress Classification; Subject Classification (Brown); Universal Decimal Classification.

Classification System. A particular scheme of classification. *See also Classification Scheme.*

Classificationist. 1. One who makes a scheme of classification. Called by Bliss and Savage a 'classifier'. 2. A theorist who organizes and divides documents according to specific criteria. *See also Classifier.*

Classified Arrangement. The arrangement of books in a library according to some scheme of classification.

Classified Catalogue. A catalogue in which the entries are arranged in classified order of subjects, whether logically, in systematic order, exhibiting hierarchical relationship between subjects as in the SYSTEMATIC CATALOGUE (*q.v.*) – the more usual, or alphabetically, as the ALPHABETICO-CLASSED CATALOGUE (*q.v.*). It is usually in two parts: the classified file of entries in systematic order, and the alphabetical subject index to the classified file. Also called 'Classed catalogue', 'Classified subject catalogue'.

Classified Catalogue Code. The code of practice for assembling classified catalogues, with rules to apply to dictionary catalogue compilation. Formulated by S. R. Ranganathan and first published in 1934.

Classified File. The entries, in systematic order, of the CLASSIFIED CATALOGUE (*q.v.*). This is one (the main) part of this kind of catalogue, the other part being the alphabetical subject index. Also called 'Systematic file'. *See also Feature Heading.*

Classified Index. 1. One in which entries are not arranged in one strict alphabetical sequence, but under general headings, e.g. the names of binders would be arranged alphabetically, under the heading 'binders' and not in their correct places in the alphabetical sequence. 2. An index characterized by sub-divisions of hierarchic structure. An index using or displaying genus-species (class-sub-class) relationships. *See also Classified Catalogue, Correlative Index.*

Classified Library. A library in which the books are arranged according to a recognized scheme of classification. Also called a 'Classed library'.

Classified Material. Memoranda, reports and other documents emanating from government departments, industrial and other corporations, research associations, etc., which are of a secret and confidential nature. They are classified as 'top secret', 'secret', 'confidential' and 'restricted' in a descending order of secrecy. also called 'Classified information'.

Classified Order. The arrangement of books and other materials, or of entries in a catalogue, in order according to a scheme of classification.

Classified Subject Catalogue. *See Classified Catalogue.*

Classifier. As used by Bliss and Savage, one who names and defines classes and co-ordinates them into tables to form a scheme of book classification. The process of compiling the tables is called 'classifying'. These terms have also generally related to the allocation of classification numbers to books. *See also Classer, Classificationist.*

Classify. To classify is to bring individuals with the same or similar characteristics together actually, or mentally, that is, conceptually. Also, in a secondary sense, to arrange classes in a classification, and to allocate the appropriate CLASS NUMBER (*q.v.*) to a book or other document according to a scheme of classification. *See also Class.*

Classifying. The act of fitting books or other material into an existing scheme of classification. Called by Bliss, Savage and Sayers 'classing'. *See also Classer, Classing, Classificationist, Classifier, Facet, Focus, Phase.*

Classing. As used by Bliss, Savage and Sayers, allocating class numbers to books according to a scheme of classification. *See also Classer, Classifying.*

Classroom Collection. 1. A temporary, or semi-permanent, collection of books deposited in a schoolroom by a public, or a school, library. 2. A number of books sent by a college library to a classroom for use by students and teachers (American).

Clay Tablets. Cuneiform clay tablets were the earliest form of books, and were protected by an outer shell of clay which was inscribed with a copy, abstract, or title, of the contents.

Clean Proof. One having very few, or no, printer's errors.

Clear Base. *See Film Base.*

Clearinghouse. An organization that collects and maintains records of research, development, and other activities being planned, currently in progress, or completed; it provides documents derived from these activities, and referral services to other sources for information relating to these activities.

Clearinghouse for Federal Scientific and Technical Information. *See CFSTI.*

Clements Library, William L. In 1923 William L. Clements deposited the library of Americana which he had been collecting for over twenty years with the University of Michigan, Ann Arbor. It is primarily a 'collection of the sources of American history' and has been extended over the years by the addition of books and documents which promote that study.

Clerical Assistant. A person who performs work requiring ability in routines, but not knowledge of the theoretical or scientific aspects of library work. *See also Library Clerk.*

Cliché. 1. A common and stereotyped journalistic or literary phrase. 2. An electrotype or stereotype plate.

Clichograph. *Synonymous with* KLISCHOGRAPH (*q.v.*).

Clift (David H.) Scholarship. An award made by the ALA Office for Library Personnel Resources.

Clinical Librarian. A person who, by aptitude, training and experience, is qualified to participate in the remedial, therapeutic and rehabilitative care of individuals in hospitals and institutions.

Clip. The metal eye, of whatever form, fixed to one of the covers of a book in a mediaeval chained library, and to which the book's chain was fastened.

Clipping. A piece clipped, or cut from a newspaper or periodical (American). Called in England a 'Cutting', 'Press cutting'.

Clipping Bureau.   A commercial organization which clips, or cuts, items from newspapers and periodicals on specific subjects and sends them to subscribers (American). Called in England a 'Cuttings bureau'.

Clipping Service.   The cutting of news items, etc. daily from newspapers and periodicals in an industrial, commercial or other organization, and sending them to officials who will find them useful. This is often undertaken in the library or information department.

Clippings File.   A collection of cuttings from newspapers and periodicals, used to supplement the information to be found in books, and usually kept in classified or subject order in folders in a vertical file. Also called 'Cuttings file'.

Clogged.   A half-tone, or line block, the impression from which has become smudged by the spaces between the dots or lines of the block becoming filled with ink. It may be due to dirty ink, dust, over-inking or the incorrect damping of a lithographic plate. Also known as 'filling in'.

Cloisonné.   Enamelled bindings made during the eleventh century, mainly by Greek and Italian craftsmen. The design was first outlined by soldering thin strips of metal on to a metal plate and then filling the compartments so formed with coloured enamels. *See also Champlevé.*

Close.   The second of a pair of punctuation marks, e.g.')]. *See also Circular Brackets, Square Brackets.*

Close Classification.   1. The arrangement of books in a classification system in as minute sub-divisions as possible; i.e. the full application of a scheme. Also called 'Exact classification', 'Depth classification', 'Bibliographic classification'.   2. Arrangement of works in conformity with the provisions of such a scheme. *See also Broad Classification.*

Close Matter.   Lines of type set without leads, or thinly spaced.

Close Roll.   A parchment roll upon which LETTERS CLOSE (*q.v.*) were enrolled at the Chancery.

Close Score.   A musical score in which the music of more than one part or instrument is written on one stave. Also called 'Short score', 'Compressed score', 'Condensed score'.

Close Up.   (*Printing*) To place lines or characters together by removing spacing-out leads or intervening letters.

Closed Access.   The obsolete method of keeping readers from the book shelves; this necessitated the provision in lending libraries of printed catalogues and indicators to inform readers which books were 'in' or 'out'. Also called 'Closed shelves', and 'Closed library'. In archive administration, archives which are not available to the general public due to the existence of a confidentiality restriction. They are said to be 'open' when the period of restriction has expired. *See also Access.*

Closed Bibliography.   One which has been completed. The opposite of PERIO-DICAL BIBLIOGRAPHY (*q.v.*). *Synonymous with* RETROSPECTIVE BIBLIOGRAPHY. *See also Bibliography, Current Bibliography.*

Closed Entry.   1. The catalogue entry for all the parts or volumes of a serial publication or work in several volumes, containing complete bibliographical information. Until the library has acquired a complete set, the bibliographical details are recorded in an OPEN ENTRY (*q.v.*). 2. A catalogue entry in which blank spaces are not left in the body of the entry or in the collation so that additional particulars of holdings may be entered subsequently.

Closed File. 1. One containing documents on which action has been finalized and to which further material is unlikely to be added. 2. One to which access is limited or denied because of the confidential nature of its contents.

Closed Indexing System. One in which the terms comprising the AUTHORITY LIST (*q.v.*) or File, or CONTROLLED TERM LIST (*q.v.*) may not be added to when new knowledge, or the indexing of a new document, would make the addition of new terms appear appropriate. A new edition of the approved list or an amendment sheet must be awaited. An Open Indexing System permits the addition of terms as necessary. *See also Open-ended Term List.*

Closed Joint. (*Bookbinding*) The type of joint which is obtained when cover boards are laced on. Also called 'Tight joint'. *See also French Joint.*

Closed Library. *See Closed Access.*

Closed Shelves. *See Closed Access.*

Closed Up. When typesetting is divided between several compositors and each has completed his allocation, the matter is closed up.

Closed User Group. Within any viewdata/videotex system, pages of information that can be accessed only by members of an organization, or subscribers to a particular part of the service.

Cloth. A generic term applied to material which is not leather or paper used for covering books. It was originally a material made of natural fibres of some kind. It was first used for this purpose in about 1820. *See also Cloth Binding.*

Cloth Binding. Used to describe a book which is bound entirely in cloth. A book so bound is called 'Cloth bound'.

Cloth Boards. *See Boards.*

Cloth-Centred. A duplex board or paper having a core, or centre, of muslin, linen or canvas (i.e. a cloth with paper on both sides), and used for maps, tables, etc. Cloth-faced, -lined, or -mounted paper or card indicates that the cloth is not a core but is pasted on one side only, and is termed linen- or canvas-lined (-backed) according to the kind of cloth used.

Cloth Joint. Piece of cloth used to cover the joints on the inside of very heavy or large books.

Cloth-Lined Paper (Board). Paper or board which is reinforced with muslin or cloth affixed to one side. *Cloth centred paper, or board,* is made up of two sheets or furnish layers with muslin or cloth between them.

Cloth Sides. A book which has cloth sides but leather at the spine and possibly at the corners as well.

CLR. Council on Library Resources, Inc. (*q.v.*).

CLSI. Computer Library Services International; a company offering a full range of library automation services in the UK, Europe, and worldwide.

CLTA. Canadian Library Trustees' Association (*q.v.*) (a Division of the Canadian Library Association).

Club Line. (*Printing*) The last line of type on a page when it begins a new paragraph. Printers try to avoid this, as they do a WIDOW (*q.v.*), because of its unsightliness.

Clump. A thick piece of type metal, ranging in width from 5 pt. upwards, but usually 6 pt. or 12 pt., and of the height of leads. Clumps are used in whiting out, and as footlines at the bottoms of columns and pages.

Cluster. (*Information retrieval*) A group of related documents.

CLV. Constant Linear Velocity; a mode of operation of optical disk equipment. Unlike the CAV FORMAT (*q.v.*) only continuous playback is possible and individual frames cannot be separately accessed. The playing time is about double that of the CAV format.

CML. Central Music Library (*q.v.*).

CNAA. *See Council for National Academic Awards.*

CNLA. Council of National Library and Information Associations (*q.v.*).

CNRS. Acronym for Centre National de la Recherche Scientifique et Technique. The most important centre in France for scientific documentation; it was set up in 1939 under the aegis of the Ministry of Education. Abbreviated CNRS. *See also INIST.*

Coarse Screen. *See Screen.*

Coated Paper. 1. A general term for papers such as chromo, art, enamel, which have been prepared for different printing processes by applying a mineral such as china clay after the body paper has been made. Also called 'Surface paper'. 2. Any paper whose surface is coated with a mixture of clay and glue made of casein to give it a smooth surface. The term is used to distinguish it from loaded papers in which the clay is mixed with the pulp during manufacture. *See also Art.*

Coating. A thin layer of light-sensitive chemical applied to a base material such as cloth, paper, or transparent plastic, or a mineral such as china clay to a printing paper. *See also Coated Paper.*

COBOL. Abbreviation for COmmon Business Oriented Language, a high-level computer programming language designed for commercial and business applications.

Cock. The middle portion of a BRACE (*q.v.*), when cast in three pieces as

Cock-up Initial. An initial letter that extends above the first line of text but aligns with the foot of it.

Cockle. (*Paper*) A puckered effect on paper, produced either naturally or artificially during the drying process. Paper and board will cockle and get out of shape with excessive heat or moisture; to prevent this these materials must be kept under temperature- and humidity-controlled conditions.

COCRIL. Acronym of the Council of City Research and Information Libraries. The Council evolved from the Group of City Librarians which was formed after the 1955 Library Association Conference. Represents the interests of large city libraries with research and large-scale information provision responsibilities.

cod. Abbreviation for CODEX (*q.v.*).

CODATA. Abbreviation for Committee on Data for Science and Technology, an interdisciplinary committee of the International Council of Scientific Unions (ICSU), which deals with data of importance to science and technology, their compilation, critical evaluation, storage and retrieval. Formed in 1966, it seeks to provide co-ordination and guidance for worldwide data-computing projects. Its scope includes quantitative data on the properties and behaviour of matter, characteristics of biological and geological systems, and other experimental and observational data. Publishes *CODATA Bulletin*.

codd. Abbreviation for codices. *See Codex*.

Code. 1. A standardized system of symbols, which may be visual, acoustic, magnetic, etc. by which information in a normal, common, source language can be converted into an artificial format for a specific purpose; typically such a system would be used to convert information into a format that could be accepted and handled by a computer. 2. A set of rules for carrying out a function in a standardized manner, for example, a code of cataloguing rules. *See also Algorithmic Code, Description, Non Semantic Code, Semantic Code, Tabulated Code*.

Code Comparison. (*Information retrieval*) In human searching, the matching of search words with words in a DESCRIPTOR FILE (*q.v.*).

Code Index. (*Information retrieval*) Any list of headings which directs the searcher, by means of a code number, to information required.

Code Mark. An indication of purchase made in code on the back of a title-page.

Code of Ethics. *See Professional Ethics*.

Coded Tape. A strip of paper, film, or other material containing an electronic or punched code for the activation of typewriter, typesetter or other machinery.

Coden. 1. A code classification assigned to a document or other library item consisting of four capital letters followed by two hyphenated groups of arabic numerals, or of two arabic numerals followed by two capital letters or of some similar combination. 2. The combination of letters, numbers and symbols assigned as a result of applying coding rules in order to produce a bibliographical citation. *See also Bishop's Rules*. The *ASTM coden for periodical titles* uses five-letter codes for the titles of periodicals and serials; the first four letters of each coden have some mnemonic relation to the title, and the fifth letter is arbitrary and will assist in maintaining as many mnemonic relationships as possible for similar periodical titles. The ASTM CODEN system was transferred on 1 January 1975 by the American Society for Testing Materials (ASTM), which had sponsored the system since 1955, to Chemical Abstracts Service (CAS). The CODEN serves as a unique and unambiguous permanent identifier for a specific title, and is used in lieu of full or abbreviated titles of publications in processing and storing bibliographical data in many computer-based information handling systems.

Codex. (*Pl.* Codices). An ancient book composed of pieces of writing material fastened so as to open like a modern book as distinct from the SCROLL or

VOLUMEN (*qq.v.*) which it superseded. The name was originally given to two or more tablets of metal, wood or ivory, hinged together with rings; the inner sides were covered with wax and these were written on with a stylus. Later 'Codex' was given to books of this type made of papyrus, vellum or parchment, and later still to volumes consisting of many leaves of parchment or vellum, e.g. *Codex Alexandrinus.* Codices became general for law-books in classical Rome, and were used largely for MS. copies of the scriptures and classics. Codex means a block of wood, probably from the wooden covers. When a codex of the original form consisted of two leaves, it was called a Diptych, of three, a Triptych, and of more, a Polyptych. Abbreviated cod. (*Pl.* codd.). There are a number of codices of the Bible, and these are often named after the place of discovery. The four most important of these are *Codex Sinaiticus* (4th or beginning of the 5th century – in the British Library), *Codex Vaticanus* (4th Century – in the Vatican), Codex Alexandrinus (5th century – in the British Library) and the palimpsest *Codex Ephraemi* (5th century Greek text overwritten in a 12th-century hand – in the Bibliothèque Nationale, Paris). These originally contained the whole Greek text of the Old and New Testaments, but are now incomplete. The *Codex Bezae* (5th ot 6th century – at Cambridge) containing only the *Gospels* and *Acts* is another important early copy of the *Bible.* All were written in uncials (i.e. capitals) and without breaks between words. The term 'codex' was also used for a collection of Roman laws; these included *Codex Theodosianus* and *Codex Justinianeus.*

Codex Alexandrinus.   This codex was given to Charles I in 1627 by the Patriarch of Constantinople, and formerly Patriarch of Alexandria. It has been in the British Museum (now British Library), since 1757. *See also Codex.*

Codex Amiatinus.   One of three codices written by order of Ceolfrid, who bedcame Abbot of Jarrow in 690, and taken by him on a journey for presentation to Pope Gregory II in 716. It is written in Latin uncials, and is one of the Vulgate. At one time it was preserved at Monte Amianta in the Abruzzi Mountains and is now in the Laurentian Library, Florence. *See also Codex.*

Codex Argenteus.   The remains of the fifth- and sixth-century MSS. of the translation of the Bible into the Gothic tongue by Wulfilas (or Ulfila), Bishop of the Visigoths. It is written mainly in Greek, but with some roman and runic characters, in gold and silver on purple-stained parchment. On 187 leaves, it contains most of the New Testament, and has been in the library of Uppsala University, Sweden, since 1669. Other fragments are in Milan and Wolfenbüttel.

Codex Bezae.   On vellum, this codex was presented to Cambridge University Library by Theodorus Beza who acquired it from the Monastery of St. Iremaeus at Lyons. *See also Codex.*

Codex Laudianus.   This codex contains the Book of the Acts of The Apostles in Greek and Latin, and was brought from Italy to England in the seventh century, probably by Benedict Biscop. It is now in the Bodleian Library at Oxford. *See also Codex.*

Codex Rescriptus Aphraëmi. A fifth century palimpsest MS. of the Bible with some works of Ephrem Syrus overwritten in the twelfth century. Fragments are in the Bibliothèque Nationale, Paris. Also known as *Codex Ephraemi.* *See also Codex.*

Codex Sinaiticus. The oldest extant Greek vellum codex, the text being written on 48-line columns. It was discovered in 1844, and the portion of 347 leaves (or an estimated total of 730) containing part of the Old Testament and all the New Testament was acquired by the British Museum (now British Library) in 1933. A further 43 leaves is in the Leipzig Library and is known as the *Codex Frederico-Augustaneus. See also Codex.*

Coding. (*Information retrieval*) 1. The translation of the names of specific subjects or of recorded information into written symbols according to a pre-arranged system or code; it must be legible to the eye or by machine and must have three characteristics: it must (1) suit the retrieving device used, (2) be capable of representing all likely subject descriptions, (3) be as compact as possible. 2. A list of successive computer operations in code for solving a given problem. Also, the act of writing a prepared list in code. *See also Code, Notation, Program.*

Coding Quires. *See Cassie.*

Coding Sheet. (*Information retrieval*) A sheet of paper on which is listed, in the form of the symbols of a code, the results of the analysis of a document.

Co-extensiveness. Intensive classification to coincide with the specific nature of the subject of a book.

Coffee Table Book. A sumptuously produced illustrated book, intended to be browsed through at leisure rather than purposefully read.

Coffin. A square frame in a hand printing press in which is bedded a stone on which the FORME (*q.v.*) is placed.

CoFHE. *See Colleges of Further and Higher Education.*

Coil Binding. *Synonymous with* SPIRAL BINDING (*q.v.*).

Coiled Binding. *Synonymous with* SPIRAL BINDING (*q.v.*).

Cold Composition. (*Printing*) Any method of composition which does not involve the casting of metal type. Typewriter, filmsetting and photographic methods are included. 'Cold type' is sometimes used to distinguish this method from 'hot metal' typesetting.

Cold Type. Composition by a composing machine which does not require hot metal, such as photographically, on a typewriter, or by computer keyboard.

Cole Size Card. A graduated card for determining the sizes of books (not by measurement but by bibliographical description) when writing catalogue and bibliography entries. This size card, which was first issued in 1889 by the Library Bureau, was based on the size rules of the American Library Association, the more uniform and accurate use of which the size card was intended to achieve. The card was named after its designer, Dr. George Watson Cole (1850–1939), who was Librarian of the Henry E. Huntington Library from 1915 to 1924. *See also Huntington Library.* A description of the card may be read in *The Library Journal,* **14**, 1889, pp. 485-6.

Collaborator.   One who is associated with another, or others, especially in the writing of books, being responsible for some aspect of, or contribution to, a work, but not responsible for the content as a whole.

Collage.   A picture or visual arrangement made partly or entirely of pieces of paper, wallpaper, illustrations, photographs or any other textured or figured material.

Collate.   1. To examine a book, whether bound or in the process of being bound, to see if the sections are complete and in the right sequence and to make sure that no maps, illustrations, etc., are missing.   2. To collect, compare and examine minutely and critically books and manuscripts to determine whether or not two copies are identical or variants.   3. Used in connection with tabulation machines to indicate the combining or merging of record cards into a desired sequence.   4. To transfer corrections marked on one proof to another marked proof, e.g. from a proofreader's proof to an author's proof.

Collateral Arrays.   (*Classification*) Arrays of the same order. *See also Array.*

Collateral Classes.   (*Classification*) Classes of the same order but not belonging to the same array. *See also Array.*

Collateral Reference.   One which in an alphabetico-specific subject catalogue links two headings belonging to the same hierarchical level under a common generic term, and which would stand side by side if arranged in a classification scheme.

Collateral Term.   (*Indexing*) A word which forms a constituent part of a BOUND TERM (*q.v.*) and which is also found in association with another word, both being used as a heading in a subject index. *See also Generic Term.*

Collating Mark.   A quad mark having a printing surface about 12-point deep by 5-point wide, which is printed so that after folding and gathering, the marks appear in descending order on the back of each section in such a way that the omission or duplication of a section becomes immediately apparent. Also called BACK MARK, BLACK STEP (*qq.v.*), 'Quad mark'.

Collation.   1. That part of a description of a book, apart from the contents, which describes the book as a physical object by specifying the number of volumes, pages, columns, leaves, illustrations, photographs, maps, format, size, etc. In a bibliographical description of an old book the number, which is expressed by the signature letters (*see Signature 2*), and composition of the sections is important. A *collation by gatherings* records the make-up of a book by stating the signature letters, e.g. A^4, $*^2$, $B-2A^4$, etc.; a *collation by pagination* records the make-up by the page numbers, e.g. [1]–[12], 1–374, etc.   2. The process of examining a new book to check its completeness, presence of all the illustrations, etc.   3. To check that a book is complete before binding or re-binding.   4. To compare two or more texts, either (a) to ascertain which is the first edition of a printed work, or (b) to establish a definitive or standard text.   5. to merge and combine two or more similarly ordered sets of items to produce an ordered set.

Collator.   1. A fitting consisting of trays or divisions into each of which is put a number of small printed or duplicated sheets of paper in a required order so that one of each may be arranged in sequence quickly when required. 2. In electric accounting machines, one which combines or merges files of cards into any desired sequence.

Collectanea. Passages selected from one or more authors, generally for instruction. A collection or miscellany.

Collected Edition. An edition of an author's works published in one volume or in a number of volumes in a uniform style of binding.

Collected Works. All the writings of an author, including those which have not been printed previously, published in one volume or a number of volumes in a uniform style of binding, usually with an inclusive title.

Collecting Drum. A revolving drum which is fitted to a high-speed printing press or paper-making machine to catch the sheets of paper coming out of the machine and collect them in groups of from five to ten so that final delivery can be at a slower speed. They are then delivered together as a group which can be passed on at only a fifth of the speed otherwise required.

Collection. 1. A number of books or other items on one subject, or of one kind, or collected by one person or organization. 2. (*Bibliography*) A number of works, or parts of them, not forming a treatise or monograph on a single subject, and regarded as constituting a single whole, as a collection of plays, essays, etc. 3. (*Cataloguing*) If written by one author, three or more independent works, or parts of works, published together; if written by more than one author, two or more independent works, or parts of works, published together but not written for the same occasion or for the same publication.

Collection Development. The process of planning a stock acquisition programme not simply to cater for immediate needs, but to build a coherent and reliable collection over a number of years, to meet the objectives of the service. The term demands a depth and quality of stock, and includes associated activity towards exploitation of the collection through publicity, staff training, etc.

Collection Number. In the Colon Classification, a suitable symbol to be determined by each individual library, and added to the CLASS NUMBER (*q.v.*) and BOOK NUMBER (*q.v.*) to indicate the collection to which the book belongs.

Collective Biography. A volume, or volumes, consisting of separate accounts of the lives of people.

Collective Cataloguing. The cataloguing of minor and fugitive material by (a) assembling a group of such items and assigning it a heading and a collective title; (b) cataloguing it by form but stating the corporate or personal authorship and giving the class number or other retrieval identification. *See also Form Entry, Form Heading.*

Collective Entries. In selective cataloguing, several entries on one card for pamphlets on the same or related subjects. They may be either author or subject entries.

Collective Title. 1. A title under which articles written separately by several authors are published together. If there is no recognized author, compiler, or editing body, the main catalogue entry appears under the title of the work. 2. The title given to a work as a whole when that work consists of several works, each with its own title.

Collector. One who puts together several works or parts of works. Usually called an editor.

College Libraries, Standards for. *See Standards for Library Services.*

College Library. A library established, maintained, and administered by a college to meet the needs of its students and faculty.

Colleges, Institutes and Schools of Education. Formerly a sub-section of the UNIVERSITY, COLLEGE AND RESEARCH SECTION (*q.v.*) of the LIBRARY ASSOCIATION (*q.v.*), then an independent Group. Became the Education Librarians' Group in 1981. Publishes *ELG News* (3 p.a.). Abbreviated CISE.

Colleges of Further & Higher Education Group. A Group of the (British) Library Association formed in 1979; formerly the Colleges of Technology and Further Education Group. Publishes *Bulletin* (3 p.a.). Abbreviated CoFHE.

Colleges of Technology and Further Education. Formerly a sub-section of the UNIVERSITY, COLLEGE AND RESEARCH SECTION (*q.v.*) of the LIBRARY ASSOCIATION (*q.v.*), since January 1970 an independent Group. Became the Colleges of Further and Higher Education group in 1979. Abbreviated CTFE.

Collocation. The arrangement of sub-classes of a classification by degrees of likeness.

Collocative *v.* Direct Cataloguing. The principle of entering books written by one author using several pseudonyms under his real name (collocative) or under the name used for each individual title (direct).

Collography. A similar production process to collotype except that a film base wrapped around a cylinder is used instead of a flat glass plate.

Colloplas. Trade name for a process for making non-etched gravure cylinders in which a rubber surface on which the printing image is impressed hydraulically is substituted for the copper-coated etched cylinders used in photogravure.

Collotype. A variety of photogravure. A print which gives accurate gradation of tone; it is made by a photo-mechanical process directly from a hardened emulsion of bichromated gelatine on glass. Phototype, Albertype, Artotype, Heliotype and Lichtdruck are forms of collotype. William Henry Fox Talbot, an English pioneer of photography, discovered in 1852 that a chromate gelatine layer was case-hardened by exposure to light, and the first person to employ this process for the production of printing plates was Alphonse Louis Poitevin in 1855. By coating a plate with chromated gelatine and printing and developing a photographic image on it, a surface could be obtained which, when damped, responds to ink in the same way as a lithographic stone. Also called a 'gelatine print'.

Colombier. Drawing and plate paper size 24 × 34½ inches. Also spelled 'Columbier'.

Colon. 1. A device used in the Universal Decimal Classification to link related class terms. 2. A device used in the Colon Classification to separate succesive foci. Later, in the Colon Classification, a device to introduce the energy facet. 3. A punctuation symbol.

Colon Abbreviations. A scheme devised by C. A. Cutter to save the writing out in full of authors' foremanes. It consists of the initial letters of the most used Christian names in each letter of the alphabet followed by a colon (vertically for men, horizontally for women), e.g.:

H: (Henry)
J: (John)
M. . (Mary)

Colon Book Number. A book number used in connection with the COLON CLASSIFICATION (*q.v.*). The numbers are based on the facet formula as follows: L the language of exposition (taken from the CC Language Schedule); F the number for the form of exposition (from the CC Form Schedule); T the number for the year of publication (from the CC Chronological Schedule); SN the serial number, used to distinguish the different books in the same ultimate class and having the same language and form numbers; V the volume number (from the book itself); S the number for the supplement (from the book itself); C the copy number, other than the first (made serially as for the SN); EVN the evaluation number for pseudo classics. Usually only three numbers are used to provide the Book Number: only the year of publication is used for individualizing each document, and the other provisions in the formula are seldom needed. *See also Book Number.*

Colon Classification. An elaborate, scholarly scheme designed by S. R. Ranganathan especially for Indian libraries. It is based on the classification of any subject by its uses and relations, which are indicated by numbers divided by the colon ':'. In this classification, ready-made class numbers are not provided for most topics, but are constructed by combining in assigned permutations and combinations the classes of the various unit schedules of which the scheme consists, colons separating the different units. Special schedules are provided for Geographical Divisions (a Local List), Language Divisions, and Chronological Divisions (Space Isolate, Language Isolate, and Time Isolate respectively). A schedule of common sub-divisions (Common Isolate), using the lower-case letters of the alphabet as its primary symbol is also provided. It was the first example of an analytico-synthetic classification, in which the subject field is first analysed into facets, and class numbers are then constructed by synthesis. *See Book Number 2, Colon Book Number.*

Colophon. (Gr. 'finishing, end'). 1. Particulars of printer, place and date of printing, title, name of author, and publisher's or printer's device, found at the end of early printed books. It was first used in printed books by Fust and Schoeffer in the 'Mainz Psalter' of 1457, and gradually became common, but was superseded towards 1600 by the Publisher's Imprint. Its use in MSS. was occasional; it then gave the scribe's name and the date. *See also Imprint.*   2. A current, but incorrect, meaning is the publisher's device, e.g. Benn's *horse*, Heinemann's *windmill* or Thames and Hudson's *dolphins*.

Colophon Date.   The date given in the COLOPHON (*q.v.*), and so described when used in a catalogue and bibliography.

Colour Coding.   The visual presentation, by means of coloured signals, of information in a conventional card catalogue, e.g. the colours indicating in a catalogue of periodicals the frequency, language, subject, etc., of each title.

Colour Gravure.   The process of producing coloured illustrations in colour by PHOTOGRAVURE (*q.v.*). This method is used principally for mass circulation colour magazines and packaging materials. The colour picture is usually of almost continuous tone, the dark and light shades being obtained by varying depths of the etched cells.

Colour Lithography.   A method of printing in colour by lithography using separate stones or plates for each colour.

Colour Printing.   The art of producing pictures, designs, etc., in a variety of colours, shades and tones by means of printing from plates, or by lithography; chromatic printing.

Colour Process.   A set of two or more half-tones made by colour separation. Half-tone colour printing is commonly called process colour work.

Colour Separation.   The process by which colours of an original work of art or colour print are analysed into the basic colours in such a way that printing plates may be prepared in order to print in succession and finally yield a print of correct colouring. This is done by placing filters in front of the camera lens when making negatives.

Colour Separation Negative.   A negative for use in colour printing which, by the use of a colour filter, has recorded a primary colour.

Colour Transparency.   A positive colour photograph on a transparent support, usually film.

Colour Under Gilt.   The edges of a book coloured (usually red) before gilding. Usually found in Bible binding. *See also Edges, Red Under Gold Edges.*

Colour Work.   Printing processes used to print in two or more colours, such as two-, or four-colour half-tone; planographic and intaglio work in colour. Often called according to the number of plates used, 'Three-colour Process', 'Four-colour Process'.

Coloured Edges.   *Synonymous with* SPRINKLED EDGES (*q.v.*).

Coloured Plate.   A whole-page coloured illustration produced by any process.

Coloured Printings.   A cheap paper, having a high content of mechanical wood pulp; it is used, among other purposes, for the covers of pamphlets.

Colporteur.   A travelling bookseller or agent, usually of a religious group or society, who sells tracts and copies of the scriptures at low prices.

COLT.   Expanded title; Council on Library/Media Technicians. Founded 1965; present name adopted 1989. Based in Chicago. Aims to improve the education of technical assistants and other non-professional or para-professional employees. Publishes *COLT Newsletter* (m.), and directories.

Columbian. An out-of-date name for a size of type equal to about 16 point.

Columbian Press. A printing press designed by George Clymer of Philadelphia and brought to England in 1817 where it became more successful than in the United States. The press derived its power from a system of levers which converted the lateral movement of the bar to the vertical movement of the iron beam from which the platen was suspended. The most conspicuous feature of the press was a cast-iron eagle which acted as an adjustable counter weight.

Columbier. *See Colombier.*

Column. 1. A narrow division of a page of a book formed by vertical lines or spaces to form two or three columns of type. 2. A narrow block of letterpress arranged in the form of a column. 3. (*Printing*) A vertical line or square bracket.

Column Inch. (*Printing*) *See Agate Line.*

Column Picture. Picture in a mediaeval illuminated manuscript the width of a column of text, whether at the head of a page, or interrupting the text at intervals.

Column Rule. (*Printing*) A metal rule used to separate columns of type in the text or in tables. *See also Rule.*

Columnar. A series or classification in which the terms, or classes, are arranged in a column. The classes may be co-ordinate, or they may be regarded as subordinate, each to that above it. *See Horizontal, Tabular Classification.*

COM. Abbreviation for computer output microfilm/microfiche; instead of a paper output, a computer system may print out directly in a microformat, at a smaller cost than on paper, and at higher speeds.

Comb Pattern. A pattern produced on marbled papers or other surfaces from a vat in which colours have been combed to form a pattern. *See also Marbled Paper.*

Combination Order. (*Cataloguing, Classification, Information retrieval*) The order in which facets in a compound subject heading are to be arranged, e.g. the order of Decreasing Concreteness (*q.v.*). *See also Descriptor Sequence, Distributed Facets.*

Combination Plate. One in which both half-tone and line methods have been used.

Combination System. *Synonymous with* Correlative System (*q.v.*).

COMLA. Commonwealth Library Association (*q.v.*).

Comma. A punctuation mark. *See also Quotes, Turned Comma.*

Command Papers. *See Parliamentary Papers.*

Commentary. 1. Explanatory or critical notes on an Act of Parliament, a literary text or some other work. It may accompany the text or be issued separately. 2. A spoken script to a film, videotape, or tape/slide presentation.

Commercial Library. Similar to a commercial section but on a much larger scale and housed in a separate unit from the reference library, and sometimes in a separate building.

Commercial Section. The section of a reference library devoted to providing material and information for business and commerce.

COMMETT. Community Action on Co-operation between Universities and Enterprises for Training and Technology; a European Community programme examining distance learning, collaborative training partnerships, and IT implications. Initial period of operation 1990–1994.

Commission of the European Community. *See European Community.*

Commission on Preservation and Access. Set up in 1986 in the USA and funded by the Council on Library Resources; a high profile body whose work is based on three principles: the creation of a new master copy, the use of the appropriate technology for the discipline involved, and the development of a co-ordinated programme of minimum standards. Supported by the NATIONAL ADVISORY COUNCIL ON PRESERVATION (*q.v.*).

Committee for Information and Documentation on Science and Technology. A European Community organization designed to facilitate discussion on proposals from the Commission of the EC. Its relevance is limited and its demise is likely.

Committee of Directors of National Libraries. An international meeting place for directors; at present much concerned with networking arrangements and licensing schemes for national bibliographic records.

Committee on Data for Science and Technology. *See CODATA.*

Committee on International Scientific and Technical Information Programmes. *See CISTIP.*

Committee on Scientific and Technical Communication. *See SATCOM.*

Committee on Scientific and Technical Information. *See COSATI.*

Common Auxiliaries. *See Universal Decimal Classification.*

Common Facets. Facets or terms which may occur in more than one field in a general classification.

Common Folio. *See Folio.*

Common Isolates. Symbols attached to many classes in the Colon Classification and indicating literary form, e.g. *a* bibliography; *c* concordance; *v* history; *y*2 syllabus, P*v* history of linguistics; Plll*v* history of English linguistics. When attached to a host class number without a connecting symbol, as in the examples given, they are called *Anteriorising Common Isolates*, but when needing a connecting symbol *Posteriorising Common Isolates*.

Common Ruling. Term used to denote the vertical lines (rules) printed on account-book paper. *See also Feint Ruling.*

Common Subdivisions. Form divisions which are used throughout a classification to sub-divide any subject. These have distinctive names in different classifications, e.g. AUXILIARY TABLES (*q.v.*) in Dewey and the Universal Decimal Classification; CATEGORICAL TABLES (*q.v.*) in Brown's *Subject classification*, and SYSTEMATIC SCHEDULES (*q.v.*) in Bliss's *Bibliographic classification*.

Commonwealth Agricultural Bureaux. This organization was set up to act as a clearing-house for information for scientists and research workers in agriculture throughout the world. The organization covers all the agricultural sciences, including forestry and animal health, and operates three Institutes and ten Bureaux. Abbreviation CAB.

Commonwealth Library Association. COMLA was founded in 1972 with a membership of 20 national library associations in Commonwealth countries. It is one of more than 25 Commonwealth Professional Associations (CPAs) sponsored by the Commonwealth Foundation since 1966, when this agency was established by the Commonwealth Heads of Government for the 'nurturing of professional activity throughout the Commonwealth as an important component of the developmental process'. The aims of COMLA are to support and encourage library associations in the Commonwealth; to forge, maintain and strengthen professional links between librarians; to promote the status and education of librarians and the reciprocal recognition of qualifications in librarianship; to improve libraries; and to initiate research projects designed to promote library provision and to further technical development of libraries in the Commonwealth. There are now 52 COMLA members, comprising 40 national library associations and 12 major library institutions in countries that do not yet have a national association. Publishes *COMLA Newsletter* (q.).

Commonwealth Poetry Prize. *See Dillons Commonwealth Poetry Prize.*

Commonwealth Scientific and Industrial Research Organization. Established in Australia by the Science and Industry Act of 1949; it replaced the Council for Scientific and Industrial Research established in 1926. It exists to provide the Australian community and industry with the technology to meet present and future challenges; it is grouped into six institutes covering information and communications technologies; space science and applications; industrial technologies for manufacturing; materials; chemicals and polymers; biotechnology; minerals and energy exploration technology; mining; processing and products; research for the construction industry; animal production, health and processing; human nutrition; crop production, protection and processing; forestry; the environment: atmosphere, wildlife, oceans and land water. Abbreviated CSIRO.

Commonwealth Writers' Prize. Annual awards sponsored by the Commonwealth Foundation and administered by the Book Trust, for works of fiction in a number of categories.

Community Antenna Television. Cable television system in which subscribers receive the service via a master antenna serving a local area. Abbreviated CATV.

Community Information. Material collected to provide a local information service to a small geographical area; the information will relate to any topics that affect the life of the community, for example social, domestic, health or educational facilities, details of local cultural activities, clubs and societies, and the range of local authority or governmental services. Material is usually in pamphlet or loose-leaf format; such a service may be provided in a public branch library, or via a special unit set up by a local authority, voluntary agency or advice group.

Community Information Project. The Community Information Project, which was originally funded in 1977 for a period of three years by the British

Library Research and Development Department, was set up by the Library Association in conjunction with such organizations as the National Consumer Council and the National Association of Citizens Advice Bureaux. The British Library funding enabled the Library Association to appoint a Research officer and a Research Assistant to work on the Project. The present aims of the Project are to collect information on research, practice and developments in information and advice work; to provide an advisory and consultation service to researchers, practitioners and anyone planning to set up an advice service: to carry out relevant research and promote co-operation between networks of agencies by sharing knowledge within the field. The Project is now independent, and operates from Bethnal Green Library, London. Publications include *Knowhow, Computer Benefits, Village Contacts,* etc. Abbreviated CIP.

Community Library.   Usually a branch library (although maybe a central or mobile service) intended to provide advice-centre functions and local information for the whole of its community, rather than only offering a bookstock to readers.

Community Profile.   A demographic study of the community served by a library, including information on social, economic and educational factors, average ages, levels of employment, numbers of children, old-peoples homes, etc., that the service should take account of in planning, and in purchasing stock.

Community Services Group.   A group of the (British) Library Association formed in 1982 to provide an opportunity for co-operation between all members interested in providing and promoting library and information services to groups within the community whose needs are not adequately met by traditional library services, especially multi-cultural, and disadvantaged users. A new constitution was adopted from the beginning of 1989, and regional groups are being formed. Publishes *Community Librarian* (3 p.a.).

Compact Disk.   Commercial sound recordings introduced in March 1983; the five-inch diameter disk is scanned by a laser beam, and reproduction is an improvement on conventional discs or tape as there is no contact with the playing surface and consequently no wear or surface noise. Abbreviated CD. *See also CD–ROM.*

Compact Disk Interactive.   *See CD–I.*

Compact Storage.   The storing of books on rolling or swinging stacks which have to be moved into another position to permit consultation, or of books or other material placed in drawers built into shelving and opening into a stack aisle. Such shelving is used normally in stack rooms. *See also Compactus, Draw-out Shelves, Rolling Bookcase, Rolling Press, Swinging Bookcase.*

Compactus.   Trade name for a particular design of shelving invented by Ingold, a Swiss engineer. Steel bookcases are placed against one another and are moved sideways for consultation of the books by operating a lever which activates a clutch on a revolving cable set in the floor, or by pressing a switch which operates an electric motor. The books on one side of each of two cases are exposed to view by this means. Also called 'Ingold-Compactus'.

Company File. A file, kept especially in commercial, industrial, research and learned or professional association libraries, containing information relating to individual firms. The type of information kept depends on the type of library and the needs of its users but may include reports, company reports, house journals, catalogues, booklets, cuttings, advertisements, stock exchange listings, etc. Also called 'Corporation file'. *See also Extel Card Services.*

Comparative Librarianship. The study of library services in various countries, reflecting differing national, cultural, political or societal environments. The comparison of similarities and analysis of differences leads to a better understanding of the general principles involved, and mature consideration of the success of varying approaches.

Compartment. 1. In a book stack, sets of shelves arranged vertically between two uprights and placed back to back. (American.) 2. (*Bibliography*) A group of decorative borders comprising (a) a single carved or engraved piece with the centre portion cut out so as to resemble a picture frame into which the letterpress of a title or other matter is set; (b) a piece originally carved or engraved as (a) but later cut into four or more pieces; (c) four or more pieces cut or engraved separately but intended to form a single design when assembled; (d) such borders made from four pieces of cast type-ornaments but with ends cut obliquely to help form a border. *See also Frame.*

Compartment Picture. An illumination, in a mediaeval illuminated manuscript, divided into sections each of which contains a picture.

Compass Map. *See Portolan Chart.*

Compatibility of Thesauri. (*Information retrieval*) The quality of two or more thesauri which are compiled by the same methods and in which the descriptors can be interchanged, and which may be used to index, or for searching, in equivalent subject fields.

Compend. A subject treated briefly, or in outline only.

Compendium. A work containing in a small compass the substance or general principles of a larger work; a brief, comprehensive summary.

Compensation Guards. Short stubs bound into a volume to balance the space taken up by folded maps or other bulky material so that this can be incorporated without distorting the shape of the book. Also called 'Filling-in guards'. *See also Guard, Stub.*

Compilation. A work compiled by assembling material from other books.

Compiler. 1. A collector or editor of written or printed material gleaned from various sources or from one or more authors; and who arranges it for publication. 2. One who produces a musical work by collecting and putting together written or printed matter from the work of several composers. Also, one who chooses and combines into one work selections and excerpts from one or more composers.

Compiler Entry. A catalogue entry for the compiler of a work.

Complete Bibliography. *See Bibliography.*

Complete Specification. *See Patent, Specification.*

Completion. *See Continuation.*

Complex Array Isolate. (*Classification*) An array isolate which is found by combining two or more array isolates to form one array in order to express the relation between them.

Complex Class. *Classification*) A class which is formed by combining two or more isolates to form one facet in order to express the relation between them.

Complex Isolate. (*Classification*) An isolate which is formed by the combination of two or more isolates to form one FACET (*q.v.*) in order to express the relationship between them.

Complex Subject. In classification, one which reflects more than one distinct conventional class.

Complutensian Polyglot. The polyglot *Bible* in six volumes printed between 1514 and 1517 at Alcalá de Henares, a small town near Madrid, by Arnald Guillen de Brocar. It was the first of the great multi-lingual Bibles, and is by far the most important landmark in Spanish printing. The text is in Hebrew, Aramaic, Greek and Latin. Called Complutensian Bible because Complutum is the Roman name for Alcalá de Henares. *See also Polyglot.*

Component. An individual constituent word in a compound subject heading.

Compose. To set type-matter ready for printing. *See also Computer Typesetting.*

Composer. One who composes, especially music.

Composer Entry. 1. An entry in a catalogue for a musical composition under the name of the composer as the heading. Normally this is the main entry but it may be an added entry. 2. Sometimes used for the composer heading chosen for the entry, and not the entry itself.

Composing Room. A room in which printing type is set, or composed, and made up into formes for printing. *See also Compositor.*

Composing Rule. A flat strip of steel or brass placed by the compositor between each line of type in his composing stick when setting type. Rules provide a flat surface for each line of type and facilitate the handling of the composed type. Also called 'Setting rule'.

Composing Stick. Also called STICK (*q.v.*).

Composite Authors. Name given to the several authors contributing to one work. Not to be confused with JOINT AUTHOR (*q.v.*).

Composite Book. 1. A book of a composite nature, where an editor has brought together several works by different authors into one volume. 2. A book on more than one subject. 3. A COMPOSITE WORK (*q.v.*).

Composite Classification. A method of classifying whereby specific subjects are represented by coupling two or more elementary terms from the classification schedules as indicated at COMPOSITE SUBJECT (*q.v.*).

Composite Heading. (*Cataloguing*) A heading consisting of more than one element each of which is to be distinguished by punctuation, or typographically, for filing purposes.

Composite Subject. (*Classification*) One which consists of more than one element, e.g. the design of furniture for children's libraries.

Composite Work. 1. A literary production on a single subject written by two or more authors in collaboration, the contribution by each forming a distinct section or part of the complete work. 2. A musical composition in which two or more composers collaborate similarly, each contribution forming a distinct section or part of the complete work.

Composition. Type setting: hence Compositor.

Composition Fount. Loosely used to indicate any type-face of a size of 14-point or less, used for book printing and 'tapped' on a type-composing machine.

Compositor. One who sets printer's type. A typesetter.

Compound. (*Information retrieval*) A pattern of data units showing all the features which are possessed in common by a given set of items.

Compound Catchword. In indexing, a hyphenated word which must be treated as if the hyphen did not exist.

Compound Class. In the Colon Classification, a class made of a Basic Class (i.e. Main, or Canonical, Class) and one or more Isolates.

Compound Heading. (*Information retrieval*) A number of general terms arranged together in a co-ordinate relationship to designate a complex idea. *See also Main Heading.*

Compound Name. A name made of two or more proper names, generally connected by a hyphen, conjunction or preposition.

Compound Subject. 1. (*Cataloguing*) One which requires more than one word in the subject heading to express its meaning. A compound subject may consist of a phrase or a combination, the separate words of which are divided by punctuation. 2. (*Classification*) One which reflects more than one facet within a conventional class, for example, within the class Building, Wooden Floor is a compound, reflecting both a material and a part.

Compound Subject Heading. A heading which consists of (a) two words joined by a conjunction, as 'Punch and Judy'; (b) a phrase, as 'Council of Trent'; (c) words which are always associated together; e.g. 'Capital Punishment'; 'Political Economy'.

Comprehensive Bibliography. One which lists, as far as possible, everything published on the subject. *See also Current Comprehensive Bibliography.*

Compresence. A linked set of FEATURES (*q.v.*) describing a given ITEM (*q.v.*), or of items defining a given feature.

Compressed Full Score. *See Score.*

Compressed Score. *Synonymous with* CLOSE SCORE (*q.v.*). *See also Score.*

Computer. An electronic machine which can accept data, store it, manipulate it as instructed in a program, retrieve it and convey the result to a user. The division into mainframes, mini-computers, micro-computers which held good in the early 1980s is now superseded by a variety of terms. As miniaturization increases and the technology develops, smaller machines can now carry out functions that only very large installations could cope with five years ago. Microcomputers/personal computers, and microprocessors have become very widely used, and for library applications larger machines are usually unnecessary.

Computer Database Advice Centre. Operated as a research project at Ealing College of Higher Education (UK). Initially funded for 1986–1988, it aims to introduce and demonstrate publicly accessible databases. Abbreviated CDAC.

Computer Input Microfilm. *See CIM.*

Computer Output Microfilm. *See COM.*

Computer Typesetting. Use of a computer to set up a page of printing; the operator can set the text on a display screen, adjust the layout, incorporate graphic material, insert page numbers, running headlines, etc., and the final product can be stored by the computer for output when required either onto printing plates or via high quality laser printers. *See also Desktop Publishing.*

CONARLS. The Circle of Officers of National and Regional Library Systems, is an informal group which reviews current issues in inter-lending and library co-operation and endeavours to give practical support to the effective development and operation of co-operative services. It examines topics in detail as considered necessary or when referred to the Circle by the Library and Information Co-operation Council (LINC). The membership of the Circle consists of the Directors/Librarians of the nine regional library systems of the United Kingdom and the Library Council/An Chomhairle Leabharlanna of the Republic of Ireland and also a representative from Northern Ireland, the British Library Document Supply Centre and the British Library Bibliographic Services. Each region hosts the Annual Meeting in turn and at least one other meeting is held each year. CONARLS has published *Inter-lending and Library Co-operation in the UK and Republic of Ireland* which gives details of all the library co-operatives involved. *See also Regional Library Co-operation (UK).*

Concept Co-ordination. 1. A system of multi-dimensional indexing with single concepts to define a document uniquely. 2. A system of co-ordinate indexing for information retrieval. *See also Co-ordinate Indexing, Uniterm Concept Co-ordinate Indexing.*

Concept Indexing. 1. The process of deciding which are the concepts in a particular document that are of sufficient importance to be included in the SUBJECT INDEX (*q.v.*). 2. The use of a standard description for each concept (whether it has been used by the author of the text or not) and using it as a subject heading whenever appropriate.

Concertina Fold. A method of folding paper, first to the right and then to the left, so that it opens and closes in the manner of a concertina. Also called 'Zig-zag fold'. *See also Accordian Fold.*

Concilium Bibliographicum. A bibliographical work begun by Herbert Haviland Field at Zurich in 1895. Cards were printed and distributed as soon as published for all publications (primarily periodical articles, with some books and pamphlets) on zoology, palaeontology, general biology, microscopy, anatomy, physiology and kindred subjects, from all countries. It thus formed a complete bibliography. After the death of the founder in 1921, the Rockefeller Foundation made a grant for five years, hoping that the organization would receive finance internationally. The enterprise continued on subscriptions alone until 1940 when it ceased to function. It is often referred to as the ZURICH INDEX.

Concise Description, Principle of. The avoidance of duplication or unessential information in a catalogue entry. *See also Cataloguing, Principles of.*

Concordance. 1. A book arranged so as to form an alphabetical index of all passages, or of all the more important words, in any work, with indications of the context of such passages and phrases in the text. 2. In machine indexing, an alphabetical index of words in a document, each word present in the text being an index entry.

Concreteness, Principle of Decreasing. *See Decreasing Concreteness, Principle of.*

Concretes and Processes. A method of indexing devised by K. Kaiser in which the main (first, or leading) word of the subject-entry is the main, 'concrete', subject, and the later one/s the secondary (or aspect) 'processes' subdividing it.

Condensed Score. *Synonymous with* CLOSE SCORE (*q.v.*). *See also Score.*

Condensed Type. Type which is narrow in proportion to its height. This is an example.

Conditioning. The maturing of paper, carried out in the paper mill by drying out or adding moisture to it so as to bring it 'into balance' with what is accepted as normal printing-room atmosphere and to enable it to be used on fast-running machines without danger of cockling. The process is carried out in a temperature of 60°–65°F, and a relative humidity of 65%; the paper will then contain about 7% moisture evenly distributed over the sheet, and the fibres will remain stable during printing.

Conductor's Part. The printed music for an instrumentalist who also simultaneously conducts a concerted work. Also called 'Conductor's score'. *See also Score.*

Conductor's Score. *Synonymous with* CONDUCTOR'S PART (*q.v.*). *See also Score.*

Confederation of Information Communication Industries. *See CICI.*

confer. (*Lat.* 'compare'.) To compare or refer to. Usually used in the abbreviated form (cf.).

Conference of Directors of National Libraries. Formed 1975 as an adjunct to the IFLA Section of National Libraries, and meets during IFLA Conferences. A forum for international action, it has been particularly effective in promoting the development of the MARC network.

Conference of European National Librarians. Formed 1987 to coordinate reaction of national libraries to CEC activities. *See also Conspectus.*

Conference of Southeast Asian Librarians. *See CONSAL.*

Confidential File. Material in a library which is kept securely, and apart from other material, and is only used under certain conditions. *See also Classified Material.*

Configuration. The physical layout and relationship of the various component parts of a computer system.

Conger.   A group of from ten to twenty wholesale booksellers who combined to share the publishing and selling of books, and to protect the sale of their books from undercutting and piracy. Congers were a feature of the London book trade in the late seventeenth and early eighteenth centuries.

Congress, Library of, Classification.   *See Library of Congress Classification.*

Conjoint Authorship.   *See Joint Author.*

Conjugate.   (*Bibliography*) This term is applied in two leaves which can be traced into and out of the back of a book and found to be one piece of paper.

Conjunction.   (*Classification*) In the Colon Classification, a symbol used to couple two substantives.

Conjunctive.   Pertaining to the joining or coupling of two documents, words, phrases, or elements of information in order to express a unity. Being neither disjunctive nor collateral.

Connecting Symbols.   *See Class Number* and *Fundamental Categories.*

Connective Catalogue.   *Synonymous with* SYNETHETIC CATALOGUE (*q.v.*).

Connotation.   A term in classification indicative of all the qualities conveyed by, or comprised in, a class name; e.g. 'man' in connotation means the qualities (mammalian structure, upright gait, reason, etc.) that go to make up man, as opposed to *denotation*, where the term merely marks down or indicates. The phrase: 'That man is really a man' shows the denotative followed by the connotative use of the word. Connotation and denotation may be considered synonymous with intension and EXTENSION (*q.v.*).

Connotative.   *See Connotation.*

CONSAL.   Abbreviation for Conference of Southeast Asian Librarians, a regional library association which was created on the initiative of the Malaysian and Singapore library associations.

CONSER.   The Co-operative Online Serials Program, based at the Library of Congress, which provides technical and administrative support. Originally planned in 1973 as a US/Canada project with the title 'Co-operative Conversion of Serials', and funded by the Council on Library Resources, CONSER was based on the Minnesota Union List of Serials file and the OCLC network was added. An enormous database of serials titles is gradually emerging, and recent participants in the program have been included to add extra information to records already authenticated.

Conservation.   The process of ensuring the survival of library or archive materials; at the simplest level this may mean basic repair or strengthening work, but increasingly publishers and producers of materials are urged to ensure the durability and longevity of paper and other components. Also termed preservation. In the UK the British Library has established a NATIONAL PRESERVATION OFFICE (*q.v.*) after the findings of the RATCLIFFE REPORT (*q.v.*). Similar facilities have been established in other national centres.

Consistent Characteristics.   *See Characteristic of a Classification.*

Console.   *See Terminal.*

Consolidated Index.   An index, in one sequence, to several volumes, a long run of a periodical or other serial publication, or to several independent works or serial publications.

Consolidated System. A system of libraries established by the decision of several municipal governing bodies, or by the action of voters, and governed by the Board of Trustees of the system. The individual library units operate as branches of the system. (American).

'Consonant' Code. (*Information retrieval*) One of several systematic methods of abbreviating words.

Consortium of University Research Libraries. *See CURL.*

Conspectus. Conspectus is an instrument for libraries to describe their existing collection strengths and current collecting intensities by assigning a set of simple alpha-numeric codes, within the basic framework of the Library of Congress subject classification. Conspectus was conceived in 1979 to support the efforts of the Research Libraries Group (RLG) in the United States to co-operate and share resources in a more comprehensive way than had previously been attempted. As members gathered information about their collections and submitted it to the RLG, the data was made available through the Research Libraries Information Network. In 1983 the RLG and the Association of Research Libraries joined forces to work on the North American Collections Inventory Project (NCIP), a co-operative effort intended to provide data on-line about the collections of a large number of libraries throughout North America, using Conspectus as the basis for collection assessment. NCIP has been growing steadily.

While some Canadian libraries have been submitting their data to NCIP, the Canadian Association of Research Libraries and the National Library of Canada have been working on the Canadian Collections Inventories Project, using a bilingual Conspectus and covering a wide range of libraries.

In Australia the National Library has accepted Conspectus methodology, and there has also been much interest from the university and state libraries.

The British Library, eleven Scottish research libraries led by the National library of Scotland, and the National Library of Wales have completed Conspectus surveys. The British Library is now discussing the best way to bring more university libraries into the national system.

After the first meeting of the Conference of European National Librarians in February 1987, the National Libraries Conspectus Group was established. The membership comprises representatives from the national libraries of France, the Federal Republic of Germany, the Netherlands, Portugal and the United Kingdom, which currently provides the Chair and the Secretariat at the British Library. The Group has been principally concerned with increasing support for the European Conspectus initiative from the European Commission.

The LIBER Executive Committee, meeting in Bremen in November 1987, decided to set up a Conspectus Group. Its members come from research libraries in France, the Netherlands, the Federal Republic of Germany, Norway, Austria, Switzerland, Spain and Portugal. The Chairman is from Scotland and the British Library provides the Secretariat. The Group has been very active in preparing for the implementation of Conspectus in the member countries.

Constable Trophy. A biennial competition for an unpublished novel from the north of England; administered by Northern Arts, UK; publication by Constable & Co. Ltd. forms a part of the award.

Constance Lindsay Skinner Award. *See Women's National Book Association.*

Constant Mnemonics. *See Mnemonics.*

Consultancy and Research Unit. *See Centre for Research in User Studies.*

Consultant. *See Library Consultant, Information Consultant.*

Contact. A copy of a photograph or document made in direct contact with the original.

Contact Copying. A non-optical copying process whereby the original and the material of reproduction are brought into close contact during exposure. The resulting copy can be described as a 'contact copy' or 'contact print'. The opposite of OPTICAL COPYING (*q.v.*). *See also Contact Printing, Reflex Copying, Transmission Copying.*

Contact Printing. Any form of photographic or other copying method in which a sheet of sensitized material is held in firm and even contact with the original photographic negative or original document during exposure. The copying may be done by the direct or transmission method, or by the reflex method; the resulting print may be termed a 'contact copy'. *See also Contact Copying, Reflex Copying, Transmission Copying.*

Container Library Service. A service for providing library facilities in small urban communities as an alternative to a small static branch library or visits from mobile libraries or trailers. The containers are special portable buildings 36′ 6″ long and 8′ wide which are built to International Container Standards to withstand frequent loading and unloading. They are moved from site to site on a trailer drawn by a tractor (being off-loaded by two lifting arms (cranes) working simultaneously) and stay at each site – a car park – for two days at a time; each container serves three communities a week. The system was first used by the Cornwall County Library UK in 1973. *See also Mobile Library.*

Contemporary Binding. One that is contemporary with the printing of the book.

Contemporary Scientific Archives Centre. The aim of the Centre is to locate, preserve and make accessible the personal papers of contemporary scientists and technologists in all fields of work in science, engineering and medicine. A small management committee is concerned with administrative and financial control of the Centre, but its main task is to identify men of science who might have papers of historical importance and whose families might welcome a rescue service of this kind. Names are submitted to a Joint Committee on Scientific and Technological Records of the Royal Society and the Royal Commission on Historical Manuscripts which was formed in 1967 and which sponsored a pilot scheme.

Contents. Strictly, a 'table of contents' but seldom used in this form. 1. A list of the 'preliminaries' and chapter headings of a book in their correct order, or of articles in a periodical, with the numbers of the pages on which they begin. 2. A list of the musical works contained in a printed collection of music or in an album of recordings or of those recorded on a single record or cassette. 3. A list of items recorded on videotape.

Contents List. 1. The contents page of a periodical, or other publication. *See also Current Contents.* 2. *Synonymous with* CONTENTS (*q.v.*).

Contents List Bulletin. A periodical bulletin consisting of reproductions of copies of the contents pages of selected periodicals, and assembled into some form of cover. *See also Current Awareness Journal.*

Contents Note. A note appearing after the catalogue entry giving the headings of the chapters, parts, or volumes. In a descriptive bibliography it will indicate what is printed on each page included in the collation by gatherings.

Contents Page. The page, usually in the PRELIMINARIES (*q.v.*) of a book on which the table of contents is printed.

Context. (*Indexing*) The parts of a title of text that precede or follow the KEYWORD (*q.v.*), usually influencing its meaning.

Continuation. 1. A book only partly written by the original author and continued by someone else. 2. A work issued as a supplement to one already published. 3. A part issued in continuance of a serial, series or book. An order to supply subsequent parts as issued is called a 'Continuation Order'.

Continuation Card. 1. A card used for ordering a CONTINUATION (*q.v.*). 2. A CONTINUATION LIST (*q.v.*). 3. An EXTENSION CARD (*q.v.*).

Continuation List, Continuation Record. A list of all books such as annuals, series, and works issued in parts for which there are standing orders.

Continuation Order. An order to supply each succeeding issue of an annual or serial publication – a 'continuation' of an item already in stock. *See also Continuation.*

Continuation Register. *Synonymous with* CONTINUATION LIST (*q.v.*).

Continuing Education for Library and Information Management. *See CELIM.*

Continuity File. (*Archives*) *See Reading File.*

Continuous Feed. The action of an automatic sheet feeder attached to a printing press, folding, or other machine, so that the supply of sheets can be replenished without interrupting the operation of the machine.

Continuous Flow Camera. Apparatus for taking photographs, which automatically moves the originals and the film to be exposed after each exposure. Also called 'Flow camera', 'Rotary camera'.

Continuous-form Loan Records. Continuous stationery used where copies of the records of loans are required in non-public libraries. A carbon, or self-carbon paper is used, and the sets of paper are supplied printed and perforated. After each loan is recorded the set of papers is torn off and the separate pieces of paper are filed in different sequences under author, borrower's name, accession number, date, etc. as desired. Each piece is usually of a distinct colour to enable insertion in the correct file to be done easily.

Continuous Pagination. The use of one sequence of page numbering throughout a book or several parts or volumes.

Continuous Printer. A photographic printing apparatus for the reproduction of an original, from either a negative or positive on to sensitized film or paper, by a continuous movement of the material through the exposing and processing stages. During the exposing process, the film being copied and a roll of paper or film, are synchronized to move at the same speed past the printing aperature. *See also Optical Printer.*

Continuous Processing. Processing photographs or films in machines which automatically transport the photographic material through the required solutions, finally drying the product.

Continuous Revision. A multi-volume work, such as an extensive encyclopaedia, which is not completely revised and published as a new edition. Minor alterations or extensive additions or revisions are carried out for each printing, replacement and additional pages being inserted within the existing pagination by the addition of 'A, B, C,' etc. to the page numbers.

Continuous Stationery. Print-out paper used by computer installations; usually supplied many metres in length, folded and perforated at intervals of 28-30 cms. in full size configurations, but may be smaller in recent microcomputer systems.

Contour Line. One drawn on a map to connect points having the same elevation.

Contours. Lines drawn on a map to join all places at the same height above sea level. The intervals between contours may represent height differences from 50' to several thousand feet dependent on the scale of the map. On physical maps the areas between contours are often shown in different colours progressing from various shades of green for lowlands through browns to red and finally white. Depths of the sea bed are indicated by ISOBATHS (*q.v.*).

Contract Services. Items appearing in a library's statement of income and expenditure to record funds (a) received from a governmental, library, or other, agency for specific services rendered; (b) for services rendered to the library by individuals or agencies on the basis of a specific contract; (c) a library or information service provided for the use of members of a firm or organization by a local library service on contract for a fee.

Contraries. Any impurities in the waste paper, rags or other materials such as silk, feathers, wool, string, bones, pins, rubber, etc., to be used for paper- or board-making, and which are likely to be injurious.

Contrast. The difference between the high and low densities in a print, negative, or television picture.

Control Field. A FIELD (*q.v.*) in a machine-readable record which identifies a particular part of the data within that record. It may contain a TAG (*q.v.*).

Controlled Circulation. *See Routeing.*

Controlled Circulation Serial. A serial publication which is usually issued without charge and is only available to those whom the author or those responsible for its publication specify.

Controlled Indexing. Implies a careful selection of terminology so as to avoid, as far as possible, the scattering of related subjects under different headings. *See also Word Indexing.*

Controlled Term List. A term used in the indexing aspects of information retrieval which is equivalent to the AUTHORITY LIST (*q.v.*) in cataloguing; it is a list of terms which have a fixed and unalterable meaning, and from which a selection is made when indexing data or items in documents. The list may not be altered or extended. *See also Controlled Indexing, Open-ended Term List, Term.*

Convenience File. (*Archives*) Duplicates of documents, PERSONAL PAPERS (*q.v.*), or books, assembled for easy access and reference.

Convention Application. A patent application filed within ten months of the first application, and made for protection of the invention in any one of the countries signatory to the Paris Convention of 1883, and claiming priority accordingly. *See also Patent of Addition, Priority Date.*

Convention Concerning the Exchange of Official Publications and Government Documents Between States. A multilateral convention which was adopted by the General Conference of Unesco in December 1958, and came into force on 30 May 1961.

Convention Country. A country which is a signatory to the 1883 Paris Convention for the Protection of Industrial Property, and which is thereby bound to observe the international rules for protecting patents.

Convention Date. The date on which disclosure is made in an application for patent protection in any CONVENTION COUNTRY (*q.v.*) and therefore the date for which priority can subsequently be claimed when application is made in any other of the convention countries.

Conventional Foliage. A bookbinding ornament which is often quite unrealistic but obviously suggested by foliage.

Conventional Name. A name, other than the real or official name, by which a person, corporate body, thing or place has come to be familiarly known.

Conventional Title. A UNIFORM TITLE (*q.v.*) which is constructed from terms describing the form or subject of a work, and arranged in a generally accepted sequence. It is used mostly in cataloguing music, where, e.g. terms are arranged in the order given to describe the musical form of the composition, its instrumentation (sonata, concerto, trio, piano quartet, etc.), its position in a sequence of the composer's works, its key, its opus (or equivalent) number, and descriptive title or soubriquet.

Conversion. The process of changing the representation of information to a form which is usable by a computer, e.g. converting it to machine 'language'.

Cooks (Kathleen) Bequest. A substantial bequest (£50,000) made to the Library Association in 1982 by Kathleen Cooks, librarian of Llandudno

1947–73. Half of the Bequest is administered by the Welsh Library Association in support of Welsh library projects.

Cooper (Duff) Memorial Prize.   An annual UK award for a literary work of biography, history, politics, or poetry in English or French.

Co-operation.   *See Co-operative.*

Co-operative.   An association of libraries and similar institutions formed for mutual assistance and undertaking functions where the sharing of resources or division of costs can be advantageous and efficient. *See also Co-operative Training, Network, Regional Library Co-operation (UK).*

Co-operative Acquisition.   A system for organizing and co-ordinating acquisitions between two or more documentary organizations (library, archive or documentation centre) at a local, regional, national or international level to ensure that one copy of each publication is held in the geographical area concerned.

Co-operative Automation Group (UK).   Formed in 1980 to ensure the best structuring of services provided by the British Library and the automation co-operatives in the interests of libraries of all types. Representatives included members from the B.L., BLCMP, LASER, SCOLCAP, SWAL-CAP, Library Association, Aslib, SCONUL and COPOL. One study group was the Working Party on Access to the National Database (WAND) which examined problems of inter-computer communication. Proposed a UK Library Database System (UKLDS *q.v.*).

Co-operative Cataloguing.   The sharing by a number of libraries of the cost and/or labour of cataloguing to avoid the duplication of effort common to each. Not to be confused with CENTRALISED CATALOGUING (*q.v.*).

Co-operative Library Agency for Systems and Services.   CLASS, originally the California Library Authority for Systems and Services, is a national US library support-services marketing operation. Based in San Jose, California.

Co-operative of Indic Language LASER Libraries.   *See CILLA.*

Co-operative Publishers.   *See Vanity Publishers.*

Co-operative Purchasing.   An arrangement between several libraries whereby one of them, or a separate organization, purchases books for all of them in order to obtain books at a cheaper rate than is possible for individual libraries, because of the smaller number of copies, and therefore the less-advantageous terms, which the small libraries obtain.

Co-operative Training.   Schemes of co-operation between various types of libraries in a region, or similar libraries in a wider area, in the provision of TRAINING (*q.v.*). Co-operative training may be one function within the activities of a CO-OPERATIVE (*q.v.*) (UK examples include EMALINK [East Midlands Libraries in Co-operation]) or be the sole function of a training co-operative (UK examples include Welsh Libraries Training Group and SALCTG [Scottish Academic Libraries Co-operative Training Group]). *See also Regional Library Co-operation (UK).*

Co-ordinate.   (*Classification*) Specific terms subordinated to the same genus. *See also* CO-ORDINATE CLASSES.

Co-ordinate Classes. (*Classification*) 1. Classes which are correlated so that classes leading up to a subject come before it and those which develop from it, or are next in likeness or character, come after it. 2. Classes which are of the same order of SPECIFICATION (*q.v.*) and grade of division in a classification. (*Bliss*). 3. Classes belonging to the same ARRAY (*q.v.*).

Co-ordinate Indexing. 1. An indexing scheme whereby the inter-relations of terms are shown by coupling individual words. 2. A system of information retrieval in which the indexing or recording of information in, or characteristics of, a document are accomplished by entering a reference number (page number, report number, etc.) on a card (or a column of a card) which is reserved for, and bears the heading of, an individual term to which it is devoted. Also called 'Concept Co-ordination', 'Correlative indexing', 'Enriched co-ordinate indexing', 'Multiple aspect indexing', 'Synthetic indexing'. In 'grouped co-ordinate indexing', the accession number becomes the identifying number of a group of documents all of which are indexed by the same set of features. *See also Free Indexing, Uniterm Concept Co-ordination Indexing.*

Co-ordinate Relation. (*Information retrieval*) The relation between terms which are subordinate to the same term.

Co-ordination of Terms. The modulation from one term to another by gradual steps in order that the process of evolving a classification may exhibit its hierarchy or schedule.

Copal. A resinous substance obtained from various tropical trees, and used in the manufacture of varnish and printing inks.

COPANT. Abbreviation for the Pan American Standards Commission which was founded in 1961; it comprises national standards bodies in the USA and eleven Latin American countries. It is a co-ordinating organization concerned with the regional implementation of International Standards Organization and International Electro-technical Commission recommendations.

COPOL. The Council of Polytechnic Librarians was formed in 1970 to coincide with the designation of the majority of the thirty Polytechnics in April of that year. Its full members are the Chief Librarians of the 29 English polytechnics and of the Polytechnic of Wales. There are six Associate Members who are the Chief Librarians of the Scottish central institutions and two corresponding members, Hong Kong and Singapore Polytechnics. The Council (abbreviated to COPOL) is a forum for the exchange of ideas, information and expertise. It also acts as a pressure group on behalf of the polytechnic libraries, maintaining contacts with the Committee of Directors of Polytechnics, the Office of Arts and Libraries, the Library Association, the Joint Consultative Council, and LISC. It is represented on a wide range of professional committees and maintains particularly close links with SCONUL. Publishes *COPOL Newsletter* (3 p.a.), Directories, Working Papers, etc.

Copper Engraving. *See Engraving.*

Copper Plate. A plate used for ENGRAVING (*q.v.*) in which the drawing is incised with a burin.

Copperplate. A carefully written cursive script often used when inscribing the captions under engravings and used until recent times by writing masters as models for their pupils to copy.

Copy. 1. Matter for the printer to set up in type. 2. A single specimen of a printed book. 3. The material to be reproduced by photographic or other means; also the result of a reproduction process.

Copy Edit. The checking of a MS. by a publisher or printer before marking it up for the typesetter, for accuracy of facts, grammatical construction, possible libel, HOUSE STYLE (*q.v.*), etc.

Copy Fitting. (*Printing*) Adjusting 'copy' to the space available by changing the space allotment, the length of copy, or the size of type. *See also Copy 1.*

Copy Number (or Copy Letter). A figure or letter added to the call number of a book to distinguish different copies of the same book. *See also Book Number, Volume Number, Work Mark.*

Copy Preparation. (*Printing*) The act of preparing for the compositor a MS. which has been 'copy edited', by making the MS. legible and accurate, indicating printing style, type to be used, etc.

Copy-preparer. (*Printing*) One who is employed by a printer to translate a publication designer's typographical specification into instructions on the typescript.

Copy Reader. An employee at a printing works whose task is to prepare the copy for composition by marking the measure, sizes of type to be used for text, quotations, footnotes, etc. and check the author's consistency in the use of capitals, citation, spelling, punctuation and sentence structure.

Copy Slip. *See Process Slip.*

Copy-tax. *See also Legal Deposit.*

Copyholder. 1. A device attached to composing machines or used in conjunction with a typewriter to hold a MS. or 'copy'. 2. An assistant who reads the 'copy' to a proof reader. 3. A device which may be a simple board or an elaborate vacuum frame designed to hold the copy before the camera.

Copying Process. A process for making copies of documents on sensitized material. *See also Contact Copying, Diazotype Process, Electrophotographic Processes, Optical Copying, Positive Process, Rapid Copying, Reflex Copying, Thermal Process, Transmission Printing.*

Copyist. A person who transcribed MSS. prior to the introduction of printing.

Copyright. A procedure whereby the originator of a piece of intellectual property (book, article, piece of music, etc.) receives due recompense for the inventiveness or imagination expended. In England copyright was originally used by the Stationers' Company to protect publications issued by one member from piracy by another; it was a marketable commodity and could be traded or assigned between members. An author usually sold his rights to a publisher. In the US the right of the author was given greater emphasis. The changing world and multiplicity of items led to substantial changes in copyright legislation and international agreements; current technological advances (databases, video-recordings) have put copyright law under stress again. Four interests are now recognized: that of the creator, the publisher/distributor, the consumer, and society at large. The Universal Declaration of Human rights (Article 27, 2) states: 'Everyone has the right to protection of the moral and material interests resulting from any scientific, literary or artistic production of which he is the author'. The European viewpoint grants copyright to the creator by natural right only; Anglo-American law treats it as a privilege that can be passed on to successors in ownership; Eastern Europe sees the state as the ultimate beneficiary and minimizes the special interest of the creator.

International regulation between these groups and with the special needs of developing countries poses great difficultues. *See Copyright International.* In the UK the new *Copyright Design and Patent Act 1988* came into effect in 1989.

Copyright, International. International copyright is regulated by a number of agreements: these include (a) Berne Convention (The International Convention for the Protection of Literary and Artistic Works) concluded in 1886 and now ratified by 71 states. Revised 1948 (Brussels) and 1967 (Stockholm); the latter conference helped to integrate the system into the World Intellectual Property Organisation (WIPO) (*q.v.*). *See also Berne Copyright Union.* (b) Inter-American Conventions (Montevideo 1889, Mexico City 1902, Rio de Janeiro 1906, Buenos Aires 1910, Havana 1928, Washington 1946). (c) Universal Copyright Convention; convened by Unesco in 1952, came into effect in 1955. UCC agreed that copyright should be secured by the simple procedure of a single notice comprising the symbol ©, the name of the copyright proprietor, and the year of first publication. (d) Paris revision (1971) A reworking of (c) that came into effect in 1974. The Commission of the European Community issued a green paper *Copyright and the Challenge of Technology* in June 1988. *See also IGC, ICIC.*

Copyright Clearance Center (US). The Center was established in 1977 in response to the (US) Copyright Act of 1976 by a group of authors, publishers and users of copyright material. The Center, based at Salem, Mass., acts as a mechanism so that authorizations to photocopy copyright material can be readily obtained from copyright owners. A computerized royalty fee collection and distribution system invoices users at fee rates set by the publishers. Abbreviated CCC.

Copyright Date. The date copyright was granted for an individual work. This is usually printed on the verso of the title page of books. If several dates are given, they signify changes in the text, or renewals of copyright. The first copyright date indicates the date of the first edition of a book and corresponds to the imprint date of the original edition. *See also Berne Convention, Copyright, Copyright, International.*

Copyright Deposit. The deposition of free copies of a book or musical composition in a COPYRIGHT LIBRARY (*q.v.*) according to law. *See also Legal Deposit.*

Copyright Fee.   Fee paid to the holder of a copyright for the right to use his material for a particular purpose, e.g. to include a poem in an anthology or to read it in public, or to play a piece of music, or a record of the same, in public.

Copyright Libraries Shared Cataloguing Programme.   The six UK Copyright Deposit Libraries began a pilot programme in 1989 to examine co-operative creation of bibliographic records for the national UKMARC and BNBMARC files. A full operational programme is planned for 1991.

Copyright Library.   A library which is entitled under copyright laws to receive a free copy of any or every book published in the country. In the UK, Section 15 of the Copyright Act, 1911 provides that the publisher of every book (including 'sheet of letterpress, sheet of music, map . . .'), is, within one month after publication, to deliver, at his own expense, a copy of the book to the British Library, and also if written demand is made before the expiration of twelve months after publication, to send a copy to the Bodleian Library, Oxford; the University Library, Cambridge; the National Library of Scotland, Edinburgh – except that law books are to be transmitted to the Faculty of Advocates to be vested in their Law Library (National Library of Scotland Act, 1925); Trinity College, Dublin, and with certain exceptions, the National Library of Wales, Aberystwyth. These exceptions are designed to exclude books published in small editions unless they are written in Welsh or relate wholly or mainly to the Welsh or other Celtic peoples or to the natural history of Wales. In October 1972 the British copyright libraries, other than the BRITISH LIBRARY (*q.v.*) agreed in principle that they would attempt, as a last resort, to satisfy requests that the British Library Document Supply Centre was unable to meet from its own and the other non-copyright library resources to which it had access.

Copyright Licensing Agency (UK).   Set up by publishers and authors as a collecting agency to receive notional fees from Local Education Authorities for photocopying of copyright material. An experimental period began late in 1984 and a permanent scheme started in April 1986. Abbreviated CLA.

Copyright List.   A list of the books deposited in a library under the copyright laws.

Copyright Users Forum.   An informal grouping of major users of copyright materials brought together to safeguard user rights during current activities of the Copyright Licensing Agency. Members include Aslib, CET, Library Association and the Royal Society. *See also Educational Copyright Users Forum.*

Copywriter.   A writer of advertisements.

Coranto.   1. The earliest form of newspaper, consisting of one leaf in small folio, the text being in two columns on each side of the leaf. Published first in Holland and Germany, and in England in 1620 and 1621, such publications were known by the name coranto, whether published in England or on the continent. They were issued at least once a week as a half-sheet in folio, and only foreign news was printed.   2. Sometimes the word Coranto is used to include Newsbooks which were published until 1642. *See also Newsbook,*

Relation. Nathaniel Butter began a *Newes* on 2 August 1622, and in October 1622 commenced publishing with Nicholas Bourne and William Sheffard *A Coranto*; these were numbered serially.

Cording Quires. *See Cassie.*

Cordonnier Cards. *See Peek-a-boo.*

Cordovan Leather. Goatskin, originally tanned and dressed at Cordova, Spain. Used for MUDÉJAR BINDINGS (*q.v.*), and often dyed red. The English name is 'Cordwain'.

Cords. Heavy strings to which the sections of large and heavy books are bound. Sometimes called BANDS (*q.v.*). *See also Tapes.*

Cordwain. *Synonymous with* CORDOVAN LEATHER (*q.v.*).

Core. *See Memory.*

Corner-marked Card. A catalogue card bearing in the top right-hand corner information such as language, date of publication, editor, or translator, or a combination of these where there are many entries under the same heading. The purpose is to facilitate rapid perusal of a number of cards at one reading. Sometimes the original title of a translated work is written in the upper right-hand corner so that original and translations may be filed together.

Corner Marking. The original title of a translated work placed in the upper right-hand corner of a catalogue card so that the original and the translation will be filed together. A reference is required from the translation title to the original. Alternatively, translations may be entered on the same card as the original title, or in other words the original title may appear above the translation, a reference under the translation title being optional but desirable.

Cornerpiece. 1. (*Binding*) An ornament, usually arabesque, designed to be used at the corners of a bound book, usually to match a centre-piece or other decoration. Also used of metal corners attached to the binding. Also called 'Cornerstamp'. 2. (*Bibliography*) Interlacing bars, 'cusping' or other separate ornament at the corner of a border around type, or lettering of an illuminated manuscript.

Corners. 1. The leather over the corners of a book in 'half' binding. *See also Library Corner, Mitred Corner, Square Corner.* 2. In printing, ornamental type metal connecting borders. 3. Pieces of metal or pasteboard to slip over the corners of a book to protect them in the post. Also called 'Cornerpieces'.

Cornerstamp. *Synonymous with* CORNERPIECE (*q.v.*).

Corporate Author. A corporate body such as a government or government department, a society (learned, social, etc.), or an institution which authorizes the publication of documents, and under the name of which, as the author, the documents will be entered in a catalogue. In certain kinds of corporate authorship, entries are made under the *place* followed by the *name* of the body.

Corporate Body. An institution, organized body, or assembly of persons known by a corporate or collective name.

Corporate Entry. A catalogue entry made under a government, government department, society or institution or other body, of a work issued by that body, or under its authority.

Corporate Name. The name by which a corporate body is known.

Corporate Publishing. *See Desktop Publishing.*

Corporation File. *See Company File.*

Corrected Edition. A new edition of a book in which errors, etc., have been corrected.

Corrected Proof. A printer's proof on which errors in typesetting have been marked, using the generally accepted code of correction-marks. *See also Proof, Proof Corrections.*

Correction Marks. The signs used on a printer's proof to mark errors in typesetting. These are set out in British Standard 5261: Part 2: 1976 *Copy preparation and proof correction. See Proof Corrections.*

Correlation. A systematic or reciprocal connexion – sometimes, the establishment of a mutual or reciprocal relation.

Correlation of Properties. In classification the likeness between the various qualities which are common to all the things comprised by a genus.

Correlative Index. An index enabling selection of documents or of references to them by correlation of words, numbers, or other symbols which are usually unrelated by hierarchic organization. *See also Classified Index, Co-ordinate Indexing.*

Correlative System. A non-conventional indexing or retrieval system in which any descriptor can be combined with any other, to indicate the subject content of a document.

Correspondence Management. (*Archives*) The application of the techniques of archive administration to correspondence.

Corrigenda. (*Sing.* Corrigendum). A printed list of corrections of errors which were noticed after matter was printed. It is usually printed on a slip and inserted among the PRELIMINARIES (*q.v.*) but sometimes a blank page is used. Also called 'Errata'. *See also Paste-In.*

Corrupt a Text. To tamper with a text by omission, addition, or alteration in order to convey a meaning which was not intended by the original author. This is sometimes done to standard or modern works for political propaganda.

Cortex. A microcomputer based system developed by the British Library to support information retrieval and cataloguing services on BLAISE.

COSATI. Acronym of the Committee on Scientific and Technical Information of the Federal Council for Science and Technology (FCST). *See also SATCOM.* It was set up by the US Government as the principle mechanism by which the views of individual agencies can be obtained and a consensus reached on desirable Federal programmes.

COSINE. Co-operation for Open Systems Interconnection Networking in Europe; a working party of major European research network users, aiming to facilitate an advanced communications network for scientific and industrial research institutes.

COSTED. Committee of Science and Technology in Developing Countries; a part of the International Council of Scientific Unions (ICSU) formed to encourage and co-ordinate international efforts to assist scientific development in third-world countries.

Costeriana. Fragments of books, having the appearance of early printing and asserted to have been printed before 1473, and consisting mostly of editions of the *Donatus*, or the *Doctrinale*. These were supposed to have been printed by Laurens Janszoon Coster of Haarlem (1405–84) who was thought at one time to have invented printing with movable types in or about 1440.

Cottage Binding. *Synonymous with* COTTAGE STYLE (*q.v.*).

Cottage Style. A decorative binding in which the centre panel was often given a gable at head and foot, and the spaces filled with a variety of interlacings, sprays, and small 'tools'. Although this style may have originated in France, it is most characteristic of English bindings of the late seventeenth century to 1710. Also called 'Cottage binding'. *See also Mearne Style.*

Cotton Linters. The short fibres adhering to the cotton seed after ginning (separating the seeds from the fibre), and also obtained as 'recovered' fibres from the cotton seed oil and cake factories. When purified it is used for paper-making. It can be used to replace 5–35 per cent of the rag content of fine papers without lessening the strength of the paper; it improves uniformity and the colour properties of the paper, and provides a cleaner, bulkier sheet. It is also used in the cheaper kinds of blotting paper used for interleaving diaries and account books.

Couch Roll. That part of a Fourdrinier paper making machine which removes some of the moisture from the sheet of paper during manufacture.

Council for National Academic Awards (UK). The Council awards degrees and other academic qualifications, comparable in standard with those granted by universities, to students successfully completing approved courses in Polytechnics and other institutions of higher education. Abbreviated CNAA.

Council of City Research and Information Libraries. *See COCRIL.*

Council of Europe. Established in 1949 to work for greater European unity, uphold democracy and human rights and improve living standards. The 22 members are Austria, Belgium, Cyprus, Denmark, Finland, France, West Germany, Greece, Iceland, Ireland, Italy, Liechtenstein, Luxembourg, Malta, Netherlands, Norway, Portugal, Spain, Sweden, Switzerland, Turkey, and UK. Unlike the EUROPEAN COMMUNITY (*q.v.*), the Council of Europe depends on voluntary co-operation; the institutions are the Committee of Ministers, the Secretariat, and the Parliamentary Assembly. Headquarters are in Strasbourg, France. Library-related matters fall to the Council for Cultural Co-operation, the executive body of the European Cultural Convention which has been ratified by all member states and by San Marino, the Vatican, and Yugoslavia.

Council of National Library and Information Associations. Founded in 1942 'to promote a closer relationship among the national library associations of the United States and Canada by providing a central agency to foster co-operation in matters of mutual interest, by gathering and exchanging information among its member associations, and by co-operating with learned, professional and scientific societies in forwarding matters of common interest'. Membership is open to national associations of the USA and Canada as well as those in related fields. Abbreviated CNLA. *See also* Z39.

Council of Planning Librarians.   Founded in the USA in 1960 by a group of planning librarians associated with schools of planning and planning agencies during the annual convention of the American Institute of Planners. Abbreviated CPL.

Council on Bibliographic Data Transfer.   Proposed new name for the NATIONAL FORUM ON BIBLIOGRAPHIC STANDARDS (*q.v.*); under discussion early 1989.

Council on Library/Media Technical Assistants.   *See COLT.*

Council on Library Resources.   A US foundation established in 1956 to put 'emerging technologies to use in order to improve operating performance and expand library services'. After an exploratory period, the thrust of that mandate was gradually concentrated on the application of computers to bibliographic processes and has since expanded to include the utilization of technology in all aspects of library operations. Over the years, additional program components have been added. Library management began to receive serious attention when universities entered the period of growth that dominated the 1960s and made libraries the costly and complex enterprises they are today. Subsequently, other topics, including the academic role of libraries, international aspects of library operations, professional and continuing education for librarians, preservation of library materials, consortial undertakings, and specialized bibliographical services have been added to the Council's agenda. As an operating foundation, CLR both manages programs and grants funds to others – academic institutions, organizations, and individuals.

Counter.   1. *Synonymous with* CIRCULATION DESK (*q.v.*).   2. (*Printing*) The interior 'white' of a letter; it may be entirely enclosed by a bowl as in 'O' or it may be the sunken part of the face as 'M' 'E' 'n'. The angular corner is known as the 'crotch'. The distance from the face to the bottom of the counter is known as the 'depth of counter'.

Counter Duty.   Duties performed in the counter area of a library.

Countermark.   A smaller and subsidiary WATERMARK (*q.v.*) found in antique papers, usually in the centre, or lower centre of the second half of a sheet and opposite the watermark. Border or corner positions are not uncommon. It usually comprises the name or initials of the maker (in the UK), and in later times, the mill number and the date (first in 1545) and place of making, although small devices such as a small post-horn or cabalistic signs have been found.

Countersunk.   A binding having a panel sunk or depressed below the normal level of the binding to take a label, inlay or decoration.

County Headquarters.   The administrative centre for a county library system.

County Libraries Group. A Group of the (British) Library Association; it existed until January 1975 to unite the interests of those working in county libraries of the UK, to provide for the expression of opinion and for liaison with the parent body. It was formed in 1927 as the County Libraries Section, the name being changed when the present constitution of the Library Association came into operation in 1963. This Group combined with the PUBLIC LIBRARIES GROUP (*q.v.*) from January 1975.

County Library. A library provided to supply the reading needs of people dwelling in a county. In America, a free public library service provided for county residents and financed from county tax funds; it may be administered as an independent agency or in co-operation with another library agency.

County Record Office. A RECORD OFFICE (*q.v.*) which is required by law to be set up in England by every county council.

County Schools Library. An instructional materials library maintained in America by a county superintendent of schools who provides materials and services to contracting schools.

Courants. Dutch news publications, related but not numbered, known to have existed since the year 1607. *See also Coranto, Newsbook.*

Court. A standard size for cards, $3\frac{1}{2} \times 4\frac{1}{2}$ inches; envelopes are $3\frac{3}{4} \times 4\frac{3}{4}$ inches.

Court Baron. Court held by the Lord of a Manor in virtue of his right as a land holder, in which offences against the customs of the manor could be published but no punishments involving the life or limbs of the subject could be inflicted.

Court Hand. 1. Style of writing used in legal and other public documents. Generally used of 'hands' from about 1100 to the end of the sixteenth century. 2. Sometimes used to mean legal hands of the same period only.

Court Leet. Court of Record to punish all offences under High treason, not incidental to a manor, but frequently held by a Lord of a Manor by virtue of a special grant.

Court Roll. A roll on which records of cases in private courts such as a Court Baron or Court Leet were kept.

Courtesy Storage. *See Deposit.*

Cover. 1. That which is placed securely on a sewn or stapled publication to protect it in use; it may be of paper or cloth, or board covered with paper, cloth or leather. The cover of a 'hard cover' book (as distinct from a 'paperback') is known as a 'case' or 'publisher's case'. 2. The outside sheet of a pamphlet, or the case of a book, used to protect the body of the work. 'Front cover', and 'back cover' relate to the side pieces or outsides of the boards of the cover.

Cover Date. The date which appears on the cover of a publication, usually a pamphlet.

Cover Paper. A generic term usually indicative of a strong, coloured paper with good folding qualities suitable for brochure, booklet, pamphlet and price-list covers. Cover papers are available in a variety of embossings as well as plain. Sizes:

	inches
Cover Double Crown	$20\frac{1}{2} \times 30\frac{1}{2}$
Cover Medium	$18\frac{1}{2} \times 23\frac{1}{2}$
Cover Royal	$20\frac{1}{2} \times 25\frac{1}{2}$
Double Crown	20×30
Double Medium	23×36
Double Royal	25×40
Imperial	22×30
Quad Crown	30×40

Cover Pocket. *Synonymous with* POCKET (*q.v.*).

Cover Title. The title of a book placed on a publisher's case, or as distinguished from that printed on the title-page. Not to be confused with the BINDER'S TITLE (*q.v.*). *See also Back Title.*

Cover to Cover Translation. A serial publication which contains in each issue a translation of the whole, or a major part, of an issue of a serial publication in another language.

Covers Bound in. The original covers of a publication bound in, or to be bound in, when a book is re-bound.

CPL. COUNCIL OF PLANNING LIBRARIANS (*q.v.*).

CPU. *See Central Processing Unit.*

Crabs. Books returned to a publisher by a bookseller because he had been unable to sell them. Also called 'Returns'.

Crackle. *See Rattle.*

Cradle Books. *See Incunabula.*

Cranfield Project. *See Aslib Cranfield Research Project.*

Crash. *Synonymous with* MULL (*q.v.*).

Crash Finish. A cover paper which is similar to Linen Finish (*q.v.*) but has a coarser texture.

Crawshay (Rose Mary) Prize. An annual award made by the British Academy for an historical or critical work by a woman on English literature.

Crayon Drawing. A drawing made with a soft, black crayon, usually for strong or impressionistic effects. It is suitable for illustrations, portraits, etc., and may be reproduced by half-tone.

Crayon Engraving. A similar process to STIPPLE (*q.v.*) but aiming to produce the effect of a chalk drawing. Various specially grained roulettes, etching needles, and a *mattoir* (a form of miniature cudgel) are used through the etching ground to prepare the printing plate for biting with acid. The graver and roulette may be used afterwards directly on the surface of the plate. Also called 'Chalk engraving'.

Creasey (John) Memorial Award. *See Crime Writers' Association.*

Creasing. 1. A linear indentation made by machine in a card or thick paper. By compressing the fibres it provides a hinge and increases the number of times the paper can be flexed at the crease before breaking. *See also Scoring.* 2. A printing fault, seen as deep creases; it may result from storing the paper at an incorrect humidity, or from other causes.

Credit. A statement of the authorship, cast, and those associated with the production of a radio, television, film or videotape programme.

Credit Line. A statement giving the name of an artist, photographer, author, agency, or owner of an original or of copyright, and printed under a photograph, drawing, article or quotation which is reproduced or published.

Cresting Roll. A ROLL (*q.v.*) which has, on one side of the design, a series of crests or tufts, the other side being approximately straight. *See also Heraldic Cresting.*

CRG. Classification Research Group (*q.v.*).

CRIB. *Current Research in Britain*; British Library produced title, issued annually in four volumes; formerly *Research in British Universities, Polytechnics and Colleges* (*RBUPC*).

Criblé Initial. A decorated initial used at the beginning of a chapter, specially by the sixteenth-century French printer Geoffrey Tory, in which the capital appears on an all-over ground of small dots, or sieve-like pattern.

Criblé Metal Cut. A soft metal used late in the fifteenth century for block printing instead of wood, the metal being punched with holes (criblé) to relieve the black mass. *See also Manière Criblée.*

CRILIS. *See Current Research in Library and Information Science.*

Crime Writers' Association. A UK organization responsible for several annual literary awards, viz: Cartier Diamond Dagger Award (outstanding title), John Creasey Memorial Award (best crime novel by an unpublished author), Gold and Silver Dagger Awards for Fiction (best crime novels published in the UK), and Sunday Express Magazine/Veuve Cliquot Short Story Competition (best unpublished short story).

Critical Annotation. *Synonymous with* EVALUATION (*q.v.*).

Critical Apparatus. *Synonymous with* APPARATUS CRITICUS (*q.v.*).

Critical Bibliography. 1. The comparative and historical study of the make-up of books (*Besterman*). 2. The science of the material transmission of literary texts (*Greg.*) Also called 'Analytical' or 'Historical' bibliography. *See also Bibliography.*

Critical Edition. A scholarly text of a work, established by an editor after original research, and the comparison of manuscripts, documents, letters and earlier texts. This editorial work is considerable, especially in textual criticism. The edition is characterized by the APPARATUS CRITICUS (*q.v.*) included. *See also Standard Edition, Variorum Edition, Definitive Edition.*

Criticism Number. *See Associated Book.*

CRL. CENTER FOR RESEARCH LIBRARIES (*q.v.*).

Crocketed Cresting. (*Binding*) A frame formed by roughly rectangular stamps ornamented with crockets (small curved designs) or with roughly triangular stamps, which, placed together and pointing outwards, give a cresting effect.

CRONOS. *See EUROSTAT.*

Cropped. 1. In bookbinding, a term applied to a book when too much of its margin, especially the head-margin, has been trimmed off and the type area mutilated. *See also Bled, Cut, Shaved, Trimmed, Uncut.* 2. A photograph of which a part of the top, bottom or sides is omitted from its reproduction, in order to bring it into proper proportions for the space it is to occupy.

Cropper. A small printing machine working on the platen principle; so named after the English manufacturer H. S. Cropper & Co. who produced the 'Minerva' machine in 1867; this was similar to the 'Franklin Press' manufactured by George Phineas Gordon, a small master printer of New York.

Cropping. (*Printing*) Masking, or trimming off portions of an illustration to eliminate unimportant detail and to obtain desired proportion.

Cross-bars. Metal bars used to divide a CHASE (*q.v.*) into sections of equal size, each of which contains the same number of pages. They enable the pages to be locked up more securely, and also make corrections in one section easier while not disturbing the others.

Cross Classification. 1. The action of dividing when forming a scheme of classification by more than one characteristic in a single process of division, leading to confusion of ideas and terms and resulting in the parts having no real relationship to one another, and in placing related subjects in different divisions. 2. A TABULAR CLASSIFICATION (*q.v.*), or one that is reducible to tabular form, in which the classes or sub-classes of each series are crossed by the terms of a secondary series of specifications, so that the resulting sub-classes have the specifications of both series and are therefore common to both.

Cross Direction. Said of paper which is cut across, that is, cut at right angles to the direction in which the web of a paper machine moves. The cross direction of the paper is much weaker, and expands more, than in the direction parallel to the flow of the pulp on the machine. *See also Against the Grain, Grain Direction, With the Grain.*

Cross Division. *Synonymous with* CROSS CLASSIFICATION (*q.v.*).

Cross Hatching. (*Binding*) Two sets of parallel lines executed in opposite directions so that the lines cross.

Cross-Head. A short descriptive heading placed in the centre of a type line to divide the sections of a work, or the chapters of a book. Cross-heads are separated from the text by one or more lines of space, and normally indicate primary sub-divisions of a chapter. Subsequent sub-divisions are: shoulder-heads and side-heads. *See also Heading 4, Shoulder Head, Side Head.*

Cross-Index. To make an index entry under several headings, where appropriate, for the same item.

Cross-Reference, General. *See General Reference.*

Cross-Reference Card. The catalogue card on which a cross-reference is entered.

Cross-Reference Sheet.   A record on a pro forma sheet recording the filing of related material in other files. It may refer to (a) a specific publication, (b) part of a publication, (c) specific facts in a given publication.

Cross-References.   In indexing and cataloguing, references or directions from one heading to another.   1. *Single* (*see* —). An instruction to look elsewhere for *all* items relating to the subject matter which is sought.   2. *Reciprocal* (*see also* —). An instruction to look elsewhere for *other* items relating to the subject matter sought.   3. *Multiple* (*see also* —). An instruction to refer to several other places, usually to more specific entries.   4. References in the text of a book to other parts of the same book. *See also General Reference.*

Crotch.   (*Printing*) The angular corner of the Counter (*q.v.*) of a type letter.

Crown.   A sheet of printing paper measuring 15 × 20 inches.

Crown Copyright.   Copyright that is vested in the British Crown when any work, whether published or unpublished, has been made by, or under the direction or control of, the Sovereign or any Government department.

Crown Octavo.   A book size, 7½ × 5 inches. *See also Book Sizes.*

Crown Quarto.   a book size 10 × 7½ inches. *See also Book Sizes.*

CRUS.   *See Centre for Research in User Studies.*

Crushed Levant.   A large-grained Levant (*q.v.*) leather binding with a smooth, polished surface, caused by crushing down the natural grain.

Crushed Morocco.   Morocco, the grain of which has been smoothed by hand. *See also Glazed Morocco.*

Cryptography.   Writing in cipher.

Cryptonym.   A secret name.

Cryptonymous Book.   One in which the name of the author is concealed under an anagram or similar device, e.g. Mesrat Merligogels (Master George Mills).

CSIRO.   Commonwealth scientific and industrial research organization (*q.v.*).

CSL.   Circle of state librarians (*q.v.*).

CSLA.   Church and Synagogue Library Association (*q.v.*). Canadian School Library Association (*q.v.*) (a Division of the Canadian Library Association).

CTFE.   Colleges of technology and further education (*q.v.*). (A Group of the Library Association.)

CTI.   *See Current Technology Index.*

Cue System.   A system, proposed to be used in bibliography and indexing, consisting of alphabetical codes placed above an entry to indicate the chronological, topical, and geographic aspects of the article referred to.

CUG.   *See Closed User Group.*

Cuir Bouilli.   Book decoration in which the leather cover is soaked in hot water, modelled and hammered to raise the design in relief; it sets very hard, and in the ninth century it was found to be so hard that boards were unnecessary.

Cuir-Ciselé Binding. A binding with a design cut into dampened leather instead of being stamped or tooled on it. A relief effect was then obtained by punching the leather around the design. Hammering from the back gave an embossed effect. A widely-practised method in fifteenth-century Germany.

CUKT. *See Carnegie United Kingdom Trust.*

Cul-de-lampe. A form of decorative printing practised in the sixteenth century which used arabesque title-borders and tail-peices strongly suggestive of metal lantern-supports. A tail-piece. J. B. M. Papillon (1698-1776), the most distinguished member of a family of French wood-engravers, was renowned for the delicacy in his minute floral head- and tail-pieces (culs-de-lampe), which decorate many mid-eighteenth-century French books.

Cullen Report. *See BTECC.*

Cum Licentia. *Synonymous with* CUM PRIVILEGIO (*q.v.*).

Cum Privilegio. (*Lat.* 'with permission') Printed by authority, either secular or ecclesiastical. Sole authority for printing.

Cumdach. A rectangular box (usually of bronze, brass or wood, and plated with ornamented silver or gold), which was made for the preservation of precious books. Also called 'Book shrine'.

Cumulated Volume. A publication consisting of entries for a bibliography, catalogue, index, etc., which have previously appeared in periodically published parts, and re-assembled into one sequence.

Cumulation. The progressive inter-filing of items arranged in a predetermined order and usually published in periodical form, the same order of arrangement being maintained.

Cumulative Book Index. An author-title-subject international bibliography of books published in the English language. Published eleven times per year, with an annual cumulation, by the H. W. Wilson Company of New York. Available also online, and on CD–ROM. Abbreviated CBI.

Cumulative Index. One which is built up from time to time by combining separately published indexes into one sequence.

Cumulative List. A list of books published separately and afterwards incorporated in other similar lists which in their turn may have been compiled in the same way.

Cuneiform Writing. Wedge-shaped letters in which Old Persian and Babylonian inscriptions were written, so termed from their wedge-like appearance and made by pressing the end of a stick or reed into the soft clay of the tablet at an angle and continuing the stroke in a straight line with constantly diminishing pressure.

Cunningham Memorial Fellowship. A fellowship offered by the Medical Library Association (USA) to qualified medical librarians outside North America to enable them to spend a six-month period in the USA or Canada.

Curator. The superintendent of a museum, art gallery, etc.

Curators. Name given to boards of people responsible for managing the various institutions of Oxford University. The Curators of the Bodleian Library, for example, number eighteen, namely, the Vice-Chancellor, the Proctors or their deputies, seven members of Congregation elected by that

House, six professors elected by the professors of the various faculties, and two members of Congregation elected by Council, one of whom must be a Curator of the Chest; these are elected to serve for ten years, and are entrusted with the general control of the affairs of the library, including the appointment of a librarian, and of other officers, subject to the approval of Convocation, and are responsible for the expenditure of all sums accruing to them through the University Chest or otherwise.

Curia Regis. Under feudal organization a court of justice, or administration was called a 'curia'; Curia Regis was the Court of the Norman Kings of England.

Curiosa. Term used in describing books of curious and unusual subject matter. Sometimes used euphemistically as a classification for *erotica*.

CURL. A deformation of a sheet of paper or board over its whole surface so that it tends to roll up into the form of a cylinder.

CURL. Consortium of University Research Libraries (UK); a grouping of very large academic libraries formed in 1982 to facilitate development of their common interests. Members are the libraries of the Universities of Cambridge, Edinburgh, Glasgow, Leeds, London, Manchester, and Oxford. In 1988 a two-year programme was initiated with University Grants Committee funds to create a CURL database using the bibliographic records of the seven members; access would be via JANET and the target date for full operation is mid 1990.

Current Awareness. A system, and often a publication, for notifying current documents to users of libraries and information services, e.g. selective dissemination of information, bulletin, indexing service, current literature. The term is sometimes used synonymously for SDI.

Current Awareness Journal. A periodical consisting of reproductions in facsimile of contents tables of many individual journals.

Current Bibliography. A list of books which is compiled at the same time as the books are published. It is usually published as a periodical. Sometimes called 'Open bibliography'.

Current Complete National Bibliography. A complete list of published or issued records of a nation; such a list can be complete only to a specified date. A current national bibliography is a listing of publications compiled at the time of publication and falling within the definition of a NATIONAL BIBLIOGRAPHY (*q.v.*).

Current Comprehensive Bibliography. The technique of making available, through current bibliographical services, informative lists of the totality of publications in particular categories defined solely by (a) recency of publication; (b) type of issuing agency; (c) the geographical area or political jurisdiction within which they were produced; but not by their contents (e.g. literary form or subject-content) or distribution (e.g. location of copies). *See also Current Selective Bibliography.*

Current Contents. A registered trade mark of the Institute of Scientific Information; used in their publications which reproduce the contents pages of periodicals.

Current Number.   The last-issued number of a newspaper or serial publication and bearing the most recent issue number and/or date. Also called 'Current issue'.

Current Publication Survey.   *See Literature Survey 2.*

Current Records.   The records which are necessary for conducting the day-to-day work of an office or business, and which must therefore be kept readily accessible.

Current Research in Library and Information Science.   A quarterly publication of the (British) Library Association recording research activity in the fields of librarianship, information science, documentation and archives, including academic research, and investigations, studies and surveys organized by libraries, etc. The fourth part of each volume is an annual cumulation. Available via DIALOG, and on CD–ROM. Contributions regularly included from 31 countries, and the UN and EEC. Abbreviated *CRILIS*. (Replaced *Radials Bulletin*, and began publication in 1983.)

Current Selective Bibliography.   The technique of making available, through current bibliographical services, informative lists of publications in particular categories defined by (a) recency of publication, (b) some one or more characteristics of the publications. The usual characteristics are content (e.g. literary form, subject), distribution (e.g. location of copies), and value. *See also Current Comprehensive Bibliography, Select Bibliography.*

Current Technology Index.   The successor to *British Technology Index*; began 1981; published 12 times per year, with an annual cumulation, by the Library Association, this index covers the fields of general technology, applied science, engineering, chemical technology, manufactures and technical services. Abbreviated CTI. An additional feature is the Catchword and Trade Name Index (CATNI) which provides a quick reference, non-technical index. CATNI is published four times per year as a supplement to *Current Technology Index*, the fourth part being an annual cumulation. Available online with DIALOG, and on CD–ROM.

Currently Received.   Periodicals which are received on publication.

Curriculum Materials Center.   A centre, usually located in an American school central administration building, in which are kept professional books, current and back numbers of teaching professional periodicals, microfilms, recordings, supplementary textbooks, art prints mounted on cardboard, pamphlets, fabrics, filmstrips, models, and possibly high school and elementary school books (which may be borrowed for the children). The materials are issued to teachers only.

Cursive.   1. Running writing, letters within words being joined.   2. Sometimes used to differentiate smaller 'hands' from uncial.   3. A class of type face which is based on handwriting. It may be ITALIC (*q.v.*) in which there is a version of almost every named type face or script which is drawn to look as though handwritten. Kaufman Script, Trafton Script and Typo Script are names of script type faces. *See also Type Face.*

Cursor.   On a VDU screen, a cursor is a point of light which can be moved by the user via a keyboard, to indicate characters needing amendment or removal, or to specify where a new character is to appear.

Curves. ( ) Signs used to denote inserted explanatory or qualifying words, phrases, clauses or remarks. To be distinguished from BRACKETS (*q.v.*). Also called 'Round brackets' and PARENTHESES (*q.v.*). *See also Brackets, Circular Brackets.*

Custodian. A person in charge of a special collection or of a building in which exhibits are displayed.

Custom-bound. (*Binding*) A book which is bound to specific instructions, not in accordance with general instructions.

Cut. (*Noun*) 1. A design cut or engraved on wood, copper, or steel from which a print is made. 2. The impression from such a printing block. 3. An engraving, or plate, printed on the text page. 4. (*Verb*) To trim the edges of a book. 5. (*Adjective*) Of a book having cut edges. *See also Cut Edges, Opened, Plate.*

Cut Corner Pamphlet File. A free-standing box file which has the upper back corners of the sides cut away to half the height of the box; the upper half of the back as well as the top are unenclosed. Such boxes are used for containing pamphlets on the shelves.

Cut Dummy. Complete proofs of the illustrations of a book, arranged in proper sequence and containing the figure and galley numbers.

Cut Edges. (*Binding*) The top, fore, and tail edges of a book cut solid by a guillotine. When gilt they are known as 'gilt edges'. *See also Edges.*

Cut Flush. A book having its cover and edges quite even, the cutting operation having been done after the cover (usually paper-boards or limp cloth) had been attached to the book. Also called 'Stiffened and cut flush'. A book so made is described as with 'flush boards'.

Cut In-boards. A book which has had the head, tail and fore-edge trimmed after the boards have been secured. *See also Cut Out-of-Boards.*

Cut-in-Heading. A paragraph or section heading set in a bold or otherwise distinguishing type in a space made available against the outer margin but within the normal type area. Also called 'Incut heading'. *See also Incut Note.*

Cut-in Index. *Synonymous with* THUMB INDEX (*q.v.*).

Cut-in Letter. One of a large size, and occupying the depth of two or more lines of type as at the beginning of a chapter or paragraph. See also Cock-Up Initial, Drop Letter.

Cut-in Note. *Synonymous with* INCUT NOTE (*q.v.*).

Cut-in Side Note. *Synonymous with* INCUT NOTE (*q.v.*).

Cut Line. Matter appearing below an illustration. More often called a 'Caption'.

Cut-out Half-tone. *See Half Tone.*

Cut Out-of-boards. A book which has had its edges cut or trimmed before the boards are affixed. This method is used for books with a hollow back, the boards of which are not laced on but fit closely in the grooves. *See also Cut In-Boards, Lacing-In.*

Cut to Register. Watermarked paper which has been so cut that the watermark appears in the same position in each sheet.

Cutter Author Marks. A system of author marks devised by C. A. Cutter, and consisting of from one to three letters at the beginning of an author's name, followed by numbers which increase as the names proceed along the alphabet. Author's names beginning with a consonant other than S have one letter, with S or a vowel have two letters, and Sc have three letters, followed in each case by a number, e.g.:

AB2	Abbot	G42	Gilman	SA1	Saint
AL12	Aldridge	SCH51	Schneider	SW1	Swain
G16	Gardiner	SCH86	Schwarts		

Their purpose is to enable books to be arranged alphabetically by using a relatively brief symbol. *See also Author Mark, Book Number, Cutter–Sanborn Three-figure Table, Three Number Author Table.*

Cutter Classification. *See Expansive Classification.*

Cutter Numbers. *See Cutter Author Marks.*

Cutter–Sanborn Three-figure Table. An extension of the Cutter Author Marks for individualizing authors by using a combination of letters and three numbers (two for J, K, Y, Z, E, I, U, O; one for Q and X) in numerical order. For example:

Rol 744	Roli 748	Roman 758
Role 745	Roll 749	Romani 759
Rolf 746	Rolle 751	
Rolfe 747	Rollo 755	

Cutter's Objects. The 'objects' of a dictionary catalogue as adumbrated by Charles Ammi Cutter in his *Rules for a dictionary catalogue*, 1875, are: (i) to enable a person to find a book of which either (a) the author, (b) the title, (c) the subject is known; (ii) to show what the library has (d) by a given author, (e) on a given subject, (f) in a given kind of literature; (iii) to assist in the choice of a book (g) as to its edition (bibliographically), (h) as to its character (literary or topical).

Cutting. A piece cut from a newspaper or periodical. Also called 'Clipping' (American), 'Press cutting'.

Cuttings Bureau. *See Clipping Bureau.*

Cuttings File. *Synonymous with* CLIPPINGS FILE *(q.v.).*

Cybernetics. The science of control and communication processes in animals and machines.

Cyclic Classified Catalogue. *See Rotated Catalogue.*

Cyclic Index. *Synonymous with* ROTATED INDEX *(q.v.).*

Cyclopaedia. *Synonymous with* ENCYCLOPAEDIA *(q.v.).*

Cylinder Dried. Paper which has been dried on the papermaking machine by being passed over steam-heated cylinders, as distinct from other methods of drying. Also called 'Machine-dried'.

Cylinder Press. A printing press which makes the impression by cylinder as opposed to platen. It has a revolving impression cylinder under which is a flat bed containing the type of plates which moves backwards and forwards. These presses can be of two types; the Wharfedale or stop-cylinder press in which for every sheet printed, the cylinder makes almost one complete revolution and stops while the bed returns, an opening in the cylinder allowing the bed to return freely, and the Miehle or two-revolution press in which a smaller and continuously revolving cylinder revolves once to print one sheet then rises and revolves once more while the type bed slides back into position. This type of machine is the best letterpress machine for colour-printing and book-work. *See also Flat-Bed Press, Platen Press, Rotary Press.*

Cyril Barnard Memorial Prize. *See Barnard Memorial Prize, Cyril.*

Cyrillic Alphabet. The form of writing used for the Russian language. Originally used by the Eastern Church and supposedly devised by St. Cyril.

Dagger. (†). The second reference mark in footnotes, coming after the asterisk. When placed before an English, or after a German, person's name, it signifies 'dead' or 'died'. *See also Reference Marks.*

Daguerreotype. A means of making a photographic image on a copper plate coated with a light-sensitive layer of silver. The process was invented by Louis Jacques Mandé Daguerre (1789–1851) in 1833 following the death of J. N. Niepce, with whom he had been in partnership, but not made public until 1839. The earliest daguerreotypes are unique in that they cannot be copied, but the process was superseded in the 1850s by a negative positive process by which an unlimited number of copies may be made. The process is considered to be the first really practicable photographic method. Daguerre was a French scene-painter who became well known as a result of the diorama he built in Paris in 1822; after 1826 he devoted himself to developing photographic processes.

Daily. A serial publication issued every day, except perhaps on Sunday.

Dainton Lecture. Initiated by the British Library Science, Technology and Industry division in honour of Lord Dainton, who himself gave the first of the annual series in 1987.

Dainton Report. The Report of the (British) National Libraries Committee of which Dr. F. S. (later Sir Frederick, then Lord) Dainton was chairman, was published in June 1969. The main recommendations were incorporated in a White Paper, entitled *The British Library*, and published on 13 January 1971. The subsequent *British Library Bill* implemented these proposals, which were mainly: (i) a board comprising a chairman and up to 13 members, would be created to manage and develop the British Library resulting from the amalgamation of the library departments of the British Museum, including the National Reference Library of Science and Invention, with the National Central Library, the National Lending Library for Science and Technology, and the *British National Bibliography*; (ii) councils would be appointed to advise on the needs of the Library's users. *See also British Library.*

Damaged Letter. A piece of type, the printing surface of which has been damaged. When appearing in a printer's proof it is marked by an X in the margin. Also called 'Bad letter', 'Battered letter', 'Broken letter', 'Spoiled letter'.

Dampers. The damping rollers which are an important part of lithographic printing presses; they damp the printing plate after each impression with a fluid, known as a damping mixture, the composition of which varies according to the material used for the forme (stone, zinc, steel, aluminium, etc.), in order to prevent the ink adhering to the plate, which it would do if the plate became too dry. In a hand-press damping is done with a sponge.

Dandy Roll. A cylinder of wire gauze which presses upon the drained but still moist pulp just before it leaves the wire cloth of the paper-making machine for the rollers. The weaving of the wire of the dandy roll leaves its impression on the paper and determines whether it is to be wove paper (with the impression of fine, even gauze) or laid paper (with the impression of parallel lines). When devices or monograms are worked into the fine wire of the roll, 'watermarks' are produced.

Daniel Press. A private printing press established by the Rev. C. H. O. Daniel at Frome in 1846, revived at Worcester College, Oxford, in 1874 and used until he died in 1919 for the private publication of family verses as well as small pamphlets and books. In 1877 he discovered the punches, matrices and types which had been used by Dr. Fell at the University Press between 1667–74 and used them at his press. *See also Fell Types.*

Danish Library Association (Danmarks Biblioteks-Forening). Formed 1905. Based in Copenhagen. Aims to further the development of libraries in Denmark. Publishes *Bogens Verden* (10 p.a.), yearbook and directory.

Dartmouth Medal. An annual award for achievement in creating new reference works of outstanding quality and significance. Presented under the auspices of the American Library Association. First awarded 1974.

Dash. A short strip of rule cast in the following lengths, and used for punctuation: the two-em dash ——; the one-em dash —; the en rule –; and the hyphen -. These may be used for decoration or for the clearer laying out of printed matter, but usually longer rules or ornamental rules are more often used for these purposes. *See also Border, French Rule, Rule, Swung Dash.*

Dash Entry. Said of an entry for a book – following one or two long dashes (one for the author, the second for the title) – which continues, indexes, or supplements a monograph. Such an entry follows the entry for the main work in a printed bibliography or catalogue.

Data. A general term for information; particularly used for information stored in a database.

Databank. Usually synonymous with DATABASE (*q.v.*) but sometimes used to specify collections of numeric data only.

Database. Information stored on computer files, or on CD-ROM. A database might contain bibliographic data, or numerical, statistical material, etc., and may be assembled and marketed commercially, or by an organization, library, or individual. Data is generally structured so that it can be sought and retrieved automatically. Access to an online database may be obtained via a 'host'. *See also Data Protection.*

Database Management Systems. Software packages for the creation and maintenance of databases. Abbreviated DBMS.

Data Compilation. The regular and systematic recording of information discovered in a variety of miscellaneous publications.

Data Processing. The handling or manipulation of data by computerized means.

Data Protection (UK). In 1970 the British Government appointed the Younger Committee on Privacy to examine the threat to privacy by the rapid growth in the use of computers, with their ability to process and link at high speed information about individuals. The Committee reported in 1972, and certain principles were set out.

In 1975 the Government issued two white papers: *Computers and Privacy* (Cmnd. 6353) and *Computers: safeguards for privacy* (Cmnd. 6354); a Data Protection Committee under the chairmanship of Sir Norman Lindop was appointed to advise on legislation, and reported in 1978 (Cmnd. 7341). The British Government in 1981 signed the Council of Europe Convention on Data Protection, and the OECD guidelines on privacy protection. In 1982 the Home Office presented the white paper *Data Protection: the Government's proposals for legislation* (Cmnd. 8539). The *Data Protection Bill* was presented in March 1983, but was abandoned with the calling of the General Election. A revised Bill was introduced in July 1983. This new Bill was enacted as the *Data Protection Act 1984*, subtitled 'an Act to regulate the use of automatically produced information relating to individuals and the provision of services in respect of such information'. The Act which runs to 44 pages, provides for the appointment of a Data Protection Registrar to operate the mechanism of data protection, and requires any organization collecting personal data to register. Libraries using mechanized files need to register: catalogues and databases are included under the Act, as well as data on staff and users. The Registry is based at Wilmslow, Cheshire. The 'appointed day' marking the commencement of registration was 11 November 1985.

Data Storage and Retrieval System. One which stores items for later re-use rather than modification, and which usually maintains the file items unaltered.

Data Validation Routine. (*Information retrieval*) A program written to check the validity or the consistency of data.

Datacentralen. *See DC.*

Data-Star. A SWISS-BASED HOST (*q.v.*) providing a large range of databases at a competitive price.

Dataview. Swedish videotex system.

Date. The statement in a book, either at the foot of the title-page, or on the reverse thereof, of the year in which the book was published. (*Cataloguing*) A filing element appearing in a heading and consisting of the date(s) of birth and/or death of a person whose name is the main element in the name heading. *See also Colophon, Copyright Date, Dedication Date, False Date, Imprint Date, Mainz Psalter.*

Date Card. *See Date Label.*

Date Due. The date on which a book is due for return to a library.

Date Guide.   A guide bearing numerals representing the dates on which books are due for return and placed in front of the appropriate charges in the issue trays, when using the Browne system.

Date Label.   The label placed in a lending library book and dated to indicate when it is due for return. In a few libraries dates of issue are used instead. Also called in America a 'Date slip' or 'Dating slip'. Sometimes a loose card, called a 'date card', is used. *See also Transaction Card.*

Date Line.   The line in any paper or magazine on which the date of issue appears.

Date of Issue.   The date on which a book was issued.

Date of Publication.   1. The year in which a book was published. it is usually printed at the foot of, or on the back of, the title-page. In old books a date often formed part of the colophon.   2. The day and/or month and year of publication in the case of a newspaper or other periodical.   3. The exact date a document was released to the public. *See also Copyright Date.*

Date Slip (Dating Slip).   A DATE LABEL (*q.v.*).

Date Stamp.   1. The date a library book is due for return (or of issue) which is stamped on a transaction card or date label.   2. The machine or dater used to make the impression.

Datum.   (*Information retrieval*) The smallest element of information. A BIT (*q.v.*).

David Committee.   The Committee of Enquiry into School Book Supply (Chaired by Baroness David) was convened by the Booksellers and Publishers' Associations (UK) in 1979. The Report 'The Supply of Books to Schools and Colleges' was published in 1981, and considered methods of direct supply of books to local authorities from publishers.

Dawson Award for Innovation in Academic Librarianship.   A biennial award open to professional staff in academic libraries for any aspect of library activity. Sponsored by Wm. Dawson and Sons Ltd., and first presented in 1988.

Day of Publication.   *See Publication Day.*

dBase.   A microcomputer-based software package for the creation, maintenance, updating and searching of databases. There have been several revised versions; popular in small libraries for housekeeping routines.

DBI.   *See Deutsches Bibliotheksinstitut.*

DBMS.   *See Database Management Systems.*

DBS.   *See Satellite Broadcasting.*

d.c.   Abbreviation for a page of printed matter set in Double Column; Double Crown (paper 20 × 30 inches); Double Cap (i.e. double foolscap) printing paper, 17 × 27 inches.

DC.   1. Decimal Classification (*q.v.*).   2. Datacentralen, a Danish host connected to DATAPAK (Danish packet switching network), offering a range of services from its Copenhagen base.

DDC.   1. Defense Documentation Center.   2. Dewey Decimal Classification (*qq.v.*)

De Luxe Binding. A fine leather binding, lettered and tooled by hand. So-called de luxe bindings are often machine products.

De Luxe Edition. An edition of a book in which especially good materials and fine workmanship have been used.

De Vinne. A type face cut for Theodore Low De Vinne, 1828–1914, a distinguished American printer. He was a co-founder with Robert Hoe in 1884 of the Grolier Club and printed its first publication, a reprint of the *Star Chamber Decree*, 1637. He encouraged New York printing house owners to form a union which, when combined with similar groups from other cities, became known in 1887 as the United Typothetae.

De-acidification. The process which raises the pH value for paper documents to a minimum of 7.0 to assist in their preservation. This process is usually carried out before thermoplastic lamination of documents. *See also pH Value.*

Dead File. In acquisition work, a file containing (1) cards for books received and catalogued, (2) cards for books not available as gifts or by purchase despite considerable correspondence, (3) completed or filled cards for serial publications.

Dead Matter. (*Printing*) Type matter or plates which have been used for printing but are not to be used again and may therefore be distributed or melted. *See also Good, Killing, Live Matter, Matter.*

Decalcomania. 1. A transfer or design printed on special paper for transfer to pottery or some other permanent base. 2. The paper for printing such transfers on. 3. The process of printing illustrations on glass, wood, pottery, etc. Abbreviated DECAL.

Decimal Classification. There have been several schemes which have employed decimals in some way but the one usually referred to by this name is that compiled by Melvil Dewey and published in 1876, in which it is the notation that is used decimally. In this scheme it is possible to extend the printed scheme at any point to any desired extent. It divides knowledge into ten main classes and is the most used classification for general libraries. Abbreviated DC. *See also Abridged Decimal Classification, Dewey Decimal Classification, Universal Decimal Classification.*

Decimal Division. The expansion of a portion of a classification schedule and giving the resulting terms a numerical notation on the decimal principle.

Decimal Notation. A notation used to identify subjects in a scheme of classification; it consists of numerals used decimally so as to permit the logical subdivision of subjects, or a chain of classes, indefinitely. The notation of the Dewey Classification is of this kind. *See also Notation.*

Decimal Number. The number of a book, or of a term, in a classification schedule, which is determined by the decimal principle. This method is used in both the Dewey Classification and the Universal Decimal Classification.

Decimo-octavo. *Synonymous with* Octodecimo, Eighteen-mo (*q.v.*).

Decimo-sexto. *Synonymous with* Sexto-Decimo (*q.v.*).

Deck. One floor of a stack containing book shelves, lifts, and workrooms (American).

Deckle.   1. Abbreviation for DECKLE EDGE (*q. v.*), and for deckle strap.   2. The frame or border, usually of wood, which confines the paper pulp to the mould when making paper by hand.   3. In the paper-making machine, the distance between the two deckle straps.

Deckle Edge.   The feathery edge at the borders of a sheet of handmade or mould-made paper; it is caused by the deckle or frame which confines the paper pulp to the mould. It is also found in machine-made papers, being caused in these by the rubber deckle straps at the sides of the paper machine, or by artificial means such as a jet of water. Also called 'Feather-edge'.

Deckle Straps.   Endless rubber bands which run on both sides of the wire cloth of a paper-making machine in order to keep the wet pulp within the desired limits of width. Also called 'Boundary straps'.

Declassify.   To remove a secret or confidential document from a security classification under proper authorization. *See also Downgrade.*

Decoder.   In information retrieval, the locater which searches and extracts items from the DOCUMENT STORE (*q. v.*).

Decorated Cover.   The front cover of a book which bears distinctive lettering or an illustration or design.

Decorative.   A class of type faces which have exaggerated characteristics of the other three classes, ABSTRACT, CURSIVE and ROMAN (*qq. v.*), or distinctive features which preclude them from being included in those classes. They are usually fussily ornamental, but included in this group is OLD ENGLISH (*q. v.*).

Decreasing Concreteness, Principle of.   A general principle for choosing an order of application of the characteristics of a classification. Ranganathan has developed a general facet formula which reflects this principle and is popularly known by the abbreviation PMEST standing for the five 'fundamental categories' Personality, Matter, Energy, Space and Time.

Dedicated Line.   A telephone line reserved for connecting a terminal directly to a computer.

Dedicated Space.   (*Information retrieval*) Space, left empty in a computer memory for the representation of new data integrated into an information retrieval system.

Dedication.   The author's inscription to a person or persons testifying respect, and often recommending the work to his (or their) special protection and favour, it usually appears on the recto of the leaf following the title-page. In sixteenth- and seventeenth-century books the dedication often took the form of a dedicatory letter written by the author to his patron.

Dedication Copy.   A copy of a book presented by the author, and so inscribed, to the person to whom the work is dedicated.

Dedication Date.   The date given at the beginning or end of a dedication.

Dedicatory Letter.   *See Dedication.*

Deep-Etched Half-Tone.   *See Half-Tone.*

Deep Etching.   In photo-engraving, additional etching made necessary to secure proper printing depth where this cannot be accomplished by routing, as in places where dense black lines are used, or where line negatives and half-tone negatives are combined in the same place. *See also Etching.*

Defaulter. A reader who fails to return a book or pay a fine.

Defence Research Information Centre. *See DRIC.*

Defense Documentation Center. *See Defense Technical Information Center.*

Defense Technical Information Center (USA). In October 1979 the Defense Documentation Center became the Defense Technical Information Center (DTIC) and its role was redefined. While still responsible for the interchange of Department of Defense (DoD) scientific, technical and management information, the main role of the DTIC is now to provide new and improved technical information services to the defense research and development community. Issues newsletters, and operates a getaway service to 400 DoD databases.

Deferred Cataloguing. The postponement by a library of the full cataloguing of less important material, brief catalogue entries being made and possibly separately arranged temporarily to serve as a finding medium.

Definition. (*Classification*) Concise description in distinct terms for essentials and characteristics.

Definitive Edition. The final authoritative text of the complete works of an author – the nearest possible approach to what the author intended – edited usually after the author's death. It is characterized by its editorial introduction, notes and sometimes APPARATUS CRITICUS (*q.v.*). Not to be confused with a VARIORUM EDITION (*q.v.*). Applies also to the works of a composer of music.

Degradation. In a computer database, the quality of the records held may be adversely affected by poor imputting, lack of checking, erroneous deletions; such loss of quality is termed degradation.

Degressive Bibliography. Varying the details of a bibliographical description according to the difference in the period treated or the importance of the publication described.

Degressive Description. *Synonymous with* SELECTIVE CATALOGUING (*q.v.*).

del, delt. Abbreviation for delineavit (*Lat.* 'he or she drew it'). Used on engravings, maps, etc. and followed by the name of the artist or cartographer responsible for the original drawings. *See also Fecit, Sculpt.*

Delayed Discharging. Delaying the cancellation of a loan until after the reader returning a book has left the counter. This is done as a normal part of the routine in some libraries, but in others discharging is only delayed during very busy periods, it being the usual practice to discharge books immediately they are returned. *See also Cheque Book Charging Method, Islington Charging System, Transaction Card Charging.*

dele. *See Delete.*

deleatur (*Lat.* 'delete'). *See Delete.*

Delete. To blot out, to erase, to omit. A mark, like the Greek letter δ, used in correcting proofs, is put in the margin to show that certain letters or words crossed through are to be deleted. Often abbreviated 'del', 'dele', or δ (representing the lower case initial letter of the Latin 'deleatur').

Deletion Mark. The mark used in correcting a proof to indicate matter to be omitted. Also called 'Cancellation mark'. *See also Delete.*

Deletion Record. (*Information retrieval*) A new record which will replace, or cause the removal of, an existing record in a MASTER FILE (*q.v.*).

Delimiter. (*Information retrieval*) A symbol (i) separating data elements within a FIELD (*q.v.*) or (ii) separating fields.

Deliquescence. Tendency to absorb atmospheric moisture.

Delivery Desk. *Synonymous with* CIRCULATION DESK (*q.v.*).

Delivery Room. In American libraries, the room in which books are returned and issued.

Delivery Station. A library service point at which no books are shelved but to which books requested by readers are sent to await collection.

Deloitte-Bookseller Award. An annual competition for the best book cover design; presented at the London International Book Fair.

Delphes. A French network of economic information, concentrating on markets, industry, products, companies, French and international economy: scans 800 French and international periodicals. Produced under the direction of the French Chambers of Commerce and Industry.

Delphi. In contemporary operations research, a prophetic method of forecasting technique whereby experts solicit the opinions of a group of advisers through a series of carefully designed questionnaires. The experts reply to the questionnaires, receive statistical feedback and resubmit their estimates. The process is repeated more than once. This Delphi approach has been used to predict trends for periods as far as fifty years ahead, e.g. an environmental forecast for research libraries in Sweden. The name originates from the Delphic Oracle of classical times, presided over by Apollo, the god of the sun, prophecy, music, medicine and poetry.

DELTA. Development of European Learning through Technological Advance. A European Community programme covering learning systems research and training efficiency; initial phase 1988–90 will probably be followed by a main plan.

Demco Self-Charging System. A simplification of the NEWARK CHARGING SYSTEM (*q.v.*) in which reader's tickets are not used. The borrower enters his ticket number on the next vacant line of the book card; this is checked by the assistant who stamps the date label.

Demonym. A popular or ordinary qualification used as a pseudonym, as 'An Amateur', 'A Bibliophile'.

Demopleth Map. A type of CHOROPLETH MAP (*q.v.*) which shows distribution by civil divisions.

Demy. A standard size of printing paper, 17½ × 22½ inches, and of writing and drawing paper (also called 'small demy') 15½ × 20 inches. *See also Octavo, Paper Sizes.*

Demy Octavo. A book size, 8¾ × 5⅝ inches. *See also Book Sizes.*

Denotation. *See Connotation.*

Denotative. See Connotation.

Densitometer. A photoelectric instrument for measuring the density, or degree or blackness, of a photographic image. A reflection-densitometer is used to measure the density of an opaque surface (print) before setting the camera and screen for half-tone exposure. Measuring the optical density of ink films during printing is done with a similar instrument.

Density. In documentary reproduction, the degree of photographic opacity. The degree of opacity of films and blackness of prints (the light-absorbing quality of a photographic image); it is usually expressed as the logarithm of opacity.

Dentelle. Lace-like tooling on the borders of a book cover, placed near the edges and pointing towards the centre. The most notable binders working in this style were the Derome family and Pierre-Paul Dubuisson who was appointed binder to Louis XV in 1758.

Dentelle à l'oiseau. Dentelle bindings in which birds are introduced into the design of the borders; chief executant was N. D. Derome. *See also Derome Style.*

Denudation. (*Classification*) The formation of a chain of classes by the application of successive characteristics of division.

Department. 1. A section of a library devoted to one subject as in a DEPARTMENTALIZED LIBRARY (*q.v.*), or to one kind of service, as a 'Reference library'. 2. An administrative section of a library which has one function or series of functions, such as 'Cataloguing department'. In America sometimes called a 'Division'.

Department of Technical Processes. *See Processing Department.*

Departmental Catalogue. A catalogue consisting of entries for books in one department only of a library.

Departmental Library. A library in a college or university which is apart from the main library and restricted to one subject or group of subjects. Also called 'Branch library', 'Faculty library', 'Laboratory collection', 'Office collection', 'Seminar collection'.

Departmental Publications. Those Non-Parliamentary Publications published and made available from the Departments of the British Central Government or through HM Stationery Office, whether printed by HM Stationery Office as the Government's printer or not.

Departmental Publishing. *See Desktop Publishing.*

Departmentalized Library. A large library in which all the material on each broad subject, whether for reference or lending, is kept in separate rooms or clearly defined sections. Also called SUBJECT DEPARTMENT (*q.v.*).

Dependent Work. A term used by cataloguers to indicate a work which is related in some way to a work by another author already published. It may be a modification, adaptation or amplification of the earlier work; the term includes such writings as abridgements, commentaries, continuations, dramatizations, librettos, parodies, revisions, selections, sequels and supplements.

Deposit. Documents which have been placed in a record office, usually for reasons of security but also to make them more readily avialable for consultation, the depositor retaining ownership. Sometimes called 'courtesy storage'.

Deposit Collection. A collection of materials from a single publisher, or owner, placed in a library organization as a collection and so that they may be made available to the public. The depositor often prescribes regulations for access.

Deposit Copy. A copy of a newly published book, pamphlet or periodical, etc., which is sent to one or more libraries, as required by law, and sometimes to complete copyright protection in the country. *See Depository Library.*

Deposit Library. 1. (*Archives*) A library in which documents are deposited under special conditions. 2. A library to which books and other publications are sent by the publishers for permanent preservation under the provisions of national copyright or legal deposit legislation; also called a COPYRIGHT LIBRARY (*q.v.*).

Depositors. Readers who pay a deposit, in lieu of obtaining a guarantee, to enable them to borrow books from a library.

Depository Catalogue. A copy of a national library catalogue, such as that of the Library of Congress, which is deposited in selected libraries.

Depository Library. In the UK, a library which is entitled by law to receive a free copy of every book published. In America, a library which is entitled to receive all, or selected, United States government publications. *See also Copyright Library, Deposit Library.*

Depth Classification. 1. Classifying so minutely that the most specific subject in all its aspects is identified and dealt with fully and accurately. 2. Classification schedules that have been sufficiently worked out to meet the needs of MICRO-THOUGHT (*q.v.*), of libraries for specialist materials and users, and of documentation. *See also Close Classification.*

Depth Indexing. Indexing as fully as possible by making specific entries for all the subjects, persons, places, books, etc. mentioned in the text.

Depth of Strike. *See Bevel.*

Deputy Librarian. The chief assistant librarian. One who becomes acting chief librarian in all absences of the principal. Also called 'Sub-librarian'. Sometimes called 'Associate librarian' in America.

Dequeker System. (*Information retrieval*) The first information searching system to be introduced. It consisted of cards with rows of holes punched in the body of the cards and filed on their edges in a cabinet. Rods were inserted through the holes corresponding to the codes for the subject of an enquiry, and a half-turn of a handle operated a mechanism to raise slightly above the level of the remainder of the cards those bearing the codes required. *See also Edge-notched Cards, Marginal-hole Punched Cards, Punched Card.*

Derivative Bibliography. Used synonymously for selective or subject bibliographies of the secondary type, and sometimes for retrospective bibliographies. *See also Bibliography, Primary Bibliography, Retrospective Bibliography, Secondary Bibliography.*

Derivative Work. A WORK (*q.v.*), e.g. extracts, anthology, abridgement, adaptation, translation, revision, compilation, arrangement of a musical work, which is the result of adapting, arranging, translating or transforming an INTELLECTUAL WORK (*q.v.*). The copyright of a derived work is protected without affecting the copyright of the original, provided that the choice, the presentation, or the form, represents the personal work of the author.

Derome Style. A style of book decoration practised by the Derome family in France in the eighteenth century. It is mainly confined to symmetrical corner tooling of a very richly engraved floreated scroll work, pertaining very closely to the roccoco style of the Louis period. Nicholas Denis Derome (1731–88) who worked for Count Hoym is famous for his Dentelle borders. *See also Dentelle.*

Descender. The vertical descending stem of lower-case letters such as j, p, q, etc.; that part which extends below the 'X'-HEIGHT (*q.v.*). *See also Ascender.*

Descriptive Bibliography. The area of bibliography which makes known precisely the material conditions of books, that is, the full name of the author, the exact title of the work, the date and place of publication, the publisher's and printer's names, the format, the pagination, typographical particulars, illustrations and the price, and for old books, other characteristics such as the kind of paper, binding, etc. Also called 'Analytical bibliography', 'Physical bibliography'. *See also Historical Bibliography.*

Descriptive Cataloguing. That part of the cataloguing process which is concerned with the choice and form of entries, transcription of title-page details, collation, etc. The term was coined by the survey committee at the Library of Congress in 1940. *See also Subject Cataloguing.*

Descriptive List. (*Archives*) A list of documents, with a brief description of the contents of each, sufficient to enable the researcher to determine whether it is likely to provide the information needed.

Descriptor. (*Information retrieval*) 1. An elementary term used to identify a subject. 2. A simple word or phrase used as a subject. 3. A word, translatable into a code, or symbol, which is given to a document to describe it and by means of which it can be discovered when required. Also called 'Code', 'Semantic factor'. It may be a subject heading or a class number. 4. (*Cataloguing. Indexing*) A descriptive designation added to a heading in a catalogue entry or index entry to distinguish otherwise identical headings. A type of ADDITIONAL DESIGNATION (*q.v.*). *See also Subject Heading, Thesaurus, Unit Record.*

Descriptor Association List. (*Information retrieval*) A list of descriptors associated with a particular descriptor, or with a group of particular descriptors, in an information retrieval system.

Descriptor Field. (*Information retrieval*) The area of subject matter covered by descriptors. *See also Descriptor Group.*

Descriptor File. A file, or sequence, of Unit Records (*q.v.*), i.e. DESCRIPTORS (*q.v.*) followed by their relevant supplementary information.

Descriptor Group. (*Information retrieval*) A subdivision of a DESCRIPTOR FIELD (*q.v.*).

Descriptor Language. A standardized indexing vocabulary comprising descriptors and used to describe documents, or their contents. A controlled descriptor language economizes on the number of symbols used in the descriptor file, standardizes subject description, maximizes the probability of retrieving all documents relative to an enquiry and none that are irrelevant, and provides for specific reference and generic survey to the extent needed by the users.

Descriptor Network. (*Information retrieval*) A diagram illustrating the logical relations between descriptors.

Descriptor Sequence. (*Information retrieval*) A controlled COMBINATION ORDER (*q.v.*) of descriptors. *See also Distributed Facets.*

Desensitization. Applying a solution, called an 'etch' (of nitric acid and gum arabic for stone; gum arabic, chromic acid and phosphoric acid for zinc; gum arabic and phosphoric acid for aluminium) to a lithographic printing plate after an image has been transferred to it, to desensitize the non-image areas, remove stray traces of grease from them, and increase the moisture-retaining capacity.

Desiderata. 1. A list of subjects on which the author of a book requires information. If only one is required the singular form 'desideratum' is used. 2. A list of books required.

Design. (*Verb*) To plan the entire format of a book. (*Noun*) The specification for the format of a book.

Designation Mark. Letters corresponding to the initial letters of the title of a book, and the volume number (if any), which are sometimes printed alongside the SIGNATURE MARK (*q.v.*) on each section to help the binder identify the sections belonging to a particular title. *See also Direction Line.*

Desk. *Synonymous with* CIRCULATION DESK (*q.v.*).

Desk Schedule. A schedule arranged to show the assignments of staff to each desk or department in a library. (*American.*)

Desktop Publishing. A combination of software and hardware which enables the production of professional standard documents at a fraction of the cost of traditional methods. It comprises word processing facilities, graphic design capability and printing techniques, and all input can be viewed and manipulated on a microcomputer display screen. Also called office publishing, in-house publishing, departmental publishing, corporate publishing. Abbreviated DTP. ELECTRONIC PUBLISHING (*q.v.*) is not to be confused with DTP although the terms are sometimes used synonymously.

Destination Slips. Pieces of paper which project from books in the Order Department or Cataloguing Department to indicate by their colour or marking to which libraries they are allocated.

Destruction Schedule. A list of documents, or of types of document, which may be destroyed as of no further value after the expiry of a specified term of years, the promulgation of the list being authority to destroy.

Detroit Self-Charging System. A simplified form of the NEWARK CHARGING SYSTEM (*q.v.*), the borrowers themselves making some of the records.

Deutsche Gesellschaft für Dokumentation. Founded in 1948 and based in Frankfurt am Main; 1200 members comprise authors, publishers and other information suppliers, archives, libraries, documentation departments, hosts, information agencies, software producers, information and system consulting agencies, organizers of education and training, and all other participants in the field of knowledge processing. DGD promotes research in documentation, development of methods and tools, and promotes education and training of information specialists. Specialized committees cover classification and thesaurus research, artificial intelligence, patent documentation, terminology, technical communication, economic efficiency, etc. Publishes *Nachrickten für Dokumentation* (6 p.a.) and reports of conferences and meetings.

Deutsches Biblioteksinstitut. The German Library Institute, based in West Berlin, is funded by the Federal Government and is principally concerned to develop and test software systems for library applications. DBI also offers host facilities for various bibliographic databases, especially those of the Staatsbibliothek Preussicher Kulturbesitz in Berlin.

Device. An emblem or monogram used by a printer or publisher to identify his work. It is usually used as part of the printer's IMPRINT (*q.v.*) or publisher's name on the title-page or spine.

Devil. *See Willow.*

Dewey Decimal Classification. The classification devised by Melvil Dewey (1851–1931) in 1873, and first published anonymously in 1876, since when it has been revised nineteen times. Knowledge is divided into the following main classes: 0, General works; 1, Philosophy; 2, Religion; 3, Sociology; 4, Philology; 5, Natural Science; 6, Useful Arts; 7, Fine Arts; 8, Literature; 9, History. The notation is a pure one, being based on three figures and used decimally. Sub-division by form is facilitated by the use of a table of common sub-divisions; the linguistic numbers from 420–499 and the geographical numbers from 940–999 are used mnemonically to subdivide by language and place. The relative index is original, and shows the relation of each subject indexed to a larger subject (or class or division), or after the entry word the phase of the subject is indicated. The schedules were considerably extended in each successive edition until the fifteenth 'Standard' Edition (1951) which was published after Dewey's death and was a much attenuated edition, being designed for a small library. In this, the simplified spelling which Dewey had always used was discontinued. The sixteenth edition was published in 1958, the seventeenth in 1965, the eighteenth in 1971, the nineteenth in 1979, and the twentieth in 1989. DDC is published by Forest Press, formerly a division of the Lake Placid Foundation, but acquired by OCLC in 1988. There is an Editorial Policy Committee representing the libraries using DDC, and the actual editing is done under contract by the Library of Congress. *See also Add Instructions, Divide Like The Classification, Division of DDC, Universal Decimal Classification.*

Dewey Medal, Melvil. Donated by Forest Press, Inc., this annual award, consisting of a medal and citation of achievement, is made to an individual or a group for recent creative professional achievement of a high order, particularly in those fields in which Melvil Dewey was so actively interested, notably library management, library training, cataloguing and classification, and the tools and techniques of librarianship. The award is administered by the ALA Awards Committee which appoints a jury of five to make the selection. The Medal was first awarded (in 1953) to Ralph R. Shaw.

DGD. *See Deutsche Gesellschaft für Dokumentation.*

DG XIII. *See Directorate-General XIII.*

Diachronous.   In user and citation studies, referring to changes that occur with the passage of time as revealed by observations made on two or more separate occasions. *See also Synchronous.*

Diacritical Mark.   A mark, such as an accent, placed over or under a letter to express some special phonetic value.

Diaeresis.   Two dots placed over the second of two consecutive vowels to show that they are to be pronounced separately, as Chloë, coöperate. In English it is now an obsolescent symbol, having been replaced by the hyphen (co-operate).

Diagonal Fraction.   The separation of the numerator from the denominator by an oblique stroke instead of a horizontal one, e.g. 1/2.

diagr.   (*Pl.* diagrs.) Abbreviation for DIAGRAM (*q.v.*).

Diagram.   As distinct from an illustration proper, a diagram gives only the general outline or plan of the thing represented. Abbreviated diagr.

DIALOG.   A major US HOST (*q.v.*) offering over 300 databases; set up in 1972, DIALOG was for many years the front-runner in online retrieval. A number of registered trade and service marks are used in the DIALOG organization, amongst them being DIALINDEX, DIALORDER, DIALOGLINK, DIALMAIL, and DIALNET. Introductory courses and advanced seminars are run worldwide, and a newsletter *Chronolog* is issued (m).

DIALTECH.   *See IRS-DIALTECH.*

Dial-Up Access.   Access from terminal to computer via the public telephone system, using a MODEM (*q.v.*) to convert the signals.

Diamond.   An out-of-date name for a size of type equal to about 4½ point.

DIANE.   *See Euronet.*

Diaper.   A binding pattern consisting of a simple figure constantly repeated in geometrical form: the pattern may consist of figures separated by the background only, or of compartments constantly succeeding one another, and filled with a design. The design is done with a 'diaper roll'.

Diaphragm Control.   A device for indicating the correct aperture for any camera extension and screen ruling when using a PROCESS CAMERA (*q.v.*).

Diapositive.   A positive copy (of a document) made on transparent material. *See also Negative, Positive.*

Diazo.   A contraction of diazonium, the chemical compound used in ammonia-developing reproduction papers, cloths and films which will reproduce anything printed, drawn, or written on a translucent or transparent material when exposed to ultra-violet light and developed in ammonia fumes. *See also Diazotype Process.*

Diazotype Process.   A copying process whereby paper treated with a diazo compound is placed against the document to be copied and an exposure made by means of powerful arc lamps. The exposed paper is developed by passing it through a chamber containing ammonia fumes or over rollers damped with a specially prepared solution.

Diced.   Binding with tooling to resemble dice or small diamond squares.

Dichotomy, Classification by.   *See Bifurcate Classification.*

Dickman Charging System.   A slightly simplified and mechanized development of the Newark system to obviate the necessity for making records in longhand, thus lessening the possibility of mistakes.

Dictionary. 1. A book explaining the words of a language, the words being arranged in alphabetical order; it usually gives the orthography, pronunciation and meaning of each word. A dictionary of the words in a restricted field of knowledge usually gives only the meaning. 2. In information retrieval, *synonymous with* THESAURUS (*q.v.*).

Dictionary Catalogue. A catalogue in which all the entries (author, title, subject, series, etc.) and references are arranged in a single alphabet – like a dictionary. As distinct from other alphabetical catalogues, subject entries are made under specific subjects. In some instances, the arrangement of sub-entries may depart from a strictly alphabetical order to provide a logical, or other convenient, arrangement, the main headings still retaining the alphabetical order. For the 'objects' of a dictionary catalogue, *See Cutter's Objects.*

Dictionary Code. The use, as a code, of words and terms in the alphabetical order of a dictionary.

Dictionary Index. A series of entries with verbal headings arranged in alphabetical order. Also called 'Alphabetico-specific subject catalogue'.

Didone. A category of type face having a sharp contrast between the thick and thin strokes. The axis of the curves is vertical, the serifs of the lower-case ascenders are horizontal and there are no brackets to the serifs. Examples are Bodoni, Corvinus, Extended and Modern. The term Didone has replaced MODERN FACE (*q.v.*).

Didot. A MODERN-FACE (*q.v.*) type cut in 1784 by Firmin Didot (1764–1836) the most famous of a French family which is important in the history of printing. Most eminent as a typefounder, he was mainly responsible for developing the type which is now familiar. He revived and developed the stereo-typing process, and produced singularly perfect editions of many classical English and French works. He and other members of his family fixed the standard for book types in France in the nineteenth century.

Didot Normal. The standard on the Continent of Europe for the height of type from the feet to the printing surface. It is 0.9278 inches. *See also Type Height.*

Didot Point. *See Didot System.*

Didot System. A system of type measurement originated by François Ambroise Didot (1730–1804), the French typefounder, in 1775. One Didot point equals 0·0148 inches; one English point equals 0·013837 inches. The Didot System was generally adopted in France early in the nineteenth century and by German typefounders between 1840 and 1879. *See also Cicero, Point.*

Die. An engraved stamp used for stamping a design.

Die Sinking. The process of making dies; die cutting.

Die Stamping. A printing process that gives a raised effect. Sometimes the die does not carry the ink, and the raised paper alone makes the letter discernible. *See also Embossing.*

Die Sunk. A depression produced by the application of a heated die or block.

Difference. *See Predicables, Five.*

Differential Facet.   A facet which applies only to the limited group of terms in the facet enumerated.

Diffuse Facets.   (*Information retrieval*) Facets representing very general and abstract subjects without specification of primary substance.

Digest.   A methodically arranged compendium or summary of literary, historical, legal, scientific, or other written matter.

Digester.   (*Paper*) The vessel in which rags, esparto or wood are boiled, with chemicals, often caustic soda, to break down the fibres. *See also Boiler.*

Digit.   1. Each of the symbols comprising a BOOK NUMBER (*q.v.*) in the Colon classification.   2. In classification, a distinctively recognizable configuration of marks (e.g. letters – both capital and lower case – numbers, punctuation marks and any other symbols), or code elements, included in a notation, therefore synonymous with 'sort'.   3. In computer codes, each item comprising a symbol; in the symbol ABA553 there re six digits but only four 'sorts' or 'characters' (A, B, 3, 5). Each conventional set of sorts is called a 'species' (the capitals, the numerals). *See also Code.*   4. The printers' symbol ☛. Also known as 'Fist', 'Hand' or 'Index'.

Digital.   Representation of data or information in combinations of separate groups of digits suitable for processing by a computer.

Digital Computer.   A computer which operates symbolically, by reducing all its input to binary digits ('bits'). *See also Bit, Digit 3, Analogue Computer, Binary Code.*

Digital Optical Disk.   *See Optical Digital Disk.*

Digital Typography.   *See Computer Typesetting.*

Digital Video Interactive.   *See DVI.*

Digraph.   *Synonymous with* DIPHTHONG (*q.v.*).

Dillons Commonwealth Poetry Prize.   An annual prize awarded by the Commonwealth Institute, London, from 1972. In 1988 Dillons Bookstore agreed to sponsor the prize, and their name was added to the title. The prize is also supported by the Office of Arts and Libraries' Business Sponsorship Incentive Scheme.

DIMDI.   Deutsches Institut für Medizinische Dokumentation und Information; founded in 1969, based in Cologne, and funded by the Federal German Government. Offers HOST (*q.v.*) facilities on behalf of a number of German agencies, particularly in the health care, life sciences and social science fields. Over 50 databases are available.

Dime Novel.   An American term for a type of paper-covered fiction which was popular during the second half of the nineteenth century. A cheap, sensational, novel.

DIN.   The characters used before figures to identify standards issued by the Deutscher Normenausschuss (DNA), the German standards institution. The DIN standards for sizes of paper were later adopted by the International Standards Organization.

DIP.   *See Document Image Processing.*

Diplomatic.   The science of the critical study of official as opposed to literary sources of history, i.e. of charters, acts, treaties, contracts, judicial records, rolls, chartularies, registers and kindred documents.

Diphthong.   Two letters joined together and representing one sound, as æ, Æ, œ, Œ. Also called 'Digraph'.

Diptych.   *See Codex.*

Direct Broadcasting by Satellite.   *See Satellite Broadcasting.*

Direct Cataloguing.   *See Collocative v. Direct Cataloguing.*

Direct Contact Copying.   A process for documentary copying which requires the action of light on a sensitized coating on paper.

Direct Entry.   (*Indexing*) An entry for a multi-word subject in its normal word order, as opposed to inverted word sequence.

Direct Printing.   Printing in which the impression is made direct from forme to paper, as in letterpress, and is not offset on to the paper from another medium. *See also Letterpress, Offset.*

Direct Purchasing Organizations.   Local authority purchasing of goods can be more economically carried out if all the authority's requirements are channelled through one organization. Consortia of several local authorities can buy on even better terms. In the early 1980s some Direct Purchasing Organizations began bulk purchasing of books at trade terms from individual publishers, thus causing problems in the Net Book Agreement. The Booksellers' Association has fiercely resisted these inroads into their trade.

Direct Sub-division.   When determining subject headings for a dictionary catalogue in repect of a book limited to one locality, the heading is sub-divided by the name of a county, province, city or other locality without the interposition of the name of the country; e.g. GEOLOGY – SURREY. Indirect sub-division interposes the name of the country; e.g. GEOLOGY – ENGLAND – SURREY.

Direction des Bibliothèques de France.   This organization, which is under the control of Le Ministère de l'Éducation Nationale was founded in 1945 when it took over from the Ministry the responsibilities for the employment and training of professional librarians. It is responsible for the administration and functioning of the French national libraries and the municipal libraries as well as the libraries of the University of Paris and 15 other universities. The Direction provides instruction and issues certificates and diplomas to staff employed in libraries which come under its control.

Direction Line.   Used to indicate the line of characters when the abbreviated title of a book called DESIGNATION MARK (*q.v.*) follows the signature mark, or letter, which is printed at the foot of the first page of each sheet, to guide the binder when gathering. Originally, the line on which a CATCHWORD (*q.v.*) was printed. Also called 'Signature line', 'Title signature'. *See also Designation Mark, Signature and Catchword Line.*

Direction Number.   The number which appears on the DIRECTION LINE (*q.v.*) at the bottom of a leaf of an old book, i.e. below the lowest line of type.

Direction Word.   *See Catchword.*

Directorate-General XIII.   The section of the Commission of the European Community concerned with library matters; its coverage is defined as 'telecommunications, information industries and innovation'. Much of its work is directed towards information technology, and of the six components it is DG XIIIB that is responsible for the information industry and the information market. *See also IMPACT, Plan of Action (EC).*

Directory.   A book containing lists of names of residents, organizations or business houses in a town, a group of towns or a country, in alphabetical order, and/or in order of situation in roads, or of firms in trade classifications arranged in alphabetical order; or of professional people, manufacturers or business houses in a particular trade or profession. *See also Trade Directory.*

DIRS.   DIMDI Information Retrieval Service. *See DIMDI.*

Dirty Proof.   A proof containing many errors or typographical imperfections; a proof that has been returned to the printer with many corrections.

DIS.   *See Distributing.*

Disc.   (also spelt Disk). A storage format, consisting of a circular piece of plastic of various types, and of various diameters. As a computer storage medium, CD-ROM (*q.v.*) is a common format, while microcomputers use *diskettes* or *floppy disks.* Higher capacity can be obtained on a *hard disk* or *Winchester disk.* Video discs (laser-discs) are a less commonly found format. Audio recordings (gramophone/phonograph records) were marketed generally on black vinyl discs, but COMPACT DISCS (*q.v.*) are now becoming equally common.

Disc Drive.   That part of a computer system that manipulates the DISC (*q.v.*) and inputs and extracts data from it.

Disc Inking.   The inking system which is found particularly in some platen printing machines. A round disc revolves on its own gearing at the head of the machine and the inking rollers pass over the disc before descending on the type-forme. *See also Platen Press.*

Disc Number.   A symbol, consisting of letters and numbers allocated to a DISC (*q.v.*) by the manufacturer for purposes of identification. It is printed on the label on the disc and is used in lists and catalogues as a means of identification.

Discard.   A book that is withdrawn from circulation in a library.

Discharge.   (*Verb*) The act of cancelling the record of the loan of a book or other item on its return to the library. *See also Charge.*

Discharging Counter.   The staff area which is set aside for the work of discharging books, i.e. cancelling the record of a loan.

Discharging Desk.   *See Circulation Desk.*

Discography.   A list of sound recordings (discs) giving details of composer, title, performer/s, maker, and maker's catalogue number.

Discontinued Number.   (*Classification*) A number from a preceding edition of a scheme of classification vacated because its content has been moved back to a more general number.

Discount.   The reduction from the list price of goods. With regard to UK published books this is limited to 10% off the published price to those who sign the NET BOOK AGREEMENT (*q.v.*) although some booksellers who do not sign the agreement offer more. It is only available to libraries which provide a free service to the whole of a community. In the USA discounts are much greater; each publisher has his own discount schedule which is applicable to wholesalers, retailers, schools, libraries, etc.

Discourse. *Synonymous with* RELATION (*q.v.*).

DISISS (UK). The DISISS (Design of Information Services in the Social Sciences) project was created to carry out research and gather information necessary for the effective design of information services in the social sciences. The project was carried out between 1971 and 1975 under the direction of Maurice Line and with funding from the British Library Research and Development Department, formerly the Office for Scientific and Technical Information (OSTI). The main research team was based at the University of Bath and was supported by researchers at the Open University and the School of Librarianship, Polytechnic of North London. *See also INFROSS.*

Disjoined Hand. Handwriting in which the letters are not connected to one another. Also called 'Script writing'. The opposite of JOINED HAND (*q.v.*).

Disjunct Leaf. The stub which remains in a book after the removal of the remainder of the leaf because it contained matter which could not be allowed to remain. *See also Cancellation.*

Disk. *See Disc.*

Diskette. *See Disc.*

Display. The presentation of data from online or videotex systems via a VISUAL DISPLAY UNIT (*q.v.*).

Display Stand. A piece of furniture built to stand on the floor of a library on which to display books.

Display Type. Large or heavy-faced type used for headings, title-pages, posters or advertisements. They may include sizes between 18 and 24 pint but usually comprise 30, 36, 42, 48, 60, 72 and more exceptionally 84 and 96 point.

Display Work. The setting of short lines in varying faces and sizes of type, as distinct from a solid area of type. Advertisements, titles and headings are 'display' work.

Displayed. (*Printing*) Matter which has been set on separate lines and distinguished from the remainder of the text by being set in a smaller or larger size of type, or by its position in relation to the margin (by being full out, indented or centred). Such matter is normally further emphasized by being preceded and followed by additional space. Long quotations, mathematical equations and headings are examples of displayed matter.

Disposal List. In archives mangement, a list of types of document with instructions for their disposal, i.e. destruction or permanent preservation.

Disposition. (*Archives*) The action taken after the APPRAISAL (*q.v.*) of non-current documents. This may include transfer to a records centre or archive depository for temporary or permanent storage, reproduction on microfilm, or destruction.

Dissection. (*Classification*) The formation of an array of co-ordinate classes.

Dissemination of Information. The distribution, or sending, of information whether specifically requested or not, to members of an organization by a librarian or information officer. The means used normally include news bulletins, abstracts, individual memoranda or letters, and personal interviews or telephone calls, but may also include notes accompanying articles, memoranda, cuttings or reports and the underlining of sentences or marking of paragraphs in same. *See also SDI.*

Dissertation, Academic. A thesis or treatise prepared as a condition for the award of a degree or diploma.

Distance Learning. *See Open Learning.*

Distinctive Title. One that is peculiar to a particular publication.

Distinguished Library Award for School Administrators. An award made by the AMERICAN ASSOCIATION OF SCHOOL LIBRARIANS (*q.v.*) to record outstanding achievement in library development by a school administrator.

Distributed Facets. (*Classification, Information retrieval*) In a compound subject, facets which are scattered throughout a classification consequent upon the COMBINATION ORDER (*q.v.*) applied. Also called 'Distributed terms'. *See also Descriptor Sequence.*

Distributed Network. A network in which files of data or processing functions are located at different points in the system.

Distributed Relatives. A secondary aspect of a subject which is used to show a relationship when classifying a document, and which will not be used as the main, but as a subordinate, subject when determining the class number. The same sub-heading may be used to subdivide many headings.

Distributed Terms. *Synonymous with* DISTRIBUTED FACETS.

Distributing. 1. Putting loose type back into their respective boxes and cases after use, or for melting, after use in the forme. This is done after machining and when type is not to be kept standing for reprints. Commonly called 'dissing'. Abbreviated 'dis'. *See also Break.* 2. In presswork, the uniform spreading of ink on the face of the printing forme.

Distribution Copy. (*Reprography*) A microcopy from which further copies of equal legibility can be obtained.

Distribution Imprint. The statement on the verso of the title-page of a book, which names the branches or representatives through which the publisher's books are distributed.

Distributor Rollers. The rollers on a printing press which spread ink on the ink slab, roll it to the correct consistency and transfer it to the rollers which ink the type-forme. They are made wholly of metal, or of rubber or composition on a metal core. Also called 'Distributing rollers'.

District. (*Public Libraries*) A part of the Library area other than a REGION or AREA (*qq.v.*) and usually comprising a town and its adjacent rural area organized as a library unit.

District Library. 1. *Synonymous with* BRANCH LIBRARY (*q.v.*) in an urban library system. 2. In a British county library system, a branch situated in a market town or other focal area. *See also Regional Branch, Regional Headquarters.*

District Materials Center. *Synonymous with* CURRICULUM MATERIALS CENTER (*q.v.*).

Dittogram. A printed character, or group of printed characters, repeated in error.

Diurnal. A periodical which is published or issued every day.

Duirnall. *See Newsbook.*

Divide Like the Classification. The mnemonic use after the decimal point of symbols from various parts of a classification schedule in order to sub-divide a subject, as e.g. in 016 of Dewey's *Decimal Classification*:

016	Bibliography of special subjects
016.1	„ of philosophy
016.17	„ of ethics
016.22	„ of the Bible
016.54	„ of chemistry

The 'divide-like' notes which were used in the 17th and earlier editions of the Dewey Decimal Classification were replaced in later editions by ADD IINSTRUCTIONS (*q.v.*).

Divided Catalogue. A catalogue in which the entries are separated into two or more sequences in order to simplify filing and consultation, which may become complicated in a large dictionary catalogue. All subject and form entries and their necessary references may form an alphabetical subject catalogue and the remaining entries form an author-title catalogue. *See also Split Catalogue.*

Dividing Stroke. *Synonymous with* LINE DIVISION MARK (*q.v.*).

Divinity Calf. A plain dark brown calf binding often used in the mid-nineteenth century for theological or devotional books. The boards were sometimes bevelled and the edges red.

Divinity Circuit. The American equivalent of Yapp, or CIRCUIT EDGES (*q.v.*).

Divinity Edges. *See Circuit Edges.*

Division. 1. In some libraries, a section of a Department. 2. In some libraries, a Department. 3. A unit in a library system which is concerned with a particular function, as a 'Catalogue division', or with a definite subject, as 'Science division'. 4. In the American Library Association and the Special Libraries Association, sections of the membership which exist to further the work of libraries and librarianship and the well being of librarians within the limitations of each division. These divisions may represent a type of organization or a subject field; each has its own officers and organizational machinery. *See also Branch, Group, Section.*

Division. (*Classification*) 1. The process of dividing classes or groups of a classification scheme into their more minute parts. 2. The result so formed. 3. A subject or topic which is subordinate to a class. 4. Breaking down a FACET (*q.v.*) into its foci. *See Focus. See also Exhaustive Division, Main Class.*

Division Library. In an American university or college, a collection of books attached to, and administered by, a division or a group of related departments, usually with some form of co-operative arrangement with the general library, or as a part of the library system.

Divisional Title.   A page preceding a section or division of a book, and bearing the name or number of the section or division. The reverse is usually blank.

Divisional Title-pages.   *See General Title.*

DLAI.   Documentation, library and archives infrastructures – the subject of an inter-governmental conference held in September 1974 at Unesco in Paris.

DMC.   District Materials Center. *See Curriculum Materials Center.*

do.   Abbreviation for ditto, the same.

DOBIS/LIBIS.   A co-operative cataloguing and information retrieval network, based originally at Leuven and Dortmund; now maintained and developed by IBM.

DOCDEL.   A programme funded by the EC and intended to further research and development in the fields of ELECTRONIC PUBLISHING (*q.v.*) and DOCUMENT DELIVERY SERVICES (*q.v.*). *See also APOLLO.*

DOCMATCH.   A study of the problems of linking full text and bibliographic databases with particular reference to electronic ordering and delivery of documents. The British Library and the University of Bradford collaborated in the initial project, started in 1985, as a part of the DOCDEL (*q.v.*) programme. This work has now been superseded by DOCMATCH 2, an experimental implementation of the original software. The system uses USBC (*q.v.*) and ADONIS (*q.v.*) identifiers.

Doctoral Dissertation Fellowship.   An award of the ASSOCIATION OF COLLEGE AND RESEARCH LIBRARIES (*q.v.*).

Document.   1. A record which conveys information; originally an inscribed or written record, but now considered to include any form of information – graphic, acoustic, alphanumeric, etc. (e.g. maps, manuscripts, tape, video-tapes, computer software).   2. (*Archives*) Things admissible to archives (*see* ARCHIVES 2) being manuscripts made of any suitable materials, scripts produced by writing machines or by means of type, type-blocks, engraved plates or blocks, or film, together with all other material evidence whether they include alphabetical or numerical signs which form part of or are annexed to, or may reasonably be assumed to have formed part of, or been annexed to, a manuscript or script record, and which were drawn up or used in the course of an administrative or executive transaction (whether public or private) of which they formed part, and which were subsequently preserved in the custody of the person or persons responsible for that transaction and for their legitimate successors. For the preservation of documents, *see Archives. See also Archival Document.*

Document Address.   (*Information retrieval*) A class number or other symbol indicating the whereabouts of a document in a STORE (*q.v.*). *See also Unit Record.*

Document card.   A UNIT CARD (*q.v.*). A card carrying all the bibliographic and index information for an item.

Document Case.   A container, usually made of stout cardboard and approximately 15 × 10 × 3 inches, for the filing flat of archives or manuscripts.

Document Delivery Services.   HOSTS (*q.v.*) enable users to order copies of materials retrieved by online searches, either by direct despatch of items by the Host, or via an agent. Such document delivery services may also be offered online to the users' terminals, rather than in hard copy, or via electronic mail.

Document Image Processing.   The scanning by optical character recognition and storage of information from paper into a digitalized optical format, which can then form the basis for various computer handling of the data and selective output. Abbreviated DIP. *See also Optical Information Systems.*

Document Retrieval System.   One which provides a complete copy of a required document instead of merely a citation or reference. An aspect of INFORMATION RETRIEVAL (*q.v.*).

Document Store.   In information retrieval, a place where documents are kept.

Document Supply Centre.   That part of a large library or similar organization that handles the actual delivery of materials to clients. Especially the British Library Document Supply Centre (BLDSC) at Boston Spa (known until 1985 as the British Library Lending Division, BLLD).

Document System.   A method of machine indexing that presumes a discrete record, e.g. a piece of film, or a length of tape which represents a single document and contains, in searchable form, all of the results of an analysis of a single document. Also called 'Item entry system'. *See also Aspect System, Item Entry.*

Documentalist.   One who practises documentation. An information officer or intelligence officer who is concerned with the collection and dissemination of knowledge, rather than the librarian who is concerned with the techniques of handling records of knowledge, making them available and possibly exploiting them. He is concerned with assembling information contained within documents together with data from other sources to form a new compilation.

Documentary Information.   Information about documents, or information recorded in documents. Either kind of information may be 'retrieved' according as to whether the purpose of the retrieval is to indicate where the needed information can be found, or what it is.

Documentary Reproduction.   The copying of documents or pages of books by photographic or non-photographic means so that the copy has the appearance of the original.

Documentation.   The study of the acquisition, handling, and communication of information, particularly relating to scientific reports, semi-published material, statistics, etc. *See also Informatics.*

Documentation, Library and Archives Infrastructures. *See DLAI.*

Documentation Centre.   A place where publications are received, processed, preserved, summarized, abstracted and indexed; where bulletins relating to such material are prepared for distribution to those interested; where research is undertaken, bibliographies prepared, and copies or translations made.

Documentation Centre for Education in Europe.   Founded as a tool for inter-governmental co-operation in education, it is financed by the Council of Europe. Publishes *Newsletter* (6 p.a.), *Information Bulletin* (3 p.a.), surveys and studies (all dealing with aspects of education in Europe) and also publications of EUDISED (*q.v.*).

Documents Depository.   In America, a library which is legally designated to receive without charge copies of all or selected US government publications.

Dog-eared   Said of a book, portfolio, or similar article having the corners of the leaves turned down and soiled by careless or long continued usage.

Domicilary Services Subject Group.   Established in the UK in 1985 to cater for those working with the housebound or elderly. Produces a newsletter *Housecalls* and organizes activities and meetings. Secretariat at Lewisham Library, London. A part of the MEDICAL HEALTH AND WELFARE LIBRARIES GROUP (*q.v.*).

Donation Record.   A record of gifts. It may be kept in a book or on cards.

Donatus de Octo Partibus Orationis.   *See Block Books.*

Dorking Conference.   *See International Conference on Classification for Information Retrieval.*

Dormitory Library.   A collection of books placed in a dormitory of an American college or university. The books are usually intended for recreational reading but may also be recommended texts.

Dorse.   The reverse side of a MEMBRANE (*q.v.*).

DOS.   Disc Operating System; the program that controls a computer's inputs and outputs. Also called system software, or by type PC-DOS, MS-DOS, etc.

Dos-à-dos Binding.   Two or more books – usually small ones – bound back to back so that the back cover of one serves as the back cover of the other and the fore-edges of one are next to the spine of the other.

Dot and Matrix Printer.   *See Matrix Printer.*

Dot-Etching.   *Synonymous with* RETOUCHING (*q.v.*).

Dot Map.   One which shows density of distribution by dots of uniform size, each dot representing a given quantity.

Dotted Rule.   A strip of metal of type height with a face showing a dotted line which may vary from fine dots close together to a sequence of short dashes. *See also Rule.*

Dotting Wheels.   Small hand-tools of varying shapes used by artists when engraving metal plates.

Double.   1. In printing, a word, etc., erroneously repeated.   2. A sheet of paper twice the unit size, e.g. double crown (20 × 30 inches), ordinary crown being 15 × 20 inches. *See also Paper Sizes.*

Double-Book.   A book printed on half sheets.

Double Columned.   A page of printed matter set to half the width of a normal page line, with an em or more space, or a RULE (*q.v.*), between the columns. Abbreviated d.c. Also said to be set in 'Half-measure'. Double columns are used in such works as dictionaries, encyclopaedias and Bibles.

Double Crown.   A sheet of paper measuring 20 × 30 inches.

Double Dagger (‡).   The third reference mark for footnotes, coming after the DAGGER (*q.v.*). Sometimes called a 'Double obelisk'. *See also Reference Marks.*

Double Elephant. *See Elephant.*

Double Entry. Entry in a catalogue under more than one subject, or under subject and place, and under the names of subordinate contributors such as joint authors, editors, illustrators, translators, etc., using the same form of entry with suitable headings added. Also, entry for a pseudonymous work under the real name of the author as well as under the pseudonym.

Double Kwic Indexing. A variation of the KWIC (*q.v.*) indexing method whereby two words in the title (the entry word and another) instead of one are rotated. The effectiveness of the index is thus theoretically doubled but indexes compiled by this method are about four times as long as ordinary KWIC indexes.

Double Leaded. *See Leaded Matter.*

Double Leaves. The leaves of CHINESE STYLE (*q.v.*) books. These are recorded in a catalogue entry in the form '18 double 1' or '36 pp. (on double leaves)'. Should the leaves be unnumbered, each is counted as two pages, as: [36] pp. (on double leaves).

Double Letter. *Synonymous with* LIGATURE (*q.v.*).

Double Numeration. A system of numbering whereby illustrations, charts, etc., are related to the chapter, the numbers of which are the key numbers, e.g. Fig. 7.5 indicates the fifth figure in the seventh chapter.

Double Obelisk. *Synonymous with* DOUBLE DAGGER (*q.v.*).

Double Pica. An out-of-date name for a size of type equal to about 22 points.

Double Plate. An illustration which stretches across two pages of a book when open. *See also Folding Plate.*

Double Printing. Two impressions on the same sheet.

Double Quotes. Pairs of superior commas " . . . " used to indicate quoted matter. *See also Single Quotes, Turned Comman.*

Double Register. Two ribbons fastened in a book to serve as book-markers.

Double Row Coding. (*Information retrieval*) A method using edge-notched cards which have a double row of holes at the edges.

Double Rule. A RULE (*q.v.*) having two lines of different thickness of face. *See also Parallel Rule.*

Double Spread. Two facing pages on which printed matter is spread across as if they were one page. When printing an illustration this way two blocks must be used unless the spread comes in the middle of a section. *See also Conjugate, Opening.*

Double Title-page. Used where a work has both a right-hand and a left-hand title-page. Usually one of these serves for the series or the complete volumes of a set, and the other is limited to the individual volume.

Double Weight Paper. Sensitized photographic paper between 0.0112 and 0.0190 inches inclusive. *See also Photographic Papers.*

Doublette. *See Replica.*

Doublure. 1. An ornamental inside lining of a book cover of leather or silk, usually with a leather hinge, and often elaborately decorated. 2. Ornamental end-paper. Also called 'Ornamental inside lining'.

Doubtful Authorship.   Authorship ascribed to one or more persons with no convincing proof. *See also Attributed Author.*

Doves Press.   One of the most famous British private presses. It was directed by T. J. Cobden-Sanderson, who founded it with Sir Emery Walker, at Hammersmith, London, in 1900. Their partnership was dissolved in 1909 but Cobden-Sanderson continued to operate until 1916. The most important publication was the Doves Bible, published in five volumes between 1903–5. The name 'Doves' was taken from Doves Place, a passage off the Upper Mall, Hammersmith. The name was first used for the Doves Bindery which Cobden-Sanderson started in 1893 at 15 Upper Mall.

Down.   A term used to signify that a computer system is out of operation.

Down Time.   Time when a computer or system is out of operation.

Downgrade.   To assign a secret or confidential document to a less restricted security classification under proper authorization. *See also Declassify.*

Downloading.   A process by which computer programs are transferred from one source to another, typically taking items from a commercial service on payment of a fee for personal or library use.

Downward Reference.   A direction from a more- to a less-comprehensive heading in an alphabetico-specific subject catalogue. The reverse of UPWARD REFERENCE (*q.v.*).

DPB.   Department of Printed Books; *see British Library.*

Dragon's Blood.   Any of several resinous substances, mostly dark red in colour. It is used in powered form in photo-engraving for etching line plates. Dragon's blood powder is brushed up against the slightly raised lines of the image or design on the metal plate from four sides, and 'burned in', thus protecting these lines against the action of the etching solution or acid.

Dramatic Work.   An INTELLECTUAL WORK (*q.v.*) which expresses dramatic action. Copyright in performance arises when the work is staged for presentation before the public.

DRAW.   Direct Read after Write. A trade name for the Philips optical disc system, but used in the USA also in a generic sense. *See Optical Digital Disk.*

Draw-Out Shelves.   A form of compact storage consisting of shelves wide enough to take two rows of books, one facing each way, fixed across, or in place of, ordinary shelves. When it is desired to consult the books these shelves are drawn out, as if they were drawers, into the gangway.

Drawer Handle.   A tool of a Corinthian volute which was commonly used in English Restoration book decoration. So called from its similarity to the handle of a small drawer.

Draw-on Covers.   The binding of square-backed magazines and paperbacks, the cover being attached by glueing to the spine of the book. When the end-papers are pasted down, it is said to be *drawn-on solid.*

Dressed Forme.   A forme of pages of type with furniture between and around them, the page-cord having been removed. *See also Forme, Naked Forme.*

Dressing.   1. Fitting the FURNITURE (*q.v.*) between and around the pages in a chase prior to locking up the FORME (*q.v.*).   2. Fitting an illustration block into type so that text and illustration can be printed together.

DRIC. Acronym of Defence Research Information Centre, which is the central facility of the Ministry of Defence for acquiring unpublished scientific and technical reports from the UK and overseas sources. Its primary function is to serve the Ministry of Defence establishments and branches and also defence contractors.

Drive Out. (*Printing*) 1. Said of type-matter which is spaced widely between the words so as to occupy more lines. 2. An instruction to the compositor to insert wide spaces between words. *See also Keep In.*

Drop. (*Printing*) To unlock a forme and remove the furniture and chase after printing, the type then being either distributed or 'kept standing', i.e. tied up and stored.

Drop-Down Title. The short title on the first page of text. It should be the same as the RUNNING TITLE (*q.v.*). *See also Caption Title.*

Drop Folio. A folio number or page number at the bottom of a page.

Drop Guides. *See Feed Guides.*

Drop Initials. *See Drop Letter.*

Drop Letter. Large initial used at the beginning of a chapter or article, and running down two lines or more. *See also Cock-Up Initial, Cut-In Letter.*

Drop-out. (*Information retrieval*) The total number of documents identified by a retrieval system in answer to a search question. (*Printing*) A HALF- TONE from which all, or some, of the dots have been removed. Also called a 'Highlight'.

Drop Slip. Publications ordered from a JOBBER (*q.v.*) but sent direct, at the jobber's request, by the publisher to the library. (American.)

Dropped Head. The first page of a chapter or book where the first line commences a third or more down the page.

Dropped Letter. A character which becomes removed during the course of printing and drops out of the forme causing an omission in the matter when printed.

Dropping Fraction. (*Information retrieval*) The fraction of the file of records in an edge-notched card system which are delivered after needle-sorting.

Dry Ammonia Process. The ammonia process of reprography. Also called DRY PROCESS (*q.v.*).

Dry end. The drying end of a paper-making machine. The other end is known as the WET END (*q.v.*).

Dry Flong. *See Flong.*

Dry Offset. 1. Printing by letterpress onto a rubber cylinder from which the impression is offset on to paper. The resulting advantages are reduced make-ready, the possibility of using uncoated paper for fine half-tones, etc. The process is not lithographic and no water need be used. 2. A printing process by which photo-engraved plates are printed by the offset transfer principle, the inked impression from a relief-etched magnesium plate being made on a rubber blanket cylinder and offset from this on to the paper as this is carried round the impression cylinder.

Dry-Point Etching. An etching made directly on copper by means of a sharp needle called a point. In dry-point work, the etching is all done by hand and not by a mordant applied to a wax-covered plate in which the design has been cut, as is the rule in ordinary etching. Etchings often have dry-point lines, which have been added after the acid etching has taken place. The beauty of this method is due to the burr caused by the point on each side of the channel being left and not removed as in an engraving. The effect of this in printing is to produce the velvety line which is characteristic of a dry-point.

Dry Process. A method for producing copies of documents which does not employ wet chemicals. Some diazotype prints are made by a dry process. The usual developing process used in electro-photography is dry. *See also Documentary Reproduction, Dust Development.*

Dry Silver. A silver halide copying process in which the latent image is made visible by the application of heat rather than the use of chemicals. *See also Silver Processes.*

Drying End. The end of a paper-making machine where there are the steam-heated drying cylinders over which the damp web of paper (containing about 70 per cent of water) is passed before it reaches the calender rolls.

D.S. (document signed). A document in which only the signture is autographic.

DTIC. *See Defense Technical Information Center.*

DTP. *See Desktop Publishing.*

Dual Programming. *Synonymous with* MULTI-PROGRAMMING (*q.v.*).

Ducali Bindings. Venetian bindings of the decrees of the Doges which are decorated with a combination of Oriental and Western techniques. The method was to cover the board with a paper composition, the centre and corners being recessed, then to paste on thinly pared leather and add a coating of colour lacquer to complete the background. Gold-painted arabesques provided the final decoration.

Duck-Foot Quotes. The common name for Continental quotes or inverted commas. The form $<<>>$ is used by French printers, but the Swiss and German printers use them in reverse, i.e. $>><<$. They were first used in 1546 by Guillaume Le Bé of Paris, and are consequently also known as 'Guillemets'.

Dudley (Miriam) Award for Bibliographic Instruction. An award for contribution to the advancement of bibliographic instruction; administered by the ASSOCIATION OF COLLEGE AND RESEARCH LIBRARIES (*q.v.*).

Dull-Coated. Paper which is coated but not polished: it is suitable for fine half-tones, being smooth but having no gloss. The term 'dull finish' is sometimes applied to the low or natural finish of COATED PAPER (*q.v.*) or uncoated papers which have not been glazed; practically identical with 'matt art' paper. *See also Art.*

Dull Finish. *See Dull-Coated.*

Dummy. 1. A copy, generally made up of blank leaves, trimmed and sewn but not bound, to represent the actual bulk of a book about to be published. 2. A complete layout of a job showing the arrangement of matter to be printed on every page, and giving particulars of type, illustrations, etc. 3. A temporary catalogue card, usually handwritten and distinctively coloured, which serves as a substitute while a main or other entry, or a block of cards, are out of the catalogue for amendment. *See also Shelf Dummy.*

Dummy Bands.   Imitation RAISED BANDS (*q.v.*) on the spine of a book. Also called 'False bands'.

Dummy Make-up.   A DUMMY (*q.v.*) with page proofs, or galley proofs cut up, and pasted in position.

Dunn and Wilson/National Preservation Office Conservation Competition.   An annual award first made in 1988 for a policy statement on conservation/preservation, relevant to an organization and capable of realistic implementation. The title 'Keeping our words' is sometimes used for the competition.

Dunn and Wilson Prizes.   A sum of money presented annually by the library binding firm of Dunn & Wilson Ltd., to each of the British Schools of Librarianship, to be used at the Schools' discretion as prizes to students.

Duodecimo. (12 mo.)   1. A sheet of paper folded four times to form a section of twelve leaves (24 pp.). As a sheet cannot be folded for binding without a portion being cut, the smaller cut-off portion has to be inserted after folding into the larger folded portion to provide the page sequence. Alternatively a sheet and a half sheet can be used. If the printer lays down two rows of six pages the result is known as 'Long twelves', but if three by four pages, 'short' or 'square' twelves. Where the width of the pages is greater than the height, the term 'broad twelves' is used. Also called 'Twelvemo'.   2. A book printed on paper folded to form sections of twelve leaves. *See also Oblong.*

Duotone.   Two-colour half-tone printing.

Duotype.   Two half-tone plates of the same black and white original, both made from the same half-tone negative, but etched separately so as to give different colour values when superimposed during printing.

Duplex.   A communications link between a computer and a remote terminal operating in both directions simultaneously. A link operating alternately in one direction or the other, but not both simultaneously is termed *Half-duplex. See also Simplex.*   2. Photographic paper which has a coating of emulsion on both sides.   3. An image-positioning technique used in rotary camera microfilming, whereby the use of mirrors or prisms enables an image of the front side of a document to be photographed on one half of the film, while an image of the back of the same document is photographed simultaneously on the other half of the film.   4. Any make of camera which will copy as described in 3.

Duplex Half-Tone.   A screen reproduction in two printings from half-tone blocks made from a monochrome original, one being used as a colour tone. The method is used in both letterpress and offset work to give the impression of a mellow monochrome picture, being richer and better toned than is possible from a single-colour half-tone block.

Duplex Ledger.   *See Ledger Weight.*

Duplex Paper.   1. Paper having two different coloured surfaces.   2. Any paper composed of two sheets pasted together. Duplex papers are usually made by bringing the two layers, generally of different colours or quality, together in the wet state and pressing or rolling them together, thus forming a homogeneous mass. *See also Twin Wire Paper.* If three papers are brought together in the way described the resulting paper is known as Triplex.

Duplicate.   A second, or subsequent, copy of a book already in stock. Strictly it should be identical in edition, imprint, etc., but the kind of library and the intrinsic value placed on variations of bibliographical details or contents determines the exact meaning of 'duplicate' in specific libraries.

Duplicate Entry.   Entry in an index or other form of record of the same subject matter under two or more distinct aspects of it or under two headings.

Duplicate Paging.   Description of a book which has paging in duplicate, as e.g. a book with the original text on the verso and the translation on the recto.

Duplicate Title.   Used of a reprint which has a reproduction of the original title-page in addition to its own.

Duplicated Signatures.   Two sets of signatures which are identical.

Durable Paper,   *Synonymous with* PERMANENT PAPER (*q.v.*).

Durham Book.   *See Lindisfarne Gospels.*

Dust Cover.   *Synonymous with* BOOK JACKET (*q.v.*).

Dust Development.   A development process used in document copying by which latent electrostatic images are made visible by treatment with a developing powder. *See also Xerography.*

Dust Jacket.   *Synonymous with* BOOK JACKET (*q.v.*).

Dust Wrapper.   *Synonymous with* BOOK JACKET (*q.v.*).

Duster.   *See Willow.*

Dutch Gold.   *Synonymous with* DUTCH LEAF (*q.v.*).

Dutch Leaf.   A thin sheet obtained by beating an alloy of copper and zinc; it is sometimes used in tooling as a substitute for gold leaf. It quickly discolours. Also called 'Dutch gold'.

Dutch Paper.   *Synonymous with* VAN GELDER PAPER (*q.v.*).

DVI.   Digital video interactive; an application of compact discs to give full motion video and audio display for INTERACTIVE VIDEO (*q.v.*) contexts. More sophisticated than CD-I (*q.v.*), but commercially viable machines are unlikely to appear before 1992.

d.w.   Abbreviation for dust wrapper. *See Book Jacket.*

Dwarf Book.   *Synonymous with* BIBELOT (*q.v.*).

Dyadic Alphabet.   A two-letter alphabet.

Dye-line Process.   *Synonymous with* DIAZOTYPE PROCESS (*q.v.*).

Dynamic Map.   One which expresses movement such as transport, migration, or military manoeuvres. The symbols used are mainly flow lines and arrows but change is sometimes expressed by isopleths or choropleths.

Eaolug.   *See East Anglia Online User Group.*

Early Map.   *See Map.*

EARN.   European Academic Research Network; established 1985 by IBM Europe and open to all European academic, education and research institutions. Provides facilities for electronic mail, computer conferencing, database enquiries and data exchange. Linked to the US academic network BITNET.

Earthworm Children's Book Award. An annual UK award of Friends of the Earth Trust to promote environmental awareness in children's literature.

East Anglia Online User Group. An informal forum for online users in the East Anglia region of the UK. Abbreviated EAOLUG.

East London Business Information Network. *See ELBIN.*

East Midlands Branch (of the (British) Library Association). Previously known as the North Midland Library Association and later the North Midland Branch of the Library Association (1929–70). The area of the Branch is now the administrative counties of Derbyshire, Leicestershire, Lincolnshire, Northamptonshire and Nottinghamshire. Publishes *Nemcon* (3 p.a.) in association with Groups of the L.A. in the area and *East Midlands Bibliography* (previously *North Midlands Bibliography*) (2 p.a.); currently behind schedule. Abbreviated EMBLA.

Eastern Branch. A Branch of the (British) Library Association; members of the Association living or working in the counties of Cambridgeshire, Norfolk and Suffolk are automatically members of the Branch. Publishes *The Easterner* (q.).

EC. *See European Community.*

ECARBICA. Acronym of the East and Central Africa Regional Branch of the International Council on Archives. Publishes *ECARBICA Journal. See also International Council on Archives.*

ECCTIS. Acronym for Education Counselling and Credit Transfer Information Service, a project undertaken at the Open University, and funded by the Department of Education and Science. Aims to maintain a computerised databank about further and higher education courses in the UK. *See TAPS.*

ECDIN. Environmental Chemicals Data and Information Network; an EC databank including regulations on packaging, classification, labelling of dangerous substances, impact of chemicals on the environment, and carcinogenicity.

ECHO. The European Commission Host Organization, based in Luxembourg, and offering online access to the increasing number of EC databases. Set up in 1980.

Écrasé Leather. Leather which has been crushed mechanically to give it a grained appearance.

ECU. Abbreviation for European Currency Unit; the artificial unit of currency used to express the budgets of the European Community, and reflecting the values of all currencies of the member states. Large amounts are expressed in MECU, millions of ECU.

Ed. (edit). Abbreviation for EDITED, EDITION, EDITOR (*qq.v.*).

EDC. *See European Documentation Centres.*

Edge Decoration. The application of ink, coloured (sprayed, sprinkled or marbled), or gold leaf to the edges of a book.

Edge Fog. Light or dark areas along the edge of a developed film or print, caused either by the unintentional admission of light to the sensitive material, or to the effects of age or unsatisfactory storage conditions.

Edge-notched Cards. Punched cards which have up to four rows of holes drilled round the edges. These are punched out to record information; the cards fall off the needle when it is inserted in the hole reserved for the information required. One edge-notched card is allocated to each document and each punchable position is reserved for one feature. Also called 'Edge-punched cards'. *See also Feature Card-System, Marginal-Hole Punched Cards.*

Edge-punched Cards. *Synonymous with* EDGE-NOTCHED CARDS (*q.v.*).

Edge-rolled. Said of leather-bound books the broad edges of which have been tooled 'blind' or 'gold' with a FILLET (*q.v.*). *See also Tooling.*

Edges. (*Binding*) The three outer edges of the leaves of a book; they may be finished in a number of ways. *See also Cut Edges, Edge-Rolled, Gauffered Edges, Gilt Edges, Gilt Top, Marbled Edges, Red Edges, Red Under Gold Edges, Sprinkled Edges, Tooled Edges, Trimmed 2, Uncut, White Edges.*

EDI. Electronic Data (or Document) Interchange; the development of standards to permit rapid exchange of data between organisations and companies. EDI should improve the speed and efficiency of all business communications, from production, stock control, to sales and marketing. National administrations will need to adapt their procedures, particularly in their relationship with industry.

EDIFACT. Electronic Data Interchange for Administration, Commerce and Transport: an international programme to oversee the development of standards for companies and organizations wishing to interchange documents electronically (EDI *q.v.*). Interested bodies include the United Nations, and Directorate General XIII of the Commission of the European Community.

Edit. 1. To amend a computer record or programme; especially to amend or upgrade a computerized bibliographic record. 2. To prepare or arrange a document for publication.

Edited. 1. A literary work by one author, or several authors, which has been prepared for publication by one or more persons other than the author of the whole work. 2. A work consisting of separate items, often written by different people, which has been assembled or prepared for publication by an EDITOR (*q.v.*).

Editio Minor. A lesser, but important, edition of a book or work previously printed, but sometimes the first separate printing of a work previously included in a larger volume. *See also Editio Princeps.*

Editio Princeps. 1. The first edition of a book printed from the old manuscript, when printing first began. *See also Editio Minor.* 2. The first edition of any new work, but for this the term 'first edition' is more commonly used.

Edition. 1. All the copies of a work published in one typographical format, printed from the same type or plates, and issued at one time or at intervals. An edition may comprise a number of impressions. 2. One of the various versions of a newspaper printed at different times on the same day, or periodically summarizing the news of the period since the previous edition was issued, or to celebrate some particular event.   3. One of the successive forms in which a musical composition is issued and in which alterations have been incorporated either by the composer or by an editor. *See also Abridged Edition, Autographed Edition, Definitive Edition, Expurgated Edition, Fine Paper Copy, First Edition, Grangerizing, Impression, Issue, Large Paper Edition, Library Edition, Limited Edition, New Edition, Numbered and Signed Edition, Parallel Edition, Polyglot, Reprint, Revised Edition, Subscribers' Edition, Title Leaf, Unexpurgated Edition, Variorum Edition.*

Edition Bindery.   A bindery in which books are bound for publishers; one in which EDITION BINDING (*q.v.*) is undertaken. *See also Case, Publisher's Cover.*

Edition Binding.   A binding, usually a casing, ordered and paid for by the publisher as a part of the normal publishing of trade editions, and used for all the copies of a title published by him, as distinct from individual binding carried out for the bookseller or purchaser. Also called 'Publisher's binding'.

Edition de Luxe.   A special edition of a book containing extras not in ordinary editions, such as additional plates, or printed on large paper, etc.

Edition Statement.   That part of a catalogue entry which relates to the edition of the book catalogued, as: 2nd rev. ed.

Editor.   1. A person, employed by a publisher, who prepares someone else's work for publication. The editorial work may be limited to mere preparation of the matter for printing, or may involve considerable revisionary and elucidatory work, including an introduction, notes and other critical matter. 2. A person who is responsible for the contents of a newspaper, journal, or periodical and sometimes its publication.

Editor Reference.   A reference in a catalogue from the name of an editor, or from an entry under an editor's name to another entry where more complete information is to be found.

Editorial.   An article expressing a paper's own policy and beliefs on current matters.

Editorial Copies.   Copies of a new publication sent out by the publisher for review, notice, or record. *See also Advance Copy, Review Copy.*

Editorial Processing Centre.   A system of using information technology in journal and book production, by converting a manuscript into machine-readable form initially and carrying out further editing, re-typing and typesetting work by computer. Abbreviated EPC.

EDP.   *See Electronic Data Processing.*

Education Advisory Services Project.   Funded by the British Library and the Advisory Council for Adult and Continuing Education. Reports issued have included the potential for educational guidance by public libraries. Abbreviated EASP.

Education Counselling and Credit Transfer Information Service.   *See ECCTIS.*

Education Librarians Group.   A Group of the (British) Library Association formed in 1981; formerly the *Colleges, Institutes and Schools of Education Group.* Publishes *ELG News* (2 p.a.) Abbreviated ELG.

Education Library Service/Department.   *See School Libraries Department.*

Educational Copyright Users Forum (UK).   A body set up under the terms of the Copyright, Designs and Patents Act, 1988, to monitor existing and future licensing arrangements and to provide advice and guidance to educational users and to rights owners on licensing matters. The members include local authorities, universities, polytechnics and teacher unions and the members collectively have considerable experience of negotiating and applying licensing schemes. It is hoped that reference to the Forum at an early stage will help to ensure that licensing schemes are relevant, fair and workable.

Educational Film Library Association.   Founded in the USA in 1943 to promote the production, distribution and utilization of educational films and other audio-visual materials. Publishes *EFLA Evaluations, Sightlines* (5 p.a.), *Film Evaluation Guide* (supplemented every 3 years). Abbreviated EFLA.

Educational Low-priced Books Scheme.   Title of a recent development of the ENGLISH LANGUAGE BOOK SOCIETY (*q.v.*), which preserves the same acronym – ELBS.

Educational Research Library.   *See NIE.*

Educational Resources Information Center.   *See Eric.*

Edwards, (Alun R) Memorial Scholarship.   A biennial scholarship in memory of A. R. Edwards, former Dyfed County Librarian (UK), pioneer of Welsh books and cultural services. The scholarship is based at the College of Librarianship Wales, and is funded by HTV Wales, of which company Edwards was a Board member from its inception to his death in 1986. A broad theme is specified each time the scholarship is offered.

Edwards of Halifax.   *See Fore-Edge Painting.*

EFLA.   EDUCATIONAL FILM LIBRARY ASSOCIATION (*q.v.*).

EFLC.   *See European Foundation for Library Co-operation.*

e.g.   Abbreviation for *exempli gratia* (*Lat.* 'for example'). Also for 'edges gilt'.

Eggshell.   A paper with a non-glossy, soft, smooth finish. Most antique papers have an eggshell finish.

Egmont.   A light-faced roman type-face designed by S. H. De Roos and available from Intertype since 1937. It has a very small x-height, with tall ascenders and short descenders; there is vertical stress, rather thin flat serifs extending both ways on the top of the ascenders. For a specimen alphabet, *see Type Face.*

Egyptian.   A group of display faces having slab-serifs and little contrast in the thickness of the strokes. They developed from the Antique face cut by Vincent Figgins prior to 1815 and were extensively used by jobbing printers in the nineteenth century. Early sans serif types were also known as Egyptians but the name gradually became limited to slab-serif types, 'grotesque' being given to sans serifs. Modern Egyptian faces are Beton,

Cairo, Karnak, Luxor, Playbill, Rockwell, etc. these are also called block-serif abstract faces. *See also Bold Face, Clarendon.*

Egyptian Association for Scientific and Technical Libraries and Information Centres. Established 1988 with advice and support of the British Council, Egypt. Aims to encourage co-operation, and promote liaison abroad.

EHOG. *See European Host Operators' Group.*

EIAJ. An open-reel videotape format devised by the Electrical Industries Association of Japan.

EIC. *See European Information Centres.*

Eichner Dry Copy. A method of producing facsimile copies of single-sheet documents by feeding them through a machine in contact with copying paper. *See also Thermography.*

Eighteen-mo. 1. A book in which the sections are folded four times so that each leaf is an eighteenth of the sheet. Also called 'Octodecimo'.   2. A sheet of paper so folded.

Eighteenth Century Short-title Catalogue. *See ESTC.*

EIIA. The European Information Industry Association was formed in 1988 from the union of EURIPA (*q.v.*) and the European Host Operators Group (EHOG) (*q.v.*). Operation commenced in 1989, and the new body aims to be a comprehensive industry voice which matches the needs of a single market in the EC, and gives the European information market place an effective presence beside parallel USA and Japanese organizations. Headquarters in Wilmslow, UK.

EIMDG. *See European Information Market Development Group.*

EISSWA. Acronym for Experimental Information Services in two Social Welfare Agencies. This British Library funded project began in 1977 and ran for three years. EISSWA was an action research project, the aims of which were to set up, monitor and evaluate a variety of experimental services designed to meet the information needs of Social Welfare Practitioners. Two Action Papers were published in 1978 and 1979.

Ejector. In the Linotype and Intertype casting machines, the mechanism for ejecting cast lines.

ELAG. *See European Library Automation Group.*

ELAN. An enhanced Local Area Network (*q.v.*).

ELBIN. Acronym for East London Business Information Network; formed 1984 to co-ordinate business information provision in the London boroughs of Hackney, Newham, Tower Hamlets and Waltham Forest.

ELBS. English Language Book Society (*q.v.*).

Eleanor Farjeon Award. *See Children's Book Circle.*

Electors' Roll. *Synonymous with* Register of Electors (*q.v.*).

Electric Stylus. An electrically heated stylus used over a strip of metallic foil to impress the Call Number (*q.v.*) on to the spine of a book.

Electro. Abbreviation for Electrotype (*q.v.*).

Electrographic Process. *Synonymous with* Electrophotographic Process. *See Xerography.*

Electronic Archives. *See Knowledge Warehouse.*

Electronic Composition. *See Computer Typesetting.*

Electronic Data Processing. The use of computers to manage data, by offering high speed handling, logical functions, and arithmetical operations. Abbreviated EDP.

Electronic Document Delivery. The transfer of information from publisher or library to user by electronic means, such as videotex, e-mail, online network, or via CD-ROM, by-passing traditional paper publishing and distribution. The ADONIS (*q.v.*) project is an example of current research in this area.

Electronic Journal. *See Electronic Publishing.*

Electronic Mail. A method of sending messages, mail, information, datafiles, etc. by electronic means. Personal exchange, conferences, and newsletters may be communicated quickly and relatively cheaply, using a variety of interlinked computers and their associated telecommunications networks. Commercial examples, such as *Telecom Gold*, complement institutional facilities, such as JANET, EARN, LA-NET etc. Abbreviated e-mail.

Electronic Photo-engraving Machines. Machines which produce half-tone plates automatically. The engraving is done on metal or plastic by a cutting or burning stylus used in conjunction with a scanning device which traces the original by means of a photographic cell. They utilize the action of light to give instructions, through electronic apparatus, to a mechanical instrument which removes unwanted areas of the plate. Trade names of such machines are: Elgrama, Fairchild Scan-a-Graver, Luxographe, Klischograph, Photo-Lathe.

Electronic Publishing. The use of electronic means of communication to make information available. Publication and dissemination avoids traditional paper formats, and uses electronic databases, videotex, e-mail, electronic newsletters, etc. *See also Adonis, Electronic Document Delivery.* (Not to be confused with DESKTOP PUBLISHING (*q.v.*).)

Electrophotographic Process. *See Xerography.*

Electrostatic Processes. *Synonymous with* ELECTROPHOTOGRAPHIC PROCESS.

Electrotype. A facsimile plate of a type forme or another plate, produced by taking an impression in wax, lead or plastic, depositing in this mould a thin shell of copper and other metal by an electro-plating process, backing it with type metal, and mounting it type high on wood. Half-tones (except the very coarsest) demand electros, which may also be made from line blocks and composed type. Abbreviated 'Electro'.

Element. (*Cataloguing*) 1. A unit of data appearing in a record which can be, or needs to be, distinguished for filing purposes, or which, representing a distinct item of bibliographic information, forms part of an area of a bibliographical description within a catalogue entry. 2. A portion of an AREA (*q.v.*) of a catalogue entry, e.g. a parallel title.

Elementary and Secondary Education Act. *See Library Law.*

Elephant. A size of paper varying from 28 × 23 inches to 34 × 28 inches. 'Double elephant' printing and writing papers vary from 36 × 24 inches to

46 × 31 inches; drawing papers are 26¾ × 40 inches (not an exact multiple of 'Elephant'). 'Long elephant' is a term employed for wallpaper 12 yards long and usually 22, 22½ or 30 inches wide.

Elephant Folio. A folio volume larger than an ordinary folio but not so large as ATLAS FOLIO (*q.v.*). about 14 × 23 inches and formerly used for service books, maps, etc.

ELG. *See Education Librarians Group.*

Elgin (Mary) Award. An annual UK award made by Hodder & Stoughton Ltd. to encourage new writers of fiction.

'Eliminate and Count' Code. (*Information retrieval*) One of several systematic methods of abbreviating words.

Eliot Prize Essay Award, Ida and George. Offered by the (American) Medical Library Association for the essay published in any journal during the previous year which has done most to further medical librarianship.

Eliot (T. S.) Centenary Fund. A memorial fund set up in 1988 by the London Library to raise revenue to enable needy students and scholars to pay their library subscriptions at a reduced rate. T. S. Eliot was President of the London Library 1952–1964, and championed the cause of those who needed to be library members but found the subscription burdensome.

Elision. The contraction of pairs of numbers, e.g. 93–98 becomes 93–8; 1974–1975 becomes 1974–5.

Elision Marks. *Synonymous with* OMISSION MARKS (*q.v.*).

Elite. The smaller of the two common sizes of typewriter type, having twelve characters to the inch as against ten for the larger 'pica' size.

Ellipsis. *Synonymous with* OMISSION MARKS (*q.v.*).

ELP. *See European Librarians and Publishers, Working Group of*

Elrod. *See Ludlow.*

Elzevier. Name of the house of Elzevier, Dutch booksellers and printers; founded by Lodewijck (Louis) Elzevier (1542–1617) at Leyden in 1583 it continued until 1791, being directed by members of the Elzevier family. Of the books emanating from this firm, the most famous are the 32 mo. pocket-sized editions of the Latin classics begun in 1629. Books of this size printed elsewhere were known as 'Elzevirs'. Also spelled Elsevier and Elzevir. The distinctive type-face they used had a great influence on book design.

Em. The square of the body of any size of type; the printer's unit of square measure. A standard unit of typographic measurement, for which a 12 point em is the basis. This equals 0.166 inch, and there are approximately six 12-point ems to one inch. Sometimes called 'Pica'. This unit is used for computing the area of a printed page no matter what size of type is to be used for setting the text; thus if the area is 20 ems wide and 30 ems deep, the width is 240-point and the depth 360-point. It is also used to indicate the amount of indenting required. So called because the space taken up by the letter m is usually square. If the printer is instructed to indent paragraphs one, two or three ems, the indention will be approximately the width of one, two or three lower-case *m*'s of the type used. *See also En, Pica.*

Em Dash. The dash — as here — used in punctuation. *See also Dash.*

Em Quadrat. A square of metal used to fill out short lines of type to the required length; its width is equal to the BODY (*q.v.*). It is a type body cast less than type height, and is always the square of the size of type it accompanies, e.g. an em quadrat of 12-point type is 12 × 12 points. Em quadrats are often made in multiple. Used normally before the first of a new paragraph. Usually called 'Em quad' or 'Mutton' (slang). *See also En Quadrat.*

Emage. The area of a block of text, or of a text page, measured in terms of ems of its type size.

E-Mail. *See Electronic Mail.*

EMBLA. EAST MIDLANDS BRANCH (*q.v.*) (of the Library Association).

Emblem Book. A type of book in which designs or pictures called emblems, expressing some thought or moral idea, were printed with accompanying proverbs, mottoes, or explanatory writing; or in which verses are arranged in symbolic shapes such as crosses.

Embossed. 1. (*Binding*) A design which is raised in relief. 2. (*Printing*) Lettering, or a design, which is raised above the surface of the paper.

Embossed Book. A book in which the text is printed in embossed characters, such as Braille, for the use of the blind.

Embossing. Relief printing by the use of a sunken die and a raised counterpart, called female and male, the surface of the paper being raised in relief. It may also be done by the use of certain substances dusted on the printed surface and caused to be raised by heating. Also called 'Process embossing', 'Relief printing', 'Bas relief printing'. *See also Die Stamping, Thermography.*

Embossing Plate. A plate cut or etched below its surface and used for producing a design, usually lettering, in relief on a sheet of paper. *See also Embossing.*

Embossing Press. A machine used in binderies for impressing lettering and designs on book covers.

Embroidered Binding. Binding in which the covering material is embroidered cloth. Also called 'Needlework binding'.

Emil Award. An award organized by the Book Trust and given annually for the children's book 'in which text and illustration are both excellent and perfectly harmonious'; now combined with the MASCHLER (KURT) AWARD (*q.v.*).

EMMA. Extra-MARC material. Item for which no record exists in the official MARC data-bases. Includes most pre-1950 material and some non-United Kingdom and non-United States imprints. The term BLDMARC (*q.v.*) or 'external MARC record' is now preferred.

Empty Digits. (*Classification*) 1. Symbols, e.g. punctuation marks used in a notation solely to separate meaningful characters (or groups of characters) forming part of a composite notation, which themselves have no meaning but merely convey structure. 2. A digit (*see* DIGIT 1) having ordinal value but without representing any specific idea.

Emptying Digit. A digit (*see* DIGIT 1) having ordinal value but depriving the preceding digit of its focal idea.

Emulsion. The chemicals with which a photographic film or paper is coated.

En. A unit of printer's measurement that is half of the EM (*q.v.*) in width but the same as the em in depth; thus a 12-point en quad is 12 by 6 points, a 10-point en is 10 by 5 points, and an 8-point en is 8 by 4 points.

En Point. A point, i.e. dot, set midway along a piece of printer's type as wide as an en, so that when printed it will appear with space on either side of it. It may be on, or above, the BASE LINE (*q.v.*).

En Quadrat. A square of metal half the width of the body of a type, and half an EM QUADRAT (*q.v.*), usually inserted after a punctuation mark when not ending a sentence. Usually called 'En quad' or 'Nut' (slang).

En Rule. A dash the width of an en space. *See also Dash.*

Enamel Paper. A highly finished paper coated on one side.

Enamelled Bindings. *See Champlevé, Cloisonné.*

Enchiridion. (*Pl.*, – ons or – a). A hand-book, specifically a manual of devotions.

Encode. 1. To put into symbolic form. 2. In information retrieval, to transform a document, message or abstract by means of a specific notation.

Encoding. (*Information retrieval*) A process whereby a message is transformed into signals that can be carried by a communication channel.

Encryption. The mechanism of coding data transmitted by various telecommunication systems so that only authorized users may have access to it; this may be relevant for sensitive information (for example, drug data to pharmacists) or to ensure that only those paying for a certain service can obtain it.

Encyclopaedia. A work containing information on all subjects, or limited to a special field or subject, arranged in systematic (usually alphabetical), order. Encyclopaedias may be in one volume, in which case very brief information will be given, or they may be in many volumes in which the various matters will be comprehensive, usually written by experts, and sometimes containing bibliographies and illustrations. The term was first used in a book title in Johann Henrich Alsted's *Encyclopaedia cursus philosophici*, Herborn, 1608. It was one of the last encyclopaedias written in Latin and compiled on a systematic plan; in future they were to be in the vernacular languages with the entries in alphabetical order. The first of this kind to be published in English was John Harris's *Lexicon technicum, or, An universal English dictionary of the arts and sciences*, London, 1704. One of the earliest encyclopaedias was the Spanish Archbishop Isidore of Seville's *Etymologiarum sive originum libri XX* which was completed in 623. More than a thousand manuscripts of this have survived, and in printed form it had an undiminished appeal as late as the seventeenth century.

End a Break. An instruction to the compositor that the last line of a TAKE (*q.v.*) or section or copy is to be filled out with quad spacing after setting the last word. *See also Break-Line, End Even, Run On.*

End Even. An instruction to the compositor that the last line of type in a TAKE (*q.v.*) or section of copy is to be spaced out so that the last word is at the end of a line. *See also Break-Line, End a Break, Run On.*

End Leaf. The piece of paper covering the turned-in covering material and the joint, or hinge reinforcement, or a re-bound book. (American).

End-matter. The items which follow the text of a printed book. These include appendices, bibliography, notes, supplements, indexes, glossary, imprint or collation, advertisements. *See also Back Matter.*

Endnotes. Notes printed at the end of a chapter or end of a book.

Endpaper. A sheet of paper at each end of a book which is inserted by the binder to help fasten the sewn sections to the cover. One half, the 'paste-down endpaper', is pasted on to a cover of the book (with the tapes between); the other, the 'free endpaper' or 'fly-leaf' is pasted with a narrow strip of paste at the fold to the end leaf of a section. *See also Doublure, Map Endpapers.*

Engine-Sizing. Hardening paper by adding a moisture-resistant substance such as casein, starch or resin to the pulp before the stuff flows on to the machine wire. This is the usual method of sizing the cheaper papers and produces a weaker paper than TUB-SIZING (*q.v.*). Engine-sized paper is abbreviated ES. *See also Surface Sizing.*

English. An out-of-date name for a size of type equal to about 14 point.

English Finish Paper. A calendered paper with a smooth but not highly glossy finish.

English Language Book Society. A non-profit making publishing organization financed by the British Government through the Overseas Development Administration and administered by the British Council with the object of making books of an educational nature – provided both publisher and author are British – available through the usual trade channels. The titles are chosen by a Committee and are printed in very large quantities. Since 1960 when the scheme was launched more than 15,000,000 books have been sold at a third or sometimes less of their normal price in seventy-nine scheduled developing countries of Asia, Africa, the West Indies and the Pacific. These editions cannot be purchased except in the scheduled countries. Abbreviated ELBS. The Society also now uses its acronym to designate its *Educational Low-Priced Book Scheme.*

English Stock. A group of publications of which the STATIONERS' COMPANY (*q.v.*) held the sole rights of printing and distributing. Perpetual rights were given in a patent granted in 1603 by James I to the Master, Wardens and Assistants of the Company. The publications included almanacs, ABC primers, prognostications, psalters, psalms in metre and catechisms and were sold in large numbers.

Engraved Title-page. A supplementary title-page usually wholly engraved on copper which faces the usual printed title-page. These were popular in the seventeenth century and were frequently elaborate allegorical pictures or symbolic designs.

Engraver's Proofs. Proofs of engravings used for verifying the quality of the work and for dummying up in pages.

Engraving. 1. The art or process of making letters or designs on wood, metal or other substances, by cutting or etching, for the purpose of printing or stamping by an intaglio or recess process on paper or other material. 2. An engraved plate, or an impression made from an engraved plate. 3. An engraved inscription. 4. The act of taking an impression from an engraved plate. *See also Aquatint, Etching, Line Engraving, Mezzotint, Wood Engraving.*

Enhanced Local Area Network. A more sophisticated development of the LOCAL AREA NETWORK (*q.v.*).

Enlarged Edition. *Synonymous with* REVISED EDITION (*q.v.*).

Enlargement. A copy, usually of a photograph or microphotograph, having a larger scale than the original. Also called 'Blowup', 'Projection print'.

Enrolled Account. An account which has been entered on a roll, usually for audit.

Enrolment. Entry of a document upon a roll.

ENSLA. Eastern Nigeria Division School Libraries Association. *See Nigerian Library Association.*

Entity. 1. The name of a country, dependency, or other area of special geopolitical interest (BS 5374: 1976, ISO 3166 – 1974 *Codes for the representation of names of countries*). 2. In co-ordinate indexing a material object mentioned as subject matter.

Entropy. The unavailable information in a group of documents. The degree of disorganization in an informational assemblage.

Entry. 1. The record of a book publication, or other item in a catalogue or other library record. In a catalogue it may be the main entry or an entry under subject, or an ADDED ENTRY (*q.v.*) or an INDEX ENTRY (*q.v.*). It may give a description of the item and also the location. 2. Sometimes used to indicate the cataloguing process which is concerned with determining the headings to be used for the BODY OF THE ENTRY (*q.v.*) or that part of the description of an item which follows a heading. 3. (*a*) A unit of an index consisting of a heading (and qualifying expression, if any) with at least one reference to the location of the item in the text or with a 'See' cross-reference. (*b*) In a complex entry, when references are numerous enough for systematic grouping sub-headings are used to introduce sub-entries, each with the relevant reference(s). 4. An item in an index to a literary composition (MS., book, periodical, etc.) which refers to a single specific place in the text, and possibly indicates the nature of the material to be found there. 5. The physical form of record on which entries are made; in information retrieval sometimes called a TALLY (*q.v.*). 6. (*Classification*) In schedules and tables, a self-contained unit of the text consisting of a number or span of numbers, a heading, and often one or more notes. *See also Added Entry, Analytical Entry, General Secondary, Heading, Main Entry, Reference, Series Entry, Title Entry.*

Entry-a-line Index. *See Line-by-Line Index.*

Entry Word. 1. The first word, other than an article, of a heading in a catalogue; the one by which the entry is arranged. *See also Heading.* 2. The word determining the place of an entry or group of related entries in the catalogue.

Enumerative Bibliography. A list of recorded items compiled within limits set by the compiler; these may be geographical, chronological or topical.

Enumerative Classification. A classification which attempts to list specific subjects. Owing to the difficulty of enumerating all possible specific subjects, most of such classifications are necessarily selective. The Library of Congress Classification is of this kind.

Enumerative Indexing Language. Subject terms used as headings for both single and composite concepts and providing a closed system (i.e. a list of terms allowing of no insertions) which the classifier could use. *See also Synthetic Indexing Language.*

Enumerative Notation. *Synonymous with* FENCED NOTATION (*q.v.*).

EPC. *See Editorial Processing Centre.*

Ephemera. 1. Pamphlets, cuttings and other material, of ephemeral interest and value. 2. Such material of earlier periods which has acquired literary or historical importance.

Ephemera Society (UK). An association devoted to the preservation of ephemera, particularly the organization of collections of ephemera in museums and libraries. Awards the *Samuel Pepys Medal* for outstanding contributions to ephemera studies.

Ephemerides. *See Ephemeris.*

Ephemeris (*Pl.* Ephemerides). 1. An almanac or calendar. 2. An obsolete term for a diary. 3. A title-word of many seventeenth and eighteenth century periodicals. 4. An astronomical almanac giving the daily positions of stars and other heavenly bodies.

Epigraph. A quotation in the preliminary pages or at the commencement of the chapter of a book to indicate the sentiment or idea.

Epistemology. The science of organized ideas in their exact correspondence with outward things, or knowledge.

Epistolaria. A liturgical book containing the Epistles.

Epithalamium. A poem or song in honour of a wedding, or of a bride and bridegroom.

Epithet. A descriptive, significant name; an additional name or title expressing an attribute of the person referred to, and used to distinguish him from others of the same name. In catalogue entries, the epithet follows the personal name under which the entry is made.

Epitome. A work that has been abridged or summarized from some larger work for a particular purpose, the essential matter of the original being retained. To be distinguished from an ADAPTATION (*q.v.*).

EPO. European Patents Office – a HOST (*q.v.*) based in Holland and providing access mainly to patent databases.

Eponym. 1. One who gives, or is supposed to give, his name to a people, place or institution; also the name of that personage. 2. A distinguishing title formed from the name of a person to designate a period, people or place, e.g. Victorian era.

Epopee. An epic poem. Epic poetry.

Equality Award.   A cash award given to an individual or group for an important contribution towards promoting equality between men and women in the library profession. Administered by the American Library Association Awards Committee, and donated by Scarecrow Press Inc.

Equivalence Relation.   (*Information retrieval*) A horizontal relationship between descriptors having the same meaning.

Erasmus.   European Action Programme on the Mobility of University Students; established by the European Community in 1987 to encourage mobility by operating a university network, introducing a system of grants, advancing recognition criteria, and providing various support mechanisms.

ERIC.   Educational Resources Information Center, a national organization supported financially by the Office of Educational Research and Improvement of the US Department of Education. ERIC acquires, selects, catalogues, abstracts, and indexes educational research documents in the widest sense, and functions through a network of 16 clearing houses. The Information Resources clearing house (ERIC/IR) based at Syracuse University, New York, is responsible for library and informatics-related work. ERIC publications include *Resources in Education* (m) and *Current Index to Journals in Education* (m).

EROMM.   *See European Register of Microform Masters.*

Erotica.   Indecent or obscene books.   *See also Curiosa, Facetiae.*

Errata.   (*Sing.* Erratum). *Synonymous with* CORRIGENDA (*q.v.*).

E.S.   Abbreviation for engine-sized. *See Engine-Sizing.*

ESA/IRS.   Acronym for European Space Agency/Information Retrieval Service. A HOST (*q.v.*) offering access to databases via its computer in Frascati, Italy.

Escapist Literature.   Light literature such as thrillers, adventure stories and romances which are read for entertainment, as a relief from more serious reading, and as a distraction.

Esdaile Memorial Fund, Arundell.   This Fund was opened in 1958 in memory of a former Secretary of the British Museum and a Past-President of the Library Association, in order to endow a lecture to be given periodically as a memorial to the late Dr. Arundell Esdaile in commemoration of his unique services to librarianship and bibliography.

Esparto.   A coarse grass, also termed 'Alfa', growing in countries around the Mediterranean, particularly southern Spain and northern Africa, which is used for making the better (but not the best) grades of book paper, featherweight and coating papers. The best grade is known as 'Spanish', the cheaper grades as 'Tripoli'. Esparto papers are distinguished by their refined silky texture and bulk, and their close uniform surface or finish. Their finish is their chief characteristic; this together with their bulkiness makes them eminently suitable for fine printings and other papers required to take a good impression from plates.

ESPRIT.   The European Strategic Programme of Research and Development in Information Technology. Began in pilot phase in 1983; the main programme 1984–89 had a budget of 750 million ECUs from the European

Community on a 50% cost sharing basis with companies, universities and research centres. The major aims were to improve Europe's IT capability, to reinforce technological co-operation and pave the way to internationally accepted standards. A second phase of the ESPRIT programme building on the achievements of the first has been proposed; it will have a budget envelope of 1600 MECUs and concentrate on three sectors: micro-electronics and peripheral technologies; information processing systems and IT application technologies.

Essay Periodical.   A periodical publication, prevalent in the fifteenth century, each issue of which usually consisted of a single essay. The *Spectator* and the *Rambler* are examples.

Essential Characteristics.   *See Characteristic of a Classification.*

Established.   Said of a catalogue heading when an authority card or catalogue entry or any kind is made for it.

ESTC.   The Eighteenth Century Short-Title Catalogue comprises a record of some 135,000 books, pamphlets and ephemera printed in Britain and its colonies, and any item printed in English anywhere in the world between 1701 and 1800. The British Library is responsible for compilation, and the project which began in 1977 will continue for several years. In 1982 the ESTC file became available on-line, through BLAISE-LINE (*q.v.*), or RLIN in the USA.

Esther J. Piercy Award.   *See Piercy Award, Esther J.*

Estienne, Robert.   Born 1503 and son of Henry Estienne who founded in 1501 the famous firm of Parisian scholar-printers. Founded his own business in 1524, and was appointed in 1539 and 1540 printer to the king in Latin, Greek and Hebrew. The fine press-work of his books matches the careful editing of the classical texts, dictionaries and translations. From 1550 until his death in 1559 he worked at Geneva, where he printed several of Calvin's works. The most important member of the greatest family of scholar-printers of all ages, his chief and most secure claim of many to immortality, is that based on his Thesaurus, *Dictionarius sive Latinae thesaurus,* Paris, 1531. He established the principle, contrary to his mediaeval predecessors, that a Latin dictionary must be based on classical authorities. He undertook the compilation of a series of Latin-French and French-Latin dictionaries which helped to create the classical French language: these were translated into German, Dutch and English, and were the progenitors of all bilingual dictionaries.

Estimates.   Annual calculations of amounts of money needed to provide a service. *Special estimates* are those for completely new items which could not be anticipated when the annual estimates were prepared. *Supplemental estimates* (sometimes called *supplementary estimates*) are those made during the course of the financial year for amounts in excess of the figure which was included in the annual estimates and are due to a variety of causes such as an increase in the cost of materials or labour, or unanticipated difficulties in the carrying out of work, or urgent and unanticipated developments in the service.

Estray. (*Archives*) The legal term applying to a document not in the custody of the original records creator or its legal successor. *See also Replevin.*

et al. Abbreviation for *et alii* (*Lat.* 'and other people'). Used in footnotes in a second or subsequent reference to a work. If follows the name of the first of three or more collaborators whose work has previously been cited. Also for *et alia* 'and other things', *et alibi* 'and elsewhere'.

et infra. (*Lat.* 'and below'.) Used to indicate that something which follows may be of smaller size, as '24 vols., 8vo. *et infra*', meaning that the largest is 8vo. *See also infra.*

et seq. Abbreviation for *et sequens* (*Lat.* 'and the following one'). *Pl. et seqq.* abbreviation for *et sequentes, et sequentia* 'and those that follow'. *See also seq.*

etc. Abbreviation for *et cetera* (*Lat.* 'and the other, the rest'). Also abbreviated '&c'.

Etching. 1. The process of producing a design upon a plate of steel, copper, glass or zinc by means of drawing lines with an etching needle through an acid-resisting wax coating upon the polished surface of the plate, and then covering this surface with an acid which corrodes the metal in the lines thus laid bare. 2. A plate with an etched design upon its surface. 3. The art of producing impressions on paper or other material from an etched plate. 4. The impression produced by 3. *See also Deep Etching, Dry-point Etching.*

Ethics. *See Professional Ethics.*

Ethnic Numbers. Numbers added to a classification symbol so as to arrange books by language or race. They are usually applicable throughout a classification scheme. Also called 'Linguistic numbers'.

Ethnomusicology. The study of the native music of a people or of a race.

Etruscan Alphabet. The most significant offshoot from the Greek alphabet and adapted to the language of the Etruscans. It developed, probably in the eighth century B.C. and lasted until the first century A.D. The Latin alphabet was derived from it.

Etruscan Style. A calfskin binding style, so called becuse of the contrasting colours or shades of leather (light brown or terracotta) and decoration (dark brown or black tooling); the terracotta shades and decoration combined represent Greek and Etruscan vases. Such bindings usually have a rectangular central panel on each cover, or occasionally a plain oval with a classical urn in the middle and are tooled in black, surrounded by a border of Greek palmated leaves in black, with outer borders of classical design (Grecian key or Doric entablature) tooled in gold. The spines also are decorated with classical ornaments. This style was used by and probably originated by William Edwards of Halifax towards the end of the eighteenth century, and was practised until about 1820.

EUDISED. Abbreviation for the European Documentation and Information System for Education, a programme of the Council of Europe. It has been in existence since 1970, and has produced a number of reports and technical studies.

EURIPA. European Information Providers' Association: a group formed in 1980 to promote the interests of European based database producers, hosts and other information industry companies. Now *see EIIA*.

EURODICAUTOM. European Dictionaire Automatique; a database of specialized terms maintained by the EC to provide ready translation of scientific and technical material between European languages.

EURODOCDEL. A research project sponsored and funded by the EC to improve the ease and speed of access to documents, publications, specifications, and legal drafts issued by EC institutions. The system stored documents in full text on digital optical disks, continuously updated, and delivered electronically to videotex terminals or high speed facsimile printers. The system ran experimentally during 1985. *See also APOLLO, ADONIS*.

EUROLIS. The title given to the *Report on Library and Information Services Activity in the European Community and the Council of Europe* prepared by George Cunningham and published by the Library Association in November 1988.

EUROLUG. *See European Online User Group*.

EURONET/DIANE. Euronet was a data transmission system, within the European Economic Community, jointly operated by the PTT (post, telegraph and telephone) services of the member states. Ceased to function 1984, replaced by national PSS networks. DIANE (Direct Information Access Network for Europe) was an information retrieval service superimposed on the Euronet telecommunications system.

European Academic Research Network. *See EARN*.

European Association of Health Information and Libraries. Formed in 1986 and now having 500 members from medical libraries, pharmaceutical industry, hospitals, and other health services. 1988 Conference (Bologna) attracted over 600 participants from 24 countries. Secretariat in Brussels.

European Association of Research Libraries. *See LIBER*.

European Association of Scientific Information Dissemination Centres. *See EUSIDIC*.

European Commission Host Organization. *See ECHO*.

European Community. The union of European countries that has grown out of the European Coal and Steel Community (founded 1951), the European Atomic Energy Community and the European Economic Community (both founded 1957). The founding treaty is the Treaty of Rome (1957); in 1986 the Single European Act prepared the way for closer social and political unity. The 12 members are: France, West Germany, Italy, Belgium, Netherlands, Luxembourg, UK, Denmark, Ireland, Greece, Spain, and Portugal. The main institutions comprise the Council of Ministers, the Commission (civil service), the European Parliament (consultative) and the Court of Justice. Library and information matters are the responsibility of the DIRECTORATE-GENERAL XIII (*q.v.*). *See also Council of Europe, Plan of Action (EC)*.

European Council on Library Resources.   A body proposed at a meeting held November 1984 in Luxembourg, and sponsored by the EC, Council of Europe, and European Cultural Foundation. It was porposed that steps should be taken in 1985 to set up the Council, and that there should be three main initial areas of concern: conservation, electronic publishing, and electronic document supply. *See European Foundation for Library Co-operation.*

European Documentation Centres.   Depository libraries entitled to receive a full range of European Community publications. Forty-five UK university and polytechnic libraries are so designated. Abbreviated EDC. An ASSOCIATION OF EDC LIBRARIANS (*q.v.*) was formed in 1981.

European Foundation for Library Co-operation.   A body founded in 1985, and sometimes referred to as the Group of Lausanne; the only product so far of the initiative launched under the name European Council on Library Resources (*q.v.*). Objectives are to support library co-operation, and support appropriate projects. Efforts initially concentrated on resource sharing, networking, and promotion of a European perspective in training and education. Major conference on 'Automation and Networking' held Brussels, May 1990. Controlled by a Board of 18 invited members; secretariat in Brussels. Abbreviated EFLC.

European Host Operators Group.   The first assembly of the European Host Operators Group (EHOG), was held on 6 October 1982. The group was formed from European information centres providing online public services over Euronet and other telecommunication networks. The European Commission had encouraged the information centres, the hosts, to form an association to support the information industry. EHOG developed the environment and market for online information services and improved the internal service elements and standards of EHOG members. Now *see EIIA.*

European Information Centres.   A network of EC sponsored in all Community countries, intended to provide small and medium-sized companies with advice and information on legislation, finance, research, etc. 189 centres are now open, of which twenty are in the U.K. Abbreviated EIC.

European Information Industry Association.   *See EIIA.*

European Information Market Development Group.   Established in 1984 to replace the Euronet launch team and ECHO; the new EC Parliament five year plan for information seeks to develop the information market in Europe, and the Group is responsible for implementing the Plan in contact with representatives of the online community in each EC Country. Abbreviated EIMDG. *See also IMPACT.*

European Information Market Observatory.   *See IMPACT.*

European Institute for Information Management.   A public establishment under the supervision of the Luxembourg Ministry of National Education. Founded 1982, it provides post-graduate training for future specialists in the field of information management. The teaching staff is international, and the languages of instruction are French and English.

European Librarians and Publishers. Working Group of. A group set up in the early 1980s at the request of the CEC to address joint problems and issues. The group is independent and members are co-opted. Major statements have been issued on *Libraries Acquisition Budgets* (1982), *Impact of Electronic Technology* (1984), *Use of optical media for publication of full text* (1987), *One world of information: OSI and EDI* (1989), *Barriers to the flow of books* (1990).

European Library Automation Group. An informal group, based at the Royal Library in Brussels, organizing meetings and workshops to discuss various aspects of automation. Aims to hold an annual, extended meeting with opportunities for discussion and exchange of experience. Abbreviated ELAG.

European Marine and Freshwater Sciences Librarians, Information Scientists and Documentalists. An Association of European librarians which held its first meeting early in 1988. Based currently at Plymouth Marine Laboratory (UK).

European Online User Group. An association of European libraries and database users, formed to encourage co-ordinated responses to manufacturers developments. UKOLUG (*q.v.*) has a representative on this body. Abbreviated EUROLUG.

European Organization for Nuclear Research. Established on 29 September 1954 'to provide for collaboration among European states in nuclear research of a pure scientific and fundamental character, and in research essentially related thereto'. Governments may become members. Publishes *CERN Courier* (m.). Abbreviated CERN.

European Register of Microform Masters. A European Community initiative to facilitate the preservation of rare books in European libraries. An initial study was completed in 1989; LIBER (*q.v.*) has been closely involved in the project. Abbreviated EROMM.

European Space Agency. *See ESA/IRS.*

Eurostat. The Statistical Office of the European Community is located in Luxembourg and is one of the Directorates-General of the Commission. Its task is to collect and process statistical data on the EC Member States and their main trading partners to serve as a basis for the policy decisions that have to be taken at Community level. Various databanks are created, including *CRONOS* containing macro-economic figures from the 1950s to date, *Regio* providing regional figures, and *Eurostatus* giving main indicators for the members states, USA and Japan.

Eurotra. An automatic translation system, designed to work between several languages, using a central pivot language. The system is under development by the EC and is intended to facilitate rapid publication of all Community papers in all necessary languages.

EUSIDIC. Originally an acronym for European Scientific Information Dissemination Centres, founded 1970, but now used as a name in its own right. Currently 180 members from 21 countries, mainly European, make up this neutral forum for all those concerned in the information industry – users, information providers and service providers. Holds regular meetings and publishes a bimonthly journal *Newsidic*.

Evaluation. The process of measuring the performance of a service or system, and assessing its effectiveness in meeting established objectives.

Evaluative Abstract. *See Abstract.*

Eve Style. *See Fanfare (Flourish) Style.*

Even Page. A page of a book bearing an even number; usually the VERSO (*q.v.*).

Even Right-hand Margin. Said of typewritten matter where the lines have been justified and all have the same length, thus giving an even right-hand margin as well as the usual even left-hand margin.

Even Small Caps. An instruction to the compositor that all the copy so marked is to be set in small capitals without any large capitals as would be done in 'caps and smalls'. Abbreviated even s. caps, or even s.c. Also called 'Level small caps'.

Even Working. The setting of 'copy' so that it will occupy a full sheet of, say, 32 pages. If an additional portion of a sheet is required for completion, this is called 'uneven working'. *See also Oddments.*

Evolutionary Order. (*Classification*) The method by which subjects are shown in the order of their history or development, 'in natural history putting the parts of each subject in the order which that theory assigns to their appearance in creation. As science proceeds from the molecular to the molar, from number and space through matter and force to matter and life, etc., etc.' (*Cutter*) Cutter's Expansive Classification follows this order, as also in a rough way does Brown's Subject Classification. No scheme is, or can be, evolutionary throughout.

Ewart-Biggs (Christopher) Memorial Prize. A biennial prize for a work in English or French that contributes to peace and understanding in Ireland, or to co-operation between members of the European community.

ex libris. 1. Latin phrase, meaning *from the books* (i.e. from the library of); frequently used on book plates, the owner's name being written or printed after 'ex libris'. 2. Surplus books from a subscription or other library.

Exact Classification. *Synonymous with* CLOSE CLASSIFICATION (*q.v.*).

Exact Size. The measured size of a book expressed by centimetres or inches rather than by a signature symbol. Also called 'Absolute size'.

Excerpt. A verbatim extract from a book, or piece of music, whether printed or manuscript. An extract or selection.

Excerpta Medica. A series of databases operated by Elsevier Science Publishers to provide medical and health professionals with access to basic research and clinical literature. Several information services, abstract bulletins and bibliographies are available in highly specialized areas. Titles of the databases include EMBASE, EMDRUGS, EMHEALTH, etc. Some services are now available also on CD-ROM.

Exchange. 1. The exchange by barter or trade of duplicate material with other libraries. 2. An arrangement whereby an organization exchanges its publications for those of another organization.

Exchange Centre. An administrative office which negotiates the exchange of books between libraries, arranging for books to be sent from libraries where they are surplus to libraries where they are needed.

Exchange Librarian. One who is responsible for the exchange of the library's publications with those of another library or organization.

Exchequer Series. *See Liberate Roll.*

Exhausted Edition. An edition which has become out-of-print.

Exhaustive Division. Dividing as exhaustively and minutely as possible in order to give specific places in a scheme of classification.

Exhibits Round Table Award. Offered by the Exhibits Round Table of the American Library Association to an individual or group for aiding or improving some aspect of librarianship or library service on the basis of need in the profession or in the operation of professional library associations. This award has been renamed the John R. Rowe Memorial Award.

Exit Counter. The side of an issue desk at which readers leave a library and have books issued or 'charged' to them.

Ex-Library Copy. A catalogue description of a book originally in a library.

Exotics. A general name used in the printing industry for Cyrillic, Arabic and other non-Latin letter-forms.

Expansion. (*Classification*) The development of a concept or series of concepts in the schedules or tables to provide for more minute subdivision.

Expansive Classification. The scheme of classification devised by C. A. Cutter, which began to appear in 1891; it is one of the most minute and scholarly of schemes for a general library, but it is now out-of-date. It consists of seven expansions (the seventh, uncompleted, being very detailed and suitable for a very large library) each of which covers the whole field of knowledge but in varying detail, and can be used according to the size of the library. Later expansions cannot be used in the same library, however, without re-classifying a number of the books, as the fundamental symbols had to be altered as the expansions progressed. The order of the schedules is evolutionary, the main classes being:

A	General Works.	R	Useful Arts, Technology.
B	Philosophy.	V	Athletic and Recreative Arts.
Br	Religion.	Vv	Fine Arts. Music.
D	Historical Sciences.	X	Arts of Communication by
H	Social Sciences.		Language.
L	Sciences and Arts.		

The intervening letters in the above schedule are given to the more important divisions. The notation is a pure alphabetical one, permitting subdivision at any point in the scheme by the use of the alphabet, but form divisions and the Local List for sub-dividing geographically have numerical notations which can be used mnemonically.

Expert System. A computer system that in part replicates human decision-making; ARTIFICIAL INTELLIGENCE (*q.v.*) developments allow some memory and reasoning functions to be superimposed on normal calculation functions so that information can be handled in an enhanced manner. Present developments include a simple classification software package. Also called a 'knowledge based system'.

Explanatory Guide Cards. Guide cards giving an explanation of the arrangement of the catalogue cards and placed at the beginning of groups of cards for voluminous authors, anonymous classics, sacred books, etc.

Explicit. The closing phrase of a manuscript or early printed book indicating its completion and sometimes giving the author's name and the title of the work. It is the author's or scribe's colophon taken over from the manuscript, and may appear instead of, or in conjunction with, the printer's colophon. It is a contraction for *explicitus est* 'it is unfolded'.

Expressive Notation. One of Ranganathan's canons of notation – that the notation should be designed to show that two terms are in the same array, or the same chain.

Expurgated Edition. An edition with those parts left out that might be objected to on moral or other grounds. *See also Abridged Edition, Bowdlerized, Unexpurgated Edition.*

Extended Score. *Synonymous with* OPEN SCORE (*q.v.*). *See also Score.*

Extender. That part of a type letter which projects above or below the main body of the letter. Also called 'Extruder'. *See also Ascender, Descender.*

Extension. (*Classification*) The extension of a term or class indicates all the different items included in the term; in other words, the compass of the term. The intension indicates their *qualities*. Extension and intension vary conversely; when one is great the other is small.

Extension Agencies. Activities of the library services which are undertaken outside the main library buildings.

Extension Card. Second and subsequent catalogue cards used when the entry is too long to go on one card. It contains the classification number and the entry word from the first card, and is numbered 2, 3, etc. Also called a 'Continuation card', 'Run-on card'.

Extension Centre Library. A branch library which is placed in an American University or college extension centre where college-level classes or other educational services are provided, usually through a specific division of an educational institution.

Extension Work. Activities which are undertaken with the object of reaching groups of people who might otherwise be unaware of the library, such as lecture societies, reading circles, discussion groups; and the provision of books for prisons, clubs, hospitals, literary societies, etc. *See also Outreach.*

Extent. (*Publishing*) The length of a book expressed in terms of the number of pages.

External Bibliography. *See Historical Bibliography.*

External Reader. A person who is permitted to use a library provided primarily for the use of privileged persons, such as the members of a professional body or association.

Extra Binder. A craftsman who uses the best materials and employs the soundest methods of construction; he usually decorates each binding with a design specially made for it.

Extra Binding. In binding, a trade term for the best work. Applicable to any book well 'forwarded', lined with marbled or other special paper, silk head-bands, and gilt with a narrow roll round the sides and inside the 'squares'.

Extra-illustrated. A book which has had additional illustrations and printed matter inserted since publication. *See also Grangerizing.*

Extra Lightweight Paper. Sensitized photographic paper between 0.0023 and 0.0031 inches inclusive. Also called 'Ultra thin paper'.

Extra Thin Paper. Sensitized photographic paper between 0.0032 and 0.0037 inches inclusive. *See also Photographic Papers.*

Extra Ticket. *Synonymous with* SUPPLEMENTARY TICKET (*q.v.*).

Extract Type. Type which is different from that used for the text, normally being smaller, and used to enable quoted (or extracted) material such as poems, bibliographies, extracts, etc., to be easily distinguished from the text itself.

Extracted Article. *Synonymous with* SEPARATE (*q.v.*).

Extrapolation. (*Classification*) The addition of new subjects to the end of an ARRAY (*q.v.*). This flexible aspect of notation is facilitated by the OCTAVE DEVICE (*q.v.*). *See also Interpolation.*

Extruder. *Synonymous with* EXTENDER (*q.v.*).

Extruders. The collective term for the ASCENDERS and DESCENDERS (*qq.v.*).

Exxon Awards Preservation Grant. An award of $1.5 million given to the COUNCIL ON LIBRARY RESOURCES (*q.v.*) to establish long-term research projects to preserve the holdings of American research libraries. CLR received the award early in 1985 and formed a Preservation Committee to co-ordinate the work.

f. Abbreviation for 'following'. *Pl.* ff.

Faber (Geoffrey) Memorial Prize. An award in alternate years for a volume of verse, and a volume of prose fiction of the best literary merit by young Commonwealth or UK authors.

Fabriano Paper. An Italian paper used for special and fine editions.

Fabric Binding. One in which a fabric has been used instead of leather and vellum. Velvet, silk, satin, and canvas have been the most popular materials, and have been used more frequently in England than elsewhere. Velvet, a most extensively used fabric, was plain, embroidered, or even gilt-tooled. Embroidered bindings, in a form of split-stitch work known as *opus anglicanum* on satin, were popular in the fifteenth century.

fac. Abbreviation for FACSIMILE and FACTOTUM (*qq.v.*).

Face. . The entire unbroken front of shelving on one side of a double case or on one side of a room or gallery. 2. (*Printing*) The printing surface of type. It comprises STEM, BOWL, SERIF, COUNTER, CROTCH and KERN (*qq.v.*). Measured set-wise, i.e. left to right, a face may be condensed (compressed) or extended (expanded); measured body-wise, it may be small, ordinary, medium or large, according to the actual size of the short and long letters. Also, the printing surface of any kind of printing plate. 3. (*Printing*) A particular design or style of a fount of type. *See also Type Face.*

Face Up. (*Printing*) Said of full-page illustrations which are printed on the right-hand side of an opening, i.e. on the recto of a leaf.

Facet. In classification, the whole group of divisions or foci (*see* FOCUS *noun*), produced when a subject is divided according to a single characteristic. Five kinds of facet are discernible in any class: these relate to personality, matter, energy, space and time. Facets may be divided into *Subfacets* (called by Ranganathan 'arrays'). *Dependent facets* do not appear in the classification except as a further division of a more fundamental facet. Modifications of basic facets are called *differential facets*. Each division of a facet is said to be an Isolate Focus, or simply an Isolate. Sometimes used to denote any single ISOLATE (*q.v.*) or any basic class. Also called 'Category'. *See also Auto-bias Device, Characteristic of a Classification, Subordination.* 2. An aspect, or orientation, of a topic.

Facet Analysis. (*Classification*) The analysis of any subject to determine what characteristics should be used to divide it, relating them to the five fundamentals. *See also Facet, Fundamental Categories.*

Facet Formula. (*Classification*) A formula for the application of division; used so that the order of applying characteristics may be consistently maintained. *See also Citation Order.*

Facet Indicator. A symbol which separates parts of a notation of a scheme of classification and indicates exactly what facet is to follow. Facet indicators were made possible in the Colon Classification by adopting the five FUNDAMENTAL CATEGORIES (*q.v.*), each of which is introduced by its own symbol. It may be a different kind of character in a mixed notation, e.g. a letter whereas other characters in the notation are figures, in which case every letter would indicate a facet. *See also Notation.*

Facet Interpolation. (*Classification*) The insertion of a new facet into a MAIN CLASS (*q.v.*).

Faceted Classification. 1. A scheme of classification which reflects in its structure the analysis of subjects according to a number of fundamental concepts, particularly those denominated: personality, matter, energy, space, time. It lists constituent parts of specific subjects, which parts must be assembled in a predetermined order to express the specific subjects. All modern schemes of classification are faceted to a certain degree: e.g. they provide tables of constant numbers for divisions relating to time and to space. A classification scheme which allows the classifier to build up the notation for a particular book from various unit schedules is called a 'faceted', 'synthetic' or 'analytico-synthetic' classification. 2. Classification schemes whose terms are grouped by conceptual categories and ordered so as to display their generic relations. These categories or 'facets' are standard unit-schedules and the terms, or rather the notation for the terms from these various unit-schedules, are combined at will in accordance with a prescribed order of permutation or combination.

Faceted Initial. In a mediaeval illuminated manuscript, an initial letter given the appearance of being faceted, that is cut like a gem.

Faceted Notation. (*Classification*) A NOTATION (*q.v.*) representing the classification of a book in which a distinctive symbol is used to separate the facets which comprise it.

Facetiae. Coarsely witty books; objectionable or indecent works collectively. *See also Curiosa, Erotica.*

Facing Pages. The two pages which are visible when a book is open. An OPENING (*q.v.*).

facsim. Abbreviation for FACSIMILE (*q.v.*). Also abbreviated 'fs.', 'fac.'.

Facsimile. 1. A copy of an original, reproduced in its exact form and style. 2. Used in cataloguing to indicate that the book catalogued contains a facsimile. Abbreviated 'facsim.', 'facsims.' (pl.) and sometimes 'fs', 'fac'. 3. An electronic system for transmitting pictures and graphic materials. *See Facsimile Transmission.*

Facsimile Binding. A binding which closely resembles an older binding.

Facsimile Catalogue. One which incorporates facsimiles of maps, pictures, designs, etc., as part of each catalogue entry which is made on larger cards than the normal size, or in loose leaf binders.

Facsimile Edition. An exact copy of a book made photographically, by xerography, or by an offset process. Used to avoid the cost of setting up type in order to produce a new edition of an out-of-print book. Previously, a copy, as near the original as possible typographically, published to make widely available a book which existed only as an incunabulum or as a manuscript.

Facsimile Reprint. A reproduction of a work, however printed, and reproducing exactly the appearance of the original.

Facsimile Transmission. A process whereby a representation of a document in its entirety can be transmitted over a telecommunications link. The recipient therefore does not obtain merely the information on the document but a complete copy of the original. Recent developments have made it possible for a digital system to turn the original copy into binary code thus greatly reducing transmission time. The abbreviation FAX is commonly used.

Factotum. An ornament of wood or metal having a space in the centre for the insertion of a capital letter of an ordinary fount of type; used to print ornamental initial letters at the commencement of a chapter. It is sometimes called a 'Factotum initial'. Abbreviated fac.

Faculty Library. *Synonymous with* DEPARTMENTAL LIBRARY (*q.v.*).

Faculty of Advocates, Edinburgh. *See National Library of Scotland.*

Fair Calf. *Synonymous with* LAW CALF (*q.v.*).

Fair Copy. A carefully made typescript or manuscript without mistakes or corrections, made after examining a draft.

Fall-out Ratio. (*Information retrieval*) In the testing of an information retrieval system, a measure expressing the ratio of the number of non-relevant documents retrieved to the total number of non-relevant documents in the file.

False Bands. *Synonymous with* Dummy Bands (*q.v.*).

False Combinations. (*Information retrieval*) A Noise (*q.v.*) which is produced by simple correlation of descriptors. Also called 'False sorts'. *See also Marker.*

False Date. A date given wrongly, either intentionally or in error. In a catalogue entry the correct date is given in brackets following 'i.e.'.

False Drop. (*Information retrieval*) 1. Citation that does not pertain to the subject sought. An alien, usually in a manipulative or co-ordinate index. 2. An irrelevant reference made in indexing documents for concept co-ordinate indexing. Also called 'False co-ordination'. *See also Uniterm Concept Co-ordination Indexing.*

'False First' Edition. An edition of a book said to be the first when in fact there had been an edition published previously by another publisher.

False Hyphen. One placed by the printer between two parts of a word which is broken at the line end.

False Imprint. *Synonymous with* Fictitious Imprint (*q.v.*).

False Link. (*Classification*) In chain indexing, a step in the notational hierarchy where the notational chain is lengthened by a symbol without an appropriate term being supplied. In the Dewey Decimal Classification, for example, where a zero is needed to introduce a standard sub-division or geographical table number, the zero having no verbal equivalent, but being merely an indicator that a form or geographical division is about to be employed. *See also Unsought Link.*

False Sorts. *Synonymous with* False Combinations (*q.v.*).

Falstaff. A fat face type. *See Fat Faces.*

Family. The complete group or collection of all the sizes and styles of type of the same design: they have common characteristics and differ only in size, set or thickness of lines, e.g. the Univers family, comprising: Univers Medium, **Univers Bold**, Univers Light, **Univers Bold Condensed**, **Univers Extra Bold**.

Family Name. A surname.

Fan. A book decoration style characteristic of Italian bindings in the seventeenth century, and of Scottish bindings, in which a design like a fan is tooled on the sides making a full circle in the centre, and often quarter circles in the corners. It is a development of the centre and cornerpiece bindings.

Fancy Type. Printing type of various sizes, ornamental in design; usually used for display purposes.

Fanfare Style. The later Eve style of decorating bookcovers, being a complication of geometrical interlacings and a multitude of scrolls, wreaths, sprays and flowers, filling all available space on back and sides of the book. It was practised in the late sixteenth century. Also called 'Flourish style'.

Fanzines. Uncommercial, non-professional, small-circulation magazines which deal with fantasy literature and art.

Farjeon Award, Eleanor. *See Children's Book Circle.*

Farmer (Prudence) Award. An annual UK award made for the best poem published in the *New Statesman* magazine.

Farmington Plan. A scheme whereby over sixty American research libraries agreed co-operatively to purchase books published in foreign countries in order to ensure that at least one copy of new books and pamphlets likely to interest research workers was acquired by an American library. Such books were promptly listed in the Union Catalogue at the Library of Congress and made available by inter-library loan or photographic reproduction. The plan was drawn up at Farmington, Connecticut, by K. D. Metcalf, J. P. Boyd and Archibald Macleish, and began to operate in January 1948.

Farries Public Relations Award, T. C. *See Library Association/ T. C. Farries Public Relations Award.*

Fascicle. Parts of a work which for convenience of publishing or printing, is issued in small instalments. They are usually incomplete in themselves and do not necessarily coincide with the formal division of the work into parts. They usually consist of sections, or groups of plates, protected by temporary wrappers, and may or may not be numbered or designated as a 'part', 'fascicule', 'lieferung', etc. Also called 'Fascicule', 'Fasciculus'.

Fascicule. *Synonymous with* FASCICLE *(q.v.).*

Fasciculus. *Synonymous with* FASCICLE *(q.v.).*

Fast Back. *Synonymous with* TIGHT BACK *(q.v.).*

Fat Faces. Type faces which have extra thick perpendicular strokes whether straight or curved, such as Elephant, Ultra Bodoni, and Falstaff.

Fat Matter. 'Copy' which can be set up in type easily since many lines of type will not be full. Novels which are largely dialogue are 'fat'. This is the opposite to difficult copy which is known as 'lean matter'. *See also Matter.*

Faulty Margin. An unequal margin due to imperfect registering.

Favoured Focus. Any simple of compound FOCUS *(q.v.)* which represents the subject of specialization of a library or the isolate in which its collection is more numerous than in other co-ordinate sub-classes.

Favoured Language. The language in which most of the books in a library are written.

Fawcett Library (UK). A collection of literature and information on feminism, the women's movement, and women in general. Maintained by the City of London Polytechnic Library.

Fawcett Society Book Prize. An annual award (alternate years for fiction and non-fiction) for a book that has contributed to the understanding of women's position in society. All submitted work is placed in the FAWCETT LIBRARY *(q.v.).*

FAX. *See Facsimile Transmission.*

Faxon (F. W.) Scholarship. An award to cover the cost of an internship for a student; administered by the ALA Office for Library Personnel Resources.

Feather-Edge. *Synonymous with* DECKLE EDGE.

Feather Ornament. *(Binding)* Engraved ornament which resembles feathers, on clasps or catches.

Feathering. 1. A fault in printing which results in a feathering effect visible when ink spreads beyond the printed impression via the fibres of the paper. It is caused by an excess of solvent in the ink, or an unsuitable paper.

2. Thinning down the overlapping edges of two pieces of paper which are to be joined when repairing a book.

Featherweight Paper. Light, bulky, printing paper with 75% air space; it is made largely from esparto and has little or no calendering. It is slightly porous and not easy to handle. *See also Antique.*

Featherwork. A type of book decoration which originated in Irish eighteenth century bindings, in which curved lines formed freehand with a gouge radiate from one point to produce a delicate and very rich pattern resembling feathers.

Feature. A characteristic of a thing indexed. *See also Characteristic of a Classification, Compresence, Item, Term.*

Feature Card. A plain or punched card allocated to a 'feature' in CO-ORDINATE INDEXING (*q.v.*) – a characteristic of the document indexed – on which are recorded the different items in a Set of Documents which have this same characteristic. Also called 'Term card' because a feature referring to subject matter is known as a 'term'.

Feature Card System. A method of information retrieval in which a card is reserved for a feature (variously called 'aspect'), 'dimension', 'facet'), characteristic, or piece of information. Each card is printed with the same grid of punchable positions, which are numbered, and each of these corresponds to a particular document. The document number is punched in each appropriate feature card. When it is required to know which document, or documents possess certain features, or combination of features, the feature cards are withdrawn from the file and placed one on the other. Light shining through the holes will reveal the documents possessing the features required. The number of features can be increased indefinitely simply by adding an additional card but when the number of documents exceeds the number of punchable positions (numbering 10,000 on cards of manageable size) a new set of feature cards must be commenced. *See also Edge-Notched Cards, Marginal-Hole Punched Cards.*

Feature Heading. The verbal part of a subject heading used in the systematic file of a CLASSIFIED CATALOGUE (*q.v.*), i.e. that part which is a translation into words of the last element of a classification symbol. The verbal part usually follows the symbol, and may be utilized to specify subjects for which no exact notation is provided in the scheme of classification.

Featuring. The provision in a classified catalogue of the hierarchic 'chain', setting out the classificatory steps (class, number and heading) leading to the individual entries at any particular number.

fecit. (*Lat.* 'he or she made (did) this'). Frequently added after the artist's name on a drawing, engraving or sculpture. *See also del., sculpt.*

Federal Librarians Association. A non-profit-making association which was formed in the USA in 1972. Aims: to (a) provide members with a variety of communication channels within and outside the library profession, including meetings and publications; (b) provide members with a service organization to help them in their professional development and advancement; (c) increase the usefulness and advance the standards, ideals, and welfare of the library profession. Membership is open to all persons retired from, or holding professional positions in USA federal libraries. Abbreviated FLA.

Federal Librarians Round Table.   Established by the Council of the ALA on 28 February 1972 to: (1) promote library services and the library profession in the federal community; (2) promote the appropriate utilization of federal library resources and facilities; (3) provide an environment for the stimulation of resources and development relating to the planning, development and operation of federal libraries. Publishes *Federal Librarian* (q.). Abbreviated FLRT.

Federal Library and Information Center Committee.   Founded in 1965 as the Federal Library Committee, a US body that co-ordinates activity and makes recommendations on and for the 2500 libraries and information centres in the federal sector. There are 39 designated members of the Committee, including representatives of the national libraries. Operates the FEDLINK network of 1200 libraries, linked into OCLC. Publishes *FLICC Newsletter* (q.) and *FEDLINK Technical Notes* (m.). Abbreviated FLICC.

Federal Micrographics Council.   *See FGMC.*

Federation Internationale de Documentation.   *See International Federation for Documentation.*

Federation Internationale des Archives du Film.   *See FIAF.*

Federation of Children's Book Groups.   Formed in the UK in 1968 the Federation exists to promote an awareness of children's literature, principally among parents, and to encourage the wider distribution and availability of a large range of books for children. It also acts as a channel for negotiations with publishers, libraries and any other official body concerned with children and books. The Federation wants to see a Children's Book Group in every village, town and city in the British Isles. In addition the Federation promotes National Tell a Story Week and Story-Aid, presents 'The Children's Book Award' annually, organizes Annual Conferences, publishes book lists and information leaflets, circulates a *Newsletter*, gives support, encouragement and practical help to its Groups and provides advice and information generally.

Federation of Local Authority Chief Librarians.   *See FOLACL.*

FEDLINK.   *See Federal Library and Information Center Committee.*

Feed Board.   The platform on a printing machine on to which single sheets of paper are passed from the pile on the stock table and from which they are passed to the impression cylinder.

Feed Guides.   One, or more, of several kinds of device for holding a sheet of paper in a uniformly straight position before it is taken, possibly by the grippers, to the place at which it will come into contact with the printing surface. On a cylinder press these are called 'Drop guides'.

Feedback.   1. (*Information retrieval*) Partial reversion of the effects of a given process to its source. Control of a system by the output of the system – that is, a self-correcting or self-compensating control.   2. User or client response to, or opinion on, a service.

Feeder. The various pieces of automatic apparatus by means of which sheets of paper are fed to, and positioned on, printing presses and paper processing machines of various kinds.

Feet. The base of a piece of movable type formed by the 'groove' or 'heel-nick' which runs set-wise across the bottom surface of the body. Type not standing squarely is said to be 'off its feet'.

Feet of Fine. In law, the foot of a fine was that one of the parts of a tripartite indenture recording the particulars of a fine, which remained with the court, the other two being retained by the parties. When the undivided sheet was placed so that this counterfoil could be read, it was actually at the foot of the parchment.

Feint Ruling. Term used to indicate the horizontal lines (rules), or cross-rules, printed on account-book paper or exercise books. *See also Common Ruling.*

Fell Types. Types cut by the Dutch typefounder Walpergen between 1667 and 1672 and introduced by Dr. John Fell to Oxford University Press during and after 1671 when this press was revived. Dr. Fell was Dean of Christ Church and later Bishop of Oxford. The beautiful Fell types which are used by the OUP for books requiring an OLD STYLE (*q.v.*) type are still cast from the collection of type-punches and matrices made by Dr. Fell, having been re-discovered by the Rev. C. H. O. Daniel in 1877, and used by him on his private press at WWorcester College. Dr.Fell was the second of the Press's great patrons, the first being Archbishop Laud. He took charge of printing and publishing on behalf of the University from 1672 until his death in 1686.

Fellowship. The highest professional qualification awarded by the (British) Library Association; candidates must satisfy certain conditions of length of membership, and present an acceptable thesis, or published work, or evidence of professional achievement. Abbreviated FLA.

Felt Mark. An imprint left on paper by the felt of the papermaking machine due to the pressure of the felt on it.

Felt Side. The side of a sheet or roll of paper which has not come in contact with the wire during manufacture; therefore the smooth side of a sheet instead of the WIRE SIDE (*q.v.*). Also known as the 'Top side'.

Feminist Library (UK). A collection of fiction, non-fiction and journals, with a register of research, maintained by the London Borough's Grant Unit after the demise of the Greater London Council. Late in 1988 its future seemed uncertain.

Fence. (*Classification*) Part of the NOTATION (*q.v.*) which merely separates facets without indicating the type of facet which is to follow. These were replaced in the fourth edition of the Colon Classification with FACET INDICATORS (*q.v.*).

Fenced Notation. A type of notation which separates two or more terms by a connective symbol, or FENCE (*q.v.*) in order to combine them. Also called 'Enumerative notation'.

Fere-Humanistica. *See Gothic or Black Letter, Type.*

Festoon Drying. A method of drying paper in a drying chamber in which warm air is circulated. The paper is hung in loops over rods which travel slowly through the chamber.

Festschrift. A memorial or complimentary volume usually consisting of a number of contributions by distinguished persons, often students and colleagues of a person and issued in his honour. The subject matter of the various contributions is usually concerned with the subject in which the individual distinguished himself. It may also honour an institution or society especially on the occasion of an anniversary. Also called 'Memorial volume'.

ff. Abbreviation for *folgende Seiten*) *Ger.* 'following pages'); for a proper name (e.g. ffolkes); for *fecerunt* (*Lat.* 'they made it); for folios (e.g. 200ff., i.e. 200 leaves, not pages) and foliation.

FGMC. Abbreviation for the Federal Government Micrographics Council which was formed under the sponsorship of the (American) General Services Administration, the National Archives, and the Records Service, to serve as a 'continuing forum for the interchange of information regarding micrographic systems and program management'.

FIAB. Fédération Internationale des Associations de Bibliothécaires. *See entry under International Federation of Library Associations and Institutions.*

FIAF. The Fédération Internationale des Archives du Film (FIAF) was founded in 1938 to promote the preservation of the film as art and historical document throughout the world and to bring together all organizations devoted to this end; to facilitate the collection and international exchange of films and documents related to cinematographic history and art for the purpose of making them as widely accessible as possible; to develop co-operation between its members; and to promote the development of cinema art and culture. The word 'film' in FIAF's name was later broadened to include all forms of the moving image, in concurrence with developments in the media. The founding members were the Department of Film of the Museum of Modern Art (New York), the National Film Archive (London), the Cinémathèque Française (Paris) and the Reichsfilmarchiv (Berlin). The first general assembly was held in 1939 in New York. FIAF now has 53 members and 33 observers from a total of 56 countries. Extensive publishing programme includes *International Index to Film Periodicals*, and *International Index to Television Periodicals*.

Fibres. The plant cells, largely composed of cellulose, which are contained in the rag, grass, wood or other vegetable matter from which paper is made. The length and strength of these fibres, and the way in which they are interwoven, determine the quality and strength of the paper.

Fiche. A card. *See also Microfiche.*

Fiction. Prose novels and stories, of which the action and/or characters are the product of the writer's imagination.

Fiction Reserve. *See Joint Fiction Reserve.*

Fictitious Imprint. An imprint that is misleading with the object of evading legal or other restrictions, concealing the anonymity of the author, or concealing a piracy publication, etc. Also called 'False imprint'. Fictitious and imaginary imprints may be given in catalogue entries (1) as given, or (2) in the conventional form. When the real imprint is known, it is given in [] after the fictitious one.

FID. *See International Federation for Documentation.*

Fidler (Kathleen) Award. An annual award administered by Book Trust Scotland for a children's novel by a new author.

Field. 1. A fixed column or group of columns in a punched card allocated for punching specific information. The total area of a punched card available for information storage. 2. (*Cataloguing*) Normally considered to mean an Element (*q.v.*) or a group of elements. Used in some systems, e.g. Marc, to mean a group of one or more subfields. *See also Filing Code.* 3. (*Classification*) A group of things, or concepts, or their representations, having one or more characteristics in common. Sometimes used in contradiction to Class (*q.v.*) when class is defined as a group formed by consideration of characteristics used in drawing up a strictly conventional hierarchy, then 'field' is defined as a group formed in Array (*q.v.*) by consideration of secondary characteristics. In this sense, a field is a group formed by consideration of characteristics other than those used in drawing up a classification schedule. 4. A broad group of related subjects. 5. (*Information retrieval*) In machine-readable records, the position of a data element, or a set of data elements, regarded as a single descriptive element; it may be allocated a unique identification symbol in the record format. 6. A particular section of a computer record, e.g. in a bibliographic record, the author, or the publication date, of a document. Fields may be of fixed or of variable length.

Figure. 1. An illustration, map, chart, graph, etc., forming part of a page of text with which it is printed from a block imposed with the type, as distinct from a Plate (*q.v.*). Figures are usually numbered consecutively by means of Arabic numerals. 2. A graphic symbol or character to represent a number. *See also Marginal Figure.*

Figure Initial. In a mediaeval illuminated manuscript, an initial letter which is made by representations of the bodies of human beings or animals.

Figured Bass. On a music score, a line of bass notes with figures under or over them from which indications the player of a harpischord or organ could tell what chords the composer intended to be used, and could construct his own accompaniment. This is known as realization. Also called 'Basso continuo', 'Thorough bass'.

Figures, Old Style. *See Hanging Figures, Old Style, Ranging Figures.*

FIInfSc. Fellow of the Institute of Information Scientists (*q.v.*).

File. (*Noun*) 1. A collection of written, typed, printed or machine-readable material or information arranged in some systematic order. 2. A holder or cabinet designed to hold such material. 3. A homogeneous collection of a single type of file items. *See also Advertisement File, Biography File, Company File, Confidential File, Geographic Filing Method, Job File, Lateral Filing, Legal File, Map File, Media File, Open Back File, Organization File, Patent File, Suspension File, Transfer File, Vertical File. (verb)* To arrange written, typed or printed material in order.

File-As-If. An instruction to file an entry consisting of, or beginning with, a symbol, an abbreviation, or a numeral, as if that which is represented by the filing element were spelled out in the letters of the alphabet.

File Item. The smallest module or piece of information to be handled as a unit in a file.

Filigree. Initials and borders decorated with fine lines around the edges.

Filigree Letter. An initial letter with a decorated or filigree outline or background.

Filing. The action of arranging papers, non-book materials and other documents, and records of such, or other, items, into predetermined sequences; also the subsequent insertion of additional items in their correct places.

Filing Cars. Desks on casters with a small table and a chair on a swivel, used when filing cards in catalogues. (*American*).

Filing Code. A code of rules for arranging entries in a catalogue, or other material in a file. Such codes may cover manual sorting, or may be intended for computer sorting. ALPHABETIZATION (*q.v.*) will be included, and the order of other data elements, for example punctuation symbols used in UDC. Terms used in filing codes may comprise the following: *Filing entry.* All of the fields that may be considered in determining the filing position of an item in a catalogue (e.g. an author heading, title and imprint date). *Field.* A major component of a filing entry that comprises one or more elements (e.g. a heading; a title). *Element.* One or more words that make up an integral part of a field (e.g. the surname in a personal name heading). An element and a field are identical when the field contains only one element (e.g. a title). The first element in a field is called the *leading element*, the others are called *subordinate elements.* For example, in a heading consisting of a surname, forename and birth and death dates, the surname is the leading element, the forename and the dates are subordinate elements. *Word.* One or more characters forming a meaningful group and separated from others by spaces and/or marks of significant punctuation. *Character.* A letter, digit, symbol, or mark of punctuation. *Significant punctuation* is a mark of punctuation that marks the end of an element, e.g. (a) period after a direct order corporate name such as 'London University Library'; (b) the comma after a surname as 'Wilson, Woodrow'; (c) parentheses surrounding a qualifying term in a subject heading, as 'Mass (Physics) – Measurement'.

Filing Entry. *See Filing Code.*

Filing Epithet. An EPITHET (*q.v.*) which is added to a personal name to assist in the filing sequence as well as to distinguish between persons whose names would otherwise be identical. A kind of DESCRIPTOR (*q.v.*). *See Honorific Epithet.*

Filing Medium. That part of the entry or an added heading-word, phrase or symbol under which a card is filed. Also called ENTRY WORD (*q.v.*), FILING TERM, FILING WORD.

Filing Order. The order (usually alphabetical, but also by classification notation, or some other appropriate sequence such as makers' catalogue number) for arranging books, documents, records, including catalogue entries. *See also Simplified Filing.*

Filing Practice. The sequential arrangement of entries in a library catalogue. To ensure consistency, this is best carried out in accordance with a recognized code. *See also Filing Code.*

Filing Rules.   Explicit directions, preferably based on a recognised code, and provided in written or printed form, for the filing of entries in catalogues. *See Filing Code.*

Filing Significance.   (*Cataloguing*) 1. An attribute of an element of data which makes it necessary to take account of the data when filing entries.   2. The sum of the attributes of one or more elements of data, which determines the position in a filing order of the entry or record which contains them.

Filing Term.   *Synonymous with* FILING MEDIUM (*q.v.*).

Filing Title.   1. The title under which are filed catalogue, or bibliography, entries for work known by a number of different titles.   2. The portion of a title which is longer than an essential part by which the book is well known,, and under which the catalogue etry is filed, e.g. *David Copperfield*, the full title of which is *The personal history of David Copperfield.* The filing title is indicated by putting a small stroke under the filing letter – in this case the 'D'. Augmented headings, conventional titles in the entries for music scores, and corner markings, are all forms of filing title. *See also Uniform Title.*

Filing Word.   *Synonymous with* ENTRY WORD (*q.v.*).

Fillet.   1. A plain line or lines impressed upon the back or side of a book-cover. A 'French fillet' is three gilt lines unevenly spaced.   2. The wheel-shaped tool, with which lines are impressed. Also called 'Roulette' or 'ROLL' (*q.v.*). *See also Tooling.*

Filling In.   A printing fault in which the spaces in type characters, or the spaces between the dots of a half-tone block, fill with ink. This may be caused by using too much, or an unsuitable, ink, the forme being too high or the rollers incorrectly set, or by using an unsuitable paper, especially one which gives off fluff. *See also Clogged.*

Filling-in Guards.   *Synonymous with* COMPENSATION GUARDS (*q.v.*).

Film Base.   The plastic material which is coated with chemicals to make it sensitive to light. Called 'Clear base' before being coated with photographic emulsion. *See also Base Stock.*

Film Clip.   A strip of film cut specially to illustrate something specific.

Film Jacket.   A transparent holder into which individual frames, or strips, of 16 or 35 mm microfilm may be inserted for storage.

Film Library.   A collection of films and video recordings; preservation of older film bases is a particular problem in such libraries.

Filmsetting.   The setting of type by photographic means using film as a medium. Each key on a filmsetting machine operates the placing of a negative of a letter of the alphabet (or other character) in position to be printed photographically in its correct order on a sheet of film. This sheet of film represents whole pages which can then be imposed in the proper position and printed down on to the lithographic printing plate. *See also Computer Typesetting.*

Filmstrip.   A strip of 16 mm or 35 mm film varying in length up to about fifty frames and bearing pictures, text or captions. The positive images, in black and white or in colour, and usually on 35 mm film, are projected one at a time by means of a film strip projector. Some film strips are equipped with a tape or a recording that contains not only the narration but also a subsonic signal that activates a solenoid to advance the filmstrip to the next frame on being given a cue.

Filmstrip Projector. An electrically operated machine designed to accept and project filmstrips, usually 35 mm. Some also have slide holders to take 35 mm and larger mounted single transparencies. They are available with manual and/or remote control.

Final Proof. Also called 'Page proof'. *See Proof.*

Final Title Strip. The wording at the end of a film which indicates its contents.

Financing our Public Library Service*: A consultative Green Paper published by the UK Minister for the Arts in February 1988 which led to a widespread professional debate.

Finding Aids. Classification schemes, catalogues, indexes of various kinds and of different varieties of library materials, etc., which have been devised to enable stored material, or information, to be obtained (retrieved) when required.

Finding List. A very brief list of books and documents in a library system, usually limited to author, title and class mark or location symbol.

Finding List Catalogue. A catalogue which contains only brief author entries consisting of author's surname, title (possibly abbreviated), date of publication, and possibly edition number if not the first. The absence of bibliographical particulars results in its use merely as a finding list of books, the authors of which are known. *See also Berghoeffer System.*

Finding Unit. The catalogues, bibliographies and circulation and information desks, which are usually grouped together in a university library. *See also Library Keys.*

Fine. A charge made for retaining a book longer than the time allowed.

Fine Copy. Used to describe a second-hand book the condition of which is better than 'good' but poorer than MINT (*q.v.*).

Fine Edition. *Synonymous with* DE LUXE EDITION (*q.v.*).

Fine-Face Rule. A printer's brass RULE (*q.v.*) of hair-line thickness.

Fine Paper Copy. Name applied to a book printed on better and larger paper than the ordinary edition.

Fine Screen. A screen with ruling above 120 lines per inch. *See also Screen.*

Finis. (*Lat.*) The end, conclusion. Frequently printed at the end of a book.

Finish. 1. (*Paper*) The degree of smoothness of the surface of paper; printing papers may be described as, e.g. antique or supercalendered, writing and drawing papers as vellum or rough. 'Hot pressed' (H.P.) means plate glazed finish. *See also Not, Paper Finishes.* 2. (*Block-making*) The treatment of the outer edges of blocks as e.g. squared up, vignetted. 3. (*Binding*) Ornamenting and lettering a bound book.

Finisher. 1. A bookbinding craftsman who performs the processes (polishing the leather, lettering, embellishing) which are carried out on a hand-bound book after the sections have been secured within the case. 2. A machine which applies varnish, lacquer, liquid plastic or other fluid to cover materials by spraying, by roller, or by a printing plate.

Finishing. That branch of binding concerned with the book after it has been put into its cover. Includes tooling, lettering, polishing. The workman who does this is called a 'finisher'. *See also Forwarding.*

Finishing House. *Synonymous with* SALLE (*q.v.*).

Finishing Room. *Synonymous with* SALLE (*q.v.*).

Finnish Library Association (Suomen Kirjastoseura/Finlands Biblioteksforening). Founded 1910. Based in Helsinki. Aims to promote the development of public library services in Finland, and enhance the professional status of librarians. Publishes *Kirjastolehti* (m.) and handbook.

FIRST. Forum for Information Resources in Staffordshire (UK); a co-operative initiative started in 1986 to maximize access to publicly available information. Earlier local schemes – MISLIC and LINOSCO – have been replaced by FIRST; at present (1989) there are 80 member libraries and related organizations.

First Assistant. In American libraries, a member of the professional staff of a department, division or branch having a minimum staff of three professional persons.

First Edition. The whole number of copies first printed from the same type and issued at the same time. Later printings from the same type are known as Reprints. Sometimes small typographical errors in a first edition are corrected during the printing, qualifying the later printings for the classification 'Corrected Edition', 'New Edition' or 'Revised Edition', but described as 'First issue of the first edition'. *See also Edition, Impression, Issue, New Edition, Reprint, Revised Edition.*

First English Edition. The first edition published in England of a book written in English and which had already been published abroad.

First Generation Microfilm. *Synonymous with* CAMERA MICROFILM (*q.v.*).

First Impression. All the copies of a book printed at the first printing and before any alterations or additions have been made to the text. Subsequent printings made soon after the first, and before a reprint is made after a lapse of time, are called 'Second impression', 'Third impression', etc.

First Indention. The eighth typewriter space from the left edge of a catalogue card, or the first, or outer, vertical line on a catalogue card ruled for handwriting. It is at this position that the author heading begins; should it run over the line, it continues at the 'Third indention'. Also called 'Author indention' and 'Outer indention'. *See also Second Indention, Third Indention.*

First Line Index. An index in which the first lines of poems, hymns, songs are arranged in alphabetical order.

First Lining. The piece of mull which is glued with a flexible glue to a book after it is sewn and nipped; it extends to within ¼ in. from the head and tail of the book and projects 1¼ in. on either side for affixing to the end-papers to give strength and firmness to the book. A strip of brown paper, the full size of the spine, is then stuck over it; this is known as the 'second lining'. The purpose of this lining is to give strength and firmness to the back of the book.

First Name.   The first of the forenames or Christian names; a personal name as distinct from family or clan name.

First Printing.   The first quantity of a book to be printed; equivalent to FIRST IMPRESSION (*q.v.*).

First Proof.   A proof of type-set matter which is read by the printer's reader and corrected before the galley proof is made. *See also Proof.*

First Published Edition.   The first edition published for sale to the public, and implying that it was preceded by an edition printed for private, official or otherwise restricted, circulation.

First Reproduction Microfilm.   A microfilm copy made from the CAMERA MICROFILM (*q.v.*). Also called 'Second generation microfilm'. *See also Generation.*

First Separate Edition.   The first edition to be printed within its own covers, of a publication which had previously been published with other matter.

First Vertical.   The left of the two vertical lines printed on a catalogue card intended for hand writing and serving as a guide to where the author heading and the second and subsequent lines of the entry should begin. *See also First Indention, Second Vertical.*

First Word Entry.   Entry under the first word of a book's title other than an article.

Firsts.   First editions.

Fist.   *Synonymous with* HAND (*q.v.*).

FIT.   Fedération Internationale des Traducteurs. *See entry under International Federation of Translators.*

Five Laws of Library Science.   1. Books are for use.   2. Every reader his book.   3. Every book its reader.   4. Save the time of the reader.   5. A library is a growing organism. (*S. R. Ranganathan.*)

Five Predicables.   *See Predicables, Five.*

Fixed Field Coding.   (*Cataloguing, Information retrieval*) In computer cataloguing, the allocation of as many areas of the record as there are particular parts of a catalogue entry, including the classification notation. With 'fixed symbol', or 'variable field' coding each part of the entry is 'tagged' with a special symbol (e.g. a punctuation mark) to indicate which part of the entry is to follow. *See also Tag.*

Fixed Fields.   In information retrieval, locations on a search medium, that are reserved for information of a particular type, form or length. *See also Free Fields.*

Fixed-Function Planning.   Planning a building in such a way that each room or department is designed and constructed for its specific purpose, thus giving the architect opportunities for displaying his architectural abilities. Walls dividing the rooms are permanent, and normally an essential part of the structure. The opposite of modular planning. *See also Modular Construction.*

Fixed Location.   An antiquated method of arrangement by marking a book with shelf and other marks so that its position on a particular shelf should always be the same. The bookcases, tiers and shelves are each marked distinctly to make finding easy and these markings are often incorporated in the book number. Also called 'Absolute location'. The opposite of RELATIVE LOCATION (*q.v.*).

Fixed Shelf. One which cannot be adjusted.

Fixed Symbol Coding. *Synonymous with* VARIABLE FIELD CODING. *See Fixed Field Coding.*

fl. Abbreviation for *flores* (Lat. 'flowers'), *floruit* (*q.v.*).

FLA. *See Fellowship.*

FLA. FEDERAL LIBRARIANS ASSOCIATION (*q.v.*).

FLAG. *Synonymous with* MASTHEAD (*q.v.*).

FLAI. FELLOW OF THE LIBRARY ASSOCIATION OF IRELAND (*q.v.*).

Flange. The margin round a half-tone plate or line block to provide for fixing to the block.

Flat. (*Printing*) The sheet containing offset negatives or positives in the proper arrangement, from which the printing plate is made. Also, a flat printing plate.

Flat Back. A book which has not been rounded before being placed inside its CASE (*q.v.*), its back being at right angles to the sides. Also called 'Square back'. *See also Backing, Round Back, Rounding.*

Flat-bed Camera. *Synonymous with* PLANETARY CAMERA (*q.v.*).

Flat-bed Cylinder Press. A printing machine with a flat bed on which the forme is placed under a rotating cylinder.

Flat-bed Press. A printing machine having the printing forme on a bed with a flat surface, as distinct from a press with a curved surface.

Flat-bed Web Press. A machine for printing from a flat forme on to an endless roll of paper.

Flat Copy. A photograph having no contrast and therefore normally unsuitable for process work. *See also Process Engraving.*

Flat Display. A book display which features the front covers rather than the spines of the books.

Flat Proof. A print made from each plate in a colour series, using the colour in which that plate is to be printed in the series. *See also Proof, Progressive Proof.*

Flat Pull (Rough Pull). The proof taken on the machine without UNDERLAY or OVERLAY (*qq.v.*).

Flat Stitched. A publication which is sewn by the FLAT STITCHING (*q.v.*) method.

Flat Stitching. Sewing a pamphlet or book, which must have a flat back, in such a way that the wire or linen thread used passes through the inner margins as close to the folds of the sections as possible from the front right through to the back. *See also Saddle Stitching, Side-stitch.*

Flatness. A condition of paper or board when it has no COCKLE, CURL (*qq.v.*) or wave.

Fletcher (*Sir Banister*) Award. An annual UK prize of the SOCIETY OF AUTHORS (*q.v.*) for the best book on architecture or the arts.

Fletcher Index. Inflation indexes for academic library purchases, widely admired by UK polytechnic librarians. Described in the *Library Association Record* 89(8) August 1987.

Fleur-de-lis Lozenge.   A lozenge stamp consisting of a flower with fleur-de-lis, or a variation of this design, filling the corners.

Fleuron.   A conventional flower or an anomalous type of ornament of floral or foliage character, generally of roughly lozenge shape, used in decorating book-bindings. *See also Flowers.*

Flexibility.   *See Flexible Classification.*

Flexible Binding.   A binding that allows the book to lie flat when open. This is largely achieved by using a FLEXIBLE SEWING (*q.v.*) and flexible glue.

Flexible Classification.   A classification which permits the insertion of new subjects without destroying the sequence or logic of the arrangement. Flexibility is mainly a function of the notation.

Flexible Notation.   A NOTATION (*q.v.*) which has the quality of allowing, by the addition of one or more symbols, the insertion of any new subject into any place in the classification without dislocating the sequence of either the notation or the classification schedule. *See also Notation.*

Flexible Plate.   A plastic or rubber printing plate.

Flexible Sewing.   Sewing a book on raised bands or cords, passing the thread entirely round all the bands which are then laced through the boards. It is the strongest form of sewing. A style of binding which allows the book to lie quite flat when open.

Flexional Symbol.   A symbol in a notation system, in which the meaning of each component character is dependent on those which precede it.

FLICC.   *See Federal Library and Information Center Committee.*

FLIRT.   FEDERAL LIBRARIANS ROUND TABLE (*q.v.*).

Floating Library.   A mobile library accommodated on a boat which takes books to isolated residents or hamlets on islands and places which are inaccessible except by river or sea.

Flong.   A pulp-like board used for making the moulds for casting stereotypes. *Wet flong* is made (usually in the foundry of a printing establishment) from layers of tissue paper and blotting paper pasted together with a special paste and beaten onto the type or blocks in the forme and then dried. *Dry flong* is a similar material which, either in a completely dry state, or damp, is placed together with the forme in a hydraulic press. The use of paper in place of plaster of paris for moulding was introduced by Genoux of Lyons in 1829; a British patent, based on this method, was taken out by Moses Poole in 1839.

Floor Case.   *Synonymous with* ISLAND STACK (*q.v.*).

Floppy Disk.   *See Disc.*

Florence Agreement.   The 'Agreement on the importation of educational, scientific and cultural material' reduces tariff and trade obstacles to the international circulation of the following groups of materials, thereby permitting organizations and individuals to obtain them from abroad with less difficulty and at less cost: 1. books, publications and documents; 2. works of art and collectors' pieces of an educational, scientific or cultural character;   3. visual and auditory materials of an educational, scientific or cultural character;   4. scientific instruments or apparatus;   5. articles for the blind. Contracting states undertake not to apply customs duties on any of the materials covered by the Agreement; they also undertake, *unconditionally*, to grant licences and/or foreign exchange for a variety of categories of books and publications. The Agreement, which was adopted unanimously by the General Conference of Unesco at its Fifth Session held in Florence in July 1950, was brought into force on 21 May 1952. It is of major interest to libraries, making it easier to import such materials, reducing tariff and trade obstacles to the international circulation of these materials and permitting organizations and individuals to obtain them from abroad with less difficulty and at less cost.

Florentine Woodcuts. These are often characterized by the combination of black-line and white-line methods in the same block; e.g. black is used as the colour of the ground, any stones, plants or other objects being represented by white lines on a black ground, while the upper part of the illustration follows the Venetian style of black lines on a white ground.

Floret. 1. A binder's finishing tool with a flower or leaf design. 2. A flower or leaf-shape type used to separate sentences or paragraphs.

floruit. (*Lat.* 'he or she flourished'). The period during which a person, whose birth and death dates were not exactly known, was believed to have been alive or flourished. Indicated by 'fl' before the dates or period.

Flourish. 1. A mark or flourish after a signature, often made as a protection against forgery. Also called a 'Paraph'. 2. A curved line or ornament, made of brass or cast metal, and used with lines of type.

Flourish Style. *Synonymous with* FANFARE STYLE (*q.v.*).

Flow Camera. *Synonymous with* CONTINUOUS FLOW CAMERA (*q.v.*).

Flow-line Map. One which shows movement, the direction or route followed being indicated by a line representing the railway or waterway concerned, while the width of the line represents the quantity of material conveyed.

Flower-headed Rivet. (*Binding*) A rivet with an ornamental head with a design resembling a daisy.

Flowers. Printer's ornaments which can be made up into decorative borders, strips, head and tail pieces. They may be floral, arabesque, geometric or pictorial in design. The best of them derive from bookbinders' arabesque stamps. *See also Fleuron, Type Flowers, Type Ornaments.*

Flush. (*Printing*) Denotes the absence of INDENTION (*q.v.*). The instruction 'set flush on left' means that the matter is to be set evenly at the left margin, 'flush right' that all lines align at the right margin.

Flush Binding. A binding in which the covers do not project beyond the leaves, the whole having been placed in a guillotine and trimmed after the covers were secured.

Flush Boards. A style of binding in which boards are glued to the paste-downs and a paper cover glued to the boards. The whole is then put into a guillotine and CUT FLUSH (*q.v.*). *See also Flush Trim.*

Flush Paragraph. A paragraph having no indention, spacing being used to separate paragraphs.

Flush Trim. A style of binding in which the top, fore and bottom edges are cut after the paper, board or lining cloth covers have been put on. The covers are thus flush with the edges and do not overlap. Such books are said to be 'cut flush'. Also called 'Flush work'. *See also Flush Boards.*

Flush Work. *Synonymous with* FLUSH TRIM (*q.v.*).

Fly-leaf. A blank leaf at the beginning or end of a book, being the half of an ENDPAPER (*q.v.*), which is not stuck down to the board, or cover, of a book. Also called 'Free endpaper'. The half which is stuck down to the board, is called a PASTE-DOWN (*q.v.*). If there are other blank leaves, these are parts of the end sections – not fly-leaves although they are sometimes known as such.

Fly-sheet. 1. A two- or four-page tract. 2. An endpaper.

Fly-title. *Synonymous with* HALF TITLE (*q.v.*).

FNZLA. FELLOW OF THE NEW ZEALAND LIBRARY ASSOCIATION (*q.v.*).

fo. Abbreviation for FOLIO (*q.v.*).

Focus. (*Classification*) (*Noun*) 1. A generic term used to denote an ISOLATE (*q.v.*) or a class or any of its equivalents in the other PLANES (*q.v.*). 2. Any specific division (*see* DIVISION 4) of the subject according to one characteristic, i.e. any single division of a FACET (*q.v.*). (*Verb*) To decrease the EXTENSION (*q.v.*) and increase the intension within any facet, and so to arrive at a specific division of a facet. *See also Classifying, Facet, Phase.*

Foil. Metal or pigment forming a very thin film on a thin backing material which is used with a stylus of a block when lettering or BLOCKING (*q.v.*) a book.

Foil Blocking. *See Blocking Foil.*

fol. Abbreviation for FOLIO (*q.v.*). Less usual than 'fo', or 'Fo'.

FOLACL. Federation of Local Authority Chief Librarians; set up in 1986 to speak on behalf of all public chief librarians in England and Wales, by the Association of London Chief Librarians, Association of Metropolitan District Chief Librarians, and the Society of County Librarians. Recent activities have included representations to the Minister, officers of the OAL and members of the standing committee on proposals in the Local Government and Housing Bill affecting public libraries, evidence to the Office of Fair Trading on the Net Book Agreement, correspondence with DES on the impact of the Education Reform Act on school library services, work on public library statistics, discussions with the Chief Executive of the British Library on the strategic plan, etc.

Fold. *Synonymous with* BOLT (*q.v.*).

Fold Symbols. The symbols used to indicate the way the paper of which a book is made is folded, and consequently the number of leaves in the section. These are F., Fo (Folio); 4to (Quarto); 6to (Sexto); 8vo (Octavo); 12mo (Duodecimo, Twelve-mo); 16mo (Sextodecimo, Sixteen-mo); 18mo (Octodecimo, Eighteen-mo); 24mo (Vicesimoquarto, Twenty-fourmo); 32mo (Trigesimo-secundo, Thirty-twomo); 64mo (Sexagesimo-quarto, Sixty-fourmo). They are often used to indicate the size of modern books.

Fold to Paper. An instruction that a sheet of printed paper is to be folded so that the edges of the leaves and the bolts are all level. *See also Bolt, Fold to Print.*

Fold to Print. An instruction that a printed sheet is to be folded in register, i.e. the edges of the printed areas are to be placed over one another exactly before the sheet is folded. *See also Fold to Paper.*

Folded Book. One consisting of a long strip of paper folded like a sheet map, concertina fashion, the ends being attached to stiff covers. Used commonly in the Orient, but in the rest of the world mainly for books of a pictorial character giving views of places or panoramas. Also called 'Folding book'.

Folded Leaf. A leaf of a bound book which is so large that it has to be folded one or more times to keep it within the area of the page size. The abbreviation *fold.* is added to the appropriate term in the collation to indicate that illustrative matter is folded, as: 80 *l.* (*3 fold.*); *fold.frontis*; 2 *fold.family trees*; 60 *maps* (2 *fold. in pocket*). *See also Folding Plate, Gatefold, Throw Out.*

Folder. 1. A publication consisting of one sheet of paper folded to make two or more leaves but neither stitched nor cut. 2. A large sheet of stout paper, usually manilla, folded once, and having a projection or tag for a heading at the top of the back portion, into which papers are placed for storage in a filing box or cabinet.

Folding. The folding of flat printed sheets into sections. The number of pages in a folded sheet is always a multiple of four (i.e. two leaves). After the last folding all the sections are secured by SEWING (*q.v.*) or stapling.

Folding Book. *Synonymous with* FOLDED BOOK (*q.v.*).

Folding Guides. Short lines printed on imposed sheets to indicate where they are to be folded.

Folding Machine. A machine for folding printed sheets to make sections for bookbinding. *See also Buckle-folder, Knife-folder.*

Folding Plate. An illustration bound into a book but folded so as not to project beyond the pages of the book. Called a 'folded plate' by cataloguers. *See also Double Plate.*

Folding Stick. A strip of white bone used when folding paper by hand to crease the paper without damaging it. *See also Bone Folder.*

Foldings. A general term referring to printed sheets which have been folded to form sections. The following table gives the usual foldings.

Folio	(fo)	Folded once	giving	2	leaves	4	pages
Quarto	(4to)	„ twice	„	4	„	8	„
Sexto	(6to)	„ three times	„	6	„	12	„
Octavo	(8vo)	„ three	„	8	„	16	„
Duodecimo (twelve-mo)	(12mo)	„ four	„	12	„	24	„
Sextodecimo (sixteen-mo)	(16mo)	„ four	„	16	„	32	„
Octodecimo (eighteen-mo)	(18mo)	„ five	„	18	„	36	„
Vicesimo-quarto (twenty-fourmo)	(24mo)	„ five	„	24	„	48	„

Trigesimo-secundo									
(thirty-twomo)	(32mo)	„	five	„	32	„	64	„
Trigesimo-sexto								
(thirty-sixmo)	(36mo)	„	six	„	36	„	72	„
Quadrigesimo-octavo								
(forty-eightmo)	(48mo)	„	six	„	48	„	96	„
Sexagesimo-quarto								
(sixty-fourmo)	(64mo)	„	six	„	64	„	128	„

Foldout. *Synonymous with* THROW OUT (*q.v.*).

Folger Shakespeare Library. Research centre for advanced scholars opened in Washington, DC, in 1932. It contains the world's largest collection of research materials on William Shakespeare and one of the Western Hemisphere's finest collections of materials on the British civilization of the sixteenth and seventeenth centuries. The stock numbers 250,000 volumes. Henry Clay Folger, an American industrialist and his wife Emily Jordan Folger selected the material forming the original collection. The collection was bequeathed to the American people, together with an endowment which was sufficient to maintain and expand it. The trust is administered by the Trustees of Amherst College, Folger's alma mater. The library is a modern building on Capitol Hill although the interior preserves the architectural conventions of the Tudor period. Holdings accessible via RLIN (*q.v.*).

Foliaged Staff. A bookbinding ornament consisting of a staff or branch entwined with foliage.

Foliate. To number the leaves of a book.

Foliate Initial. In a medieval illuminated manuscript, an initial letter decorated with, or composed of, foliage.

Foliated. Used to describe the marking of every leaf – not page – of a manuscript or printed book with a consecutive number, or foliation.

Foliation. (*Verb*) Allotting folio or section numbers or other markings to pages. (*Noun*) The numbering of leaves of a MS. or book. Foliation was comparatively rare until the last quarter of the fifteenth century: it consisted originally of the word 'Folio', or an abbreviation thereof, followed by a roman numeral. Arabic figures were used in Italy between 1475 and 1500, and outside Italy after 1500. Eventually the Arabic figures stood alone. Sometimes columns of print were numbered instead of leaves. The numbering of pages (pagination) began to replace foliation towards the end of the sixteenth century but was not finally established until the eighteenth century. Abbreviated ff.

Folio. 1. Relates to the format of a book; a book printed on sheets of paper folded once, each sheet making two leaves or four pages. For an accurate indication, the paper size should also be stated, e.g. *crown folio*. In practice, a double-size sheet could be used and folded twice, or a quad-size sheet folded three times to give the same size pages. *See Foldings.* 2. The individual leaf of a book. A sheet is usually folded into two parallel with the narrow way (i.e. halving the long side) and when so folded is called 'regular', 'common', or 'broad' folio.   3. An indication of the size of a book, usually 30 cm. The actual size depends on the size of the sheet of paper and on the way it is folded. Abbreviated *Fo., fo., fol., or 2°. See also Book Sizes, Elephant Folio.*   4. A sheet of paper in its full size, i.e. flat unfolded, hence a folio ream is a ream of paper supplied flat.   5. The number of a leaf written or printed at the top or more usually, the bottom of the RECTO (*q.v.*).   6. One sheet of MS (which should be written, typed or printed on one side only) supplied to a printer's compositor for setting. Folios are numbered consecutively from 1 with arabic numerals to indicate correct sequence, and bear no relation to subsequent page numbering of the resultant print.

Folio Edition.   One issued in FOLIO (*q.v.*) form.

Follow Copy.   When written on a MS. this is a direction to the compositor to follow precisely the spelling and punctuation, however incorrect it may appear. When written on printed matter it indicates that the style and setting of the original are to be followed as closely as possible.

Follow Through.   *Synonymous with* the 'letter-by-letter' system of ALPHABETI-ZATION (*q.v.*).

Follow-up File.   An American term for a chronological file of cards, correspondence or copies of orders sent, to facilitate checking overdue orders or letters.

FOLUSA.   *See Friends of Libraries USA.*

Fonds.   The chief archive unit in the continental system and the basis of all rules as to arrangement of the contents of archives. An archive group consisting of archives resulting from the work of an administration which was an organic whole, complete in itself, capable of dealing independently, without any added or external authority, with every side of any business which could normally be presented to it.

Font.   *See Fount.*

Foolscap.   A sheet of printing paper measuring 13½ × 17 inches, usually folded to give a size of 13½ × 8½ inches. Formerly known as 'large foolscap'.

Foolscap Folio.   A book size 13½ × 8½ inches. *See also Book Sizes.*

Foolscap Octavo.   A book size 6¾ × 4¼ inches. *See also Book Sizes.*

Foolscap Quarto.   A book size 8½ × 6¾ inches. *See also Book Sizes.*

Foot.   1. The bottom edge of a book. *See also Head.*   2. The margin at the bottom of a page of type.   3. The under-surface of type. The plane, parallel to the face on which the BODY (*q.v.*) rests. *See also Feet.*

Footline.   1. The line at the bottom of a page, especially the blank line or DIRECTION LINE (*q.v.*) i.e. the line containing the folio, signature, or page number just below the lowest line of type.   2. The horizontal ruled line near the bottom of a ruled page or sheet.   3. Supplementary material at the bottom of a page to be used in connection with matter appearing above it.

Footnote.   A note at the foot of a page, usually in smaller type than the text, giving a reference, an authority, or an elucidation of matter in the text above. Footnotes are usually referred to by SUPERIOR FIGURES (*q.v.*) or symbols in the text. *See also Reference Marks.* Also called 'Bottom note'.

Footprint. The area in which the signal from an orbiting telecommunication satellite can be received. Footprints can now be focused in small areas if required. *See also Satellite Broadcasting.*

Footstick. *See Chase.*

Fore-edge. The front edge of a sheet of paper or of the sections of a book opposite the folded edge through which the sewing passes. Also called 'Front edge'.

Fore-edge Fold. *See Bolt.*

Fore-edge Margin. The space between the type matter and the fore-edge of a book or periodical. Also called 'Outside margin'. *See also Margin.*

Fore-edge Painting. A picture painted on the fore-edges of a book which is seen to the best advantage when the pages are splayed out. A 'double fore-edge' has two paintings which can be seen singly by fanning the leaves first one way, and then the other. Gold is usually applied after the paintings have been done. A 'triple fore-edge' has a visible painting in addition. This form of decoration is particularly associated with William Edwards of Halifax, a binder who opened a bookshop in London for his sons James and John in 1785, although the earliest known *dated* disappearing fore-edge painting is on a Bible dated 1651, where the painting of the Leigh arms is signed 'Lewis fecit, Anno Dom. 1653'. Edwards pioneered the idea of painting landscapes on fore-edges, first of all in brown or grey monochrome, and later in a full range of colours.

Fore-edge Title. A title hand-written on the fore-edge of a book so that it could be identified when standing on a shelf with its fore-edge outwards, the normal position in the sixteenth century.

Forel. 1. Heavy, rough parchment used for covering old books. Also called 'Forrel', 'Forril'. 2. A case or cover in which a book or MS. is kept for protection, or into which it is sewn.

Forel Binding. English book-bindings in which oak boards were covered with roughly dressed deerskins. They were made by monks in the eighth and ninth centuries.

Forename. A name that precedes the family name, clan name, or surname. A Christian, or personal, name. It is a name or part of a name which designates a person as an individual and distinguishes him from others bearing the same family name, surname or clan name. Also called GIVEN NAME (*q.v.*), 'Personal name'.

Forename Entry. The entry in a catalogue for a book under the author's forename or personal name instead of the surname or family name as is usual. Books by the following are so entered: saints, popes, persons known by the first name only, sovereigns, ruling princes and members of the immediate families of sovereigns.

Foreword. *Synonymous with* PREFACE (*q.v.*).

Form. 1. A classification term applied to the manner in which the text of a book is arranged, as a dictionary, or the literary form in which it is written, as drama, poetry, etc. *See also Form Classes, Form Divisions.*   2. *Form in music* indicates the structure of a musical composition which may be indicated by 'sonata', 'symphony', etc.   3. American spelling for FORME (*q.v.*).

Form Classes.   Those parts of a classification in which the books are arranged according to the form in which they are written, e.g. poetry, drama, fiction, essays, etc., the subjects of the books being ignored.

Form Divisions.   Adjuncts to a classification which enable books to be arranged (within their subject) according to the form in which they are written. They usually have a mnemonic notation which can be applied to any part of a scheme. There are two kinds of form division: OUTER FORM indicates books of which the contents are arranged in a particular way, such as in classified or alphabetical order as in dictionaries, or according to the form of writing or presentation, as essay, bibliography, periodical. Subjective, or INNER FORM, indicates modes of approach such as the theory, history, or philosophy of a subject.

Form Entry.   An entry in a catalogue under (1) the name of the form in which a book is written, e.g. Poetry, Drama, Fiction, or (2) the form in which the subject material is presented, e.g. Periodicals.

Form Heading.   1. A heading used in a catalogue for a FORM ENTRY (*q.v.*), e.g. 'Encyclopaedias'. Also called 'Form subject heading'.   2. A heading derived from and describing the category of document entered under it rather than its author, title or subject, e.g. Encyclopaedias.

Form Number.   (*Classification*) A symbol used to indicate the literary form in which a work is written. It is obtained in connection with the Colon Classification by translating the name of the form of exposition into appropriate symbols in accordance with the Scheme's Form Schedule, and may be used as part of the BOOK NUMBER (*q.v.*).

Form Subheading.   1. A subheading used for sub-arranging in a catalogue entries for books on the same subject by their literary or practical form, e.g. Electronics – Bibliography.   2. A subheading, not consisting of an author's name or of a title, designed to delimit a group of entries according to some common characteristic of form, e.g. Laws, Treaties, under the name of a country.

Form Subject Heading.   *Synonymous with* FORM HEADING (*q.v.*).

Formal Anonyma.   Works, like periodicals, which do not involve the idea of concealed authorship. These are catalogued by Library of Congress and many other libraries in the style known as HANGING INDENTION (*q.v.*). *See also True Anonyma.*

Format.   1. A term used to describe the appearance and make-up of a book; its size, shape, paper, type, binding, illustrations, etc.   2. Strictly, the number of times a sheet of paper has been folded to form a section of a book, e.g. quarto (folded twice giving four leaves).   3. The layout or presentation of items in machine-readable form or in a machine printout.   4. The physical type of an audio-visual item, e.g. a slide transparency, or a particular specification in any given type, e.g. a *VHS* video tape.   5. The general style, or make-up, or the general plan of physical organization, or arrangement, of an index. *See also Foldings, Folio.*

Forme. The combination of chase, furniture and type when 'locked up' ready for machining; i.e. the pages imposed in a chase. The forme containing the text, which will be on the inside pages of a printed sheet when folded, is called the 'inner forme' and that which contains those on the outside, the 'outer forme'. Spelt in America without the 'e'. *See also Dressed Forme, Naked Forme.*

Forme Gauge. *See Gauge.*

Forrel. *Synonymous with* FOREL *(q.v.).*

Forril. *Synonymous with* FOREL *(q.v.).*

Fortnightly. A serial publication issued every second week. Also called 'Bi-weekly', 'Semi-monthly'.

Forty-eightmo. (48mo). A sheet of paper folded six times to form a section of forty-eight leaves (96 pp). Also called 'Quadrigesimo-octavo'.

Forum for Information Resources in Staffordshire. *See FIRST.*

Forum for Interlending. A UK group concerned with all aspects of inter-library loans and document supply. Formed 1989. Intends to issue a *News-letter.* Initially based at Aston University.

Forwarding. The processes of binding a book after it is sewn until it is about to be placed in its cover ready for FINISHING *(q.v.).* The workman doing this is called a 'Forwarder'.

Fotosetter. A machine for typesetting by photography, constructed by the Intertype company and introduced in 1947. A keyboard releases matrices from the magazines in which they are stored. A matrix, known as a *Fotomat,* has a photographic negative character embedded in its side; type lines are made up of separately photographed characters, justification being pre-arranged and automatic, and interlinear spacing obtained by adjusting the film feed dial as necessary.

Foul Case. A case of type in which some of the separate pieces of type have been put into wrong compartments.

Foul Proof. One with many corrections marked on it. In America a proof pulled after corrections have been made.

Founder's Type. Type cast by a type-founder as distinct from type cast by the printer on such machines as the Monotype, Linotype, Ludlow or Intertype.

Foundry. The department of a printing works where matrices are made from the type-formes and blocks, and where stereo plates are cast. Other operations concerned with the casting or fabricating of type and other printing surfaces are also carried out here; the casting and routing machines, type-metal, stereo-metal and similar materials and the necessary tools are to be found here.

Foundry Proof. A proof pulled before the forme is sent to the foundry to be stereotyped.

Foundry Type. *Synonymous with* FOUNDERS' TYPE *(q.v.).*

Fount. 1. A full set of type of one style and size containing the correct number of the various characters, i.e. upper and lower case, numerals, punctuation marks, accents, ligatures, etc. A type family includes founts of roman, italic, semi-bold, semi-bold condensed, and sanserif. *See also Sort, Type Face 2.* 2. The whole collection of tools used by a binder's finisher.

Fount Scheme. *See Bill of Type.*

Four-Colour Process. An extension of the *Three-Colour Process* (*q.v.*), by adding black or grey to give greater depth or solidarity. Also called 'Full colour'.

Fourdrinier Machine. The first machine for making a continuous roll of printing paper. It was invented by Nicolas Louis Robert in 1797, developed in England by Bryan Donkin on behalf of Henry and Sealy Fourdrinier but not perfect until 1804. The principle of this machine is the basis for contemporary machines. The fluid pulp flows from a tank to a moving wire mesh belt during which it is strained and the fibres shaken into a web by agitation. This web of pulp then passes between couch rolls which give it enough strength to be transferred from the wire-cloth to an endless felt on which it passes through successive pairs of press rolls and so to drying cylinders. Thus all the separate processes carried out in the vat, mould, couch and press are combined in one machine. Originally the paper was then cut into sheets and loft-dried in the traditional way, but later additions to the Fourdrinier machine enabled the web of paper to be passed round a series of heated drums and so dried before being drawn through the rolls of a calender to impart the desired finish.

Fournier. A type face cut about 1730 by the French engraver and type-founder Pierre Simon Fournier *the younger* (1712–68). A Modern Face (*q.v.*) type which is characterized by its very fine hair-line serifs. For a specimen alphabet *see Type Face.*

Fournier Point. A unit of type measurement, one point being 0.0137 inch, established by P. S. Fournier in 1737. It was superseded by the Didot Point. *See also Didot System.*

Foxed. 1. Prints and pages of old books with yellowish-brown spots caused by dampness. 2. A mechanical gluing technique sometimes used to make up shortrun multiple snap-apart forms.

Foxing. *See Foxed.*

Fractional Scanning. (*Information retrieval*) Scanning a file by a series of stages. *See also Binary Search.*

Fragmenting. (*Information retrieval*) Determining a number of appropriate terms or descriptors, to indicate adequately the various aspects of a document.

Fraktur. (*Printing*) The group name for German blackface type or bold face type. *See also Bold Face.*

Frame. 1. A wooden stand with a sloped top on which cases of type are placed for the compositor's use. 2. (*Binding*) Ornamentation consisting of a simple hollow rectangle placed some distance from the edges of the cover of a book. To be distinguished from Border (*q.v.*). 3. (*Bibliography*) The complete borders which are not Compartments (*q.v.*). They comprise (a) enclosures made up of separate cuts or ornaments which show no evidence of having been carved or engraved for use together as a border; (b) those made up of separate cast type-ornaments, commonly used for book decoration. 4. (*Reprography*) An area containing an image in a film or microprint. 5. A geometric subdivision of the microfiche grid. A micro-image and its margins are contained within a frame. The standard size of a microfiche frame is 11.25 mm × 16 mm (single) or 23 mm × 16 mm (double). 6. In microcopying, cinematography, and videotaping, portion of film exposed to light through the camera optical system for one image.

Frame Margin. (*Reprography*) The non-image area between the micro-image and the frame. *See also Frame 4.*

Framed-cut. A completely carved decorative full-page cut except for a small panel into which is set a letterpress title. Also called 'compartment', 'title-cut' or 'woodcut title-page with panel'.

FRANCIS. *See INIST.*

Francis Joseph Campbell Citation. *See Campbell Citation, Francis Joseph.*

Fraternity Library. A library in a fraternity on an American college or university campus. It may be one of a circulating collection from the main library, or it may be owned by the fraternity.

Free. 1. In CO-ORDINATE INDEXING (*q.v.*), alone, not bound or joined to a separate modifier. *See also Bound 2.* 2. (*Binding*) Said of a stamp, of whatever form, which has no boundary line, or frame, round it; such stamps may be in intaglio or relief.

Free Acquisition. A procedure enabling an organization to acquire a publi-cation or document, or a series of same, without buying them.

Free Endpaper. That portion of an endpaper which is not pasted down to the cover but adhered to the end section of a book. Also called 'Fly-leaf'. *See also Endpaper.*

Free Field Coding. (*Information retrieval*) The use of a complete coding field, the entry of codes not being restricted to fixed positions.

Free Fields. In information retrieval, location on a search medium which is not reserved for information of a particular type, form or length. *See also Fixed Fields.*

Free Hand. Writing of any period not conforming to definite rules such as the regular use of set abbreviations.

Free Indexing. In CO-ORDINATE INDEXING (*q.v.*), the assignment as index terms for a given document, of words or phrases chosen from a set of words or phrases considered by the indexer to be appropriate indexing terms even though they may not appear in the document.

Freelance. Term used to indicate a style of self-employment in which the individual sells a service to a number of different agencies for a fee. Journalists, photographers or information workers may operate on this basis. Compare also INFORMATION BROKER, INFORMATION CONSULTANT, LIBRARY CONSULTANT.

Free Term List. (*Information retrieval*) A list of terms or descriptors not rigidly defined, and to which other terms or descriptors can be freely added.

Free Text Searching. Online searching in which all aspects of the records may be used as sought terms; natural language is used rather than a controlled vocabulary.

Free Text System. An indexing/information retrieval system that uses the actual words of the text as its indexing words, and not recommended terms from a thesaurus. Abbreviated FTX.

Freedley Memorial Award, George. Established in 1968 by the THEATRE LIBRARY ASSOCIATION (*q.v.*) to honour the late founder of the Association, theatre historian and first curator of the Theatre Collection of the New York Public Library. The award, in the form of a plaque, is made on the basis of scholarship, readability, and general contribution to knowledge. It was first awarded (in 1969) to Louis Sheaffer for his *O'Neill, son and playwright.*

Freedom to Read Foundation. Founded in 1969 by the ALA, the Foundation has a two-part objective: to (a) support and defend librarians whose jobs are jeopardized because they challenge violations of intellectual freedom; (b) provide a means through which librarians and others can set legal precedent for the freedom to read. As a non-profit group, it is supported entirely by membership contributions: there are no special criteria for membership. Publishes *Freedom to Read Foundation News* (q. membs. only). Abbreviated FTRF.

French Federation for Inter-library Co-operation (Fédération Française de Co-opération entre Bibliothèques). Set up in 1985 to co-ordinate the regional structures of co-operation in France. Encourages development of bibliographic databases, arranges conferences and publicity. Based in Paris.

French Fillet. *See Fillet.*

French Fold. A sheet printed on one side only and then folded into a section, the bolts being left uncut. *See also Orihon.*

French Japon. *See Japanese Paper.*

French Joint. A joint formed by keeping boards a short distance from the back, splitting the boards and placing tapes between, thus allowing greater play at the hinge and permitting the use of a much thicker leather or cloth than otherwise. *See also Closed Joint.*

French Rule. (*Printing*) A rule made of brass or type metal and widening to a diamond shape in the middle.

French Sewing. (*Binding*) Sewing without TAPES (*q.v.*).

Fret. A continuous border pattern made up of interlaced bands or fillets. Such patterns may be used for the decoration of pages or tooled on book covers.

Friar. A light patch left on a forme or printed sheet due to imperfect inking. *See also Monk.*

Friedman-Jeffreys Report. A survey of cataloguing and classification in fifty-one British university libraries and published by the University of Sheffield Postgraduate School of Librarianship, under the auspices of SCONUL in 1967, with the title *Cataloguing and classification in British University libraries: a survey of practices and procedures.*

Friends of Libraries. A UK charitable trust set up in 1987 which aims to build up a permanent fund from which it will give grants to help libraries in the public and academic domain; its target is £100 million in its first decade. The Board of Trustees includes eminent figures from the fields of libraries, bookselling and finance.

Friends of Libraries USA. An association to encourage and support volunteer action and sponsorship for libraries. Operates from ALA Headquarters and makes awards each year for State Friends Organization; Large Public Library Friends; Small Public Library Friends; Academic Library Friends.

Friends of the British Library. An organization established in 1988 to widen public awareness of the British Library and encourage special relationships for fund-raising and joint ventures.

Fringed Foliage Ornament. (*Binding*) A finisher's ornament of roughly lozenge shape, with a design of conventional foliage, the characteristic feature of which is a shallow fringe round its edge.

Frisket. A light rectangular iron frame about the size of a TYMPAN (*q.v.*) which is covered witth brown paper and attached to the upper part of the tympan. The frisket sheet folded over the tympan, the centre part of the brown paper which would otherwise cover the printing surface being cut out, before the tympan is turned over the forme. Its purpose is to prevent the sheet of paper being dirtied or blackened by the CHASE (*q.v.*), and FURNITURE (*q.v.*), to hold the sheet to the tympan and to lift the sheet from the FORME (*q.v.*) after printing.

front. (frontis.). Abbreviation for FRONTISPIECE (*q.v.*).

Front Board. The piece of millboard or strawboard which is used for the front cover of a book.

Front Cover. *Synonymous with* OBVERSE COVER (*q.v.*).

Front Edge. *Synonymous with* FORE-EDGE (*q.v.*).

Front Matter. *Synonymous with* PRELIMINARIES (*q.v.*).

Front-Projection Reader. A reader in which an enlargement of a microform is projected onto the front of an opaque screen and read by reflected light. *See also Back-projection Reader.*

Frontispiece. Any pictorial representation at the front of a book, usually facing the title-page, and as a rule unnumbered and unpaged. *See also Illustrations.*

Fry (Maxwell) Book Fund. Set up 1988 by the British Architectual Library of the Royal Institute of British Architects to enable special purchases to be made.

fs. Abbreviation for FACSIMILE (*q.v.*).

FTR. *See Full Text Retrieval.*

FTRF. FREEDOM TO READ FOUNDATION (*q.v.*).

FTX. *See Free Text System.*

Fugitive Colours. Coloured printing inks which change or fade when exposed to normal light. Reds, greens and blues are particularly susceptible to fading.

Fugitive Facts File. A file of facts which it has been difficult to obtain in answer to readers' inquiries, and which are likely to be asked for again. (American).

Fugitive Material. Such publications as pamphlets, programmes and duplicated material produced in small quantities and of immediate, transitory or local interest.

Fulda MS. A MS. of the Gospels and other books of the New Testament written in Latin uncials and dating from *c.* 546.

Full Binding. A binding in which the covering material covers back and sides. Usually applied to a leather bound book. A book so bound is described as 'full bound' or 'whole bound'. *See also Half Leather, Quarter Leather, Three-quarter Leather.*

Full Bound. A book wholly covered with leather.

Full Cataloguing. The style of cataloguing in which the entries give all the information provided for by the rules of the code adopted.

Full Colour. When an ample amount of ink has been used in printing; in distinction from grey colour, when only a small quantity of ink is used.

Full Face. Sometimes used *synonymously with* BOLD FACE (*q.v.*). Also used to denote FULL ON THE BODY (*q.v.*).

Full-Gilt. A book with all edges gilded.

Full Leather. *See Full Binding.*

Full Measure. Type set throughout the whole length of a line, whether of type column or page. *See also Measure.*

Full Music Edition. *See Score.*

Full Name. The names of an individual given in full.

Full-name Note. The full name of an author which is given in the bottom right-hand corner of Library of Congress catalogue cards when a short form of the name (e.g. omitting an indication of a Christian name or giving only the initials) is used for the heading. Similar notes are given in the same position for the name in religion, the original name, a pseudonym which covers joint authors, the real name, secular name, or stage name.

Full on the Body. A fount of capitals designed to occupy the complete body area, AS THIS. Also called 'Full face'.

Full Out. (*Printing*) To commence printed matter flush without indention.

Full Point. The punctuation mark used at the end of a sentence, between figures to mark decimals, and elsewhere in typography. Also called a 'Full stop'.

Full Score. *See Score.*

Full Stop. *Synonymous with* FULL POINT (*q.v.*).

Full-term Co-ordination. A PERMUTED TITLE INDEX (*q.v.*) in which all significant words in the title are co-ordinated with every other significant word.

Full Text Retrieval/Searching. Online searching in which every word of the source documents is on the record and can be retrieved. Abbreviated FTR. *See also Free Text System.*

Full Title. *Synonymous with* MAIN TITLE (*q.v.*).

Fundamental Categories. (*Classification*) Personality, Matter, Energy, Space, and Time (PMEST) are the five fundamental categories of facets which Ranganathan has developed into a general facet formula which represents the PRINCIPLE OF DECREASING CONCRETENESS, Personality being regarded as the most concrete category and Time as the most abstract. *See also Category.* 'Each facet of any subject, as well as each division of a facet, is considered as a manifestation of one of the five fundamental categories' (*Ranaganathan*). Placed in reverse order to that given above they would be in the order of increasing sequence of concreteness. The Connecting Symbols and Symbols of the Facet are as follows:–

Fundamental category (FC)	Connecting symbol (CS)	Symbol for the Facet
Personality	,(comma)	[P]
Matter	;(semicolon)	[M]
Energy	:(colon)	[E]
Space	.(dot)	[S]
Time	.(dot)	[T]

See also Decreasing Concreteness, Principle of.

Furnish. The materials from which a paper is made, e.g. the furnish of a litho paper might be: esparto, 60 per cent; chemical wood, 30 per cent; loading, 10 per cent.

Furnish Layer. Paper or board made up of one or more plies of the same furnish, combined while still moist, without the use of adhesive. Two, three, or more furnish layers similarly combined are known as 'Two-layer, Three-layer, or Multi-layer paper or board' (in some countries as 'Biplex' or 'Duplex', 'Triplex', or 'Multiplex' respectively) according to the number of layers. The external furnish layers of the three-layer papers may be of the same composition, while the multi-layer papers may have two or more furnish layers of the same composition.

Furniture. The wood or metal material used by the printer to form margins and to fill in large gaps between the type matter especially where there is a small amount of type to a page as on a dedication or title-page, and to help secure the printing material in the CHASE (*q.v.*).

Futhark. *See Runes.*

'Futures' Report. *See Library Association.*

Gale Research Financial Development Award. An award presented to a library organization for outstanding achievement in securing and carrying out a library financial development project. Administered by the American Library Association Awards Committee.

Galley. A long narrow and shallow steel tray about 22 inches long and open at one end, into which type is transferred from the compositor's stick or from the typesetting machine to await making up into pages. It is from the type in this galley that the galley proof (also called a 'galley') is taken. *See also Proof.*

Galley Press. A printing press made for the pulling of galley proofs. *See also Proof.*

Galley Proof. *See Proof.*

Garalde.   A category of type face in which the axis of the curves is inclined towards the left. There is generally more contrast between the relative thickness of the strokes than in the Humanist designs (*See Humanist 1*), the serifs are bracketed, the bar of the lower-case 'e' is horizontal, and the serifs of the lower-case ascenders are oblique. These designs are based on those of Aldus and Garamond, and were formerly called OLD FACE or OLD STYLE (*qq.v.*). Bembo, Caslon and Vendôme are garalde faces.

Garamond.   An elegant OLD FACE (*q.v.*) type named after Claude Garamond (d. *circa* 1561), a pupil of Geoffroy Tory, and the first, and perhaps the finest, of the French letter-cutters and typefounders. Garamond types are very legible and unusually pleasing; the face is of light and clean design, showing a very slight difference between the thick and thin strokes. For a specimen alphabet, *see Type Face.*

Garfield (Eugene) Lecture.   An annual lecture sponsored by the Institute of Scientific Information (ISI) and hosted by the Department of Information Science at the Strathclyde Business School, Scotland.

Gascon. *See Le Gascon Style.*

Gatefold.   An illustration, map, or other insert which is larger than the page of the publication into which it is bound, so that it must be unfolded for viewing. (American.) *See also Folded Leaf, Folding Plate, Throw Out.*

Gateway.   A software package allowing a user to access a host via a network; four types of gateway can be found, firstly *host to host* (moving from one host computer to another), secondly *network level gateways* (use of a network for a choice of services), thirdly *common command or search gateways* (access to a service that performs a search on the user's behalf having obtained the specification) and fourthly *network front-end gateways* (using a network as the access service to a variety of hosts). Levels of sophistication vary, and the user may well not be aware what kind of gateway is in use.

Gathering.   (*Verb*) The process of assembling and arranging in correct order the various sections which go to make up a book, preparatory to SEWING (*q.v.*). (*Noun*) Synonymous with SECTION 1 (*q.v.*).

Gauffered Edges.   The gilt edges of the leaves of a book which have been decorated by impressing heated engraved tools to indent a small repeating pattern. This style was popular in the sixteenth and seventeenth centuries. Also called 'Chased', 'Gauffred', 'Goffered'.

Gauffering.   The decoration of the gilded edges of a bound book with heated finishing tools which indent a small repeating pattern. Also called 'Chased edges', 'Goffered edges'.

Gauge.   (*Printing*) A strip of metal or wood with a notch which is used by the make-up man to denote the exact lengths of pages or widths of margins. Also called 'Forme gauge'.

Gazette.   A record of public events which is published periodically. A journal or newsheet. A publication issued by a government or university to convey official information, decisions or statements.

Gazetteer. A geographical dictionary with a varying amount of descriptive, geographical, historical or statistical information.

g.e. Abbreviation for GILT EDGES (*q.v.*).

GEAC. A major supplier of automation 'services to libraries; particularly renowned for stand-alone, turnkey systems that do not involve networks or supplied data.

Geddes Prize, (Philip). A memorial prize for journalism, first awarded 1985, named after the *Daily Express* reporter killed in the Harrod's bombing, 1983.

Gelatine Print. Another name for COLLOTYPE (*q.v.*).

Genealogical Table. A representation of the lineage of a person or persons in tabular or diagrammatical form.

General Abstract. *See Abstract.*

General Bibliography. *See Bibliography.*

General Classification. A classification which arranges the whole field of knowledge – the visible and invisible universe – in logical order.

General Cross-reference. *Synonymous with* GENERAL REFERENCE (*q.v.*).

General Information Programme. A programme sponsored by UNESCO to provide news of activities in the fields of scientific and technological information, and of documentation, libraries and archives by and for member states. A part of the programme is the UNISIST project, for the development and co-ordination of scientific and technological information. Publishes *GIP/UNISIST Newsletter* (irreg.). *See also ISORID, UNISIST, Office of Information Programmes and Services.*

General Information Reference. A general reference in a catalogue from a specific subject on which there are no individual books to a more general subject which includes the specific subject.

General Reference. A *See also* reference in an index or catalogue which directs the user to a number of headings under which entries on specific subjects may be found. These are often used to avoid bulking out the catalogue with a number of specific references. Also called 'Geneal cross-reference', 'Information entry', 'Multiple reference'. *See also Cross-References, Specific Reference.*

General Search. *Synonymous with* HIERARCHICAL SEARCH (*q.v.*).

General Secondary. An entry for a person or a corporate body whose connection with the publication catalogued cannot be indicated in the heading by the use of some specific designation as arranger, editor, etc.

General Special Concept. A subdivision of a topic according to a characteristic which has general applicability to other subdivisions that are based on different characteristics, e.g. the division of diseases by the process of diagnosis, which applies to kinds of diseases, such as liver diseases.

General Title. One which is provided for a book consisting of several works which have previously been published separately and whose title-pages are called 'Divisional title-pages'.

General Works. A group name, sometimes used as a heading in a scheme of classification, for books of a general nature, i.e. dealing with many different subjects. Sometimes called a GENERALIA CLASS (*q.v.*).

Generalia Class. The main class of a classification which is reserved for books on many subjects such as encyclopaedias.

Generation. (*Reprography*) An indication of the remoteness of a copy from the original document. The original picture of the document is called a 'first generation' microfilm (camera microfilm); copies made from this are called 'second generation', and copies made from this, 'third generation', etc.

Generic. Pertaining to a genus or class of related things.

Generic Coding. (*Classification*) The encoding of descriptors in such a way as to preserve generic relations, e.g. encoding by hierarchical class numbers, or with characteristics, replacing each descriptor by a compound of its characteristics.

Generic Descriptor. A DESCRIPTOR (*q.v.*) related to a genus or class of related things.

Generic Relation. (*Classification*) 1. The relationship between *GENUS* and *SPECIES* (*q.q.v.*). 2. The relationship between a class term and the members of that class, where all the members have certain characteristics defined by the class term. 3. The relation between classes in a chain of subordinate classes, where each fore-going member includes all the following members of the chain. 4. (*Information retrieval*) The relationship between two concepts or classes of a classification where one is the genus and one the species. *See also Relation.*

Generic Searching. (*Information retrieval*) In machine searching for indexed material, where the machine has a memory which will hold references to allied ideas, searching under broader headings than the more specific ones under which a document is indexed.

Generic Term. (*Indexing*) A single word which is a constituent part of a BOUND TERM (*q.v.*). *See also Collateral Term.*

Geneva Bible. A version of the English Bible, translated by William Whittingham, Anthony Gilby, Thomas Sampson and possibly others, and printed by Rouland Hall, Geneva, 1560. It was produced by Marian exiles and was never sanctioned by the Archbishop of Canterbury; after the death of Archbishop Matthew Parker in 1575, it was openly printed in London (first English edition, 1576) and was the Englishman's private Bible until Cromwellian times. The General Assembly of the Scots Kirk adopted the Geneva Bible (1579) as its official version. Being the first English Bible printed in roman type it did much to help the English reading public to become familiar with the roman face. It was the first Bible in English to be divided into verses. Because of the rendering of Genesis iii. 7, 'They sewed fig leaves together and made themselves breeches', it is sometimes referred to as the *Breeches Bible*. It is also called the *Whig Bible* because a printer's error causes Matt: 5:9 to read 'Blessed are the place makers, for they shall be called the children of God'.

Geneva Convention. Popular name for the Universal Copyright Convention. *See Copyright, International.*

Genus. *See Predicables, Five.*

Geographic Division.   Sub-division in classification or in subject headings by country, region or locality. *See also Area Table.*

Geographic Filing Method.   Arranging material, or entries in a catalogue, list or bibliography, according to place, either by place-names or by a geographic classification scheme. Also sub-arrangement by place (either alphabetically by place-name or by classification) in any method of filing. Alphabetical filing may be by specific place.

Geographical Entry.   The name given to catalogue entries for topographical books and geographical guides, which go under the name of the district to which they refer.

Geographical Numbers.   Numbers added to a classification symbol to arrange the books geographically. They are usually applicable throughout a classification scheme. *See also Area Table.*

Geological Survey.   An organization which publishes geological maps of Britain through the ORDNANCE SURVEY (*q.v.*).

Geometric.   A group of LINEALE (*q.v.*) type faces which are based on a circle, a triangle or on geometric shapes. They are usually MONO LINE (*q.v.*), and the 'a' is often single-storey.

Geo-ref.   The machine-readable file of citations covering the world literature in the geosciences. It is developed and maintained by the American Geological Institute.

George Freedley Memorial Award.   *See Freedley Memorial Award, George.*

German Library Association (Deutscher Bibliotheksverband).   Founded 1949. Based in Berlin. Aims to promote library services and professional librarianship. Publishes *Bibliotheksdienst* (m.) handbook, conference proceedings and reports.

German Library Institute.   *See Deutsches Bibliotheksintitut.*

German Society for Documentation.   *See Deutsche Gesellschaft für Dokumentation.*

Germanic Handwriting.   A pre-Carolingian, or pre-Caroline handwriting, which was greatly limited in time and space (eighth to ninth centuries A.D.). A 'national' style of handwriting which developed after the dissolution of the Roman Empire, and was a development of the Latin cursive. *See also Cursive, Handwriting.*

Get En Mol.   *See Jeté En Moule.*

Get In.   1. To set 'copy' in less space than estimated.   2. To set type very close, or to set it so that it will fit within a required area by using thin spacing.

Ghost Writer.   One who writes or prepares a book such as an autobiography, or articles for, and in the name of, another (usually well-known) person.

Giant Book.   A three-dimensional cardboard blow-up of the outside of a book for purposes of display. *See also Blow-Up.*

Gift Binding.   Any book bound in leather for presentation such as a school prize, or part of an edition bound in leather at the publisher's order for the gift market.

Gift Book.   *See Keepsake.*

Gift Card.   A record made for each gift; it corresponds to an order card made for a purchased book.

Giggering.   Polishing a blind impression on a leather binding by rubbing a small hot tool on it.

Giles (Louise) Minority Scholarship.   An award made by the ALA Office for Library Personnel Resources, to a student from an ethnic minority community.

Gill.   A type-face named after Eric Gill (1882–1940) the English sculptor, artist and type designer; it is characterized by the absence of serifs and is therefore known as 'Gill Sans'. Although excellent for display captions it is not wholly suitable for book work as it becomes tiring to read after a time. Gill designed two type faces which are excellent for this purpose: 'Joanna' (1930) and 'Perpetua' (1929–30), the last being his most widely-used type. This most pleasing type is used for display as well as for text. In 1934 he designed a special type for Sterne's *Sentimental Journey* published by the Limited Editions Club of New York. This was the basis for Linotype's 'Pilgrim' which appeared in 1953. For alphabet specimens, *see Type Face.*

Gilt Edges.   (*Binding*) The edges of a book which have been trimmed by a guillotine, covered with gold leaf and burnished. 'Antique gold edges' are those which have an unburnished gilt finish. Edges are sometimes tooled with a diapered pattern after binding. *See also Edges.*

Gilt Extra.   (*Binding*) A binding with more than the normal amount of gilt ornamentation.

Gilt in the Round.   A book, the fore-edges of which have been gilded after rounding, the fore-edge appearing as a solid gilt surface.

Gilt in the Square.   A book, the fore-edges of which have been gilded before rounding with the result that there is a tendency for the sections at the beginning and the end of the book to show a white edge.

Gilt on the Rough.   Gilding on the uncut edge of a book, or on one that has not been cut solid. It provides the elegance of gold without any sacrifice of margin but does not, like smooth gilt edges, keep the dust out. This was a popular style in France in the nineteenth century and continues to be found. *See also Marbling Under Gilt, Rough Gilt Edges, Solid Gilt.*

Gilt Top.   The top edge of a book trimmed smooth and gilded, the remaining edges being trimmed only. Also called 'Top edges gilt'. Abbreviated g.t., g.t.e., or t.e.g. *See also Edges, Gauffered Edges, Solid Gilt.*

GIP.   *See General Information Programme.*

Girdle Book.   A book used in the middle ages and early Renaissance which had secured to it an extra protective cover of soft leather made in such a way that the book could be hung from the girdle or habit cord of a cleric.

Given Name.   The personal name (in Western races the 'Christian' name) given to an individual to distinguish him from other members of his family or clan.

GK III.   Conventionally an abbreviation for the British Library General Catalogue of Books to 1955, completed in 1966. Now superseded by a new edition with supplements and corrections, issued 1987, and a CD-ROM version currently in progress.

GKD Notation.   An abbreviation for the Gordon-Kendall-Davison notation which is used simply to describe structural formulae in chemistry. Also called the 'Birmingham notation'. *See also Wisweisser Line Notation.*

Glaire.   An adhesive substance (made by heating up the white of eggs and vinegar or water) used as a size to retain gold in 'finishing' and edge-gilding books.

GLASS.   Acronym for the Greater London Audio Specialization system, which is a subject specialization scheme, with inter-lending facilities, for audio materials. The scheme became operational on 1 April 1972, and embraces the thirty-two London Boroughs (excluding originally the City of London and the Upper Norwood Joint Library), which comprise the Greater London areas. Aims: to (a) ensure that at least one copy of all issues within scheduled composer/jazz artist/subject fields is purchased and preserved for public lending within the region; (b) avoid over-purchase of records with low loan potential within the region; (c) make each specializing library within the region the discographical reference point for its particular subjects; (d) issue accessions lists, and where the subject warrants it, printed catalogues of holdings. Records of classical music, jazz and spoken word are covered by the Scheme. The purchase and collection of classical music is allocated to the libraries by composer, and of jazz by performer; records by these composers/performers withdrawn from stock in other libraries in the Scheme may be sent to the 'specializing' libraries for preservation.

Glassine.   A transparent glossy-surfaced paper obtained by excessive beating of the stock, or by acid treatment. It is made in white and a variety of colours, and is used for panels for window-envelopes, as jackets to protect new books, and for general wrapping purposes.

Glazed Morocco.   Morocco, the grain of which has been smoothed by calendering to impart a polished appearance. *See also Crushed Morocco.*

GLCLG.   Acronym of the Greater London College Librarian's Group which was formed in December 1966 to facilitate the meeting of, and exchange of information with librarians working in further and higher education in the Greater London area.

Glenerin Declaration.   A tri-national statement resulting from a series of meetings of information specialists from Canada, UK and USA, convened by the Institute for Research on Public Policy (Canada), British Library, and National Commission on Libraries and Information Service (USA). (The relevant meeting was held at the Glenerin Inn, Mississauga, Ontario, Canada, in 1988.) The Declaration aims to foster understanding of the role of information in the economy and society, and develop an agenda to maximize the benefits to society of the changing role of information and the information industry. The text can be found in *FID News Bulletin* v 38(5) 1988 pp. 37–38.

Glenfiddich Awards.   An annual series of awards for writers on food and drink in the UK.

Gloss.   In ancient MSS. an explanation or interpretation of a word or expression, placed in the margin or above the line, often in a more familiar language. Also used for an explanation inserted in the margin or text of a book to clarify a foreign or difficult passage. *See also Side Note.*

Gloss Ink. A printing ink consisting of a synthetic resin base and drying oils; this composition ensures that penetration and absorption into the paper is retarded and that it dries with a brilliant, glossy surface. Specially suitable for use with coated papers and for printing by letterpress or lithographic methods.

Glossarial Index. An index to a book which gives a description or definition of the word indexed as well as its page number.

Glossarist. *Synonymous with* GLOSSOGRAPHER (*q.v.*).

Glossary. 1. An alphabetical list of abstruse, obsolete, unusual, technical, dialectical or other, terms concerned with a subject field, together with definitions. 2. A collection of equivalent synonyms in more than one language.

Glossator. A writer of glosses to texts; a commentator; especially a mediaeval commentator on the texts of civil and canon law. *See also Glossographer.*

Glossist. *Synonymous with* GLOSSOGRAPHER (*q.v.*).

Glossographer. A writer of glosses to a text, or of commentaries on a text; an annotator. Also called a 'Glossarist', 'Glossist', 'Glottographer'. *See also Glossator.*

Glossography. The writing of glosses or commentaries; the compiling of glossaries.

Glossy Print. A photographic print with a shiny surface. These are necessary for the making of satisfactory half-tone blocks.

Glottographer. *Synonymous with* GLOSSOGRAPHER (*q.v.*).

Gluing Off. The process of applying glue to the spine of a book, either after sewing, or instead of sewing, and just prior to placing it within its case.

Glyphic. Styles of type face which are chiselled, rather than calligraphic, in form. Of such are Albertus, Augustea and Latin.

Glyphography. A process of making printing plates by engraving on a copper plate covered with a wax film, then dusting with powdered graphite, producing a surface that is used to make an electrotype.

Go List. (*Indexing. Information retrieval*) A list of terms or characters which one wishes to include in a printout. A Go List makes it possible to select specific items from a very large number forming a group. The opposite of a STOP LIST (*q.v.*).

Goatskin. Leather manufactured from the skins of goats; the best skins come from the River Niger, the Levant or Morocco, and are named after the places from which they come.

Godort. *See Government Documents Round Table.*

Goffered Edges. *Synonymous with* GAUFFERED EDGES (*q.v.*).

Gold. Used in the form of thin leaves or foil for lettering or tooling books.

Gold and Silver Dagger Awards for Fiction. *See Crime Writers' Association.*

Gold Cushion. A pad, used by binders' finishers, to which a sheet of gold leaf adheres and from which the finisher takes the small pieces required for each book. The pad is usually filled with blotting paper, felt, or similar material, and covered with leather.

Gold Knife.   A knife used by binders' finishers, to cut gold leaf while on the gold cushion. It has a long, flat blade, and is sharpened on both sides.

Gold Stamped.   A book with a design stamped in gold on the binding by means of a stamp. *See also Block 3, Panel Stamp, Tooling.*

Gold Tooling.   *See Tooling.*

Golden Cockerel Press.   An English private press, founded in December 1920 by Harold Midgely Taylor at Waltham Saint Lawrence, Berkshire, to print and publish (in a co-operative manner, and under the conditions of a 'village industry') new works of literary significance by young authors; and to print and publish fine editions of books of established worth. When Mr. Taylor retired in January 1924 owing to illness, the Press was purchased by Robert Gibbings, illustrator and woodcutter who operated it until 1933. The press is still active. Most of the printing is done in Caslon Old Face.

Golden Type.   The first of three types cut by William Morris for his Kelmscott Press. It was a 14-point roman based on an early fount used by Nicholas Jenson and was first used in 1891. In 1891 he designed the TROY and, in 1892 the CHAUCER, types (*qq.v.*). *See also Kelmscott Press.*

Gone to Bed.   *See Gone to Press.*

Gone to Press.   A term used to indicate that formes or plates have been sent for machining and that it is too late to make any but vital corrections or alterations. Any which occur at this stage are often included in corrigenda. In a newspaper office the term 'Gone to bed' is generally used.

Gore.   A triangular piece of paper or thin card on which is printed a section of a map of the world, bounded by meridians and tapering to the Poles; twelve or twenty-four of these can be stuck to a sphere and so make a complete printed globe.

Gothic Minuscule.   The style of handwriting which, by the end of the twelfth century, had degenerated from the Carolingian Minuscule into a hand consisting of long, angular pointed letters. It was on this that most of the early European printers based their first types.

Gothic Type.   Type resembling the Gothic script used as a book hand in the later middle ages. Gothic types are usually divided into four groups: (1) *Text, Lettre de forme* (Lat. *textura*), or (pointed) church type; (2) *Gothico-antiqua, lettre de somme* (Lat. *fere-humanistica*), the simple round gothic; (3) *Rotunda*, the ordinary round text-type; (4) *Bastard, lettre bâtarde* (Lat. *bastarda*), or cursive type. It is now loosely used to include all bold sans serif and grotesque type faces. Also called 'Black letter type'.

Gothico-antiqua.   *See Gothic Type.*

Gottlieb Prize, Murray.   Offered by the (American) Medical Library Association for the best essay submitted on some phase of medical history.

Goudy.   A type face named after the American type designer, Frederic W. Goudy who flourished in the early years of the present century. Probably his most famous type is Kennerley.

Gouffered.   *See Gauffered Edges.*

Gouge.   A bookbinder's finishing tool used for producing a curved line on a book cover at a single application. It has a set of arcs of concentric circles.

Government Document. A publication issued at government expense or published by authority of a governmental body. As used in America, any publication in book, serial or non-book form bearing an imprint of a government, whether federal, state, local, or foreign, and of inter-governmental organizations, such as UNESCO, etc. *See also Official Publication.*

Government Documents Round Table. A discussion group permanently sponsored by the American Library Association. Abbreviated GODORT.

Government Libraries Group. Founded in 1977, this Group of the (British) Library Association aims to unite and represent those employed in central government department libraries, national libraries, museums and galleries. Publishes a *newsletter.*

Government Libraary. A library maintained out of central government funds. Government libraries normally fall into three broad groups: National libraries, departmental libraries and the libraries of rsearch stations.

Government Publications. Publications of an official character, or of an instructional, descriptive, or historical nature, which are published by the government publishing department for parliament or one of the government departments. *See also Parliamentary Publications.*

Grabhorn Press. Founded by the Grabhorn brothers, Edwin and Robert, of San Francisco, this press has established a leading reputation for gifted and original work since their first commission from the Book Club of California in 1921. The Grabhorns' work is lively and virile and they are particularly skilful in colour-printing, especially from wood-blocks.

Gradation in Speciality. Bliss's 'principle by which the several sciences and studies distinguished by their conceptional scope and their relations to the real order of nature, are arranged in serial order from the most general to the most special.' The modulation of more fundamental classes into their derivatives in the same way that special sciences depend on, and to some extent are derived from, the general sciences.

Grain. The direction in which the fibres lie in a sheet of paper. *See also Against the Grain, Machine Direction, With the Grain.*

Grain Direction. The direction in which the majority of the fibres in a sheet of paper lie. The moving web of a paper-making machine causes the fibres in the pulp to lie parallel with one another in the direction of the web movement. Also called 'Machine direction'. It is important to determine the 'direction' of paper used for lithography, postage stamps, account books or close register work, to avoid differences in expansion. Hand-made papers expand or shrink equally in all directions due to the shaking which occurs during manufacture and which felts the fibres in all directions. *See also Against the Grain, With the Grain.*

Grained Leather. A tanned skin on which the natural grain (visible on the side on which the hair grew) has been worked up to raise and accentuate it. Graining is also artificially produced by stamping a skin with engraved metal plates.

Graining.   1. The process of producing the natural grain markings of leather by boarding, i.e. the pushing or pulling of a fold in the skin with the aid of a board covered with cork, which grips that portion of the skin with which it is in contact.   2. The art of producing an artificial grain on leather by stamping it with metal plates or passing it through rollers on which the desired grain markings are engraved.

Gramophone Record.   A sound recording made on a flat, black vinyl disc; the US term is 'phonograph record'; popularly termed 'disc'. Increasingly superseded by audio tape and compact disc recordings.

Grangerizing.   The practice of inserting in a bound volume illustrations, letters, documents, etc., not issued as part of the volume but referred to in the text. Such additional matter is mounted or inlaid on sheets of good quality paper and inserted in the appropriate parts of the book which is usually re-bound. The practice dates from 1769, when James Granger published a 'Bibliographical History of England' with blank leaves for the reception of illustrations. Such a volume is said to be 'Extra-illustrated' or 'Grangerized'.

Graph.   A pictorial representation of numerical data. Graphs may take various forms and are described as pictograms or as bar, line, broken-line or circular, graphs.

Graphic.   Styles of type faces which suggest that the characters have not been written but drawn. Of such are Cartoon, Libra and Old English (Monotype).

Graphic Length.   A characteristic of the length of notation symbols used in a scheme of classification, whereby there is ability to remember easily a sequence because of their visual appearance. *See also Phonic Length.*

Graphics.   Non-verbal material, e.g. diagrams, drawings, photographs, graphs.

Graticule.   A system of lines representing meridians and parallels on a map. Not to be confused with grid which is a network of parallel lines drawn at right angles on a map to represent fixed distances.

Graver.   A Burin (*q.v.*).

Gravure.   A French word, meaning cutting or engraving; used as a continuing word, like photogravure, rotogravure, etc. An abbreviation for Photogravure (*q.v.*).

Great Primer.   An out-of-date name for a size of type equal to about 18 point.

Greater London Audio Specialization Scheme.   *See GLASS.*

Greater London College Librarians' Group.   *See GLCLG.*

Greek Fashion.   Book bindings with raised Headbands (*q.v.*), i.e. those which project beyond the boards at the head and tail of the spine. The Greek technique of forwarding was used in the West only for Greek books.

Green Book.   An official report published by the Italian government; so called because bound in a green paper cover. *See also Blue Book.*

Green Paper.   A document issued by any Department or Ministry of the British Government. It has green covers, and sets out government propositions so that full consultation and public discussion may take place while policy is still in a formative stage. Green Papers are intended to meet the need for better communication between Government and public rather than to present proposals as in a White Paper. *See also Blue Book, Parliamentary Papers, White Paper.*

Greenaway (Kate) Medal. An award, made by the (British) Library Association annually with the intention of recognizing the importance of illustrations in children's books, to the artist who in the opinion of the Library Association has produced the most distinguished work in the illustration of children's books during the year preceding the award. The work must have been originally published in the United Kingdom. It was first awarded in 1956 to Edward Ardizonne for *Tim all alone.* A list of books awarded the medal is published in the Library Association *Year book.*

Gregory (Eric) Trust Fund. Administered by the SOCIETY OF AUTHORS (*q.v.*) for the encouragement of young UK poets.

Gregynog Press. A private press founded in 1922 within the cultural centre formed by the Misses Gwendoline and Margaret Davies at Newton, Wales. The press ran from 1923–40 under a succession of controllers; wood engraving was a speciality, and Kennerley, Bembo, and Poliphilus types were much used. Bindings were varied in style. The press was willed to the University of Wales, and re-started operation in 1978.

Gregynog Prize. Biennial awards to Welsh publishers for high standards in book production, for adult books, and for children's books.

Grey Literature. 'Semi-published' material, for example reports, internal documents, theses etc. not formally published or available commercially, and consequently difficult to trace bibliographically. *See also SIGLE.*

Grid. (*Binding*) An ornament which is frequently used on heads-in-medallions rolls, and consists of two horizontal lines with a few short vertical bars between them, the sides having a foliage character. (*Cartography*) A referencing system using distances measured on a chosen projection. Not to be confused with GRATICULE (*q.v.*).

Grid Reference. The position of a point on a map expressed in grid letters and co-ordinates, or co-ordinates alone. *See also Grid.*

Grigg Committee. Popular name of the (British) Committee on Departmental Records of which Sir James Grigg was Chairman. It was set up in 1952 by the Master of the Rolls and the Chancellor of the Exchequer to review the arrangements for the preservation of Government Department's records and to make recommendations. The Committee's report was presented in 1954, and the recommendations it contained were accepted by Government in principle; the Public Records Act 1958 which came into force on 1 January 1959 repealed the former acts of 1838, 1877 and 1898. This Act transferred the direction of the Public Record Office from the Master of the Rolls to a Minister of the Crown, the Lord Chancellor, who was given a general responsibility for public records. *See also Modern Public Records.*

Gripper Edge. *See Lay Edges.*

Grolier-Americana Scholarships. Donated by the Grolier Foundation, and made to two library schools, one of which is a graduate library school and the other with a programme of library education at undergraduate level, for scholarships for a student in each institution who is in training for school librarianship. It is awarded annually, and administered by the American Association of School Librarians.

Grolier Foundation Award.   Donated by Grolier Inc., this award is made annually to a librarian in a community or in a school who has made an unusual contribution to the stimulation and guidance of reading by children and young people. It 'is usually given for outstanding work with children and young people through high school age, for continued service, or in recognition of one particular contribution of lasting value'. Selection of the recipient is made by a jury of five appointed by the ALA Awards Committee (which administers the Award), and representing the following ALA divisions: AASL, ALSC, YASD and one member representing the ALA Awards Committee who serves as chairman.

Grolier National Library Week Grant.   Donated by Grolier Inc., and offered by the ALA Committee on National Library Week to the state library association sponsoring the most effective statewide Library Week programme.

Grolieresque.   The style of binding which is associated with Jean Grolier (1479–1565). It depends for its effect on light and graceful geometrical 'strapwork' (interlaced double fillets), and influenced ornate binding for two centuries. *See also Maioli Style.*

Groove.   The cut-out portion of the base of a piece of movable type. Also called 'Heel-nick'. It has no particular purpose in printing. *See also Feet.*

Grooves.   (*Binding*) 1. The shoulders formed on the sides of books in backing, to allow the boards to lie even with the back when secured.   2. Incisions in the back edge of a board to take the cords on which the sections are sewn.

Grotesque.   Sans serif display types of unconventional design. A name given at the beginning of the nineteenth century to the earliest SANS SERIF (*q.v.*) types, which have been revived and come into favour for display work. During the 1920s and 1930s the following sans serif faces became popular: Futura, Gill, Granby, Vogue. These are a group of LINEALE (*q.v.*) type faces with nineteenth-century origins. Some contrast in the thickness of the strokes exists, and there is a squareness in the curves. The ends of the curved strokes are usually horizontal. The G is spurred and the R usually has a curled leg. *See also Neo-grotesque.*

Ground.   An acid-resisting compound used on etching plates to protect the non-image-bearing portions from the action of the acid. It is composed of beeswax, asphaltum, gum mastic and pitch.

Groundwood Pulp.   *Synonymous with* MECHANICAL WOOD (*q.v.*).

Group.   A section of the membership of the (British) Library Association, and formally constituted in accordance with the bye-laws of the Association. Each group is concerned with a particular subject interest in librarianship. *See also Branch, Division, Library Association, Section.* Aslib also has subject Groups.

Group Notation Device. The device of using ordinal decimal fraction numbers of two or more digits (but the same number of significant digits) to represent a number of co-ordinate isolates or array-isolates, when they are too many to be represented economically by SECTOR DEVICE (*q.v.*) alone.

Group of Lausanne. *See European Foundation for Library Co-operation.*

Growing Flower. A common ornament on bookbinders' finishers' rolls, consisting usually of a flattened elliptical base from which springs a stem bearing leaves and at the top two flowers, the tops of which curl outwards.

Grub Street. According to Dr. Johnson, 'originally the name of a street near Moorfields, much inhabited by writers of small histories, dictionaries, and occasional poems . . .'

C.S.G.S. Series of Maps. A series of maps published by the Directorate of Military Survey of the British War Office (formerly known as the General Staff, Geographical Section) covering Europe, Africa and Asia, and the East Indies.

g.t. (or g.t.e.). Abbreviation for GILT TOP (*q.v.*).

Guard. 1. A strip of linen or paper pasted by a binder (1) on to or into the sections of a book to prevent the sewing tearing through the paper, (2) on the inner edge of an illustration, the guard being sewn through. 2. One or more pieces of paper or linen placed together to equalize the space taken by a folded map or other insert or by material pasted to the pages of cuttings book. Also to enable additional illustrations, maps or leaves to be added after binding. Also called 'Stub'.

Guard Book Catalogue. *See Page Catalogue.*

Guard Sheet. A sheet of paper, usually thinner (and often transparent) than that on which the book is printed, bearing a letterpress description or an outline drawing to protect and/or elucidate the illustration which it accompanies. The guard sheet is not normally included in the pagination.

Guardian Award for Children's Fiction. An annual prize instituted in 1967 by the *Guardian* Newspaper for an outstanding work of fiction for children written by a British or Commonwealth author.

Guardian Fiction Prize. An annual award made by the *Guardian* newspaper for a work of fiction published by a British or Commonwealth writer.

Guarding. Fixing a guard to a section, maap or illustration, etc. Strengthening the fold between two conjugate leaves with an adhesive, pasted, or glued-on strip of paper.

Guide Card. A card with a projecting tab used in a card catalogue or file to indicate the arrangement and to facilitate reference.

Guide-Letter. A letter printed in the space to be filled by the rubrisher or illuminator or an early printed book as a guide to prevent him inserting a wrong letter.

Guide Slip. *See Proces Slip.*

Guiding. A system of signs, signpostings, maps, plans, shelf-labels or symbols devised to assist a user in finding services, categories of stock etc., in a library.

Guillemets. *See Duck-foot Quotes.*

Gum Arabic. A solution used to preserve offset plates, and in lithographic printing. *See also Desensitization.*

Gumming Up. Applying a solution of gum arabic to an offset plate to protect it from grease and oxidation.

Gutenberg Bible. *See Mazarin Bible.*

Gutter. 1. The adjoining inner margins of two facing pages of type; the margins at the sewn fold of a section. 2. (*Binding*) The trough between the edge of the board and the backed spine of a bound book. *See also BBacking, Groove, Joint 3, Spine.* 3. In a permuted title, index, or similar mechanically-produced listing, a vertical column of one or more spaces at which point the index words are positioned to provide a readil-viewable alphabetical order.

Gutter Margin. *Synonymous with* BACK MARGIN (*q.v.*).

Guttering. The ridges that sometimes occur (as a result of use) along the spine of a binding which has a tight or a flexible back.

Gypsographic Print. *Synonymous with* SEAL PRINT (*q.v.*).

Habilitationsschrift. A probationary treatise embodying the results of original research that is submitted in order that its author be recognized as a Privatdozent at a university. (German).

Hachures. Vertical and horizontal lines used on a map to indicate by their length and closeness the direction and steepness of variations in height of the earth's surface, the lines being crowded together to represent the steepest slopes. *See also Hatching.*

Hagar Press. The German counterpart of the ALBION PRESS (*q.v.*).

Hagionym. The name of a saint taken as a proper name.

Hague Scheme. A scheme of book classification compiled by Dr. Greve. *See also SISO.*

Hair Line. A thin stroke of a letter or type character.

Hair Space. (*Printing*) The thinnest spacing material. It is cast less than type height and is used between letters or words. Hair spaces vary in thickness from eight to twelve to an em, according to body size, thus in 6pt. the hair space is ½pt.; in 12pt. it is 1½pts.; in 18pt. it is 2pts.; and in 24pt. it is 3pts. T h i s s e n t e n c e i s h a i r s p a c e d .

Hale Award, Sarah Josepha. A medal awarded to a distinguished author whose work and life reflect the literary tradition of New England. Donated by the friends of the Richards Free Library.

Half Bands. Ridges on the spine of a bound book, at the top and bottom, smaller than bands. They usually mark the position of the KETTLE STITCH (*q.v.*).

Half Binding. *See Quarter Binding.*

Half Bound. *Synonymous with* HALF LEATHER (*q.v.*).

Half Cloth. A book with a cloth spine, usually with the title printed on a paper label, and having paper covered 'board' (i.e. strawboard) sides. May also be called 'Half linen'.

Half-dark Type. *Synonymous with* MEDIUM FACE (*q.v.*).

Half-Duplex. *See Duplex.*

Half Frame. The use of a mask in the gate of a camera to reduce the image to half size, e.g. to 24 × 18 mm. from 24 × 36 mm.

Half Leather. A term used to describe a book with a leather spine and corners, but with the rest of the sides covered in cloth. *See also Leather Bound, Quarter Leather.*

Half-Line Block. A printing block made by interposing a half-line screen (i.e. parallel lines without cross-lines) between the original line drawing and the negative. The result is lighter in tone than the original.

Half-linen. *See Half Cloth.*

Half-measure. *See Double Columned.*

Half Monthly. A periodical issued twice a month, or fortnightly.

Half See Safe. An expression used by a bookseller when ordering copies of a book from a publisher to indicate that, while all copies will be paid for, he may ask the publisher to take back half of them in exchange for copies of another title. *See also See Safe.*

Half-sheet Imposition. *Synonymous with* HALF-SHEET WORK (*q.v.*).

Half-sheet Work. Printing (with two machinings) a sheet of paper on both sides with the same forme, laid out in such a way that the paper may then be cut in half to give two copies. *See also Sheet Work.* Also called 'Half-sheet imposition'.

Half-stamp. (*Binding*) A finisher's stamp the design of which is the same as, or similar to, one half of a fleuron, pineapple, etc. It is generally used for the compartments at the edges of the frame in lozenge compartment bindings. Sometimes used back to back to form the lozenges in the centre.

Half-stuff. (*Paper*) Partially broken and washed STOCK (*q.v.*) which has been reduced to a fibrous pulp, usually before it is bleached. The finished pulp, ready for the vat or paper machine is termed 'whole-stuff'. *See also Pulp, Stock, Stuff, Whole-stuff.*

Half-title. The brief title of a book appearing on the recto of the leaf preceding the title-page. It serves to protect the title-page and help the printer to identify the book to which the first sheet belongs. The wording of long titles is often abbreviated. The use of such a page dates from the latter half of the seventeenth century although a blank sheet had been used to protect title-pages for a very long time. It is often abbreviated h.t. Also called 'Bastard title', 'Fly-title'. *See also Second Half-title.*

Half-tone. The name given to the process by means of which photographs, drawings, designs, etc., are reproduced in tone as opposed to solid black and white: also to the actual prints made by it. The printing plate is of copper or zinc and the image is reduced to a series of dots varying in intensity with the tone values of the original. This is done photographically in conjunction with a mechanically ruled screen which is coarse with few dots to the square inch for printing on coarse papers, and many to the square inch for fine, smooth papers. Etching removes the background, leaving the dots representing the image to be printed by relief process. *A Squared-up half-tone* is one finished with straight sides at right angles. Half-tones are also finished as Circles or Ovals. A *Vignetted half-tone* is one which has no sharp edge to the design, and 'fades' out. A *Cut-out half-tone* is one from which the background is entirely removed. A *Deep-etched half-tone* is one from highlights of which the dots characteristic of a half-tone are entirely removed, leaving the paper virgin white in the reproduction. A *Highlight*, or *Drop-out*, is one from which the dots have been removed.

Half-tone Paper. An ART (*q.v.*), imitation art, or other super-calendered or coated paper suitable for the printing of half-tones.

Half-tone Screens. Transparent plates of glass used for making half-tone blocks. They are ruled diagonally with opaque lines usually, but not necessarily, at right angles to each other, the thickness of the lines and of the intervening spaces being approximately equal. The number of lines to the inch varies, 'fine' screens having more than 'coarse' ones. The smoother the paper used, the finer must be the half-tone block. *See also Screen.*

Half Uncial. The last stage in the development of the Roman period of Latin manuscript handwriting, being a somewhat informal kind of letter based on minuscule forms and used from the fifth to the ninth centuries. It is specially associated with the calligraphic revival by Alcuin in the ninth century. Most of the letters were miniscules, only a few of the capitals, such as N and F, remaining.

Half Yearly. A periodical which is issued at six-monthly intervals. Also called 'Semi-annual'. *See also Bi-annual.*

Hall (G. K.) Award for Library Literature. An award administered by the ALA.

Hammond Incorporated Library Award. An annual Award donated by the C. S. Hammond Company, and made to a librarian who has effectively encouraged the use of maps and atlases or promoted an interest in cartography. The Award is administered by the ALA Awards Committee.

Hand. The printers' symbol ☞. Used to attract attention. Also called 'Digit', 'Fist', 'Index'.

Hand Composition. The setting up of printer's type by hand as distinct from machine setting.

Hand Gravure. A method of copperplate printing. After inking and before each impression is taken, the surface is wiped by hand.

Hand-made Paper. Paper made by dipping a mould into the pulp vat and taking up sufficient 'stuff' to form a sheet of paper of the required substance. A shaking movement causes the fibres to mix together. The pulp is composed of rag fibres; when the best linen rags are used the resulting paper is the most durable obtainable. Also called 'Vat paper'.

Hand Press. A press in which the forme is inked, the paper fed and removed, and the pressure applied, by hand; used to distinguish it from one worked by power; often used in printing offices to pull proofs by hand and for short runs on small sheets of paper. It is the direct descendant of the earliest type of printing press.

Hand Roller. *See Brayer.*

Hand Set. Type which has been set by hand, as opposed to type set by machine.

Hand Sewing. The sewing by hand through the folds of sections of a book, using a sewing frame. *See also Sewn.*

Hand Stamp. A brass letter, or motif, set in a wooden handle, and used by a binder's finisher in lettering the cover of a hand-bound book.

Handbill. A poster, or placard, printed by hand.

Handbook. A treatise on a special subject; often nowadays a simple but all-embracing treatment, containing concise information, and being small enough to be held in the hand; but strictly, a book written primarily for practitioners and serving for constant revision or reference. Also called a 'Manual'.

Handwriting. Books were produced by writing by hand before the use of wood blocks early in the fifteenth century (*see Block Book*). After European countries had shaken off the political authority of the Roman empire, and the educated communities had been scattered and dissolved, the Latin 'cursive' or 'running' script changed and several 'national' hands, or style of the Latin cursive minuscule developed. The five principal national hands are South Italian or Beneventan, Merovingian (in France), Visigothic (in Spain), Germanic pre-Carolingian, and Insular (in Ireland and England). The earliest of the five periods into which Latin manuscript handwriting can be divided is the Roman period (second to eighth centuries) and this can be divided into five groups: *Quadrata*, or *Square capital*, hand; *Rustic capital* hand; *Uncial* hand. *Later cursive* hand; and *Half uncial* hand (*qq.v.*).

Hanging Figures. The numerals of certain type-designs which range within the limits of the EXTRUDERS (*q.v.*), e.g. the Caslon figures 3456789 as distinct from the 12 and 0 of the same face. Old-face types usually have hanging figures, although in some, e.g. Plantin, RANGING FIGURES (*q.v.*) are available as an alternative. *See Old Style Figures.*

Hanging Indention. 1. A paragraph of which the first line is set to the full width of the measure, the second and all subsequent lines of the paragraph being indented one or more ems from the left-hand margin as for this definition. *See also Em, Paragraph Indention.* Also called 'Hanging paragraph'. 2. In cataloguing, the form of indention in which the first line begins at the 'author indention' ('first indention') and succeeding lines at the 'title indention' ('second indention'). This method is used by the Library of Congress and many other libraries for 'formal anonyma', i.e. works like periodicals which do not involve the idea of concealed authorship. It is a method which tends to emphasize the first word of the title.

Hanging Paragraph. *Synonymous with* HANGING INDENTION (*q.v.*).

Hans Christian Andersen Award. *See Andersen Award, Hans Christian.*

'Hansard'. *See Parliamentary Papers.*

Hard Bound. Bound in cloth- or paper-covered boards. Also called 'Hard cover'.

Hard Copy. 1. A human-readable copy produced from information that has been transcribed to a form not easily readable by human beings. 2. A record on card or paper, to distinguish it from a record on microfilm or magnetic tape. It may be a contact copy of an enlargement.   3. A printed copy of machine output in readable form.

Hard Cover. *See Hard Bound.*

Hard Packing.   Thin card, or hard or stiff paper, used to cover the cylinder of a printing press in order to obtain a sharp impression, with little indentation of the paper, when printing on smooth hard paper.

Hardback.   A book published in stiff covers. The opposite of PAPERBACK (*q.v.*).

Hardware.   Apparatus used in information retrieval, data processing, the audio-visual field, or required for the consultation of all non-book materials which are not readable by the unaided eye. More specifically, the physical devices of which a computer consists. *See also Software.*

Harkness Fellowships.   Fellowships for twelve to twenty-one months' study and travel in the United States are offered annually to candidates from the United Kingdom. Applicants may propose an American programme which best suits their personal and professional needs, with unrestricted choice of university or other institution at which to work. 'The Harkness Fellowships of the Commonwealth Fund of New York' was incorporated in the State of New York, and the endowment derives entirely from the estates of the founder, Mrs. Stephen V. Harkness, and of Mr. & Mrs. Edward S. Harkness.

Harleian Style.   An English style of book decoration with a centre motif composed of small tools usually arranged in a lozenge-shaped design, and having an elaborate if sometimes rather narrow border decorated by means of one or more rolls. These 'Harleian' bindings were made by Thomas Elliott for Robert and Edward Harley, the First and Second Earls of Oxford.

Harris Award, John.   Offered by the New Zealand Library Association 'for the written record of notable library work, whether in the bibliographical, critical, historical or administrative fields, which will be a contribution to New Zealand librarianship'. It was first made to W. J. McEldowney, a former Honorary Secretary of the NZLA, in 1963.

Hart's Rules.   A classic rule book for compositors and proofreaders, compiled in 1903 by Horace Hart.

Harvard System.   A method of citing papers from scientific books and periodicals. The items making up a reference are as follows: (i) author's name and initials; (ii) year of publication, in parentheses, with *a*, *b*, etc. if more than one paper in the year is cited; (iii) full title of paper (roman type); (iv) name of periodical, contracted as in the *World List of Scientific Periodicals* (italic type); (v) volume number (in bold arabic figures); (vi) number of first page of paper; e.g.

Gregory, P. H. (1940). The control of narcissus leaf disease. *Ann. appl. Biol.* **27**, 338.

Jensen, H. L. & Betty, R. C. (1943). Nitrogen fixation in leguminous plants. *Proc. Linn. Soc.* N.S.W.**68**.I.

One of the chief advantages of this system is that footnotes can be dispensed with, a list of references being printed at the end of the article in alphabetical order of authors' names. In the text, references are given by printing the author's name and the date of publication in parentheses as (Gregory, 1940), (Jensen and Betty, 1943), but if the author's name is part of the text the date only is given in (). When three or more authors have collaborated in a paper, all the names are given in the first citation, but subsequently only the first name followed by '*et al.*' need be used.

Hash. The sign # commonly found on alphanumeric keyboards for computer or viewdata use.

HASL. *See Hertfordshire Association of Special Libraries.*

Hatching. A row of parallel, diagonal lines. Often found on the half bands or on the heads and tails of the spines of bindings from the sixteenth century onwards. Also used for the 'azured' shading on the centres of finishers' tools. *See also Cross Hatching, Hachures.*

Hawnt Report. The Report on *The public library service in Northern Ireland*, 1966, (Belfast HMSO, Cmd, 494), so named after Dr. J. S. Hawnt, the Chairman of the Advisory Committee appointed in September 1964 by the Minister of Education, Government of Northern Ireland, 'to consider the public library service . . . and make recommendations for its development, having regard to the relationship of public libraries to other libraries'.

Hawthornden Prize. An annual award by the Hawthornden Trust for a work of imaginative literature by a young British author.

Head. 1. The margin at the top of a page. 2. The top of a book or of a page. 3. The top of the spine of a book where the headband is placed. 4. The top edge of a book. *See also Foot.*

Head and Tail. The top and bottom edges of a book.

Head (Francis) Bequest. Administered by the SOCIETY OF AUTHORS (*q.v.*) to help British authors during illness or disablement.

Head Margin. The blank space above the top line of printed matter. 'Heads' relates to the top margins.

Head Ornament. An ornament specially designed for the top of a page: it may incorporate the lettering of the chapter heading, or provide an *island space* in which to print it. It is sometimes called a 'Headband' or 'Head piece'. *See also Tail Ornament.*

Head Piece. *Synonymous with* HEAD ORNAMENT (*q.v.*).

Head Title. The title, even in abbreviated form, given as a heading above a page or on the first page of a piece of music. *See also Headline.*

Headband. (*Binding*) The band, usually of coloured silk threads, at the head of a book, sewn or glued to the folds of sections, placed between the sections and the cover, and projecting slightly beyond the head. Originally it was a cord or leather thong similar to the ordinary bands, around which the ends of the threads were twisted, and laced-in to the boards. Nowadays headbands are usually made of coloured silks and are sewn on after the book has been forwarded thus having no purpose other than decoration. The two were formerly distinguished as 'headband' and 'tailband' but both are now called 'headbands' or 'heads'. *See also Tailband.* 2. (*Printing*) A printed or engraved decorative band at the head of a page or chapter. Also called 'Head piece, 'Head ornament'.

Headcap. The thickened end of the spine at head and tail of the leather spine of a book; this is caused by placing a piece of sized Italian hemp inside the turn-in at the head and tail of the spine after the leather has been fitted to the book. If headbands are used, they are left visible. *See also Headband, Tailcap.*

Heading. 1. (*Cataloguing*) The first sequence of characters (forming a number, name, word of phrase) at the beginning of a catalogue entry – usually written or printed on a separate line and sometimes in larger type than the remainder of the entry – to (a) determine the exact position of an entry in a catalogue, (b) keep group-related entries together in a catalogue. A third function of a heading is to display entries either singly or in groups. This function has become more important in the various forms of printed catalogues that have become common in recent years. The heading is generally the author, subject, or first word not an article, of the title, but may be the class number. *See also Entry Word, Form Heading, Form Sub-heading, Sub-heading, Uniform Heading.* 2. (*Information retrieval*) The word, name or phrase at the beginning of an entry to indicate some special aspect of the document (authorship, subject content, series, title, etc.). 3. (*Indexing*) The word(s) or symbol(s) selected from, or based on, an item in the text, used as an additional part of an entry; this includes any qualifying expression or epithet. Such words or symbols express the subject or idea to which reference is given and appear at the beginning of the entry. 4. The entry word followed by any other (or others) necessary for its meaning. 5. The word or words at the top of a page, chapter or section. 6. (*Book production, Printing*) Sub-headings which divide chapters and comprise CROSS-HEADS, INCUT NOTE, MARGINAL NOTES, SHOULDER-HEADS, SIDEHEADS (*qq.v.*).

Headline. The heading at the top of the page giving the title of the book (usually on the verso) or the subject of the chapter or of the page (usually on the recto). Also called 'Page head'. *See also Caption Title, Half-title, Page Headline, Running Title, Section Headline.* When giving the title of the book, even in abbreviated or different form, it may be called 'Head title'.

Heads. *See Head Margin.*

Health Care Libraries. A generic term covering medical, nursing, and hospital library services, together with specialized resources in ancillary fields.

HEBIS. Hessisches Bibliotheksinformations-system; West German bibliographic network, linking university and research libraries for co-operative cataloguing, and inter-loan functions. Founded 1987 and based at Frankfurt am Main. Eight members at present.

Heel-nick. *See Groove.*

Heidelberg. The name of a fully automatic printing press made by the Schnellpressenfabrik A.G., Heidelberg. The first press was a platen press made in 1914, in which the paper was fed by revolving wings. The Cylinder Heidelberg, first marketed in 1936, is a single-revolution machine in which the cylinder, moving at a constant speed, makes one revolution for each impression.

Height to Paper.   The exact height of type from the bottom (or feet) of the type to the printing surface. Types of the exact height will print evenly; those which are too high receive too much pressure while those too low receive little or no pressure. Also called TYPE HEIGHT (*q.v.*).

Heiligenbilder.   *See Helgen.*

Helgen.   Woodcuts printed on paper at the end of the fourteenth century and beginning of the fifteenth. They were usually very simple black-line pictures, often hand-coloured, with little or no shading, and consisted of pictures of the saints or other religious subjects. They were intended to illustrate the teachings of the wandering monks who distributed them to the illiterate peasantry. Also called 'Heiligenbilder'.

Heliograph.   A print made by Albrecht Breyer of Berlin who used the REFLEX COPYING (*q.v.*) process in 1839. He placed silver chloride papers in contact with the printed pages to be copied.

Heliography.   1. An obsolete name for photography.   2. In photo-engraving, the art of fixing the images produced by the *camera obscura*.

Heliogravure.   Any photo-engraving process by which intaglio engravings are made.

Hellbox.   (*Printing*) The box into which damaged or broken type made on a casting machine is thrown for melting down and re-casting.

Helpful Order.   The order of items in a classification schedule which displays the subjects in such a way that the order itself leads the user to the specific subject needed.

HELPIS.   Acronym of Higher Education Learning Programmes Information Service, a British project which was begun in 1970 by the National Council for Educational Technology at the request of the Department of Education and Science and the University Grants Committee to take responsibility for the exchange of information about teaching and learning materials produced in all sections of higher and further education. Publishes a *Catalogue*. HELPIS can be accessed via BLAISE-LINE.

Hemi-celluloses.   (*Paper*) Impure forms of cellulose consisting of organic substances, comprising, in the main, sugars, starches and carbohydrates. These are associated with cellulose (which is formed from the elements carbon, hydrogen and oxygen, and obtained from the atmosphere by the process known as photo-synthesis) in plant fibres. A high hemi-cellulose content in pulp is desirable as this provides a paper with good bonding and folding qualities.

Hemp.   A fibre derived from the tissue of an annual plant which is grown extensively in America, Asia and many parts of Europe. Hemp, hemp refuse, twines and old ropes are used to make brown wrapping paper and cable insulating paper.

Henne (Frances) Award.   An award to enable a young school library media specialist to attend an AMERICAN ASSOCIATION OF SCHOOL LIBRARIANS (*q.v.*) conference, or an ALA Conference.

Her Majesty's Stationery Office.   The government publisher in Britain, variously named 'Her Majesty's' or 'His Majesty's' according to whether the ruling monarch is a queen or king. HMSO prints all parliamentary publications and many others but arranges with commercial printers to print much that is published. The printing of stationery and the purchase of books is undertaken for government departments and libraries as well as the publishing for all government departments. It is also the agency in the United Kingdom for publications of Unesco, the United Nations, OECD, and some other international bodies and governments. *See also Non-Parliamentary Publications, Parliamentary Papers, Parliamentary Publications.*

Heraldic Cresting. Cresting on bindings, the projections of which terminate in heraldic (usually Tudor) emblems. *See also Cresting Roll.*

Hermes Project. A feasibility study undertaken by the National Physical Laboratory and PIRA to develop an electronic mail and document delivery service using teletex. First results were announced in 1982. Abandoned 1985, but *see Teletex.*

Hertfordshire Association of Special Libraries. A loose, informal co-operative of libraries in Hertfordshire (UK). Abbreviated HASL.

Hertfordshire County Council Technical Information Service. *See HERTIS.*

HERTIS. Abbreviation for Hertfordshire County Council Technical Information Service. A scheme, conceived in 1956, and based on the resources of Hatfield Polytechnic UK. Its 180 industrial and commercial members receive a range of services including in-depth literature reviews, online search services, and reference library facilities under contract.

Heures. *See Book of Hours.*

Heuristic Searching. The searching for information or a document by the user of a library, the search being modified as it progresses, each piece of information or document found tending to influence the user's continuing search.

Heuristic Techniques. In machine indexing, simulations of human methods of learning and problem solving. Functionally heuristic programmes are designed to discover solutions to problems by setting up goals and sub-goals, which are then put in order and tested to determine whether any of the solution sequences satisfy the requirements of the problem.

Hierarchic. 1. Arranged in serial rank rather than ordinal position. 2. Pertaining to a generic classification or organization of materials.

Hierarchical Classification. 1. A scheme of classification in which the schedules are developed systematically, every term, descriptor, or isolate (*See Isolate 3*) showing a logical relationship to each preceding and following term. 2. A scheme of classification in which the terms are arranged according to a hierarchical principle and are consequently arranged in subordination to other terms. The Dewey Classification is of this kind. The opposite of an ENUMERATIVE CLASSIFICATION (*q.v.*).

Hierarchical Force. (*Classification*) The property by which headings and certain notes apply to all subdivisions of the topic described and defined.

Hierarchical Notation.   (*Classification*) A NOTATION (*q.v.*) which is designed to show that two terms are in the same array, chain, hierarchy or facet. The chains and arrays of symbols reflect the hierarchy of terms. All main classes are represented by symbols of equal length, and new main classes are inserted by the introduction of new digits. Also called 'Expressive notation', 'Structural notation'.

Hierarchical Relation.   (*Information retrieval*) Relationship between two concepts or classes in a classification scheme in which one is subordinate to the other. *See also Relation.*

Hierarchical Search.   An examination of entries in a subject catalogue under heads which constitute a CHAIN (*q.v.*): it is conducted in an upward direction from the most, to the least, specific heading. Also called 'General search'. *See also Alphabetical Collateral Search, Substitution Generic, Systematic Collateral Search.*

Hierarchy.   The order of precedence in which subjects are set out in the schedule of a scheme of classification. Where each element in a sequence of terms has a unique predecessor, this is known as *strong hierarchy*; In a *weak hierarchy* an element may have more than one predecessor; a given descriptor (e.g. plastic transparency tray) may be immediately subordinate to more than one generic descriptor (plastic tray, transparency tray).

Hieroglyph.   A character, originally in the form of picture-writing engraved in stone by the ancient Egyptians, to convey thoughts or information. Any symbol or character used in any form of picture-writing. The meaning of the ancient Egyptian symbols was discovered in 1799 by Champollion when he deciphered the Rosetta Stone, now in the British Museum, on which was a parallel text in hieroglyphics, demotic script and Greek.

Hieroglyphics.   1. Ancient Egyptian picture-writing; hence symbols or characters used in any picture-writing.   2. The form of communicating information or ideas by hieroglyphs.

Hierogram.   A sacred character or written symbol.

Hierographic.   Pertaining to sacred writing.

Hieronym.   A sacred name used as a surname.

Higham (David) Prize for Fiction.   Administered by the BOOK TRUST, and awarded for a first novel or book of short stories by a UK or Commonwealth author.

Higher Education Learning Programmes Information Service.   *See HELPIS.*

Highlight.   The white, or light, parts of a photograph, drawing or half-tone block. Also called 'Drop-out half-tone'.

Hinge.   (*Binding*) A strip of paper or fabric, placed between the two halves of an endpaper, where the body of the book is fixed to the covers, to give strength. In America this term is used to indicate the part of the book identified by the groove along the front and back covers when they join the back strip or spine, allowing the book to be opened easily. *See also Joint.*

Hinged.   Plates, maps or other separate sheets to be inserted in a book, which have been given a narrow fold on the inner edges so that there is little chance of the sheets tearing away from those to which they are attached; also so that they will lie flat, and turn easily in use, when bound.

Hinged and Jointed Plates. Two adjoining plates from which a strip has been cut away at the binding edge and then joined together by means of a common strip of linen or paper to form a hinge and joints.

Historiated Initial. An initial, capital or border of a mediaeval MS. or early book decorated with figures of men and/or animals, rather than illuminated with flowers or conventional designs; a representation of a person or scene, illustrating the text it introduces. *See also Inhabited Initial.*

Historical Bibliography. Dealing with the history and methods of book production – printing, binding, paper making, illustrating and publishing. Also called 'analytical', 'applied', 'critical', 'descriptive', 'external', or 'material' bibliography.

Historical Manuscripts Commission. Founded in the UK in 1869 to discover and publish papers of historical importance. Until recently its principal activity was the publication of printed Reports and Calendars. Since 1945, and especially since the new warrant of 1959, its activities have proliferated: it maintains the NATIONAL REGISTER OF ARCHIVES (*q.v.*); new series of publications are appearing, including a list of *Record repositories in Great Britain*, joint publications in conjunction with record societies, publication of papers of nineteenth-century prime ministers, a guide to scientists' papers under a joint Royal Society/HMC committee, and a summary guide, list by list, to the contents of the National Register of Archives.

History Card. A card inserted in a catalogue and giving particulars, under the name of a corporate body, of dates of foundation, incorporation, changes of name, affiliation with other bodies, etc. Also called 'Information Card'.

History Entry. An entry in a catalogue which gives changes of name, affiliations, etc., concerning a person or corporate body, or in the wording of a title, together with significant dates. Such entries precede specific entries under the appropriate headings.

History File. *Synonymous with* ORGANIZATION FILE.

Hit. In searching a computer database, a hit is the successful location of a relevant item.

HMSO. HER MAJESTY'S STATIONERY OFFICE (*q.v.*).

Holding Area. (*Archives*) Space assigned for storing semi-current records temporarily.

Holdings. 1. The stock (books, pamphlets, periodicals, audio-visual items, micro-records, software and other material) possessed by a library. 2. Specifically, the volumes, or parts of serial publications, possessed by a library.

Holdings Card. A catalogue card which shows the volumes or parts of a work which the library has. It is usually the main entry card.

Holing. The drilling, or punching, of holes in the boards of a book to take the slips or cords ready for lacing. Also called 'Holing out'.

Holing Out. *Synonymous with* HOLING (*q.v.*).

Holkham Bible Picture Book. A MS. probably made in London for a Dominican patron between 1326 and 1331 and now in the British Library. It has no contemporary title and consists of forty-two leaves all but two of which are illustrated with 231 pictures.

Hollander. (*Paper*) A beater or beating engine of the type made in Holland towards the end of the seventeenth century.

Hollow. The space between the back of a book itself (i.e. the folded and sewn sheets) and the spine of a HOLLOW BACK (*q.v.*) book.

Hollow Back. A binding in which there is a space between the back of the book itself and the cover, caused by the leather, cloth or other material being attached at the joints, and not glued to the back of the book itself. Also called 'Loose back', 'Open back'. Sometimes a tube of thin card or paper is flattened and pasted between section folds and spine-covering. A publisher's case binding is of this type. *See also Case.* When the cover is glued to the back it is known as a TIGHT BACK (*q.v.*).

Hollow Quads. Large quads which are cast with hollow parts to make them lighter and save metal. Also used of type which is occasionally cast similarly for the same reason.

Hologram. Alternative term for HOLOGRAPH (2) (*q.v.*).

Holograph. 1. A document or manuscript wholly in the handwriting of its author. Hence, holograph reprint, a reproduction of a MS. by mechanical means. 2. A recording on photo-sensitive film, made without the use of lenses, by combining two or more laser beams of different colour to form a single beam. When the holograph is viewed in white light a three-dimensional, multicolour picture is revealed.

Holography. The process of making holographs. *See Holograph 2.*

Holotheme. All the notions (things or characteristics mentioned as subject matter) considered as subject-matter.

Holtby (Winifred) Memorial Prize. An annual award of the Royal Society of Literature for the best regional work of fiction or non-fiction by a UK or Commonwealth author.

Home Bindery. 1. A binding department maintained by a library. 2. A method of developing the book-buying habit in Asia. It is run by a single publisher who has a strong and varied list of publications, or by a wholesale bookseller, and incorporates features of book clubs in the West.

Home Reading Department. *Synonymous with* LENDING DEPARTMENT (*q.v.*).

HOMER. A microcomputer-based, interactive, multi-user system for text information retrieval based on ASSASSIN (*q.v.*).

Homograph. One of several words having the same spelling but a different meaning, e.g. Birmingham (Alabama), Birmingham (England); skate (fish), skate (sport); game (sport), game (fowl). These should be avoided in subject headings and indexes where possible, but when unavoidable, a qualifying, or defining word or phrase should be added to each in order to clarify the meanings and to separate entries on different subjects. *See also Homonym, Homophone.*

Homology. The principle used in forming schedules in a classification which uses the similarity of essential characteristics as a basis of division.

Homonym. 1. An identical name (surname and forenames) for two or more people. A namesake. Also an identical corporate, or other, name. 2. One of several words which may have a different origin and meaning but the same sound and possibly a different spelling, e.g. pail (bucket), pale (stake), pale (wan).

Homonymic, Homonymous. Having the same name.

Homophone. A word with a different spelling and meaning as another but with the same pronunciation, e.g. rough, ruff.

Homotopic Abstract. An abstract of an article published in the same issue of a journal as the article abstracted.

Honorific Epithet. (*Cataloguing. Indexing*) A title of honour or of rank which is appended to a heading (and so becomes part of it) for identification but which may or may not be used as a FILING EPITHET (*q.v.*).

Honorific Title. A title conferred on a person to indicate royalty, nobility, rank, or an honour. The whole name is sometimes incorporated with that of an organization or activity with which the person was associated. Examples: John XIV, *Pope*; Mountbatten *Earl, Field-Marshal*; Princess Mary Home; Bishop Creighton House; Sir Halley Stewart Trust; Lord Roberts Workshops. A 'title of honour'.

Hooked on own Guard. The method of securing a single-leaf illustration by folding its binding edge, so as to form a guard, around the fold of the section before sewing. *See also Guard 1 (2), Plate Guarded and Hooked.*

Horae. *See Book of Hours.*

Horizontal. A series or classification in which the terms, or classes, are arranged in a horizontal line. The several classes are then usually regarded as co-ordinate; but a series of successively subordinate classes and sub-classes might also be so arranged, instead of in a column. *See also Columnar, Tabular Classification.*

Horn Book. A children's primer which appeared towards the end of the sixteenth century. It consisted of a thin sheet of vellum or paper mounted on an oblong piece of wood and covered with transparent horn. The wooden frame had a handle by which it was hung from the child's girdle. The sheet bore the alphabet, the vowels in a line followed by the vowels combined with consonants in tabular form, the Roman numerals, the Lord's Prayer, and the exorcism 'in the name of the Father and of the Sonne and of the Holy Ghost, Amen!' A simpler and later form of Horn book, consisting of the tablet without the horn covering, or a piece of varnished cardboard, and resembling a horn book without the handle, was called a battledore.

Hors texte. Illustrations to a book which are without text matter. A plate. They are usually numbered with roman numerals to avoid confusion with numbered illustrations in the text (which are usually in line) and with the pagination of a book.

Hospital Libraries and Handicapped Readers Group. A group of the (British) Library Association which was formed in 1962 following the activities of the Guild of Hospital Librarians between 1934 and 1953 and sporadic meetings of hospital librarians subsequently. In 1978 reformed as the MEDICAL, HEALTH AND WELFARE LIBRARIES GROUP (*q.v.*).

Hospital Library. A library provided for the use of hospital patients and sometimes the staff, either by the hospital authority, a voluntary organization, or a public library.

Hospitality. (*Classification*) The quality of a notation which enables new subjects to be inserted in their appropriate place. A feature of the notation of the Colon Classification in which it is virtually infinite, and is achieved by combining the decimal fraction principle with the faceted principle. *Hospitality in array* i.e. the ability to accommodate co-ordinate topics, is achieved by (1) the octave device, (2) group notation, (3) the chronological device, (4) the subjects device, and (5) the alphabetical device. *Hospitality in chain*, i.e. the simultaneous specification of all the facets of a subject, if necessary, and the ability to specify new facets in their correct sequence, is secured by (1) decimal fractions, (2) faceted notation, (3) the apportionment of 'sectors', or zones, of notation to a different array within the same facet, (4) auto-bias, (5) intra-facet relation and (6) phase relations.

Host. A host makes available, on a commission or rental basis, access to any number of databases via its own computer, and using a common command language.

Host Book. As used in connection with the Colon Classification, a book about which another is written, as e.g. a criticism or a reply; the latter is called an ASSOCIATED BOOK (*q.v.*).

Host Document. A MACRO-DOCUMENT (*q.v.*) when considered from the point of view of a document forming part of it; e.g., a periodical would be considered a macro-document, and each article in it a micro-document; the periodical would then be the host document for each of the articles in it.

Hot Melt. In bookbinding, a glue which is applied hot and sets immediately when used on a cool surface.

Hot-Metal Typesetting. A method of typesetting which uses a process for casting type from molten metal (e.g. Intertype, Monotype, Linotype) as distinct from COLD COMPOSITION (*q.v.*).

Hot-Pressed. Good quality rag paper which is given a glazed, smooth finish by being pressed with hot metal plates. Abbreviated HP. *See also Finish, Not, Rough.*

House Corrections. Corrections, or alterations, made to a script or proof by the publisher or printer's proof reader, as distinct from those made by the author.

House Journal. A periodical produced by a commercial or industrial organization, either for internal distribution amongst the staff and employees or externally to customers.

House Magazine. *See House Journal.*

House of Commons Bills. Public Bills, printed by HMSO on pale green paper for consideration in the House of Commons. *See also Private Bills.*

House of Commons Papers. Reports and returns which have to be presented to the House under the provisions of various Acts of Parliament, reports from government departments compiled by direct order of the House, and reports of the Standing Committees and Select Committees of the House.

House of Lords Papers and Bills. A series of publications consisting almost entirely of Public Bills but also a few Papers. Public Bills are printed by HMSO on pale green paper.

House of Lords Record Office. Contains over 1,500,000 records of Parliament as a whole dating back to 1497. They are in the custody of the Clerk of the Parliaments. The Search Room is open to the public who may also be granted access to the Journals of the House of Commons (from 1547), and to the other surviving records of the Commons (from 1572). Records of Parliament prior to 1497 are preserved in the PUBLIC RECORD OFFICE (*q.v.*).

House Organ. *See House Journal.*

'House' Papers. *See Parliamentary Papers.*

House Style. The typesetting style normally used in a printing establishment or publishing house. *See also Style Manual, Style of the House, Style Sheet.*

Housekeeping. Routine and continuing library operations, such as book ordering, accessioning, cataloguing, processing, and the circulation, etc. of documents and other library materials. In computer operations, it is generally contrasted with information retrieval.

h.t. Abbreviation for HALF-TITLE (*q.v.*).

HULTIS. The Humberside Libraries Technical Information Service is centered on the Library of Science, Technology and Commerce in Hull Central Library UK. Industrial, academic and other specialized libraries in the area agree to co-operate; a *Members' Handbook and Directory* provides more detailed information on individual members with an index of their specialized interests.

Humanist. 1. A group of type faces, formerly known as 'Venetian' and derived from the fifteenth-century style of minuscule handwriting characterized by a varying stroke thickness achieved by means of an obliquely-held broad pen. In faces in this group the cross stroke of the lower case 'e' is oblique, the axis of the curves is inclined to the left, there is little contrast between thin and thick strokes, the serifs are bracketed, and the serifs of the ascenders of the lower case letters are oblique. Examples of this category of type faces are Verona, Centaur and Kennerley. *See also Type Face.* 2. Also a group of LINEALE (*q.v.*) type faces based on the proportions of roman capitals and Humanist or GARALDE (*q.v.*) lower-case letters, rather than on the early grotesques which are another group of Lineales. They have some contrast between the thick and thin strokes, and the 'a' and 'g' are two-storey.

Humanistic Hand. A mediaeval handwriting less angular than Gothic, based on Old Roman capitals and the Carolingian minuscule. It was a result of the Renaissance in the fifteenth century which brought a general awakening of interest in classic, and pre-Christian literature. Also called 'Neo-Caroline'.

Humberside Libraries Technical Information Service Scheme. *See HULTIS.*

HUMBUL. Humanities Online Bulletin Board for computing in the humanities; an electronic current awareness service for those wishing to apply computing to research and teaching in the Arts and Humanities fields. HUMBUL I ran 1985/86 at the Primary Communications Research Centre and the Office for Humanities Communication at the University of Leicester, UK, funded by the British Library Research and Development Department. HUMBUL II, open to any interested user via JANET (*q.v.*) was launched in 1986.

Humphry (John Ames)/Forest Press Award for a Significant Contribution to International Librarianship. An annual award made by the International Relations Committee of the ALA.

Hundred Rolls, of A.D. 1274. Public records of great importance for local history, containing an inquisition into the state of every hundred (a division of a county) and answers, on oath, to questions relating to the public exchequer.

Hunt Report (UK). Report of the inquiry into cable expansion and broadcasting policy; Chairman: Lord Hunt of Tanworth. (Cmnd. 8679) HMSO 1982. *See also Cable Systems.*

Huntington Library. One of the most famous of scholars' libraries of Americana and English literature. It is situated in San Marino, California, USA, and is surpassed only by the British Library and the Bodleian in the quality and importance of its British books. The library is in a building which was opened in 1920 and was especially designed to protect and preserve the valuable collection of books in the grounds of Huntington House (formerly the home of Henry Edwards Huntington, 1850–1927). The collections contain 2.2 million manuscripts, 336,000 rare books and 253,000 reference books, concentrated in the fields of British and American history, literature and art, and stretching in time from the eleventh century to the present. *The R. Stanton Avery Conservation Center*, completed in 1981, has up-to-date equipment for the repair and preservation of rare books, manuscripts and photographs in the Huntington collections. *The Library Exhibition Hall* has on exhibition 200 of its most oustanding rare books and manuscripts. Among the finest treasures of the Huntington are: the beautifully illuminated Ellesmere manuscript of Chaucer's *Canterbury Tales* (c. 1410); a Bible printed by Gutenberg (c. 1450–55); an unexcelled collection of the early editions of Shakespeare; and letters and manuscripts of famous Americans. Original materials from the Revolutionary period represent the most extensive collection west of the Atlantic seaboard. First editions and manuscripts by authors such as Pope, Blake, Wordsworth, Shelley, Mark Twain, Thoreau, Stevens and London are on display. In addition, several changing exhibitions from the collections are mounted each year. There are also magnificent art collections and botanical gardens.

Hydrographic Chart. A chart of coasts and harbours.

Hypertext. A methodology for organizing information in an electronic database, according to a structural framework into which data is inserted, in preference to the conventional system whereby the structure of the data forms the structure of the database. By means of hypertext, links would automatically be made between data sources rather than needing to access each source separately. At present, hypertext is mainly used for small, personal or local databases; the costs and complexity of its application to large databases are very great. *Hypercard* is an alternative format; *Hypermedia* a generic term for the concept.

Hyphen.   The shortest rule used for punctuation. It is used to join compound words, or as the link at the end of a line to join the parts of a word which cannot be set in one line. *See also Dash.*

Hyphen Stringing.   (*Indexing*) The process of using hyphens to bind terms in order to convey more information, as well as for filing purposes.

Hypo.   Abbreviation for hyposulphite of soda (formerly known as sodium thiosulphate) which is used in photography for fixing prints.

Hypsometric Map.   One on which the successive altitudes are indicated by the system of colour tints.

I & R.   Information and referral service.

IAALD.   International Association of Agricultural Librarians and Documentalists (*q.v.*).

IAC.   An INFORMATION ANALYSIS CENTRE (*q.v.*).

IACBDT.   Abbreviation for the Unesco International Advisory Committee on Bibliography, Documentation and Technology.

IACDT.   Abbreviation for the Unesco International Advisory Committee for Documentation and Technology.

IACODLA.   Acronym of the International Advisory Committee on Documentation Libraries and Archives which was established in 1967 to advise the Director-General of Unesco at his request, on questions of documentation in general, and in particular on those related to subject fields of interest to Unesco.

IALL.   International Association of Law Libraries (*q.v.*).

IAML.   International Association of Music Libraries (*q.v.*).

IANI.   Intelligent Access to Nordic Information Systems; a PC program developed by NORDINFO, the Nordic Council for Scientific Information and Research Libraries (*q.v.*) and giving easy access to three Nordic hosts – FEK (Computer Department of the Office of the National Librarian, Denmark), LIBRIS (Royal Library, Sweden) and VTKK (State Computer Centre, Finland). Other services are being added.

IAOL.   Acronym of the International Association of Orientalist Librarians. Founded in 1967 to promote better communication between Orientalist librarians and libraries throughout the world; provide a forum for the discussion of problems of common concern; improve international co-operation among institutions holding research resources for oriental studies. Members: librarians in oriental studies and others who have an interest in the activities of the Association. Publishes *IAOL Newsletter* (2 p.a.), directory, and conference proceedings.

IASA.   INTERNATIONAL ASSOCIATION OF SOUND ARCHIVES (*q.v.*).

IASL.   INTERNATIONAL ASSOCIATION OF SCHOOL LIBRARIANSHIP (*q.v.*).

IASLIC. Acronym for Indian Association of Special Libraries and Information Centres. Founded in September 1955 with the following aims: to encourage and promote the systematic acquisition, organization and dissemination of knowledge; to improve the quality of library and information services and documentation work; to co-ordinate the activities of, and to foster mutual co-operation and assistance among, special libraries, scientific, technological and research institutions, learned societies, commercial organizations, industrial research establishments, as well as other information and documentation centres to the fullest extent; to provide contact for libraries, information bureaux, documentation centres, scientists, research workers, specialists and others having a common interest; to improve the technical efficiency of the workers in special libraries and information and documentation centres, and to look after their professional welfare; to act as a centre of research in special librarianship and documentation techniques; to act as a centre of information in scientific, technical and other fields. Publishes working papers irregularly, technical pamphlets and monographs; also *IASLIC Bulletin* (q.).

IATUL. INTERNATIONAL ASSOCIATION OF TECHNOLOGICAL UNIVERSITY LIBRARIES (*q.v.*).

ib., ibid. Abbreviation for *ibidem* (*Lat.* 'in the same place', 'the same reference'). Used in a footnote reference to avoid repeating the title of a work referred to immediately above. It can be used in successive references to the same work.

IBBD. Acronym for the Instituto Brasiliero de Bibliografia e Documentação (Brazilian Institute of Bibliography and Documentation); situated in Rio de Janeiro, it is the country's national bibliographical information centre.

IBBY. Abbreviation for INTERNATIONAL BOARD ON BOOKS FOR YOUNG PEOPLE. Founded by Jella Lepman in 1953 in Zurich to promote international understanding through children's books. It is composed of national Sections from many countries which work within their own countries to promote children's books. Awards the Hans Christian Andersen Medal for important contributions to children's literature. International Children's Book Day (ICBD), originated by Jella Lepman, is a well-known activity of the Board observed each year throughout the world on 2 April which is Hans Christian Andersen's birth date. The Board's secretariat is at Basle, Switzerland. The IBBY Documentation Centre of Books for Disabled Young People was established in 1985 at the Norwegian Institute of Special Education. IBBY has links with Unesco and Unicef, and is a member of IFLA and the International Book Committee. Publishes *Bookbird* (q.) in co-operation with the INTERNATIONAL INSTITUTE FOR CHILDREN'S LITERATURE AND READING RESEARCH (*q.v.*).

IBE. INTERNATIONAL BUREAU OF EDUCATION (*q.v.*).

IBI–ICC. Abbreviation for the Intergovernmental Bureau for Informatics – International Computation Centre. Established as an intergovernmental institution by international treaty which became effective as from 11

November 1961. Aims: to promote research, education and utilization of informatics at government level. With this objective, the Bureau operates in a number of ways to further the use of informatics in economic and industrial planning and development. It operates from Rome. Publishes *IBI–ICC Newsletter* (6 p.a.), *International Directory of Computer and Information systems* (a).

IBIS Information Services Ltd. A subject-coded file of information on libraries and academic staff of universities and polytechnics, maintained by several leading UK publishers of academic books. The file covers most countries of the world, and has a reciprocal arrangement with a US equivalent.

IBY. Acronym of the International Book Year which was organized by Unesco and held on a worldwide basis in 1972 to promote books and encourage reading. *See also International Book Award, International Book Committee.*

ICA. INTERNATIONAL COUNCIL ON ARCHIVES (*q.v.*).

ICAE. Acronym of the International Council for Addult Education, a non-governmental oganization whose chief function is to facilitate development and exchange of experience in adult education, including many associated fields such as functional literacy, publishing and libraries, anpower training, labour education and 'learning at a distance'. The Council does not duplicate the work of existing institutions but works with and through them in order to build upon and support their activities. The Secretariat is in Toronto. Publishes *Convergence* (q.) *Newsletter* (irreg.).

ICBA. INTERNATIONAL COMMUNITY OF BOOKSELLERS' ASSOCIATIONS (*q.v.*).

ICBD. International Children's Book Day. *See entry under IBBY.*

ICC. INTERNATIONAL CHILDREN'S CENTRE (*q.v.*).

ICC–IBI. International Computer Centre – Intergovernmental Bureau for Informatics. *See entry under IBI-ICC.*

ICCP. INTERNATIONAL CONFERENCE ON CATALOGUING PRINCIPLES (*q.v.*).

ICCSTI. *See Interdepartmental Co-ordinating Committee for Science and Technical Information.*

ICIC. Acronym of the International Copyright Information Centre, at Unesco Headquarters, Paris; approved at the 16th Session of Unesco in 1970. Functions: to: (a) collect copyright information on books that can be made available to developing countries on terms as favourable to them as possible; (b) arrange for the transfer to developing countries of rights ceded by copyright holders; (c) help in the development of simple model forms of contracts for translation, reprint and other rights required by developing countries; (d) study ways and means of securing copyright and other rights as well as methods of financing the rights required where foreign currency is not available; (e) promote arrangements for the adaptation and publication of works, particularly those of a technical and educational nature; (f) encourage the formation of national copyright information centres in both developed and developing countries, and act as a link between them; (g) provide assistance to developing countries for the organization of training courses for translators and covering all aspects of the publishing industry, for the provision of fellowships and equipment, for the joint publication of technical works, and for bringing together pedagogical authorities to develop adaptations of works. Publishes *Information Bulletin* (irreg.) which gives information on the centres and serves as a link for the exchange of information and ideas on copyright activities.

ICIREPAT. Abbreviation for the Paris Union Committee for International Co-operation in Information Retrieval among Patent Offices, which is part of the World Intellectual Property Organization (WIPO). Aim: to promote international co-operation in the field of storage and retrieval of technical information needed in connection with the search or examination of applications for patents, inventors' certificates or other similar documents. It was established in Munich in 1962 and became in 1968 a Committee of Experts of the Paris Union; it was visualized as an organization to help patent offices throughout the world solve their search problems co-operatively and to avoid duplication of effort. The Secretariat operates at WIPO in Geneva. *See also INPADOC.*

ICLG. Acronym of the International and Comparative Librarianship Group. A Group of the (British) Library Association, formed in 1968 with the object of uniting librarians concerned with international and comparative librarianship and fostering relations with librarians abroad. The Group arranges meetings which are addressed by foreign librarians and at which problems of international librarianship may be discussed. Publishes *Focus on International and Comparative Librarianship* (3 p.a.).

Icon. Symbol used on computer display screens to show the user the available options and thus avoid the use of command statements.

ICLS. Irish Central Library for Students (*q.v.*).

Iconography. 1. The study of the portraits, statues, coins, and other illustrative material relating to a person, place or thing. 2. The detailed listing of such material. 3. The art of illustrating, or representing, by figures, images, diagrams, etc.

ICSSD. International Committee for Social Sciences Documentation (*q.v.*).

ICSTI. *See International Council for Scientific and Technical Informtion.*

ICSU. International Council of Scientific Unions (*q.v.*).

id. Abbreviation for *idem* (*Lat.* 'the same [author or publication]'). Used in footnotes to avoid repeating an author's name, or other identity of a book or periodical when being referred to successively.

id est. (Lat. 'that is to say'). Abbreviated i.e.

Id. Abbreviation for Identifier; a group of characters input to the computer to identify a user or a terminal.

Ida and George Eliot Prize Essay. *See Eliot Prize Essay, Ida and George.*

Ideal Arrangement. (*Classification*) The mental operation resulting in placing things in order corresponding to an idea, or series of ideas, in the mind and in accordance with the mental picture of the things to be arranged. *Actual arrangement* is the physical placing in order, of specimens which can be seen or touched, such as botanical specimens, postage stamps or books.

Identification. (*Bibliography*) The discovery of the date of an undated book, or the determination of the precise edition, impression, issue or state of a given copy or series of copies of a book. (*Information retrieval*) A classification number, code number or code name which identifies a record, file, document or other unit of information.

Identification Caption. (*Reprography*) The identification symbol or phrase, both on the document and on the frame of microfilm or fiche, which is visible to the unaided eye.

Identification Card. Used in place of a borrower's ticket in the Newark Charging System (*q.v.*) and Transaction Card (*q.v.*) systems generally.

Identifiers. (*Information retrieval*) Terms, such as acronyms, projects, proper names of persons, geographical locations, the number of a patents specification or of a national 'standard', or any part of a bibliographical description, test names, and trade names which provide subject indexing, in addition to descriptors. Also called 'Identifying factors'. *See also Id.*

Identify. (*Information retrieval*) To allocate and attach a unique code, or code name, to a unit of information.

Identifying Factors. *See also Identifiers.*

Ideogram. *Synonymous with* Ideograph 2 (*q.v.*).

Ideograph. 1. An individual signature or trade mark. 2. A symbol or picture used in writing, e.g. in Chinese, to represent an object or an idea, and not, as in the phonetic system, the sounds which make up the name of these.

Ideography. The representation of ideas by graphic symbols ('ideograms'). A highly developed form of picture-writing in which ideas are conveyed by pictorial representation.

i.e. Abbreviation for *id est* (*Lat.* 'that is').

IEAB. Acronym for the Internacia Esperanto-Asocio de Bibliotekistoj (International Association for Esperanto-speaking Librarians) which was formed in 1972. Amongst its aims are: (a) the promotion of Esperanto for use in library affairs; (b) the building of Esperanto collections, both instructional and literary, in all major world libraries; (c) the promotion of Esperanto-language sections in the various national library associations; (d) the encouragement of bibliographical and literary projects, and the compilation of Esperanto bibliographies and translations of important technical literature (in the library field) into Esperanto.

IFD. International Federation for Documentation (*q.v.*).

IFIP. International Federation for Information Processing (*q.v.*).

IFLA. Acronym for International Federation of Library Associations and Institutions (*q.v.*).

IFRT. *See Intellectual Freedom Round Table.*

IFRT State Program Award. An annual award presented to the state intellectual freedom committee that has produced the most successful and creative project; awarded by the Intellectual Freedom Round Table (*q.v.*).

IGC. Abbreviation for Intergovernmental Copyright Committee which was established in Geneva on 6 September 1952; it is administered by Unesco. Aims: to study the problems concerning the operation of the Universal

Copyright Convention of 1952; make preparations for periodic revisions thereof; study any other problems concerning the international protection of copyright (or which may affect copyright) in co-operation with the various interested international organizations. It works jointly with the Berne Convention which is basically concerned with copyright. *See also Copyright, International.*

IIA. *See Information Industry Association.*

IIB. Institut International des Brevets. *See entry under International Patent Institute.*

IIS. *See Institute of Information Scientists.*

IKBS. Intelligent knowledge-based systems. *See Expert Systems.*

ILA. INDIAN LIBRARY ASSOCIATION. ISRAEL LIBRARY ASSOCIATION (*qq.v.*).

ILAM. *See Institute of Leisure and Amenity Management.*

ILL. Abbreviation for INTER-LIBRARY LOAN (*q.v.*)

ill. (illus.). Abbreviation for illustrated, ILLUSTRATIONS (*q.v.*). *ill* is the recommended form of the abbreviation for use in the collation area of a cataloguing entry.

Illative Abstract. *See Abstract.*

Illuminated Binding. A term used for all bindings which included extra colours, but particularly to those where a design was blocked in blind and the outline afterwards filled in with colour. Originally a French innovation, this style was practised in Britain from about 1830 to 1860.

Illuminated Book. A book or manuscript, usually on vellum, decorated by hand, with designs and pictures in gold, silver and bright colours, not primarily to illustrate the text, but to make with it a unified whole.

Illuminated Initial. A first letter of a word or paragraph decorated with colours, especially gold.

Illumination. The painting of initial letters at the commencement of a chapter of a MS. in gold, silver, or colour.

illus. Abbreviation for illustrated, illustration, illustrator.

Illustrations. Photographs, drawings, portraits, maps, plans, plates, tables, facsimiles, diagrams, etc., placed in a book to elucidate the text.

Illustrations Collection. A collection of photographs, prints, drawings or reproductions of pictures assembled either for general use in public libraries or in institutions as an aid to their work. *See also Picture File, Picture Collection.*

Illustrator. A person who makes drawings and designs to illustrate a book or periodical.

Illustrator Entry. A catalogue entry for an illustrator whose work is of sufficient importance to be catalogued.

ILY. *See International Literacy Year.*

I'M. *Information Market*: a newsletter published by the DIRECTORATE-GENERAL XIII (*q.v.*) of the European Community.

IMAC. *See International Marc Network Advisory Committee.*

Image. 1. A design or picture to be reproduced by a printing process as an illustration. 2. (*Reprography*) That area within the frame (*see also*

Frame 4) which, after exposure and processing, contains the whole of the representation of the original.

Imbrication. A style of book decoration in which the pattern consists of overlapping leaves or scales.

IMC. International Micrographics Congress. Irish Manuscripts Commission (*qq.v.*).

IMCE. Acronym of the International Meeting of Cataloguing Experts which met in Copenhagen in 1969 (prior to the IFLA Conference) to examine closely *inter alia* an annotated edition, in a provisional form, of the *Statement of principles* with a view to the preparation of a definitive edition. Another workkin party was formed to prepare the International Standard Bibliographic Description to serve the needs of catalogues and national bibliographies, and which would include all the bibliographical data required for catalogues, bibliographies and other records, e.g. book orders. *See also International Conference on Cataloguing Principles, ISBD, Paris Principles.*

Imitation Art. *See Art.*

Imitation Binding. A modern binding made to represent an old style.

Imitation Embossing. *Synonymous with* THERMOGRAPHY (*q.v.*).

Imitation Leather. Paper or cloth embossed or finished to represent leather.

Imitation Parchment. A variety of tough paper first made by W.E. Gaine in 1857. It may be (a) rendered transparent, strong, grease-proof, and sometimes water-proof, by prolonged beating of the pulp, or (b) passed through a bath of sulphuric acid which 'toughens' the fibres.

Immroth (John Phillip) Memorial Award. An annual award to honour intellectual freedom fighters, made by the INTELLECTUAL FREEDOM ROUND TABLE (*q.v.*) of the ALA.

IMMY Awards. A series of awards presented annually by the INFORMATION INDUSTRY ASSOCIATION (*q.v.*). The awards recognize exceptional efforts in marketing, promotion and sales, and are judged on the basis of originality, creativity, impact, clarity, and excellence of design. The awards are presented at the IIA Annual Convention and Exhibition.

IMO. (European) Information Market Observatory. *See IMPACT.*

IMP. *See International MARC Programme.*

IMPA. *See Information Management Professionals Association.*

IMPACT. The Information Services Market Programme of the European Community which runs 1988–1990 has been titled IMPACT – Information Market Policy Actions. Funding will be allocated to pilot demonstration projects to show the potential of advanced information systems. The European Information Market Observatory is a part of this programme, and will monitor demand through a user panel. Eleven transnational projects are now in hand. IMPACT 2 (1991–95) is to concentrate on a further series of strategic projects.

impensis. (*Lat.* 'at the expense of'). Used in an IMPRINT (*q.v.*) or COLOPHON (*q.v.*) of an early printed book to indicate the publisher, or bookseller or patron who was financially responsible for its publication.

Imperfect. A book which is found to have pages or sections omitted, duplicated, misplaced or inserted upside down, damaged or missing.

Imperfections. Printed sheets rejected by the binder as being in some respect imperfect, and for which others are required to make the work complete.

Imperial. A sheet of printing and drawing paper measuring 22 × 30 inches.

Imperial War Museum Library. One of the national libraries maintained by the British government. It is concerned only with collecting material relating to World Wars 1 and 2 and other military operations involving Great Britain and the Commonwealth.

Import. A book published in one country and imported into another. The importer may act as one of several importers or may have sole distribution rights over a given area. He may or may not arrange to have his own name placed on the title page as distributor or publisher either in addition to or in place of the original publisher's name, and he may do this by means of a small label.

Imposing Stone. *See Stone.*

Imposition. The arrangement of the pages of type in the chase so that they will read consecutively when the printed sheet is folded. On correct imposition depends not only the right order of the pages but also REGISTER (*q.v.*).

Impressed Watermark. A watermark produced, not by the usual method, but by placing a stereo, in bronze, rubber, or other substance, on the press roll of the paper-making machine, and so leaving a design in the paper where it was more compressed. *See also Watermark.*

Impression. 1. (*Printing*) The copies of a book printed at the same time from the same type or plates. A *new impression* is one taken from the same standing type, or stereotype, as the original. An edition may consist of several impressions providing no alterations are made. Also called a 'Printing'. 2. All those copies of an edition printed at one time. *See also Edition, First Edition, Issue, Reprint, Revised Edition.* 3. The pressure applied to a forme of type by the cylinder or platen. 4. (*Binding*) The effect of impressing a block or type into the cover of a book. 5. A single copy of a print or map. 6. (*Illustration*) A print taken, by means of the special engraving press, from an engraved plate. *See also State.*

Impression Cylinder. The roller of an offset printing press which presses the paper into contact with the blanket cylinder; or any cylinder around which the paper is carried during its contact with type or plates.

imprimatur (*Lat.* 'let it be printed'). The licence for publication, granted by a secular or ecclesiastical authority, carrying the name of the licenser, and the date (which may differ from that of the imprint). Usually printed at the beginning of a book: when on a separate leaf this is called a 'licence leaf'. Now rarely found except in the form of the words 'permissu superiorum' on works by Roman Catholic priests. This is distinct from copyright. Where state or church censorship exists, the imprimatur becomes an approval of what has been published.

Imprint. 1. The statement in a book concerning the publication or printing of a book. Also called 'Biblio'. The PUBLISHER'S IMPRINT is the name of the publisher and the date and place of publication, it usually appears at the foot of the title-page, and sometimes more completely on the back. The PRINTER'S IMPRINT gives the printer's name and the place of printing, it usually appears on the back of the title-page, on the last page of text, or on the page following. *See also Colophon, Distribution Imprint.* 2. (*Cataloguing and bibliography*) That part of an entry which gives the above particulars, though it is customary to omit the *place* of publication if it is the capital city of the country. When the imprint is covered by a label (usually giving the name of a publisher or agent in a country other than that of origin) the date for the catalogue entry is taken from the label. 3. (*Binding*) The name of (a) the owner; (b) the publisher appearing at the bottom of the spine; (c) the binder stamped on the cover of a book, usually at the bottom of the inside of the back board. 4. (*Printing*) The name of an OLD FACE type which is much used for book work. For a specimen alphabet *see Type Face.*

Imprint Date. The year of publication as specified on the title-page. *See also Date of Publication.*

IMS. INTERNATIONAL MUSICOLOGICAL SOCIETY (*q.v.*).

In Boards. 1. When a book is cut after the mill-boards are attached, it is said to be cut in boards. *See also Boards.* 2. A cheap style of binding common in the eighteenth and early nineteenth centuries, consisting of pasteboards covered with paper (usually blue sides and white spine). It was superseded by cloth. Occasionally used in the early twentieth century.

In Galley. Type which has been set and is in a galley awaiting correction and making up into pages.

In Pendentive. (*Printing*) Typesetting in which successive lines are set in decreasing width, the first (and possibly second) line being set to the full measure, the subsequent ones being indented left and right of a central axis so that the last line of a page or paragraph is only a single word. It has the effect of a triangle resting on its apex.

In Print. Said of a book which is available from the publisher.

In Progress. A term used in catalogues and elsewhere to indicate that a work in several volumes is not complete but still in course of publication. *See also Check-list.*

In Quires. A book in unbound sheets. *See also In Sheets.*

In Sheets. Printed sheets of a book, either flat or folded, but unbound. This term is gradually replacing 'in quires' with which it is synonymous. *See also Sheets.*

In Slip. Matter set up and proof-pulled on galleys before being made up into pages.

In Stock. Said of a book, copies of which are held by a bookseller for sale.

In the Press. A book which is in the actual process of being printed.

In the Trade. Books published by, and obtainable from, commercial publishing firms rather than from government or private presses.

Incentive Funding. An initiative promoted in the UK by LISC and the Library Association to encourage the formation of new partnerships between the public and private sectors in funding joint ventures in information provision, sub-contracting some elements of library services etc. The LIPS (*q.v.*) will tend to indicate scope for such collaboration. Little evaluation has yet been carried out, but the initiative does not seem to be very successful. *See also Public Library Development Incentive Scheme.*

Incidental Music.   Music written for performance during the presentation of a theatrical play or film whether it has an essential connection with the plot, or story, or not.

incipit   (*Lat.* 'here begins'). The commencement of a mediaeval MS. or early printed book. The identity of the work and of the author may be found here if it is not given on the title-page or in the colophon.

Inclusion Note.   (*Classification*) An enumeration of subordinate topics under a heading (and which are not obviously part of it) that have not yet been given separate provision. Such notes do not have HIERARCHICAL FORCE (*q.v.*).

Incomplete.   Said of a book from which a part has been omitted during manufacture.

Incunabula.   (*Sing.*, INCUNABULUM; Anglicized, INCUNABLE). Books printed before 1500, this date limitation probably deriving from the earliest known catalogue of incunabula: an appendix to Johann Saubert's *Historia bibliothecae Noribergensis . . . catalogus librorum proximis ab inventione annis usque ad a. Chr. 1500 editorum,* 1643. 'Incunabula' derives from the Latin 'cunae' (cradle) and indicates books produced in the infancy of printing; more specifically those which were printed before the use of loose type was common.

Incunabulist.   One who is well versed in a knowledge of incunabula.

Incut Heading.   *See Cut-In Heading.*

Incut Note.   A side note which is let into the outer edge of a paragraph of text instead of appearing in the margin. Usually set in smaller and heavier type than the text. Also called 'Cut-in note', 'Cut-in side note', 'Let-in note'. *See also Centre Note.*

Indent.   To begin a line of type a little way in, as at the beginning of a fresh paragraph.

Indented Style.   In book indexes, the typographical setting which allows sub-headings to be indented, usually one em, the main heading being set flush to the lefthand margin. Sub-subheadings are further indented. *See also Run-on Style.*

Indention.   1. (*Printing*) The leaving of a blank space at the beginning of a line or a new paragraph. *See also Em, Hanging Indention.*   2. (*Cataloguing*) The distances from the left edge of a catalogue card at which the various parts of the entry begin. *See also First Indention, Second Indention, Third Indention.*

Indenture.   A document drawn up in duplicate and divided so as to leave a tooth-like edge on each part.

Independent Research Libraries Association.   *See IRLA.*

Independents.   Books or pamphlets published separately and afterwards bound together.

Index.   1. A detailed alphabetical list or table of topics, names of persons, places, etc., treated or mentioned in a book or series of books, pointing out their exact positions in the volume, usually by page number (sometimes with an additional symbol indicating a portion of a page) but often by section, or entry, number.   2. A much broader connotation is now given to this term due to contemporary practices of compiling finding-guides to the contents of, and shelved position of, material in a library collection, sometimes using mechanical methods for this purpose. From many points of view an index is synonymous with a catalogue, the principles of analysis used being identical, but whereas an index entry merely locates a subject, a catalogue entry includes descriptive specification of a document concerned with the subject. 3. (*Information retrieval*) That which specifies, indicates or designates the information, contents or topics of a document or a group of documents. Also a list of the names or subjects referring to a document or group of documents.   4. (*Verb*) To prepare an organized or systematic list which specifies, indicates or designates the information, contents or topics in a document or group of documents. *See also Auto-Abstract, Controlled Indexing, Index Librorum Prohibitorium, Kwic Index, Permutation Indexing, Society of Indexers, Uniterm Concept Co-ordination Indexing, American Society of Indexers, Word Indexing.*   5. The printers symbol ☛. Also called 'Digit', 'Fist', 'Hand'.

Index Board.   A quality of single-or twin-wire pulp board, white or coloured, used for cutting into standard sizes for index cards and record work generally. They may be described as pulp board with a good, even and well-finished surface suitable for writing. They are smooth, hard-sized and of even Look Through (*q.v.*). Sizes: Index Royal 20½ × 25½ inches, Index Royal and a half 25½ × 30½ inches.

Index Entry.   The entry which is included in an index.

Index Expurgatorius.   An index to passages to be expunged or altered in works which are otherwise permitted. This term is loosely used for the list of books that the Roman Catholic Church forbade its members to read, or permitted them to read only in expurgated form – the Index Librorum Prohibitorum (*q.v.*).

Index Language.   The language that is used in the subject index which is part of an information retrieval system. It may be an alphabetical or classified arrangement of terms, or a variation of these. Each term or heading actually used in the index language, of whatever kind, is called an 'index term'. Also called 'Descriptor language'. Its 'vocabulary' is the complete collection of sought terms in the natural language.

Index Librorum Prohibitorum.   A list of books which Roman Catholics were prohibited by ecclesiastical authority from reading or keeping without permission. Such books could not be imported into countries where Roman Catholic control was considerable. The list was commonly called the 'Index' or 'Roman Index', and was also known as 'Index Expurgatorius'. The *Index* was printed first by Antonio Blado in Rome in 1559 and is the classic example of censorship. From late Roman times there had been censorship of books considered to be dangerous to religion and morals, and although bishops, universities and inquisitions had circulated lists of prohibited books this was the first really effective means of censorship. The 'Congregation' which was first set up in 1558 to prepare the *Index* continued to be responsible for its publication. The Index was last brought up to date in 1947; Cardinal Ottaviani, pro-perfect of the Doctrinal Congregation declared in April 1965 that no more books would be put on the Index. On 14 June 1966 the Vatican announced that it had been abolished; although it ceased to be legally binding, Roman Catholics were reminded of their duty to avoid reading books dangerous to faith and morals.

Index-map. A small-scale key map to an atlas or series of maps, which shows how the total area has been divided up by the individual maps.

Index Tab. A small piece of paper, card or fabric attached to, and projecting from, the fore-edge of a leaf and bearing in progressive order from top to bottom letters or words. Its purpose is to assist the speedy finding of the information required. *See also Thumb Index.*

Index Term. *See Index Language.*

Indexing. The art of compiling an INDEX (*q.v.*). *See also American Society of Indexers, Society of Indexers.*

Indexing at Source. The publication of indexing data simultaneously with (often at the head of) a periodical article.

Indexing by Exclusion. A system of automatic indexing based on the isolation and exclusion of non-significant or meaningless words. All words which have not been so excluded are processed as indexing words.

Indexing Language. A set of indexing terms as used in a particular retrieval system. The 'language' can be 'natural' (the language of the documents indexed) or 'structured' or 'controlled' (classified or having classificatory features). *See also Artificial Indexing Language, Natural Language, Thesaurus.*

Indexing Service. A periodical publication which regularly and systematically indexes the contents of periodicals and sometimes other forms of publication, either of a general nature or within specified subject fields.

India Office Library and Records. (IOLR). The IOLR comprises the records of the East India Company (1600–1858), the Board of Control (1784–1858), the India Office, and the Burma Office, together with the Library which was founded in 1801. The collection includes books, prints, drawings, paintings, sculpture, furniture, stamps, coins, maps, medals and photographs. IOLR is housed at Orbit House, Blackfriars Road, London; in April 1982 responsibility for the collection passed from the Foreign and Commonwealth Office to the BRITISH LIBRARY (*q.v.*).

India Paper. Originally a soft absorbent paper, cream or buff in colour, imported from China for proofs of engravings. In 1875 the name was used for a thin opaque paper made from hemp or rag. *See also Bible Paper, Cambridge India Paper, Oxford India Paper.*

India Proof. A proof of an engraving taken on India or other fine paper. Sometimes wrongly applied to the whole first edition.

India Proof Paper. *See also China Paper.*

Indian Association for Special Libraries and Information Centres. *See IASLIC.*

Indian Bible. The first Bible printed in the American Colonies was a translation by John Eliot into the Indian language.

Indian Ink. A very black waterproof writing and drawing fluid having great density, used for drawings designed for reproduction and for records where permanence is desired.

Indian Library Association. Founded in 1933, with the following objects: the furtherance of the library movement in India, the promotion of the training of librarians, and the improvement of the status of librarians. Published *Abgila* (= annals, bulletin and granthalaya of the Indian Library Association) (q.).

Indicative Abstract. *See Abstract.*

Indicator. 1. A frame, glazed on the public side, which indicated the numbers of the books 'in' and 'out' in a closed access library. 2. A dye used to evaluate the active acidity of paper. 3. (*Printing*) A 'superior' number or symbol in the text which indicates a foot-note at the bottom of the page (or at the end of the chapter, or at the end of the textual matter) to the word or sentence. *See also Superior Figures (Letters).* 4. A data element associated with a field supplying further information about the contents of the field, the relationship between the field and other fields in the record, or the action required in certain data manipulation processes.

Indicator Digit. A symbol used in the notation of a scheme of classification to announce a change of method of division. *See also Division 4.*

Indicography. The compilation of an index.

Indirect Subdivision. *See Direct Sub-division.*

Indirect Subject Heading. (*Indexing*) A subject heading which merely refers to another subject heading by means of a *See* reference. *See also Mixed Subject Heading.*

INDIS. Abbreviation of Industrial Information Service, a function of UNISIST (*q.v.*).

Individual Entry. Entry in a catalogue under a person or place as subject.

Industrial Group. Formed in May 1971, this Group of the (British) Library Association aims to represent librarians and information workers employed in industry and commerce. Publishes *LAIG Newsletter.*

Industrial Libraries. Libraries provided by, and in, industrial firms.

Inedita. Unpublished works.

Inedited. A work published without editorial changes; it may contain indelicate passages which might have been altered or omitted in editing.

Inevitable Association, Principle of. In descriptive cataloguing, the principle that applies to any name, whether it be of person, book (title), corporate body, periodical, etc., that contains a word that will inevitably be remembered by anyone who asks for that person, book, subject, corporate body or periodical. The principle dictates that the entry chosen for that name will be the word inevitably remembered. *See also Cataloguing, Principles of.*

Inferior Characters.   Small figures and letters cast below the level of the base line, as in chemical formulae, thus: $H_2 SO_4$. Also called 'Subscript'. *See also Base Line, Superior Figures (Letters).*

Infima Species.   The class with which the division of a classification ends. *See also Subaltern Genera and Summum Genus.*

Influence Phase.   One of Ranganathan's three main 'phase relations'; it is the relationship of one subject influencing another. The other two are BIAS PHASE and TOOL PHASE (*qq.v.*). The process of determining the appropriate class for a document; where one thing influences another, the document is classified under the thing influenced. *See also Phase.*

Infoline.   A British HOST (*q.v.*), operated by Pergamon-Infoline Ltd.

Informatics.   1. The processes, methods and laws relating to the recording, analytical-synthetical processing, storage, retrieval and dissemination of scholarly information, but not the scholarly information as such which is the attribute of the respective science or discipline.   2. The study of the structure of knowledge and of its embodiment in information-handling systems.   3. The study of the handling and communication of information, particularly by automated and electronic methods.

Informatics Group.   A technique group of ASLIB (*q.v.*); In 1986 the name was extended to: Aslib Informatics – the Advanced Information System Group.

Information.   An assemblage of data in a comprehensible form capable of communication.

Information Analysis Centre.   A formally structured organizational unit specifically (but not necessarily exclusively) established to acquire, select, store, retrieve, evaluate, analyse and synthesize a body of information and/or data in a clearly defined specialized field, or pertaining to a specific mission, with the intention of arranging and presenting the material in a most authoritative and useful form. Abbreviated IAC.

Information and Referral Service.   A service set up in NEIGHBOURHOOD INFORMATION CENTRES (*q.v.*) in America which receive, mainly over the telephone, enquiries for information of all kinds and refer the enquirers instantly to a community or agency, or individual capable of providing the answer.

Information Area.   (*Reprography*) The printed, or written, area of a document or micro-print which contains the information; it usually excludes the margins.

Information Broker.   An information worker who sells a personal service on a commercial basis, probably operating as a FREELANCE (*q.v.*) self-employed individual, offering information gathering, research, and information-marketing services.

Information Card.   *Synonymous with* HISTORY CARD (*q.v.*).

Information Centre.   Usually an office, or a section of a bibliographical centre, research bureau or documentation centre, which gives information about books or on a subject with which the organization providing the facilities of the centre is concerned. Staffing varies, but may include any or all of the following: research officers, librarians, bibliographers or trained information officers. It may include the functions of a special library and extend its activities to include collateral functions such as: technical writing, abstracting, SDI, and library research for clients.

Information Centre for Terminology. *See INFOTERM.*

Information Clearing House. A name sometimes given to a special library possessing a limited amount of published material, but which collects and gives information by telephone, correspondence and the use of other libraries (American).

Information Consultant. A generic term used by self-employed FREELANCE (*q.v.*) individuals operating on a commercial basis in the areas of information handling, research, data handling and related fields. *See also Library Consultant.*

Information Department. The department of an organization, the primary function of which is to give information when requested.

Information Desk. A desk in a library or other building staffed by one or more persons whose function is to give information. This may vary from little more than directions to various parts of the building to a full information service (even if only of a quick-reference nature) based on an appropriate collection of reference books and other appropriate material.

Information Entry. *Synonymous with* GENERAL REFERENCE (*q.v.*).

Information File. 1. A list of sources of information which is not readily found and which may in the first instance have been difficult to obtain. 2. Extracts, illustrations, pamphlets, and articles taken from periodicals and other fugitive material filed in some systematic order for ready reference.

Information Handling. The storing, processing and retrieval of information from acquisition to user.

Information Industry Association. Established 1968 and now a major US organization for commercial firms in the information market. A regional structure covers the USA. Abbreviated IIA.

Information Management Professionals Association. Based at the Asian Institute of Technology, Bangkok; seeks to promote the advancement of knowledge in information management amongst librarians and others by organizing meetings, seminars and conferences. Issues a *Newsletter*. Abbreviated IMPA.

Information North. A development agency for library and information services in the Northern Region (UK) County Durham, Cumbria, Northumberland, Cleveland, Tyne and Wear. Serves public, private, and voluntary sectors, and is supported by the Northern Regions Councils Association, and the Office of Arts and Libraries. Set up in 1988/89 with headquarters in Newcastle-on-Tyne. It grew out of the LIP (*q.v.*) for the area, and the PUBLIC LIBRARY DEVELOPMENT INCENTIVE SCHEME (*q.v.*). Publishes a health information series, directories, network guides, local databases etc. Issues a newsletter *IN*.

Information Officer. One whose function is to give information; he or she often works in close co-operation with a librarian, giving information from their own knowledge (often being specialists in the field of knowledge concerned) and from published materials which are collected, administered and made available by a librarian.

Information Processing. *See Processing 1.*

Information Provider. In interactive videotex systems, an individual firm, or agency acting for others, that provides pages of information. Abbreviated IP.

Information Retrieval. Finding documents, or the information contained in documents, in a library or other collection, selectively recalling recorded information. Methods of retrieval vary from a simple index or catalogue to the documents, to a computer-based system. Classification, indexing and machine searching are all systems of information retrieval. *See also Data Processing, Retrieval.* Abbreviated IR.

Information Science. The study of the use of information, its sources and development; usually taken to refer to the role of scientific, industrial and specialized libraries and information units in the handling and dissemination of information.

Information Science Abstracts. First published in 1969, developed from *Documentation Abstracts* which began in 1966. An abstract service covering journals, books, proceedings, reports and patents. At present published monthly by Plenum Publishing Corporation, after a confused earlier history. Founded by the American Society for Information Science, the Division of Chemical Information of the American Chemical Society, and the Special Libraries Association. Currently guided also by the American Library Association (ALA), the American Society of Indexers (ASI), Association of Information and Dissemination Centers (ASIDIC), Association of Library and Information Science Education (ALISE) and the Medical Library Association (MLA). Abbreviated *ISA.* Available online via DIALOG.

Information Scientist. Originally an INFORMATION OFFICER (*q.v.*). Emphasis is now more on providing the *science* of an information service than with a knowledge of a traditional science. The concern is therefore more with acquiring, processing and retrieving information than with the content of the information possessed. *See also Institute of Information Scientists.*

Information Service. A service provided by, or for, a special library which draws attention to information possessed in the library or information department in anticipation of demand; this is done by preparing and circulating news sheets, literature surveys, reading lists, abstracts, particulars of articles in current periodicals, etc. which it is anticipated will be of interest to potential users of the service.

Information Services Group. A group of the (British) Library Association; the title was adopted in 1985, and the group had formerly been known as the REFERENCE, SPECIAL AND INFORMATION SECTION (*q.v.*). Abbreviated ISG.

Information Specialist. A person who is primarily concerned with the processing of data in a particular area of knowledge rather than with the control of documents.

Information System. An organized procedure for collecting, processing, storing, and retrieving information to satisfy a variety of needs.

Information Technology. *See IT.*

Information Technology Centre. *See Library and Information Technology Centre.*

Information Technology Group. A Group of the (British) Library Association formed in January 1983 with a view to: promoting the lilbrary and information profession's role in information technology, and to educate and advise the profession on the social and working implications of information technology; advising the Library Association on information technology and related matters; liaising closely with all relevant bodies, including other Library Association groups and branches; providing a forum for discussion and facilities for the dissemination of ideas and experience; establishing links with the various sections of the information industry; promoting access to sources of specific expertise and interest; encouraging the provision of appropriate education and training.

Information Work. The collection, evaluation and organized dissemination of information; it may include abstracting, translation, editing, indexing, literature searching, preparation of bibliographies, assembling of databases, and general subject advice and support. *See also Information Science.*

Information UK 2000. A British Library Research and Development Department project detailing trends in information generation, handling, storage and use over the next decade. Began 1989 with the report expected at the end of 1990. Eleven task forces are examining social trends, technology, archives and libraries, recording, communications infrastructure, publishing and distribution, domestic use of information, organizations, education and training, policy for users, policy for providers.

Informative Abstract. *See Abstract.*

INFOTERM. Abbreviation for International Information Centre for Terminology. Established in 1972 within the framework of UNISIST (*q.v.*) with the assistance of Unesco, and affiliated to the Austrian Standards Institute in Vienna, this Centre has as its main objective to enhance and co-ordinate terminological work. As the co-ordinator of terminological activities carried out throughout the world, its documentation and information functions include: (a) collecting terminological publications from all over the world, particularly terminological standards and principles, and specialized dictionaries; (b) providing information on terminological libraries and their sources; (c) extensive dissemination of information on terminological publications in existence or in preparation; (d) providing information on terminological courses; (e) investigating the possibility of interconnection of terminological word banks. A network of terminological activities – Termnet – was established. Two Symposia have been held in Vienna, in 1975 and 1985.

INFOTERRA. The International Referral System for Sources of Environmental Information, initiated at the UN Conference on the Human Environment, Stockholm, 1972. A world-wide network designed by experts from various countries under the auspices of the UN Environment Programme (UNEP), which began operating in 1975 and is a decentralized system based on existing environmental information services; the central UNEP Headquarters in Nairobi, Kenya co-ordinates activities with an international system of national, regional and sectoral focal points.

infra. (*Lat.* 'below'). Used in footnotes and sometimes in the text to refer to an item mentioned subsequently. *See also supra.*

INFROSS. The INFROSS (Information Requirements of the Social Sciences) project was carried out at the University of Bath during the period 1967 to 1970. The aim of the project was to obtain an overall view of information requirements in the social sciences. The information needs of four specific groups of workers were studied: 1) Researchers in the Social Sciences. 2) Social Scientists in Government Departments. 3) College of Education lecturers and schoolteachers. 4) Social workers. The project was backed by the Office for Scientific and Technical Information (now the British Library Research and Development Department) and the results of the research were published as a series of reports. INFROSS was succeeded by the DISISS PROJECT (*q.v.*).

Ingo-Pact. Ingold's world patent for compact shelving. *See Compactus.*

Ingold-Compactus. *See Compactus.*

Ingrain. A rough and shaggy quality of tinted paper used for pamphlet covers and wall hangings.

Inhabited Initial. In a mediaeval illuminated manuscript, an initial letter containing figures of human beings, beasts, or both. *See also Historiated Initial.*

Inhouse. The system of provision of particular services or activities within a company or organisation from its own resources, rather than from outside agents or contractors.

In-House Publishing. *See Desktop Publishing.*

INISS. Project INISS is a shortened acronym for 'Research project on information needs and information services in local authority social services departments'. Originated at a research forum held in 1974 at the Department of Library and Information Studies, Sheffield University, UK. The work has been supported by the British Library Research & Development Department.

INIST. Institut de l'Information Scientifique et Technique; created 1988 to replace the Centre de Documentation Scientifique et Technique (CDST) and the Centre de Documentation Sciences Humaines (CDSH). INIST is directly attached to the CNRS (*q.v.*). Direction de l'Information Scientifique et Technique. Aims to disseminate scientific knowledge by database development, document delivery systems, and research programmes. New premises opened 1989 in Nancy. Major databases are PASCAL and FRANCIS.

Initial Letter. A capital letter, being the first letter of a word, sentence or paragraph, larger than the subsequent letters, and so set to give emphasis or for decoration. In typography, its size is indicated by the number of lines of body type it occupies, as '3-line initial'. Sometimes called 'Ornamental initial'. *See also Factotum.*

Initialism. *Synonymous with* ACRONYM (*q.v.*).

Ink Ball. A large, round sheepskin or buckskin pad stuffed with wool, or horsehair and cotton, and fastened to a wooden handle. It was used from the fifteenth century until about 1820 (when superseded by rollers) for inking set-up type in the forme. The pressman used them in pairs holding one in each hand.

Ink Block. A piece of beech wood fastened to the hind-rail of a printing press and used for spreading the ink. *See also Ink Slab.*

Inkjet Printer. Non-impact computer output printer that squirts droplets of ink onto the paper in a matrix to form an image.

Ink Slab. The part of some printing machines, consisting of a large, flat, steel bed, on to which the ink is placed and from which the distributing rollers take, mix and spread it, before transferring it to the forme. *See also Ink Block.*

Inlaid. 1. A piece of printing, a MS., or an illustration, which is inset in a frame or border of paper, the overlapping edges having first been shaved thin in order to prevent bulkiness at the joints. 2. A leather binding with leather of another colour or kind set in the cover.

Inlay. 1. The paper used to stiffen the spine of a book when being re-bound. 2. A picture or decoration inlaid in the cover of a book. *See also Onlay.* 3. A MS., letter, leaf, plate or document mounted in a cut-out frame to protect it and permit both sides to be read.

Inlaying. In bookbinding, pasting down a differently coloured leather to that of the cover as part of the decoration; usually within an outlined tool form, border or panel. *See also Onlay.*

Inline Letters. Jobbing and display work letters in which hand-tooling of the main strokes results in a white line forming their central part when printed. This gives the effect of blackness relieved by white. *See also Open Letters.*

Inner Cities. The decaying centres of older towns and cities, presenting urgent housing and social problems. Such areas often have a need for unconventional services in library terms – particularly advice-centre and information functions. In the UK special funds have been made available to local authorities to improve conditions.

Inner Form. *See Form Divisions.*

Inner Forme. A forme containing the pages of type which will, when printed, become the inside of a printed sheet in SHEET WORK (*q.v.*). The reverse of 'outer forme'.

Inner Indention. *Synonymous with* SECOND INDENTION (*q.v.*).

Inner Margin. *Synonymous with* BACK MARGIN (*q.v.*).

INPADOC. Abbreviation for International Patent Documentation Centre. Established by the Austrian Government in collaboration with WIPO (*q.v.*) in 1972, and as a result of the signing (at a Diplomatic Conference held in Washington in 1970) of the Patent Co-operation Treaty (PCT). It aims to furnish to national or regional patent offices, and also to make available to industry, bibliographic data concerning patent documentation in machine-readable form, as well as services identifying patent documents relating to the same invention or to a given branch of technology. *See also ICIREPAT.*

Input.   (*Information retrieval*) That which is put in – that is, the information transferred from external storage to the internal storage of a computer or database.

Input Devices.   (*Information retrieval*) Equipment that provides the means by which data and programs are entered into a computer. It includes various devices employing a keyboard, optical character equipment, light pen, etc.

Inscribed Copy.   *See Presentation Copy.*

INSDOC.   The Indian National Science Documentation Centre was founded by the Indian Government in 1952 with the following objects: (1) to receive and retain all scientific periodicals; (2) to inform scientists and engineers of articles of interest by means of a monthly bulletin of abstracts; (3) to answer specific enquiries; (4) to supply photocopies or translations to individual workers; (5) to be a national depository for published and unpublished Indian scientific reports; (6) to be a channel through which Indian scientific work is made known and available to the rest of the world. The Centre comes under the Council for Scientific and Industrial Research and has been placed under the administrative control of the Director, National Physical Laboratory. Publishes *Insdoc list of current scientific literature.*

INSELTEL.   Spanish videotex system.

Insert.   An additional sentence or a paragraph added to a proof to be inserted in a revise or final proof.

Insertion Mark.   *Synonymous with* CARET (*q.v.*).

Insertion Motif.   An ornament such as a pillar or a bar, etc., dividing two columns of text, or one scene from another, in a mediaeval illuminated manuscript.

In-service Training.   A scheme whereby trainees or the more junior members of a staff are given instruction in the routines carried out in the library and on wider and more general aspects of librarianship. *See also Training.*

Inset.   1. An illustration, map or other item, not part of the printed sheets, included when binding a pamphlet or book. They may or may not be sewn in.   2. A folded sheet laid inside another. It may be part of a printed sheet cut off before folding and inserted in the middle of the folded sheet to complete the succession of the pages. If so, it is also called 'offcut'.   3. An advertisement or separate leaf, not an integral part of the publication inserted in a magazine or booklet.   4. An extra page or set of pages inserted in a proof, or a book.   5. A small map, illustration, etc., set within the border of a larger one.

Inset Map.   A small map printed within the border of a larger one.

Inside Lmning, Ornamental.   *Synonymous with* DOUBLURE 1 (*q.v.*).

Inside Margin.   *Synonymous with* BACK MARGIN (*q.v.*).

INSPEC.   The abstracting and indexing service of the (British) Institution of Electrical Engineers (originally an acronym of Information Services for the Physics and Engineering Communities). Services are available in printed form and online, and centre on four areas: physics; electrical engineering and electronics; computers/computing and control technology (including software engineering and desktop publishing); and information technology.

INSPEL. The quarterlyy journal of the IFLA Division of Special Libraries; published in co-operation with the German Special Libraries Association. Articles usually in English, with abstracts in several languages.

inst. Abbreviation for instant, and meaning 'of the current month' when following a date. *See also ult.*

Instalment. A part of a literary work, published serially in a periodical; sometimes a portion of a work whih is published in 'parts' or 'numbers'.

Institut de l'Information Scientifique et Technique. *See INIST.*

Institut International de Documentation. Formerly the Institut International de Bibliographie. Now the Fédération Internationale de Documentation. *See Universal Decimal Classification.*

Institut International des Brevets. *See International Patent Institute.*

Institut National des Techniques de la Documentation. French school for the training of information scientists; based at the Conservatoire National des Arts et Métiers, Paris. Abbreviated INTD.

Institute for Documentation. (Institut für Dokumentationswesen). Established in Frankfurt-Niederrad, Federal Republic of Germany in 1961 as part of the Max Planck Gesellschaft zur Foerderung der Wissenschaften (Max Planck Society for the Advancement of Science), comprises forty-seven institutes and is the largest research organization in the Federal Republic of Germany. It is mainly a co-ordinating, advisory and financing body with planning and administrative functions in scientific and technical information. The Centre for Documentation at Frankfurt/Main, which is an agency of the Institute, is a training, advisory, equipment-testing, and information centre.

Institute for Scientific Information. A profit-making, multi-national corporation providing a range of information services to scientists. Publications include *Current Contents, Science Citation Index* and *Social Science Citation Index.* Abbreviated ISI.

Institute of Arab Manuscripts. Founded in April 1946 by the Arab League to make more widely known the Arab contribution to universal culture which is to be found in more than three million volumes scattered in public and private libraries throughout the world. Microfilms and enlargements have been made of over 15,000 rare and valuable manuscripts. These are available for consultation at the Institute in Cairo, through inter-library loans or by providing enlargements.

Institute of Information Scientists (UK). A professional organization formed in 1958 to promote and maintain high standards in scientific and technical information work and to establish a professional qualification for graduates engaged therein. The Institute claims that there is a clear distinction between the work of a librarian and of an information officer, arising from the latters' use of specialized scientific knowledge in evaluating, interpreting and collating information. There are over 2000 members; five branches are in operation (Northern; Southern; Midlands; Irish; Scottish) and there are three Special Interest Groups – Small Business Group; UK Online User Group (UKOLUG); Patent and Trade Mark Group. A London head office was set up in 1985, and considerable rethinking and re-organization has taken place in recent years. Publishes *Inform* (m), *Journal of Information Science* (6 p.a.) and newsletters; arranges seminars and an annual conference. Abbreviated IIS.

Institute of Leisure and Amenity Management. Formed 1983 in the UK from the merger of the Institute of Recreation Management, Institute of Park and Recreation Management, and the Association of Recreation Managers. Aims to be the professional association for leisure and recreation services staff. Publishes *Leisure Manager* (m.) and a *Yearbook*. Abbreviated ILAM.

Institute of Librarians. A national voluntary organization of professional librarians in India which was formed in 1975; the Institute is located at the Department of Library Science, University of Calcutta. Publishes *Indian Journal of Library Science* (q.). Abbreviated IOL.

Institute of Reprographic Technology. (UK). Inaugurated in 1961, the objects of this professional association are to provide for the professional and technical advancement of all those (whether users, suppliers or advisers) concerned with: (a) photocopying and duplicating; (b) the reproduction of engineering drawings; (c) inplant printing; (d) photography and visual aids; (e) micrographics and micropublishing; (f) office systems; (g) mechanized addressing and mailing. Apart from the central administration in London, there are fifteen regional units (to which members are automatically allocated) which organize meetings and visits to places of reprographic interest. The Institute is an examining body and awards the qualifications AMIRT and MIRT. There are five grades of membership. Text books are published as well as *Repro* (q.). Abbreviated IRT.

Instituto Brasileiro de Dibliografia e Documentação. Founded in 1954 in Rio de Janeiro with the assistance of Unesco. It is a unit of the Conselho Nacional de Pesquisas, and provides a science reference library and documentation training courses. Abbreviated IBBD.

Instituto de Documentación e Información Cientifica y Tecnica. A national documentation centre established in 1963, with the technical assistance of Unesco, at Havana, Cuba, being attached to the Comisión Nacional de la Academia de Ciencias de la República de Cuba. Publishes a *Boletín*.

Instruction. (*Information retrieval*) A machine word consisting of characters which are recognized by the computer and therefore capable of causing machine action. A set of characters which specifies an operation and usually indicates the location of the data to be processed.

Instruction Note. (*Classification*) A note directing the user to take some specific step which is not obvious from the heading and its context or from the general notes.

Instructional Materials Center. A room, in an American elementary or high school, in which all learning materials (books, periodicals, vertical file materials, slides, films, filmstrips, transparencies, tapes, models, art reproductions, etc., and any necessary machinery to operate them) are kept and from which they may be borrowed, or used, by teachers or pupils. Also called 'Learning Resources Center'. *See also Curriculum Materials Center.*

Instrumental Cues. Abbreviations and/or thematic indications in a music score or PART (*q.v.*) and serving as a guide to the instrumentation, or as an entry signal, for the performer. These are common in 'parts' of concerted music and essential in the scores for piano-conductor. *See also Score.*

Insular Handwriting. The beautiful national style of handwriting which developed from the semi-uncial book hand of the early Christian missionaries to the British Isles and, unlike the Continental styles, from the cursive minuscule. The two principal varieties of this script are (a) the Irish hand which was used from the sixth century to the Middle Ages and developed into the modern Irish script, and (b) the Anglo-Saxon semi-uncial style which developed from (a) in the seventh and eighth centuries. *See also Cursive, Handwriting.*

Intaglio. 1. (*Printing*) A design engraved or incised in the surface of a hard plate. An intaglio plate for printing is usually of copper and has the design engraved with a graver or etched by acid. Photogravure is an intaglio process. 2. (*Binding*) The impression of a ROLL (*q.v.*) in which the sunk part of the leather forms the design.

Intaglio Printing. Printing done from an intaglio (incised) plate, into which the design or image is countersunk or depressed; after being inked and wiped, leaving ink only in the engraved parts, it is placed with a damp sheet of printing paper on the press, layers of felt are added, and pressure applied. The thickness of the ink transferred to the paper varies with the depth of the incisions on the plate; this ink being layered on the plate can be felt on the resulting print (as distinct from the planographic and letterpress methods) and is a means of identifying the method of printing. Copperplate printing, steel die embossing and impressions taken from dry-point plates are forms of intaglio printing, as are etchings, line engravings, mezzotints, aquatints, photogravures and dry-point etchings. The opposite of LETTERPRESS (*q.v.*) and RELIEF PRINTING (*q.v.*).

INTAMEL. The International Association of Metropolitan City Libraries, a sub-section of IFLA (*q.v.*) which was formed in 1968 with the object of encouraging members (libraries in metropolitan areas serving not less than 400,000 population) (a) to participate in international co-operation; (b) to exchange books, staff, and information particularly in connection with deposits and collections of international and foreign literature; (c) to participate in IFLA and its Public Libraries Section. Publishes *INTAMEL Newsletter* (irreg.).

INTD. *See Institut National des Techniques de la Documentation.*

Integer Notation. One in which the notation of a scheme of classification consists of whole numbers as opposed to decimal *fraction notation*. There is no method of allowing for interpolation of new subjects in an integer notation except by leaving gaps where it is estimated that future expansion might take place.

Integral. A leaf which is part of a section, as distinct from one which is printed independently from a section but inserted in it.

Integral Notation. The NOTATION (*q.v.*) of a scheme of classification which uses numbers arithmetically (as does the Library of Congress scheme) and not decimally. Also called an 'arithmetical' notation.

Integrated Database. A database assembled from several sources in such a way that duplicated, redundant material is excised.

Integrated Library System. An automated package of services provided for librarians, in which a common core of data is assembled, and used for all required subsystems. For example, a circulation control system will use the same bibliographic database as the cataloguing system.

Integrated Services Digital Network. *See ISDN.*

Integrity of Numbers. The view that the numbers or other symbols used to denote items in a scheme of classification should not be drastically altered in later revisions of the scheme.

Intellectual Freedom Award. An award made by the AMERICAN ASSOCIATION OF SCHOOL LIBRARIANS (*q.v.*) to recognize a school library media specialist who has upheld the principles of academic freedom.

Intellectual Freedom Round Table. A group of the ALA. Abbreviated IFRT.

Intellectual Level. An indication of the presumed age-range and intelligence of the potential readers of a book; such information could be included in code form in a bibliographical description, to avoid confusion for example between a children's book, general monograph, or specialised treatise with similar titles. The development of such a code was investigated by Unesco in the late 1970s.

Intellectual Work. (*Copyright*) A creation resulting from intellectual activity covering all forms of expression, and possessing the characteristics of NOVELTY (*q.v.*) or ORIGINALITY (*q.v.*).

Intelligent Knowledge-based Systems. *See Expert Systems.*

Intelligent Terminal. A terminal which can hold programs for processing data.

Intension. *See Extension.*

Interactive Video. The convergence of computer and audiovisual technologies, whereby a computer is linked to a videodisc, or videotape, player via an interface. The video programme is controlled by the computer program, but the ultimate control of both is vested in the user, who must indicate decisions or progress via a keyboard to enable the video programme to proceed.

Inter-availability of Tickets. Arrangements whereby the membership tickets of one library may be used to borrow books from another library.

Intercalation. The act of inserting a heading for a new subject between two existing headings of a classification.

Intercalation Device. (*Classification*) The part of a NOTATION (*q.v.*) which indicates the incorporation of part of a notation from a different scheme of classification.

Interdepartmental Co-ordinating Committee for Science and Technical Information. ICCSTI is a British government organization consisting of representatives of government departments, professional bodies and non-government organizations, set up in 1974; recently keen to provide a response mechanism to European Community proposals originating from DIRECTORATE-GENERAL XIII and CIDST (*qq.v.*). *See also National Focus on European Library Co-operation, and Plan of Action (EC).*

Interest-Profile. A list of terms selected from a thesaurus indicating the area of interest of the user of an information service; it is used in the selection of documents in a Selective Dissemination of Information System. Also called USER-PROFILE. *See also SDI.*

Interests Record. A record of the interests of individuals habitually using a library. It is compiled from statements made on their membership application forms, from requests for books or information, deliberate interviews, or contacts, and in an organization of fixed and limited numbers such as a firm or research laboratory, by reading correspondence. It is maintained, usually in subject order, to determine what current matter shall be routed or abstracted and to whom lists of additions and other information shall be disseminated.

Interfix. (*Information retrieval*) 1. A device to signal relationships between concepts. Thus for a series of compounds, A, B, C, . . . insertion of the interfixes 1 and 2 (for example A_1, B_1, B_2, C_2 . . .) signals that the compounds with the same numerical interfix are in one mixture and those with a different one are in a different mixture. *See also Links, Modulant, Roles.* 2. A neutral symbol attached to a DESCRIPTOR (*q.v.*) to indicate other descriptions with which it is interlocked.

Intergovernmental Bureau for Informatics – International Computer Centre. *See IBI–ICC.*

Intergovernmental Computation Centre. *See IBI–ICC,*

Intergovernmental Copyright Committee. *See IGC.*

Interlacing. Ornament composed of bands, etc., woven together.

Interlay. An UNDERLAY (*q.v.*) consisting of a sheet of paper or other material placed between a printing plate and its mount in order to raise the plate to its proper height for good printing.

Interleaf. An extra leaf, usually blank, inserted between the regular leaves of a book. The blank leaves may be provided for the writing of notes, or if they are thin tissues, to prevent the text and illustrations from rubbing. The latter may be pasted to the inner mmargins, or they may be loose. The plates so protected are know as tissued plates. Such a book is said to be interleaved.

Interleaving. Tissue or blank paper used for interleaving illustrations and letterpress. Also thin blotting paper used for interleaving diaries.

Interlending. Schemes whereby users of one library or information system may request their service point to borrow from other library systems materials not held in their own library system. Most libraries participate in interlending schemes, which may be locally, regionally, nationally or internationally organized. Many requests will be lodged with library services set up to act as interlending bases, for example the British Library Document Supply Centre.

Inter-library Loan. A book or other item lent between libraries. *See Interlending.*

Interlinear Blank. *Synonymous with* INTERLINEAR MATTER (*q.v.*).

Interlinear Matter. Characters providing explanations, translations or subsidiary matter, written or printed in smaller characters between the ordinary lines of text to which they relate.

Interlinear Space. Space between lines of type. Also called 'Interlinear blank'.

Interlinear Translation. A translation printed between the lines of the original text to which it relates.

Interlit. A working party formed 1986 to bring together the Council of Regional Arts Associations, the Book Trust, the Book Marketing Council, the Booksellers Association, and the Library Association. Encourages collaboration, and understanding of contemporary writing. *See also National Book Committee.*

Intern. In America, a graduate who works in a library full-time while attending a school of librarianship. *See also Interne.*

Internacia Esperanto-Asocio de Bibliotekistoj. *See IEAB.*

International Advisory Committee on Documentation, Libraries and Archives. *See IACODLA.*

International and Comparative Librarianship Group. *See ICLG.*

International Association for Esperanto-speaking Librarians. *See IEAB.*

International Association for the Development of Documentation, Libraries and Archives in Africa. Founded in 1960 and known as the International Association for the Development of Libraries in Africa until 1967 when the name was changed to indicate the expanded aims of: promoting and establishing in all African countries a public archives service, a national system of libraries, documentation centres and museums. Membership is open to individuals. It has national sections in four countries. This Association was developed from the Association for the Development of Public Libraries in Africa which was founded in 1957. Abbreviated AIDBA (Association Internationale pour le Développement de la Documentation des Bibliothèques et des Archives en Afrique).

International Association for the Development of Libraries in Africa. *See International Association for the Development of Documentation, Libraries and Archives in Africa.*

International Association of Agricultural Librarians and Documentalists. Founded 1955 to promote internationally, and nationally, 'agricultural library science and documentation as well as the professional interest of agricultural librarians and documentalists'. It succeeded the International Committee of Agricultural Librarians (founded 1935). Publishes *Quarterly Bulletin of the IAALD.* Abbreviated IAALD.

International Association of Bibliophiles. Founded 10 October 1963 in Barcelona. Aims to establish permanent links between bibliophiles in all parts of the world. Membership is open to individuals, societies and libraries in any country. Publishes *Bulletin du bibliophile.*

International Association of Documentalists and Information Officers. Founded 1962 in Paris to promote contacts between people of all nationalities whose work concerns the problems of documentation, and to defend their professional interests. Individuals may become members. Abbreviated AID (Association Internationale des Documentalistes et Techniciens de l'Information).

International Association of Law Libraries. Founded in New York in 1959 'to promote on a co-operative, non-profit and fraternal basis the work of individuals, libraries, and other institutions and agencies concerned with the acquisition and bibliographic processing of legal materials collected on a multinational basis, and to facilitate the research and other uses of such materials on a world-wide basis.' Publishes *International Journal of Law Libraries* (3 p.a.) formerly *IALL Bulletin.* Abbreviated IALL.

International Association of Metropolitan City Libraries. *See INTAMEL.*

International Association of Music Libraries, Archives and Documentation Centres. Founded in Paris in 1951, the object of this Association is 'to constitute a representative international organization charged with stimulating and co-ordinating all the activities, national and international, of music libraries, and to study and facilitate the realization of all projects dealing with music bibliography and music library science'. It aims to arrange for co-operation in the compilation of music bibliographies, exchange material, and train music librarians. Publishes *Fontes artis musicae* (3 a year). Abbreviated IAML. It has a British branch which was founded in 1953 and was primarily responsible for inaugurating the *British catalogue of music* (1957); publishes *Brio* (q.). *See also RISM.*

International Association of Orientalist Librarians. *See IAOL.*

International Association of Scholarly Publishers. Formed at the International Conference on Scholarly Publishing, held in Toronto in 1972, to associate university presses with other publishers of scholarly works. Aims: to encourage the dissemination of the fruits of scholarship and research; to exchange ideas and advice relating to scholarly publishing. The headquarters of the Association was established at Toronto University Press. An Asian Group is based on the University of Tokyo Press, Japan.

International Association of School Librarianship. Founded in 1969 (originally as a Committee of the World Confederation of Organizations of the Teaching Profession) to promote school library provision all over the world. Financed by the subscriptions of individual members and associations. Publishes *Newsletter* (4 p.a.). Abbreviated IASL.

International Association of Schools of Information Science. Founded 1977, sponsors workshops and conferences. Secretariat at the University of Montreal. Abbreviated AIESI, from the French title.

International Association of Sound Archives. A non-governmental Unesco affiliated organization. It was established in 1969 in Amsterdam to function as a medium for international co-operation between archives where preserve recorded sound documents. The Association is actively involved in the preservation, organization and use of sound recordings, techniques of recording and methods of reproducing sound in all fields in which the audio medium is used; in the exchange of recordings between archives and of related literature and information; and in all subjects relating to the professional work of sound archives and archivists including acquisition, documentation, copyright, access, distribution, preservation, and the technical aspects of recording and playback. Membership of the Association is open to all categories of archives and other institutions which preserve sound recordings, and to organizations and individuals having a serious interest in the purposes or welfare of IASA. The Association includes members representing archives of music, history, literature, drama and folklife recordings; radio and television sound archives; collections of oral history, natural history, bioacoustic and medical sounds; recorded linguistic and dialect surveys. IASA holds an annual conference which includes a General Assembly to report the business of the Association to the members, working sessions for IASA committees, and sessions on topics of general interest. The Association has over 400 members, individual and institutional, in more than 50 countries.

International Association of Technological University Libraries.   Founded in Brussels in May 1955 to act as an organ for international co-operation between member libraries and to stimulate and develop library projects of international and regional importance. It is a section of IFLA. 150 members are drawn from 40 countries; regular conferences are held, and research sponsored. Publishes *IATUL Quarterly* (q). Abbreviated IATUL.

International Board on Books for Young People.   *See IBBY.*

International Book Award.   Instituted at the first meeting of the INTERNATIONAL BOOK COMMITTEE (*q.v.*) held at Bogatá, Colombia, in 1973, the Award is designed to accord recognition for outstanding services rendered by a person or institution to the cause of books in such fields as authorship, publishing, production, translation, bookselling, encouragement of the reading habit and promotion of international co-operation. The Award is an honorary distinction bestowed in the form of a diploma or other means decided upon by the International Book Committee at regular intervals on the nomination of the Committee. It was first awarded to Mr Herman Liebaers, Royal Librarian of Belgium, President of IFLA, and Chairman of the Preparatory Meeting, the Planning Committee and the Support Committee which organized IBY (*q.v.*) 'in recognition of his outstanding contribution to International Book Year, 1972'.

International Book Committee.   The Committee was originally organized in 1971 in Paris as a support body for Unesco's International Book Year, 1972 (*see IBY*). Comprised of representatives of six international nongovernmental organizations and other international experts concerned with books and reading, the Committee adopted the slogan 'Books for All', and helped plan the Programme of Action, not only for the International Book Year, but also for the ensuing decade. International Book Year 1972 was extremely successful. A climate of solidarity nourished by the support committee brought the book world solidly behind the Unesco initiative. The Secretariat was pleased with this result, and recommended that a broadly representative inter-professional body be established to promote book development, distribution and use. This became the International Book Committee. Plenary sessions have been held at approximately yearly intervals, and new statutes were approved in 1985. *See also International Book Award.*

International Book Year. *See IBY.*

International Bureau of Education. A co-operative abstracting service of Unesco's specialized centre for comparative education, was put into full effect in 1971, and was later extended to cover all Member States, thus enabling participating centres to select and summarize important national documents on educational policy worthy of being communicated to other countries. The Bureau acts as an international centre of information and educational research, and provides for a wide exchange of data so that each country may be encouraged to profit by the experience of others. Abbreviated IBE.

International Catalogue Card. The size of card which has been adopted internationally for use in card catalogues: it is 5 × 3 inches (7.5 × 12.5 centimetres).

International Centre for African Economic and Social Documentation. Founded January 1961 to gather together and co-ordinate documentation on economic and social material concerning Africa with a view to facilitating and promoting the progress of the Continent in these fields. Publishes *Bibliographical index* (a).

International Children's Book Day. *See IBBY.*

International Classification. The brief name for Fremont Rider's scheme of classification for a general library, *International classificationn for the arrangement of books on the shelves of general libraries*, first published in 1961. Its main outline is similar to the Library of Congress classification; form and geographical sub-divisions are enumerated in each main class; the notation consists of three letters and can be extnded by 'book numbers' which are a combination of letters from the BISCOE DATE TABLE (*q.v.*) plus the initial letter of the authors name; no auxiliary tables are provided, neither are alternative locations. The schedules have 14,000 places.

International Committee for African Social and Economic Documentation. *See CIDESA.*

International Committee for Social Sciences Documentation. Founded in November 1950 in Paris at a meeting called by Unesco following recommendations of two committees of experts in 1948 and 1949. Registered in accordance with French law. Collects, keeps up-to-date and disseminates information on the different documentation services in the social sciences, and helps establish bibliographies and documentary tools which its surveys show to be necessary. It initiated, with the help of the Nuffield Foundation, investigation into the need for, and production of, a scheme of classification for the four Unesco bibliographies dealing with sociology, political science, economics, and social anthropology. The Kyle Classification for Social Sciences was the result. The membership consists mainly of representatives of international associations specializing either in the social sciences or in documentation and bibliography. It is financed by a grant from Unesco, and its activities include the compilation of current bibliographies and directories. Abbreviated ICSSD.

International Community of Booksellers Associations. Founded in 1956. Aims: co-operation between all booksellers and associations of booksellers of countries which enjoy freedom of thought and expression with a view to the exchange of experience and the discussion of common commercial problems. Abbreviated ICBA.

International Conference on Cataloguing Principles. An outstanding conference of cataloguers, bibliographers and library officers with cataloguing expertise was held in Paris, 9–18 October 1961, consequent upon a proposal made by the council of IFLA in 1957 to seek agreement on certain basic cataloguing principles. It was sponsored by IFLA with the object of reaching 'agreement on basic principles governing the choice and form of entry in the alphabetical catalogue of authors and titles'. The definitive annotated edition of the *Statement of principles*, known as the PARIS PRINCIPLES (*q.v.*), which was an outcome of this Conference and was mainly written by Dr Eva Verona, was published by the IFLA Committee on Cataloguing, London, in 1971. *See also IMCE.* Abbreviated ICCP.

International Conference on Children's Literature. Annual conferences have been held in Austrian cities beginning in 1965, and organized by the INTERNATIONAL INSTITUTE FOR CHILDREN'S LITERATURE AND READING RESEARCH (*q.v.*). An international exhibition of children's books has been held on each occasion.

International Conference on Classification for Information Retrieval. Held at Dorking, England, 13–17 May, 1957. The *Proceedings* of the Conference were published by Aslib who organized it as the British member of FID in co-operation with the Classification Research Group and the University of London School of Librarianship and Archives. Further Conferences have been held in Elsinore (1965), Bombay (1975), and Augsburg (1982).

International Conference on Information Processing. Held 15–20 June 1959 in Paris; organized by Unesco with the help of experts from various countries, with the object of bringing experts together to share their knowledge and experience. The conference was mainly concerned with the workings and uses of computers. The International Federation of Information Processing Societies was set up and was later known as the INTERNATIONAL FEDERATION FOR INFORMATION PROCESSING (*q.v.*).

International Co-operation in Information Retrieval Among Patent Offices. *See ICIREPAT.*

International Copyright. *See Copyright, International.*

International Copyright Act, 1886. This was passed to enable the original Berne Convention to be carried out in the Dominions. *See Copyright, International.*

International Copyright Information Centre. *See ICIC.*

International Council for Building Documentation. Abbreviated CIDB. *See International Council for Building Research, Studies and Documentation.*

International Council for Building Research, Studies and Documentation. Founded in 1953. Superseded the International Council for Building Documentation (CIDB) which had been established in 1950. Aims to encourage, facilitate and develop international co-operation in building research, studies and documentation, covering technical, economic and social aspects of building. Abbreviated CIB. Has published *ABC: abridged building classification for architects, builders and civil engineers: a selection from the Universal Decimal Classification system by the International Building Classification Committee* in single language editions in English, Dutch, French, German, Hungarian, Italian, Norwegian, Serbo-Croatian, Swedish and Danish. Publishes also the 'CIB Directory' – in full: *Directory of building research and development organizations; Organizations in Europe; CIB member organizations outside Europe; International organizations,* and *Building Research and Practice* (bi-m.) bilingual English/French.

International Council for Scientific and Technical Information. Established 1984 as successor to the International Council of Scientific Unions Abstracts Board (ICSU/AB). Exists to widen access to and awareness of scientific and technical information. In 1985 its scope was extended to cover electronic publishing and document delivery. Abbreviated ICSTI.

International Council of Scientific Unions. ICSU is a federation of 20 International Scientific Unions, 74 national academies, research councils or other national scientific bodies and 26 Scientific Associates, one of which is IFLA; others in the information field are FID, IFIP, IFSEA, ICSTI, and IATUL. The Council was established in 1931 from the earlier International Research Council (created in 1919). The main objectives of ICSU are: to encourage, for the benefit of humankind, international scientific activity which will serve scientific and technological development and so help to promote the cause of peace and international security throughout the world; to facilitate and co-ordinate the activities of the International Scientific Unions; to stimulate, design and co-ordinate international interdisciplinary scientific research projects, and scientific education; to facilitate the co-ordination of the international scientific activities of its National Members. One of the most recent developments in ICSU concerning information is the creation of an ICSU Press, which provides members of the ICSU family with advice on publication problems and also publishes books and journals. Based in Paris; publishes a *Yearbook,* and numerous specialist journals. Abbreviated ICSU. *See also International Council for Scientific and Technical Information.*

International Council on Archives. Founded in June 1948 by professional archivists meeting in Paris under the auspices of Unesco. Aims to hold periodical international congresses (Montreal, 1992), establish and maintain relations among archivists of all nations, and among all professional agencies and institutions whose activities relate to the conservation, organization or administration of archives; to further technical and administrative aspects of public and private archives wherever located and to facilitate access to archives, their objective study and the knowledge of their contents. There are nine regional branches including: ARBICA, ECARBICA, SARBICA and SWARBICA (*qq.v.*). Liaison committees with IFLA and FID were established in 1974. Guides to the sources of the history of nations are being published in three series: 1. Latin America; 2. Africa; 3. North Africa, Asia and Oceania. Publishes *Archivum* (a.), *Bulletin* (2 p.a.) in English and French editions. 850 members in 140 countries; Paris-based secretariat. Abbreviated ICA.

International Federation for Information and Documentation. The English title of the Fédération Internationale d'Information et de Documentation (FID). This organization exists (a) to group on an international basis, organizations and individuals interested in the problems of DOCUMENTATION (*q.v.*) and to co-ordinate their efforts; (b) to promote the study and practice of documentation in all its branches and forms, and to create an international network of documentation; (c) to establish guiding principles for the member organizations in their work; (d) to organize the exchange of information relevant to the work of member organizations; (e) to convene conferences dealing with the problems of documentation; (f) to publish, sell and distribute periodical and non-periodical publications dealing with documentation; (g) to co-operate with other international organizations concerned with related subjects; (h) to take such other legal and appropriate measures as may be conducive to the attainment of the above objects. The development of the UNIVERSAL DECIMAL CLASSIFICATION (*q.v.*) is a major activity. Five major programme areas are currently in progress: availability and applicability of information; developing the information market place; tools for information work; understanding of properties of information; professional development. Various Committees operate specialized activities, for example FID/ET (Education and Training Committee), FID/EEII (Executive Expert Information in Industry), and FID/CR (Classification Research). Regional groupings include FID/CLA (Commission for Latin America), FID/CAO (Commission for Asia and Oceania). Since 1971 FID has published monthly *R & D projects in documentation and librarianship* as a current awareness service for on-going and projected research and development in the fields of library, documentation and information sciences and related areas of interest. Publishes *International Forum on Information and Documentation* (q.), *FID News Bulletin* (m.), *Newsletter on Education and Training Programmes for Specialised Information Personnel* (q.). *See also Standard Reference Code, ISORID.*

International Federation for Information Processing. Formerly the International Federation of Information Processing Societies which was set up as a result of an international congress on information processing organized by Unesco and held in Paris in 1959. The members of the Federation are national societies, the adhering society in the United Kingdom being the

British Computer Society. Aims: to sponsor international conferences and symposia on information processing; to establish international committees to undertake special tasks falling within the scope of member societies; to advance the interests of member societies in international co-operation in the field of information processing. Publishes *IFIP Summary*. Abbreviated IFIP.

International Federation of Film Archives. *See FIAF.*

International Federation of Library Associations and Institutions (IFLA). Founded 1927, and now having over 1200 members in 120 countries. Headquarters in The Hague, Netherlands; its objectives are: (a) To promote international understanding, co-operation, discussion, research and development in all fields of library and information service activity. (b) To promote the continuing education of library personnel. (c) To provide an organization through which librarianship can be represented in matters of international interest. (d) To develop, promote and maintain guidelines for various types of library activity, including compilation of statistics, recording and communication of bibliographic data, preservation and conservation of library materials, etc. IFLA is represented on several international bodies (including ISO, ICSU, WIPO) and has consultative arrangements with many more (eg. SIBMAS, FID, ICA, IASA, IPA, IBBY, etc.). It is organized into 8 divisions, comprising the 31 Sections, and 10 Round Tables, thus:

1. General Research Libraries (includes National Libraries, University Libraries and other General Research Libraries, and Parliamentary Libraries).

2. Special Libraries (includes Administrative Libraries, Social Science Libraries, Geography and Map Libraries, Science and Technology Libraries, Biological and Medical Science Libraries, and Art Libraries).

3. Libraries serving the general public (includes Public Libraries, Children's Libraries, School Libraries, Disadvantaged Users, Blind *and* Round Tables for Documentation on Children's Literature, INTAMEL (*q.v.*), ROTNAC (*q.v.*), Mobile Libraries, Ethnic and Linguistic Minorities).

4. Bibliographic Control (includes Cataloguing, Bibliography, and Classification and Subject Cataloguing).

5. Collections and Services (includes Acquisition and Exchange, Interlending and Document Delivery, Serial Publications, Official Publications, Rare and Precious Books and Documents).

6. Management and Technology (includes Conservation, IT, Buildings and Equipment, Statistics, *and* Round Tables on Audiovisual Media, Management of Library Associations, and Newspapers).

7. Education and Research (includes Library Schools and other Training Aspects, Theory and Research, *and* Round Tables on Library History, of Editors of Library Journals, and on Research in Reading).

8. Regional Activities (includes groups for Africa, Asia and Oceania, and Latin America and Caribbean).

IFLA's major undertaking is the operation of six core programmes; these are: (1) Universal Bibliographic Control (UBC) (*q.v.*), (2) Universal Availability of Publications (UAP) (*q.v.*), (3) International MARC Programme

(IMP) (*q.v.*), (4) Preservation and Conservation (PAC) (*q.v.*), (5) Universal Data Flow and Telecommunications (UDT) (*q.v.*), (6) Advancement of Librarianship in the Third World (ALP) (*q.v.*). (Nos. 1 and 3 were combined in 1986 into UBCIM – Universal Bibliographic Control and International MARC). A medium term plan covering the years 1986–91 was published in 1988. *See also Vosper (Robert) Fellowships.* Publishes *Libri* (q.) *IFLA Journal* (q.), *IFLA Directory* (annual), *International Cataloguing* (q.) standards, monographs and proceedings.

International Federation of Translators.   Founded in Paris with Unesco support in December 1953 to bring together representative groups of translators in order to defend their material and moral interests, encourage the establishment of such groups in countries where they do not exist, represent translators at the international level, follow the development of theoretical and practical questions relating to translation, and contribute to the spread of culture. Organizes congresses and pursues various projects through committees relating to terminology, registers of specialist translators, copyright, training, etc. Abbreviated FIT.

International Information Centre for Standards in Information and Documentation.   *See ISODOC.*

International Information Centre for Terminology.   *See INFOTERM.*

International Information System on Research in Documentation.   *See ISORID.*

International Institute for Children's Literature and Reading Research.   This Institute, which operates in Vienna, is a non-profit-making association; it also serves as the office of the Austrian Section of the International Board on Books for Young People (IBBY *q.v.*). Founded in 1965, it endeavours to create an international centre of work and co-ordination in the field of children's literature and to take over documentation in this area. Publishes *Bookbird* (q.) in co-operation with the IBBY and *Jugend und Buch* (q. *in German*) in co-operation with the Austrian Children's Book Club.

International Librarian of the Year.   An annual award made in recognition of a significant contribution to good relations between British libraries or librarians and those overseas. Administered by the Library Services Trust at Library Association HQ.

International Literacy Year.   1990 has been so designated by the United Nations; the lead organization for activity is Unesco, which is using the year to launch a Plan of Action to eradicate illiteracy by 2000.

International MARC Network Advisory Committee.   A consultative body of libraries using MARC for national bibliographic networks; members include British Library, Bibliothèque Nationale, Library of Congress, etc. Abbreviated IMAC.

International MARC Programme (IMP).   A core programme of IFLA (*q.v.*) responsible for the testing and development of UNIMARC. Now combined into the UB programme; *see Universal Bibliographic Control.*

International Meeting of Cataloguing Experts.   *See IMCE.*

International Micrographics Congress. An international federation of national societies of the world which are engaged in furthering the progress and application of the micro-recording and micro-reproduction art. The congresses are held annually. Aims to: stimulate development of new methods and devices; provide an international clearinghouse for information of developments and facilities for exchange of publications and papers among member societies; promote and encourage the establishment and use of international standards; promote international exhibitions and conventions. National microfilm societies and individuals in countries without national societies may join. Publishes *IMC Journal* (q., distributed through national associations), and *The International Directory of Microreproduction Equipment*. Abbreviated IMC.

International Millionth Map. A 'map' of the world on a 1:1,000,000 scale; so far, about 300 of the projected 1,500 sheets have been completed.

International Musicological Society. Founded in Basle, 1927, by amalgamating the *Internationale Musikgelleschaft* and the *Union Musicologique*. Reconstituted in 1949, the Society aims to establish relations between musicologists in different countries; serves as a central information and bibliographical office. Publishes *Acta Musicologica* (q.), and congress reports. Abbreviated IMS. *See also RISM.*

International Organization for Standardization. Constituted in London under its present statues in October 1946 to replace the pre-war International Federation of National Standardizing Associations (ISA) and the United Nations Standards Co-ordinating Committee. Aims to promote development of standards in the world with a view to facilitating international exchange of goods and services, and to develop mutual co-operation in the sphere of intellectual, scientific, technological and economic activity. Over 100 technical committees of experts appointed by national standard bodies who are members formulate recommendations to national member associations. Publishes *ISO Bulletin* (m.), *ISO Catalogue* (a.) and *ISO Memento* (a.). Abbreviated ISO.

International Packet Switching Service. A switched data service, providing a link between terminals and computers in different countries, which may be using apparently incompatible equipment. Abbreviated IPSS. *See also Packet Switching, PSS.*

International Paper Sizes. The international 'A' series of paper sizes, now widely used throughout the world. In Britain many organizations have adopted them and there is both a British Standard (BS 4000) and an international recommendation (ISO/R 216) covering them. *See also Paper Sizes* for details of dimensions.

International Patent Documentation Centre. *See INPADOC.*

International Patent Institute. Aims to provide technical reports on novelty of inventions, undertake documentary research in all fields of science and technology. Financed by the eight member governments (Belgium, France, Luxembourg, Monaco, Netherlands, Switzerland, Turkey, UK) and by payment for services provided. Situated at The Hague. Abbreviated IIB (Institut International des Brevets).

International Publishers Association. Founded in Paris in 1896 as International Publishers Congress to consider problems common to the publishing and bookselling trades, and to uphold and defend the right to publish and distribute the work of man's mind in complete freedom, both within the frontiers of each country and among the nations; to secure international co-operation among themselves and to overcome illiteracy, the lack of books and other means of education. Congresses are held periodically in different countries. A permanent office is maintained at Geneva. Membership is open to professional book and music publishers associations. Activities include help to secure signatories to the BERNE CONVENTION and UNIVERSAL COPYRIGHT CONVENTION (*qq.v.*) and to keep the flow of books between countries free of tariffs and other obstacles, provision of aid to emerging countries, and consideration of international copyright and translation rights. Publishes reports and congress proceedings. Publishes a newsletter (q.). Abbreviated IPA.

International Reading Association. Founded in the USA on 1 January 1956 to encourage the study of reading problems at all levels, and also to stimulate and promote research in developmental, corrective and remedial reading. There are 60,000 members in 65 countries. Publishes *The Reading Teacher, Journal of Reading* (both 8 p.a.), *Reading Research Quarterly* and about twenty different works annually. Abbreviated IRA. *See also United Kingdom Reading Association.*

International Serials Data System. *See ISDS.*

International Society for Knowledge Organization. Founded July 1989 in Frankfurt, FRG, to unite personal and institutional members interested in 'research, development and application of all methods for the organization of knowledge in general or of particular fields by integrating especially the conceptual approaches of classification research and artificial intelligence.' First major conference held Frankfurt, FRG, August 1990. Abbreviated ISKO.

International Society for Performing Arts Libraries and Museums. Founded in September 1954 at Zagreb with the object of developing co-operation among libraries, as well as museums, public, private and specialized collections concerned with the theatre, dance, cinema, marionettes, mime, festivals, son et lumière, radio and television. Publishes *Spectacles-Documents* (bulletin) in *Theatre Documentation* (3 a year). Congress proceedings. Now titled SIBMAS (*q.v.*).

International Standard Bibliographic Description. *See ISBD.*

International Standard Book Number. *See ISBN, Standard Book Number.*

International Standard Music Number. *See ISMN.*

International Standard Serial Number. *See ISSN.*

International Standards. Of several international standards organizations the two most important are International Organization for Standardization (ISO) and International Electro-technical Commission (IEC). ISO seeks to achieve worldwide agreement on international standards with a view to the expansion of trade, the improvement of quality, the increase of productivity and the lowering of prices. The ISO Information Network came into operation officially on 1 January 1974 in order to link the ISO Information Centre at the Central Secretariat in Geneva with information centres nominated by the national standards organizations throughout the world, so as to create a fast and efficient technical information service for all questions relating to standardization. *See also American National Standards Institute, Inc., British Standards Institution, DIN, International Organization for Standardization, Copant, Z39.*

International Translations Centre. The Centre, based at Delft, Netherlands, and formerly known as the European Translations Centre, founded 1961, provides a central index of translations held by European organizations. Since 1987 ITC has covered all scientific and technical translations into European languages. Translations notified to ITC are listed in the monthly journal *World Translations Index,* which is available online via ESA/IRS and DIALOG, and the directory *Journals in Translation* (4th ed., 1989) published with BLDSC. *See also National Translations Center.*

International Union for the Protection of Literary and Artistic Works. Founded 9 September 1886 to ensure effective protection to authors of literary and artistic works, and to ensure and develop the international protection of literacy and artistic works. Membership is open to governments. Organizes diplomatic conferences. Publishes *Le droit d'auteur* (m.), *Copyright* (m.).

International Youth Library. An associated project of Unesco; founded 1949 in Munich out of the first post-war exhibition of international children's books organized 1946 by Jella Lepman (1891–1970). From 1982 housed in Schloss Blutenburg, near Munich. Abbreviated IYL.

Interne. *See Intern.*

INTERNET. Originally founded in 1969 as ARPANET to link academic, military and commercial organizations in North America. Currently being transformed into a new network – INTERNET – which will segregate its users into groups according to their organizational activities; the educational and research group remains a major inter-university network.

Interpolated Note. An explanation or description added to an entry by the compiler of a catalogue or bibliography to clarify the original material. Such information is inserted within SQUARE BRACKETS (*q.v.*).

Interpolation. (*Classification*) The insertion of a new topic at any point in a scheme of classification. A non-structural type of notation renders this readily possible. *See also Extrapolation.*

Inter-regional Subject Coverage Scheme. Under this scheme each of the British Regional Bureaux became responsible on 1 January 1959 for seeing that one library in its area purchases every new book and pamphlet published in the United Kingdom, which is included in the *British National Bibliography*; the allocation of sections of the Dewey Classification is as follows:

000–099	Northern	400–499	East Midlands
100–199	Wales	800–899	,, ,,
200–299	South-Western	500–599	West Midlands

300–349	Yorkshire	600–699	North-Western
350–399	Scotland	700–799	London
		900–999	South-Eastern

The books purchased under this scheme are intended to be provided primarily for preservation.

Interrogation Mark.   A punctuation sign (?) placed at the end of a direct question. Also used between parentheses to indicate an author's questionin the accuracy of a statement. Also called 'Interrogation point', 'Mark of interrogation', 'Question mark'.

Intersecting Frame.   (*Binding*) One or more decorative frames, the sides of which (or some of them) are extended, where they meet each other, to the edges of the cover.

Interspacing.   *Synonymous with* LETTER SPACING (*q.v.*).

Intertype.   A typesetting machine casting type in a slug, similar to, but differing in detail from, the LINOTYPE (*q.v.*).

Intra-facet Relation.   *See Phase.*

Intrex.   *See Project Intrex.*

Intrinsic Value.   (*Archives*) In the appraisal of manuscripts, the worth of a document as affected by some unique factor such as its age, an attached seal, a signature or the handwriting of a distinguished person, or the circumstances regarding its creation. *See also Appraisal.*

Introduction.   1. A short essay or statement, usually being a general survey of the subject preparing the reader for the treatment to follow, of a commendatory nature, and written by an authority in the field with which the book deals. Its order in the PRELIMINARIES (*q.v.*), is after the Preface and immediately before the first page of text. Sometimes it is the first chapter. 2. Included in the title of a book, it indicates that it is an introductory book on the subject, intended for students, and possibly a popular treatment, but not as elementary as a PRIMER (*q.v.*).

Introduction Date.   The date given at the beginning or end of an INTRODUCTION (*q.v.*).

Inversion, Principle of.   In classification, placing the facets in schedule order in such a way that the most concrete, intensive or significant is last.

Inversion of Title.   The turning about of a title to bring a particular word to the front. This practice is frequently adopted in dictionary catalogues.

Inverted Baconian Scheme.   A scheme of classification in which the order of the main classes in Francis Bacon's philosophical system outlined in his *The advancement of learning* (1605) history, poesy, philosophy – are inverted, as in the Dewey Decimal Classification.

Inverted Commas.   Pairs of superior commas, or sometimes single commas, placed at the beginning and end of quotations. *See also Quotes.*

Inverted Entry.   An index entry which has been re-arranged to bring the most important word or words to the front. For example, 'CO-EFFICIENT OF EXPANSION, APPARENT'. The opposite of DIRECT ENTRY (*q.v.*).

Inverted Heading.   A catalogue heading which has had the order of the words inverted to bring the most important word to the front, as CHEMISTRY,

ORGANIC. Also called 'Indirect heading'.

Inverted Title.   *See Inversion of Title.*

IOL.   Institute of Librarians (*q.v.*).

IOLR.   *See India Office Library and Records.*

Ionometer.   *See pH Value.*

IP.   *See Information Provider.*

IPA.   INTERNATIONAL PUBLISHERS ASSOCIATION (*q.v.*).

IPS.   *See Office of Information Programmes and Services.*

IPSS.   *See International Packet Switching Service, PSS.*

i.q.   Abbreviation for *idem quod* (*Lat.* 'the same as').

IR.   INFORMATION RETRIEVAL (*q.v.*).

IRA.   Acronym for INTERNATIONAL READING ASSOCIATION (*q.v.*).

Irish Central Library for Students.   Founded by the Carnegie United Kingdom Trust in 1923; control was transferred to An Chomhairle Leabharlanna (The Library Council) in 1948. Supplements the regular library services of local authorities, educational institutions and learned societies, and the services of public and special libraries generally, by providing books for study and research both from its own stock and by means of inter-library loans. Abbreviated ICLS.

Irish Manuscripts Commission.   Set up in October 1928 (under a warrant of the President of the Executive Council of Saorstát Éireann) to report on collections of manuscripts and papers of literary, historical and general interest, relating to Ireland, whether in private or public ownership, and also to arrange for and supervise the execution of programmes of publication. Since September 1970, the Commission has been responsible for a Survey of Business Records throughout the Republic of Ireland. Financed by government vote under the Department of Education. Publishes *Analecta Hibernica* (irreg.) and many books of calendars, abstracts, reports etc. Abbreviated IMC.

Irish Society for Archives (Cumann Cartlannaiochta Eirann).   Founded in December 1980 'to stimulate, encourage and co-ordinate the work of the many individuals, authorities and societies interested in the conservation and use of archives in Ireland'. Membership is available to students, individuals and organizations. Financed by members' subscriptions. Publishes *Irish Archives Bulletin* (a.). Abbreviated ISA.

Irish Style.   An eighteenth-century style of book decoration distinguished by a large centre lozenge of inlaid fawn leather.

IRLA.   Independent Research Libraries Association; an association of American major research collections, formed in 1972 to safeguard the interests of members, and promote their development. Members are: American Antiquarian Society, American Philosophical Society, Folger Shakespeare Library, Hagley Museum and Library, Linda Hall Library, Historical Society of Pennsylvania, Huntington Library, Library Company of Philadelphia, Massachusetts Historical Society, Pierpoint Morgan Library, Newberry Library, New York Academy of Medicine, New York Historical Society, New York Public Library, Virginia Historical Society.

IRS-Dialtech.   The UK link to the ESA-IRS HOST (*q.v.*).

IRT.   INSTITUTE OF REPROGRAPHIC TECHNOLOGY (*q.v.*).

ISA.   International Federation of National Standardizing Associations. *See entry under International Organization for Standardization.*

ISA.   *See Information Science Abstracts.*

Isadore Gilbert Mudge Citation.   *See Mudge Citation, Isadore Gilbert.*

Isarithms.   *Synonymous with* ISOPLETHS (*q.v.*).

ISBD.   The International Meeting of Cataloguing Experts (Copenhagen, 1969) organized by IFLA, established a basis for internationally uniform descriptive cataloguing practices, and set up a Working Group to develop an International Standard Bibliographic Description (ISBD). The first edition of this appeared in 1971, and in subsequent years further specialist groups were formed. The ISBD programme has been IFLA's major contribution to bibliographic standardization, and is a central part of the programme for UNIVERSAL BIBLIOGRAPHIC CONTROL (*q.v.*).

Published ISBDs are
ISBD(M) (Monographs) 1978 (revised edition)
ISBD(S) (Serials) 1977
ISBD(G) (General) 1977 [The framework document]
ISBD(CM) (Cartographic Materials) 1977
ISBD(NBM) (Non-book Materials) 1977
ISBD(A) (Antiquarian) 1980
ISBD(PM) (Printed Music) 1980
ISBD(CP) (Component Parts) 1988
ISBD(CF) (Computer Files) 1989

Each ISBD takes descriptive information from the item itself, and not according to a rigid code; ISBDs have been adopted and incorporated into several cataloguing codes, including AACR 2 and recent German and Japanese equivalents. The texts of the ISBD's appear in sixteen languages. In order to maintain the ISBDs the IFLA Section on Cataloguing agreed at the IFLA Conference (Manila, 1980) to a five-year review, so that the various texts will be co-ordinated, and will form the basis for descriptive cataloguing worldwide.

ISBN.   Acronym for International Standard Book Number. A number which is given to every book or edition of a book before publication to identify the publisher, the title, the edition and volume number. The ISBN consists of ten digits (arabic 0 to 9) the first group of which is a group identifier and indicates a national geographical, language or other convenient group. The other digits comprising the ISBN are grouped to indicate the publisher and the title or edition of a title; the final digit serves as a check digit. Each group of numbers is separated by a space or a hyphen. The ISBN system was a development of the STANDARD BOOK NUMBER (*q.v.*) system and was recommended for international use by the International Organization for Standardization (ISO) in October 1969 being accepted by the delegates to the plenary session then and circulated to all member bodies in 1970. The numbers comprising the ISBN are the same as a national SBN plus a preceding group identifier, and are allocated by the appropriate national standard book numbering agency. *See also ISSN, Standard Book Numbering Agency.*

ISDN. Integrated Services Digital Network; the latest technological advance in the development of the public telecommunications network. High quality rapid date and facsimile transmission will be feasible, and such services as video-conferencing. Satellite services form a part of the ISDN concept. A regular service was established in West Germany in 1988 and there are ambitious plans for development both there and in France.

ISDS. Acronym for INTERNATIONAL SERIALS DATA SYSTEM. An international network of operational centres (established in 1973 within the framework of the UNISIST (*q.v.*) programme) which are jointly responsible for the creation and maintenance of computer-based data banks. Objects: to (a) develop and maintain an international register of serial publications containing all the necessary information for identifying the serials; (b) define and promote the use of a standard code (ISSN – *q.v.*) for identifying each serial; (c) facilitate retrieval of scientific and technical information in serials; (d) make this information currently available to all countries, organizations or individual users; (e) establish a network of communication between libraries, secondary information services, publishers of serial literature and international organizations; (f) promote international standards for bibliographic description, communication formats, and information exchange in the area of serial publications. The system has an International Centre (IC) in Paris and also national and regional centres; the International Centre delegates to the national and regional centres (when these have been formed) allocation of ISSNs in respect of serials published in their respective areas. The British Library is the national centre for the UK, and the Library of Congress for the US. The IC handles the input of ISDS from countries that do not yet have a national centre. *See also ISSN.* The IC publishes *ISDS Bulletin* (q.).

Isephodic Map. One which shows the equal cost of travel, places of equal freight rates being connected by isephodes similar to isochrones.

ISG. *See Information Services Group.*

ISI. *See Institute for Scientific Information.*

ISI Award. An award offered annually to the author of the best paper published in each volume of the *Journal of Information Science.* The award is made by the Institute for Scientific Information.

Island Bookcase. *See Island Stack.*

ISKO. *See International Society for Knowledge Organization.*

Island Case. A bookcase (usually double-sided) which is so placed that readers can walk all around it.

Island Stack. A book STACK (*q.v.*) which is placed away from the wall so that readers can walk all round it. Also called 'Island bookcase'.

ISLIC. *See Israel Society of Special Libraries and Information Centres.*

ISMN. International Standard Music Number; a consultative document was issued in August 1986 by the International Association of Music Libraries (UK) as a draft standard. In 1983 the Trade and Copyright Sub-committee of IAML (UK) began a full investigation of ISBN's applied to music, and found there was no possibility of complete coverage of music; plans for the ISMN followed from this investigation.

ISO. INTERNATIONAL ORGANIZATION FOR STANDARDIZATION (*q.v.*).

Isobars. Lines on a map which connect places with the same barometric pressure.

Isobaths. Lines on a map joining points on the sea bed which have an equal depth. Such lines show the relief of the sea bed, just as CONTOURS (*q.v.*) show the relief of the land by joining places of equal altitude. Areas between isobaths are coloured in varying shades of blue.

Isochronic Map. One which shows possible progress of travel in all directions from a given centre in certain specified time intervals.

Isocrymes. Lines on a map which connect places with the same degree of frost.

ISODOC. Abbreviation for International Information Centre for Standards in Information and Documentation which was established by agreement between Unesco and ISO and is located at the Secretariat of ISO/TC 46. The Centre is designed to facilitate and promote the availability and application of standards in the area of information and documentation and related fields by (a) collecting, evaluating and storing information on standards, (b) disseminating this information.

Isogones. Lines on a map which connect places with equal angles of magnetic variation. Also called 'Isogonic lines'.

Isogonic Chart. One which shows lines connecting places of equal magnetic declination or variation.

Isograms. *Synonymous with* ISOPLETHS.

Isohalines. Lines on a map joining points in the oceans which have equal salinity.

Isohels. Lines on a map which connect places with the same amount of sunshine over a certain period.

Isohyets. Lines on a map which connect places with the same amount of rainfall over a certain period.

Isohypses. Lines on a map which connect places with the same elevation.

Isolate. (*Classification*) 1. A generic term applicable to all the three planes – Idea, Notation, Words – in the Colon Classification, and indicating a division of a FACET (*q.v.*). Also called 'Isolate focus'. In addition to COMMON ISOLATES (*q.v.*), there are Time, Space and Language isolates used to indicate periods of time, geographical division, and languages respectively. 2. The name of anything that can exist and behave as a unit or a word expressing its behaviour. Isolates are taken from the literature of a subject. 3. A single component ('ingredient') of a compound subject.

Isonephs. Lines on a map which connect places with the same amount of cloud over a certain period.

Isopleth Map. A quantitative aerial map on which the geographical distribution of the elements is shown by lines of equal value, such as contours, isobars, isohyets and isotherms. *See also Isopleths.*

Isopleths. Lines on a map which connect places of equal density or value of distribution of any specific element. Also called 'Isarithms' and 'Isograms'. If they connect places of equal temperature they are called 'isotherms'; of equal rainfall, 'isohyets'; of barometric pressure, 'isobars'; of magnetic variation, 'isogones'; of sunshine, 'isohels'; of frost, 'isocrymes'; of clouds, 'isonephs'; of equal elevation, 'isohypses'. They connect an average number of individual units. Lines which connect a continuous value, such as temperature, are called 'isarithms'.

ISORID. The International Information System on Research in Documentation established by Unesco in co-operation with FID, is charged with collecting, organizing, analyzing, storing and diffusing information on research and development in the fields of information, documentation, libraries and archival records management. In order to achieve the objectives of ISORID more effectively the following policy has been adopted and approved by the Intergovernmental Council for the General Information Programme of Unesco:

- the extension of co-operation with the FID with a view to avoiding the duplication of activities between FID and Unesco;
- the extension of ISORID by adding Member States which do not yet participate and by the inclusion in the system of information on research in the archive field;
- the improvement of the system's functioning in order to allow specialists maximum use of reported research results.

Consequently, Unesco and FID have concluded an arrangement on co-operation in order to eliminate competition and duplication of efforts. This arrangement covers the following points:

(a) all information on research is sent directly to FID;
(b) FID assigns descriptors to this information using the *UNESCO Thesaurus*;
(c) all relevant information received is published by FID in its periodical bulletin *R & D Projects in Documentation and Librarianship*.

Isoseismal Lines. Lines on a map joining places which have suffered an equal intensity of shock from an earthquake. Such lines usually form closed curves round their seismic focus.

Isotherms. Lines on a map which connect places with the same temperature at a particular instant or having the same average temperature over a certain period.

Israel Library Association. Founded in 1952 to raise professional standards of all types of libraries and improve the working conditions of librarians. Membership is open to anyone who has held a permanent position in a library for one year or who has graduated from the Graduate Library School of the Hebrew University in Jerusalem. Publishes *Yad-la-kore (The*

Reader's Aid) – contains abstracts in English of the main articles. Abbreviated ILA.

Israel Society of Special Libraries and Information Centres.   Registered in August 1966 to encourage and promote efficient utilization of knowledge through special libraries and information centres, to facilitate written and oral communication among its members, and to co-operate with other bodies with similar or allied interests in Israel and abroad. Publishes *Bulletin* (3 p.a.) *Contributions to information science* (irreg.). Abbreviated ISLIC.

ISSN.   Acronym for International Standard Serial Number – an internationally accepted code for the identification of serial publications; it is precise, concise, unique and unambiguous. The ISSN consists of seven arabic digits with an eighth which serves to verify the number in computer processing. A letter code indicating the country of publication may precede as an additional identifier; this is optional. The International Organization for Standardization Technical Committee 46 (ISO/TL 46) is the agency responsible for the development of the ISSN. The organization responsible for the administration and assignment of ISSN is the International Centre (IC) of the International Serials Data System (ISDS) – (*q.v.*); this is supported by the French government and Unesco, and is situated in Paris. National and regional centres of ISDS are assuming responsibility for the registration and numbering of serials, but where these have not yet been established, this function is being performed by the IC. An ISSN is the tool for communicating basic information about a serial title with a minimum of error, and may be used by subscription agencies and publishers for such processes as ordering, invoicing and inventory control; authors may use it for copyright. It can be used by librarians for a number of administrative purposes. A serial may have an ISBN (*q.v.*) as well as an ISSN if the publication is one of a monographic series (each work being issued separately under a common title, generally in a uniform format with numeric designation), an annual or other work is a separately edited written publication related only to other works by having some relationship in content and similarity in format. The ISSN is assigned to the serial title whether 'dead' or 'alive' while the ISBN is assigned to each individual title or monograph in the series. *See also ISBN.*

Issue.   1. All the charges or other records representing books and other items on loan.   2. The number of items so issued.   3. The copies of a book in which the original sheets are used but which differ in some respects from copies previously issued (e.g. a new title-page, an additional appendix, the inclusion of a list of publisher's announcements, or different format paper edition).   4. The number of impressions (copies) of an old map or print made at a given time without any change being made in the plate.   5. A particular publication, complete in itself, of a serial or periodical which is issued at intervals or in parts. *See also Edition, First Edition, Impression, New Edition, Reprint, Revised Edition.*

Issue Date.   1. The date on which a publication was issued to a reader.   2. (*Publishing*) The specified day, date, month or period by which the date of publication of a particular issue of a serial may be identified.

Issue Desk. *See Circulation Desk.*

Issue Guides. Pieces of card, plastic or metal which project above the Issue (1) (*q.v.*) (the projection being numbered or lettered according to the method of arrangement) to facilitate the finding of records of books on loan. *See also Charge.*

Issue Number. The number given to a separately issued part of a serial to distinguish it from other issues. Numbers may run consecutively from the first issue onwards, but if the issues are divided into volumes, a new sequence of issue numbers commences with each volume; in this case they are printed on the cover, and also in each issue immediately after the volume number.

Issue Systems. *See Charging Methods, Circulation Control Systems.*

Issue Tray. A tray containing the Issue (1) (*q.v.*).

IT. Information Technology; a generic term to cover the acquisition, processing, storage and dissemination of information – textual, numerical, pictorial and vocal. The term is restricted to systems dependent on a microelectronics-based combination of computing and telecommunications technology.

ital. Abbreviation for italic.

Italian Libraries Association (Associazione Italiana Biblioteche). Founded 1930; based in Rome. Aims to promote library education, library services, improve status of librarians, and foster international co-operation. Publishes *Bollettino di Informazioni* (q.), and *AIB Natizie* (m.).

Italian Style. *See Aldine (Italian) Style.*

Italic. Sloping type, as distinguished from the normal, upright, Roman type, used to emphasize any special point, or for the names of publications, etc. It was first used by Aldus Pius Manutius in 1501, and was originally called Aldine or Chancery, and was based on a humanistic Italian handwriting of a somewhat earlier period. *This is italic* and is indicated in a MS. prepared for the printer by a single underlining. Abbreviated *ital.*

ITAP Report. A report produced in 1981 by the Information Technology Advisory Panel on *Wideband Cable Systems.* The Hunt Report (*q.v.*) was a response to this document.

ITC. *See International Translations Centre.*

Item. (*Information retrieval*) In an index, the reference to the document. Also the document itself, whether a book, serial, abstract, article, photograph or microform, etc. *See also Compresence, Feature, Term.*

Item Cards. Cards used to record information by means of coloured tabs, holes or notches in connection with some form of Co-ordinate Indexing (*q.v.*). *See also Feature Card.*

Item Entry. In information retrieval, the entry of particulars of a document under a heading or symbol identifying the document. This is the traditional method used in library catalogues. It is also the method used on edge-slotted cards. Also called 'Document system'. *See also Term Entry.*

Iterative Searching. The searching for information or a document by a librarian for a user, the librarian finding such material as will meet the user's needs. A subsequent search, or searches, may be required, based on the use made of this material and the user's further request/s. This kind of search is modified at intervals and not continuously as with HEURISTIC SEARCHING (*q.v.*).

IV. *See Interactive Video.*

Ivory Board. A good quality card, made from wood, and used for printing.

IYL. INTERNATIONAL YOUTH LIBRARY (*q.v.*).

J. D. Stewart Travelling Bursary. *See under Stewart Travelling Bursary, J.D.*

Jacket. *Synonymous with* BOOK JACKET (*q.v.*).

Jacket Band. A strip of paper wrapped round a book-jacket to emphasize some sales aspect.

Jacketed Film. Microfilm which has been inserted in a FILM JACKET (*q.v.*). *See also Microfilm Jacket.*

Jaconet. Cotton material, glazed on one side, and used to line and strengthen the spines of books.

James Report. The Report of a British Committee of Enquiry into Teacher Education and Training, of which Lord James of Rushden was Chairman, was published in January 1972. It produced recommendations which were incorporated in the White Paper published on 6 December 1972, entitled *Education: a framework for expansion* (Cmnd. 5174).

Jane Addams Award. *See Addams Award, Jane.*

JANET. Acronym for the Joint Academic Network; an extensive network linking UK universities, polytechnics, research councils and the British Library. The network can be used to send commands, mail and data files from most participants to most others. It can also log on interactively to a remote machine, and thus access library catalogues.

JANET User Group. Started 1987 to support the activities of JANET (*q.v.*). Abbreviated JUGL. In 1989 a major initiative – Project Jupiter – was launched to ensure that all UK university libraries are linked to JANET and have staff trained in its use and services. The University of Glasgow has contracted to run Project Jupiter.

Jannon, Jean. A master printer in Paris in 1610, who, due to his Protestant leanings, went to Sedan where he printed for the Calvinist Academy and issued one of the finest and earliest of French specimen books in 1621.

Jansenist Style. A very simple binding named after Cornelius Jansen, the seventeenth century Bishop of Ypres, decorated only by a centrepiece (often armorial) and corner fleurons, or devoid of ornamentation on the outside of the covers, but with elaborate DOUBLURES (*q.v.*) tooled with DENTELLE (*q.v.*) borders.

Japan Information Center of Science and Technology. *See JICST.*

Japan Library Association (Nippon Toshokan Kyokai). Founded 1892. Based in Tokyo. Aims to develop library services, unite librarians, and encourage research in librarianship. Publishes *Toshokan Zasshi* (m.).

Japanese Paper. A paper, or tissue, in varying substances, having a silky texture; it is handbeaten from the bark fibres of the mulberry tree, or in imitation thereof. Used for printing, etchings, photogravures, books; also used for binding. 'French Japon' is a good imitation, it is less expensive but not so strong.

Japanese Style. *See Chinese Style.*

Japanese Vellum. An extremely costly, strong hand-made Japanese paper with a firm glossy surface, and a creamy tint. It is much used for engravings, and diplomas, or where a very durable paper is required. It will not withstand india-rubber, and must be handled very carefully. An imitation is made by treating thick ordinary paper with sulphuric acid.

JCC. *See Joint Consultative Council.*

Jeffreys Report, Friedman. *See Friedman-Jeffreys Report.*

Jenkins Bibliographical Award, John H. This award is offered annually by Union College, Schenectady, New York, for a bibliographical work of unusual merit bearing an imprint date two years before the year of the Award. It is named after John H. Jenkins, bookseller, of Austin, Texas, who returned to Union College the $2000 reward given him for the recovery of J. J. Audubon's 'elephant folio' of the *Birds of America* which had been stolen from Schaffer Library, Union College, in June 1971, on condition that the College match it and establish a bibliographical prize.

Jenson. A type face named after Nicolas Jenson (1420–80), a French printer who went to Venice in 1468 and had his own printing works there. 'The world's first great type designer, perhaps the greatest in all typographical history' – *McMurtrie*. He used his 'perfect roman letter' in *De praeparatione evangelica* by Eusebius, 1470; this served as the model for Morris's Golden type and for Benton's Cloister. Jenson was working in Venice, and his type became a pattern for all future type designs. The Monotype Centaur, designed by Bruce Rogers, is based on Jenson. The letters are open, dignified, clear and legible, of even colour and perfect harmony. The contrast between thick and thin strokes is slight; the serifs are blunt with very small brackets.

Jessup Report (UK). *A Report on the Supply and Training of Librarians* prepared by the Library Advisory Councils for England and Wales under the chairmanship of F. W. Jessup. (HMSO 1968.)

Jeté en Moule. ('Cast in a mould'). Mould metal type for use in printing. Also called 'Get en mol'.

Jewett's Code. A code of cataloguing rules prepared by Charles Coffin Jewett, Librarian of the Smithsonian Institution, Washington, and published as the second part of *The Smithsonian report on the construction of catalogues of libraries, and their publication by means of separate stereo-titles*, 1852.

Jewish Librarians Association. Founded in 1946 in the USA to advance the interests of Jewish libraries and the professional status of Jewish librarians; to promote publications of Jewish bibliographical interest. Abbreviated JLA. It was merged in June 1966 with the Jewish Library Association to form the ASSOCIATION OF JEWISH LIBRARIES (*q.v.*) of which it is an autonomous Division.

Jewish Library Association.   Founded in 1962 in the UUA 'to promote and improve library service and standards in Jewish communities; to serve as a centre for the dissemination of Judaica, library information and guidance; to encourage the establishment of new Judaica libraries'. Published *Newsletter* (3 a year). It was merged in June 1966 with the Jewish Librarians Association to form the ASSOCIATION OF JEWISH LIBRARIES (*q.v.*) of which it is an autonomous Division.

JFR.   Joint Fiction Reserve (*q.v.*).

JICST.   The Japan Information Center of Science and Technology, set up in 1957 to co-ordinate information activities in Japan for the advancement of science and technology. JICST collects 14,000 scientific periodicals from some 50 countries, and disseminates this information through JOIS (JICST Online Service) set up in 1986, published abstract services, and a range of other facilities. JOIS files include Science and Technology, Medical Science, Current Research, and Government Reports, as well as more specialized databases and imported files. JICST is also the Japanese base for STN INTERNATIONAL (*q.v.*) and co-operates with other national organizations in the information industry, for example FID, ICSTI, ASIS and INIST.

Jigsaw Puzzle Library.   *See British Jigsaw Puzzle Library.*

JLA.   Jewish Librarians Association (*q.v.*).

JMRT.   *See Junior Members Round Table.*

Joanna.   A light roman type designed by Eric Gill in 1930. It is remarkable for its small capitals which do not reach the height of the ascenders, themselves not tall.

Job Audit.   *See Staff Appraisal.*

Job Description.   *See Job Specification.*

Job File.   A collection of SEARCH RECORDS (*q.v.*). The record of the results of the enquiries may be kept separately from the search records. In either case they serve as a record of information and may save searching on a subsequent occasion when the enquiry is repeated.

Job Press.   A small platen printing press which is used for producing small items such as handbills.

Job Printer.   One who prints small items such as labels, leaflets, forms, stationery, handbills, etc., in small quantities.

Job Sharing.   A system whereby a vacant job may be offered to two people who will divide the hours of attendance between them. Administratively the post remains one full-time job, but the system encourages the employment of people who would be unable to consider full-time employment. Unlike ordinary part-time work job sharing confers contractual rights on each employee.

Job Specification.   A detailed paper laying down objectives for a post, with criteria for achieving them, and suggesting methods of evaluating success. A less specific outline may be termed a *job description. See also Personnel Specification.*

Jobber. In America, a wholesale bookseller who stocks many copies of various kinds of books issued by different publishers and supplies them to retailers and libraries. There are two types of jobber (1) those who stock mainly current text-books, trade, and technical books, and (2) those who stock only remainders.

John Carter Brown Library. *See Brown Library, John Carter.*

John R. Rowe Memorial Award. The new name of the EXHIBITS ROUND TABLE AWARD (*q.v.*).

John Rylands University Library of Manchester (UK). The magnificently endowed John Rylands Library, Manchester, with its special collections of books including those of incunabula, manuscripts, and rare books, was merged administratively in 1972 with the existing large research library of the University to form the University Library with this title. The collection now comprises over 2,000,000 books; some 8000 periodical titles are currently taken, and over 300,000 titles are on microfilm. The extensive holdings of MSS., early printed and rare books are housed in the superb Deansgate building, the home of the original John Rylands Library, and an additional building.

Joined Hand. Handwriting in which the letters are all joined to one another. The opposite of DISJOINED HAND (*q.v.*).

Joiner's Press. The name given to the earliest hand printing presses which were introduced about 1440. Made of wood, they were similar to wine presses, the pressure needed to press the paper on to type being applied by means of a screw turning on to a flat platen.

Joint. 1. One of the two parts of the covering material that bend when the covers of a book are opened. 2. The strips of cloth, leather or other material that are used to reinforce the end-papers. 3. The grooves, formed by the backing process, which are made to receive the boards when binding a book. *See also Hinge.*

Joint Author. One who writes in collaboration with another, or several other writers. The parts written by each are not always indicated; in fact, the contribution of each is usually not distinguishable.

Joint Authorship. (*Cataloguing*) Describes the authorship of books in which two or more persons collaborate, the parts written by each not being specified.

Joint Board. Two or more British library authorities which are authorized by an order of the Secretary of State made after consultation, and with the agreement of the authorities concerned, to be a library authority and provide a library service covering the areas of the separate library authorities before the formation of the joint board. Provision for their formation is made in Section 5 of the Public Libraries and Museums Act, 1964. *See also Library Authority.*

Joint Catalogue. One containing entries for the books in two or more libraries.

Joint Consultative Council (UK). A forum for librarianship organizations to discuss common issues; members are Aslib, Institute of Information Scientists, Library Association, Society of Archivists, SCONUL and COPOL (*qq.v.*). Abbreviated JCC.

Joint Enterprise. *See PUPLIS.*

Joint Fiction Reserve (UK). A scheme whereby a number of libraries agree to hold novels permanently. The authors are allocated according to alphabetical sequence amongst the co-operating libraries by agreement. The first scheme of this kind was started in London and included the keeping of all copies which were redundant in Metropolitan libraries as well as buying all new titles by the allocated authors. A similar scheme was adopted in the Northern Regional Bureau and on 1 January 1962 a National Joint Fiction Reserve scheme (abbreviated NJFR) which is as co-operative effort of all regional bureaux outside London and the South-Eastern area began to operate. Each region is responsible for a certain section of the alphabet. This scheme provides only for the purchase and retention of new publications and is not retrospective. Allocation by author amongst the regions is as follows:

A-C	North-Western	K-M	West Midlands
D-F	Northern	N-S	Yorkshire
G-J	East Midlands	T-Z	South Western

See also Association of Metropolitan Chief Librarians, Library Association of Ireland.

Joint Work. A work by two or more authors in which the individual contributions are not distinguishable.

JOIS. *See JICST.*

Jones (Mary Vaughan) Award. Awards by the Welsh National Centre for Children's Literature for various categories of Welsh and English children's literature.

Jordan Report (UK). A survey: *Working Conditions in Libraries*, edited by P. Jordan, and published by the Association of Assistant Librarians, 1968.

Joseph W. Lippincott Award. *See Lippincott Award, Joseph W.*

Journal. 1. A newspaper or periodical. Particularly a periodical issued by a society or institution and containing news, proceedings, transactions and reports of work carried out in a particular field. 2. A record of a person's activities day by day.

Journalese. Words and phrases commonly used by journalists. Hackneyed phrases.

Journalism. The profession of compiling, writing for and editing newspapers, periodicals, etc.

Journalist. One who edits or contributes to a newspaper or periodical.

Journal of the House of Commons and of the House of Lords. *See Parliamentary Papers.*

Judicial Writ. One issuing from a Court of Law.

JUGL. JANET USER GROUP (*q.v.*).

Jumbled Type. *Synonymous with* PIE (*q.v.*).

Junior Assistant. A library assistant who does not supervise the work of other assistants.

Junior Book. A book for children.

Junior Department. *Synonymous with* JUNIOR LIBRARY and CHILDREN'S LIBRARY (*q.v.*).

Junior Librarian. One who works with children, or in a children's library.

Junior Library. *Synonymous with* CHILDREN'S LIBRARY (*q.v.*).

Junior Members Round Table. A group of the ALA. Abbreviated JMRT.

Juris. The information retrieval and inquiry system of the US Department of Justice.

Justification. (*Cataloguing*) The provision of data, especially in the form of a note, introduced into an added entry, cross-reference, or subject heading for the sole purpose of making clear why the particular entry was provided. An entry treated in this way is said to be justified.

Justifying. (*Printing*) In typesetting, equally spacing out letters and words to a given measure, so that each line will be of the same length.

Jute. A plant which contains weaker and less durable fibres than flax or hemp and which are somewhat easily rotted by water. Jute paper was originally made from old rope, burlap, jute or manilla clippings, but is now usually made from sulphite stock (woodpulp used for making kraft paper) and is the material from which heavy wrapping paper and large bags for such materials as cement, coal and potatoes are made. 'Jute tissue' is made from old sacks and similar material and is used for tailors' patterns.

Jute Board. A strong, light-weight board, made from jute fibres, and used for binding books.

Juvenile Book. Trade name, now rarely used, for a book for children.

Juvenile Department. *Synonymous with* CHILDREN'S LIBRARY (*q.v.*).

Juvenile Library. *Synonymous with* CHILDREN'S LIBRARY (*q.v.*).

K. Abbreviation for *kilo*; i.e. 1000. *See Byte.*

Kaiser Index. *See Kaiser's System.*

Kaiser's System. A method of subject indexing propounded by J. Kaiser in his *Systematic indexing*, 1911.

Kaula Gold Medal, Professor P. N. A major international award, started in 1975, and presented to outstanding figures in the world of librarianship and documentation. Awarded by the International Awards Committee of the Professor Kaula Endowment for Library and Information Science. Professor Kaula was head of the library school at Benares Hindu University for many years. Recipients of the medal include Bernard Palmer, Jesse Shera, and Preben Kirkegaard.

KC. The Kyle Classification. *See entry under Classification for Social Sciences.*

Keep down. (*Printing*) To use capitals sparingly.

Keep in. (*Printing*) 1. To set matter closely so that it does not take up more space than necessary. 2. Type matter with narrow openings between the words. *See also Drive Out.*

Keep out. (*Printing*) To set matter widely spaced so that it takes up as many lines as possible.

Keep standing. An order not to distribute the type after running off, pending possible reprinting.

Keep up.   (*Printing*) To use capitals freely.

Keepsake.   1. A lavishly printed and ornately bound gift book, often consisting of poetry; many such books were issued annually in the first half of the nineteenth century.   2. Printed commemorative publications issued by clubs or other organizations for special occasions.   3. Before the end of the seventeenth century it was the custom in some English printing establishments to honour visitors by printing their names and the date in an ornamental style – usually in a framework of flowers and rules – and present it to them as a memento. The guest witnessed the setting of the type and pulled the press. The practice became more general during the eighteenth century but declined in the last quarter; it was reserved for distinguished persons in the nineteenth century, for the most exalted of whom the printing was done on silk or satin.

Kells, Book of.   An illuminated MS. of the Latin Gospels, found in the ruins of the Abbey of Kells, Ireland, and thought to date from the eighth or early ninth century. It has been in the Library of Trinity College, Dublin, since 1661. It is an important example of Hiberno-Saxon art.

Kelmscott Press.   A private press founded and directed by William Morris between 1891 and his death in 1896, although the Press continued until 1898. The three founts of type used (Golden, 1890; Troy, 1891; Chaucer, 1892) were designed by Morris and cut by E. P. Prince in the years stated but not used until 1892. The books issued were excellent examples of book production. The Golden Type face was named after Caxton's *Golden Legend* in which it was to have been used first. It was, however, first used in 1891, and for six books, before the *Golden Legend* was printed in 1892. *See also Jenson.*

Kent (*Sir* Peter) Conservation Book Prize.   An annual award administered by the Book Trust for a book on environmental issues published in the UK.

Kenyon Report.   The 'Report on public libraries in England and Wales' by the Public Libraries Committee (Chairman Frederic G. Kenyon), presented by the Board of Education to Parliament in 1927. (HMSO, 1927) (Cmd. 2868). The Committee had been asked to enquire into the adequacy of library provision under the Public Libraries Acts, and the means of extending and completing such provision.

Kept Book.   *Synonymous with* RESERVED BOOK (*q.v.*).

Kerfs.   Shallow saw-cuts, about 1/32 inch deep, made between 1/4 and 1/2 inch from the ends of the gathered sections of a book. The loops of the kettle stitches formed by the sewing of the section, or the cords, fit snugly into the kerfs and leave the back of the sewn sections smooth.

Kern.   (*Printing*) Any part of the face of a type letter which extends over the edge of the body and rests on the shoulder of the type adjacent to it, as *fi, fl.*

Kerned.   Said of a type letter which has part of the face projecting beyond the metal body on which it is cast.

Kettle Stitch.   The stitch made at the head and tail of a book in hand sewing, by which the thread of one section is fastened to the thread of the one on each side. The term is frequently regarded as being a corruption of 'catch up stitch', but it may be derived from the German *Ketten-stich* (chain stitch) or *Kettel stich*, (the stitch that forms a little chain). Also called 'Catch stitch'.

Key. 1. The block or FORME (*q.v.*) in letterpress printing, and the plate or stone in lithography, which acts as a guide for position and registration of the other colours. Also called KEY PLATE (*q.v.*). 2. A binder's tool for securing the bands when sewing. 3. An explanation of the conventional signs or symbols used on a map or diagram.

Key in. The action of inserting a note in the margins of the typescript of a book to indicate the exact or approximate position where illustrations, or other items not incorporated in the text, are to appear.

Key-Letter-in-Context. *See KLIC.*

Key Plate. 1. The plate of maximum detail in a set of colour plates to which other plates in the same set are registered during the printing process. 2. Any printing plate that is used to get others into register. Also called KEY (*q.v.*).

Key Term. *Synonymous with* KEYWORD (*q.v.*).

Keyboard. (*Verb*) To type (or otherwise record by depressing keys) data or information, usually for direct computer input and processing.

Keyboard. (*Noun*) Device containing keys and connected to a computer. The most usual means of communicating with a computer.

Keyboarding. Producing type, proofs, tape or film by manual operation of a keyboard machine.

Keypad. A hand-held device with numerical keys, used to input signals by infra-red rays to control electronic equipment (e.g. remote control of television).

Keypunch. A manually operated mechanical device which punches holes in pre-determined positions to record information on punched cards.

Keys, Library. *See Library Keys.*

Keyword. (*Information retrieval*) Grammatical element which conveys the signficant meaning in a document. Word indicating a subject discussed in a document. In a PERMUTED TITLE INDEX (*q.v.*), the word considered to be most indicative of the title is to be used as an ACCESS POINT (*q.v.*), and therefore is the keyword of the subject content of the document. *See also Catchword, KWAC.*

Keyword-and Context. *See KWAC.*

Keyword-in-Context. *See KWIC.*

Keyword-out-of-Context. *See KWOC.*

Keyword-out-of-Title. *See KWOT.*

Kier. The part of paper-making machinery used to boil the raw material (e.g. rags, esparto) especially under steam pressure. Also called 'Boiler'.

Kill. (*Printing*) Direction to the printer to melt down, or distribute, composed type matter which is no longer wanted. *See also Dead Matter, Live Matter.*

Killing. (*Printing*) Distribution of set-up type after use so that it may be used again.

Kilobyte. *See Byte.*

Kinderbox. A box about 2 feet square and 8 inches deep, divided into four compartments and standing on short legs. It holds large-page books for young children. Called in the USA a 'Cart'.

Kinetic Relation. (*Information retrieval*) A phase relation expressing motion, e.g. a person can move to, from, into, out of, through, off, onto, etc. *See also Phase.*

King (Coretta Scott) Awards. Annual awards, established 1970, given for the most outstanding text, and most imaginative illustrations by a black author and illustrator for children's books. Presented by the American Library Association.

King (Martin Luther) Memorial Prize. An annual UK award for a literary work reflecting the ideals of Dr. King, published in the UK.

King Report. The report of a committee of which Dr. Gilbert W. King was chairman, set up in 1961 to survey the application of automatic devices to the work of the Library of Congress and other general research libraries. The Report *Automation and the Library of Congress: a survey sponsored by the Council on Library Resources, Inc.* was published by the Library of Congress in January 1963. The MARC (Machine Readable Cataloguing) project was a result of this. *See MARC.*

KIS. Acronym for the Kirklees Information Service which was originally formed in 1959, as the Huddersfield and District Information Service (HADIS), and membership was confined to organizations in Huddersfield and its immediate vicinity. However, since local government reorganization in 1973, the service has been extended to cover the metropolitan district of Kirklees, UK.

KLIC. Acronym of Key-Letter-In-Context, a method which was first developed by UKCIS (*q.v.*) for producing permuted term lists wherein all terms are sorted on each letter in every term with the balance of the term displayed. This method is useful for selecting truncation fragments.

Klischograph. A German electronic photoengraving machine for producing plastic, zinc, copper or magnesium half-tone plates. Blocks can be engraved for monochrome and for three- and four-colour printing. The machine was invented by Dr. Rudolph Hell of Kiel and is also known in Great Britain as the 'Clichograph'.

Knife-folder. A folding machine which has a blunt-edged knife parallel with and above the slot formed by two parallel and constantly revolving rollers. When a sheet of paper is placed above these with an edge against a stop the knife descends and presses the sheet between the rollers which carry it away, the fold being made where the knife made contact. *See also Buckle-folder.*

Knowledge-based System. *See Expert System.*

Knowledge Classification. A classification used for any branch of knowledge, but which cannot be adapted for classifying books until a generalia class, form classes and divisions, a notation, and an index have been added.

Knowledge Industry Publications, Inc. Award for Library Literature. A cash award made to an individual for an outstanding contribution to the literature of librarianship. Administered by the American Library Association Awards Committee.

Knowledge Warehouse.   A project supported by British Library, Department of Trade and Industry, and Publishers Databases Ltd, which investigated the technical, legal and commercial aspects of archiving and exploiting a collection of machine-readable publications. Report issued 1987.

Korean Library Association.   Founded on 16 April 1955 to contribute to cultural advancement and social improvement in Korea by accelerating the spread of libraries and the betterment of the library service. Its objects are: to study the principles of library organization and administration; to publish books and other materials about library services; to train library personnel and improve their working conditions; to provide guidance to any individual or organization in planning a library; to prepare selected lists of Korean books; to activate the national reading movement; to devise specifications for standard library furniture and equipment; to organize and operate a professional reference library; to co-operate with international organizations concerned with library services. Publishes *KLA Bulletin* (m). Abbreviated KLA.

Kraft Paper.   A strong calendered brown paper of medium colour and with prominent chain-lines (*see Laid Paper*) used specially for wrapping purposes. It is sometimes strengthened with hessian or tar to make waterproof wrapping paper of great strength. *See also Bleached Kraft.*

Kursiv.   *See Cursive.*

Kurzweil Reading Machine.   A combination of a camera, computer and voice synthesizer which converts the printed word into spoken word for the benefit of blind people.

KWAC.   Acronym for Keyword-and-Context. An index of titles of documents permutated to bring each significant word to the beginning, in alphabetical order, followed by the remaining words which follow it in the title, and then followed by that part of the original title which came before the significant word. *See also KWIC, KWOC.*

KWIC.   Acronym for Keyword-in-Context. 1. A method of Permutation Indexing (*q.v.*) which uses a computer to permute automatically words in periodical article titles, and to group titles in which the same words occur. When the index is printed, the keywords in each index line are printed at the middle of the type measure and thus appear under one another in alphabetical order in a column. The full measure of the line is filled by printing as much of the title immediately before and after the keyword as can be accommodated.   2. A listing, usually of title, or significant sentences from an abstract, with the keywords put in a fixed position within the title or sentence and arranged in alphabetic order in a column.   3. An index based on the cyclic permutation of words; each 'substantive' term being brought to a predetermined position and alphabetized. *See also Co-ordinate Indexing, KWAC, KWOC, WADEX.*

KWOC.   Acronym for Keyword-out-of-Context, a refinement of KWIC (*q.v.*). Titles are printed in full under as many Keywords as the indexer considers useful; these may be chosen from a thesaurus or list of standard headings as well as from the title, and there is no limit to the source of Keywords. The Keywords are separated from the title on a line of their own and act as subject headings. *See also WADEX.*

KWOT. Acronym of Keyword-out-of-Title, a KWOC (*q.v.*) index, which is computer-produced by ABACUS (AB Atomic Energy Computerized User-oriented Services), the result of co-operation between the Royal Institute of Technology (Stockholm) and AB Atomenergi (Sweden).

Kyle Classification. *See Classification for Social Sciences.*

LA. LIBRARY ASSOCIATION (*q.v.*).

LA DDC Committee. *See Library Association Dewey Decimal Classification Committee.*

LAA. LIBRARY ASSOCIATION OF AUSTRALIA (*q.v.*).

Label. 1. A small strip of leather, usually of a different colour to that used for the binding of a book, placed on the spine and displaying one or more of the following: title, author's name, volume number, date. Also called 'Lettering pieces'. When two labels are used they are described as 'double lettering pieces'. Labels of paper were used on books bound in boards covered with paper. 2. (*Information retrieval*) In a machine-readable record, one or more characteristics which are written or attached to a set of data which contains information about the set, including its identification. *See also Tag.*

Label Title-page. The title and author's name printed near the top of an otherwise blank page, or protecting leaf, at the beginning of a book. Often called 'Label title', the name is given to the first form of title-page in early printed books (1470–1550). The earliest extant example is a Papal Bull of Pius II, printed in 1463 at Mainz, probably by Fust and Schöffer.

Labelled Notation. The style of the notation used in the COLON CLASSIFICATION (*q.v.*). Each main class is labelled with a letter, and each facet is first symbolized by combining the main class letter with a facet indicator; simple terms are represented by numerals.

Laboratory Collection. *Synonymous with* DEPARTMENTAL LIBRARY (*q.v.*).

LACAP. Acronym for Latin America Co-operative Acquisitions Program. Organized in 1960 as a result of the extension of the FARMINGTON PLAN (*q.v.*) to Latin America and the organization of the SALALM (*q.v.*) which recommended its formation; it is a co-operative enterprise that provides its participants with a steady flow of the printed materials currently published in all the countries of Latin America. The University of Texas, the New York Public Library and Stechert-Hafner Inc. were the initiators of the scheme.

Lace Border. *See Lacework 2.*

Laced On. *See Lacing-In.*

Lacework. 1. A border decoration on bindings, done by tooling, to represent lace. *See also Dentelle.* 2. Borders framing whole-page illustrations in nineteenth-century French books, the border-decoration consisting of punching the pattern out of the paper as in paper doyleys.

Lacing-In. (*Binding*) Attaching the boards by the operation of passing the slips or cords on which the book is sewn, and after they have been splayed out and moistened with paste, through holes pierced in the boards.

LACIRS. *See INCIRS.*

Lacuna. (*Pl.* LACUNAE). Gaps in the stock of a library, which await filling.

LAD. *See Office of Information Programmes and Services.*

LADSIRLAC. Abbreviation for Liverpool and District Scientific, Industrial and Research Library Advisory Council which was sponsored by the Liverpool City Council UK in 1955 to develop and improve information services to industry. One of three co-operative bodies entrusted with the co-ordination of an LIP (*q.v.*).

LAI. LIBRARY ASSOCIATION OF IRELAND (*q.v.*).

Laid In. Used in a note to a catalogue entry to indicate the inclusion in a record album or musical publication, of a leaflet or pamphlet relating to the music and its performance.

Laid Paper. Paper which, when held up to the light, shows thick and thin lines at right angles. They are caused by the weave of the dandy roll, or in hand-made paper by the mould having long thin wires placed very close together and fastened to thicker ones at intervals of about one inch. The horizontal thin ones are called 'wire-lines' or 'wire-marks' and the vertical thick ones 'chain-lines', 'chain-marks' or 'wide-lines'. To obtain the best impression when printing the wire-lines should run across the page and the chain-lines down it. *See also Watermark.*

LAIG. Library Association Industrial Group. *See Industrial Group.*

LAMA. LIBRARY ADMINISTRATION AND MANAGEMENT ASSOCIATION (*q.v.*) – division of ALA.

Lambert Scholarship, (Nancy Stirling). Established by Blackwell's, the Oxford booksellers, to encourage the investigation of matters of common concern to libraries and the book trade. The Scholarship takes its name from the grandmother of Sir Basil Blackwell, President of the firm. It was first awarded, in 1974, to Alastair John Allan.

Lambskin. A bookbinding leather with a smooth finish; it is similar in appearance to calf but less durable.

Laminated. A sheet of paper to which a sheet of clear plastic has been permanently adhered on one or both sides. Book jackets, leaves of books, or paper covers are treated in this way to strengthen them.

Lamination. A method of preserving frail papers or the thin or perishing leaves of books by placing them between two sheets of thin transparent thermoplastic material which when subjected to heat under pressure protects the paper by making it impervious to atmospheric conditions. *See also Silking.*

Lampblack. Pure carbon deposit; formerly the most important black pigment used in manufacturing printing inks. It was produced by burning pitch resin in a vessel in a tent made of paper or sheepskins. The smoke was deposited on the inside of the tent which was then beaten to cause the black to fall on to the floor. Impurities were removed by heating it several times until red-hot in an iron box with a small aperture at the top.

Lampoon. A satirical attack generally of a scurrilous but humorous character, upon a person, and written in prose or verse.

LAMSAC. Acronym of Local Authorities Management Services and Computer Committee which was established in 1967 to help advise members of the Local Authority Associations and River Authorities in England, Scotland and Wales on the introduction and use of management services and computers. Much of the research work carried out for the benefit of local government is undertaken by various 'panels' but LAMSAC undertakes some research through its staff, and commissions work to be executed by other specialist organizations and local authorities. It organizes general appreciation and specialist training courses on management services and computer services.

LAMSAC Report (UK). *The staffing of public libraries* 3 vols. 1976, published by the Department of Education and Science as No. 7 in their Library Information Series. It has been welcomed by the LA as a positive step forward in the assessment of staffing needs.

LAN. *See Local Area Network.*

LANCET. The LA/NCET (Library Association/National Council for Educational Technology) rules were published in 1973 as an effort to establish authoritative cataloguing standards for non-book materials. The rules were developed by the Library Association's Media Cataloguing Rule Committee with considerable support from NCET and the Aslib Audio-visual Group. They have now been superseded by later developments in the cataloguing of non-book materials.

LA-NET. Electronic mail network operated by the Library Association; launched 1988. *See also ALANET, LIBNET.*

L&HCB. LONDON AND HOME COUNTIES BRANCH (*q.v.*) (of the Library Association).

Landscape. A book or document that is wider than its height; one that is designed to be read with its longer edges towards the reader. More often called 'Oblong'.

Landscape Binding. A type of binding which has landscape views on its covers, the landscape views being drawn freehand with Indian ink or acid and later coloured, or printed by some means. They date between 1777 and 1821.

Landscape Page. A page on which graphs, tables, illustrations, etc. are printed so that their foot is parallel to the fore-edge of the page. Also called 'Broadside page'. *See also Turned.*

Lane (Allen) Award. *See Mind Book of the Year.*

Language Number. A facet which may form part of a BOOK NUMBER (*q.v.*) in the Colon Classification. It is obtained by translating the name of the language in which the book is written into appropriate symbols in accordance with the language schedule given in Chapter 5 of the Schedules. *See also Ethnic Numbers.*

Language of the Text. The language in which the text of a book is printed and which is not determinable from the title, e.g. *Faust.* In such a case the cataloguer may (1) add a note, e.g. 'Text in German and English'; (2) integrate a translator statement, e.g. 'Tr. into English by . . .'; (3) augment the heading, e.g. 'Goethe, Johann Wolfgang von. Faust. English'.

Language Sub-division. (*Classification*) Sub-division of a subject according to the language in which it is written, or sub-division of a language division in the philological class of a scheme of classification.

Lanston. *See Monotype.*

LANW. Library Association, North Western Branch. *See entry under North Western Branch.*

Lapidary Type. A fount of capital letters similar to those on Roman monumental inscriptions. Examples were cut by Erhard Ratdolt at Augsburg in 1505. *See also Square Capitals.*

Laptop. Small portable computer; usually battery-operated to be used on trains, planes etc.

LARC Association. Abbreviation for The Association for Library Automation Research Communications (formerly Library Automation, Research and Consulting Association), an international non-profit organization established in July 1969. In 1976 merged into WISE (*q.v.*).

Large Folio. A general term to indicate a large-sized folio book. *See also Folio 3.*

Large Paper Copy, or Edition. An impression of a book printed on larger and better quality paper than the usual trade edition, thus having wider margins. *See also Fine Paper Copy, Limited Edition, Small Paper Copy.*

Large Post. A sheet of printing paper measuring 16½ × 21 inches.

Large Royal. A sheet of printing paper measuring 20 × 27 inches.

LARRIE. Local Authorities Race Relations Information Exchange; a UK body set up in 1984 and jointly funded by the Local Government Training Board, Commission for Racial Equality, Home Office and the Department of the Environment. Acts as a clearing-house for documents on race issues produced by UK local authorities.

LAS. LIBRARY ASSOCIATION OF SINGAPORE (*q.v.*).

LASER. *See London & South Eastern Region.*

Laser Disc. *See Optical Digital Disk.*

Laser Optical Disk. *See Optical Digital Disk.*

Laser Printer. A printer which uses a laser beam to form an image on paper. It produces higher quality printing than traditional lineprinters, and can print on both sides of the paper.

Laser Viewdata Information Service. Operated by LASER (*q.v.*) initially with a grant from the British Library, aims to provide an information and consultancy service about viewdata and related topics. Abbreviated L-VIS.

Last Fold. *See Bolt.*

Later Cursive. A Latin manuscript handwriting which came in sequence between UNCIAL and HALF UNCIAL (*qq.v.*). Its main characteristics are ligatures (joined letters) and the uneven height of the letters, some of which ascended or descended beyond the normal letter limits – which had not previously occurred. This distinction between tall and small letters marked the first stage in the development of minuscules (lower-case letters).

Lateral Filing. Equipment which consists of pockets of tough paper, or linen, which are suspended (and usually move laterally within limits) from two rails placed one behind the other and running from left to right. They are made into fittings which will rest on shelves or as a complete filing cabinet.

Laterally Reversed. In documentary copying, reflecting the original as in a mirror. Also called 'Left-to-right-reversed'. *See also Right Reading.*

Lattice. (*Information retrieval*) The network of inter-relationships between specific subjects. A partially ordered system in which any two elements have a greatest lower bound and a least upper bound. *See also Bound.*

Lattice Stamp. (*Binding*) A decorative ornament, the distinguishing feature of which is a central diamond formed of lattice or criss-cross work.

Lattice Structure. (*Information retrieval*) The algebraic structure of an information file described as a network, or lattice, of units of information which are linked to each other and to document references.

Laura Ingalls Wilder Medal. *See Wilder Medal, Laura Ingalls.*

Law Binding. *See Law Calf.*

Law Calf. A leather binding using plain uncoloured calf or sheepskin. Mainly used for law books but now largely superseded by buckram cloth. Also called 'Fair calf', 'Law sheep'.

Law of Scattering. A 'law' deduced by Dr. S. C. Bradford (and later corrected by B. C. Vickery) who found that about a third of the articles on a subject are printed in the journals devoted to that subject, a further third appear in a larger number of journals devoted to related subjects, and the remaining third in an even larger number of journals in which such articles would not normally be expected to be published. According to the law of scattering, if Tx represents the number of journals having x references, T_2x the total number of journals having $2x$ references, etc., then: $Tx:T_2x:T_3x = 1:n:n^2$ where n may be any number depending on the value chosen for x.

Law Sheep. *Synonymous with* LAW CALF (*q.v.*).

Lay Edges. The edges of a sheet of paper which are laid against the front and side lay gauges of a printing or folding machine. The front edge is known as the 'gripper edge'.

Layout. 1. A plan, prepared for or by a printer, to show the arrangement of the matter, type faces, sizes of type, position of illustrations and captions, for a piece of printing. 2. The plan of an entire book.

Laystool. A stool on which white paper and printed sheets were laid close to the printing pressman's hand. By the nineteenth century a 'horse' with a sloping top had been evolved to take the paper and make it easier to pick sheets off the heap.

Lazerow (Samuel) Fellowship for Research in Acquisitions or Technical Services. An award of the ASSOCIATION OF COLLEGE AND RESEARCH LIBRARIES (*q.v.*).

LBI. LIBRARY BINDING INSTITUTE (*q.v.*).

LC. *See Library of Congress.*

l.c. Abbreviation for lower case. *See Lower Case Letters.*

LCF. Acronym of LIBRARIANS' CHRISTIAN FELLOWSHIP (*q.v.*).

LCLA. Lutheran Church Library Association (*q.v.*).

LCMARC. Library of Congress Machine Readable Cataloguing. Machine-readable tapes containing bibliographic records for United States publications. The tapes are compiled at the Library of Congress and are available on-line in the United Kingdom via Blaise-line. *See also MARC.*

Le Gascon Style. Modified Fanfare (*q.v.*) bindings of the early seventeenth century, in which the strapwork is retained, the enclosed spaces differentiated by inlaid leather of different colours, and the sprays lighter. Fine dotted scrolls are frequently enclosed in the geometrical compartments and often extended into lines and curves of remarkable lustre and elegance. These scrolls and other ornaments are given dotted lines known as pointillé, instead of unbroken lines. Not practised after about 1660.

Leab (Katherine and Daniel) American Book Prices Current Award. An award for bibliographic catalogues to exhibitions, administered by the Association of College and Research Libraries (*q.v.*).

Lead. (*Verb*) To insert leads between type or re-set on a larger body. A page of printed matter where the lines are well spaced out is said to be 'well leaded'.

Lead Moulding. A process for making electros or half-tone plates in which the base is lead instead of wax. Soft lead is forced into the forme under great (hydraulic) pressure and a mould of fine quality obtained. A copper shell is then deposited on the mould in the same manner as in wax moulding.

Leaded Matter. (*Printing*) Having the lines of type separated by 'leads', or cast on a larger body, as 8 pt. type on 9 pt. body, to achieve the same effect. In the latter case, the type is called 'Longbodied'. Type without 'leads' is said to be 'set solid'. 'Double-leaded' means a double space (usually 4 points) between lines of type. *See also Em, Leads, Pica, Solid Matter.*

Leader. 1. A short newspaper article expressing views or comments, and usually indicating the policy or editorial views of the proprietors of the paper. Fully, a leading article. 2. A portion of film at the beginning of a roll of film, and which is used for the threading of the film in a camera, processing machine, or projector. 3. (*Information retrieval*) In machine-readable records, the part of the record which precedes the information content, and which carries data needed to manipulate, identify or locate the information content.

Leader Writer. The writer of newspaper editorials, or leaders.

Leaders. A sequence of dots or hyphens to lead the eye from one word to another as in tabular work, or across a page as in a table of contents.

Leading Line. The top horizontal line on a standard ruled catalogue card; the one on which the author heading is entered.

Leads. Thin strips of lead which are less than type high, used to separate lines of type or to space them further apart. Type set on a larger body, such as 8 point on a 9 point body to give the same effect without the use of separate leads between each line, is called *long-bodied type*. Leads are usually made 1, 1½ (thin), 2 (middle) which is the usual leading, 3 (thick), and 4 points – known as 'double leaded' thick; when 6 point or more they are called 'clumps' and may be of wood or metal. When clumps are made of wood they are called 'reglets'. Spacing material of greater dimensions than 18 point is known as 'furniture'. *See also Leaded Matter, Solid Matter.*

Leaf. A sheet of paper, printed, and folded once forms a section of two leaves or four pages, and is called folio; folded twice, it forms a section of four leaves or eight pages and is called quarto. A leaf consists of two pages, one on each side, either of which may or may not be printed on. Usually the recto has an odd number, and the verso the subsequent number, but in reprints this may not be the case. Books with un-numbered leaves or pages may be described in a catalogue or bibliographical entry as containing a specific number (ascertained by counting) of pages or leaves – preferably the latter if the book was published before pagination was general – in the form '320 1'. *See also Foldings, Foliation, Plate, Section.*

Leaflet. A small sheet of paper folded once and printed on to make two to four pages following in the same sequence as in a book, but not stitched or bound. Often used to indicate a small, thin PAMPHLET (*q.v.*).

League of European Research Libraries. *See LIBER.*

Lean-Face Type. Type, the stems and other strokes of which have not their full width.

Lean Matter. *See Matter.*

Learning Resources Centre. A designation given to a school or college library in which the storage, loan and use of audio-visual items and the associated hardware are regarded as of equal importance as the service based on books and journals. *See also Instructional Materials Center.*

Learning Resources Development Group. Formed 1977 following the emergence of colleges and institutes of higher education as an identifiable group in the UK. Linked with the Standing Conference of Principals. Membership now open to all colleges, polytechnics and universities. Promotes discussion of learning resources, and is concerned with standards and levels of spending. Holds meetings, seminars, demonstrations, visits. Publishes *Learning Resources Journal* (3 p.a.). Abbreviated LRDG.

Leather. The cured and dyed hide of goat, pig or sheep. Used extensively for binding books.

Leather Bound. A book bound in leather, either FULL, HALF, QUARTER, or THREE-QUARTER (*qq.v.*).

Leather Joints. Leather inner joints affixed (usually stuck in but sometimes sewn) to the endpapers of large hand-bound books to give greater strength. They were occasionally used in the seventeenth century in Europe; between 1750 and 1800 they were a fairly common feature of the best English morocco and russia bindings, and were usually heavily decorated with fillets, rolls and small tools.

Leathercloth. A fabric or plastic material which has been finished to simulate leather.

Leatherette. Paper or cloth having a surface in imitation of leather.

Leaves of Plates. *See Plate.*

LEC. LONDON EDUCATION CLASSIFICATION (*q.v.*).

Lectern. A sloped wooden ledge on which books were laid flat and chained, and at which they were consulted, in mediaeval libraries.

Ledger Catalogue. *Synonymous with* PAGE CATALOGUE (*q.v.*).

Ledger Charging. An antiquated method of recording books on loan by entering book-numbers against names or ticket numbers in adjacent vertical columns on loose sheets or in a bound ledger.

Ledger Weight. (*Reprography*) Photographic paper of moderately heavy weight; used when greater body and mechanical durability are required. 'Duplex ledger' is coated on both sides for reproducing books; the paper used may have a wood, fibre or rag (linen ledger) base.

Left-to-Right Reversed. *Synonymous with* LATERALLY REVERSED (*q.v.*).

Legal Deposit. A method whereby certain libraries are entitled by law to receive one or more copies of every book or other publication which is printed or published in the country. Also called 'Copyright deposit', 'Copytax'. *See also Copyright Library.*

Legal File. A collection of material relating to law cases; it may include briefs, decisions, or histories of cases.

Legend. 1. The title or short description printed under an illustration or engraving, or on a coin or medal. Also called 'Caption' and 'Cut-line'. 2. An explanation of symbols on a map or diagram. 3. A story based on tradition.

Legislative History. A chronological account of the stages through which a particular bill has passed before enactment as a law. This would include all 'readings', committee debates and decisions, and 'floor' debates in both houses. The events leading to the bill, the efforts of organizations concerned in furthering it, any evidence given, and any history subsequent to enactment are also sometimes included.

Leighton Library. The library of Robert Leighton, Bishop of Dunblane and later Archbishop of Glasgow (1611–84), founded in Dunblane in 1688 for the benefit of local clergy under the term of Leighton's will, and still housed in its original building. In 1734 the library was reconstituted as one of the earliest public libraries in Scotland. A British Library grant to Stirling University has aided production of a catalogue of the collection, and grants have also been given by the Pilgrim Trust and the Historic Buildings Council for Scotland.

Lemma. The argument or subject written at the head of a literary composition.

Lemonnier Style. A style of book decoration practised by Jean Christophe Henri Lemonnier, who worked for Count Hoym in France in the eighteenth century. It is characterized by pictorial mosaics of landscape, bouquets, etc.

Lending Department. The department of a library containing books for home-reading. Called a 'Circulation department' in America.

Lending Desk. *See Circulation Desk.*

Lending Library. *Synonymous with* LENDING DEPARTMENT (*q.v.*).

Lenin State Library. The Lenin State Library, probably the largest library in Europe, is the national library of the USSR. Its book collection totals some

30 million items, originally housed in the Pashkov House, close to the Kremlin in Moscow. Its national functions commenced in 1925, and massive new buildings were completed in 1941. The library is under the jurisdiction of the Ministry of Culture, and is the national centre for research in library science.

Lesbian and Gay Librarians Group.   An informal group for all grades of UK library staff; re-established 1985 after several years of inactivity.

Let-in Note.   *Synonymous with* INCUT NOTE (*q.v.*).

Letter Book.   A book in which correspondence was copied by some means resulting in a facsimile copy. This was often done by writing the original letter with copying ink, placing it against a dampened sheet of thin paper (leaves of which comprised the book) and applying pressure. Such books were sometimes known as letterpress copybooks. Also, a book of blank or ruled pages on which are written letters, either drafts written by the author or fair copies made by the author or by clerks. The term is also used for a book comprising copies of letters which are bound together, or of one into which such copies are pasted onto guards or pages.

Letter-by-Letter.   *See Alphabetization.*

Letter Spacing.   The insertion of spaces between the letters of a word or words to lengthen the MEASURE (*q.v.*), improve the appearance of the setting, or in special instances emphasize a word or sentence. T h i s   i s   l e t t e r s p a c e d.

Letter Writer.   1. One who writes letters for illiterates.   2. A writer who has become famous for the letters he has written and possibly published.

Lettera Fonda.   *See Antiqua.*

Lettered Proof.   The proof of an engraving in which the title and the names of the artist, engraver, printer, etc. are printed under the illustration.

Lettering.   The emplacement of the library CALL NUMBER (*q.v.*) on the spine of a book.

Lettering on the Spine.   When the lettering on the spine of a book or bookjacket does not go across it, the direction may be up or down according to the choice of the publisher with consequent inconvenience to library users. In 1926 the Publishers Association and the Associated Booksellers of Great Britain and Ireland recommended that 'when a volume stands on the shelf the lettering reads from bottom to top', but in 1948 reversed their decision, recommending that the lettering should be downward so that the title can be easily read when the book lies flat, face upward. *Periodicals of reference value* . . . (B.S. 2509:1959) recommends that the lettering of periodicals should be 'across the spine if the title is short enough; otherwise along the spine in such a way as to be readable when the publication is lying flat with the *front* cover uppermost'.

Lettering Piece.   A piece of leather secured to the spine of a book to receive its title. *See also Label.*

Letterpress.   1. The text of a book as distinguished from its illustrations.   2. Matter printed from type as distinct from plates.   3. A method of relief printing as opposed to intaglio or planographic.

Letterpress Copybook.   *See Letter Book.*

Letters Close.   Letter addressed usually by the sovereign to some individual or group of individuals and closed with a seal.

Letters Patent.   An open letter issued generally under the great seal of the sovereign or some other magnate as a guarantee to the person or corporation named therein.

Lettre Bâtarde.   *See Gothic Type.*

Lettre de Forme.   *See Gothic Type.*

Lettre de Somme.   *See Gothic Type.*

Lettre Ronde.   *See Antiqua.*

Levant.   A high-grade Morocco leather used for binding books, and made from the skin of the Angora goat.

Level.   (*Classification*) A measure of the degree of complexity or generality of a concept, term or class.

Level Small Caps.   *Synonymous with* EVEN SMALL CAPS (*q.v.*).

Lever Press.   Any printing press on which the impression is made by moving a lever, but the term is usually applied to the type of press used for proofing, etc., in which the lever is pulled down.

Levigation.   The action of using the LEVIGATOR (*q.v.*).

Levigator.   A heavy steel disc which is rotated by hand over a lithographic stone when preparing its surface, sand and water being used as the abrasive.

Lexeme.   A word, particle or stem which denotes the meaning.

Lexicographer.   The compiler of a dictionary.

Lexicographist.   A LEXICOGRAPHER (*q.v.*).

Lexicography.   The act, or process, of compiling a dictionary.

Lexicology.   The branch of knowledge which is concerned with words, their history, form and meaning.

Lexicon.   A dictionary of the words of a language, the words being arranged in alphabetical order; especially one giving the meaning in another language. It is chiefly applied to a dictionary of Greek, Syriac, Arabic or Hebrew but is also used for encyclopaedias and subject dictionaries.

Liability Slip.   A slip recording the loan of a book for use on the library premises. It is cancelled, or returned to the reader, when the book is returned.

LIAC.   LIBRARY AND INFORMATION ASSISTANT'S CERTIFICATE (*q.v.*).

LIB 1.   Economic and statistical survey of European libraries carried out for the CEC 1985–88. The survey pointed out density of resources, regional variations, and the overall size of the library market. The private sector was not included.

LIB 2.   A major study funded by the Commission of the European Community on 'the state of the art of the use and impact of technology in libraries and information centres across Europe'. Twelve parallel studies were undertaken and these are now being considered in policy formulation for co-operative activities between libraries in the Community.

LIB 2 UK.   The British contribution to LIB 2 (*q.v.*). Undertaken April–August 1986 by the Library Association and the Library Technology Centre, submitted November 1986.

LIB 3. Unpublished CEC-funded investigation of the technical requirements for the interconnection in an OSI/ISDN environment of standards designed for library applications.

LIBER. Acronym of Ligue des Bibliothèques Européennes de Recherche (League of European Research Libraries). This Association was founded in March 1971 by a steering group set up through the National and University Libraries Section of IFLA at the Council of Europe's headquarters in Strasbourg. Its purpose was to bring together the large libraries of Austria, Belgium, Cyprus, Denmark, Finland, France, the Federal Republic of Germany, Greece, Holy See, Iceland, Ireland, Italy, Luxembourg, Malta, Netherlands, Norway, Portugal, Spain, Sweden, Switzerland, Turkey and the UK, and thereby to establish close co-operation between European research libraries, particularly national and university libraries, and also to help in finding practical ways of improving the quality of the services these libraries provide. Also, to organize research into librarianship on a European scale, and set up working parties in well-defined and circumscribed subjects. It desires to facilitate international loans and exchange of publications and to find corresponding members in each country. Membership consists of 170 research libraries (mostly university libraries, some national libraries and other large research libraries) in Western Europe. Financed by members' subscriptions with some assistance from the Council of Europe in respect of meetings. The possibility of expansion to cover Eastern Europe is being considered. Current working groups are: Conspectus; library architecture; library automation; library history; library management; manuscripts and rare books; maps. Publishes *LIBER Bulletin* (2 p.a.), monographs, directory of bibliographic networks. *See also Conspectus, European Register of Microform Masters.*

Liberate Roll. A record of the writs authorizing delivery of money out of the Treasury. Chancery Liberate are rolls of letters issued, and the Exchequer series rolls of letters received; both are copied from the same originals.

Libertas. An integrated library automation system developed and marketed by SWALCAP LIBRARY SERVICES LTD (*q.v.*).

LIBEX. A bureau to facilitate exchange arrangements between library staff of different countries. Sponsored by ICLG (*q.v.*) and based at the College of Librarianship Wales.

LIBGIS. *See National Center for Education Statistics.*

LIBIS. A library bibliographic network based at the University of Louvain/Leuven, Belgium. Established 1977; ten members at present. *See also DOBIS/LIBIS.*

LIBNET. The electronic mail service of the Australian Library and Information Association. *See also ALANET, LA-NET.*

Librarian. One who has the care of a library and its contents, selecting the books, documents and non-book materials which comprise its stock, and providing information and loan services to meet the needs of its users.

Librarian-in-Charge. The librarian placed in charge of a particular department.

Librarians' Christian Fellowship. Formed 1973, and officially constituted 1976; operates in liaison with the (British) Library Association. An interdenominational group aiming to bring together Christians, to discuss issues relating to librarianship, and to exert a positive influence on professional affairs. Publishes *Christian Librarian* (a.) and *Newsletter* (3 p.a.).

Librarians of Institutes and Schools of Education. *See LISE.*

Librarianship. The profession of the librarian. *See also Library Science.*

Libraries Open and Free. *See LOAF.*

Librarii. Used in mediaeval times to signify scribes.

Library. 1. A collection of books and other literary material kept for reading, study and consultation. 2. A place, building, room or rooms set apart for the keeping and use of a collection of books, etc. 3. A number of books issued by one publisher under a comprehensive title as the 'Loeb Classical Library', and usually having some general characteristic such as subject, binding, or typography. 4. A collection of films, photographs and other non-book materials, plastic or metal tapes and discs, computer tapes, disks and programs. All of these, as well as printed and manuscript documents, may be provided in departments of one large library or they may be in collections restricted to one type of material.

Library Acts. *See Library Law.*

Library Administration & Management Association. A division of the American Library Association. Aims to encourage the study of administrative theory, and improve management practice. Responsible since 1974 for LIBRARY TECHNOLOGY PROGRAM (*q.v.*). Publishes *LAMA Newsletter* (q.), proceedings, bibliographies. Abbreviated LAMA.

Library Advisory Councils. The formation of national advisory councils, one for England (excluding Monmouthshire) and the other for Wales and Monmouthshire, was provided for by Section 2 of the Public Libraries and Museums Act 1964. In 1981 they were merged, and retitled the LIBRARY AND INFORMATION SERVICES COUNCIL (*q.v.*).

Library Agreement. *See Net Book Agreement.*

Library and Information Assistant's Certificate (UK). A sub-professional qualification intended for unqualified library assistants; operated by the City and Guilds of London Institute. Abbreviated LIAC.

Library and Information Co-operation Council. Set up in 1989 to replace the National Committee on Regional Library Co-operation, and to continue and develop its work. Main objective is to promote co-operation and partnership as a means of improving the effectiveness of the library and information sector in the UK. Reviews and facilitates all types of co-operation between the British Library, the Regional Library Systems, and other organizations and institutions in the library and information community. Detailed aims for 1990 included promotion of LIPs, IT and interlending, performance indicators, statistics, and co-ordination of activities on CEC initiatives. Abbreviated LINC.

Library and Information Plans. *See LIPs.*

Library and Information Research Group.   Founded in 1977 to cater for the needs and interests of those concerned or active in library and information research. Makes an annual award, (*see Clark Award, Daphne*) and publishes *Library and Information Research News* (irreg.). Abbreviated LIRG. Operates in association with the (British) Library Association.

Library and Information Science.   The study and practice of professional methods in the use and exploitation of information, whether from an institutional base or not, for the benefit of users. An umbrella term, abbreviated LIS, and used to cover terms such as library science, librarianship, information science, information work etc.

Library & Information Science Abstracts.   An extended and enlarged form of LIBRARY SCIENCE ABSTRACTS (*q.v.*); it commenced publication in January 1969 by the Library Association jointly with Aslib, which organization withdrew in 1980. Published bi-monthly until the end of 1982, then monthly. Abbreviated LISA. Available on-line via DIALOG, and on CD-ROM.

Library and Information Services Council (UK).   The Library Advisory Council (England) was set up by the 1964 Public Library Act; by the late 1970s it was clear that some revision of structure and function was necessary. In the autumn of 1979 the Council issued a report *Future development of libraries; the organisational and policy framework* which suggested strengthening the Council, raising its profile, and securing a greater involvement of the library and information community in policy making.

In 1980 the House of Commons Select Committee on Education, Science and the Arts produced a report *Information storage and retrieval in the British library service* (HMSO 1980) chaired by Christopher Price, MP, and sometimes referred to as the *Price Report*, which sought machinery to co-ordinate library and information policy on a national basis, and recommended a standing commission representing a wide range of interests concerned with the provision of information.

In April 1981 the British Government responded in a white paper *Information storage and retrieval in the British library service* (Cmnd. 8237) (HMSO, 1981) which agreed to treating libraries and information together, gave responsibility to the Minister for the Arts, and in accepting the need for a committee, considered that the Library Advisory Council (England) would suffice, but should be reformed and redesignated the Library and Information Services Council (LISC). In July 1981 Prof. W. Saunders was appointed the first chairman. LISC operates within the Office of Arts and Libraries of the Dept. of Education and Science; its aims are to advise the Minister, review issues, react to developments, and give access for outside organizations to its agenda and discussions (its papers are generally not confidential). It has an important function to present an annual report to Parliament.

Information is also fed into LISC by its Welsh counterpart (LISC-W) – another statutory body – by the Scottish Library and Information Services Committee, which advises the Secretary of State for Scotland, and LISC for Northern Ireland (these two last organizations are not statutory).

Papers from groups and individuals are permanently invited, and an annual meeting is held with the profession at large. Major concerns have included manpower/education/training, co-operative arrangements, and electronic publishing. LIPS (*q.v.*). are a currently important area of interest.

Library and Information Statistics Unit. Set up in 1987 at Loughborough University (UK) and funded until 1991 by the British Library Research and Development Department. Will continue the work of CLAIM (*q.v.*). Abbreviated LISU.

Library and Information Technology Association. Division of the American Library Association. Founded 1966. Concerned with the development and application of automated systems, electronic data processing techniques, communications technology; promotes research and organises standards. Publishes *Information Technology & Libraries* (q.) *LITA Newsletter* (irreg.). Abbreviated LITA.

Library and Information Technology Centre (UK). Established at the Polytechnic of Central London in 1982 with funding from the Department of Trade and Industry, and the British Library Research and Development Department. Initially entitled the *Information Technology Centre*, it changed its name in 1984 to the *Library Technology Centre*, and adopted its present title in 1987. The Centre demonstrates systems, offers an enquiry service, issues two key journals, *VINE* and *Library micromation news*, publishes information packs, and runs seminars and workshops.

Library, Archives and Documentation Services (LAD). *See Office of Information Programmes and Services.*

Library Assistants' Association. *See Association of Assistant Librarians.*

Library Assistant's Certificate. *See Library and Information Assistant's Certificate.*

Library Association. The British professional association, for the regulation of the profession of librarianship, for the promotion of the better administration of libraries and the encouragement of bibliographical study and research and for the accumulation and dissemination of information concerning libraries. It was founded as the Library Association of the United Kingdom on 5 October 1877 at the conclusion of the First International Conference of Librarians, which was held at Brussels from 2–5 October under the presidency of Mr. John Winter Jones, the joint secretaries being E. W. B. Nicholson and H. R. Tedder. The *American Library Journal* was adopted as the official journal, the word 'American' being dropped. Publication of the *Monthly Notes* was commenced on 15 January 1880 and *The Library* was adopted as the official journal on 10 December 1880. On 30 January 1896 the name of the Association was changed to The Library Association, and the Association was granted its Royal Charter on 17 February 1898. The *Library Association Record* commenced publication as the official journal of the Association in January 1899. It became a wholly professional association in 1962 when new bye-laws came into operation. Members are automatically allocated to membership of one of twelve branches (these include the Scottish and Welsh Library Associations) according to their place of residence, and may become members of two groups (more by paying a small annual fee).

The Groups are as follows: Association of Assistant Librarians, Audovisual Group, Branch and Mobile Libraries, Cataloguing and Indexing, Colleges of Further and Higher Education, Community Services, Education Librarians, Government Libraries, Industrial Group, Information Services, Information Technology, International and Comparative Librarianship, Library History, Local Studies, Medical, Health and Welfare Libraries, Personnel, Training and Education, Prison Libraries, Public Libraries, Publicity and Public Relations, Rare Books, Reference, Special and Information Section, School Libraries, Training and Education, University, College and Research, Youth Libraries. There are 24,000 members.

The Association's motto is *Ingenia hominum res publica* (The thoughts of mankind are the common wealth). The responsibility for the Association's library was transferred to THE BRITISH LIBRARY (*q.v.*) on the official formation of that Library on 1 April 1974 (*see BLISS*). The Association operates the Register of Chartered Librarians and oversees professional education in the UK. Publishes a *Yearbook, Directory,* and a range of monographs under its own imprint and that of Clive Bingley. In 1990 its serial publications (including *BHI, CTI, ASSIA, CRILIS, LISA*) were sold to Bowker-Saur Ltd. Abbreviated LA.

Library Association Dewey Decimal Classification Committee. Established 1971, aims to encourage discussion of DDC, co-ordinate, formulate criticism, consider draft schedules, and liaise with the Library of Congress DC Office and Forest Press. The Committee consists of 6 members nominated by the LA Cataloguing and Indexing Group, and three members nominated by British Library Bibliographic Services. Abbreviated LA.DDC.

Library Association Literacy Medal. A medal which may be awarded annually by the Library Association for an item of outstanding published material for adults developing basic reading skills. The item must have been produced in English during the previous three years.

Library Association of Australia. Founded in 1949, being re-constituted from the Australian Institute of Librarians which had been founded in 1937. In 1989 the name was changed to the AUSTRALIAN LIBRARY AND INFORMATION ASSOCIATION (*q.v.*).

Library Association of Ireland. Founded 1928, incorporated 1952. This Association represents the profession of librarianship in Eire; it provides postal tuition for, and conducts examinations for, the professional qualification (FLAI). Membership is open to all engaged in, or interested in, the profession of librarianship in Ireland or elsewhere. Abbreviated LAI. With the March 1972 issue (NS Vol. 1 No 1) of *An Leabharlann* (q.), it became the joint journal of the LAI and of the Northern Ireland Branch of the Library Association with the title *An Leabharlann: The Irish Library*. Conferences of the two bodies have been held since 1961, and there is a standing liaison committee between them. A successful joint fiction reserve scheme has been in operation for several years, and an agreed format for compiling Irish county bibliographies is in use.

Library Association of Malaysia.   Founded on 6 May 1960 to (a) unite all persons engaged in library work or interested in libraries in Malaysia; (b) promote the better administration of libraries; (c) encourage the establishment, development, and use of libraries in Malaysia; (d) encourage professional education and training for librarianship; (e) publish such information as will be of service to members; (f) undertake such activities, including the holding of meetings and conferences, as are appropriate to the attainments of the foregoing objects. Individual membership is open to all persons engaged in library work or interested in libraries in Malaysia; institutional membership is open to all libraries and other institutions which share the objects of the Association; honorary membership is conferred on persons who have distinguished themselves in library work. The association was known as the Library Association of the Federation of Malaya from 6 May 1960 to 8 July 1964. Publishes *Perpustakaan* (semi-a.). Abbreviated PPM (Persatuan Perpustakaan Malaysia).

Library Association of Singapore.   Founded in 1954 as the Malayan Library Group and successively known as: Library Association of Malaya & Singapore (from November 1958); Library Association of Singapore (1960); Library Association of Malaysia, Singapore Branch (from January 1965); Library Association of Singapore (since January 1966). The objects of the Association and membership conditions are similar to those of the LIBRARY ASSOCIATION OF MALAYSIA (*q.v.*). Publishes *Singapore Libraries* (a.), *LAS Newsletter* (irreg.). Abbreviated LAS.

Library Association/T. C. Farries Public Relations and Publicity Awards.   Annual awards sponsored by the Scottish library suppliers T. C. Farries, in association with the Library Association Publicity and Public Relations Group, open to all public, academic, school and special libraries in the UK. There are five categories, ranging from a total public relations programme to personal PR achievements, and including a category for Branches and Groups.

Library Authority (UK).   The local government unit responsible for the provision of public library services. In *England and Wales* there are two tiers of authorities – Counties and Districts. The Public Libraries and Museums Act 1964 is administered outside London by District Councils in the urban areas and by County Councils in the more rural counties. For the Greater London area, the London boroughs formed under the London Government Act 1963 are the library authorities. In the City of London, the Common Council is the library authority. In *Wales* they are (a) the council of a county, (b) the council of a district which has been constituted a library authority, (c) the joint board in the area which has been the subject of a joint board order. In *Scotland* there are local government areas known as Regions, each of which contains local government areas known as Districts; Orkney, Shetland and the Western isles were designated island areas. For the purposes of the Public Library (Scotland) Acts 1887–1955 (which were in some respects superseded) the Islands and District Councils became the library authorities except that within the Highlands, Borders, and Dumfries and Galloway regions, the appropriate Regional Council became the library authority. School libraries became functions of the Regional Education Committees. *See also Paterson Report.* In *Northern Ireland* libraries are no longer a local authority responsibility. An Education and Libraries Bill to establish education and library services in five areas, with a board having statutory responsibility for the local administration of library service, was presented to the Northern Ireland Parliament on 17 February 1972 and was given a second reading in the House of Commons on 15 March. But before the bill became law, direct rule from Westminster was introduced and the Northern Ireland Parliament was prorogued. The legislative proposals of the Education and Libraries Bill were, however, enshrined in the Education and Libraries (Northern Ireland) Order 1972. This Order repealed all library legislation dating back to the mid-nineteenth century; it became effective on 1 October 1973, and provided that one of the primary duties of a board is 'to provide a comprehensive and efficient library service'. Virtually, the librarians and their staffs immediately became civil servants. Whereas the HAWNT REPORT (*q.v.*) favoured the amalgamation of counties, the five new library areas ignored all long-standing county boundaries; each serves between a quarter and a half-million people. Under this Order, five area Education and Library Boards were established, each of which became the local education authority and library authority for its area. The areas are Belfast; South-Eastern (five districts); Southern (six districts); Western (five districts); North-Eastern (nine districts). The Order repealed the Public Libraries Acts (Northern Ireland) in so far as they relate to libraries. Those Acts and the Museums and Gymnasiums Act 1891 are still in force, however, in their application to museums and art galleries.

Library Bill of Rights. The American Library Association's basic policy on intellectual freedom. First adopted in 1939, a completely revised version was adopted in 1948, with amendments in 1961, 1967, and 1980. Affirms the librarian's right to purchase and provide appropriate materials without restriction, and the user's right of access. The full text, and several interpretative appendices, were last published in the *Intellectual Freedom Manual*, 2nd ed. American Library Association, 1983. In 1984 further interpreted to cover films and video materials.

Library Binding. A specially strong binding to enable library books to withstand considerable use. This is achieved by a number of means, but particularly by guarding sections, sewing the sections on tapes and using specially durable cloth.

Library Binding Institute. An American non-profit trade organization, founded in 1935 'to: (a) develop a spirit of mutual helpfulness and co-operation among those engaged in library binding and related industries; (b) encourage and direct activities leading to constructive co-operation between the industry and its customers . . .; (c) help sustain the highest possible standards of fair dealing between library binders, their customers, their employees and their competitors; (d) raise and sustain standards of craftsmanship and quality; (e) improve the methods of the industry and stimulate its progress through research and the exchange of experience; (f) give the fullest aid and support to the libraries of the nation and to the profession which makes them possible'. Membership is open to commercial library binders capable of doing work meeting the LBI standard, suppliers to library book binders, and those interested in the preservation of books and periodicals. Members' dues finance the Institute. Publishes *Library Scene* (q.) and various technical papers and brochures. Abbreviated LBI.

Library Boards. *Synonymous with* BOARD OF LIBRARY TRUSTEES (*q.v.*).

Library/Book Fellows Program. A system of grants to place US library and publishing professionals in working situations overseas; jointly administered by ALA and USIA.

Library Campaign. A UK pressure group which seeks to increase awareness of the importance of library services, monitor local campaigns, and oppose financial constraints. In 1988 a part-time paid Campaign Director was appointed to develop activities, and lobby more extensively. Holds an annual conference; issues *The Library Campaigner* (6 p.a.).

Library Centre. *See Branch Library.*

Library Clerk. One who performs duties involving simple tasks related to library functions but limited to strict adherence to specific routines and procedures. The work is carried out under close supervision of a librarian or LIBRARY TECHNICAL ASSISTANT (*q.v.*) (American).

Library Collection. The total accumulation of material of all kinds assembled by a library for its clientele. Also called 'Library holdings', 'Library resources'.

Library Commission. 1. An American organization created by an act of legislature, operating in one state but independent of the state library. It exists to promote library services by establishing, organizing and supervising public, and sometimes school, libraries, and by lending books and other material to communities which do not possess libraries. 'State Library Agency' is replacing this term. 2. Occasionally, a Board of Library Trustees.

Library Committee. The committee responsible for the provision of a library service.

Library Consultant. An individual offering a range of professional skills and advice relevant to the operation of libraries. Usually these skills will be marketed on a commercial basis by a FREELANCE (*q.v.*) self-employed person who is not directly employed by the library concerned, but retained on contract for a fee. The term INFORMATION CONSULTANT (*q.v.*) is loosely used to cover this and other types of consultancy occupations.

Library Corner. (*Binding*) The turning in of cloth at the corners of books so as to take up the excess in two diagonal folds, one under each turn-in. In this way the cloth is not cut, and the corner given additional strength. *See also Mitred Corner, Square Corner.*

Library Co-operation. *See Co-operative.*

Library Council. (An Chomhairle Leabharlanna) A Republic of Ireland body set up in 1947 to advise local authorities and the Minister for the Environment on the development of public library services, and since 1961, to provide financial assistance for such development under the Public Library Grant Scheme; and to administer the interlending system for Ireland and to promote library co-operation between all sectors of the library and information scene. (*See also Irish Central Library for Students.*) In practice this includes involvement in matters as wide ranging as public library planning, education and training, library automation, standards for mobile libraries, library equipment, union catalogues of serials holdings, etc. The three broad divisions within An Chomhairle's organization reflect its main activities: library development, interlending and library co-operation, information and research.

Library Discount. Discount on the cost of books purchased for a library.

Library Documentation Centre. This Centre was established in November 1970 and is part of the Public Services Branch of the National Library of Canada in Ottawa. It serves as a collection centre for up-to-date documentation on library and information science in Canada for both the Library staff and the Canadian library community. It functions as Canada's national information transfer centre for ISORID (*q.v.*).

Library Economy. The practical application of library science to the founding, organizing and administering of libraries.

Library Edition. 1. A vague term indicating the edition of a book, series or set of books, often all the works of an author, in a substantial and uniform format to distinguish it from another less substantial edition, possibly in paper covers. Sometimes called 'Cabinet edition'. 2. An edition printed on good paper and in a specially strong binding for library use.

Library Education Group. *See Personnel, Training and Education Group.*

Library Extension. The provision of lectures, film shows, etc. in the library, arranging talks, book-displays, etc. outside the library buildings in order to draw attention to the library services and book stocks. In America, the promotion of libraries and the development of library services by state, regional or local agencies.

Library Hand. A handwriting used by librarians with the object of achieving uniformity and legibility in manuscript catalogues and other records. The formation of letters and the slope were determined with clarity in mind, and many librarians used this handwriting before the use of typewriters became common.

Library History Group. A Group of the Library Association, formed in 1962 to unite members interested in the history of libraries in order to further the aims set forth in the Charter of the LA, to encourage the discussion of, and promote interest in, all matters relating to library history, and encourage original work in the history of librarianship in the British Isles. Publishes *Library History* (2 p.a.).

Library Holdings. *Synonymous with* LIBRARY COLLECTION (*q.v.*).

Library Improvement Act. 1988 United States legislation. *See Library Law.*

Library Instruction. *See User Education.*

Library Keys. Said of the card catalogue, the circulation and information desks, the bibliographies and indexes to periodicals, etc., grouped together in what is called a 'Finding unit' in university libraries.

Library Law. The legal framework which establishes and governs libraries in any given country or state. In the UK the adoptive acts were the Public Libraries Act 1892, Public Libraries (Amendment) Act 1893, Public Libraries Act 1908, Public Libraries Act 1919; in 1964 the Public Libraries and Museums Act replaced earlier legislation and remains the current Act covering England and Wales. (For preliminary work on this Act *see Baker Report, Bourdillon Report, Roberts Report.) See also Library Authority.* The British Library Act 1972 is the relevant legislation covering the national libraries.

In the US the *Library Services & Construction Act* controls public library activities, state library services, and inter-library lending; the *Elementary and Secondary Education Act* Title II School Library Resources, the *Higher Education Act* and the *Medical Library Assistance Act* are other important statues. The 1988 *Library Improvement Act* seeks to increase library impact on education and learning, especially to the disadvantaged and handicapped, and promote resource sharing and research support. *(See also NCLIS.)* Each State also has its own legislation covering libraries.

Library Literature. An index to the literature of librarianship and information science, published by the H. W. Wilson Company. *Library Literature* first appeared in 1934, produced by the American Library Association's Junior Members Round Table, and covered 1921–32. H. W. Wilson Company took it over thereafter; publication is six times p.a. with cumulated annual volume, and two-year cumulations. Some 220 journal titles are scanned, of which 140 are of US origin. Available on-line via WILSONLINE, and on CD-ROM.

Library Management. The technique of organizing priorities, motivating staff, securing resources, and evaluating performance in order to obtain the optimum efficiency and benefit from a library service.

Library of Congress (USA). The Library of Congress provides library and information services by authority of Congress, is responsible to Congress for giving priority in its services to Congress, and although not officially a national library provides services appropriate to a national library, and at a higher level than most other specifically designed national libraries. Abbreviated LC. Aims to develop a comprehensive national collection of printed literature, maps, films, music, audiovisual materials and manuscripts. It is responsible for the production of the national bibliography. LC has no interlending role, nor any role in library co-ordination although much has been achieved through voluntary co-operation. LC developed machine-readable cataloguing (MARC) data bases for bibliographical records, is the national centre for the exchange of MARC data, and the national agency for CIP, ISBNs and ISSNs. The MARC database now holds over 10 million items.

Divisions of LC include a Collections Development Office, CIP Division, Processing Services, Special Materials Cataloguing, Office for Descriptive Cataloguing Policy, Automation Planning and Liaison, Automated Systems, Cataloguing Distribution Service, General Reading Rooms, Preservation Policy (including the Mass De-acidification Project in Houston, Tx.), Rare Books and Special Collections. There are over 5000 staff and an annual budget of $250 million (1987). Special services include the Congressional Research Service, Copyright Office, Law Library, American Folklife Center, Center for the Book and Children's Literature Center, National Library Service for the Blind and Physically Handicapped. There is an extensive programme of publishing, concerts and other performances. *See also CONSER.*

LC has published the *National Union Catalog* (NUC) and the *National Union Catalog of Manuscript Collections* (*qq.v.*).

Library of Congress Card. A printed catalogue card on which a full catalogue entry is given, also notes, tracings, and Dewey and L. of C. classification numbers. Such cards have been issued by the Library of Congress since 1901, and are available for purchase. Each card bears a serial number which is used by libraries when ordering printed cards for their catalogues. These numbers are printed in the respective books if published in the USA, usually on the back of the title-page. *See also Cataloguing in Publication.*

Library of Congress Classification. The scheme of classification used in the main national library of the USA. The outline of the scheme was drawn up by Dr. Herbert Putnam, in 1897, and is based in some respects on the Dewey Decimal and Cutter's Expansive schemes, the schedules being worked out by specialists in the various subjects. The main tables have been published, each with its own relative index, as completed, and revised from time to time. The result is a series of special schedules of greater detail than any other scheme. The outline, which is purely arbitrary, is as follows:

A	General Works, Polygraphy.
B	Philosophy, Religion.
C	Auxiliary Sciences of History.
D	Universal and Old World History [and Topography] (*except America*).
E-F	America.
G	Geography, Anthropology. Folk-lore. Manners and Customs. Sports and Games.
H	Social Sciences. Economics. Sociology.
J	Political Science.
L	Education.
M	Music.
N	Fine Arts.
P	Language and Literature.
PN-PZ	Literary History. Literature.
Q	Science.
R	Medicine.

S	Agriculture. Plant and Animal Industry. Fish Culture and Fisheries. Hunting. Sports.
T	Technology.
U	Military Science.
V	Naval Science.
Z	Bibliography and Library Science.

The scheme does not conform to the theoretical rules for classification, being compiled to meet the needs of the library's huge collection of books. It typifies the enumerative method of classification and retains all powers of growth in the hands of the compiler. It is too detailed and complex for use in any but the largest library but the subject schedules are most useful for special and university libraries. There are no tables for sub-division by form or place which can be used in any part of the scheme. The notation is mixed, consisting of two letters and four figures used arithmetically, blanks being left in the alphabet and in the numbers for future insertions. The schedules are undergoing constant amendments and updating; these amendments are published in *LC Classification – additions and changes* and the schedules of whole classes are reprinted from time to time.

Library of Congress Subject Headings. *See Subject Headings.*

Library of Deposit. Under the UK Copyright Act 1911, a library which is entitled to receive free copies of books published in the UK. Often referred to as a COPYRIGHT LIBRARY (*q.v.*) and wrongly as a DEPOSIT LIBRARY (*q.v.*).

Library of Tomorrow. A demonstration collection of software, CD-ROM, videodisc, and other advanced technology formats, opened 1988 at the Library of Congress. Officially titled the Machine-Readable Collections Reading Room.

Library Orientation. *See User Education.*

Library Processing. *See Processing.*

Library Promotion Fortnight. First run in November 1990 on the initiative of certain Library Association groups and the Library Campaign; intended to raise the profile of libraries and act as a framework for local activities.

Library Public Relations Council. Founded in the USA in 1939 to investigate, discuss, and promote every phase of library public relations. Abbreviated LPRC.

Library Rate. The amount of money per unit of currency of rateable value of a local authority area which is required to provide a public library service.

Library Research Bursary. *See 3M/Library Association Library Research Bursary.*

Library Research Round Table. A group within the ALA. Abbreviated LRRT.

Library School. An organized course, or courses, in librarianship attended by full-time and/or part-time students. It may be a separately managed institution in its own building but is usually a department of an institution for higher education, or a faculty within a university. Abbreviated LS.

Library Science. A generic term for the study of libraries and information units, the role they play in society, their various component routines and processes, and their history and future development. Used in the United States in preference to the British term *librarianship*.

Library Science Abstracts. A publication of the Library Association (quarterly since January 1950) giving abstracts of books and articles in periodicals on librarianship published throughout the world. Abbreviated LSA. Expanded in 1969 and renamed *Library & Information Science Abstracts* (*q.v.*).

Library Science Classification. A fully faceted scheme, prepared in draft by members of the Classification Research Group (UK) and entitled *Classification of library science*, was published in 1965. An amended version of this scheme is used in *LIBRARY AND INFORMATION SCIENCE ABSTRACTS*. A later version with the title *A classification of library and information science* was published in 1975.

Library Service. The facilities provided by a library for the use of books and the dissemination of information.

Library Services and Construction Act. *See Library Law.*

Library Services Trust. A trust fund owned and administered by the (UK) Library Association and the London and Home Counties branch of the Association. The Trust provides financial assistance for Association members wishing to attend professional courses and meetings, and operates the STEWART (J.D.) BURSARY (*q.v.*).

Library Shelving. Shelving which is made to meet the special needs of libraries.

Library Society of Puerto Rico. Sociedad de Bibliotecarios de Puerto Rico. Founded to extol the position of the librarian and to promote a greater recognition of the profession in Puerto Rico; to obtain a better qualification for its associates, and to promote an interest in the profession with the object of drawing the best talent into it, and also to strive to get the authorities concerned to make available the means to offer courses in library science in the country; to work for a greater expansion of the library services in Puerto Rico, and to advocate for the establishment of public libraries in all the communities in the island; to stimulate a greater exchange among the librarians both local as well as from abroad. Publishes *Bulletin of the Library Society of Puerto Rico*.

Library Stamp. A rubber stamp bearing the name of the library; this is used to indicate the ownership of books, periodicals and other publications.

Library Technical Assistant. One whose duties are based on skills required by a library clerk, but, in addition, possesses a proficiency developed in one or more functional areas or in certain limited phases of library services. Such an assistant works under the supervision of a librarian, and may supervise and direct library clerks or clerical staff. *See also Library Clerk* (American).

Library Technology Centre. *See Library and Information Technology Centre.*

Library Technology Program. Established 1959 as the Library Technology Project, based at the American Library Association headquarters, and financed by grants from the Council on Library Resources. Promoted standardization of equipment, an evaluation programme, a research and development programme, and provided a technical information service. Retitled Library Technology Program in 1966; dissolved in 1972 and the staff and its publication *Library Technology Reports* transferred to the LIBRARY ADMINISTRATION AND MANAGEMENT ASSOCIATION (*q.v.*) – a division of the ALA. Abbreviated LTP.

Library Ticket.   One indicating membership of a library and serving as the authority for borrowing books.

Library Trustees.   *Synonymous with* BOARD OF LIBRARY TRUSTEES (*q.v.*).

Library Week.   A week designated by the principal library associations in a country, state, region, or internationally, for the promotion of public awareness of libraries and library services, by exhibitions, tours, events, media coverage, etc.

Librettist.   The author of the text of an opera or other extended choral composition.

Libretto.   The words to which an opera or other lengthy musical composition for voices is set.

Libri Manuscripti.   Books written by hand, as were all books before the invention of printing.

LIBRIS.   Library Information System; a bibliographic network serving some 70 Swedish research libraries, and responsible for the Swedish National Bibliography. Based in Stockholm, and established in 1972; 400 members at present.

LIBTRAD.   Abbreviation for the Working Party on Library and Book Trade Relations, a basically non-profit-making organization which was formed in London in 1965 to investigate and report on matters of common concern to publishers, booksellers and librarians. It is independent of the official associations connected with the world of books; membership is small, restricted by invitation to: large and small publishing firms, large and small bookselling firms, public and academic librarians, library suppliers. Biennial conferences, known as 'Holborn' conferences (after the place where they were held), are organized to consider a problem area of general concern to libraries and the book trade.

Licence Leaf.   *See Imprimatur.*

Licentiateship (UK).   In the mid 1980s the first stage in professional qualification in the UK. *See also Associateship.*

Lichtdruck.   A kind of COLLOTYPE (*q.v.*).

Lifted Matter.   Type or blocks removed from the forme and put on one side for use in other pages or in another job.

Ligature.   Two or more letters joined together, or differing in design from the separate letters, and cast on one type body, as ﬆ, ﬅ, ffl, ff, fi, fl to save space, avoid the unsightly juxtaposition of st, ct, ffl, ff, fi, fl, and to reduce the risk of damage to kerned letters. The term also refers to the joining stroke which connects the characters. Also called 'Double letter', 'Tied letter'. *See also Logotype.*

Light Face.   The weight of type-face which is lighter than medium – the ordinary book weight – having thinner strokes. The opposite of BOLD FACE

($q.v.$). Most type families are made in varying weights, usually called light, medium, bold, extra bold; but 'medium' is normally understood when referring to a type face and is therefore only expressed when it is essential to distinguish it from the other weights.

Light-pen. A pen or stylus with a light sensor, which can be used to mark a position on a VDU screen. Also sometimes used loosely to mean a BAR-CODE ($q.v.$) scanner.

Lightweight Paper. Sensitized photographic paper between 0.0044 and 0.0059 inches inclusive. *See also Photographic Papers.*

Ligue des Bibliothèques Européennes de Recherche. *See LIBER.*

Likeness. The quality of similarity or alikeness which is used in classification in order to group together objects or ideas according to their likeness.

Lilliput Edition. *See Miniature Book.*

Limitation Notice. The statement in a book published in a LIMITED EDITION ($q.v.$) indicating the number of copies printed which comprise the edition, or part of the edition. The statement would define the special character of the edition, such as printed on 'large paper' or hand-made paper, and provide for the number of the individual copy to be written in.

Limited Cataloguing. A term used by the Library of Congress for the standard of descriptive cataloguing which began to be applied in 1951 by the Library of Congress to certain categories of books in order to speed up cataloguing processes. Limited cataloguing is practised in order to reduce the work and time involved in recording more details than are required to identify and locate works which are not of sufficient bibliographic and reference utility to compensate for the time expended.

Limited Edition. An edition, printed on special paper and often with a special binding, which is printed in limited numbers (seldom more than 1500, usually about 200 to 500, but often as few as ten) and sold at a higher price. Each copy bears a printed certificate (usually facing the title-page) indicating the size of the edition on which is written the actual copy number. Sometimes copies are signed by the author.

Limited Editions Club. An American subscription book club, founded in 1929 by George Macy, which produces well-designed and well-printed books.

Limp Binding. Said of a book which is not bound in boards but with flexible cloth or leather.

Limp Cloth. A term used to describe a style of publisher's binding. *See also Limp Covers.*

Limp Covers. Thin flexible book covers made of plastic, or of other material, without boards and covered with cloth or leather.

Limp Leather. A full leather binding made without using stiff boards and therefore flexible. Often used for Bibles.

LINC. *See Library and Information Cooperation Council.*

Lindisfarne Gospels. Written in Latin, this is the earliest and most beautiful extant manuscript in English half-uncials; it is supposed to have been written by Eadfrith, Bishop of Lindisfarne, about 700. Also known as the 'Durham Book'.

Lindop Committee.   A British government committee under the chairmanship of Sir Norman Lindop which investigated the security of information on computers. (*Report of the committee on data protection*. Cmnd. 7341 HMSO 1978). *See also Data Protection.*

Line.   1. The imaginary base-line of a piece of movable type, running set-wise on or about which all the characters are positioned. *See also Set 2.*   2. A row of printed or written characters extending across a column or page. *See also Measure.*   3. A FILLET (*q.v.*) used in bookbinding.   4. Reproduction of a drawing which prints only solid areas and lines, there being no tones.

Line Block.   A metal printing block made photographically direct from a black and white drawing without any intermediate tones other than tints, and mounted type-high for letterpress printing. *See also Zincography.*

Line-by-line-index.   An entry in an index, with its page or other reference, which is printed on a single line. Also known as an 'Entry-a-line-index'. Where the entries consist of titles which are similarly confined to one line, it is known as a 'Title-a-line Index'.

Line-casting Machine.   A type-casting machine which casts a line of type in one slug. Intertype and Linotype are machines of this kind.

Line Copy.   A copy of a document which has no tone values. Also called 'Line reproduction'. *See also Line Original.*

Line Cut.   *Synonymous with* LINE ENGRAVING (*q.v.*).

Line Division Mark.   A mark, usually a vertical or oblique line, used in bibliographical transcription to indicate the end of a line of type in the original.

Line Drawing.   A black ink drawing made in line or stipple with indian ink, pencil, crayon, or brush, from which a line block may be made. An impression of grey is achieved by using a tint.

Line End Stroke.   *Synonymous with* LINE DIVISION MARK (*q.v.*).

Line-ending.   1. Term used to indicate the last letter of a line of type when giving an exact bibliographical description of a title-page, the ending of each line being indicated by a vertical or oblique stroke or two such strokes.   2. An ornament (of which there are a great variety) filling the space at the end of a line in a mediaeval illuminated manuscript. Also called 'Line-filling'.

Line Engraving.   1. Engraving in which the effects are produced by lines of different width and proximity, cut into copper, steel, zinc or other similar material.   2. A plate produced by the line engraving process.   3. A picture printed from a line engraving.

Line Etching. *Synonymous with* ETCHING (*q.v.*).

Line-filling.   *Synonymous with* LINE-ENDING (*q.v.*).

Line Management.   Line managers are those within an organization who have authority to take decisions affecting the organization. The antitheses are *staff* posts which have an advisory, data-collecting, information giving role, but cannot take decisions.

Line Original.   An original document for copying, and having no tone values. A copy of such an original may be called a 'Line copy' or 'Line reproduction'.

Line Printer. The standard device for printing the output from a computer.

Line Reproduction. *Synonymous with* LINE COPY (*q.v.*). *See also Line Original.*

Lineale. Styles of type face where the characters have no serifs. Such faces were formerly known as 'sans-serif'. They may be sub-divided into GROTESQUE, NEO-GROTESQUE, GEOMETRIC AND HUMANIST (*qq.v.*)

Lined. Said of a book which has a piece of material (strips of parchment which overlapped the joints and were pasted down under the end-papers of seventeenth- and eighteenth-century bindings) lining the spine to give it strength.

Linen. A cloth made from flax for covering books.

Linen Faced. Paper with a linen finish on one or both sides.

Linen Finish. Paper, the surface of which is made to resemble linen by placing it between plates of zinc and sheets of linen under pressure. *See also Crash Finish.*

Linen-grained. A book-cloth which is patterned to resemble linen.

Linen Paper. 1. Paper made from rags; originally from linen rags. 2. LINEN FACED (*q.v.*).

Linguistic Numbers. *Synonymous with* ETHNIC NUMBERS (*q.v.*).

Lining. A piece of material, usually mull, placed in the spine of a book when binding it to give it strength. Also called 'Back-lining'. *See also First Lining, Second Lining, Triple Lining.*

Lining, Ornamental Inside. *Synonymous with* DOUBLURE 1 (*q.v.*).

Lining Figures. (*Printing*) Arabic numerals which do not have ascenders or descenders, but which are the same size as capital letters, stretching from base-line to cap line thus: 1234567890. Also called 'Ranging figures'. *See also Hanging Figures.*

Lining Paper. 1. That portion of an endpaper which is pasted down on the inner cover of a book. The other portion of the endpaper is known as the 'free endpaper'. *See also Endpaper.* 2. Coloured or marbled paper used as an ENDPAPER (*q.v.*).

Lining-up Table. *Synonymous with* REGISTER TABLE (*q.v.*).

Link Letters. *See Links.*

Linked Books. Separately bound books where the relationship between each other is indicated in various ways, such as collective or series title-pages; continuous paging, series or signatures; mention in contents or other preliminary leaves.

Linked Systems Project. An arrangement to link the Library of Congress, Research Libraries Information Network (RLIN), Western Library Network (WLN) and OCLC, enabling the users of any one of the systems to search all the others without new search commands. Provides interactive facilities for the large centralized database systems, and interaction with local systems at individual institutions. The first phase was completed in 1987. Abbreviated LSP.

Links. In co-ordinate indexing, grouping devices; generally but not necessarily, symbols appended to item numbers. They show that terms are related. Also called 'Interfixes', 'Link letters', 'Punctuation', 'Association'.

Linocut.   1. A piece of linoleum engraved by hand, mounted on a wooden block at type height and printed from as if from a woodcut. Linocut blocks are very durable and can be electrotyped. Illustrations comprising broad flat masses and bold lettering are suitable for this method.   2. The impression made from a linocut block.

Linofilm.   A photo-composing machine built by the Mergenthaler Linotype Co., of New York and demonstrated in 1954.

Linoleum Block.   An engraved piece of linoleum from which a LINOCUT (*q.v.*) is made.

Linoleum Dry-point.   An impression made from a linoleum block on which the design has been made with a dry-point tool.

Linotype.   A typesetting machine casting a line of type in a slug. It was invented by Ottmar Mergenthaler (1854–99). The machine carries a large number of single matrices in a magazine; these are released as the keyboard is operated and assembled in sequence with double-wedge spaces separating the words. The spaces are used to justify the completed line as it is brought to the orifice of a mould, and there cast in a type-high slug. Linotype machines have been in use since 1890, and were the kind most used for printing newspapers.

Linotype Caledonia.   *See Type Face.*

Linson.   The trade name for a particularly tough variety of paper used extensively for publisher's casing. It can be embossed to represent linen and is available in a wide variety of colours and finishes. It is used increasingly as an alternative to cloth, being much cheaper. It is one of a number of binder coverings made by Grange Fibre of Leicester.

Lint.   Dust, or loose fibres, which separate from the raw material during paper-making.

Lippincott Award, Joseph W.   Donated by Joseph W. Lippincott in 1937, and suspended between 1940 and 1947, this annual Award is made to a librarian for distinguished service in the profession of librarianship, such service to include outstanding participation in the activities of professional library associations, notable published professional writing, or other significant activity on behalf of the profession and its aims. The Award is administered by the ALA Awards Committee, the selection being made by a jury of five appointed by the ALA Awards Committee. The first recipient was Mary U. Rothrock in 1938.

LIPs.   Library and Information Plans; a UK series of regional surveys and analyses of library and information services. A first phase has been followed by a second round, and ten such plans have now been undertaken under the auspices of LISC, OAL, and the British Library Research and Development Department. Several of the plans cover more than one local authority area, and three of them are led by co-operative organizations. The five-year management plans examine all services, both public and private, and may reveal possibilities of inter-sector contracts to make the best use of an area's resources. It is hoped that the plans will encourage closer working relationships, joint activities in fields such as local data and training. Cooperative ventures, such as INFORMATION NORTH (*q.v.*) would be one possible outcome. The LIBRARY AND INFORMATION COOPERATION COUNCIL (*q.v.*) has placed a contract with Information North (1990/91) to monitor and evaluate the LIP's achievements.

LIRG. *See Library and Information Research Group.*

LIS. *See Library and Information Science.*

LISA. *See Library and Information Science Abstracts.*

LISC. *See Library and Information Services Council.*

LISE. Acronym of Librarians of Institutes and Schools of Education (UK). Formally inaugurated in 1954 to co-operate in the provision of library services and in bibliographic work in the field of education.

List, Publisher's. A list of books published by one publisher and still in print.

List of Contents. A contents-list or list of 'preliminaries'. *See Contents.*

List of Illustrations. This follows the 'Table of Contents' and indicates the position in the book of the illustrations, both full-page and 'in the text'. *See also Preliminaries.*

List of Signatures. *See Register 2.*

List Price. The price of a book as quoted by the publisher in his catalogue.

LISU. *See Library and Information Statistics Unit.*

LITA. Library and Information Technology Association (*q.v.*) – division of ALA.

LITA/CLSI Scholarship. A cash award made annually to a student on an ALA-accredited study programme with an emphasis on library automation. Supported by CLSI Inc., and administered by the ALA Library and Information Technology Association (LITA) Education Committee.

LITA/Gaylord Award for Achievement in Library and Information Technology. An annual award administered by the LIBRARY AND INFORMATION TECHNOLOGY ASSOCIATION (*q.v.*). Recognizes development of technology or application, or research, or publication.

Literal. An error made in setting type, usually through confusion of similar letters or an unclear manuscript, and involving no more than a letter-for-letter correction, such as a full point for a comma, or a transposition.

Literal Mnemonics. *See Mnemonics.*

Literary Agent. One who arranges the sale and publication of authors' work with publishers of books, newspapers and periodicals, and who negotiates subsidiary rights such as dramatic, broadcasting, and film rights. An agent also acts for publishers by arranging for the writing of scripts which they need. The author pays the agent on a commission basis.

Literary Guild. One of the original American book clubs; it manufactured its own editions.

Literary Manuscript. A record or document produced by hand and indicating literary rather than textual excellence. Also called 'Textual manuscript'. *See also Artistic Manuscript.*

Literary Property. The product of an author's creative effort in the form of manuscripts or published work which have an existing or potential financial value.

Literary Warrant. 1. The volume of books which have been written on any topic. 2. (*Classification*) The quantity of expressed and embodied knowledge in any given field, waiting to be organized.   3. (*Information retrieval*) A subject which has appeared in the literature, is represented by the descriptors used in the retrieval system if it is desired to retrieve documents specifically relevant to that subject, and with minimum 'dilution' by other documents.

Literary Work.   A work, other than a SACRED WORK (*q.v.*), written in a literary form, e.g. a poem, drama, novel, etc. and having outstanding qualities such as beauty of form, emotional or intuitive appeal.

Literature Review.   A survey of progress in a particular aspect of science over a given period (e.g. one, five, or ten years); it may range from a bibliographical index or mere list of references, to a general critical review of original publications on the subjects covered.

Literature Search.   A systematic and exhaustive search for published material on a specific subject, together with the preparation of annotated bibliographies or abstracts for the use of the researcher. This is an intermediate stage between reference work and research, and is differentiated from both. It is often the first step in a research project, patent search, or laboratory experiment and sometimes reveals that the proposed action is unnecessary, having been carried out previously by others; if this is not the case the search usually gives valuable information on similar or identical work previously undertaken. In some libraries a separate room called a 'search room' is set aside and equipped with appropriate bibliographical 'tools' such as volumes of abstracts, periodical indexes, etc. for the carrying out of searches. *See also Online Searching.*

Literature Survey.   1. A bibliography relating to a specific subject and listing material either in a given collection, or in more than one library, or literature on the subject.   2. A listing, with full bibliographical references, of recently published books and articles on a given subject in current journals, prepared usually by librarians or information officers in industrial organizations or research associations for the information of members of, or users of, the organization. It serves to keep those to whom it is circulated up-to-date in the literature of the subjects with which they are concerned. Brief annotations are often provided. Also called 'Current publication survey'.

Litho Crayon.   A special crayon for drawing on lithographic plates.

Litho Papers.   Papers made especially for lithographic printing. Made basically from esparto, they have dimensional stability to ensure correct register, and are usually placed the narrow way across the printing machines, for any stretch must be the narrow way of the sheet.

Lithograph.   A print or illustration produced by LITHOGRAPHY (*q.v.*).

Lithographic Press.   A press for printing from a lithographic stone or plate. It is similar in appearance to a stop-cylinder press used for bookwork, and operates in much the same way.

Lithographic Printing.   A planographic printing process whereby the areas of the printing surface (the non-image areas) are hydrophilic (i.e. have an affinity for water) and the printing (image) areas are hydrophobic (i.e. repel water and attract grease). *See also Lithography.*

Lithographic Ribbon. A special ribbon used for typing direct on to lithographic plates.

Lithography. The process of drawing designs on stone with a special greasy crayon, chalk, paint or ink, and of producing printed impressions therefrom; also any process based on the same principle in which a thin flexible metal plate or plastic is used instead of stone. The stone is saturated with water, the printing ink is then applied and adheres only to those portions covered by the crayon or other drawing medium. A separate drawing is required for each colour in the resulting print. In direct lithography the drawing is in reverse; in offset lithography the drawing is first made the right way round on transfer paper, printed on to a rubber-covered cylinder and 'offset' on to the paper. Lithography was invented by Aloys Senefelder, a Bavarian, in 1798. From the Greek 'Lithos' = stone. *See also Auto-lithography, Offset Lithography, Offset Printing, Photo-lithography, Photo-offset.*

Lithogravure. A process of photo-engraving on stone.

Litho-offset. *See Lithography, Offset Printing.*

Lithophotography. *Synonymous with* PHOTO-LITHOGRAPHY (*q.v.*).

Lithoprint. *Synonymous with* OFFSET PRINTING (*q.v.*).

Lithotint. An obsolete method of lithography by which the effect of a tinted drawing was produced. Also a picture so produced.

Litterae Venetiae. *Synonymous with* BOLOGNESE LETTERS (*q.v.*).

Live Matter. A form of letterpress or illustrations, ready for printing, electrotyping or stereotyping. It may be held for future use. *See also Good, Matter, Standing Type.*

Livres à Vignettes. Books printed in the eighteenth century which were illustrated by vignette copper-plate engravings. The kind of engraving used was a mixture of etching with some gravure work.

LIW. Library and information work; employment in the area of LIBRARY AND INFORMATION SCIENCE (*q.v.*).

ll. Abbreviation for leaves of a book, lines of type, *leges* (laws).

Loaded Paper. *See Coated Paper.*

Loading. The adding of clay, chalk, or similar materials to STUFF (*q.v.*) when in the beater of a paper making machine, or flowed into the stock as it goes through the sluice-gate of the Fourdrinier machine. It fills the spaces between fibres and so imparts solidity to the paper and provides a better printing surface.

LOAF. Acronym for Libraries Open and Free; a pressure group started in Hertfordshire in 1980, with support from other areas arising from time to time. The Group is opposed to charges for library services, and to reductions in opening hours caused by poor resource provision.

Loan. A book, or a number of books, on loan to an individual, a group of persons, an institution or a library.

Loan Collection. A collection of books, prints or pictures which are available for use at home as distinct from a collection which may only be referred to on the premises.

Loan Department. A department from which loans of books and other materials are made, or in which such materials are kept. *Synonymous with* LENDING DEPARTMENT (*q.v.*).

Loan Desk. *See Circulation Desk.*

Loan Fee. A charge made for the use of library materials.

Loan Period. The period which is allowed for reading a book away from a library.

loc cit. Abbreviation for *loco citato* (Lat. 'in the place already cited'). Used in a footnote reference to avoid using the title or short title of the periodical referred to. It should be used less sparingly than *op. cit* (*q.v.*).

Local Area Network. A data transmission system linking computers and other devices within a restricted geographical area; abbreviated LAN.

Local Authorities Management Services and Computer Committee. *See LAMSAC.*

Local Authority. The unit of administration in Britain which is responsible for providing, either on its own behalf and as it is entitled to do by law, or on behalf of the central government, certain services within the area of its geographical boundaries. Not all of the various services may be provided by each kind of local authority. A local authority with power to provide public libraries is called a LIBRARY AUTHORITY (*q.v.*). *See also Local Government Boundaries.*

Local Bibliography. A bibliography of books and other forms of written record relating to a geographical area smaller than a county. It normally includes books by and about people born in, or who have resided in, the area, as well as books relating strictly to the geography, natural history, architecture and social history of the area.

Local Collection. A collection of books, maps, prints, illustrations and other material relating to a specific locality, usually that in which the library housing the collection is situated. *See also Local Government (Records) Act, 1962.*

Local Directory. A directory relating to a specified locality; it may be limited in scope in any way, e.g. to telephone addresses or businesses, but usually includes particulars of residents and businesses, the entries being arranged in street order with 'trade' entries in classified order in addition.

Local Government Boundaries (UK). Under the Local Government Act 1972, the boundaries of most local authorities (excluding Greater London where local government was reorganized in 1965 – *see London Boroughs Committee*) in England and Wales were changed on 1 April 1974. County Boroughs, Cities, Boroughs, Urban Districts and Rural Districts ceased to exist as such; they were all regrouped to form larger administrative units. Some counties were regrouped, at least one was absorbed, all were changed in some degree. There were now six Metropolitan Counties covering the main centres of population, and within these, thirty-six Metropolitan Districts; the Metropolitan Counties and the Greater London Council (GLC) ceased to exist on 1 April 1986. In the rest of England there are 39 Counties and within these 296 Districts; in Wales, eight Counties and within these, 37 Districts. The services provided by local authorities were re-allocated. Now, public library services outside the former GLC area are provided *only* by the councils of the Counties, and Metropolitan Districts. *In Scotland*, a somewhat similar re-arrangement of boundaries came into effect on 15 May 1975 under the provisions of the Local Government (Scotland) Act 1973. In consequence of the passing of this Act, Scotland (other than Orkney, Shetland and the Western Isles which became three 'Island areas') was divided into nine Regions which in turn were subdivided into 53 Districts. On 16 May 1975 all 430 existing local government authorities (counties, cities of counties, large and small burghs, and districts) ceased to exist and were incorporated in the newly formed areas. *See also Bains Report, Library Authority* (for changes in the provision of public libraries in the United Kingdom and Northern Ireland), *Maud Report, Redcliffe-Maud Report, Wheatley Report.*

Local Government (Records) Act, 1962 (UK). This Act amends the law relating to the functions of local authorities respecting records in written or other form. It (1) empowers local authorities to promote the adequate use of their records by allowing inspection, copying, indexing, publication, exhibition, etc.; (2) enables local authorities to acquire local records by gift or purchase – or accept on deposit – records which, or (in the case of a collection) the majority of which, appear to be of local interest, and may deposit them with itself or other authorities; (3) authorizes the appointment of sub-committees to deal with records; (4) provides funds for dealing with records of local interest whether under the authority's control or not. The clerk to the council is custodian 'subject to any direction which the council may give'. *See also Modern Public Records.*

Local Government (Scotland) Act. *See Local Government Boundaries, Library Authority, Wheatley Report.*

Local List. 1. A list prepared by W. P. Cutter and appended to his *Expansive classification*, giving geographical and political divisions, with numbers, for use in arranging material geographically or to indicate relationship. 2. A list of places which may be used to permit sub-division by place in a scheme or classification. 3. A list of books relating to a particular locality.

Local Studies Group. Group of the (British) Library Association; formed in 1977. Concerned with the furtherance of local history libraries by interchange of ideas, promotion of standards, staff training, elementary conservation techniques. Publishes *Local Studies Librarian* (2 p.a.).

Local Unit Card. The basic catalogue entry, or UNIT CARD (*q.v.*), which is made at a library normally purchasing printed catalogue cards, for a book which is to be catalogued locally, either temporarily until printed cards are received, or permanently.

LOCAS. *See BLAISE-LOCAS.*

Location. 1. The place on the shelves or elsewhere in which required material may be found. It is indicated on records, for example on catalogue entries, by the LOCATION MARK (*q.v.*). 2. That part of an index entry which enables the user to locate the document, or part of a document, to which the entry refers. It may be a book, line, column, page, abstract, patent, report, accession number, classification number, or a more or less complete bibliographic citation. It can be a component in a machine documentation system.

Location Index. A record used in county libraries for tracing the whereabouts of particular books. It consists of book cards bearing the names or numbers of the centres to which the books have been sent, and is arranged in alphabetical order.

Location Mark. A letter, word, group of words or symbols used on a catalogue entry, book list or bibliography, sometimes in conjunction with the CALL NUMBER (*q.v.*), to indicate the collection, library or position at which the book or item in question is shelved. Also called 'Location symbol'.

Location Register. A collection, or list, of records of books, documents, or other items, which are arranged by the FIXED LOCATION (*q.v.*) method or in a CLOSED ACCESS (*q.v.*) library. The arrangement of the items on the register may be by author, title, or accession number.

Location Symbol. *See Location Mark.*

Locative Abstract. *See Abstract.*

Locking Up. (*Printing*) Tightening up a forme of type matter in the metal frame known as a chase, preparatory to putting it on the press.

locus sigilli. (*Lat.* 'the place of the seal'). Usually abbreviated LS and printed within a circle at the place for a signature on legal documents.

Loft-dried. Hand- or mould-made papers which are dried by suspension in a dry, airy loft.

Log. A registry of items, e.g. on an accession list.

Logical Arrangement. (*Cataloguing*) A departure from the normal alphabetical order so as to arrange entries by principles associated with the subject matter or type of the entries, e.g. chronological, hierarchical, numerical.

Logical Notation. One in which each symbol of a classification scheme may be divided without limit by a sequence of similar symbols, each having the same value but representing a further step in the sub-division of the subject as represented by the preceding symbol or group of symbols.

Logical Sequence. (*Cataloguing*) A group of entries, in the filing of which, implicit rather than alphabetical criteria have been used. *See also Logical Arrangement.*

Logo. *Synonymous with* MASTHEAD (*q.v.*).

Log-off. *See Log-on.*

Logogram. An initial letter or number used as an abbreviation.

Logograph. A symbol that stands for a whole word.

Logographic Writing. The earliest form of picture writing in which a single symbol was used to represent an entire word.

Logography. A method of casting logotypes. It was first patented by Henry Johnson in 1780 who had a fount of 3500 words and syllables, but the idea never developed owing to opposition from compositors of the time.

Logon. (*Information retrieval*) That which enables one new distinguished group or category to be added to a representation.

Log-on. In accessing a computer file, or using an on-line database, the log-on procedure is that set of operations and routines that the user must complete to obtain access. The closing operation or routine is termed 'log-off'.

Logotype. Several letters, or a word, cast on one type, or as a single matrix. Used in the printing of directories or other works in which such combinations are frequently repeated. *See also Ligature.*

LOLUG. *See London Online User Group.*

Lombardic Handwriting. An offshoot of the Italian semi-cursive minuscule which was derived from the Roman cursive style used throughout Italy in the seventh to ninth centuries. *See also Cursive, Handwriting.*

London and Home Counties Branch. The largest and oldest Branch of the (British) Library Association, having been formed in July 1923.

London and South Eastern Region (LASER). Formed early in 1969 by the amalgamation of the London Union Catalogue and the South Eastern Regional Library System (both of which were formed 40 years earlier) consequent upon the reorganization of the London Borough boundaries in 1965. LASER is currently incorporated as a company, and has 42 public library and 14 non-public library members. It has access to 40 million or so volumes in the stock of member-libraries for interlending, photocopying and reference purposes. Its union catalogue contains entries for some 2.5 million titles, 2 million of which are recorded in machine-readable form and maintained in an on-line minicomputer system. Access to fiction in English and less-used foreign languages is available through special collected schemes. Self-sufficiency in British books is assisted by a Subject Specialization Scheme. Access to serials is available through the maintenance of a manual regional union catalogue of periodicals. Catalogues of play sets and sets of music scores are also maintained and a catalogue of sets of vocal scores was published in 1979 and 1989. On-line access is available for members to the LASER database via VISCOUNT (*q.v.*).

London Boroughs Committee. The committee on which are represented all the 32 London Boroughs (which were formed after the borough boundaries were revised, and the London County Council and the Middlesex County Council ceased to exist, on 1 April 1965) plus the Common Council of the City of London. It performs similar functions to the Metropolitan Boroughs Standing Joint Committee which it superseded, viz. the co-ordination of local government services throughout Greater London. (The Greater London Council ceased to exist on 1 April 1986.)

London Declaration. The Unesco World Congress on Books held in London, 7–11 June 1982 and attended by representatives of 86 countries issued a declaration under the heading 'Towards a Reading Society', and endorsed a series of recommendations which seek to create an environment in which the role of the book is reinforced. The text of the Declaration is given in the *Library Association Record* 84(6) June 1982, page 213.

London Education Classification. A faceted classification scheme designed for use in the library of the University of London Institute for Education, where it has been used since 1962. The second edition, 1974, referred to as

LEC 2, is a thesaurus/classification combining the advantages of faceted classification and thesauri and was used as the basis for the EUDISED Multilingual Thesaurus. The alphabetical index of LEC 2 is in the form of a thesaurus. Abbreviated LEC. *See also EUDISED.*

London Housebound Services Group. A sub-group of the ASSOCIATION OF LONDON CHIEF LIBRARIANS (*q.v.*).

London Online User Group. Established 1985 as an informal forum for discussion on all aspects of online use; in 1989 a new committee took control and instigated a regular programme of evening meetings in central London. Abbreviated LOLUG.

London Union Catalogue. The union catalogue of the (London) Metropolitan Public Libraries. From 1 November 1934 until the reorganization of the London boroughs on 1 April 1965 it was controlled by the Metropolitan Boroughs Standing Joint Committee which levied on all metropolitan libraries a like amount of money for its upkeep, and administered by the Association of Metropolitan Chief Librarians on behalf of the MBSJC. It was maintained at the premises of the National Central Library, and although not strictly a regional bureau, functioned as one, arranging for the loan of books between the London libraries and other libraries throughout the country. *See also London & South Eastern Library Region.*

Long. *See Broad, Oblong.*

Long-bodied Type. Type which is cast on bodies larger than usual, e.g. 10-point on 12-point. This avoids the use of LEADS (*q.v.*).

Long Descender. Letters g, j, p, q and y with extra long descenders; these are available as alternatives in some faces as, for example, Linotype Caledonia and Times Roman. *See also Ascender, Descender.*

Long Elephant. *See Elephant.*

Long Grain. Paper in which the fibres lie in the longer direction of the sheet. *See also Grain Direction, Short Grain.*

Long Index. A very full index to a work in one or more volumes where the text is of such a nature that a very large number of entries and references is required.

Long Letter. A character, such as f, j or k, which has either ASCENDER OR DESCENDER (*qq.v.*) or both. *See also Short Letter*, which has neither.

Long Page. A page of a book with more lines of type than most of the others. *See also Short Page.*

Long Primer. An old name for a type size, about 10 point.

Long Ream. 500 or 516 sheets of paper. *See also Ream, Short Ream.*

Look-through. The examination of paper by holding it up against strong light. By this means, the dispersion of fibres can be seen, and consequently the strength of the paper judged; it is also a means of seeing whether the paper is laid or wove, and if its texture is marred by impurities. *See also Wild Look-through.*

Loose. A book, the sections of which are badly loosened from the case, the sewing having broken.

Loose Back. *Synonymous with* HOLLOW BACK (*q.v.*).

Loose Leaf Binding. A binding which permits the immediate withdrawal and insertion of pages at any desired position, as in a ring binder.

Loose Leaf Catalogue. A SHEAF CATALOGUE (*q.v.*).

Loose-leaf Service. A serial publication which is revised, supplemented, cumulated, and indexed by means of new replacement pages inserted in a loose-leaf binder; such publications are used where the latest statements and revisions of information are important, as with legal, political, social and scientific material. *See also Serial Service.*

Low Priced Book Scheme. *See Educational Low Priced Book Scheme.*

Lower Case Letters. Minuscules or 'small' letters such as a.b.c.; those other than capitals. The name originated from the fact that printers kept their type in two large cases, one above the other, each divided into sections containing one SORT (*q.v.*). The upper case contained the capital letters, majuscules, and the lower one the others. Abbreviated l.c. *See also Capitals, Small Capitals, Upper Case Letters.*

Lower Cover. *Synonymous with* REVERSE COVER (*q.v.*).

Lower Edge. The TAIL (*q.v.*) of a book. Also called 'Bottom edge', 'Tail edge'.

Lower Margin. *Synonymous with* TAIL MARGIN (*q.v.*).

Loxodrome. *See Portolan Chart.*

Lozenge. (*Binding*) A diamond-shaped figure, or a square figure, placed on one of its corners; it is usually decorated.

l.p. Abbreviation for LARGE PAPER COPY or EDITION (*q.v.*).

LPRC. Library Public Relations Council (*q.v.*).

LRDG. *See Learning Resources Development Group.*

LRRT. *See Library Research Round Table.*

LS. (1) Abbreviation for LIBRARY SCHOOL (*q.v.*) and LIBRARY SCIENCE (*q.v.*). (2) *See locus sigilli and ALS.*

LSA. *Library Science Abstracts* (*q.v.*).

LSCA. Library Services and Construction Act (American). *See Library Law.*

LSP. *See Linked Systems Project.*

LTP. LIBRARY TECHNOLOGY PROGRAM (*q.v.*).

Lubavitch Lending Library. A library of some 10,000 volumes on spiritual, philosophical and halachic subjects built up since 1973 by Svi Rabin, and housed in Stamford Hill, London.

Lubetzky Code. A draft, issued in 1960, under the title of *Code of Cataloguing rules, author and title entry.* This was written on entirely fresh lines (but firmly grounded in the Panizzi and Cutter traditions) under the direction of the (American) Catalog Code Revision Committee. Seymour Lubetzky was at the time the specialist in bibliographic and cataloguing policy at the Library of Congress.

Ludlow. A machine which casts slugs for display work. Composing is done by hand, a special composing stick being used; when the characters are all in position, the stick is placed into the machine which casts a line as a slug. It is frequently used in conjunction with the Elrod machine which casts rules, leads, borders and plain slugs.

LULOP. *London Union List of Periodicals.* First issued in 1951, this publication records the periodicals available in the municipal and county libraries in Greater London. It gives the extent of the permanent files of periodicals possessed, and also a guide to places where files or current issues only are available.

Lumbecking. The PERFECT (*q.v.*), or flexible, method of binding whereby the separate sheets are not kept together by sewing but by adhesive only.

Luminotype. The original name for the ÜHERTYPE (*q.v.*) photocomposing machine.

Lumitype. A method of FILMSETTING (*q.v.*).

Lundia Shelving. A patented design of adjustable shelving of Swedish origin made under licence in a number of countries.

Lutheran Church Library Association. Founded in 1958 in the USA 'to promote the growth of church libraries in Lutheran congregations by publishing a quarterly journal, *Lutheran Libraries*, furnishing booklists, assisting member libraries with technical problems, providing meetings for mutual encouragement, assistance and exchange of ideas among members'. Abbreviated LCLA.

Luttrell Psalter. An English Psalter of the East Anglian School, illuminated (as was usual at the time) by mainly grotesque beasts and monkeys (babewyns) but also with agricultural scenes, games and sports, and also incidents from the lives of the saints. It was written about 1340 for Sir Geoffrey Louterell of Lincolnshire who is depicted on a charger, his wife and daughter being in the same group. It is in the British Library.

Lux. The metric measurement of light value, one lumen or foot-candle being equal to 10.76 lux.

Luxury Binding. *Synonymous with* DE LUXE BINDING (*q.v.*).

l.v. Abbreviation for *locis variis* (*Lat.* 'various places').

L-VIS. *See Laser Viewdata Information Service.*

Lyonese (Lyonnaise) Style. A style of binding with broad interlaced geometrical strapwork usually painted, lacquered, or enamelled in different colours; so called because it appeared on books bound at Lyons in the latter part of the sixteenth century. Also a style in which the binding is decorated with large corner ornaments and with a prominent centre design, roughly lozenge shaped, the all-over background being filled in with dots.

M. 1. Abbreviation for *million* in computing terminology. 2. Roman figure for 1000 used as an abbreviation by printers.

MacBride Report. The report *Many voices, one world: report of the International Commission for the Study of Development Problems* (Unesco, 1980) which is concerned with global communications problems.

McCarthy Award. Awarded by Kodak (UK) Ltd., to a firm judged to have made an outstanding contribution to the application of microfilming.

McColvin Medal. Awarded annually by the Library Association for an outstanding reference book first published in the United Kingdom during the preceding year.

McColvin Report (UK). The report: *The Public Library System of Great Britain*, including proposals for post-war development, by L. R. McColvin. (Library Association, 1942).

Machell (Roger) Prize. Sponsored by Hamish Hamilton Ltd., and administered by the SOCIETY OF AUTHORS (*q.v.*); for a UK published non-fiction book on any of the performing arts.

McLeod (Enid) Prize. An annual award of the Franco-British Society for a book contributing to Franco-British understanding.

Macmillan Silver Pen Award. An annual award for an outstanding UK novel; sponsored by Macmillan, and administered by the English Centre of PEN INTERNATIONAL (*q.v.*).

McVitie's Prize. An annual award for a literary work in any form by a Scottish resident; submission in English, Scots, or Gaelic.

Machine Coated. (*Paper*) Paper which has been coated with clay or a similar substance during the actual making of the paper to give it a smooth printing surface. When the coating is applied as a separate and later operation, it is called 'brush coated'.

Machine Composition. Type-setting by machine as distinct from setting by hand.

Machine Direction. The direction in which paper travels through a paper-making machine. Most of the fibres lie in this direction; therefore paper folds more easily along the machine direction (said to be 'with the grain'), and a sheet of paper when wetted expands mainly across this direction, with a corresponding shrinkage of the paper on drying. *See also Against the Grain, Grain, Grain Direction.*

Machine-dried. *Synonymous with* CYLINDER DRIED (*q.v.*).

Machine Finish. Paper which has been made smooth, but not glossy, by receiving the normal finish of a Fourdrinier paper-making machine: this passes the paper over heated drums and through steel calendering rollers. Abbreviated MF. This is the normal paper for letterpress printing where half-tones are not to be used. *See also Paper Finishes.*

Machine Glazed. Said of a paper in which the 'glaze' or polish is produced on the paper-making machine, and not by means of super-calenders or a glazing machine. The only paper-machine which glazes in the process of making is the single-cylinder machine or 'Yankee' in which the web of paper is dried on the one large steam-heated cylinder with a highly polished surface. Machine-glazed papers are identified by being glazed on only one side (the under), the other being in the rough condition to which it comes from the wet end of the machine. Papers made on such machines are very varied in character and uses, for example, manillas for envelopes; litho, poster, kraft and sulphite bag papers and cheap wrappings and tissues. Abbreviated MG.

Machine Indexing. A process whereby the indexing processes are accomplished by mechanized means.

Machine Language. Information in the physical form that a computer can handle.

Machine-made Paper. The continuous web, or roll, of paper made on cylinder machines or on the Fourdrinier machine.

Machine Proof. A proof taken when corrections which were marked on galley and page proofs have been made, and the forme is on the printing machine. This proof affords the last opportunity for correcting mistakes before machining takes place. Also called 'Press revise'.

Machine Readable. Information in a form that can be directly assimilated by computer input equipment.

Machine Readable Data Files. Files of information held in a form which can be directly input into a computer. Abbreviated MRDF.

Machine Revise. A proof printed when the forme is on the printing machine, in order that a comprehensive revise may be made of the whole of the details of workmanship, including those which the reader has not had an opportunity of verifying. Also called 'Machine proof'.

Machine Translation. Automatic translation from one representation to a different one. The translation may involve codes or other systems of representation. Computer programs now exist to enable a natural language text to be translated without human intervention, but the results are crude and suitable only for weather forecasts or other simply structured and unambiguous material. The EEC has pioneered a term bank, EURODI-CAUTOM (*q.v.*) as an assistance to machine-aided human translation (MAHT), or machine-aided translation (MAT) (also known as computer-aided translation, or computer-assisted translation) (CAT). *See also Mechanical Translation, Target Language.*

Machine Wire. *Synonymous with* WIRE (*q.v.*).

Machining. (*Printing*) 1. That part of printing concerned with actually printing on the paper. The other major processes in producing a book are composition and binding. Called 'Press work' in America. 2. The actual process of printing by running the forme through the machine to give the paper an impression from the printing surface.

Mackle. A printed sheet with a blurred impression, owing to some mechanical defect in the printing.

Macro-document. A book, treatise, or document embodying macro-thought. *See also Macro-thought, Micro-document.*

Macroform. A reproduction of a document which can be read with the unaided eye. *See also Microform.*

Macrograph. A photographic reproduction of an object that may be slightly reduced, or of natural size, or magnified up to about ten diameters.

Macro-thought. (*Classification*) A subject of great extension, usually embodied in the form of a book. *See also Macro-document, Micro-thought.*

MAD. *See Manual of Archival Description.*

Made-up Copy. A book which has had imperfections made good by the insertion of portions from other copies of the same edition.

Made-up Set. A work in a number of volumes which is made up by assembling volumes of more than one edition. It is catalogued as a regular set except that the various editions are specified in a note unless they can be mentioned in the body of the entry.

Magazine. 1. A periodical publication as distinct from a newspaper, separate issues being independently paginated and identified by date rather than by serial number. 2. A receptacle above the keyboard of a Linotype, or similar type-casing machine, for containing the matrices ready for assembling into lines of type or slugs. 3. A container for the automatic projection of photographic slides. 4. A container for roll microfilm which both protects the film and facilitates its loading into a reader.

Magazine Case. A cover for periodicals, usually having some contrivance for holding the magazine – cord, rod, etc. Also called 'Periodical case' and 'Reading case'.

Magazine Rack. A fitting for displaying magazines.

Magazine Room. A room used exclusively for the reading of periodicals. Sometimes called 'Periodical room'. *See also Newsroom.*

Magnetic Disc. *See Disc.*

Magnetic Master Track. The track obtained from combining a number of separate sound tracks into a single magnetic track.

Magnetic Storage. A storage device that utilizes the magnetic properties of materials to store data, e.g. magnetic films, tapes, discs and cones.

Magnetic Tape. Plastic tape coated with a magnetic material on which information can be recorded and identified by computers and other machines.

MAHT. Machine-Aided Human Translation; *see Machine Translation.*

Mailbox. *See Electronic Mailbox.*

Main Card. The catalogue card bearing the MAIN ENTRY (*q.v.*).

Main Catalogue. A colloquialism for what may be considered the most important catalogue in a library; it is usually the one with the most entries or the 'main entries'; it may be the classified catalogue without the author and subject indexes.

Main Class. The principal division of a scheme of classification, e.g. in Brown's *Subject Classification*: Matter, Life, Mind, Record; or Dewey's General works, Philosophy, Religion, Social Sciences, Language, Pure science, Technology, The Arts, Literature, History. These are divided into 'Divisions' which are divided into 'Subdivisions' which are in turn divided into 'Sections', each division proceeding by gradual steps, and each new heading becoming more 'intense'.

Main Entry. 1. The basic catalogue entry; the main entry has the fullest particulars for the complete identification of a work. In card catalogues – especially dictionary ones – the main entry bears the TRACING (*q.v.*). It may bear in addition the tracing of related references and a record of other pertinent official data concerning the work. For music, the entry under the composer's name. 2. The entry chosen for the basic entry, whether it be a personal or corporate name, or the title of an anonymous book, collection, composite work, periodical or serial, or a UNIFORM TITLE (*q.v.*).

Main Heading. 1. (*Indexing*) A description sometimes used (for a heading) in contradistinction to a subheading. 2. (*Cataloguing*) The first part of a composite heading which includes one or more subheadings. That part of a heading which precedes a subheading.

Main Library. *See Central Library.*

Main Stroke. The principal stroke, heavy line, or stem of a type letter.

Main Subject. A book may treat of several subjects, or may be considered by classifier or cataloguer to need cross references from a subsidiary to the one most important subject. The subject which is given priority and to which references are made is the 'main subject'.

Main Title. That part of the title which precedes the SUB-TITLE (*q.v.*).

Main Title-page. The title-page from which the details for a catalogue entry are taken. *See also Added Title-page, Half Title.*

Mainframe. A term indicating a large computer, as distinct from a minicomputer or microcomputer. Now needed only for the very largest applications.

Mainz Psalter. In Latin, this famous masterpiece of printing was printed by Johann Fust and Peter Schoeffer in Mainz and is dated 14 August 1457. It is the first printed book to give the name of the printer and the date of printing. *See also Mazarin Bible.*

Maioli Style. The style of book decoration executed for Thomasso Maioli or Mahieu, (actually Thomas Matthieu a Frenchman), a contemporary of Grolier, in the middle of the sixteenth century. A distinguishing characteristic is that the Arabic ornaments are frequently in outline, whereas those of Grolier are ajuré, and of Aldus, solid. The style is generally composed of a framework of shields or medallions, with a design of scrollwork flowing through it, portions of the design usually being studded with gold dots.

Majuscule. Large letter whether capital (upper case) or UNCIAL (*q.v.*). *See also Minuscule.*

Make-ready (Making-ready). The process of preparing a forme ready for printing. Levelling up and lining up by patching with paper, or cutting away on the impression cylinder or platen BED (*q.v.*) and by underlaying or interlaying the blocks so that the impression from type and blocks on paper will be clear, clean and of uniform colour. The amount and position of make-ready is determined by a trial pull. The time which this process takes is an important item in every printing bill. It is upon the care with which a job is made-ready that the quality of the printing depends. Make-ready is of paramount importance in colour and half-tone work. *See also Overlay and Underlay.*

Make-up. (*Printing*) 1. A general term for taking the type from the galleys, putting it into page form, insetting illustrative cuts, dividing the matter into page lengths, and adding running heads, titles of sub-divisions, folios, footnotes, etc., and securing with page-cord. The pages of type are then ready for locking in the CHASE (*q.v.*). 2. Sometimes used instead of 'layout' to indicate the dummy showing the desired arrangement of letterpress and illustrations. 3. A list of the contents of a book supplied by the publisher to the binder to serve as an instruction as to the positioning of plates, plans, folded leaves, map endpapers, etc. 4. (*Archives*) The particular method and order in which the leaves, or membranes of a document are fastened together to constitute a complete volume or document, or the manner in which a single leaf or membrane is folded. *See also Make-up Copy, Publisher's Binding.*

Make-up Copy. A set of folded sheets, plates, plans, etc. in correct order and sent by the publisher as an instruction to the binder. *See also Make-up.*

Managed Data Network Service. A project of the European Community, to make feasible interconnection of the computer systems of European researchers. A part of the ESPRIT programme (*q.v.*), and a major need identified by COSINE (*q.v.*). Abbreviated MDNS.

Management. *See Library Management.*

Management by Objectives. *See Objectives.*

Management Information System. A system designed to use all data collected by an organization to provide management with the information needed for decision making. Abbreviated MIS.

Manière Criblée. A fifteenth-century 'relief' method of producing illustrations by means of a plate of soft metal such as copper, pewter or zinc in which the drawing was made with a graver and which, being sunk below the level of the plate, would appear as white lines on a black ground when printed. Intermediate tones were produced by punching dots in the surface of the plate at more or less regular intervals. Also called 'Schrotblatt'.

Manilla Paper. A superfine tough quality of wrapping and label paper made from manilla hemp; also applied to cheap imitations made from wood pulp.

Mann Citation, Margaret. Instituted in 1950, and administered by the Cataloging and Classification Section of the Resources and Technical Services Division (now ALCTS) of the American Library Association, this citation is made to a librarian in recognition of distinguished contributions to librarianship through publication of significant professional literature, participation in professional cataloguing associations, or valuable contributions to practice in individual libraries. The first recipient of the Citation was Miss Lucile M. Morsch in 1951.

Manorial Courts. Administrative and legal courts concerned with matters affecting a particular manor. The *Court Customary* was principally concerned with the agricultural organization of the township, while the *Court Leet* had a minor criminal jurisdiction.

Manorial Documents. Documents relating to manors and the management of estates. Manorial Documents Rules were made in 1926 (S.R. & O. 1926, No. 1310) to implement the provisions of the Law of Property Act, 1922, as amended, by which the Master of the Rolls has power to transfer manorial documents to the Public Record Office or a public library, museum, or historical or antiquarian society.

Manual. *Synonymous with* HANDBOOK (*q.v.*).

Manual Input. (*Information retrieval*) The insertion of data by hand into a machine or other device at the time of processing.

Manual of Archival Description. A product of the British Library funded archival description project based at the University of Liverpool, initially 1986–88. MAD includes specialized format descriptions, such as letters, photographs, plans, sound archives and machine-readable formats. A format suitable for electronic transmission is also envisaged, with further work on a second manual – MAD 2.

Manuale. A case to protect a VOLUMEN (*q.v.*). *See also Capsa.*

Manuscript. A document of any kind which is written by hand, or the text of a music or literary composition in hand-written or typescript form, and which, in that form, has not been reproduced in multiple copies. An *illuminated manuscript* is one which has been decorated as described under ILLUMINATED BOOK (*q.v.*). Abbreviated MS. (*Pl.* MSS.).

Manuscript Catalogue. One written by hand.

Manuscript Librarian. A librarian who has charge of a collection of manuscripts of all kinds, i.e. unprinted materials (whether written by hand or typed) other than books written by hand before the invention of printing (*libri manuscripti*).

Manuscript Music Book. A book of MUSIC PAPER (*q.v.*).

Manuscript Note. A handwritten note in a book.

Manuscript Society. *The Manuscript Society* was founded in 1948 as the *National Society of Autograph Collectors*, and has grown to an international membership of over 1400, including dealers, private collectors, scholars, authors, and caretakers of public collections, such as librarians, archivists, and curators. There are also many institutional members, such as historical societies, museums, special libraries, and academic libraries. Publishes *Manuscripts* (q.), and a newsletter.

Map. A plane representation of the earth's surface, or a part of same, indicating physical features, political boundaries, etc. Also a similar representation of the heavens, showing the position of the stars, planets, etc. Also called an 'Astronomical map'. The first book to contain a printed map or diagram of the whole world was Isidore of Seville's *Etymologiarum sive Originum libri XX*, Augsburg, 19 November 1472. The earliest and most important maps to be printed from engraved copper plates in England were those of Christopher Saxton, who issued county maps between 1574 and 1579. An 'early map' is considered to be one made before 1825. For different kinds of maps, *see Artistic Map, Average Slope Map, Astronomical Map, Cadastral Map, Cartogram, Choro-chromatic Map, Chorographic Map, Choropleth Map, Choro-schematic Map, Demopleth Map, Dot Map, Dynamic Map, Flow-line Map, Hypsometric Map, International Millionth Map, Isephodic Map, Isochronic Map, Isogonic Chart, Isopleth Map, Relative Relief Map.*

Map Curators Group. A sub-section of the British Cartographic Society, providing a forum for map librarians. Affiliated to the Library Association.

Map Endpapers. Endpapers on which maps are printed. *See also Endpaper.*

Map File. A sequence of sheet or folded maps arranged in classified order, or alphabetically by place name. Sheet maps are kept in shallow drawers, often with hinged fronts which fall down and so reduce wear when consulting the maps, or in specially made vertical cabinets. *See also Plan Cabinet.*

Map Paper. *See Plan Paper.*

Map Projection. The arrangement of parallels and meridians so as to enable part, or the whole, of the spheroidal surface of the earth to be represented on a plane-surface.

Map Room.   A room devoted to the storage and consultation of maps.

Marbled Edges.   The three edges of a book cut solid, and stained to resemble marble. *See also Edges, Sprinkled Edges, Stained Edges, Stippled Edges.*

Marbled Paper.   Surface-colour paper used by bookbinders. Marbling is done by floating white paper, or dipping the edges of a sewn book before inserting into the cover, on a bath of gum tragacanth, the surface of which has been sprinkled with various colours, and combed out to a desired pattern.

Marbling.   The process of colouring the endpapers and edges of a book in imitation of marble.

Marbling Under Gilt.   Marbled edges of a book overlaid with gold. Usually the marbling is not very noticeable until the edges are fanned out. The style was first used in France in the seventeenth century, its invention being accredited to Le Gascon. Sometimes it is found in English bindings of the middle of the eighteenth century and later. *See also Gilt on the Rough, Rough Gilt Edges, Solid Gilt.*

MARC.   The MARC format was developed to provide an internationally acceptable standard for the exchange of bibliographic data in machine-readable form. *Machine-Readable Cataloguing* began in 1966 as a pilot scheme operated by the Library of Congress. Bibliographic records on machine-readable tape were distributed weekly to sixteen American libraries who then used their own computing facilities to process them. At this stage the most usual form of output was the conventional catalogue card. By 1967 the MARC II format had been introduced and the service extended to some fifty libraries. The original MARC format had revealed certain limitations which the MARC II format was specifically designed to overcome. Each record can accommodate a large quantity of bibliographic data in machine-readable form. In addition to a full AACR 2 description, the record may contain Dewey Decimal Classification numbers, Library of Congress Classification numbers, Precis subject headings and Library of Congress subject headings. Any of the these individual elements may be used to access the MARC file of bibliographic records. Subsequently the British National Bibliography (now part of the Bibliographic Services Division of the British Library) began to develop UKMARC and by 1969 tapes were being distributed to British libraries. The MARC format is available for many different types of library materials (monographs, serials, audio-visual materials) and has become an international standard. It is used in many countries other than the United Kingdom and the United States, notably Australia, Canada, France and Scandinavia. *See also BLDMARC, BLMARC, BNBMARC, UKMARC, UNIMARC.*

MARC format.   The structure of a machine-readable bibliographic record resulting from the application of ISO 2709 for the purpose of transmitting or communicating library catalogue data. There is a 'family' of MARC formats including the UKMARC format, the USMARC format, the UNIMARC format, etc. *See MARC.*

Margin.   1. The unprinted area between printed or written matter and the edges of a page. The proportional width of the margins is a very important element in a properly balanced book-page. A good ratio is: head (top) margin 2; fore-edge (outside) 3; tail, also called 'lower' or 'bottom' (bottom) 4; back (inside) 1½.   2. The area of a map, drawing or print, between the line enclosing the information area and the edge of the paper.   3. On microfilm, the area of background between the line enclosing the information area and the edge of the film frame.

Marginal Figure.   A figure printed in the margin of a book to indicate the number of a line of type for purposes of easy reference. *See also Runners.*

Marginal Heading.   A heading printed at the side of the type area.

Marginal-hole Punched Cards.   Cards which have rows of holes punched round the margins or over a large part of the card's area. These holes are notched or slotted to record information which is obtained, when required, by inserting needles, in the holes and allowing cards on which the required information is recorded to fall away. *See also Dequeker System, Edge-notched Cards.*

Marginal Note.   A note or GLOSS (*q.v.*) written or printed on the margin of a page opposite the portion of text to which it refers. Notes are called *footnotes* when printed at the bottom of the page, and *Shoulder-notes* when printed at the top corner of the page. Also called 'Marginal Heading', 'Marginalia'. *Synonymous with* SIDE NOTE (*q.v.*).

Marginalia.   *Synonymous with* MARGINAL NOTES (*q.v.*).

Marine Librarians Association.   Formed in 1971 in London to promote contact and co-operation between librarians and information workers in the marine field, and to develop a body of professional expertise concerning the literature and information sources relevant to the marine field. Membership is on an individual basis, and includes librarians and information officers working for a variety of organizations having major or minor interests in subjects ranging over the broadest interpretation of 'marine' topics. These subject interests include marine science and technology, shipping, shipbuilding, marine engineering and telecommunications, maritime law and economics, ports and cargo handling, fisheries, off-shore activities etc. Publishes a *Newsletter* (3 p.a.) and various guides.

MARIS.   Materials and Resources Information Service: a project of the Open Tech, based at the National Extension College, Ely, Cambs. *See also TAPs.*

Marked Proof.   *See Proof.*

Marker.   (*Information retrieval*) A symbol which is used to separate more than one independent subject description assigned to the same item in order to guard against FALSE COMBINATIONS (*q.v.*).

Markers.   1. In American libraries, members of the staff who process books by writing call numbers on the spines, insert book pockets, labels, etc.   2. Sensitized strips placed in books as part of a system to obviate their unauthorized removal from libraries.

Market Letter.   A bulletin issued by a stockbroker or investment house at regular intervals.

Marking.   1. The placing of call numbers on books and other library materials.   2. The placing of a mark of ownership, with a note about disposition, on each item of a serial publication, as each is checked.

Marking-up. In book-binding, dividing the spine into equal portions and marking the position of the cords.

Markov Process. *See Stochastic Process.*

Marks. *See Code.*

Marks of Omission. *Synonymous with* OMISSION MARKS (*q.v.*).

Marks of Reference. *See Reference Marks.*

Martin (Allie Beth) Award. An annual award to recognize outstanding bibliographic knowledge and ability to communicate that knowledge; made by the PUBLIC LIBRARY ASSOCIATION (*q.v.*) of the ALA.

Maschler (Kurt)/Emil Award. Administered by the BOOK TRUST (*q.v.*), an annual UK award for 'a work of imagination in the children's field in which text and illustration are of excellence and so presented that each enhances, yet balances the other'.

Masefield (John) Memorial Trust. Administered by the SOCIETY OF AUTHORS (*q.v.*), the Trust makes occasional grants to professional poets.

Masking. (*Printing*) The placement of an opaque cut-out overlay or a transparent overlay on which lines have been lightly drawn, over a photograph or drawing, or lines drawn on the back thereof, in order to indicate areas at the sides which are not to be reproduced.

Mass Book. *See Missal.*

Master. The plate, or stencil in duplicating processes, from which copies are made.

Master Catalogue. A catalogue in which every main entry is a master card forming the official, complete and up-to-date record of catalogued stock, and providing essential information for the cataloguers who maintain it. Being the union catalogue of the whole system it is usually kept in the cataloguing department or in the central library.

Master File. (*Information retrieval*) 1. A file containing relatively permanent information. 2. A main file of information.

Master Film. Any film, but usually a negative, which is used for making further copies.

Masthead. The statement of the title, ownership, address and frequency of publication, printer's name and address, and sometimes postage and subscription rates of a periodical publication. It is usually on the last or the editorial page of a newspaper, and on the editorial or contents page of a magazine. Also called 'Flag' and 'Logo'.

MAT. Machine-aided translation. *See Machine Translation.*

Matching. In computer technology, the comparison of two sets of codes to ascertain their similarity or difference. It is the basic operation in selecting, sorting or collating.

Material Bibliography. *See Historical Bibliography.*

Mathematical Order. (*Classification*) Used by E. C. Richardson to indicate a possible order for terms in an ARRAY (*q.v.*) which forms a series of co-ordinate classes. Order by means of a NOTATION (*q.v.*). *Synonymous with* S. R. Ranganathan's CANONICAL ORDER (*q.v.*).

Matrix. (*Pl.* MATRICES). (*Printing*) 1. The mould from which a stereotype (stereo) or electrotype (electro) is made. The mould is made by placing wet flong (a material, about ¹⁄₁₆ inch thick, made of alternate layers of tissue paper and blotting paper) over the type of which an impression is needed and then beating it with a stiff brush. It is then subjected to pressure, removed and dried.   2. A mould from which type is cast in a typesetting machine.   3. A copper mould which has been struck with a punch and from which individual type letters are cast. Also called a 'strike'. *See also Electrotype, Stereotype.* 4. (*Information retrieval*) A rectangular array of elements . . . used to facilitate the study of problems in which the relation between these elements is fundamental.

Matrix Printer.   A computer-output printer which forms each character from a series of overlapping dots. This technique produces a potentially infinite range of characters. Also called *dot (and) matrix printer.*

Matt Art.   *See Art.*

Matter.   1. Type, whether in the process of setting up, or standing. It may be *live* matter (not yet printed from) or *dead* matter (awaiting distribution), *open* matter (leaded) or *solid* matter (without leads). The ancient terms, *fat* and *lean* matter, are still used to indicate the proportion of open spaces or break lines.   2. Manuscript of copy to be printed. *See also Good.*

Maud Report (UK).   The report of the Committee on the Management of Local Government which was set up by Sir Keith Joseph, when Minister of Housing and Local Government, on 3 March 1964; so named after Sir John Maud, the Chairman. The terms of reference of the Committee were 'to consider in the light of modern conditions how local government might best continue to attract and retain people (both elected representatives and principal officers) of the calibre necessary to ensure its maximum effectiveness'. The report itself occupies volume 1 of the 5 volumes the overall title of which is *Management of local government*; volumes 2–4 are enquiries carried out for the Committee and entitled *The local government councillor, The local government elector* and *Local government administration abroad* Volumes 1–4 were published in May 1967; volume 5 *Local government administration in England and Wales*, comprising further research enquiries carried out for the Committee, was published in July 1967. Sir John Maud was created a life peer in 1967 and then took the title of Baron Redcliffe Maud. *See also Redcliffe-Maud Report.*

Maugham (Somerset) Trust Fund.   Administered by the Society of Authors (*q.v.*), the fund makes awards for young writers to travel.

Mazarin Bible.   The 42-line Bible printed in Latin by Johann Gutenberg Johann Fust and Peter Schoeffer at Mainz between 1450–55 and one of the earliest books to be printed from movable type. So called because the copy which first attracted the attention of bibliographers was discovered by Debure the French bookseller, in 1760, among the books of Cardinal Mazarin (1602–61) who was a well-known bibliophile. Mazarin's library i now in the Collège Mazarin, Paris. Forty-eight copies of this Bible are known, of which 36 are printed on paper and 12 on vellum; 21 in all are perfect. The British Library possesses one of each, both perfect. Also known as the 'Gutenberg', or '42-line Bible'. *See also Mainz Psalter.*

MB. Megabyte. *See Byte.*

MbO. *See Objectives.*

MBSJC. Metropolitan Boroughs Standing Joint Committee. *See entry under Association of Metropolitan Chief Librarians.*

Mbyte. Abbreviation for Megabyte. *See Byte.*

MDNS. *See Managed Data Network Service.*

Mean Line. (*Printing*) An imaginary line running along the top of all x-height letters, i.e. those without ascenders, a, c, e, etc. *See also Ascender Line, Base Line, Cap Line, Superior Figures (Letters).*

Meaning. (*Information retrieval*) The relation of formal equivalence between symbols (codes).

Mearne Style. The style of book decoration used during the seventeenth and early eighteenth centuries in England. This style is named after Samuel Mearne, the stationer and binder to Charles II and is a development of the Fanfare and Le Gascon styles. Red and black inlay was used with great effect, and the centre panel was often in the COTTAGE STYLE (*q.v.*). The ALL-OVER STYLE (*q.v.*) was also often used. Also called 'Restoration style'. *See also Rectangular Style.*

Measure. The width to which printed matter is set, i.e. the length of line. It is usually counted in 12-point ems. *See also Didot System, Em, Point.*

Mechanical Binding. A binding which uses a mechanical device such as a spiral binding of metal or plastic to hold the pages together.

Mechanical Overlay. *See Chalk Overlay.*

Mechanical Preparation. The preparation of books and other library materials for use. It includes rubber stamping and other forms of ownership marks, pasting labels, book pockets, and, where preparation is carried out in a cataloguing department, includes lettering books with class numbers and making out book-cards. (*American*) *See also Processing Center.*

Mechanical Tints. *Synonymous with* TINT (*q.v.*).

Mechanical Translation. A generic term for language translation by computer. *See also Machine Translation.*

Mechanical Wood. The lowest grade of wood pulp used in the manufacture of paper, and prepared by the purely mechanical process of grinding. This method produces a higher yield than the chemical process but the resulting pulp is less pure. It is suitable only for newsprint: it has good printing qualities and is opaque but impermanent. Also called 'Groundwood pulp'. *See also Chemical Wood.*

Mechanical Wood Pulp. *Synonymous with* SEMI-CHEMICAL PULP (*q.v.*).

Mechanization. *See Automation.*

Mechanized Indexing. The accomplishment of indexing operations by mechanical means. This includes the preparation and compilation of indexes, and the sorting, assembling, duplication and interfiling of catalogue cards carrying index entries. *See also Automatic Indexing.*

MECU. *See ECU.*

Media. 1. A generic term to denote methods of public communication – the press, radio, television etc. 2. A loosely defined term for non-print items held by a library: for example, audio-visual materials, software and possibly maps.

Media Aide.   An individual engaged in clerical or secretarial duties in a MEDIA CENTRE (*q.v.*).

Media Centre.   Sometimes used for a school library, or learning resources centre in a school, where a range of print and audio-visual media, necessary equipment, and the services of a media specialist, are accessible to students and teachers.

Media File.   Information prepared for buyers of advertising space in newspapers and periodicals, and giving particulars of circulation, column and type sizes and rates. Also termed *media pack*.

Media Programme.   All the instructional and related services provided for students and teachers by a MEDIA CENTRE (*q.v.*) and its staff.

Media Resources.   Collections of non-book MEDIA (*q.v.*).

Media Specialist.   An individual who has broad professional preparation in educational media.

Media Staff.   The personnel who carry out the work of a MEDIA CENTRE (*q.v.*) and its programme.

Media Technician.   An individual who has training in the preparation of materials and the operation and maintenance of apparatus.

Mediaan System.   A Belgian system of line measurement used in conjunction with the Fournier system of measuring type bodies; 12-point equals 0.1649 inch or 4.18 mm.

Mediamobile.   A vehicle which carries various forms of media, in addition to books, for loan to the public.

Medical, Health and Welfare Libraries Group.   A group of the (British) Library Association formed in 1978 by the merger of the Hospital Libraries and Handicapped Readers Group, and the Medical Section; the group is a focus for librarians working in many types of libraries within the health service. Publishes *Health Librarian Review* (3 p.a.). *See also Reading Therapy Sub-group.*

Medical Library Assistance Act.   *See Library Law.*

Medical Library Association.   Founded in the USA in 1898 to foster medical and allied scientific libraries, and exchange medical literature among its institutional members; to improve the professional qualifications and status of medical librarians; to organize efforts and resources for the furtherance of the purposes and objects of the Association. There are several subject groups and regional groups. Membership is of various categories (Active, Association, Student, Life, Institutional). Publishes *Bulletin of the Medical Library Association* (q.), *MLA news* (q.), *Directory of the Medical Library Association* (a.). Abbreviated MLA.

Medical Section.   Formed on 24 September 1948 as a Section of the (British) Library Association. It established the CYRIL BARNARD Memorial Prize (*q.v.*). In 1978 reformed with the MEDICAL, HEALTH AND WELFARE LIBRARIES GROUP (*q.v.*).

Medium.   1. The weight of type-face midway between light and bold. This is the kind normally used for periodicals and book work.   2. An alternative name for Ben Day tint. *See Ben Day process.* 3. The liquid, usually linseed oil, in which the pigment of printing ink is dispersed and by means of which it leaves an impression on paper. 4. A standard size of printing paper, 18 × 23 inches. 5. A finish given to paper that is neither highly calendered nor antique, but intermediate between the two extremes. Also called 'Medium finish'. 6. In music, the means (instrument/s or voice/s) by which musical sounds are produced, as indicated in the score. *See also Media.*

Medium Face. The weight of type-face half-way between light and bold. It is the kind that is normally used for periodicals and book work. Also called 'Half-dark type'.

Medium Finish. *See Medium 5.*

Medium Weight Paper. Sensitized photographic paper between 0.0084 and 0.0111 inches inclusive. *See also Photographic Papers.*

MEDLARS. Acronym for Medical Literature Analysis and Retrieval Service which is a collection of databases operated and maintained by the NATIONAL LIBRARY OF MEDICINE (*q.v.*). MEDLARS contains over 10 million records in its 25 databases, and covers the whole field of biomedical literature. CD-ROM formats are available in addition to online access; there are over 14,000 institutional users.

MEDLINE. MEDLINE is the MEDLARS online service, available also on CD-ROM. The current file contains articles abstracted from 3400 journals from 70 countries. Subject arrangement is based on MeSH (*q.v.*).

Megabyte. *See Byte.*

Meilleur Report (UK). The report MEILLEUR: *Mobility of Employment International for Librarians in Europe*, prepared by Anthony Thompson (LA 1977).

MELA. Acronym of The Middle East Librarians' Association which was formed in the USA in November 1972 with the aim of increasing communication and co-operation among members, especially in acquisitions and in development of bibliographic controls.

Melody Edition. *See Score.*

Melvil Dewey Medal. *See Dewey Medal, Melvil.*

Membership Voucher. An application voucher for membership of a lending library.

Membrane. A single skin of parchment or vellum either forming part of a roll, or complete in itself. Skins of goats, sheep or calves are used; they are scraped free of hair and reduced in thickness, soaked, stretched, smoothed and dried. This produces a thin, smooth and white parchment, the flesh side being whiter and shinier than the hair side, which is known as the Dorse.

Memoir. 1. A biography of a person written by someone else. 2. A monograph, or dissertation, on some noteworthy subject.

Memoirs. 1. A narrative of events based on the observations, experiences and memories of the writer; an autobiographical record. 2. A collection of researches and accounts of experiments, or dissertations on a learned subject, published by a learned society, especially in the form of a record of proceedings or transactions.

Memorial. 1. A written statement of views in the form of a petition for submission to an authoritative body. 2. Usually in pl., a chronicle or document containing a historical narrative.

Memorial Volume. A publication, often consisting of contributions by several writers, in memory of a person or event. Also called 'Festschrift'.

Memorialist. A person presenting, or signatory to, a memorial.

Memory. The storage capacity of a computer system, comprising operations software, application software, and peripheral storage devices. *See also RAM, ROM.*

Mending. Minor repairs to the leaves of a book not involving the replacement of any material or separation of the book from the cover. Not to be confused with REPAIRING (*q.v.*).

Mentefacts. (*Classification*) A group of 'artificial' entries, i.e. those which do not occur naturally, and which are abstract, e.g. systems of belief and products of the imagination. The other group is said to be ARTEFACTS (*q.v.*).

Menu. A technique whereby available options offered to a computer user are displayed on a VDU and can be selected by number: the Menu system avoids the need for the user to learn several command codes.

Mercator's Projection. A chart enabling a mariner to steer a course by compass in straight lines; invented by Gerardus Mercator, all the meridians are straight lines perpendicular to the equator and all the parallels are straight lines parallel to the equator. It was first used by Mercator in a world map in 1569, and made navigation by dead reckoning easier. Edward Wright made its use practicable by publishing a set of tables for constructing the network of charts, and this development has made it possible to use Mercator's projection for all nautical charts.

Mercurius Intelligence. *See Newsbook.*

Merge. (*Information retrieval*). (*Verb*) To combine two files, already in sequence, into a single file.

MERLIN. Machine Readable Library Information. The British Library's proposed online remote access MARC database, plans for which were cancelled in mid-1979 due to lack of funds.

Merovingian Handwriting. The style of handwriting used in France from the sixth to the eighth centuries; a national style of cursive minuscule script which developed from the Latin cursive after the dissolution of the Roman Empire. *See also Cursive, Handwriting.*

Merrill Alphabeting Numbers. A scheme devised by W. S. Merrill for arranging books in rough alphabetical order. The table is reprinted in the Introduction to Brown's *Subject Classification* and consists of 100 numbers allocated as the following first sixteen from the table show:

01	A	09	Beno		
02	Agre	10	Bix		
03	Als	11	Bou	The numbers
04	Ap	12	Brim	are applied
05	Ash	13	Bum	fractionally.
06	B	14	C		
07	Ban	15	Carr		
08	Bax	16	Chan		

Merrythought. (*Binding*) A finisher's stamp in the form of a merrythought, or wishbone, usually decorated with cusps or foliage ornament.

MeSH. Acronym for Medical Subject Headings, the 'vocabulary' of the (American) National Library of Medicine; it is used in connection with MEDLARS (*q.v.*), the Library's catalogue and the *Index Medicus*.

Metabolic Map. A map which shows the interrelations and correlations of biochemical reactions in metabolic sequences.

Metal Furniture. *See Furniture.*

Metalanguage. A language that is used to specify another language. In documentation, this term is used in classification and indexing.

Metallography. A lithographic process in which metallic plates are used instead of stone.

Metalwork. (*Binding*) A decorative ornament which is an imitation of wrought and curved ironwork.

Methodical Catalogue. *Synonymous with* SYSTEMATIC CATALOGUE (*q.v.*).

Metonymy. The use of an attribute of a thing instead of the thing, e.g. 'crown' for a king. Reversed metonymy, i.e. the use of a descriptor naming the thing to indicate the attributes of the thing, is common.

Metric Book Sizes. The following are the metric book sizes recommended in *Page sizes for books* (BS 1413:1970).

	Trimmed sizes in mm	Untrimmed sizes in mm	'Quad' Paper sizes in mm
Metric Cr. 8vo.	186 × 123	192 × 126	768 × 1008
Metric Lge. Cr. 8vo.	198 × 129	204 × 132	816 × 1056
Metric Demy 8vo.	216 × 138	222 × 141	888 × 1128
Metric Royal 8vo.	234 × 156	240 × 159	960 × 1272
A5	210 × 148*	215 × 152.5	860 × 1220*

The trimmed and untrimmed sizes of case-bound books are those of a folded sheet after and before trimming 3 mm from the edges of a page (head, tail and foredge). The measurements followed by a * are ISO sizes. The ISO sizes which are internationally recommended for general printing are not suitable for books and cannot, in practice, be used. The trimmed page size for a paperback should be 180 × 110 mm.

Metron. A unit of metrical information which supplies one element (i.e. of evidence) for a pattern.

Mezzotint. 1. A process of engraving on copper or steel in which the entire surface of the plate is slightly roughened, after which the drawing is traced and the plate smoothed in places by scraping, burnishing, etc., to produce the desired light and shade effect. 2. An engraving produced by the mezzotint process.

MF.   (*Paper*) Abbreviation for MACHINE FINISH (*q.v.*).

MG.   (*Paper*) Abbreviation for MACHINE GLAZED (*q.v.*). *See also Paper Finishes.*

Michel Style.   The style of book decoration practised during the nineteenth century by Marius Michel and his son in France. The designs are often based on natural forms and the ornament is generally expressed in colour, outlined in blind, and very often without the use of gold.

Microbibliography.   The production of subject bibliographies or indexes pro-·vided with supplements containing the full text in micro-print of the material they list.

Microcard.   1. A term, trade-mark of the Microcard Corporation and covered by an American patent, which refers exclusively to 5 × 3 inch cards with images arranged in a specific manner.   2. The term is more generally used to indicate an opaque card of varying size on which microcopies have been reproduced photographically. A micro-card resembles a MICROFICHE (*q.v.*) in that the microcopies are arranged in rows and catalogue details, readable with the naked eye, are at the top of the card. It differs from other microforms in that the prints are positive as well as being opaque, and cannot be directly reproduced. A microcard is not readable without optical aid in the form of a specially-made reader.

Microchip.   *See Chip.*

Microcomputer.   A generic term for a computer suitable for small operations; usually a desk-top machine with various abilities from simple word-processing to sophisticated library housekeeping routines, CD-ROM handling, etc.

Microcopy.   A copy of a document, or image, the scale of which is greatly reduced (compared with the original) by means of an optical device, and which needs an enlarger to enable it to be legible to the unaided eye. Also called 'Microrecord'.

Microdensitometer.   A densitometer designed to measure the density of very small areas of a photographic image.

Micro-document.   Communication on a specialized topic, and usually short, e.g. a periodical or newspaper article, news-cutting, separate, or pamphlet which embodies micro-thought. *See also Macro Document, Micro-thought.*

Microfiche.   A flat sheet of photographic film standardized (BS 4187:1981 at 1978) at 105 × 148 mm (nominally 4 × 6 inches) and 75 × 125 mm (nominally 3 × 5 inches), displaying at the top a catalogue entry, or title, readable with the naked eye, and bearing in horizontal and vertical rows micro-images of the text of a publication. The standard size of a frame is 11.25 × 16 mm (single) and 23 × 16 mm (double). Where a document is too long to be recorded on one microfiche, each subsequent one is called a 'Trailer' microfiche. Microfiche can be (a) a positive copy printed from strips of microfilm, (b) an actual frame cut from microfilm (usually 70 mm film), or (c) made directly with a step-and-repeat camera. Such sheets may be stored vertically like catalogue cards but require envelopes to protect them from damage. *See also Ultra-microfiche, CIM, COM.*

Microfilm. A microphotograph on cellulose film. It may be negative or positive and may be 16 or 35 mm wide and of any length, depending on the number of exposures thereon. For special purposes, e.g. copying newspapers, or engineering drawings, or the preparation of MICROFICHE (*q.v.*), film of 70 mm width may be used.

Microfilm Flow Camera. A flow camera for taking microcopies automatically, usually on film. *See also Continuous Flow Camera.*

Microfilm Jacket. A transparent holder into which individual strips of film may be inserted for protection.

Microfilm Print. An enlarged print made, normally on paper, from microfilm.

Microfilm Reader. Apparatus for the reading of microrecords by means of their enlarged projection on an opaque or transparent ground-glass screen; printing facilities may be included.

Microfilm Roll. A roll of MICROFILM (*q.v.*).

Microfilm Strip. A short length of MICROFILM (*q.v.*). *See also Microstrip.*

Microfolio. A sheet of optically clear acetate that holds rows of microimages by a special adhesion process.

Microform. A generic term indicating any form of micro record, whether on flat or roll film, paper or other material.

Micrograph. 1. A graphic record of the image, formed by a microscope, of an object. 2. An instrument constructed for producing extremely small copies of writing, printing or engraving, or for executing minute writing or engraving.

Micrographics. The science and technique of reproducing documents in so small a scale that enlargement is necessary to make them legible.

Micro-image. *Synonymous with* MICROCOPY (*q.v.*).

Micronet. A Prestel closed user group for microcomputer owners who wish to download software.

Micro-opaque. A copy of the whole, or part, of a book or other document made by means of microphotography, the print being on opaque paper or card. May be made solely by photographic means or by a printing method. Also called 'Opaque microcopy'. *See also Microcard.*

Micro-opaque Reader. A device for reading a MICRO-OPAQUE (*q.v.*).

Micro-opaque Tape. A form of microtext which can be stuck on index cards used as a filing medium.

Microphotography. Photography on so reduced a scale that a visual aid is required to discern the features of the resulting microphotograph; 16 mm or 35 mm cellulose film is used, and the final form of the microcopy may be MICROFICHE, or MICROFILM (*qq.v.*). The opposite of PHOTOMICROGRAPHY (*q.v.*).

Microprocessor. Microprocessors are computer processing units which can be contained, together with their control circuiting, on a single circuit board a few inches square. To be used as a microcomputer they must be supplemented by ancillary mechanical equipment. *See Microcomputer.*

Microrecord. A copy of a document, the scale of which is reduced compared with the original, and which needs an enlarger to enable it to be legible. Also called 'Microcopy'.

Microrecording. A form of photocopying in which the copy, either on film or paper, is reduced in size so much that it must be read in a 'reader' or by projection. The resultant copy may be made on roll film, sheet film or opaque paper, and is sometimes called 'Microtext'. *See also Microcard, Microfiche, Microform.*

Microreproduction. 1. The process of making microcopies of documents, the images being too small to be read by the unaided eye, on either opaque or transparent materials. 2. The copies so produced.

Microscopic Edition. *See Miniature Book.*

Microsecond. A millionth of a second; a unit of measurement used to determine the speed at which a computer operates. *See also Nanosecond.*

Microslide. A single frame of microfilm which has been mounted for use in a microfilm projector.

Microstrip. 1. Micro-images made from 16 mm or 35 mm film on to a roll of gummed paper, cut into sections and stuck on to standard size cards. 2. A strip of microfilm about 8 inches long which has been cut from a roll of film. It usually contains ten pages of text together with a title sheet. Also called 'Microfilm strip', 'Strip microfilm'.

Microtext. *See Microrecording.*

Micro-thought. (*Classification*) A subject of small extension, and therefore of great intension, usually embodied in the form of an article in a periodical, or of a section or a paragraph in a book, or of a pamphlet. *See also Extension, Macro-document, Macro-thought.*

Microxerography. The creation of micro-images by means of xerography. Negative as well as positive images are possible.

Middle East Librarians' Association. *See MELA.*

Middle Space. *See Quad.*

Midwest Inter-library Center. Founded on 4 March 1949 to (1) provide more adequate research materials for the needs of mid-western scholarship and research; (2) provide for economical and efficient utilization of resources to avoid needless duplication and expense. The Midwest Inter-Library Center which was formed to carry out these objectives operated over a central block of twelve mid-western states and had as its two initial activities: (1) the co-operative collecting and housing of little-used material for the use of the region as a whole; (2) the development of a programme for filling out and enriching the resources of the region. Over twenty libraries (mainly university) co-operated in this scheme. Abbreviated MILC. Its name was changed on 25 January 1965 to the CENTER FOR RESEARCH LIBRARIES (*q.v.*).

Miehle. (*Printing*) The commonest type of TWO-REVOLUTION MACHINE (*q.v.*). Robert Miehle, a young Chicago machine-minder (d. 1932), made an important contribution to printing machine design by controlling the momentum of the bed (with the forme on it) at the instant of reversal by means of an enlarged star wheel and rack.

MILC. MIDWEST INTER-LIBRARY CENTER (*q.v.*).

Mildred L. Batchelder Award. *See Batchelder Award, Mildred L.*

Millboard. A kind of strong PASTEBOARD (*q.v.*) but made from old rope, sacking, wood pulp, and paper. Used for the covers of books which are heavy or have to stand hard wear. Also called 'Binder's board'.

Mimeograph. A trade name for a duplicator using wax stencils, and made by A. B. Dick Co. of America.

Mind Book of the Year/Allen Lane Award. An annual award administered by the UK charity MIND for a book which furthers public understanding of mental illness.

Miniature. 1. A coloured initial letter or picture in an ill·minated manuscript. 2. A greatly reduced copy of a document which is usually read or reproduced by means of optical aids. 3. A small highly-detailed drawing, painting, or portrait, especially on ivory or vellum.

Miniature Book. A very small book, generally 3 inches (10 cm) or less in height, conceived as a whole on a tiny scale, printed with small type on suitable paper, bound in a binding which is tooled delicately, and, if illustrated, having drawings or reproductions which are in keeping with the size of the book. Many distinguished printers and publishers have issued such books. They include Bibles, books of devotion, almanacs, the poets, the classics, books for children, etc. Also called 'Lilliput edition', 'Microscopic edition'.

Miniature-painter. A painter of miniatures. Also called a 'MINIATURIST'.

Miniature Score. *See Score.*

Miniaturist. *Synonymous with* MINIATURE-PAINTER (*q.v.*).

Minicomputer. Smaller and cheaper than a mainframe computer, but having less storage capacity. Technical advances have resulted in minicomputers being able to handle processes that were recently only possible on a mainframe. Minicomputers may be isolated 'stand-alone' systems, or linked with other minis to provide a centralized computing resource in an organization, or as a 'front-end' system controlling communcations between remote terminals and a mainframe computer.

MINICS. Abbreviation for the Minimal-Input Catalogue System developed at Loughborough University of Technology; a multi-purpose local file structure simpler than MARC (*q.v.*).

Minim. Single downstroke of a pen.

Minimal-input Catalogue System. *See MINICS.*

Minion. An out-of-date name for a size of type equal to about 7 point.

Minister's Accounts. Accounts rendered by stewards, bailiffs or other manorial officials to the lord of the Manor.

Minitel. *See Teletel.*

Minitext Edition. Microprint version of a document whose text layout has been arranged to fit a given size page.

Mint. A book which is in the same condition as when it came from the publisher.

Minuscule. 1. A small type of writing developed from cursive. 2. LOWER CASE LETTERS (*q.v.*).

Minute Classification. *Synonymous with* CLOSE CLASSIFICATION (*q.v.*).

Minute Mark. A printer's symbol ' to represent feet (measurement) and minutes; it is also placed after a syllable on which the stress falls.

Minutes of Proceedings of the House of Lords. *See Parliamentary Papers.*

MIS. *See Management Information System.*

Misbound. A LEAF (*q.v.*), leaves or a SECTION (*q.v.*) which has been folded wrongly or misplaced by the binder.

Miscellanea. *Synonymous with* MISCELLANY (*q.v.*).

Miscellany. A collection of writings by various authors or on a variety of subjects. Also called 'Miscellanea'.

Misleading Title. One which does not indicate the subject-matter, or the form, of the work. In cataloguing when such a title is not clarified by the TRACING (*q.v.*), it can be amplified in the catalogue entry as: (a) *Doctor Zhivago, a novel*; (b) *A life of one's own* [autobiography]; or an explanatory note may be added.

Misprint. A typographical error.

Missal. A book containing the service for the celebration of the mass throughout the year. Sometimes loosely used for any book of devotions. Before the invention of printing, the writing of missals was a branch of art which reached a high state of excellence in the monasteries. The books were written upon vellum in the most beautiful style of penmanship, and were adorned with the utmost magnificence. Also called 'Mass book'. *See also Book of Hours.*

Misses. (*Information retrieval*) Relevant documents which were not retrieved in a search.

Mistletoe Tool. (*Binding*) A finisher's tool which appears to have been first used on Irish bindings in about 1766; it is particularly common on the panels of spines of Irish bindings about 1780. In some forms it is embossed, and seems to be a feather rather han a mistletoe leaf.

Mitred. (*Binding*) A junction of lines at an angle of 45 degrees such as is necessary at the turn-in of covering material on the inside of the covers. Lines, in finishing, which meet each other at right angles without over-running. The connection at the angles of an outer FRAME 2 (*q.v.*) to an inner frame of PANEL 1 (*q.v.*) by the diagonal use of FILLETS 1 (*q.v.*) or a ROLL (*q.v.*).

Mitred Corner. (*Binding*) Turning the covering material over the inside of the board in such a way, by cutting, that the turn-ins meet without overlapping. *See also Library Corner, Square Corner.*

Mixed Notation. *See Notation.*

Mixed Subject Heading. (*Indexing*) A subject heading which, in addition to being followed by a number of entries or references, refers (by means of *see also* references) to other subject headings. *See also Indirect Subject Heading.*

MLA. 1. MEDICAL LIBRARY ASSOCIATION. 2. MUSIC LIBRARY ASSOCIATION (*qq.v.*)

Mnemonic Characteristic. The use of symbols in such a manner that they have a more or less constant meaning when applied anywhere in a classification scheme.

Mnemonics. Symbols of the notation of a classification. When they are drawn from lists of divisions, tables or parts of schedules they are called by Ranganathan 'scheduled mnemonics'. Related ideas or 'associations' as used by Ranganathan in classifying, are called 'unscheduled mnemonics' or 'seminal mnemonics' to distinguish them from 'scheduled mnemonics'. Mnemonics may be *constant*, i.e. always denoting the same aspects or form wherever used throughout a scheme of classification, or *variable*, i.e. occasionally alternated or altered to suit the special needs of a specific subject. Dewey's common form divisions now called 'Standard subdivisions' are variable whereas the form marks of the Universal Decimal Classification are constant. *Systematic* mnemonics are those which reflect a consistent order; they are mainly a result of synthesis. *Literal* mnemonics depend on the use of letters in notation in such a way that the symbol for a class is the initial letter of the same class.

Mobile Branch Library. *See Travelling Library.*

Mobile Librarian. A librarian whose duties are mainly carried out in a travelling or mobile library.

Mobile Library. A vehicle devised, equipped and operated to provide a service comparable to a part-time branch library. *See also Container Library Service.*

Modelled Initial. In a mediaeval illuminated manuscript, an initial letter given a rounded or three-dimensional aspect.

Modem. Modulator-demodulator; a device that converts a digital signal from a computer to an audible analogue sound that can be transmitted on a telephone line, and similarly decodes replies into digital form to input into the computer.

Modern Face. Printers' types, French in origin dating from 1698; but not popular until after the Revolution when Didot (France), Bodoni (Italy), Figgins, Thorne and Fry (England) cut various versions. 'Modern' were popular throughout the nineteenth century. They are characterized by vertical emphasis, there being a considerable difference between thick and thin strokes and curves thickened in the centre. The fine bracketed serifs are at right angles to the strokes. Examples are: Bodoni (most foundries); Walbaum (Monotype). The following is in 12 pt. Bodoni:

ABCDEFGHIJKLMÑOPQRSTUVWXYZ
abcdefghijklmnopqrstuvwxyz   1234567890

For specimen alphabets of other faces, *see Type Face.* It is characteristic of modern type faces that the numerals stand on the BASE LINE (*q.v.*), but in some type faces the numerals are available in both forms, e.g. Bookprint. The term 'Didone' has superseded 'Modern face' for this category of type faces. *See also Arabic Figures, Old Face, Transitional.*

Modern Public Records (UK). *Modern public records: the Government response to the Report of the Wilson Committee.* A white paper presented by the Lord Chancellor's Department to Parliament in March 1982 (Cmnd. 8531. HMSO, 1981). *See also Wilson Committee.*

Modification. (*Cataloguing*) Variation in the presentation of information in catalogue entries by, for example, inversion of the initials of a manufacturing firm to bring the last name to the front, the omission of the first part of a geographic name if it indicates a type of governmental administration, the use of a uniform title (perhaps a translation from an original 'foreign' form) to bring all entries for the same work together. (*Indexing*) A word or phrase(s) inserted after a heading to indicate an aspect or character of the information given in the text at the place referred to, to limit its meaning or subdivide the entries.

Modifiers. *See Roles.*

Modulant. An INTERFIX (*q.v.*); a standardized suffix added to the root of a word to bring out the different aspects of a word's basic meaning (US Patent Office). *See also Roles.*

Modular Planning. Planning a building so that it consists of a number of modules (units), having no permanent internal walls dividing the floor area into rooms. Each floor is supported by pillars at regular intervals and these pillars are often partly hollow to accommodate plumbing, electric wiring and air conditioning ducts. Except for core service areas (lifts, staircases, etc.) which are enclosed by permanent walls, the whole of the floor area can be subdivided into rooms and departments by placing free-standing book cases, partitions and furniture where desired, and can be varied at will.

Modulation of Terms. A phrase used to indicate the development of terms, or headings, of a classification. A term should modulate into the term following it.

Mohonk Statement. A summary of an international conference on the Role of Books and other Educational Materials in meeting the educational and economic goals of developed and developing countries, held 10–13 December 1972 at Mohonk Mountain House, New Paltz, New York. It is reproduced in *IFLA News,* No. 43, March 1973.

Moncrieff (Scott) Prize. An annual UK award of the Translators' Association for the best translation published of a French twentieth century work.

Monitor. A television-type display of video signals, usually of a finer quality than a receiver which first converts all signals to radio frequency; used for video playback, and as a computer VDU.

Monk. An ink blot or splash on a printed sheet; the term originated in the days when formes were inked with ink balls. *See also Friar.*

Monochrome. Any illustration in one colour.

Monograph. A separate treatise on a single subject or class of subjects, or on one person, usually detailed in treatment but not extensive in scope and often containing bibliographies. Frequently published in series. In cataloguing, any publication which is not a SERIAL (*q.v.*).

Monograph Series. A series of monographs with a series title as well as individual titles; often issued by a university or society. *See also Series 3.*

Monographic Publication. A non-serial publication, consisting of text and/or illustrations, either complete in one volume or intended to be completed in a specified number of volumes.

Monoline. A type face in which all the strokes of the characters appear to be of the same thickness. Most LINEALE and SLAB SERIF (*qq.v.*) types are of this kind. *See also Geometric.*

Monophonic. Relating to a sound transmission system in which only a single signal exists.

Monophoto. Trade name for a photo-typesetting, or film-setting, machine manufactured by the Monotype Corporation which produces characters on films instead of metal. *See also Filmsetting.*

Monotype. Separate paper-perforating and type-founding machines invented by Tolbert Lanston for composing and casting single types. Individual types are cast on the casting machine from paper rolls perforated on the perforating machine in which a keyboard is incorporated.

Montage. The combination of several photographs, drawings, or parts of pictures, blended to form a single illustration for decorative, display or advertising purposes. *See also Photo-Montage.*

Monthly. A periodical which appears once a month.

Moon Type. A system of reading for the blind in which the letters are formed by raised lines based on a greatly modified form of Roman capital letters. It is more easily learned than Braille and is consequently used by adults who have become blind late in life and find it difficult to master Braille. It is named after Dr. William Moon, a blind clergyman.

Mordant. Acid or other corrosive, used in etching plates.

Morgue. A collection of obituary notices of famous living people kept up to date in newspaper offices.

Morocco. 1. Leather manufactured from the skins of goats and largely used in bookbinding. 'Niger' morocco is tanned with a vegetable tannin, and being durable, flexible and relatively thin, is suitable for bookbinding. 'Persian' morocco lacks strength and durability and is unsuitable for bookbinding. 2. Leather made from sheepskin and lambskin but finished to look like goatskin.

Mortice (Mortise). An open space cut out of a printing plate or block so that type may be inserted in it. A block so prepared is said to be 'pierced'.

Mosaic. A book decoration formed by inlaying or onlaying small pieces of leather of various colours to form a pattern. The technique is particularly associated with the work of the eighteenth-century French binders Padeloup le Jeune and Le Monnier.

Mosaic Map. A photographic representation of the earth's surface and the buildings, etc. thereon, made from two or more aerial photographs placed side by side.

Mother Goose Award. An award given to the most exciting newcomer to British Children's book illustration. Instituted by the specialist firm of booksellers 'Books for Children'. The award was first made in March 1979.

Motorized Shelves. A form of compact shelving in which the bookcases are moved by electrical, or mechanical, power.

Mottled Calf. A calf binding which has been mottled with colour or acid dabbed on with sponges or wads of cotton.

Mottled Finish.   A paper with a variegated colour surface produced by mixing two slightly differently dyed shades of fibres, or by a drip of colour on the wet pulp.

Mould.   1. (*Paper*) A rectangular wooden frame over which brass wires or wire cloth is stretched to serve as a sieve in order to permit water to drain away from the pulp fibres to form a sheet of paper. A wooden frame called a DECKLE (*q.v.*) fits round the edges of the mould and forms a tray with raised edges; this keeps the required thickness of pulp fibre on the wires until the excess water has drained away.   2. (*Printing*) A device in two parts used for casting movable type.

Mould-made Paper.   An imitation hand-made paper made from rag FURNISH (*q.v.*) on a machine.

Mount.   A card or paper on to which something is pasted to protect, preserve, or display it.

Mounted.   A cutting, print, photograph, page, or similar item which is pasted on a mount.

Mounted Plate.   An illustration printed on a separate sheet of paper and pasted to a page of a book.

Mouse.   Handheld device, rolled across a desktop, which causes a pointer to move on a computer display screen.

Movable Location.   *See Relative Location.*

Movable Type.   (*Printing*) Type cast as single units as distinct from slugs or blocks on which are a number of characters. It was the use of movable type towards the end of the fifteenth century, instead of engraved blocks, which led to the rapid development of printing. *See also Incunabula, Slug, Xylography.*

MPRC.   *See Music Performance Research Centre.*

MRDF.   *See Machine Readable Data Files.*

MS.   Abbreviation for MANUSCRIPT (*q.v.*).

MSC.   Metropolitan Special Collection. *See entry under Association of Metropolitan Chief Librarians.*

Mudéjar Bindings.   Spanish bindings in Cordovan leather, done between the thirteenth and fifteenth centuries by Moorish inhabitants of Spain known as mudéjares who were allowed religious freedom and to practise their crafts, of which bookbinding was one. The main design was a blind-tooled pattern of double outline interlacings with stamped strips of dots, curves, rings, etc. to form a background.

Mudge Citation, Isadore Gilbert.   Instituted in 1958, and administered by the Reference Services Division of the American Library Association, this Citation is given annually to a person who has made a distinguished contribution to reference librarianship. This contribution may take the form of an imaginative and constructive programme in a particular library, the writing of a significant book or articles in the reference field, creative and inspirational teaching or reference services, active participation in professional associations devoted to references services, or in other noteworthy activities which stimulate reference librarians to more distinguished performance. The first person to receive the Citation was Mary Neill Barton in 1959.

Muehsam (Gerd) Award. *See ARLIS/NA.*

MUGOLIS. Acronym for the Manchester User Group for Online Information Systems (UK).

Mull. A thin loosely woven cotton cloth glued on to the backs of books to help hold the sections together. Known as 'super' in America.

Multicounty Library. A library established by the joint action of the governing bodies, or by vote of the residents, of the counties concerned, and governed by a single board of library directors. (American.)

Multi-Dimensional Classification. The characterization of each document from more than one point of view. This can be accomplished for the physical placing of documents only when there are as many copies as there are classificatory points of view. When classification schemes also serve as guides to the physical collection of documents, as in a classified catalogue, copies of catalogue cards (each representing a document) are placed at the different numbers for each point of view. Although each catalogue card represents a single document, one such document may be represented by several cards. *See also Rigid Classification.*

Multi-layer Paper. *See Furnish Layer.*

Multi-level Access. (*Information retrieval*) A form of access to files in which entries or blocks of entries are arranged in a definite order of subject symbols. The symbols can arrange the entries systematically as effectively as in an alphabetical index, or as the notation of a classification can arrange the entries of as classified card catalogue.

Multi-level Indexing. The indexing of a document by the appropriate broader generic terms as well as the narrower term.

Multimedia. 1. A collection, or the record of a collection, of materials in various MEDIA (*q.v.*), including non-book material, audio-visual material and non-print material, with or without books and other printed material. 2. Information presented through a combination of different communication techniques, either simultaneously or sequentially. 3. Emerging technology based on CD-ROM to enable a disc to carry a combination of text, graphics, sound, etc. For example, a CD-ROM of an encyclopedia might include text of articles, moving maps, animations, historic photographs, recordings of speeches, music, etc. The British Library will host a major international conference on this topic in 1991.

Multiple Approach, Principle of. A fundamental fact that books may be approached from the points of view of author, title, subject, series, etc.,; this always has to be borne in mind by cataloguers. *See also Cataloguing, Principles of.*

Multiple Entry. (*Information retrieval*) The filing of as many descriptors (terms, entries) in an ITEM ENTRY (*q.v.*) system as have been made in respect of a document.

Multiple Meaning. *Synonymous with* POLYSEMIA (*q.v.*).

Multiple Reference. *Synonymous with* GENERAL REFERENCE (*q.v.*).

Multiplexer.   A device used to divide a data channel into two or more independent channels of lower speed. Simple networks can be created by such division. Multiplexers may operate by frequency division, or time division (transmitting each channel for a fixed duration). Statistical multiplexers are more sophisticated versions of time division systems.

Multi-programming.   Computers which have large storage units and which can accommodate more than one program and the input information for them. Also called 'Dual programming'.

Multi-tier Stack.   A self-supporting metal framework extending from basement to roof and designed to carry the weight of the deck floors and the book load. The columns are placed close together and permit the use of thin slab concrete or metal plate floors as well as shelf supports.

Multi-user Microcomputers.   A facility to allow a number of users to share the same computer power; terminals are usually not intelligent, or in cases where they are, data files must be transferred to a control machine before other terminals can access them. Not to be confused with a LOCAL AREA NETWORK (*q.v.*).

Multivalued Words.   (*Information retrieval*) Words which have different meanings in different contexts, whether they be homographs or homophones.

Multi-volume Publication.   A non-serial publication issued in a number of physically separate parts known to have been conceived and published as an entity; the separate parts may have differing authorship and their individual titles as well as an inclusive title.

Municipal Library.   A public library serving an urban area; the use of the word 'municipal' is becoming less common, and has no legal meaning or connection. In America, one which may also be similarly provided by a village or school district. In Australia, a public library.

Muniment Room.   A room in which archives are kept.

Murray Gottlieb Prize.   *See Gottlieb Prize, Murray.*

Music Library.   A library specializing in music; the stock will comprise printed music and musical reference works, catalogues, textbooks, biographies of composers and general instructional and historical works relating to the subject. Such a library may also stock sound recordings of music.

Music Library Association.   Founded in the USA in 1931; the purposes of the Association are to promote the establishment, growth, and use of music libraries; to encourage the collection of music and musical literature in libraries; to increase the effectiveness of music library services; and to further studies in music bibliography. Publishes *Notes* (q.); *Music Cataloguing Bulletin* (m.); *Newsletter* (q.). Abbreviated MLA.

Music Paper.   Paper ruled with staves of five lines for the writing of music. When made up into a book it is called a manuscript music book.

Music Performance Research Centre.   Initiated by the Musicians' Union, the Centre has been recording non-broadcast concerts and opera since 1987 to preserve British performance heritage. Personal conversations with performers are also made. The Centre opened listening premises in the Barbican Library, London, in 1989.

Music Score. *See Score. See also Bibliographical Information in Printed Music.*

Musical Description. A description of the separate parts for instruments or voices used *simultaneously* during a musical performance. To be distinguished from a BIBLIOGRAPHICAL DESCRIPTION (*q.v.*) which is only concerned with *successive* parts and/or volumes (i.e. the various editions) of a musical composition.

Musical Work. A composition to be played by one or more musical instruments or to be sung by one or more human voices.

Musicology. The study of music as a branch of knowledge or field of research.

Musikriter. A machine that will type music scores. It was invented by Lily Pavey of London, and first manufactured by the Imperial Typewriter Co. in 1964.

Muskett (Netta) Award. An annual award for the best unpublished romantic novel, given by the Romantic Novelists Association (UK).

Mutton. *See Em Quadrat*

NAB. *See National Advisory Body for Local Authority Higher Education.*

NACAB. National Association of Citizens' Advice Bureaux. The co-ordinating and policy-making body overseeing the work of CITIZENS' ADVICE BUREAUX (*q.v.*).

NACL. Acronym for NATIONAL ADVISORY COMMISSION ON LIBRARIES (*q.v.*).

NACO. *See Name Authorities Co-operative.*

NAG. *See National Acquisitions Group.*

NAG Award. An award founded 1989 for the National Acquisitions Group (UK) for an outstanding piece of written work on the selection, acquisition or supply of library materials.

Naked Forme. Pages of type secured by page-cord. *See also Dressed Forme, Forme.*

NALGO. NATIONAL AND LOCAL GOVERNMENT OFFICERS ASSOCIATION (*q.v.*).

Name Authorities Co-operative. A group of major US libraries sending potential authority records for names to the Library of Congress for addition to computer files. Abbreviated NACO.

Name Authority File. The list of name headings used in a given catalogue, and the references made to them from other forms. *See also Authority List, Subject Authority File.*

Name Catalogue. A catalogue arranged alphabetically by names of persons or places, or both, whether used as authors or subjects.

Name Entry. In indexing, an entry under the name of a person, place, or institution.

Name Index. An index of names of authors or other persons.

Name Pallet. *See Binder's Ticket.*

Name Reference. Where alternative forms of names are available, a reference to the one adopted for the heading in a catalogue.

Nancy Stirling Lambert Scholarship. *See Lambert Scholarship, Nancy Stirling.*

Nanosecond. A billionth of a second, a unit of measurement used to determine the speed at which computers operate. *See also Microsecond.*

NAPLIB. *See National Association of Aerial Photographic Libraries.*

NARA. *See National Archives and Records Administration.*

Narration. *Synonymous with* RELATION (*q.v.*).

Narrow. A book whose width is less than two thirds its height.

Narrower Term. (*Information retrieval*) A term which denotes a concept which is narrower than that of a term with a broader, more general, meaning, e.g. *Chairs* is narrower than *Furniture. See also Broader Term, Related Term.*

NASIG. North American Serials Group, formed mid-1985 to discuss, resolve and communicate issues relating to serials management. The Group seeks to bring together educators, librarians, publishers and agents and is independent of any other bodies.

National Acquisitions Group (UK). Formed 1986 and now has 400 members in libraries, publishing, bookselling, etc. Seeks to bring together those concerned in acquisitions work (production, selection, purchase, supply of books and other printed materials, equipment and software for use in libraries and information units) and to act on a pressure group or other organizations. Holds an Annual Conference, and issues a *Newsletter.*

National Advisory Body for Local Authority Higher Education (UK). Established in 1982 to control and co-ordinate public expenditure on higher education outside the universities. Abbreviated NAB. *See now Polytechnics and Colleges Funding Council.*

National Advisory Commission on Libraries. Established in the USA by Executive Order on 2 September 1966, and issued by President Johnson. The Commission was charged to make a comprehensive study and appraisal of the role of libraries as sources of scholarly pursuits or centres for the dissemination of knowledge, and make recommendations designed to ensure an effective and efficient library system for the nation. The report was submitted to President Johnson on 15 October 1968. It recommended that it be declared national policy, enunciated by the president and enacted into law by Congress, that the American people should be provided with library and informational services adequate to their needs, and that the Federal Government, in collaboration with State and local governments and private agencies, should exercise leadership assuring the provision of such services. Abbreviated NACL.

National Advisory Council on Preservation. A US organization set up in 1987 and representing 20 bodies in the academic, scholarly, archival and library communities. Works closely with the COMMISSION ON PRESERVATION AND ACCESS (*q.v.*).

National Afro-Caribbean Library Association. The National Afro-Caribbean Library Association was formed as the result of a meeting convened at Hornsey Library, London on 3 December 1981. It was felt that such a group was needed since there were certain issues pertinent to Black people and Black librarians which were best resolved and discussed collectively. The Association liaises with organizations that are committed to combatting racism, particularly in books and library services, and the promotion of positive multicultural materials and relevant activities.

National Agricultural Library.   One of the three national libraries in the USA, the others being the Library of Congress and the National Library of Medicine. It was formed as a result of the Organic Act of 1862 which placed upon the Department of Agriculture the duty of 'acquiring and preserving all information concerning agriculture', the nucleus of the library being the transfer of the book and journal collection amounting to 1000 volumes from the Agricultural Division of the Patent Office. The library was designated the National Agricultural Library in 1962. Its services are provided to personnel of the Department of Agriculture in Washington, state agricultural agencies, agricultural colleges and universities, research institutions, industry, individual scientists, farmers and the general public in every part of the world. In 1969 the library moved to a fifteen-storey building in Beltsville, Maryland. The Library's database – AGRICOLA – is available online and on CD-ROM, and a co-operative agreement is in operation with OCLC. Abbreviated NAL.

National and Local Government Officers Association (UK).   The trade union to which most public librarians and other officers employed by local authorities belong. Abbreviated NALGO.

National Archival Collections of Audio-visual Material Forum.   A UK Forum started 1986 to examine what provision is at present made for retention of audio-visual materials. Aims to co-ordinate the national effort, make proposals for directories, cataloguing needs, training, conservation, and legislation. Secretariat at BLDSC. Abbreviated NAVF.

National Archives and Records Administration.   A grouping of five co-ordinate offices: the Office of Federal Records Centers, the Office of the Federal Register, the Office of the National Archives, the Office of Presidential Libraries, and the Office of Records Management. It supersedes the National Archives Establishment, founded in 1935, and is responsible for identifying, preserving and making available to the federal government of the USA and to the public all forms of government record not restricted by law, which have sufficient historical, informational or evidential value to warrant preservation. Publishes *Prologue : Journal of the National Archives* (q.). Abbreviated NARA.

National Art Library.   The library of the Victoria and Albert Museum in South Kensington, London. One of the national libraries maintained by the British government.

National Association of Aerial Photographic Libraries.   Formed 1989 in the UK to safeguard and preserve aerial photographs. The Association will offer guidance on storage, indexing, and operate a publicity programme to make the public aware of the value of such photographs for archaeological, land use, and social purposes. Abbreviated NAPLIB.

National Association of Citizens' Advice Bureaux. *See NACAB.*

National Association of News Librarians.   *See Association of UK Media Librarians.*

National Bibliography.   A bibliography which lists all the books and other publications published, or distributed in significant quantity, in a particular country. Sometimes the term is used in respect to the new publications published within a specific period, and sometimes in respect to all those published within a lengthy period of many years. It is also used to indicate a bibliography of publications about a country (whether written by its nationals or not) and those written in the language of the country as well as those published in it.

National Biography.   A publication containing biographies of nationals of one country.

National Book Awards.   Bestowed in the USA to honour books worthy of a distinguished role in general and cultural life. They are not intended for outstanding research, scholarship or scientific achievement in themselves, or to recognize works written for professional or otherwise specialized audiences, but rather to recognize distinction of thought and spirit, and their creative, literary expression. The awards are presented annually for books written by American citizens and published in the United States in the preceding two calendar years. The prizes are contributed by six American book industry associations. From 1960 until 1974 the awards were administered by the NATIONAL BOOK COMMITTTEE (*q.v.*). When the NBC was unable to continue its activities, the National Institute of Arts and Letters took over the Awards Programme in 1975, reducing the prize categories to five: arts and letters; contemporary affairs; fiction; history and biography; and poetry. The Association of American Publishers' General Trade Division and other organizations including the Exxon, IBM, and Xerox corporations are financing the Awards. *See also National Medal for Literature.*

National Book Centre.   *See British National Book Centre, National Central Library.*

National Book Committee (US).   An American non-profit, educational society of citizens devoted to the use of books. Founded in 1954, its purpose was 'to keep books free, make them widely available, and encourage people to read them'. The two principal continuing projects were the NATIONAL BOOK AWARDS (*q.v.*) and the National Library Week Program. On 4 May 1965 it instituted the annual presentation of the NATIONAL MEDAL FOR LITERATURE (*q.v.*).

National Book Committee (UK).   Formed in August 1975 by the leading British organizations concerned with the printed word, for the purpose of furthering the production and use of books, particularly the resistance to the recent reduction of funds available to libraries for the purchase of books. *See also INTERLIT.*

National Book Council.   An Australian organization, formed in 1973 'to bring together bodies and individuals who privately or professionally have an interest in or concern for books; to encourage the free flow of books, and for this purpose (inter alia): to (a) publish and circulate information about books and to encourage the ownership and use of books; (b) assist in the development of a healthy book industry in all aspects, including authorship, publishing, bookselling, and library use; (c) persuade Federal, State and Local Governments to give every support to the book trade and to ensure its freedom from undesirable imposts and restrictions; (d) generally do everything to increase the permeation of books, recreationally and educationally throughout Australia'. There are five categories of membership: corporate, institutional, book trade, associate, and individual. The Council is financed by membership fees and grants; it is known by the acronym NBC and has its office in Melbourne. Publishes *Newsletter* (m., membs. only) and occasional booklists.

National Book Development Council. At a series of regional meetings convened by Unesco, it was recommended that a council or similar body should be established by every nation with the following objectives: to (a) serve as an intermediary between the book professions and the government so as to ensure the integration of book production and distribution into overall economic and social plans; to act as spokesman for the industries in questions of finance, taxation, customs regulations involving the government; (b) initiate measures that would help prevent or correct conditions prejudicial to book development and to promote activities and plans for national book development; (c) encourage the formation of professional associations relating to reading material where none exist and to strengthen such as are already in being; (d) promote, assist, and, where necessary, co-ordinate plans for concerted action on such questions as the training of personnel; (e) establish suitable machinery for promoting the reading habit and conduct research essential to the full development of book industries; (f) provide information related to the book trade and practices which can serve the development of books and reading generally; (g) undertake such additional activities as would ensure the balanced production and distribution of books and reading materials. The Unesco Secretariat has drawn up a model constitution for such a council.

National Book League. *See Book Trust.*

National Braille Association. *See NBA.*

National Bureau of Standards. *See National Institute of Standards and Technology.*

National Cartographic Information Center. *See NCIC.*

National Catalogue. A list of books in a number of libraries in a country. *See also National Bibliography.*

National Center for Education Statistics (US). The Center is concerned with the use of academic libraries; school libraries and media centres, and public libraries; it developed in 1974 a Library General Information Survey (LIBGIS) to provide uniform statistics nationwide on school library/media centres and public libraries. Abbreviated NCES.

National Central Library. Formerly the Central Library for Students; the national centre for lending books for study, and the clearing house for loans of books and periodicals between public, university and special libraries of all types, working in co-operation with Regional Library Bureaux, and with special libraries known in this connection as OUTLIER LIBRARIES (*q.v.*). The Library ceased to exist as an independent organization on its absorption into the Lending Division of the BRITISH LIBRARY (*q.v.*), and thereby lost its identity. Abbreviated NCL. *See also Regional Bureaux.*

National Centre for Information Media and Technology. Formerly National Reprographhic Centre for Documentation (NRCD); name revised 1984. Based at Hatfield Polytechnic (UK). Promotes and advises on the application of reprographic, micrographic and video technology; evaluates equipment, runs short curses and seminars. Publishes Technical Evaluation Reports (*TER*) and *Information Media and Technology* (q.) formerly *Reprographics Quarterly*. Abbreviated CIMTECH.

National Centres for Library Services. Organizations of various types which offer a range of services to libraries within a country or region. For example: Nederlands Bibliotheck en Lektuur Centrum, Deutsche Biblioteksintitut, Bibliotekscentralen (Denmark), Centre for Public Libraries, Israel. The term is used probably only for convenience in the IFLA ROUND TABLE OF NATIONAL CENTRES FOR LIBRARY SERVICE (*q.v.*).

National Commission on Libraries and Information Science. *See NCLIS.*

National Commission on New Technological Uses of Copyrighted Works. *See CONTU.*

National Committee on Regional Library Co-operation. A body funded by the British Library, Office of Arts and Libraries, and the Library Association to investigate and develop regional co-operation. A report was commissioned to be ready late 1987, and action on this led to re-titling of the body to LIBRARY AND INFORMATION CO-OPERATION COUNCIL (*q.v.*) Abbreviated NCRLC. As the earlier National Committee on Regional Library Co-operation, formed 1931, it had instituted the INTER-REGIONAL SUBJECT COVERAGE SCHEME, and the PROVINCIAL JOINT FICTION RESERVE (*qq.v.*). *Now see Library and Information Co-operation Council.*

National Co-ordinated Cataloguing Programme. During 1987 the Library of Congress, the Research Libraries Advisory Committee to OCLC, and the Research Libraries Group planned a US national programme to co-ordinate cataloguing. The resulting NCCP is a two-year pilot 1988–90 to test the effect of such co-ordination. Participants are the Library of Congress, and the universities of Chicago, California (Berkeley), Harvard, Illinois (Urbana-Champaign), Indiana, Michigan, Texas (Austin) and Yale. Records will appear on the LC database and be distributed to members of OCLC, RLG, WLN and via LSP (*qq.v.*)

National Council for Educational Technology (UK). Formed in 1988 from the union of the earlier Council for Educational Technology (CET) and the Micro-electronics Education Support Unit (MESU). It aims to improve education and training through the use of educational technology, and therefore provides advice, co-ordination, and acts as a focal point for the collection and dissemination of information. Publishes *NCET News* (3 p.a.). Abbreviated NCET.

National Discography. A centralized online database of all commercially recorded UK audio materials, both current and deleted. A joint project of the NATIONAL SOUND ARCHIVE (*q.v.*) and the Mechanical Copyright Protection Society; expected to be available in 1990.

National Endowment for the Humanities. A US funding body founded in 1965, which aims to support research, education, and public understanding of the humanities through grants to individuals, organizations, and institutions – many of these being library-related. An Office of Preservation is a major current focus. Abbreviated NEH.

National Federation of Abstracting and Information Services. A confederation of major abstracting and indexing service organizations. Founded in the USA in 1922 and incorporated in January 1958 as the National Federation of Science Abstracting and Indexing Services to encourage and improve the documentation (abstracting, indexing, and analysing) of the world's scientific and technological literature so as to make it readily available to all scientists and technologists by: (a) encouraging the development of abstracting and indexing for the specialized subjects fields not covered by such services, and the further development of such services; (b) seeking greater uniformity in such matters as journal citations and abbreviations and transliteration of foreign titles; (c) co-operation, education, research, and the pursuit of mutually useful enterprises, to strive for the best possible research information services for science and technology in the US and abroad. The scope of the Federation's activities was enlarged to include the social sciences and the humanities, and the word 'science' was consequently omitted from its name on 1 October 1972. 'Indexing' was changed to 'Information' in 1982. The aims of the Federation are to help to improve members' services and operations and to advance their prestige nationally and internationally; to undertake specific projects on behalf of members that would be broadly useful to most of the member services but which they could not undertake alone; to act as a national spokesman for the member services. Publishes *NFAIS Newsletter* (bi-m.). Abbreviated NFAIS.

National Film Archive. *See British Film Institute.*

National Focus on European Library Co-operation. A UK consultative body set up in 1986 by the Office of Arts and Libraries to ensure that the library profession and other interested parties are aware of European Community proposals and can make a response. Representatives are invited from professional groups and non-governmental bodies. *See also Plan of Action (EC).*

National Forum on Bibliographic Standards. A discussion group operated by the (British) Library Association, comprising representatives from 33 organizations. Two meetings are held each year. Fully reviewed in 1988 with support from the BNB Research Fund; a new name is possible – Council for Bibliographic Data Transfer.

National Framework Study. An Office of Arts and Libraries model currently in progress to study the interaction between various kinds of library and information organizations. The model should show the flows of information, transactions, the user communities, costs, and quality of service.

National Handwriting. *See Handwriting.*

National Information Policy (UK). A strategy for the co-ordinated development of library and information services, recognizing the challenges and opportunities of new technology, and the scope for resource sharing. The (British) Library Association held seminars to discuss the formation of a policy, building on the Report *The future development of library and information services 2: working together within a national framework* issued by LIBRARY AND INFORMATION SERVICES COUNCIL (*q.v.*). Abbreviated NIP.

National Information Standards Organization. The body responsible for preparing standards in library, information, and related fields, formerly a part of the AMERICAN NATIONAL STANDARDS INSTITUTE INC. (ANSI) (*q.v.*) but now independent. Abbreviated NISO. The body is more generally referred to as Z39 (*q.v.*).

National Information Systems. *See NATIS.*

National Information Transfer Centres (NITCs). *See ISORID.*

National Institute of Arts and Letters. Chartered by Congress in 1898 'to further literature and the fine arts in the United States', this, the highest honour society of the arts in the USA, now awards the NATIONAL MEDAL FOR LITERATURE (*q.v.*) and the NATIONAL BOOK AWARDS (*q.v.*).

National Institute of Education. *See NIE.*

National Institute of Standards and Technology. The focal point in the American Federal Government for providing measurements, calibrations and quality assurance to commerce and industry, and assisting in the development of technology and procedures to improve quality, and encourage products based on new technological discoveries. Extensive publication programme. Abbreviated NIST. (Until 1988 titled National Bureau of Standards.)

National Interactive Video Centre. The Centre was established in September 1984 as the world's first independent centre for interactive technology. The Centre's work covers the full range of interactive communication from interactive video disc and tape to emerging technologies such as interactive compact disc. The NIVC offers objective, impartial advice and information on all aspects of interactive media for training, education, marketing and communications. It maintains a display collection in central London, and has an extensive programme of courses and publications. Funding is provided by the UK Dept. of Trade and Industry and corporate sponsors.

National Jazz Foundation Archive. A UK collection of historical jazz material housed at Loughton Library, Essex.

National Joint Fiction Reserve. *See Joint Fiction Reserve.*

National Lending Library for Science and Technology. Founded (as a consequence of a recommendation in the *Eighth Annual Report* of the Advisory Council on Scientific Policy, 1955) in 1962 and based on the library of the Department of Scientific and Industrial Research with books and bound periodicals from the Science Museum Library and other sources. This library ceased to function as an independent organization, and also lost its identity, on its absorption into the BRITISH LIBRARY (*q.v.*) in 1973, becoming a major part of the Document Supply Centre of the British Library.

National Librarians Association. *See NLA.*

National Libraries Authority. The name for the body which the *National Libraries Committee Report* recommended should be used for the administrative body responsible for the provision and administration of national libraries in the United Kingdom. *See also Dainton Report.*

National Libraries Conspectus Group. Set up in 1987 to increase support for Conspectus initiatives from the CEC. Members include representatives of the national libraries of France, West Germany, Netherlands, Portugal, and the UK. *See also Conspectus.*

National Libraries Committee. *See Dainton Report.*

National Libraries Task Force. *See US National Libraries Task Force on Co-operative Activities.*

National Library. A library maintained out of government funds and serving the nation as a whole. Usually, books in such libraries are for reference only. They are usually copyright libraries. The function of such a library is to collect and preserve for posterity the books, periodicals and newspapers published in the country. This is best done by a law requiring publishers to deposit copies of all publications issued by them, and by purchasing books published in other countries. A copyright act normally has penalty clauses to enable the act to be enforced. *See also Copyright, Legal Deposit.* The functions of national libraries vary considerably. They may compile union catalogues, produce a national bibliography, publish a retrospective national bibliography, or act as a national bibliographical centre. National libraries in the United Kingdom are: British Library, Imperial War Museum Library, National Art Library (situated at the Victoria and Albert Museum), Science Museum Library, the National Library of Scotland and the National Library of Wales. For those which receive books under the Copyright Act, *see Copyright Library*. National libraries in the United States are: Library of Congress, National Agricultural Library (formerly the National Library for Agriculture) and National Library of Medicine.

National Library and Information Centre on Books, Reading and the Handicapped Child. A project sponsored by the Enid Blyton Trust for Children in co-operation with Margaret Marshall; set up in 1985 to bridge the gap between children with disabilities and those who create, supply and promote children's books. Maintains a library, information services and technical aids. Initially located in Tavistock Square, London. Also known as the *National Library for the Handicapped Child* and as the *Blyton Handi-Read Centre*.

National Library for the Blind. Britain's principal source of general reading in Braille and Moon, the library provides for the blind as nearly as possible what the public library does for the sighted. Its service is completely free and open to all who need it. Begun in 1882, it now houses a third of a million volumes in a specially-adapted modern building. The Library is also a source of books in large print, making available many titles whose potential readership is too small to warrant the cost of typesetting, and which would otherwise never be available. This series is usually lent through public libraries. Publishes catalogues, and *NLB Bulletin* (6 p.a.). Abbreviated NLB.

National Library for the Handicapped Child. *See National Library and Information Centre on Books, Reading and the Handicapped Child.*

National Library of Australia. The National Library Act of 1960 (which created a statutory authority – the National Library Council – to manage the National Library which was then separated from the Parliamentary Library) was amended in 1973 in order to facilitate a major developmental programme and to create new library-based information services. The National Librarian was also redesignated Director-General and was nominated as the executive member of the Council. A new building was erected in Canberra on a site on which it was planned eventually to house 11,000,000 volumes and their related services.

National Library of Canada. Established in 1953, this Library together with the Public Archives were accommodated in a new building in Ottawa in 1967. The Library is concerned mainly with material in social and behavioural sciences and the humanities, the sciences being served by the Canada Institute for Scientific and Technical Information (CISTI *q.v.*). A new National Library Act came into force on 1 September 1969; amongst other provisions, this assigned co-ordinating powers to the National Library and enabled it to provide active and effective leadership to the libraries of the federal government. The National Library of Canada has a three-fold mandate: to gather, preserve and make known the Canadian literary and musical heritage; to promote the development of library services and resources in Canada; and to support resource sharing among Canadian libraries. There are three operating branches: Public Services; Acquisitions and Bibliographic Services; and Information Technology Services. The National Library produces *Canadiana*, the national bibliography, which provides full English and French cataloguing copy for current Canadian publications and foreign publications of Canadian interest. There is an extensive programme of publishing, and cultural events.

National Library of China. Founded in Beijing (Peking) in 1909, and moved into new premises in 1987. The new building is thought to be the largest single library building in the world, and gives 140,000m^2 of floor space, with 22 storeys and additional basements. Stock exceeds 14 million items, and there are 3000 seats in 33 reading rooms. There are 1600 staff, and a CLSI circulation system is in use.

National Library of Ireland. Originally the library of the Royal Dublin Society, a semi-public, grant-aided institution; it became known as the National Library of Ireland in 1877. It benefits from Irish (but not English) legal deposit, and is controlled by the Irish government. It is the principal centre for research into Irish literature and history and contains 500,000 books, as well as collections of periodicals, newspapers, maps, prints, drawings, manuscripts, films and photographs, all relating to Ireland. It was the first library in the British Isles to adopt the Dewey classification.

National Library of Medicine. Founded in 1836 as the Library of the Surgeon General's Office, United States Army, re-named the Army Medical Library in 1922, again re-named the Armed Forces Medical Library in 1952 and finally re-named in 1956 when it became a part of the Public Health Service of the Department of Health, Education and Welfare. Situated in Bethesda, Md., the National Library of Medicine (NLM) is the world's largest research library in a single scientific and professional field. The Library collects materials exhaustively in all major areas of the health sciences and to a lesser degree in such areas as chemistry, physics, botany and zoology. The collections today stand at 4 million items – books, journals, technical reports, manuscripts, microfilms, and pictorial materials. Housed within the Library is one of the world's finest medical history collections of old (pre-1914) and rare medical texts, manuscripts, and incunabula. NLM serves as a national resource for all US health science libraries. Lending and other services are provided through a Regional Medical Library Network consisting of 4000 'basic unit' libraries (mostly at hospitals), 125 Resource Libraries (at medical schools), 7 Regional Medical Libraries (covering all geographic regions of the US), and the NLM itself as a national resource for the entire Network. Some 2 million interlibrary loan requests are filled each year within this Network. Abbreviated NLM. *See also MEDLARS, MEDLINE.*

National Library of New Zealand. Formally established in 1966 following the National Library Act of 1965; formed from the Alexander Turnbull library bequeathed in 1918, and the General Assembly (now Parliamentary) library, which was subsequently (1986) returned to the Parliamentary service. New building opened 1987 in Wellington; 14 district offices and regional centres assist in providing support services to all types of libraries, and an interlending service. The New Zealand Bibliographic Network, a licensee of the WESTERN LIBRARY NETWORK (*q.v.*) operates from the Library, together with the Kiwinet database host. *See also SATIS.*

National Library of Quebec. Formed in 1967, this Library performs all the modern functions of a national library, including legal deposit and the compilation of current and retrospective bibliographies relating to the Province of Quebec. Based on the Library of Saint Sulpice, founded 1915 and acquired by the government of Quebec in 1941.

National Library of Scotland. Founded as the Advocates' Library in 1682, it became the National Library of Scotland by Act of Parliament in 1925, when the Faculty of Advocates transferred to the nation all but its legal collection. The Library has held the British Copyright Privilege since 1710. Its collections of printed books and MSS., augmented by gift and purchase, are very large, and it has an unrivalled Scottish collection. A new building was opened in 1956. In 1974 the Scottish Central Library was incorporated to become Lending Services (NLSLS), and is the Scottish counterpart of the DOCUMENT SUPPLY CENTRE (*q.v.*) of the British Library. A new building to house the Scottish Science Library opened in 1989. Publications include: *Bibliography of Scotland* (annually), *Directory of Scottish Newspapers* (1984), *Catalogue of Manuscripts* (7 vols), *General Catalogue of Printed Books on microfiche* (1988). Abbreviated NLS.

National Library of Wales. A government-financed library which was founded in 1909 following the granting of a Royal Charter in 1907. It specializes in manuscripts and books relating to Wales and the Celtic peoples, and has a stock of over 3 million printed books, 30,000 manuscripts, 3.5 million deeds and documents, and numerous maps, prints and drawings. It is a Copyright Library in respect of books in the Welsh language or dealing with Wales.

National Library Week. Sponsored by the (American) NATIONAL BOOK COMMITTEE and the AMERICAN LIBRARY ASSOCIATION (*qq.v.*) National Library Weeks have been held inn the USA for over 30 years. Their object has been to attempt to reduce illiteracy and increase interest in books, reading and libraries but their effectiveness was dependent on the extent to which state library associations and agencies and individual libraries organized and developed programmes for their own purposes. From 1975 the (American) National Library Week is organized by the American Library Association. *See also National Book Committee.* In 1966 and since similar weeks have been organized in the UK but not annually; they have been planned by a national committee on which appropriate associations have been represented. In the early 1970s their character was broadened and the emphasis was on books rather than libraries.

National Manuscripts Fund. Established in 1989 by the British Government, and administered by the British Library Research and Development Department, the Fund is intended to assist record offices, libraries, owners of archives, manuscripts, and documents accessible to the public, where a need can be shown for financial support beyond the applicant's normal resources.

National Medal for Literature. An award made annually to a living American author for the whole body of his or her work; it was first presented to Thornton Wilder on 4 May 1965. The Medal is made possible by a grant from the Guinzburg Fund, honouring the late Harold K. Guinzburg, founder of the Viking Press, and was instituted by the NATIONAL BOOK COMMITTEE (*q.v.*). *See also National Book Awards.*

National Micrographics Association. Founded in the United States in 1943 as the National Microfilm Association (the name being changed in 1975) to 'promote the lawful interests of the micro-reproduction industry in the direction of good business ethics, the liberal discussion of subjects pertaining to the industry; technological improvement and research; standardization; the methods of manufacturing and marketing; the education of the consumer in the use of microfilm and related technique'. The Association operates through Chapters in about 25 American states. In 1973 the Board of the Association approved a plan for the development of a Resource Center in the field of micrographics, the purpose of which is to provide access to all current and relative material to all interested persons. Publishes *Journal of Micrographics* (bi-m. to membs.), *Micro-news Bulletin* (bi-m. to membs.), *Proceedings of the Annual Convention* (a. to membs.). Abbreviated NMA.

National Peace Book Week. *See BAND.*

National Preservation Advisory Committee. Independent group of experts set up to advise the National Preservation Office. Includes representatives from national, research, and public libraries, archives, record offices, SCONUL, LISC, etc. Abbreviated NPAC.

National Preservation Office.   Established 1984 by the BRITISH LIBRARY (*q.v.*) and intended to initiate research in the area of document and book conservation and preservation. Issues *Library Conservation News* (q.). The examination of security has also been added to its area of concern. *See also Ratcliffe Report.* Abbreviated NPO.

National Program for Acquisitions and Cataloguing.   An acquisitions and cataloguing project initiated in the financial year 1966 and implemented in the following financial year, whereby the Library of Congress seeks to acquire abroad, catalogue immediately, and disseminate cataloguing data rapidly, all current monographs, as well as monographic series, of research value, in order to meet the current needs of American libraries through a national cataloguing effort. To avoid unnecessary duplication of cataloguing already accomplished in other countries, SHARED CATALOGUING (*q.v.*) techniques have been adopted wherever possible in co-operation with the producers of foreign national bibliographies. The House Appropriations Committee received a critical report from congressional staff investigators on this Program and on Shared Cataloguing in February 1974; this was reported in *American Libraries* 5, (8), Sept. 1974, pp. 406–7. Abbreviated NPAC.

National Reference Library of Science and Invention.   Formed by amalgamating the Patent Office Library which was transferred to the British Museum in May 1966, with books on science in the British Museum in separate buildings apart from the British Museum. When the BRITISH LIBRARY (*q.v.*) was formed in 1973 this Library was denominated the Science Reference Library and became part of the Reference Division. Abbreviated NRLSI.

National Referral Center for Science and Technology.   Usually referred to as the National Referral Center. Formed in 1963, and functioning at the Library of Congress as a clearing house to provide comprehensive, co-ordinated access to the USA's resources of scientific and technical information. It has as its four major areas of responsibility: (1) the identification of all significant information resources in the fields of science and technology; (2) the acquisition, cataloguing, and correlation of substantive and procedural data defining the nature, scope, and capabilities of these resources; (3) the provision of advice and guidance about these resources to any organization or individual requiring access to them by responding to requests for referral assistance, and by publishing directories and guides in selected subject fields; and (4) the exploration, through actual operating experience, of the roles and relationships that exist or should exist among the many elements of the scientific and technical information complex. Abbreviated NRC.

National Register of Archives.   Since 1945 the HISTORICAL MANUSCRIPTS COMMISSION (*q.v.*) has built up this collection of lists and related personal, subject and topographical indexes of non-official records in private custody and in libraries and record offices. The lists (over 20,000), some summary, others detailed, cover a wide variety of accumulations from family and estate papers to the archives of institutions, political parties and businesses. The Register may be consulted without charge at the offices of the Historical Manuscripts Commission. The *Bulletin* (1–14, 1948–67) is now discontinued; the *List of Accessions to Repositories* appears annually; and duplicated subject source lists are being issued. Abbreviated NRA.

National Reprographic Centre for Documentation. Established January 1967 with a grant from OSTI. In 1984 the name was changed to NATIONAL CENTRE FOR INFORMATION MEDIA AND TECHNOLOGY (*q.v.*).

National Science Foundation. A United States federal agency established by Congress in 1950 'to promote the progress of science to advance the national health, prosperity and welfare; to secure the national defence; and for other purposes'. In carrying out these broad objectives, the Foundation supports research and education through grants and fellowships, fosters the exchange of scientific information among scientists in the US and foreign countries, and surveys the nature and extent of scientific research and development activities in the US. Abbreviated NSF. *See also OSIS.*

National Serials Data Program. Established on 17 April 1972 in the USA as Phase 3 of a co-ordinated effort to implement a system for identifying and controlling serial publications. Its immediate concern was to develop a corporate authority file (a serials data base) to take into consideration the various authorities used by the three National Libraries (Library of Congress, National Library of Medicine, National Agricultural Library); the assignment of ISSNs to prospective periodical titles published in the USA from 1971 onwards and listed in *New Serial Titles*, and assigning ISSNs to titles in science and technology mentioned in Bowker cumulations. Phase 1 resulted in the identification of data elements needed for the control of serials by machine methods and the development of the MARC (*q.v.*) serials format. Phase 2 was the creation of a machine-readable file of live serial titles in science and technology and the production of a variety of listings. In April 1972 it became the US national centre for ISDS (*q.v.*), and assumed responsibility for allocating International Standard Serial Numbers. *See also ISSN.* Abbreviated NSDP.

National Sound Archive (UK). From April 1983 the British Institute of Recorded Sound merged with the British Library to form the National Sound Archive. The Institute has departmental status within the Library, with its own Director. Publication of a national discography is envisaged. The collection includes music, drama, literature, language, dialect, speeches, events and wildlife. NSA is housed at 27 Exhibition Road, London SW7. A Northern Listening Service operates at the British Library Document Supply Centre at Boston Spa.

National Technical Information Service. *See NTIS.*

National Toy Libraries Association. *See Play Matters.*

National Translations Center. An international depository and referral centre for helping users locate unpublished translations of foreign-language literature in scientific, technological, and social science fields. Translations made by societies, libraries, government agencies etc. are deposited at the Center, whose holdings are now included in *World Translations Index*. Located at the Library of Congress 1989 onwards, after a move from the University of Chicago. Abbreviated NTC.

National Union Catalog, The. *The National Union Catalog, a cumulative author list* represents Library of Congress printed cards and titles reported by other American libraries. It commenced publication in 1948. The sequence of printed catalogues is as follows: *A catalog of books represented by Library of Congress printed cards issued to July 31, 1942* (167 vols.). *Supplement: cards issued August 1, 1942–December 31, 1947* (42 vols.), 1948. *Library of Congress author catalog; a cumulative list of works represented by Library of Congress printed cards, 1948–1952* (24 vols.), 1953. *Library of Congress catalog – books: authors, 1953–June 1956*. This was continued under the title *National union catalog: a cumulative author list representing Library of Congress printed cards and titles reported by other American libraries 1953–1957* (28 vols.), 1961. These volumes include one on music and phonorecords and one on motion pictures and film strips. This series was continued by one covering the years 1958–1962 and published in 1963; it comprised 54 volumes including two on music and two on motion pictures. This series is continuing with at least four volumes each year, being cumulations of monthly parts which are also cumulated quarterly. Meanwhile a series was published with the title *National union catalog, 1952–1955 imprints (*30 vols.), a similar author list, in 1961. The *National union catalog, pre-1956 imprints* began publication in 1968 and was concluded in 1981. The *Library of Congress catalog – books: subjects* began publication in 1950; 1950–54 (20 vols., 1955); 1955–59 (22 vols., 1960); 1960–64 (25 vols., 1965); and then annually with a minimum of three volumes per annum. Current availability is more common in the monthly cumulating microfiche service, with annual cumulations; online availability is possible as LCMARC, from 1968 onwards. Abbreviated NUC.

National Union Catalog of Manuscript Collections. A grant (the first of several) from the Council on Library Resources in 1959 enabled a commencement to be made on a large co-operative project to produce and bring together in a central file printed catalogue cards presenting uniform descriptions of some 24,000 manuscript collections in about 90 participating libraries and archives, and of some 3000 collections in the Library of Congress. Planning for automation is well advanced. Abbreviated NUCMC.

NATIS. Abbreviation for National Information Systems, the formation of which in most countries is being encouraged; these encompass all services involved in the provision of information for all sectors of the community and for all categories of users. The objectives for the establishment of NATIS were discussed at the Intergovernmental Conference on the Planning of National Overall Documentation, Library and Archives Infrastructures which was attended by representatives from 86 countries in September 1974 when held in Paris. Its proposals were approved at the eighteenth session of the General Conference of Unesco held in Paris in October and November 1974 with a view to encouraging the creation, development or improvement of documentation, library and archives infrastructures in its Member States. The NATIS concept implies that national, state or local governments should maximize the availability of all relevant information through these services. At a meeting with FID, IFLA and ICA, held in April 1975, Unesco's Department of Documentation, Libraries and Archives asked these non-governmental organizations to make proposals for Unesco's long-term programme for NATIS, in consequence of which an *ad hoc* NATIS Working Group was formed.

Natural Classification. One in which qualities which are essential to the existence of the thing or things to be divided is adopted as the 'difference' (*see Predicables, Five*) or characteristic of arrangement. One which exhibits the inherent properties of the things classified, and which groups or separates them according to their likeness or unlikeness. *See also Artificial Classification, Characteristic of a Classification.*

Natural Language. (*Information retrieval. Indexing.*) 1. A language the rules of which reflect current usage without being specifically prescribed. 2. The language of the documents indexed. *See also Artificial Indexing Language; Indexing Language.*

Nautical Almanac. A publication which tabulates the position of the sun, moon, planets and navigational stars for each date at any time of day or night.

NAVF. *See National Archive Collections of Audio-visual Material Forum.*

NBA. Acronym of the National Braille Association, a non-profit-making American organization founded in 1945, which exists to produce and distribute Braille and large type publications and tape recordings for blind and partially sighted readers in the USA, particularly students in elementary and secondary schools, colleges and universities. This material is produced by volunteers. The Association also operates the Braille Book Bank, the prime source of current college textbooks in Braille for blind students.

NBC. NATIONAL BOOK COMMITTEE (America). NATIONAL BOOK COUNCIL (Australia, UK) (*qq.v.*).

NBL. National Book League. *See Book Trust.*

NBM. NON-BOOK MATERIALS (*q.v.*).

NBS. National Bureau of Standards. *See National Institute for Standards and Technology.*

n.c. Abbreviation for 'not catalogued'; relates usually to a volume of miscellaneous pamphlets which are not individually catalogued.

NCCP. *See National Co-ordinated Cataloguing Programme.*

NCES. NATIONAL CENTER FOR EDUCATIONAL STATISTICS (*q.v.*).

NCET. *See National Council for Educational Technology.*

NCIC. Acronym for the National Cartographic Information Center which was established by the Department of the Interior of the US Geological Survey in July 1974. It provides a national information service to make cartographic data more easily accessible to the public and to federal, state and local agencies. Thirty federal agencies collect and prepare cartographic material of all kinds, including space photography and related data on the US and possessions and these form the basis of the Center's material resources numbering over 1.5 million maps, twenty million aerial and space photographs, and 1.5 million geodetic control points. The function of NCIC is not to obtain all of the cartographic data from the holders but to act as a central information agency by collecting and organizing descriptive information about the data and arrange for its availability. It is anticipated that 'NCIC willl not form a network of information centres across the country but that local participating organizations will provide local users with direct access to NCIC information.

NCL. NATIONAL CENTRAL LIBRARY (*q.v.*).

NCLIS. Acronym of National Commission on Libraries and Information Science, a permanent and independent agency within the Executive Branch, and established by Congress in July 1970; it has the primary responsibility for developing and recommending overall plans for providing library and information services adequate to meet the needs of the people of the USA. Aims to: (a) ensure that all local communities are provided with basic, adequate library and information services; (b) provide adequate suitable services to special user constituencies; (c) strengthen existing statewide resources and systems; (d) develop the human resources required to implement a national programme; (e) co-ordinate existing federal library and information programmes; (f) make the private sector a more active partner in the development of a national programme. Recent emphases have been on planning for a second WHITE HOUSE CONFERENCE (*q.v.*), action on the GLENERIN DECLARATION (*q.v.*), access to government information, and the impact of new technology.

NCR Award. An award of £30,000 sponsored by the computer manufacturers NCR for a new work of non-fiction. First awarded 1988.

NCRLC. *See National Committee on Regional Library Co-operation.*

n.d. *See No Date.*

Near Print. A general term for substitute printing processes, the basic techniques being typewriter composition and offset printing.

Near Letter Quality. Output from a dot-matrix printer of a superior quality to the fastest draft printing.

Neat Line. A line, usually a GRID (*q.v.*) or GRATICULE (*q.v.*) bounding the borders of a map.

Neck. *Synonymous with* BEVEL (*q.v.*).

Nederlands Bibliotheek en Lectuur Centrum (NBLC). (DUTCH CENTRE FOR PUBLIC LIBRARIES & LITERATURE). Founded 1972. Based in The Hague. Aims to promote public librarianship, encourage co-operation and provide a centre to improve quality and efficiency of library work. Publishes *Bibliotheek en Samenleving* (11 p.a.), reports and proceedings.

Need to Know. A basic principle of security which restricts access to classified documents and information to those whose duties make such access essential, no person being permitted to have access merely by virtue of rank or appointment.

Needlework Binding. *Synonymous with* EMBROIDERED BINDING (*q.v.*).

Negative. 1. In photographing with a camera, a negative image normally results when a film is developed; in this the tones are reversed black being white and vice versa. A positive print, in which the tones are again reversed and then seen as with the naked eye, can be produced from the negative either by contact or by enlargement. 2. In printing, reversed image and light values appear on half-tone blocks of illustrations, and these stand in the same relationship to the resulting print as do negatives in the ordinary photographic process.

Negative Selection. *Synonymous with* WEEDING (*q.v.*).

NEH. NATIONAL ENDOWMENT FOR THE HUMANITIES (*q.v.*).

Neighbourhood Information Centers. A project carried out between 1971 and 1974 at five major public library systems in the USA (Houston, Detroit, Cleveland, Atlanta and Queens Borough) and partly funded by a federal grant. Reports on the results indicated that the INFORMATION AND REFERRAL SERVICE (*q.v.*) is best carried out by libraries and that the demand for it is overwhelming. Abbreviated NIC.

NELINET. Abbreviation for New England Library Information Network, a large regional network of diverse membership; supplies computing services and OCLC access. Based at Newton, Massachusetts.

Neo-caroline. *Synonymous with* HUMANISTIC HAND (*q.v.*).

Neo-grotesque. A group of LINEALE (*q.v.*) type faces derived from the GROTESQUE (*q.v.*) group compared with which they have less contrast in the thickness of the strokes, and are more regular in design. The ends of the curved strokes are usually oblique and the g often has an open tail. Of such are Edeh/Wotan, Helvetica and Univers.

NEPHIS. Acronym for Nested Phrase Indexing System. A computer-assisted system for the production of printed indexes. The indexer decides on appropriate subject descriptions and translates them into input strings. The NEPHIS program then generates the required permutations.

Net Book. One which is subject to the Standard Conditions of Sale of Net Books which are set out in the Net Book Agreement, 1957, which stipulates that a book shall not be sold at less than the 'net' price stated by the publisher other than in certain circumstances (e.g. to libraries) licensed by the Council of the Publishers Association.

Net Book Agreement. An agreement drawn up in 1929 (and revised in 1957) between the Publishers Association, the Booksellers Association, and the Library Association, enabling rate-supported libraries and other libraries admitting the public without charge throughout the usual opening hours to receive a discount of 10 per cent on all new books purchased, provided the library applies for a licence. In consequence of the Library Association becoming a professional association it has discontinued its functions under the Library Licence Agreement, and handed them over to the authorities responsible for public libraries and for libraries in universities and colleges.

Network. 1. A bookbinding design made of intersecting lines forming squares set lozengewise. 2. A system of physically separate computers with tele-communication links, allowing the resources of each participating insti-tution to be shared by each of the others. *See also Local Area Network, Wide Area Network, Value Added Network.*

Neutrality. In subject cataloguing, a situation in which user preference cannot influence one course over another because it is unascertainable or because it does not exist. Catalogues of general libraries are mostly neutral in this sense whereas those in special libraries may reflect the viewpoints of a homo-geneous clientele.

New-book Card. A temporary main entry catalogue card, made on a coloured card, and inserted in the catalogue until a permanent card is ready.

New-book Number. A temporary number assigned to a book which it is desired should be circulated before it is catalogued because it is in great demand or because of temporary shortage of staff. The number is from a special sequence, or preceded by some symbol, as: N.B., and the book is catalogued and finally processed subsequently. A temporary main entry is used in the catalogue.

New Edition. An issue of a book in which misprints noticed in an earlier edition have been corrected. The BS 4719:1971 *Title leaves of a book* states that in current publishing practice, reprints which are made a substantial number of years after the original edition are regarded as new editions, and that a new edition is created when the type is re-set even if the text remains the same as in the earlier edition, but that such cases are best described as '2nd '(etc.) edition re-set'. *See also Edition, First Edition, Impression, Issue, Reprint, Revised Edition.*

New England Deposit Library, Inc. A storage library opened on 2 March 1942, housing books in three types of rental storage: (a) material classed as permanent with books available on request, the largest depositor being Harvard University Library which sends part of its current additions to store, (b) temporary and (c) 'dead' stock; (b) and (c) are not available for general use. A union catalogue is maintained, and the books stored are available for loan to member libraries, and, with the permission of the owning library, to the inter-leading system. The large windowless storage warehouse is owned and operated by seven libraries – Massachusetts State Library, Massachusetts Institute of Technology, Massachusetts Historical Society, Boston Public Library, Boston Athenaeum, Boston University and Harvard University Library – each paying rent for the space occupied in order to cover operating costs. The scheme was proposed in 1937. Abbre-viated NEDL.

New Impression. *See Impression.*

New Zealand Library Association. A society incorporated by Act of Par-liament in 1939 (The New Zealand Library Association Act 1939). Founded at a conference held in Dunedin in March 1910 as the Libraries Association of New Zealand. At a conference in 1935 the name was changed to New Zealand Library Association, and a new constitution adopted; this allowed among other things the formation of Branches and Sections. Publishes *New Zealand Libraries* (6 p.a.), *Newsletter* (m. to membs.). Abbreviated NZLA.

Newark Charging System. An American method of recording book issues whereby the book cards are inscribed with the borrower's number and dated, so becoming the time record. The reader possesses a membership card which he retains whether he borrows books or not, and which enables him to borrow an unlimited number of books from any library in a system. *See also Detroit Self-charging System.*

Newberry Library. A free reference library established in Chicago, Illinois, USA, in 1887 and maintained by a moiety of the estate of Walter Loomis Newberry (1804–68), a Chicago merchant. This bequest is supplemented by subsequent gifts and by the continuing programme of the Newberry Library Associates. The stock totals 900,000 volumes on many subjects but mainly the humanities, certain subjects being relatively unrepresented by agreement with the Chicago Public Library and the John Crerar Library. The Library is particularly strong on Americana, American Indians, history of printing, Western Europe, Great Britain until the early twentieth century, Latin America, Portuguese discoveries and music, and there are treasures in each of the subject divisions. The first Librarian was William Frederick Poole (1887–95), compiler of *Poole's index to periodical literature, 1802–81*, 2 vols.

Newbery (John) Medal. The Newbery medal has been awarded annually since 1922 under the auspices of the Association for Library Services to Children of the American Library Association. Donated by the Frederic G. Melcher family, the award is made to the author of the most distinguished contribution to children's literature published in the United States during the preceding year. Winner must be citizen of or resident in the United States. Named after John Newbery (1713–67) the famous British publisher of St. Paul's Churchyard who was the first to publish books for children; he was part-author of some of the best of those he published. The medal was first awarded (in 1922) to Hendrik Willem Van Loon for *The story of mankind. See also Caldecott Medal.*

Newsbook. A publication printed in a small 4to volume of up to twenty-four pages, and containing news. Newsbooks were first published in 1622, being dated and numbered, and although calling themselves 'weekly', were published at irregular intervals and never on a fixed day of the week. They contained all kinds of news from all over the world but were strictly forbidden to print home news. They were not numbered until 1641 and dealt almost exclusively with the Thirty Years War. Their publication was considerably diminished after the outbreak of the Great Rebellion towards the end of 1641, and ceased in 1642. At first they comprised one sheet of quarto, and later two. Variously called Diurnall, Mercurius Intelligence. *See also Coranto, Relation.*

Newsletter. 1. A manuscript report of current happenings, written for special subscribers and issued irregularly or weekly in the sixteenth and seventeenth centuries. 2. A similar report published in the seventeenth century and sometimes set in script-like type and imitating the appearance of the earlier manuscript newsletter. 3. A brief publication conveying news. Frequently issued by societies or business organizations.

Newspaper. A publication issued periodically, usually daily or weekly, containing the most recent news. The word 'newspaper' was first used in 1670. Previously the word was CORANTO and later NEWSBOOK (*qq.v.*).

Newspaper File. *See Stick 2.*

Newspaper Library. 1. A collection of reference books, pamphlets, reports, press cuttings and government publications provided to serve the needs of the staff of a daily newspaper. 2. *See British Library.*

Newspaper Rack. A fitting for displaying newspapers. Also called 'Newspaper stand'.

Newspaper Rod. *See Stick 2.*

Newspaper Stack. Shelving designed to accommodate bound newspapers in which they lie flat.

Newspaper Stand. A fitting on which one or more newspapers are displayed for consultation. Also called 'Newspaper rack'.

Newspaper Stick. *See Stick 2.*

Newsplan. A programme maintained by the British Library Newspaper Library to preserve UK local newspapers held in local libraries and archives throughout the country. The pilot study (published as *Newsplan* by BLRDD, 1986) found that deterioration of originals was far advanced and that microfilming resources were scarce and of poor quality; the programme has initiated regional investigations and aims to assess the problem and recommend action.

Newsprint. The lowest grade of paper: it is made mostly from wood pulp and used for newspapers.

Newsroom. The department of a library in which current newspapers may be read. *See also Magazine Room.*

NFAIS. Acronym for NATIONAL FEDERATION OF ABSTRACTING AND INFORMATION SERVICES (*q.v.*).

NIC. Neighbourhood Information Centers (*q.v.*).

Nick. The groove which is cut on the BELLY of a piece of movable type. Its purpose is to enable the compositor to set type the right way up without looking at the face of the type, and also (by reason of the position and number of nicks for each type size and face) to know immediately when a wrong SORT (*q.v.*) has come to hand. Also called 'Groove'. *See also Body.*

Nickel-faced Stereo. A stereo which is given a facing of nickel in order to lengthen its effective life.

Nickname. A fanciful appellation given by others, in addition to, or in place of, a proper name, as, for example, Scaramouche to Tiberio Fiorella. Also called 'Byname', 'Sobriquet'.

Nickname Index. A list of 'nicknames', or popular names, for places, persons, official reports, laws or organizations and giving the full, proper, or official names or titles. It is usually arranged alphabetically.

NIE. Acronym of National Institute of Education. The research, development and dissemination arm of education in the USA federal government. Formed in 1972 and operating as a separate agency within the Department of Health, Education and Welfare (HEW), its functions are 'to conduct educational research, collect and disseminate the findings of educational research . . . assist and foster such research, collection, dissemination or training, through grants or technical assistance to, or jointly financed co-operative arrangements with, public or private organizations, institutions, agencies or individuals . . .' The NIE Educational Research Library began to function as the principal Federal Library in the field of education; it has been formed by the merger of the library of the Center for Urban Education in New York City and the education portion of the Office of Health, Education and Welfare Library. NIE is responsible for ERIC (*q.v.*).

Niger Morocco. Leather produced on the banks of the River Niger from native-tanned goatskin. Often abbreviated to 'Niger'.

Nigerian Library Association. Founded as the West African Library Association in August 1953 as an outgrowth of the Unesco Seminar on the Development of Public Libraries in Africa; it was superseded by the Ghana Library Association, and the Nigeria Library Association in 1963. Publishes *Nigerian Libraries* (3 a year), *NLA Newsletter* (membs. only). Abbreviated NLA.

nihil obstat. (Lat. 'nothing hinders'). Sanction for publication given by a Roman Catholic censor and usually found on the verso of the title-page or the following leaf.

Nijhoff (Martinus) International West European Specialists Study Grant. An award administered by the ASSOCIATION OF COLLEGE AND RESEARCH LIBRARIES (*q.v.*).

Ninety-one Rules. A cataloguing code comprising 91 rules which was compiled at the instigation, and with the guidance, of Sir Anthony Panizzi, as a guide to cataloguing the printed books in the British Museum. It was the first major code for the consistent cataloguing of books, and set the pattern for good cataloguing practice. It was approved by the Trustees of the British Museum in 1839 and was published in 1841.

NIP. Acronym for NATIONAL INFORMATION POLICY (*q.v.*).

Nipper. *Synonymous with* BUMPER (*q.v.*).

NISO. *See National Information Standards Organization.*

NIST. *See National Institute of Standards and Technology.*

NITC. Acronym for National Information Transfer Centres. *See ISORID.*

NIVC. *See National Interactive Video Centre.*

NJFR. National Joint Fiction Reserve. *See entry under Joint Fiction Reserve.*

NLA. The National Libraries Association, formed 1975 and currently based at Alma, Michigan. NLA's mission is to provide librarians with the means by which they can support and contribute to the advancement of the profession. Members of NLA are interested in increasing their professional knowledge, working towards the welfare of the profession, and sharing experience as well as expertise with their peers. Librarians from all around the country and from all types of libraries are finding that NLA provides a forum where they may voice their professional concerns. NLA members are addressing such issues as professional standards; competence in the practice of librarianship; career development; pay-equality; the image, status and dignity of librarians; the quality of library education; and the identification of unprofessional trends. Publishes *National Librarian* (q.).

NLB. NATIONAL LIBRARY FOR THE BLIND (*q.v.*).

NLC. NATIONAL LIBRARY OF CANADA (*q.v.*).

NLL. Acronym for NATIONAL LENDING LIBRARY (FOR SCIENCE AND TECHNOLOGY) (*q.v.*).

NLLST. Acronym for NATIONAL LENDING LIBRARY FOR SCIENCE AND TECHNOLOGY (*q.v.*).

NLM. NATIONAL LIBRARY OF MEDICINE (*q.v.*).

NLQ. *See Near Letter Quality.*

NLS. NATIONAL LIBRARY OF SCOTLAND (*q.v.*).

NLSLS. National Library of Scotland Lending Services. *See entry under National Library of Scotland.*

NMA. NATIONAL MICROGRAPHICS ASSOCIATION (*q.v.*).

No. Abbreviation for number (*It.* 'numero'.). *Pl.* Nos.

'No conflict' Policy. The policy of adopting new cataloguing rules only when they do not conflict with existing headings in the catalogue. Also called 'Superimposition' policy.

No Date. Abbreviation: n.d. Indicates that the date of publication is not known. If the book bears no indication of date of publication but this has been obtained from bibliographical or other sources, it is expressed in a bibliographical or catalogue entry within [ ].

No More Published. A phrase used in a note to a catalogue entry for a work which was intended to be published in several volumes but the publication of which was not completed.

NOC. Abbreviation for Notation of Content. *See KWOC.*

Node. A central switching point in a telecommunications network.

Noise. 1. In information retrieval, items selected in a search which do not contain the information desired, or items delivered by a search through accidental code combinations. 2. In interacting with a computer, or searching a computer-held database, interference in the communication process, resulting in mistaken commands or nonsensical responses.

Nom de Plume. *Synonymous with* PSEUDONYM (*q.v.*).

Noma Award. A prize awarded by the Japanese publishing firm Kodansha to African writers whose work is published in Africa. The award is intended to encourage the African publishing industry. Founded 1979 and named after Shoichi Noma, the firm's founder.

Nomenclature. A system of names for a system of classes, or classification; its terms.

Non-book Materials. Those library materials which do not come within the definition of a book, periodical or pamphlet and which require special handling, e.g. audio-visual materials, vertical file materials, microforms or computer software.

Non-current Records. (*Archives*) Those which are no longer required by current business and which can therefore be appraised for preservation in an archival depository, or destroyed.

Non-distinctive Title. One that is common to many serials, e.g. *Bulletin, Journal, Proceedings, Transactions.*

Non-expressive Notation. *See Notation.*

Non-fiction. Books that are not prose fiction.

Non-lining Figures. (*Printing*) Arabic numerals which have ascenders and descenders. Also called 'Hanging figures', OLD STYLE FIGURES (*q.v.*).

Non Net. A book usually a school text, likely to be sold in large numbers at one time which is not subject to the minimum selling price of the Net Book Agreement. *See also Net Book.*

Non-parliamentary Publications. Those published by HMSO (UK) (*q.v.*) but which are not PARLIAMENTARY PUBLICATIONS (*q.v.*). Prior to about 1925 when this heading began to be used in HMSO catalogues, such publications were known as 'Official Publications' or 'Stationery Office Publications'. These can be roughly grouped into (a) Statutory Instruments, (b) Reports, (c) other publications. Statutory Instruments are government orders or regulations made by a Minister under the authority of a specific Act of Parliament. They are numbered according to the calendar year in which they are made, a new sequence beginning each year. Prior to 1948 they were known as Statutory Rules and Orders. 'Reports' include a variety of departmental, committee and working party reports which are prepared for submission to, or for the information of, Parliament. 'Other publications' include the immense range of publications which are issued by HMSO.

Non-periodical. A publication which is published at one time, or at intervals, in complete, usually numbered, volumes, the total number of volumes being generally determined in advance.

Non-print Materials. *See Non-book Materials.*

Non-relief Type. Engraved or incised type in which the printing surface is not the character but the typeface around the incised character. This results in a white letter on a printed background.

Non-resident Member. A person who is permitted to use a library in a district other than the one in which he resides, by paying a subscription, or because he owns property in, is employed in, or studies in, the district.

Non-semantic Code. In information retrieval, one in which the notation does not carry meaningful information beyond that which is inherent in the spelling of the word in the source language for which it stands as the equivalent. *See also Semantic Code.*

non. seq. Abbreviation for *non sequitur* (*Lat.* 'it does not follow logically').

Non-Structural Notation. *See Structural Notation.*

Nonesuch Press. A publishing house founded in 1923 in London by Miss Vera Mendel with Francis Meynell to supervise book production and David Garnett to publish fine editions of scholarly works to be sold at modest prices through normal trade channels. After a period of inactivity during the Second World War production was resumed in 1953 with the Nonesuch Shakespeare in four volumes. Nearly all the books were machine set by various printers but were designed by Meynell. Many 'Monotype' matrices were specially designed for this Press. The press publishes its own books but does not do the actual printing.

Nonet. A combination of nine singers or musicians; the music for same.

Nonpareil. 1. An out-of-date name for a type size of about 6 point. 2. A 6-point lead.

NORDFORSK. Abbreviation for Nordiska Samarbetsorganisationen för Teknisk-Naturvetenskaplig Forskning – Scandinavian Council for Applied Research (formerly referred to as SCAR). Founded jointly by Iceland, Denmark, Finland, Norway and Sweden on 4 June 1947 to promote and organize co-operation in the field of scientific and industrial research and in the utilization of research results in the five countries. Members: scientific and industrial research councils and academies of engineering sciences in the countries concerned. Has a special committee on technical information – NORDINFO (*q.v.*).

NORDINFO. The Nordic Council for Scientific Information and Research Libraries; founded 1976 as an inter-governmental agency by Denmark, Finland, Norway, Sweden and Iceland, to improve the transfer and use of scientific information and documentation within the Nordic countries, and to support activities that make information of Nordic origin more accessible to users outside the area. Publishes a newsletter: *NORDINFO-NYTT* (q.) and a monograph series. Headquarters at Helsinki University of Technology Library.

Norsk Samkatalog. Norwegian bibliographic network operating a union catalogue; founded 1983 and has 300 members. Based at the University of Oslo.

North Midland Library Association. Formed in March 1890, and covering the counties of Nottingham, Derby, Leicester, Northampton and Lincoln. It became a Branch of the (British) Library Association in 1929 and was known as the North Midland Branch of the Library Association until 1970 when it was changed to East Midlands Branch.

North Western Branch. A Branch of the (British) Library Association. Founded in 1896 at Manchester. The 'Librarians of the Mersey District' had been formed in 1887 but was disbanded in 1905 to become absorbed in the Branch. Membership entitlement is residence or employment in the North Western geographical area, comprising Lancashire, Cheshire, the metropolitan counties of Merseyside and Greater Manchester, and the Isle of Man. Publishes *North Western Newsletter* (m.) and occasional books and booklets. Abbreviated LANW.

Northern Branch. A Branch of the (British) Library Association, all members of which who live or work in the counties of Cleveland, Cumbria, Durham, Northumberland, and the Metropolitan County of Tyne and Wear, automatically become members.

Northern Ireland Branch. A Branch of the (British) Library Association formed in 1929. It is now associated with the LIBRARY ASSOCIATION OF IRELAND (*q.v.*) in the joint publication of *An Leabharlann* (q.).

Northern Libraries Colloquy. An international group of librarians, archivists and information specialists representing libraries and institutions of all kinds either located in the Arctic or Sub-Arctic or physically in milder latitudes but whose interests are wholly polar. Formed in June 1971, in which year the first of the annual colloquies was held; the organization publishes *Northern Libraries Bulletin* (2/3 p.a. free to members) and has published a *Directory of northern libraries.* Financed by the annual colloquy fees, and based on the Scott Polar Research Institute, Cambridge, England.

Northern Listening Service. A facility based at the British Library Document Supply Centre at Boston Spa, to enable users to hear recordings held by the Library's National Sound Archive in London.

Norwegian Library Association. (Norsk Bibliotekforening (NBF).) Originally founded in 1913, in 1972 the four Norwegian professional library associations combined to form one body which unites all types of library. Membership is open to individuals and institutions. The Association comprises four sections: (1) special and research librarians; (2) public librarians; (3) part-time librarians; (4) public and school librarians.

Not. A FINISH (*q.v.*) given to good quality rag papers – not glazed or hot pressed. Those with no finish are called 'rough'; 'not' is less rough but 'not-smooth'. *See also Hot-pressed, Machine Glazed, Rough.*

Notation. 1. The symbols which stand for the divisions in a scheme of classification. The purposes of notation are (a) to mechanize the order headings in a scheme of classification, (b) to serve as a short-hand sign for the easy arrangement of documents on shelves or in drawers or files, and also for entries in respect of them in catalogues and indexes (the alternative to which would possibly be cumbersome and not easy-to-remember sequences of words), and (c) to provide easily memorized links between catalogues and the storage position of documents. Symbols must be brief and easily extended. If the notation consists of two or more kinds of symbols it is called a 'mixed notation'; if of one kind only, a 'pure notation'. The notation may be expressive or non-expressive. Expressive notation reveals the hierarchical structure of the classification scheme, in addition to mechanizing the order of the headings. The notation must be (a) hospitable, i.e. enable symbols for additional subject to be added at any position, (b) easily comprehensible, i.e. consisting only of roman letters and/or arabic numbers, and (c) easily memorized, written and spoken. A 'flexible notation' is one which expands with the classification, and permits the insertion of new subjects without any dislocation. 2. In information retrieval, a symbolism which is not in natural language but humanly legible, as distinct from CODING (*q.v.*). 3. An arbitrary device to indicate the contents or location of a document. 4. In machine searching as part of information retrieval, the designation of a particular set of symbols used to represent a code; the physical representation of a code. *See also Facet Indicator, Faceted Notation,*

Fence, Graphic Length, Hierarchical Notation, Intercalation Device, Labelled Notation, Phonic Length, Pronounceable Notation, Retro-active Notation, Structural Notation, Syllabic Notation.

Notational Plane. (*Classification*) The plane of symbols representing concepts.

Note. 1. An explanation of the text of a book or additional matter, appearing usually with other notes at the foot of a page, at the end of a chapter or at the end of the book. Where numbers are not used to separate and distinguish the notes, REFERENCE MARKS (*q.v.*) are used in a recognized sequence. Also called FOOTNOTE (*q.v.*). 2. A concise statement, following particulars of collation in a catalogue or bibliographical entry, giving added information such as the name of the series, contents, or bibliographical information. The term is sometimes limited to the information which appears below the collation and the main body of an entry. Notes should only be made to supply significant additional data in order to amplify a catalogue entry or be helpful to a reader.

Nothing Before Something. Alphabetizing 'word by word', counting the space between one word and the next as 'nothing'. *See also Alphabetization.* A word files before another word having the same letters plus additional ones, these additional ones being considered 'something'.

Notion. In co-ordinate indexing, an ENTITY (*q.v.*) or an ATTRIBUTE (*q.v.*).

Noun Order. (*Information retrieval*) An order of nouns in a compound heading, the order being determined by one of several rules, e.g. concrete – process (*see Concretes and Processes*) by using OPERATORS (*q.v.*) or by using facet citation chains.

Novel. A long fictitious story of imaginary people and events.

Novella. A short prose narrative, generally with a structural centre represented by a surprising event.

Novelette. A short novel.

Novelist. One who writes novels.

Novelty. (*Copyright*) The quality of a new INTELLECTUAL WORK (*q.v.*).

Noyes Award, Marcia C. This Award consists of a silver tray, and is given, not necessarily every year, to a medical librarian, anywhere in the world, for outstanding achievement in his chosen field. It was first awarded in 1953, to Mary Louise Marshall.

n.p. 1. Abbreviation for no place of publication, no printers name, no publisher's name. 2. Abbreviation for 'new paragraph'; an instruction to the compositor that a new paragraph is to be begun. It is indicated in a manuscript or proof by the letters 'n.p.' in the margin and [or // in the text before the first word of the new paragraph. 3. Also used in book reviews and elsewhere as an abbreviation for 'no price'.

NPAC. 1. NATIONAL PROGRAM FOR ACQUISITIONS AND CATALOGUING (*q.v.*). 2. NATIONAL PRESERVATION ADVISORY COMMITTEE (*q.v.*).

NPO. *See National Preservation Office.*

NRC. NATIONAL REFERRAL CENTER FOR SCIENCE AND TECHNOLOGY (*q.v.*).

NRCd. NATIONAL REPROGRAPHIC CENTRE FOR DOCUMENTATION (*q.v.*).

NRLSI. National Reference Library of Science and Invention (*q.v.*).

NSA. *See National Sound Archive.*

NSDP. National Serials Data Program (*q.v.*).

NSF. National Science Foundation (*q.v.*).

NTBL. Abbreviation for Nuffield Talking Book Library for the Blind which was established in 1935 as the Talk Book Library for the Blind, the name being changed in 1954. In 1960 the Nuffield Foundation gave a grant to convert the information then on records on to tape. The Library is administered by the Royal National Institute for the Blind and St. Dunstan's through their joint Sound Recording Committee, and maintained by the funds of these two voluntary charities. Membership is free and open to blind persons over the age of 21 who are registered with their local Blind Welfare Authority. The 'books' are specially recorded in the Committee's own studio; they are mainly fiction but a number of recordings of biographies, travel books and other non-fiction subjects are also produced. The 'books' are lent free and played on special recording machines which are non-commercial and rented from the Library. Now known as the British Talking Book Service for the Blind.

NTC. *See National Translations Center.*

NTIS. Acronym of National Technical Information Service which was formed in 1970 by the US Department of Commerce to simplify and increase public access to federal publications and data files of interest to the business, scientific and technical communities. It is the American clearinghouse for the collection and dissemination of scientific, technical, and engineering information. Previously known as the Office of Technical Service (OTS), it is a central source for the public sale of government-sponsored research, development and engineering reports and other analyses, information being brought together from hundreds of federal sources. Some 2 million titles are on sale, and a bibliographic database is maintained. The service is self-supporting, and privatization has been an issue in recent years. A series of weekly newsletters is issued, covering 26 subject areas announcing details of research reports and other documents newly acquired.

NUCMC. *National Union Catalog of Manuscript Collections* (*q.v.*).

Nuffield Talking Book Library for the Blind. *See NTBL.*

Number. 1. A single numbered or dated issue of a periodical or serial publication. 2. One of the numbered fascicules of a literary, artistic or musical work issued in instalments, ordinarily in paper wrappers, and called 'number' by the publisher. 3. In extended vocal works such as cantatas, oratorios and operas (especially the latter), one of the distinct and separate sections into which the composition is divided, each of which is complete in itself and in a specific form, such as aria, duet, chorus. 4. Any item in the programme of a concert or other entertainment. *See also Opus Number.*

Number Building. (*Classification*) The process of making a number more specific by adding segments taken from other parts of the classification.

Numbered and Signed Edition. An edition of a work the copies of which are numbered, and signed by the author. *See also Limited Edition.*

Numbered Column. Where the text of a book is printed in two or more columns to a page, and these instead of the pages are numbered consecutively. Where this is done a note to this effect normally appears at the head of the index.

Numbered Copy. A copy of a limited edition of a book which bears the copy number, usually on the page facing the title-page.

Numbered Entry. One of the entries in a printed bibliography or catalogue in which the entries are numbered consecutively.

Numbering. Placing (a) the call number on the spine of, or (b) the charging symbol in, a library book.

Numeral. A graphic symbol or character to represent a number of a group of numbers. A figure. *See also Arabic Figures, Hanging Figures, Ranging Figures, Roman Numerals.*

Numerals. The correct printer's term for figures and fractions.

Numeration. (*Cataloguing*) A number, roman or arabic, appearing in a heading, indicating the sequence of the person (as e.g. monarchs bearing the same forename) or another element in the heading (e.g. chemical formulae), and so affecting the filing sequence. *See also Character Significance Sequence, Logical Arrangement.*

NUT. *See En Quadrat.*

n.y.p. Abbreviation for 'not yet published'.

OAL. *See Office of Arts and Libraries.*

Oasis. An area in a university or college library where students may read or undertake research. Less formal than a CARREL (*q.v.*) and more economic of space.

Obelisk. Alternative name for the dagger (†) reference mark. Similarly a double dagger (‡) is also called a 'Double obelisk'. *See also Reference Mark.*

Oberly Award for Bibliography in Agricultural Sciences. Established in 1923, this Award is made by the Oberly Memorial Award Committee of the ACRL Division of the American Library Association every two years to the American citizen who compiles the best bibliography in the field of agriculture or the related sciences in the two-year period preceding the year in which the Award is made.

Objective Classification. A classification of the sciences according to the attributes of the relative scientific subjects.

Objectives. A set of specific aims or targets established as desirable that a given service or system should achieve, *Management by Objectives* (MbO) functions as a management technique by constantly re-defining and monitoring the achievement of agreed objectives in a participative environment.

Oblique. The sign / commonly found on alphanumeric keyboards for computer and viewdata systems.

Oblong. 1. Of a book that is wider than its height. Hence oblong folio, oblong quarto. This is the result of folding a sheet of paper across the long way (i.e. halving the short side). Also called 'Cabinet size', 'Landscape', 'Long'. The opposite of BROAD (*q.v.*). *See also Narrow, Size, Square.* 2. Applies to a

BROAD (*q.v.*) sheet of paper halved lengthways. A quarto size used with the longest dimension at the foot of the page, or sheet, is termed 'oblong quarto' and is the reverse of 'upright'.

Obverse Cover. The upper cover of a book. Also called 'Front cover', 'Upper cover'. *See also Reverse Cover.*

OCLC. Online Computer Library Center, a not-for-profit corporation. The acronym originally stood for Ohio College Library Center, established 1967 to share resources and reduce costs of academic libraries in the state of Ohio. In 1973 members were admitted from outside Ohio, and a rapid expansion ensued. The new name was adopted in 1981, and in the same year a European marketing campaign was launched. There are now 8000 members. The OCLC network database consists of MARC records and records created by member libraries for material not covered by the MARC files. A range of other services is also provided, including a micro-computer based serials control system, a circulation control system, and an online public access (OPAC) system.

OCR. OPTICAL CHARACTER RECOGNITION (*q.v.*).

OCR-A. A specific typeface intended for OPTICAL CHARACTER RECOGNITION (*q.v.*). There is also a variant known as OCR-B.

Octave Device. In classification, the name given by Ranganathan to a method of extending the decimal base of arabic numerals to infinity, by setting the figure 9 as an extender to bring in a further eight figures at the end of the first eight. The series thus reads: 1, 2, 3, 4, 5, 6, 7, 8, 91, 92, 93, 94, 95, 96, 97, 98, 991, 992, and so on, the figure 9 never being used unsupported. The figure 9 is known as the Octavizing Digit. This device, which was first used by Ranganathan in his *Colon Classification*, and adopted by the UNIVERSAL DECIMAL CLASSIFICATION (*q.v.*) in 1948, can be extended to letters, z (or any last letter of any other alphabet) being used in the same way. By this means the octave device provides hospitality in array.

Octavizing Digit. *See Octave Device.*

Octavo. (8vo). 1. A sheet of paper folded three times to form a section of eight leaves, or sixteen pages. The following sizes (in inches) of printing papers are usually used to produce an octavo page:

		Double	*Quad*	*Size of 8vo*
Foolscap	13½ × 17	17 × 27	27 × 34	6¾ × 4¼
Crown	15 × 20	20 × 30	30 × 40	7½ × 5
Large Post	16½ × 21	21 × 33	33 × 42	8¼ × 5¼
Demy	17½ × 22½	22½ × 35	35 × 45	8¾ × 5⅝
Medium	18 × 23	23 × 36	36 × 46	9 × 5¾
Royal	20 × 25	25 × 40	40 × 50	10 × 6¼
Super Royal	20½ × 27½	27½ × 41	41 × 55	10¼ × 6⅞
Imperial	22 × 30	30 × 44	44 × 60	11 × 7½

2. A book having sections of eight leaves, or sixteen pages. 3. Any book whose height is betwen 6¼ and 10 inches. *See also Book Sizes, Paper Sizes.*

Octavo Edition. One issued in OCTAVO (*q.v.*) form.

Octodecimo   (18mo). *See Eighteen-mo.*

Odd Fellows (Manchester Unity) Social Concern Book Award.   An annual award for a book or pamphlet within a specified area of social concern; administered by the BOOK TRUST (*q.v.*).

Odd Folios.   The page-numbers which come on the first, or recto, side of each leaf, the right hand of each OPENING (*q.v.*), 1, 3, 5, 7, 9, 11, etc.

Odd Page.   The page of a publication bearing an odd number; the right-hand page of an OPENING (*q.v.*), and the recto of a LEAF (*q.v.*).

Odd Part.   One part of a serial publication, or of a work published in a number of parts, which is separately issued and isolated from the others.

Odd Sorts.   Characters not normally included in a standard fount of type. Also called 'Side sorts'. Such characters can be used on a machine which sets lines of type in SLUGS (*q.v.*) but the matrices from which they are cast must be inserted by hand in the correct position by the typesetter.

Odd Volume.   One volume of a work in several volumes which is the only one possessed.

Oddments.   1. The items of a printed book which precede and follow the text. These are known as the PRELIMINARIES (*q.v.*) and the END-MATTER (*q.v.*).   2. When the pages of a book make an exact multiple of sixteen (or thirty-two if the sections are of 32 pages) it is said to make an even working. If an odd eight pages or so are needed to complete the printing it is termed 'uneven working' and the additional pages are said to be oddments.

O.E.   Abbreviation for OLD ENGLISH (*q.v.*).

'Off its Feet'.   Type which has been cast in such a way that its base is not true, with the result that it does not stand firm in the galley.

Offcut.   1. That part of a sheet which has to be cut off after 'imposition', as in the case of a 12mo., so that the sheet may be correctly folded, the cut off piece being folded and inserted in the larger piece after folding. The cut off piece is then called an 'inset' and usually bears a signature mark to indicate its proper place in the gathering.   2. A piece cut off a sheet of paper to reduce it to the size required for a particular job.   3. Remainders of reams which have been cut down to a smaller size.

Office Collection.   *Synonymous with* DEPARTMENTAL LIBRARY (*q.v.*).

Office for Library Networking.   Set up in 1990 at the Centre for Bibliographic Management, University of Bath, UK. Funded by the British Library Research and Development Department, and intended to represent the needs of libraries to the computing and telecommunications industries, and promote the effective use of existing and developing networks. Abbreviated OLN.

Office for Scientific and Technical Information.   *See OSTI.*

Office of Arts and Libraries (UK).   The section of the Department of Education and Science responsible for libraries. Until 1981 known as the DES Arts and Libraries Branch. The Office reports to the Minister for the Arts, and is advised by the LIBRARY AND INFORMATION SERVICES COUNCIL (*q.v.*).

Office of Information Programmes and Services.   A Unesco directorate set up in 1988 by the merger of the General Information Programme (PGI) and the Library, Archives and Documentation Services (LAD). It comprises four divisions: General Information Programme (IPS/PGI); Software Developments and Applications (IPS/SDA); Unesco Information Services (IPS/UIS); Operational Activities (IPS/OPS).

Office of Libraries and Learning Resources.   One of the provisions of the (US) Education Amendments of 1974 (HR 69) which became Public Law 93–380 on 21 August 1974 and amends and extends the existing Elementary and Secondary Education Act (ESEA), was the setting up of this office, the function of which is to administer all programmes related to 'libraries, information centers, and education technology'. The Office is within the US Office of Education.

Office of Management Studies.   A major study, carried out by Booz, Allen and Hamilton for the (US) Council on Library Resources Inc., and published as *Problems in university management* in 1970, called for the creation of an office of University Library management within the Association of Research Libraries. This was begun in 1970 with financial support from the CRL, working with interested university libraries and concentrating on the development of a policy or administrative manual on the use of policy as a management tool in large libraries. Abbreviated OMS.

Office Publishing.   *See Desktop Publishing.*

Official Catalogue.   A union catalogue for the use of library staff only, and usually kept in the cataloguing department.

Official Gazette.   A periodical publication issued by, or on behalf of, a government or university to convey official news, statements or decisions.

Official Name.   The legal name of a corporate body, office or government department.

Official Publication.   One issued by a government or government department it may be in a series or isolated. The Unesco Convention Concerning the Exchange of Official Publications and Government Documents between States, 1958, considered the following, when they are executed by the order and at the expense of any national governmental authority, to be official publications: parliamentary documents, reports and journals and other legislative papers; administrative publications and reports from central federal and regional governmental bodies; national bibliographies, State handbooks, bodies of law, decisions of the Courts of Justice; and other publications as may be agreed.

Official Title.   The title of a book appearing on the title-page, and which is accepted, either in whole or in part, by the cataloguer for purposes of cataloguing.

Off-line Equipment.   (*Information retrieval*) The peripheral computer equipment, or devices, not in direct communication with a computer's central processing unit.

Off-line Operation.   (*Information retrieval*) The accomplishment of functions which are not a part of the main processing operations.

Offline Print.   Printing of search results after the searcher has disconnected from the computer.

Offprint. *Synonymous with* SEPARATE (*q.v.*).

Offset. 1. The printing process in which the impression is transferred from a litho stone or plate to a rubber-covered cylinder, and thence offset by pressure on to the paper. *See also Offset Printing.* 2. Sometimes erroneously used to describe the unintentional transfer of ink from one sheet to another; this is correctly called 'set-off'. *See also Slip Sheet.*

Offset Foil. A printing plate used for making prints (copies of documents) by the offset process.

Offset Lithography. A method of printing in which a drawing is made on transfer paper the right way round, printed on to a rubber-covered cylinder and 'offset' on to paper. *See also Transfer.*

Offset Paper. Paper especially made for use on an offset press. It should lie flat, be free from lint, and stretch as little as possible.

Offset-photo-lithography. *See Photo-offset.*

Offset Printing. An adaptation of the principles of stone lithography, in which the design is drawn or reproduced upon a thin, flexible, metal plate which is curved to fit one of the revolving cylinders of the printing press; the design from this plate is transferred or 'offset' to the paper by means of a rubber blanket which runs over another cylinder and which has received its impression from the plate.

OFTEL. Office of Telecommunications (UK); a non-ministerial government department, which is responsible for supervising telecommunications activities and developments in the UK.

Oghamic Character. *See Runic Letters.*

Oghamic Scripts. Inscriptions, peculiar to the Celtic population of the British Isles, usually found on wooden staves but sometimes also on shields or other hard material. They are also found on tombstones. Used for writing messages and letters. The alphabet consisted of twenty letters which were represented by straight or diagonal strokes varying from one to five in number and drawn, or cut, below, above or through, horizontal lines, or to the left, or right, of, or through, vertical lines.

Ohio College Library Center. *See OCLC.*

Okapi. An experiment in the provision of OPACs (*q.v.*) conducted at the Polytechnic of Central London (UK).

Ola Books. Books made in Sri Lanka from olas, or strips of young leaves of the Talipat or Palmyra palm which are soaked in hot water and pressed smooth. They are cut into strips about 3 inches wide and from 1 to 3 feet long. A cord is passed through holes pierced at the ends of each so as to secure the leaves between two lacquered wooden boards. Writing is done with an iron stylus, and the incisions made more easily readable by rubbing in a mixture of charcoal and oil. The aromatic and preservative nature of the oil is believed to have enabled the books to survive from pre-Christian days. Buddhist monks still make ola books in Sri Lanka. Also called 'olla books'.

Old English. An angular type of the black-letter group; abbreviated O.E. This is an example of Old English:

This is 12 point Old English

Old Face. The majority of book types in England belong to this family of types. Its origin is generally attributed to Garamond (Paris, first half of sixteenth century) who modelled his design on the roman types of the Venetian printer Aldus Manutius which were actually cut in 1495 for Aldus by Francesco Griffo who also cut the famous Aldine italic. The Old Face group of letters is characterized by oblique emphasis, lightness of colour, comparatively small differences between thick and thin strokes and fairly substantial bracketed serifs. The capitals are slightly lower than the ascending lower case letters and the descenders are long. The modern versions of Old Face have a comparatively small X-Height (*q.v.*) and a narrow set. Examples are, Caslon Old Face (Stephenson Blake and others); Bembo, Fournier, Imprint, Plantin, Van Dijck (Monotype); Garamond (Monotype and Intertype). The figures of Old Face do not all stand on the line: 1234567890. The following is in 12-point Bembo:

This is BEMBO type face.

There is at present a revival of old faces, the most famous of recent years being Eric Gill's *Perpetua* which is effective and useful both as a book type, because it is narrow, (see example in TYPE FACE), and especially at titling. The term 'Garalde' has superseded 'Old face' for this category of type faces. *See also Arabic Figures, Hanging Figures, Modern Face, Ranging Figures, Transitional.*

Old Style. A modification of OLD FACE (*q.v.*), the ascenders and descenders being shorter. Examples are: Old Style (Stephenson Blake); Old Style Antique (Miller & Richard); Bookprint (Linotype); Bookface (Intertype). Old Style capitals, lower case letters and figures are as follows:

ABCDEFGHIJKLMNOPQRSTUVWXYZ
abcdefghijklmnopqrstuvwxyz   1234567890

Old Style Figures. (*Printing*) Numerals, three of which are of x-height, the others having ascenders and descenders as in the specimen under OLD STYLE (*q.v.*). Also called 'Non-Lining figures'. *See also Arabic Figures, Modern Face.*

Oldman Prize. An annual prize awarded by the UK Branch of the International Association of Music Libraries for the best British book on music librarianship or bibliography. Commemorates C. B. Oldman (1894–1969), Principal Keeper of Printed Books in the British Library 1947–59.

Oleograph. A reproduction of an oil painting, printed by lithography, mounted on canvas, sized and varnished, the irregularities of the oil painting and canvas being reproduced by an embossing process.

Oleography. The lithographic process used to produce an OLEOGRAPH (*q.v.*).

Olin Book Number. An author number from a scheme devised by Charles R. Olin. The use of Olin Numbers enables collective biography to be separated yet to be brought into close relation at the same class number. They convert all authors' or compilers' surnames into A followed by figures, thus enabling collective biographies to be arranged before the individual biographies bearing Cutter Author Marks. The following is section S from the Table:

Sa	A77	Scr	A79	Sia	A82	Sq	A84
Sch	A78	Sea	A81	Sma	A83	Sva	A85

Strickland's *Queens of England* would be A84 (Olin number) and be arranged before a life of Queen Anne, An 7 (Cutter Author Mark). The Olin Book Numbers and the Biscoe Time Numbers were printed in the 11th, 12th and 13th editions of the Dewey Classifications.

Olympus. A satellite launched in 1989 by the European Space Agency; for a two-year period any educational institution in Europe will be permitted to experiment with innovatory programmes without charge for transmission facilities.

OMB. *See One Man Band.*

Omissible. Something which may be omitted if required, necessary or desirable.

Omission Marks. Three dots, thus . . . , used on the BASE LINE (*q.v.*) in quoted text, or a catalogue entry, to indicate that something in the original has been omitted. Also called 'Ellipsis'.

Omnibus Book. A volume containing reprints of short stories by various authors or of novels or other works by one or more authors.

Omnibus Review. One which discusses a number of books of one type or field of literature.

OMS. OFFICE OF MANAGEMENT STUDIES (*q.v.*).

On Approbation. *Synonymous with* ON APPROVAL (*q.v.*).

On Approval. Applied to a transaction whereby a customer may have the opportunity of examining goods before deciding whether to purchase them, and to return same within a short specified time if he decides not to keep them. Abbreviated: on appro. 'On approbation' has the same meaning.

On Sale. Books supplied to a bookseller under an agreement that they may be returned if unsold. Also known as 'On sale or return'. *See also Half See Safe, See Safe.*

One Man Band. An Aslib membership group for those employed as the sole member of staff in special libraries and information units. Abbreviated OMB.

One Place Index. *See Specific Index.*

One Place Theory. The classifying of material on various aspects of a subject at one place only.

One Sheet On. *Synonymous with* ALL ALONG (*q.v.*).

One Shot. 1. The reprinting in one issue of a periodical of the full text, or an abridgement, of a book, as distinct from a serialized reprint. 2. A magazine of which only one issue has been published. 3. Single issue rights, where the whole of a literary work or an abridgement of it, appears in a periodical.

One Side Coloured. Paper or board which has been intentionally coloured during manufacture.

Onion Skin. A thin, glazed, transparent paper.

Onlay. A decorative panel of paper or other material glued to the cover of a book without preparing the cover to receive it. *See also Inlay.*

On-line. A general term for devices and peripherals which are interacting directly and simultaneously with a computer in real time.

On-line Computer Library Center. *See OCLC.*

Online Information Retrieval. A means whereby a searcher at a remote terminal can access and interrogate databases containing bibliographical or other data. Such databases, produced by commercial firms, government departments, professional bodies, research organizations etc. and usually made available via a HOST (*q.v.*). *See* for example DIALOG, DATA-STAR, INFOLINE etc. The searcher accesses the database using a telecommunications link, and quoting a password to establish authenticity and facilitate billing.

Online Public Access Catalogue. An automated catalogue system. The catalogue is stored in machine-readable form, and accessed online by the library clientele via a terminal and employing user-friendly software. Abbreviated OPAC.

Online Searching. *See Online Information Retrieval.*

Onymous. The exact opposite of ANONYMOUS (*q.v.*).

O.P. Abbreviation for OUT OF PRINT (*q.v.*).

op. cit. Abbreviation for *opere citato* (Lat. 'in the work cited'). Used in a footnote reference to avoid using the title or short title of the work referred to. It should not be used if there is more than one book by the author concerned, and preferably not if another book has been referred to since the first citation.

Op. no. Abbreviation for OPUS NUMBER (*q.v.*).

OPAC. *See Online Public Access Catalogue.*

OPAC Research Group. A group set up by the British Library Research and Development Department to co-ordinate OPAC research, facilitate exchange between research teams, and keep the whole programme under review.

Opacity. The quality of non-transparency in book papers. Creamy or off-white papers are more opaque than bright white ones, and a matt finish gives a greater opacity than a glazed finished.

Opaque Copy. A copy of a document on opaque, or non-transparent, material.

Opaque Microcopy. A microcopy made on opaque, or non-transparent, material, usually paper or card. Also called 'Micro-opaque'.

Opaque Projector. A projector which can project small opaque printed images such as maps, post-cards, illustrations, photographs, pages of books, etc., but much enlarged on to screens or walls.

Opaquing. Painting a negative with an opaque liquid to block out pin-holes and other defects, or render certain parts unprintable.

Open Access. Applied to a library where readers are admitted to the shelves.

Open Back. (*Binding*) *Synonymous with* HOLLOW BACK (*q.v.*).

Open-back Case. *Synonymous with* SLIP CASE (*q.v.*).

Open Back File. A box file for holding pamphlets and similar material, consisting of a five sided box the shape of a book. The sixth side (the back) is open to allow the easy insertion – and more easy removal – of material.

Open Bibliography. *Synonymous with* CURRENT BIBLIOGRAPHY (*q.v.*).

Open Edge. Any edge of a section of a book which is open and not enclosed by a BOLT (*q.v.*).

Open-ended. Being possessed of the quality by which the addition of new terms, subject headings, or classifications does not disturb the pre-existing system.

Open-ended Term List. A list of terms to which, in contrast to a CONTROLLED TERM LIST (*q.v.*), terms may be added as required, provided that the terms in the existing list are not altered. Also called 'Open indexing system'. *See also Closed Indexing System.*

Open Entry. A catalogue entry which leaves room for the addition of information concerning a work which is in course of publication, or of which the library does not possess a complete copy or set, or concerning which complete information is lacking. Open entries usually occur in respect of serials still in course of publication, the date of the most recent issue and last volume number being omitted in the case of works in several volumes which are still in course of publication; or of living authors, in catalogues in which birth and death dates are given. Space may be left elsewhere than in the main part of the entry, e.g. in the notes, for particulars of publications or of the library's holdings. *See also Closed Entry.*

Open Learning. A process of teaching and learning by which students study in their own homes or local centres using materials mailed or broadcast from a central unit. Tutorial work may be handled by correspondence with the central unit, or on a regional basis.

The emphasis is on opening up opportunities by overcoming barriers of geographical isolation, personal or work commitments, and conventional course structures, which have often prevented certain categories of people from gaining access to educational and training facilities. British examples include the Open University, Open College; many traditional educational institutions are moving rapidly into the field. The term *distance learning* is practically synonymous.

Open-letter Proof. A proof of an engraving with the caption engraved in outline letters, whereas the finished engraving has solid letters.

Open Letters. Jobbing and display type which have the centres of the strokes of the characters incised, and so beyond the reach of the inkers; this gives the impression of white areas rather than black. Also called 'Outline letters'. *See also Inline Letters.*

Open Matter. Type which has been generously 'leaded'. *See also Leaded Matter.*

Open Order. In book acquisition in North America, two types of order: (1) those made up of items listed individually, some or all of which have not been supplied, hence the orders are not closed or completed; (2) those which approximate to open requisitions, as they ear-mark sums of money with booksellers to be spent on a particular subject or category.

Open Score. The printed or written music for two or more voices or parts each of which is separately displayed one above another. Also called 'Extender score'. *See also Score.*

Open Shelf Library. *See Open Access.*

Open Systems Interconnection. Work on OSI began in 1977, and its aim is to enable all types and sizes of computers to communicate directly with each other on a worldwide basis. OSI therefore specifies international standards to which most major equipment manufacturers are committed. ISO 7498 (also BS 6568), the basic *Reference Model of OSI*, was issued in 1983 and has been followed by many dozen standards and recommendations; principally these emanate from ISO (INTERNATIONAL ORGANIZATION FOR STANDARDIZATION *q.v.*) and from CCITT (*q.v.*). The UK Department of Trade and Industry Information Technology Division promotes OSI through a special section, and has set up a showcase site at the University of Aston.

Opened. A book of which the top, fore, and sometimes bottom, edges have not been cut in manufacture but opened with a paper knife before being read.

Opening. Two pages facing one another. *See also Conjugate, Double-spread.*

Operation Code. That part of an instruction in a computer programme designating the processing step to be performed.

Operators. (*Classification*) Categories of relation, indicated by symbols, to mark steps of progression in analysing complex subjects. An analysis set down in this way is called an 'Analet'. *See also Relational Indexing (q.v.).*

Opisthographic. Applied to early-printed books printed on both sides of the paper and to manuscripts or parchments with writing on both sides. *See also Anopisthographic Printing, Block Book.*

Optical Character Recognition. A technique for machine recognition of characters by their images, whereby printed characters are read directly by light-sensitive devices. Special forms of type have been designed for the purpose. Abbreviated OCR.

Optical Coincidence. *Synonymous with* UNITERM CONCEPT CO-ORDINATION INDEXING (*q.v.*). *See also Batten System, Co-ordinate Indexing, Peek-a-boo, Peephole Card.*

Optical Copying. 1. Making a copy of a document on photographic material in the same scale, or one different from the original. 2. A print made by such a means may be called an 'optical copy'. 3. A term used in REPROGRAPHY (*q.v.*) for a photograph made by means of an optical system. *See also Contact Copying.*

Optical Digital Disk. A disc normally made of plastic with a reflective metal coating which is capable of storing either audio signals, video information or high-volume computer data. The playback system uses a small laser beam in the playing head. Read-only optical disks ('videodiscs' or 'laser-discs') have been used for home entertainment and industrial training; CD-ROM (*q.v.*) has become the most relevant term for library purposes. *See also WORM.*

Optical Fibres. *See Fibre-optic Cables.*

Optical Information Systems. The use of optically encoded formats for information storage. CD-ROM (*q.v.*) and Video discs are the most common media. *See also Document Image Processing.*

Optical Photocopying Device. A machine for making 'optical copies' of an original, i.e. copies on photographic material of the same, or a different, scale by means of an optical system.

Optical Printer. A CONTINUOUS PRINTER (*q.v.*) for the production of copies (prints) by optical means.

Optical Stencil Card. A card used in information retrieval in which holes are punched in certain positions to indicate files or documents containing particular information; a heading word is placed at the top of the card, and is chosen from a thesaurus which is specially compiled for the subject matter of the organization's material. Several cards are placed together so that light can shine through the punched holes and so indicate which files contain the information indicated by their heading words. These cards are used in Uniterm systems. *See also Peek-a-boo, Uniterm Concept Co-ordination Indexing.*

Optical Videodisc. *See Optical Digital Disk.*

Option. The privilege to buy rights in a manuscript or book if required.

Optional Provision. (*Classification*) In the Dewey Decimal Classification, a variation from the preferred provision; it is offered to users in the printed schedules and tables of the scheme, but not used in centralized classification as supplied by the Library of Congress.

Opus Anglicanum. A form of split-stitch embroidery on satin; used as a decorative binding in the fifteenth century. *See also Fabric Binding.*

Opus Number. A number assigned to a musical work or collection of works, usually in the order of composition. The numbers are assigned by the composer or by the publisher. An opus number may refer to one work or to a group of works of similar form and for the same medium; each has a secondary number. Abbreviated Op. no.

Opuscule. (*Pl.* Opuscula). 1. A lesser or minor literary or musical work or composition. 2. A small book or treatise.

OR. 1. Abbreviation for ORIGINAL (*q.v.*). 2. Operational Requirement; the specification of the required features of an automated system, given to the computer manufacturer by the client.

ORACLE. The TELETEXT (*q.v.*) service provided by the Independent Broadcasting Authority (UK). Originally probably an acronym for Optical Reception of Announcements by Coded Live Electronics. *See also* VIDEOTEX.

ORBIT. ORBIT Search Service, a division of Pergamon ORBIT Infoline, is a major international online information retrieval service. This host specializes in patents, materials science, chemistry, engineering, energy, health and safety; over 100 databases are available.

Orchestral Score. *See Score.*

Order Book of the House of Commons. *See Parliamentary Papers.*

Order Card. The card used for recording orders placed, and later, the delivery of the material and payment for it: the official record of each individual order.

Order Department. The department of a library which deals with the ordering and sometimes processing of books and periodicals. *Also called* 'accession department', 'acquisition department'.

Order File. The file containing records of the books on order from booksellers.

Order Information. Data concerning the placing of orders for books and other library materials, and also of their receipt. It includes (1) entering an order, order number, date of order, name of supplier, and fund to which cost will be charged, and (2) after delivery of the goods, date of receipt, cost, and date of invoice.

Order Section. *Synonymous with* ORDER DEPARTMENT (*q.v.*) except that it may be a section of another department, e.g. Cataloguing Department, rather than being an independent department.

Order Slip. *See Order Card.*

Ordered File. (*Information retrieval*) In mechanized systems, one in which the contents are arranged in a predetermined manner to facilitate reference.

Ordinal Notation. (*Classification*) One which merely provides order and does not express hierarchical relations. Also called 'Non-expressive notation'. *See also Hierarchical Notation, Notation.*

Ordnance Survey. A department of the British government, founded 1791, which exists to make an accurate map survey of the British Isles. Maps of various kinds are published in scales varying from ¼ to 50 inches to a mile, and a metric series. Maps of Ireland were issued until April 1922, since when the government of Eire has issued its own. Abbreviated OS.

Organ-vocal Score. *See Score.*

Organization File. A file of written or published material by or about the organization of which a special library is a part. It may include official minutes, proceedings, records and other archive material, items prepared for the guidance or instruction of the staff, publicity material, information publications, etc. whether published for limited or for general distribution, periodical and newspaper articles about the organization, etc. Also called 'History file'.

Orient. (*Verb*) To write extracts in such a way as to meet the needs of a particular 'audience'.

Original. 1. Finished art work (drawing, painting or photograph) as completed by the originator, and ready for reproduction. 2. In the author's own words or other original medium. 3. In the author's own language or as written by him. 4. A first copy. 5. A process block (half-tone or line) as distinct from a duplicate block (stereotype or electrotype). Abbreviated: Or. or Orig. 6. In documentary reproduction, an object, or document, to be reproduced.

Original Binding. The binding that was first put on a specific book.

Original Parts. A first edition of a work which appeared serially in a number of parts, each provided with a paper wrapper, and numbered.

Original Sources. *See Primary Sources.*

Original Writ. One issuing from the Chancery.

Originality. (*Copyright*) The quality of an *intellectual* work which seems to be significantly different from any other work, either in form or in content. A work may possess originality even when not dealing with new material.

Orihon. 1. A book composed of a continuous, folded, uncut sheet or, of small single sheets, folded but uncut. It is held together by cords laced through holes stabbed down one side. This form is used in China and Japan where the paper is so thin that it can only be printed on one side. 2. A 'stabbed binding' of Oriental origin. 3. A manuscript roll on which the text was written in columns running the short way of the paper; the roll was not cut but folded down the margins between the columns of text. *See also French Fold.*

Ornamental Initial. *See Initial Letter.*

Ornamental Inside Lining. *Synonymous with* DOUBLURE 1 (*q.v.*).

Ornaments. Printers' ornaments are little designs used to decorate printed matter. They are often arranged as borders, headpieces, tail-pieces, etc. Also called 'Printer's ornament'.

Orthographic Coding. (*Information retrieval*) 1. A statistical analysis of the spelling of the descriptive headings used, as a device to increase the efficiency of single-field superimposed coding systems. 2. A superimposed coding system using pairs of letters in a single field.

Orthography. Spelling correctly, or according to accepted usage.

O.S. 1. Abbreviation for OUT OF STOCK (*q.v.*). 2. Abbreviation for ORDNANCE SURVEY (*q.v.*).

Osborne Collection. A collection of Early English Children's Books which was assembled by Mr. E. Osborne, a former County Librarian of Lancashire, UK. It is owned by the Toronto Public Libraries, Canada.

OSI. *See Open Systems Interconnection.*

OSI/NM Forum. Open Systems Inter-connection Network Management Forum; established 1988 to improve the development of co-ordinated and compatible products, by eight companies, including British Telecom and STC plc from the UK.

OSIS. Acronym of the Office of Science Information Service which operates within the (US) NATIONAL SCIENCE FOUNDATION (*q.v*). In 1976, following the reorganization of the NSF, OSIS was re-named the Division of Science Information. *See also Science and Technology Information and Utilization Corporation.*

Osmosis, Method of. The classification by a newly adopted scheme, of all literature received after a given date, and the reclassification of the older literature in stock, as and when able to do so.

OSTI. The Office for Scientific and Technical Information; set up by the Department of Education and Science to handle funds for research and development into information and information science. Now absorbed into the Research and Development Department of the BRITISH LIBRARY (*q.v.*).

Other Award. An alternative award established in 1975 by the Children's Rights Workshop and now administered by Children's Book Bulletin. Awards are given to an unspecified number of non-biased books of literary merit.

Other Title. (*Cataloguing*) A title, other than the title proper, or a parallel title, which appears in a publication – e.g. a SUB-TITLE (*q.v.*), an ALTERNATIVE TITLE (*q.v.*).

Other Title Information. Any phrase (other than a title, a statement of authorship, or an edition statement) which appears in the PRELIMINARIES (*q.v.*) of a book, and which indicates the character or contents of the publication, or the motive for, or occasion of, its production.

Oustinoff System. A method devised by Helen Oustinoff, Assistant Director of the University of Vermont Library, to reduce work and ensure accuracy in the ordering of books. By using a Polaroid Camera, copies of bibliographical entries in books or catalogues, are made; these are passed to ordering clerks for making up orders and subsequently filed with the orders.

Out of Print. A book is out of print when the publisher has no more copies for sale and no intention to reprint. Abbreviation O.P.

Out of Stock. Not available from the publisher (although in print) until his stock has been replenished. Abbreviated: O.S.

Outer Form. *See Form Divisions.*

Outer Forme. The forme for the side to be printed first; it bears the SIGNATURE MARK (*q.v.*). *See also Inner Forme.*

Outer Indention. *Synonymous with* FIRST INDENTION (*q.v.*).

Outguide. A form card on which is recorded the loan of material from a file, or the file itself. It is submitted for the material lent, and being large enough to project above the folder, immediately indicates material on loan and possibly overdue.

Outlier Library. A library of a research institution, or one devoted to a particular subject, which did not generally participate in the work of a regional bureau, but whose stock was available to other libraries through the NATIONAL CENTRAL LIBRARY (*q.v.*). *See also Regional Bureaux.*

Outline. 1. Usually a popular treatment of an extensive subject, e.g. H. G. Wells *The outline of history.* 2. (*Printing*) A type face in which the shape of the character is outlined in a continuous line of more or less consistent width. *See also Inline Letters.*

Outline Letters. *Synonymous with* OPEN LETTERS (*q.v.*).

Output. (*Information retrieval*) The product of a process – that is, the information transferred from the internal storage of a computer to output devices for external storage.

Output Devices. Computer peripherals which convert the result of the computer's activities into a comprehensible form, e.g. a VDU or line printer.

Outreach. The process whereby a library service discovers the true nature of the community it serves and becomes fully involved in supporting community activities, whether or not centred on library premises.

Outsert. An extra double leaf placed round the outside of a printed section of a book, and forming part of it. *See also Wrap Rounds.*

Outside Margin. *Synonymous with* FORE-EDGE MARGIN (*q.v.*).

Outside Source. An idiom used, often by special librarians, to indicate a source of information outside their own organization which may be drawn upon when the resources of the library are inadequate to deal with enquiry needs. Such sources are often listed in the catalogue under appropriate subject headings or in a separate SOURCE INDEX (*q.v.*).

Oval Half-tone. *See Half Tone.*

Ovals, In. A binding with an oval arabesque centrepiece impressed in the centre of the top and lower covers. A common style in the late sixteenth and early seventeenth centuries, and found both in gold and blind.

Over Matter. Matter set ready for printing but held over through lack of space.

Over-run. (*Printing*) 1. To turn over words from one line to the next for several successive lines as necessary after an insertion or a deletion. 2. Copies printed in excess of the number ordered.

Over-running. Re-adjusting a paragraph of type which has been set up, due to corrections affecting the length of a line or poor make-up, or to avoid a RIVER (*q.v.*) or the unsatisfactory division of words. Words set in one line are carried forward or backward to adjacent lines as necessary.

Overcasting. *Synonymous with* OVERSEWING (*q.v.*).

Overdue. Colloquialism for an overdue book and also for an OVERDUE NOTICE (*q.v.*).

Overdue Book. A library book which has been retained longer for home reading than the period allowed.

Overdue Notice. A request to a reader asking for the return of a book which has been kept out beyond the time allowed.

Overhead Projector. A device for projecting images or transparent material of about nine inches square on to a screen in front of, or to one side of, the audience while the operator faces them. The transparency is known as an 'overhead transparency'. *See also Overlay 2.*

Overlay. 1. The placing of pieces of paper on the tympan or impression cylinder of a printing machine, by manipulation of which an even impression is obtained from the matter after it has been levelled as far as possible by UNDERLAY (*q.v.*). 2. A group of transparent or translucent prints or drawings which can be superimposed on one another to form a composite print or slide. This method is often used in overhead projectors. 3. (*Information retrieval*) A technique for bringing routines into high-speed storage from some other form of storage during processing so that several routines will occupy the same storage locations at different times. Overlay functions when the total storage requirements for instructions are in excess of the main storage which is available. 4. Also, a transparent sheet bearing additional or alternative information which registers over another sheet. *See also Routine.*

Overplus. (*Printing*) Additional sheets printed in excess of the number actually ordered to allow for getting exact position, testing colour, determining register and for spoilt sheets so that on completion of a job the number ordered is available. These are usually known as 'overs'. Bibliophiles also apply the term to limited editions, copies of which are numbered serially.

Overprint. 1. To revise printed matter by blocking out unwanted matter and printing a revision above it. 2. To print over matter which has already been printed whether blocked out or not. 3. To add information in a space, or in a Box (*q.v.*), on something which has already been printed. This frequently occurs with circulars, catalogues and advertising leaflets where a name and address are inserted to give the impression that the printed matter appears to originate from this source. *See also Separate.* 4. More copies printed than needed, or ordered. 5. In colour printing, to obtain required colours by printing with one colour superimposed over another.

Overprinting. 1. Printing in a primary colour over printing already carried out in a different colour in order to obtain a compound shade. 2. Application of a varnish or lacquer to matter printed from type or by a litho process, by means of a brush, spray or roller. 3. In blockmaking, superimposing one negative over another on the coated metal plate before developing. *See also Overprint.* 4. The printing of additional material, as e.g. the name and address of a retailer on to a sheet or page that has already been printed.

Overs. 1. Extra sheets issued from the paper warehouse to the printing room, to allow for make-ready, testing colour, and for spoilt sheets, so that on completion of a job the number ordered is available. 2. Sheets or copies of a work printed in excess of the number ordered to make up spoiled copies, and to provide review and presentation copies. Also called 'Overplus'.

Oversewing. The act or process of sewing over and over the leaves of a book, usually done when it consists of single leaves or when the paper is too poor or too heavy for normal sewing to be satisfactory. Called 'whip-stitching' in America.

Oversize Book. One which is too large to be shelved in normal sequence.

Ownership Mark. A rubber-stamp impression, perforation, embossment, or other mark of ownership in a book.

Oxford Bible. *Synonymous with* VINEGAR BIBLE (*q.v.*).

Oxford Corners. In book finishing, border rules that cross and project beyond each other.

Oxford Decimal System. A scheme of classification based on the Universal Decimal Classification. It was worked out at the School of Forestry of Oxford University and is restricted to the field of forestry.

Oxford Folio. *See Vinegar Bible.*

Oxford Hollow. A tube-like lining which is flattened, and one side stuck to the folded and sewn sections of the book and the other to the inside of the spine of the cover.

Oxford India Paper. An INDIA PAPER (*q.v.*) about 8lb demy (480) used by the Oxford University Press mainly for Bibles and prayer books, and made from selected rag stock according to a secret formula at their Wolvercote Mill since 1857. It is similar to an India paper first brought to Oxford in 1841, being very thin and opaque (one thousand sheets making less than an inch in thickness), and is a proprietary article. *See also Bible Paper, Cambridge India Paper.*

Oxford Rule.   A rule with one thick and one thin line running parallel with each other.

Oxidation.   The action which occurs when air contacts the unprotected areas of a lithographic plate which has been inadequately gummed. *See also Gumming Up.*

OZDB.   Österreichische Zeitschriften Datenbank; a library bibliographic network based at the Austrian National Library, Vienna, and specializing in handling serials records of scientific libraries. Founded 1984; members include all Austrian universities, colleges, museums, and state libraries, and numerous special libraries.

p.   Abbreviation for page; pp., pages.

P-Slip.   A slip of paper 5 × 3 inches. P-slips are often made up into pads. (American).

PA.   *See Publishers Association.*

PAC.   1. Public Access Catalogue; identical to OPAC (*q.v.*).   2. *See Preservation and Conservation.*

Packet Assembler – Disassembler.   *See PSS.*

Packet Device.   The symbol used in building classification numbers to connect class numbers from two parts of the classification schedules, the second one being used to show an aspect of the subject indicated by the first number.

Packet Notation.   The use of a connecting symbol, e.g. in the Colon Classification a bracket, or in the Universal Decimal Classification square brackets, to divide an isolate number by a number drawn from another schedule. Such a digit can be used as an octavizing digit (*see Octave Device*) to extend the hospitality of an array.

Packet Switch Stream.   *See PSS.*

Packet Switching.   A method of dividing data into small *packets* for transmission between computers, terminals, networks; each packet is separately routed, and thus large quantities of data can be transmitted simultaneously by various routes. Data is split either at an initial stage, or at an exchange point, and needs reassembling by the receiving device. *See also PSS.*

PAD.   Packet Assembler/Disassembler. A device for making up packets from data, and converting the packets back to data in a packet-switching system. *See also PSS.*

Padding.   Blank leaves added at the back of a thin pamphlet when binding it to form a sizeable volume.

Padeloup Style.   A style of book decoration practised by the Padeloup family in France in the eighteenth century. It is mainly characterized by its inlays of coloured leathers of diapered simple geometrical form, devoid of any floreation.

Page.   *See Leaf.*

Page Break.   The point in the text of a book where one page ends and the next begins.

Page Catalogue.   One in which only a few entries are made on a page at first, with spaces left for the insertion of subsequent entries in correct order. Also called 'Guard book catalogue', 'Ledger catalogue'.

Page Cord.   A cord which withstands water, specially made for printers, and used to tie up pages of type prior to imposition or distribution.

Page Headline.   A summary of the contents of a page, or an OPENING (*q.v.*), or of the main topic of a page or opening, appearing on both left- and right-hand pages, or on one side only in conjunction with a section headline on the other page. Also called 'Page head'. *See also Headline, Running Title, Section Headline.*

Page-on-galley Proof.   A galley proof with the type already made up into pages. This is done to avoid the necessity for supplying page proofs after correcting galley proofs.

Page Proof.   *See Proof.*

Page Reference.   In bibliographies, the number of the page on which the article, etc., indexed is to be found in a particular volume or volumes.

Pagination.   1. That part of a catalogue entry or bibliographical description specifying the number of pages in a book.   2. The system of numbers by which consecutive pages of a book or MS. are marked to indicate their order. Pagination is rare until 1500 and not really common until 1590.

Painted Edges.   *See Fore-edge Painting.*

Pakistan National Scientific and Technical Documentation Centre.   This organization was established in Karachi in 1957, with the technical assistance of Unesco. Abbreviated PANSDOC.

Palaeography.   The study and description of ancient and mediaeval manuscripts, documents and systems of writing, including the knowledge of the various characters used at different periods by the scribes of different nations and languages, their usual abbreviations, etc.

Palimpsest.   Manuscript in which a second writing has been superimposed upon the original text, which has been wholly or partially obliterated.

Pallet.   1. A tool used to decorate the panels on the spine of a bound book. Pallets are usually used to make straight lines (sometimes decorative) but are also used to impress a whole word such as the author's name or title.   2. A bookbinder's typeholder.

Palm Leaf Book.   Manuscript books consisting of strips of Palmyra or Talipat palm leaf from 16 to 36 inches long and from 1½ to 3 inches broad. Writing was done by scratching with an iron stylus and ink prepared from oil and charcoal rubbed over the surface to fill the incisions. The strips were then bound by piercing a hole in the middle of each and stringing them on cords or a piece of twine, and attaching them to a board. They were made in India, Burma and Sri Lanka. The Palmyra and Talipat palm leaves which are thick but long and narrow, were the only writing material for books in ancient Odra and other parts of the Central Provinces of Southern India; they were also used to some extent in Sri Lanka, Burma, Thailand and Northern India. Sacred works were written on Talipat palm leaves in Thailand, the edges of the leaves being gilded, or painted with vermilion, and the leaves threaded on strings and folded like a fan.

Pamphlet. A non-periodical publication of at least five but not more than 48 pages, exclusive of the cover pages. (General Conference of Unesco, 1964). *See also Book.* It usually has an independent entity, not being a SERIAL (*q.v.*), but it may be one of a series of publications having a similarity of format or subject matter.

Pamphlet Binding. 1. Binding done by, or for, a printer, in which the sheets as they come from the press, are wire-stitched. The term applies both to pamphlets and to magazines. 2. The manner in which such publications are bound when they come from the publisher, being WIRE STITCHED, SIDE-STITCHED or SADDLE STITCHED (*qq.v.*).

Pamphlet Box. A box, usually of cardboard covered with cloth, or of steel, or plastic, for holding pamphlets and other unbound material. *See also Box File, Solander Case, Transfer Box, Transfer File.*

Pamphlet-style Library Binding. A style of binding for a thin pamphlet or a group of thin pamphlets which are expected to be used infrequently.

Pamphlet Volume. A volume consisting of a number of pamphlets bound together with or without a title-page or table of contents.

Pan American Standards Commission. *See COPANT.*

Pancatalogue. French union catalogue of research monographs, established online in 1988. Anticipated membership by 1990 is 65, with a relevant stock of 2 million items. At present operated by the Serveur Universitaire National pour l'Information Scientifique et Technique (SUNIST) but the structure is not yet finalized.

Panel. 1. A compartment of the external cover of a book enclosed in a BORDER 2 (*q.v.*) or FRAME 2 (*q.v.*). 2. The space between two bands on the back of a book. 3. The list of books 'by the same author' facing the title-page. This is more for bibliographical than for advertising purposes and may therefore include out-of-print titles and those issued by other publishers.

Panel Back. In hand binding, a volume finished with panelled borders between the raised bands on the shelf-back.

Panel Stamp. A large piece of metal, engraved intaglio, used for impressing a design on the sides of book covers. Some of the stamps used for the early leather bindings were of quarto and folio size, but often book covers of these sizes were impressed two, three, four or more times with small panel stamps. A popular form of ornamentation in the early sixteenth century. *See also Blocking.*

Panizzi Club. Founded in 1914 (first honorary secretary, E. W. Hulme, Librarian of the Patent Office Library) 'to provide opportunities for social intercourse between the Senior Officers of Reference and Research Libraries and to promote all measures tending to their higher efficiency'. Librarians of all kinds of library were admitted to membership. It is not known when the Club ceased to function, but it was the foundation on which the CIRCLE OF STATE LIBRARIANS (*q.v.*) was built.

Panoramic Catalogue. The endless chain principle adapted for displaying catalogue entries.

PANSDOC. THE PAKISTAN NATIONAL SCIENTIFIC AND TECHNICAL DOCUMENTATION CENTRE (*q.v.*).

Pantone. A photo-engraving method of printing from a flat (planographic) plate with letterpress equipment, having the advantage over letterpress half-tone in that it can print from a screen up to 400 lines on antique paper and other rough surfaces. It is based on the principle that a printing plate bearing an image that is not in relief can be made to repel ink in the bare parts by treating them with mercury, while the printing parts will take up ink.

Paper. 1. A fibrous material made by breaking down vegetable fibres, purifying them, interweaving them into a compact web and pressing them into thin sheets. Book papers are made from MECHANICAL WOOD (*q.v.*) pulp (used for the cheapest publications and newspapers), CHEMICAL WOOD (*q.v.*) pulp (for most books), ESPARTO (*q.v.*) or rags, which make the best quality hand-made papers (for fine books). 2. A brief, literary composition, especially one to be read at a public meeting. 3. Contraction for newspaper. 4. To insert the end papers and fly-leaves of a book before inserting in its cover.

Paper-backed. *Synonymous with* PAPER-BOUND (*q.v.*).

Paper Boards. *See Boards.*

Paper-bound. Bound with a paper cover. Also called 'Paper backed'. A book so bound is called a PAPERBACK (*q.v.*).

Paper Covered. A pamphlet or small book which is not bound in boards, but covered with a stiff paper which is usually pasted on to the book or sewn through. If the paper covers are pasted down on to thin boards, cut flush at the head and tail, flaps turned over, the style is called 'Stiffened paper covers'.

Paper Finishes. *Antique*: a rough uneven surface. *Eggshell*: slightly finished surface, having the appearance of the shell of an egg. *Machine*: smoother than antique with a slight gloss, but not suitable for half-tone illustrations, excepting those of coarse-screen finish. *Smooth antique*: an antique slightly rolled. *Super-calendered*: smooth finish without lustre; this will print half-tone blocks up to 100-screen. *American*: a finish with medium gloss and suitable for half-tone illustrations up to 100-screen. *Enamel* or *coated*: has a very high gloss, being coated in the making with china-clay, satin white, and casein which fills in the pores; takes illustrations of the finest screen. *Dull coated*: has the coating as on a coated paper, but is calendered for smoothness only, not for gloss; it has a perfect surface of mellow softness for the finest cuts.

Paper Sizes. The dimensions of a sheet of paper or board (generally rectangular shape) as supplied by the manufacturer, the width (the smaller dimension) being given first. The British Standards Specification for writing and printing paper is as follows:

	millimetres	*inches*
Foolscap	343 × 432	13½ × 17
Foolscap, Double	432 × 686	17 × 27
Foolscap, Oblong Double	343 × 864	13½ × 34
Foolscap, Quad	686 × 864	27 × 34
Pinched Post	368 × 470	14½ × 18½
Post	387 × 483	15¼ × 19
Post, Double	483 × 775	19 × 30½
Large Post	419 × 533	16½ × 21
Large Post, Double	533 × 838	21 × 33 ·
Demy	445 × 572	17½ × 22½
Demy, Double	572 × 890	22½ × 35
Demy, Quad	890 × 1144	35 × 45
Medium	457 × 584	18 × 23
Medium, Double	584 × 914	23 × 36
Medium, Quad	914 × 1168	36 × 46
Royal	508 × 635	20 × 25
Royal, Double	635 × 1016	25 × 40
Crown	391 × 508	15 × 20
Crown, Double	508 × 762	20 × 30
Crown, Double Quad	1016 × 1524	40 × 60
Crown, Quad	762 × 1016	30 × 40
Imperial	559 × 762	22 × 30
Imperial, Double	762 × 1118	30 × 44

Other sizes are:

	millimetres	*inches*
Pott	318 × 394	12½ × 15½
Pott, Double	394 × 635	15½ × 25
Post, Small	400 × 495	15¾ × 19½
Royal, Large	508 × 686	20 × 27
Royal, Super	521 × 698	20½ × 27½

A sheet of 'quad' gives four times the number of sections as a sheet of ordinary size, a 'double' sheet twice the number. Papers for other purposes differ in size. *See also Book Sizes, Octavo.*

The American practice is not to use names but to specify the size of paper by inches and its weight per ream. The ordinary sizes of book papers in the USA are:

22 × 32	28 × 44	34 × 44	44 × 56
24 × 36	29 × 52	35 × 45	44 × 64
25 × 38	30½ × 41	36 × 48	All the
26 × 39	32 × 44	38 × 50	above measurements
26 × 40	33 × 44	41 × 51	are in inches.
28 × 42	33 × 46	42 × 56	

The German DIN A series of paper sizes is widely used in Europe. DIN stands for Deutsche Industrie Normen, and indicates standards agreed by Deutscher Normenausschuss (Committee for Standards), a similar body to the British Standards Institution. The A is to distinguish this standard from others known as B and C which apply to related poster and envelope sizes. The chief features of the DIN A series are that they apply to all types of paper, and that the proportions of a sheet remain constant when it is cut or folded in half across the long side. The letters A0 indicate a basic size of 1 square metre. A sheet of paper half this size is indicated by A1, half this size by A2 and so on. A larger sheet than A0 is indicated by a figure before the A; thus a sheet twice the size of A0 is indicated by 2A. The following table shows 7 trimmed sizes in the DIN A series which correspond to the British sizes from 8-demy to demy 8vo.

	Millimetres	Inches (approx.)	Demy sizes
2A0	1189 × 1682	46¹³⁄₁₆ × 66³⁄₁₆	45 × 70
A0	841 × 1189	33⅛ × 46¹³⁄₁₆	33 × 45
A1	594 × 841	23⅜ × 33⅛	22½ × 35
A2	420 × 594	16⁹⁄₁₆ × 23⅜	17½ × 22½
A3	297 × 420	11¹¹⁄₁₆ × 16⁹⁄₁₆	11¼ × 17½
A4	210 × 297	8¼ × 11¹¹⁄₁₆	8¾ × 11¼
A5	148 × 210	5⅞ × 8¼	5⅝ × 8¾
A6	105 × 148	4⅛ × 5⅞	
A7	74 × 105	2¹⁵⁄₁₆ × 4⅛	
A8	52 × 74	2¹⁄₁₆ × 2¹⁵⁄₁₆	
A9	37 × 52	1½ × 2¹⁄₁₆	
A10	26 × 37	1 × 1½	

There is also a 4A0 size: 1682 and 2378 mm.
(Continental practice is to state the smaller dimensions first.)
Series B is intended for posters, wall charts and other large items, and C for envelopes, particularly where it is necessary for an envelope in the C series to fit into another envelope. The International Organization for Standardization (ISO) adopted the A series for trimmed sizes for administrative, commercial and technical uses, and printed matter such as forms, professional periodicals and catalogues; the sizes to not necessarily apply to newspapers, published books, posters, continuous stationery or other specialized items. These sizes are sometimes referred to as 'ISO-A' sizes. The B sizes have also been adopted by ISO and are sometimes referred to as 'ISO-B' sizes, but, unlike the A series, have not been adopted by the British Standards Institution. The ISO recommends that these sizes are intended for use in exceptional circumstances, when sizes are needed intermediate between any two adjacent sizes of the A series. The C sizes have not been adopted by the ISO. *See also Periodical, Untrimmed Size.*

Paperback. A book bound in heavy paper or light card covers trimmed to the size of the pages. Originally used for novels in the late nineteenth century. In 1935 Allen Lane founded Penguin Books in England and began publishing large editions of paperbacks at a very low price. Paperbacks now form the bulk of the personal book buying market, both for fiction and non-fiction.

Paperless Society. A term expressing the potential ultimate result of ELECTRONIC PUBLISHING (*q.v.*).

Papers. (*Archives*) 1. An assemblage of personal and family material of miscellaneous nature as distinct from formal records. 2. A general term used to include more than one type of manuscript or typewritten material.

Papyrology. The study of ancient documents and literary manuscripts on papyrus.

Papyrus. 1. A giant water-reed from the stem of which the Egyptians made a writing material. 2. The material itself. 3. A manuscript written on papyrus.

Paradigms. In subject analysis, a term used by J. C. Gardin to indicate subjects which have a permanent relationship (e.g. aluminium; polyethylene) whereas syntagmas are those in which subjects which are normally distinct are brought together to form a composite more specific than any of its elements considered separately.

Paragraph Indention. (*Cataloguing*) *Synonymous with* SECOND INDENTION (*q.v.*). (*Printing*) Setting the first line of a paragraph one em or so in from the margin. Also called 'Paragraph indentation'. *See also Hanging Indention.*

Paragraph Mark. 1. The reversed or 'blind' P sign (¶) used in a MS. or proof to indicate the commencement of a new paragraph. 2. The sixth reference mark for footnotes, coming after the parallel. *See also Reference Marks.*

Parallel. (*Information retrieval*) Pertaining to the simultaneous handling of all the elements in a group. *See also Serial* 3. (*Printing*) The printer's sign ‖; it is used as the fifth reference mark. *See also Reference Marks.*

Parallel Arrangement. Separating books of varying sizes to economize shelf space by arranging larger books by one of the following methods: (a) in a separate sequence on the bottom shelves of each tier; (b) in a separate sequence at the end of each class; (c) in a complete separate sequence of the whole classification.

Parallel Classification. Material classified by the same scheme is said to be placed in parallel classification when it is again divided by size, character, etc., e.g. there may be four perfectly classified sequences for octavos, folios, pamphlets and illustrations; thus giving four parallel classifications.

Parallel Edition. A publication in which different texts of the same work are printed side by side, e.g. the Authorized and Revised versions of the Bible, or an original and a translation into another language, or two or more versions of a work.

Parallel Index. A system of indexing books by providing index terms or cross references in small type at the side of a page to give a lead into or onwards from the main text of the page.

Parallel Mark. (‖). The fifth reference mark for footnotes, coming after the section mark. *See also Reference Marks.*

Parallel Processing. New technique of computer construction avoiding problems of size, speed of memory transfer, heat, etc. Several processors are linked to provide great power when required; problems are split up and eventually recombined. Such a system is at present usually only applicable to very large applications, but systems involving microcomputers are likely. The technology is based on the transputer chip; not to be confused with a network.

Parallel Publishing. The production of publications simultaneously in print-on-paper and electronic formats.

Parallel Rule. A RULE (*q.v.*) having two lines of the same thickness. *See also Double Rule.*

Parallel Text. *See Parallel Edition.*

Parallel Title. The title proper, given in a publication, but in another language, or in another script, than that used for the text. *See also Added Title-page.*

Parallel Translation. A text, with a translation into another language, both printed in parallel columns.

Paraph. A mark or flourish after a signature, made often as a protection against forgery, and especially used by notaries. Also called a 'Flourish'.

Paraphrase. 1. An arrangement, transcription or imitation of a vocal or instrumental work in a form for voices or instruments other than was originally intended. 2. An abridgement of a literary work.

Parchment. 1. Sheepskin or goatskin dressed with alum and polished. It is not so strong as vellum (calfskin) which it resembles, and from which it can be distinguished by its grain. It is used for documents of a permanent nature and for binding large and heavy volumes. The term is now sometimes applied to fibrous imitations. 2. In the paper trade, wrapping paper with a high resistance to grease and atmospheric humidity.

Parchment-paper. *See Parchment 2.*

Parentheses. Curved lines ( ) used to include words inserted parenthetically. Used in cataloguing to enclose explanatory or qualifying words or phrases to set off some item in the entry, such as a series note. Also called 'Round Brackets' or 'Curves'. *See also Square Brackets.*

Parenthesis. A short explanatory clause inserted in a sentence, usually between parentheses. Abbreviated paren.

***Parents Magazine* Best Book for Babies Award.** An annual prize administered by the Book Trust for the best UK book for the under-fours.

Paris Principles. (*Cataloguing*) The twelve principles on which an author/title entry should be based. So named as the International Conference on Cataloguing Principles (ICCP), at which they were drawn up, was held in Paris in October 1961. The Conference, which was organized by IFLA, was intended to serve as a basis for international standardization in cataloguing. The principles apply only to the choice and form of headings and entry words in catalogues of printed books (and other library materials having similar characteristics) in which entries under authors' names, or the titles of works, are combined in one alphabetical sequence. The foregoing is a summary of part of the first Principle. The subject matter of the others are: (2) functions of the catalogue; (3) structure of the catalogue; (4) kinds of entry; (5) use of multiple entries; (6) function of different kinds of entry; (7) choice of uniform heading; (8) single personal author; (9) entry under corporate bodies; (10) multiple authorship; (11) works entered under title; (12) entry word for personal names. Since these principles were formulated, at least twenty cataloguing codes have been drawn up which have these principles as their common basis; one of these is AACR 2.

Parish Library. One which was provided by a parish council.

Parliamentary Papers (UK). A term which when used in the scholars' narrow sense means a particular group of Parliamentary Publications, e.g. (a) House of Lords Papers and Bills, (b) House of Commons Bills, (c) House of Commons Papers, (d) Command Papers, and not all the publications issued by Parliament and published by HMSO which alone has authority to publish on behalf of Parliament. *See also Parliamentary Publications, Sessional Papers.*

Parliamentary Publications (UK)

1. GENERAL DEFINITION. Papers printed for parliamentary purposes and placed on sale to the general public through HMSO. These comprise:

House of Lords Papers
   ,,   ,,   ,,   Bills
   ,,   ,,   ,,   Journals
   ,,   ,,   ,,   Debates
   ,,   ,,   ,,   Minutes of Proceedings

House of Commons Papers
   ,,   ,,   ,,   Bills
   ,,   ,,   ,,   Journals
   ,,   ,,   ,,   Debates
   ,,   ,,   ,,   Votes and Proceedings
Command Papers
Public General Acts
Local and Private Acts
Measures passed by the National Assembly of the
Church of England.

2. 'HOUSE' PAPERS. Documents presented either to the House of Lords or to the House of Commons under statute or by order of the House and 'ordered to be printed'. The sessional number appears at the bottom left hand corner of the title-page. House of Lords Paper and Bill numbers (in a common series) are printed in parentheses; House of Commons Bill numbers are in square brackets; House of Commons Paper numbers are not enclosed in brackets. 3. COMMAND PAPERS. Papers presented by a Minister to both Houses of Parliament by Command of Her Majesty. Occasionally, a Paper has been presented by Command to one House only, but with the exception of estimates (House of Commons Papers) the practice is now rare. The series is limited to documents relating to matters likely to be the subject of early legislation, or regarded as otherwise essential to Members of Parliament to enable them to discharge their responsibilities.

They were first published as Appendices to the House of Commons Journal but since 1836 have been numbered serially as follows:

1833–1869	[1]–[4222]
1870–1899	C.1–C.9550
1900–1918	Cd.1–Cd.9239
1919–1956	Cmd.1–Cmd.9889
1956–	Cmnd.1–

4. 'HANSARD'. The official verbatim reports of the debates of both Houses of Parliament. The debates of the House of Commons and of the House of Lords (issued separately) are published daily while Parliament is sitting. They are named after Luke Hansard (1752–1828) and his descendants who printed these reports from 1811–91. The issue of an officially authorized edition began in 1892, and in 1909 HMSO assumed the responsibility for printing and publication.

5. VOTES AND PROCEEDINGS OF THE HOUSE OF COMMONS. These are issued daily while the House is sitting and comprise six parts, each separately paged. They are:

Proceedings of the previous day;
Private business;
Questions, notices of Motions, Orders of the day;
Papers delivered to the House, notices of sittings of Public Committees;
Proposed amendments to Bills;
Proceedings in Standing Committees (each Committee's Proceedings are paged separately);
Divisions.

In addition, a list of the Public Bills which have been introduced during the Session, showing progress made, is circulated weekly with the Votes and Proceedings, and a similar list of Private Bills is included periodically in the private business section.

6. MINUTES OF PROCEEDINGS OF THE HOUSE OF LORDS. These, also, are issued daily while the House is sitting and contain:

The proceedings of the previous day;
Notices of judicial business;
Agenda for the day (including questions);
Notices of future questions and business;
Divisions;
A list of Bills showing the stages reached.

7. THE JOURNALS OF THE HOUSE OF COMMONS AND OF THE HOUSE OF LORDS, containing a complete record of Parliamentary proceedings, are published separately at the end of each Session.

8. THE ORDER BOOK OF THE HOUSE OF COMMONS is a consolidation of the business appearing in the Votes and Proceedings. It is issued daily for the convenience of Members and is not generally available to the public.

See also Green Paper, Non-Parliamentary Publications, Parliamentary Papers, White Paper. All parliamentary publications are published by HMSO.

Parliamentary Session (UK). A parliamentary year which begins with the opening of Parliament and normally ends with its prorogation. It usually begins in the first week of November, immediately after the old session, and does not correspond either with the calendar year or with the government's financial year. Also called a 'Session'. *See also Sessional Papers.*

Parry Report (UK). The *Report of the Committee on Libraries* (HMSO 1967) which was set up in 1963 by the University Grants Committee; so named after Dr. Thomas Parry, Principal of the University College of Wales, Aberystwyth, who was the chairman. It surveys libraries in British universities and makes recommendations on improving these and developing the British Museum Library as the chief functionary in the provision of library and bibliographical services.

Part. 1. A portion of a work in one or more volumes issued by a publisher as the work is completed for publication. Parts may be issued at frequent, regular intervals, as fortnightly, or at monthly, yearly, or irregular intervals, according to the nature of the work and its compilation. It usually has a separate title, half title, or cover title, and may have separate or continuous paging. It is distinguished from a FASCICLE (*q.v.*) by being a unit rather than a temporary portion of a unit. 2. A division of work (*See Work* 1) according to its content. 3. The music for any one of the participating voices or instruments of a musical composition. 4. The manuscript or printed copy of the music for such a participant. *See also Volume.* 5. A separately published number of a SERIAL (*q.v.*). Parts usually have paper covers bearing the title of the serial, the volume numbers (if any), issue number and date of issue. This information usually appears also on the first page of the text if the cover does not have textual matter on it, and nowadays often at the foot of each page in addition, the title usually being in an abbreviated form.

Part Publications. Long works which are issued in separate parts at regular intervals.

Part Title. *Synonymous with* DIVISIONAL TITLE (*q.v.*).

Partial Bibliography. One in which a limit has been put on the material included; e.g. periodicals only, books or articles of a certain period or in a certain country or library. *See also Select Bibliography.*

Partial Contents Note. A note which gives only the more important items in the contents.

Partial Title. One which consists of only a secondary part of the title as given in the title-page. It may be a CATCHWORD TITLE (*q.v.*), SUB-TITLE (*q.v.*) or ALTERNATIVE TITLE (*q.v.*).

Partial Title Entry. A catalogue entry made under a PARTIAL TITLE (*q.v.*).

PASCAL. *See INIST.*

Password. In accessing a computer file, or using an on-line database, the user may be required to give to the computer a word or code that identifies the right to access or use the system. This word or code is referred to as a password.

Paste-down. That part of an endpaper which is pasted down to the inner surface of the cover or boards of a book. Also called 'Board paper'. The free half of the endpaper forms a fly-leaf.

Paste-down Endpaper. *See Endpaper.*

Paste-grain. Split sheepskin hardened by coating with paste and given a highly polished surface.

Paste-in. 1. A correction or addition to the text supplied after the sheets have been printed, and tipped into the book opposite the place to which it refers. *See also Corrigenda.* 2. A separately printed illustration or map, cut to the size of the book, and the inner edge pasted into the text before gathering.

Paste-up. An arrangement on sheets of paper of proofs of a number of pages in order to plan the positioning of blocks, legends, illustrations and text.

Pasteboard. The material, made by pasting sheets of brown paper together, and lined on both sides with paper, which is used for printing and also for the covers of books. *See also Millboard, Strawboard.*

Pastiche. A musical or artistic composition consisting of a medley of passages or parts from various sources; usually satirical.

Pasting Down. The action of attaching a sewn book to its case or cover.

Pastoral. A book relating to the cure of souls.

Pastoral Letter. A letter from a spiritual pastor, especially from a bishop to the clergy or people of his diocese.

Patent. 1. A specification concerning the designs or manufacture of something which is protected by letters patent and secured for the exclusive profit of the designer or inventor for a limited number of years which varies in different countries from fifteen to twenty years. The department which controls the registration of patents is called a 'Patents office'. 2. A publication, issued by such an office, which gives details of designs and processes. 3. In the field of patents, a 'provisional specification' is a patent application which is merely to establish a date for disclosure of an inventive concept to the Patent Office. It does not include a claim to the monopoly sought; this is made in a 'complete specification' which describes at least one preferred way in which the invention may be performed, and which sets out a claim or claims for the protection sought.

Patent Base. A device for raising the level of the bed of a printing press so that the electrotypes or stereotypes need not be mounted on wood.

Patent Express. Title of the patent and industrial property collections held at the British Library Science Reference and Information Service (SRIS).

Patent File. Patent specifications and drawings which may be arranged by country and number, name of patentee or subject, or an index of such material similarly arranged.

Patent of Addition. A patent which represents an improvement in, or modification of, the invention of another patent in the same name, and for which no renewal fees are necessary to keep it in force. It expires when the other patent expires. *See also Convention Application.*

Patent Office Library.   Founded in London in 1855 to stimulate developments in the field of invention my making relevant information on applied science freely and readily available to all. On incorporation within the British Museum Library to form the NATIONAL REFERENCE LIBRARY OF SCIENCE AND INVENTION (*q.v.*), its scope was widened to include developments and discoveries in any branch of the natural sciences and technology. Since incorporation within the Reference Division of the BRITISH LIBRARY (*q.v.*) in 1973, it has been known as the SCIENCE REFERENCE AND INFORMATION SERVICE (SRIS) (*q.v.*).

Patent Roll.   A parchment roll upon which royal letters patent were enrolled at the Chancery.

Patentee.   The person or persons entered on the register of patents as grantee or proprietor of a patent according to the appropriate national procedure.

Patents Information Network.   *See PIN Bulletin.*

Paterson Report.   The report (of a working group appointed by the Scottish local authority associations and supported by the Secretary of State for Scotland) *The new Scottish local authorities: organization and management structures* (Edinburgh: HMSO 1973). The Chairman of the Steering Committee was J. F. Niven and of the Advisory Group, I. V. Paterson.

PATRA.   Abbreviation for Printing, Packaging and Allied Trades Research Association. *See Printing and Allied Trades Research.*

Patristics.   A publisher's series on the writings of the Fathers of the Christian Church, e.g. *The Library of Christian Classics* and *Ancient Christian Writers.*

Pattern.   A specimen volume, or rubbing, sent to a binder to indicate the style of lettering to be used.

Pattern Board.   A board maintained by a binder on which is mounted a specimen of the covering material to show titling layout, colour, size, etc., to ensure uniformity in the binding of a series.

Pattern Recognition.   (*Information retrieval*) Machine-sensing or identification of visible patterns (shapes, forms and configurations).

Pattern Rubbing.   A rubbing made to ensure that subsequent volumes in a series are lettered in the same style. *See also Rub.*

Paulin Report (UK).   The Report of the (Library Association) Working Party on the Future of Professional Qualifications. (L.A. 1977). Chairman; Miss L. V. Paulin.

Payne Style.   The style of book decoration practised by Roger Payne in England in the eighteenth century. It consisted of the repetition of small floral forms in borders or radiating corners, the background being formed with dots and circles.

PC.   *See Personal Computer.*

PCFC.   *See Polytechnics and Colleges Funding Council.*

PCMI System.   The Photo-Chromic-Micro-Image system, developed by the National Cash Register Company for data recording. It was demonstrated at New York World's Fair in 1964, and enables 1245 pages to be recorded on a 2 × 2 inches film. *See also Ultra-Microfiche.*

PDL. *See Publishers Databases Ltd.*

P.E.N. International. An international fellowship open to all writers of standing, which aims to promote freedom of expression and understanding between nations. Founded in 1921, the acronym originally stood for Poets, Playwrights, Editors, Essayists, Novelists, but creative writers of any genre are eligible for membership.

P.E. Notes. In an attempt to speed up decisions on extensions to the Universal Decimal Classification the International Commission sends out *P.E. notes* (Projets d'extensions) which invite criticisms to be submitted within four months, and *P.P. notes* (projets provisoires) which are intimations of provisional 'revolutionary suggestions'.

Peacock Roll. (*Binding*) A finisher's roll which includes a peacock in its ornamentation. It is characteristic of some English Restoration bindings, and also appears on eighteenth century Irish bindings.

Pearl. An out-of-date name for a size of type equivalent to 5 point.

Pear Tree Press. A private printing press, begun in Essex in 1899 by James Guthrie. It moved to Flansham in 1907.

Pebbling. *See Stippling.*

PEBUL (UK). Acronym for the *Project for evaluating the benefits from University Libraries*, published by the University of Durham in 1969.

Pedestrian Work. (*Classification*) A work which is not a SACRED WORK (*q.v.*), a CLASSIC (*q.v.*), or a LITERARY WORK (*q.v.*), and is not treated as if it were a class or a subject in usage.

Peek-a-boo. A principle of punching ASPECT CARDS (*q.v.*) to record information which is represented by certain positions on the card. Such cards are sorted by machine or are searched by placing several in front of the source of light, possibly in a light box. Wherever light shows through there is a coincidence of document-number punches and this identifies documents as possessing the aspects indicated by the position of the hole. The cards used in this system are also called 'Cordonnier cards' or 'Batten cards' after G. Cordonnier of France and W. E. Batten of Britain who were early exponents of the system. They are also called 'Optical co-incidence cards'. *See also Batten System.*

Peephole Card. One with holes punched in it to represent information or characteristics possessed; it is used with a system of CO-ORDINATE INDEXING (*q.v.*). Also called 'Aperture card', 'Optical coincidence card'. It may also have an opening specifically prepared to mount one or more frames of a microfilm.

Pellet's Process. A blueprint process suitable only for the reproduction of line drawings whereby the prints have blue lines on an almost white background. It was introduced in 1877.

Pen International. *See P.E.N. International.*

Pen-name. *Synonymous with* PSEUDONYM (*q.v.*).

Penny-dreadful. A thrilling story magazine for children sold at a very low price. A morbidly sensational story.

Pepys (Samuel) Medal. *See Ephemera Society.*

Perfect. (*Binding*) A method of binding by which the folds of the sections forming the back of the book are cut away; the edges of the loose sheets so formed are then coated with a very flexible but strong adhesive and covered with paper, mull or other material. The book is then inserted into covers by ordinary methods employed when sections are not sewn on tapes. Also called 'Lumbecking'. *See also Caoutchouc Binding.*

Perfect Copy. A sheet of paper which has been printed on both sides from an 'inner forme' and also from an 'outer forme'.

Perfecter. A printing machine which prints on both sides of the paper at the same time whereas stop-cylinder presses and two-revolution machines print on one side only. Also called a 'Perfecting machine' or 'Perfecting press'. The first machine of this kind was made in 1816 by Koenig and Bauer and was called by the maker a 'completing machine'.

Perfecting. Printing the second side of a sheet. A perfecting press is one that prints both sides of a sheet in one operation. Also called 'Backing up'.

Perfecting Machine. *See Perfecter.*

Perforating Stamp. A punch or stamp which perforates a mark of ownership through the page of a book.

Performance Index. A method of evaluating the service provided by a library.

Performing Arts Library. Sponsored jointly by the Library of Congress and the John F. Kennedy Center for the Performing Arts, opened at the Kennedy Center early in 1979. It serves as a reference centre and introduction to the collection of music, theatre, dance and film materials in the L. C. and provides a service for the Kennedy Center archival materials.

Pergamon-Infoline. *See Infoline.*

Perinorm. A European compendium of standards and technical regulation information issued on CD-ROM. Up-to-date and detailed bibliographic entries on all current and draft standards, and specifications are included for the UK, France and the Federal Republic of Germany (from BSI, AFNOR, and DIN) together with European and international standards.

Period Bibliography. One limited to a certain period of time.

Period Division. 1. A division of a classification scheme for works covering a limited period of time. 2. A sub-division of a subject heading in a catalogue which indicates the period covered.

Period Printing. Producing books in a style which is similar to that used when they were first published.

Periodical. A publication with a distinctive title which appears at stated or regular intervals, without prior decision as to when the last issue shall appear. It contains articles, stories or other writings, by several contributors. *Newspapers*, whose chief function is to disseminate news, and the *memoirs, proceedings, journals*, etc. of societies are not considered periodicals under the cataloguing rules. *See also Serial.* At the General Conference of Unesco, held at Paris on 19 November 1964, it was agreed that a publication is a periodical 'if it constitutes one issue in a continuous series under the same title, published at regular or irregular intervals, over an indefinite period, individual issues in the series being numbered consecutively or each issue being dated'. In statistical records, a periodical publication with a single system of numeration whether or not the title has changed. Where a change of numeration occurs, a new sequence starting at one irrespective of any change of title, is considered to be a separate unit.

Periodical Bibliography. One which is published in parts and revised or extended by the cumulative method. *See also Closed Bibliography, Current Bibliography.*

Periodical Case. *Synonymous with* MAGAZINE CASE (*q.v.*).

Periodical Index. 1. An index to one or more volumes of a periodical. 2. A subject index to a group of periodicals; usually issued at short intervals and cumulated.

Periodical Rack. A fitting for accommodating current and possibly a few recent issues of periodicals, either horizontally or perpendicularly without displaying the covers. Each compartment has a label bearing the title of the periodical. *See also Periodical Stand.*

Periodical Stand. A piece of furniture for displaying periodicals so that much of the cover is visible. Sometimes the display fitting on which current issues are placed is constructed at an angle of 15 to 30° and is hinged to accommodate back numbers on a shelf immediately behind the slope.

Periodicals Collection. A library collection of periodicals, newspapers, and other serials whether bound, unbound, or in microform, treated like periodicals; usually kept as a collection and separate from other library materials.

Peripherals (Peripheral Units). (*Information retrieval*) A general term for the various devices used with computers, and operating under computer control. They include input, output and storage devices.

Permanent Paper. A term which is applied to pH neutral papers. Also called 'Durable paper'. *See also pH Value.*

Permanent Record Film. Photographic material made and treated in such a way that both the image and the base will have the maximum archival quality when stored in ordinary room conditions.

Permission. Authority from the owner of copyright to quote passages or reproduce illustrations from a work.

Permutation Index. *Synonymous with* KWIC index. *See KWIC.*

Permutation Indexing. Indexing by selecting as entry headings words, phrases or sentences which the author has emphasized as important by using them in the title, introduction, section headings, conclusion, summary, etc. This method has been developed to become a technique of machine indexing; each entry in the index being a cyclic permutation of all the words in the original titles, each term being brought to a predetermined position for alphabetizing. *See also KWIC.*

Permuted Title Index. The result of a method of indexing, which can be carried out by a machine, whereby entries are made for every important word in a title. The document identification code follows each entry. Types of such indexes are KWIC, KWOC and WADEX (*qq.v.*).

Permuted Title Word Indexing. Also called 'Keyword-in-Context (KWIC) Indexing', 'Permutation Indexing'. *See also KWIC.*

Permuterm. An indexing procedure which provides permitted pair combinations of all significant words within titles to form all possible pairs of terms. 'Permuterm' is a contradiction of the phrase 'permuted terms'.

Perpetua. Eric Gill's most popular typeface (named after St. Perpetua, a female saint who was martyred at Carthage in A.D. 203). Cut in 1929, it is one of the most distinguished types, being not only used effectively for books, where dignity, repose and stateliness are required, but also for book jackets where the related Bold, and Bold Titling, are specially useful. The serifs are small, firmly pointed, sharply cut and horizontal. For a specimen alphabet, *see Type Face.*

Persian Morocco. A badly-tanned leather derived from Indian goat and sheep. It is an inferior leather unsuitable for binding books, being fairly strong but not durable.

Personal Authorship. Authorship of a work in which its conception and execution is entirely the responsibility of an individual and carried out in his personal capacity, not by virtue of any paid or voluntary office held by him within a corporate body.

Personal Catalogue. A catalogue in which entries are made under an individual's name for books both by him and about him. *See also Name Catalogue.*

Personal Computer. A microcomputer marketed for home users or individual low-level business use. Distinction between standards of microcomputers is becoming increasingly blurred as technology advances and prices fall.

Personal Name. *Synonymous with* FORENAME (*q.v.*).

Personal Papers. (*Archives*) The private documents accumulated by, and belonging to, an individual, and subject to that person's disposition.

Personal Subject. The name of an author who is well known in connection with one particular branch of knowledge, and which is used as a subject heading in selective cataloguing.

Personnel Specification. A statement of the qualities, abilities and responsibilities considered to be necessary in a person who might be appointed to a job. The specification is prescriptive, and concentrates more on personal attributes of staff than on the technical requirements of the job – these would be detailed in a job description or job specification.

Personnel, Training and Education Group. New title adopted 1988 by a group of the (British) Library Association. Previously the Training and Education Group (formed 1983) and prior to that the Library Education Group (formed 1970). Publishes *Training and Education* (3 p.a.).

pf. Abbreviation for portfolio.

PGI. *See General Information Programme.*

pH Value. Measurement of the acid and alkaline content of paper, as recorded on a scale. pH7 is neutral; a figure lower than 7 indicates acid quality, higher than 7 indicates alkaline quality, the strengths being indicated by the respective distances from 7 and extending from 1 to 14. The measurement is determined by an electrical apparatus called an Ionometer. pH is an abbreviation for 'hydrogen-ions concentration'. The scale is logarithmic. *See also Permanent Paper.*

Phase. In classification, that part of a complex subject (i.e. a sub-class representing the interaction of an original subject on another separate subject, e.g. the influence of the Bible on English literature) derived from any one main class of knowledge: that part of a complex subject derived from one distinct field of knowledge: any one of two or more classes brought into relation to one another in a document. The interaction of two normally distinct subjects is called a Phase Relation. So far five kinds of phase-relation have been isolated. (1) Form phase (the method of presentation); (2) Bias phase (one subject presented for the requirements of another): (3) Influencing phase (one subject influenced by another); (4) Comparison phase (one subject compared with another); (5) Tool phase (one subject used as a method of expounding another). Ranganathan suggests that Form is not a phase relation, that it is more closely allied to the individual book than to the subject, and that it should accordingly be shown as part of the book number, not the class number. *See also Classifying, Facet, Focus.* Where relations occur between foci in the same facet, these are called 'Intrafacet relations'.

Phase Relation. *See Phase.*

Philosophical Classification. *See Knowledge Classification.*

Phloroglucin. A chemical which is used in conjunction with hydrochloric acid and alcohol as a test solution to detect mechanical wood in paper, which it turns red.

Phoenix Schedule. (*Classification*) A completely new development of the schedule for a specific discipline. Unless by chance, only the basic number for the discipline remains the same as in earlier editions, all other numbers being freely re-used.

Phonetic Writing. A form of writing in which the signs or symbols represent sounds or groups of sounds, rather than objects or ideas as they did in earlier forms of writing such as ideography or pictography. Each element corresponds to a specific sound in the language represented. Phonetic writing may be syllabic or alphabetic, the latter being the more advanced of the two.

Phonic Length. A characteristic of the length of a sequence of notation symbols in a scheme of classification, whereby there is ability to remember them easily by reason of their pronounceability. *See also Graphic Length.*

Phonogram. A symbol used to express a sound or idea; it can represent a complete word, a syllable, or the sound which a syllable represents.

Phonograph. An obsolete instrument for recording sounds on cylindrical wax records and reproducing them.

Phonograph Record. *Synonymous with* GRAMOPHONE RECORD (*q.v.*).

Phonorecord. Any object on which sound has been recorded.

Phonoroll. A perforated roll, usually of paper, which is used to activate a player-piano, or player-organ.

Phonotape. *Synonymous with* AUDIOTAPE (*q.v.*).

Photocharging. The recording of the loan of books by photographing on 35mm film details of the book borrowed, the reader's identification card and a transaction card which is then placed in the book and taken by the reader.

Photochromic Micro-image. *See PCMI System.*

Photochromic Substance.   One which changes its colour when subjected to radiation from different light sources. Such substances are used in the PCMI SYSTEM (*q.v.*) or reprography.

Photo-composing Machine.   (*Printing*) A machine for setting solid text by photographic means, as distinct from metal-type composition. The following are makes of such machines:

Fotosetter, Hadego, Highton, Huebner, Linofilm, Monophoto, Orotype, Photon, Rotofoto and Uhertype.

Photocomposition.   Setting type by means of a photo-composing machine, i.e. placing type images on photographic film or paper.

Photocopy.   The reproduction of the information on a sheet of paper or the page of a book etc. by various types of photographic process.

Photo-electrostatic Reproduction.   *Synonymous with* XEROGRAPHY (*q.v.*).

Photo-engraving.   Any photo-mechanical process for reproducing pictures or the like in which the printing surface is in relief, as distinguished from photo-lithography and photo-gravure. It includes the half-tone process, zinc etching and other processes for making line cuts, the swelled-gelatine process, etc. *See also Electronic Photo-engraving Machines.*

Photo-gelatine Process.   Any of the gelatine processes of photo-mechanical printing, as Collotype, Lichtdruck, Phototype, Albertype, Artotype, Heliotype, etc.

Photographic Papers.   These are graded in thickness as follows:

Ultra thin (also called 'Extra lightweight')	between 0.0023 and 0.0031 inches inclusive
Extra thin	between 0.0032 and 0.0037 inches inclusive
Thin	between 0.0038 and 0.0043 inches inclusive
Lightweight	between 0.0044 and 0.0059 inches inclusive
Single weight	between 0.0060 and 0.0083 inches inclusive
Medium weight	between 0.0084 and 0.0111 inches inclusive
Double weight	between 0.0112 and 0.0190 inches inclusive

Photography.   A basic printing process in which the normal principles of photography are used at some stage, e.g. photo-engraving, photo-offset, photo-lithography.

Photogravure.   1. Any of the various processes for producing prints from a plate prepared by photographic methods. Also called 'Heliogravure'. 2. A print so produced. *See also Rotogravure.*

Photo-lithography.   The process of reproducing a picture or design photographically on to metal for lithographic printing.

Photo-mechanical Process. *See Process Engraving.*

Photo-montage. A picture made by the combination of several photographs or portions of photographs into one large composite photograph, or parts of photographs cut out and pasted together to achieve a particular effect. Other methods are to make a number of exposures on the same negative, or to project a number of negatives to make a composite print.

Photomosaic. An assembly of parts of aerial photographs joined together to form a map.

Photo-offset. Offset printing in which the image is reproduced on a metal plate by photography. Also called 'Photo-litho-offset', and 'Offset-photo-lithography'.

Photon. A photo-typesetting machine made in the USA by Photon Inc. and used since 1954. Photographic negatives or positives are produced and these may be used for lithography, gravure or to make letterpress blocks.

Photoscope. A small illustrated poster.

Photosetting. (*Printing*) The setting of type by a photographic means. FOTOSETTER, LINOFILM, MONOPHOTO and PHOTON (*qq.v.*) are trade names of such methods and apparatus. *See also Filmsetting, Computer Typesetting.*

Photostat. 1. A trade name of a machine for reproducing photographically pages of printed, drawn or written matter on sensitized paper without films or plates. 2. A copy made by such a machine; it is optical and right-reading.

Phototype. A form of collotype, being a plate with a printing surface usually in relief, obtained from a photograph.

Photo-typography. Any photo-mechanical process in which the printing surface is produced in relief so that it can be used with type. *See also Computer Typesetting.*

Photo-zincography. A method of reproducing pictures, drawings, etc., by using a zinc plate on which the design has been produced by photographic means.

Phrase-Pseudonym. A pseudonym consisting of a phrase, as 'A Gentleman with a Duster'.

Phylactery. A narrow band or scroll on which a name or a speech was inscribed. Sometimes seen in block books, illuminated manuscripts or incunabula where they are drawn as if issuing from the mouths of characters, or held in the hand. They also appear in contemporary comics and comic strips as 'balloons' coming from the mouths of characters.

Physical Bibliography. *See Descriptive Bibliography.*

pi. 1. (*Bibliography*) The Greek letter π used to denote an unsigned gathering or leaf which precedes signed gatherings, and in respect of which no signature can be inferred. *See also Chi.* 2. (*Printing*) (*Verb*) To mix up type. (*Noun*) Type which has been mixed up. (American). *See also Pie.*

Piano-conductor Score. *See Score.*

Piano Reduction. An arrangement for piano of the voice parts of a work for unaccompanied voices for use as an accompaniment during rehearsal, such accompaniment not being intended by the composer for performance. Such music may be indicated by some such designation at the head of the score as 'Piano, for rehearsal only'.

Piano Score. *See Score.*

Piano-vocal Score. *Synonymous with* VOCAL SCORE. *See Score.*

PIC. *See Publishers Information Card Services Ltd.*

Pica. 1. A standard of measurement , approximately ⅙ inch; in the Point System .166 inch, equal to 12 point. *See also Em.* 2. Pica type, the largest size ordinarily used for books; 12 point, six lines to an inch, as this.

PICA. Centre for Library Automation; a Dutch Library bibliographic network based at The Hague. Established 1969, with over 350 members.

Pick Up. Type which has been kept standing since first used, ready to be 'picked up' for further use when required.

Pickup. *See TAPs.*

PICT. The Programme for Information Technology and Communication; a research initiative funded by the Economics and Social Research Council (ESRC) with co-operation from the British Library Research and Development Department.

Pictogram. *See Pictography.*

Pictograph. A pictorial sign or simple illustration which tells a story instantaneously by representing an object or an idea. A primitive form of writing consisting of pictographs.

Pictography. The most primitive stage of true writing, in which a picture or sketch represents a thing, or a sequence of pictures, drawings or symbols (each of which is termed a 'pictogram') tells a narrative. Pictography is a semantic representation, not a phonetic one. *See also Alphabetic Writing.*

Pictorial Map. A map which contains pictures indicating the distribution of physical and biological features, and social and economic characteristics, etc.

Picture Book. A book consisting wholly or mostly of pictures.

Picture Collection. A collection of pictures, or of reproductions of pictures. *See also Illustrations Collection, Picture File.*

Picture File. A collection of illustrations, prints, reproductions of pictures, and possibly cuttings; small enough to be filed rather than needing to be displayed. They may be arranged by subject, artist, etc. This is American usage. *See also Illustrations Collection, Picture Collection.*

Picture-writing. *Synonymous with* PICTOGRAPHY (*q.v.*).

Pie. 1. A table, or collection, of ecclesiastical rules used before the Reformation in England to determine (from each of the 35 possible variations in the date of Easter) the proper service or office for the day. Also called 'Pye'. 2. An alphabetical index or catalogue, to count rolls and records (obsolete); usually called a 'pye book'. 3. (*Printing*) Type matter that has been mixed accidentally.

Piece. (*Archives*) 1. The basic unit of archival arrangement and description which is produced from the repository as an entity under its own reference. For example, a file is a piece, but a single sheet on that file is not; however, a single document, once forming part of an original file would be a piece in this context. Also called 'Item'. 2. A fragment, or part, of a document, separated from the whole in any manner, such as cutting or detaching.

Piece Fraction. (*Printing*) A fraction that is made by using two or more pieces of type due to the fraction on one piece of type, as ¼ not being available. A SOLIDUS (*q.v.*) is used between the two groups of figures as 43/50.

Pierced. *See Mortice.*

Piercy Award, Esther J. Established by the Resources and Technical Services Division (now ALCTS) of the American Library Association to honour the late editor of *Library Resources & Technical Services.* The Award is given annually 'to recognize the contribution to librarianship in the field of technical services by younger members of the profession', and consequently it is restricted to those with not more than ten years of professional experience. First awarded to Richard M. Dougherty in 1969.

Pierpoint Morgan Library. Assembled by John Pierpoint Morgan (1837–1913), inherited by his son J. P. Morgan, Jr. (1867–1943), who expanded it and in February 1924 conveyed it to six trustees to administer as a public reference library for the use of scholars. Subsequently the State of New York incorporated the collection and dedicated it to 'the advancement of knowledge and for the use of learned men of all countries'. The collection comprises about 55,000 books and manuscripts, and in addition, cuneiform tablets, drawings, prints, Italian medals, and Greek and Roman coins. The collection of mediaeval illuminated manuscripts is unique for its geographical and linguistic coverage.

Pigeonhole Classification. *Synonymous with* RIGID CLASSIFICATION (*q.v.*).

Pigskin. A strong leather made from the skin of a pig; it has good lasting qualities and is used for covering large books.

PIN Bulletin. Acronym for Patents Information Network Bulletin, an information service operated by the Science Reference and Information Service (SRIS) (a part of the British Library).

Pin Holes. 1. Minute and almost imperceptible pits in the surface of art papers, due to frothy coating material. 2. Minute holes in paper, caused by fine particles of sand, alum, etc., being crushed out during the calendering process, leaving a hole. 3. Tiny transparent dots which appear in a litho plate after development and which, unless covered with an opaque medium, will appear in resulting prints.

Pin-mark. A small depression on one side of the body of a piece of movable type. It is made by the pin which ejects the types from the moulds of certain casting machines and sometimes bears the number of a body-size of the fount.

Pin Seal. A binding leather from the skin of a very young, or baby, seal, having much finer grain and a more lustrous finish than ordinary SEALSKIN (*q.v.*). Used for expensive bindings.

Pineapple. (*Binding*) An ornament bearing some likeness to a conventional pineapple, and used in the same position as a FLEURON (*q.v.*). *See also Twisted Pineapples.*

Pipe Roll. A parchment roll upon which a record of the audit at the exchequer was kept.

PIRA. Originally the Printing Industry Research Association. *See Printing and Allied Trades Research.*

Piracy. The publication in a foreign country of a literary work without the permission of, or payment to, the author.

PIRATE. Public Information in Rural Areas Technology Experiment. A microcomputer based community information service providing a local database, and commercial information. Set up in 1984 in Devon County Libraries with funding for four years from the British Library Research and Development Department, and the Rural Development Commission. Enthusiastically received, and now locally funded after BLRDD support expired in 1988.

Pirated Edition. *See Unauthorised Edition.*

Pivoted Bookcase. *Synonymous with* SWINGING BOOKCASE.

Pixel. Abbreviation for picture element; the individual dots generated by a computer and which make up the picture on the display screen.

pl. (*Pl.*pls.) Abbreviation for PLATE (*q.v.*) (illustration), also place.

PLA. PRIVATE LIBRARIES ASSOCIATION. PUBLIC LIBRARY ASSOCIATION (*qq.v.*).

Placard. A large, single, sheet of paper, usually printed, but sometimes written, on one side with an announcement or advertisement, for display on a wall or notice board. Also called a 'Poster'.

Placard Catalogue. A list of books displayed on a large sheet, or sheets, and hung up for consultation.

Place of Printing. A bibliographer's or cataloguer's term for the name of the town in which a book is printed.

Place of Publication. A bibliographer's or cataloguer's term for the name of the town or other locality in which the office of a publisher who issues a book is situated.

Plagiarism. To copy the writings of another person and publish the same as original work.

Plain Text. An edition of a classic without notes, or possibly even an introduction, and intended for study in a class or with a tutor.

Plan. 1. The representation of anything drawn on a plane, as a map or chart; the representation of a building or other structure, landscape design, arrangement of streets or buildings, or arrangement of furniture in a room or building, in horizontal plane. 2. Acronym of the Public Library Automation Network which was funded by the American Library Services and Construction Act (LSCA); it sought to indicate how users in different sizes and types of community benefit from a computerized system. The libraries participating were Los Angeles Public, Los Angeles County, Marin County, Orange County, San Francisco Public, Santa Clara County and Sutter County.

Plan Cabinet. A piece of furniture designed to accommodate plans, architectural drawings, or reproductions, either suspended or resting in a pocket vertically, or flat in shallow drawers. Also called 'Plan file'.

Plan File. A container for filing plans and maps either vertically or horizontally. Also called 'Plan cabinet'.

Plan Paper. A thin, tough, paper which is made specially for printing maps, plans, etc. It is subject to much wear by constant handling and folding. Also called 'Map paper'. *See also Chart Paper.*

Planes. (*Classification*) In the Colon Classification these are three in number: Idea, Notation (or Notational) and Words (or Verbal); within which the designing or application of a scheme has to be done.

Plan of Action (EC). The Plan of Act for Libraries in the European Community was issued in draft form for comment in 1988, intended to improve the infrastructure particularly through co-operation. There were five action lines in the Plan: library source data projects (national bibliographies, union catalogues etc.); linking of systems; innovation through IT; development of commercially viable products, services and tools; exchange of experience and dissemination. Action line 5 was subsequently dropped, being subsumed into the other lines. An original budget of 33 mecu over 5 years now seems likely to be reduced considerably. Final approval of the Plan is still awaited (June 1990) and it may be subordinated to a larger information industry development plan.

Guidelines for participative projects were issued in February 1990. In the UK the Office of Arts and Libraries established a National Focus (Focal Point) to co-ordinate reaction, and is currently setting up a new Advisory Committee on the European Library Plan.

Planetary Camera. A camera used for photocopying in which the document being copied and the film are stationary during exposure. After each exposure the document is changed manually and the film is moved on one frame automatically. Also called a 'Flat-bed camera' or 'Stepwise operated camera'.

Planograph. *Synonymous with* OFFSET PRINTING (*q.v.*).

Planographic Printing. *See Planographic Process.*

Planographic Process. 1. A generic term for all printing which depends on chemical action, and in which the printing surface is a plane, merely transferring its image, as in lithography, collotype and offset. 2. The method of printing from flat surfaces, the parts to be printed accepting ink from the rollers while the non-printing areas reject it. The printing, or image, areas are greasy, the rest moist. Printing is by even pressure of a hand-roller or cylinder over the flat plate, or by offsetting the image from a curved plate on to a rubber roller and so to the paper. It is one of the six basic principles of printing, the others being relief, intaglio, stencil, photography and xerography. Also called 'Surface printing'.

Planography. Printing processes which are dependent on the antipathy of oily ink and water, using methods of printing from flat surfaces other than stone. The term replaces 'zincography' and 'aluminography'. *See also Planographic Process.*

Plantin. A type face designed by Christopher Plantin (1514–89) one of the world's most distinguished printer–publishers, whose house and printing equipment now form the Plantin-Moretus Museum at Antwerp. This OLD FACE (*q.v.*) is characterized by the thickness, and consequent black appearance, of all the strokes. For a specimen alphabet, *see Type Face.*

Plaster of Paris Mould. One made by placing a thin film of plaster of Paris mixed with water to a fluid consistency on a sheet of paper which is then transferred face downwards to the forme and subjected to moderate pressure after several sheets of an absorbent type of paper are placed on the paper-backed plaster of Paris. It is used for reproducing illustrations by half-tone and three- and four-colour half-tone processes.

Plastic Binding. A type of binding used for pamphlets, commercial catalogues, etc. which are printed on unfolded leaves. These leaves and the separate front and back covers are kept together by means of a piece of curved synthetic plastic which has prongs, or combs, which pass through slots punched near the binding edge of the leaves and curled within the cylinder thus formed by the plastic. *See also Spiral Binding.*

Plasticizer. *(Archives)* A substance added to, for example, a synthetic resin, to increase its flexibility. If the plasticizer is in some measure chemically combined with the resin, it is said to be an 'internal' plasticizer.

Plasticizing. Putting a plastic cover or sleeve on to a book or BOOK JACKET (*q.v.*), either by securing a loose cover or by laminating the plastic by means of heat.

Plastocowell. A lithographic process introduced by W. S. Cowell, Ltd., of Ipswich, in which a plastic sheet is used as a substitute for stone or metal, and is easier and more convenient for the artist to work than the ordinary forms of auto-lithography.

Plat. A map or chart, such as a precise and detailed plan, showing the actual or proposed divisions, special features, or uses of a piece of land, e.g. a town or town site. (American.)

Plate. 1. An illustration, often an engraving taken from a metal plate, printed separately from the text of the book with one side of the leaf blank, and often on different paper. Plates may be bound into a book or they may be loose in a portfolio. They are not generally included in the pagination. *See also Figure.* 2. A flat block of wood or metal, usually of copper, nickel or zinc, on the surface of which there is a design or reproduction of a type forme, to be used for printing, engraving, embossing, etc. The method of printing may be relief, intaglio, or planographic. 3. To make an electrotype or stereotype from printed matter. *See also Illustrations, Leaf.*

Plate Cylinder. The roller of an offset printing machine which bears the printing plate. *See also Offset Printing.*

Plate Guarded and Hooked. An illustration printed on a separate piece of paper and stuck to a narrow strip of paper or linen to form a guard which is then placed around, or hooked-in, a section before sewing. *See also Hooked on own Guard.*

Plate Line. *Synonymous with* PLATE MARK (*q.v.*).

Plate Mark. A line marking the boundary edge of a plate used in making an engraving; it is caused by the pressure used to make the impression on the sheet of paper. The part of the paper on which the plate rested is depressed and more smooth than the surrounding portion.

Plate Number. One or more figures, or a combination of letters and figures, assigned serially to each musical composition on preparation for printing, being copied by the engraver at the bottom of each page and sometimes on the title-page also. If on the title-page only, it is better designated as 'Publisher's number'.

Plate Paper. A superfine soft rag paper of good substance, made for steel-plate or photogravure printing. Of recent years cheaper esparto qualities have been introduced.

Platen. The flat part of a printing press which presses the paper on to the forme. *See also Platen Press. (Reprography)* A mechanical device which holds the film in position in a camera, or copying apparatus, in the focal plane during exposure.

Platen Press. A printing press which has a flat impression, not a cylindrical one. The type is normally fixed on the bed in a vertical or almost vertical position, and the platen bearing the paper is swung up and pressed against the type. Such machines are usually used for jobbing work. *See also Cylinder Press.*

Plates Volume. In a work of several volumes, the one which consists of illustrations to the text, and has no printed matter other than that relating specifically to the illustrations.

Plating. The process of pasting book plates and other labels in library books.

Plaquette. A small metal relief, like a classical cameo, which is inlaid into Italian book bindings of the sixteenth century.

Play Matters. The working title of the UK National Toy Libraries Association; has 700 members; London based.

PLDIS. *See Public Library Development Incentive Scheme.*

Plea Roll. A parchment roll on which a record of cases heard in the King's Court was entered.

Plenum Publishing Corporation Award. Offered by the Corporation 'to a member of the Special Libraries Association for an outstanding original paper, not previously published or presented, covering any aspect of special libraries or special librarianship'. The Award was first made in 1977.

Plessey. Originally known as a company offering computer charging systems to libraries, but now offering other aspects of systems automation.

PLR. PUBLIC LENDING RIGHT (*q.v.*).

PLRG. *See Public Libraries Research Group.*

Plough. The tool used for cutting the edges of a book.

PMEST Formula. Ranganathan's five FUNDAMENTAL CATEGORIES (*q.v.*) – Personality, Matter, Energy, Space, Time – or facets, which, in this order, are arranged by decreasing concreteness.

Pochoir. French for 'stencil'. A hand-coloured illustration process which, although dating from the eighteenth century, is still used in France, and is similar to SILK SCREEN (*q.v.*) except that paper, celluloid or metal stencils are used and the colour is dabbed through, rather than drawn across, the stencil. It is an expensive method, and is used for editions de luxe. 2. A method of reproducing gouache paintings. The design, necessarily simplified is preprinted by collotype and the ink applied with stencil and brush.

Pocket. A wallet-like receptacle made from linen or stiff paper inside a cover of a book (usually the back cover) to hold loose music parts, diagrams, or maps. Also called 'Cover pocket'. *See also Book Pocket.*

Pocket Card Charging. The recording of loans of books by using a card kept in a corner pocket stuck to the inside of the cover of a book. The best-known method is the BROWNE BOOK CHARGING SYSTEM (*q.v.*).

Pocket Edition. A small edition of a book, already printed in an octavo edition, of 6¾ × 4¼ inches or less. Sometimes these are paperbound but they are then usually called 'paperbacks'.

Pocket Part. A separate publication which is issued to bring a book up-to-date, and is usually kept in a pocket on the inside of the back cover.

Pocket Score. *See Score.*

Poetry Library. A national collection of poetry, comprising some 35,000 volumes published in the English language since 1912. Also stocks journals, cassettes, photographs and cuttings; opened in new premises at the Royal Festival Hall, London, at the end of 1988. A small theatre, known as the Voice Box, is available for poetry readings.

Point. 1. The unit of measure for printer's type: approximately 1/72 (0.013837) of an inch. Thus 12 point type is 12/72 or 1/6 of an inch in the body. One inch equals 72.25433 points and 72 points equal 0.9962 of an inch. Each body size is an exact multiplication of the point size. Type bodies are measured in points. The width of a line of type (or 'measure') is determined in pica (12-pt.) ems – called 'picas' in America. The depth of a page of type is similarly measured in ems or picas. After a fire at the typefoundry of Marder, Luse & Co. in Chicago in 1872, this firm began to supply type the bodies of which were multiples of 1/12 part of a typical Pica measuring 0.166 inch. The United States Type Founders' Association recommended this system to its members in 1886, and British typefounders conformed to the American point-system in 1898. The standard measurements according to the British-American Point System are:

5-point	0.0692 in.	14-point	0.1937 in.
6-point	0.0830 in.	16-point	0.2213 in.
7-point	0.0968 in.	18-point	0.2490 in.
8-point	0.1107 in.	24-point	0.3320 in.
9-point	0.1245 in.	30-point	0.4150 in.
10-point	0.1383 in.	36-point	0.4980 in.
11-point	0.1522 in.	48-point	0.6640 in.
12-point	0.1660 in.		

See also Didot System. 2. Any mark of punctuation. A full point (full stop).

Point System. *See Point.*

Pointillé. A binding decoration in gold done with tools with a dotted surface.

Points. 1. Small holes made in the sheets during the printing process which serve as guides in registering when the sheets are folded by machinery. 2. The bibliographical peculiarities of a printed book, the absence or presence of which determine whether the book is a first or other edition, or a particular issue of an edition, or a variant, etc.

Polaire. The leather case or satchel in which the ancient monks placed their books. Polaires were usually made without decoration unless for a wealthy man in which case they bore a design stamped in relief.

Polis (UK). Acronym for the Parliamentary On-Line Information System; a database compiled by the House of Commons Library, and consulted there and in the European Parliament.

Polish Library Association. Founded in 1917 as the Alliance of Polish Librarians – and Archivists' being added after the end of the Second World War until the archivists formed a separate organization in 1953, when the present name was adopted.

Polish Library in London. The Lanckaroński Foundation Collection of Polonica amounting to some 3000 books and over 500 etchings, drawings and engravings was received in 1969. This collection includes 16th- to 19th-century books, calendars, MSS., as well as more recent books, serials and pamphlets, and is the most outstanding of the bequests, gifts and legacies to be received by the Library from Poles all over the world. The Library originated in 1942 and functioned since 1943 as the Library of the Polish Government in London, its aim being to act as a central collection and bibliographical agency for Polish books published outside Poland since 1 September 1939 and also to acquire other material in Polish or in other languages concerning Poland and Polish affairs. From 1948 to 1953 it acted as the library of the Polish University College, and since then has concentrated on expanding its collection of books on Polish arts and humanities, and acting as a bibliographical centre for books in Polish or relating to Poland which are published outside that country. Of the Library's stock of about 100,000 volumes, 65% are in Polish. The Library has a reading room and lending library. Membership is free and is open to students and researchers.

Polonym. A work by several authors.

Polydecimal. A classification developed by L. Melot, which uses both letters and numbers in the notation.

Polyglot. A book giving versions of the same text in several languages, generally arranged in parallel columns. The first of the great Polyglot bibles was the so-called COMPLUTENSIAN POLYGLOT (*q.v.*). The second of the famous polyglot Bibles was printed between 1569 and 1573 by Christopher Plantin, with the patronage of Philip II of Spain. It was in eight folio volumes, the text being in Hebrew, Greek, Latin, Chaldaic, and Syriac. The Paris polyglot Bible, 1654, in nine volumes edited by G. Michel Le Jay and others added

Arabic and also Samaritan to Plantin's text. The *Biblia sacra polyglotta* published in six volumes in London between 1655–57 was in nine languages.

Polygraphic. Written by several authors.

Polygraphy. Books consisting of several works or extracts from works by one or a number of authors.

Polyhierarchic. (*Classification. Information retrieval*) Pertaining to an organizational pattern involving a multiplicity of facets or aspects.

Polynomial. A work by several authors.

Polyonymal. Having several, or different, names.

Polyonymous. Possessing many names.

Polyptych. *See Codex.*

Polysemia. The provision of instructions to an indexing machine as to how a significant word in a document is used in that document. Also called 'Multiple meaning'.

Polysemy. (*Information retrieval*) The quality of a term having two or more independent or overlapping meanings.

Polytechnics and Colleges Funding Council. The UK co-ordinating body for the financing of polytechnics and higher education colleges by governmental and other means. Replaced the National Advisory Body for Local Authority Higher Education in 1989.

Polyterms. An extension of UNITERM CONCEPT CO-ORDINATION INDEXING (*q.v.*) whereby a group heading, instead of one simple basic idea, is used on each uniterm card. Also called 'Unit concepts'.

Polytopical. Treating of several subjects.

Polyvalent Notation. A system of notation wherein each digit represents one of the characteristics of division. SEMAPHORE INDEXING (*q.v.*) is a polyvalent notation.

POPSI. Postulate-based Permuted Subject Index; a method of subject indexing devised by S. Battacharyya which uses classification scheme headings as lead terms followed by subject terms linked in a standard order derived from the categories in the *Colon Classification*. Groupings for various subject fields are made in accordance with twenty postulates (rules which control the order).

Popular Copyrights. Used at the beginning of this century to denote books published by firms specializing in low-priced editions, who used, with the permission of the copyright owners, the plates made for the original editions.

Popular Edition. An edition of a book published on poorer paper, possibly without illustrations, and in a paper cover or a less substantial cloth binding than the normal edition, and sold at a cheaper price.

Popular Library. A department containing books of general interest for home-reading, those of special interest, or of an advanced character being placed in SUBJECT DEPARTMENTS (*q.v.*). *See also Browsing Room.*

Popular Name. An abbreviated, shortened, or simplified form of the name of a government department, society or other corporate body, by which it is usually known.

PORBASE. Base Nacional de Dados Bibliographicos; Portuguese biblio-graphic network established in 1988 and currently at the development stage. Based at the National Library, Lisbon.

Porcelain. A sheet of paper consisting of a sheet of blotting-paper pasted to one of coated stock. (American.)

Pornography. Writings of an obscene or licentious character: originally applied only to treatises on prostitutes and prostitution. It comes from the Greek words meaning 'writing about harlots'. Many catalogues of old and rare books include such items under the term *Erotica*.

Porphyry, Tree of. A device for abstracting the qualities of terms. It is, in a rough sense, a sub-dividing of the term Substance, by adding differences at different steps; thus Substance, by the addition of the difference Corpore-ality, divides into Corporeal and Incorporeal Substance; then (neglecting the Incorporeal), to corporeal is added the difference 'Body' which results in Animate and Inanimate. This method of division is known as bifurcate (or division in pairs, positive and negative). The Tree is used to illustrate the FIVE PREDICABLES (*q.v.*).

port. (*Pl.* ports.) Abbreviation for PORTRAIT (*q.v.*). 2. A socket for connec-ting peripherals to a computer system.

Portfolio. A case for holding loose paintings, drawings, illustrations, diagrams, papers or similar material. Usually made of two sheets of strawboard, covered with paper or cloth with a wide cloth joint to form the 'spine', often with cloth flaps attached at the edges of one board to turn in and so protect the papers, and with tapes at fore-edges to secure the contents. Abbreviated pf.

Portico Prize. A prize established in 1985 for a work of fiction, non-fiction or poetry set wholly or partly in the North-West of England. The prize is sponsored by Manchester's Portico Library, a subscription library founded in 1806.

Portolan. *Synonymous with* PORTOLAN CHART (*q.v.*).

Portolan Chart. An early type of chart produced, often in MS., between the thirteenth and seventeenth centuries to guide mariners in coastwise sailing. Such charts were based on estimated bearing and distances between the principal ports or capes. They are believed to have been first produced by the admirals and captains of the Genoese fleet during the second half of the thirteenth century and maybe earlier, and are sometimes called 'Compass maps' or 'Loxo-dromes', but wrongly so, as they were used before com-passes. Originally a harbour book or written sailing instructions, but the name has come to be used for a sea chart. In England a portolan became known as a 'ruttier' or 'rutter of the sea' (from 'route'). Also called 'Portolan', 'Portulan', 'Portolano'.

Portolano. *Synonymous with* PORTOLAN CHART (*q.v.*).

Portrait. 1. A representation of a person, made from life, especially a picture or representation of the face. 2. When portraits are a feature of a work they are indicated in the collation part of a catalogue entry as *ports*. Otherwise they are subsumed. *See also Illustrations*. 3. (*Publishing*) An illustration, or a book, is referred to as 'portrait' when its height is greater than its width.   4. (*Printing*) A table is said to be 'set portrait' when set upright on the page with the bottom of the table parallel with the bottom edge of the page. *See also Landscape.*

Portulan. *Synonymous with* PORTOLAN CHART (*q.v.*).

Portway Reprints.   A scheme arranged by the (British) Library Association and Messrs. Cedric Chivers for the reprinting of out-of-print books. This scheme was started in 1971 and is the successor to an arrangement by the London and Home Counties Branch of the LA and Messrs. Chivers.

Positive.   In photography and documentary reproduction, the film or print which has the same tones as the original. It is sometimes made from a NEGATIVE (*q.v.*) in which the image and the tones are in reverse compared with the original.

Positive Copy.   In documentary reproduction, a copy prepared by a POSITIVE PROCESS (*q.v.*) and having the same tones and image as in the original. Also called 'Positive print'.

Positive Microfilm.   A film bearing microcopies with tone values corresponding to those of the originals.

Positive Print. *Synonymous with* POSITIVE COPY (*q.v.*).

Positive Process.   A documentary reproduction, or copying, process, in which the tones and the image are the same as in the original. *See also Positive.*

Post.   (*Information retrieval*) 1. To transfer an indicial notation from a parent or main entry to individual analytic entries – for example, to type the proper catalogue entry and number at the top of a group of catalogue cards.   2. In co-ordinate indexing, to put the accession number of a document under each entry representing a co-ordination term.

Post-a-book.   A service of the British Post Office, in association with the Book Marketing Council and the Booksellers' Association. For a small charge a book purchased as a gift may be mailed directly to the recipient with a bookmark as a greetings card.

Post-Co-ordinate Indexing System.   One in which the indexer or cataloguer is concerned only with simple concepts as headings with a number of entries under each, providing a device or devices whereby the user can combine them to create the compound subjects in which he is interested. The BATTEN SYSTEM, PEEK-A-BOO AND UNITERM (*q.v.*) systems are of this kind. *See also Pre-co-ordinate Indexing System.*

Post-dated.   A book which bears a date of publication which is later than the actual date. The opposite of 'Ante-dated'.

Post Octavo.   A book size, 8 × 5 inches. *See also Book Sizes.*

Poster. *Synonymous with* PLACARD (*q.v.*).

Posthumous Work.   One which is first published after the death of the author.

Posting Up.   An indexing practice whereby terms describing the content of a document are also indexed by broader terms.

Postings.   The number of records retrieved by a search statement.

Postings List.   (*Information retrieval*) An alphabetical list of descriptors with the identification numbers of documents using the descriptor posted against it.

Pot Casśe Device. A device consisting of a broken jar, or urn, pierced by a wimble (Fr. *toret*) and usually accompanied by the motto 'non plus'. It was used by Geoffrey Tory the French printer on his title-pages. It was also used as part of the design for decorating book covers.

Pott. An obsolete name of a size of paper varying from 15 × 12½ inches to 17¼ × 14¼ inches, and being the smallest of the original (uncut) hand-made papers; the name is probably derived from a water-mark design of a pot. *See also Paper Sizes.*

Pounce. (*Binding*) An adhesive used under gold or colours.

Powder. (*Binding*) An heraldic term signifying a diaper design of small figures (sprays, flowers, leaves, etc.) frequently repeated by the use of one to three small tools at regular intervals over the greater part of a binding, producing a powdered effect. Sometimes there is a coat of arms, or some other vignette, in the centre, or even at each corner; there may be a lightly tooled fillet around the side of the cover. Also termed *semé, semée* or *semis*.

Power Press. A printing press in which the operation of the machine was done by some form of power other than the human being. It was introduced in the nineteenth century and superseded the HAND PRESS (*q.v.*) for rapid operation.

p.p. Abbreviation for PRIVATELY PRINTED (*q.v.*).

PPBS. Abbreviation for Planning Programming Budgeting System; a management and financial system that requires identification of goals, examination and costing of alternative means of securing those goals, specifying necessary activities for each alternative, and overall evaluation. The emphasis of PPBS is on planning, and improvement of the decision making process.

PPRG. *See Publicity and Public Relations Group.*

Practile. (*Information retrieval*) The percentage of useful documents retrieved per search.

Praeses. The person or persons who open an academical disputation by propounding objections to some tenet or proposition, usually moral or philosophical, as distinguished from the RESPONDENT (*q.v.*) who defends it.

Prebound. *Synonymous with* PRE-LIBRARY BOUND (*q.v.*).

Precatalogued Book. One which is accompanied by catalogue cards when supplied, the cards obtained by purchase, contract, or agreement from a commercial supplier.

Precedent Epithet. An epithet which both in common usage and in cataloguing practice precedes a person's forename(s), e.g. 'Mrs', 'Sir'.

PRECIS. Acronym of the PREserved Context Index System. A subject indexing system in which the initial string of terms, organized according to a scheme of role-indicating operators, is computer-manipulated so that selected words function in turn as the approach term. Entries are restructured at each step in such a way that the user can determine from the layout of the entry which terms set the appropriate term into its context and which terms are context-dependent on the approach term. This system was developed initially in the British National Bibliography and has been used in its publications since January 1971. It is also used by the *Australian National Bibliography* and by library servics in Canada. *See also MARC.*

PRECIS Vocabulary Fiche. Formerly known as the RIN file, an alphabetical listing of all the indexing terms used as entry points in the PRECIS indexes produced by British Library Bibliographic Services since 1974.

Precision Ratio. (*Information retrieval*) The ratio of retrieved relevant documents to the total number of retrieved documents. *See also Relevance Ratio.*

Pre Co-ordinate Indexing System. (*Information retrieval*) A system by which terms are combined at the time of indexing a document, the combination of terms being shown in the entries. This is the system known as PRECIS (*q.v.*) and is used for the entries in the *British National Bibliography*. Such a system co-ordinates terms to form compound classes at the indexing stage, and is used with classification schemes, the classified catalogue and the alphabetical subject catalogue. *See also Post-Co-ordinate Indexing System.*

Predicables, Five. A series of logical terms and notions, first explained by Porphyry in his treatise on Aristotle's *Topics*, and forming the basis of the science of classification. They are: 1. GENUS – a main class, or group of things, which may be divided into sub-groups called 2. SPECIES, the groups into which the genus is divided. 3. DIFFERENCE – a characteristic which enables a genus to be divided, e.g. add to the genus 'books' the difference 'method of production' and the species 'MS. books', and 'printed books' result. 4. PROPERTY – some quality of a thing or group of things which, although common, is not exclusive to them, e.g. 'jealousy' is common to 'human beings' and 'animals'. 5. ACCIDENT – a quality which is incidental to a class, which may or may not belong to it, and which has no effect on the other qualities of the class. *See also Porphyry, Tree of; Bifurcation.*

Preface. The author's reasons for writing, and his afterthoughts. It indicates the scope, history, and purpose of the book and the class of readers for whom it is intended, and expresses thanks to helpers. It is usually written by the author, follows the DEDICATION (*q.v.*), and precedes the INTRODUCTION (*q.v.*). It is usual to write a new preface to a new edition, outlining the extent of changes and additions. Sometimes called 'Foreword'.

Preface Date. The date given at the beginning or end of the preface.

Preferred Order. The order in which the facets in a faceted classification schedule are arranged. Once this preferred order has been decided it is invariable. The purpose of preferred order is to display the relations between the terms to the best advantage.

Preferred Term. In a thesaurus, a preferred term is used to gather in one place other nearly synonymous terms that would lead to scattered entries in a catalogue, etc.

Pre-library Bound. Books bound in a LIBRARY BINDING (*q.v.*) before being sold. Called 'prebound' for short.

Preliminaries. Those parts of the book which precede the first page of the text. The order should be: half title, frontispiece, title, history of book (date of first publication, dates of subsequent reprints and revised editions) and imprint, dedication, acknowledgements, contents list, list of illustrations, list of abbreviations, foreword or preface, introduction, errata. All except the frontispiece, which faces the title-page, and the history and imprint which are on the verso of the title page, should begin on right-hand pages, but the errata may be placed on the left-hand or be printed on a separate slip and pasted in. They are usually printed last on a separate sheet or sheets, and paged separately, usually in Roman figures. Sometimes abbreviated to 'prelims'. When they are printed on leaves conjugate with leaves bearing part of the text, it is often an indication in very old books of an issue later than the first. Also called 'Front matter', 'Preliminary matter'. *See also Subsidiaries.*

Preliminary Cataloguing. The making of preliminary catalogue entries by typists utilizing data supplied by clerical officers or junior assistants who search the card catalogue for entries. These entries are examined with the books by the cataloguer, who is thus saved clerical work, being enabled to concentrate on professional work requiring judgment and decision. *See also Searching.*

Preliminary Edition. An edition issued in advance of the ordinary edition. This is sometimes done in order to obtain criticisms of the text before the final edition is published. Also called 'Provisional edition'.

Preliminary Leaf. One of the unnumbered leaves, printed on one or both sides, which appear before the numbered leaves at the beginning of a book.

Preliminary Puff. *See Puff.*

Prelims. Abbreviation for PRELIMINARIES (*q.v.*).

Pre-natal Cataloguing. *See Cataloguing-in-publication.*

Pre-natal Classification. Classifying material before it is published, classification numbers (L. C. and Dewey) being printed on the back of the title-pages of books. *See Cataloguing-in-publication.*

Pre-print. A portion of a work printed and issued before the publication of the complete work. A paper submitted at a conference which is published prior to the holding of the conference.

Pre-processed Book. One which is delivered by the book supplier with all the necessary processing completed.

Pre-publication. The practice of disseminating small numbers of duplicated copies of scientific or technical papers or documents, etc., prior to publication by normal routines in printed serial publications.

Pre-publication Cataloguing. Cataloguing books at a national library or national bibliographic centre from gathered and folded sections or review copies of books which are submitted for the purpose by the publishers. *See also Cataloguing-in-Publication.*

Pre-publication Price. The price at which a book would be sold if ordered prior to a specified date (which is before the publication date) after which the book would cost substantially more.

Prescribed Books. Those which are prescribed for a course of reading.

Presentation Copy. 1. A copy of a book bearing a presentation inscription, usually by the author. 2. A copy of a book presented by the publisher. Only a book that is spontaneously presented properly qualifies for this description; one that is merely autographed at the request of the owner should be called an 'inscribed copy'.

Preservation. The provision of adequate care and maintenance facilities to ensure the safe survival of library stock or archives. Generally synonymous with CONSERVATION (*q.v.*).

Preservation Advisory Committee. Established 1985 by the Council on Library Resources to guide initial work on long-term preservation work at US libraries.

Preservation and Conservation (PAC). An IFLA core programme started in 1984, and based at the Library of Congress. The programme envisages research into different methods of preservation, the formulation of policy and strategy at national and international levels; the co-ordination of the work in this field carried out by related national and international agencies; and co-operation with information producers in order to assure for the future the use of permanently durable materials.

Preserved Context Index System. *See PRECIS.*

Presidential Libraries. The papers of each US President since Hoover are placed in a separate research library operated and maintained by the National Archives. There are at present eight libraries: Herbert Hoover Library, West Branch, IA; F. D. Roosevelt Library, Hyde Park, N.Y.; Harry S. Truman Library, Independence, MO.; Dwight D. Eisenhower Library, Abilene, KS.; John F. Kennedy Library, Boston, MA.; L. B. Johnson Library, Austin, TX.; Gerald R. Ford Library, Ann Arbor, MI.; Jimmy Carter Library, Atlanta, GA. The Ronald Reagan Library is to be built at Thousand Oaks, near Los Angeles, CA.

Press. 1. A double-sided bookcase of not less than four tiers (i.e. two each side), called in America, a 'Range'. In America a single-sided bookcase with more than two tiers placed end to end; formerly, a 'Bookcase'. *See also Book Press, Book Stack, Bookcase, Tier.* 2. The machine, or apparatus, used to press the paper on to the type, plate, engraving or block. In printing there are three methods of imparting this pressure: (a) by the PLATEN PRESS; (b) by the FLAT-BED CYLINDER PRESS; (c) by the ROTARY PRESS (*qq.v.*). *See also Printing Press.* 3. A simple piece of machinery, possibly a 'screw press', used to keep a book or books in position under pressure to effect adhesion of pasted or glued surfaces, or for some other purpose, during the binding process. *See Presses 1.* 4. A popular name for the trade, and craft, of writing for, and publishing, newspapers and periodicals.

Press à un Coup. A hand printing press on which the operator could lower the platen on to the type in a single movement. It was invented by François Ambroise Didot (1720–1804), the elder son of François Didot (1689–1759).

Press Agent. One who arranges for editorial publicity in the press (*see Press 4*) for individuals, institutions, etc.

Press Book. One issued by a private press.

Press Copy. *Synonymous with* REVIEW COPY (*q.v.*).

Press Cutting. A piece cut from a newspaper or periodical. Also called 'Clipping' (American), 'Cutting'.

Press Errors. Errors made by a compositor when setting type. These are corrected at the printer's cost. Also called 'Printer's errors'.

Press Mark. The symbol given to a book to indicate its location. Used in old libraries to indicate the *press* in which the book is shelved, not the book's specific place. This is not so precise as the CALL NUMBER (*q.v.*). Press marks are usually written on the spine of a book (often on a label or tag), on the endpaper, on the front or back of the title-page and against the entry in the catalogue. *See also Class Mark, Class Number, Fixed Location.*

Press Notice. A short statement of specific information in a newspaper – including an 'obituary notice' – announcement of a death, notice of an engagement, birth or marriage, or a reference to, or a review of, a new book, or a criticism or commentary on an artistic performance of music, ballet, etc.

Press Number. A small figure which in books printed between 1680 and 1823 often appears at the foot of a page, sometimes twice in a gathering (once on a page of the outer forme and once on a page of the inner), the page on which it appears being apparently a matter of indifference, though there is some tendency to avoid a page bearing an ordinary signature. The press number is believed to have been used to indicate on which press the sheet was printed.

Press Photographer. One who takes and supplies photographs for publication in the press.

Press Proof. The final proof passed by the author, editor, or publisher for printing.

Press Queries. Obscurities in a MS. referred to the author by the printer's proof reader.

Press-ready. Sometimes used as a synonym for MAKE-READY (*q.v.*) but also to indicate other machine preparations than that of the forme, such as of the inking, paper-feed, and paper delivery mechanisms.

Press Release. An official statement giving information for publication in newspapers or periodicals.

Press Revise. An extra proof taken from type in which corrections marked on earlier proofs have been made, and when machining is about to take place. The press revise is submitted to the machine reviser who finally passes it for press. Also called 'Machine proof'.

Press Run. The number of copies to be printed rather than the number ordered: it is usually larger than the number ordered to allow for spoilage.

Presses. 1. In bookbinding, there are several kinds, namely, lying, cutting, standing, blocking and finishing. 2. In printing, the printing machines. In England, 'printing presses' refers to hand-operated apparatus, 'machines' to those operated by power. In America the term 'presses' refers to both. *See also Press.*

Presswork. Making an impression on paper from matter set up in type; in modern usage, the care and attention devoted to this as indicated by the quality of the result. It includes the preparation of the printing surface for even printing and the control of inkflow during the running of the press. *See also Machining.*

PRESTEL. The *interactive* VIDEOTEX (*q.v.*) system marketed by British Telecom.

Price Committee (UK). The Education, Science and Arts Committee of Parliament, Chairman: Christopher Price. Its fourth report for 1979/80 was entitled *Information Storage and Retrieval in the British Library Service.* (HMSO 1980). *See also Library and Information Services Council.*

Presumed Author. *Synonymous with* SUPPOSED AUTHOR (*q.v.*).

Prima. 1. The first word of the next page, sheet or slip being read, and printed (repeated) at the right hand of the measure immediately below the last line. 2. A mark made on copy where reading is to be resumed after interruption. 3. Program for Research Information Management; a wide-ranging investigation of information sources within and outside traditional library areas, part of the activities of RLG (*q.v.*).

Primary Access. (*Information retrieval*) Access to a particular entry (or block of entries) in a file; it may be simultaneous, sequential, fractional or random access. *See also Scanning, Secondary Access.*

Primary Bibliography. 1. An original, 'extensive' or 'general' bibliography dealing with books unrelated in subject matter. 2. One which is the original record of the whole, or part of, a publication. *See also Secondary Bibliography.*

Primary Binding. The style of binding used for a book when it is first published.

Primary Distribution. The initial despatch of a document from its originator, or publisher, to more than one destination, especially in accordance with a mailing or distribution list.

Primary Name Heading. (*Cataloguing*) An author heading which is provided for an entry where one person or body has primary intellectual responsibility for the existence of a work.

Primary Publication. A publication which contains mainly original (new) matter, e.g. papers describing the results of original research, as distinct from SECONDARY PUBLICATION (*q.v.*). Also called 'Primary Journal'.

Primary Sources. Original manuscripts, contemporary records, or documents which are used by an author in writing a book or other literary compilation. Also called 'Source material' and sometimes 'Original sources'. *See also Secondary Sources.*

Prime. A personnel consultancy, recruitment and placement service for top information professionals; operated by Aslib, and started in 1989.

Primer. A simple introduction, of an elementary nature, to a subject, possibly intended as a school class book. *See also Introduction 2, Long Primer.*

Principles of Classification. The rules formulated by logicians and classifiers by which a scheme of classification is made.

Print. 1. (*Noun*) A reproduction of a picture or drawing by any printing process. Generally applied to etchings, engravings, mezzotints, etc. 2. (*Verb*) To apply ink and then paper to blocks, plates or types to make an 'impression' or a 'print' of the image.

Print Collection. A collection of prints such as engravings, etchings, etc.

Print Film.   A fine grain, high resolution film which is used primarily for making contact film copies.

Print Room.   A room in a large library in which the collection of prints is kept.

Print Run.   The number of copies printed.

Printed.   Broadly, any representation of characters which are reproduced on any material by any method of mechanical impression, whatever it may be.

Printed as Manuscript.   *See Printed but not Published.*

Printed Book.   A book produced from type or by a similar process. *See also Book, Publication.*

Printed but not Published.   Printed, but not put on sale, and therefore not published. This fact may be so noted on the title-page. Also called 'Printed as manuscript'.

Printed Catalogue.   A catalogue, printed and issued in book form as distinct from a card, or other, form of catalogue.

Printed Edges.   Matter which is printed by means of rubber type on the cut edges of books. This is done on the fore-edge in order to aid speedy reference to the contents, but also here and on the top and bottom edges for the purposes of advertising.

Printed Matter.   A literary composition in the sense of an intelligible, rather than a stylish, arrangement of words which has been set up in type and printed.

Printer.   1. The person or firm responsible for printing a book or other publication, as distinguished from the publisher or bookseller. Of considerable importance in old books. In cataloguing rare books, the printer statement, even when it includes a number of names, is given in the imprint. Added entries may be given under printers' names. When no publisher's name is given on the title page, the printer's may be given in the imprint.   2. Equipment for producing computer output in paper copy.

Printer's Device.   *See Device.*

Printer's Devil.   An apprentice to the printing trade, especially to a compositor. The origin of the term is said to be that in 1561 a monk published a book called *The Anatomy of the Mass*, and although it had only 172 pages, fifteen more were needed to correct the many typesetting mistakes. These were attributed to the special instigation of the devil, but they turned out to be the work of an apprentice learning the trade.

Printer's Errors.   *Synonymous with* PRESS ERRORS (*q.v.*).

Printer's Flower.   *See Flower.*

Printer's Imprint.   *See Imprint.*

Printer's Keepsake.   *See Keepsake* 3.

Printer's Mark.   *See Device.*

Printer's Ornament.   *See Ornament.*

Printer's Pie.   *See Pie.*

Printer's Reader.   *See Reader* 1.

Printing.   *See Impression.*

Printing and Allied Trades Research.   The activities of the former British Paper and Board Industry Research Association (BPBIRA) and of the

Printing, Packaging and Allied Trades Research Association (PATRA) are now undertaken by PIRA, the Research Association for the Paper and Board, Printing and Packaging Industries. Situated at Leatherhead, Surrey, PIRA is organized into four operating divisions – paper and board; printing; packaging; information, training and techno-economics. It provides technical enquiry, testing and consultancy services. Its worldwide monitoring of information and its computer-based data bank provide the basis for a number of services. A non-profit making organization, its sources of income are: membership subscriptions, government contracts and direct fee income from the sales of consultancies and services. Publishes *PIRA News* (m.), *Printing Abstracts* (m.), *Paper and Board Abstracts* (m.), *Packaging Abstracts* (m.), *PIRA Management and Marketing Abstracts* (m.), *Newsbrief* (for newspaper management) (bi-w). Contributes to *LISA*.

Printing Block.   A general term for any kind of BLOCK (*q.v.*) used in printing.

Printing Historical Society.   Founded in 1964 'to encourage the study of, and foster interest in, the history of printing; to encourage the preservation of historical equipment and printed matter; to promote meetings and exhibitions; to produce publications in connection with these aims'. Publishes *Journal* (a.).

Printing Industry Research Association.   The name by which the Printing, Packaging and Allied Trades Research Association was known until 1930. *See Printing and Allied Trades Research.*

Printing Press.   A machine for making impressions from a plate, block or type which has been inked, on paper or some other material. *See also Cylinder Press, Flat-bed Press, Intaglio, Letterpress, Lithography, Offset, Platen Press, Rotary Press.*

Printings.   A general term for papers which are specially suitable for printing as distinct from other purposes.

Printout.   A statement printed automatically from data stored in a computer.

Priority Date.   The date when the basis of the claim was first disclosed to a patent office; it is usually the date on which a provisional or complete specification was filed, or a convention date. It is the date on which a patent claim relies if it is challenged. *See also Convention Application, Patent of Addition.*

Prison Library.   A library maintained in a prison for the use of prisoners. In many prisons in Great Britain the libraries are provided by the local authority.

Prison Libraries Group.   A Group of the (British) Library Association; formed in 1984, but it had existed since 1975 as the Prison Libraries Subject Group of the Medical, Health and Welfare Libraries Group. Aims to unite all those interested in the operation of libraries in penal establishments, and promote such libraries by meetings and publications.

Privacy.   *See Data Protection.*

Private Bills.   Bills published by their promoters for submission in the House of Commons.

Private Libraries Association. An international society of authors, publishers, booksellers, librarians and private book collectors – collectors of rare books, fine books, single authors, reference books on special subjects, and above all collectors of books generally for the simple pleasures of reading and ownership. Its functions include the organizing of lectures on subjects of bibliographical interest and visits to famous libraries, printing works, binderies, etc. running an Exchange Scheme enabling members to dispose of surplus material and advertise for desiderata; issuing publications of interest to members. Publishes a *Newsletter, Exchange List* and *The Private Library* (q.). Abbreviated PLA.

Private Library.   One which is owned by a private individual. Also a library owned by a society, club or other organization, to which members of the public have no right of access.

Private Mark.   Some indication of ownership, usually the name of the library impressed with a rubber stamp, which is always placed in a particular part of a library book.

Private Press.   A printing establishment which undertakes only the work of the owner, or of publishing clubs who may be supporting it financially, or prints only those books (usually not first editions) which the proprietor fancies. Private presses are usually small establishments using hand presses or small letterpress machines, and producing well-printed books in limited editions on hand-made paper. Eric Gill, writing to the *Monotype Recorder* in 1933, said that such a press prints solely what it chooses and not what its customers demand of it, which is the case with a 'public' press, and that 'the distinction has nothing to do with the use of machinery or with questions of the artistic quality of the product'. Of such were the Kelmscott, Essex House, Doves, Vale, Gregynog, Ashendene, Cuala, Eragny, and Pear Tree.

Private Publisher.   One who has works printed by a commercial or private printer and publishes them himself, mainly to ensure the publication of work which might not otherwise be published and/or to achieve a high standard of physical production.

Privately Printed.   This term is given to books printed for the author or a private individual, usually for distribution gratis. It is also applied to books printed on a PRIVATE PRESS (*q.v.*). When printed on a public press it is often described as being printed at the author's expense, or by private subscription. Abbreviated p.p.

PRO.   PUBLIC RECORD OFFICE (*q.v.*).

Probable Association, Principle of.   The principle that the heading chosen for a catalogue entry (whether for a person, subject, place, organization, etc.) should be one most users of the library are likely to look under. *See also Cataloguing, Principles of.*

Procedure Manual.   *Synonymous with* STAFF MANUAL (*q.v.*) except that in an American special library it may be more detailed, and personnel matters are omitted if they are contained in the employee handbook. Also called 'Work manual'.

Proceedings. The published record of meetings of a society or institution, frequently accompanied by the papers read or submitted, or by abstracts or reports. *See also Transactions.*

Process. (*Verb*) 1. To manipulate data by mechanical means. 2. To prepare books and other documents for a collection, especially physical preparation such as labelling and giving marks of ownership.

Process Block. A metal printing surface produced with the aid of photography and a chemical or mechanical process.

Process Camera. One used for the production of a photographic intermediate (usually film – either negative or positive) necessary for making an image on a material from which prints can be made, e.g. an offset-litho plate.

Process Colour Printing. *See Colour Work.*

Process Embossing. *Synonymous with* EMBOSSING (*q.v.*).

Process Engraving. Any of the processes for reproducing pictures, print, etc. that uses plates or blocks prepared by photographic, mechanical or chemical action rather than by hand. Also called 'Photo-mechanical process', and 'Process work'.

Process Photography. The reproduction of line copy as distinct from continuous tone copy, e.g. a line drawing compared with a photograph. Materials of great contrast are used with this method.

Process Publications. Those which are produced by a duplicating process other than ordinary printing. The output may be single sheets or complete books.

Process Record. Usually a card record of a book or other item received at a library and in process of being added to library records.

Process Slip (Accession Slip, Copy Slip, Guide Slip, Routine Slip). A slip or card bearing author's name, title, imprint, collation, tracings, and allocations of copies to libraries or departments. It accompanies the book throughout the cataloguing department and is generally used as the copy for the typist or printer. Called also, in America, 'Rider slip'.

Process Stamp. A rubber stamp impression on the back of the title-page of a book to give the library history of the book.

Process Work. *See Process Engraving.*

Processes, Department of Technical. *Synonymous with* PROCESSING DEPARTMENT (*q.v.*).

Processing. 1. Strictly, the carrying out of the various routines such as stamping, labelling, numbering, etc., before a book is ready for the shelves, but it may include *all* the processes involved in so preparing a book. Also called 'Book preparation', 'Book processing'. 2. Preparation of index entries for manual or mechanized systems from books, journal articles or other items of information. 3. In photography and documentary reproduction, the carrying out of such processes as are necessary after the projection of the image to be copied on to the sensitized material. *See also Mechanical Preparation.* 4. (*Archives*) The actions connected with the description, arrangement and preservation of archival material, and undertaken with a view to facilitating the use of the documents.

Processing Center.   In America, a building in which the processing of books for a number of libraries is carried out. Such centers have developed by co-operation of librarians in adjoining areas, often being initiated under the provisions of the Library Services Act. Sometimes they operate from an existing public library, from a state library agency, as an entirely separate enterprise on a contract or other co-operative basis among a group of libraries, or as a commercial project.

Processing Department.   1. A combined book-ordering (or acquisition) and cataloguing department.   2. In some libraries, a department in which the work of preparing books for circulation, other than cataloguing and classification, is carried out. *See also Cataloguing Department, Technical Services Department.*

Proctor Order.   The system of classification of incunabula named after the order used by R. G. C. Proctor in his *Index of early printed books in the British Museum*, 1897–1903.

Product of the Year Award.   An annual award started in 1988 and presented by Online Inc., publisher of the journals *Online, Database* and *Laserdisk Professional*. Judging is done by the advisory boards of the three journals, and recognizes innovation and usefulness to the consumer. The award is announced at the US Online Conference.

Professional Assistant.   A member of the professional staff performing work of a nature requiring training and skill in the theoretical or scientific parts of library work as distinct from its merely mechanical parts.

Professional Ethics, Code of.   A document setting out the norms of professional conduct and behaviour required of members of a professional association. The American Library Association issued a Code of Ethics adopted at its Council meeting June 30 1981 (The text is reproduced in *American Libraries* 13(9) October 1982, p. 595) and a paper 'Ethics for Reference Librarians' in 1978; the (British) Library Association issued a Code of Ethics in 1980, and this was ratified by the Association's AGM in September 1983.

Professionalism.   The character and conduct of those working in a profession. *See also Professional Ethics.*

Profile.   1. A biographical account combined with a description and assessment of the subject's achievements.   2. (*Information retrieval*) A set of indexing terms which characterize the interests of an individual or a group using a selective dissemination of information service. Also called an INTEREST-PROFILE (*q.v.*), this is matched with the terms by which each document is indexed in the system.

Pro-forma Invoice.   1. An invoice received for checking and approval prior to receiving the formal invoice.   2. An invoice provided to facilitate payment before the despatch of materials, to avoid the cost of chasing outstanding payments.

Program.   (*Information retrieval*) (*Noun*) An outline giving the schedule of actions to be followed or the order and arrangement of such a schedule. A series of instructions expressed in symbols which a machine system can accept and understand. A sequence of steps or coded instructions to be executed by the computer to solve a given problem. (*Verb*) To determine the steps and plan the procedures necessary for the computer to solve the problem.

Programmer. A person who is skilled in the writing of computer programs.

Programming Language. A stylized method of writing instructions (a 'program') which instruct a computer what to do. All programming languages differ from natural language in being non-ambiguous. BASIC and FORTRAN are examples.

Progress, In. *See In Progress.*

Progressive Proof. A proof showing the sequences and effect at each stage of a colour-printing process as each colour is added. *See also Flat Proof.*

PROI. PUBLIC RECORD OFFICE OF IRELAND (*q.v.*).

Project INISS. *See INISS.*

Project Intrex. A long range programme, established in January 1964 by the Massachusetts Institute of Technology, for the application of the principles and methods of information processing to library operation, with the specific object of establishing the bases upon which the technical library of the future may be modelled. Intrex stands for Information Transfer Exchange.

Project Jupiter. JUGL University Project for Information Transfer, Education and Research. *See JANET User Group.*

Project Leer. A joint undertaking by the Books for the People Fund, Inc. and the Bro-Dart Foundation for the compilation and publication of annual lists of children's books and elementary reading materials for adults which are available in the Spanish language, and for the encouragement of the production and use of such reading materials.

Project Quartet. Based on the work a BLEND (*q.v.*) this project will examine further potentials of electronic publishing, networking, CD-ROM, and optical digital disks. The Universities of Birmingham and Loughborough, Hatfield Polytechnic, and University College London are partners in the Project, which is scheduled to end in June 1989. The investigation has centred on the use of new technology to improve information exchange within the academic research community. Application areas examined have included electronic mail, computer conferencing, online database access and document delivery. The Underlying technologies include CD-ROM, ISDN, and hypertext systems.

Projected Books. Microfilmed books intended for projecting on to a ceiling, wall or screen for the benefit of physically-handicapped people.

Projection. The method used by a cartographer for representing on a plane the whole, or part, of the earth's surface, as Mercator's Projection.

Projection Print. In documentary reproduction, a copy having a larger scale than the original: an enlargement. Also called a 'Blow-up'.

Projection Printing. A method of obtaining a photographic copy by exposing a photosensitive surface by projecting an image through an optical system.

PROLOG. A computer language used in the development of EXPERT SYSTEMS (*q.v.*).

Prompt. Symbol on a computer display screen; an indication that the user should make a response.

Prompt Book. *Synonymous with* PROMPT COPY (*q.v.*).

Prompt Copy. The copy of a play used by a prompter, showing action of a play, cues, movements of actors, properties, costumes, and scene and light plots.

PRONI. Public Record Office of Northern Ireland (*q.v.*).

Pronounceable Notation. (*Classification*) A notation, which for ease of memorizing consists of letters which as a group can be pronounced. Also called SYLLABIC NOTATION (*q.v.*).

Proof. 1. In bookbinding: the rough edges of certain leaves left uncut by the plough are proof that the book is not cut down. 2. An impression made from type before being finally prepared for printing. Proofs are made on long sheets of normal page width (GALLEY or SLIP PROOF) for the author's inspection and correction but not until after a *First Proof* has been made, corrected by the printer's reader and returned to the compositor. When the printer has made the corrections the type is divided up into pages, the page numbers inserted, and a further proof submitted to the author. This third proof is called the *Page Proof*. A *Marked Proof* is one marked by the printer's reader, corrected by the author and again read by the printer's reader, and a *Revise* or *Revised Proof* is a further one embodying corrections made by the author/or reader to the first proof. *See also Author's Proof, Clean Proof.* 3. A preliminary impression taken from an engraved plate or block, or a lithographic stone. Usually called 'Trial proof'. 4. An impression taken from a finished plate or block before the regular impression is published and usually before the title or other inscription is added. Also called 'Proofprint' or 'Proof impression'.

Proof Before Letters. A proof of an engraving, etching or other illustration process made before the addition of title, artist's and engraver's name, date, dedication or other matter.

Proof Corrections. Signs used by proof readers on printers' proofs to indicate corrections to be made in the typesetting. These have become established over the centuries and the British code is published in *British Standard* 5261: Part 2: 1976. The American Standard is Z 39.22–1974. A British Standard for colour printing was published in 1972–BS 4785: 1972 *Colour proof correction symbols. See also Standard Generalized Markup Language.*

Proofpress. A small or medium-sized press operated electrically or by hand on which proofs from type of other relief surfaces are made.

Proof Reader. A person who reads printers' proofs to discover errors in type, punctuation, statement and so forth, and marks the corrections on the proof while the 'copy' is read out to him by the copyholder.

Proof Reader's Marks. *Synonymous with* PROOF CORRECTIONS (*q.v.*).

Proof Reading. The process of reading a printer's proof and comparing it with the MS. or COPY (*q.v.*) in order to detect errors in typesetting. Errors are marked on the proof in accordance with generally accepted signs and the resulting 'corrected proof' is returned to the printer so that the necessary corrections may be carried out. *See also Proof, Proof Corrections.*

Proof Sheet. A sheet of paper on which a proof of type-matter, plate, or block, is made by a printer. *See also Proof.*

Proper Name. A name used as the designation of a single person, place or thing, e.g. Leonard, Wimbledon, Festival Hall.

Property. *See Predicables, Five.*

Proprietary Information. Information which is owned by reason of discovery or purchase, and is private or confidential to a specific firm or organization.

Prospectus. 1. A leaflet or pamphlet issued by a publisher and describing a new publication. 2. A publication written to inform, arouse interest in, and encourage the reader to take some action concerning, a book about to be published, a school or other education institution, or the issue of stock or shares of a company, etc.

PROSPO. PUBLIC RECORD OFFICE OF IRELAND (*q.v.*).

Protection. (*Copyright*) The legal guarantee of copyright in an INTELLECTUAL WORK (*q.v.*) which is given by the law of a country. This protection is usually given either from the date of its deposit with a national organization or its date of publication.

Protocol. Agreement on methods of coding data for use on several communicating devices.

Provenance. A record or indication of previous ownership of a book or manuscript. A special binding, book plate, or inscription may indicate previous owners, collections or libraries through which a particular book has passed. (*Archives*) 1. In archival theory, the principle that the archives of a given records creator must not be intermingled with those of different origin. 2. In general archival usage, the originating entity which created or accumulated the records; also the source of PERSONAL PAPERS (*q.v.*) and manuscript collections. 3. Information concerning the successive changes of ownership or custody of a particular document.

Provincial Joint Fiction Reserve (UK). A national scheme for the co-operative preservation of books, similar to the scheme initiated by the former Association of Metropolitan Chief Librarians. It commenced on 1 January 1962; each Regional Bureau outside London and the South East, which already had schemes, is responsible for a part of the alphabet. The scheme provides only for the purchase and retention of new publications and is not retrospective, although offers of older novels are sometimes made to the responsible library. Allocation by author amongst the regions is as follows:

A–C	North Western	K–M	West Midlands
D–F	Northern	N–S	Yorkshire
G–J	East Midlands	T–Z	South Western

See also Joint Fiction Reserve.

Provisional Edition. A book which is published in a small edition, possibly by some near-print process, and circulated to selected individuals or sold in the ordinary way, so that observations, criticisms and suggestions may be submitted and considered before a final edition is published. Also called 'Preliminary edition'.

Provisional Specification. *See Patent, Specification.*

Prussian Instructions. The German cataloguing code; an English translation was published by the University of Michigan Press in 1938.

Psalm-book. A PSALTER (*q.v.*).

Psalter. The Book of Psalms in which the Psalms are arranged as in the Book of Common Prayer for use in a religious service, whether to be spoken or sung; in the latter case they may be in a metrical version.

Pseudandry. The use by a woman author of a masculine name as a pseudonym. *See also Pseudonym.*

Pseudepigraphy. The attributing of false names to the authors of books.

Pseudo Abstract. An abstract that was written in anticipation that an article, or 'paper' would be written in the future, but has not been, and might never be, written. Such an abstract is written by a speaker invited to address a meeting of a professional association and is published prior to the delivery of the full 'paper' which may, in the event, be spoken extempore and never published or otherwise recorded.

Pseudograph. A literary composition falsely attributed to a particular writer.

Pseudonym. A name used by an author, which is not his real name. Also called a 'Pen name' or 'Nom de plume'. *See also Syncopism, Telonism, Titlonym.*

Pseudonymous Works. Those written by persons who have used a name other than their real name on the title-page in order to conceal their identity. *See also Pseudonym.*

Pseudo-weeding. *See Weeding.*

PSS. Acronym for Packet Switch Stream, a service of British Telecom; a subscriber may use the service to connect one computer to any other on a network. Additionally, by using a PAD (Packet Assembler-Disassembler) it is possible to access any computer on a network from a simple terminal or microcomputer. This is a standard method of accessing online databases, as only a local telephone call is necessary.

PTEG. *See Personnel, Training and Education Group.*

Public Catalogue. A catalogue issued for the use of the public as distinct from one issued for use by officials. *See also OPAC.*

Public Documents. The regular official publications of a government, containing reports, statistics, etc.

Public Domain. Material not copyrighted, or for which copyright has expired.

Public Lending Right. A subsidy paid to authors in respect of books issued from public libraries. It has been in operation in Denmark, Sweden and Norway for many years and in Finland since 1961. The UK situation is as follows:- Registration of authors and titles began on 1 September 1982. Rules to determine the eligibility of books and authors are complex but very specific. Authors and illustrators named on the title page can apply for PLR providing they are alive at the time of registration and are UK residents. Translators, editors, compilers, and revisers are not eligible. Books have to be more than 32 pages long (24 pages for poetry and drama), to have been put on sale, and to have been the work of one to three individual authors/illustrators. Magazines, journals, and periodicals do not count nor do corporate and conference titles. Books in reference sections of libraries are not included nor are books lent out from university and specialist libraries. The language of the book and place of publication are not criteria, provided its author is a citizen of an EC country and resident in the UK.

The collection of loans data began on 1 January 1983; by collecting loans data from ten 'principal' service points, mostly with issues over 500,000 per annum and from six 'ordinary' service points with fewer issues, the Public Lending Right Office will accumulate and process some 6–7m issues a year. This represents 1.2% of all public library lending.

For each of the seven regions (London, Metropolitan Boroughs, English Counties-South, English Counties-North, Wales, Scotland, Northern Ireland) loans are added and then grossed up according to total regional issues (from CIPFA statistics). They can then be added together to give notional national issues for every title.

The computer will then identify those books registered by their authors for PLR. The others are ignored for the calculation of payment to authors, which is worked out by the computer to spread a given sum of money among registered authors in proportion to the popularity of their books measured by library issues. The money is at present £2m each year from which has first to be deducted the administrative expenses in operating the Scheme both at the PLR Office at Stockton-on-Tees and in local authorities. The funding is provided entirely from central government.

Public Libraries Acts.   *See Library Law.*

Public Libraries Group.   A group of the (British) Library Association. Formed in November 1974 'to establish an organization to unite members engaged or otherwise interested in public libraries with a view to increasing the effectiveness of Public Libraries and furthering the objects set forth in the Charter of the Library Association'. Membership is open to any member of the LA, and also to duly nominated and approved representatives of those authorities in affiliated membership. The County Libraries Group ceased to function after December 1974 in order to combine its functions with those of the Public Library Group which took over this former Group's publications programme and also its series of weekend schools.

Public Libraries Research Group.   Established in early 1970 the Public Libraries Research Group (PLRG) was originally part of the London and Home Counties Branch of the Library Association. Now an independent body informally linked to the Library Association, the Group fosters and carries out research relevant to the UK public library field. The Group membership consists mainly of public librarians, library school lecturers and researchers. The Group holds workshops and seminars on relevant topics and publishes research reports.

Public Library.   A library provided wholly or partly from public funds, and the use of which is not restricted to any class of persons in the community but is freely available to all.

Public Library Association.   A Division of the American Library Association under this name since 1958; originally organized in 1951, it is 'concerned with the improvement and expansion of public library services to users of all ages and in all types of communities, and with increasing professional awareness of the social responsibilities of the library to its public'. Publishes *PLA Newsletter* (q.). Abbreviated PLA.

Public Library Automation Network. *See Plan.*

Public Library Development Incentive Scheme. An initiative of the Office of Arts and Libraries (UK) to encourage private sector organizations, co-operatives, and non-public libraries to put forward proposals for schemes and projects in partnership with public libraries. The administration is co-ordinated by the British Library Research and Development Department. Announced 1987, and scheduled to run initially over three financial years, 1988–91. Abbreviated PLDIS. *See also PUPLIS.*

Public Library Manifesto. A document published by Unesco first in 1949, revised in 1972 (text in *IFLA News,* No. 41, July 1972 and in the May–June 1972 issue of *Unesco Bulletin for Libraries*) and published in all the major languages of the world for wide distribution, particularly in developing countries. It sets out the basic services which public libraries should provide, how they should be provided, administered and financed. By July 1973, with the help of IFLA member associations and individuals, the Manifesto had been translated into 35 languages, and the USSR was translating it into Russian and the 14 major regional languages.

Public Record Office. The depository for British Official documents; it con-tains documents from the twelfth century to date. The Public Records Act 1958, much of which was based on the report of the Committee on Departmental Records (the 'Grigg Report') transferred the direction of the PRO from the Master of the Rolls to a Minister of the Crown, the Lord Chancellor, who now has a general responsibility for public records; he is authorized to appoint an Advisory Council on Public Records, of which the Master of the Rolls is the Statutory Chairman; this Council is particularly concerned with those aspects of the work of the PRO which affect members of the public making use of the facilities provided. The Act places on govern-ment departments a duty to select records for permanent preservation and to pass them to the PRO within thirty years of their creation. They were open to public inspection when they were 50 years old until 1 January 1968 when the period was reduced to 30 years. The Lord Chancellor has power to appoint for any class of records a special place of deposit; this enables public records accruing in local courts and offices to be kept in local repositories, and those of a technical character to be kept in appropriate specialist institutions. The 1958 Act declares that 'records' includes not only written records but those conveying information by any other means whatsoever. *See also Modern Public Records.*

Public Record Office of Ireland. Founded by provisions of the Public Records (Ireland) Act 1867 in order to preserve and render readily accessible the non-recurrent records of Government and the courts, and other archival material of importance. The Office, which is situated in Dublin, is provided by Government and open to the public. Abbreviated PROI; often PROSPO (Public Record Office and State Paper Office). Publishes reports (annual) of the Deputy Keeper of Public Records. The Deputy Keeper of the PROI is also the Keeper of State Papers. The State Paper Office, which was established in 1706, aims to preserve and make accessible to researchers the state papers of Ireland, in particular the records of the Chief Secretary's Office; it i situated in Dublin Castle. The Reports of the Keeper appear as appendices tc the Reports of the Deputy Keeper of Public Records, Ireland, 1–59 (1869- 1962). Abbreviated SPOI.

Public Record Office of Northern Ireland. Formed in 1924 to provide for the reception and safe keeping of the records of the Northern Ireland Govern ment, the Courts of Justice, the local authorities and other public bodies. The Office also encourages the depositing of documents by private individual and institutions so that the public may have access to all material of social economic and historical interest. Approximately 100 million documents have been deposited. This office is provided by Government and is open to the public. Abbreviated PRONI. Publishes many calendars, facsimiles, book and Deputy Keeper's reports on accessions; these are available from HMSC bookshops.

Public Records. Records made in the process of government and including those made by any means whatsoever, not only those which are written. *See also Modern Public Records.*

Public Records Act 1958. *See Public Record Office.*

Public (Service) Area. That portion of the area of a library to which the public are admitted but which is occupied by fixed furniture used by both staff and public (circulation desk, information, enquiries or registration desks, etc.) catalogues, exhibits and displays.

Publication. 1. A work (*see Work 1*) issued to the public in the form of a document or book. 2. The act of issuing a book to the public. 3. A defined in Article VI of the Universal Copyright Convention 1971, 'the reproduction in tangible form and the general distribution to the public o copies of a work from which it can be read or otherwise visually perceived'.

Publication Date. *Synonymous with* DATE OF PUBLICATION (*q.v.*).

Publication Day. 1. The day of the week or month on which a periodical i issued. 2. The first day on which a book may be sold to the public.

Publicity and Public Relations Group. Group of the (British) Library Associ ation; formed in 1984, it aims to make the profession aware of the importance of continuous and planned public relations, encourage the interchange o ideas, and promote co-operative initiatives. Publishes *Public Eye* (3 p.a.) Abbreviated PPRG.

Publish. 1. The action of a publisher in issuing and offering for sale to the public, a book or print produced on some kind of printing, copying o photographic reproducing machine. 2. The action of an author, artist, o composer of music, in creating something, and arranging for it to be reproduced in quantity and offered for sale.

Published. A document which has been reproduced in a number of copies and made available to the public to whom it may be sold or distributed free o charge and whether or not it is intended to have a restricted readership such as to members of parliament, of a learned, professional or political organi zation.

Published Price. The retail price at which a book is published.

Publisher.   A person, firm, or corporate body responsible for placing a book on the market, as distinguished from the printer. Publisher and printer may be the same, but in modern books usually is not. Relates also to publication of music, reproduction of works of art and of maps and photographs. A firm which undertakes publishing is sometimes referred to as a 'Publishing house' or 'Publishing firm'.

Publishers Association.   A trade association which was founded in Britain in 1896. Membership is open to any publisher in the United Kingdom whose business, or an appreciable part of it, is publishing books, journals or electronic publications. The original object of the Association was to maintain the prices of net books, and while this is still a matter of consider-able interest, the Association is largely engaged in assisting its members to secure a greater, and more efficient, distribution of books, and in the education of publishers' staffs. It deals with problems which face publishers as a whole, regulates conditions of employment within the trade, supplies its members with information and advice on all matters of technical, economic and legal aspects of publishing, and represents publishers in discussions or negotiations with the government, EC, local authorities, and public and trade bodies. Two education councils (Educational Publishers Council, and University, College and Professional Publishers Council) are directed speci-fically towards the presentation of even more evidence of the true value of books to children, students and the cost-efficiency of the education system and the generation of greater financial resources for book purchasing. National and regional campaigns aim to persistently heighten public and professional awareness in this area. Specific committees oversee policies on copyright, school book supply, public relations, educational software, mar-keting, further education, and serial publishing. Surveys, submissions and delegations are quickly organized and pursued to effective and profitable conclusions for participating companies. The PA's market development work is administered by the Book Development Council (BDC) securing international markets, and Book Marketing Council (BMC) for home trade markets. Abbreviated PA.

Publisher's Binding.   The binding in which a publisher issues a book.

Publisher's Case.   *Synonymous with* PUBLISHER'S COVER (*q.v.*).

Publisher's Catalogue.   A list of books issued for sale by a publisher.

Publisher's Cloth.   Used to indicate a book as issued by the publisher in a cloth binding.

Publisher's Cover.   The cover for a book that is provided by a publisher for the normal trade edition of a book. Also called 'Publisher's case'. *See also Case, Edition Binding.*

Publishers Databases Ltd.   Launched in December 1984, a project to initiate viable commercial electronic and database publishing projects, and to operate a research service in this field. Initially information will be available only to shareholding companies. Abbreviated PDL.

Publisher's Device.   *See Device.*

Publisher's Dummy.   A dummy book made up of the right number of sections of plain paper, and sometimes cased, to indicate the size of a proposed book.

Publisher's Imprint. *See Imprint.*

Publishers Information Card Services Ltd. Produces and mails standard format cards giving information on new books to major libraries, bookseller and academic staffs. Over 100 publishers now use the service, which began in 1968. Abbreviated PIC.

Publisher's List. A list of books published by one publisher and still in print

Publisher's Mark. *See Device.*

Publisher's Number. *See Plate Number.*

Publisher's Reader. One whose work is the reading, judging and criticizing of manuscripts offered for publication.

Publisher's Series. The name given to a series of books which usually have been published previously, and comprising standard or current books on related or unrelated subjects, issued in a uniform style and at the same price, and bearing a series title such as *World's Classics*, or *Everyman's Library*. Each volume contains one or more distinct works, and some series include books published for the first time. Also called 'Trade series'. Series which comprise only books previously published are sometimes called 'Reprint series'.

Publishing. The trade of publishing books; this includes negotiations with authors or their agents, design of books in conjunction with printers, book production, publicity and sales through book wholesalers and retailers. In addition to books it relates to music, reproduction of works of art and of photographs and maps. *See also Desktop Publishing.*

Puff. A term, in use since the seventeenth century, for exaggerated praise for a book, usually written by the author or publisher for use in advertisements and on the book's jacket. A 'Preliminary puff' is supplied to the publisher' travellers as pre-publication publicity. *See also Blurb.*

Pugillares. From two to eight small wooden writing tablets of ivory, wood, or metal and covered with wax on one side upon which writing could be scratched with a stylus. Sometimes the tablets were hinged together with rings or leather cords down one side to form a tablet book. Notebooks of this sort were known as *pugillaria. See also Codex.*

Pull. A trial print taken from type of a block before an edition is printed.

Pulled. In bookbinding, a book the cover of which has been removed and all the sheets separated. *See also Take Down.*

Pulled Type. Type letters which have been pulled out of the forme by ink-balls

Pulling. (*Binding*) Stripping the old covers off a book, separating the sections and removing any old glue prior to rebinding.

Pullout. (*Book production*) *Synonymous with* THROW OUT (*q.v.*).

Pulp. The mechanically or chemically prepared mixture made from vegetable fibres which becomes paper when passed over wire and dried. *See also Chemical Wood, Hand-made Paper, Mechanical Wood.* 2. A cheap magazine printed on newsprint.

Pulp Board. Board manufactured in one thickness, or by bringing two or more thicknesses of board or paper together into a single structure on a multiple wire machine, as distinct from boards made by laminations of paper pasted together and called 'Pasteboard'.

Sizes:

	inches
Imperial	22 × 30
Postal	22½ × 28½
Pulp Royal	20½ × 25

Pulp Magazine. A cheap magazine printed on newsprint and containing stories of adventure, mystery or love, usually of poor quality.

Punch. A piece of steel on which a type character is engraved. After hardening it is used as a die to strike the matrices from which type is cast.

Punch Engraving. A method of book illustration which had previously been used by goldsmiths and ornament engravers. The tools used consisted of a dotting punch, a small pointed punch set in a wooden handle and used by hand pressure, and larger punches with either grained or plain striking surfaces intended for use with a hammer.

Punched Card. A lightweight card which has holes punched in certain positions either round the edges (edge-punched) or in the body of the card (body-punched) to represent specific pieces of information. Edge-punched cards are sorted manually with the aid of a 'needle' and body-punched cards usually by machine.

Punched Card Charging. A TRANSACTION CARD CHARGING (*q.v.*) system whereby a punching machine is used to punch two transaction cards simultaneously, to record book number, reader's number, main class number and date for return. One card is placed in the book and is taken away by the reader; it has a readable date due for return stamped on it. The other is retained. *See also Charging Methods.*

Punctuation. *See Dash, Filing Code, Links, Quotes.*

Punctuation Symbols. A device used in co-ordinate indexing to associate terms or symbols in order to indicate relationship. For example, a double dot (..) may be used before each associated set to words to indicate that they are to be considered together.

PUPLIS. The working acronym of the LISC/BLRDD Working Party on the Roles and Relationships of the Public and Private Sector in the Provision of Library and Information Services. Set up in 1985, PUPLIS produced a major report *Joint Enterprise: roles and relationships of the public and private sectors in the provision of library and information services* (HMSO 1987). The report fed into the Green Paper on Public Libraries (1988). Case studies have been commissioned by the Office of Arts and Libraries. *See also Public Libraries Development Incentive Scheme.*

Pure Bibliography. The type of bibliography which treats of the value of the contents of books, including textual criticism.

Pure Notation. *See Notation.*

Pustaka. A book consisting of long strips of the thin bark of trees or of a kind of paper made from tree bark; it may deal with magic medicine, domestic remedies, or 'the art' of destroying life. The Sanskrit word 'pustaka' is used for this kind of book in North Sumatra, Java and other countries, but in South Sumatra 'pustaha' is used; here such books were used as divination texts, for codes of law and for legends. Pustakas were written in a brilliant ink on long strips of writing material, folded concertina-fashion and tied together with a string of woven rushes.

Put to bed.   *See Bed.*

Putnam Award, Herbert W.   An award made to an American librarian for the purpose of travel or writing to further the library profession. Administered by the American Library Association Awards Committee and presented at irregular intervals.

'Putting Knowledge to Work'.   The slogan of the (American) SPECIAL LIBRARIES ASSOCIATION (*q.v.*).

Putwiths.   Acknowledgements and other consequential papers such as corrigenda and addenda relating to documents already filed in a correspondence or similar file, and which in themselves are of no significance from a filing or indexing point of view.

Pye.   An alternative spelling of PIE (*q.v.*).

Pye Book.   *See Pie (q.v.).*

Pyes.   A kind of ecclesiastical calendar.

q.v.   Abbreviation for *quod vide* (*Lat.* 'which see'); *Pl. qq.v. (quae vide).*

Quad.   Abbreviation for QUADRAT. 1. A piece of metal, lower in height than type, and used for spacing.

> An em quad (mutton), the square of the body.
> An en quad (nut), ½ the body or 2 to an em.
> A thick space, ⅓ the body or 3 to an em.
> A middle space, ¼ the body or 4 to an em.
> A thin space, ⅕ the body or 5 to an em.
> A hair space, 1/12 the body approximately.

See also Em Quadrat, En Quadrat, Paper Sizes. 2. Prefix to standard paper-size names to indicate a sheet four times the size of a single and twice the size of a double, sheet. *See also Octavo, Paper Sizes.*

Quad Mark.   *Synonymous with* BACK MARK, BLACK STEP, COLLATING MARK (*q.v.*).

Quadrat.   A term which is never used in its full form, but in the abbreviated version QUAD (*q.v.*).

Quadrata.   An early style of Latin manuscript writing; it was practised from the second to the fifth century A.D. and was characterized by a square capital letter based on formal inscriptions cut with a chisel in stone. Also called 'Square capital' hand.

Quadrigesimo-octavo.   *See Forty-eightmo.*

Quadrille.   Paper ruled so as to form a very large number of small squares; it is used for graphs, etc.

Qualification.   The addition of one or more words in parentheses to a subject heading, usually in dictionary catalogues, indicating the sense in which the heading is being used. Also used in indexes to the scheme of classification. Chiefly used to distinguish homonyms.

Qualified Heading.   A heading followed by a qualifying term which is usually enclosed in parentheses, e.g. Composition (Art), Composition (Law).

Qualified List.   Produced by deleting False and Unsought links of the chain (when using the chain procedure to produce subject index entries) and adding qualifiers to the remaining terms. It is the second stage of the conversion of a classification symbol to a verbal subject heading, the first being BASIC ANALYSIS (*q.v.*).

Qualifier.   A sub-heading in a subject index which has been constructed by CHAIN PROCEDURE (*q.v.*). (*Indexing*) A word, or words, added to a heading, after punctuation or within parentheses, in order (a) to distinguish it from identical headings which have different meanings, or (b) to identify the heading, e.g. by using an epithet or honorific title. *See also Access Point.*

Quarter Binding.   A binding in which the spine and a very small part of the sides is covered with a stronger material than the rest of the sides. 'Half-binding' has the corners covered with the same material as the spine. In 'three-quarters binding' the material used on the spine extends up to half the width of the boards.

Quarter Bound.   *Synonymous with* QUARTER LEATHER (*q.v.*).

Quarter Leather.   A term used to describe a book with a leather spine and cloth sides. *See also Half Leather, Leather Bound, Three-quarter Leather.*

Quarterly.   A periodical published once every quarter.

Quartet.   *See Project Quartet.*

Quaternion.   Paper or vellum folded into a section of four leaves.

Quarto.   1. A sheet of paper folded twice to form a section of four leaves. The sheets given under the definition OCTAVO are folded twice to give the following quarto book sizes in inches. Double size sheets folded three times would give the same size sections but would be described bibliographically as octavos, not quartos.

Foolscap	8½ × 6¾
Crown	10 × 7½
Large Post	10½ × 8¼
Demy	11¼ × 8¾
Medium	11½ × 9
Royal	12½ × 10
Large Royal	13½ × 10
Super Royal	13½ × 10¼
Imperial	15 × 11

Abbreviated 4°, 4to.   2. A book having sections of four leaves, or eight pages.   3. A book over 10 and under 13 inches high. This is the popular, or book trade, definition.

Quarto Edition. One issued in QUARTO (*q.v.*) form.

Quarto Shelving. Shelves to accommodate quarto books.

Quasi-facsimile Bibliography. One which attempts to reproduce the kind of type used in the original – roman, italic or gothic, etc.

Query. The symbol ? written in the margin of a proof by the printer's reader to indicate to the author that he is required to check some detail. Sometimes 'Qv' is used.

Question Mark. *Synonymous with* INTERROGATION MARK (*q.v.*).

Questioned Document. A document, the origin or authorship of which has been challenged and is in doubt.

Quick-reference Books. Books which are essentially of a reference character, such as directories, dictionaries and gazetteers.

Quinternion. A GATHERING (*q.v.*) of five sheets folded once to form ten leaves or twenty papers.

Quire. 1. 24 sheets of paper and one 'outside', making 25; the twentieth of a ream; 25 copies of a newspaper or periodical. 2. A gathering, section or signature, especially when unfolded. Books in sheets, unbound, are said to be 'in quires'. *See also Section.* For 'Cording quires', *see Cassie.*

Quoins. Wedges of metal or wood, used to lock the matter in the CHASE (*q.v.*).

Quotation Marks. *See Quotes.*

Quotations. (*Printing*) Very large quads, used for filling up large areas of space in printed matter: they are usually hollow, simply four walls, sometimes strengthened by one or more internal girders. Also called 'Quotes'.

Quotes. The inverted commas " " placed at the beginning and end of quotations. *See also Quotations.* Sometimes called 'Double quotes' to distinguish them from 'Single quotes': ' . . .'. *See also Double Quotes, Duck-foot Quotes, Single Quotes, Turned Comma.* In Germany and Austria they are printed thus „ . . .". although some German printers now prefer the French guillemets but pointing inwards (». . .«). Spanish printers prefer the guillemets («. . .») pointing outwards.

Qwerty. The standard typewriter keyboard arrangement used in the UK and USA, placing the letters q.w.e.r.t.y. from the left on the top row. *See also Azerty.*

RACE. A European Community programme, Research and Development in Advanced Communications in Europe is designed to help create the telecommunications channels and infra-structure for the mid 1990s on. Such a broadband network will allow the digital transmission of both images and data. The 18 month definition phase, launched in 1985, studied the challenges and problems of the project itself. The main RACE programme will establish the technological base for the introduction of a Community wide integrated broadband communications network, the equipment necessary and the definition of new standards. The main programme was launched at the end of 1987, on the basis of 550 mecus from the Community budget over five years.

Rack. A shelf, or group of shelves, or a case, usually built on to a wall or into a piece of furniture, for displaying books, magazines or periodicals, and distinguished as Book Rack, Magazine Rack, according to the special use of the fitting.

Radial Routeing. *See Routeing.* Also called 'controlled circulation'.

Radials Bulletin. RADIALS was an acronym for *Research and Development-Information and Library Science.* The Bulletin was issued twice a year by the (British) Library Association, and covered research in its widest sense, including investigations, studies, surveys and evaluated innovations. Work was included if carried out in the UK, or done by British nationals abroad, or where British institutions or funds were involved. From 1982, student theses and dissertations were included in a separate section. The Bulletin first appeared in 1974, as a development of the Register of Research formally included in the *Library Association Yearbook.* In January 1983 replaced by *Current Research in Library and Information Science (q.v.).*

Radiating Stacks. Island stacks arranged like a fan, the point being towards the staff area thus enabling all readers on both sides of every stack to be visible to the staff.

Radix Notation. The significance of digits in the representation of numeric data which is governed by their relative position with respect to 'period' (.).

Rag Paper. Paper made from rags, especially cotton rags.

Ragged. In typesetting, uneven layout or lack of justification; left or right-hand margins may be ragged, or both.

Raised Bands. When the cords, on which the sections of a book are sewed, are not embedded in their backs and consequently show as ridges, they are called raised bands. The opposite of SUNK BANDS (*q.v.*).

Raised-letter Printing. *Synonymous with* THERMOGRAPHY (*q.v.*).

Ralph R. Shaw Memorial Award. *See Shaw Memorial Award, Ralph R.*

RAM. Acronym for *random access memory*; a computer memory facility in which data stored at any point can be accessed without delay regardless of its position.

Ramean Tree. *Synonymous with* Tree of Porphyry. *See Porphyry, Tree of (q.v.).*

Ramie. China (Chinese) grass which has been used for paper making in China since the third century A.D. In Europe it is normally used only for textiles and banknotes.

Ramifying Classification. *Synonymous with* BRANCHING CLASSIFICATION (*q.v.*).

RAMP. Records and Archives Management Programme; a component part of Unesco's General Information Programme.

Randolph J. Caldecott Medal. *See Caldecott Medal, Randolph J.*

Random Access. (*Information retrieval*) A storage device not restricted to sequential scanning. Book indexes, card catalogues, magnetic drums and cards, magnetic or optical discs, and photographic strips are all of this kind. With this method, access to any location in the file is equally rapid; it is also quicker than sequential scanning. *See also Scanning.*

Random Access Memory. *See RAM.*

Random Access Storage. A storage technique in which the time required to obtain information is independent of the location of the information – that is, items do not have to be processed in sequence. Also called 'Direct access'.

Random File. A series of records on cards, or other material, which are not maintained in any recognizable sequence, but are 'mixed up'.

Ranfurly Library Service. A service started by the Earl and Countess of Ranfurly in 1954 for collecting books from individuals and institutions in the UK and sending them to overseas countries in the fight against illiteracy and where there is an urgent need for English books. Books are sent to a central point in each country whence they are distributed to libraries and other institutions in over 80 countries. In 1988 some 650,000 books were distributed overseas to 65 countries; about 70 per cent of the total go to Africa. Increasingly it directs its long term strategy towards the encouragement of local publishing in the developing countries.

Ranganathan Award for Classification Research. This award is offered by the Committee on Classification Research of the International Federation for Documentation (FID) in honour of Dr. R. S. Ranganathan, the Indian classificationist. It is made every two years for an outstanding contribution in the field of classification, and was first awarded in 1976 to Derek Austin in recognition of his achievement in designing PRECIS.

Range. An American term for a bookcase, equivalent to the English PRESS (*q.v.*).

Ranging Figures. The numerals of modern type faces which do not have ascenders or descenders but extend from the base line to the cap line, e.g. the Times New Roman figures 1234567890. Also called 'Lining figures'. *See also Hanging Figures.*

Rank. 1. (*Information retrieval*) A measure of the relative position in a series, group, classification or array. (*Classification*) 2. (*Noun*) A measure of the relative position of terms in a series, group, classification, or array. 3. (*Verb*) To arrange terms in an ascending or descending series according to importance.

Rare Books Group. A Group of the (British) Library Association. It was formed (on the initiative of the then University and Research Section) in October 1967 'to unite librarians, who are concerned with the custody of collections of rare books and similar materials, and other members of the Library Association who are interested in rare books, and to promote the study and discussion of questions relating to the acquisition, maintenance and use of such collections'. A *Newsletter* began publication in March 1974.

RASD. Acronym of REFERENCE AND ADULT SERVICES DIVISION (*q.v.*) of the American Library Association.

Ratcliffe Report. 'Preservation policies in British Libraries; report of the Cambridge University Library conservation project', (BLRDD Library and Information Report 25, 1984). Chairman Dr. F. W. Ratcliffe. The report revealed a very unsatisfactory national picture of preservation, and led to the establishment of the NATIONAL PRESERVATION OFFICE (*q.v.*).

Rate, Library. *See Library Rate.*

Rating Authority (UK). The local authority responsible for levying and collecting rates and community charge; it is the council of the authority or the Common Council of the City of London.

Rattle. The sound produced by shaking or snapping a sheet of paper; it is indicative of hardness (due to the degree of wetness or hydration) and, generally speaking, of quality. Called 'crackle' in the USA. Linen rags will give a toughness and rattle to papers which is distinctive from those made from cotton.

Raw Data. (*Information retrieval*) Data, in machine-sensible form or otherwise, which has not been processed.

Raw Paper. *Synonymous with* BODY PAPER (*q.v.*).

Read-Only Memory. *See* ROM.

Reader. 1. A person employed by a printer to read through proofs with the 'copy' to make sure that corrections have been properly made. *See also Publisher's Reader.* 2. A person who makes use of literary material in a library; a member of a lending library is frequently called a Borrower. 3. In an American special library or information department, the member of staff who scans current publications to select articles, news items, etc., pertinent to the work of individuals and departments of the organization of which the library is a part, for subsequent dissemination. 4. In a newspaper library, the member of the library staff who scans the several editions of the paper and marks articles for cutting and filing. *See also Dissemination of Information.* 5. In reprography, a device for projecting a readable image of a microcopy on to a screen within the device or on to a separate portable screen or suitable surface which may be opaque or translucent. *See also Microfilm Reader.* 6. In an educational institution, a member of the faculty whose role is primarily in research.

Reader Area. That portion of the total floor space of a library which is allocated for use by readers.

Reader for the Press. A printer's reader. *See Reader 1.*

Reader-interest Classification. A very simple and broad classification, intended to reflect the special interests of readers rather than the subject contents of books as such.

Reader-printer. In documentary reproduction, a microform reader which can also be used to make prints automatically, normally to A4 size from a single frame.

Reader Services. A part of a library's establishment devoted to the provision of assistance, advice, and other services to the library's users. Usually found in tandem with a TECHNICAL SERVICES unit (*q.v.*), and most common in academic libraries.

Readers' Adviser. An experienced and tactful member of the staff who is detailed for advising readers on their choice of books, interesting casual readers in more systematic reading, recording results of interviews, maintaining a close touch with local educational agencies and generally furthering the use of books.

Reader's Card. The card issued to a reader when registering to use a library.

Reader's Proof. The first proof which is made from composed type; it is read by the printer's reader and sent to the compositor who makes any necessary alterations before the second proof is pulled and which is the first one sent to the author.

Reader's Register. A register giving details of the members of a library.

Reader's Set. A set of proofs in which corrections are to be made, usually so marked on the proofs by the printer's reader.

Reader's Ticket. The ticket issued to a reader on joining a library.

Reading Case. *Synonymous with* MAGAZINE CASE (*q.v.*).

Reading Circle. A group of people who meet regularly to read, study or discuss books.

Reading Copy. A copy of a book offered for sale in poor condition the text being complete and legible. Also called 'Binding copy'.

Reading File. (*Archives*) A file containing copies of documents arranged in chronological order. Also known as 'chronological file', 'Chronfile' and in Canada as a 'Continuity file'.

Reading List. A list of recommended books and/or periodical articles in some special order and on a particular subject, often with guidance as to their purpose and features. It may be added to an encyclopaedia article or a chapter in a book in order to suggest matter for further study. *See also Source List.*

Reading Room. A room set aside for the reading of periodicals or books.

Reading Shelves. Examining books to see that they are in correct order on the shelves. Also known as 'Shelf tidying', 'Shelf checking' and in American practice as 'Shelf reading' and 'Revising shelves'.

Reading Therapy Sub-group. Formed 1985 within the Library Association Medical, Health and Welfare Libraries Group. Reading therapy is used to help elderly people, psychiatric patients, children with learning difficulties, offenders and other client groups.

Ready Reference. Reference work concerned with questions of a factual nature which can be answered readily, often from QUICK-REFERENCE BOOKS (*q.v.*) which in many libraries are shelved together with standard reference books, sometimes in a separate area reserved for dealing with questions of this nature.

Real Time. A computing term indicating that the computer response to commands is simultaneous with the input. *See also On-line.*

Realia. Three-dimensional objects such as museum materials, dioramas, models and samples which may be borrowed or purchased by a school library and used in connection with class lessons.

Realization. In music, the written expression, by an editor, on music staves of a full harmonization which is indicated by a figured bass on the original score The realization may also be made in performance from the FIGURED BASS (*q.v.*).

Ream. A pack of 500 identical sheets of paper. A ream contains twenty quires. In the UK, packs of 480 sheets for special classes of papers, such as wrapping papers and blotting paper, are recognized. A ream of hand-made and drawing papers may contain 472, 480 or 500 sheets. Originally a ream contained 516 sheets. A 'short ream' has 480 sheets, a 'long ream' 500 or 516 sheets.

Rear Projection. The projection of an image on a transparent or opaque material through an appropriate type of projector on to a translucent screen from the side opposite to that from which the image is viewed.

Re-back. To repair a book by providing a new spine without re-covering the sides or re-sewing. *See also Backed.*

Re-bound. Said of a book the original binding of which has been replaced with another, usually after re-sewing the sections.

Rebus. 1. A form of riddle, in which words or their syllables, names, mottoes, etc., are represented by objects or by a combination of objects, letters or words. 2. An enigmatical representation of a name, word or phrase by figures, pictures, arrangement of letters, etc., which resemble the intended words or syllables in sound.

REBUS. Réseau des Bibliothèques utilisant. SIBIL; users of SIBIL are grouped into the REBUS bibliographic network. (SIBIL – Système Informatisé pour Bibliothèques is a record format most used for shared cataloguing). Five centres are at present involved: Lausanne, St. Gallen and Basle (Switzerland), Montpellier (France) and Luxembourg.

REBUS Luxembourg. Based at the Luxembourg National Library, a bibliographic network established 1985 as a part of REBUS (*q.v.*).

Recall. 1. (*Verb*) To request the return to the library of a book or other item which is on loan. 2. (*Noun*) The retrieval of a required document or reference from an information store.

Recall Notice. A notice sent to a reader requesting the return of a book or other item which is overdue or required for use by someone else. *See also Overdue Notice.*

Recall Ratio. An information retrieval, the number of documents actually recalled from an index in response to a question on a given theme, in proportion to the number of documents on that theme which are known to be indexed. Also called 'Sensitivity'. *See also Relevance Ratio.*

Re-casing. The re-insertion of a book into its original cover, with or without re-sewing.

Receiving Desk. *See Circulation Desk.*

Recension. A revision. Used to indicate a scholarly edition of a work, for instance of a classic, in which the existing text is thoroughly re-edited, revised and re-examined by collation with all known sources of textual emendation. *See also Redaction.*

Recess Printing. Intaglio, photogravure and other processes whereby the ink is obtained from cavities or recesses in the printing plate or cylinder.

Recommendation Card. *Synonymous with* SUGGESTION CARD (*q.v.*).

Recommended Input Standard. A standard proposed 1983 to be used by libraries in sharing bibliographic records; the Standing Group on Bibliographic Standards of the Co-operative Automation Group published the proposal, and after its good reception embarked on a programme to extend the standard to all types of library material. In addition to printed books, an enlarged standard was issued in 1985 to cover audiovisual material, music, cartographic material, and serials.

Recommending Committee. A (library) committee which recommends its proposals to the local council for approval.

RECON. Abbreviation for *remote control* or for *retrospective conversion* (e.g. of serial records to an automated form).

Record.   1. A document preserving an account of fact in permanent form, irrespective of media or characteristics.   2. The data relating to a document on which a catalogue or other entry is based.   3. (*Information retrieval*) To preserve information, typescript, or coded form.   4. A unit of information preserved in writing, typescript or coded form. A set of data elements forming a unit. Records are combined to form files.   5. In automatic data processing, a collection of related items of data, which for purpose of operating systems, is treated as representing a unit of information.   6. A GRAMOPHONE RECORD (*q.v.*).

Record Mark.   (*Information retrieval*) A character which is used to terminate each record within a machine-readable file. Also called 'Record terminator'.

Record Office.   An office in which contemporary official records concerning local government and also earlier records of all kinds relating to the respective area which have been obtained by purchase, gift, or on deposit, are preserved and made available to persons desiring to consult them. *See also County Record Office.*

Records.   All recorded information setting out facts or events, irrespective of media, characteristics or origin, which is maintained by an institution or organization in the transaction of its normal business or in pursuance of its legal obligations. Also referred to as 'Documents'. *See also Archives.*

Records Centre.   An institution or building providing accommodation for the inexpensive but efficient storage and further processing of records which are no longer frequently used but which must be preserved, and for the provision of a reference service.

Re-covering.   The process of making a new book cover and affixing it to a volume without re-sewing the sections.

Rectangular Style.   Bindings executed for Charles II while Samuel Mearne was the Royal Bookbinder. Their design consists of a simple three-line gilt rectangular panel with a crown or similar emblem at each corner. Crimson morocco was mostly used.

Recto.   1. A right-hand page of an open book or manuscript, usually bearing an odd page number. Sometimes called an uneven page.   2. The first side of a printed or ruled sheet of paper when folded and bound, as distinct from the 'verso' which is the reverse side. *See also Verso.*

Red Edges.   The edges of a book cut, coloured red, and burnished.

Red Ochre.   A powder used by type casters to coat the inner surface of their moulds when casting very small sorts to make the metal flow more easily.

Red Printing.   Printing in a second colour (usually red) for headings, capitals, etc. This is usually performed on a separate machine after the text has been printed.

Red under Gold Edges.   The three edges of a book cut, coloured red, and then gilt. *See also Edges.*

Redaction.   1. The editing, arranging, or revision for publication of a literary work which was left by the author incomplete or in a state unsuitable for publication. *See also Recension.*   2. A new, or revised, edition of a work.

Redcliffe-Maud Report. The Report *Royal Commission on local government in England, 1966–69*, 3 vols., 1969. The Royal Commission was set up in 1966 'To consider the structure of local government in England outside Greater London . . . and to make recommendations for authorities and boundaries, and for functions and their division, having regard to the size and character of areas in which these can be most effectively exercised and the need to sustain a viable system of local democracy'. Sir John Maud was nominated as chairman and was created a Life Peer in 1967 when he chose the title Baron Redcliffe-Maud. A similar Commission on local government in Scotland was appointed at the same time under the chairmanship of Lord Wheatley. Its Report *Royal Commission on local government in Scotland, 1966–69* was published in 2 vols. in 1969. *See also Library Authority, Local Government Boundaries, Maud Report.*

Reduction. 1. In documentary reproduction, a copy the scale of which is reduced compared with the ORIGINAL (*q.v.*). 2. In music, an arrangement of a musical work for a smaller group of instruments than for which it was originally written.

Reduction of Numbers. (*Classification*) Dropping by the classifier of one or more digits at the end of a notation number given in the schedules or tables. This results in a shorter number with a more inclusive meaning, and thus in broader classification. *See Broad Classification.*

Reduction of Schedules. (*Classification*) Dropping by the editors of some or all of the previous subdivisions of a number in a classification scheme with resultant classification of these concepts in a higher number. This results in notation for the topic that is one or more digits shorter than it was in the immediately preceding edition.

Redundancy. (*Information retrieval*) The use of more words or symbols than are necessary to convey a meaning (thought, word or idea). It may be planned repetition in order to overcome NOISE (*q.v.*) in the system.

Redundant Indexing. The use of more than one term, the meanings of which are not clearly distinguishable, for indexing the same information in a document.

Re-edition. A publication which is distinguished from previous editions by changes made in contents (revised edition) or layout (new edition).

Reel Fed. A printing press which prints on paper in a reel instead of single sheets.

Reel to Reel. The playback or projection from one reel or spool of film or audiotape to a separate take-up reel or spool.

Re-enlargement. An enlarged reproduction from a MICROCOPY (*q.v.*) .

'Refer from' Reference. An indication, in a list of subject headings, of the headings from which references should be made to the given heading; it is the reverse of the indication of a 'See' or 'See also' reference.

Referee. An independent expert who assists the editor of a journal in evaluating the acceptability of contributions submitted for publication.

Reference. (*Cataloguing*) 1. A direction from one heading to another. References may be *general* to indicate a class, giving an individual heading only as an example, as

ANIMALS, *see also under the names of animals as* LION.

or *specific* by stating the exact heading to which reference must be made, as ANIMALS, *see* LION.

CLEMENS, S.L., *see* TWAIN, MARK.

They may be made between (a) synonymous headings – *see* references, and (b) related headings – *see also* references.   2. A partial registry of a book, omitting the imprint and collation, under subject or title, but referring to the main entry.   3. (*Information retrieval*) An indication referring to a document or passage.   4. An indication of where to find specific information, e.g. a page, column or other part of an entry in a book index, an author's name, classification number or other IDENTIFICATION (*q.v.*), mention of a document or of information contained in a document. *See also Collateral Reference, Cross-References, Downward Reference, Upward Reference.*

Reference and Adult Services Division.   A Division of the American Library Association; it was formed in 1972 by the amalgamation of the Adult Services Division and the Reference Services Division. The goal of the Division is to stimulate and support full access to library services which are user-oriented, concentrating on identifying and evaluating media and services which meet the educational, informational, recreational, research, and social needs of library users. Publishes *RQ*(q.). Abbreviated RASD.

Reference Assistant.   An assistant librarian, working in a reference library.

Reference Books.   1. Books such as dictionaries, encyclopaedias, gazetteers, year books, directories, concordances, indexes, bibliographies and atlases, which are compiled to supply definite pieces of information of varying extent, and intended to be referred to rather than read through.   2. Books which are kept for reference only and are not allowed to be used outside the library.

Reference Card.   A catalogue card bearing a cross-reference. *See also Cross References.*

Reference Center.   In the USA, a scheme, which is stimulated through Library Service Act funds, whereby a number of small public libraries in a given geographical area contribute funds to a large library in the area having a good reference library which is willing to expand its resources and services to meet the reference and information needs of enquirers throughout the whole area. 'Information services' and 'bibliographic centres' undertake similar functions.

Reference Collection.   A collection of books which may not be borrowed for use outside the library.

Reference Department.   The department of a library containing books which may not be taken away but are for consultation in the library only.

Reference Edges.   The left-hand and bottom limits of a microfiche grid.

Reference Librarian.   A librarian in charge of, or undertaking the work of, a reference library.

Reference Library.   A library or department containing books which may not normally be used elsewhere than on the premises.

Reference Marks. 1. Printers' marks used to indicate references to other books or passages or to footnotes on the page. Where more than one reference is given on a page the order of the marks is as follows: *(asterisk or star), † (dagger or obelisk), ‡ (double dagger or double obelisk), § (section mark), ‖ (parallel mark), ¶ (paragraph mark). If more than six notes are required to a page, these signs are given first in single, then double and afterwards in treble sequence. Letter and figures in alphabetical or numerical order are more often used for the same purpose. 2. A set of suitable marks, usually fine line crosses, which provide reference points for registration in printing of art work, image location on printer-readers, etc.

Reference Material. Books and other library materials which may not be borrowed for use out of the library, either because their nature is such that they are prepared for brief consultation rather than for continuous reading, or because they belong to a reference collection from which items may not be borrowed.

Reference Matter. *See Subsidiaries.*

Reference Retrieval System. One which provides a complete reference to a document in response to a general research request. A card catalogue or other index is such a system. An aspect of INFORMATION RETRIEVAL (*q.v.*).

Reference Room. *Synonymous with* REFERENCE DEPARTMENT (*q.v.*).

Reference Service. The provision and organization by a library of REFERENCE WORK (*q.v.*).

Reference Source. Any publication which is used to obtain authoritative information.

Reference, Special and Information Section. A Group of the (British) Library Association. It was formed on 6 October 1950 and had as its objects 'to unite members engaged or interested in the work of reference and special libraries and information departments, to foster their interests within the Library Association, and to increase the usefulness of all reference and special libraries and information departments'. Abbreviated RSIS. The title of the section was changed in 1985 to the Information Services Group.

Reference Work. 1. That branch of the library's services which includes the assistance given to readers in their search for information on various subjects. 2. The work of the Reference Library. 3. A book, or work, compiled to be referred to rather than for continued reading. 4. Personal assistance given by the librarian to individual readers needing information.

References. A list of publications to which an author has made specific reference; usually placed at the end of an article or chapter, or at the end of a book, sometimes in chapter order. The entries are usually arranged in number order, corresponding numbers appearing in the text. *Also called* 'Citations'. *See also Harvard System.*

Referral Centre. An organization for directing researchers for information and data to appropriate sources such as libraries, agencies, documentation centres and individuals. A referral centre does not supply data or documents.

Reflex Copying. A process for reproducing photographically copies of documents which are opaque or printed on both sides. The light-sensitive emulsion on the paper is placed against the document: light is passed through the sensitized paper and reflected back from the light parts of the document – not from the dark or printed parts. The reversed negative which results máy then be used to print a positive by transmitted light on the same kind of paper.

Regina Medal. Established in 1959 by the (American) Catholic Library Association 'to dramatize its standards for the writing of good literature for children'. The award has been made possible through the generosity of an anonymous donor, and is given without regard to the recipient's religion, country, or birth, or the nature of the contribution (author, publisher, editor, illustrator, etc.) and in recognition of a lifetime contribution to the field of children's literature, which has been most representative of Walter de la Mare's philosophy 'Only the rarest kind of best in anything can be good enough for the young'. It was first awarded to Eleanor Farjeon.

REGIO. *See Eurostat.*

Region. *(County Libraries)* (UK) A part of the County Library area including branch libraries, centres, travelling libraries and other facilities administered from a REGIONAL HEADQUARTERS or REGIONAL BRANCH (*qq.v.*) as a library unit within the county library system.

Regional Bibliographic Center. A clearing-house for regional co-operation among library groups in the USA, locating books required and facilitating their loan between libraries, directing research workers and students requiring materials on particular subjects and possibly compiling complete or partial union catalogues.

Regional Bibliography. *See National Bibliography.*

Regional Branch. A library which, because of its larger size and greater resources, answers reference enquiries, supplies bibliographical information, display material, and books in bulk or individually, for a group of smaller libraries in a large county or urban system, as well as serving the public. Sometimes also called a 'Regional library'.

Regional Bureaux (UK). The offices which act as clearinghouses for request for particular books which are not in stock where asked for, and pass on the requests to other libraries in their own regional areas. *See Regional Library Co-operation (UK).*

Regional Catalogue. 1. A catalogue of the books in libraries situated in a given geographical region. 2. A catalogue of books relating to, or written by, people living in a given geographical region.

Regional Classification. Classification by place rather than by subject.

Regional Headquarters. Premises from which are administered the library service points in its region but at which the public may or may not be served directly. It provides the control, bookstock, postal services and other facilities which are normally available from headquarters in a centralized system. *See also Area Headquarters.*

Regional Librarian. One who is responsible for the administration of a REGIONAL BRANCH library, and also the distribution of books to service points in a REGION (*q.v.*) centred on that branch.

Regional Library. *Synonymous with* REGIONAL BRANCH (*q.v.*).

Regional Library Co-operation (UK). Ten UK regional library systems form the basis of library co-operation; the systems are North-Western; South Western; East Midlands; West Midlands; London and South Eastern (LASER *q.v.*), Northern; Yorkshire and Humberside; Scotland; Wales; and Northern Ireland. Each regional library system consists of members from all types of libraries and information services, and offers a range of co-operative services. Some systems have become involved in the VIS-COUNT project (*q.v.*); officers from the systems meet at CONARLS (*q.v.*), the Circle of Officers of National and Regional Library Systems. *See also Co-operative, Co-operative Training.*

Regional Library System. *See Regional Bureaux.*

Regional Officer. A librarian who is responsible for the development and administration of all aspects of library service throughout a REGION (*q.v.*), but not combining with this the functions of a Branch Librarian. *See also Regional Librarian.*

Register. 1. The ribbon attached to a volume to serve as a bookmarker. 2. A list of signatures attached to the end of early printed books, or printed above the colophon or on a separate leaf, for the guidance of the folder or binder. A 'registrum'. 3. In printing, a term used when the type area on the recto coincides exactly with that on the back of the verso. The adjustment of colour blocks so that the colours are superimposed with absolute accuracy. Register is of tremendous importance in multi-colour process work. When properly adjusted the work is said to be 'in register', when not, 'out of register'. 4. A catalogue or bibliography; particularly, an official list of enumeration.

Register of Electors (UK). A printed list of persons who are entitled to vote at a local government or parliamentary election. A new register is prepared each year and comes into force on 16 February. Also called 'Voters' list' and 'Electors' roll'.

Register Table. A table with an opaque-glass top and a box-like interior fitted with lights and painted white. It is used to position negatives on positives together with any accompanying type matter, on a layout sheet. It is also used for other purposes, e.g. register work in colour printing. Also called a 'Lining-up Table', 'Shining-up Table'.

Registered Reader. One who has become a member of a library, and is entitled to borrow material.

Registration. 1. The process of filing readers' application forms and making out membership tickets. This may be done at one library in a system (centralized registration) or at each library. 2. The entering of particulars of books added to a library in the ACCESSIONS REGISTER (*q.v.*).

Registration Card. A membership, or identity, card which is issued to members entitling them to use, or borrow books from, a library.

Registration Department. The unit which is concerned with maintaining records of membership and issuing membership tickets.

Registration Marks. (*Printing*) Pairs of marks, usually in the form of a cross, to show the relative position and exact orientation of two pieces of artwork that are to be superimposed in printing.

Registration Period. The period during which a REGISTERED READER (*q.v.*) is entitled to use library services before being required to re-register.

Registrum. *See Register 2.*

Reglet. A strip of wood, about the height of leads, used to separate lines of type, thus saving leads, lightening the forme and making it easier to handle. They are chiefly used in poster work. *See also Leads.*

Regnal Numbers. In Brown's classification, the first divisions of each block of numbers devoted to a country relate to the country's historical development, by reigning monarch or other ruler. These numbers provide for all royal biographies, State papers, histories and special monographs, or any event of a historical nature.

Regular Folio. *See Folio.*

Rehearsal Score. *See Score.*

Reimposition. The rearrangement of pages of type matter in a forme, consequent upon the addition of new matter to type already arranged in pages, or to the use of a different type of folding machine.

Reinforced Binding. Publisher's binding strengthened by a library bookbinder, usually by adding a cloth strip to the HINGE (*q.v.*) and resewing with strong thread.

Reinforced Union Paper. UNION PAPER (*q.v.*) which has a lining between the two sheets of which it is made, in order to increase its mechanical strength.

Reinforcing-piece. (*Binding*) The paper or parchment, on which for greater strength, the backs of some or all of the sections are sewn, and part of which shows under the paste-downs. *See also Paste-down.*

Re-issue. A re-publication at different price, or in a different form, of an impression, or edition, which has already been issued, usually from standing type or plates.

Rejection Slip. A printed acknowledgement sent out by a publisher or magazine editor, when returning a MS. to an author informing him that the MS. has not been accepted for publication.

Rejects. Copies of printed matter which are rejected by publisher or customer because of inferiorities.

Related Term. (*Information retrieval*) A term which is co-ordinate (i.e. equal in status or specificity) to another term, e.g. Blind person is related to Partially-sighted person. *See also Broader Term, Narrower Term.*

Related Title. A title which has a relationship to another by being a subsequent book in a series, or a commentary on, or a 'reply to' an earlier work. In the eighteenth century many anonymous pamphlets of this kind were published. Such books are catalogued under their title with an added entry under the title of another book included therein.

Related Work. (*Cataloguing*) A work which has some relationship to another. It may be a continuation, supplement, index, concordance, manual, sequel, scenario, choreography, libretto, special number of a serial, collection of extracts from serials, a work produced by the editorial staff of a serial, or a work in a subseries.

Relation. 1. A non-periodical pamphlet published in England and describing a battle or some other event. A forerunner of the newspaper. Also called a 'Discourse' or a 'Narration'. *See also Coranto, Newsbook.* 2. (*Information retrieval*) Relationship between two concepts or between class numbers of a classification. For different kinds of relationship, *See Equivalence, Generic-, Hierarchical-, and Semantic Relation.*

Relation Marks. Symbols used in an agreed order when building up the classification numbers of the UNIVERSAL DECIMAL CLASSIFICATION (*q.v.*) in order to separate the various parts and also to indicate their meaning.

Relational Indexing. (*Information retrieval*) In facet analysis and indexing: 1. Any system which involves a formal statement of the relationship between terms and in particular one in which complex subjects are represented by terms connected by symbols indicating their notational relations. 2. Such a system in which the structure of complex subjects is represented by the inter-position of symbols between terms to denote particular relations. The symbols are known as 'relational symbols' or 'operators'.

Relational Symbols. *See Relational Indexing.*

Relative Classification. Classification which shows, as most modern schemes do, the relationships between subjects.

Relative Index. An alphabetic index to a classification scheme in which all relationships and aspects of the subject are brought together under each index entry. An index to a scheme of classification also translates a natural language term into a class number; this it does by putting the class number after the natural language term. Such an index is provided for the Dewey Decimal Classification. *See also Specific Index.*

Relative Location. An arrangement of books according to their relation to each other and regardless of the shelves or rooms in which they are placed and allowing the insertion of new material in its proper relation to that already on the shelves. Also called 'Movable Location'. The opposite of FIXED LOCATION (*q.v.*).

Relative Relief Map. One which shows the relative height of land areas by colour or shading, but not the steepness of slope: this is shown by an AVERAGE SLOPE MAP (*q.v.*).

Relativity. That property of the index to a scheme of classification which reverses the subordination of subject to discipline, thus bringing together from all disciplines the various aspects of individual subjects.

Relator. (*Cataloguing*) A word or words in a heading indicating the relationship of the person named in the heading to the work specified in the remainder of the entry, e.g. editor, illustrator.

Relevance Ratio. In information retrieval, the number of documents which are actually wanted in proportion to the number of documents retrieved in response to a question on a given theme. *See also Recall Ratio.* Later known as PRECISION RATIO (*q.v.*).

Relevant Characteristic. *Synonymous with* 'essential characteristic'. *See Characteristic of a Classification.*

Relief. (*Binding*) Said of a finisher's tool which is made in such a way that the design, when impressed on the leather, appears in relief.

Relief Map. One which represents elevations of the earth's surface by various methods.

Relief Model. (*Cartography*) A scaled representation in three dimensions of a section of the earth's crust or of another heavenly body. Usually the vertical scale is exaggerated compared with the horizontal in order to accentuate mountains and plateaus. Known in the USA as a 'terrain model'.

Relief Printing. Printing from characters or designs that are raised above their surrounding surface, such as type, plates, etc., as distinguished from INTAGLIO PRINTING (*q.v.*). It includes woodcuts, wood engravings, zinc etchings, and half-tones.

Remainders. When books have ceased to sell well, the publisher's stock remaining is sold off by auction or at a price, to a wholesaler or bookseller. Such books are then known as remainders.

Remake. To re-page a book, either partly or completely. To re-arrange typographic elements in a page or publication.

Remarque Proof. *See Artist's Proof.*

Remote Access. A keyboard which is linked with a distant computer and is able to communicate directly with it.

Remote Terminal. A VDU or printer geographically separated from the computer which it is accessing.

Removal Slip. A card inserted in a catalogue to indicate that an entry has been removed for alteration. It bears sufficient information for the book to be identified, and indicates the whereabouts of the permanent card.

Removes. Quotations, passages or notes set, usually at the foot of a page, and in smaller type than that of the text.

Renaissance Ornament. (*Binding*) Conventional decorative ornament, apparently suggested by columns, urns, vases, beasts, birds, garlands and foliage which appear in Renaissance architecture.

Renew. To extend the period (a) for which a book or other item is on loan; (b) during which a library membership ticket is valid; (c) for supplying a periodical on subscription.

Renewal. 1. The extension of the time allowed to the same borrower for reading a book. 2. The re-registration of a reader at the expiry of a period of library membership.

Renewal Slip. A form on which is recorded information necessary to renew a loan or a membership ticket.

Repairing. The repair of a worn binding including restoring the cover and reinforcing the joints. Not to be confused with MENDING (*q.v.*).

Répertoire Internationale des Sources Musicales. *See RISM.*

Repertory Catalogue. A catalogue of books in more than one library.

Replacement. 1. A book bought to take the place of a worn-out copy of the same title. 2. The routine involved in substituting a volume for one which has been withdrawn.

Replevin. (*Archives*) 1. The recovery of property such as archives, documents, manuscripts, by an institution or organization which claims ownership. 2. The writ and legal action by which a person or institution secures such property. *See also Estray.*

Replica. A copy or reproduction of a work of art, especially one made by the artist himself, and assumed to be of equal quality to the original. A doublette. A facsimile or nearly exact copy.

Report. A publication giving a formal or official record, as of the activities of a committee or corporate body, or of some special investigation, or the proceedings of a governmental body. *See also Technical Report.*

Report Literature. A general term which includes reports of all kinds, which give the results of research or development work, and which are associated with the name of the sponsor within a numbered sequence. The publications may include technical notes and memoranda, preprints, conference proceedings and papers, research and development reports, as well as formal reports.

Reporting Committee. A (library) committee which reports its actions to the local council.

Repository. 1. A book store belonging to one library system, or a number of co-operating library systems prepared to inter-lend the books deposited therein. 2. A store for archives belonging to a RECORD OFFICE (*q.v.*).

Representative Fraction. The ratio between distance measured on a map and the corresponding distance on the ground. Thus a map on the scale 1 inch to 1 mile has a representative fraction of 1 : 63,360 there being 63,360 inches in a mile.

Reprint. 1. A copy of a book, made from the same type or stereotype as the original, with which it is identical except for possibly a new title-page and a note on the verso of the title-page of the number and date of reprinting and the correction of minor errors. *See also Edition, Facsimile Reprint, First Edition, Impression, Issue, New Edition, Revised Edition, Separate.* 2. Setting up type and printing again, using a previous printing as 'copy' as distinct from manuscript 'copy'. 3. A contribution to a periodical, afterwards issued separately, though not necessarily from the same type as the original. Sometimes called a SEPARATE (*q.v.*). 4. A British Standard (BS 4719: 1971) defines a reprint as 'All those copies of an edition reproduced at an interval after the original printing of the edition. In current practice this term is frequently preferred to impression'. In recent years, arrangements have been made between publishers to print copies of out-of-print books which are in demand, but which the original publisher does not wish to reprint himself, or by firms specializing in the reproduction of very old and/or scarce books. Photographic reproduction methods are used, and the original text remains unchanged.

Reprint Series. A series of books, which have been published previously by one or more publishers, in the same format by one publisher and bearing a series name. The books need not be related in either subject matter or treatment. *See also Publisher's Series.*

Reprinted Article. One which has been reprinted, but with its own pagination. *See also Separate.*

Reproduction Proof.   A proof copy of a work of art, photograph, tabulation, etc., of the highest quality which may be used for reproduction purposes by means of a printing block or plate.

Reprographic Marking.   The reprographic transfer of workshop drawings directly on to the materials, e.g. sheets of metal, to be fashioned.

Reprography.   The reproduction in facsimile of documents of all kinds by any process using light, heat or electric radiation – photocopies, micro-copies, blueprints, electro-copies, thermo-copies, etc.; also reproduction by methods of duplicating and office printing.

Republication.   1. The re-issuing of a publication by a publisher other than the original, without changes in the text. Sometimes used of reprints made in another country.   2. Broadly, re-issuing a work, with or without textual changes, or as a new edition.

Request Card.   *Synonymous with* SUGGESTION CARD (*q.v.*).

Request Form.   A form, or card distributed to the users of a special library to request information or material from the library. It can be so designed as to show the progress of steps taken to meet the request, record and borrowing of material from another library and record the loan of material to the user.

Requisition Card.   *Synonymous with* SUGGESTION CARD (*q.v.*).

Requisition Form.   *Synonymous with* CALL SLIP (*q.v.*).

Re-registration.   The re-registering (automatic or otherwise) of persons whose library tickets have expired.

Research and Development Report.   A document which formally states the results of, or progress made with, a research and/or development investigation, which, where appropriate, draws conclusions and makes recommendations, and which is initially submitted to the person or body for whom the work is done. A report is usually one of a series and commonly carries a report number which identifies both the report and the producing, disseminating or sponsoring organization.

Research Book.   In film studio research libraries, a scrapbook made up of sketches, abstracts, and other information relating to the settings, architecture, costumes, etc., which are gathered in advance of the production of a particular picture in order to ensure that the presentation is historically and artistically accurate.

Research Carrel.   *Synonymous with* CARREL (*q.v.*).

Research Librarian.   A title often used in respect of the librarian in a special library who undertakes the work of a RESEARCH SERVICE (*q.v.*) as distinct from one who undertakes the work normally carried out in a reference library. *See also Information Officer.*

Research Libraries Group.   *See RLG.*

Research Libraries Information Network.   *See RLIN.*

Research Library.   A library consisting of specialized documents, and providing facilities for undertaking exhaustive investigation. It may also provide referral services in support of studies in subject fields connected with development, tests, engineering and evaluation as well as research. *See also Centre, Referral Centre, University Research Library.*

Research Room. *Synonymous with* SEARCH ROOM (*q.v.*).

Research Service. A service rendered by special librarians by examining, appraising and summarizing information obtained from written sources and from individuals and organizations considered to be authorities in the appropriate fields. This implies giving the solutions to problems, providing statistics and other information as distinct from supplying publications from which the information may be obtained. The information assembled is usually presented in tabular, report or memorandum form. Also called 'Search service'. *See also Literature Search.*

Research Stall. *Synonymous with* CARREL (*q.v.*).

Research Ticket. *Synonymous with* SUPPLEMENTARY TICKET (*q.v.*).

Réseau Romand. Swiss library bibliographic network, founded 1982, with 40 members – mainly university and special libraries. Based in Lausanne; a member of REBUS (*q.v.*).

Réseau Sibil France. French library bibliographic network; founded 1987 as a part of REBUS (*q.v.*).

Reservation. A request for a specific book or other item to be reserved for a reader as soon as it becomes available on completion of processing, or on its return from the binder or another reader.

Reserve Card (Form, Slip). A card on which borrowers enter particulars of books to be retained for them when available for borrowing.

Reserve Collection. 1. Library materials for which there is infrequent demand and which consequently is not kept on open shelves, but individual items of which are obtained on request. 2. In academic libraries, material which is in great demand because of being placed on reading lists and set on one side for very short limited periods, or for an academic term, and then only for use on the premises or overnight. Also known as SHORT LOAN COLLECTION.

Reserved Book. One which after having been returned by another reader is held on payment of any necessary fee for a certain length of time at a reader's request and until he can call and collect it for home reading.

Reservoir Library. *Synonymous with* STORAGE CENTRE (*q.v.*).

Re-set Edition. One printed from newly set type but without revision of the text.

Re-setting. Setting type again, because of corrections, additions, changes of layout, etc.

Resist. A coating of glue, enamel or shellac used to protect a plate from acid corrosion during the etching process.

Resolution. 1. In documentary reproduction, the measure of the ability of an emulsion to record fine line detail or of a lens to record minute lines or points clearly, distinctly and separately. Also called 'Resolving power'. 2. In photography, a measure of the sharpness or visibility of an image; it is usually measured in line pairs per mm. 3. The measurement of the number of onscreen dots that a monitor or VDU can accommodate; the greater the number, the better the clarity of the image.

Resolving Power. *Synonymous with* RESOLUTION (*q.v.*).

Resource Centres. Collections of books and non-book materials of all kinds, which are relevant sources of information and instruction in schools, colleges and institutions of higher education. They are developments of libraries in such centres of learning.

Resources and Technical Services Division. *See Association for Library Collections and Technical Services.*

Resources Scholarship Award. An award first offered in 1976 by the Resources Section of the Resources and Technical Services Division of the American Library Association 'to honour the author or authors of a monograph, published article, or original paper on acquisitions pertaining to college and university libraries'.

'Respect des Fonds'. (*Archives*) The cardinal principle to be followed in archival arrangement, namely that the original grouping of documents must be preserved so that there shall be no impairing of their archival value and significance.

Respondent. The candidate for a degree who, in an academical disputation, defends a tenet or thesis against the objections proposed by the PRAESES (*q.v.*). The respondent is also the defendant.

Response Frame. A viewdata frame or page that enables a user to send a reply or order to an information provider.

Response Time. The time taken by the computer to respond to a command.

Restoration Style. *Synonymous with* MEARNE STYLE (*q.v.*).

Restricted Loan. A loan of library material with some form of limitation, as on period of loan, or number of volumes allowed at one time.

Ret. The second side of a sheet of paper.

Retouching. 1. Hand etching or improvements carried out to a photographic print or negative used in PROCESS ENGRAVING (*q.v.*). 2. The hand-correcting of colour separations used in the photo-engraving and photo-lithographic processes. Called 'Dot-etching' in America.

Retree. Slightly defective sheets of paper. Derived from the French *retiré*, 'withdrawn'.

Retrieval. 1. The act of finding again, recovery, retrospective searching and securing of documents. The act of going to a specific location or area and returning therefrom with an object or document. 2. The act and means of obtaining (a) facts and other information which is recorded and indexed in some way by subject, or (b) the documents containing the required facts. *See also Retrieval Device.*

Retrieval Device. A record of documents or information which is consulted in order to obtain what is needed and recorded as being in the STORE (*q.v.*). An abstracts journal, a text-book, a library catalogue, a mechanical selector or an electronic data processor used to select documentary information, are all retrieval devices.

Retrieval System. A sequence of actions which result in obtaining (retrieving) required information. The system requires such components as a SELECTOR (*q.v.*) which enables the information to be identified in the STORE (*q.v.*).

Retro-active Notation. (*Classification*) 1. A NOTATION (*q.v.*) in which FACET INDICATORS (*q.v.*) and intra-facet connectors are eliminated by using one species of characters indicating the construction of the notation (and thereby the subject matter of the material) in reverse order to the schedules. 2. A notation in which compounds are specified merely by adding earlier numbers to later ones. The notation to Dewey's Decimal Classification is of this kind, where, e.g. the form number 08 is used as a facet indicator to indicate the literary form in which a work is presented.

Retrospective Bibliography. A bibliography which lists books published in previous years as distinct from a 'current' bibliography which records books recently published. Also called 'Closed bibliography'. *See also Bibliography.*

Retrospective Conversion. (*Information retrieval*) The partial or complete conversion of an existing catalogue into machine-readable form, as opposed to converting records created currently.

Return Desk. *See Circulation Desk.*

Return Key. A key on a terminal keyboard that is used at the end of each command or entry procedure to indicate the end of inputting. Use of this key causes the computer to accept the input and make a response.

Returns. Unsold publications which are returned by a bookseller to the publisher. Also called 'Crabs'.

Re-use of Numbers. (*Classification*) A total change in the meaning of a given number as between one edition and another.

rev. Abbreviation for revise, revised, revision. *See also Revised Edition.*

Reveal. A facility in a viewdata system to display on the screen information previously excluded, for example answers to jokes or quiz questions.

Revenue Stamps. Stamps which were stuck on English newspapers in accordance with the Stamp Act, 1712. The paper had to be stamped before printing. The duty was the same irrespective of the size of the newspaper, and the Act, which was repealed in 1855, consequently had the effect of increasing the size of newspapers.

Reversal Process. Developing in such a manner that the material exposed in the camera shows a positive instead of a negative image. The reversal process is used extensively in colour photography, and for producing duplicate negatives.

Reverse Browne. A method of issuing books which is similar to the BROWNE BOOK CHARGING SYSTEM (*q.v.*) but which uses a pocket book-card and a card ticket.

Reverse Cover. The lower cover of a book, i.e. that nearest to the last leaf. Also called 'Back cover', 'Lower cover'. *See also Obverse Cover.*

Reverse Left to Right. (*Printing*) To reverse a design, etc., so that it prints as if a mirror image.

Reverse Out. (*Printing*) When making a plate or block, reversing black to white so that the final appearance of the print is of white printed on black (or another colour) instead of the normal black on white.

Review. 1. A periodical publication which is devoted largely to critical articles and reviews of new books. 2. An evaluation of a literary work published in a periodical or newspaper. *See also Omnibus Review.*

Review Copy. A copy of a book sent by the publisher to a newspaper or magazine for the favour of a review. Sometimes called 'Press copy'.

Revise. *See Proof.*

Revised Edition. A new edition of a book in which errors have been corrected, and possibly new material added. Sometimes wrongly called 'Enlarged edition'. *See also Edition, First Edition, Impression, Issue, New Edition, Reprint.*

Revised Proof. *See Proof.*

Revising Shelves. *Synonymous with* READING SHELVES (*q.v.*).

Revolving Bookcase. One having shelves on four or more sides; built around a central cylinder it rotates in either direction on a spindle.

Rhondda (Margaret) Award. A triennial award of the SOCIETY OF AUTHORS (*q.v.*) given to a woman journalist to fund research.

Rhys (John Llewellyn) Memorial Prize. An annual award administered by the Book Trust, and offered to a young UK writer, poet or dramatist.

Ribbon Arrangement. A method of arranging books in a public library with non-fiction on upper shelves and novels on lower shelves, or vice versa, or novels on middle shelves and non-fiction above and below, the object being to disperse the readers around the library and avoid congestion at the fiction shelves.

Rice Paper. Paper made from the pith of a small tree, *Aralia* (also *Fatsia*) *papyrifera*, grown in Taiwan.

Rider. An additional MS. added to a proof.

Rider Slip. *Synonymous with* PROCESS SLIP (*q.v.*).

Ridge. One of the two projections along the sides of a rounded and backed volume against which the board is fitted. Also called 'Flange' or 'Shoulder'. (American). *See also Binding Edge.*

Right. The printer often needs to know which is the right side of a sheet of paper owing to differences in surface, and the undesirable effect of using sheets laid one way mixed with those laid another way in the publication. Flat papers are usually packed with the right side uppermost; if folded, the right side is outside. In handmade papers, the right side touches the wire cover of the mould; the 'wire' side is therefore known as the right side. In blue and azure papers the right side is usually darker than the other. In machine-made papers, it is the upper side which is the right side, i.e. the one on which the couch roll acts and not the wire. A WATERMARK (*q.v.*), in both hand-made and machine-made paper is read from the right side. Thus, it can be taken that in hand-made papers, the 'wire' side is the right side, but in machine-made papers this is the wrong side.

Right Reading. (*Reprography*) An image which is legible in a normal reading position as opposed to being a mirror image, i.e. LATERALLY REVERSED (*q.v.*).

Right to Read. A programme inspired, introduced in the early 1970s and organized by Dr. Ruth Love Holloway in the USA with the object of eliminating illiteracy. It has been implemented by the public school systems in over forty states. Parents are admitted to classrooms as ancillary teachers, and help in the teaching of reading and writing.

Rights. The privileges of entitlement to permit the publication, performance, or adaptation of authorship and receive payment for same. *Volume rights* give the publisher 'the exclusive rights to publish a work in volume form' within the territorial area for which he makes himself responsible. These include the right to reprint in paperback form, in book club or school editions, or to negotiate these on behalf of the author. Digest rights, ONE SHOT (*q.v.*) rights and anthology rights – are also included. *Subsidiary rights* include foreign publication, and film, TV, translation, serial, dramatic and mechanical reproduction rights; these may or may not be handled by the original publisher of the work.

Rigid Classification. 1. The classification of books relative to their positions on shelves rather than according to a scheme of book classification. Such methods of classification were used before the formation of modern schemes of bibliographical classification, and resulted in the allocation of numbers to books according to the shelf, in a given tier of a particular press, or alcove, in a specific room. Another form of rigid classification is the arrangement of books in broad subjects according to size and accession number. 2. The characterization of each document from a single point of view and thereby the allocation of only one classification symbol to it. When a document is shelved or stored, and only one copy is available, one single physical location must be provided: this is indicated by a symbol representing one point of view, usually the most important, or major, one. Sometimes called a 'Pigeonhole classification'. *See also Multi-dimensional Classification.*

RIN File. *See PRECIS Vocabulary Fiche.*

RIP. Rest in Proportion; an instruction in reprography or printing to enlarge or reduce material by an agreed amount.

Rising Space. *Synonymous with* WORK UP (*q.v.*).

Rising Type. Type which rises up in the forme, usually in the centre, when locked up too tightly. Spaces and quads rise and print due to poor justification or loose lock-up.

RISM. Acronym for Répertoire Internationale des Sources Musicales; published under the auspices of the International Musicological Society, and the International Association of Music Libraries. Aims to list all available bibliographies of musical works, writings about music and textbooks on music published up to 1800, with locations. Publication started 1960, and eventually 30 volumes are envisaged. Series 'A' (currently nine volumes) covers composers; series 'B' (currently 11 volumes) covers subjects and forms. Series 'C' consists of a *Directory of music research libraries*: planned as six volumes of which four have appeared to date.

River. What appears to be a streak of white running vertically or diagonally through printed matter. It is caused by spaces between words occurring almost one below the other in several lines of type. Rivers are avoided by re-setting the type and varying the spacing or placing a very short word on a line above or below.

RLG. Acronym of the Research Libraries Group, Inc., a consortium of major universities and research institutions in the United States. 96 members (early 1989) collaborate in operating a set of ongoing programs and developing new initiatives to enhance access to research information. RLGs programs and technical resources focus on collecting, organizing, preserving, and providing information necessary to education and scholarship. RLGs automated information system, RLIN, combines data bases and computer systems to support the partnership's co-operative programs. RLIN is a nationwide network, serving the materials processing and public services requirements of RLG's members and many non-member institutions. Headquarters moved 1989 from Stanford to Mountain View, California. Special programmes include: archives, manuscripts and special collections; art and architecture; East Asia studies; Hebrew and Middle Eastern studies; law, medical and health sciences; information management; music. Issues *RLG News*.

RLG Conspectus. *See Conspectus.*

RLIN. Research Libraries Information Network formed by RLG (*q.v.*) members in 1974 and originally an outgrowth of BALLOTS (*q.v.*). RLIN is now used by over 400 libraries, and contains records for over 35 million items.

Roan. A thin sheepskin used for binding books.

Roberts Report. Popular name for the Report of the 'Roberts Committee' which was set up by the Minister of Education in September 1957 under the chairmanship of Sir Sydney Roberts, 'to consider the structure of the Public Library Service in England and Wales, and to advise what changes, if any, should be made in the administrative arrangements, regard being had to the relation of public libraries to other libraries'. The Report is entitled *The Structure of the Public Library Service in England and Wales*, 1959. Cmnd. 660. This Report resulted in the setting up of working parties by the Minister of Education in 1961. *See also Baker Report, Bourdillon Report.*

Robinson Medal (UK). Awarded for firms and individuals – librarians or not – for originality shown in devising new and improved methods in library technology and any aspect of library administration. Funds for the award come from a bequest by the late Frederick Robinson, formerly Deputy Librarian at Colchester who left to the Library Association a trust fund from the proceeds of which a Medal and prize are awarded every two years.

Role Directors. *See Roles.*

Role Factors. *See Roles.*

Role Indicators. *See Roles.*

Roles. In CO-ORDINATE INDEXING (*q.v.*), generally but not necessarily, symbols appended to terms or term numbers and thereby narrowing the definition of the terms by designating the role of a word in its context. They describe the use of a term in its context, not how terms are related. Also called 'Modifiers', 'Modulants', 'Role Factors', 'Role directors', 'Role indicators', 'Scope notes'.

Roll. 1. A bookbinder's tool consisting of a brass wheel about 3 inches in diameter secured in a long handle which rests against the shoulder when being used. The edge of the wheel is engraved so as to impress a continuous line or repeating pattern as it revolves under pressure. Also called 'Fillet'. 2. The design impressed by the tool referred to. *See also Scroll, Tooling.*

Roll Cassette. A light-proof container for roll film on a spool. Also called a 'Roll magazine'.

Roll Magazine. *Synonymous with* ROLL CASSETTE (*q.v.*).

Roll Microfilm. Microcopies on roll film as distinct from those on sheet microfilm, as MICROFICHE (*q.v.*).

Rolled Edges. Edges of book covers decorated with a roll, or 'roulette', a finishing tool having a brass wheel with a design on its rim.

Roller Shelves. Deep shelves which rest on a series of rollers or ball bearings and are drawn out so that folio volumes such as bound volumes of newspapers can be lifted off instead of being dragged off with possible damage to the binding. Also a series of rollers placed horizontally behind one another and which support large books; they revolve on their spindles as the volumes are pushed on and off.

Rolling Bookcase. A metal bookcase secured to a framework on wheels, which runs on metal rails or wheels, and placed as close as possible to others side by side, so as to permit maximum storage in a book stack. The bookcases are rolled from one position to another to permit access to the books. *See also Compact Storage.*

Rolling Press. 1. A bookcase suspended from overhead tracks or running on rails let into the floor enabling cases to be placed very close together and pulled out to permit consultation of the books. 2. A hand press, for printing from incised or etched plates. Power is applied by passing the plate and paper, covered by thick blankets, between oak rollers held in a rigid frame. The upper roller which is turned by a capstan, carries the plate through the press.

Rom. Abbreviation for ROMAN (*q.v.*).

ROM. Acronym for Read-Only Memory; a computer memory facility from which data can be retrieved, but which cannot be altered or up-dated. *See also CD-ROM.*

Romains du Roi. A series of roman and italic types made for use in the Royal Printing Office of Louis XIV in the Palace of the Louvre, Paris, between 1694 and 1745. They were based on drawings which accompanied a report made to Louis XIV, and are characterized by being condensed letters with thin, flat, unbracketed serifs. Designed by Philippe Grandjean, they were first used in 1742 for *Médailles sur la événements du règne de Louis-le-Grand.*

Roman. Ordinary type as distinct from italic, being vertical instead of sloping and having graduated thick and thin strokes and serifs. It is based on the Italian Humanistic or Neo-Caroline hand of the fifteenth century and was first used by Adolf Rusch in Strasbourg in 1464, and perfected by Johannes da Spira, a German who used roman type for the first book to be printed in Venice, in 1469, and by Nicholas Jenson, a Frenchman, also in Venice, 1470. The use of roman types was greatly expanded in Italy in the last quarter of the fifteenth century; they may be divided into three main groups, VENETIAN TYPE, OLD FACE and MODERN FACE (*qq.v.*). Written in full, or in its abbreviated form 'Rom', the word 'Roman' is used on printer's copy or on a proof to indicate that the matter is to be set up in Roman, i.e. not italic type. *See also Antiqua, Egyptian, Italic, Roman Numerals, Transitional, Type Face.*

Roman à clef. A novel in which one or more characters are based on real people but are given fictitious names.

Roman Index. *See Index Librorum Prohibitorum.*

Roman Numerals. Capital letters which are used as numbers in books for chapter headings and for the designation of part numbers, appendixes, on title-pages for date of publication, etc., and in lower-case form for the pagination of preliminary pages. The roman capitals most commonly in use as numerals are:

1	5	10	50	100	500	1000
I	V	X	L	C	D	M

A complete sequence to 20 in capitals is: I, II, III, IV, V, VI, VII, VIII, IX, X, XI, XII, XIII, XIV, XV, XVI, XVII, XVIII, XIX, XX, and in tens from 30 to 100: XXX, XL, L, LX, LXX, LXXX, XC, C. The numerals from x to xx indicate the method of building numbers. Italic figures 1 to 20 are: *i, ii, iii, iv, v, vi, vii, viii, ix, x, xi, xii, xiii, xiv, xv, xvi, xviii, xix, xx*. Combinations of numbers are made up by addition and subtraction, e.g. XX = 20; XIX = 19; XXIV = 24; MCMLVII = 1957. 1000 was first represented by the Greek letter, *phi* ɸ, which in lettering and in architectural inscription became CIↃ; this soon became M. 500 was half a *phi* a IↃ, and soon became D. 100 was represented by the symbol θ (*theta*) which became ϵ then C, and 50 by the Chalcidian form of the letter *chi* χ which became ⊥ and later L. The following table includes most of the known numerals.

B	300	IↃↃ	5000
C	100	L	50
CIↃ	1000	M	1000
CIↃCIↃ	2000	N	900
D	500	Q	500
E	250	R	80
F	40	T	160
G	400	V	5
H	200	X	10
I	1	χ	1000
IↃ	500	∞	1000

A bar or dash placed over a letter increases its value a thousand times. Roman numerals were used by the earliest fifteenth-century printers because they had no arabic figures, and were normally used in early printed books. *See also Chronogram.*

Romanization. The representation of 'picture writing' characters, such as Chinese, Japanese and Korean in the Roman alphabet. *See also Transliteration.*

Romantic Novelists' Association. *See Muskett (Netta) Award.*

Romantic Style. A bookbinding decoration with an informal, non-classical style in which fancy predominates.

Ronde. An upright angular form of script type. Being based on French manuscript it has the appearance of upright handwriting.

Root Thesaurus. Published in 1981 by the British Standards Institution the *Root Thesaurus* was designed to be used as a basic indexing tool and act as a guide to technical terminology. Being computer-generated, this faceted thesaurus is easy to update and manipulate and makes possible the production of thesauri on specialized topics by searching the main file. The thesaurus itself consists of a subject display and a complete alphabetical list of subject terms. Terms in the alphabetical list are linked to the subject display by means of an alphabetical notation. Each entry in the subject display contains descriptors, synonyms, related narrower and broader terms, non-preferred terms and notes which outline the scope of each term. The use of a subject display allows an identical layout when terms are translated into a foreign language. A second edition appeared in 1985.

Rotaprint. An offset lithographic printing and duplicating machine made by the Rotaprint Co.

Rotary Camera. *Synonymous with* CONTINUOUS FLOW CAMERA (*q.v.*).

Rotary Card File. A filing cabinet in which cards are placed on their edges in a wheel- or drum-like container. The container revolves on an axle in the side of the drum in such a way that the cards are always on their edges, those in the lower half being prevented from falling out by a fixed retaining strap of webbing or other material. Up to four containers may be placed side by side in a cabinet. Another type consists of large round trays which revolve on a pivot, each tray being divided up so as to provide several rows of cards side by side. Each fitting or cabinet will hold up to five such trays one above another.

Rotary Gravure. *Synonymous with* ROTOGRAVURE (*q.v.*).

Rotary Press. A style of press that prints from curved electrotype or stereotype plates held on a cylinder, the paper being fed from a continuous roll and passing between this cylinder and another one which makes the impression. It is used for printing newspapers, periodicals or large editions and occasionally for books of a large run. There are also 'sheet-fed rotary presses'. All printing presses are rotary in principle except the flat-bed press and the platen press which are largely used in letterpress work. Where printing is done from the original flat forme on an endless web of paper, this is called a 'flat-bed web press'. Also called a 'Web press' when the paper is fed from a continuous reel. *See also Cylinder Press, Flat-Bed Press, Platen Press.*

Rotated Catalogue. A classified catalogue in which entries are made under each integral part of the classification symbol, instead of making an entry under the class number with merely references from headings or parts comprising the composite symbol. Also called 'Cyclic classified catalogue'.

Rotated Entry. An entry in an index to documents, or a classified catalogue, where full information and not merely a reference is given under each heading.

Rotated Index. An index to a catalogue of documents classified by a faceted classification whereby entries are made under every heading and inverted heading which comprises part of the classification symbol. Also called 'Cyclic index'.

Rotated Indexing. The indexing of documents classified by a faceted classification whereby a full entry, and not a reference, is made under each heading representing, or being, a part of the classification symbol. Also called 'Cyclic indexing'.

Rotational Indexing. The making of a CORRELATIVE INDEX (*q.v.*) wherein each term is 'rotated' so as to file in the first position.

ROTNAC. *See Round Table of National Centres for Library Services.*

Rotogravure. 1. An intaglio or photogravure printing process for rotary presses, in which the impression is obtained from an etching made on a copper cylinder which is automatically inked as it revolves. 2. An illustration produced by this process.

Rotunda. *See Gothic Type.*

Rough. Rag paper that has not been given a finish. *See also Finish, Hot-Pressed, Not.*

Rough Calf. A calf skin prepared with a nap similar to suede leather; used for bookbinding from the seventeenth century.

Rough Edges. A widely used term to indicate paper with rough edges whether because they are UNCUT (*q.v.*) or a result of the way the paper was made. *See also Deckle Edge.*

Rough Gilt Edges. A book which has been 'cut rough' and the edges gilded, or which has been cut solid and gilded before sewing so that when the book is later sewn the edges are slightly uneven. This method has been widely used by English binders, specially by non-trade binders who dislike the solid-block-of-metal appearance of solid gilding. *See also Gilt on the Rough, Marbling Under Gilt, Solid Gilt.*

Rough Pull. *Synonymous with FLAT PULL (q.v.).*

Roulette. *Synonymous with FILLET (q.v.).*

Round Back. 1. The back of a thin booklet of which the folded sheets have been inserted inside each other and wire-stitched, sewn, or corded to the cover from the centre. 2. A book which has been rounded during the binding process and so given the familiar round back. The opposite of 'Flat back'. *See also Backing, Flat Back, Rounding.*

Round Brackets. *Synonymous with PARENTHESES (q.v.).*

Round Letter. *See Antiqua.*

Round Table. A group of members of an organization having a similar area of interest. Round Tables are opportunities for informal meetings and discussions and are unlikely to be an administrative part of the parent body.

Round Table of National Centres for Library Services.   An IFLA group, for co-operative organizations serving a range of libraries in individual countries and termed for this purpose 'NATIONAL CENTRES' (*q.v.*). Abbreviated ROTNAC.

Rounded Corners.   In library bookbinding the sharp corners of the boards are sometimes cut and slightly rounded as a preventative against wear.

Roundel.   (*Binding*) A decoration consisting of a double ring, usually with a centre dot.

Rounding.   The bookbinding process which gives the book a convex spine – and consequently concave fore-edges. It is achieved by a forwarder hammering the spine of a book, after it has been sewn and had its first coat of glue, with a round-headed hammer while gripped between backing boards at the same time as the book is backed. This operation can be done by machine. In Britain and America books are backed (to provide joints) as well as rounded. In most European countries backing is seldom done, with the result that there are no joints. *See also Backing, Flat Back, Round Back.*

Roundlet.   A small circle in gold used by bookbind:rs' finishers as part of a book's decoration.

Routeing.   The systematic circulation of periodicals or other printed material among the staff or officers of a library or organization in accordance with their interests in order to keep them informed of new developments. *Automatic routeing* is the sending of each issue as soon as it is received to a pre-arranged list of persons. *Selective routeing*, or *selective circulation*, is sending articles and publications individually selected by a reader on the basis of an individual's known interests to the individual, usually with an ATTENTION NOTE (*q.v.*). *Circular routeing* (also called *uncontrolled circulation*) is the sending of a periodical to all who need it before it is returned to the library: this is achieved by sticking to the cover a slip with the names of persons and/or departments for rapid perusal; such slips may bear a space for the insertion of the date of onward transmission. *Radial routeing* (also called *controlled circulation*) ensures that the periodical is returned to the library by each reader before it is passed on to another reader. This method enables the librarian to keep better control of loans. *See also Routeing Slip, Selective Routeing.*

Routeing Slip.   A slip pasted on to the cover of a periodical and bearing the names of the persons (possibly with space for dates of sending) to whom it is to go. *See also Attention Note, Routeing.*

Routine.   (*Information retrieval*) A set of coded instructions arranged in proper sequence in order to direct the computer to perform a desired operation or sequence of operations. A sub-division of a program consisting of two or more instructions that are related functionally – for this reason, a PROGRAM (*q.v.*).

Routine Slip.   *Synonymous with* PROCESS SLIP (*q.v.*).

Routing.   (*Printing*) Cutting away mechanically the non-printing areas of a half-tone or line block.

Rowe Memorial Award, John R.   The new name of the EXHIBITS ROUND TABLE AWARD (*q.v.*).

Roxburghe Binding. A book with plain black leather back, without raised bands, lettered in gold near the top within a border, having cloth or paper sides, and leaves gilt at top otherwise untrimmed. So named after the third Duke of Roxburghe (Scotland), a famous book collector who adopted this style for the books in his library.

Royal. A sheet of printing paper measuring 20 × 25 inches.

Royal Commission on Historical Manuscripts. *See Historical Manuscripts Commission.*

Royalty. Payment made to an author by the publisher of a book, the basis being calculated as an agreed percentage of the retail price of the book, and paid in respect of every copy of the book sold.

R.P. Indicates that a book is not available from the publisher but is 'reprinting'. If R.P. is followed by a date as 'R.P. Jan.' it indicates when a reprint will be ready.

RSIS. REFERENCE, SPECIAL AND INFORMATION SECTION (*q.v.*) of the Library Association.

RTSD. Resources and Technical Services Division (of the American Library Association). *See now Association for Library Collections and Technical Services.*

Rub. A representation of the back or sides of a book showing the lettering bands, decoration, etc. It is done by firmly holding a piece of paper or tracing linen over the part of the binding of which an impression is to be made, and rubbing with a cobbler's heel-ball, lead pencil or soft crayon all over it until a recognizable copy of all details of the back or sides of the volume is obtained often used as a master pattern in journal binding.

Rub-off. Printing ink which has rubbed on to the fingers from a printed sheet which has not dried sufficiently.

Rubber Back Binding. A binding in which the folds of the sections are cut off and the spine dipped in rubber solution before insertion in the cover.

Rubbing. *See Rub.*

Rubric. 1. The heading of a chapter, section or other division of a book, and catchwords or marginal index words printed or written in red (the remainder of the text being in black), or otherwise distinguished in lettering, as a guide to the contents of pages. 2. A particular passage so marked.

Rubricated. A book in which rubrics have been used.

Rubrication. 1. Underlining in red the filing entries on the tracings on standard printed catalogue cards or slips. Sometimes a red diagonal line leads from the upper-left-hand corner to lead the eye to the underlining. 2. The carrying out of rubrics.

Rubrisher. One who carried out rubrication, or the plain painting of the large initial letters at the commencement of chapters of MSS. or early printed books, in red and blue. *See also Rubric.*

Rule. A strip of metal used to print lines; it is of type height of varying thickness (hair, fine, medium, 1½, 3, 4, 6, 12 point) with a face finished to a continuous line or lines. Rules which are placed at right angles to form frames or borders are said to be abutted or mitred according to whether the ends of the rule are square or mitred at an angle of 45°. A rule may also be designed to print dots or patterns. A SWELLED RULE is a line which is wide in the middle and tapers to a fine point at each end. *See also Dotted Rule, Double Rule.*

Rule Border.   (*Printing*) A frame, made up of rules, fitted around a page of type. Also called 'Rule frame'. *See also Box.*

Rule Frame.   *Synonymous with* RULE BORDER (*q.v.*).

Run.   A machinist's term for a number of impressions taken from a forme, or plate, at one time. On completion, the job is said to be 'run-off'.

Run-around.   Variation of length of lines of type to fit around blocks.

Run On.   1. A term, used in manuscripts and proof reading, to indicate to the printer that printed matter must be continuous and not broken up into paragraphs. This indication is marked by a line joining the end of one piece of matter to the beginning of the next and the writing of 'run on' in the margin.   2. To let a printing press continue to print sheets after the printing order has been completed. Sheets so printed 'run on cost' and involve little more than charges for paper and machine time.

Run-on Card.   A catalogue card which bears the continuation of an entry on the previous card. The heading is usually repeated on successive cards which are numbered 'Card 1', 'Card 2', etc. Also called 'Extension card'.

Run-on Chapters.   Chapters which do not start on a new page but run on at the end of the previous chapter. This is a style used in cheap bookwork.

Run-on Style.   In book indexes, the typographical style which allows the subheadings to be printed continuously (with their relative page references) instead of being arranged under one another, and indented, under the heading to which they relate. Called in America 'Run-in Style'. *See also Indented Style.*

Run Out and Indented.   A style of typesetting where the first line is set to the full measure, and the second and subsequent lines of the paragraph are indented.

Run Over.   The continuation of matter on to another page.

Run-up Gilt Book.   In EXTRA BINDING (*q.v.*), used to describe the running of gold lines by a fillet so that the gilt panel lines are not mitred at each band. *See also Bands.*

Runciman Award.   An annual prize offered by the Anglo-Hellenic League and administered by the Book Trust, for a literary work about Greece.

Runes.   1. The earliest Scandinavian and Anglo-Saxon alphabet. Some letter forms continued in use in English documents until the seventeenth century and even later. A notable example is the 'y' form th, which has given rise to the psuedo-archaic form 'ye' for 'the'.   2. The name given to the characters which were cut or carved on metal, stone or wood by the ancient Teutons, usually as memorial inscriptions, but also for divination and for messages, and for carving the name of the artist or for the owner of weapons or ornaments. Runic characters were used for secular documents; amongst the more important runic manuscripts are: the old Danish legal MS., *Codex Runicus* (end 13th century), *Fasti Danici* (*c.* 1348), *Codex Leidensis* at Leyden, the *Codex Sangallensis* (878) at St. Gallen, and the *Codex Salisbur-*

gensis (140). The Runic alphabet is also known as 'Futhark', from the sequence of its first seven letters.

Runic Letters.   The 'national' writing of the ancient Germanic peoples; the characters have thorny, elongated and angular shapes.

Runners.   Figures or letters printed for reference purposes at regular intervals down the margins of a book and against lines of type to indicate the particular number or position of any given line. This is usually done in long poems or in school texts of plays or of texts in foreign languages.

Running Headline (Running Head).   *Synonymous with* RUNNING TITLE (*q.v.*).

Running Number.   One, such as an accession number, which is given from a consecutive sequence to a book or other object.

Running Title.   The title that runs through a book or section of a book, repeated at the head of each page or at the top of the left-hand pages, with the chapter heading or the subject contents of both open pages on the right-hand page. Also called a 'Running head'. *See also Drop-Down Title, Headline, Page Headline, Section Headline.*

Russell Committee (UK).   The Committee of Inquiry appointed in February 1969 by the Secretary of State for Education and Science 'to assess the need for and to review the provision of non-vocational adult education in England and Wales; to consider the appropriateness of existing educational, administrative and financial policies; and to make recommendations . . .' The Committee is named after its Chairman, Sir E. Lionel Russell. The Committee's Report, *Adult education: a plan for development*, was published in 1973.

Russia.   A variety of calf leather used for bookbinding. It is specially tanned, and finished with birch oil which gives it a characteristic spicy odour. 'American Russia' is cowhide.

Rustic Capital.   1. An upper case letter with a design engraved on the face, or an ornamentally designed letter.   2. The form of roman capital letters used by early scribes as a book hand between the second and sixth centuries A.D. The letters were less formal and not so heavy as the QUADRATA or SQUARE CAPITALS (*q.v.*) from which they were derived, giving a thinner, and more condensed appearance to the page. Also called 'Scriptura actuaria'.

Rustica.   A freely-written, rather elegant fourth- and fifth-century writing used in Roman manuscripts. This style seems to have been influenced by Greek artistry and craftsmanship; it was displaced as a manuscript letter by the UNCIAL (*q.v.*), but used as initials or for emphasis in the line, in the same way that italics or small capitals are used by modern printers, in manuscripts until the eleventh century.

Ruthven Press.   An iron printing press, patented in 1813 by John Ruthven, an Edinburgh printer. In this, the bed which carried the type remained stationary while the platen was moved over it on a wheeled carriage. Springs kept the platen raised until the moment of impression, when power was applied through a series of levers which were worked by depressing a bar at the side of the press. It was not popular with the trade.

Rutland. Trade name for a fine-quality sheepskin used for bookbinding.

Ruttier. *See Portolan.*

Rylands Library, Manchester, John. *See John Rylands University Library of Manchester.*

s.a. Abbreviation for *see also* (*q.v.*).

SAA. Society of American Archivists (*q.v.*)

SAALIC (UK). Abbreviation for Swindon Area Association of Libraries for Industry and Commerce, formed in 1961 and based on the Divisional Library, Swindon, Wilts. The scheme arranges the inter-loan of books and periodicals, and the co-operative filing of periodicals, and deals with requests for information. There are no membership limitations.

SAB. Sveriges Allmänna Biblioteksförening. *See Swedish Library Association.*

Sacred Work. A basic writing of a religion, such as the *Bible, Koran, Talmud, Upanishads, etc.,* which is generally accepted as such by those who follow that religion. In classification, it is often treated as if it were a class or a subject.

Saddle Stitching. Binding a pamphlet by placing it on the saddle-shaped support of a stitching machine where it is automatically stitched with wire or thread through the centre of the fold. *See also Flat Stitching, Side-stitch.*

SALALM. Acronym for Seminars on the Acquisition of Latin American Library Materials. The first Seminar was held in 1956 'to consider the problems involved in finding, buying and controlling library materials relating to Latin America'. A Seminar has been held each year since. Publishes *SALALM Newsletter* (2 p.a.), reports and bibliographies. *See also LACAP.*

Salle. A well-lit room in a paper-mill where the paper is examined sheet by sheet, sorted, counted and arranged in reams. Also called 'Finishing house' or 'Finishing room' in a machine paper mill.

Sampleback. A strip of leather, cloth or other material made up to represent the back of a book and used as a sample for matching colour, material, lettering, etc.

Sample Pages. Selected pages of a proposed book, set by the printer as a specimen and model for the whole book.

Sanding. Rubbing down the edges of a book with sand-paper, or a sand-wheel machine, so as to remove as small an amount of paper as possible.

Sans Serif. A type face without SERIFS (*q.v.*). The best known is 'Gill Sans' designed by Eric Gill; other well-known sans serif types are Futura and Vogue. The first sans serif type, designed by William Caslon, was named Egyptian; it was afterwards re-named Sanserif.

Sarah Josepha Hale Award. *See Hale Award, Sarah Josepha.*

SARBICA. Acronym for South-East Asian Regional Branch of the International Council on Archives; it was inaugurated in Kuala Lumpur in July 1968 as the first branch of the INTERNATIONAL COUNCIL ON ARCHIVES (*q.v.*). Its membership comprises the national archival institutions of six SEA countries (Indonesia, Malaysia, the Philippines, Singapore, Thailand, and

Viet-Nam). The Secretariat is provided by the National Archives of Malaysia, Pataling Jaya. Publishes *Southeast Asian Archives* (a.).

Sarum Use. In the fifteenth century, certain Parisian presses specialized in books of Hours of the Virgin (the layman's prayer book) which were similar in format but differed slightly according to the locality in which they were to be used. To prevent the printer and binder mixing the various editions, abbreviations such as 'Sar' for 'secundum usum Sarum' or 'Par' for 'secundum usum ecclesiae Parisiensis' were placed after the signature letter. The version used mostly in England, particularly in the southern part, and in Scotland, was that of Salisbury or 'Sarum', the York use being confined to the north. Their use was discontinued after the Reformation. Sarum books were largely produced in Paris and Rouen.

SASLIC (UK). Abbreviation for Surrey and Sussex Libraries in Co-operation, an organization which came into being formally in July 1969 following a year of preparatory investigation inspired by the Report of the Scientific Library Services Committee of the Library Association in 1968. The area covered comprises the counties of Surrey, East Sussex and West Sussex. Its aims are 'to improve library resources and information services in science, technology, commerce and related subjects, by co-operative action, and to implement such recommendations of the Report mentioned "as will contribute to that end".' Membership subscriptions, training course fees, and the proceeds from the sale of publications are the only sources of income. Over sixty public library authorities, academic institutions, and special libraries of all kinds are in membership. Publishes *SASLIC Newsletter* (irreg.).

SATCOM. Abbreviation for the Committee on Scientific and Technical Communication which was set up in March 1966 at the suggestion of COSATI (*q.v.*) by the large US learned academies, the National Academy of Sciences and the National Academy of Engineering, the object of which is to provide a focus for participation by scientists and engineers, through their societies, in planning a national network of information systems.

Satellite Broadcasting. A system of telecommunications based on transmission of data, information, or entertainment material from orbiting satellites. In the UK in 1988 and 1989 several commercial channels began transmission; the library relevance of satellite services lies mainly in off-air recording for subsequent use mainly in the educational context. The OLYMPUS (*q.v.*) project is an interesting educational experiment which may increase relevant activity. As an alternative to CABLE SYSTEMS (*q.v.*) satellites can also be used for a range of telecommunication services at a local, regional, national or international level.

Satellite Television. *See Satellite Broadcasting.*

SATIS. 1. Acronym for Socially Appropriate Technology Information System. A clearing house for information and referral in the fields of alternative and appropriate technology. Set up in 1982 by 25 organizations mainly from the non-government sector. Functions internationally; secretariat in Amsterdam. 2. A semi-commercial information search and delivery service operated by the National Library of New Zealand. Offices in

Auckland, Wellington, Christchurch and Dunedin. The acronym stands for Scientific and Technical Information Service, and has developed from a service based in Auckland and started in 1968.

Saunders Report. *Towards a unified professional organisation for library and information science and services*; prepared by Professor Wilfred Saunders and published by the (UK) Library Association in 1989. The report urges the merger of the Library Association, Aslib and the Institute of Information Scientists. It was received positively by all the bodies concerned, and during 1990 representatives have been meeting to plan possible implementation.

Sawcuts. Grooves made in the back of a book with a saw to take the cords used in sewing.

Sawing-in. Sawing grooves in the back of a book for the reception of the cord in sewing.

Sayers Memorial Prize (UK). This Prize takes the form of professional books, and was created from the royalties of the *Sayers memorial volume*, and donated by the editors D. J. Foskett and B. I. Palmer. The volume was produced as a tribute to the late W. C. Berwick Sayers, Chief Librarian of the Croydon Public Libraries for many years, a former President of the Library Association, and particularly noted for his teaching and writing on classification. The Prize is awarded to the candidate gaining the highest mark in classification in the Final Examination of the Library Association. It was first awarded in 1965 to Henry Gilby.

SBN. Acronym for STANDARD BOOK NUMBER (*q.v.*).

SBN. (Italian) National Library Service; projected bibliographic network of the Central Institute for the Union Catalogue of Italian Libraries, Rome. Expects to start in 1990 with 75 members.

SBN Agency. *See Standard Book Numbering Agency.*

s.c. Abbreviation for (1) small capitals; (2) super-calendered paper.

sc. Abbreviation for *scilicet* (*Lat.* 'namely').

SCAD. The bibliographical databank produced by the Commission of the European Community; offering information on the principal Community Acts, documents and official publications, with abstracts of periodical articles relating to Community affairs. Established 1983, the databank is available on-line and in a weekly paper format – *SCAD Bulletin*.

Scale. The ratio of the distance on an architectural drawing, map, globe, model or vertical section, to the actual distances they represent.

Scaling. The process of calculating the area by which an illustration block must be altered to fit a given layout.

SCAMP. Abbreviation for the Scottish Association of Magazine Publishers which exists to promote the sale of the literary magazines receiving Scottish Arts Council grants along with any of their publications.

Scan. To examine every reference or every entry in a file routinely as part of a retrieval scheme. To examine periodicals and other materials to determine the usefulness of the information contained to the library's users, especially to the interests and work of individuals served by a special library. This enables decisions to be made as to ROUTEING (*q.v.*), the preparation of

ABSTRACTS and ATTENTION NOTES (*qq.v.*), and how cataloguing and classifying should be carried out.

Scan-column Index. A co-ordinate book-form index developed by J. O'Connor which provides for manual serial searching of terms arranged in columns. *See also Co-ordinate Indexing.*

Scan Plates. A generic term for plates made by an electronic photo-engraving machine.

Scandinavian Association of Research Librarians. Founded 1947 in Copenhagen to promote and facilitate contacts and co-operation between Scandinavian librarians and their libraries. Associations in Denmark, Iceland, Finland, Norway and Sweden are members. Abbreviated NVBF (Nordiska Vetenskapliga Bibliotekarie Förbundet).

Scanner. A computer peripheral that can convert images on paper into electronic impulses readable by a computer.

SCANNET. A Nordic co-operative project established to promote the use of Scandinavian online databases; financed by NORDINFO, the Nordic Council for Scientific Information and Research Libraries (*q.v.*) and supported by an advisory group with members from Denmark, Norway, Finland, Sweden, and Iceland. Secretariat in Helsinki, Finland. Issues *Scannet Today* (irreg.).

Scanning. In information retrieval, the examination of tallies (records). This may be done (a) *sequentially*, in sequence one after another right through a file, (b) *simultaneously*, e.g. as a batch of edge-notched cards is needled, (c) *fractionally*, in a series of separate and intermittent consultations, e.g. as a catalogue is searched.

Scarecrow Press Award for Library Literature. Presented annually by the Scarecrow Press, this Award is administered by the ALA Awards Committee, the selection being made by a jury composed of one representative of each type-of-library division of the American Library Association. The first recipient (in 1960) was Marjorie Fiske Lowenthal for *Book selection and censorship.*

Scatter. The separation of entries in an index for the same topic or concept caused by entry under both singular and plural forms, or variant forms of name, or entry in one instance under a broad heading and in another under a specific heading, or by the imprecise use of terms, or by lack of control of synonymy. *See also Bibliographical Scatter.*

Scattering. *See Law of Scattering.*

Scaul. Acronym of the Standing Conference of African University Librarians. Founded 1964. Aims to support and develop academic library services in the area, and to promote interchange, contact and co-operation among academic libraries in Africa.

Scenario. 1. The outline of a film plot. 2. Any abbreviated presentation of the personages, plot, and outline of a dramatic work, such as a play, dramatic oratorio, cantata or opera. In cataloguing music, the term is also used for a ballet plot, directions for a dance composition, etc.

Schedule. 1. A statement of the sub-divisions of a classification as set out on paper so as to show hierarchical relationship. *See also Summum Genus.* 2. A series of serial classifications, arranged in one series of co-ordinate classes, with sub-classes, if there are any, arranged in secondary series, or columns, indented to show the subordination. These secondary series may be sub-divided successively, resulting in tertiary and quaternary series. These forms are equivalent to TABULAR CLASSIFICATION (*q.v.*) of three or more dimensions. 3. In information retrieval, any list of terms used in constructing a file. *See also File 3.* 4. An appendix to an Act of Parliament or other document; an annex or supplement. 5. (*Archives*) A document attached to another document, especially in amplification.

Scheduled Mnemonics. *See Mnemonics.*

Scheme. *See Bill of Type.*

Scheme of Classification. The schedules, index, and apparatus of a classification; the complete classification tables.

Schlegel-Tieck Prize. An annual award of the Translators' Association for the best UK-published translation of a German twentieth-century work.

Scholium. (*Pl.* Scholia.) An explanatory marginal note or comment, or interpretative remark, especially an annotation on a classical text by an ancient grammarian.

School District Library. A free public library established and financially supported by action of a school district for the use of residents of the district. Such a library is supervised by a local board of education or by a separate library board appointed by a board of education. (American.).

School Edition. An edition of a book especially prepared for use in school.

School Librarian. A professionally qualified librarian employed to organize and operate a library within a school. *See also Teacher-librarian.*

School Libraries Department. A section of a public library service, or local education service, which administers a system of school libraries. Also called: *Education Library Service/Department.*

School Libraries Group. A group of the (British) Library Association, formed in 1980, which aims to unite and represent members interested in librarianship in schools, to develop the role of the qualified librarian in a school, and emphasize the contribution made to education by the school library resource centre. Publishes *SLG News* (2 p.a.).

School Libraries Section. A Section of the (British) Library Association, the formation of which was agreed by the Council of the Association on 4 December 1936. It became a constituent part of the SCHOOL LIBRARY ASSOCIATION (*q.v.*).

School Library. An organized collection of books placed in a school for the use of teachers or pupils, but usually for pupils. It may comprise books of reference and/or books for home reading, and be in the care of a professional librarian, teacher, or teacher-librarian. Variously called an *Instructional Materials Center, a Learning Resources Centre* or a *Media Centre.*

School Library Association (UK). Formally constituted on 23 January 1937, strengthened in 1945 by the adhesion of the former School Libraries Section of the Library Association, and incorporated in 1955. This Association aims to promote development of the school library as an instrument of education in schools of all kinds; to encourage efficient methods of administration and routine; and to provide opportunities for interchange of experience among school librarians and others interested in the aims of the Association. Corporate membership is open to any school, college, institute of education, or library; Personal membership is available to individuals, and Student membership to students. Publishes *The School Librarian* (4 p.a.) and various monographs. Abbreviated SLA. Liaises with the Library Association, Book Trust, and IFLA. There are currently 34 branches. *See also International Association of School Librarianship.*

School Library Association in Scotland. Formed in 1953, this Association is an integral part of the SCHOOL LIBRARY ASSOCIATION (*q.v.*). Financed by the remission of a percentage of the membership fee from the SLA and a grant from the Scottish Education Department. Has branches in the largest Scottish cities.

School Library Manpower Project. *See Knapp School Libraries Project.*

School Library Supervisor. The American term for a librarian who supervises and co-ordinates the work of several other school librarians. The American Association of School Librarians recommends one for every system having five or more schools. Duties and responsibilities vary but usually include: consulting with school administrators, providing leadership, guidance and knowledge in school librarianship to stimulate improvement in the service. Also called 'Adviser', 'Consultant', 'Co-ordinator', 'Director', 'District-Librarian', 'Head Librarian', 'Specialist'.

School of Librarianship. *Synonymous with* LIBRARY SCHOOL (*q.v.*).

School System Materials Center. A library located in the central office of a system of school libraries from which are circulated films, filmstrips, records, tapes and other audio-visual materials and equipment to the schools in the system.

Schrotblatt. *Synonymous with* MANIÈRE CRIBLÉE (*q.v.*).

Schwabacher. 1. An early variety of Gothic type used in Germany. 2. A type used in Germany today, based on early Gothic designs.

Schweizerische Vereinigung für Dokumentation. The Association Suisse de Documentation. *See ASD.*

Science and Technology Policies Information Exchange System. *See SPINES.*

Science Book Prizes. Two annual awards made by COPUS at the Royal Society, for popular non-fiction books in the field of science and technology, one for general readers, and one for young people.

Science Fiction. Imaginative fiction describing life and adventure in the future, life on other worlds, interplanetary travel, etc. It usually has a scientific or prophetic background.

Science Fiction Foundation Library. A special collection maintained by the Polytechnic of East London Library (UK).

Science Reference and Information Service (SRIS). *See British Library.*

Science-Technology Division. A division of the (American) Special Libraries Association. Often abbreviated Sci-Tech.

Scientific and Technological Information Services Enquiry Committee. *See STISEC.*

Scientific Documentation Centre Ltd. (UK). Formed in 1962 as a non-profit-making research association to provide information services for scientists. Financed from subscriptions and payment for services provided; members are entitled to use certain types of service at reduced costs. Abbreviated SDC. Publishes *SDC Bulletin* (q.), which carries continuing bibliographies on information retrieval, spectrometric applications, bibliographies and reviews.

Sci-tech. Abbreviation for the SCIENCE-TECHNOLOGY DIVISION (*q.v.*) of the Special Libraries Association.

SCL. SCOTTISH CENTRAL LIBRARY (*q.v.*).

SCOBI. *See Standing Committee on Business Information.*

SCOCLIS. Acronym of the STANDING CONFERENCE OF CO-OPERATIVE LIBRARY AND INFORMATION SERVICES (*q.v.*).

Scoggin Memorial Collections. From 1970, notable books of the year for children and young adults are selected by the Association for Library Service to Children (American Library Association) and formed into collections. They were begun by the Children's Book Council, of New York City, to honour Margaret Scoggin, an authority on books for the young. They are a project of the US Section of the INTERNATIONAL BOARD ON BOOKS FOR YOUNG PEOPLE (*q.v.*) and are presented each year to repositories in parts of the world where publishing either does not exist or is not fully developed; one collection also is given to the International Youth Library in Munich.

Scoggin Scholarship, Margaret. Offered by the Young Adult Services Division of the American Library Association to a librarian or prospective librarian working with youth. The Scholarship is offered to honour Margaret Clara Scoggin (1905–68) who was Co-ordinator of Young Adult Services in the New York Public Library from 1952 until the end of 1967.

SCOLCAP. A library bibliographic network based at the National Library of Scotland; originally founded 1973 as the Scottish Libraries Co-operative Automation Project. Membership consists of five major Scottish libraries.

SCOLE. *See Standing Committee on Library Education.*

SCOLLUL. (UK) Acronym for Standing Conference of Librarians of the Libraries of the University of London which holds periodic meetings to consider aspects of co-operation between the libraries of the University.

SCOLMA (UK). Acronym for Standing Conference on Library Materials on Africa. This organization was set up at a meeting held in Chatham House on 2 April 1962. Its aims are: to facilitate the acquisition and preservation of library materials needed for African studies; to assist in the recording and use of such materials. Publications: *African Research and Documentation* (3 p.a.), *The SCOLMA Directory of Libraries and Special Collections on Africa.*

SCONUL. The Standing Conference of National and University Libraries (SCONUL) was founded in 1950 to represent the interests of the libraries of member institutions by providing a forum for the exchange of information and the marshalling of collaborative effort; it was incorporated as a company limited by guarantee and registered as a charity in 1980. The Standing Conference, in promoting the aims of national and university libraries, also represents their interests to government, official and semi-official bodies as the need arises. The Conference holds plenary meetings twice yearly at which each member institution is represented by its chief library officer. There are a number of Advisory Committees dealing with such interests as automation policy, buildings, education, training and staffing matters, information services, investigatory projects, manuscripts, recurring expenditure, relations with the book trade and statistics. There are also Advisory Committees concerned with the interests of area specialists (e.g. in the fields of American, Latin American, Medical, Oriental and Slavonic Materials) who are thus enabled to collaborate closely with the parent body.

SCONUL Library Design Awards. An irregular series of awards for UK universities made to recognize outstanding new or remodelled buildings that put user needs first. Three awards were made in 1988; previously there had been no award since 1976.

SCOOP. Acronym for Standing Committee on Official Publications. Took over the functions of the Library Association/HMSO Services Working Party in January 1983; working groups were formed to examine certain topics, and SCOOP keeps the profession aware of work and developments in British official publishing.

SCOPAS. Acronym of the Standing Conference on Professional Activities in Scotland which was formed about 1968 to co-ordinate activities in order to avoid possible date clashes when arranging meetings, etc.

SCOPE. 1. Abbreviation for the Systematic Computerized Processing in Cataloguing system which is an automated system for the catalogue department of a university library. It is an economic system which produces spine labels, pocket labels, book cards for the circulation system, catalogue cards including shelf list, main entry, subject and added entry cards, statistics, an updated master file in machine-readable form, and an accessions file. It was developed at the University of Guelph Library, Canada. 2. Abbreviation for Systematic Control of Periodicals, a system implemented by the Technical Information Department of Pfizer, Inc. at the Medical Research Laboratories in Groton, Connecticut, and is used for a computerized serials record system.

SCOPE. (UK) Acronym for Standing Committee on Professional Education. The discussion forum between the profession and the schools of librarianship, set up by the Library Association in 1982 following implementation of the PAULIN REPORT (*q.v.*).

Scope Card. A comprehensive catalogue card indicating the extent of musical or other works possessed in one form or medium, or of an identical title by one author or composer.

Scope Note. 1. In information retrieval, a statement giving the range of meaning and scope of a subject heading or descriptor and usually referring to related or overlapping headings. 2. In co-ordinate indexing, a symbol appended to a term or term number to narrow the definition of the term rather than designate the role of a word in its context. *See also Roles.*

Score. A printed or written version of a musical work in notational form which shows the parts for the participating voices or instruments on two or more staves ('staffs' in America), one above the other. The term is not usually applied to music for one performer. A *Full Score* shows the music for each participating voice or instrument on separate staves one above the other, with the music for each solo voice, each choral part and each instrument being set out on a separate stave one above another. A *Miniature Score* has the same music as a full score but is reduced considerably in size by photographic reproduction. Miniature scores are usually so described on the title-page, but if not, can be considered to be such if the music is smaller than normal and the page size is not more than 20 cms. An *Orchestral Score* is the full score of an orchestral work. A *Piano Score* is an orchestral or vocal work reduced to a piano version. A *Piano-Conductor Score* (violin-conductor score, etc.) is a piano (or violin, etc.) part in a concerted work, with cues to indicate when vocal or instrumental performers 'come in', i.e. begin to perform. The pianist (or violinist, etc.) performs and conducts at the same time. A *Vocal Score* shows the music for voices on separate staves but the orchestral parts reduced to a piano version. This is the common version for members of choirs, of the music of cantatas, operas, and oratorios. Also called 'Piano-vocal score'. A *Close Score* has the music for more than one part or instrument on one stave. Also called 'Compressed score', 'Short score'. An *Open Score* has the music for each voice or part on a separate stave, each being placed above one another, as in a full score. Also called 'Extended score'. A *Small full score* is a photographic reduction of a *Full score*. *Pocket score* is synonymous with *Miniature score*. A *Study score* is musically identical with a *Full score*. A *Part* shows the individual instrumental or vocal lines and states the nature of the part, e.g. Chorus part, Tenor part, Violin part. A *Short Score* is one showing all the parts on the smallest possible number of staves; also called a 'Compressed Full Score'. A *Full Music Edition* is a fully harmonized version of a vocal work, especially a collection of hymns or of songs. A *Melody Edition* is the melody line only of a vocal work; it is used mainly of collections of songs and hymns. A *Chorus Score* is one showing all the chorus parts, with the accompaniment, if any, arranged for keyboard. *See also Realization, Reduction.* A *Rehearsal Score* is a compressed version of a full score, in many respects similar to a 'Short Score' but with sufficient cues to be of practical use at rehearsals. An *Organ-vocal score* is a score of a work for chorus and/or solo voices and organ, the accompaniment being a reduction of the music originally composed for an instrumental ensemble. A *piano-vocal score* is a similar work to an organ-vocal score, but for piano instead of organ. *See also Transcription.*

Scoring. Compressing the fibres of heavy paper along a line, to facilitate either folding or tearing. Scoring with a dull rule increases folding endurance. The use of a sharp rule however partially breaks the paper fibres and has a similar effect to perforating.

Scot Report. *See BTECC.*

SCOTAPLL. The Standing Conference of Theological and Philosophical Libraries in London. This Association was founded in 1948 to improve facilities for research in these subjects, and to interchange books between constituent libraries. It was merged with the Association of British Theological and Philosophical Libraries in 1964. *See also ABTAPL.*

SCOTBEC. *See SCOTVEC.*

SCOTEC. *See SCOTVEC.*

Scottish Academic Libraries Bibliographic Network. A project to investigate the linking of major academic library catalogues in Scotland.

Scottish Association of Magazine Publishers. *See SCAMP.*

Scottish Central Library. Now incorporated in the National Library of Scotland, it was the Scottish counterpart to the National Central Library; formed on 1 July 1952. It was founded in Dunfermline in 1921 as the Scottish Central Library for Students. As from 1 October 1953 it absorbed the Regional Library Bureau of Scotland (founded in 1945) and became responsible for the Scottish Union Catalogue from the same date. Abbreviated SCL. On 1 May 1974 this Library was incorporated within the National Library of Scotland, becoming the NLS Lending Services (NLSLS).

Scottish Children's Book Association. Founded 1973 to: (a) stimulate and encourage among children and others an interest in, and appreciation of, good literature for children; (b) encourage, or assist in promoting, the formation of groups of persons interested in children's books; (c) communicate information and advice about children's books; (d) promote discussion of all matters relating to children's books and their evaluation; (e) stimulate and encourage better provision of library facilities for children; (f) co-operate in furtherance of the Association's objects, with persons, institutions and organizations concerned with children. Membership is open to individuals, groups and institutions. Financed by members' subscriptions, donations and advertising in *Book Window* (3 p.a.).

Scottish Law Librarians Group. An inaugural meeting of the group was held early in 1988; acknowledges the separate legal system in Scotland and the growing professionalism of practitioners' libraries in the main cities.

Scottish Libraries Co-operative Automation Project. *See SCOLCAP.*

Scottish Library and Information Council. *See SLIC.*

Scottish Library Association. A Branch of the (British) Library Association. It was an independent association, having been formed in October 1908 at Edinburgh, until January 1931 when it was affiliated with the LA and incorporated as a Branch. There are four regional branches each of which is represented on the SLA Council. Publishes *Scottish Libraries* (6 p.a.). Abbreviated SLA.

Scottish Science Library. A part of the NATIONAL LIBRARY OF SCOTLAND (*q.v.*); opened in new premises in 1989 to serve the scientific, technological and business needs of Scottish users.

Scottish Style. An eighteenth-century style of book decoration resembling the HARLEIAN STYLE (*q.v.*), but which has for a centre-piece a straight stem from which short sprays branch at regular intervals on either side, or else consists mainly of a large wheel pattern.

Scottish Vocational Education Council. *See SCOTVEC.*

SCOTVEC. Abbreviation for the Scottish Vocational Education Council. Formed in 1985 to succeed SCOTBEC and SCOTEC. A validating body for sub-degree level commercial and technical qualifications.

Scraperboard. 1. A method of drawing for reproduction. It utilizes a 'board' coated with a chalk surface and covered with a black wash which the artist scrapes away to reveal the white lines and areas of his drawing. Black lines may be drawn in afterwards if desired. 2. A drawing made by this method. It is similar in appearance to a wood engraving.

Scratchboard. American term for paper coated with black ink which is scratched away to show the white paper underneath. The picture drawing so produced. A scraperboard.

Screamer. The printer's term for exclamation marks used for display purposes.

Screen. A grid of opaque lines cut in glass (used in making half-tone blocks) crossing at right angles, and producing transparent square apertures between the intersections which split up the image into dots; these dots are distinctive of the half-tone process. The number of lines to the inch varies from forty for a coarse screen for use with rough or poor quality paper to 250 for a fine screen for use with art paper. *See also Half-Tone.*

Screen. 1. (*Reprography*) A surface of any material on to which, or if translucent, through which, an image is projected. 2. (*Information retrieval*) To make a preliminary selection of information or documents with a view to reducing the number to be examined at a later date.

Screw Press. A press used by bookbinders to flatten paper or books in process of binding, especially after pasting or glueing. It is operated by turning a wheel or lever attached to the upper end of a large-dimension screw placed perpendicularly which has at its lower end a heavy iron plate below which, and on the bed of the press, are placed the papers or books to be pressed. *See also Press.*

Scrim. *Synonymous with* MULL (*q.v.*).

Scrinium. A cylinder-shaped container with movable lid used by the Romans to hold a number of scrolls.

Script. 1. A form of printer's cursive type resembling handwriting. 2. Any type face which is cut to resemble handwriting. 3. Handwriting, as opposed to printed characters. 4. A typescript, specially of a play, film scenario, or text of spoken matter for broadcasting.

Script Writing. *Synonymous with* DISJOINED HAND (*q.v.*).

Scriptores.　Writers who copied books by hand in Roman times.

Scriptorium.　The room in a mediaeval monastery or abbey which was set aside for the copying of manuscripts, and for writing and studying generally.

Scriptura Actuaria.　*Synonymous with* RUSTIC CAPITAL (*q.v.*).

Scroll.　1. Movement of the display on a VDU to accommodate new material; as new data appears at one edge the existing display disappears line by line at the opposite edge. Scrolling may proceed upwards, downwards, or to left or right.　2. A roll of paper or parchment, usually containing writing and rolled onto rollers. This was an early form of manuscript, called by the Romans *volumen* (roll) from which the word *volume* is derived. The scroll (or 'roll') comprised a number of sheets of papyrus or parchment glued together to form a 20- or 30-feet long strip which was wound on a cylinder with projecting ornaments or knobs in ivory or colours, and was finished with a coloured parchment cover, fastened with laces and identified with a 'sittybus', or title label. The text was written in rather narrow columns on the recto of the material, where, if papyrus, the fibres run horizontally.　3. (*Binding*) A scroll-shaped stamp used for bearing an inscription, or an ornament of similar shape, and generally used between Flowers on a roll.

sculpt.　Abbreviation for *sculpsit* (*Lat.*). Indicates on an engraving the name of the engraver, and on sculpture the name of the sculptor. *See also del., fecit.*

Scumming.　A fault in the lithographic process usually caused by plate wear, in which the water-accepting layer becomes inefficient.

SD Classification.　The scheme of classification, used by the US government's Superintendent of Documents who is responsible for the centralized control and distribution of US government documents. It is not a systematic scheme in that there is no visible subject relationship between the various parts. The notation consists of a combination of letters and numbers.

SDI.　Abbreviation for Selective Dissemination of Information, which is an automated system of information retrieval utilizing a computer for disseminating relevant information to users. An interest profile depicting and defining each area of interest is compiled for each user; it consists of terms which are likely to appear in relevant documents. Key words representing documents are matched with these interest profiles. If, for any given document and user, the terms match, its abstract is sent to the user. *See also Current Awareness.*

SDM.　Abbreviation for selective dissemination of microfiche, a system whereby large-scale microfiche users regularly receive microfiche copies of documents in selected specified subject areas.

Seal Print.　A woodcut with blind embossing around the picture, the embossing being done after the printing. Practised in the fifteenth century. Also called 'Gypsographic print'.

Sealskin.　Binding leather made from the skin of the seal; it has a coarse grain, but is soft to the touch. *See also Pin Seal.*

Search Record.　A record which shows the publications, organizations, and individuals consulted in answering an enquiry or obtaining information. The completed memorandum, information statement, or report, may be inserted on the form or attached to it, or it may form a separate record kept in a JOB FILE (*q.v.*).

Search Room. 1. A room associated with an archives or record centre in which people may carry out their searches in the documents. 2. A room in which volumes of indexes to periodicals, volumes of abstracts, and similar bibliographical and search tools are provided for users to conduct literature searches. *See also Archives.*

Search Service. *Synonymous with* RESEARCH SERVICE (*q.v.*).

Search Statement. An individual search consisting of one search term or several terms linked.

Search Strategy. The plan adopted for answering a particular enquiry, or more specifically, the search statements used to answer an enquiry.

Search Term. A word, phrase, or number input by the user to find those records on the database that contain that term.

Searching. The act of checking a book against the catalogue to determine whether it is a duplicate, another edition of a book already in stock, or a new title (to be) added to the library. In PRELIMINARY CATALOGUING (*q.v.*), the searcher notes such descriptive and subject cataloguing details as may be helpful to the cataloguer. Often, searching slips are provided to standardize the operation. The term is also applied to the checking of titles for acquisition purposes. *See also Literature Search, Online Searching.*

Second Generation Microfilm. *Synonymous with* FIRST REPRODUCTION MICROFILM (*q.v.*). *See also Generation.*

Second Half-title. A repetition of the title of a book between the preliminaries and the text.

Second Indention. The tenth typewriter space from the left edge of a catalogue card; the second, or inner, vertical line on a catalogue card ruled for handwriting. It is at this position that the title normally begins; if it runs over the line, it continues at the 'First indention', and is followed by particulars of edition and imprint. The *collation* also begins at the second indention, but without spacing between these two parts of the description. The collation is followed by a series note. The *notes* and the *contents* also begin at the second indention, but a 'blank line' is left between these and the previous parts of the description. Should either collation, notes or contents over-run the first line, subsequent lines begin at the first indention. Also called 'Title indention', 'Inner indention' and 'Paragraph indention'. *See also First Indention, Indention, Second Vertical, Third Indention.*

Second Lining. A strip of brown paper the full size of the back of a book which is glued into position after the FIRST LINING (*q.v.*) has been affixed.

Second Reproduction Microfilm. A microfilm copy made from the FIRST REPRODUCTION MICROFILM (*q.v.*). Also called 'Third generation microfilm'. *See also Generation.*

Second Vertical. The second vertical line printed on a standard ruled catalogue card and serving as a guide to where the title should begin – at the SECOND INDENTION (*q.v.*). *See also First Vertical.*

Secondary Access. (*Information retrieval*) Access from one entry to related entries in a FILE (*q.v.*). *See also Primary Access.*

Secondary Bibliography. 1. An 'intensive' or special bibliography dealing with books relating to one subject for the compilation of which primary bibliographies have been used. 2. A bibliography in which material is rearranged for convenience of research. (American.) *See also Bibliography, Primary Bibliography.*

Secondary Entry. An entry in a catalogue other than the MAIN ENTRY (*q.v.*), an ADDED ENTRY (*q.v.*). *See also General Secondary.*

Secondary Fullness. The detail with which, in full cataloguing, an author's name is given in all secondary entries, e.g. the Christian name is given in full if there is only one, but initials if there are more than one. Also called 'Subject fullness'.

Secondary Publication. 1. A document such as an abstract, digest, index to periodicals, current awareness journal, or popularization, which is prepared in order to disseminate more widely information which has already appeared in another form, particularly in a PRIMARY PUBLICATION (*q.v.*). 2. The act of publishing such material.

Secondary Service. *Synonymous with* ABSTRACTING SERVICE (*q.v.*).

Secondary Sources. Books or unpublished literary material in the compilation of which PRIMARY SOURCES (*q.v.*) have been used.

Secondary Title. An addition to the main title of a serial to distinguish an independent section.

Second-hand Book. One which has previously been owned by another person. A bookseller who deals in such books is called a 'Second-hand bookseller'. Librarians refer to such books when purchased for a library as 'Second-hand copies'.

Second-hand Catalogue. A list of second-hand books offered for sale.

Secret Literature. *Synonymous with* CLANDESTINE LITERATURE (*q.v.*).

Secret Press. *See Clandestine Press.*

Section. 1. The unit of paper which is printed, folded and sewn and which, together with other sections, goes to make up a printed book. It usually consists of one sheet of paper, but may be one and a half or two sheets, or even one sheet and an extra leaf pasted in. Also called 'Signature', 'Gathering', 'Quire', 'Stave'. Each section of a book bears a different SIGNATURE (*q.v.*). *See also Foldings.* 2. All the shelves arranged between two uprights. *Synonymous with* TIER (*q.v.*). 3. A sub-division of an administrative unit or department of a library, e.g. 'Processing section'. Sometimes called a 'Division' or 'Department'. 4. In the Dewey Classification a sub-division of a 'division'. 5. One of the separately folded parts of a newspaper, such as the 'Business section'. 6. A portion of a text of a book which can logically be divided into separate parts or sections. 7. A portion of the membership of the (British) Library Association who were interested in a particular aspect of librarianship. Under the present bye-laws of the Association these are now mostly known as Groups although some still bear the former name of Section.

Section Headline. One which consists of whatever sub-divisions (chapters, books, parts, etc.) the book may have. *See also Headline, Page Headline, Running Title.*

Section Mark. 1. The sign § used before a numeral thus: §6, to refer to a section. 2. The fourth reference mark for footnotes, coming after the double dagger. *See also Reference Marks.* It is sometimes also used in quantity for borders.

Section Title. A half title which introduces a section of a book.

Sectional Brace. *See Brace.*

Sectionalized Index. An index to a periodical split into sections such as (a) long articles of importance, (b) short paragraphs and brief news items, (c) literature abstracts, and similar well-defined groups.

Sectioning. Microfilming a very large document in two or more parts in such a way as to permit mounting the film in the same number of aperture cards.

Sections. *See Section.* For use in classification, *see Main Class.*

Sector Device. The device of using a sectorizing digit, i.e. to form another sector or stretch of co-ordinate digits by adding to it the successive digits of the species and deeming the resulting double-digited numbers as if fused into a single digit, and repeating this process to form successive sectors. *See also Group Notation Device.*

Sectorizing Device. A digit such as the Octave Device (*q.v.*) for extending the capacity of a numerical base in the Colon Classification.

Sedanoise. The smallest size type of the early seventeenth century, designed by Jannon at Sedan. *See also Jannon, Jean.*

See. (*Cataloguing*) A reference from a heading under which no entries are placed, to one or more which contain them.

See also. (*Cataloguing*) A reference often found in dictionary catalogues – and sometimes in classified ones – from one heading with entries under it, to related ones.

See Copy. An instruction written on a proof to a printer to refer to the 'copy' in order to correct a typesetting error.

See Safe. Said of books bought from a publisher by a bookseller, and paid for, but with the understanding that at some future date the publisher may be asked to exchange unsold copies for copies of another title. *See also Half See Safe, On Sale.*

Segment. Part of a computer program which carries out a specific function.

Select Bibliography. One which gives only a selection of the literature of a subject, the selection having been made with a view to excluding worthless material or to meeting the needs of a special class of people. Also called 'Selective bibliography'. *See also Bibliography 1, Current Selective Bibliography, Partial Bibliography.*

Select List. A reading list which includes a selection only of the books in the library on the subject of the list.

Select List of References. A partial list of references for material for further reading, the selection having eliminated items which for one reason or another are not particularly appropriate in the circumstances. The details included in the entries may be similar to those provided in a bibliography, although some items of a bibliographical nature may not be included, and the subject coverage would not be so great.

Selectasine. A process in silk screen printing; the term implies that one screen only is used for all the colours of a design.

Selected Term Co-ordination. (*Indexing*). The co-ordination of significant terms in titles with other selected title terms.

Selection Section. The division of a cataloguing, accessions, or order department, which deals with the selection of books.

Selective Abstract. *See Abstract.*

Selective Abstract Service. A service which abstracts only those publications and articles which are considered to be of use to a specific group of readers.

Selective Bibliography. *Synonymous with* SELECT BIBLIOGRAPHY (*q.v.*).

Selective Cataloguing. The omission of certain types of entry, or of entries for little-used books, or of parts of an entry (as for example some items of collations), in order to reduce the bulk and cost of a catalogue without impairing its efficiency.

Selective Charging. The practice of recording the loan of certain classes of books, usually non-fiction or particularly expensive books, while others are issued by a TOKEN CHARGING (*q.v.*) system.

Selective Circulation. *See Routeing.*

Selective Classification. The arrangement of large groups of little-used books either alphabetically or chronologically rather than by specific subject in order to save the expense of cataloguing and classifying.

Selective Dissemination of Information. *See SDI.*

Selective Dissemination of Microfiche. *See SDM.*

Selective Listing in Combination. *See SLIC Index.*

Selective Routeing. ROUTEING (*q.v.*) to only a selection of the staff of a library or organization.

Selector. The component in a RETRIEVAL SYSTEM (*q.v.*) which enables the information required to be identified in a STORE (*q.v.*). It may consist of, or comprise, recording media, code symbols or reading devices.

Self-charging System. Any system for recording book loans in which the borrower makes part or all of the record.

Self-cover. A pamphlet in which the same paper is used for cover and text.

Self-ends. Endpapers which are leaves forming part of the end sections of a book.

Self Positive. In documentary reproduction, a positive print which is prepared without the use of an intermediate negative. Also called 'Direct positive'.

Self-renewing Library. A phrase popularized by the ATKINSON REPORT (*q.v.*). The principle of self renovation is that a library should remain at a constant overall size, in terms of stock, by discarding material at an equal rate to its acquisition, thereby maintaining the currency of its collections, and relying on interlending services for materials seldom required.

Self-wrapper. The paper cover of a pamphlet or book which is an integral part of the sheet or sheets comprising the publication. It may or may not be printed.

'Selfdemarcating' Code. (*Information retrieval*) One of several systematic methods of abbreviating words.

Semanteme. The ultimate, smallest irreducible element or unit of meaning, such as a base or root which contains and represents the general meaning of a word or group of derivatives.

Semantic Code. 1. A linguistic system developed for use on machines designed to detect logically defined combinations; a symbol representing the concept of a word. 2. In information retrieval, one in which the notation carries meaningful information in addition to that which is carried by the source word. *See also Non-semantic Code.*

Semantic Factor. 1. In co-ordinate indexing, the separate unit of a code entry, representing one of a number of highly generic concepts. The semantic factors forming a code are arranged in alphabetical order. *See also Descriptor.* 2. A generalized concept used, with others, to construct a SEMANTIC CODE (*q.v.*). *See also Analytical Relations.*

Semantic Factoring. American term for FACET ANALYSIS (*q.v.*).

Semantic Relation. (*Information retrieval*) A general term used to indicate all types of relationship between language descriptors in a thesaurus. *See also Relation.*

Semantics. The study of the relations between linguistic symbols (words, expressions, phrases) and the objects or concepts to which they refer. Semantics relates a symbol to its meaning. *See also Syntax.*

Semaphore Indexing. A method of indexing with punched cards, each punch being shaped so as to indicate morphological changes in the subject; this is a POLYVALENT NOTATION (*q.v.*).

Semé, Semis. *Synonymous with* POWDER (*q.v.*).

Semi-annual. A periodical which is issued at six-monthly intervals. Also called 'Half yearly'.

Semi-chemical Pulp. The product of an intermediate process between Mechanical Wood Pulp (merely ground wood without the addition of chemicals or heat) and Chemical Wood Pulp which is obtained by the action of chemicals on wood chips.

Semi-current Records. (*Archives*) Records that are so infrequently required in the conduct of current business that they be moved to a holding area or to a RECORDS CENTRE (*q.v.*) (American.)

Semi-indexing. Listing a number of items to be indexed on one sheet of squared paper, bearing the letters of the alphabet at the top to serve as guide-line headings. The entries commence on the lines having the corresponding initial letters entered at the top.

Semi-monthly. *Synonymous with* FORTNIGHTLY (*q.v.*).

Semiotics. The science of signs; it is divided into three main sub-divisions: semantics, syntatics, and pragmatics, each of which (as can semiotics as a whole) can be pure, descriptive or applied. *Pure semiotic* elaborates a language to talk about signs, *descriptive semiotic* studies actual signs, *applied semiotic* utilizes knowledge about signs to accomplish various purposes.

Semi-pulp. A term applied to the product of the grinding process in paper making, the ground wood still containing impurities and large fragments of wood.

Semi-rag. Paper made partly of rags.

Semi-weekly. A serial publication issued twice a week. Also called 'Twice weekly'.

Seminar Collection. *Synonymous with* DEPARTMENTAL LIBRARY (*q.v.*).

Senior Assistant. An assistant librarian who has the supervision of the work of junior assistants but does not have the responsibility for a department.

Senior Librarians Award (UK). A cash award offered in alternate years to Chartered Librarians with at least seven years' experience since their election to the Register, who are past or present members of the London and Home Counties Branch. It is normally made for personal research into practical problems of librarianship or information work, or practical problems likely to result in improvement in library services over a wide area, either for staff or users.

Sensing Mark. (*Reprography*) A mark on film or paper which activates an electrical device to carry out automatically a function such as cutting paper.

Sensitive Paper. A paper which has been treated with light-sensitive chemicals for photographic purposes. *See also Sensitized Paper.*

Sensitivity. *Synonymous with* RECALL RATIO (*q.v.*).

Sensitized Paper. Paper used in documentary reproduction which is coated with an emulsion sensitive to light or heat as used in a thermographic process.

Separate. A copy of an article published in a periodical, specially reprinted for the author's use, but retaining the numbering of the issue from which it was taken. It may or may not have a title-page. Sometimes called 'Extracted article', 'Off-print', 'Overprint', or 'Reprint'. *See also Reprinted Article.*

Separation Negatives. Individual negatives for each colour used in colour reproductions. *See also Colour Separation.*

Separator. (*Classification*) A symbol (e.g. a point, bracket, colon) used to separate parts of a lengthy notation.

Separatrix. The diagonal stroke / , used in proof correction to mark and separate alterations.

Separatum (*Pl.* Separata). A reprint of one of a series of papers. An offprint or SEPARATE (*q.v.*).

seq. (*Pl. Seqq.*). Abbreviation (in singular) of Latin *sequens* 'the following', *sequente* 'and in what follows', *sequitur* 'it follows' and (in plural) of *sequentes, -tia* 'the following', *sequentibus* 'in the following places'. *See also et seq.*

Sequel. A literary work, usually a novel, which is complete in itself, but continues an earlier work.

Sequence of Signs. The use of recognized signs in notes (*see Reference Marks*) and especially of 'Relation marks' in the UNIVERSAL DECIMAL CLASSIFICATION (*q.v.*) to separate the different components of a classification number and at the same time indicate their meaning.

Sequential Camera.   One which produces a sequence of images in column form on one film from cards which are fed into the camera in a pre-determined sequence.

Serial.   1. Any publication issued in successive parts, appearing at intervals, usually regular ones, and, as a rule, intended to be continued indefinitely. The term includes periodicals, newspapers, annuals, numbered monographic series and the proceedings, transactions and memoirs of societies. Not to be confused with SERIES (*q.v.*).   2. A book consisting of parts or volumes published successively with a common title and intended to be continued indefinitely, not necessarily at regular intervals. (In the United States of America the term 'serial' is used to mean a periodical, regular or irregular).   3. (*Adj.*) The handling of data in a sequential fashion. *See also Parallel.*   4. A long story published in instalments.   5. As defined by the INTERNATIONAL SERIALS DATA SYSTEM (ISDS *q.v.*): for the purpose of allocating an INTERNATIONAL STANDARD SERIAL NUMBER (ISSN *q.v.*) 'a publication in print or in non-print form, issued in successive parts, usually having numerical or chronological designations, and intended to be continued indefinitely'.

Serial Catalogue.   An official, or a public catalogue of serials in a library.

Serial Classification.   A classification, the classes of which are in a series, or in an order of gradation.

Serial Number.   1. The number indicating the order of publication in a series.   2. One of the consecutive numbers appearing in front of an entry in a bibliography or catalogue.

Serial Publication.   *Synonymous with* SERIAL (*q.v.*).

Serial Record.   A record of a library's holdings of serials.

Serial Rights.   An author's rights in the publication of his work by instalments.

Serial Section.   A division of an order, or an acquisition, department that has charge of the acquisition of serials; or a sub-division of a preparation division where responsibility is taken for the cataloguing of serials.

Serial Service.   A serial publication which is revised, accumulated or indexed by means of new or replacement pages. *See also Loose-leaf Service.*

Serials Department.   The administrative unit in charge of handling serials; this may include ordering, checking, cataloguing, preparation for binding, etc.

Serials Industry Systems Advisory Committee.   Formed 1982 by common interest of serial publishers, database producers, subscription agents and librarians to foster standardization of machine-readable formats to allow mechanized handling of serials information, standardization of coding of serial articles, and general development of the automation of library serials control. Abbreviated SISAC.

Serials Librarian.   One who is responsible for the receipt of serials and for the maintenance of the relative records.

Series.   1. Volumes usually related to each other in subject matter, issued successively, sometimes at the same price, and generally by the same publisher, in a uniform style, and usually bearing a collective 'series title' on the HALF TITLE (*q.v.*) or the cover, or at the head of the TITLE-PAGE (*q.v.*).   2. Succeeding volumes of essays, etc., issued at intervals or in sequence.   3. A type of serial publication (*See Serial 1*) in which the parts (a) have, in addition to a constant title, a distinctive title for each part; (b) consist of a single work; (c) are not issued at predetermined intervals. The successive parts may, or may not, be given systematic or sequential numbering. This type of series is also called 'Monographic Series', 'Monograph Series'.   4. (*Archives*) A folder (*see Folder 2*) holding documents related to a particular subject or function, or documents arranged in accordance with a filing system. *See also Serial.*   5. A number of articles or stories of a similar nature or by the same author published in succession. *See also Publisher's Series, Reprint Series.*   6. (*Classification*) A succession of classes, or terms, in some relation.

Series Authority File.   A list of series entries used in a given catalogue together with the references made to them from other forms.

Series Card.   A catalogue card on which the SERIES ENTRY (*q.v.*) appears.

Series Entry.   In a catalogue or bibliography, a brief entry under the name of the series to which the publication belongs. *See also Series.*

Series Note.   In a bibliography or in a catalogue, a note following the collation, and giving, in parentheses, the name of the series to which a book belongs.

Series Number.   The number assigned by a publisher to an individual book or piece of music published in a series. The series may contain titles which are unrelated, or they may be related to one another by subject, musical form, medium of performance (musical), or the titles may be unrelated. *See also Publisher's Series.*

Series Statement.   1. The information on a publication which names the series to which it belongs and gives the number, if any, of the publication in the series.   2. (*Cataloguing*) The statement in a catalogue entry, of the name of the series to which the document belongs, and the number, if any, of the publication in the series. This usually appears within curved brackets at the end of the entry.

Series Title.   The title of a series to which a book belongs. It may appear on the half-title page, title-page, or a page following the title-page.

Serif.   A fine finishing stroke or grace, drawn at right angles to, or obliquely across, the ends of stems or arms of a letter. Letters without serifs are usually described as 'sans serif'.

Serigraphy.   *Synonymous with* SILK SCREEN (*q.v.*) process.

Serrated Square.   (*Binding*) A stamp, more or less square with concave serrated sides, and usually a cruciform centre; often used in a group and giving the effect of a number of circles with serrated inner edges.

Service Basis.   A method of determining prices for a publication or series of publications issued periodically and cumulated at regular intervals. The prices are scaled for individual libraries according to book expenditure, circulation and anticipated potential use to the subscriber. For periodical indexes, it is based on the number of indexed periodicals taken in a library.

Service Points.   Places at which the public are served. Include branches (inclusive of mobile branches and travelling libraries, each halt to count as a separate service point), centres, school libraries, hospital libraries, youth clubs, prisons, lighthouses, colleges, military camps, etc. The characteristic denoting a Service Point is that provision is intended to be permanent and/or continuous, is of a relatively wide subject range, and is located at a definite place. Does not include the supply of collections of books to adult classes, choral and dramatic societies, and for other similar purposes where the use of the collection is intended to be limited in duration and where the books cover a relatively narrow subject range.

SESAME. An EC database covering the work of two programmes of the Directorate-General for Energy – the Hydrocarbon Technology Programme and the Community Energy Demonstration Programme.

Session. *See Parliamentary Session.*

Sessional Papers. Two series (*House of Commons Sessional Papers* and *House of Lords Sessional Papers*) of Parliamentary Papers arranged (and probably bound) in sessional sets. The *House of Commons Sessional Papers* consist of the *House of Commons Bills*, the *House of Commons Papers* and the *Command Papers.* The *House of Lords Sessional Papers* consist of the series called the *House of Lords Papers and Bills.*

Set. 1. A series of publications associated by common publication or authorship, and which form one unit, being issued in a uniform style. They may be by one author, or on one subject, or they may be a file of periodicals or be unrelated but printed and bound uniformly. 2. (*Printing*) The distance between the left- and right-hand sides of a piece of movable type. Type is said to have a wide or narrow set according to the width of the BODY (*q.v.*); a figure is used to indicate the comparative width of a Monotype design, e.g. 12-point 10½ set, is narrower than 12-point 12 set. 3. To compose type.

Set Flush. 1. An instruction to the typesetter to set the type right up to the left-hand margin, avoiding indentions at the beginning of paragraphs. 2. Matter so composed.

Set Hand. Writing which conforms to definite rules, such as styles of abbreviations. Not generally applied to hands later than the seventeenth century.

Set of a Fount. (*Printing*) The measurement of the widest letter, described by the point-system, as e.g. 12 point 11¼ set.

Set of a Letter. (*Printing*) The width of a piece of type across its shank (i.e. the piece of metal bearing the face, or printing-surface).

Set-off. 1. The accidental transfer of ink from one printed sheet to another. 2. Any kind of paper placed between a sheet after printing to prevent theink from one sheet soiling another. Also called 'Slip sheet'. *See also Offset.*

Set Solid. Type matter with no leads between the lines.

Setting Rule. *Synonymous with* COMPOSING RULE (*q.v.*).

Setting Type. Composing type either by hand or by machine so that it is ready for printing.

Sevensma Prize, The. A money prize awarded for an essay written on a prescribed subject to a member, under forty years of age, of any member-association of IFLA (*q.v.*). The Prize honours T. P. Sevensma, the Dutch librarian who was successively Director of the Public Library of Amsterdam of the League of Nations Library, and of the University Library in Leyden In 1929 he became Secretary of IFLA, and in 1939 on the occasion of his completing ten years in this honorary office, also on the occasion of his sixtieth birthday, the President of IFLA announced the establishment of the prize bearing Dr. Sevensma's name. The subject of the essay is set every two years and is on some aspect of libraries in their relation to practical life.

Seventy-twomo (72mo).   A sheet of paper folded into seventy-two leaves making 144 pages.

Sewed.   In cataloguing, a pamphlet stitched without covers.

Sewing.   When the sections of a book have been gathered and collated, they are sewed together, one by one, with thread, usually by machinery. In job binding they are usually sewed by hand. *See also All Along, Stabbing, Stitching, Thread Stitched, Wire Stitched.*

Sewing Frame.   The frame on which cords or tapes are attached and stretched taut, and to which the sections of a book are sewn by hand.

Sewing on Tapes.   When the sections of a book are sewn together and two or more tapes are used to secure the book to the covers, some of the loops pass over the tapes thus also securing the sections to them. In LIBRARY BINDING (*q.v.*) and hand-sewing, each section is sewn to every tape.

Sewn.   A book is said to be sewn when the sections are fastened together with linen threads passing round tapes or cords.

Sexagesimo-quarto.   *Synonymous with* SIXTY-FOURMO (*q.v.*).

Sexto (6to).   A sheet of paper folded three times to form a section of six leaves or twelve pages; a half-sheet of twelves.

Sexto-decimo (16mo).   A sheet of paper folded four times to form a section of sixteen leaves (thirty-two pages); a half-sheet of thirty-two. Now called foolscap 8vo. Also called 'Sixteen-mo'.

s.f.   Abbreviation for *sub finem* (*Lat.* 'towards the end').

SfB.   A classification system for trade literature, periodicals, and information concerning the building industry. The letters stand for the initials of the Swedish committee which originated it, Sanarbetskommittèn för Byttnads-frågor.

SGML.   *See Standard Generalized Markup Language.*

Shackleton Report (UK).   The *Report of the Committee on University Libraries*, 1966, so named after R. Shackleton, the Chairman of the Committee which examined the structure of the three different types of library in Oxford: 1. direct grant libraries (Bodleian, Ashmolean and Taylorian); 2. libraries financed by the General Board (mainly faculty libraries); 3. college libraries. The report made many recommendations with regard to buildings, administration and services.

Shaded Tools.   (*Binding*) Finisher's tools partly in outline and partly solid.

Shadow.   A type face which gives a three-dimensional effect.

Shagreen.   A type of leather with a rough, granular surface. When used for bookbinding it is usually prepared from sharkskin.

Shaken. A cataloguing term used in the USA to describe copies of books which have loose leaves and/or binding.

Shank. The rectangular body of a type letter, on which are the NICK, or nicks, PINMARK, BELLY and BACK (*qq.v.*). Also called BODY (*q.v.*) and STEM (*q.v.*). The piece of metal on which the shoulder bearing the FACE (*q.v.*) or printing surface of a type-letter is supported. *See also Shoulder.*

Shape. Books which are not of normal proportions are described as 'oblong' or 'landscape' when the width of the page exceeds its height, 'narrow' when the width is less than $^3/_5$ of the height, and 'square' if more than $^3/_4$. *See also Size.*

Shapiro Report (UK). The report *Organisational and Policy Framework* submitted by the Library Advisory Council (England) to the Minister for the Arts in 1979. Chairman: D. M. Shapiro. Published as part one of *Future Development of Libraries and Information Services* (HMSO 1982). *See also Library and Information Services Council.*

Shared Authorship. A work which is produced by the collaboration of two authors, compilers, editors, translators, collectors, adapters, etc.

Shared Cataloguing. A form of cataloguing undertaken by the Library of Congress and other agencies responsible for national bibliography. The L. of C., under the United States Higher Education Act, 1965 was charged with '(a) acquiring so far as possible, all library materials of value to scholarship currently published throughout the world; and (b) providing catalogue information, for such materials promptly after receipt . . .' and in order to achieve these objects arranged with other national agencies to send catalogue entries for all works published in their country to the L. of C.

Sharpness. In photography, the density-gradient at an edge of an image.

Shaved. A book which has been trimmed by the binder so closely that the lines of print have been grazed, without actually being cut into. *See also Cropped.*

Shaw Memorial Award, Ralph R. Established in 1974 by the University of Hawaii Foundation; it consists of monetary awards to individuals, particularly from Hawaii and the Pacific area, to provide further education through scholarships at accredited library schools, fellowships, conferences, institutes and workshops.

Sheaf Binder. A case or binder to hold a sheaf of papers to form a loose-leaf catalogue or other record. The sheets of paper are punched with holes to go over posts which keep the sheets in position, and there is some form of locking device to keep the covers and the sheets securely in position.

Sheaf Catalogue. A catalogue made on slips of paper, as distinct from one made on cards, and fastened into a sheaf binder which permits the insertion of new material in correct order.

Sheaf Holder. *Synonymous with* SHEAF BINDER (*q.v.*).

Sheepskin. The skin of a sheep prepared as a bookbinding material. Such skins have been used for bookbinding in the United Kingdom since about 1400. The boards they covered were usually of oak. *See also Alaska Seal, Law Calf, Roan, Rutland, Skiver, Smyrna Morocco.*

Sheet. 1. A large piece of paper as manufactured. Also used of the sheet after it has been printed and folded to form a section of a book or pamphlet; to avoid confusion, a folded sheet is best called a SECTION (*q.v.*). Sheets of paper bearing the same size name can be had in double ('double') or quadruple ('quad') size. *See also Octavo, Paper Sizes.* 2. An individual map printed (usually) on one side of a sheet of paper. Also called 'Sheet map'.

Sheet-feed. Said of a printing press which takes paper cut into sheets instead of paper in a continuous roll.

Sheet Index. (*Cartography*) An index, usually based on an outline map showing the layout, numbering system, etc. of map sheets which cover an area.

Sheet Map. A map printed on one side of a sheet of paper. Also called a 'Sheet'.

Sheet Music. Printed music which is not bound into stiff covers. There is no limit on the number of pages. *See also Score.*

Sheet Stock. A stock of unbound printed sheets of a block which are kept in stock by the printer until the publisher orders them to be bound up. This method of binding books as required to meet orders, is done to spread the cost of production.

Sheet Work. Printing one side of a sheet of paper from an 'inner forme' and the other from an 'outer forme'. Also called 'Work and back'. When both sides have been printed, the sheet is known as a 'Perfect copy'. By this method, one sheet is used to print one copy using two formes. *See also Half-Sheet Work.*

Sheets. The printed pages of a book, either flat or folded, but unbound. *See also In Sheets.*

Sheetwise. A method of printing in which a separate forme is used for printing each side of a sheet of paper. *See also Work and Turn.*

Sheffield Local Co-operation Scheme. Library Co-operation in Sheffield (UK) has a long history; the Sheffield Interchange Organization (SINTO) was formed in 1932. The Sheffield Libraries Co-ordinating Committee which was very active in the 1980s is now replaced by a new Board for Library and Information Services in Sheffield. One of the three co-operative bodies entrusted with the co-ordination of an LIP (*q.v.*).

Shelf. A flat piece of wood, steel or other material, which is placed horizontally between two uprights, or supported on brackets, to hold books. Shelves may be constructed of rollers to save wear on the binding of very heavy and large books. The normal length of shelves is 3 feet or 1 metre from centre to centre of the uprights supporting them.

Shelf-back. *Synonymous with* SPINE (*q.v.*).

Shelf Capacity. The capacity of a library for storing books on shelves; it is generally expressed by the total number of books which can be so accommodated or by the number of linear feet or metres available for housing books or other library materials.

Shelf Checking. *Synonymous with* READING SHELVES (*q.v.*).

Shelf Classification. A classification which is designed for use in arranging books on shelves rather than for minute precision in designating subject areas and relationships.

Shelf Department. The administrative unit of a library responsible for the care of books on the shelves, and sometimes for other work such as classification and shelf-listing.

Shelf Dummy. A piece of wood or cardboard placed on a shelf to indicate a specific book which is shelved out of sequence.

Shelf Guide. A guide placed on the edge of a shelf to indicate its contents. Also called 'Shelf label'.

Shelf Height. The vertical distance between two shelves.

Shelf Life. The length of time which sensitized materials used in photocopying or documentary reproduction may be kept before exposure without loss of efficiency.

Shelf List. A list of the books in a library, the entries being brief and arranged on cards or sheets in the order of the books on the shelves, and forming, in effect, in a classified library, a subject catalogue without added entries, analytics and cross-references.

Shelf Mark. *Synonymous with* SHELF NUMBER (*q.v.*).

Shelf Number. With FIXED LOCATION (*q.v.*) a number given to a shelf to assist in the finding of books by indicating the one on which any individual book will be found. This number is incorporated in the BOOK NUMBER (*q.v.*). *See also Call Number.*

Shelf Reading. *Synonymous with* READING SHELVES (*q.v.*).

Shelf Register. *Synonymous with* SHELF LIST (*q.v.*).

Shelf Support. 1. The upright part of a book stack which holds the shelves, either directly or by means of a bracket. 2. The small fittings which fit into slots in the uprights and actually support the shelves. These may be pins, studs or brackets.

Shelf Tidying. *Synonymous with* READING SHELVES (*q.v.*).

Shell. (*Printing*) The electro plate before it is backed with metal.

Shelving. 1. All the shelves in a library. 2. The act of putting books away in their proper places on the shelves of a library.

SHEMROC. Acronym for the Sheffield Media Resources Organizing Committee; formed to co-ordinate purchase and arrangement of audio-visual materials by the libraries and art gallery in Sheffield, UK.

Shera (Jesse H.) Award for Research. An award made by the LIBRARY RESEARCH ROUND TABLE (*q.v.*) for the best paper presented by an author at an LRRT meeting.

Shiner. A mineral impurity in paper seen as a shining speck on the surface of the paper; sometimes it is due to mica in the china clay which is used as LOADING (*q.v.*) being compressed into a translucent spot during passage through the calenders. Hard, brittle materials fall out and leave 'pinholes'.

Shining-up Table. *Synonymous with* REGISTER TABLE (*q.v.*).

Shipping Room. The room of a library where parcels of books, etc., are unpacked and distributed to the various departments, and from which the outgoing material is despatched. (American.)

Shoes. (*Binding*) Metal attached to the edges only at the corners of the covers of books, and sometimes at the base of the spine, to protect the leather binding.

Shooting Stick. A tool of metal or hardened wood used to hammer wooden quoins into position against the side of a chase when locking up a forme.

Shop Library. A library opened in a former shop, usually as a temporary measure and until permanent premises can be built. Sometimes such accommodation is taken for a short time to test the best site for a permanent library.

Short And. *See Ampersand.*

Short Cataloguing. The style of cataloguing in which the entries give author, main title, and date only.

Short Descenders. Lower case letters with descenders (g, j, p, etc.) which are shorter than usual; these can be obtained with certain founts of type.

Short Form Cataloguing. *See Short Cataloguing.*

Short Grain. Paper in which the fibres lie in the shorter direction of the sheet. *See also Grain Direction, Long Grain.*

Short Letter. A character, such as a, o, s, which has neither ascender nor descender. *See also Long Letter.*

Short-loan Collection. *See Reserve Collection 2.*

Short Page. A page of type matter with fewer lines of type than there is room for, or than has been specified. In bookwork the space at the foot is left blank or it may be filled with a decorative piece. *See also Long Page, Type Page.*

Short Ream. 480 sheets of paper. *See also Long Ream, Ream.*

Short Score. *Synonymous with* CLOSE SCORE (*q.v.*). *See also Score.*

Short Story. A complete story of from 1000 to 8000 words in length.

Short Title. 1. The abbreviated title by which an Act of Parliament is known and officially designated. 2. Enough of the title of a book to enable it to be identified in a catalogue or bibliography.

Short-title System. A system of bibliographical references in publications which uses a shortened form of the title of a book or periodical article after the first full mention.

Shorts. 1. The copies of different sheets needed to complete an imperfect edition. 2. Books ordered from, but not delivered by, a bookseller owing to their not being in stock.

Shoulder. The top of the shank of a piece of movable type. Its parts are the BEVEL (or neck), BEARD, LINE and SIDE BEARING (*q.v.*). The FACE (*q.v.*) is above the bevel.

Shoulder-head. A short descriptive heading, which precedes a paragraph; it is set in large or small capitals, or in italics, flush to the left-hand margin occupying a separate line and with a line of leading between it and the following paragraph. It marks the second division of text within the chapter, subsidiary to the CROSS-HEAD (*q.v.*) and superior to the SIDE HEAD (*q.v.*). *See also Marginal Note.*

Show Through. Printed matter which shows through from the other side of a printed leaf, due to ink penetration because of the paper being insufficiently opaque or to improper pressure during machining. *See also Strike Through.*

SI Units. Abbreviation for units of the Système International d'Unités which are now normally used in science and mathematics books, and are receiving general acceptance. The basic SI units for physical quantity with their appropriate symbols are:

length: metre m
mass: kilogram kg
time: second s
electric current: ampère A
thermodynamic temperature: kelvin K
luminous intensity: candela cd
amount of substance: mole mol

SIBIL. Système Informatisé pour Bibliothèques. *See REBUS.*

SIBMAS. Acronym of the Société Internationale des Bibliothèques et des Musées des Arts du Spectacle; this international association was formed during the tenth international congress of the IFLA Section of Libraries and Museums of the Theatre Arts, held in Brussels in October 1972 during the annual IFLA Council when the former International Society for Performing Arts Libraries and Museums restructured itself in this way. SIBMAS is concerned with all matters relating to performing arts collections in libraries, archives and museums. An International Council is held every two years. There are several active national branches. *See also International Society for Performing Arts Libraries and Museums.*

sic. (*Lat.* 'so, thus, in this manner') Usually printed in [ ] to indicate that an exact reproduction of the original is being made.

Side. 1. The right hand or left hand of a piece of type when the printing surface is uppermost and facing the viewer. The front is called the 'belly' and the back the 'back'. 2. The front or back cover of a bound book.

Side Bearing. The amount of 'shoulder' on either side of a piece of movable type; it controls the amount of white space left between characters when composed into lines.

Side Head (Side Heading). A short descriptive sub-heading dividing sections of a chapter, indented one em and usually printed in italics (but maybe in caps, large and small, or in bold), not occupying a separate line, and placed at the beginning of a paragraph with the matter running on. It is the third division of text within a chapter, subsidiary to the SHOULDER-HEAD (*q.v.*). *See also Cross-Head, Heading 4.*

Side Lettering. *Synonymous with* SIDE TITLE (*q.v.*).

Side Note. A marginal note outside the type page, and usually set in narrow measure in type several sizes smaller than the text of the page. *Synonymous with* MARGINAL NOTE (*q.v.*). Also called 'Hanging shoulder note'. Sometimes it is a substitute for a CROSS-HEAD (*q.v.*), but more usually provides a gloss on the text, or running commentary, which does not interrupt the argument; if read with continuity, side notes give an abstract of the whole book.

Side Sewing. *See Side-Stitch.*

Side Sorts. *Synonymous with* ODD SORTS (*q.v.*).

Side Stick. *See Chase.*

Side-stitch. (*Binding*) To stitch a booklet or pamphlet of two or more folded signatures from back to front through the leaves or sections (not through their folds), and near their binding edges, using thread or wire. Also called 'Flat stitching', 'Side sewing', 'Stab-stitch'. When wire is used the process is called 'Wire-stabbing'. *See also Saddle Stitching, Singer Sewing.*

Side Title. A title impressed on the front cover, or side, of a bound book.

Side-wire. To side-stitch a pamphlet with wire staples.

Siderography. The process of producing steel engravings and making prints therefrom.

SIG. SPECIAL INTEREST GROUP (*q.v.*).

Sigil. A chronological CODEN (*q.v.*) in which the first characters would represent the date of publication followed by those representing the title.

Sigillography. The science or study of seals, being a branch of diplomatics. Also called 'SPHRAGISTICS'.

Sigla. Symbols; it is sometimes printed at the head of a table of these.

SIGLE. Acronym for *System for Information on Grey Literature in Europe;* an EC scheme to improve the accessibility of GREY LITERATURE (*q.v.*). Accessible via BLAISE-LINE since 1984.

Sign Manual. A signature written with the person's own hand, especially the signature of a sovereign or head of state, to give authority to a state document.

Signal Poetry Award. This award recognizes particular excellence in poetry for children published during the previous year. The award was first made in 1978 to Ted Hughes.

Signature. 1. A folded printed sheet, forming part of a book; a section. 2. The letter or number, or combination of letters and numbers, printed at the foot of the first page, and sometimes on subsequent leaves of a section, as a guide to the binder in arranging them in their correct order. These were written or stamped in until 1472 when Johann Koelhoff of Cologne, printed a signature as the last line of a text page. The binders of MSS. usually cut off the signature letters. Each section has a different signature and when letters are used, as is usual, they progress in alphabetical order, J, V and W usually being omitted to avoid confusion. There is also a historical reason for the omission of these letters: MSS. and early printed books were usually written in Latin, in which alphabet I stands for both I and J, and V for both U and V, and there is no W. When the alphabet has been used up a lower case sequence or a new sequence of double letters followed by one of treble letters, or sequences combining capital and lower case letters are used. If the same sequence is used again it is known as a duplicated or triplicated signature. Signatures are usually omitted in American books. Also called 'Signature mark'. *See also Collation, Collating Mark, Designation Mark, Direction Line, Section, Title Signature, Volume Signature.* 3. The name or initials, written in a person's own hand to authenticate a document.

Signature and Catchword Line. The line of type which in an old book bears both the signature and the catchword. It is usually below the lowest line of text. Also called 'Direction line'; should the signature and catchword be on separate lines, the lower is called the direction line.

Signature Mark. The letter or number, or a combination of both, placed at the left of the tail margin of the first page of each section of a book. *See also Signature 2.*

Signature Title. *Synonymous with* TITLE SIGNATURE (*q.v.*).

Signatures, List of. *See Register 2.*

Signed Edition. *Synonymous with* AUTOGRAPHED EDITION (*q.v.*). *See also Limited Edition.*

Signed Page. The first page of a section – the one bearing the SIGNATURE (*q.v.*).

'Significant Letter' Code. (*Information retrieval*) One of several systematic methods of abbreviating words.

Significant Punctuation. *See Filing Code.*

Significant Words. In a PERMUTED TITLE INDEX (*q.v.*), words which are permitted to be indexed by reason of their absence on a STOP LIST (*q.v.*).

Silhouette. 1. To remove non-essential background from a half-tone to produce an outline effect. 2. A print, illustration, drawing, or other form of artistic reproduction from which background has been removed.

Silicon Chip. *See Chip.*

Silk Paper. Produced at Baghdad in the Middle Ages and famous throughout Persia. It was prepared from linen. The term is also used for papers containing a quantity of short, coloured silk fibres, or even one or more strands of silk or metal running through the sheet; this is used for bank notes, and is difficult to counterfeit.

Silk Screen. A stencil process for multiplying an original design and for lettering in colours which is used for posters and other jobs requiring short runs and for which lithography would be too expensive. Bolting silk, organdie, phosphor bronze or steel gauze are tightly stretched over a wooden frame. A stencil bearing the design is fixed to the underside of the silk or other material and paint is forced through the silk at the open parts of the stencil with a rubber squeegee on to the paper, silk, metal, glass, wood or other material to be printed.

Silked. A leaf of a book which has been repaired by backing it on both sides with transparent silk.

Silking. The application of silk chiffon to one or both sides of a sheet of paper as a means of repairing or preserving it. *See also Lamination.*

Silver Book Award. A little silver book mounted on a plaque; it is awarded by the (American) Library Binding Institute on the nomination of a Certified Library Binder to people who have made some significant or outstanding contribution to the field of library science.

Silver Halide Paper. A paper used in lensless copying machines. It is necessary to use the traditional photographic developing processes of making negatives (i.e. developing, rinsing, fixing, washing, drying) before making positive copies.

Silver Processes. A group of processes using silver halide sensitized materials for document copying.

SilverPlatter. Trade name of SilverPlatter Information which was founded in the UK in 1983 and was one of the first organizations set up specifically to publish using CD-ROM technology. Now has offices in London and Boston, an international distributor network, and a user base of many thousands. Some 30 databases are available at present, with access via SPIRS, the SilverPlatter Information Retrieval System, specifically designed for use with microcomputers.

Silvered.   The edges of a book which are treated with silver instead of gold.

Simple Heading.   *See Main Heading.*

Simplex.   A communications link between a computer and a remote terminal operating in one direction only. *See also Duplex.*

Simplified Cataloguing.   The elimination of some of the information normally given in full catalogue entries to reduce the work involved in cataloguing and thereby the cost, or to make the catalogue simpler to use. *See also Full Cataloguing, Limited Cataloguing, Short Cataloguing.*

Simplified Filing.   A method of filing cards in a catalogue or entries in an index of any type, that deliberately ignores detailed rules of filing in the interests of greater speed of filing or ease of access. For example tickets in a manual charging system may be filed by author's name and accession numbers only, ignoring initials and titles. *See also Finding List Catalogue.*

Simulation.   In the examination of operational or organizational problems, or solutions to problems, or alternative paths of action, simulation is the construction of a fictional model system, which may be computer-based, on which experiments can be carried out to plot likely outcomes of particular decisions.

Simulator.   A provision in some computers which allows the acceptance of a program written for a computer of a different type.

Simultaneous Scanning.   (*Information retrieval*) A method of scanning a File (*q.v.*).

Sin File.   *See Subject Authority Fiche.*

sine loco.   (*Lat.* 'without a place') used in a catalogue entry, in the abbreviated form (s.l.) for no place of publication.

sine nomine.   (*Lat.* 'without a name') used in a catalogue entry, in the abbreviated form (s.n.) for no known publisher.

Singer Sewing.   Side-stitching with thread, the sewing extending the full length of the volume. *See also Sewing, Stabbing, Thread Stitched.*

Single Look-up.   An index to items embracing bibliographical references which give full bibliographical details, thus avoiding the need to refer to another section of the index.

Single Quotes.   Superior commas used to indicate quoted matter already within quoted matter. '. . .' So named to distinguish them from double quotes ". . .", the more common form of quotation mark. *See also Double Quotes.*

Single-revolution Machine.   A letterpress printing machine in which the continuously running cylinder, having a diameter twice that of the Two-revolution Machine (*q.v.*), runs at a constant speed. During the first half-rotation the bed moves forward and the impression is made; during the second half-rotation the bed returns. Some makes of this type of machine have varying speeds for the bed and/or cylinder.

Single Weight Paper. Sensitized photographic paper between 0.0060 and 0.0083 inches inclusive. *See also Photographic Papers.*

Sinkage. Space left at the top of a printed page in excess of the normal margin, for example at the beginning of a new chapter.

SINTO. Abbreviation for Sheffield Interchange Organization. This is the earliest British scheme of local library co-operation, having been commenced in 1932. *See Sheffield Local Co-operation Scheme.*

SISAC. *See Serials Industry Systems Advisory Committee.*

SISO. A Dutch 'scheme for the classification of the subject catalogues in public libraries' which was published in 1958 by the Central Association of Public Libraries of Holland. It is basically Dr. Greve's 'Hague Scheme' first published in 1931; it has a decimal notation, and the schedules resemble the Universal Decimal Classification and Dewey.

Site Librarian. The librarian in charge of one of a number of libraries within a group but which does not include 'branch' or 'district' in its name, e.g., a library in one of a number of separate teaching units which are part of an educational institution such as a polytechnic or college.

Sittybus. A title label which identified papyrus rolls. *See also Scroll 1.*

Sixteen-mo. *See Sexto-decimo.*

Sixth Form College Libraries Group. Formed 1977 as a focal point for librarians working in Sixth Form Colleges and Tertiary Colleges. Holds regular meetings and publishes a *Newsletter* (m). In 1981 became a Group in Association with the (British) Library Association.

Sixty-fourmo (64mo). A sheet of paper folded six times to form a section of sixty-four leaves, making 128 pages. Also called 'Sexagesimoquarto'.

Size. 1. (*Cataloguing*) The size of a book is measured by its height; a book is called 'narrow' if the width of the cover is less than $^3/_5$ of the height; 'square' if more than $^3/_4$; and 'oblong' or 'landscape' if the width of the cover is greater than the height. Width is usually given only when unusual, or for old books. When both height and width are given, the height is given first. Measurements are usually given in centimetres in bibliographies and catalogues, although often in inches in the latter. The fold symbol (e.g. f°, 4°, 8°, 12°) is often used as an indication of approximate size. *See also Book Sizes, Fold Symbol, Foldings, Type Sizes.* 2. (*Paper*) A mixture of gelatine, alum and formaldehyde through which paper is passed, after coming from the paper-making machine, in order to produce a better surface and to repel water. 3. (*Binding*) A bonding material placed between binding material and lettering.

Size Copy. A thickness or dummy copy. *See also Dummy 1.*

Size Letters. The symbols (F, Q, O, D, etc.) used to indicate the size of books. *See also Fold Symbols, Foldings.*

Size Notation. The method of indicating the size of a book: it may be by measurement in centimetres or inches, by FOLD SYMBOLS (*q.v.*) or by SIZE LETTERS (*q.v.*).

Size Rule. A rule graduated in inches and/or centimetres with fold symbols and corresponding size letters marked at the proper places; it is used for measuring books.

Sized Paper. Paper which has been treated to make it less receptive to water Blotting paper is unsized: writing paper is hard-sized. The treatment consists of adding resin to the stuff in the beater or to the surface of the paper or board (surface sizing) so that the finished paper will be non-absorbent Animal glue, starch or casein may be used as alternatives. *See also Size* (*Paper*).

Sizing. 1. The act of applying size. 2. (*Book Production*) Marking the reduction, or final, size on the original of an illustration as an instruction to the block maker. *See Size 2, 3.*

Skeleton. The cross-bars which separate the pages of type in a forme, the 'furniture' (pieces of wood or metal) which form the page margins, and the running titles, which are left in position when the pages of type have been removed after printing for breaking up, ready for the emplacement of the next pages of the same volume.

Skeleton Abstract. (*Information retrieval*) An abbreviated stylized abstract.

Skeleton Catalogue Card. An outline catalogue card bearing the names of the parts of an entry to show a student of cataloguing the proper placing of the various parts.

Sketch. 1. A drawing. 2. A brief description of a person or event. 3. A short musical or dramatic play.

Skinner Award, (Constance Lindsay). *See Women's National Book Association.*

Skiver. A leather made from the hair or grain side of split sheepskin; it is often embossed and finished in imitation of various leather grains.

Skiver Label. A paper-thin skiver used for a title panel on the spine of a book.

Skolnik Award. An annual award recognising outstanding contributions to and achievements in the theory and practice of chemical information services. The Herman Skolnik Award is presented by the Division of Chemical Information of the American Chemical Society.

s.l. Abbreviation for *sine loco* (*Lat.* 'without a place'). Used in cataloguing entries when the probable place of publication cannot be ascertained.

SLA. SCHOOL LIBRARY ASSOCIATION. SCOTTISH LIBRARY ASSOCIATION. SPECIAL LIBRARIES ASSOCIATION (*qq.v.*).

Slab Serif. (*Printing*) A serif consisting of a plain horizontal stroke which is not bracketed to the upright stroke of a latter.
Glypha, Clarendon and Playbill are faces of this kind.

Slanted Abstract. An abstract giving emphasis to a particular aspect of the contents of a document so as to cater for the interests of a particular group of readers.

Sleeve. 1. A transparent, plastic jacket made to fit over a BOOK JACKET (*q.v.*) to protect the book from wear and at the same time preserve the information printed on the book jacket. 2. A plasticized, printed case made of thick card (*see Boards 3*) to slip over and so protect a gramophone record.

SLIC. Scottish Library and Information Council; a new body planned to replace LISC (Scotland) (*q.v.*) in 1991. Unlike LISC(S) which is funded in part by the Scottish Office, relies on voluntary effort, and secretarial support from the National Library of Scotland, SLIC will be a limited company independent of official ties, and able to sponsor research and consultancy as well as comment on legislation and professional matters. The body will be financed by members' subscriptions.

SLIC Index. An index compiled on the principle of Selective Listing In Combination. It consists of deriving every combination of terms from the set of alphabetically ordered terms assigned by the indexer, selecting from these combinations only those which do not form the beginnings of longer combinations, and listing these selected groups in alphabetical order. Not more than five terms are assigned as a set, but these can be re-arranged so as to give a total of sixteen entries.

Slick. A large-circulation consumer magazine printed on coated stock and usually characterized by articles chosen for popular appeal and fiction limited to formulized stories with happy endings. The authors of the material published receive a higher rate than for the 'pulps'. Also called 'Slick paper'. *See also Pulp 2.*

Slide. A visual positive image on transparent material, usually film, mounted in rigid format designed for projection. This term is tending to be superseded by TRANSPARENCY (*q.v.*).

Slide Box. *Synonymous with* SLIP CASE (*q.v.*).

Slide Case. *Synonymous with* SLIP CASE (*q.v.*)

Slide-tape. *See Tape-Slide.*

Sliding Shelves. Large shelves for the flat storage of folios; designed so that they may be pulled forward to facilitate handling and save wear and tear on the bindings.

Slip. (*Verb*) 1. To discharge a book. *See Book Card, Discharging Books.* 2. To list books on separate slips of paper, one for each book. (*Noun*) A small piece of paper, usually of standard 5 × 3 inches size, used to record briefly author and title, etc., as part of the book-preparation processes, or for some temporary recording purpose. The master catalogue entry or the catalogue entry for a typist to copy, may be written on such a slip. *See also P-Slip, Slips.*

Slipcancel. A small piece of paper bearing a printed correction and pasted over the incorrect matter in a printed book.

Slip Case. 1. A cardboard box made to fit one or more volumes published together, and open at the front to show the titles. Also called 'Open-back case', 'Slide box', 'Slide case', 'Slip-in case'. 2. (*Archives*) A box usually open-fronted, sometimes with a soft fabric lining, used to protect a book or set of books.

Slip Catalogue. *Synonymous with* PAGE CATALOGUE (*q.v.*).

Slip-in Case. *Synonymous with* SLIP CASE (*q.v.*).

Slip Proof. *See Proof.*

Slip Sheet. A sheet of paper which is placed between sheets as they come from the printing machine to prevent offset. *See also Set-off.*

Slipping Books. The American term for DISCHARGE (*q.v.*) of books.

Slipping Desk. *See Circulation Desk.*

Slips. 1. The pieces of sewing cord or tape which project beyond the back of the book after it is sewn, and which are afterwards attached to the boards. Also called 'Tabs'. 2. The paper slips on which are written the instructions to the binder. 3. Applied to matter not set up into pages, but pulled as proofs, on long slips of paper called galley proofs. *See also Proof.*

Sloping Shelves. *Synonymous with* TILTED SHELVES (*q.v.*).

Slotted Shelving. A form of adjustable steel shelving whereby the shelves slide into slots running through the uprights from back to front.

SLS. *See SWALCAP Library Services Ltd.*

Slug. 1. A line of type set solid on a composing machine. 2. A metal bar the length of a line of type characters, to print an entire line, having the appearance of a solid line of type and serving the same purpose.

Slug-casting Machine. A machine for setting up type in the form of cast lines or slugs. These include INTERTYPE, ITALTYPE, LINOTYPE, LUDLOW and TYPO-GRAPH (*qq.v.*).

Slugset. Type which has been set in slugs, e.g. lines of type cast in one piece.

Slur. A letterpress machine printing fault caused by an irregular movement of the paper while the impression is being taken, and resulting in the distortion of dots in a half-tone or a double impression of the type characters.

Small Capitals. The smaller capital letters (as distinct from the full capitals) of which they are about ⅔ the size, thus: A, B, C; the same size as the X-HEIGHT (*q.v.*) of a letter. Indicated in a MS. or proof by two strokes underneath. Abbreviated s.c., s.cap., sm.cap., s.caps, small caps (*pl.*). *See also Capitals, Lower Case Letters, Upper Case Letters.*

Small Demy. *See Demy.*

Small Firms Information Centre (UK). The Small Firm Service is run by the Department of Employment and is available to anyone intending to set up a small business. There are 14 Small Firms Information Centres throughout the country which provide comprehensive information, literature and a counselling service.

Small Full Score. *See Score.*

Small Paper Copy. A copy, or an edition, of a book which is printed on paper of a smaller size than a LARGE PAPER COPY (*q.v.*) or large paper edition. Also called 'Small paper edition'.

Small Pica. An obsolete size of type, about 11 point.

Small Type. (*Printing*) Strictly, type which is intermediate in size between that used for the main text of a book and that used for the footnotes. Colloquially, type of any size except large. Abbreviated s/t.

Smalt. A species of glass, usually deep blue through the use of oxide of cobalt, and finely pulverized for use as a colouring medium in paper making. It is usually used as a 'loading', and as it is resistant to acids, alkalis, heat and moisture, it is a very permanent colouring material. As it has a low colouring power it is expensive, and is used mainly for hand-made and the better machine-made azures for writings. Having a high specific gravity, it usually sinks through the pulp and colours one side more than the other.

Smarties Prize. An award organized by the Book Trust, and given for a children's book in three age categories.

Smasher. *Synonymous with* BUMPER (*q.v.*).

Smashing Machine. A machine used in binderies for compressing folded signatures to render them more compact for binding by expelling the air from between the pages.

Smith (W. H.) Illustration Award. An annual award first made in 1987 by the UK national bookselling chain W. H. Smith. The award is successor to the five-yearly Francis Williams Award run by the Victoria and Albert Museum.

Smith (W. H.) Literary Award. A cash award which has been offered by W. H. Smith & Son Ltd. annually since 1959 when Patrick White received it for *Voss*. The Award is made to the Commonwealth author whose book (originally written in English and published in the United Kingdom within the 24 months ending on 31 December preceding the year of the award) makes, in the opinion of the judges, the most outstanding contribution to literature.

Smooth Antique. *See Paper Finishes.*

Smyrna Morocco. A sheepskin finished with a grain to imitate MOROCCO (*q.v.*). *See also Sheepskin.*

Smyth Sewing. Sewing through the sections of a book; done by a Smyth sewing machine. The usual kind of sewing in Edition binding (*q.v.*), usually without tapes. (American.) *See also Case.*

s.n. Abbreviation for *sine nomine* (*Lat.* 'without a name'). Used in catalogue entries when the name of the publisher is unknown.

Snag File. A file into which are placed items that will not fit into the organization of a main file, either because of certain weaknesses or deficiencies in the main file organization, or because the file system must perform a function which is not part of the original design.

SNI. *See Standard Network Interconnection.*

Sobriquet. A nickname: a fanciful appellation. As these names are usually better known than the real names, books by or about them are often entered in catalogues under the sobriquet. *See also Nickname.*

Social Concern Book Award. *See Odd Fellows (Manchester Unity) Social Concern Book Award.*

Société Internationale Des Bibliothèques – Musées Des Arts Du Spectacle. *See SIBMAS .*

Society of American Archivists. Founded in 1936, this is the world's largest professional association of those individuals and institutions interested in the preservation and use of archives, manuscripts, and current records. The Society's membership includes over 2600 persons serving in government, academic institutions, historical societies, businesses, museums, libraries, religious organizations, professional associations, and numerous other institutions. Nearly 800 institutions also hold membership in the Society, and 800 subscribers to *The American Archivist* (q.) complete the membership. Eleven sections and numerous round tables enable SAA members to meet, exchange information with, and work with colleagues with similar concerns and needs. Abbreviated SAA.

Society of Archivists. Founded in 1947 to foster the care and preservation of archives and to enable archivists to discuss common problems and interchange technical knowledge in Great Britain and the Commonwealth. Publishes *Journal* (two p.a.).

Society of Authors. A UK body that gives advice to members on business matters, publishes guides to contracts, copyright, VAT, etc., administers a trust fund for authors, organizes special interest groups and pursues campaigns on behalf of the profession. Issue *The Author* (q.).

Society of County Librarians. The organization representing the librarians of the (UK) shire counties (that is, the non-metropolitan counties). Formed 1954; advises, comments and initiates research in public library matters. *See also FOLACL.*

Society of Indexers. Founded in London in 1957 with the aim of improving standards of book indexing and securing some measure of uniformity in its technique, advising publishers and editors on the qualification and remuneration of indexers, and safe-guarding their interests. Publishes *The Indexer* (2 p.a.), *Indexers Available* (a.), *Newsletter* (q.). *See also Index, Wheatley Medal, Carey Award.*

Society Publication. An official publication issued by, or under the auspices of, a society, institution or association.

Soda Pulp. (*Papermaking*) Chemical wood pulp which is prepared by digesting the wood fibres under pressure with a solution of caustic soda. This process is usually applied to straw and soft or deciduous trees such as aspen, poplar, etc., which cannot be treated by the sulphite process (*see Sulphite Pulp*) usually confined to coniferous woods.

Soft Cover. *Synonymous with* PAPERBACK *and* PAPER-BOUND (*qq.v.*).

Soft-Ground Etching. One in which the ground commonly used is softened by mixing with tallow, the design being made with a pencil on a piece of fine-grained paper stretched over the ground. This, when etched with acid, gives the effect of pencil or chalk lines in the printed impression.

Software. A generic term for computer programs (both system programs which operate the computer, and applications programs which relate to the particular organization or job in hand). Physical formats include tape, disks, CD-ROM, etc. *See also Hardware.*

Solander Case. A book-shaped box for holding a book, prints, pamphlets or other material, named after its inventor, Daniel Charles Solander (1736–82). It may open at the side or front with hinges, or have two separate parts, one fitting over the other. Its most developed form has a rounded back, projecting SQUARES (*q.v.*) like a book, and possibly one or more spring catches. Also called 'Solander', 'Solander box', 'Solander cover'.

Solid Filing. Synonymous with letter-by-letter filing. *See Alphabetization.*

Solid Gilt. A book the edges of which have been gilded 'in the round', i.e. after the book has undergone ROUNDING (*q.v.*). *See also Gilt on the Rough, Marbling Under Gilt, Rough Gilt Edges.*

Solid Matter. Type which has been set without 'leads'. Matter so set is said to be 'Set solid'. *See also Leaded Matter, Leads.*

Solidus. An oblique stroke used for various purposes, e.g. to indicate line endings in a bibliographical description of a title-page, as An/address/to the/ . . . Also called 'Virgule'.

SOLINET.   Abbreviation for the Southeastern Library Network, one of the largest US regional library network organizations. Based in Atlanta, Georgia.

Sombre.   A binding with both BLIND (*q.v.*) and coloured TOOLING (*q.v.*).

Sorority Library.   A library in a sorority on an American college or university campus. It may be a circulating collection from the main library, or owned by the sorority, a girls' or women's club.

Sort.   A single type-letter. The complete muster of sorts, made up in the correct proportion of characters, is called a 'fount'. Also called 'Character'. *See also Code, Digit, Special Sorts.*

Sort of Symbol.   (*Information retrieval*) A constituent part of a symbol, e.g. in the symbol ABA 553 there are six digits but only four sorts or characters (A, B, 3 and 5).

Sound Library.   A collection of audio records such as gramophone records, tape, and sound film.

Sound Recordings Group.   A Group of the Library Association which was formed in 1964. *See Audio-Visual Group.*

Source.   1. Any document which provides the users of libraries or of information services with the information sought.   2. Any document which provides information reproduced in another document.   3. The data or records providing the basis for an informational search.

Source Document.   (*Information retrieval*) A document from which data is extracted. *See also Source.*

Source Index.   A card, or other, index to sources of unusual and elusive information. This is usually built up in the process of dealing with enquiries.

Source Language.   The natural language in which a document is originally written. *See also Code.*

Source List.   A list of references appended to a treatise to show the sources used by the author. *See also Reading List.*

Source Material.   *See Primary Sources.*

South African Institute for Librarianship and Information Science.   Name adopted in 1979 by the South African Library Association to form it into a multi-racial organization. The original Association was founded in July 1930 as a result of a conference held at Bloemfontein in 1928. Abbreviated SAILIS. Publishes *South African Libraries* (5 p.a.) and *Newsletter* (m.). A number of branches have been formed to function in geographical areas.

South-East Asian Regional Branch of the International Council on Archives.   *See SARBICA.*

Southeastern Library Network.   *See SOLINET.*

South Eastern Regional Library System (UK).   An inter-lending organization which was formed in 1933. Its member libraries were all the public urban and county libraries in South Eastern England excepting those of the Metropolitan boroughs (i.e. in the then London County Council) area – these functioned as a bureau under the name of the LONDON UNION CATALOGUE (*q.v.*). After the alteration of the local government boundaries which became operative in 1965, the System and the London Union Catalogue were combined to form the LONDON & SOUTH EASTERN LIBRARY REGION (LASER) (*q.v.*).

South West Academic Libraries Co-operative Automation Project.   *See SWALCAP.*

South Western Branch.   A Branch of the (British) Library Association. Covers the counties of Avon, Cornwall, Dorset, Devon, Gloucestershire, Hampshire, Somerset, Isle of Wight and Wiltshire.

Space.   (*Printing*) A small rectangular block of metal not bearing a character, which is used between letters or words to provide spacing. Spaces are less than type height, cast in point sizes and smaller than an em quad (mutton), the square of the body. The usual sizes are:

en quad (nut), ½ body or two to the em;
thick space (⅓-em space), ⅓ body or three to the em;
middle space (¼-em space), ¼ body or four to the em;
thin space (⅕-em space), ⅕ body or five to the em;
hair space (1/12-em space), 1/12 body or twelve to the em.

Space.   (*Information retrieval*). 1. A unit of area on a record, i.e. an area that may contain only one printed character.   2. To remove from one place to another according to a prescribed format (*see Format 3*), e.g. to remove horizontally to the right, or vertically, on a printed page.   3. A place intended for the storage of data, e.g. a location in a storage medium, or on a printed page.

Space Dot.   *Synonymous with* CENTRED DOT (*q.v.*).

Space Lines.   Strips of brass which are often used in place of LEADS (*q.v.*).

Space to Fill.   Space left in a printing layout through insufficient COPY (*q.v.*) being provided.

Spacebands.   Wedge-shaped pieces of metal used in line-casting machines such as LINOTYPE and INTERTYPE (*qq.v.*) to separate words and at the same time automatically justify lines of type.

Spacing.   The distribution of printed matter on a printed page or pair of pages so that it is aesthetically satisfactory. It relates to the space between letters, words, lines, and any decorative or illustrative matter.

Spanish.   The best grade of esparto grass. Cheaper grades grown in North Africa are known as Tripoli.

Spanish Calf.   A light-coloured calf on which brilliant effects can be obtained by staining.

Spearhead.   A British Government database set up to provide industry with information relevant to the European single market planned for 1992.

Special Bibliography.   *See Bibliography.*

Special Classification.   A scheme of book classification which is applied to a section of knowledge; for example:

Barnard's *Classification for medical and veterinary libraries.*
Vernon, K.D.C. and Lang, V. *The London classification of business studies.*
Moys, E.M. *A classification scheme for law books.*

Special Collection. A collection of books connected with local history, celebrities, industries, etc., or on a certain subject or period, or gathered for some particular reason, in a library which is general in character.

Special Edition. 1. An edition of a work or works, re-issued in a new format, sometimes with an introduction, appendix, or illustrations, and having a distinctive name. 2. An edition which differs from the normal edition by some distinctive feature, such as better paper and binding or the addition of illustrations. 3. An extra or enlarged number of a newspaper or periodical, such as an anniversary, Christmas, or souvenir number.

Special Estimate. *See Estimates.*

Special Interest Group. A group of members of an organization formed to represent a focus on a specific area of activity; probably more applicable to a small area than a 'division' or 'section'. Abbreviated SIG.

Special Issue. 1. *Synonymous with* SPECIAL NUMBER (*q.v.*). 2. The loan of a book to a person who does not possess a membership ticket, or a loan for an unusual period.

Special Librarian. One who is in charge of, or is employed in, a special library; should have a knowledge of the literature of the field covered by the library (not necessarily a special knowledge of the field itself) and also of the means of organizing it for use.

Special Librarianship. The branch of librarianship which is concerned with selecting, administering, and evaluating books and non-book materials in specific and limited fields of knowledge, and disseminating the information contained therein to meet the needs of the particular institution or its clientele.

Special Libraries Association. Founded in the USA in 1909; the objectives of this 'not-for-profit corporation' are to: 'provide an association of individuals and organizations having a professional, scientific or technical interest in library and information science, especially as these are applied in the recording, retrieval and dissemination of knowledge and information in areas such as the physical, biological, technical and social sciences and the humanities; and to promote and improve the communication, dissemination and use of such information and knowledge for the benefit of libraries or other educational organizations'. It has as its slogan 'Putting knowledge to work'. The work of the Association is carried out through many subject divisions and geographical chapters. There are currently 12,000 members in special libraries and information centres serving business, research, government, universities, newspapers, museums, and institutions that use or produce specialized information. The Professional Development Program is a current priority. Abbreviated SLA. Publishes *Special Libraries* (11 p.a.), *Specialist List* (m) and an extensive range of monograph titles.

Special Library. 1. (a) A library or information centre, maintained by an individual, corporation, association, government agency or any other group; or, (b) a specialized or departmental collection within a library. 2. A collection of books and other printed, graphic or record material dealing with a limited field of knowledge, and provided by a learned society, research organization, industrial or commercial undertaking, government department or educational institution. It may also be a special branch of a public library serving certain interests or occupational groups, such as a technical library; or a subject library meeting the needs of all enquirers on a given subject, such as a music library. A special library is broadly one which is neither academic, commercial, national nor public. It is intended to serve the needs of a portion of the community requiring detailed information respecting a limited subject field.

Special Number.   A special issue (usually enlarged in size) of a periodical devoted to a special subject or occasion. More routine occasions to which issues of periodicals are wholly or partly devoted are: (a) directory issue containing a directory of the trade or group served by the periodical; (b) membership list containing a list of members; (c) proceedings issue containing papers read at a conference, or a summary of the same; (d) an annual review, or annual report, issue surveying the past year and giving tables of statistics, possibly with forecasts relating to the following year; (e) yearbook (handbook, or almanac) issue combining any or all of the foregoing types, together with general data kept up to date by annual revisions. *See also Special Edition.*

Special Sorts.   Type characters which are not usually included in a FOUNT (*q.v.*), and are supplied on request, such as fractions, musical signs, superior and inferior letters and figures, etc.

Special Title-page.   A title-page, usually with imprint, preceding a single part of a larger work. Also one preceding the normal title-page of a complete work which is issued or re-issued as part of a collection, series, or serial publication.

Specialized Information Market Programme.   A European Community programme set to run 1984–89; examined document delivery, electronic publishing, CD-ROM databases, etc. *See also IMPACT.*

Species.   1. In classification, the groups into which a genus is divided. *See also Predicables, Five.*   2. In computer coding, each conventional set of 'sorts' comprising a symbol. *See also Digit.*

Specific Classing.   Allocating a book to the most specific or detailed place in a scheme of classification.

Specific Cross-reference.   A reference in a catalogue to a specific heading or headings.

Specific Differences.   (*Classification*) Differences which characterize some individuals as a *specific* sub-class within a more comprehensive *generic* class.

Specific Entry.   An entry in a catalogue under the actual subject, as distinct from one under some broader heading embracing that subject. It should be as specific as, but not more specific than, the content of the document. This is the principle for entry of subjects in a dictionary, subject or classified catalogue. *See also Cataloguing, Principles of.*

Specific Index.   An index such as that to Brown's *Subject Classification*, which has one entry only to each subject. Also called 'One-place index'. *See also Relative Index.*

Specific Reference. (*Cataloguing*) One which states the exact heading to which reference must be made as (in a dictionary catalogue): AUTOMOBILES *see* MOTOR CARS, whereas a general reference would be: ANIMALS see also under the names of individual animals, as ANTELOPE. In the subject index to a classified catalogue references are usually specific as: RELIGION 200, METHODISTS 287. *See also General Reference.*

Specific Subject. (*Classification*) The most precise, and therefore least general, subject heading that is appropriate for a particular document. *See also Close Classification.*

Specification. 1. Instructions prepared for a binder, printer or builder setting out the details of work to be carried out. 2. (*Information retrieval*) The cataloguing, bibliographical, or similar description, of a document. *See also Unit Record.* 3. (*Classification*) Definition by SPECIFIC DIFFERENCE (*q.v.*) in characters. 4. In the field of patents, a concise statement of a set of requirements to be satisfied by a product, a material or a process, indicating, whenever appropriate, the procedure by means of which it may be determined. A *provisional specification* is a specification field with a patent application merely to establish a date for disclosure of an inventive concept to the Patent Office; it does not include a claim to the monopoly sought. A *complete specification* is a patent specification which describes at least one preferred way in which the invention may be performed, and which sets out a claim or claims for the protection sought. 5. (*Book Production*) A book designer's specification listing typeface and size, style for headings, margins, illustration type and position, etc.

Specificity. (*Information retrieval*) In the testing of an information retrieval system, a measure expressing the ratio of the number of non-relevant documents not retrieved to the total number of non-relevant documents in a file.

Specificity Rule. (*Cataloguing*) This rule provides that an entry in a subject catalogue should be made under the specific subject of a document, not under a more general one which includes that specific subject.

Specimen Pages. Printed pages which are submitted by the printer to show the proposed style of setting. They usually number four and include a chapter opening with any sub-headings.

Speckled Sand Edge. A bound book the top-, fore-, and bottom-edges of which have been rubbed down with sandpaper and sprinkled or sprayed with colour.

Speculum Humanae Salvationis. *See Block Books.*

Sphragistics. *Synonymous with* SIGILLOGRAPHY (*q.v.*).

Spine. The part of the cover of a book which conceals the folds of the sections. It normally bears the title, author and (when in a publisher's case) the publisher's name. Also called 'Back', 'Backbone', 'Shelf-back', 'Backstrip'.

Spine Title. The title which appears on the spine of a book. It is often shorter than the title as given on the title-page.

SPINES. Abbreviation for Science and Technology Policies Information Exchange System. Following the results of a feasibility study, it was agreed at the 18th Session of Unesco held in 1974 to authorize the Director-General to elaborate a programme for the international exchange of information on literature relating to science and technology policies. This programme included the preparation of a report and a resolution at the 19th Session on the establishment of SPINES and the publication of the English source version. This appeared in 1976 as *SPINES Thesaurus: a controlled and structured vocabulary of science and technology for policy-making, management and development.* (Unesco Press, 1976). Latest revision is the *SPINES Thesaurus: a controlled and structured vocabulary for information processing in the field of science and technology for development* (2 vols), 1988.

Spinner. *See Host.*

Spiral Binding. A type of binding used for pamphlets, art reproductions, commercial catalogues, and occasionally books, printed on separate leaves, usually of art paper. These leaves are drilled or slotted near the binding edge to take a spiral-twisted wire or strip of plastic, which is drawn through the apertures. A tendency for the wire to be torn through the holes makes this style unsuitable for publications likely to be subject to much, or to careless, handling. Also called 'Coil binding', 'Spirex binding'. *See also Plastic Binding.*

SPIRS. SILVERPLATTER (*q.v.*) Information Retrieval System.

Splice. A join made by cementing or welding together two pieces of film or paper so that they will function as one when passing through a camera, processing machine, projector or other apparatus. Lap splices are those in which the two pieces overlap and are cemented together. Butt slices are those in which the two pieces are placed together without overlapping and welded.

Split Boards. The boards normally of MILLBOARD (*q.v.*) forming the covers of a book, which are split to receive the ends of the tapes on to which the sections are sewn.

Split Catalogue. A library catalogue in which the different varieties of entry – e.g. subject, author, title – are filed in separate alphabets. Sometimes called a 'Divided catalogue' (*q.v.*).

Split Fractions. Type for setting fractions cast in two parts which when combined make the complete fraction. The upper half contains the upper figure and the lower half the dividing line and the lower figure. Fractions may be set horizontally, e.g. $\frac{3}{8}$ or diagonally, e.g. ⅜ or 3/8.

Split Leather. Leather which has been divided into two or more thicknesses.

Spoiled Letter. *Synonymous with* DAMAGED LETTER (*q.v.*).

Spoiled Sheets. Printed sheets which bear imperfections; it is to allow for such that additional sheets, called 'overs', are issued to the printer. Often called 'Spoils'.

Spoils. *See Spoiled Sheets.*

Spongy Paper. *Synonymous with* FEATHERWEIGHT PAPER (*q.v.*).

Sponsor. A person or corporate body subsidizing or otherwise encouraging the production of a book.

Spread. A pair of facing pages.

Spreadsheet. A set of computer programs used for financial forecasting and control. Many software houses market such packages under a variety of tradenames.

Sprinkled Edges. The three cut edges of a book which have been finely sprinkled with colour to prevent them becoming, or appearing to be, soiled. *See also Edges.*

SPRINT. A programme of the Commission of the European Community, Directorate-General XIII–C, designed to facilitate the transfer of technology throughout the Community, to give better use of the results of research and technological innovations. The initial programme ended in 1988, and a new programme has been launched for 1989–93. Each member state supports SPRINT through a Technology Transfer Network; harmonization of standards is a priority area.

Squabble. A printing fault caused by one or more letters being pushed into an adjacent line.

Square. Said of a book the width of a cover of which is more than three-quarters its height. *See also Narrow, Oblong.*

Square. (*Binding*). The boards of a book are cut slightly larger than the bound sections after trimming so as to leave an even projection over the HEAD, TAIL, and FORE-EDGE (*qq.v.*). This projection of the boards is called the 'square'.

Square Back. *Synonymous with* FLAT BACK (*q.v.*).

Square Brackets. Signs [ ] used in a catalogue or bibliographical entry to indicate that whatever appears within them does not appear in the original, but has been supplied by the copier. Not to be confused with PARENTHESES (*q.v.*).

Square Capitals. The alphabet used as a book hand from the third to the fifth centuries, being adapted from the Roman lapidary capitals. The letters had square serifs instead of being sharply pointed as were those cut in stone. Also called 'Capitales quadrata' and 'Quadrata'. *See also Lapidary Type, Rustic Capital.*

Square Corner. (*Binding*) Folding the covering material over the boards in such a way that after cutting a wedge-shaped piece at the corner, one turn-in may neatly overlap the other. *See also Library Corner, Mitred Corner.*

Square Up. To trim, or adjust, illustrations so that all corners are right angles.

Squared Up Half-Tone. *See Half-Tone.*

Squares. The portions of the boards of a bound book which project beyond the paper on which it is printed.

S.R. Abbreviation for the Register of the STATIONERS' COMPANY (*q.v.*).

SRC. Acronym of Subject-field Reference Code (taking the place of the name Broad System of Ordering, BSO), a UNISIST (*q.v.*) project.

SRIS. *See British Library* (Science Reference and Information Service).

SRL. *See British Library* (Science Reference Library).

S/S. Abbreviation for same size; an instruction, written on the illustration, to the blockmaker to make a block the same size as the copy.

s/t. Abbreviation for SMALL TYPE (*q.v.*).

Stab Marks. Punctures made in folded sheets of printed paper preparatory to sewing.

Stab-stitch. *See Side-Stitch.*

Stabbed. *See Stabbing.*

Stabbing. Binding together one or more sections of a book with wire or thread passed through holes stabbed through the back edge of the folded sheet. This method prevents the book from lying flat when open. A book so bound is said to be 'stabbed'. Piercing the boards with a bodkin for the slips to pass through is sometimes termed 'stabbing'. *See also Stitching.*

Stack. 1. A piece of furniture containing at least four tiers of shelves back to back. 2. The space equipped for the storage of books on one or more floors; more properly, the self-supporting structure of steel book cases, often extending for several floors, or decks, and independent of the walls of the building. For American terms used in connection with book stack equipment, *see Compartment, Deck, Press, Range, Section.* 3. A stack room usually adjoining a public department, containing lesser-used books, and to which only the staff have access.

Stack Room. *See Stack.*

Staff. American spelling for a STAVE (*q.v.*) in music. *Pl.* Staffs.

Staff and Line Management. *See Line Management.*

Staff Appraisal. The technique of monitoring the performance of individual members of staff, having agreed objectives and criteria with the individuals at the outset, and discussing the findings with them during and after evaluation. Staff appraisal is a continuous process, and is usually used as a basis for staff development programmes, promotion opportunities, etc. Can be used to reconcile the individual's view of his job with the organization's view: such a use is sometimes termed *job audit.*

Staff Development. *See Training.*

Staff Enclosure. That part of a public department of a library such as a junior, lending, or reference library, which is restricted to the use of the staff. *See also Circulation Desk.*

Staff Manual. A guide book indicating the correct procedures and processes to be followed by the staff in the various departments or branches of a library system. Called in the USA a PROCEDURE MANUAL (*q.v.*).

Staff Room. A room reserved for the use of the staff for purposes of rest, refreshment and recreation.

Staff Training. *See Training.*

Stained Edges. The edges of a book which have been stained with colour. Where only the top edges have been stained the term 'stained top' is used. *See also Edges.*

Stained Label. A coloured panel painted or printed on the spine of a book as a background for lettering, and to simulate a leather label.

Stained Top. *See Stained Edges.*

Stalls. In old libraries, combined book shelves and reading desk, or LECTERN (*q.v.*), the books being stood upright on shelves (of which there were three) above the reading desk. The fore-edges of the books faced outwards, and the books were chained. This type of shelving was first used by Sir Thomas Bodley at the Bodleian Library, Oxford, and replaced the mediaeval lectern.

Stamp. *See Blocking, Panel Stamp, Tooling.*

Stamp Acts. Towards the end of the seventeenth century duties were imposed on certain legal documents, and paper, vellum and parchment. The Stamp Act of 1712 added to the list of dutiable articles, e.g. essay periodicals like the *Spectator*, and from time to time the list increased. The notorious Stamp Act of 1765 ordered a stamp to be applied to all legal documents in the colonies; it met with great opposition in North America, and was repealed the following year. The subsequent history of the duties is of innumerable variations, generally increasing in the eighteenth, and declining in the nineteenth and twentieth centuries.

Standard Author. An author whose writings have sufficient literary merit to justify a place in the literature of the country, and which, it is hoped, will not become out of print.

Standard Book Number. The use of a sequence of nine digits to individualize titles, editions or volumes. The digits comprising the first group are allocated to UK and Northern Ireland publishers, the remainder – except the last which is a check number to guard against mistakes when feeding into a computer – are allocated to identify individual titles, editions or volumes. The system was prepared by the Publishers Association of Great Britain so that identification and recording could be done by computers if desired, and came into operation on 1 January 1968. The numbers appear against entries in *The Bookseller*, in the *British National Bibliography* and in publishers' catalogues. The British Standard *Specification for book numbering* is BS 4762:1971, the American, Z39. 21. *See also Standard Book Numbering Agency.* Early in 1969, at a meeting sponsored by ISO, this book numbering principle developed internationally with the result that the International Standard Book Number system was adopted, for which *see ISBN.* For the International Standard Serial Number for journals, *see ISSN.*

Standard Book Numbering Agency. A company which is formed in each participating country to operate the International Standard Book Number system. Its duties are to allocate where necessary, verify, record and publish International Standard Book Numbers and maintain master files which are kept on magnetic tape form for computer use. In the UK, the Standard Book Numbering Agency Ltd. was jointly sponsored by J Whitaker & Sons Ltd., the Council of the British National Bibliography Ltd. (later incorporated within the Bibliographic Services Division of the British Library) and the Publishers Association. In the USA the R.R. Bowker Company performs this function. *See also ISBN, Standard Book Number.*

Standard Edition. The edition of an author's books, so called by the publisher, to suggest a good quality of book production which is better than that used for a cheaper edition. It may contain notes and an introduction but need not be a CRITICAL EDITION nor a DEFINITIVE EDITION (*qq.v.*). *See also Uniform Edition.*

Standard Generalized Markup Language. A draft publishing industry standard for the preparation, coding and processing of author-generated electronic texts, drawn up to be applicable to any typesetting system. Gradually being adopted worldwide, e.g. BS 6868. Abbreviated SGML.

Standard Network Interconnection. The Research Library Group, Western Library Network and the Library of Congress worked on this system to permit interconnection. Abbreviated SNI. *See now Open Systems Interconnection, Linked Systems Project.*

Standard Reference Code. A superstructure to be worked out by the Central Classification Committee of FID, primarily for the identification and location of information blocks or collections by the UNISIST network.

Standard Size Card. A card used for cataloguing and other purposes, of the internationally agreed size of 5 × 3 inches (7.5 × 12.5 centimetres in Continental countries). The American Standard (Z85.1–1969 USA Standard for Permanent and Durable Catalog Cards) gives 2.95 × 4.92 inches (75mm × 125mm) with a recommendation that the hole should be 5/16 in. (7.9mm) in diameter and that the lower edge of the hole should be 3/16 in. (4.8mm) from the bottom edge of the card. *See also A7 Library Card.*

Standard Title. The title under which copies of a work, or musical composition, appearing under different titles, is entered in a catalogue. Also called 'Conventional title', 'Uniform title'.

Standard Work. A book recognized as of permanent value.

Standards for Library Services. A statement of the criteria by which a given type of library service can be evaluated; such statements may be specific in quantitative detail, or may be intended as a stimulus towards an ideal, in which case they may be rather entitled *guidelines* or *mission statements*. In some areas of work, notably US Public Libraries, standards as such are being replaced by the concept of planning procedures and output measurement as better indicators of efficiency and effectiveness. The Canadian Library Association's *Project Progress* is on similar lines.

The principal US standards are:

ALA standards for college libraries, 1975.

ACRL statement on quantitative standards for two-year college learning resources programs, 1979.

ARL/ACRL standards for university libraries, 1978/79.

AASL: Media Program: district and school, 1975.

PLA Mission statement, 1977, and A planning process for public libraries, 1980.

(A full discussion of the US position occupies the whole issue of *Library Trends*, vol. 31, no. 1. Summer, 1982).

The principal UK standards are:

Convention of Scottish Local Authorities; public library service in Scotland, 1987.

LA: guidelines for reference and information services to public libraries in England and Wales, 1981.

LA: college libraries: guidelines, 1982.

LA: library resource provision in schools, 1977.

SLA: the way ahead, 1980.

LA: guidelines for library provision in the health service, 1978.

LA: prison libraries: guidelines, 1981.

LISC (Wales): public library services, 1988.

Prison Dept: library facilities for people in custody. HMSO, 1978.

Domiciliary Services Subject Group of the Medical, Health and Welfare Libraries Group, and London housebound Services Group of the ALCL: national standard on housebound library services.

Standing Committee on Business Information. A part of the INFORMATION SERVICES GROUP (*q.v.*) of the (British) Library Association. Abbreviated SCOBI.

Standing Committee on Library Education. A Standing Committee of the AMERICAN LIBRARY ASSOCIATION (*q.v.*) concerned with the development of professional education. Abbreviated SCOLE.

Standing Committees. Committees which local authorities may set up to carry out particular and continuing functions, or manage departments, or provide services.

Standing Conference of African University Libraries. *See SCAUL.*

Standing Conference of Co-operative Library and Information Services (UK). Formerly the Standing Conference of Commercial and Technical Library Co-operative Services. Formed in 1964 to further co-operation between schemes of local library co-operation, to investigate the possibilities of procuring government grant-in-aid for the work of the schemes, and to further the dissemination of commercial and technical information by joint action where necessary. In 1988 awarded a small BLRDD Grant to investigate the potential impact of LIPs (*q.v.*) on existing arrangements. Abbreviated *SCOCLIS.*

Standing Conference of Librarians of Libraries of the University of London. *See SCOLLUL.*

Standing Conference of National and University Libraries. *See SCONUL.*

Standing Conference on Library Materials in Africa. *See SCOLMA.*

Standing Conference on Professional Activities in Scotland. *See SCOPAS.*

Standing Conference on Theological and Philosophical Libraries in London. *See SCOTAPLL.*

Standing Formes. *See Standing Type.*

Standing Order. 1. An order to supply each succeeding issue of a serial, periodical or annual publication, or subsequent volumes of a work published in a number of volumes issued intermittently. 2. One which is to be acted upon until countermanded. Also called 'Continuation order' and (in America) a 'Till-forbid order'.

Standing Press. A larger press than a BENCH PRESS (*q.v.*). It stands on the floor and is used to press cased books. Pressure is applied by a platen which is screwed down with a crow bar. *See also Building-in Machine* which dries and presses books in a few seconds.

Standing Type. The type from which a book has been printed and is kept 'standing' exactly as it came from the machine, to be used again if further copies are to be made. Also called 'Live matter', 'Standing formes'.

Stanford (Winifred Mary) Prize. A biennial award offered by Hodder & Stoughton for a UK-published book inspired by the Christian faith.

Stanhope Press. The first all-iron printing press introduced in 1800 by Charles Mahon, 3rd Earl Stanhope (1753–1816). The platen, which covered the whole forme, was operated by a screw which had several levers thus enabling a satisfactory impression to be obtained with less physical effort than with previous machines.

Star. *Synonymous with* ASTERISK (*q.v.*). *See also Reference Marks.*

Star Map. A map of the heavens. Also called an 'Astronomical map'.

Star Signature. A signature indicating an off-cut (part of a sheet) and distinguished by an asterisk placed with the signature letter or figure of the main part of the sheet. This part of a section is usually placed inside the part bearing the plain signature.

Starch. The original material for sizing paper. It is now used in addition to other sizing agents as a loading agent in order to give a hard 'rattle' and an improved 'finish' to paper.

Starr. A Hebrew deed, covenant, contract, or obligation, anciently required to be filed in the royal exchequer, and invalid unless so deposited. The name was applied to all agreements between Jews and Christians and, occasionally, to other Jewish documents before the expulsion of the Jews from England in 1290. Starrs were written in two languages, Latin or Norman-French, with an acknowledgement in Hebrew at the foot.

Start. Leaves of a book are said to 'start' when the sewing is defective, causing the leaves to become loose.

Starter. (*Classification*) The first curve, used in the Colon Classification to enclose the Subject Device Number. The second, or closing, curve is called the 'Arrester'. *See also Brackets, Circular Brackets, Curves.*

State. An impression of an engraving taken from a plate at any stage in the perfecting process. Various states include *open letter proof* and *publication state*. An *early impression* is one of the first copies to be taken; it is consequently sought after by collectors as representing a print taken when the plate is in its best condition.

State Document Centre. A library that has the responsibility of collecting, preserving and organizing as complete a file as possible of the public documents of the state in which it is situated. (American.)

State Library. In America, a library maintained by state funds, which preserves the state records and provides books for the use of state officials, books relating to the history of the state, books published by authors living in the state, and newspapers published in the state. In many states, all classes of books are purchased in order to supply any resident's needs for books or information. *See also National Library.*

State Library Administrative Agency. A term used in the (American) Library Services Act, 1961, to mean the official State agency charged by

State law with the extension and development of public library services throughout the State.

State Library Agency. An American state organization existing to extend and improve library services in the state. It should be free from partisan politics and political interference of all kinds, led by professional librarians, supported by law, and adequately financed. Amongst its functions are the planning of a state-wide public library service, promotion of the development of these libraries supervising library provision with a view to improving services by formulating and enforcing minimum standards; providing a consulting and advisory service to librarians, boards of library trustees and citizen groups; administering a state system of grants-in-aid as well as federal grants-in-aid to libraries; providing supplementary services such as inter-library loans of books and non-book materials, travelling libraries; providing a centralized information and bibliographic service; centralized cataloguing; providing library services to schools, clubs and individuals where no public library services exist.

State Library Associations. In the United States of America each state has a local library association. The standard and size of these organizations vary enormously. Most issue a newsletter, and some produce more substantial journals.

State Paper Office of Ireland. *See Public Record Office of Ireland.*

Stationarii. Men commissioned by universities in mediaeval times to attend to the production and distribution of books.

Stationer. From *Lat. stationarius* 'one who stands' (i.e. at a stall). One who sells stationery. Originally used to mean a bookseller.

Stationers' Company. The authority which regulated and organized printing and the book trade in England. It was established by a Royal Charter from Queen Mary in 1557, created a livery company in 1560, and until the passing of the Copyright Act in 1842 had an absolute monopoly, as all apprentices to the printing trade were obliged to serve a member of the Company, and every publication was required to be 'Entered at Stationers' Hall' as proof of registration. The *Registers* which commenced in 1554 are of great value in the history of English literature.

Statistical Bibliography. 1. The assembling and interpretation of statistics relating to books and periodicals in order to: (a) demonstrate historical movements; (b) determine the national or universal research use of books and journals; (c) ascertain in many local situations the general use of books and journals. 2. To shed light on the processes of written communication and of the nature and course of development of a discipline by means of counting and analysing the various facets of written communication.

STATUS. An information retrieval package developed at the Atomic Energy Research Establishment, Harwell, UK. The package combines in one integrated whole a command language, data input and output facilities, and storage/retrieval facilities.

The storage/retrieval function works on the free text principle – any machine-readable form may be stored – and STATUS creates a file of all meaningful words either individually or in logical combinations, including truncations, synonyms and numerical data, from which retrieval can take place. There are facilities for on-line editing or updating of stored material and the system can be integrated with many storage devices, including CD-ROM, and is suitable for many screen formating and validation tools, and word processing packages. Harwell Computer Power Ltd was set up in 1986 to place development on a commercial footing. Uses of STATUS include the assembling and management of data bases comprising texts of abstracts, reports, legal opinions, flight-safety reports, inventories, toxic chemical data, etc., also bibliographic databases, and library housekeeping routines featuring subject codes, keywords, or classification numbers. A STATUS User Group was formed in 1981.

STATUS/IQ. A software system for use with STATUS which understands questions phrased in plain English and can rank its findings according to their importance to the perceived needs of the user. The Intelligent Query package was introduced in March 1989.

Statutory Instruments (UK). Documents by which the power to make, confirm, or approve Orders, Regulations, or other subordinate legislation, conferred by an Act of Parliament on Her Majesty in Council or on a Minister of the Crown, is exercised. Prior to 1 January 1948, when the Statutory Instruments Act, 1946, came into operation, they were known as *Statutory Rules and Orders*. Although Statutory Instruments are frequently required to be laid before Parliament, they rank as Non-Parliamentary Publications.

Statutory Reference. In the British patents field, a reference placed at the end of a patent specification as a Statutory act by the Comptroller to direct attention to another specification.

Stave. 1. The five horizontal lines on which musical notation is written or printed. Spelt 'staff' in America. 2. *Synonymous with* SECTION 1 (*q.v.*).

STC. Abbreviation for *A short-title catalogue of books printed in England, Scotland, and Ireland, and of English books printed abroad, 1475–1640*, by A.W. Pollard and G.R. Redgrave, London, Bibliographical Society, 1926.

Steel Engraving. *See Engraving.*

Stem. 1. The outline of the design of a type letter; the bare lines apart from the serifs, which indicate most clearly the character and height of the letter. The main stroke of a letter. 2. The body of a type letter between the face and the foot. Also called the SHANK (*q.v.*) or BODY (*q.v.*). 3. A string of letters which occur at the beginning of several related words, e.g. LIBR for library, libraries, librarians, etc.

Stencil. 1. The basic principle of printing, in which a wax, silk or other stencil is used. The ink is applied to the back of the printing image carrier (i.e. the stencil) and reaches the front through the image areas which are porous and open. *See also Silk Screen.* 2. The 'master' or image area which carries the image, and by means of which the printing is done. 3. A thin cut metal plate which allows the transfer of a design, etc., to paper when an ink roller or brush is passed over its surface.

Stencil Duplicating. A method of producing multiple copies from a specially prepared wax master. A particular kind of ink is forced through the cuts made by a typewriter in the stencil and transferred to the paper.

Step-and-repeat Camera. A microfilm camera which provides a series of latent image frames in a predetermined pattern on a single sheet of film.

Step-and-repeat Machine. A machine for multiple copying (on offset plates, etc.), with devices for the adjustment of each copy. Intended specially for reproduction in colour in which the printing plates for each colour must be superimposed precisely when printing.

Stepwise Operated Camera. *Synonymous with* PLANETARY CAMERA (*q.v.*).

Stereo. *See Stereotype.*

Stereophonic. Relating to a sound transmission system in which is realized the illusion of auditory perspective.

Stereoscopic Slide. A pair of positive photographic prints made from negatives taken from two slightly different viewpoints to give a three-dimensional effect when viewed through a specially made viewer.

Stereotype (Stereo). A metal printing plate carrying a printing surface in relief, made by pouring stereotype metal into a papier-mâché (called 'flong'), or plaster of paris, mould of the original type, line block or very coarse half-tone. Future printings are made from the resulting 'stereos'. The whole process is known as stereotyping. Curved stereos are used on rotary presses for high-speed work, particularly newspaper printing. The process was patented in 1725 by William Ged, a Scottish printer, who was commissioned by Cambridge University to stereotype prayer books and bibles. *See also Matrix.*

Stereotype Metal. An alloy of tin, antimony, and lead; used for casting stereos.

stet (*Lat.* 'let the matter stand'.) Written in the margin of printer's copy or proof to denote the cancelling of any correction marked thereon. Dots under the words indicate the correction to which the 'stet' refers.

Steward. Agent and representative of the lord of a manor.

Stewart Bursary, J.D. Founded in 1958 as a testimonial to J.D. Stewart's outstanding and continuous service to the London and Home Counties Branch of the (British) Library Association. It is awarded annually to fund a research project or professional investigation.

Stick. 1. The tool used by the compositor for setting or forming into lines the types as he picks them out of the CASE (*q.v.*). It usually contains about twenty lines of 8 point type. 2. A device like a small-diameter walking stick divided down its length, used for holding from one to about six copies of a newspaper. Also called 'Newspaper file', 'Newspaper rod', and 'Newspaper stick'.

Stiff Back. *See Tight Back.*

Stiffened and Cut Flush. *See Cut Flush.*

Stiffened Paper Covers. *See Paper Covered.*

Stigmatypy. The use of small type-units to design and print a picture or portrait.

Stigmonym. Dots instead of the name of the author. Used on the title-page and elsewhere in a book. Where the authorship of such books cannot be traced, they are catalogued under their titles.

Still Frame. A single image on a videotape held on the display screen.

Stipple. A printing surface of a copper plate used for making illustrations; it consists of dots, instead of lines. The process is to cover the plate with ordinary etching ground, and through this to sketch the contours and lightly indicate the main shadows with dots by means of the etching needles and a roulette. The portions of the plate thus uncovered are bitten with acid, after which the drawing is completed and given brilliance by flicking or dotting directly on to the surface of the plate with a specially curved graver or roulette. The dots may be fine or coarse, to give effects of light and dark. Although this method was used by W.W. Ryland (1732–83) the Royal engraver, it was first made popular in the eighteenth century by Francesco Bartolozzi, an Italian painter and engraver who came to London in 1764 from Venice and worked for the publisher John Boydell. Half-tones are a kind of stipple engraving.

Stippled Edges. The edges of a book which have been spotted irregularly with colour to prevent them appearing to be soiled. *See also Edges, Marbled Edges, Sprinkled Edges, Stained Edges.*

Stippling. 1. (*Paper*) A roughened finish, also called 'Pebbling'. 2. (*Printing and art*) A gradation of light and shade produced by dots.

Stitching. The operation of fastening a pamphlet consisting of a single section, with wire or thread passed through the centre of the fold. *See also Sewing, Stabbing, Thread Stitched.*

STN International. The Scientific and Technical Information Network (STN) International is a worldwide integrated computer network system for scientific and technical information, establishing Service Centres at three database producers – JICST (Japan), Chemical Abstracts Service (CAS) located in Columbus, Ohio, USA and Fachinformationszentrum Karlsruhe (FIZ Karlsruhe) located in Karlsruhe, the Federal Republic of Germany, where the same type large-scale computer facilities are installed, linking each centre through international dedicated telecommunication lines and operated by common softwares. Online services have been available from 1984, and over 70 databases are now offered.

Stochastic Process. A system which produces a sequence of discrete symbols according to certain probabilities, as for example the sequence of letters which makes up a passage of printed English. If the probabilities depend on previous events in the series this is called a 'Markov process' after the Russian mathematician.

Stock. 1. (*Printing*) Paper or other material for printing upon. 2. (*Paper*) The material (rags, waste-paper, esparto, ropes, etc.) used for making paper; the term is applied at any stage of manufacture, whether to untreated materials or the finished paper. *See also Half-Stuff, Pulp, Stuff, Whole-Stuff.* Also, the printing trade term for paper. 3. All the books and other items in a library. 4. All the books available for sale by a bookseller or publisher.

Stock Book. *Synonymous with* ACCESSIONS REGISTER (*q.v.*).

Stock Editor. A member of the staff of a library who is responsible for maintaining the book stock in good physical condition and up-to-date as well as for ensuring that the latest and most useful titles are available in adequate quantities.

Stock Revision. A part of the stock management process; the stock of a particular library or a total library system is examined by subject area on a regular basis with regard to its adequacy to meet user needs, and is improved by the purchase of new material, or extra copies, or by discarding old material as appropriate.

Stockholding Bookseller. A retail bookseller who keeps a varied and large stock of books on his shelves.

Stocktaking. The process of taking stock by checking records of books possessed with copies on the shelves or records of books on loan.

Stone. Usually a steel-top table (originally it was stone) on which the imposing work – that is, the assembling of the various parts of a printing job – is done. It is on the stone that the type, blocks, etc., are locked in the chase and levelled with mallet and planer. *See also Imposition.*

Stone Engraving. Engraving on blue or grey lithographic stone (fine-grained, compact limestone); a hand process which is used chiefly for script and line drawings in which sharpness and precision of line are more important than artistic expression. The outline is traced and then deeply scored with a steel or diamond pen. As the number of copies which can be made on a hand press is small, it is usual for a stone engraving to be made as an original for transferring to a plate for use on a printing press. Also used to indicate a print made from an engraved stone.

Stone Proof. One made after the forme has been locked up for press, but before it has been put on the press.

Stop-cylinder Press. A type of printing machine in which a cylinder (which is placed over a reciprocating bed on which rests the forme) revolves once during which the impression is made on paper fed underneath the cylinder, and stops until the forme is again in position for printing the next sheet. Often called a 'Wharfedale' press. *See also Miehle, Perfecter, Single-Revolution Machine, Two-Revolution Machine.*

Stop List. (*Indexing. Information retrieval*) A list of words or terms, or roots of words, which are considered to be meaningless or non-significant for purposes of information retrieval, and which are excluded from indexing. The opposite of GO LIST (*q.v.*).

Stopping Out. Painting with varnish such parts of an etching plate as are not to be further etched by acid during repeated dipping in the acid bath. In blockmaking, painting out of the screen or the negative, parts of the subject which are not required to be printed.

Stopword. A word which cannot be used as a search term on a particular database.

Storage. A source from which documents or information of specified descriptions may be supplied. A receptacle for information. *See also Memory.*

Storage and Retrieval. The recording of the holdings of library material of various kinds and of information recorded in such material, and the means of ascertaining the whereabouts of the material or information by means of catalogues, indexes, and mechanized methods.

Storage Area. That portion of the total floor area of a building which is allocated to the storage of materials, furniture, equipment and supplies not in current use.

Storage Centre. A library or library agency in which co-operating libraries store little-used library materials, and which are readily available on request. Also called 'Deposit library', 'Reservoir Library'. (American.)

Storage Devices. (*Information retrieval*) Equipment used to store both data and program instructions; (a) the main memory, which is usually the internal store of the computer, i.e. immediate access store; (b) the backing store which is of larger capacity but offers slower access than the main memory.

Storage Shelving. Shelving which is intended for accommodating little-used books or stores. It may consist of wooden slat or fixed steel shelves. *See also Adjustable Shelving, Library Shelving.*

Store. 1. In information retrieval, the set of all codes which have been physically recorded in some medium. 2. A collection of books or other documentary information which are the subject of records: it may be a library but it may well be a single publication such as a textbook or abstracts journal. An index, or catalogue to a store, can be called a 'Retrieval device'.

Story Hour. A definite period (which is usually about half an hour) set aside for telling stories to the youngest members of a junior library. The stories are told by members of the staff, particularly the children's librarians.

Straight-grain Leather. A leather that has been dampened and rolled, or 'boarded', to make the grain run in straight lines. An innovation credited to Roger Paine.

Straight-grain Morocco. Morocco leather in which the natural grain has been distorted by elongated lines or ridges all running in the same direction.

Straight Matter. Text uninterrupted by illustrations, tables or any special settings.

Straightening. The task (usually performed daily in a busy library) of arranging tidily books in correct classified order.

Strap Binder. A binder fitted with thin steel strips which pass through the staples of the periodicals.

Strapwork. (*Binding*) Interlaced double lines, usually forming a geometrical pattern.

Strawberry Hill Press. The private press on which Sir Horace Walpole, fourth Earl of Orford, printed his own and other books. The Press functioned between 1757 and 1789, and the printers included William Robinson, Thomas Kirgate, Benjamin Williams, and others. The Press was situated at Walpole's estate at Strawberry Hill, Twickenham, Middlesex, UK.

Strawboard. A coarse yellow board, made from straw and used for the covers of books.

Streamer. A printed poster used in shop or window advertising.

Street Index. An index of streets in a town showing the number of houses and the number of persons therein who hold membership tickets for a public library. Also, an alphabetical list of streets in any given area.

Stress. The thickened part of a curved stroke or letter.

Strike. *See Matrix 3.*

Strike-on Composition. The preparation of camera-ready copy on an electric typewriter or other machine operated by a similar principle.

Strike Through. A fault in printing when ink printed on one side of a sheet penetrates to the other. *See also Show Through.*

Strip Cartoon. Small drawings, fewer than about eight or ten in number, about 2 inches square, appearing side by side in a row in a newspaper or periodical. They are usually serials and tell a continuing story or relate the adventures and experience of the characters.

Strip Film. A length of microfilm which is too short to be conveniently wound on a reel.

Strip In. To combine one photographic record with another, or others, or a photograph and lettering, preparatory to using all in making a printing plate. In lithography the operation of stripping is analogous to the operation of imposing in letterpress.

Strip Index. A form of visible index in which entries are made on strips of card shallow enough to take only one line of typewriting. These strips are placed in a metal frame and the surface of the whole of each strip is visible and may be typed or written on.

Striped Film. Cinematograph film edged with a narrow band of magnetic coating for carrying sound.

Stripping. The removal, and subsequent destruction of documents of no further importance, from files which it is decided to preserve.

Strong. (*Printing*) A term used by some printers to indicate a printed page with too many lines of type on it.

Structural Notation. A notation to a classification which indicates the hierarchy or structure of the scheme. A non-structural notation does not do this. *See also Hierarchical Notation.*

Structured Indexing Language. The use of words in non-literary order to construct succinct meaningful subject headings (e.g. 'libraries, university', for university libraries 'Greenhouses: heating, Natural gas-fired', for natural gas-fired heating of greenhouses). *See also Artifical Indexing Language, Natural Language.*

Stub. 1. The part of an original leaf which is left after most of it has been cut away to insert a correct one (*see Cancel*). 2. A narrow strip of paper or linen sewn between sections of a book for attaching folded maps or other bulky items. *See also Compensation Guards, Guard.*

Study Issue. Books issued to students in excess of the usual number and for a longer period than usual.

Study Score. A musical score, similar to a MINIATURE SCORE (*q.v.*) but of a somewhat larger size due to the work being fully scored, i.e. having music for so many instruments that it would be difficult to read if reduced to the normal miniature score size. *See also Score.*

Stuff. The pulp in the paper-maker's vat prior to its being removed to the mould. *See also Half-Stuff, Pulp, Stock 2. Waterleaf, Whole-Stuff.*

Style Book. *Synonymous with* STYLE MANUAL (*q.v.*).

Style Manual. A set of rules drawn up by a printing establishment for the guidance of its staff to ensure that details of typography, spelling, capitalization, punctuation and other matters about which opinions and customs differ, are in accordance with the prevailing practice of that establishment. Such rules are known as the 'style of the house'. *Rules for Compositors and Readers of the Oxford University Press* are a standard set followed by many printers and authors.

Style of the House. (*Printing*) The practice of a printing establishment with regard to capitals, italics, spelling, punctuation, etc. It is called a 'Style manual' or 'Style book' when printed as a guide for use.

Style Sheet. 1. A guide to a printer's HOUSE STYLE. 2. A list of types and their sizes, style of setting, etc., proposed for a given publication. *See also Style Manual, Style of the House.*

Stylus, Style. A writing instrument, pointed at one end, which was used in ancient and mediaeval times for writing on wax or clay. *See also Electric Stylus.*

Subaltern Genera. The intermediate classes of a classification between the SUMMUM GENUS (*q.v.*) and the INFIMA SPECIES (*q.v.*).

Sub-branch. A small branch library open a few hours each day. A part-time library. *See also Branch Library.*

Sub-committee. A committee formed from members of a larger committee to consider one or more matters on behalf of the larger committee to which it reports its deliberations.

Subdivision. 1. The word commonly used to denote the process of dividing a scheme of classification into its parts. 2. The result of such subdivision.

Sub-entry. In indexing, the part of the entry following the entry-word or heading which is used to subdivide a large number of references into a group of related items, i.e. the whole entry minus the entry-word or heading.

Subhead. *See Subheading.*

Subheading. 1. A secondary heading, used in the subdivision of a subject. In a verbal heading it is the second or subsequent word, separated from the preceding by punctuation. 2. A word or group of words added to a heading and designed to delimit a particular group of entries under the heading, or to designate a part of the entity named in the heading. Subheadings may be subjected to modification, and if there is more than one modification of a subheading, each of the modifications is then known as a sub-subheading. Each group of sub- and sub-subheadings is indented in printing to make the meaning clear. The terms sub- and sub-subheadings are often abbreviated to 'subhead' and 'sub-subhead'.

Sub-index. An index within an index.

Subinfeudation. The granting or sub-letting of lands by a feudal vassal to an undertenant on the same terms as he held them from his overlord. Abolished in England in 1290, but the principle still survives in Scotland.

Subject. 1. The theme or themes of a book, whether stated in the title or not. 2. (*Indexing*) A unit concept found in, or derived from, manuscript or published literary material. It may be found, or expressed, as a theme, name, date, first line of a poem, title of a book, or be an expression coined to convey the gist of the material indexed, etc.

Subject Analytic. *See Analytical Entry.*

Subject Arrangement. Books arranged in order of subject, either alphabetically or according to some scheme of classification.

Subject Authority Card. A card which, in addition to citing the authorities consulted in determining the choice of a given heading, also indicates the references made to and from related headings and synonymous terms.

Subject Authority Fiche. A British Library service, formerly known as the RIN/SIN fiche, offering a comprehensive package for subject indexing. Access is via an alphabetical listing of PRECIS index entries. The fiche contain subject index entries for books entered in BNB from 1974, English language books indexed by BL Bibliographic Services from 1976, foreign language books indexed by the British Library Department of Printed Books 1976–81, audio-visual materials recorded in the *British Catalogue of Audiovisual Materials* from 1979 and periodical articles indexed for *British Education Index.*

Subject Authority File. The list in a book, or on cards, of subject headings used in a given catalogue, and the references made to them. Also the entries made for the classified list of class symbols or numbers and the appropriate subject index entries made when first allocating a book to a particular position in the classification. An entry is made for each step taken when indexing by the chain indexing method. *See also Authority Card, Authority List, Chain Index, Name Authority File.*

Subject Bibliography. A list of material about a particular subject or individual.

Subject Card. A catalogue bearing a subject entry.

Subject Catalogue. Any catalogue arranged by subjects, whether in alphabetical or classified order, which directs users to the documents dealing with them. *See also Alphabetico-specific Subject Catalogue, Alphabetico-classed Catalogue.*

Subject Cataloguing. 1. That part of cataloguing which involves the allocation of subject headings to entries for specific books or other documents. 2. The branch of cataloguing which is not concerned with DESCRIPTIVE CATALOGUING (*q.v.*) but with the provision of subject headings.

Subject Classification. The scheme devised by J.D. Brown in 1906, in which the main classes are Matter and Force, Life, Mind, and Record. The notation is mixed (letter and figure) and does not permit of easy extension although the CATEGORICAL TABLES (*q.v.*) enable a certain amount of subdivision.

Subject Concepts. (*Classification*) The terms which result when a subject is divided by a single characteristic. The group of terms which so results is called a 'Facet'.

Subject Department. A department in a large general library in which are shelved all the books on a particular subject, e.g. science, whether intended for reference or for home-reading. Where such departmentalization exists there is usually a POPULAR LIBRARY (*q.v.*) containing a selection of books of interest to the 'general reader'. Also called 'Departmentalized library'.

Subject Device. Ranganathan's term for the process of dividing by the whole classification. It is one of the distinctive principles of the Colon Classification for determining the sequence of subjects and is used in the Dewey Classification when a subject such as 016 Subject Bibliography is divided by the whole classification.

Subject Device Number. In the Colon Classification, that part of an Isolate Number which is contributed by the SUBJECT DEVICE (*q.v.*).

Subject Entry. 1. In a catalogue, an entry under the heading adopted to indicate a book's subject. In a subject catalogue it is the basic unit, and includes the description of the document, and its location. In the classified file of the CLASSIFIED CATALOGUE (*q.v.*) the heading may also be the LOCATION MARK (*q.v.*). Subject entries for music are entered under the medium of performance (*see Medium*) or the form (*see Form 2*) in which the music is written. They may also be given under the subject described in the music. 2. In an index, an entry relating to a subject as distinguished from one beginning with the name of a person.

Subject Fullness. *See Secondary Fullness.*

Subject Guide. A guide to the shelves of a library, showing where books on particular subjects may be found. Also called 'Topic guide'.

Subject Heading. The word or group of words under which books and other material on a subject are entered in a catalogue in which the entries are arranged in alphabetical order. The heading may include punctuation to which an arranging significance may be assigned. In a classified catalogue the subject heading consists of a classification symbol with or without its verbal meaning. It may also include entries for all material on the same subject in an index or bibliography, or arranged in a file. Lists of headings are used by some cataloguers to aid them in their choice of appropriate subject headings and to achieve uniformity.

Subject Heading Language. The terms used as subject headings and under which entries are made, as well as those from which references are merely made to other subject terms.

Subject Index Entry. An entry in the subject index of a classified catalogue which directs to the class number under which entries for books on the required subject will be found.

Subject Index Illusion. The term used by H.E. Bliss for the alphabetical arrangement of subjects in a scheme of classification according to the first letter of the subject name, etc., e.g. Q Quartos, R Roman antiquities, S Science, T Technology, U Unclassified. As subjects are subdivided similarly, an alphabetical index is essential to determine the position of any subject in the sequence, and Bliss wrote 'no index, however convenient or necessary, can convert an arbitrary or disordered arrangement into a systematic classification'.

Subject Libraries. *See Subject Department.*

Subject Reference. A reference from one subject to another whether a synonym or a related heading.

Subject Series. A number of books published in a named series by one publisher and dealing with different phases of a single subject or with a particular field of knowledge. The books are usually written by different authors, are not usually reprints, and are uniform in textual and physical characteristics. Similarly, a number of musical compositions dealing with different phases of music, media of performance, form, etc.

Subject Specialization. A scheme of co-operation whereby public libraries in a restricted geographical area purchase books on a specific subject. In some schemes the libraries act as depositories for preserving little-used books on their particular subject which might otherwise be discarded.

Subject Style. The use of red for headings in catalogue entries to indicate subjects. As an alternative (owing to the tendency of red ink or red typescript to fade) black capitals are sometimes used. *See also Author Style.*

Subject-Word Entry. Entry in a catalogue under a word of the title of a book indicative of its subject matter.

Sub-librarian. *See Deputy Librarian.*

Subordination. The allocation of a subject term to its right place in the classification schedules; its order of precedence in the HIERARCHY (*q.v.*). In a FACETED CLASSIFICATION (*q.v.*) the placing of a term belonging to one FACET (*q.v.*) after a term belonging to another facet, in a CITATION ORDER (*q.v.*).

Sub-professional Assistant. In American libraries, one who undertakes, under the immediate supervision of professional staff members, work largely concerned with the lighter routine processes which are peculiar to library work and which require some knowledge of library procedure.

Subscriber. A person who pays a subscription to receive a periodical as published, or to a society.

Subscribers' Edition. An edition prepared for circulation only to persons who have agreed to purchase on announcement and before publication. It may differ from the ordinary 'trade edition' by the inclusion of a list of subscribers, by being printed on hand-made or other special paper and having larger margins, or by being sumptuously bound.

Subscript. 1. An indexing notation. 2. A small letter or figure put below the level of the foot of a full-size lower case character as in H_2O. Usually called an 'Inferior' character. *See also Superscript.*

Subscription Agent. A firm or organization which arranges, at the order of an individual or library, for the regular delivery of serials as published, and handles the financial records.

Subscription Books. 1. Those published at intervals by societies and issued to subscribing members. 2. Individual books of limited appeal, the publication of which depends to some extent on subscriptions promised prior to publication, and the price of which is raised after publication.

Subscription Edition. One which is published after enough subscriptions have been received to ensure financial success.

Subscription Library. A commercial lending library the members of which pay subscriptions entitling them to borrow books during the period of the validity of their subscription. They were first formed in England in the late seventeenth and early eighteenth centuries. *See also Circulating Library.*

Subscription Price. The price at which books are sometimes offered for sale before they are published. The price is usually lower than the after-publication price. This is done to give the publisher some guidance as to the potential sales of the book and therefore of the number to be printed.

Subseries. A series of publications, the title of which is distinctive and is dependent on the title of another series.

Subsidiaries. The parts of a book in addition to the text and including notes (whether placed in the pages or massed at the end of a book), bibliographies, appendices, glossaries, plates, indexes, imprint, colophon, blank leaves, end-papers and book jackets. Sometimes called 'Reference matter'. Also called 'End-matter', 'Back matter'. *See also Preliminaries.*

Subsidiary Rights. An author's rights to literary property other than the original one of first publication. These include dramatic, film, translation and serial rights.

Subsidy Publishers. *Synonymous with* VANITY PUBLISHERS (*q.v.*).

Substance. The weight of paper expressed in terms of weight per ream of sheets of a given size; the weight of a ream of a particular size and number of sheets is known as the 'substance number'. The 'substance' of the paper is the product of the density, i.e. the degree of dilution of the stuff flowing on to the machine wire, and the speed at which it is permitted to flow, plus the speed of the machine wire.

Substitution Generic. In a HIERARCHICAL SEARCH (*q.v.*), a situation in which two headings in the alphabetico-specific subject catalogue, each with the same number of subheadings, represent concepts in hierarchical relationship, i.e. the heading and the first subheading are identical, the second subheading being different. *See also Alphabetical Collateral Search, Systematic Collateral Search.*

Sub-subheading. *See Subheading.*

Subtitle. A secondary or subordinate title, usually explanatory, and often following a semicolon, 'or', 'an', or 'a'.

Suggestion Card. A printed card which is filled in by a reader with particulars of a book suggested for addition to a library. All appropriate bibliographical information is entered, and in some libraries it subsequently serves as an ORDER CARD (*q.v.*). Also called 'Recommendation card', 'Request card', 'Requisition card', 'Suggestion slip'.

Sulphate Pulp. (*Papermaking*) Chemical wood pulp which has been prepared by cooking wood chips under pressure and high temperature in a solution consisting mainly of sulphate of soda (Glauber's salt). The resulting paper is strong, and is often used unbleached, but it can be bleached white. The process was introduced by Dahl in 1883–4. *See also Soda Pulp.*

Sulphite Pulp. (*Papermaking*) Chemical wood pulp which has been prepared by submitting the wood fibres to the action of sulphurous acid and its acid salts (bisulphite of lime, magnesia, or soda) at high pressure and in closed vessels. The process was invented by B.C. and R. Tilghmann in 1863–6 and is usually used with coniferous woods. *See also Soda Pulp.*

Summum Genus. The first, comprehensive class from which the division of a classification commences. The terminology of schedule construction, as used by Ranganathan is: *universe* (= *summum genus*) an aggregate of *entities* (things or ideas) under consideration which is *divided* by a succession or *train* of *characteristics* each of which gives rise to an *array* of classes. The *order* of a class is the number of characteristics used to divide it out of the universe; the *rank* of a class is its position in its array. A *chain* is a series of classes in successive subordination, each one being subordinate to the preceding one. *See also Infima Species, Subaltern Genera.*

Sunday Express Book of the Year. A substantial annual award for the most stylish, literate and readable UK published work of fiction.

Sunday Express Magazine/Veuve Cliquot Short Story Competition. *See Crime Writers' Association.*

Sunday Times Small Publishers Award. An award sponsored by the *Sunday Times* newspaper, open to independent publishers producing between five and forty titles each year. Administered by the Book Trust, and first awarded in 1988.

Sunk Bands. (*Binding*) Cords or bands (in old books, often of leather) which are placed in grooves sawn into the backs of sections of a book to give a smooth back or spine. The sewing of the sections passes round the bands. The opposite of RAISED BANDS (*q.v.*). Also called 'Sunk cords'.

Super. *See Mull.*

Super Royal. A sheet of printing paper measuring 20½ × 27½ inches.

Super-calender. A machine, separate from the paper-making machines, which consists of a stack of from five to sixteen rolls. Paper is passed through under pressure to be given a highly glazed finish; it is then known as 'Super-calendered'. *See also Calendered Paper.*

Super-calendered Paper. Paper which is given an extra smooth, glossy surface by rolling between 'calenders' (metal rollers) in a super-calender machine.

Super-caster. An instrument for casting large sizes of type for hand-composition.

Superimposed Coding. A system of coding which uses more than one code symbol per concept, the combination of code symbols being such that the number of random combinations is minimal.

'Superimposition' Policy. *See 'No Conflict' Policy.*

Superintendent of the Reading Room. The librarian responsible for the service to readers in the reading room of a national, university or research library.

Superior Figures (Letters). Very small characters aligning with the top of the next text type, usually as reference marks to footnotes or notes at the end of the chapter or text, or in a margin. They are cast on the mean line, and often on the same body as the type with which they appear. Also called 'Superiors', 'Superscript'. *See also Inferior Characters, Mean Line, Reference Marks.*

Superordinate Class. (*Classification*) A class which is of more general extension or higher grade, or rank: a more general class. *See also Co-ordinate Classes.*

Superscript. (*Printing*) A small character aligning with the top of a full-size lower case character; superscripts are usually used as reference marks to footnotes or notes at the end of the chapter or text. Usually called 'Superior' characters. *See also Subscript, Superior Figures (Letters).*

Supplement. 1. Additional matter continuing, or adding new matter to that already published. It is usually issued separately. 2. An extra sheet, section, or number accompanying a normal issue of a newspaper or periodical. *See also Addendum.*

Supplemental Estimate. *See Estimates.*

Supplementary Publication. *See Auxiliary Publication.*

Supplementary Ticket. A library ticket which is issued to students, teachers, and others in addition to the number usually allowed.

Supplied Title. The title composed by the cataloguer to indicate the nature and scope of the monographic work under study.

Supposed Author. One to whom is attributed by some authoritative source the authorship of a work published anonymously or of which the stated authorship is doubted. Also called 'Attributed author', 'Presumed author'. Such a book is catalogued under the name of the supposed author which phrase appears after the name to qualify it. The authority for the supposition is given in a note.

Supposititious Author. One who is substituted for the genuine author with intent to defraud.

Suppressed. 1. Withheld from publication or circulation by author, publisher, government, or ecclesiastical authority because of unreliability, inaccuracy or moral tone. 2. (*Bibliography*) Of a leaf which has been cancelled because of some inaccurate, imperfect, or objectionable feature.

supra. (*Lat.* 'above'). Used in footnotes and sometimes in the text to refer to an item previously mentioned. *See also infra.*

Surface Paper. *Synonymous with* COATED PAPER (*q.v.*).

Surface Printing. *Synonymous with* PLANOGRAPHIC PROCESS (*q.v.*).

Surface Sizing. The addition of resin or other materials to the surface of a sheet of paper or board to render it more resistant to liquids, especially writing ink. *See also Engine-sizing.*

Surname. A family name which a person uses in conjunction with his or her personal names. It is the name used as a heading for entries in a catalogue or bibliography.

Surname Indexing. The allocation of symbols to surnames so that they may be arranged in order other than by strict alphabetization.

Surrey and Sussex Libraries in Co-operation. *See SASLIC.*

Survey. An account of some research, examination, or enquiry which has been done by a scientific or organized method.

Suspension File. Loops of tough manila, the full width of a filing cabinet drawer, which are attached to, and suspended from, rigid metal or plastic bars which at their extreme ends rest on a cradle, or framework, contained in the drawer. Into these loops are placed files or wallets containing documents, papers, photographs, etc.

Suspension Shelving. Shelves affixed to, or between, shelf-ends having lugs which engage in slots in uprights fixed to the wall. No support other than the shelf-end is provided at the front of the shelves. The shelf-ends are the full depth of the shelf and serve as book supports. Also called 'Bracket shelving'. *See also Cantilever Shelving.*

SVD. Schweizerische Vereinigung für Dokumentation/Association Suisse de Documentation. *See ASD.*

SWALCAP (UK). Acronym for South West Academic Libraries Co-operative Automation Project. The participating libraries were (1969) the Universities of Bristol, Exeter and University College, Cardiff; *now see SWALCAP Library Services Ltd.*

SWALCAP Library Services Ltd. A commercial venture, based initially on SWALCAP (*q.v.*), providing to its readers shared cataloguing and library management services. There are some 25 members; the integrated system LIBERTAS is a part of the service offered.

Swann Report. *Education for All*, the Report of the Committee of Inquiry into the Education of Children from Ethnic Minority Groups, chaired by Lord Michael Swann. (HMSO, 1985) (Cmnd. 9453).

SWARBICA. Acronym for South and West Asian Branch of the INTER-NATIONAL COUNCIL ON ARCHIVES (*q.v.*).

Swash Letters. Italic capitals and lower-case letters with tails and flourishes, as
B G N F A W P T R₀ Nᵢ

Swedish Binding. *Synonymous with* CUT FLUSH (*q.v.*).

Swedish Institute for Children's Books. Opened in 1967; aims at acquiring literature which is unobtainable, or rarely found, in Swedish Libraries. It also serves as a documentary centre for children's books built up on an international basis; and to supply individuals and libraries with the information and material they need.

Swedish Library Association (Sveriges Allmänna Biblioteksförening). Founded in 1915, one of the association's principle tasks is to act as a gathering agency, a common platform for Swedish library co-operation. There is at present no other organization capable of representing Swedish research, public and school libraries. Publishes *Biblioteksbladet* (18 p.a.).

Swelled Rule. *See Rule.*

Swinging Bookcase. A form of compact book storage whereby two presses consisting of hinged three-foot tiers are placed one on each side of one fixed press. When the books on either side of the fixed press or on the inner sides of the two outside presses are to be consulted, the hinged tiers are swung out into the gangways. Also called 'Pivoted bookcase'.

Swiss Librarians' Association. *See Association of Swiss Librarians.*

Switching. The process of connecting machines, terminals, users, etc., via a telecommunications link.

Swung Dash. A curved dash ~ similar to a TILDE (*q.v.*).

Sydney Ltd.   An integrated library housekeeping system first marketed in the UK in 1985. The micro-based system is popular in small libraries; a user group has been formed.

Syllabic Notation.   A notation using the letters A–Z to produce pronounceable syllables, each of which signifies a CONCEPT. The three symbol letter notation is used in D.J. Foskett's London Education Classification, e.g. Jip = Assessment, Mob = Sciences; Ser = Further education. Such class marks are easy to say and remember. Also called PRONOUNCEABLE NOTATION (*q.v.*).

Syllabic Writing.   The middle stage in picture writing in which a symbol was used to represent each syllable or vowel when this constitutes a syllable in the spoken language; thus, a combination of signs representing a group of syllables conveys a spoken word. A syllabic form of writing is known as a syllabary. *See also Phonetic Writing.*

Syllabication.   *Synonymous with* SYLLABIFICATION (*q.v.*).

Syllabification.   The action or method of dividing words into syllables. Also called 'Syllabication'.

Symbol.   A substitute or representation of characteristics, relationships, or transformations of ideas or things.

Symposium.   1. A volume of the papers or addresses originally presented at a conference.   2. The conference itself.   3. A collection of articles specially written on a given theme.

Synchronous.   In user and citation studies, referring to changes that reflect the influence of age as shown in observations made on a single occasion. *See also Diachronous.*

Syncopism.   Applied to a pseudonym where dots take the place of certain letters. Such books are catalogued under their titles when the author's full name cannot be ascertained, with added entries under the leading initials of the syncopism. *See also Pseudonym.*

Syndetic.   Having entries connected by cross references. In information retrieval, co-ordination of two or more related documents.

Syndetic Catalogue.   A dictionary catalogue that connects entries by a scheme of cross-references to form a co-ordinated whole. References are made from broad subjects to those that are less broad, and from these to still more subordinate subjects, and sometimes *vice versa*.

Syndetic Index.   An index in which relationships between headings are provided, e.g. by the indexing sequence (classified or other subject arrangements), the use of subheadings and cross-references.

Synecdoche.   A figure of speech in which a species is used for the whole genus (e.g. 'bread' for food in general) or the genus for a species. As applied by C.L. Bernier to information retrieval, the use of a GENERIC DESCRIPTOR (*q.v.*) to represent a set of included words.

Synopsis.   1. A brief outline of the plot, setting, or important points of a play, book or serial.   2. A factual summary of an article or paper contributed to a learned journal, suitable for use as an abstract published in accompaniment with the article, presumed to be prepared by the author of the article but in any case subjected to the same editorial scrutiny and correction which is given to the full article.

Synoptic Journal. A journal which publishes brief resumés, abstracts, diagrams, etc., of full articles, which are not themselves published, but made available if requested.

Synoptic Table. A classification 'map' showing interconnections between terms.

Syntactics. A theory dealing with the formal relations between signs or expressions and the formal properties of language, distinct from their meaning or interpreters.

Syntagmas. *See Paradigms.*

Syntax. Concerned with the relations between symbols without reference to their meanings. *See also Semantics.*

Synthetic Classification. *See Faceted Classification.*

Synthetic Indexing. *Synonymous with* CO-ORDINATE INDEXING *(q.v.).*

Synthetic Indexing Language. A list of subject terms used as headings together with rules for the construction of headings for composite subjects. *See also Enumerative Index Language.*

System for Information on Grey Literature. *See SIGLE.*

Systematic Auxiliary Schedules. Twenty schedules provided in Bliss' *Bibliographic classification* to serve as tables of common subdivision. Only the first three – form divisions (*see Anterior Numerical Classes*), geographical subdivision, subdivision by language – are of general application throughout the scheme, the remainder being applicable to groups of classes, to single classes, or to sub-classes. Symbols from these schedules are added to those from the main tables of the classification which indicate subject matter. Auxiliary tables are also provided in the UNIVERSAL DECIMAL CLASSIFICATION *(q.v.).*

Systematic Bibliography. The enumeration and classification of books. The assembling of bibliographical entries into logical and useful arrangements for study and reference.

Systematic Catalogue. A classified catalogue. One in which the classes and subjects are arranged in a logical order according to some scheme of book classification.

Systematic Collateral Search. An examination of entries under headings which, in a scheme of classification, would be co-ordinate with, and stand next to, each of the headings covered in the HIERARCHICAL SEARCH *(q.v.).* *See also Alphabetic Collateral Search, Substitution Generic.*

Systematic Computerized Processing in Cataloguing. *See SCOPE.*

Systematic Control of Periodicals. *See SCOPE.*

Systematic File. *Synonymous with* CLASSIFIED FILE *(q.v.).*

Systematic Mnemonics. *See Mnemonics.*

Systematic Schedules. *See Systematic Auxiliary Schedules.*

Systems Analysis. The examination and investigation of routines and administrative processes, typically using flowcharts to pinpoint obstructions. Often carried out prior to automation.

T-Card Charging. Abbreviation for TRANSACTION CARD CHARGING (*q.v.*).

Tab. (*Binding*) A small piece of paper, card, plastic or fabric attached to the outer edge of a card, or leaf of a book, and bearing one or more characters to serve as a guide or index.

Tabbed. A GUIDE CARD (*q.v.*) which has tabs projecting from the upper edge. They are called 'three-, four- or five-tabbed' according to the portion of the card which projects. A 'three-tabbed' card is one, the tab of which is a third the length of the card.

Table. 1. An arrangement of written words, numbers or signs, or of combinations of them, in a series of separate lines or columns. 2. A synoptical statement or series of statements; a concise presentation of the details of a subject; a list of items. *Synonymous with* FILE 3 (*q.v.*).

Table Book. 1. An ancient writing book comprised of wax-covered tablets of metal, ivory or wood and fastened together at the back by rings or thongs of leather. The writing was done with a stylus. 2. An obsolete name for a note-book. 3. An elaborately decorated edition of a book, often covered in velvet or silk, for display on a drawing-room table. Popular in the nineteenth century. *See also Coffee-Table Book.*

Table of Contents. *See Contents.*

Table of Precedence. (*Classification*) A statement of the correct citation order under a subject that the schedules subdivide according to several characteristics.

Tablet. An ancient writing material made of clay (used when moist and afterwards baked), stone, lead, wood or ivory and covered with wax. Also called 'Tabula'. *Cum tabula* (*Lat.* 'with plates').

Tabular Classification. A classification or table consisting of several columns and several horizontal series, some of which may not be of equal numbers of terms. The terms need not recur as in cross-classifications. A tabular classification may be less regular and less complete than a cross-classification. *See also Columnar, Horizontal.*

Tabular Work. (*Printing*) Figures and other matter arranged vertically in columns, with or without rules.

Tabulated Code. In machine sorting as part of information retrieval, one that requires a code book or dictionary to provide code equivalents for source words and vice versa. Also called an 'Arbitrary code'. *See also Code.*

Tachygraphy. A system of shorthand invented by Thomas Shelton and used by Samuel Pepys when writing his *Diary* (14 January 1660 – 31 May 1669).

Tack Marks. Small dots incorporated in imposing schemes for sheets printed by the WORK AND TURN (*q.v.*) method. One dot is used for the first side printed and two for the second.

Tag. (*Information retrieval*) 1. A character or digit which is attached to a record, or to a FIELD (*q.v.*) in a record, as a means of identification. 2. An identification label ('identifier') to signal the computer what is coming next. 3. In a machine-readable record, one or more characters attached to a set of data that contains information about the set.

Tagged (Tagging). (*Cataloguing. Information retrieval*) 1. With Variable Field Coding (*see Fixed Field Coding*), the use of symbols to indicate what part of an entry is about to follow. 2. The attaching of characters or digits to a record, or to a field in a record, as a means of identification.

Tail. 1. The bottom or lower edge of a book. The term is applied both to the margin below the text and to the cover of the book. 2. In typography, the lower portion of letter *g* and the projection on the *Q*.

Tail Edge. *Synonymous with* LOWER EDGE (*q.v.*).

Tail Fold. *See Bolt.*

Tail Margin. The space below the bottom line of a page of type matter. Also called 'Lower margin'. *See also Margin.*

Tail Ornament. An ornament appearing at the foot of a page or the end of the matter occurring on it, especially at the end of a section, chapter or book. It is sometimes called a 'Tail piece'. *See also Head Ornament.*

Tail Piece. *Synonymous with* TAIL ORNAMENT.

Tailband. A decorative band similar to a HEADBAND (*q.v.*) but placed at the tail of a book.

Tailcap. The fold of leather at the foot of the spine of a book to protect the TAILBAND (*q.v.*).

Tailed Letter. A digraph consisting of a letter and a full stop, which gives the impression of being a letter with a horizontally tailed last stroke. *See also Swash Letters.*

$$e \quad m \quad nt$$

Take. The amount of copy taken at one time by a compositor to set up in type. *See also Break-Line, End a Break, End Even.*

Take Down. (*Binding*) To take a book to pieces and reduce it to its original sections. *See also Pulled.*

Taking out Turns. Inserting the correct type character where the twin black footmarks (as ■ ■) on a galley proof indicate that the correct one was not available. *See also Turned Sort.*

Talbotype. *Synonymous with* CALOTYPE (*q.v.*).

Talking Book. A 'book' for the blind recorded on tape. *See also NTBL.*

Talking Newspapers. Cassettes containing news and short magazine articles; they are prepared locally and circulated amongst visually handicapped persons. First made early in 1974; within a year, 35 were being produced in the UK where there is a National Association of Talking Newspapers.

Tall Copy. A book that has lost nothing of its original height in binding.

Tally. (*Information retrieval*) 1. The form of a record, or unit, on which may be made one or more entries. *See also Entry 5, File 3.* 2. Notched piece of wood used as a receipt for money or goods, both public and private, from the early Middle Ages until about the third decade of the nineteenth century.

Tape. (*Data processing*) 1. A plastic strip coated or impregnated with magnetic or optically sensitive substances, used for data input, memory or output. 2. A paper or plastic strip with punches or other arbitrary signs

representing alphabetic or numerical data and operations.   3. Loosely for
AUDIOTAPE or VIDEOTAPE (*qq.v.*).

Tape Cassette.   *See Cassette 2.*

Tape Mark.   (*Information retrieval*) A special configuration recorded on magnetic tape, to indicate the boundary between files and labels (*see File, Label
5*), and also between certain label groups.

Tape Reader.   (*Information retrieval*) A device which senses information
recorded on paper or magnetic tape.

Tapes.   The pieces of tape to which the sections of a book are sewn, the ends
being pasted to the boards or between the split boards which form the
covers.

Tape-Slide Presentation.   A co-ordinated and synchronized programme of
transparencies and audiotape.

TAPPI.   Technical Association for the Pulp and Paper Industry (US); a body
concerned in the development of permanent/durable paper and deacidifi-
cation processes.

TAPs.   Training Access Points; a UK government initiative undertaken
through the Training Agency to build a network giving access to information
on local educational facilities, supported by three national databases –
PICKUP (short-course data), MARIS-NET (self-study materials and
trainer support) and ECCTIS (national higher education and further education courses). TAPs are accessible on-line, on CD-ROM, e-mail, PRES-
TEL, and microfiche from public libraries, job centres and colleges.

TARGET.   In microcopying, any document or chart containing identification
information, coding or resolution test patterns.

Target Language.   (*Information retrieval*) A language that is an output from a
given automatic translation process. *See also Machine Translation.*

Tarred Brown Paper.   Wrapping paper consisting of one or more sheets of
paper coated or impregnated with coal- or wood-tar or bitumen and so given
some degree of waterproofing. *See also Union Paper.*

Tauber Report.   A report, *Resources in Australian libraries*, written by
'Maurice F. Tauber, Melvil Dewey Professor of Library Service at Columbia
University, New York, of a systematic survey of the total library resources of
Australia. It was published in 1963.

Taxonomy.   The science of classification. Also, the study of the names and
naming of items in generic assemblies.

TDF.   Transborder Data Flow. *See now Universal Dataflow and Telecommunications.*

Teacher-Librarian.   A title indicating a member of a school's staff with specific
teaching commitments, but who is allocated a number of hours per week to
organize and maintain a school library. *See also School Librarian.*

Teacher's Book.   An explanatory handbook issued with a series of textbooks or
a single textbook for the use of teachers. It sometimes has a 'key' or answers
to questions and problems.

Team Librarianship.   The organization of professional staff into small groups
responsible for various service functions or for several functions, within a

certain geographical area or over the whole of a library system. Team librarianship removes professional staff from the daily routine of responsibility for a service point, and provides opportunites for organizational and individual development through joint setting of priorities and solving of problems.

Tear Sheet. A sheet of paper torn from a publication; when the item consists of more than one sheet, it is called a 'clipped article' or 'clipping'. *See also Cutting.*

Technical Abstract Bulletin. A periodical containing indicative and/or information abstracts of newly published or released technical literature. The abstracts are usually arranged in subject order, and alphabetical subject and/or author indexes are provided.

Technical Association for the Pulp and Paper Industry. *See TAPPI.*

Technical Information Centre. An organization for acquiring, processing and disseminating technical information. Such a centre usually has a library and a staff of scientists and engineers for extracting, evaluating and indexing technical literature.

Technical Information System. A network of information services providing facilities for the processing of information and data, and transmitting same to the enquirer.

Technical Journal. A journal which is devoted to a particular branch of technology. Also called a 'Technical periodical'.

Technical Library. A library containing mostly books of a technical nature. When connected with a public library, it may be a section of the reference library, a separate department in the central building, or a separate building.

Technical Periodical. *Synonymous with* TECHNICAL JOURNAL (*q.v.*).

Technical Processes, Department of. *Synonymous with* PROCESSING DEPARTMENT (*q.v.*).

Technical Report. A scientific paper, article, translation, probably recording the current position of scientific research and development, etc., whether security classified, unclassified or declassified.

Technical Services. All the activities and processes concerned with obtaining, organizing and processing library material for use.

Technical Services Department. A department of a library where the functions of book acquisition, cataloguing, classification and processing are carried out. Also called 'Technical services division'.

Technician. A sub-professional grade in North American libraries; technicians normally held a qualification and are thus at a higher level of responsibility than unqualified library staff.

Technology Reports Centre. *See TRC.*

Teenage Libraries. Libraries intended to serve young adult readers who are not attracted to adult libraries, but have outgrown libraries for children.

TEG. Training and Education Group. *See now Personnel, Training and Education Group.*

t.e.g. Abbreviation for top edge gilt. *See Gilt Top.*

Teldata. Danish videotex system.

Telecine. The process of transferring films and slides onto a videotape format.

Telecom Gold. The British Telecom electronic mail system.

Teleordering. A process whereby booksellers store orders daily, usually identified by ISBN, which are overnight automatically communicated to a central computer and thence directed to the terminals of participating publishers. Other publishers receive orders in the post. Confirmation, or errors are reported back to the bookseller's terminal.

Telescoped Notation. (*Classification*) The assignment of more than one facet to a single notation sequence, in an otherwise expressive notation.

Telesoftware. Software (computer operating instructions and programs) transmitted either to an intelligent videotex terminal or to a microcomputer programmed to act as a videotex terminal.

Teletel. The French videotex service. The terminals are called minitels. *See also Antiope.*

Teletex. A system was introduced in 1985 by British Telecom enabling text messages to be relayed over telephone lines. This system developed from the HERMES PROJECT (*q.v.*). Abandoned in the UK in 1988, but still popular elsewhere in Europe.

Teletext. The generic term for *Broadcast* VIDEOTEX (*q.v.*). British examples are CEEFAX and ORACLE.

Teletypesetting. The process of setting type with a teletypesetter apparatus, which automatically operates a keyboard slugcasting machine consisting essentially of a separate keyboard that perforates a tape which is fed into an attachment to the slugcasting machine, or into a sender that transmits electrical impulses telegraphically to any number of re-perforators, with the perforated tape causing the slugcasting machine to set type by automatic operation of the keyboard. Abbreviated TTS.

Telidon. A private Viewdata system originating in Canada. This system has the ability to produce high-quality graphics very quickly and at comparatively low cost. At present Telidon is aimed at the advertising market.

Telonism. Terminal letters of an author's name used as a pseudonym, as N.S. (John Austis). *See also Titlonym.*

Telset. Finnish videotex system.

Temporary Card. A card, bearing brief particulars of a book, which is inserted in a catalogue in place of the usual card during its temporary removal for emendation. Also called 'Temporary slip'.

Temporary Slip. *Synonymous with* TEMPORARY CARD (*q.v.*).

Term. (*Information retrieval*) In an index, the subject heading or DESCRIPTOR (*q.v.*). *See also Feature Card, Heading 2, Item.* (*Indexing*) A heading consisting of the word(s) or symbol(s) selected from, or based on, an item in the text of a document, and used as an indexing unit, identifying an item in a classification scheme, or catalogue, or any form of information retrieval. *See also Heading 2, Indirect Subject Heading, Mixed Subject Heading.* Also (in patents literature) a word, phrase or sentence (which is the officially recommended form of international systems of indexing patents material) which is descriptive of the subject-matter content, or part of the subject-matter content, of a document. *See also Authority List 1, Controlled Term List, Open-ended Term List.*

Term Card. *Synonymous with* ASPECT CARD, FEATURE CARD (*qq.v.*).

Term Entry. In information retrieval, the 'inverted' form of entry used by UNITERM (*q.v.*), peephole card, and other co-ordinate indexes, in which a TALLY (*q.v.*) is made and filed under a term chosen to describe a characteristic of information kept by the library or information centre, and on which are recorded symbols representing all the documents possessing this characteristic. Also called 'Aspect system'. *See also Item Entry.*

Term Indexing. Choosing words used in the text as headings of the index to the text. *See also Concept Indexing.*

Terminal. A combination of VDU and Keyboard, often a microcomputer, used to contact a remote computer or network.

Terminal Digit Posting. Arranging and recording serial numbers of documents on the basis of the last digit of the serial number.

Terms. The headings – words or combinations of words – used in a scheme of classification for classes, divisions, subdivisions, or sections. The *names* of any subjects that may be included in the classification.

Ternion. Three sheets folded together in folio.

Terrain Model. *Synonymous with* RELIEF MODEL (*q.v.*).

Terrapin Reska Travel Award. First introduced in 1972, these annual awards are available only to students at the College of Librarianship Wales; they are designed to develop and further students' interest and knowledge of library systems, especially in Scandinavia.

Test Question. (*Information retrieval*) A 'proving' question, based on a document known to be in the collection, for testing the retrieval efficiency of a system.

Tetraevangelium. A book containing the four Gospels.

Tetralogy. A set of four related dramatic or literary compositions, said especially of three Greek tragedies and a satyric comedy.

Text. 1. The body of a work following the PRELIMINARIES (*q.v.*). 2. The type matter on a page as distinct from the illustrations. 3. In the conservation of documents, that part of a sheet of paper or membrane of a document covered by writing, printing or drawing.

Text Area. *Synonymous with* TYPE AREA (*q.v.*).

Text Comparator. A machine that presents the images of two documents so that they appear to lie exactly on top of each other. Tiny discrepancies in apparently identical pages thus become noticeable.

Text Hand. A style of writing employed for books, treatises and the headings of business documents from about 1100 to 1500.

Text Title. *Synonymous with* CAPTION TITLE (*q.v.*).

Text Type. Type used for setting the text of a book or periodical, or other large amounts of copy. It is seldom larger than 14 point.

Textbook. A book written specifically for use by those studying for an examination in any particular system.

Textile Binding. An ornate style of binding using fabrics. It was popular in France and England during the Renaissance. Coloured satin and velvet, often embellished with many-coloured silk embroidery and gold and silver threads, was frequently used.

Textual Bibliography. The study and comparison of texts and their transmission through different printings and editions.

Textual Manuscript. *See Literary Manuscript.*

Textual Records. (*Archives*) Manuscript or typescript documents as distinct from cartographic, audiovisual, and machine-readable archives.

Textura. *See Gothic, or Black Letter, Type.*

Thames Board. A British-made board used in EDITION BINDING (*q.v.*). Each side is covered with brown kraft paper to give equal tension, and thus rigidity.

Theatre Library Association. Based in New York, the Association is a non-profit organization established in 1937 to advance the interests of all those involved in collecting and preserving theatrical materials and in utilizing those materials for purposes of scholarship. The membership is international and includes public and private institutions as well as librarians, curators, private collectors, historians, professors, theatre designers, writers, and other interested persons. Publishes *Broadside* (q), *Performing Arts Resources* (a.); awards the GEORGE FREEDLEY MEMORIAL AWARD (*q.v.*), and the Theatre Library Association Award for an outstanding American book in the field of recorded performance (established 1974).

Theatre Museum Library. A branch collection of the UK National Art Library at the Victoria and Albert Museum; at present housed in the new Theatre Museum, Covent Garden, but intended to form part of a planned new study centre in West London.

Thematic Catalogue. One containing a list of one or more composers' works and the opening themes or passages of each composition, or for each section of lengthy musical compositions. Entries are usually arranged in chronological order, or by categories.

Theme. *Synonymous with* TOPIC (*q.v.*).

Thermal Process. A process for copying documents without the use of liquid chemicals. Heat sensitive paper is used to make copies from an original having carbon or metallic writing or printing inks.

Thermographic Copy. A copy of a document made by a THERMAL PROCESS (*q.v.*), or thermography. Also called a 'Thermic copy'.

Thermography. 1. Any printing process which involves the use of heat; specifically that method of printing from ordinary type or plates on an ordinary press and in which a special ink is used, the type impression being sprinkled while still wet with a special powder and then subjected to a heating process which causes the particles to adhere to the printed surface and fuse together to give the printing a raised effect. Also called 'Raised-letter printing', 'Imitation embossing' and 'Virkotype process'. 2. THE THERMAL PROCESS (*q.v.*) of document copying.

Thermoplastic Binding. A method of binding a book without sewing. The folds are cut off, the edges roughened and glued and the covers stuck on.

Thermoplastic Process. A microfilming process whereby an electrostatic image is made to produce a permanent deformation of a plastic film layer. Recording can be made by optical projection, electron beams, or computer print-out devices. Thermoplastic systems also have a higher capacity than magnetic tape for carrying coded information for use with computers.

Thesauri (*Pl.*). *See Thesaurus.*

Thesaurofacet. A faceted classification with a fully structural thesaurus as index. It was developed from the English Electric Company's faceted classification for engineering.

Thesaurus. 1. Literally, a storehouse, or treasury, of knowledge. A term which is best known through its use in the title *Thesaurus of English words and phrases* by P.M. Roget, first published in 1852 and frequently revised. 2. A lexicon, more especially where words are grouped by ideas; a grouping or classification of synonyms or near synonyms; a set of equivalence classes of terminology. 3. A compilation of groups of words, consisting of the links between words used in documents and words used as DESCRIPTORS (*q.v.*), prepared for consultation by a machine used in information retrieval. They display relations within the vocabulary based on semantics, not on orthography. A number of thesauri of the most commonly used terms in various fields have been published in order to achieve a unity of indexing terminology in their respective fields. 4. A thesaurus may be defined either in terms of its function or of its structure. In terms of function, it is a terminological control device used in translating from the natural language of documents into a more constrained system language (documentation language, information language). In terms of structure, a thesaurus is a controlled and dynamic vocabulary of semantically and generically related terms which covers a specific domain of knowledge. 5. A list of descriptors. Also called 'Dictionary' or 'Words authority file'. 6. A terminological control device used in translating from the natural language of documents into a more constrained 'system language'. It is a controlled and dynamic vocabulary of semantically and generically related terms which covers a specific domain of knowledge. (Adopted by Unesco and published in *Guidelines for the establishment and development of monolingual thesauri*).

Thesis. *Synonymous with* DISSERTATION (*q.v.*).

Thick Space. (*Printing*) A space whose width is one-third of its own body.

Thickness Copy. *Synonymous with* DUMMY (*q.v.*).

Thin Paper. Sensitized photographic paper between 0.0038 and 0.0043 inches inclusive. *See also Photographic Papers.*

Thin Space. (*Printing*) A space whose width is one-fifth of its own body.

Third Generation Microfilm. *Synonymous with* SECOND REPRODUCTION MICROFILM (*q.v.*). *See also Generation.*

Third Indention. The twelfth typewriter space from the left edge of a card, and the second space from the second or inner vertical line on a ruled card. The distance from the left-hand edge of a catalogue card at which certain parts of the description begin or continue. It is generally as far to the right of the SECOND INDENTION (*q.v.*) as this is from the FIRST INDENTION (*q.v.*). *See also Indention.*

Thirty-sixmo (36mo). A sheet of paper folded to form 36 leaves, making 72 pages. Also called 'Trigesimo-sexto'.

Thirty-twomo (32mo). A sheet of paper folded five times to form a section of 32 leaves (64 pages) each leaf being one thirty-second of the sheet. Also called 'Trigesimo-secundo'.

Thomas (Dylan) Award. Offered annually by the Poetry Society (UK) for poetry and short stories in alternate years.

Thorough-bass. *Synonymous with* FIGURED-BASS (*q.v.*).

Thread Stitched. A booklet that is fastened with thread through the section fold. *See also Sewing, Side-stitch, Wire Stitched.*

Three-colour Process. Printing by photo-mechanical colour separation in half-tone, which will reproduce colour in the copy in three printings of yellow, red and blue. *See also Two-colour Process, Two-colour Reproduction.*

Three-decker. A novel published in three volumes during the latter half of the nineteenth century.

Three Dots. Used on the type BASE LINE (*q.v.*) thus . . . in quoted text, or a catalogue entry, to indicate that some part of the original has been omitted. Called 'Omission marks'.

Three Number Author Table. A table initiated by G.C. Makkar whereby numbers are allocated consecutively to sequences of not more than four letters of authors' names arranged alphabetically. The numbers serve to arrange books (which have been classified) or records of books alphabetically by authors' names.

Three-quarter Binding. *See Quarter Binding.*

Three-quarter Leather. A book bound similarly to one in HALF LEATHER (*q.v.*), but with the leather of the spine projecting across a third of the sides. *See also Leather Bound, Quarter Leather.*

Thriller. A novel of a sensational character, usually dealing with crime and criminals.

Throw Out. Maps, tables, or diagrams likely to be much consulted during the reading of a book, are sometimes 'thrown out' by the binder. This is done by making the 'guard' the size of the page, or printing the map on extra large paper, and pasting it at the end of a book or beyond the text which refers to it, so that the whole of the map, etc., when opened out, may remain in view during reading.

Thumb Book. *Synonymous with* BIBELOT (*q.v.*).

Thumb Index. A series of rounded notches cut into the fore-edges of a book, with or without tabs let in and bearing in progressive order from top to bottom the letters or words showing the arrangement. Usually provided for Bibles and dictionaries.

Tied Down. (*Binding*) Where the fillets which flank the bands of the spine are carried on to meet at a point near the hinge.

Tied Letter. *Synonymous with* LIGATURE (*q.v.*).

Tied Up. Said of type-matter that has been made up into pages and tied up with page-cord to secure it until imposition.

Tier. A set of shelves one above another between two uprights and reaching from the floor to the top of the shelving: a section of a PRESS (*q.v.*). *See also Book Press, Book Stack, Bookcase, Press.*

Tier Guide.   A guide to the contents of a TIER (*q.v.*).

Ties.   1. Silk, leather, cord, tape, ribbon or other slips attached, usually in pairs, to the outer edges of boards of books for a decorative purpose, or to prevent sagging by holding the covers together.   2. Terminations to tooled lines on each side of projecting bands on the spine of a bound book and carried over on to the covers to form ornamental features.

Tighe Report.   A report by F.C. Tighe and based on a national survey of the conditions of service of assistant librarians in British public libraries. The *Recommendations on welfare and working conditions of public library staffs*, based on this report, were approved by the Council of the Association of Assistant Librarians and adopted by the Council of the Library Association in May 1953. *See also Jordan Report.*

Tight Back.   A binding in which the cover of leather or other material is pasted or glued to the spine of the book, so that it does not become hollow when open. The pages do not lie flat when the book is open unless the paper used is thin and not stiff, as e.g. India paper. This is therefore a less satisfactory form of binding than either Flexible or Hollow. Also called 'Fast back', 'Stiff back'. *See also Flexible Sewing, Hollow Back.*

Tight Joint.   *Synonymous with* CLOSED JOINT (*q.v.*).

Tilde.   (*Printing*) An accent in the form of a wavy line as used over letters in Spanish and Portuguese: – ñ; õ. Also used in mathematics.

Till-forbid Order.   *Synonymous with* STANDING ORDER (*q.v.*).

Tilted Shelves.   The bottom or lower two or three shelves of a bookcase which are arranged in a sloping position to render the examination of titles easier.

Time Lapse Cinematograph Film.   Cinematograph film exposed frame by frame over a considerable time interval in order to record motion or growth in an extremely accelerated form.

Time-Life Silver Pen Award.   An annual prize for an outstanding work of UK-published non-fiction; administered by the English Centre of PEN INTERNATIONAL (*q.v.*).

Time Numbers.   A series of numbers or letters designed to facilitate the arrangement of books in chronological instead of author or alphabetical order. *See also Biscoe Time Numbers, Merrill Alphabeting Numbers.*

Time-schedule.   *See Time-Sheet.*

Time-sharing.   (*Information retrieval*) Being able to use a device for more than one purpose in the same time period. This process is accomplished by the automatic interspersing of different operations by the computer.

Time-sheet.   A schedule showing the exact hours each day that each member of staff is scheduled to be on duty. Also called 'Time-schedule'.

***Times Educational Supplement* Information Book Awards.**   Two annual awards for authors of the best information books for children published in the UK or Commonwealth. One award is for a book for children up to the age of nine, the other for a book for children aged 10–16.

Times Educational Supplement Schoolbook Award.   An annual award for the best school textbook; age range and subject area varies each year.

Times – Europa.   A new type, designed by Walter Tracy for *The Times*, largely to replace TIMES NEW ROMAN (*q.v.*) which had been in use for forty years. Tracy was manager of the typographic department of the Linotype Co. and designed five newspaper text faces: Jubilee (1954); Adsans (1958) a 4¾ pt. sans-serif face; Maximus; Linotype Modern (1961). It was first used by *The Times* on 9 October 1972.

Times New Roman.   A type face designed under the direction of Stanley Morison by the Monotype Corporation for *The Times* newspaper in 1932 and later extensively used in book work. Usually called 'Times Roman'. For a specimen alphabet, *see Type Face*.

Tint.   (*Printing*) 1. A ready-made dotted, hachured or other pattern, available in various densities, which can be applied by a draughtsman, blockmaker or printer to an illustration in order to give an impression of grey to a line drawing. Usually called 'Mechanical tint'.   2. A solid panel in a second colour.

Tipped In.   A single leaf, errata slip or illustration, inserted in a book at the inner edge with a narrow edge of paste against the following page.

Tipping Machine.   A bookbinding machine for the gluing of single plates and end-papers on to folded sheets or sewn sections. Some models also glue paper covers on to the folded and sewn sections.

Tips.   Very thin millboards used for book-binding.

Tissue-Papers.   Sheets of superfine thin paper placed in front of illustrations to protect them from set-off while the ink is fresh. These are often removed after the ink has dried, but sometimes they are to be found tipped-in, and they frequently bear a typographical description of the illustration.

Tissued Plate.   An illustration in a book which has a thin tissue placed between it (either loose or pasted to the inner margin) and the text page to protect it from SET-OFF (*q.v.*). Sometimes the tissue bears the caption relating to the illustration or an appropriate quotation. *See also Interleaf.*

Tithe Documents.   Documents relating to tithes. The Tithe Act, 1936, as amended, provides that the Master of the Rolls may direct that sealed copies of tithe documents shall be transferred to the Public Record Office or to any public library or museum or historical or antiquarian society willing to receive them. On the transfer of such documents the governing body of the library, museum or society assumes responsibility for their proper preservation. The Tithe (Copies of Instruments of Apportionment) Rules were made in 1946 (S. R. & O., 1946, No. 2091) to implement the provisions of the Act.

Title.   The word or words by which an intellectual work is designated on its title-page, and distinguished from any other work. In its fuller sense, it includes any sub-title, alternative title, or associated descriptive matter, but excludes the name of the author and/or editor, translator, etc. (unless the name forms a grammatically inseparable part of the title) and the edition, but not the imprint. In statistical records, the name of a document exclusive of any alternative title, subtitle or other associated descriptive matter on the title, which is catalogued separately. Thus a periodical which suffers a change of title is counted once under each; each monograph with an individual title is counted as well as any series title to which it belongs. *See also Back Title, Binders Title, Collective Title, Cover Title, Short Title, Spine Title.*

Title-a-line Catalogue. A catalogue in which the entries occupy only a single line of type.

Title-a-line Index. *See Line-by-line Index.*

Title Analytic. *See Analytical Entry.*

Title Area. (*Reprography*) The portion of a MICROFICHE (*q.v.*) which is specifically allotted for title and other bibliographical information.

Title Backing. The material, or treatment, applied to the back of the title area (i.e. the area extending the full width of the film and above the micro-images) of a microfiche so that the title can be more easily read by reflected light. It is usually applied to a distribution MICROFICHE (*q.v.*) not intended to be used for the reproduction of additional microfiches.

Title Card. A catalogue card bearing an entry under the title of a work.

Title Catalogue. A catalogue consisting only of title entries.

Title-cut. *Synonymous with* FRAMED-CUT (*q.v.*).

Title Entry. A record in a catalogue, bibliography or index, usually under the first word of a title not an article.

Title Indention. *Synonymous with* SECOND INDENTION (*q.v.*).

Title Index. *Synonymous with* Key-word-in-context, or KWIC (*q.v.*) index.

Title Leaf. The leaf at the beginning of a book, the recto of which is the title-page. The verso usually bears bibliographical details of printer, copyright date, the ISBN (*q.v.*), etc. and any earlier editions. The BS 4719: 1971 *Title leaves of a book* defines title leaves as 'The initial printed leaves of a book. They normally consist of two leaves, the half-title leaf followed by the title leaf, but there may be only one leaf of more than two title leaves'. This BS is based on ISO Recommendation R 1086 *Title leaves of a book*, and lists 15 items of bibliographical and other information which should be given on the title leaves.

Title List. A periodical publication in which important and relevant articles are selected from periodicals and listed by title and grouped in subject order.

Title of Honour. A title which denotes superior rank or station, or special distinction of any kind.

Title-page. Usually the recto of the second leaf which gives the title in full, sub-title (if any), author's name in full together with particulars of qualifications, degrees, etc., edition, publisher's name and address, and date of publication. The verso may give particulars of edition, printer's name and sometimes his address, binder's name, details of type and paper used in making the book, owner of copyright, and CIP information. If there is more than one page giving particulars of the title, the title-page is that which gives the fullest information. The information which should be given on the title leaves of a book is given in BS 4719: 1971 *Title leaves of a book* and on the title page of printed music, in BS 4754: 1971 *The presentation of bibliographical information in printed music*. *See also Title Leaf, Double Title-page, Engraved Title-page, Second Half-title, Section Title.*

Title-page Border. A frame, at first a woodcut, and later made of heavy type ornaments, surrounding the matter on the title-page.

Title-page Title. The title of a book as it appears on the title-page. It is the authority for the correct reference to the book; other versions of the title as given on the spine, cover, half-title, top of the pages or jacket may vary slightly.

Title Piece. A leather label, sometimes coloured, pasted on the back of a binding, and bearing the title of the book.

Title Proper. The title appearing on the title-page, or elsewhere in a publication which does not possess a title-page, but which is obviously the chief title. It is the chief title of a publication and includes any ALTERNATIVE TITLE (*q.v.*) but excludes parallel titles and any other title.

Title Sheet. The first printed sheet of a book containing the title-page and other preliminary matter.

Title Signature. The title (often abbreviated to initial letters) placed on the signature line of signed pages to prevent the binder mixing up the sheets of various books. Also called 'Direction line'. *See also Signature and Catchword Line.*

Title Space. The area specifically allotted on a microfiche or microcard for title information. *See also Title Backing.*

Title Strip. Wording at the beginning of a FILM STRIP (*q.v.*) or other sequence of microcopy frames giving the title or indicating their contents.

Title Wrap-around. A feature of the KWIC (*q.v.*) index whereby unused space is filled by allowing the remainder of the imprinted title at the end of the type-line to appear at the beginning of the same line, providing space is available there. Also called 'Title recirculation', 'Title snap-back'.

Titling. Capital letters of modern Roman type which are cast 'fullface' on the BODY (*q.v.*); there are thus no BEARD (*q.v.*) or LOWER CASE letters (*q.v.*). They are used for headlines, titles, jackets or posters.

Titlonym. A quality or title used as a pseudonym, as 'A Barrister'. If the author's name cannot be determined, such books are catalogued as if they were anonymous, entry being made under the title. An added entry is made under the titlonym. *See also Telonism.*

T.L.S. *See A.L.S.*

Toggle Press. The Albion press which was introduced in 1823 and allowed the platen to be lowered and given great pressure by means of a toggle-jointed lever instead of the screw method. A toggle-jointed lever is one with an elbow-shaped joint with two arms known as the chill and the wedge. When the joint is straightened so that chill and wedge form a straight line, great endwise pressure is produced.

Token Charging. A system of issuing books whereby the borrower on entering the lending department of a library is given a token which is exchanged for a book on leaving.

Tom-Gallon Trust. Awards made biennially by the UK SOCIETY OF AUTHORS (*q.v.*) to fiction writers of limited means.

Tome. A volume, or book, especially a heavy one.

Tool Phase. In classification, where one discipline is used to assist the investigation of another, the document is classified under the thing investigated, not under the tool of investigation. It is one of Ranganathan's three main 'phase relations', the other two are BIAS PHASE and INFLUENCE PHASE (*qq.v.*).

Tooled Edges. The edges of a book which have been impressed with designs. *See also Edges.*

Tooling. The impressing of designs – by means of finishing tools such as rolls – into a leather or cloth binding. The tools used may be 'embossed' in which case there is modelling on the top surface (i.e. the bottom of its impression), 'outline', 'shaded' or 'azured'. When this is done through gold leaf it is called 'gold tooling', when neither leaf nor pigment is used it is called 'blind tooling'. When the entire cover design is a single piece, it is called a 'stamp'. Gold tooling is believed to have been introduced by Thomas Berthelet, royal binder to Henry VIII. *See also Azure Tooling, Block 3, Edge-rolled.*

Top Edges Gilt. The top edges of a book cut smooth and gilded. Abbreviated 't.e.g.'. Also called 'Gilt top'.

Top Margin. The space between the top line of type of a book or periodical, and the edge of the page. *See also Margin.*

Top Side. *Synonymous with* FELT SIDE (*q.v.*).

Topic. In co-ordinate indexing, a group of terms describing a given subject. Also called 'Information item' and 'Theme'.

Topic Guide. A shelf guide; it is usually a narrow block of wood or piece of cardboard bearing the subject and class number, placed on the shelf at the beginning of the books on the subject. Also called 'Subject guide'.

Topical Bibliography. A subject bibliography, consisting of short lists of books or references placed at the ends of chapters.

Topographical Catalogue. A catalogue of books relating to places.

Topographical Index. An index of places arranged in alphabetical order.

Topographical Map. One which shows physical or natural features of an area.

Tory Style. A style of binding executed in the sixteenth century for Geoffroy Tory the famous French printer, wood-engraver and designer. Distinguished by arabesque panels, borders and ornaments.

TOSCA. Acronym for Total Online Searching For Cataloguing Activities: Library of Congress cataloguers in 1983 ceased to check LC card catalogues and now rely on machine-readable files.

Town Plan. A map of a town showing the organized arrangement of streets, open spaces, etc. *See also Plat.*

Toy Libraries Association. *See Play Matters.*

Toy Library. A collection of toys available on loan.

TPI. Abbreviation for Title-page, Index. Used to refer to the separately published title-page and index to a volume of a serial which may often have to be separately ordered for insertion in a bound volume.

Tr. (trans). Abbreviation for TRANSACTIONS (*q.v.*), translated, TRANSLATION (*q.v.*), TRANSLATOR (*q.v.*).

Tracing. An indication on the front or back of a main entry catalogue card showing under what additional headings added entries appear. Also, the record (on the main entry card, or on an authority card) of all the related references made. Specially important in a dictionary catalogue in order to ensure that in case of change, correction or removal, all the cards referring to a given book may be traced and the change applied to all of them. In co-ordinate indexing, a list of descriptors, Uniterms, etc., applied to a specific document.

Tracing Paper. Paper treated with a coating of Canada balsam in turpentine, or a solution of castor oil or linseed oil in alcohol. The papers chosen for this treatment must have excellent transparency, high tearing strength, and be resistant to erasure; they must contain no loading and be engine-sized. Tracing papers cockle readily on absorbing moisture from the atmosphere and must therefore be wrapped in waxed or other waterproof paper.

Tract. 1. A pamphlet containing a short propagandist discourse, especially on a religious, political or social subject. 2. A pamphlet printed on a single sheet and imposed in pages.

Trade Bibliography. *See Bibliography 1, Trade Catalogue 1.*

Trade Binding. 1. The binding in which a publisher issues a book. Also called 'Publisher's binding'. 2. Plain calf or sheep bindings which were used in England by publishers from the fifteenth–eighteenth centuries; only rarely did they carry lettering on the spines. Until the nineteenth century, purchasers usually bought books unbound or enclosed in wrappers, and had them bound to order.

Trade Book. A common US publishing term for a book intended for general readership. It is neither a children's book, a textbook, nor a technical treatise, but a book which would interest anybody, and be published by a commercial publisher as distinct from one published by a society, institution, governmental agency or other non-commercial group.

Trade Catalogue. 1. A list of the books in print published in a country, and frequently of books published abroad, for which the home publishers are agents. 2. A publication containing particulars of goods manufactured by, or sold by, a firm; frequently illustrated and containing prices.

Trade Directory. A DIRECTORY (*q.v.*) which is concerned with one trade or a group of related trades.

Trade Edition. Copies of a book which are regularly printed and supplied to booksellers by publishers at the appropriate wholesale rates. *See also Large Paper Edition, Subscribers' Edition*, especially such an edition contrasted with a de luxe, paperback, library-bound, or book club edition.

Trade Information. *Synonymous with* BIBLIOGRAPHIC INFORMATION (*q.v.*).

Trade Journal. A periodical restricted to the interests of a trade or industry and including all or some of the following: news items, articles and descriptions of goods, products and manufactured articles, lists of new publications, statistical data, patents, personal notes, legislative activities, etc. Also called 'Trade paper'.

Trade List. A list of publications in print, which is issued by a publisher for the information of the bookselling trade, often providing space for ordering the various titles and giving particulars of the terms under which the books are sold to booksellers.

Trade Paper. *Synonymous with* TRADE JOURNAL (*q.v.*).

Trade Series. *See Publisher's Series.*

Trade Terms. The provision of facilities for retailers to obtain goods at a discount for re-sale to the public. In the book trade, the discounts may vary according to the kind of book (general, children's, educational, technical, etc.) but they are fairly standard. Export terms are usually different from those for the home market.

Trade Union Information Group. The Group was set up in 1980 in the UK, and aims to stimulate and encourage the development of library and information services to serve trade unionists. Membership is open to library staff and others interested in the provision of information within the trade union and labour movements. The Group holds meetings, provides speakers, and publishes an irregular *Newsletter*. Abbreviated TUIG.

Traditional Abstract. *See Abstract.*

Traditional Format. The format of oriental books, consisting of double leaves with folds at the fore-edge and with free edges sewn together to make a fascicle. Usually several fascicles are contained in a cloth-covered case.

Trailer. A portion of developed but unexposed copying material, such as film strip, at the end of a sequence of exposures, which is not cut off; it serves to protect the exposed portion and assists projection.

Trailer Card. A microfiche card which follows another, and is provided to give additional data, information or pages of a document.

Trailer Microfilm. *See Microfiche.*

Trailer Record. A record which follows a group of similar records and contains pertinent data related to the group of records.

Training. The process of developing the skill, awareness or expertise of staff, both professional and non-professional. Training may consist of induction into a system or routine, organization of new skills or attitudes, or development of existing skills towards greater efficiency, job satisfaction, commitment, interchangeability, co-operation, or promotion. It is important that training should be carefully prepared in response to needs, and its effectiveness monitored. Libraries may join *co-operative training* groups to reduce costs and spread expertise. Training specifically aimed at promotion opportunities may be termed *staff development*.

Training Access Points. *See TAPs.*

Training and Education Group. *See Personnel, Training and Education Group.*

Training Co-operative. *See Co-operative Training.*

Transaction Card. A card which is inserted in a book, the loan of which is recorded by a TRANSACTION CARD CHARGING (*q.v.*) method.

Transaction Card Charging. Book issue methods in which the records of loans are kept in the order in which they are made, transactions being given numbers in consecutive order. At the time of recording the loan a numbered 'transaction card' is inserted in the book and remains there until the book is returned to the library when it is withdrawn. Transaction cards for all returning books are then put into number order, any missing ones indicating overdue books. The transaction cards usually have the date the books are due for return stamped on them. Photo-charging, Audio Charging (*q.v.*) and Punched Card Charging (*q.v.*) and the Bookamatic (*q.v.*) systems are transaction card charging methods. Abbreviated T-card charging.

Transaction Room. A room to which books issued by a method using transaction cards are taken on their return by readers, for examination, checking with lists of reserved books, or sorting for shelving. The manual sorting of transaction cards may also be done here, punched transaction cards being sent to the machine sorter.

Transactional Analysis. The scientific study of the behaviour of individuals or groups of individuals in the process of communication with other individuals or groups.

Transactions. The published papers read at meetings of a society or institution, or abstracts of the same. *Also sometimes synonymous with* Proceedings (*q.v.*). A general distinction made between Transactions and Proceedings is that the Transactions are the papers presented and the Proceedings the records of meetings.

Transbinary Group on Librarianship and Information Studies. Set up early 1985 by the University Grants Committee and the National Advisory Body for Public Sector Higher Education; the terms of reference were: 'to advise on the current provision of, and likely needs for, library and information courses at institutions within the responsibilities of the UGC, the NAB and the WAB, (Welsh Advisory Board), taking account also of institutions within the responsibility of the SED (Scottish Education Department) and the DENI (Department of Education, Northern Ireland), and to make recommendations for action. This will involve a review of likely future demand (both in terms of numbers and of expertise) for library and information professionals and of the course provided by each of the library and information science schools, bearing in mind the changing nature of library and information work'. A report back to the UGC and NAB was made mid-1986. The acronym TYGLIS is sometimes used.

Transborder Data Flow. An IFLA project established in 1985 to promote the electronic transfer of data between libraries across national boundaries. The project is based at the National Library of Canada. Four main issues are under consideration: privacy and data protection; the role of the European Community; the role of Eastern bloc countries; Third World reaction to the domination of the system by the industralized nations. Abbreviated TDF. Retitled 1986 Universal Dataflow and Telecommunications (*q.v.*).

Transcribe. (*Information retrieval*) To copy from one external storage medium to another.

Transcript. 1. A copy made from an original, particularly of a legal document. 2. Also, a written record of words usually spoken, e.g. of court proceedings, or of a broadcast. In the archives field, an exact reproduction, so far as the resources of script or typography allow, of an original document, with the single exception that abbreviations may be extended providing their interpretation is unquestionable.

Transcription. 1. An expression in one notation that is equivalent to an expression in another. 2. In music, the arrangement for one musical medium of music originally composed for another, e.g. an organ piece from an orchestral overture. 3. An arrangement in which some liberty is taken by way of modification or embellishment. *See also Version.*

TRANSDOC. A European Community project for document delivery using optical digital discs and microforms as storage media. *Now see ADONIS.*

Transfer. A chemically prepared paper for transferring drawings direct on to lithographic stone or a rubber-covered cylinder used in offset lithography.

Transfer Box. A box, somewhat similar to a PAMPHLET BOX (*q.v.*) but of less durable construction and serving to store lesser used pamphlet material which is transferred from the current sequence.

Transfer File. 1. A container of some kind (box-like or folder) of a less sturdy type and cheaper, to contain older material which must be filed but which is seldom referred to and encumbers current files. 2. The material itself which is removed from current files.

Transfer Printing. *See Decalcomania.*

Transformer. In information retrieval, the selector which searches the DESCRIPTOR FILE (*q.v.*).

Transitional. A name sometimes given to the type face designed about 1760 by John Baskerville, and those based on it. Transitional types retain the bracketed serifs of old face and suggest by their precision the engraved quality of modern face types. The faces are more angular, with sharper contrast between the thick and thin strokes. *See also Egyptian, Modern Face, Old Face, Type Face.* The following is in 12 point Baskerville:

ABCDEFGHIJKLMNOPQRSTUVWXYZ
abcdefghijklmnopqrstuvwxyz 1234567890

Bell is a 'transitional' type face, as are also Fournier, Caledonia and Columbia.

Transitional Face. *See Transitional.*

Translated Title List. A periodically issued bulletin which lists, usually in a systematic order, the translated titles of periodical articles and documents which are likely to be of interest to its readers.

Translation. 1. The act of turning a literary composition from one language into another. 2. The work so produced. *See also Machine Translation.*

Translation Pool. A centrally held collection of translations acquired from a variety of sources, and available for use on a co-operative basis.

Translation Rights. The right to allow or refuse the publication of any literary production in another language is a part of COPYRIGHT (*q.v.*).

Translator. One who translates from one language into another.

Transliteration. The representation of the ordinary characters of a language by those of another, as from Russian, Arabic, Cyrillic, Irish or Greek into Roman, each digit or letter being transcribed independently of the others. British Standards for transliteration are: BS 2979:1958 *Transliteration of*

Cyrillic and Greek characters and BS 4280:1968 *Transliteration of Arabic characters. See also Romanization.*

Translucent Copy. In documentary reproduction, a copy on translucent material.

Translucent Screen. A sheet of glass treated in some way (ground, opal, coated, etc.), or of plastic, on to which an image is projected in a microfilm reader.

Transmission Copying. In documentary reproduction, making a photocopy by passing light through a one-sided original which is in contact with sensitized paper. Included in this method are blue-print and Diazo or dyeline processes and the use of silver halide paper in contact with single-sided document which is thin enough to permit light to pass through it.

Transmission Print. A copy of a document made by TRANSMISSION PRINTING (*q.v.*).

Transmission Printing. The making of contact prints by passing light through the original and on to the material of reproduction. *See also Contact Copying, Transmission Copying.*

Transparency. An image, in black and white or colour, on transparent base-stock, usually film, which may be viewed by transmitted light, usually with the aid of a projector.

Transparent Vellum. A method (patented in 1785) used by Edwards of Halifax which rendered the vellum to be used in bookbinding transparent. A painting or drawing was done on the underside and the whole then lined with white paper.

Transpose. To change over the positions of letters, words or lines of type. This is marked on a proof by putting a loop round the characters to be changed and writing 'trs.' in the margin.

Transposing Instrument. A musical instrument for which the music is written in a key or in an octave other than its actual sound, but which (mechanically and without thought on the part of the player) transposes the music to a higher or lower pitch.

Trask (Betty) Awards. Annual awards administered by the SOCIETY OF AUTHORS (*q.v.*) to enable young Commonwealth authors to travel abroad.

Travelling Card. A catalogue card on which subsequent issues of annuals or other serial publications (*see Continuation 3*) are entered and which is passed to each department or library in turn for the appropriate addition to be made to the catalogue entry. On completion of the addition to all the catalogues, this card is filed in the official catalogue, or in a special sequence, to await subsequent publications when the process is repeated.

Travelling Library. A motor vehicle equipped with shelves, which visits districts where there is no other library service at specified times on a certain day or days of the week. The public may choose their books from the shelves. In the UK there is a tendency to describe such a vehicle as a 'Mobile Branch Library' or 'Mobile Library' and to use the term 'Travelling Library' for a small vehicle which is shelved or otherwise equipped to provide a service to villages, and isolated farms and houses, with short stops for issuing books. *See also Mobile Library*. In America, the term also refers to a small collection of selected books sent by a central library agency for the use of a branch, group or community, during a limited period.

Travelling Mould. *See Wire.*

Tray Label. A label inserted in the holder provided on the front of a catalogue drawer to indicate its contents.

TRC. Acronym of the Technology Reports Centre, which was a research and technical information centre, processing and making available for industry and research centres exploitable and unpublished research and development reports arising from UK Government programmes and those of overseas governments. Operated by the Department of Industry until 1982, when control was transferred to the British Library.

Treatment of Correspondence. *See Correspondence Management.*

Tree Calf. A calf binding which has had acid poured on it in such a way as to form stains resembling a tree-like pattern.

Tree of Porphyry. *See Porphyry, Tree of.*

Tree Structure. An hierarchical system used in database construction to organize material from general (root) to specific (leaf) concepts. Searching in such a structure proceeds via only one path subdividing at a series of branches.

Trial Binding. A sample of the proposed cover for a book submitted by the binder or casemaker to the publisher.

Trial Issue. A few copies of a book printed for circulation to critical friends prior to the printing of the edition for publication which is printed without re-setting of the type. If re-setting occurs then the preliminary edition is known as a 'trial edition'.

Trial Proof. *See Proof.*

Trigesimo-secundo (32mo). A sheet of paper folded five times to form a section of 32 leaves (64 pages). Also called 'Thirty-twomo'.

Trigesimo-sexto. *Synonymous with* THIRTY-SIXMO (*q.v.*).

Trilogy. A set of three related dramatic or literary compositions.

Trimmed. 1. Paper which has been trimmed on one or more sides to ensure exactness of corner angles and to reduce to the size required. 2. (*Binding*) The top edge untouched, and only the inequalities removed from the others, the folds not being opened. *See also Edges.*

Trimmed Page Size. The size of a sheet after folding and trimming.

Trimmed Size. The final dimensions of a sheet of paper. British papermakers may interpret this term as 'guillotine trimmed'. *See also Paper Sizes, Untrimmed Size.*

Trinity College Library, Dublin. The oldest library in Ireland; it was established by Royal Charter in 1592 and in 1801 was granted the right to receive a copy of every publication issued in the United Kingdom. It is rich in manuscripts, its best-known treasure being the *Book of Kells*.

Triple Lining. A method of LINING (*q.v.*) used to give added strength. It is used in better-quality cased books and consists of providing a strip of crêpe manila lining, with head-and-tailbands if desired. All the lining processes used in this instance number seven and can be carried out mechanically.

Triplex Paper. *See Duplex Paper.*

Tripoli. The cheaper grades of esparto grass, grown in North Africa. *See also Esparto.*

Tripper. (*Reprography*) A device, operated mechanically or electronically, to control lights, film advance, or the beginning or end of the operation.

Triptych. *See Codex.*

Troy Type. A type cut by William Morris in 1892; it was an 18-point Gothic type based on the early types of Schoeffer, Mentelin and Zainer. *See also Chaucer Type, Golden Type.*

trs. Abbreviation for Transpose (*q.v.*); in proof correcting it is written in the margin to indicate that the position of the words, letters or lines around which a loop is drawn are to be exchanged.

True Anonyma. Books which could be catalogued under the author's name if their authors were known. These are catalogued in the Library of Congress and some other libraries with the author line left blank so that it can be entered without re-typing the whole entry should the authorship be discovered. This method is known as 'hanging indention'. *See also Formal Anonyma.*

Truncation. 1. The process of shortening or cutting off part of a keyword or a title in a Permuted Title Index (*q.v.*). A truncated title lacks one or more words or syllables at the beginning or end. 2. Shortening of a search term so that it will match related terms starting with the same stem, e.g. LIBR: will match library, libraries, librarian, librarianship, etc.

T.S. Abbreviation for typescript and tub-sized. *See also Tub-Sizing.*

TTS. Abbreviation for Teletypesetting (*q.v.*).

Tub-Sizing. Dipping sheets of Waterleaf (*q.v.*) into a tub of animal glue, gelatine, a prepared starch, or a combination of these, drying on cow-hair ropes or hessian, and then glazing them. Tub-sized paper (abbreviated 'T.S.') is strong and has a high resistance to moisture. Also called 'Animal Tub-sized' (abbreviated 'A.T.S.'). *See also Engine-sizing.*

TUIG. *See Trade Union Information Group.*

Tumbler Scheme. The method of perfecting sheets to be printed from a forme imposed in the oblong, or landscape, manner. In order to obtain correct page sequence, the sheet must be turned or tumbled, in its short direction. *See also Work and Turn.*

Turn-in. 1. That portion of the material covering the boards of a book which overlaps the head, tail and fore-edges of the boards and is turned-in over these edges of the boards. 2. To make use of type matter which is already set. 3. The turned-over end of a book jacket which is folded around the cover.

Turn Over. 1. Printed matter extending beyond the allotted space. 2. The part of an article continued from a preceding page. Also called Run Over (*q.v.*). 3. The second and subsequent lines of a paragraph.

Turned. (*Printing*) A printed impression of a graph, table or illustration, etc., which is turned at right angles so that its foot is parallel to the fore-edge of the page. *See also Landscape Page.*

Turned Comma.   A comma which is used upside down and in a superior position, i.e. on the MEAN LINE (*q.v.*); it is used at the beginning of quoted matter ' . . . ' and in the abbreviation of the Scottish 'Mac', as in M'Gregor.

Turned Letter.   A letter used upside down such as a 'u' for an 'n'.

Turned Sort.   A type letter used foot uppermost for one not known or not available. This is very conspicuous in galley proof. When turned sorts are replaced with the correct letters, the process is called 'taking out turns'.

Turnkey System.   A computer system supplied complete for a specific purpose. No preparation is required on the part of the purchaser other than to turn the key to commence.

Turnover Lines.   The second or subsequent lines of type in a paragraph. Called 'Run-in lines' in America.

Turns.   *See Taking Out Turns.*

Tutor Librarian.   A librarian of an educational institution who gives lectures to students on the library and how to make the best use of it, and sometimes on academic subjects, as well as having responsibility for the administration or functioning of the library.

Twelvemo.   *See Duodecimo.*

Twenty-fourmo   (24mo). A sheet of paper folded to form a section of 24 leaves (48 pages). Also called 'Vicesimo-quarto'.

Twentymo   (20mo). A sheet of paper folded into 20 leaves, making 40 pages.

Twice Weekly.   A periodical which is published twice a week. Also called 'Semi-weekly'.

Twin Wire Paper.   A DUPLEX PAPER (*q.v.*) made by bringing the two wet webs together, WIRE SIDES (*q.v.*) innermost, to form a single sheet with two top or FELT SIDES (*q.v.*) and no wire side or 'underside'. Such paper is particularly suitable for offset printing. *See also Right.*

Twisted Pineapples.   (*Binding*) The form of ornament used on a number of English and French finishers' rolls, and consisting of twisted stems with conventional pineapples at intervals. *See also Pineapple.*

Two-colour Half-tones.   Two half-tone plates in which one of the plates is made with the line of the screen as in a one-colour half-tone, and the other with lines at a different angle, usually about 30°. The colours tend to blend into one another in different tones.

Two-colour Press.   A machine which prints in two colours at one operation. The principle is applicable to letterpress, lithographies and offset machines. Most offset printing is carried out on two-colour presses.

Two-colour Process.   A photo-mechanical process in which the printing is done in two colours.

Two-colour Reproduction.   Printing in two colours instead of the more usual three. The colours used are normally green or blue, and orange; subjects have to be carefully chosen or the resulting prints may be not true to the original, or they may be crude.

Two-layer Paper.   *See Furnish Layer.*

Two-line Letter.   (*Printing*) A capital letter having a depth of body (or height of letter on the printed page) equal to double that of the size specified, as 'two-line pica'. Three- and four-line letters are used similarly. They are often used as the initial letter for the first word of a chapter.

Two On.   Printing two sheets, jobs, page, etc., at the same time. The printing of small jobs in duplicate is done to facilitate the work and economize in time and costs.

Two-page Spread.   *Synonymous with* DOUBLE SPREAD (*q.v.*).

Two-revolution Machine.   A printing machine in which the cylinder, over which the paper is fed, does not stop after traversing the forme but continues to revolve, rising slightly during its second revolution so that it cannot come into contact with the type, and descending when the forme is again in position for printing. During its second revolution, the bed with the forme returns and the sheet is delivered. The earliest machine of this kind was made by Koenig in 1814. *See also Miehle, Perfecter, Single-Revolution Machine, Stanhope Press, Stop-cylinder Press.*

Two Sheets (Sections) On.   The method of sewing books when two sections are treated as one. In hand-sewing two sheets at a time are placed on the sewing-frame; the thread is passed from the kettle stitch of the lower section, and brought out at the first tape or cord, when it is inserted in the upper section, and so on. Thus, two sections receive only the same number of stitches one would do by the ALL ALONG method (*q.v.*). Although a weaker method than the 'all along', it helps to reduce the swelling in the back in the case of very thin books.

Two Sides Coloured.   Paper or board both sides of which have been coloured intentionally during manufacture.

Two-up.   1. Printing two texts, or duplicate stereos made from the same forme, side by side on the same sheet of paper. It is an economical way of machining short runs.   2. The processing of two books as a single unit from the forme through all the binding processes until they are separated by the trimmer. A method which is sometimes used for mass-producing PAPERBACKS (*q.v.*).

Two-way Paging.   The system of page numbering used for a book with the texts in two languages, one of which reads from left to right (as English) and the other from right to left (as Hebrew or Arabic); the texts being in two sections with page sequences from opposite ends of the book.

Twopenny Library.   A circulating library, usually in shop premises, for which the charge for borrowing a book was twopence a week. The charge became much greater but the name persisted.

TYGLIS.   *See Transbinary Group on Librarianship and Information Studies.*

Tying-up.   The tying of a volume after the cover has been drawn on, so as to make the leather adhere better to the sides of the bands; also for setting the headband.

Tympan.   A kind of leaf consisting of a thin frame of metal over which is stretched parchment or cambric, and which is hinged to the carriage bearing the forme of a printing press in such a way that it places the paper resting on it in the exact position for printing.

Type.   (*Classification*) *See Characteristic.* (*Printing*) A small rectangular block of metal or wood, having on its upper end a raised letter, figure, or other characters. *See also Type Face, Type Sizes.* For purposes of nomenclature, a single movable type character has always been considered as a human being standing erect, and having a BODY (but no head), a FACE, BEARD, NECK, SHOULDER, BACK, BELLY, FEET. Type letters are formed within three imaginary lines: the 'base line' on which the bases of capitals rest, the 'mean line' running along the top of the lower-case letters which are without ascenders, the 'cap line' which runs across the top of the capital letters. *See also Body, X-height.*

Type Area. The area, or part, of a page of a book, periodical or other publication which will be, or has been, filled with printed matter.

Type-casting Machine. Originally, one which cast single type units which were then set up in a stick by hand. More modern machines such as *Monotype, Linotype* and *Intertype* both set and cast.

Type Face. 1. The printing surface of the upper end of a piece of type which bears the character to be printed. 2. The style, or design, of characters on a set of pieces of type, comprising all the sizes in which the particular design is made. There are four classes of type face: ABSTRACT, CURSIVE, DECORATIVE, ROMAN (*qq.v.*), and they may also be divided in the following nine categories: HUMANIST, GARALDE, TRANSITIONAL, DIDONE, SLAB SERIF, LINEALE, GLYPHIC, SCRIPT AND GRAPHIC. The following is a selection of type faces (nearly all in 12-point):

12 pt Antique
ABCDEFGHIJKLMNOPQRSTUVWXYZ -
abcdefghijklmnopqrstuvwxyz - 1234567890

12 pt. Baskerville
ABCDEFGHIJKLMNOPQRSTUVWXYZ–abcd
efghijklmnopqrstuvwxyz–1234567890 –1234567890
*ABCDEFGHIJKLMNOPQRSTUVWXYZ – abcdefg
hijklmnopqrstuvwxyz–*

12 pt. Bell
ABCDEFGHIJKLMNOPQRSTUVWXYZ–abcdefg
hijklmnopqrstuvwxyz – 1234567890 –*ABCDEFGHI
JKLMNOPQRSTUVWXYZ – abcdefghijklmnopqrst
uvwxyz*

12 pt. Bembo
ABCDEFGHIJKLMNOPQRSTUV WXYZ – abcdefghijk
lmnopqrstuvwxyz – 1234567890–*ABCDEFGHIJKLMNO
PQRSTUVWXYZ – abcdefghijklmnopqrstuvwxyz*

.12 pt. Poliphilus & Blado
ABCDEFGHIJKLMNOPQRSTUVWXYZ – abcde
fghijklmnopqrstuvwxyz– 1234567890–*ABCDEFGHIJK
LMNOPQRSTUVWXYZ – abcdefghijklmnopqrstuvwxyz*

12 pt. Bodoni
ABCDEFGHIJKLMNOPQRSTUVWXYZ – abcde
fghijklmnopqrstuvwxyz – 1234567890 –*ABCDEFG
HIJKLMNOPQRSTUVWXYZ – abcdefghijklmno
pqrstuvwxyz*

12 pt. Bookprint
ABCDEFGHIJKLMNOPQRSTUVWXYZ– abc
defghijklmnopqrstuvwxyz – 1234567890– 1234567
890 – *ABCDEFGHIJKLMNOPQRSTUVWXYZ
·· abcdefghijklmnopqrstuvwxyz*

12 pt. Caslon
ABCDEFGHIJKLMNOPQRSTUVWXYZ – abcde
fghijklmnopqrstuvwxyz – 1234567890 – *ABCDEFGH
IJKLMNOPQRSTUVWXYZ – abcdefghijklmnopqrstu
vwxyz*

12 pt. Centaur
ABCDEFGHIJKLMNOPQRSTUVWXYZ – abcdefghijkl
mnopqrstuvwxyz – 1234567890 – *ABCDEFGHIJKLMNOPQ
RSTUVWXYZ – abcdefghijklmnopqrstuvwxyz – 1234567890*

12 pt. Clarendon
ABCDEFGHIJKLMNOPQRSTUVWXYZ – ab
cdefghijklmnopqrstuvwxyz – 1234567890

12 pt. Cochin
ABCDEFGHIJKLMNOPQRSTUVWXYZ –
abcdefghijklmnopqrstuvwxyz – 1234567890 –*ABCD
EFGHIJKLMNOPQRSTUVWXYZ – abcdefghijk
lmnopqrstuvwxyz*

10 pt. Cornell
ABCDEFGHIJKLMNOPQRSTUVWXYZ – abcdefghijklmn
opqrstuvwxyz – 1234567890 – *ABCDEFGHIJKLMNOPQR
STUVWXYZ – abcdefghijklmnopqrstuvwxyz*

12 pt Egmont
ABCDEFGHIJKLMNOPQRSTUVWXYZ—abc
defghijklmnopqrstuvwxyz—1234567890
*ABCDEFGHIJKLMNOPQRSTUVWXYZ—abc
defghijklmnopqrstuvwxyz—*

12 pt. Ehrhardt
ABCDEFGHIJKLMNOPQRSTUVWXYX – abcdefg
hijklmnopqrstuvwxyz–1234567890 –1234567890 –*ABCD*
EFGHIJKLMNOPQRSTUVWXYZ–abcdefghijklmno
pqrstuvwxyz

12 pt. Fournier
ABCDEFGHIJKLMNOPQRSTUVWXYZ – abcdefghijk
lmnopqrstuvwxyz – 1234567890 – *ABCDEFGHIJKLMN*
OPQRSTUVWXYZ – abcdefghijklmnopqrstuvwxyz

12 pt. Garamond
ABCDEFGHIJKLMNOPQRSTUVWXYZ – abcdef
ghijklmnopqrstuvwxyz–1234567890 –*ABCDEFGHI*
JKLMNOPQRSTUVWXYZ – abcdefghijklmnopqrstuv
wxyz

12 pt. Georgian
ABCDEFGHIJKLMNOPQRSTUVWXYZ – abcdefg
hijklmnopqrstuvwxyz – 1234567890 – 1234567890 – *A*
BCDEFGHIJKLMNOPQRSTUVWXYZ – abcdefghi
jklmnopqrstuvwxyz

12 pt. Gill
ABCDEFGHIJKLMNOPQRSTUVWXYZ – abcdefghij
klmnopqrstuvwxyz – 1234567890 – *ABCDEFGHIJKLM*
NOPQRSTUVWXYZ – abcdefghijklmnopqrstuvwxyz

12 pt. Goudy
ABCDEFGHIJKLMNOPQRSTUVWXYZ - abcde
fghijklmnopqrstuvwxyz - 1234567890 - ABCDEF
GHIJKLMNOPQRSTUVWXYZ - *abcdefghijklmn*
opqrstuvwxyz

12 pt. Granjon
ABCDEFGHIJKLMNOPQRSTUVWXYZ — abcdefghi
jklmnopqrstuvwxyz — 1234567890 — *ABCDEFGHIJKL*
MNOPQRSTUVWXYZ – abcdefghijklmnopqrstuvwxyz

11 pt. Grotesque 215   (12 pt. not cut)
ABCDEFGHIJKLMNOPQRSTUVWXYZ – abcdefghij
klmnopqrstuvwxyz – 1234567890 – *ABCDEFGHIJKLMN*
OPQRSTUVWXYZ – abcdefghijklmnopqrstuvwxyz

12 pt. Imprint
ABCDEFGHIJKLMNOPQRSTUVWXYZ – abcd
efghijklmnopqrstuvwxyz – 1234567890–*ABCDEFG*
HIJKLMNOPQRSTUVWXYZ – abcdefghijklmnop
qrstuvwxyz

12 pt. Juliana
ABCDEFGHIJKLMNOPQRSTUVWXYZ – abcdefghij
klmnopqrstuvwxyz–1234567890 – ABCDEFGHIJKLM
NOPQRSTUVWXYZ–abcdefghijklmnopqrstuvwxyz

12 pt. Modern
ABCDEFGHIJKLMNOPQRSTUVWXYZ – abcd
efghijklmnopqrstuvwxyz–1234567890–ABCDEF
GHIJKLMNOPQRSTUVWXYZ – abcdefghijklm
nopqrstuvwxyz

11pt Pastonchi
ABCDEFGHIJKLMNOPQRSTUVWXYZ , abcdefghijklmno
pqrstuvwxyz , 1234567890 , ABCDEFGHIJKLMNOPQRST
UVWXYZ , abcdefghijklmnopqrstuvwxyz

12 pt. Perpetua
ABCDEFGHIJKLMNOPQRSTUVWXYZ – abcdefghijklmn
opqrstuvwxyz–1234567890 – ABCDEFGHIJKLMNOPQRST
UVWXYZ–abcdefghijklmnopqrstvwxyz–

12 pt. Pilgrim
ABCDEFGHIJKLMNOPQRSTUVWXYZ – abcdefghijkl
mnopqrstuvwxyz – 1234567890 – ABCDEFGHIJKLM
NOPQRSTUVWXYZ – abcdefghijklmnopqrstuvwxyz

12 pt. Plantin
ABCDEFGHIJKLMNOPQRSTUVWXYZ – abcd
efghijklmnopqrstuvwxyz–1234567890–ABCDEFGH
IJKLMNOPQRSTUVWXYZ – abcdefghijklmnopqrs
tuvwxyz

12 pt. Rockwell
ABCDEFGHIJKLMNOPQRSTUVWXYZ – abcdef
ghijklmnopqrstuvwxyz – 1234567890 – ABCDEF
GHIJKLMNOPQRSTUVWXYZ–abcdefghijklmno
pqrstuvwxyz

12 pt. Scotch
ABCDEFGHIJKLMNOPQRSTUVWXYZ–abcd
efghijklmnopqrstuvwxyz – 1234567890 – ABCDE
FGHIJKLMNOPQRSTUVWXYZ – abcdefghijk
lmnopqrstuvwxyz

12 pt. Times
ABCDEFGHIJKLMNOPQRSTUVWXYZ–abcd
efghijklmnopqrstuvwxyz–1234567890–ABCDEFG
HIJKLMNOPQRSTUVWXYZ – abcdefghijklmnop
qrstuvwxyz

12pt. Van Dijck
ABCDEFGHIJKLMNOPQRSTUVWXYZ– abcdefghijklmno
pqrstuvwxyz– 1234567890-*ABCDEFGHIJKLMNOPQRSTU*
VWXYZ – abcdefghijklmnopqrstuvwxyz

11D on 12 pt. Walbaum
ABCDEFGHIJKLMNOPQRSTUVWXYZ – abcdefghijklm
nopqrstuvwxyz – 1234567890 – *ABCDEFGHIJKLMNOP*
QRSTUVWXYZ – abcdefghijklmnopqrstuvwxyz

Type Facsimile. A reprint in which a printed original is copied exactly.

Type Flowers. Conventional designs cast in type metal of type height and used to decorate a book as an alternative to using blocks. *See also Flowers.*

Type Gauge. A rule marked off in ems, points and inches and used for measuring width of type, page depths, etc.

Type Height. 1. The standard height to which type bodies are cast. In the UK and the USA this is 0.918 of an inch from the feet, on which the type rests, to the printing surface, except for the Oxford University Press which works to 0.9395 inches. On the continent of Europe the standard height is 'Didot Normal' (0.9278 inches). 2. The height to which a printing plate is mounted for use in letterpress work; it must be the same height as the letterpress.

Type-high. A printing block or plate which has been mounted on wood or metal to the same height as type for use on a printing machine.

Type Metal. (*Printing*) An alloy of tin, lead, antimony and sometimes copper which is used for casting type.

Type Ornaments. Conventional designs cast in type metal, being larger than TYPE FLOWERS (*q.v.*) and used to ornament chapter heads and tails, and title-pages.

Type Page. The part of a page that is printed upon; i.e. the type area, the margins being excluded.

Type Size. The measure of the dimensions of type, taken from the body of the individual type rather than the actual printing area. Also called 'Body size'. The following are the type sizes normally used in book-work:

	Old Name
5 point	Pearl
6 point	Nonpareil
7 point	Minion
8 point	Brevier
9 point	Bourgeois
10 point	Long Primer
11 point	Small Pica
12 point	Pica
14 point	English
16 point	Columbian

18 point   Great Primer
22 point   Double Pica

Larger sizes exist, but these are used for display and not book work. Other, mostly discarded, sizes with their names are:

	Old Name
3½ point	Minikin (or Brilliant)
4 point	Brilliant
4 point	Gem
4½ point	Diamond
5½ point	Ruby (or Agate)
6½ point	Emerald
16 point	Two-line Brevier
20 point	Paragon
24 point	Two-line Pica
28 point	Two-line English
36 point	Two-line Great Primer
40 point	Two-line Paragon
44 point	Two-line Double Pica
48 point	Four-line Pica (or Canon)
60 point	Five-line Pica
72 point	Six-line Pica

British Standard 4786:1972 *Metric typographic measurement* describes a system employing the conventional millimetric scale, intended first as a viable alternative to present systems and later as a replacement. It recommends a basic unit of 0.5 mm having twenty sub-multiples of 0.025 mm for calculation of character width, the expression of line length in millimetres, and interlinear spacing in multiples of 0.25 mm. It recommends the measurement of lettering from BASE LINE (*q.v.*) to base line.

Typescript.   Typewritten matter; a typed manuscript. Abbreviated T.S.

Typesetter.   One who sets type; a compositor.

Typesetting.   The arrangement of printing types in order for printing, including the operation of Intertype, Linotype, Ludlow or Monotype machines. *See also Computer Typesetting.*

Type-setting Machine.   A machine for selecting, assembling and spacing typefounders' letterpress printing types which are arranged in channels instead of cases. *See also Type-casting Machine.*

Typewriter Setting.   Typesetting by means of a typewriter made specially for the purpose, such as an IBM Composer, Justowriter or Varityper; such machines enable word spacing to be varied and justifying to be achieved.

Typical Characteristic.   *See Characteristic of a Classification.*

Typical Class.   *See Characteristic of a Classification.*

Typograph.   Trade name for a typecasting, setting and distributing machine which casts a slug or line of type, similar to the LINOTYPE (*q.v.*) machine.

Typographer. One who is responsible for the lay-out and appearance of printed matter.

Typographical Error. A mistake made by the typesetter.

Typography. 1. Printing, or taking impressions from movable letter-units or 'types'. The art of printing. The opposite of XYLOGRAPHY (*q.v.*). 2. The character and appearance of printed matter.

Typometer. A gauge for measuring the body and thickness of type and comparing them with a standard.

UAI. *See Universal Availability of Information.*

UAP. *See Universal Availability of Publications.*

UBC. *See Universal Bibliographic Control.*

UBCIM. Universal Bibliographic Control and International MARC. *See Universal Bibliographic Control.*

UCC. Universal Copyright Convention. *See entry under Copyright, International..*

UCRS. *See University, College and Research Section.*

UDACE. Unit for the Development of Adult Continuing Education; set up at the National Institute of Adult Continuing Education, Leicester, UK, to guide and develop provision in all areas of adult education, but with particular emphasis on information technology.

UDC. UNIVERSAL DECIMAL CLASSIFICATION (*q.v.*).

UDT. UNIVERSAL DATAflow AND TELECOMMUNICATIONS (*q.v.*).

UFC. *See Universities Funding Council.*

UFOD. Acronym for Union Française des Organismes de Documentation (French Union of Documentary Organizations). Provides professional training for assistants in documentation services. Publishes *Informations UFOD* (irr.), *Documentation en France* (6 p.a.), *l'Aide-Mémoire du Documentaliste*.

UGC. *See University Grants Committee.*

Ühertype. A photo-composing machine built in 1928 by Edmund Üher, a Hungarian. It was first called Luminotype.

UK Association for Information and Image Management. Formed in 1989 by leading industrial concerns (3M, Olivetti, Kodak, Racal Imaging, Wang) to act as a forum for the discussion and promotion of the uses of electronic document imaging systems and other similar developing technologies. Abbreviated UKAIIM; affiliated to the USAIIM.

UK Serials Group. Formally established in 1978, the UK Serials Group is an autonomous organization which brings together all parties interested in serials. It is not exclusively a group for academic librarians – membership is open to any organization or individual having an interest in serials. The current membership includes representatives from publishers, agents, industry and many different types of libraries and information units. The aims of the Group include promoting discussion about serials and related areas between interested parties; developing and maintaining links between the producers and users of serials; encouraging research in the field of serials management. The Group seek to achieve these aims by holding meetings and conferences, by the issuing of publications and by encouraging exchange of information. European expansion is envisaged.

UKAIIM. *See UK Association for Information and Image Management.*

UKLDS. Expanded title: United Kingdom Library Database System. A proposal made by the CO-OPERATIVE AUTOMATION GROUP (*q.v.*) to provide for general access to a common database of both cataloguing and location records. The British Library signalled its intention to develop its online services in a form suitable to support UKLDS, but financial support was not forthcoming.

UKMARC Format. The British national MARC format as specified and described in the British Library UKMARC Manual. This carries the implication that only the communications format, using the ISO 2709 structure, may be termed UKMARC. Internal input formats which use the MARC format content designation within a different structure, and which are therefore sometimes referred to as 'MARC compatible', should be referred to as 'local MARC formats'; these include the LOCAS format, the formats used in the ESTC and ISTC programmes and numerous non-British Library formats. *See MARC.*

UKOLN. UK office for Library Networking. *See Office for Library Networking.*

UKOLUG. UK Online User Group; formed 1978 as a special interest group of the Institute of Information Scientists, but open to all. Acts as a forum for all users of online information systems, and as a consumer group representing its members with organizations such as British Telecom, hosts, and database producers. Encourages local groups. Publishes a newsletter (6 p.a.). Represented on European Online User Group.

UKRA. UNITED KINGDOM READING ASSOCIATION (*q.v.*).

UKSG. *See UK Serials Group.*

ult. Abbreviation for *ultimo* (*Lat.* 'last'). Used for 'last month'. *See also inst.*

Ultimate Class. The class of the smallest extension admitted by the scheme of classification, into which a document can be placed.

Ultra-microfiche. A MICROFICHE (*q.v.*) with such small images that 3000 page-images can be accommodated on one 4 × 6 inch fiche. Also known as 'Ultrafiche'.

Ultra Thin Paper. Sensitized photographic paper between 0.0023 and 0.0031 inches inclusive. Also called 'Extra light-weight'. *See also Photographic Papers.*

Ulverscroft Munford Research Fellowship. An award offered every two years for research into the supply of books or other media to the disadvantaged. Formerly the Frederik A. Thorpe Travelling Fellowship, the award is funded by Ulverscroft Large Print Books, and administered by the (UK) Library Association.

Ulverscroft Series. A series of books printed in large type (18 pt.) and published by F.A. Thorpe, of Ulverscroft, with whom the (British) Library Association has co-operated in the selection of titles for this venture which has proved very successful. The volumes are available to public libraries, welfare organizations and blind agencies direct, and not through the book trade.

U-Matic. ¾in. video-cassette format marketed by the Sony Corporation which has become the standard for industrial and commercial applications although some educational institutions also use it.

Unauthorized Edition. An edition issued without the consent of the author, his representative or the original publisher. The responsibility to the author would be moral, not legal. A PIRATED EDITION is an unauthorized reprint involving an infringement of copyright.

Unbacked. Printed on only one side of the paper.

Unbleached Paper. Special paper made from unbleached STUFF (*q.v.*). Such papers do not usually have a good colour; they retain the colour of the original white rags, no bleaching during the process of manufacture having taken place. The paper is consequently stronger as bleaching weakens the pulp.

Unbound. A publication the leaves or sections of which have not been fastened together.

Uncial. Style of majuscule writing, resembling capitals in some letter forms, but with rounder curves. This was a more flowing cursive form of Latin manuscript handwriting and was used for commercial and everyday writing. In use generally from the fourth to the eighth centuries.

Uncut. A book is described as being 'uncut' when the edges have not been trimmed or cut by a guillotine, thus leaving 'bolts' which have to be opened with a paper knife. Until this has been done the book is described as being unopened. Also called 'Unploughed', 'Untrimmed'. *See also Edges.*

Undergraduate Library. In academic libraries, pressure on space and the disturbance caused by large numbers of users, may be alleviated by providing separate facilities in an undergraduate library for students who require access only a basic collection and space to work, leaving research collections in a quieter environment.

Underground Literature. *Synonymous with* CLANDESTINE LITERATURE (*q.v.*).

Underground press. A printing press which secretly prints leaflets, pamphlets, periodicals or books which have as their object the overthrow of the government, or of authority, or the propagation of subversive or generally unacceptable political views.

Underlay. Work done on the printing machine by placing paper, thin card, etc., under the matter in the forme so as to level it up as much as possible for printing, before the final touches are put on by means of OVERLAY (*q.v.*).

Underline. A line or series of lines placed under parts of 'copy' or proof to indicate style of type to be used: a single line indicates italic; a double line, small capitals; a treble line, capitals; a wavy line (which can be placed under any of the aforementioned) bold face. Called 'Underscore' in America. *See also Caption 2.*

Underrun. A shortage in the number of copies printed.

Underscore. *Synonymous with* UNDERLINE (*q.v.*).

Undifferentiated Entries. In a Permuted Title Index (*q.v.*), a series of similar entries with no discriminating features.

UNDIS. Acronym of the United Nations Documentation Information System, the computer-based information storage and retrieval system developed and operated by the United Nations Library to facilitate access to information on official documents and publications of the United Nations.

Unesco. Abbreviation for United Nations Educational, Scientific and Cultural Organization, an international body which exists to further the development of emerging nations. Constituted 16 November 1945 in London by representatives of 44 governments; an agreement between the United Nations and Unesco was approved by the General Assembly of the UN in New York at its October–December 1946 session. It is financed by Member States of the UN who are eligible for membership. The Unesco Press was established in 1974 to continue the publishing and distribution functions of the former Office of Publications. *See also Public Library Manifesto, General Information Programme, ISORID, Office of Information Programmes and Services.*

Unesco Coupons. A form of international currency enabling foreign payments to be made for education, scientific and cultural materials without the tedious and time-consuming procedures of making payments through the normal machinery of banks, and the involvement of currency control regulations. The government of a country wishing to use Unesco coupons nominates a body to distribute the coupons against local currency payment to organizations or individuals who send them to suppliers of goods who then obtain cash for them. The currency is entitled 'Unum' (Unesco Unit of Money).

Uneven Pages. Those which bear the odd page-numbers. The right-hand, or recto, pages.

Uneven Working. *See Even Working.*

Unexpurgated Edition. An edition of a work in which the full text is given, including any objectionable material which normally would be omitted. *See also Expurgated Edition.*

Ungathered. The printed sheets of a book which have not been gathered, or collected, into order.

Uniform Edition. The individual works of an author published in an identical format and binding. *See also Standard Edition.*

Uniform Heading. The form of a heading adopted for use in the catalogue for an author (personal or corporate), title, or for any other heading.

Uniform Title. The distinctive title by which a work, which has appeared under varying titles and in various versions, is most generally known, and under which catalogue entries are made. Also called 'Conventional title', 'Filing title', 'Standard title'.

UNIMARC. Universal machine-readable catalogue – a standard format developed under the auspices of a Working Group set up by IFLA. UNIMARC specifies the tags, indicators and subfields to be assigned to bibliographic records in machine-readable form. Its primary purpose is to facilitate the international exchange of bibliographic data in machine-readable form between National bibliographic agencies. *See also Universal Bibliographic Control, MARC.*

Union Catalogue.   A catalogue of stock in the various departments of a library, or of a number of libraries, indicating locations. It may be an author or a subject catalogue of all the books, or of a selection of them, and may be limited by subject or type of material. *See also Centralized Cataloguing, Co-operative Cataloguing.*

Union Finding List.   American term for a complete record of the holdings of a given group of libraries. It may be of materials of a given type, in a particular field, or on a particular subject.

Union Française des Organismes de Documentation.   *See UFOD.*

Union List.   A complete record, usually printed, of holdings of material in a certain field, on a particular subject, or of a given type such as of periodicals or annuals, for a group of libraries.

Union of International Associations.   Founded in Brussels in 1907 as the Central Office of International Associations and became a federation under its present name at the first World Congress of International Organizations in 1910. Serves as a documentation centre on international governmental and non-governmental organizations, their activities and meetings.

Union Paper.   Two sheets of wrapping paper stuck together with tar, bitumen, or some similar material with a waterproofing property. *See also Reinforced Union Paper, Tarred Brown Paper.*

Unique Entry, Principle of.   (*Cataloguing*) The entry for a book under a heading chosen (from more than one alternative) for person, subject, organization, place, etc., cross-references being provided from the other words which might have been used as alternatives. *See also Cataloguing, Principles of.*

UNISIST.   Abbreviation for United Nations Information System in Science and Technology, resulting from a feasibility study undertaken by Unesco and the International Council of Scientific Unions (ICSU), and approved by the 17th session of the General Conference of Unesco in November 1972. It comprises five main objectives: '(a) improving tools of systems interconnection; (b) improving information transfer; (c) developing specialized information manpower; (d) developing science information policy and national networks; (e) special assistance to developing countries.' UNISIST's most embracing and far-reaching activity is the establishment of a standardization programme for all phases of information handling, the ultimate goal being the evolution of a worldwide science information system. UNISIST National Committees have been formed in many Member States and governmental agencies nominated to act as national focal points for questions relating to the UNISIST programme. The focal point for the UK is at the British Library (*q.v.*); for the USA, at the Office of Science Information Service, National Science Foundation, Washington, DC; for Canada at the National Library of Canada, Ottawa; for India at the Department of

Science and Technology, New Delhi; and for Ireland at the National Science Council, Dublin. Publishes *UNISIST Newsletter* (q.). *See also BSO, INFOTERM, ISDS, ISSN, General Information Programme.*

Unit Abstract Card. A card, or other record, bearing an abstract prepared for use in a selective dissemination of information, or other current awareness, system. *See also SDI.*

Unit Bibliography. A bibliography of different editions of a book with the same title.

Unit Card. A basic catalogue card, in the form of a main entry, a duplicate of which may be used as a unit wherever an entry for that particular book is required in any catalogue, after the addition of any heading which may be necessary.

Unit Concept Co-ordinate Indexing. (*Information retrieval*) A system based on a combination of the Colon Classification structure with the techniques of the Uniterm system.

Unit Concepts. *Synonymous with* POLYTERMS (*q.v.*).

Unit Entry. A basic catalogue entry which gives the fullest information – a MAIN ENTRY (*q.v.*) – and which, being reproduced by printing or other duplication method, is used for all ADDED ENTRIES (*q.v.*), usually with the addition above the entry of appropriate headings (subject, author, title, series, editor, illustrator, translator, etc.).

Unit Record. The records comprising a descriptor file. Each consists of (a) descriptors (e.g. subject headings or class numbers) appropriate to the subject of the documents, (b) specifications of the documents (e.g. author, title, publisher, date, pagination, etc., plus possibly an annotation or abstract), (c) a document address, i.e. class number, call number, shelf number, file number, accession number or other indication of its whereabouts in the STORE (*q.v.*).

United Kingdom Library Database System. *See UKLDS.*

United Kingdom Reading Association. A non-profit-making professional organization which was founded in 1964 to: (a) encourage the study of reading problems at all educational levels; (b) stimulate and promote research in reading; (c) study the various factors that influence progress in reading; (d) publish the results of pertinent and significant investigations and practices; (e) assist in the development of teacher-training programmes; (f) act as a clearing-house for information relating to reading; (g) disseminate knowledge helpful in the solution of problems relating to reading; (h) sponsor conferences and meetings planned to implement the purposes of the Association. Membership is open to anyone interested in the teaching of reading. There are four categories of membership – Individual, Student, Institutional, Overseas. Publishes *Newsletter* (3 p.a.); *Reading* (3 p.a.). Affiliated to the parent body, The International Reading Association. Abbreviated UKRA.

United Nations Documentation Information System. *See UNDIS.*

United Nations Information System in Science and Technology. *See UNISIST.*

United States Government Printing Office. Created by a Congressional Joint Resolution on 23 June 1860, the Government Printing Office executes orders for printing and binding placed by Congress and the departments, independent establishments, and agencies of the federal government; it distributes government publications as required by law, and maintains necessary catalogues and a library of these publications; it also prints for sale to the public, documents which are of a non-controversial nature.

United States Information Agency. Abbreviated USIA. An arm of US foreign policy which receives its foreign policy guidance from the President of the US and the Department of State. It has public information missions in 120 countries. The responsibilites of USIA include explaining those activities of American domestic agencies which have significance in the foreign field. The functions of USIA are (a) to explain abroad US foreign policies and programmes; (b) to disseminate accurate information about the US; (c) to counter and correct propaganda distortions and lies about US policies and intentions; (d) to administer cultural and educational exchanges and programmes as the cultural and educational arm of the Department of State. Gives financial assistance in the publishing of American books in foreign languages, arranges for such translation to be undertaken; publishes books in English overseas; arranges with US publishers to publish books in paperback and simplified editions for distribution overseas; supplies books to USIS libraries, to foreign libraries, bi-national centres, schools and other institutions.

United States Information Service. *See USIS, United States Information Agency.*

United States of America Standards Institute. *See American National Standards Institute, Inc.*

Uniterm Concept Co-ordination Indexing. With this system, invented by Mortimer Taube in 1953, periodical articles or other documents to be indexed are scanned to see their subject contents. Aspects of the subject, called 'concepts', are expressed in one or two simple basic words called 'keywords' (which are to be found in the *Thesaurus* (*q.v.*) containing all the keywords likely to be used in the literature of the subject) and the accession number of the document recorded (by punching holes in numbered squares) on cards on which are entered as headings the 'keywords' or 'uniterms', sometimes called 'descriptors'. The cards are arranged in alphabetical order of uniterms, and the information is retrieved by placing the cards several at a time (for a separate card is punched for each aspect of the document's subject) over an illuminated glazed frame so that the light shines through the holes showing which documents have all the required terms. 'Uniterm' is a trademark of the developer of the system, Documentation, Inc., Washington, DC, and is the abbreviation for Uniterm Concept Co-ordination System. *See also Co-ordinate Indexing.*

Uniterm Index. A method of indexing which involves the selection of 'key words' from graphic records. Keywords represent the content of the record or document that is being indexed. It is not necessary to create or maintain a list of approved headings since a list is compiled as the work proceeds. The keywords must be predicted when analysing a question in order to provide searching clues.

Universal Availability of Information. Adopted as the theme of the 1985 IFLA Conference in Chicago; a natural development of Universal Bibliographic Control (UBC) and Universal Availability of Publications (UAP) – two recent IFLA programmes. Abbreviated UAI.

Universal Availability of Publications. Universal Availability of Publications (UAP), is a programme initiated by IFLA and supported by Unesco, and its objective is the widest possible availability of published materials (in whatever form or format) to users wherever and whenever they need it, as an essential element in economic, social, educational and personal development. The programme covers all levels of activity, local to international, and all stages from initial publication to retention of final copies for future needs. Authors, publishers, distributors, librarians, and users are thus all involved.

UAP functions by identifying the constraints to availability, and supporting action to improve the situation; several research projects assessing the present position were the basis of the *Main Working Document* of a Unesco/IFLA Congress on UAP held in Paris in May, 1982. Main sessions were devoted to access and availability, production and supply, acquisition policies and planning, repository policies and planning, and interlending policies. The *Final Report* of the Congress (PGI–82/UAP/6) forms the basic strategy document for future development, which will include the study of the impact of new technology on availability, and the preparation of guidelines for national UAP planning and policy development. The IFLA International Office for UAP is housed at the British Library Document Supply Centre, Boston Spa, UK. Publishes *UAP Newsletter* (irreg.) of which the first issue appeared February 1983. *See also Universal Bibliographic Control.*

Universal Bibliographic Control (UBC). The International Meeting of Cataloguing Experts (Copenhagen, 1969) organized by IFLA, envisaged a system for the international exchange of information by which the standard bibliographic description of each published item would be determined and distributed by a national agency in the country of origin. The IFLA conference held in Grenoble in 1973 had Universal Bibliographic Control as its theme, and in 1974 IFLA launched the UBC project as its contributory gesture to the Unesco Intergovernmental Conference on the Planning of National Documentation, Library, and Archive Infrastructures.

UBC is the worldwide system for the control and exchange of bibliographic information, promptly and universally supplied in an internationally acceptable form, providing basic data on all publications in all countries. Its success relies on efficient national bibliographic control, and each national agency must therefore ensure that it can have sight of all new publications issued in its country, must establish a definitive record, publish its data promptly and distribute it efficiently (on cards, magnetic tape or other format) must agree to receive and distribute other countries' data, and eventually seek to produce a retrospective national bibliography.

The UBC network internationally must ensure the acceptance of each national part within the network, and devise an international standard on form and content of the bibliographic record; progress so far in this latter field is as follows: for the *heading* the IFLA Office for UBC has published Names of Persons (3rd ed., 1977; and supplement, 1980); for the *description* of each item IFLA Working Groups have been producing INTERNATIONAL STANDARD BIBLIOGRAPHIC DESCRIPTIONS (ISBD) (*q.v.*); for the *subject approach* the Dewey Decimal Classification has been recommended; *international numbering schemes* such as ISBN, ISSN have been incorporated, but other materials such as maps, sound recordings and printed music are not yet covered by any scheme; for the *machine readability* of the record UNIMARC (*q.v.*) is a possible basis, and at present a Working Group of the Unesco General Information Programme is examining a Common Communication Format, which could be introduced here: transliteration of various alphabets remains an unsolved problem.

UBC is a complementary programme to the UNIVERSAL AVAILABILITY OF PUBLICATIONS (UAP) (*q.v.*). The International MARC Programme (IMP) was amalgamated in 1986 with the UBC programme, and the whole operation is entitled UBCIM – Universal Bibliographic Control and International MARC. The programme has been based at the British Library Bibliographic Services Division, but moved in 1990 to the Deutsche Bibliotek, Frankfurt, FRG.

Universal Bibliography.   A bibliography of the world's books. None exists at present, but an attempt has been made by the Fédération Internationale de Documentation (formerly the Institut International de Documentation and the Institut International de Bibliographie). *See also International Federation for Documentation.*

Universal Copyright Convention.   *See Copyright, International.*

Universal Dataflow and Telecommunications (UDT).   An IFLA core programme established 1985 as Transborder Data Flow (TDF) and re-titled 1986. Hosted by the National Library of Canada, it aims to promote among libraries the electronic transfer of data across borders both for storage and for processing by computer. Databases may provide information on all essential subject areas and cover reference data as well as source data, including full text. It is intended that economic and policy issues should be taken into account at national and international levels, and that aspects such as legislation, tariff policy, government inspection, technical facilities and their cost-effectiveness, should be covered. It will be centred on raising awareness of the subject at the level of government and library associations; the formulation of policies and guidelines and the furthering of library focal points for issues relating to transborder data flow; co-operation; communications with different groups involved in transborder data flow at national and international levels; and the improvement of access to computerized databases, including access to full text bases through library networks.

Universal Decimal Classification (UDC).   French abbreviation: CDU; German: DK. A general scheme of classification covering the whole field of knowledge. It is an elaborate expansion of the Dewey Decimal Classification which was first suggested by Senator Henri La Fontaine and Paul Otlet at the first International Conference of Librarians held at Brussels in 1895, and carried out by the Institut International de Bibliographie, now called the Fédération (formerly Institut) Internationale de Documentation. It has been called the International Classification, is constantly under revision, and is extremely flexible. In application, the three-figure notation of Dewey is simplified where possible (usually by the omission of 'unit') and extended by auxiliary signs or Relation Marks sometimes called 'Common auxiliaries' which are recommended to be filed in the following 'Standard' order:

SYNOPSIS OF AUXILIARIES (IN ORDER OF FILING)
  a. Aggregation signs + and / (*preceding the simple class number*)
  b. Relation signs : and [ ]
  c. Language auxiliaries = . . .
  d. Form and presentation auxiliaries (o . . .)
  e. Place, region, country auxiliaries (1/9)
  f. Race, people nationality auxiliaries (= . . .)
  g. Time, date, period auxiliaries '. . .' (alternatively before e.)
  h. Alphabetical and numerical (non-UDC) auxiliaries A/Z, No. 1 to . . .
  i. Point of view subdivisions .00 . . .
  k. Special auxiliaries –. . . and .0. . .

The object of the scheme is to arrange and individualize, by the use of the subdivisions tabulated above, the entries in a great general catalogue or bibliography, or the written or printed material, however detailed, in a specialized library, in order that users may, to some extent, judge the material without actually handling it. It has been adopted by the International Organization for Standardization (ISO) which has recommended it for adoption by the national standards bodies which are members of ISO for the classification of their published standards. It has therefore become the most widely used of all classification systems. Full editions of the whole, or of sections, have been published in French, English, German, Japanese, Spanish, Polish and Portuguese. The publication of the English translation of the complete second edition (BS 1000), in sections, is in progress. It incorporates all authorized extensions and modifications up to the date of publication. A medium version of the whole scheme is also available (BS 1000 M. Part 1:1985; Part 2:1988). The guide to the UDC is published as BS 1000 C:1963 (1980). *See also CCC, International Council for Building Research Studies and Documentation.*

Universal Information System in Science and Technology.   *See UNISIST.*

Universal Standard Bibliographic Code.   *See USBC.*

Universities Funding Council.   The UK co-ordinating body of the financing of universities by governmental and other means. Replaced the University Grants Committee in 1989.

University and Research Section.   Former name for the UNIVERSITY, COLLEGE AND RESEARCH SECTION (*q.v.*) of the Library Association.

University, College and Research Section. A section of the (British) Library Association; formerly the University Research Section. It was the first 'section' of the Library Association to be formed (in 1927). The objects of the Section are to increase the usefulness of national, university, and other academic libraries serving research. There are several regional groups and sub-sections. Publishes a *Newsletter* (3 p.a.). Abbreviated UCRS.

University Grants Committee (UK). *See Universities Funding Council.*

University Library. A library or group of libraries established, maintained, and administered by a university to meet the needs of its students and members of the academic staff.

University Research Library. A RESEARCH LIBRARY (*q.v.*) differing from other university libraries by virtue of the size, range, depth and quality of its collections, necessary general background stock to support its special areas, and large-scale holdings amassed over a long period of time to form a concentration of materials important enough to attract scholars world-wide.

Unjustified. (*Printing*) Type which is set with equal word spacing resulting in text lines of different length. *See also Justifying.*

Unlettered. A book without the title or the author's name on the spine.

Unopened. When the 'bolts' or folded edges of the sections of a book, have not been opened with a paper-knife. Not be confused with UNCUT (*q.v.*).

Unpaged. Pages of a book which do not bear page numbers. These usually occur amongst the PRELIMINARIES (*q.v.*), if referred to in a catalogue or bibliography, the total number, or the page numbers which the individual pages would have been given, are entered within [ ].

Unprocessed Paper (or Board). Paper or board in sheets or reels as supplied to the printer or stationer.

Unscheduled Mnemonics. *See Mnemonics.*

Unscheduled Records. (*Archives*) Those for which no final decision has been made as to their disposition.

Unsewn Binding. *Synonymous with* PERFECT (*q.v.*).

Unsigned. A book, the sections of which bear no signature letters or figures, and are therefore 'unsigned'.

Unsought Link. (*Classification*) In chain indexing, a step in a notational hierarchy which is unwanted for indexing purposes, either because no enquirer is likely to search under the appropriate verbal term, or because of faulty subordination in the classification scheme itself. *See also Chain Index, False Link, Subordination.*

Untrimmed Page Size. The size of a sheet after folding and before trimming.

Untrimmed Size. The dimensions of a sheet of paper, untrimmed and not specially squared, sufficiently large to allow a trimmed size to be obtained from it as required. British papermakers may interpret this term as 'not guillotine trimmed'. *See also Paper Sizes, Periodical, Trimmed Size.*

Unum. Unesco Unit of Money. *See Unesco Coupons.*

Updated Version. A DERIVATIVE WORK (*q.v.*) resulting in modifying an INTELLECTUAL WORK (*q.v.*) by removing items of information and substituting for them, or adding, new or more up-to-date knowledge.

Upper Case Letters. Capital letters, i.e. those contained in the upper of the two cases of printer's type. Their use is indicated in a MS. or proof by underlining with three lines. Abbreviation: u.c. *See also Capitals, Lower Case Letters, Small Capitals.*

Upper Cover. *Synonymous with* Obverse Cover (*q.v.*).

Upright. 1. A book that is taller than its width. 2. A sample of print or a printing job, that is set to an upright size. *See also Broad.*

Upward Reference. A direction from a less to a more comprehensive subject heading in an alphabetico-specific subject catalogue. The reverse of Downward Reference (*q.v.*).

Urban Library. A public library provided by a local authority to serve an urban area.

URICA. Integrated library automation system produced by McDonnell Douglas Information Systems Ltd; the name first appeared in 1984 when various earlier activities were re-grouped.

US National Libraries Task Force on Co-operative Activities. Established in 1967 by the Directors of the Library of Congress, the National Library of Medicine and the National Agricultural Library to 'improve access to the world's literature in all areas of human concern and scholarship, so that comprehensive access to the materials of learning can be afforded to all citizens of the United States'. In 1972 the Task Force membership was expanded, a structural reorganization implemented, and formal operating procedures adopted. The principal areas for investigation were also identified as: (a) the relationship of the national libraries to the national information system; (b) co-operation in and co-ordination of public service functions . . .; (c) co-operation in and co-ordination of technical service functions . . . and co-operation in the National Serials Data Program (*q.v.*).

US National Standards Association. A co-ordinating body for United States government standards and specifications. *See also American National Standards Institute, Inc.*

USA Standards Institute. *See American National Standards Institute, Inc.*

USASI. Abbreviation for United States of America Standards Institute, now the American National Standards Institute, Inc. (*q.v.*).

USBC. Universal Standard Bibliographic Code was the subject of a feasibility study undertaken for the British Library by the University of Bradford, and aims to eliminate the duplication of bibliographic records when large files are merged. USBC is a fixed length code unique to each item recorded and is derived by computer algorithm directly from bibliographic details. *See also DOCMATCH 2.*

User Education. A programme of information provided by libraries to users, to enable them to make more efficient, independent use of the library's stock and services. A programme of user education might include tours, lectures, exercises and the provision of support materials. Also termed '*library instruction*' and '*library orientation*'.

User-friendly. Used to describe a software package or computer system designed to be very easy to operate, even by untrained users. A Menu system (*q.v.*), helpful prompts, and simple commands would be features of such a system.

User Group. Users of a HOST system (*q.v.*) or of a particular computer or software systems may band together to share experiences, pass on hints, and provide feedback to the host or manufacturer.

User ID. A group of characters input by a user from his terminal which identify him to the computer system.

User-profile. *Synonymous with* INTEREST-PROFILE (*q.v.*).

User Relevance. The appropriateness of information retrieved for a user even if it is not exactly what was requested.

USGPO. UNITED STATES GOVERNMENT PRINTING OFFICE (*q.v.*).

USIA. UNITED STATES INFORMATION AGENCY (*q.v.*).

USIS. Abbreviation for the United States Information Service which provides libraries in overseas countries as part of the work of the UNITED STATES INFORMATION AGENCY (*q.v.*).

USSR Library Council. Founded 1959. Based at the State Lenin Library, Moscow. Aims to improve library services in USSR. Is under the jurisdiction of the Ministry of Culture. Has numerous sections, committees, standing conferences, etc. Publishes *Bibliotekar* (m.), *Biblioteki* (m.) and others via VINITI (*q.v.*).

ut infra. (Lat. 'as below'.)

ut sup. Abbreviation for *ut supra* (Lat. 'as above').

UTLAS. University of Toronto Library Automation System: originally developed as a Canadian equivalent of BALLOTS (*q.v.*) and later expanded into a full network in Canada with extensions to the USA.

v. Abbreviation for verse, *versus* (against), *vide* (see), *vice* (in place of), *violino* (violin), *voce* (voice) and VOLUME (*q.v.*).

Vade-Mecum. A guide, handbook, or manual which can be conveniently carried for reference.

VADS. *See Value Added Network.*

Validation Routine. *See Data Validation Routine.*

VALUE. Valorisation et Utilisation pour l'Europe; a new (1989) ongoing programme of the Commission of the European Community, Directorate-General XIII-C, aimed at the improvement of the framework for Community research and technological development.

Value Added Network. A network which leases telecommunications links from a public utility, and supplements these with additional services, specialized features, etc. and markets the 'improved' resulting network to customers. Abbreviated VAN. The UK Department of Trade and Industry prefers to use the term 'Valued Added and Data Services' (VADS) with the same meaning.

Value Added Tax. *See VAT.*

VAN. *See Value Added Network.*

Van Gelder Paper. A brand of good-quality paper which is produced in Holland and used mainly for fine paper copies. A variety with an ANTIQUE

FINISH (*q.v.*) is used by artists for drawings, sketches and water-colour paintings. Also called 'Dutch paper'.

Vanguard. A programme operated by the UK Department of Trade and Industry to promote value added networks or VADS.

Vanity Publishers. Firms who publish and market books at authors' risk and expense. Also called 'Subsidy' or 'Co-operative' Publishers.

Variable Field Coding. (*Cataloguing. Information retrieval*). See *Fixed Field Coding.*

Variable Mnemonics. *See Mnemonics.*

Variant. A term given to corrections inserted in later printings of a book. These are frequent in hand-printed books and are accounted for by the fact that mistakes were noticed and the type altered during printing, the sheets already printed remaining untouched.

Variant Edition. The edition of a work which gives the author's variations, textual changes and alterations in the text of his work possibly from their first composition to their final appearance in a DEFINITIVE EDITION (*q.v.*).

Variorum. Abbreviation of the Latin *cum notis variorum* 'with notes by various editors'.

Variorum Edition. An edition of a work composed from a comparison of various texts which have been published previously, variations being given in footnotes, and including the notes of various commentators. In the USA, publishers tend to use this term for Definitive Edition, Textual Variant or Variant Edition.

Various Dates. Used to describe a volume containing several works of different date or a work consisting of several volumes published at different dates. Abbreviated v.d.

Varnishing. A process applied to book jackets to give them a shiny appearance.

Vat. The tank containing beaten pulp from which hand-made sheets of paper are made.

VAT. Value Added Tax is used in all European Community countries but is levied at different rates; VAT on books is charged in most EC countries, but they are zero-rated in the UK, Ireland and Portugal, on periodicals it is not levied in the UK, Belgium, Denmark and Portugal. Proposals to harmonize VAT rates have led to concern that book and periodical prices would rise and the Library Association has led a fierce campaign against imposition.

Vat Paper. Another name for HAND-MADE PAPER (*q.v.*).

Vat-sized. Said of paper when the size is added to the pulp before the pulp is used to form a sheet.

Vatican Code. The Vatican Library's *Rules for the Catalog of Printed Books* (A.L.A. 1931. 2nd ed., 1948, tr. from the 2nd Italian ed. publ. in 1938) were drawn up to provide a new general catalogue of the Library.

VCR. *See Video Cassette Recorder.*

v.d. Abbreviation for VARIOUS DATES (*q.v.*).

VDU. *See Visual Display Unit.*

Vegetable Parchment. A partially transparent wrapping paper. *See Parchment 2.*

Vellum. Calf skin dressed with alum and polished, and not tanned like leather. A smooth, fine parchment.

Vellum Parchment. A very strong hand-made vellum paper, similar in appearance to animal parchment, but almost indestructible and not as easily affected by heat, mildew and insects as are skins. Called 'art parchment' in the USA.

Vendor. *See Host.*

Venetian Type. A roman type which is characterized by heavy slab serifs, thick main strokes, and a slightly oblique calligraphic emphasis in the round forms. The bar of the small 'e' is tilted. The roman types of Nicholas Jenson (for specimen, *see* TYPE FACE) are the finest examples of this kind of type. *See also Humanistic Hand.*

Venn Diagrams. Graphic methods of sorting out the simple logical relationships between objects or classes or objects. They are named after the English logician John Venn (1834–1923).

verbatim et literatim. (*Lat.* 'word for word' and 'letter for letter'.) A literal translation or transcription.

Verbatim Report. A word for word version of a speech, lecture, or debate.

Vereinigung Schweizerischer Bibliothekare. *See Association of Swiss Librarians.*

Verification. (*Information retrieval*) The process of checking the original punching of data into an input medium for the computer.

Vernacular. The language of a country. When it is directed that a name shall be given in the vernacular, it means the form which is customary in the country concerned.

Version. 1. A rendering in graphic art form, or sequence of words, of a record, publication, or document, especially a translation of the Bible. 2. One of several intellectual forms taken by the same work. (These may be an original text and its translation, or various texts in one language based on the same original work.) 3. In music, a TRANSCRIPTION (*q.v.*) in which the original work is so changed as to be virtually a new work, either in the same or in a different medium.

Verso. The left-hand page of an open book or manuscript, usually bearing an even page number. The reverse, or second, side of a sheet of paper to be printed. *See also Recto.*

Vertical File. 1. A drawer, or number of drawers, in a case, in which papers or similar material may be filed on their edges. 2. A collection of pamphlets, cuttings, correspondence, or similar material arranged on their edges in a drawer or box.

Vertical Filing Cabinet. A cabinet of two, three or four drawers, each of which is wide enough to take quarto or foolscap files resting on their spines.

Vertical Press. A printing press in which the flat forme moves up and down instead of to and fro horizontally.

VHD. Very High Density: in optical disk technology, a type of capacitance disk in which the stylus is kept in position by tracking signals encoded on both sides of the information track. *See also Capacitance Disk.*

VHS. Abbreviation for video-home-system; ½ inch video cassette system manufactured by JVC and aimed mainly at the domestic market.

VIATEL. The Australian videotex service.

Vicesimo-quarto (24mo). *Synonymous with* Twenty-Fourmo (*q.v.*).

vid. Abbreviation for *vide* (*Lat* 'see').

vide ante. (*Lat.* 'see before').

vide infra. (*Lat.* 'see below'). ⎫

vide post. (*Lat.* 'see below'). ⎬   Used in footnotes to refer to an item mentioned elsewhere

vide supra. (*Lat.* 'see above'). ⎭

Video Cassette Recorder. Video recording and playback equipment which uses videotape cassettes. Such cassettes wholly enclose the videotape. The area of tape which contacts the playing head is covered by a flap which is opened within the machine. Abbreviated VCR.

Video Library. A collection of video-recordings, often available for hire to the public as a commercial venture.

Videodisc. *See Optical Digital Disk.*

Videoform. A textual or graphic image recorded on magnetic tape for transmission by electronic means.

Videotape Recording. An electronic recording of sound and vision on magnetic tape.

Videotel. Italian videotex system.

Videotex. A generic term for a system whereby computer based information is made available on an adapted television monitor. There are two main types: *interactive* (e.g. PRESTEL) in which information is carried by telephone line and the user can request any page from a theoretically limitless databank, and *broadcast* in which information is carried by radio waves and the user may only select from a comparatively limited number of pages (e.g. CEEFAX and ORACLE). Interactive videotex is also known as VIEWDATA.

Videotext. Strictly, a German teletext service; however this term is often confused with Videotex (*q.v.*).

Viditel. Dutch videotex system.

Viewdata. *See Videotex.*

Vignette. A small illustration or ornament used principally in book production at the beginning ends of chapters, not having a definite border but the edges shading off gradually.

Vignetted Half-tone. *See Half-Tone.*

Vinculum. In mathematics a straight, horizontal line placed over two or more numbers of a compound quality to join them. An old name for a Brace (*q.v.*).

Vine. A quarterly journal publishing up-to-date information on new work on the automation of library processes. *Vine* is supported by a grant from the British Library Board, and is based at the Library and Information Technology Centre, Polytechnic of Central London.

Vinegar Bible. A Bible printed in two volumes at Oxford by John Baskett, the King's Printer, in 1716–17; so-called from one of its misprints, the 'Parable of the vineyard' in Luke XX being rendered the 'Parable of the vinegar'.

Although the production was excellent, it was so full of errors that it became known as 'Basket(t) full of Printers' Errors'. It was also known as the 'Oxford Folio'.

Viniti. Vsesoyuznyi Institut Nauchnoi i Tekhnicheskoi Informatsii. (All-Union Institute of Scientific and Technical Information). Viniti is subordinate to the USSR State Committee for the Co-ordination of Scientific Research, Moscow and to the USSR Academy of Sciences, Moscow. It was established in 1952 and is the most important of the organizations concerned with scientific information in the Soviet Union, and has as its main tasks: (a) the preparation of abstracts in the natural and applied sciences, excluding architecture, building, medicine and agriculture; (b) the organization of instruction in scientific information in universities and institutes at undergraduate and postgraduate levels; (c) the organization and co-ordination of research into the rational organization of information activities, and the mechanical and automatic means of processing and retrieving scientific information. Publishes *Referativnyi Zhurnal* (the base Viniti publication; it is issued in twenty-four series representing various individual branches of the natural and technical sciences excluding building and architecture; over a third of the world's output of scientific and technical periodicals and a great quantity of other literature being processed, and providing the most comprehensive abstracting service in the world), *Scientific and Technical Information* (m.), *Achievements of Science* (a.).

Virgule. An oblique stroke, /, used typographically for a number of purposes, e.g. 14/18 as an alternative to 14–18; and/or; in bibliographical descriptions to indicate line-endings. Usually called 'Solidus'.

Virkotype Process. *Synonymous with* THERMOGRAPHY (*q.v.*).

VISCOUNT. Viewdata and Interlibrary Systems Communication Network; a research project aiming to achieve a coherent inter-library communications network. Funded 1985–87 by the British Library Research and Development Department. Participants in the project were a number of British regional co-operative schemes – SWRLS, LASER, NWRLS and the National Library of Scotland Lending Services. LASER now continues to run the network as a testbed for OSI between European countries, funded by the European Commission. Currently 74 members.

Visible Cloth Joint. A cloth joint used to fasten the sections of a sewn book to its covers, and visible when the book is bound.

Visible Index. 1. A frame, or series of frames, usually of metal, for holding cards or strips of card, on which records are entered. They are made so that all the headings contained in the frame are visible at the same time and so that entries may be added or extracted at will whilst maintaining the alphabetical, or other, sequence. *See also Blind Index.* 2. A record, as of periodicals or a list of subjects, contained in such a device.

Visigothic Handwriting. A Spanish form of handwriting, being a national adaptation of the Latin cursive after the dissolution of the Roman Empire. It was used in Spain in the eighth and ninth centuries, and also spread to Italy. *See also Cursive, Handwriting.*

Visual Aids. Film strips, films, and other illustrative material used as an adjunct to teaching or lecturing.

Visual Display Unit. A monitor used for the display of data from a computer; usually combined with a keyboard.

Visual Punched Card. Cards which are punched in positions to represent specifically numbered documents, each card being named according to a list of keywords, or thesaurus, and so reserved to represent a particular aspect of information. *See also Uniterm Concept Co-ordination Indexing.*

Visualtek Machine. A device enabling partially-sighted readers to scan a document with a television-type camera and project a greatly enlarged image which they can more easily read.

viz. Abbreviation for *videlicet* (*Lat.* 'namely').

Vocabulary. *See Index Language.*

Vocal Music. Music written to be sung by one or more persons: if for many people, it is known as choral music, and in its larger concerted forms of cantata, oratorio, or opera is accompanied by an orchestra, otherwise it may be unaccompanied, or a piano or organ used.

Vocal Score. *See Score.*

Vocational Education Act. Passed in 1963, this Act provides for the payment of librarians' salaries, books and other materials for libraries in American vocational and technical high schools.

vol. (*Pl.* vols). Abbreviation for VOLUME (*q.v.*).

Vollans Report. *Library Co-operation in Great Britain*, 1952, the report on the working of the national inter-lending system which R.F. Vollans wrote at the request of the joint working party set up by the National Central Library in 1949. The recommendations, together with other proposals, were incorporated in a joint memorandum, *Recommendations on library co-operation*, issued by the joint working party in 1954, and measures to implement them were taken by the National Committee on Regional Library Co-operation.

Volume. 1. A book distinguished from other books or from other volumes of the same work by having its own title-page, half-title, cover title or portfolio title, and usually independent pagination, foliation, or register. It may be designated 'part' by the publisher, and it may have various title-pages, paginations, or include separate works or portfolios, etc. The volume may be as originally issued or as bound subsequently; in this sense 'volume' as a physical, or material, unit, may not be the same as 'volume' as a bibliographical unit. A volume of music may consist of a score, of loose parts, or of a score with loose parts in pockets. 2. Whatever is contained in one binding. 3. A document or part of a document bound or intended to be bound in one cover and, normally, having its own title-page. 4. For library statistical purposes, any book, pamphlet, or document, in whatever form it exists which has been separately published and is separately catalogued and accessioned. In a catalogue entry the statement of the number of volumes relates to the physical, not the bibliographical, number, e.g. 1 *vol in* 2; 2 *v. in* 1; 8 *vols. in* 6.

Volume Capacity. *Synonymous with* SHELF CAPACITY (*q.v.*).

Volume Number. A number used to distinguish certain volumes of a work, set or series.

Volume Rights. *See Rights.*

Volume Signature. The number of the volume, as 'Vol. I', or simply 'I', or a letter, placed on the same line as the signature (*see* SIGNATURE 2) to prevent the binder mixing the sections of various volumes.

Volumen. (*Lat.* 'a thing rolled up'). The papyrus roll used in ancient Egypt, Greece and Rome, which was written on one side in ink with a reed pen, the text being in columns, the lines of which ran parallel with the length of the roll. The last sheet of the papyrus was rolled round a stick which had knobbed ends and served as a handle. The rolls were kept in boxes (CAPSA *q.v.*) or on shelves, and for purposes of distinction when placed in this position had a vellum label attached to the end of the roll. This label bore the title of the work, and was sometimes coloured. A wooden case (*Manuale*) was sometimes used to protect the edges of the roll from being frayed by the owner's toga or cloak.

Voluminous Author. An author under whose name many titles are entered in a catalogue, whether for different books or for books the various editions of which have different titles.

Voluntary Centre. A library service point which is staffed by unpaid workers.

Volute. (*Binding*) An ornament consisting of a large curl in the form of a Corinthian volute, and at the opposite end a small curl turning the other way. Found in pairs in sixteenth-century finishers' rolls of the heads-in-medallions type.

Vosper (Robert) Fellowships. A series of annual awards funded by the Council on Library Resources (CLR) to encourage involvement in the IFLA core programmes. First awards were made in 1989.

Voters' List. *Synonymous with* REGISTER OF ELECTORS (*q.v.*).

Votes and Proceedings of the House of Commons. *See Parliamentary Papers.*

Vowel-ligatures. The ligatures æ or œ are used in Old English and French words (Ælfric, Cædmon, hors d'œuvre, etc.), but the combinations *ae* and *oe* are printed as two letters in Latin, Greek and English words (Aetua, Boeotia, larvae, etc.).

v.p. Abbreviation for 'various places' or 'various publishers'. *See also l.v.*

VUBIS. An on-line cataloguing system, with relatively easy public access, based on the Free University of Brussels.

Vulgate. The Latin Bible translated by St. Jerome in the fourth century and authorized by the Roman Catholic Church.

WADEX. Abbreviation for Word and Author Index. A computerized indexing system which uses authors' names as well as titles, printing authors and significant words from titles on the left-hand margin, using them as headings and following them with the full author and title. *See also KWIC, KWOC.*

w.a.f. With all faults. An abbreviation used in booksellers' and auctioneers' catalogues to indicate that a book is, or may be, faulty and is offered for sale in this condition and therefore not subject to return because of defects.

Wall Shelving. Shelving placed against walls.

Walter Press. A rotary press which was first used in 1866 for printing *The Times*. It was constructed by J.C. MacDonald and J. Calverlye for J. Walter, owner of *The Times*. By 1880 this kind of press was in use throughout Europe.

WAN. *See Wide Area Network.*

WANDPETLS. Wandsworth Public, Educational, and Technical Library; a local scheme of co-operation set up in 1966 and including several education libraries seeking better facilities for students. One of three co-operative bodies entrusted with the co-ordination of an LIP (*q.v.*).

Wanting. This word when followed by details of parts or volumes of a publication in a catalogue entry, indicates that those items are not possessed.

Wants List. A list of books wanted, which is issued by a librarian or second-hand bookseller.

Wash Drawing. An illustration, usually in sepia or black or white, done with a brush.

Washing. When developing photographic negatives, or making prints on sensitized paper, the materials are thoroughly washed in clean running water after they have been in the fixing solution so as to remove all traces of the developing or fixing solutions.

Washington Library Network. *See Western Library Network.*

Washington Press. The American counterpart of the ALBION PRESS (*q.v.*). It was invented in 1827.

Waterleaf. Hand-made paper in its initial stage of manufacture, consisting of pulp spread and evened by shaking in the hand mould, and pressed between felts. It is semi-absorbent, being unsized, and must be sized before it is suitable for use as writing paper. *See also Engine-sizing, Tub-sizing.*

Waterleaf Paper. BODY PAPER (*q.v.*) which has been prepared for surface sizing or impregnation.

Watermark. A paper-maker's device which can be seen on any sheet of good paper when held up to the light. In handmade paper this is caused by twisting or soldering wire into the mould on which the paper is made; in machine-made paper, by a special roller called a 'dandy', which revolves over the moving pulp on the mould, impressing the mark at every revolution. The watermark is usually placed in the centre of one-half of the sheet. *See also Countermark, Impressed Watermark.*

Watermarked Paper. Paper containing a watermark.

Wave-border. (*Binding*) An eighteenth-century finisher's roll border incorporating an undulating line with other conventional ornament. Found in both English and Irish bindings.

Wavy Line. A line placed underneath words in 'copy' or proof to indicate that bold-faced type is to be used.

Wax Engraving.   A method of making electros from which to print maps in letterpress work. The outline is drawn on a wax mould and the lettering impressed by hand. On this a copper shell is then deposited.

Wayzgoose.   An annual outing or party held in summer by employees of the printing industries. Originally an entertainment given by a master-printer to mark the return to shorter hours of daylight and the necessity to re-light candles. The derivation of the word is unknown.

Web.   A large roll of paper which is fed into a printing machine.

Web Fed.   A printing machine which receives paper from a reel instead of loose sheets.

Web Perfecting Press.   A rotary press which prints consecutively on both sides of a reel of paper.

Web Press.   A printing machine on which the paper is fed from a continuous reel. A 'web perfecting press' prints consecutively on both sides of a continuous reel of paper. Also called 'Web machine'.

Weeding.   Discarding from stock books which it is considered are of no further use in the library. PSEUDO-WEEDING is transferring from one department to another, from stack to shelf and *vice versa*, or from files to bound form. Also, examining documents in an archives depository in order to discard items which appear to lack permanent value. *See also Stripping.*

Weekly.   A newspaper or periodical published once a week.

Weight.   'The degree of blackness of a typeface'. (BS.2961:1967.) The types in a FAMILY (*q.v.*) vary in weight from extra-light to ultra bold.

Weight of Face.   Comparative colour value of type faces when printed, as light, medium, bold.

Weight of Type.   Four square inches of solid type weigh approximately one pound.

Weighting Descriptors.   (*Information retrieval*) Giving a measure of relevance to a particular document or question when assigning descriptors to documents and formulating research questions. The weight 'increases' from 1/8 for 'barely relevant' to 8/8 for a 'major subject' when the term is highly specific and covers an entire major subject of the document.

Welsh Library Association.   A Branch of the (British) Library Association formed in 1931; until 1971, it was called the Wales and Monmouthshire Branch. All members of the LA who live or work in Wales are automatically members. Publishes *Y Ddolen* (irreg.).

WERTID.   The West European Round Table on Information and Documentation. An informal group of members of national associations representing the professions in the field of information and documentation from Belgium, France, Federal Republic of Germany, Portugal, Spain and the UK. Membership by invitation only.

West Midlands Branch.   A Branch of the (British) Library Association; it operates in the area of the counties of Hereford and Worcester, Salop, Staffordshire, Warwickshire and the Metropolitan County of the West Midlands. Several publications have been issued in addition to *Open Access* (3 p.a.). Abbreviated WMBLA.

Western. An adventure story set in the 'Wild West' of America.

Western Library Network. A bibliographic consortium based in Washington State (US) (and originally titled the Washington Library Network), offering an online and CD-ROM database and relevant software. Over 350 current members primarily in Washington, Oregon, Idaho, Montana, Alaska, Arizona, British Columbia, with extensions internationally, especially to the Australian and New Zealand bibliographic networks. Abbreviated WLN.

Wet End. The part of the paper-making machine where the wet pulp is formed into a web of paper, up to the first drier. The other end is known as the 'Dry End'.

Wet Flong. *See Flong.*

w.f. *See Wrong Fount.*

Wharfedale. *See Stop-cylinder Press.*

Whatman Paper. A brand of fine grade English hand-made wove drawing paper which was originally made by James Whatman from *c.* 1770 at Turkey Mill near Maidstone, Kent. Sometimes used for limited editions and privately-printed books.

Wheatley Medal. An award offered annually for an outstanding index first published in the UK. The Medal, which is named after Henry B. Wheatley (author of *How to make an index*, 1902), is awarded on the recommendation of a joint panel of the Library Association and of the Society of Indexers.

Wheatley Report. *The Report of the Royal Commission on Local Government in Scotland* 1966–1969, 2 vols. (HMSO 1969). The Commission is named after Lord Wheatley who was its Chairman; it was set up on 9 June 1966 'to consider the structure of local government in Scotland in relation to its existing functions and to make recommendations for authorities and boundaries . . . and the need to sustain a viable system of local democracy', and was the basis of the Local Government (Scotland) Act 1973. *See also Local Government Boundaries.*

Whig Bible. *See Geneva Bible.*

Whip-stitching. The American term for OVERSEWING (*q.v.*).

Whitbread Book of the Year. *See Whitbread Literary Awards.*

Whitbread Literary Awards. Annual prizes awarded to authors living in the UK or Eire for books published in those countries; five categories – novel, first novel, biography, children's novel, poetry – are selected, of which one is further declared Whitbread Book of the Year. Administered by the Booksellers Association of Great Britain and Ireland.

White Book. An official report published by the German government, so-called because issued in a white paper cover. *See also Blue Book.*

White Edges. Edges of books which have been cut but not coloured or gilded. *See also Edges.*

White House Conference on Library & Information Services (WHCLIS). In 1974 legislation authorizing a White House Conference was signed, and the National Commission on Libraries and Information Science was made responsible for its organization. Funds were forthcoming in 1977, and during 1977–79 most US library organizations held pre-White

House Conferences; two-thirds of the participants at the pre-Conferences and the Conference itself were non-librarian lay citizens, and one-third professional librarians and information workers. Over 100,000 people were involved in pre-Conference activities; five theme conferences provided the major intellectual input; *structure and governance of library networks* (Pittsburgh, 6–8 November 1978), *federal funding alternatives* (Arlington, 8–9 June, 1978 and Washington, DC 14 Sept. 1978), *libraries and literacy* (Reston, Va. April, 1979), *new communication and information technologies and their application to individual and community use* (Washington, DC 20–21 June 1979) and *international information exchange* (Washington, DC 31 July 1978). The resulting resolutions were grouped into five Conference themes: *meeting personal needs, enhancing lifelong learning, improving organisations and professions, effectively governing our society, increasing international understanding and co-operation.*

The Conference was held 15–19 November 1979 in Washington, DC; over 2000 participants attended. President Carter gave an address on 16 November. 25 major resolutions were passed to the President for submission to Congress.

The final report of WHCLIS runs to some 800 pages (US Government Printing Office, 1979) and was submitted to Congress in full by President Carter. Preparations are now in hand for another Conference in 1991. NCLIS (*q.v.*) is the planning body.

White Letter.   'Roman' type as opposed to BLACK LETTER or GOTHIC TYPE (*qq.v.*).

White Line.   (*Printing*) A line of space the same depth as a line of printed characters.

White-line Method.   *See Wood Engraving.*

White-out.   To space out composed matter, as in displayed or advertisement work.

White Paper (UK).   A term often used to denote a Report, Account or other Paper ordered by the House of Commons to be printed, or prepared primarily for debate in the House, and printed in the parliamentary series of official publications. There is a growing tendency, however, to apply the term to similar official publications not required by Parliament and published accordingly in the non-parliamentary series. *See also Blue Book, Parliamentary Publications.*

Whitfield Prize.   An annual award made by the Royal Historical Society for the best UK-published work on English or Welsh history by a young author.

Whitford Committee.   The Committee under the chairmanship of Mr. Justice Whitford that produced the *Report on Copyright and Design Law* (HMSO 1977). *See Copyright.*

Whitney-Carnegie Awards.   An award administered by the ALA to support the preparation of bibliographic aids to research.

Whole Bound.   Books bound entirely in leather.

Whole Number.   The number given by a publisher to an issue of a periodical or serial publication, and continuing from the first issue. It is distinguished from the numbers assigned for volume and part of volume, and from those assigned for series and volume.

Whole-stuff.   The pulp used in making paper after it has been thoroughly beaten and bleached, and is ready for the VAT (*q.v.*) or the paper machine. *See also Half-stuff.*

Who's Who File.   *Synonymous with* BIOGRAPHY FILE (*q.v.*).

Wickersham Quoins.   Expanding steel QUOINS (*q.v.*) which are inserted with FURNITURE (*q.v.*) at the side and foot of a CHASE (*q.v.*). They are adjusted with a key to lock and unlock pages of type in the chase.

Wide.   Any material, such as a map or illustration that is wider than the type pages.

Wide Area Network.   A data transmission system linking several organizations; maybe national or international in scope. Abbreviated: WAN. WANS are the inter-organization equivalent of LOCAL AREA NETWORKS (LANs) (*q.v.*).

Wide Lines.   *Synonymous with* CHAIN-LINES. *See Laid Paper.*

Widener Library.   Collected by Harry Elkins Widener (1885–1912) who lost his life in the steamship *Titanic* in 1912. The books, which are all 'rare', are placed in a special room in the building which was given to Harvard University in 1913 by his mother as a memorial to her son; the building, known as the Harry Elkins Widener Memorial Library, also houses the college library.

Widow.   An incomplete line of type at the top of a column or page, usually the last line of a paragraph, and avoided in good typography because of its unsightliness.

Width.   Type faces are of varying widths in the same FAMILY (*q.v.*), and are distinguished by the following (in progressive order): ultra-condensed, extra-condensed, condensed, semi-condensed, medium, semi-expanded, expanded, extra-expanded, ultra-expanded. 'Medium' is the width usually used and indicates the width which the manufacturer determines is the one representing the design and from which variants in the family have been, or may be, derived. *See also Fount, Type Face 2, Weight.*

Wiener Library.   Founded in Amsterdam by Dr Alfred Wiener in 1933, and brought to London in 1939. After financial difficulties in the late 1970s which threatened the future of the collection, some material was sent to Tel Aviv in return for support from Israel, but all such material was microfilmed first. Development of the London premises is now envisaged. The Collection comprises material on Nazi Germany and the immediate post-war years.

WIL.   *See Women in Libraries.*

Wild Look-through.   LOOK-THROUGH (*q.v.*) which is irregular and cloudy.

Wilder Medal, Laura Ingalls.   A bronze medal designed by Garth Williams, awarded by the Association of Library Services to Children (Division of the American Library Association) to an author or illustrator whose books, published in the US, have over a period of years made a substantial and lasting contribution to children's literature. It was first awarded (to Laura Ingalls Wilder) in 1954, and is now offered every three years.

William L. Clements Library. *See Clements Library, William L.*

Williams (Francis) Book Illustration Award. An award given every five years to a book illustrator who produced an outstanding book in which illustration was a major element. Photographs and illustrations of a purely technical nature were excluded from consideration for this award. Now amalgamated into the annual W.H. Smith Illustration Award.

Williams (Vaughan) Memorial Library. The English national folk-music archive and resource centre, located at the headquarters of the English Folk Dance and Song Society, London.

Willow. A machine consisting mainly of two rotating drums inside which spikes are fixed to tear out the raw material (rags, esparto, waste paper, etc.) for paper-making. Also called a 'Devil'. Often combined with a 'duster' which removes unwanted dust from the material.

Wilson Committee (UK). The Committee appointed by the Lord Chancellor in 1978 to inquire into the working of those provisions of the Public Record Acts of 1958 and 1967 which have a bearing on the selection of and access to modern public records. The Chairman was Sir Duncan Wilson and the Report was published in 1981. *See also Modern Public Records.*

Wilson Library Periodical Award. A cash award offered annually by the H.W. Wilson Company in respect of a periodical published by a local, state, or regional library, library group, or library association in the United States or Canada which has made an outstanding contribution to librarianship. Publications of the ALA, CLA, and their divisions are excluded. The Award is administered by the ALA Awards Committee, the selection being made by a jury of three, including an editor of a national library periodical and a member of the Library Periodicals Round Table. The first periodical to receive the Award (in 1961) was *The California Librarian*, the journal of the California Library Association which was then edited by William R. Eshelman. All issues for the calendar year prior to the presentation of the Award are judged on the basis of sustained excellence in both format and content, with consideration being given to purpose and budget.

Wilson Library Recruitment Award. A cash award made by the H.W. Wilson Company annually, and administered by the ALA Awards Committee. It is given to any local, state, or regional library association, any library school, or any other appropriate group concerned with recruitment to the profession. The Award is made for the development of a sustained programme of recruitment for librarianship based on a total continuing programme, not limited to one year's activity. The money comprising the Award is to be used for the continuation and further development of a recruitment programme. The first recipient (in 1966) was the Pennsylvania State Library, Harrisburg.

Wilson Library Staff Development Grant. An award made by the H.W. Wilson Company to a library organization to assist in a current or proposed programme to further stated staff development goals. Administered by the American Library Association Awards Committee.

Wilsonline. The name given to online access arrangements to the indexes published by the H.W. Wilson Company, introduced between 1984 and 1986 for most of the Wilson indexes. Wilsonline is available only directly from H.W. Wilson and not via any hosts; a CD-ROM version of many indexes is now also available.

WIMP. *Acronym for windows, icons, mouse and pointer*; four features of computer software that make for easier use.

Winchester Disk. *See Disk.*

Window. 1.(*Archives*) An opening made in repair paper or parchment to expose a small portion of text.   2. Part of a computer display screen acting like an aperture through which underlying images can be viewed.

'Window' Copy. Printed pages pasted up on sheets of paper cut to expose the type area so that both sides of each printed page are visible.

Wingate (H.H.) Prize. Two annual prizes (for fiction and non-fiction) made for UK-published books by Commonwealth authors that best stimulate an interest and awareness of themes of Jewish concern. Administered by the Book Trust.

WIPO. Acronym of the World Intellectual Property Organization, located in Geneva; it was established in Stockholm in July 1967 and became operative in April 1970 when it continued the work of the United International Bureaux for the Protection of Intellectual Property (BIRPI). Aims to: (a) promote the protection of intellectual property throughout the world through co-operation among States and, where appropriate, in collaboration with any other international organization; (b) ensure administrative co-operation between the Unions created by certain international conventions or agreements dealing with various subjects of intellectual property. WIPO is the only intergovernmental organization specializing in all subjects of intellectual property. It administers the six intergovernmental Unions, the most important of which are the International Union for the Protection of Industrial Property created in 1883 at the Paris Convention, and the International Union of the Protection of Literary and Artistic Works (including scientific works) created in 1886 at the Berne Convention. This last is basically concerned with copyright and works jointly with the IGC (*q.v.*). The Secretariat of WIPO, called the International Bureau of Intellectual Property, functions also as the secretariat of the various organs of the Union. WIPO is not only the administrative centre but also the international organization responsible for the promotion of such property throughout the world through co-operation between the States. The special organ for this purpose is its 'Conference' consisting of all 120 States party to the WIPO Convention. *See also Berne Copyright Union, Copyright International, IGC, ICIREPAT, INPADOC.*

Wire. The endless band of plain brass or bronze, tinned or leaded, or of nickel or stainless steel wires, which forms the moulding unit of a paper-making machine and carries the pulp from the breast box to the couching rolls and so felting it into a sheet, or web of paper. The mesh of the wire varies from fifty to ninety wires per inch according to the quality of paper made. Also called 'Machine wire', 'Wire-cloth', 'Wire-gauze', or 'Travelling mould'.

Wire-cloth. *See Wire.*

Wire-gauge. *See Wire.*

Wire Lines. *See Laid Paper.*

Wire Mark. *See Laid Paper.*

Wire Sewing. Sewing the sections of a book with wire staples driven through the folds of the sections and through tapes, canvas or muslin to which the staples are clinched. Also called 'Wire stitching'. *See also Saddle Stitching, Sewing, Stitching, Thread Stitched.*

Wire Side. The side of a sheet of paper which has come in contact with the WIRE of the paper-making machine during the course of manufacture. *See also Felt Side, Right, Twin Wire Paper.*

Wire Stabbing. Securing a number of leaves or sections by inserting one or more wire staples, usually from back to front (i.e. not through the fold of sections). This work is done on a stapling machine. Also called 'Side-stitching'. *See also Saddle Stitching.*

Wire Stitched. The fastening of a single section with wire driven through the centre of the fold and clinched (saddle stitched) or through the inner margin of the section (side stitched).

Wired. *Synonymous with* WIRE STITCHED (*q.v.*).

WISE. Expanded title: World Information Systems Exchange; an international collaborative project between hundreds of organizations to exchange material and data on Information Technology. It has a Library and Information Science Division, based in Tempe, Arizona, and established in 1976 by merging with the LARC ASSOCIATION (*q.v.*).

WISI. Acronym of World Information System on Informatics, which was set up following a report issued by the Intergovernmental Bureau for Informatics (IBI) in 1972. Developed in direct response to UNISIST Recommendation 1, and financed by Unesco, its long-term objectives are: the comprehensive collection of world information in the fields of computer science, operations research, mathematics, statistics, software and hardware in related areas, dissemination of information in the form of current awareness services (SDI services); dissemination of information in the form of abstracting and indexing services (continuing bibliographical services); distribution of published documents in both hardcopy and microform; special search, reference and referral services; investigation of compatibility of existing information systems and media including standardization of existing formats.

Wiswesser Line Notation. A method of representing structural details of chemical compounds by a string of characters, suitable for handling along with ordinary text material.

With the Grain. Said of paper which has been folded in the direction in which the fibres tend to lie. *See also Against the Grain.*

Withdrawal. The process of altering or cancelling records in respect of books which have been withdrawn from the stock of a library.

Withdrawals Register. A record which gives particulars of all books withdrawn from the stock of a library.

Wittenborg (George) Award. *See ARLIS/NA.*

WLN. *See Western Library Network.*

WMBLA. West Midland Branch (*q.v.*) (of the Library Association).

WNBA. Women's National Book Association (*q.v.*).

Wodehouse (P.G.) Prize. An annual award made by Century Hutchinson Ltd. for the best unpublished work of comic fiction or non-fiction.

Women in Libraries. A pressure group set up by Avril Rolph in September 1980 to work for positive change in the position of women in the library profession. The group is concerned at the under-representation of women in senior posts, and the lack of practical schemes to help women's needs (job-sharing, part-time posts, refresher courses, etc). The group works by pressuring employers, professional associations and trades unions. Publishes a newsletter: *WILpower.*

Women's National Book Association. The only professional organization in the book trade that covers a national cross-section of women engaged in all phases of the American book industry. Founded in 1917. Membership is open to all women in the world of books – booksellers, critics, editors, librarians, literary agents, writers, illustrators, those engaged in publishing, book production or other activities allied to the book trade. There are ten chapters in the USA, and affiliated groups in Japan and India. It offers the Constance Lindsay Skinner Award, as a tribute to an author and editor who was for a long time active in the affairs of the Association, to a woman for distinguished contributions to the book world. It was first awarded in 1940 to Anna Carroll Moore. Publishes *The Bookwoman* (2 p.a.). Abbreviated WNBA.

Wood Block. A block of wood, usually box, on which a design for printing from has been cut in relief.

Wood Engraving. 1. The art or process of cutting designs with a graver or burin upon the end-grain of a block of box-wood, leaving the designs in intaglio for printing. The resulting print appears as white lines or masses on a dark background; this has caused the process to be known as the 'white-line' method. This technique was introduced by Thomas Bewick. 2. A print from a wood engraving.

Wood Letter. A large type-letter of wood; used in poster printing.

Wood Pulp. Wood reduced to a pulp by mechanical or chemical means for subsequent paper-making.

Wood Type. Wood letters above 72-point used in poster work, because they are lighter and cheaper than metal.

Woodcut. An illustration made by pressing a sheet of dampened paper on a block of soft wood such as beech or sycamore which has been cut away to leave a design at the surface, so that when the block is inked an impression will be left on the paper, the cut-away parts showing white. The side-grain of a block of softer wood, such as pear or sycamore, is used for woodcuts rather than for wood engravings, and the design is executed with a knife whereas a variety of gravers are used for wood engravings. The design of a woodcut is of black lines or masses on a white background whereas that of a wood engraving is the reverse; woodcutting is therefore known as a *black-line* method whereas wood engraving is a *white-line* method. Before the invention of movable type, books (text and illustrations) were printed in this way; these are called BLOCK BOOKS (*q.v.*). When movable type came into use, only borders, capitals and illustrations were printed from wooden blocks. *See also Florentine Woodcuts.*

Woodcut Title-page with Panel. *Synonymous with* FRAMED-CUT (*q.v.*).

Wooden Boards. Said of books made before the sixteenth century which had covers made of thick wooden boards. By 1550 they had been replaced almost completely by pasteboards in England, although these had been used in the East for centuries. Leather was stretched over the boards and secured.

Woodfield Lecture. An annual lecture on an aspect of children's literature given at the Loughborough University (UK) Department of Library and Information Studies, sponsored by the bookselling firm of Woodfield and Stanley.

Woodson Book Award, Carter G. Offered by the (American) National Council for the Social Studies for the most distinguished social science book appropriate for young readers which depicts ethnicity in the USA; the purpose of this award is to encourage the writing, publishing, and dissemination of outstanding social science books for young readers which treat topics related to ethnic minorities and race relations sensitively and accurately. Dr. Woodson was a distinguished black social scientist, historian and educator who wrote books for adults and young people which told the story of the black people in the USA. The Award takes the form of a plaque and was first presented in November 1974 to Eloise Greenfield for *Rosa Parks*, the 'mother of the civil rights movement', published by Thomas Y. Crowell of New York.

Word. In information retrieval, a spoken or written symbol of an idea. In computer terminology, the contents of a storage location. *See also Filing Code.*

Word-book. A lexicon, or dictionary.

Word Break. (*Printing*) Splitting a word at the end of a line.

'Word by Word'. *See Alphabetization.*

Word Index. An index which is based on the choice of words used in a document without considering synonyms and more generic concepts related to the word selected as a heading, or term.

Word Indexing. A form of indexing which is the simplest to apply as it assumes on the part of the indexer a minimum knowledge of the subject-matter background and the least amount of technical skill. Such a type of indexing can be performed with precision by machines. *See also Concordance, KWIC, Permutation Indexing* and *Uniterm Index* which are of this kind, and *Controlled Indexing, Index, Uniterm Concept Co-ordination Indexing.*

Word Processing. The linking of a typewriter with computer facilities; text can thus be input on a conventional keyboard, usually with a visual-display check, stored on a magnetic tape memory or floppy disk, updated or amended whenever necessary, and printed out in any desired format in any quantity, incorporating individual features as required. *See also Desktop Publishing*.

Word Recognition Test. Usually a standardized test of the ability to read single words aloud. The words are graded in difficulty and the tests yield scores which can be converted into reading ages (the measure most commonly employed when standards of reading are being discussed).

Words Authority File. *Synonymous with* THESAURUS (*q.v.*).

Work. Any expression of thought in language, signs or symbols, or other media for record and communication [i.e. a work before printing or other publication]. After publication it becomes a 'published work'. *See also Document*. A work is now generally taken to mean a published DOCUMENT (*q.v.*) varying in extent from a single paper (*see* PAPER 2) or ARTICLE (*q.v.*) to a contribution to knowledge written by one or more persons and published in several volumes, or even all the published writings by one person. It is also used to include a series of related but separate series (*see Series 1, 2, 3*) or PERIODICALS (*q.v.*).

Work and Back. *See Sheet Work*.

Work and Tumble. The method of printing the second side of a sheet of paper by turning it over in its narrow direction and feeding it into a printing machine to print the reverse side.

Work and Turn. To print from a forme in which the pages have been so imposed that when a sheet has been printed on both sides and cut in half it will provide two copies. *See also Sheetwise, Tumbler Scheme*.

Work Area. That portion of a library's total floor space which is allocated for use as working space for the staff. It includes space for desks, furniture and equipment as well as rooms set aside for the exclusive use of staff members.

Work Card. A card used to record the results of bibliographical searching and checking prior to ordering a book. The SUGGESTION CARD (*q.v.*) sometimes serves for this purpose.

Work Manual. *Synonymous with* PROCEDURE MANUAL (*q.v.*).

Work Mark. A letter indicating the title, edition, etc., of a work. This is added to the normal author mark to distinguish several books by one author on the same subject, and to give each a definite location. It usually consists of the letter of the first word not an article of the title, plus, in the case of later editions, the edition number, and/or in the case of other titles beginning with the same letter and having the same class number, a figure (consecutively for each title). *See also Author Mark, Book Number, Call Number, Volume Number*.

Work Off. To print the paper; to finish printing.

Work Responsibility Schedule. A schedule concerned with the special work assigned to each member of the staff as his own individual responsibility.

Work Room. A room not open to the public in which any of the technical library routines or manual processes are carried out.

Work Slip. A card, or other form of record, that accompanies a document throughout the cataloguing and preparation processes and on which the cataloguer notes directions and information necessary to prepare full catalogue entries, cross-references, etc.

Work Space. The part of a book stack which is allotted to assistants to carry out routine duties, including the space for necessary furniture or apparatus.

Work Up. A smudge or mark on a printed page caused by a letter or piece of spacing material in an improperly locked forme working up into a printing position during a press run. Also called 'Black', 'Rising space'.

Working Group of European Librarians and Publishers. *See European Librarians and Publishers, Working Group of.*

Working Party. A group of members of an organization having similar interests, formed to meet a particular need without establishing a permanent committee or other body.

Working Party on Library and Book Trade Relations. *See LIBTRAD.*

'Working with Figures'. *See Press Number.*

World Bibliography. *Synonymous with* UNIVERSAL BIBLIOGRAPHY *(q.v.)*.

World Information System Exchange. *See Wise.*

World Information System of Informatics. *See WISI.*

World Intellectual Property Organization. *See WIPO.*

World Metal Index. The World Metal Index is a listing by grades, abbreviations or numbers of the metal compositions published in national, international and commercial specifications and trade catalogues. There is also an accompanying collection of trade literature standards and specifications covering both the United Kingdom and overseas countries. The index is compiled by and held at Sheffield City Libraries (UK). Originally it was restricted to ferrous metals but now includes both ferrous and non-ferrous materials.

Worldbook – ALA Goal Awards. Two awards made to units of the American Library Association to encourage developments in any field of professional activity.

WORM. Write Once, Read Many; acronym for CD-ROM *(q.v.)* systems that can be loaded with data once, and read as frequently as necessary. Loading of data is a specialised task that can only be handled by an experienced bureau.

Worm-bore (Wormhole). A hole or series of holes bored into, or through, a book by a book worm. A book containing such holes is said to be 'wormed'.

Wove Paper. Paper which, when held up to the light, shows a faint network of diamonds. This is caused by the weave of an ordinary DANDY ROLL *(q.v.)* (machine-made paper) or mould (hand-made paper). James Whatman was probably the first manufacturer of wove paper, and it was first used by John Baskerville in 1757 when he printed his Virgil on it. Not to be confused with LAID PAPER *(q.v.)*.

WPOM. Acronym for Word Processing Output Microfilm; an experimental system of publication-on-demand.

Wrap-around Gathering. A book in which one or more leaves at one end are printed on paper forming part of a section at the other end. This practice was used most in the last seventeenth and eighteenth centuries.

Wrap Rounds. Units of four pages of illustrations, or multiples of four, wrapped around a section of a book and sewn with it. Also called 'Outserts'.

Wrapper. *Synonymous with* BOOK JACKET *(q.v.)*.

Wrench Travelling Fellowship for Librarians, The Sir Evelyn.   Originally set up in 1965 by the founder of the English-Speaking Union, this Fellowship is now run jointly by the (British) Library Association and the ESU which is an independent organization founded to foster good relations between the USA and the Commonwealth by a programme of educational exchanges. The aims of the Fellowship are: (1) to enable the librarian chosen to enrich professional knowledge by visiting American libraries noted for their achievements in special field(s) of interest, and (2) to give an insight into, and understanding of, the American way of life. Each year the Fellowship finances one award-winner on a month-long tour of American libraries. Although the main emphasis is on American libraries, a proportion of visits may also be made in Canada. The award-winner selects the libraries he or she wishes to visit. On return, a report of professional standard on experiences and impressions received is required.

Writ.   King's precept in writing under seal commanding an official to perform or abstain from some action.

Writing Masters.   In the fifteenth century professional writers, no longer needed for literary works because of the invention of printing, became writing masters. The increase of reading led to a general demand to learn the art of writing, and these masters found employment in the universities, schools, Courts, and houses of the wealthy. 'Writing Masters' Books' giving examples of the various hands, appeared in the sixteenth century.

Wrong Fount.   A letter of a different face or size from the rest of the text. This is caused in hand-set printing by placing type in a wrong case of type when 'distributing' after a printing job. Abbreviated w.f.

Wrong Side.   (*Printing*) There is a wrong side and a right side to paper and this is important for many printing purposes. *See Right.*

WYSIWYG.   What You See Is What You Get; popular slogan extolling the simplicity of production in Desktop Publishing (*q.v.*).

X.   Series of recommendations (eg X400, X500, etc.) produced by CCITT (*q.v.*) and relating to digital telecommunications.

X-Height.   The height of that part of a lower case letter between the Ascender (*q.v.*) and the Descender (*q.v.*), i.e. the height of a lower case x. Used to describe the apparent height of a type which may vary within the same point size according to the design of the type face, e.g. in 12-point type from 0.056 to 0.08 inches. Centaur, Egmont, Perpetua and Walbaum have small x-heights, Plantin and Times Old Roman big.

Xmail.   *See ALANET.*

Xerography.   A method of making copies by the use of light and an electro-statically charged plate. It was invented by Chester F. Carlson, patented by him in 1937 and developed in the Graphic Arts Research Laboratory at the Battelle Memorial Institute. Rank-Xerox Limited, a joint company formed by the Haloid Company and Rank Organization (Rank-Xerox), exploits this process throughout the world. Smaller and larger copies than the original can be made, as also can offset plates on a paper base. This is a dry method of positive reproduction of drawn or written material (whether in ink, pencil or colour) and of printed or typewritten matter, or the representation of objects, directly on to ordinary paper which does not need a coated or emulsified surface. The process depends on the ability of static electricity to attract particles of black powder to un-exposed areas of the image. A selenium-coated surface is given a positive electostatic charge and the image is then exposed to it through a camera. Where light is reflected, the charge will be dissipated, leaving a positive charge in the image areas. When a negatively-charged black resinous powder is cascaded over the selenium it is attracted to the charged area. Paper which is then placed over the selenium and charged positively will have the powder image transferred to it, and the image is fused permanently to the paper by the application of heat.

Xylograph. 1. A block book. 2. A wood engraving.

Xylographic Book. *See Block Books.*

Xylographica. Block books.

Xylography. The art or process of engraving on wood. *See also Woodcut, Wood Engraving.*

Xylotype. Wood engraving, or a print from a wood engraving.

Yankee Machine. A machine on which machine-glazed papers are made. Its chief characteristic is one large steam-heated cylinder with a highly polished surface in place of the usual drying rolls. Machine-glazed papers are glazed on only one (the under) side, the other being in the (rough) condition in which it comes from the WET END (*q.v.*) of the machine.

Yapp Edges. *Synonymous with* CIRCUIT EDGES (*q.v.*).

YASD. Young Adult Services Division (*q.v.*) of the American Library Association.

Year Book. A volume often called an *annual*, containing current information of a variable nature, in brief descriptive and/or statistical form, which is published once every year. Often year books review the events of a year.

Year Number. A symbol used to represent the year in which a book was published. This may form part of the BOOK NUMBER (*q.v.*), as used with the Colon Classification, and is obtained by translating the year of publication into the appropriate symbols in accordance with the Scheme's Time Schedule.

Year of Young Reader. In the USA 1989 was so designated by Congress; this initiative was started by the Librarian of Congress, the Center for the Book, and the Children's Literature Center. The aim was to encourage parents, educators and librarians to observe the year with activities that focused attention on encouraging a love of books and reading among young people. The 17 state centers for the book, each affiliated with the Center for the Book in the Library of Congress, were prominent in activities; other participants included the American Booksellers' Association, the Association of Booksellers for Children, the Children's Book Council, and the International Reading Association.

Yellow Book. An official report published by the French government, so called because issued in a yellow paper cover. *See also Blue Book.*

Yellow Press. A popular name for sensational newspapers and periodicals.

Yellowback. A cheap popular novel, usually not of the first quality. So named from the fact that such books were published in shiny yellow paper covers with a picture on the front.

Yorkshire and Humberside Branch. A Branch of the (British) Library Association, formed in 1974 following local government re-organisation, and covering the counties of North, South and West Yorkshire and Humberside. Publishes *Yorkshire Library News* (4 p.a.).

Yorkshire and Humberside Joint Libraries' Committee. An organization which operates as one of a number of joint services, an inter-library lending system covering the four Metropolitan Districts in South Yorkshire, the five Metropolitan Districts in West Yorkshire, and the Counties of North Yorkshire and Humberside. It supersedes the Yorkshire Regional Library System.

Yorkshire Post **Awards.** Three annual awards made by the *Yorkshire Post* newspaper; the categories are: best work of fiction or non-fiction, work by a new author, and an 'Art and Music' award for the book that best stimulates understanding and appreciation of those subjects.

Young Adult Book. One intended for adults but suitable for adolescents.

Young Adult Services Division. Established as a Division of the American Library Association on 1 January 1957. It is interested in the improvement and extension of services to young people in all types of library, and has specific responsibility for the evaluation and selection of books and non-book materials and the interpretation and use of materials for young adults, except when such materials are designed for only one type of library. Abbreviated YASD. Publishes *Journal of Youth Services in Libraries* (q.), jointly with the Association of Library Services to Children.

Young Observer/Rank Organization Fiction Prize (UK). A prize awarded annually for a work of children's fiction; the sponsor is the *Observer* newspaper with financial support from the Rank Organisation.

Young People's Department. *Synonymous with* CHILDREN'S LIBRARY (*q.v.*).

Young Reader's Choice. An award bestowed on the author of a children's book. It takes the form of a parchment presented by Harry Hartman, a Seattle bookseller, and was first awarded in 1940 to Dell McCormick for *Paul Bunyan swings his axe.* Except for three years, it has been awarded annually; the Work with Children & Young People Division of the Pacific Northwest Library Association makes the award.

Younger Committee (UK). The Committee on Privacy set up by the British Government in 1970 under the chairmanship of Kenneth Younger. The Committee reported in 1972. *See Data Protection.*

Youth Libraries Group. A Group of the (British) Library Association; it exists to bring together all those interested in encouraging children and young people to use and enjoy books. It was founded as the Work with Young People Section in 1946 and changed its name when the present constitution of the Library Association came into operation in 1963. Publishes *Youth Library Review* (2 p.a.).

Z39. Abbreviation for National Information Standards Organization (Z39) which develops standards for the AMERICAN NATIONAL STANDARDS INSTITUTE INC. (ANSI) (*q.v.*) in the areas of library science, information sciences and related publishing practices. NISO (Z39) represents the major professional organizations, principal commercial agencies in the field, and US Government Departments; the Council of National Library and Information Associations serves as its secretariat. The Standards are all based on voluntary consensus, and the current list (December 1988) is as follows:–

Z39.1–1977　Periodicals: format and arrangement.

Z39.2–1985　Bibliographic information interchange.

Z39.4–1984　Basic criteria for indexes.

Z39.5–1985　Abbreviation of titles of periodicals.

Z39.6–1983　Trade catalogs.

Z39.7–1983　Library statistics.

Z39.8–1977　Compiling book publishing statistics.

Z39.9–1979　(Re-affirmed 1984) International Standard Serial Numbering.

Z39.10–1971　(Re-affirmed 1977) Directories of libraries and information centers.

Z39.11–1972　(Re-affirmed 1983) System for the Romanization of Japanese.

Z39.12–1972　(Re-affirmed 1984) System for the Romanization of Arabic.

Z39.13–1979　(Re-affirmed 1984) Describing books in advertisements, catalogs, promotional materials, and book jackets.

Z39.14–1979　(Re-affirmed 1987) Writing abstracts.

Z39.15–1980　Title leaves of a book.

Z39.16–1979　(Re-affirmed 1985) Preparation of scientific papers for written or oral presentation.

Z39.18–1987　Guidelines for the organization, preparation and production of scientific and technical reports.

Z39.19–1980　Guidelines for thesaurus structure, construction and use.

Z39.20–1983　Criteria for price indexes for library materials.

Z39.21–1980　Book numbering.

Z39.22–1981　Proof corrections.

Z39.23–1983　Technical report number (STRN).

Z39.24–1976　System for the Romanization of Slavic Cyrillic characters.

Z39.25–1975　Romanization of Hebrew.

Z39.26–1981　Advertising of micropublications.

Z39.27–1984　Structure for the representation of names of countries, etc., for information interchange.

Z39.29–1977　Bibliographic references.

Z39.30–1982　Order form for single titles of library materials in 3″ × 5″ format.

Z39.31–1976   (Re-affirmed 1983) Format for scientific and technical trans-
                lations.
Z39.32–1981   Information for microfiche headings.
Z39.33–1977   (Re-affirmed 1982) Development of identification codes for
                use by the bibliographic community.
Z39.34–1977   (Re-affirmed 1983) Synoptics.
Z39.35–1979   System for the Romanization of Lao, Khmer, and Pali.
Z39.37–1979   System for the Romanization of Armenian.
Z39.39–1979   Compiling newspaper and periodical publishing statistics.
Z39.40–1979   Compiling US microform publishing statistics.
Z39.41–1979   Book spine formats.
Z39.43–1980   Identification code for the book industry.
Z39.44–1986   Serials holdings statements.
Z39.45–1983   Claims for missing issues of serials.
Z39.46–1983   Identification of bibliographic data on and relating to patent
                documents.
Z39.47–1985   Extended Latin alphabet coded character set for biblio-
                graphic use.
Z39.48–1984   Permanence of paper for library materials.
Z39.49–1985   Computerized book ordering.
Z39.50–1988   OSI protocol.
Z39.52–1987   Standard order form for multiple titles of library materials.
Z39.53–1987   Codes for the representation of languages for information
                interchange.

Zero-based Budgeting.   A management and financial system that requires an
organization to identify priorities and justify activities from 'point Zero',
that is without any prior assumptions. This may lead to a re-ranking of
traditional goals, and examination of hidden costs. Abbreviated ZBB.

Zigzag Fold.   *See Accordian Fold, Concertina Fold.*

Zinc Etching.   *Synonymous with* ZINCOGRAPHY *(q.v.).*

Zinco.   1. Abbreviation for ZINCOGRAPH *(q.v.).*   2. A block made of zinc and
used as an alternative to a BINDER'S BRASS *(q.v.).* It is less durable, and the
impression made with it lacks sharpness.

Zincograph.   1. A zinc plate which is etched and mounted for use as a line block
for printing book illustrations and diagrams in black and white. The printing
method is known as Zincography.   2. A print or design made from such a
block. Abbreviated 'zinco'.

Zincography.   A photo-mechanical method of printing whereby designs or line
drawings are produced in black and white. It is a relief method, zinc being
used for the blocks, although copper is used for specially fine work.

Zincplate Litho.   *See Lithography.*

Zipf's Law.   Formulated by George K. Zipf in 1949. Zipf studied the word
counts of linguistic samples and observed that if the words appearing in a
piece of text (one of reasonable length) are counted and ranked in order of
frequency, this frequency is proportional to the rank order. *See also Law of
Scattering.*

Zone Librarian. One who has charge of a group of branch libraries, one of which provides a full range of materials (books for adults and children, a small collection of reference books, gramophone records, tapes and cassettes), the others being three or four smaller branches providing fewer or smaller services.

Zone Library. A library providing a full library service, but from which smaller near-by libraries, which provide a restricted service within the same system, are supervised and from which their resources are supplemented.

Zone of Convenience. An area for shelving which is a suitable height for readers. (American).

Zoomorphic Initial. In a mediaeval illuminated manuscript, an initial letter formed by the bodies of beasts.

Zurich Index. *See Concilium Bibliographicum.*

Zweig (Stefan) Programme. 1987 was the inaugural year of the British Library Stefan Zweig Programme. This annual series of concerts and lectures was set up by the Library in response to the gift to the nation, in May 1986, of the enormously important collection of autograph musical and literary manuscripts formed by the Austrian writer Stefan Zweig. The series aims to provide opportunities for both performers and public that might not otherwise occur.